W9-BXN-067

# THE NEW OXFORD HISTORY
# OF ENGLAND

*General Editor* · J. M. ROBERTS

# England Under
# the Norman
# and Angevin Kings

## 1075–1225

———

ROBERT BARTLETT

CLARENDON PRESS · OXFORD

2000

# OXFORD

UNIVERSITY PRESS

Great Clarendon Street, Oxford OX2 6DP

Oxford University Press is a department of the University of Oxford.
It furthers the University's objective of excellence in research, scholarship,
and education by publishing worldwide in

Oxford New York

Athens Auckland Bangkok Bogotá Buenos Aires Calcutta
Cape Town Chennai Dar es Salaam Delhi Florence Hong Kong Istanbul
Karachi Kuala Lumpur Madrid Melbourne Mexico City Mumbai
Nairobi Paris São Paulo Singapore Taipei Tokyo Toronto Warsaw

and associated companies in Berlin Ibadan

Oxford is a registered trade mark of Oxford University Press
in the UK and certain other countries

Published in the United States
by Oxford University Press Inc., New York

British Library Cataloguing in Publication Data

Data available

Library of Congress Cataloging in Publication Data

Bartlett, Robert, 1950–
England under the Norman and Angevin kings, 1075–1225 / Robert Bartlett.
—(The new Oxford history of England)
Includes Index.
1. Great Britain—History—Norman period, 1066–1154.  2. Great
Britain—History—Angevin period, 1154–1216.  3. England—
Civilization—1066–1485.  4. Normans—England—History.  5. Anjou,
House of.  I. Title.  II. Series.
DA 195.B28  1999  942.02—dc21  99–16108

ISBN 0–19–822741–8

1  3  5  7  9  10  8  6  4  2

Typeset in Ehrhardt
by Jayvee, Trivandrum, India
Printed in United States
on acid-free paper by
T. J. International Ltd.,
Padstow, Cornwall

FOR BRIAN

# General Editor's Preface

The first volume of Sir George Clark's *Oxford History of England* was published in 1934. Undertaking the General Editorship of a *New Oxford History of England* forty-five years later it was hard not to feel overshadowed by its powerful influence and well-deserved status. Some of Clark's volumes (his own among them) were brilliant individual achievements, hard to rival and impossible to match. Of course, he and his readers shared a broad sense of the purpose and direction of such books. His successor can no longer be sure of doing that. The building-blocks of the story, its reasonable and meaningful demarcations and divisions, the continuities and discontinuities, the priorities of different varieties of history, the place of narrative—all these things are now much harder to agree upon. We now know much more about many things, and think about what we know in different ways. It is not surprising that historians now sometimes seem unsure about the audience to which their scholarship and writing are addressed.

In the end, authors should be left to write their own books. None the less, the *New Oxford History of England* is intended to be more than a collection of discrete or idiosyncratic histories in chronological order. Its aim is to give an account of the development of our country in time. It is hard to treat that development as just the history which unfolds within the precise boundaries of England, and a mistake to suggest that this implies a neglect of the histories of the Scots, Irish, and Welsh. Yet the institutional core of the story which runs from Anglo-Saxon times to our own is the story of a state-structure built round the English monarchy and its effective successor, the Crown in Parliament, and that provides the only continuous articulation of the history of peoples we today call British. It follows that there must be uneven and sometimes discontinuous treatment of much of the history of those peoples. The state story remains, nevertheless, an intelligible thread and to me appears still to justify the title both of this series and that of its predecessor.

If the attention given to the other kingdoms and the principality of Wales must reflect in this series their changing relationship to that central theme, this is not only way in which the emphasis of individual volumes will be different. Each author has been asked to bring forward what he or she sees as the most important topics explaining the history under study, taking account of the present state of historical knowledge, drawing attention to areas of dispute and to matters on which final judgement is at present difficult (or, perhaps, impossible) and not merely recapitulating what has recently been the fashionable centre of professional debate. But each volume, allowing for its special approach and proportions, must also provide a comprehensive account, in which politics is always likely to be prominent. Volumes have to be demarcated chronologically but continuities must not be obscured; vestigially or not, copyhold survived into the 1920s and the Anglo–Saxon shires until the 1970s (some of which were to be resurrected in the 1990s, too). Any single volume should be an entry-point to the understanding of processes only slowly unfolding, sometimes across centuries. My hope is that in the end we shall have, as the outcome, a set of standard and authoritative histories, embodying the scholarship of a generation, and not mere compendia in which the determinants are lost to sight among the detail.

J. M. ROBERTS

# Acknowledgements

This book was written in the sympathetic and stimulating environment of the Department of Mediaeval History at the University of St Andrews. It owes a great deal to the readily shared learning, interest, and encouragement of colleagues within the Department and to the spur provided by a particularly intelligent and congenial body of students. The University itself offered valuable practical help to support the research on which the book was based. Some sections had an airing in talks at other universities and benefited from lively and informed criticism and comment on those occasions. Domesday Book statistics were kindly provided by John Palmer of the University of Hull.

Tenure of a British Academy Research Readership in 1995–7 was crucial in providing uninterrupted time for reading and writing. This is deeply valued. The scheme is a model of imaginative and whole-hearted support for scholarship.

Two individuals in particular must be mentioned with especial gratitude. John Hudson, a valued colleague and friend, has read the whole book in draft and made innumerable suggestions, comments, and criticisms, drawing on his own deep knowledge of the period. The book has been greatly improved by those hours in the Whey Pat Tavern. Finally, and most importantly, Nora Bartlett has backed this project with characteristic whole-heartedness, reading and commenting upon the entire text and giving unlimited and much appreciated encouragement.

ROBERT BARTLETT

. . . latentes rerum causas propalare nequeo sed rogatus a sociis annalem historiam simpliciter actito.

(Orderic Vitalis, *Historia ecclesiastica* 13. 16)

# Contents

# Plates

# Figures

# Maps

# Tables

# Abbreviations

| | |
|---|---|
| *AASS* | *Acta sanctorum* (Antwerp. etc., 1643– ) |
| *Abingdon Chron.* | *Chronicon Monasterii de Abingdon*, ed. J. Stevenson (2 vols., RS; 1858) |
| Ad. Eyns., *V. Hugh* | Adam of Eynsham, *Magna V. sancti Hugonis: The Life of Hugh of Lincoln*, ed. and tr. Decima Douie and D. Hugh Farmer (2 vols., NMC, 1961–2; repr. OMT, 1985) |
| Ailr. Riev., *Op. asc.* | Ailred of Rievaulx, *Opera omnia*, 1. *Opera ascetica*, ed. A. Hoste and C. H. Talbot (CCCM 1; 1971) |
| Ailr. Riev., *Rel. de Standardo* | Ailred of Rievaulx, *Relatio de Standardo*, in *Chron. Steph.* 3, pp. 179–99 |
| *Aldgate Cart.* | *The Cartulary of Holy Trinity Priory, Aldgate*, ed. Gerald A. J. Hodgett (London Rec. Soc. 7; 1971) |
| Alex. Ashby, *De modo pred.* | Alexander of Ashby, *De artificioso modo predicandi*, ed. F. Morenzoni, *Studi medievali*, 3rd ser., 32 (1991), pp. 902–35 |
| Alex. Nequam, *DNR* | Alexander Nequam (Neckham), *De Naturis Rerum*, ed. Thomas Wright (RS; 1863) |
| Alex. Nequam, *Ut.* | Alexander Nequam (Neckham), *De nominibus utensilium*, ed. Thomas Wright, in *A Volume of Vocabularies* (n.p., 1857), pp. 96–119 |
| *Ancr. Wisse* | *Ancrene Wisse*, ed. J. R. R. Tolkien (EETS 249; 1962 for 1960) |
| *Ann. Dunst.* | *Annals of Dunstable, Ann. Mon.* 3, pp. 1–420 |
| *Ann. Mon.* | *Annales Monastici*, ed. H. R. Luard (5 vols., RS; 1864–9) |
| *Ann. Wav.* | *Annals of Waverley, Ann. Mon.* 2, pp. 127–411 |
| *Ann. Wint.* | *Annals of Winchester, Ann. Mon.* 2, pp. 1–125 |
| *ANS* | *(Proceedings of the Battle Conference on) Anglo-Norman Studies* |
| Anselm, *Op.* | Anselm, *Opera omnia*, ed. F. S. Schmitt (6 vols.; Edinburgh, 1946–61) |
| *ANTS* | Anglo-Norman Texts Society |
| *ASC* | *Anglo-Saxon Chronicle*, ed. Charles Plummer, *Two of the Saxon Chronicles Parallel* (2 vols.; Oxford, 1892–9), vol. 1 |
| Baldwin, *Masters* | John Baldwin, *Masters, Princes and Merchants: The Social Views of Peter the Chanter and his Circle* (2 vols.; Princeton, 1970) |

Baldwin, *Op.*           Baldwin of Ford, *Opera*, ed. David Bell (CCCM
                         99; 1991)
BAR                      British Archaeological Reports
Barnwell Chron.          Walter of Coventry, *Memoriale*, ed. William
                         Stubbs (2 vols., RS; 1872–3), vol. 2, pp. 196–279
                         (incorporating part of the unpublished 'Barnwell
                         Chronicle')
Bart. Ex.                Bartholomew of Exeter, *Liber paenitentialis*, in
                         Adrian Morey, *Bartholomew of Exeter, Bishop and
                         Canonist* (Cambridge, 1937), pp. 175–300
*Battle Chron.*          *The Chronicle of Battle Abbey*, ed. and tr. Eleanor
                         Searle (OMT; 1980)
*Becket Mats.*           *Materials for the History of Thomas Becket*, ed. J. C.
                         Robertson (7 vols., RS; 1875–85)
Biddle, *Winchester*     Martin Biddle (ed.), *Winchester in the Early Middle
                         Ages* (Oxford, 1976)
Birch, *Seals*           W. de G. Birch, *Catalogue of Seals in the Depart-
                         ment of Manuscripts in the British Museum* (6 vols.;
                         London, 1887–1900)
*Bk. Fees*               *Book of Fees* (2 vols. in 3; London, 1920–31)
*Bk. Gilbert*            *Book of St Gilbert*, ed. and tr. Raymonde Foreville
                         and Gillian Keir (OMT; 1987)
*Bk. Seals*              *Sir Christopher Hatton's Book of Seals*, ed. Lewis
                         Loyd and Doris Stenton (Oxford, 1950)
BL                       British Library
*Borough Charters*       *British Borough Charters, 1042–1216*, ed. Adolphus
                         Ballard (Cambridge, 1913)
*Brut (RBH)*             *Brut y Tywysogyon or The Chronicle of the Princes:
                         Red Book of Hergest Version*, ed. and tr. Thomas
                         Jones (Cardiff, 1955)
Burton Cart.             G. Wrottesley, 'The Burton Cartulary', *CHS* 5/i
                         (1884), pp. 1–101
Burton Surveys           Charles G. O. Bridgeman, 'The Burton Abbey
                         Twelfth Century Surveys', *CHS* (1916), pp. 209–
                         300
*Bury Docs.*             *Feudal Documents from the Abbey of Bury St
                         Edmunds*, ed. D. C. Douglas (London, 1932)
*Caen Custumals*         *Charters and Custumals of the Abbey of Holy Trinity
                         Caen*, ed. Marjorie Chibnall (London, 1982)
*Cal. Ch. Rolls*         *Calendar of the Charter Rolls, 1226–1516* (6 vols.;
                         London, 1903–27)
*Can. Osmund*            *The Canonization of St Osmund*, ed. A. R. Malden
                         (Wiltshire Rec. Soc.; 1901)
*Canterbury Cases*       *Select Cases from the Ecclesiastical Courts of the
                         Province of Canterbury c.1200–1301*, ed. Norma

Adams and Charles Donahue (Selden Soc. 95; 1981 for 1978–9)

CCCM  Corpus Christianorum, Continuatio mediaevalis (Turnhout)

*CDF*  *Calendar of Documents Preserved in France Illustrative of the History of Great Britain and Ireland*, 1. *A.D. 918–1206*, ed. J. H. Round (London, 1899)

*Chester Charters*  *The Charters of the Anglo-Norman Earls of Chester, c.1071–1237*, ed. Geoffrey Barraclough (Record Soc. of Lancashire and Cheshire 126; 1988)

*Chichester Acta*  *Acta of the Bishops of Chichester 1075–1207*, ed. H. Mayr-Harting (Canterbury and York Soc. 56; 1964)

*Chron. Steph.*  *Chronicles of the Reigns of Stephen, Henry II and Richard I*, ed. Richard Howlett (4 vols., RS; 1884–9)

*CHS*  *Collections for a History of Staffordshire* (Staffordshire Record Soc., formerly The William Salt Archaeological Soc.)

Cole, *Docs.*  *Documents Illustrative of English History in the Thirteenth and Fourteenth Centuries*, ed. Henry Cole (London, 1844)

*Const. domus regis*  *Constitutio domus regis*, in *Dial. scacc.*, pp. 128–35

*Councils and Synods*  *Councils and Synods with Other Documents Relating to the English Church* 1 (871–1204), ed. D. Whitelock, M. Brett, and C. N. L. Brooke (2 vols.; Oxford, 1981); 2 (1205–1313), ed. F. M. Powicke and C. R. Cheney (2 vols.; Oxford, 1964)

*CRR*  *Curia Regis Rolls* (12 vols. to 1226; London, 1922–57)

D. Beccles  *Urbanus Magnus Danielis Becclesiensis*, ed. J. Gilbart Smyly (Dublin, 1939)

D. Morley  Daniel of Morley, *Liber de naturis inferiorum et superiorum*, ed. Gregor Maurach, *Mittellateinisches Jahrbuch* 14 (1979), pp. 204–55

*Danelaw Docs.*  *Documents Illustrative of the Social and Economic History of the Danelaw*, ed. F. M. Stenton (London, 1920)

Darby, *Domesday England*  H. C. Darby, *Domesday England* (Cambridge, 1977)

*DB*  *Domesday Book* (see pp. 696–7)

*Decretals*  *Decretales Gregorii IX*, ed. Emil Friedberg, *Corpus iuris canonici* 2 (Leipzig, 1879)

*De exp. Lyxb.*  *De expugnatione Lyxbonensi: The Conquest of Lisbon*, ed. and tr. Charles W. David (New York, 1936)

| | |
|---|---|
| *Dial. scacc.* | *Dialogus de Scaccario* (attrib. Richard fitz Neal), ed. and tr. Charles Johnson (NMC, 1950; OMT, 1983) |
| *Dict. Med. Latin* | *Dictionary of Medieval Latin from British Sources* (London, 1975– ) |
| Duggan, 'Equity' | Charles Duggan, 'Equity and Compassion in Papal Marriage Decretals to England', in *Love and Marriage in the Twelfth Century*, ed. Willy Van Hoecke and Andries Welkenhuysen (Mediaevalia Lovaniensia, ser. 1, studia 8; 1981), pp. 59–87 |
| Eadmer, *HN* | Eadmer, *Historia novorum*, ed. Martin Rule (Rolls Series; London, 1884) |
| Eadmer, *Tractatus* | Eadmer, *Tractatus de conceptione sanctae Mariae*, ed. H. Thurston and T. Slater (Freiburg, 1904) |
| Eadmer, *V. Anselm* | Eadmer, *Life of St Anselm*, ed. and tr. R. W. Southern (NMC, 1962; OMT, 1972) |
| *Earliest Lincs. Ass. Rolls* | *The Earliest Lincolnshire Assize Rolls (1202–1209)*, ed. Doris Stenton (Lincoln Record Soc. 22; 1926) |
| *Early Charters St Paul's* | *Early Charters of the Cathedral Church of St Paul, London*, ed. Marion Gibbs (Camden, 3rd ser., 58; 1939) |
| *Early Waltham Charters* | *The Early Charters of the Augustinian Canons of Waltham Abbey, Essex, 1062–1230*, ed. Rosalind Ransford (Woodbridge, 1989) |
| *EEA* | *English Episcopal Acta* (Oxford, 1980– ) |
| EETS | Early English Text Society (original series) |
| *EHR* | *English Historical Review* |
| *Elenchus* | *Elenchus fontium historiae urbanae 2/2*, ed. Susan Reynolds *et al.* (Leiden etc., 1988) |
| *Engl. Ben. Libr.* | *English Benedictine Libraries: The Shorter Catalogues*, ed. Richard Sharpe *et al.* (*Corpus of British Medieval Library Catalogues* 4; London, 1994) |
| *Engl. Rom. Art* | *English Romanesque Art 1066–1200*, ed. George Zarnecki *et al.* (Arts Council of Great Britain; 1984) |
| *EYC* | *Early Yorkshire Charters*, ed. William Farrer and Charles Clay (12 vols. plus index to vols. 1–3; vols. 4–12 = Yorkshire Archaeological Soc., Record Ser., extra series, 1–10; 1914–65) |
| Fantosme | Jordan Fantosme, *Chronicle*, ed. and tr. R. C. Johnston (OMT; 1981) |
| *Fasti* | John Le Neve, *Fasti Ecclesiae Anglicanae 1066–1300*, compiled by Diana Greenway (London, 1968– ) |
| Flor. Worcs. | Florence of Worcester, *Chronicon ex chronicis*, |

|  |  |
|---|---|
|  | ed. Benjamin Thorpe (English Historical Soc., 2 vols.; London, 1848–9) |
| Foliot, *Letters* | Gilbert Foliot, *Letters and Charters*, ed. Adrian Morey and C. N. L. Brooke (Cambridge, 1967) |
| Gaimar | Geffrei Gaimar, *L'Estoire des Engleis*, ed. Alexander Bell (ANTS 14–16; 1960) |
| Geoff. Monm., *HRB* | Geoffrey of Monmouth, *Historia regum Britannie*, ed. Neil Wright (Cambridge, 1984) |
| Gerald, *De reb.* | *De rebus a se gestis*, in Gerald, *Op.* 1, pp. 1–122 |
| Gerald, *Descr.* | *Descriptio Kambriae*, in Gerald, *Op.* 6, pp. 153–227 |
| Gerald, *Exp.* | Gerald of Wales (Giraldus Cambrensis), *Expugnatio Hibernica: The Conquest of Ireland*, ed. and tr. A. B. Scott and F. X. Martin (Dublin, 1978) |
| Gerald, *Gemma* | *Gemma ecclesiastica*, in Gerald, *Op.* 2 |
| Gerald, *Inv.* | Gerald of Wales (Giraldus Cambrensis), *Invectiones*, ed. W. S. Davies (*Y Cymmrodor* 30; 1920) |
| Gerald, *Itin.* | *Itinerarium Kambriae*, in Gerald, *Op.* 6, pp. 1–152 |
| Gerald, *Op.* | Gerald of Wales (Giraldus Cambrensis), *Opera*, ed. J. S. Brewer, J. F. Dimock, and G. F. Warner (8 vols., RS; 1861–91) |
| Gerald, *Prin.* | *De principis instructione*, in Gerald, *Op.* 8 |
| Gerald, *Spec. duorum* | Gerald of Wales (Giraldus Cambrensis), *Speculum Duorum*, ed. Yves Lefèvre and R. B. C. Huygens, general ed. Michael Richter (Cardiff, 1974) |
| Gerald, *Spec. eccl.* | *Speculum ecclesiae*, in Gerald, *Op.* 4, pp. 1–354 |
| Gerald, *Symb. el.* | *Symbolum electorum*, in Gerald, *Op.* 1, pp. 197–395 |
| Gerald, *Top.* | *Topographia hibernica*, in Gerald, *Op.* 5, pp. 1–204 |
| Gerald, *V. Geoffrey* | *V. Galfridi archiepiscopi Eboracensis*, in Gerald, *Op.* 4, pp. 355–431 |
| Gerald, *V. Remigius* | *V. sancti Remigii*, in Gerald, *Op.* 7, pp. 1–80 |
| Gerv. Cant. | Gervase of Canterbury, *Chronica*, in Gerv. Cant., *Works* 1 |
| Gerv. Cant., *Works* | *The Historical Works of Gervase of Canterbury*, ed. William Stubbs (2 vols., RS; 1879–80) |
| Gerv. Tilb. | Gervase of Tilbury, *Otia imperialia*, ed. G. W. Leibnitz, *Scriptores rerum Brunsvicensium* (3 vols.; Hanover, 1707–11), vol. 1, pp. 881–1004 (variant readings, vol. 2, pp. 751–84) |
| *Gesta antecess. Waldevi* | *Gesta antecessorum comitis Waldevi*, ed. F. Michel, *Chroniques anglo-normandes* (3 vols.; Rouen, 1836–40), vol. 2, pp. 104–11 |
| *Gesta Hen. II* | *Gesta regis Henrici secundi Benedicti abbatis*, ed. William Stubbs (2 vols., RS; 1867) (actually by Roger of Howden) |

| | |
|---|---|
| *Gesta Herw.* | *Gesta Herwardi*, ed. T. D. Hardy and C. T. Martin, in Gaimar, *L'Estoire des Engles* (2 vols., RS; 1888–9), vol. 1, pp. 339–404 |
| *Gesta Ric. I* | *Gesta Hen. II* 2, pp. 71–250 |
| *Gesta S. Alb.* | *Gesta abbatum monasterii sancti Albani*, ed. Henry T. Riley (3 vols., RS; 1867–9) |
| *Gesta Stephani* | *Gesta Stephani*, ed. and tr. K. R. Potter and R. H. C. Davis (OMT; 1976) |
| Glanvill | *The Treatise on the Laws and Customs of the Realm of England commonly called Glanvill*, ed. and tr. G. D. H. Hall (NMC; 1965) |
| *Gloucester Charters* | *Earldom of Gloucester Charters*, ed. Robert B. Patterson (Oxford, 1973) |
| Goscelin, *Hist. Augustine* | Goscelin, *Historia major sancti Augustini*, PL 80, cols. 41–94 |
| Gratian | Gratian, *Decretum*, ed. Emil Friedberg, *Corpus iuris canonici* 1 (Leipzig, 1879) |
| Green, *Govt.* | Judith Green, *The Government of England under Henry I* (Cambridge, 1986) |
| H. Hunt. | Henry of Huntingdon, *Historia Anglorum*, ed. Diana Greenway (OMT; 1996) |
| Hallam, *Agrarian Hist.* | H. E. Hallam (ed.), *The Agrarian History of England and Wales*, 2. *1042–1350* (Cambridge, 1986) |
| Hermann, *Mir. Laud.* | Hermann of Laon, *De miraculis sanctae Mariae Laudunesis*, PL 156, cols. 961–1020 |
| Hill, *Atlas* | David Hill, *An Atlas of Anglo-Saxon England* (Oxford, 1981) |
| *Hist. ducs Norm.* | *Histoire des ducs de Normandie et des rois d'Angleterre*, ed. Francisque Michel (Société de l'Histoire de France 18; 1840) |
| *Hist. Guill. Mar.* | *L'Histoire de Guillaume le Maréchal*, ed. Paul Meyer (3 vols., Société de l'Histoire de France 255, 268, 304; 1891–1901) |
| HMC | Historical Manuscripts Commission |
| Holtzmann and Kemp | W. Holtzmann and E. W. Kemp (eds.), *Papal Decretals Relating to the Diocese of Lincoln in the Twelfth Century* (Lincoln Rec. Soc. 47; 1954) |
| Hue, *Ipom.* | Hue de Rotelande, *Ipomedon*, ed. A. J. Holden (Paris, 1979) |
| Hue, *Proth.* | Hue de Rotelande, *Protheselaus*, ed. A. J. Holden (3 vols., ANTS 47–9; 1991–3) |
| Hugh Chanter | Hugh the Chanter, *The History of the Church of York 1066–1127*, ed. and tr. Charles Johnson (rev. edn., OMT; 1990) |

| | |
|---|---|
| Hunt, *Nequam* | R. W. Hunt, *The Schools and the Cloister: The Life and Writings of Alexander Nequam* (Oxford, 1984) |
| *Hyde Chron.* | *Chronica Monasterii de Hida*, ed. Edward Edwards in *Liber Monasterii de Hyda* (RS; 1866), pp. 283–321 |
| *ICC* | *Inquisitio comitatus Cantabrigiensis, subjicitur Inquisitio Eliensis*, ed. N. E. S. A. Hamilton (London, 1876) |
| *Itin. reg. Ric.* | *Itinerarium regis Ricardi*, ed. William Stubbs, *Chronicles and Memorials of the Reign of Richard I* (2 vols., RS; 1864–5), vol. 1 |
| J. Ford, *V. Wulfric* | John of Ford, *V. sancti Wulfrici*, ed. M. Bell (Somerset Rec. Soc. 47; 1932) |
| J. Hexham | John of Hexham, *Historia*, in Simeon, *Op.* 2, pp. 284–332 |
| J. Salisb., *Letters* | John of Salisbury, *Letters*, ed. W. J. Millor, H. E. Butler, and C. N. L. Brooke, 1. *The Early Letters (1153–61)* (rev. edn., OMT; 1986); 2. *The Later Letters (1163–80)* (OMT; 1979) |
| J. Salisb., *Policr.* | John of Salisbury, *Policraticus*, ed. C. C. J. Webb (2 vols.; Oxford, 1909) |
| J. Worcs. | *The Chronicle of John of Worcester 1118–1140*, ed. J. R. H. Weaver (*Anecdota Oxoniensia*; 1908) |
| JHSE | Jewish Historical Society of England |
| JL | *Regesta pontificium Romanorum . . . ad annum . . . 1198*, ed. P. Jaffé, rev. S. Loewenfeld *et al.* (2 vols.; Leipzig, 1885–8) |
| *Jnl* | *Journal (of)* |
| Joc. Brak. | *The Chronicle of Jocelin of Brakelond*, ed. H. E. Butler (NMC; 1949) |
| Joc. Furn., *V. Waltheof* | Jocelin of Furness, *V. sancti Waldevi*, *AASS* 1 Aug. (1733), pp. 248–76 |
| Keefe, *Assessments* | Thomas K. Keefe, *Feudal Assessments and the Political Community under Henry II and his Sons* (Berkeley etc., 1983) |
| King, *Peterborough* | Edmund King, *Peterborough Abbey 1086–1310* (Cambridge, 1973) |
| *King's Works* | R. A. Brown, H. M. Colvin, and A. J. Taylor, *The History of the King's Works: The Middle Ages* (2 vols.; London, 1963) |
| Lambeth Anon. | 'Lambeth Anonymous', in *Becket Mats.* 4, pp. 80–144 |
| Lanfr., *Const.* | Lanfranc, *Monastic Constitutions*, ed. and tr. David Knowles (NMC; 1951) |

| | |
|---|---|
| Le Patourel, *Norman Empire* | John Le Patourel, *The Norman Empire* (Oxford, 1976) |
| *LHP* | *Leges Henrici Primi*, ed. L. J. Downer (Oxford, 1972) |
| *Lib. Eliensis* | *Liber Eliensis*, ed. E. O. Blake (Camden, 3rd ser., 92; 1962) |
| Liebermann, *Gesetze* | Felix Liebermann (ed.), *Die Gesetze der Angelsachsen* (3 vols.; Halle, 1898–1916) |
| *Magd. Pont.* | *The Pontifical of Magdalene College*, ed. H. A. Wilson (Henry Bradshaw Soc. 39; 1910) |
| Map | Walter Map, *De nugis curialium*, ed. M. R. James, rev. C. N. L. Brooke and R. A. B. Mynors (OMT; 1983) |
| Marie de France, *Fables* | Marie de France, *Fables*, ed. Harriet Spiegel (Toronto, 1987) |
| Marie de France, *Lais* | Marie de France, *Lais*, ed. A. Ewert (Oxford, 1944) |
| *Melrose Chron.* | *Chronica de Mailros*, ed. Joseph Stevenson (Bannatyne Club 49; 1835) |
| *Mem. Edm.* | Memorials of St Edmunds Abbey, ed. Thomas Arnold (3 vols., RS; 1890–6) |
| *MGH* | *Monumenta Germaniae historica* |
| Mir. | Miracula (Miracles) |
| *Mir. Erkenwald* | *Mir. sancti Erkenwaldi* (attrib. Arcoid), ed. and tr. E. Gordon Whatley, *The Saint of London: The Life and Miracles of St. Erkenwald* (Binghamton, 1989), pp. 100–64 |
| *Mir. John Bev.* | *Mir. sancti Johannis Eboracensis episcopi*, ed. J. Raine in *Historians of the Church of York* (3 vols., RS; 1879–94), vol. 1, pp. 261–347 |
| *Mir. Nectan* | *Mir. sancti Nectani*, ed. P. Grosjean, 'Vie de S. Rumon. Vie, invention et miracles de S. Nectan', *Analecta Bollandiana*, 71 (1953), pp. 359–414, at 405–14 |
| *Mir. Wulfstan* | *Mir. Wulfstani*, in W. Malm., *V. Wulfstan*, pp. 115–80 |
| *Monasticon* | William Dugdale, *Monasticon anglicanum*, ed. John Caley *et al.* (6 vols. in 8; London, 1846) |
| *Mowbray Charters* | *Charters of the Honour of Mowbray 1107–1191*, ed. D. E. Greenway (London, 1972) |
| Nigel, *Spec. Stult.* | Nigel Longchamp (alias Wireker or Whiteacre), *Speculum Stultorum*, ed. John H. Mozley and Robert R. Raymo (Berkeley and Los Angeles, 1960) |
| NMC | Nelson's Medieval Classics (later Texts) |
| O. Cheriton, *Parabolae* | Odo of Cheriton, *Parabolae ex sermonibus super* |

|  |  |
|--|--|
|  | *evangeliis dominicalibus extractae*, ed. Leopold Hervieux, *Les fabulistes latins depuis le siècle d'Auguste jusqu'à la fin du Moyen Age* (4 vols.; Paris, 1884–96), vol. 4, pp. 265–343 |
| OMT | Oxford Medieval Texts |
| Orderic | Orderic Vitalis, *Historia ecclesiastica*, ed. and tr. Marjorie Chibnall (6 vols., OMT; 1968–80) |
| Osbert, *Letters* | Osbert of Clare, *Letters*, ed. E. W. Williamson (London, 1929) |
| P. Blois, *Confess.* | Peter of Blois, *De confessione*, PL 207, cols. 1077–1092 |
| P. Blois, *Letters* | Peter of Blois, *Letters*, PL 207, cols. 1–463 |
| Painter, *John* | Sidney Painter, *The Reign of King John* (Baltimore, 1949) |
| Paris, *CM* | Mathew Paris, *Chronica majora*, ed. Henry R. Luard (7 vols., RS; 1872–84) |
| *Pat. Rolls HIII* | *Patent Rolls of the Reign of Henry III* (1216–32) (2 vols.; London, 1901–3) |
| *PBKJ* | *Pleas before the King or his Justices, 1198–1202*, ed. Doris Stenton (4 vols., Selden Soc. 67–8, 83–4; for 1948–9 and 1966–7) |
| Peter Cornw., *Liber rev.* | Peter of Cornwall, *Liber revelationum*, Lambeth Palace MS 51 |
| *Petr. Chron.* | *Chronicon Petroburgense*, ed. Thomas Stapleton (Camden Soc. 47; 1849) |
| Philip, *Mir. Fridesw.* | Philip, prior of St Frideswide's, *Mir. sanctae Frideswidae*, *AASS* October 8, pp. 568–89 |
| *PL* | *Patrologia cursus completus, series latina*, ed. J.-P. Migne (221 vols.; Paris, 1844–64) |
| PR | Pipe Roll (see pp. 697–8) |
| *Priory Hexham* | *The Priory of Hexham* 1, ed. James Raine (Surtees Soc. 44; 1864) |
| PRS | Pipe Roll Soc. |
| R. Coggesh. | Ralph of Coggeshall, *Chronicon Anglicanum*, ed. Joseph Stevenson (RS; 1875) |
| R. Devizes | Richard of Devizes, *Chronicle*, ed. John T. Appleby (NMC; 1963) |
| R. Diceto, *Abbrev.* | *Abbreviationes chronicorum*, in R. Diceto, *Op.* 1, pp. 3–263 |
| R. Diceto, *Op.* | Ralph de Diceto, *Opera historica*, ed. William Stubbs (2 vols., RS; 1876) |
| R. Diceto, *Ymag.* | *Ymagines Historiarum*, in R. Diceto, *Op.* 1, pp. 289–440; 2, pp. 1–174 |
| R. Hexham | Richard of Hexham, *Historia*, in *Chron. Steph.* 3, pp. 137–78 |

| | |
|---|---|
| R. Howd. | Roger of Howden, *Chronica*, ed. William Stubbs (4 vols., RS; 1868–71) |
| R. Torigni | Robert de Torigni, *Chronica*, in *Chron. Steph.* 4 |
| R. Wend. | Roger of Wendover, *Flores historiarum*, ed. H. G. Hewlett (3 vols., RS; 1886–9) |
| *Ramsey Cart.* | *Cartularium monasterii de Rameseia*, ed. W. H. Hart and P. A. Lyons (3 vols., RS; 1884–93) |
| *Ramsey Chron.* | *Chronicon abbatiae Ramesiensis*, ed. W. Dunn Macray (RS; 1886) |
| *RBE* | *Red Book of the Exchequer*, ed. Hubert Hall (3 vols., RS; 1896) |
| *Reading Cart.* | *Reading Abbey Cartularies*, ed. Brian Kemp (2 vols., Camden 4th ser., 31 and 33; 1986–7) |
| *Rec. actes Hen. II* | *Recueil des actes de Henri II*, ed. Léopold Delisle (3 vols.; Paris, 1916–27) |
| Rec. Comm. | Record Commission |
| Reg., *Libellus* | Reginald of Durham, *Libellus de admirandis beati Cuthberti virtutibus*, ed. James Raine (Surtees Soc. 1; 1835) |
| *Reg. Osm.* | *Register of St Osmund*, ed. W. H. R. Jones (2 vols., RS; 1883–4) |
| Reg., *V. Godric* | Reginald of Durham, *Libellus de V. et miraculis sancti Godrici heremitae de Finchale*, ed. Joseph Stevenson (Surtees Soc. 20; 1845) |
| Richardson, *Jewry* | H. G. Richardson, *The English Jewry under Angevin Kings* (London, 1960) |
| Robertson, *Laws* | *Laws of the Kings of England from Edmund to Henry I*, ed. and tr. A. J. Robertson (Cambridge, 1925) |
| *Rolls Fifteenth* | *Rolls of the Fifteenth of the Ninth Year of the Reign of Henry III, etc.*, ed. Fred A. and Annarie P. Cazel (PRS, n.s. 45; 1983 for 1976–7) |
| *Rot. chart.* | *Rotuli chartarum in turri Londinensi asservati*, ed. T. D. Hardy (Rec. Comm.; 1837) |
| *Rot. dom.* | *Rotuli de dominabus et pueris et puellis de donatione regis*, ed. J. H. Round (PRS 35; 1913) |
| *Rot. Hug. Welles* | *Rotuli Hugonis de Welles episcopi Lincolniensis*, ed. W. P. W. Phillimore (3 vols., Canterbury and York Soc. 1, 3–4; 1907–9) |
| *Rot. lib.* | *Rotuli de liberatis ac de misis et praestitis, regnante Johanne*, ed. T. D. Hardy (London, 1844) |
| *Rot. litt. claus.* | *Rotuli litterarum clausarum in turri Londinensi asservati*, ed. T. D. Hardy (2 vols., Rec. Comm.; 1833–44) |
| *Rot. litt. pat.* | *Rotuli litterarum patentium in turri Londinensi asservati*, ed. T. D. Hardy (Rec. Comm.; 1835) |

| | |
|---|---|
| *Rot. obl.* | *Rotuli de oblatis et finibus in turri Londinensi asservati, tempore regis Johannis*, ed. T. D. Hardy (Rec. Comm.; 1835) |
| Round, *King's Sergeants* | J. H. Round, *The Kings Serjeants and Officers of State* (London, 1911) |
| *RRAN* | *Regesta regum anglo-normannorum*, ed. H. W. C. Davis *et al.* (4 vols.; Oxford, 1913–69) |
| RS | *Rerum britannicarum medii aevi scriptores* ('Rolls Series') (251 vols.; London, 1858–96) |
| S. Durh., *HDE* | *Historia Dunelmensis ecclesiae*, in Simeon, *Op.* 1, pp. 17–135 (with continuators, pp. 135–69) |
| S. Durh., *HR* | *Historia regum*, in Simeon, *Op.* 2, pp. 3–283 |
| S. Rouen, *Draco* | Stephen of Rouen, *Draco Normannicus*, in *Chron. Steph.* 2, pp. 585–781 |
| Sanders, *Baronies* | Ivor J. Sanders, *English Baronies* (Oxford, 1961) |
| *Sel. Charters* | William Stubbs (ed.), *Select Charters* (9th edn.; Oxford, 1913) |
| Simeon, *Op.* | *Symeonis monachi opera omnia*, ed. Thomas Arnold (2 vols., RS; 1882–5) |
| Soc. | Society |
| Stenton, *Engl. Justice* | D. M. Stenton, *English Justice between the Norman Conquest and the Great Charter 1066–1215* (Philadelphia, 1964) |
| Stenton, *First Century* | Frank Stenton, *The First Century of English Feudalism 1066–1166* (2nd edn.; Oxford, 1961) |
| Stones, *Rels.* | E. L. G. Stones (ed.), *Anglo-Scottish Relations 1174–1328: Some Select Documents* (OMT; 1965) |
| Stringer, *Earl David* | Keith Stringer, *Earl David of Huntingdon* (Edinburgh, 1985) |
| T. Chobham, *SC* | Thomas of Chobham, *Summa confessorum*, ed. F. Broomfield (Analecta mediaevalia Namurcensia 25; Louvain and Paris, 1968) |
| T. Chobham, *SP* | Thomas of Chobham, *Summa de arte praedicandi*, ed. Franco Morenzoni (CCCM 82; 1988) |
| T. Monm., *V. William* | Thomas of Monmouth, *The Life and Miracles of St William of Norwich*, ed. Augustus Jessopp and Montague Rhodes James (Cambridge, 1896) |
| *Templar Records* | *Records of the Templars in England in the Twelfth Century*, ed. Beatrice A. Lees (London, 1935) |
| *Text. Roff.* | *Textus Roffensis*, ed. Thomas Hearne (Oxford, 1720); facs. ed. Peter Sawyer (2 vols., Early English Manuscripts in Facsimile 7, 11; 1957–62) |
| Turgot, *V. Margaret* | Turgot, *V. sanctae Margaritae Scotorum reginae*, |

|  |  |
|---|---|
|  | ed. J. Hodgson Hinde, *Symeonis Dunelmensis opera*, Surtees Soc., 51 (1868), pp. 234–54 |
| V. | Vita (Life) |
| *V. Christina* | *The Life of Christina of Markyate*, ed. C. H. Talbot (rev. edn., OMT; 1987) |
| Van Caen., *Lawsuits* | R. C. Van Caenegem (ed.), *English Lawsuits from William I to Richard I* (2 vols., Selden Soc. 106–7; 1990–1) |
| Van Caen., *Writs* | R. C. Van Caenegem, *Royal Writs in England from the Conquest to Glanvill* (Selden Soc. 77; 1959) |
| *VCH* | *Victoria County History* (London, 1900– ) |
| *Vis. Eynsham* | *Vision of the Monk of Eynsham*, ed. H. E. Salter, *Eynsham Cartulary 2* (Oxford Hist. Soc. 51; 1908), pp. 255–371 |
| *Vis. Orm* | 'The Vision of Orm', ed. Hugh Farmer, *Analecta Bollandiana*, 75 (1957), pp. 72–82 |
| *Vis. Thurkill* | *Visio Thurkilli, relatore, ut videtur, Radulpho de Coggeshall*, ed. Paul Gerhard Schmidt (Leipzig, 1978) |
| W. Cant., *Mir. Thos.* | William of Canterbury, *Mir. sancti Thomae*, in *Becket Mats.* 1, pp. 137–546 |
| W. Dan., *V. Ailred* | Walter Daniel, *The Life of Ailred of Rievaulx*, ed. and tr. Maurice Powicke (NMC, 1950; OMT, 1978) |
| W. f. Stephen, *V. Thomas* | William fitz Stephen, *V. sancti Thomae*, in *Becket Mats.* 3, pp. 1–154 |
| W. Malm., *GP* | William of Malmesbury, *Gesta pontificum*, ed. N. E. S. A. Hamilton (RS; 1870) |
| W. Malm., *GR* | William of Malmesbury, *Gesta regum*, ed. William Stubbs (2 vols., RS; 1887–9); ed. R. A. B. Mynors, R. M. Thomson, and M. Winterbottom (OMT; 1998) |
| W. Malm., *HN* | William of Malmesbury, *Historia novella*, ed. and tr. K. R. Potter (NMC; 1955) |
| W. Malm., *V. Wulfstan* | William of Malmesbury, *V. Wulfstani*, ed. R. R. Darlington (Camden 3rd ser., 40; 1928) |
| W. Newb. | William of Newburgh, *Historia rerum anglicarum*, in *Chron. Steph.* 1–2 |
| Waugh, *Lordship* | Scott Waugh, *The Lordship of England: Royal Wardships and Marriages in English Society and Politics 1217–1327* (Princeton, 1988) |
| *Westminster Charters* | *Westminster Abbey Charters 1066–c.1214*, ed. Emma Mason (London Record Soc. 25; 1988) |
| *Wigmore Chron.* | 'The Anglo-Norman Chronicle of Wigmore Abbey', ed. J. C. Dickinson and P. T. Ricketts, *Trans. Woolhope Field Club*, 39 (1969), pp. 413–46 |

Wilmart, 'Maître Adam'  André Wilmart, 'Maître Adam chanoine pré-
montré devenu chartreux à Witham', *Analecta
Praemonstriana*, 9 (1933), pp. 209–32
*Worcester Cart.*  *Cartulary of Worcester Cathedral Priory*, ed. R. R.
Darlington (PRS, n.s., 37; 1968 for 1962–3)

## NOTE ON MONEY

During the period discussed in this book, there was only one English coin, the silver penny, but, in accounting, two other units, the shilling (12 pence) and pound (20 shillings or 240 pence), were also employed. Shilling is abbreviated *s.*, penny *d.* The figure £10. 10*s.* 4*d.* thus means 'ten pounds, ten shillings, and four pence'. British readers who knew the pre-decimal coinage will find this familiar.

# Introduction

England in 1075 was a conquered country. Many of those who had recently been its rulers, the Anglo-Saxon landed class, were dead, exiled, or pressed down into the ranks of the peasantry. A small armed group speaking a language incomprehensible to the majority of the population controlled virtually all the landed wealth. Members of this group were busy supervising the construction of scores of castles, designed to ensure their dominion. Everywhere the raw earth of new mounds, which formed the core of the so-called motte-and-bailey castles, served as a visible sign that the country was in the hands of new rulers. In the towns dozens of house were destroyed to make room for these intrusive fortifications. Within a few years Londoners would be looking up to the rising stone tower that has distinguished their eastern skyline ever since. The nunneries were full of Englishwomen who had taken the veil in the attempt to escape rape by Norman soldiers.[1] The tensions of newly conquered England are revealed by the so-called *murdrum* fine enforced by William the Conqueror: if an unknown man were found dead, the neighbouring villages were liable to a fine—unless they could prove that the dead man was not French but English.[2] This law is obviously intended as a deterrent against the casual knifing of Normans and the need for it shows how many shared the view of the author of the *Anglo-Saxon Chronicle*, writing of the fateful year 1066, that 'after that things became much worse'.[3] England in 1075 was a land under occupation.

The occupation endured, however. Gradually distinctions became less clear. Already by 1088 the English were fighting for their Norman king, William II, against his own French barons. Intermarriage, especially of immigrant Frenchmen with native women, diluted racial identity and promoted bilingualism. The very names of the conquerors began to be adopted by the conquered, so that by 1225 the mass of the English male peasantry bore names like William, Henry, and Richard, which, in 1075, would have been

---

[1] Eadmer, *HN*, pp. 123–4.
[2] Liebermann, *Gesetze* 1, p. 510 (Leis Wl. 22); Robertson, *Laws*, p. 264.
[3] *ASC*, p. 200 (D text).

certain indicators of Norman origin. Writing about 1178, Richard fitz Neal, the king's treasurer, was of the opinion that 'with the English and Normans living side-by-side and intermarrying, the peoples have become so mingled that nowadays one can scarcely tell—as far as free men are concerned—who is of English and who of Norman descent'.[4] The conquest of the north French dominions of the king of England in John's reign (1199–1216) severed a link across the Channel that had distinguished the top ranks of the aristocracy. By 1225 there was indeed still a strong French cultural air to the English landed elite, but that elite was now a native ruling class, not the garrison aristocracy of 1075.

The gradual lessening of the distinction between conquered English and conquering French was, however, a very slow process. Throughout the period covered by this book, the top ranks of English society were bound to northern France in a way unparalleled in any other comparable stretch of English history. The Norman and Angevin kings were not only kings of England but also rulers of large parts of France, while many of their barons, and indeed lesser vassals, held lands on both sides of the Channel. There were corresponding links between the ecclesiastical establishments in England and northern France. There was no question that England was part of Europe and it was a Europe that was undergoing relatively rapid change in this period, as demographic and economic growth was accompanied by transformations in cultural and religious life.

Yet these changes took place in a world that also exhibited profound structural continuities. Society was dominated by landed aristocrats. The French flavour of the English ruling elite in this period simply sharpened a stark class contrast that would have been present in any case. When contemporaries spoke as if society were divided into two clear-cut groups, knights (*milites*) and peasants (*rustici*), they certainly oversimplified, but the scheme did convey a basic reality—England was a peasant society dominated by a small number of military aristocrats. As in the neighbouring parts of Europe, the majority of the population were rural small-holders, working plots of land with the labour of their families, dependent for their subsistence primarily on the crops they could grow and the animals they could raise. Above them, living off the fruits of their labour, was a class of lords, some ecclesiastical but mostly lay, whose male members were trained in mounted combat.

Although the peasant labour that produced the food on which this society lived was its essential foundation, we actually know far less about farming and the lives of the rural lower classes than we do about politics and the lives of the upper classes. Literacy was limited and clerical observers wrote about what interested them—the affairs of the church or of great men. As we move

---

[4] *Dial. scacc.*, p. 53.

from the world of kings, bishops, and aristocrats, we move from the relatively well-documented to a cloudier sphere of guess and inference. Given the nature of the evidence, it makes sense to start this survey of England in the period 1075–1225 not with its foundations but with the story we can tell more fully—the doings of the powerful.

CHAPTER I

# Political Patterns

The first and fundamental issue in English politics was who should be king. In our period this question was invariably complicated by the fact that the king of England claimed also to be ruler of a large part of France. The struggle for the English succession and the politics of France are thus interwoven stories.

## 1. THE STRUGGLE FOR THE SUCCESSION 1075–1225

Between 1086, when Canute IV of Denmark was murdered while planning an invasion of England, and 1215, when rebellious English barons offered the throne to Louis, son of the king of France, there was no serious challenge to the rule of the lineage of William the Conqueror. The problem was, however, to decide which member of that line should be king (see Figure 1). Only twice in the period 1075–1225 did the English Crown pass from father to oldest surviving son: in 1189, when the famous fighter Richard 'the Lionheart' succeeded his father, Henry II, and in 1216, when Richard's brother John died in the midst of civil war, leaving the Crown to his infant son, Henry III. On three occasions the king left no surviving legitimate son: in 1100, when the childless William Rufus was struck by an arrow in the New Forest, in 1135, when the great autocrat, Henry I, died leaving as his only legitimate child his daughter, the Empress Matilda, and in 1199, when Richard I, like Rufus a century before, died from a bowshot with no direct heir. Twice there was an oldest son who did not inherit: in 1087, when the throne went to a younger son, Rufus, rather then the oldest, Robert, and in 1154, when a negotiated settlement transferred the throne from Stephen to Henry II, son of the Empress Matilda.

Collateral succession was thus far more usual in the history of the royal dynasty in this period than direct transmission of royal power from father to son. The contrast with the Capetians, who passed the French throne from father to son for over three centuries (996 to 1316) is striking, as also is that with later English medieval experience, which consisted of an unbroken

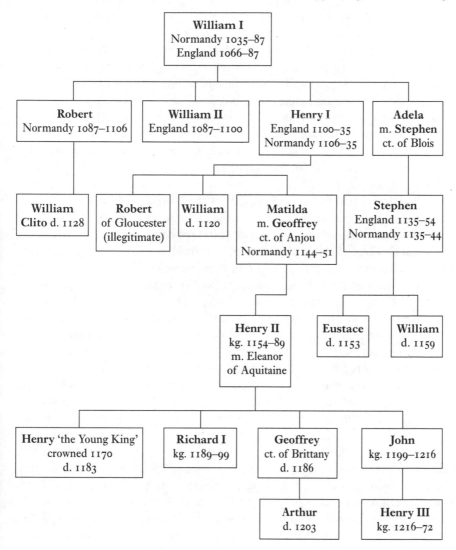

FIGURE 1. *Simplified family tree to illustrate the struggle for the succession under the Norman and Angevin kings*

chain of father–eldest son inheritance from 1216 to 1377. One consequence of the unsteady pattern of succession that prevailed in the late eleventh and twelfth centuries was frequent armed conflict between royal brothers, between uncle and nephew, and, in one solitary but devastating case (1139–53), between cousins. Hence, although there were no serious claims to the kingship from outside the lineage between 1086 and 1215, there was virtually no decade in that period which did not witness armed struggle between members of the ruling dynasty.

The English succession was so violent and unpredictable because high politics was dynastic politics, that is, the structure of political life at its highest level was the same as that of family life. The great crises and turning points of both were birth, marriage, and death. Sibling rivalry and intergenerational tensions within the ruling house determined such fundamental issues as the level of public order, the shape of aristocratic faction, and the pattern of international alliances. Success as a dynastic ruler thus rested in large part on successful family strategies. Since customary law and military requirements gave precedence to males rather than females, to secure his succession, a ruler had to father sons. Given the level of child mortality, it was prudent to father more than one. On the other hand, a batch of sons would prove troublesome to provide for and would probably quarrel, as the cases of William I's three surviving legitimate sons, or Henry II's four, demonstrate. As the sons grew up, they would flex their muscles. From their teens they would be leading armed men and exercising command and they might well come to fret at the limitations on their independence that their father created or symbolized. In this tense scene of father–son and brother–brother tension, mothers and stepmothers could throw their weight behind favoured candidates, act as mediators, or stir up trouble. Eventually the ruler would die, a son or other male heir emerge as successor, and then the cycle would recommence: the new ruler would have to placate or suppress his brothers, produce sons, and deal with them as they grew up. A successful king was one who ensured the longest gap between conflicts with his brothers and conflicts with his sons.

It was these family tensions that formed the basic pattern of political life in England in the period covered here. In a lineage with the family misfortune of the Norman and Angevin kings, a misfortune partly accidental (early deaths, childlessness), partly psychological (other royal families, like the Capetians, managed to restrain family conflict more effectively), and partly a simple consequence of having to deal with a cross-Channel dominion, then the central thread of political life was continually liable to be strained or snapped. William the Conqueror himself died while his eldest son, Robert, was in revolt against him. After Henry I had emerged victorious from his fraternal rivalry with William Rufus and Robert and had won the long war fought in northern France with Robert's son, William Clito (d. 1128), there was an insecure lull before the civil war of Stephen's reign—a particularly prolonged and vicious family feud, fought out, unusually, more on English than on French soil. The victor in that war, Henry II, cleared his brothers out of the way early and then had several years untroubled by family conflict while his children were still growing up. From 1173 to 1199, however, disputes within the Angevin family erupted continually and English political history was shaped by the recurrent clashes between Henry II and his sons and amongst his sons. The one survivor, John, then had to establish himself over the murdered body of his nephew. It is not entirely surprising that the clerical critic Gerald of Wales could describe the Norman and Angevin kings as 'princes who did not succeed one another in regular hereditary order but rather acquired violent domination through an inversion of order by killing and slaughtering their own.'[1]

In a world of dynastic politics, succession to the throne was obviously a fundamental and recurrent political problem. A ruler would die and everybody in the landed class and in the ecclesiastical hierarchy would be affected by the decision as to his successor. The beginning of a new reign was a time for changes, when both the dangers and the opportunities of political life were great. After Richard I succeeded in 1189, some of his father's ministers fell into disgrace. Stephen of Marsai, seneschal of Anjou under Henry II, was imprisoned and forced to pay 30,000 Angevin pounds, while Ranulf de Glanville, who had been chief justiciar for the previous decade and was so central a figure in the administration that he could be termed 'the governor of the kingdom and the eye of the king', was also disgraced and fleeced of 15,000 pounds of silver.[2] Waiting in the wings were men like William de Longchamps, who had served as Richard's chancellor when he was count of Poitou and now became chancellor of the kingdom.

The transitional period was a risky time: Henry I's swift coronation was excused on the grounds that otherwise 'the kingdom might have been disturbed'.[3] It was also the time when all sorts of individuals and communities—lords, monasteries, towns—would seek confirmation of rights and properties that they had possessed or claimed under the new king's predecessor. There was still very much a sense that the reigning king's word was a stronger guarantee than that of his predecessors, however strongly backed by written record or long possession. Hence the early days of the new reign would see a flurry of administrative activity. It has been calculated that something like a half of Henry II's charters date to the first two years of his reign, while over two-thirds of Richard's were issued in his first twelve months as king.[4]

Given the uncertain pattern of succession in the Norman and Angevin period, the question of the transmission of power was particularly acute and threw its shadow over large parts of every reign. When a king died leaving more than one legitimate son, as in the cases of William I, Henry II, and John,

---

[1] Gerald, *Prin.* 3. 30 (p. 320).
[2] *Gesta Hen. II* 2, p. 71; R. Howd. 3, p. 1; R. Devizes, pp. 4–5.          [3] Hugh Chanter, p. 18.
[4] Thomas K. Keefe, 'Place–Date Distribution of Royal Charters and the Historical Geography of Patronage Strategies at the Court of King Henry II Plantagenet', *Haskins Society Jnl* 2 (1990), pp. 179–88, at p. 181 and n. 8.

the central issue was which son was to be king and what was to be given to the other or others. The succession to John took place in quite exceptional circumstances, with a child heir, civil war, and foreign invasion, and necessity ensured there would be little debate, but neither of the two other instances resulted in uncontested settlements. William I's succession was not truly resolved until the death of William Clito, forty years after the Conqueror was buried, and within five years of Richard I's succession, his brother John was up in arms against him, albeit with limited success.

The succession to William I in 1087 was shaped not only by the need to satisfy or neutralize three active adult sons (Henry, the youngest, was almost 20), but by the peculiar circumstance of William's enormous conquest empire. There were two parts to his domains, Normandy and England, one acquired by inheritance, one by conquest, and they were divided by the sea. If there were to be a division, then the dividing line was relatively obvious, fraught though it might be with difficulties for the great magnates. On the other hand, it is not at all clear why there was a question of division. It was not a usual practice at this time either for west European kings or for the French princes. The chronicler William of Malmesbury, writing a generation later, was of the view that the Conqueror bequeathed Normandy to his eldest son, Robert, 'unwillingly and under pressure',[5] so it may be that William's intentions were not to divide his lands but to disinherit Robert completely and give everything to his second son, William, but that pressure from those around him on his deathbed forced him to relent and propose the compromise of division. In the division of 1087, Robert received Normandy, William England, and Henry 'treasure too great to be counted'.[6] Over the course of the next two decades conflict among the brothers was the main theme of political life in the Anglo-Norman realm. William gained temporary possession of Normandy in 1096, as a surety for money his brother Robert borrowed from him in order to go on crusade, but the king's death in a hunting accident in 1100 and the capture of Robert by Henry I at the battle of Tinchebray in 1106 brought the whole inheritance into the hands of the youngest son.

The next occasion on which a king died leaving more than one legitimate son was not until 1189, when Henry II died. Two of his four legitimate sons had predeceased him. During his lifetime he had made various proposals for dividing his territories, more than one of which had prompted violent opposition from sons who thought they were being ousted, and Henry indeed died while in the middle of a struggle with his oldest surviving son, Richard. As things turned out, Richard succeeded to the whole of his father's domains, though he made generous provision within them for his brother John. It was

---

[5] W. Malm., *GR* 3. 282 (2, p. 337); OMT edn., p. 510.
[6] *ASC*, p. 219, *s.a.* 1086 (*recte* 1087).

not until the time of Richard's captivity in Germany (1192–4) that John mustered his courage to attempt to oust his brother. The succession of 1189 was thus a very rare example in this period of the transmission of an undivided inheritance from father to son.

Even more fraught than the situation of a king's leaving more than one son was the case of a king's dying without a legitimate son. In two cases in our period (1100 and 1199) this occurrence was followed by swift seizure of the throne by a younger brother of the deceased king, though in both cases warfare followed with other claimants. The most difficult situation arose in 1135, when Henry I died leaving one legitimate daughter, Matilda, and no legitimate sons, though more bastards than any other English king. He had had bad luck. His first wife had borne him a son and a daughter before her own death in 1118, but the son, William, had drowned in the wreck of the White Ship in 1120. Henry had immediately remarried but, although both he and his new wife, Adeliza of Louvain, were fertile (she married again after his death and had children), their fourteen-year marriage was childless.

One noteworthy aspect of the succession to Henry I was that no serious consideration seems to have been given to his illegitimate sons, even though one of them, Robert of Gloucester, was respected, competent, and extremely wealthy.[7] A century earlier William the Conqueror, or William the Bastard as he was often called, had made his way to power despite this bar. In 1135, notwithstanding the excruciating dilemma of the death of a king without legitimate sons, the inheritance of a bastard seems to have been ruled out. This emphasis was already present in the arrangements over the succession made by William Rufus and Robert in 1091 and by Henry I and Robert in 1101, when it had been agreed that the surviving brother should be the heir of the other if he left no 'son by rightful marriage' or 'heir by rightful marriage'.[8] In other European kingdoms legitimacy was a less hardened concept and inheritance by sons who were not the children of a ruler by his wife was common. In contemporary Ireland and Wales sons of rulers by more than one mother, many of whom would have been deemed illegitimate by the canon law of the church, were convincing aspirants to regnal power. Perhaps an even closer parallel is to be found in the Norman kingdom of Sicily, where the illegitimate Tancred succeeded in 1190, in preference to his legitimate aunt Constance.

The objection to Matilda as heir of Henry I was partly that her second husband, Geoffrey, count of Anjou, was a traditional enemy of the Normans. Henry I had arranged the match in 1127 for immediate political ends—'to

---

[7] *Gesta Stephani* 6 (pp. 12–14), mentions a rumour that some urged Robert to seize the throne after his father's death.

[8] *ASC*, pp. 226, 237.

have peace with the count of Anjou and help against his nephew William [Clito]'.⁹ It was a deeply unpopular alliance. A marriage alliance between the Norman and Angevin dynasties was not in itself objectionable—Henry's son William, who died in 1120, had been married to the daughter of the count of Anjou—but this match between the female heir and the count himself would raise the prospect of the count of Anjou becoming virtual ruler of Normandy and England. An even stronger objection to Matilda, however, was that she was a woman. Queens regnant, ruling in their own right and not as consorts of kings, were unknown in western Europe prior to the twelfth century. The earliest was Urraca, queen of Leon and Castile, who reigned from 1109 to 1126, and would thus be known in Henry I's England. The lesson to be drawn from her troubled reign was not favourable to female rulership.

Although he had an elder brother who had to be squeezed out of the picture, Stephen of Blois had a plausible claim to the throne through heredity, being, along with that brother, one of the only legitimate, adult, male, lay descendants of William the Conqueror. It was swift and decisive action after the death of Henry I that secured that claim. If he had managed to rule as sure-footedly as he won the throne, the claims of Matilda might well have eventually been forgotten. As it was, with her powerful backers, her husband, the count of Anjou, her uncle, the king of Scots, and (eventually) Robert of Gloucester, she was able to wage a long war which, if she never won, she never lost. Her son Henry could inherit the Angevin tradition and aspiration, attaining such military superiority in England by 1153 that Stephen was forced to make peace, recognizing Henry as his heir and thus disinheriting his own son.

Although Henry of Anjou performed homage to Stephen as part of the 1153 settlement, as Henry II he never admitted the legitimacy of Stephen's reign. As late as the last few years of his life he was explaining how 'when through God's gift I attained the kingdom of England, I found that in the time of king Stephen my usurper [*ablatoris mei*] many things had been given away and alienated from the royal demesne'.¹⁰ His survey of knights' fees undertaken in 1166 carefully avoided any mention of his predecessor, asking of his barons how many knights they had at two points: firstly 'in the year and on the day that king Henry [I] was alive and dead' (i.e. in 1135) ('the old enfeoffment'), and, secondly, 'after the death of king Henry' ('the new enfeoffment'). Only one respondent was so bold or ill-informed as to list his knights 'of the new enfeoffment in the time of king Stephen'.¹¹ It became politic for Henry's subjects to refer to the late king's unhappy reign as 'the time of war'. This was a phrase used in the unctuous and grandiloquent response of the abbot of Tavistock to the inquest into knights' fees and similarly, in a charter

---

⁹ *ASC*, pp. 256–7.        ¹⁰ *Rec. actes Hen. II* 2, no. 682, p. 306.        ¹¹ *RBE* 1, p. 196.

of this same period, a grant is made of a tenement 'that was held by a certain Duva in the war' [*in guerra*].[12] The official view of the Angevin kings was that legitimate government ended in 1135 and was resumed in 1154.

The only occasion on which a minor succeeded to the throne was in 1216, when Henry III was crowned, on 28 October, at the age of 9. For the royalist opponents of Louis of France there was no other choice: Henry and his young brother Richard were the only surviving legitimate descendants of Henry II in the male line. A regency government was established, headed by the experienced and respected William Marshal, earl of Pembroke, and began the process of reconquering the country from Louis and the rebel barons. Within a year of Henry III's coronation, Louis had withdrawn and the royal government began to re-establish its routines and its rights. The king was declared of age for certain limited purposes in 1223 and unreservedly in 1227. The conventional medieval wisdom was, in the words of Ecclesiastes (10: 16), 'Woe to the land where the king is a child!' but this period of government by aristocratic and ecclesiastical committee compares well with the personal rule of many adult kings.

## 2. THE CROSS-CHANNEL REALM

The year 1066 marked the beginning of a long period in which the king of England was also ruler of a substantial territory in France. This fact was to have the profoundest consequences for English politics down to the age of the Tudors. In the period under discussion there are three distinct phases in the history of this connection. First, from 1066 to the 1140s, is the period when there was an Anglo-Norman realm and an Anglo-Norman baronage. It was a realm fought over by rival members of the ruling dynasty and a baronage often with divided loyalties, but it was nonetheless a political entity conceived of as fundamentally one, and one ruled by Frenchmen. After 1154 the accession of the Angevin, Henry II, changed the pattern. He not only inherited Anjou and its subordinate territories but had also acquired control of Aquitaine, the vast duchy extending over south-west France, by his marriage to Eleanor of Aquitaine. In consequence England was now part of a congeries of lordships that stretched from the Pyrenees to Scotland. A king such as Richard I spent far more of his life in Aquitaine than in England. Finally, the third phase involved the collapse of this extensive cross-Channel power in the face of the offensive of Philip Augustus of France. Rouen, chief city of Normandy, fell in 1204, and after that date the French lordships of the English kings consisted only of the territories south of the Loire that they could save from conquest, territories eventually to be centred around Bordeaux in the south-west.

[12] *RBE* 1, p. 251 (cf. pp. 351, 368, 369, 392, 401, 408, 409); *Danelaw Docs.*, no. 306, p. 230.

The three periods, that of the Anglo-Norman realm, the Angevin empire, and the collapse of the early thirteenth century, are markedly different, but all entailed the most intimate and continuous involvement of English kings with the politics of the French principalities. The priorities of the rulers being dynastic, they did not conceive of 'the interests of England' separate from those of their own, and they conceived of their own interests as being as closely tied up with their fortunes in France as with their position in England. Before becoming king of England William I had been duke of Normandy for thirty years and he had the instincts and priorities of a French feudal prince. Political and military life meant the constant manoeuvring for advantage in a competitive world of dukes and counts, with a king no more powerful than they. It meant the capture of territory by castle-building, the wooing of allies by gifts of lands or high-born wives, the readiness to use devastation, imprisonment, or intimidation to win one's way. A hundred years after William I's death none of this had changed. Richard I was, as well as king of England, a great French prince involved in just such a political and military world as his great-great-grandfather had inhabited.

Naturally, all the kings of England in this period spent considerable time in France. William the Conqueror was probably in Normandy for well over half of his reign (1066–87) and while his sons, William Rufus and Henry I, did not possess Normandy in their early years, once they had they acquired it—in 1096 (as a mortgage) and 1106, respectively—this is true of them too. It has been calculated that in the years 1106–35 Henry I spent 60 per cent of his time in Normandy.[13] Stephen was an exception, since after one visit as king in 1137, he never returned to the duchy, which was overrun by the Angevins, but the French involvement re-emerged and even intensified with Henry II and Richard I. Over the whole course of his reign, Henry II spent more than 60 per cent of his time in France, the balance of royal activity thus being even more firmly south of the Channel than in his grandfather's day. His son Richard, although born in Oxford, concentrated his activities and found his identity in France, especially in his mother's duchy of Aquitaine. While both Henry I and Henry II had spent continuous periods of as much as four and a half years away from England (1116–20 and 1158–63), Richard notoriously outdid them, passing a mere six months of his reign in the country that gave him his royal title. His successor John, like Stephen, was beaten out of his domains in northern France. After the great conquests of Philip Augustus, which culminated in the fall of Rouen in 1204, John's only visits to France consisted of his two military expeditions to Poitou, in 1206 and 1214, although both were relatively lengthy, lasting over six months in each case.

---

[13]  Le Patourel, *Norman Empire*, p. 330 n. 4.

The pattern is obvious. The only kings of England to spend prolonged periods in England were the military failures. Any of the Norman and Angevin rulers who were able to do so spent more time in France than England. This was probably partly policy and partly taste. They needed to control their rich, extensive, and often troublesome French lands and personal presence was essential. They also may have felt more at home in France than in England, although this is difficult to demonstrate. Both Henry I and Richard I were born in England, but they do not seem to have regarded it as their natural abode. King John was the first king after the Conquest both to be born in England and to die there.

## The Cross-Channel Aristocracy

The Norman Conquest and the subsequent distribution of English lands to the followers of William the Conqueror created not only an entirely new political situation but a new class—the cross-Channel aristocracy. Throughout the Norman and Angevin period their needs, fears, and ambitions were fundamental in shaping the character of elite life. Almost all the greater aristocratic dynasties had estates in both England and Normandy. The twelfth-century earls of Chester were also *vicomtes* of Avranches—one of the charters of Hugh, earl of Chester, is addressed to his barons and officials 'both this side of the sea and beyond the sea'.[14] The earls of Leicester were lords of the great estate of Breteuil, where they enfeoffed more than eighty knights, and other Norman lands.[15] At a level just below such magnates were barons like the Mohuns, who took their name from Moyon near St-Lô in western Normandy. After the Norman Conquest William de Mohun was given large estates in Somerset and adjoining counties, building his castle at Dunster, and his descendants continued to hold estates on both sides of the Channel. In the reign of Henry II another William de Mohun, probably grandson of the builder of Dunster castle, is recorded as owing 5 knights' service in Normandy and 46½ in England. The family monastery at Bruton in Somerset was granted churches in Normandy, at Moyon and other places under Mohun lordship. This substantial cross-Channel baronial estate was only broken into two during Philip Augustus's conquest of Normandy in 1204, when the triumphant French king granted Moyon to his new Norman seneschal. Until that time, Mohun charters addressed to all their men 'French and English' were using no empty formula.[16]

[14] *Chester Charters*, no. 141, pp. 149–50.   [15] *RBE* 2, p. 627.

[16] G. E. C(okayne), *The Complete Peerage* (rev. edn., 12 vols.; London, 1910–59), vol. 9, pp. 17–19; *DB* 1, 95b (Som. 25. 2); *RBE* 1, pp. 226–7; 2, p. 629; Keefe, *Assessments*, pp. 178, 257 n. 107; *CDF*, nos. 486–505, pp. 172–8; *Two Cartularies of the Augustinian Priory of Bruton and the Cluniac Priory of Montacute* (Somerset Rec. Soc. 8; 1894), nos. 393–7, 420–1, pp. 107–8, 112; *Recueil des actes de Philippe Auguste*, ed. H.-F. Delaborde *et al.* (4 vols. to date; Paris, 1916– ), vol. 2, no. 793, pp. 371–2.

Cross-Channel estates were not limited to holdings in England and Normandy. A few lords held not only English and Norman lands, but also properties in France beyond the Norman frontier. A notable example is provided by the counts of Meulan, who took their title from the town and castle on the Seine between Rouen and Paris. For this, they were vassals of the kings of France, but they were also vassals of the kings of England and dukes of Normandy for lands in England and Normandy. Moreover, the expansion of the Anglo-Norman aristocracy into Scotland, Wales, and Ireland, discussed below, created a yet wider sphere of activity. The great William Marshal, earl of Pembroke (d. 1219), had an estate that comprised lands in Normandy, England, Wales, and Ireland. He could, if he wished, journey from his Norman castles of Longueville and Orbec, across the English Channel to his castles of Hamstead Marshall in Berkshire, Chepstow, and Pembroke, and then across the Irish Sea to Kilkenny, centre of his lordship of Leinster.

The conquest of England in 1066 thus opened up a huge new source of patronage for the Norman aristocracy, but there were problems as well as benefits in having lands on both sides of the Channel. Absenteeism was unavoidable, with all its consequences. The management of English and French lands would require duplicate administrations. Maritime transport had to be organized. Lords who made arrangements for their burial had to plan for the eventuality of dying either in England or Normandy.[17] One unusual, but sensitive, issue is revealed in a letter of the canonist Ivo of Chartres. It contains advice to a French noble who was worrying about the paternity of his child born, as Ivo says, 'while you were spending time in England'.[18] Several Norman barons are indeed recorded as abandoning their English fiefs and returning to Normandy, for fear of what their 'lascivious wives' might be doing in their absence.[19]

Cuckoldry was not the only anxiety induced by the cross-Channel condition. Political separation of England and Normandy, which occurred in 1087–96, 1100–6, 1141–54, and finally from 1204, presented the aristocratic families who held lands on both sides of the Channel with a dangerous situation. To avoid losing either their English estates or their Norman ones, they could try to serve two lords—if their lords would have it—or they might resign themselves to the situation and allot the English lands to one branch of the family and the Norman to another. Alternatively, they might attempt to engineer a restoration of unity, for those who held lands on both sides of the Channel naturally developed pronounced 'unionist' views, trying to secure, in the words of the chronicler Orderic Vitalis, 'the union of the two realms' (*unitas utriusque regni*).[20] The recurrent succession disputes that

---

[17] e.g. *Abingdon Chron.* 2, pp. 124, 168.    [18] Ivo of Chartres, ep. 205 (*PL* 162, col. 210).
[19] Orderic 4 (2, pp. 218–20).    [20] Orderic 8. 2 (4, p. 124).

characterized English political history in this period thus galvanized this group into swift, if not always unanimous, action. When a group of nobles in Normandy was about to support the candidacy of Theobald of Blois for the English throne in 1135, they immediately abandoned him on hearing that his brother Stephen had already been crowned, deciding 'to serve one lord, on account of the great estates that the barons possessed in each region'.[21]

Both the durability and the vulnerability of cross-Channel estates are demonstrated by the story of Pevensey and the fortunes of the family that possessed it longest, the Laigles.[22] Pevensey had been one of the many prizes that came to Robert, count of Mortain, half-brother of William the Conqueror, in the aftermath of the Norman conquest. It was lost by his son in 1106 when Henry I dispossessed the supporters of his brother Robert after the battle of Tinchebray. Henry gave it to a dependable follower, Gilbert de Laigle, member of a family that took its name from a castle in southern Normandy on the river Risle. The castle had been built by Fulbert, the ancestor of the Laigles, in the first half of the eleventh century and been christened from the nest of an eagle (*l'aigle*) found during construction. Fulbert's descendants had earned some reward from the dukes of Normandy, their lords, for Fulbert's son Engenulf had been killed at the battle of Hastings and his grandson Richer died fighting for William the Conqueror in Maine about 1084.

After the death of Gilbert de Laigle, recipient of Henry I's gift of Pevensey, his son, another Richer, was eventually able to gain possession of his father's lands from the king, even though his record of loyalty was imperfect, and he held Pevensey until the start of the civil war in England under Stephen. Then, at some point in the 1140s, Pevensey was acquired by earl Gilbert fitz Richard of the house of Clare. Although he was a supporter of Stephen, and presumably received Richer's lands because of that support, earl Richard fell out with the king and, in 1147, was besieged by him in Pevensey castle. After the fall of the castle, Stephen granted the lands first to his own older son, Eustace, then to his younger son, William, whose rights were explicitly recognized in the treaty of 1153 between Stephen and Henry of Anjou.

Richer de Laigle did not abandon his claims, however, and, after the death of Stephen's son was eventually able to regain Pevensey and its appurtenant estates from Henry II. In 1166, during the great inquest into knight service, he duly filed a record of the knights he had enfeoffed upon his lands in Sussex and elsewhere when he had acquired them in the days of Henry I.[23]

---

[21] Orderic 13. 20 (6, p. 454).

[22] Sanders, *Baronies*, pp. 136–7; Orderic 3; 4; 7. 10; 12. 1, 4, 26; 13. 30, 44 (2, pp. 176, 356; 4, pp. 48–50; 6, pp. 188, 196–8, 298–300, 484, 546–8); Kathleen Thompson, 'The Lords of Laigle: Ambition and Insecurity on the Borders of Normandy', *ANS* 18 (1995), pp. 177–99.

[23] *RBE* 1, pp. 203–4.

Richer died in 1176 and was eventually succeeded by a grandson, Gilbert (II) de Laigle. This Gilbert's lifetime saw the annexation of Normandy by Philip II of France and the consequent dissolution of the political connection between Normandy and England. Gilbert rode out the storm but not without uncomfortable moments. The crisis of 1204, when Philip's armies seized Normandy, made a choice between lords unavoidable, at least for the time being. In September 1203, Gilbert is recorded in king John's service in France, but in September 1204 his English lands were seized into the king's hands because he had withdrawn from the king's service and the sheriff of Sussex was ordered to draw up an inventory of his chattels and stock.[24]

The Laigle family were luckier than most holders of cross-Channel estates. If, in 1204, it was not possible to hold Pevensey from the king of England and Laigle from the king of France, the situation changed as the opposition to John within England grew stronger and his need for friends greater. While, in 1214, the Laigle estates in England were still in the hands of the earl Warenne, to whom John had granted them, by 1216 the king could write that he 'had restored his rights to Gilbert de Laigle some time ago'.[25] This restoration did not, in the event, stop Gilbert joining the rebellion against John, but the regency government that took over after John's death was willing to be placatory. They wrote to Gilbert in December 1216 commanding him to return to his allegiance and promising that, if he did so, he would be restored to all the lands that he held before the civil war. Pevensey receives a special mention in this letter and it is clear that the regents were determined to keep the castle from falling into the hands of Louis of France, who had invaded at the rebels' request. When the war is over, the letter states, 'we will show you full justice regarding that castle'.[26] Gilbert de Laigle did indeed eventually recover Pevensey and enjoyed his large cross-Channel estates until his death, without heirs, in 1231.[27]

It is easy to see how the vicissitudes of the Pevensey estate and the Laigle family are intertwined with two other complicated stories: the struggle over the succession to the throne of England and the repeated union and separation of England and Normandy. The counts of Mortain acquired the castle and its lands as a consequence of the conquest of 1066, they lost it as a result of the 'reverse conquest' of 1106, when Henry I invaded Normandy and destroyed his brother's power there. The civil war of the 1140s saw Pevensey taken from the Laigles to be given by Stephen to one of his supporters, then taken away again for the benefit of the king's own son. After the restoration of the cross-Channel realm under Henry II, the Laigles once more enjoyed

---

[24] *Rot. litt. pat.*, p. 34; *Rot. litt. claus.* 1, pp. 9, 10, 14.

[25] PR 16 John, pp. 37, 166–7; *Rot. litt. pat.*, p. 196.      [26] *Pat. Rolls HIII* 1, p. 17.

[27] For evidence of his activities in France, see *Cartulaire Normand de Philippe Auguste, etc.*, ed. L. Delisle (Caen, 1852), nos. 206, 366, pp. 32, 57.

their cross-Channel estate. The crisis of 1204 again severed the connection. Just as Henry I's conquest of Normandy in 1106 brought Pevensey to the Laigle family, so Philip Augustus's conquest a century later meant that they lost it, as least for a decade or so.

The geography of the Laigle estates mirrored that of the Norman and Angevin realm. We can see family members crossing backwards and forwards from Normandy to England. In 1111 Gilbert de Laigle witnessed a charter of Henry I at Portsmouth 'before the crossing' (*in transitu*), and in 1140 Richer de Laigle was captured by enemies at Lire in Normandy after 'he had set out peacefully for England with fifty knights'.[28] When in London, Richer lodged with Thomas Becket's parents, who came from the Risle valley, and he took the young man hawking on his country estates.[29] A lawsuit involving Gilbert II de Laigle in 1201 turned on the question 'whether or not Gilbert was in England' at the time of the alleged offence.[30] Even at the end of his life, Gilbert was crossing and recrossing the Channel just as his forebears had done. In 1226 he was granted royal licence to travel to and fro from England to Normandy. In 1230 he was with Henry III in France, the following year in the royal army in Wales.[31] For aristocrats of his standing, Britain and northern France formed one extended theatre of action.

## English Kings and French Politics

If 1066 had created a new situation for the Norman aristocracy, it had an equally fundamental effect on the political geography of western Europe: the man who was anointed king of England in that year was already a great French duke. The potential difficulty of a king of one country being a subordinate to a king in another was in practice not so great, given the very high degree of autonomy enjoyed by the dukes and counts of eleventh-century France. Although there was theoretical recognition that there was a 'kingdom of the French' with a crowned and anointed 'king of the French', this was a period when real political and military power was in the hands of the great princes. The Capetian kings were simply players in the game—and not the ones with the best hand. Capetian power was limited to the royal domain centred on the Ile-de-France. The dukes of Normandy minted their own coins, appointed the Norman bishops, and held supreme jurisdictional authority within their duchy. Although they were vassals of the king of France, their practical obligations to their overlord were slight.

The Capetian kings were thus simply one set of rulers with whom the

---

[28] *RRAN* 2, no. 988, pp. 101–2; Orderic 13. 44 (6, pp. 546–8).
[29] Edward Grim, *V. sancti Thomae* 8 (*Becket Mats.* 2, pp. 359–60).    [30] *CRR* 1, p. 460.
[31] *Pat. Rolls HIII* 2, pp. 95–6, 361; *Close Rolls of the Reign of Henry III: 1227–31* (London, 1902), pp. 351, 544.

Norman dukes had to deal in their north French milieu. As important were the other princes with whom they might compete or ally: the counts of Flanders, Blois, Anjou, and Brittany. The vigorous Angevin dynasty, expanding its power on the lower Loire, was a particularly dangerous rival. When the counts of Anjou allied with the Capetian kings against Normandy, as they frequently did in the time of the Norman kings, the situation often became dangerous, especially since they could usually count on the support of rebels within the duchy and dissident members of the Norman dynasty. To counteract this threat, William I and his sons allied with the house of Blois, made periodic attempts to come to terms with Anjou, negotiated intermittently with Flanders and, most important of all, undertook constant, vigorous campaigning.

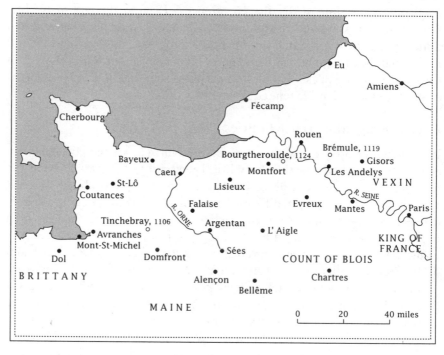

MAP 1. *Normandy and environs*

Normandy had no natural geographical frontiers. The rolling country and woodland of the duchy merged into the rolling country and woodland of its neighbours. To the west lay Brittany, a region which had not felt the hand of a dynasty with the centralizing ambitions and abilities of the Normans or Angevins and was hence the setting of a political life of great complexity and division. The Norman dukes tried to exercise overlordship there, but a more important connection with Breton affairs was provided indirectly through the existence of a section of the Breton aristocracy who participated in the Norman Conquest of England and were rewarded with English lands. A junior branch of the Breton ducal line was given huge estates in the north of England, centred on the great stone castle of Richmond, and eventually, in 1136, received the title of 'earl of Richmond'. The Bretons probably formed the second largest group among the conquest aristocracy. These Anglo-Breton lords encountered the same opportunities and dilemmas that faced the Anglo-Norman cross-Channel aristocracy.

The rebellion of 1075 against William the Conqueror provides a good example of the link that now existed between English and Breton affairs. The plot involved Roger, the Norman earl of Hereford, and Waltheof, the last surviving English earl, as well as allies from Denmark, but its main participants were Bretons, headed by Ralph de Gael, who was both earl of East Anglia and lord of Gael in Brittany. After his confederates in England had been captured and his castle of Norwich taken, Ralph continued resistance from Brittany. Joining forces with other dissident Breton nobles, he stationed himself in the castle of Dol, a mere ten miles from the Norman frontier. William I obviously had to deal with this threat and in 1077 he undertook a siege of Dol. He was unsuccessful. The defenders held out until king Philip of France could come to their assistance and 'then William retreated, losing men and horses and much of his treasure'.[32] The network of property and power spanned the Channel and a touch on the web in Norfolk or Paris could set it vibrating on the borders of Brittany.

Adjoining Brittany to the east lay Maine, chief theatre of Norman–Angevin conflict. Here the expanding spheres of the dukes of Normandy and counts of Anjou met. William the Conqueror had taken control of Maine in the early 1060s, placing it under his son Robert, although with a formal recognition of Angevin overlordship. William had to fight to keep Maine, but he managed to do so. Robert was less effective and in 1090 the barons of Maine 'threw off the Norman yoke' and soon re-established a native dynasty.[33] Elias de la Flèche ruled as count of Maine from 1092 to 1110, with a brief intermission when William Rufus occupied the county in 1098–1100. Although Elias gave valuable help to Henry I at the decisive battle of Tinchebray, he married his daughter and heir to the heir of Anjou, thus ensuring that on his death in 1110 Maine became part of the Angevin dominions. The best that Henry I could do was to win recognition that the counts of Anjou held Maine as vassals of the dukes of Normandy, a curious reversal of the situation established in the 1060s. From 1110, however, the county was clearly part of the 'Greater Anjou' made up of Anjou proper, Maine, and Touraine.

---

[32] *ASC*, p. 213 (E text), *s.a.* 1076 (*recte* 1077).    [33] Orderic 8. 11 (4, p. 192).

Just as Maine was a contested territory between the expansionist powers of Normandy and Anjou, so, on a smaller scale, was the Vexin between Normandy and the Capetian domains in the Ile-de-France. The contest here was, if anything, fiercer, for Rouen was only seventy miles downstream from Paris and control of the Vexin would bring the victor within easy reach of their rival's chief town. In the tenth century the Vexin had been split into the eastern (French) Vexin and western (Norman) Vexin, the latter forming part of the duchy of Normandy and the former with its own line of counts. When this line came to an end in 1077, the Capetian kings immediately annexed their lands. The region was critically important in the struggles between the Norman rulers and the Capetian kings. William I died from an injury sustained during his sack of Mantes in the French Vexin and his son, William Rufus, invaded the French Vexin in 1097 and 1098, while he was holding the duchy of Normandy in pawn.

The history of the wars and alliances of Henry I shows how French feudal politics had to be the central preoccupation of the kings of England in this period. Within twelve months of his coronation, Henry faced an invasion launched from France, as his brother Robert attempted to make himself ruler of the whole of the Anglo-Norman realm. A compromise was agreed in the Treaty of Alton of 1101, but did not last. Henry began the conquest of Normandy in 1105 and defeated and captured Robert at Tinchebray in 1106. He had to fight to retain the duchy. Louis VI, who succeeded to the French throne in 1108 was a vigorous fighter, eager to press his claims in the Vexin and willing to stir up opposition to Henry within Normandy. After 1110, when the counts of Anjou occupied Maine, these powerful princes had a long common border with Normandy. The biggest peril arose from an alliance of the Angevins, Capetians, and Flemings, threatening Normandy from three sides. Although Henry made treaties with the counts of Flanders in 1101 and 1110, they joined Louis VI against him in the warfare that took place in 1111–13 and 1116–20. Count Baldwin VII was indeed mortally wounded during an attack on Normandy in 1118. Henry proved able to win over or defeat his opponents. In 1119 he arranged a marriage alliance with the Angevins and, after routing Louis VI at the battle of Brémule, forced him too to accept peace. When, in the following year, the French king accepted the homage of Henry's son and heir, William, for Normandy, it looked as if a stable political situation might have been reached.

The drowning of the young prince in the wreck of the White Ship in that very year instantly transformed Henry's position. His nephew, William Clito, son of his captive brother, Robert, now seemed a much more serious competitor. Louis VI had already backed the young exile prior to 1120, but after the death of Henry's son it was easier to muster widespread support for him. Within a few years 'the storm of war arose again' and a coalition of forces

formed against Henry.[34] Among his opponents were not only the king of
France and count of Anjou but also Norman magnates such as Waleran, the
young count of Meulan, who had lands in both the duchy and the French
Vexin, and Hugh de Montfort, an important baron in central Normandy and
Waleran's brother-in-law. Hostilities began in 1123, when Henry besieged
the castles of the rebels in Normandy. Then, in 1124, his household troops
encountered the Norman rebels and their French allies at Bourgtheroulde,
fifteen miles south-west of Rouen. The rebels tried a cavalry charge but the
royalist archers shot them down before they could come to close quarters.
Waleran of Meulan and Hugh de Montfort were captured, along with many
of their vassals and followers, some of whom Henry blinded.

Henry's position was more secure in the aftermath of his victory, but in
1127 a new threat emerged, when king Louis granted William Clito the
county of Flanders. Henry responded by negotiating a marriage alliance with
Geoffrey of Anjou, who wed Henry's daughter, Matilda, and by taking the
war into France, where, in summer 1128, he camped for a week at Epernon,
between Paris and Chartres, 'as securely as if he were in his own kingdom'.[35]
William Clito was killed fighting in Flanders in that same year and his death
removed one of Henry's greatest dangers, but towards the end of his life
quarrels with his new son-in-law, Geoffrey of Anjou, began. Geoffrey allied
himself with dissident Norman barons. Among Henry's last acts were the
confiscation of rebel lands and the strengthening of strategic castles. Although he was one of the most ruthless and successful rulers of his time,
Henry I never had quiet days to enjoy his power. The perpetual turmoil of
French politics gave him a life of anxious striving.

## The Angevin Empire

Despite the relentless activity of his reign, Henry I was not able to rule from the
grave. His plans for the succession were disregarded immediately, by a man
who had benefited enormously from his patronage and who had been among
the first of his barons to swear to recognize Henry's daughter as his heir. In
1127 and again in 1131 the troubled king had insisted that all his great men take
such an oath, but within three weeks of Henry's death, Stephen of Blois had
been crowned in his place. The first big political question was whether
Normandy, as well as England, would acknowledge him. It was a question
made acute by the fact that Matilda, the jilted heiress, was married to the count
of Anjou, that ancient enemy and powerful neighbour of the Normans.

As soon as Henry I died, Geoffrey of Anjou began nibbling at Normandy.
He occupied Domfront and Argentan in the south-west of the duchy and

[34] Orderic 12. 33 (6, p. 328).        [35] H. Hunt. 7. 38 (p. 478).

allied himself with old Norman enemies of king Henry, like William Talvas of the border dynasty of Bellême. In 1136 he invaded again, reaching Lisieux, less than twenty miles from the Channel coast. Stephen at first left the defence of the duchy in the hands of one of his chief supporters, Waleran of Meulan, but in 1137 he undertook an expedition in person. It was a decisive episode and one that ruined Stephen's prospects for good. His army disintegrated around him, as his lukewarm Norman followers quarrelled with his Flemish mercenaries, and he was forced to conclude a truce with Geoffrey of Anjou, promising him also an annual payment. Stephen left Normandy in December 1137 and never returned.

The year after Stephen's departure Geoffrey of Anjou allied with earl Robert of Gloucester, who now formally withdrew his allegiance to Stephen, and this enabled the count to establish a much stronger position in western Normandy. His final triumph in the duchy did not come until some years later, however, when Stephen's capture at the battle of Lincoln in 1141 convinced many of his Norman supporters that it was hopeless to continue to back him. From 1141 to 1144 count Geoffrey systematically completed his occupation of Normandy, entering Rouen in the latter year and even receiving formal recognition of his possession from Louis VI of France. The unity of the cross-Channel realm was once again broken.

The Angevin conquest of Normandy in 1141–4 could, of course, have resulted in the permanent separation of Normandy and England rather than their union. This was not to be the case because Henry, son of Geoffrey of Anjou and Matilda, born in Le Mans, was determined to obtain his whole inheritance as he saw it. Granted Normandy by his father in 1150 and formally invested with it by the king of France in 1151, he asserted his rights as heir to the throne of England in 1153 and was crowned king the following year. His marriage to Eleanor of Aquitaine in 1152 brought control over her extensive lands in southern France. From 1154 a new political situation thus prevailed, in which Anjou and Aquitaine were added to Normandy as possessions of the man who was also king of England. Henry II had authority over half the kingdom of the French and quite eclipsed his nominal suzerain, the king of France, in wealth, territory, and power. The territorial realignment of the years 1150–4 was one of the most sudden and far-reaching ever to affect the political map of twelfth-century Europe. Normandy, Anjou, and Aquitaine, which had previously been separate, and very often competing, principalities, were now under the rule of one man. The French territories that acknowledged the overlordship of Henry II and his sons were vast, ranging from Eu in the north to Bayonne in the south, a distance of about 500 miles—roughly the length of Britain. After Henry betrothed his son Geoffrey to the heiress of Brittany and received the homage of the Breton barons in 1166, his lordship there was far more direct that any exercised by his Norman predecessors. The count of Toulouse did homage to him in 1173 and this brought the king's technical suzerainty to the shores of the Mediterranean.

This 'Angevin empire', as it is sometimes called, had no precedent and its rulers exercised power on a stage quite different from that trodden by the Anglo-Norman duke-kings. The presence of Aquitaine, in particular, with its huge distances, unruly aristocracy, and ties with the Mediterranean world and the Iberian peninsula, made the political history of the Angevin period different from that of the Norman epoch. As early in his reign as 1159 Henry II was before the walls of Toulouse in arms; his son Richard married a princess from Navarre; and, albeit perhaps fortuitously, it was to be ties between Bordeaux and the English Crown that were the longest lasting heritage of the Angevin empire. When the forces of Henry VI were expelled from Gascony in 1453, a link was broken that had lasted almost exactly 300 years.

However, the Angevin and Aquitainian territories of Henry II and his sons never became enmeshed with England in the way that Normandy was. There was no Anglo-Angevin aristocracy like the Anglo-Norman aristocracy. Although officials and courtiers might occasionally have careers and property that took them from the Loire to the Thames, they were isolated examples, not a class. The Angevin religious houses did not receive the lavish grants of English lands and revenues that the Norman monasteries had enjoyed after 1066. Moreover, the Angevin kings themselves seem to have adapted to the demands of the Anglo-Norman structure. Henry II, although he was born and died in Greater Anjou, spent only one-fifth of his reign in the Angevin and Aquitainian lands, while John, in the few years of his reign before Normandy fell, was in Anjou and Poitou for about 30 per cent of the time. Anjou was the homeland of the Angevins, but England gave them their title and wealth and Normandy was the hinge that joined the whole together.

The territorial conglomerate created in the early 1150s was to be one of the dominant features of the political landscape for the next fifty years and its eventual fate was the central issue for both the Angevin and the Capetian dynasties. For the Capetian kings of France this accumulation of territories under the Angevins was not primarily a threat to their existing position but rather a large and potentially permanent obstacle to their ever doing anything to improve it. If the lower reaches of both the Seine and the Loire were held by Henry II and his sons, there could be no expansion downstream from the Ile-de-France.

Under Louis VII (1137–80) the Capetians nibbled and probed but there was no major confrontation with the Angevins except in the exceptional crisis of 1173–4, when the French king led an alliance of Henry's enemies in a short siege of Rouen. The more usual pattern was that exemplified by the year 1167. In April of that year Henry II led an army into Auvergne and

devastated the lands of William, count of Auvergne, who had promised to
come to Henry II's court to settle a dispute with his nephew but had then
'gone off to the king of France and sowed discord between them'. Louis and
Henry met at Gisors, on the borders of Normandy and the Ile, on 4 June, to
discuss this and other disputed matters, but no agreement was reached. Both
kings gathered troops and fortified their castles. Louis burned some Norman
villages between Mantes and Pacy, Henry responded by sending his Welsh
soldiers to burn the castle of Chaumont-sur-Epte, where the French king had
concentrated his stores and supplies, and Louis then burned Gasny and the
town of Les Andelys. A truce was agreed in August, to last until the following
Easter. Henry then went off to Brittany to subdue local opposition there.[36]
This is the very stuff of Angevin–Capetian relations: local, spasmodic hostilities, consisting mainly in the devastation of towns, villages, and castles on the
borders, and punctuated by repeated truces; the endless potential for vassals
to appeal to one king over the head of the other; the endless task of enforcing
one's lordship. The only distinctive feature of the confrontations of 1167 is
king Arthur's supposed intervention on behalf of the Bretons.[37]

The accession of Philip II ('Augustus') to the throne of France in 1180
marked a change in the fortunes of the French monarchy and, in particular,
in the balance of power between the Capetians and their Angevin rivals. This
was not revealed immediately, but indications were already present in the
1180s and a spectacular crescendo was reached in the early years of the thirteenth century, with Philip's conquest of Normandy in 1204 and his celebrated victory at Bouvines in 1214, when king John had the ignominy of
being amongst the defeated without even the dignity of being present at the
decisive battle. As so often, tensions within the Angevin dynasty gave the
Capetians a lever. Just as his father, Louis VII, had been most successful when
allied with Henry's sons against their father, in 1173–4, so Philip wooed the
old king's impatient brood. In 1183 he gave secret aid to Henry 'the Young
King', the oldest son of Henry II, in his quarrels with his father, and he
courted Geoffrey of Brittany, the third son, with such apparent sincerity
that, when Geoffrey died and was buried at Paris in 1186, the French king
had supposedly to be restrained from throwing himself into the grave too. He
achieved his greatest results in 1189, by winning over Henry's eldest surviving son and presumed heir, Richard. Together the Capetian king and the
Angevin prince pursued the disheartened Henry II across the heartlands of
his dominions, burning his birthplace, Le Mans, capturing the strategic city
of Tours and forcing Henry to submit fully to their demands. Henry returned
to his castle of Chinon, muttered 'Woe, woe, on a vanquished king!' and died.

---

[36] R. Torigni, pp. 229–32.
[37] S. Rouen, *Draco* 2. 17–22, lines 941–1282 (pp. 695–707).

The death of Henry II meant, of course, the immediate dissolution of the alliance between Richard and Philip Augustus. A disgruntled and restless heir was one thing, ruler of the Angevin domains another. Successor to all his father's lands, Richard I proved a capable defender of them. The early years of his reign were dominated by the Third Crusade, in which he participated along with Philip Augustus, with whom he constantly quarrelled. Philip returned early, in 1191, but Richard stayed another year in the East and then, during the course of his return journey, was taken prisoner by another adversary, the duke of Austria. When the news of his captivity reached France and England early in 1193, Philip realized he had, temporarily at least, a free hand. Not only this, but he found a willing ally within the Angevin dynasty, John, Richard's younger brother. While Philip's troops occupied the Norman Vexin and pressed Rouen hard, John agreed to surrender eastern Normandy and the Touraine to the French king in return for the rest of Normandy, Anjou, and Aquitaine.

Richard was caged but he was not dead. Despite the efforts of Philip Augustus and John to ensure that he was kept imprisoned, arrangements were made for his ransom and, after a brief visit to England, he arrived in Normandy in May, 1194. For the next five years, until his death from a crossbow bolt in April, 1199, Richard was continuously in France and almost as continuously at war. He was a spectacular leader and a clever general. At Fréteval in 1194 he routed the French under Philip himself. His brother John, quickly cowed, served him with a nervous devotion. Yet there were territories that he never regained from the Capetian king. Most of the Vexin, including its fortress of Gisors, remained in Philip's possession. Richard raised the great castle of Château Gaillard at Les Andelys as a substitute, but this was one step closer to Rouen. Even with a soldier like Richard as its head, the Angevin empire was feeling the cold wind of Capetian pressure.

## The Loss of the Northern French Territories

'Normandy, once safe beneath king Richard's shield, but undefended now . . .'[38] So the English poet Geoffrey de Vinsauf registered the critical change of 1199, with Richard's death and his replacement by a king far inferior as a general and military leader. Moreover, John's succession was contested. His nephew Arthur, son of his deceased elder brother, Geoffrey, was recognized not only in his inherited duchy of Brittany but also by most of the barons of Anjou. Philip Augustus, who was Arthur's guardian, obviously had a vested interest in splitting the Angevin dominions in this way.

---

[38] Geoffrey de Vinsauf, *Poetria nova*, lines 368–9, ed. Edmond Faral, *Les Arts poétiques du XIIe. et du XIIIe. siècle* (Paris, 1924), p. 208.

At first things went well for John. His swift action in 1199, seizing the treasury at Chinon, being invested as duke of Normandy at Rouen and crowned king of England at Westminster, all within seven weeks, and the support of his mother, Eleanor of Aquitaine, who secured her own hereditary lands in south-west France, gave him a powerful position. Philip Augustus and Arthur were unable to make much headway and in the Treaty of Le Goulet in 1200 the French king recognized John as 'the rightful heir of his brother, king Richard'. In return John ceded Evreux to the French king and agreed to accept Arthur as his vassal for Brittany. It appeared as if John had achieved a transmission of power virtually as complete as that of 1189.

The rapid reversal of John's position in France between the Treaty of Le Goulet in 1200 and the fall of Rouen in 1204 was a political revolution as swift and complete as that of 1150–4, which had created the empire of Henry II. John's second marriage in 1200 was the catalyst. His bride was Isabella of Angoulême, heiress of an important county in Aquitaine. Her fiancé, Hugh de Lusignan, felt an understandable grievance at this development and soon the numerous Lusignan dynasty was in revolt. Denied what they saw as justice by their lord, John, the Lusignans appealed beyond him to his over-lord, king Philip. Louis VII and Philip had both been able to insist that the Angevins perform homage to them and thus become their vassals for their lands in France. Philip was now able to insist on a central juridical feature of the lord–vassal relationship: a vassal had to appear in the court of his lord when summoned. The potential difficulty of a king being a vassal of another king, that had mattered little when the Norman kings were strong enough to refuse homage and the French kings too weak to enforce it, now had to be faced. Philip summoned John as his vassal, yet John could not easily face the prospect of coming to Paris to be judged by the French king.

John's refusal to obey Philip's summons turned the Lusignan rebellion into a war between John and Philip:

The court of the king of France was assembled and adjudged that the king of England should be deprived of all the lands that he and his predecessors had hitherto held from the kings of France, because they had long disdained to perform the services that were incumbent on those lands, nor were they willing to obey their lord in almost anything.[39]

Philip launched an invasion of Normandy and granted Anjou and Poitou to Arthur, who allied with the Lusignans in order to secure them. John was not without success in this war. At Mirebeau in Poitou he captured Arthur and the leading members of the Lusignan family. Yet his treatment of them exhibits two opposite kinds of miscalculation. The Lusignans were soon

---

[39] R. Coggesh., p. 136.

released on promise and guarantee of good behaviour; they immediately rebelled again. Arthur disappeared and, according to one account, was killed by John himself in the castle at Rouen one evening after supper when the king was drunk. As suspicions of his fate spread, the Bretons took to arms. John's leniency and his brutality alike worked against him.

Philip Augustus did not have to fight hard to win Anjou and Poitou from John—they melted away as the baronage lost confidence and turned from him. Normandy was a different matter and here the French king undertook a long and often gruelling campaign of conquest. He was aided by John's absence from the duchy after December 1203. Personal leadership might have made a difference. Yet, even in Normandy, many important Norman barons had gone over to Philip Augustus by that date. The castle of Vaudreuil surrendered to Philip's forces without making any defence, because its garrison 'had no faith that help would come from their own king'.[40] Richard I's great new castle of Château Gaillard was besieged in August 1203 and surrendered, after a long, grim winter, in March 1204. The following month the death of Eleanor of Aquitaine down in the south released many Aquitainian nobles from any last shreds of loyalty to the family of Henry II. The French king now marched triumphantly through Normandy, entering Falaise and Caen, where a Breton army joined him, and laying siege to Rouen. The fall of Rouen to Philip Augustus on 24 June 1204 marked the effective end of the Angevin empire.

The momentousness of these events registered at the time:

And thus, within a short space of time, haughty Normandy and Anjou and the whole of Brittany and Maine, along with the Touraine, were subjected to the lordship of king Philip . . .

From duke William, who conquered the kingdom of the English, down to king John, who lost the duchy and many other lands across the sea in the fifth year of his reign, the kings of England had always been dukes of Normandy, holding the duchy and the kingdom together for 139 years.[41]

No one, however, was sure that the situation established in 1204 would be permanent. The English king did not formally concede Normandy, Anjou, and Poitou until the Treaty of Paris of 1259. The whole of John's reign after the fall of Normandy was dominated by attempts to recover the territories in France. Preparations for an expedition to Poitou, the preferred strategic approach, began as early as 1205. The limited success of John's expeditions there in 1206 and 1214, the heavy war taxation and disputes over military service all contributed to the crisis of his reign, culminating in Magna Carta and civil war in 1215. The Capetians were then able to bring the war to England.

---

[40] Ibid., p. 143.     [41] Ibid., p. 146.

In the twelfth century the Norman and Angevin kings had sometimes advanced to within a day's ride of Paris; in 1216 Louis of France held court in London.

The possibility of a Capetian dynasty ruling both in Paris and London disappeared with the withdrawal of Louis in 1217 but, despite his rebuff, the French prince continued to plan for the extinction of Angevin territorial power in France and, in 1224, after he had succeeded to the throne as Louis VIII, launched expeditions against the English king's possessions in Poitou and Gascony. Among the earliest preoccupations of the young Henry III of England was a counterattack in the form of an expedition to north-western France, fully in the tradition of his father. The French connection of the English Crown may have been attenuated by the conquests of Philip Augustus, but it was not severed.

## 3. COURT POLITICS

### Patronage and Faction

Petrus Alfonsi, who is reported to have been Henry I's doctor and thus knew something of court life, recorded the following shrewd judgement about royal patronage: 'A king is like a fire—if you are too close, you burn; if you are too far away, you freeze.'[42] English politics was court politics. It revolved around the ambitions, alliances, and enmities of a small group of high-born men and women who wanted to be close enough to royal patronage to enjoy its fruits, but who also had to negotiate the dangers of court life. Politics was personal, not structural. Great men did not represent sectors of society but pursued their own interests and those of their followers. The character of the individual monarch determined the tone and the pattern of the struggle for power. Henry I was confident enough to break some of his greatest baronial families, like the house of Bellême, and had the reputation of raising up lesser men in his service. By contrast, Stephen, at least at the beginning of his reign, relied upon an aristocratic group centred around the Beaumont twins, Waleran, count of Meulan, and Robert, earl of Leicester, but he was notorious for sudden coups against unsuspecting targets, arresting at his court the governmental dynasty of Roger, bishop of Salisbury, in 1139, Geoffrey de Mandeville in 1143, and the earl of Chester in 1145. John was, and is, even more renowned for the grudging and suspicious unease with which he dealt with his great men.

'Court' meant both the usual, permanent attendants and companions of the king and the great ceremonial meetings when the royal retinue would be

---

[42] Petrus Alfonsi, *Disciplina clericalis* 26, ed. A. Hilka and W. Söderhjelm (Acta Societatis Scientiarum Fennicae 38/iv; Helsinki, 1911), p. 36.

augmented by the presence of the leading aristocrats. Attendance on such occasions was an elementary sign of loyalty and refusal to attend a defiance that could not be ignored. In 1095, when William Rufus held his Easter court at Winchester, Robert de Mowbray, earl of Northumbria, 'was unwilling to come to court'. The king was furious and sent messengers to the earl, commanding him to attend his Whitsun court, 'if he wished to be in the king's peace'. When the king and his counsellors assembled in Windsor at Whitsun, however, the earl was not there, since he suspected Rufus's good faith. A royal expedition was immediately launched to Northumbria, that ended with the earl's dispossession and imprisonment.[43]

The court could dazzle and confuse. The opening words of Walter Map's *Courtier's Trifles* (*De nugis curialium*), a work produced at the court of Henry II, convey this tone of light-headedness: ' "I am in time and I speak of time", said Augustine, adding, "I do not know what time is." With a similar sense of amazement I could say that I am in the court and I speak of the court, and God knows what the court is.' The court consisted of a group of people enjoying patronage, hoping for it or losing it. It was a constantly changing and competitive environment—'stable only in its mobility'. Royal patronage was unpredictable and those at court, especially if they felt undervalued, bemoaned the apparent arbitrariness of favour: 'the court is a pleasing place only for those who obtain its favour . . . and this favour comes regardless of reason, establishes itself regardless of merit, arrives obscurely from unknown causes.'[44]

Robert Bloet, bishop of Lincoln from 1093 to 1123, would have agreed with Map's estimate of the capriciousness of royal favour. He had a long history of royal service, as chancellor and judge, but in the last year of his life he found that the protective mantle of the king's good will had been withdrawn. He, 'who had been deeply feared by all', was twice impleaded by the king and fined heavily, the indignity being compounded by the king's employment of 'an ignoble judge' as his agent. One day, after these indignities had been inflicted, Bishop Robert's archdeacon found him weeping at his dinner table. 'Once,' he lamented, 'my attendants were dressed in precious clothes; now the fines imposed by a king whose favour I have always sought mean they can wear only wool.' Even when it was reported to him that Henry had uttered praises of him, Robert could not be comforted. 'The king praises one of his own men,' he said, 'only when he wants to destroy him utterly.' Shortly after this bishop Robert suffered a stroke and died. 'King Henry,' commented the archdeacon, the chronicler Henry of Huntingdon, 'if it is right to say so, was a man of the deepest dissimulation and inscrutability of mind.'[45] It did not

---

[43] *ASC*, pp. 230–2.     [44] Map 1. 1 (pp. 2–4).
[45] H. Hunt., *De contemptu mundi* 1–2 (pp. 586–8).

make a courtier's life comfortable to be dependent on a powerful figure whose motives and intentions were unfathomable.

The instability of royal favour is illustrated yet more dramatically by the career of William de Braose, a baron who was raised up by John but then brought crashing down by him. De Braose was already a great landholder at John's accession, but in the years 1199–1205 John showed him continual favour, endowing him with lands in Wales, Ireland, and England and making his son bishop of Hereford. In 1208 a crisis occurred, brought on, according to one account, by the imprudent words of William de Braose's wife, Matilda, who is alleged to have referred to John's murder of his nephew, Arthur. William de Braose was one of the few people who knew what had happened to John's young rival. The king's reaction was to seize the Braose estates and attempt to arrest the family, but William, Matilda, and their sons were able to take flight to Ireland, where they found refuge with friends and allies. For a while they were safe, but John was determined to have them. In 1210 he launched a full-scale expedition to Ireland and was eventually able to capture Matilda and one of her sons, while William de Braose escaped to France. The too-outspoken Matilda and her boy were shut up in one of John's prisons and left to starve to death. Their fate shows that, as Petrus Alfonsi had observed, kings could burn those close to them.

One way of identifying a king's companions and inner circle is to count the frequency with which given individuals witnessed royal charters. Those who witnessed most frequently can be reasonably presumed to be among the more constant and important members of the court. The case of the first two members of the Redvers family illustrates this point. Richard de Redvers, a knight with lands in the Cotentin in western Normandy, attached himself to the service of Henry, William the Conqueror's youngest son, in the 1090s. On Henry's accession to the throne in 1100, Richard was among 'the wise and active men he summoned to his counsels'. His closeness to the centre is shown not only by the great landed estate he was given in England but also by the fact that he witnessed twenty-two of Henry's surviving charters and writs in the short period between 1100 and his death in 1107. By contrast, his son and heir, Baldwin de Redvers, witnessed only three of the king's charters between 1123, when he first occurs, and Henry's death in 1135. Baldwin was not a dissident but nor was he a close adviser and companion of the king, as his father had been. Charter attestations thus allow us to distinguish the 'courtiers' (*curiales*) from the non-curial aristocracy.[46]

Those who were close enough and important enough to be chosen as

---

[46] *Charters of the Redvers Family and the Earldom of Devon 1090–1217*, ed. Robert Bearman (Devon and Cornwall Rec. Soc., n.s. 37; 1994), pp. 2–5; Orderic 10. 16 (5, p. 298); it should be noted as a caveat that many more royal charters were issued in 1100–7 than in 1123–35.

witnesses to royal charters and other documents fall into several, sometime overlapping, groups: members of the royal family; bishops and, occasionally, important abbots; earls and other great magnates; officers and clerks of the chancery; lay holders of household office, such as the king's chamberlains, stewards, constables, and butler; and other lay aristocrats. An analysis of the men active in 1130 who are known to have witnessed at least two documents of Henry I per annum reveals thirty-one names: two earls (one of them the king's illegitimate son, Robert of Gloucester), ten bishops, fourteen officials of the household (chancellor, keeper of the seal, treasurer, stewards, constables, chamberlains, butler, and marshal) and five others, four of whom are known to have served as royal sheriffs or judges or both.[47] King John's fifty-five most regular witnesses included eleven earls, eleven bishops (all formerly royal clerks), and a large number of non-baronial royal servants.[48] The king was thus in constant contact both with men of high aristocratic birth and with those from lower in the social scale who had made themselves useful through service of some kind, usually military or administrative. Favours were given to both groups.

The patronage that the king had to offer was of very varied types. The rarest, and most painful to the giver, was a grant of royal land. Offices could also be granted, with tenure for life or a term. A more flexible and less draining source of patronage could be found in the wardships and marriages that the king had at his disposal. He claimed the right to the custody of minor heirs of those who held land directly from him and also the right to marry off their heiresses. He could thus arrange profitable marriages for the beneficiaries of royal favour or alternatively give them custody of these heirs and heiresses. The custodian of an estate would take its profits until the heir came of age, while an heiress could be sold on the marriage market, given to a relative, or taken as a wife by the guardian himself. Among the royal wards listed in a partial survey dating to 1185, 16 per cent had been entrusted to the guardianship of their mothers or stepmothers, 14.5 per cent to other kin, 22 per cent were kept directly under Crown control, but the wardship of a substantial 47.5 per cent had been granted to strangers, who thus had the temporary (although often long-term) benefit of the estate and the chance to arrange or sell the marriage.[49] Finally, in addition to such positive rewards as grants of land, office, or wardship, the king could bestow favours in the form of remission of demands or pardon for offences. Remission of taxation was common and welcome. The total amount of money that the king pardoned

---

[47] C. Warren Hollister and John W. Baldwin, 'The Rise of Administrative Kingship: Henry I and Philip Augustus', *American Historical Review*, 83 (1978), pp. 867–905, at pp. 887–8.

[48] Ralph V. Turner, *King John* (London, 1994), pp. 182–3.

[49] Waugh, *Lordship*, p. 196, calculated from *Rot. dom.*

his servants and favourites in 1130 was the equivalent of 23 per cent of the amount he actually received at the Exchequer, the annual royal audit.[50]

One of the consequences of enjoying royal favour was that one could do favours in turn. Every royal official or great lord must have been familiar with an incessant stream of requests, petitions, letters of introduction and commendation, hints more or less direct from his own entourage, endless 'cousins of my brother's wife' and 'deserving young men from my own county'. A direct record of the operation of such networks of patronage appears in the royal exchequer accounts of 1130, where certain tax remissions are described as being granted 'for love of' (*pro amore*) a named courtier. Thus Geoffrey Mauduit of Essex was pardoned two marks (£1. 6s. 8d.) of a relief (inheritance payment) of seven marks that he owed 'for love of earl Warenne', and Henry of Tringeham was excused his tax payment of 17s. 6d. in Buckinghamshire 'for love of the earl of Gloucester'.[51]

The royal patronage machine was the single most important instrument for making or breaking individual fortunes in the medieval period, rivalled only by the Church, with which it was, in any case, closely integrated. Royal service could take a man from knightly to baronial rank. Nigel d'Aubigny was the landless younger brother of a minor Norman aristocrat, but in 1101 he entered the service of Henry I, probably as a household knight, and, in the course of a lifetime of activity as royal justice, military commander, and counsellor, acquired a great feudal estate. This consisted of lands in western and southern Normandy and in the Midlands and the north of England. Most of the English lands had been part of the property of Robert de Stuteville, whom Henry I had dispossessed and condemned to perpetual imprisonment for fighting against him at Tinchebray in 1106. Many of the Norman lands came to Nigel on the occasion of his marriage to Maud de Laigle, sister of the Gilbert de Laigle discussed above and wife of the dispossessed and imprisoned earl of Northumbria, Robert de Mowbray, from whom she had to be divorced. Nigel d'Aubigny was thus enriched from the lands of the king's aristocratic enemies, rather than from the royal estates directly, but, whatever the source of his new wealth, it constituted one of the largest baronies in England.[52]

A similarly steep rise is seen in the career of Geoffrey fitz Peter, who held one knight's fee from the Crown in 1166 and died in 1213 with more than 180 and the title earl of Essex. His career in royal service can be traced from the 1180s, when he was sheriff of Northampton and Chief Forester, but he must already have served as a household knight in either the royal household or that of some other great man. In the 1190s he was active as a sheriff, royal just-

---

[50] Green, *Govt.*, p. 225.      [51] PR 31 HI, pp. 55, 102.      [52] *Mowbray Charters*, pp. xvii–xxv.

ice, and military commander besides continuing as Chief Forester. Eventually, in 1198, Richard I appointed him chief justiciar, head of the royal administration, and this was a post he held until his death in 1213. His rewards increased in step with his political ascent. Given such gifts as a house in Winchester and a payment of £15 in his early days in royal service, he soon began to acquire lands and other valuable assets, including the custody of Beatrice de Say, one of the heiresses of William de Say. He married her himself, thus acquiring a (large) share in the Say estate, as well as a claim to the earldom of Essex, that had been held by Beatrice's cousins, the Mandeville earls. Despite the competing claims of other members of the Say family, Geoffrey was granted the Mandeville lands in 1191, in return for a substantial payment, though he had to wait until John's accession in 1199 to be formally titled earl of Essex.[53]

Nigel d'Aubigny and Geoffrey fitz Peter are exceptionally dazzling cases, but the story of advancement within the aristocratic hierarchy through royal service and favour was a common one. Such success stories fuelled the dreams of other courtiers: 'The hope of royal generosity frequently cheers those who dwell in the court of the lord king. They all hope that what they see has happened to others will happen to them.'[54] Another reaction, and perhaps a more common one, was envy. 'Friendship among those who are summoned to give the king counsel and undertake his business is one of the rarest things,' wrote Arnulf of Lisieux, who himself suffered from the hard political conflicts in the court of Henry II. 'Anxious ambition dominates their minds; each of them fears to be outstripped by the endeavours of the others; so is born envy, which necessarily turns immediately into hatred.'[55] Neither did Walter Map picture the court as a joyful place: 'Greed, the lady of the court, incites us with so many sharp stings, that laughter is completely removed by care.' Court life was a life of anxious jealousy.

The limited number of places at the top and the sharpness of rivalry for them are the themes of a story told among the earls of Huntingdon about their eleventh-century ancestor, Siward, the founder of their fortune. After winning fame as a dragon-slayer, Siward had come to London and been summoned to the presence of king Edward the Confessor in Westminster:

After they had spoken together for a long time, the king retained him in his service and promised to him that he would give him the first honor [great estate] in his kingdom that should fall into his hands.

---

[53] Ralph V. Turner, *Men Raised from the Dust: Administrative Service and Upward Mobility in Angevin England* (Philadelphia, 1988), pp. 35–70.

[54] P. Blois, *Letters*, no. 14 (cols. 44–5).

[55] *Letters of Arnulf of Lisieux*, ed. F. Barlow (Camden Soc., 3rd ser., 61; 1939), no. 10, p. 14.

Subsequently Siward has a brush with Tostig, earl of Huntingdon, and he lies in wait for him.

Siward pulled out his sword and cut off Tostig's head. He went back to court, holding the head under his cloak, and asked the king, according to his promise, to confer on him the lordship and honor of Huntingdon, that he said was vacant. The king was surprised, since the earl had left him only a short time before, and thought that his words were a joke rather than the truth. Thereupon Siward asserted that the earl was dead and, as an incontrovertible sign, threw the severed head before the king's feet. According to his promise, the king at once gave him the honor of Huntingdon and invested him with it.[56]

The royal halls and palaces of Norman and Angevin England were littered with severed heads only in the imagination, but fierce competitiveness between rivals was a reality. On occasion this took a clear enough form of group rivalry that it can be termed faction-fighting. Royal absences and minorities produced predictably intense factionalism. While Richard was away on crusade in 1191, his chancellor, William de Longchamps, who dominated the absentee government, so antagonized many of the leading men that a coup was organized to remove him. He had the support of one or two of the chief members of the aristocracy, such as the earl of Arundel and William de Braose junior, who were linked to him by 'affinity'—perhaps marriage alliances— but the large majority of the baronage, headed by the king's brother, John, and Richard's special envoy, Walter of Coutances, gave its backing to a show of force that ended with Longchamps's flight from England.

The motives of the party opposed to Longchamps were scarcely 'constitutional'. As the courtier and man of letters Peter of Blois pointed out, in a letter excoriating Hugh de Nonant, bishop of Coventry, the chief spokesman of John's coup, 'Where the rancour was tending and where the envy was leading has today been made clear by the enormity of these treacherous proceedings.' When Longchamps had been entrusted with the government of England, 'you saw—and you envied; that gave birth to your rancour. Envy conceived vexation and gave birth to wickedness.'[57] Longchamps had been in power long enough to establish several relatives in reasonably secure positions of wealth and influence, but, although he retained the king's confidence, the envious reaction of the hostile faction of 1191 had ensured that his supremacy could not be re-established.

Longchamps's fall occurred in the unusual circumstances of the king's absence on crusade. The more common situation was for groups of rivals and allies to make their way by gaining the king's ear. The political crisis of 1139

---

[56] *Gesta antecess. Waldevi*, pp. 107–8.

[57] P. Blois, *Letters*, no. 89 (cols. 278–81); for the affinity between Longchamps and Arundel and Braose, Gerald, *V. Geoffrey* 2. 6–7 (pp. 400, 402).

shows the tortuous workings of court faction around the person of the king. In the early years of Stephen's reign Roger, bishop of Salisbury, and his family, the great clerical dynasty that had managed the government under Henry I, continued in power, with Roger dominating the central administration and relatives holding the posts of chancellor and treasurer, as well as two further bishoprics. Their ostentatious display of wealth and the size of their retinues aroused the animosity of Stephen's particular favourite, Waleran, count of Meulan: 'the count of Meulan, and other close and private adherents of the king, resented the magnificent glory of the bishops and, inflamed by the torch of envy, they boiled over with hostile rage against them.' The tactic these 'close and private adherents of the king' adopted was a whispering campaign. The bishops, they said, had amassed money and men and built their castles not to strengthen the king but to undermine him; it would be quite justifiable to arrest them and take their castles. Stephen was bombarded with this advice. Although he had reservations about apprehending ecclesiastics, he also considered 'that it was pernicious and wrongful not to heed those with whom he shared his private thoughts and who were amongst the first at court'. The king, 'overcome by their insistent requests and the continual, shameless pressure they applied', eventually agreed to the courtiers' plan of seizing Roger and his family.[58]

The outcome of this internal coup was the seizure of the bishops at the king's court, the confiscation of their castles, and the termination of their control over the chief offices of the royal government. Philip de Harcourt, a member of Waleran's network, was appointed chancellor in place of Roger of Salisbury's son. The arrest of the bishops, followed soon after by the landing of the empress Matilda in England, was a turning point in Stephen's reign. The dynamics at court in the period leading to the coup must, however, have been characteristic of court politics at any time in our period. The question of who was 'in' and who was 'out', the jealousies of factions, the dangers of flaunting one's good fortune, the crucial matter of who had the king's ear— this was the fabric of court life.

## The Role of Queens

Court politics revolved around the fortunes of a family, the ruling dynasty. For all but the last decade of the period discussed here the head of that family was an adult male. It was usual, too, for the pattern of political and public life to include the potentially significant figure of the queen. In the whole of the twelfth century there were no more than eight years in which there was no queen consort: 1118–21, between the death of Henry I's first wife and his remarriage; 1152–4, after the death of Stephen's queen; and

---

[58] *Gesta Stephani* 34 (pp. 72–4).

1189–91, before Richard's marriage. Taking the century and a half 1075–1225 as a whole, there were, exceptionally, two longer periods in which there was no queen, the first provided by William Rufus's failure to marry and the second by the minority of Henry III. The latter is obviously explicable, but Rufus's bachelorhood is more open to interpretation. He was in his forties when he died in 1100 and had shown no inclination to arrange a marriage. His court had a reputation for homosexuality among hostile monastic critics, although no explicit accusations were directed against the king himself.[59] With the exception of a much later story, recounting how Rufus wanted to go through two rivers in Maine with the unlikely names of Cul and Con, remarks made about the king would suggest nothing other than simple extramarital sexual activity.[60] Whatever the explanation, he reigned for thirteen years without a wife, and he thus ensured that his line could be ended by the sudden accident (if that is what it was) in the New Forest.[61]

Eight women bore the title queen in this period:

(1)  Matilda of Flanders, 1066–83;
(2)  Matilda of Scotland, 1100–18;
(3)  Adeliza of Louvain, 1121–51 (who outlived Henry I by 16 years and remarried between 1136 and 1139);
(4)  Matilda of Boulogne, 1135–52;
(5)  Eleanor of Aquitaine, 1154–1204 (who outlived Henry II by 15 years);
(6)  Berengaria of Navarre, 1191–c.1230 (who outlived Richard I by about 31 years);
(7)  Isabella of Gloucester, 1199–1200 (who was divorced by John, remarried in 1214, and died in 1217);
(8)  Isabella of Angoulême 1200–1246 (who outlived John by 30 years, remarrying in 1220).

Of these eight queens, only two came from the British Isles: Matilda of Scotland, a daughter of king Malcolm Canmore and his wife, Margaret, a descendant of the Anglo-Saxon royal line; and Isabella of Gloucester, who was married to John when his succession was very far from certain and who was discarded once he became king. The other six came from the continental elite, four of them from the kingdom of France, one from the part of the Empire bordering on France and one from Navarre. The basic continuity in the choice of royal brides over this period was the need to establish political relationships with the great princes of, under the Norman kings, northern and, under the Angevins, western France, the lands where those kings had

---

[59]  e.g. Orderic 8. 10 (4, p. 188).
[60]  Wace, Le Roman de Rou, lines 9873–88, ed. A. J. Holden (3 vols., Société des Anciens Textes Français; Paris, 1970–3), vol. 2, p. 252.
[61]  On the whole question, Frank Barlow, William Rufus (London, 1983), pp. 101–10.

their territories and frequently their cultural and social identities. Flanders, Brabant, and Boulogne, under the Normans, and Aquitaine, Navarre, and Angoulême, under the Angevins, were all critical forces in the high politics of feudal France. With the solitary exception of Isabella of Gloucester, there were no brides from the Anglo-Norman aristocracy, and neither were there any from more distant royal families. Royal marriage policy was primarily a matter of French politics.

Some of those who became queens were not consciously foreseen as such: Matilda of Flanders, Matilda of Boulogne, and Isabella of Gloucester married at a time when their bridegrooms were not yet kings and had no certain prospects of becoming one; Eleanor of Aquitaine married Henry of Anjou when his succession in England was being strongly asserted but was not a foregone conclusion; the other brides all married reigning kings. Obviously the choice of a bride for a reigning king was a different matter from that for a count or cadet. The only two queens who were themselves of royal birth (Matilda of Scotland and Berengaria of Navarre) were selected for reigning monarchs, although Stephen's wife, Matilda of Boulogne, was of royal descent, being the daughter of Mary, the daughter of Malcolm Canmore and Margaret of Scotland, and thus having as ancestors both the Scottish royal line and the Wessex kings. As the heiress to the county of Boulogne, she was a figure of major political importance and her marriage to Stephen in 1125, when he was count of Mortain, added enormously to his power and prospects. Like Matilda of Boulogne, but even more spectacularly, Eleanor of Aquitaine was a great heiress and brought with her claims to lordship over a third of France. She personifies the shift in the political geography that the Angevin succession represented and was the first queen to be chosen from the southern French aristocracy. She had a critical personal role in Aquitaine in the fifty years between the accession of Henry II to the English throne and her own death in 1204. Berengaria, her daughter-in-law, probably has the claim to be the least English of England's queens, never having visited the country, either in her husband's lifetime or during her long widowhood.

Being chosen mostly from great continental families, queens were usually outsiders in England and unlikely to align immediately or naturally with aristocratic or political factions within the country. Siding with their sons against their husbands was a different matter. Eleanor is renowned for the way she backed her favourite son, Richard, who was entrusted with the rule of Aquitaine, against her husband, Henry II, but even the harmonious relations between William the Conqueror and his wife Matilda were strained by the support she gave to her son Robert, who rebelled against his father more than once. She provided him with soldiers paid for from her queenly estates.[62]

⁶² W. Malm., *GR* 3. 273 (2, p. 331); OMT edn., p. 502.

Queens could thus be important participants in the dynastic turmoil that marked the history of the Norman and Angevin dynasties. They also perpetuated the lineage, served as regents, acted as patrons of religious and cultural life and had, moreover, substantial resources of their own to dispense or enjoy.

Henry I's wives, Matilda and Adeliza, may be taken to illustrate two variants of the queenly role.

Matilda of Scotland, who married Henry in 1100 three months after he became king, won such an enduring reputation for piety and benevolence that for many subsequent generations she was known by the nickname 'the good queen'.[63] The monastic chronicler, William of Malmesbury, writing soon after Matilda's death, gave her an approving tribute. Brought up and educated among the nuns of Wilton and Romsey, he wrote, she even wore the veil for a time and was deemed by some to be a nun; after her marriage, when she lived permanently at Westminster in royal state, she wore a hair shirt under her robes and went bare-foot to church during Lent; she washed the feet of the sick; was an enthusiastic patroness of church music and poetry; generous, to a fault, to foreigners; after seventeen and a half years as queen, she was 'snatched away from the country' by death and buried at her beloved Westminster.[64]

Matilda's reputation for sanctity was based, in part, on the zealous liturgical life of her household. As an admirer put it, 'You would think that her chapel was not a gathering of court clerks but an assembly of fervent monks.'[65] It also arose from her willingness to undergo ritual self-abasement, a humility that some of her high-born peers indeed regarded as unqueenly. Her brother David told the story how one evening he went to her bedchamber and found her washing and then kissing the feet of a group of lepers. David's response was characteristic of the male aristocrat: 'What are you doing, my lady? Certainly if the king knew about this, he would never deign to kiss your lips, polluted with corruption of lepers' feet.' Matilda replied, 'Everyone knows that the feet of the eternal king are to be preferred to the lips of a mortal one.'[66] Matilda's mother, St Margaret of Scotland, who was also known as 'the good queen' (even as early as her daughter's lifetime), was famous for her religious practices, including the ritual washing of the feet of six poor men during Lent and Advent, but the washing and kissing of the feet of lepers was a step further in the calculus of self-abnegation.[67] Matilda's genuine concern for lepers is attested also by her foundation of the leper hospital of St Giles, Holborn, a mile or so from her residence at Westminster.[68]

[63] *Aldgate Cart.*, pp. 224, 230.       [64] W. Malm., *GR* 5. 418 (2, pp. 493–5); OMT edn., pp. 754–8.
[65] *Hyde Chron.*, p. 312.       [66] Ailred of Rievaulx, *Genealogia regum Anglorum* (*PL* 195, col. 735).
[67] *ASC*, p. 236 (1100); Turgot, *V. Margaret*, p. 248.       [68] *Monasticon* 6/ii, pp. 635–6.

It may well be that king Henry did not have to make the choice to kiss Matilda's 'polluted' lips. Although she bore him children, this was within the first few years of the marriage: both their daughter Matilda and their son William were born by 1103. 'Thereafter,' wrote William of Malmesbury, 'content with having borne a child of each sex, she ceased to become pregnant or give birth, and she tolerated it with equanimity that the king was occupied elsewhere.'[69] Between 1106 and Matilda's death in 1118 Henry spent more than half his time in Normandy, sometimes being away for almost two years continuously, and, although the queen is known to have accompanied him on one occasion, this was probably an isolated occurrence.[70] The date of birth of Henry's numerous illegitimate children is not known with certainty, but the fact that three of his bastard sons were described as 'still young' in a text written about 1138 would support the idea that the king found other sexual partners during his marriage to Matilda.[71] By 1103 she had fulfilled her main task by producing a male heir and, in doing so, contributing her ancient dynastic legitimacy to the Norman line. Through her mother, as the author of the *Anglo-Saxon Chronicle* noted, she was 'of the right royal kin of England'.[72]

Yet, if reproduction was her destiny and piety her proclivity, Matilda was no background figure. When Henry was in Normandy she exercised vice-regal powers in England. The very earliest mention of the English Exchequer dates to 1110, but the second earliest, a year later, refers to a sitting of the exchequer court in Winchester at which the queen was present, 'because the king was then in Normandy', and its verdict was declared in a charter issued by the queen and sealed with her seal.[73] She sent out, in her own name, the imperious writs by which royal government was conducted:

Matilda, queen of England, to Nigel d'Aubigny, greeting. I order you to ensure that Ranulf, bishop of Durham, has his full rights against Robert de Muschamps concerning the lands of St Cuthbert [i.e. of the church of Durham] that he has occupied.[74]

Matilda, queen, to Ansfrid the steward, greeting. I order you to ensure that the ship of the abbot of St Augustine's [Canterbury], with all his property that was taken, is restored in accordance with justice . . . and I order that all his property be safe and secure, as it was on the day when the king crossed the sea, until he returns to England.[75]

At her death in 1118 Matilda was given unanimously enthusiastic obituaries. 'From the time that England was first subject to kings,' wrote one

---

[69] W. Malm., *GR* 5. 418 (2, p. 494); OMT edn., pp. 754–6. One source also mentions a son called Richard, who must have died in infancy: Gerv. Cant., p. 92.

[70] *RRAN* 2, nos. 808–9, p. 64; *Ann. Wint.*, p. 42.

[71] *The Gesta Normannorum Ducum of William of Jumièges, Orderic Vitalis and Robert of Torgni*, ed. Elisabeth Van Houts (2 vols., OMT; 1992–5), vol. 2, p. 248; for the date of composition, vol. 1, pp. lxxix–lxxx.

[72] *ASC*, p. 236 (1100).       [73] *Abingdon Chron.* 2, p. 116.

[74] Van Caen., *Writs*, p. 487, no. 143.       [75] Ibid., pp. 441–2, no. 59.

monastic historian, 'there has not been a queen like her, nor will you find her match in ages to come. Her memory will be praised and her name blessed for ever.'[76] One small sign that king Henry shared this concern for the continuing memory of his first wife is an item recorded in the only surviving royal accounts from his reign, those of 1130: 'to purchase a cloth to place on the queen's tomb, three shillings'.[77]

Adeliza of Louvain, Henry's second wife, whom he married in 1121, after almost three years as a widower, left no such reputation. The king was supposedly attracted by her beauty,[78] may have given some weight to the blood of Charlemagne she carried in her veins, and certainly had very good grounds for wanting further legitimate offspring, but there could also have been some immediate political calculation at work. Adeliza was the daughter of Godfrey, count of Louvain (1095–1139), who held the title Duke of Lower Lotharingia 1106–28 and was the ancestor of the ducal line of Brabant. Godfrey was an ally of the emperor Henry V, king Henry's son-in-law, and his lands bordered Flanders on the east. The marriage took place at a time when Flanders, which always had to be considered seriously by English kings and Norman dukes, was particularly important.

In 1118 the count of Flanders, Baldwin VII, had fought in alliance with the French king against Henry I. After Baldwin's death in the next year from a wound received while campaigning in Normandy, his cousin Charles succeeded to the county, but not without opposition. Among Charles's most powerful enemies was Clemence, Baldwin VII's mother, now remarried to Godfrey of Louvain. Relations between Henry I and Count Charles were not invariably hostile, but Charles had served in one of the French armies that Louis VI led against the Normans in 1119 and, although Henry and Charles had come to terms in autumn 1119, Henry had no reason to suppose his friendship was permanent.[79] The king's marriage to the daughter of Godfrey of Louvain, who was now married to one of Charles's chief enemies, was planned in 1120 and can plausibly be seen as part of a containment of Charles. The count of Flanders himself certainly seems to have deemed it a hostile act, since in the year after the marriage he reportedly refused to permit the empress Matilda, Henry I's daughter, to cross Flanders on her way from Germany to England.[80]

Adeliza was Henry's wife for almost fifteen years, but never bore him the son he needed. It is clear that this was a cause of grief to her. A letter consoling her on her failure to bear the king a child, written by the prelate and poet, Hildebert of Lavardin, archbishop of Tours, praises her for the care she showed for the poor:

[76] *Hyde Chron.*, pp. 312–13.      [77] PR 31 HI, p. 144.      [78] H. Hunt. 7. 33 (p. 468).
[79] Suger, *V. Ludovici Grossi regis* 26, ed. H. Waquet (Paris, 1929), p. 200; *Hyde Chron.*, p. 320.
[80] *Ann. Wav.*, p. 218.

If it has not been granted to you from heaven that you should bear a child to the king of the English, in these [the poor], you will bring forth for the king of the angels, with no damage to your modesty. Perhaps the Lord has closed up your womb, so that you might adopt immortal offspring . . . it is more blessed to be fertile in the spirit than in the flesh.[81]

It is not known how Adeliza received this consolation.

In the event she was to be fertile in both flesh and spirit, for after the king's death she remarried and had children. She also had a small but important part in the political crisis of Stephen's reign, the year 1139. By that date she was remarried to William d'Aubigny, son of one of king Henry's longest-serving officials. Stephen does not appear to have regarded either her or her husband with suspicion and indeed probably created William d'Aubigny earl of Lincoln on the occasion of the marriage (he later had the title earl of Sussex or Arundel, after the large estate that Adeliza brought to him as part of her royal dower). Until 1139, whatever Stephen's difficulties, there had not been an alternative candidate for the Crown actually present in England. That autumn, however, Henry I's daughter Matilda crossed the Channel in the company of her main champion, her illegitimate half-brother, Robert of Gloucester. Their immediate destination was Adeliza's castle of Arundel. The chroniclers who record this event do not discuss Adeliza's involvement at great length. Robert of Torigny reports that William d'Aubigny had invited the Angevin leaders, while William of Malmesbury claims that there had been frequent contact by messenger between Adeliza and Matilda and Robert while the latter were still in Normandy.[82] He makes this point, however, primarily to emphasize what he regards as Adeliza's betrayal of Matilda, for, while Robert of Gloucester was away from Arundel attempting to raise the country to his sister's cause, king Stephen besieged the castle and Adeliza surrendered Matilda to him.

The reasons for Adeliza's behaviour are not obvious. Personal relations between 'the ex-queen' and 'the ex-empress', as one contemporary neatly terms them, can only be guessed, though Matilda's own haughtiness is notorious and tension between a widowed and remarried stepmother and her stepdaughter may have existed. William of Malmesbury attributes the surrender to 'female fickleness', but this would be a natural phrase for this misogynist Angevin propagandist. John of Worcester suggests a more practical motive: 'she feared the king's majesty and worried that she might lose the great estate she held throughout England'. He goes on to give Adeliza's excuse to Stephen: 'she swore on oath that his enemies had not come to England on her account but that she had simply given them hospitality as persons

<hr>

[81] Hildebert of Lavardin, ep. 1. 18 (*PL* 171, cols. 189–91); cf. ep. 1. 14 (ibid., cols. 179–81).
[82] R. Torigni, p. 137; W. Malm., *HN* 478 (p. 35).

of high dignity once close to her'.[83] Whatever the truth behind these claims, the critical move at this juncture was Stephen's. By agreeing to give Matilda free passage to join her half-brother at Bristol he ensured civil war. Adeliza's role does not reflect well on her steadfastness, nor perhaps on her truthfulness, but she was at least successful in keeping 'the estate she held throughout England'. Neither she nor her husband figure significantly in the subsequent political and military affairs of Stephen's reign. Adeliza's most long-lasting contribution to the English political scene was the line of d'Aubigny earls of Arundel, which lasted until 1243.

Henry's queens Matilda and Adeliza emerge, as far as one can judge from the flickering light of early twelfth-century evidence, as personalities of very different types. Their circumstances, however, had much in common. Both were not only married to the king but also, in a separate ceremony, consecrated queen. This was a permanent, quasi-sacramental status, and Adeliza bore the title 'queen' throughout her life, even after Henry's death and her remarriage. This was usually the case, too, with later widowed queens. Both Matilda and Adeliza were also great landholders. Like other aristocratic women, queens could hold land of three types: inheritance, dower (allocated from their husband's land), and marriage portion (given with them at their marriage, usually by their father). It is not always possible to tell from which source any given estate held by a queen came, but sometimes the evidence is explicit, as in the case of the reference to the manor of Aston (Herts.), described as given by Henry I to Adeliza 'as his queen and wife'.[84] Some property was traditionally part of the queen's dower. Waltham in Essex, for instance, was held by both Matilda and Adeliza. Later it was also briefly in the possession of Matilda, wife of Stephen, between Adeliza's death and her own. Then it was held by Eleanor of Aquitaine. Even after the manor had been granted to the abbey of Waltham, founded in 1177, for a fixed rent, this money was paid to the queen mothers Eleanor (1189–1204) and Isabella (1216–27).[85]

Besides Waltham, Matilda had property in Northumberland, Yorkshire, Lincolnshire, Rutland, Buckinghamshire, and Devon, and, in addition to these scattered agricultural properties, a share in the growing urban and commercial revenues of England. She held Aldgate in London, took two-thirds of the revenues of the city of Exeter, and had rights in the tolls paid at Salisbury market. Her leper hospital of St Giles was assigned sixty shillings per annum from a lucrative dock on the Thames at London, originally called

[83] J. Worcs., p. 55.     [84] *Reading Cart.* 1, no. 370, pp. 301–2.
[85] *Early Waltham Charters*, nos. 3, 17, 19–21, 26 n. 6, 290, 296–8, 300, pp. 4–5, 11, 12, 16, 195, 198, 199.

Aederdeshithe or Athereshithe, but renamed Queenshithe from its royal proprietor.[86]

The Pipe Roll of 1130, an early and isolated surviving record of the royal accounts, gives some information about Adeliza's property in England. Exemption from the land-tax known as the geld was granted to many great land-holders for their demesne lands, i.e. those parts exploited directly rather than occupied by tenants. Adeliza enjoyed this favour and the list of her exemptions in 1130 shows a moderate estate in south-east England, concentrated in Essex, with smaller clusters in nearby Hertfordshire and Bedfordshire, and further lesser properties in Buckinghamshire, Berkshire, and Middlesex. In addition, she had property in Devon bringing in over £50 per annum and £13 from Ashleworth (Glos.), a component of the royal estate of Berkeley, as a gift from the king. The largest element in her endowment, however, does not appear in the Pipe Roll. In 1126 she had been given the entire county of Shropshire, which did not thereafter have to render accounts to the royal exchequer.[87]

In addition to their landed properties and urban revenues, queens could also expect their cut from the constant stream of proffers, fines, and payments that the king received. Adeliza certainly benefited from such income. After the death of earl Ranulf of Chester in 1129, Henry I was promised 45 marks of silver by the countess Lucy of Chester in return for his agreement regarding some of the arrangements she made about the succession; the king explicitly instructed that twenty marks of this should go to the queen.[88] By the reign of Henry II, the queen's share of such offers had been standardized: for every 100 marks of silver offered to the king, a mark of gold must be paid to the queen (the gold–silver ratio was 1:9). Her own officers attended the Exchequer sessions to ensure this payment was made.[89] Thus, in 1163, when Richard de Anstey offered the king 100 marks to attain the settlement of his prolonged lawsuit, a mark of gold also went to the queen.[90] It is revealing that we know this not from the royal Pipe Rolls, that record the annual audit of the king's revenues, but from Richard's own private accounts, for these payments to the queen were dealt with separately by the queen's own agent and recorded on his own rolls. Eleanor of Aquitaine, who continued to receive the queen's gold after the death of her husband, Henry II, employed a clerk of Waltham abbey for this purpose.[91] Only after 1207, when the king

---

[86] Peter Sawyer, *Anglo-Saxon Charters* (London, 1968), no. 1628; *Monasticon* 6/ii, pp. 635–6; E. Ekwall, *Street Names of the City of London* (Oxford, 1954), p. 35.

[87] PR 31 HI, pp. 60, 62, 102, 104, 126, 133, 152, 153; W. Malm., *HN* 451 (p. 3).

[88] PR 31 HI, p. 110.      [89] *Dial. scacc.*, p. 122.

[90] Patricia Barnes, 'The Anstey Case', in Patricia Barnes and C. F. Slade (eds.), *A Medieval Miscellany for Doris May Stenton* (PRS n.s. 36; 1962 for 1960), pp. 1–24, at pp. 21–2; PR 11 HII, p. 18.

[91] *Early Waltham Charters*, no. 36, pp. 26–7.

commanded that the queen's gold be audited at the Exchequer just like other royal revenues, do references to 'the queen's gold' became a regular feature of the financial records of the Exchequer.[92]

Queens thus commanded a large income and could use it to create their own network of patronage. They had families of their own, whose members could reasonably expect that the elevation of a female relative to the Crown would benefit them too. David, the younger brother of Henry I's queen, Matilda, the same who reported the story about the lepers, was himself of royal stock, son of Malcolm III of Scotland, but he was a younger son and did not expect to succeed to the throne. He made his way at Henry's court and was richly endowed by his brother-in-law. At his Christmas court in 1113 Henry gave the queen's brother the earldom of Northampton (also known as Huntingdon).[93] By the accident of succession this then became a property of the kings of Scots for the next century and a quarter.

Adeliza's brother, Jocelin, was also fortunate. He received from his sister the honor of Petworth, a large estate in Sussex dependent on her own great dower property of Arundel. He occurs in various records, as 'Jocelin of Louvain', until 1180 and obviously did well, marrying the heiress to the Percy fortune and becoming the ancestor of the later Percies—Harry Hotspur's ancestry thus goes back to this favoured brother of a foreign queen, a link symbolized by the fact that the Percy arms still bear the blue lion of Louvain. Perhaps Jocelin reflected on his fortunes during Adeliza's funeral in 1151, when she was laid beside her royal husband in Reading abbey in her brother's presence.[94] Other members of a queen's household might also expect promotion. Matilda's chancellors, Reinhelm and Bernard, became bishops of Hereford and St David's, respectively.[95] Adeliza brought with her from Louvain a cleric named Godfrey, who served as her chancellor before being rewarded with the bishopric of Bath in 1123.[96]

Queens could thus look after their own, securing lands and titles for their families, rich bishoprics for their clerks, and a host of minor favours for their retainers and tenants. They also had the resources to act as religious and cultural patrons. Queen Matilda's major act of religious patronage was the foundation of the important Augustinian priory of Holy Trinity, Aldgate. The first prior, Norman, was her confessor, and she bequeathed her collection of relics and her royal sceptre to the house on her death.[97] Her leper hospital at St Giles has already been mentioned. The host of minor gifts and favours that she extended to ecclesiastics can be represented by the golden candelabra she

---

[92] *Rot. litt. claus.* 1, p. 98.    [93] *ASC*, p. 244 (H text), *s.a.* 1114.

[94] *EYC* 11, no. 290, pp. 359–60. According to another account Adeliza retired to and was buried in Afflighem in her homeland: Antonius Sanderus, *Chorographia sacra Brabantiae* (3 vols.; The Hague, 1726–7), vol. 1, p. 45.

[95] *RRAN* 2, p. xi.    [96] *ASC*, p. 252.    [97] *RRAN* 2, no. 897, p. 83; *Aldgate Cart.*, p. 230.

sent to Hildebert of Lavardin, at that time bishop of Le Mans.[98] Adeliza, unlike her predecessor, founded no major house, but, especially after the king's death, she did make pious benefactions to very varied recipients—the canons at her dower manor of Waltham, king Henry's foundation of Reading, Chichester cathedral, the canons of Osney by Oxford, the black monks of Eynsham, the crusading order of Templars, the newly arrived Cistercians of Waverley (Surrey), the abbey of St Sauveur in the Cotentin—as well as founding a tiny priory at Pynham on the causeway by her main castle at Arundel.[99]

Both queens had literary as well as religious interests and Matilda, in particular, was renowned for her own level of literary education and for the patronage she extended to writers. She is the first queen of England from whom any letters survive. Major Latin poets, such as Hildebert, sent her poems and letters. Historical writing was an area of especial interest to her, for Matilda was proud of, and curious about, her royal Anglo-Saxon ancestry. Turgot, prior of Durham, wrote his *Life* of Margaret of Scotland, Matilda's mother, at the queen's request and the work contains a chapter tracing her descent from Edgar, the celebrated tenth-century king of the Wessex line. She commissioned a genealogy of the Wessex kings from the monks of Malmesbury and provided the impetus for the production of William of Malmesbury's *Deeds of the Kings* (*Gesta regum*), recounting English history from the coming of the Anglo-Saxons to the reign of Henry I.[100] Literature in French, just beginning to be written down at this time, was also produced for her court, for the Anglo-Norman *Voyage of Brendan*, by a poet called Benedict, was originally dedicated to her, although in later versions the dedication was altered to Adeliza, her successor.[101] Another work in French, Philip de Thaon's *Bestiary*, was also dedicated to Adeliza, who is known to have commissioned a (no longer extant) life of Henry I from a certain David, possibly David the Scot, schoolmaster of Würzburg and bishop of Bangor 1120–39.[102] The poet Serlo of Wilton was in her service in the period after Henry's death.[103]

[98] Hildebert of Lavardin, ep. 1. 9 (*PL* 171, cols. 160–2).

[99] *Early Waltham Charters*, nos. 17–18, p. 11; *Reading Cart.* 1, nos. 268, 370, 459, 534–8, pp. 225–6, 301–2, 353, 403–7; *RRAN* 3, nos. 185, 629, 921, pp. 68, 231–2, 335–6; *CDF*, no. 974, p. 347; *Cartulary of Oseney Abbey*, ed. H. E. Salter (6 vols., Oxford Historical Soc.; 1929–36), vol. 4, p. 107, no. 75; *Facsimiles of Early Charters in Oxford Muniment Rooms*, ed. H. E. Salter (Oxford, 1929), no. 45; *VCH Sussex* 2, p. 80; *Monasticon* 6/i, pp. 259–60.

[100] Anselm, ep. 395, 400 (*Op.* 5, pp. 339, 344); Elisabeth Van Houts, 'Latin Poetry and the Anglo-Norman Court', *Jnl Medieval History*, 15 (1989), pp. 39–62, at pp. 50–2; Turgot, *V. Margaret*, pp. 234, 237–8; Ewald Könsgen, 'Zwei unbekannte Briefe zu den *Gesta Regum Anglorum* des Wilhelm von Malmesbury', *Deutches Archiv*, 31 (1975), pp. 204–14; W. Malm., *GR*, OMT edn., p. 8.

[101] *The Anglo-Norman Voyage of St Brendan by Benedeit*, ed. E. G. R. Waters (Oxford, 1928).

[102] Gaimar, lines 6477–88, appendix, lines 2–5, pp. 205, 207; for identification, ibid., p. xi.

[103] A. G. Rigg, 'Serlo of Wilton: Biographical Notes', *Medium Aevum*, 65 (1996), pp. 96–101.

Both Henry's queens were thus active patrons of literature in Latin and French.

## Marriage Networks

In many ways the picture that emerges of Henry I's two queens—propertied ladies, patrons of culture and religion, fostering their families and households, with a clear procreative duty—would be true of the other queens of the period. In one sense, though, they were exceptional. Neither Matilda nor Adeliza faced the complexities of competition between their children or between their children and their husband. Matilda had only one son, who was about 15 at the time of her death, while Adeliza had no children by Henry I. Neither of them was ever queen mother. The contrast would be with Eleanor of Aquitaine, who took her motherly role to its extreme, backing her rebellious sons against their father, holding the English government together in the early years of the reign of her son, Richard, organizing forces to support the succession of her son, John, against her grandson, Arthur, in the last years of her life.

One important decision that had to be made about royal children was who they would marry. Like the marriages of kings themselves, the marriages of sons and daughters of kings were part of a political game and, as has been pointed out, that game was French politics. Relations with Normandy's neighbours, the Capetian kings and the houses of Blois and Anjou, were especially important. William I married his daughter Adela to Stephen of Blois in the early 1080s as part of an alliance directed against the aggressive counts of Anjou. The marriages of Henry I's son, William, to Matilda of Anjou and of his daughter, Matilda, to Geoffrey of Anjou were both intended to bring about a rapprochement between the Norman and Angevin dynasties. Stephen's son, Eustace, was married to Constance, daughter of Louis VI, in 1140, when the two kings were both interested in containing Geoffrey of Anjou. After the succession of Henry II, with Normandy and Anjou under a single ruler, French politics continued to be conducted partly in the idiom of marriage alliances. Henry's eldest son, Henry 'the Young King', was married to Margaret, daughter of Louis VII (1160); his second son, Richard, was betrothed to her sister Alice (1169); his third son, Geoffrey, married to Constance, heiress of Brittany (1181); and his youngest son, John, was betrothed to the heiress of the count of Maurienne in 1173, although the prospective bride died soon after.

Marriage alliances might have territorial consequences. An instance is the fortune of the Norman Vexin, that disputed border area between the lands of the dukes of Normandy and the kings of France. Geoffrey of Anjou and his son Henry, the future Henry II, had been forced to cede it to Louis VII in return for recognition as dukes in 1144 and 1151. In 1160 Henry II recovered it as the dowry of Louis's daughter, Margaret, the child bride of his infant son Henry. After the younger Henry died in 1183, his widow sold out her own claims to the Norman Vexin to Henry II, and her sister Alice, who was betrothed to Richard, Henry's next son, was endowed with it. The French marriage and betrothal of Henry's eldest and second sons thus brought concrete territorial reinforcement to the Norman frontier. Some marriages of kings' sons, especially younger sons, were obviously designed simply to ensure them landed wealth. Stephen arranged the marriage of his younger son, William, with the heiress of the great comital house of Warenne, while Henry II sought to secure the future of his youngest son, John, in a similar way, by betrothing him to the heiress to the earldom of Gloucester.

The status of the bride or groom reflected on the honour of the family making the match and Henry II must have been well pleased to arrange regal or semi-regal marriages for all three of his daughters. Matilda, the oldest, was married to the great duke of Saxony and Bavaria, Henry the Lion; the next, Eleanor, to Alfonso VIII of Castile; Joanna, the youngest, to William II of Sicily. All three matches created political entanglements of various kinds. The link with Henry the Lion began an association of the Angevins with his family, the Welfs, that was to endure for generations (see below, pp. 103–6). Alfonso VIII seems to have acquired, along with Eleanor, the promise of Gascony after the death of Eleanor of Aquitaine, and in 1204, after his mother-in-law died, he did indeed invade Gascony in order to assert his claim. The Sicilian involvement created by Joanna's marriage to William II reached its sharpest form when, in the winter of 1190–1, Richard I spent several months camped in the kingdom en route for the Holy Land, and took up arms against its ruler, Tancred, in order to enforce his widowed sister's rights to her dower. These marriages thus entailed a far-flung web of political and military action, with repercussions from Messina to Brunswick.

The marriages of the members of the royal family other than kings show much the same patterns as that of the kings themselves. Except in the case of Henry I's numerous illegitimate offspring, few connections were made with the Anglo-Norman aristocracy. Ties with French princes were the central matter and, for Henry II's daughters, links with an even wider international royal network. As a letter of Henry III puts it, reporting the views of opponents of a proposed marriage of his sister to the earl Marshal in 1224, they 'asserted that we had no greater treasure than our marriage and that of our sisters, whence it behoved us to marry our sisters so that we gained a great alliance in foreign parts'.[104]

---

[104] Pierre Chaplais (ed.), *Diplomatic Documents Preserved in the Public Record Office*, 1. *1101–1272* (Oxford, 1964), no. 140, p. 96.

## 4. PREDATORY AND PUNITIVE RULE

'God is a slow avenger, the king a swift one.'[105] This was the view of the courtier Walter Map, and his view has weight. Henry I was renowned for being 'an implacable enemy to the disloyal, scarcely ever pardoning those who were proved guilty without punishment in body, in honour or in cash. This was felt most wretchedly by the guilty ones who died in the king's chains ...'[106] The Angevin kings were notorious for their rage. The following is a description of Henry II's behaviour when annoyed by one of his court officials: 'The king, enflamed with his customary fury, threw the cap from his head, untied his belt, hurled his mantle and other garments from him, removed the silk coverlet from the bed with his own hand and began to chew the straw of the bedding.'[107] The capacity for such tantrums seems to have been hereditary. When crossed by the chancellor, William de Longchamps, John 'was more than angry, his whole body was unrecognizable. Rage furrowed his brow, his eyes glowed with flame, his rosy face became livid; I know what would have become of the chancellor if he had fallen like a ripe apple into those gesticulating hands in the hour of his anger.'[108]

This 'wrath and malevolence' (*ira et malevolentia*) did not signify merely a subjective mood. The king could decide, consciously and explicitly, to turn his disfavour against those who had offended him. It was a standard practice of twelfth-century law to apply distraint—that is, the seizure of chattels or the confiscation of land—in order to enforce compliance with judicial commands or attendance at court, but the Norman and Angevin kings often needed no such judicial pretext for their heavy grasp. King John admitted freely in one of his royal mandates that Hugh Grassus had been disseised (i.e. dispossessed) of his lands 'Because we were angry with him'.[109] The royal financial records contain many references to payments 'so that the king will remit his anger', 'to have the king's good will', 'to have peace from the king's malevolence'.[110] When some of the Cistercian abbots refused to pay the land-tax of 1200 without the consent of their Chapter-General, John turned the heat of his ill-will against their Order: 'The king was greatly angered at their answer and, in wrath and fury, he issued instructions to his sheriffs that they should harass and disturb the men of that Order by whatever means they could, neither doing justice against those who oppressed or impleaded them, nor helping them in any matter.'[111]

To be the victim of the king's malevolence in this way was virtually to be

---

[105] Map 5. 7 (p. 510).      [106] Orderic 11. 2 (6, p. 18).
[107] *Becket Mats.* 6, p. 72 (Becket Letters 253).      [108] R. Devizes, p. 32.
[109] *Rot. litt. claus.* 1, p. 48.      [110] J. E. A. Jolliffe, *Angevin Kingship* (2nd edn.; London, 1963), p. 96.
[111] R. Coggesh., p. 102.

treated as an enemy and some aspects of royal rule in our period suggest that the royal government did not always draw a sharp line between subjects and foes. The retinues of the Norman kings had a reputation for harrying the districts they passed through. While Rufus and his court were awaiting a favourable wind to cross to Normandy in 1097 'his retinue did more harm in the shires where they lay than ever retinue or army should do in a peaceable land'.[112] His successor, Henry I, was charged with a similar indifference to the distinction between subjects and prey: 'wherever the king went, his retinue harried his wretched people, burning and killing'.[113] Although the households of the Angevins seem not to have practised such open brutality, there continued to be many governmental practices which treated enemies and subjects almost on a par. The taking of hostages is one example.

'He is no king that has not hostages in chains', said the Old Irish lawcodes, and the principle was just as true in the Norman and Angevin periods.[114] Possession of one's enemies' children or friends offered a cruel sanction in the violent competition that constituted medieval politics. It was, of course, a standard feature of dealings with other political powers. When William the Lion of Scotland made his formal submission to Henry II after his defeat and capture in 1174, the terms included the surrender of five Scottish castles and the handing over of twenty-one important hostages, including the king's brother, David. David would be released once the castles were in English hands and the other hostages could then substitute a son or other close relative for themselves.[115] Such hostages faced real dangers. In 1165 Henry II ordered that the male hostages he had taken from the Welsh, some of them sons of princes, should be blinded and castrated, while the females should have their noses and ears cut off.[116] His son John hanged all his Welsh hostages during the hostilities of 1211–12.[117]

However, hostages were not only taken from potential enemies beyond the borders of England. Many of the dealings between English kings and their subjects, especially barons of whose loyalty they might have doubt, involved guarantees through hostage-taking. Henry I required hostages before he would release Waleran of Meulan, Stephen before he freed Ranulf of Chester.[118] Several of the great men of the Angevin period had known the constrictions, apprehensions, and, possibly, the excitements of life as a hostage. When Nigel, bishop of Ely, made terms with King Stephen in 1144, in addition to paying the king £200, he had to surrender his son, Richard fitz Neal, as a hostage. This was the second time the boy (probably in his early teens at

<hr>

[112] *ASC*, pp. 233–4.    [113] *ASC*, p. 239 (1104); cf. Eadmer, *HN*, pp. 192–3.
[114] F. J. Byrne, *Irish Kings and High-Kings* (London, 1973), p. 31.
[115] Stones, *Rels.*, pp. 6–8 [3]–[4].    [116] *Melrose Chron.*, p. 79; *Brut (RBH)*, p. 147.
[117] Barnwell Chron., p. 207.    [118] *ASC*, pp. 259, 267 (1129, *s.a.* 1140).

this moment) had experienced such a fate.[119] Richard, who was eventually treasurer of Henry II, author of the *Dialogue on the Exchequer* (*Dialogus de Scaccario*) and bishop of London, thus learned at first hand the importance of the political handle that hostage-taking represented. Later in Stephen's reign, the young William Marshal, perhaps 5 or 6 years old, was given as a hostage to the king by his father, John Marshal, as part of an agreement to win a truce in the siege of Newbury castle, that John held and the king had surrounded. When John breached the terms of the truce, Stephen was urged to hang the young boy, but characteristically offered his father the chance to save his life by surrendering the castle. John replied by saying that he was not concerned about the fate of his son, 'for he still had the anvil and hammer to forge better ones'. Despite the father's callous response, Stephen could not bring himself to have William Marshal killed, even resisting his counsellors' ingenious idea of having the boy thrown into the castle by a siege machine.[120] William survived and ended his days as earl of Pembroke and regent of England.

The king who made most systematic use of the practice of taking hostages from his baronage was John. Hostage-taking formed part, perhaps the most vexing part, of John's elaborate system of control, for the king's suspicious and distrustful character led him to create as thorough a web of obligations as his ingenuity could devise. Great barons were lured into debt and the debt guaranteed on their whole estate. Special charters of fealty were required, with the vassal having to promise that 'if he does not serve the king faithfully, all his land will come into the king's hand'.[121] The surrender of sons or other family members into the custody of the man who had supposedly murdered his nephew Arthur with his own hands was another iron cog in this machinery of intimidation.

Hostages were frequently held as a pledge for castles. When, at the beginning of his reign, John restored to Roger de Lacy, a great northern baron, his castle of Pontefract (Yorks.), he did so only after first taking his son and heir as a hostage.[122] William d'Aubigny retained his castle of Belvoir (Leics.) on condition that he give his son as hostage.[123] The arrangement with another northern lord, Roger de Montbegon, was 'that Roger will give to the lord king four hostages that the lord king wishes to have from him and Roger will hold his castle as long as he serves the lord king well and faithfully and, if he does otherwise, he will render to the lord king his castle of Hornby [Lancs.] and will have his hostages back'.[124] John knew how dangerous Roger de Montbegon could be, for he had been one of the most determined supporters of his own rebellion against his brother, king Richard, in 1194.

One baron who had to place his sons in John's dubious care was William

---

[119] *Lib. Eliensis* 3. 86 (p. 333).     [120] *Hist. Guill. Mar.* 1, pp. 18–22, lines 467–594.
[121] e.g. *Rot. obl.*, p. 484.     [122] R. Howd. 4, pp. 91–2.
[123] Ibid., p. 161.     [124] *Rot. obl.*, p. 275.

Marshal, the same who had himself been so narrowly saved from death as a hostage over half-a-century earlier. One can only speculate as to his emotions when John demanded first his eldest, then his second son. On the latter occasion, his wife and counsellors were not in favour of sending the boy. William determined, however, that compliance was the better policy, telling the king's messenger, 'Sir, know for certain that I would willingly send all my children to the king, if he wished', asking only, in naiveté or perplexity, 'but tell me, for the love of God, why does he have such fury against me?'[125] As the Marshal's biographer comments, John was a king 'who would never stop making one further demand'.[126] The resentment that this relentless pressure created echoes behind Clause 49 of the Magna Carta of 1215, by which John was forced to promise that 'We will immediately restore all hostages and charters that Englishmen have given us as a guarantee of peace and faithful service'. Indeed, Magna Carta can be plausibly seen as a shout of protest against a monarchy that had taken its powers of force and coercion beyond the limit.

## 5. REBELLION

The kings of England had to rule over, as well as by means of, a group of men who were themselves trained in combat, had at their disposal armed followers and the wealth to support them, and were educated with a high sense of their own dignity and honour. It is not surprising that violent opposition to the king was recurrent. It can be analysed into three basic types. First was the instinctual reaction of individual lords kicking back at real or supposed infringements or threats emanating from the royal government. Their response was as unthinking as trying to swot a fly. The rebellion of Baldwin de Redvers against Stephen in 1136 appears to have been of this type, even though he eventually joined—indeed, helped to form—the Angevin party. His initial complaint was 'that he could not have a certain honor (great estate) that he had sought from the king'.[127] This personal grievance moved him to try to establish a private lordship in and around Exeter, using the royal castle there as a base and the threat of fire and destruction as a method. It took a three months' siege for Stephen to secure the castle and even then Baldwin continued resistance, in England and subsequently in Normandy, where his cause merged with that of the Angevins.

More threatening than rebellion of this individual and visceral kind was a general movement among the aristocracy in support of a rival ruler. The recurrent divisions within the ruling family meant that there was usually a focus for opposition, in the person of the king's brother, son, or cousin. Some

---

[125] *Hist. Guill. Mar.* 2, pp. 113–14, 117–19, lines 13271–6, 13362–419.
[126] Ibid., p. 154, lines 14396–7.  [127] R. Hexham, p. 146.

of the great rebellions of the Norman and Angevin period, such as those of 1088 or 1173–4, were headed by, or in support of, members of the ruling dynasty. Rebels could thus enjoy a semi-legitimacy in their opposition and envisage a future in which a new regime would be headed by their own leader. The civil war of Stephen's reign was simply a situation of this type that, because of military deadlock, became extended over years rather than months. The goal of the participants in such general rebellions in favour of rival rulers was to replace their current lord with another. The third type of opposition went beyond this. On occasion, aristocratic rebels clearly had a programme, couched in the language of principled reform. The barons who opposed John in the period that led to, and followed, Magna Carta, possessed an ideological scheme that they wished to realize. Of course, the three types of rebellion could overlap and merge. The rebels of 1215 included many men with personal grievances and they eventually found themselves offering the throne to a rival ruler, Louis of France. There is still, however, a useful distinction to be drawn between the isolated, personal rising of a Baldwin de Redvers, the widespread, but entirely unideological, support for Robert against William Rufus in 1088, and the barons who drew up the complex and sometimes general provisions of the Articles of the Barons and Magna Carta in 1215.

## The Rebellion of 1088

The chronicler Orderic Vitalis, describing the consequences of the division of England and Normandy between Robert and William Rufus in 1087, put the following words into the mouths of the Norman magnates:

What are we to do? Now that our lord is dead, two young men have succeeded and precipitately divided the lordship of England and Normandy. How can we properly serve two lords who are so different and so distant from each other? If we serve Robert, duke of Normandy, worthily, we will offend his brother, William, and we will be stripped by him of our great revenues and large estates in England. On the other hand, if we obey king William fittingly, duke Robert will deprive us of all our inherited lands in Normandy.[128]

However fictional the speech, the dilemma was real. They resolved to form a league to depose or kill William.

The rebels of 1088 included, in the words of the *Anglo-Saxon Chronicle*, 'the most powerful Frenchmen who were in this land'.[129] Of the ten greatest baronial landholders recorded in Domesday Book (drawn up just the previous year), six joined the rebellion against Rufus, including Odo of Bayeux, William the Conqueror's half-brother, and the great magnate Roger de Montgomery. The rebellion had a wide geographical base, from Kent,

---

[128] Orderic 8. 2 (4, p. 122).     [129] *ASC*, p. 222, *s.a.* 1087.

dominated by Odo, to Northumbria, whose earl, Robert de Mowbray, was a participant, and from Norfolk, where Roger Bigod seized the royal castle of Norwich, to Bristol, held at this time by Geoffrey, bishop of Coutances, another rebel. The rebels anticipated that Robert would launch an expedition from Normandy to back them up. In the meantime they began the rebellion.

Resistance to the king could be marked by some symbolic act, such as refusing to attend a summons to his court. More concrete methods were also available and the insurgents of 1088 welcomed the coming of spring with the traditional gestures of revolt: 'They set out as soon as Easter came and harried and burned and laid waste the king's demesne farms and devastated the lands of all those men who were loyal to the king. Each of them went to his castle and manned and provisioned it as best he could.'[130] As is clear from this account, the two fundamental signals of rebellion were the activation of the castles and the wasting of one's opponents' lands. There could be a link between the two, for one of the simplest ways of provisioning a castle was to seize crops and drive off stock. Once this process had begun, a response was demanded. If no one stepped in at this point, the situation might then arise where every lord of a castle lived by plundering his neighbourhood—the classic stereotype of 'feudal anarchy'.

William Rufus was not the kind of king to ignore such a challenge. His response was threefold. First, he tried to split the opposition. He told Roger de Montgomery that

he did not understand why they [the rebels] are so wild. If they wish, they can have as much money as they want, likewise with an increase in their lands; they can have absolutely what they want. Only be careful not to upset William the Conqueror's decisions: if they set those aside they should be careful of their own positions. The same man made them dukes who made him king.[131]

Moved by this combination of promise and threat, Roger abandoned the conspiracy. Secondly, Rufus appealed to the English, promising them, in the words of the *Anglo-Saxon Chronicle*, 'the best law there had ever been in this land'.[132] The last surviving Anglo-Saxon bishop, Wulfstan of Worcester, stiffened the resistance to the rebels, who were advancing on his cathedral city, burning as they came, by blessing the royalist troops and excommunicating the insurgents. As his household knights and other soldiers loyal to Rufus marched out on a sortie, he exhorted them, 'Maintain your fidelity to the king, fight manfully to protect the people and the city'. The rebels were routed.[133]

Thirdly, and most importantly, Rufus undertook vigorous military action in person. After storming Tonbridge, he captured bishop Odo in Pevensey

---

[130] *ASC*, p. 223, *s.a.* 1087.    [131] W. Malm., *GR* 4. 306 (2, pp. 361–2); OMT edn., p. 546.
[132] *ASC*, p. 223, *s.a.* 1087.    [133] Flor. Worcs. 2, pp. 24–6.

castle after a six-week siege. Meanwhile, the forces that Robert was sending from Normandy were driven back by 'the Englishmen who were guarding the sea'.[134] Rufus now took Odo to one of the bishop's chief fortresses, Rochester, on the understanding that he would order his garrison there to surrender. In a startling manoeuvre, however, Odo's troops pulled their lord inside the defences and continued their defiance. Rufus then 'called together his Englishmen and ordered them to summon all their countrymen to the siege, unless they wanted to be called "Nithing"; the English thought this the most shameful name and flocked in troops to the king . . .'.[135] Faced by a large English army, a determined king, and the continued absence of Robert, the rebels at Rochester eventually capitulated. The rebellion was over. In the aftermath 'many Frenchmen relinquished their lands and went overseas', among them the great Odo of Bayeux.[136]

The rebellion of 1088 is a classic instance of a large-scale, coordinated, but non-programmatic rising. As their goal, the rebels sought to replace one son of William the Conqueror with another. Manning their castles and devastating the land of the king and his adherents, they threw down the gauntlet. Rufus picked it up with energy, splitting the opposition, rousing the English, and conducting a very successful campaign of castle-warfare. The revolt lasted probably between three and six months. The uncertain pattern of succession in Norman and Angevin England made crises of this type part of the expected fabric of political life.

## The Rebellion of 1173–1174

The rebellion of 1173–4 differed in several obvious ways from that of 1088: it was fought on behalf of a son of the king, not a brother, and a son whose ultimate right to inherit had been acknowledged in the most unquestionable way; it lasted longer; it drew in surrounding kings. Yet, despite these differences, the rebellious aristocrats were a group with similar motives, opposing the king on behalf of another member of the ruling dynasty, anticipating personal rewards from service to a (hopefully) rising star. Henry II's son, Henry 'the Young King', was praised by his followers for his good looks, courtly charm, and generosity,[137] but was impatient for greater autonomy than his father was willing to grant him. Married to the daughter of the king of France, crowned as joint-king in 1170 and 18 years old at the time of his rebellion, Henry the Young King was eager to be given one of the lands of the paternal inheritance—Normandy, Anjou, or England—as a territory to rule in his own right. He kept a large and glamorous retinue but felt constrained

[134] ASC, p. 224, s.a. 1087.      [135] W. Malm., GR 4. 306 (2, p. 362); OMT edn., p. 548.
[136] ASC, p. 225, s.a. 1087.      [137] e.g. Gerv. Tilb. 2. 20 (p. 947).

by lack of resources: 'he had many knights but he had no means to give rewards and gifts to the knights'.[138]

The immediate occasion for his rebellion was his father's plan to endow his youngest son, John, with territory in Anjou, as part of the arrangements made at the time of John's betrothal to the daughter of the count of Maurienne. Henry the Young King withdrew from his father's court in exasperation and went to join his father-in-law, Louis VII. This was in March 1173. Two of the Young King's brothers, Richard and Geoffrey, joined him at Louis's court, although their mother, Eleanor of Aquitaine, who was also party to the rebellion, was captured by her husband en route, and thereafter held in captivity. The Young King and his Capetian mentor now created a far-flung alliance against Henry II. Promises flowed: land and revenues in England and Anjou were offered to the counts of Flanders, Boulogne, and Blois; William the Lion, king of Scots, was to have his long-coveted Northumberland. The younger Henry planned to win his father's kingdom partly by dismembering it.

Hostilities commenced in April 1173. The counts of Flanders and Boulogne invaded Normandy from the east, the king of France and the younger Henry from the south, while the Bretons menaced the west. Each of these assaults ended in failure. The count of Boulogne lost his life, Henry II chased Louis out of Normandy, while at Dol, in Brittany, the Bretons were defeated and a large haul of captives taken, including the earl of Chester, one of the chief leaders of the rebellion among the Anglo-Norman baronage. About the same period William the Lion's desultory campaign in the north of England tailed off and soon English troops under Richard de Lucy, the chief justiciar, and Humphrey de Bohun, the constable, were ravaging southern Scotland in turn. Negotiations were opened between Henry II and his opponents near Gisors on the frontier of Normandy but these yielded no result, except, according to one report, giving the earl of Leicester, who was with the Young King, the opportunity to insult and threaten Henry II.

The insubordinate earl of Leicester now undertook to continue the rebellion in England, where his chief castle of Leicester was one of the main centres of the revolt. He raised a force of Flemish mercenaries and crossed from the continent to East Anglia, to join another of the rebel barons, Hugh Bigod, earl of Norfolk, at his great castle of Framlingham. After some limited military activity in Suffolk, the earl of Leicester determined to cross the country to Leicester, but was intercepted on 17 October 1173 at Fornham, near Bury St Edmunds, by a royalist army, led by Richard de Lucy and Humphrey de Bohun, who had hurried down from Scotland, and the loyal earls of Cornwall, Gloucester, and Arundel. Leicester and his Flemings were completely defeated, the earl and his wife, who had dressed in man's armour,

---

[138] *Brut (RBH)*, p. 161.

were captured, along with their higher status followers, while the bulk of the mercenaries were slaughtered or left to rot in captivity. As Henry II's barons supposedly remarked to him in 1173, 'It is a bad year for your enemies'.[139]

The rebellion was by no means over, however. In spring 1174 campaigning recommenced. David, brother of William the Lion of Scotland, who had been granted the earldom of Huntingdon by Henry the Young King, took possession of Huntingdon and also charge of the rebels based in Leicester. The earl Ferrers, a rebel baron whose chief castle was at Tutbury (Staffs.), burned the royal town of Nottingham, while earl Hugh Bigod likewise put Norwich to the torch. William the Lion himself undertook the conquest of the north of England. On 8 July Henry II, who had been concentrating on defeating his enemies in France, landed in England, along with his prisoners, including his wife, Eleanor. His first act was to seek the forgiveness of Thomas Becket, the archbishop of Canterbury who had been murdered by Henry's knights three and a half years earlier and canonized the previous year. At Becket's tomb in Canterbury cathedral he prayed and wept and was then beaten as a penance. The results were immediate. The day following the ceremony at Canterbury, on 13 July 1174, William the Lion and many of his knights were surprised and captured at Alnwick by a group of northern loyalists. The Scots king was sent south with his feet bound beneath his horse.

In the aftermath of Alnwick, Henry was able to sweep up the opposition. He marched to Huntingdon and Framlingham, receiving the surrender of the rebel castles there, and then on to Northampton, where there was something like a general submission, with rebels coming in to surrender their castles, promising to repatriate their Flemish mercenaries and make their peace with the king. With England secure, Henry recrossed the Channel to relieve the capital of Normandy, Rouen, which was under siege by Louis VII. Chasing the French king off with ease, Henry was now able to arrange a settlement with his enemies. Terms were agreed on 30 September, whereby 'King Henry, the king's son, and his brothers, returned to their father and to his service, as their lord'.[140]

The rebellion of 1173–4 lasted eighteen months, took place on a stage that extended from Scotland to Poitou, and left its scars on the land in the form of charred towns and tumbled castles: 'Many a castle and many a town was ruined because of this war and many a fine man . . . was killed or exiled, impoverished or brought low by this cursed turn of events.'[141] Blame tended to focus on the Young King's advisers. He had acted 'unadvisedly, by the

---

[139] Fantosme, line 150, p. 12.      [140] *Gesta Hen. II* 1, p. 77; R. Howd. 2, p. 67.
[141] *Hist. Guill. Mar.* 1, p. 81, lines 2202–9; Gerald, *Exp.* 1. 44 (p. 120).

counsel and suggestions of a treacherous faction', 'on the advice of wicked men'.[142] Even the biographer of William Marshal, who had maintained his loyalty to his lord, Henry the Young King, and joined him in rebellion, wrote, 'Cursed be the day when the traitors schemed to embroil the father and the son.'[143]

Henry II had faced a powerful opposition, including, as well as his three sons, two kings, several of the great princes of northern France and the earls of Chester, Leicester, Norfolk, and Ferrers. Each of the great barons could draw in turn on the support of tenants, vassals, and retainers. Over thirty of the tenants of the earldom of Huntingdon followed earl David, brother of William the Lion, into rebellion.[144] Bonds of loyalty worked for Henry II as well as against him, however. His illegitimate son, Geoffrey, bishop-elect of Lincoln, was steadfast and active in his support, and his uncle, Reginald, earl of Cornwall, an illegitimate son of Henry I, was one of those who won the battle of Fornham. A man like Richard de Lucy, the chief justiciar, who had risen from knightly to baronial status through service in the Angevin administration, took the opportunity of the war of 1173-4 to demonstrate that Henry's patronage had been well directed. The towns seem to have been loyal. Rouen underwent its siege with constancy and the Londoners were praised as men who 'never failed their rightful lord'.[145]

As well as being able to call on such loyalty, Henry II had enormous material resources at his disposal, to buy the allegiance of those who might not offer it freely. Many French barons were won over to 'the king who greased their palms'.[146] His war machine was well funded and he could keep large numbers of mercenaries (his 'Brabançons') in the field. Perhaps most important of all, he showed himself a confident, able, and energetic general, inspiring his followers, dismaying his enemies, and giving a clear lesson to those of doubtful loyalty. He emerged from the war with power and reputation enhanced. It was not the case, however, that any of the fundamental problems had been resolved. He still had restless sons, who grew older and more experienced year by year. He still faced the deep-seated hostility of the kings of France. When the young Philip Augustus succeeded his father, Louis VII, in 1180, and Henry's son, Richard, a brilliant general and soldier, became his heir-apparent after the death of the Young King in 1183, all the conditions were in place for a repeat performance of the rising of 1173 with the odds much more in the rebels' favour. Henry II did indeed die in despair, harried by the combined forces of his son and the French king, learning on his deathbed that his youngest and dearest son, John, had joined the rebellion.

[142] P. Blois, *Letters*, no. 2 (col. 7).    [143] *Hist. Guill. Mar.* 1, p. 81, lines 2210-12.
[144] Stringer, *Earl David*, p. 27.    [145] Fantosme, line 914, p. 68.
[146] *Hist. Guill. Mar.* 1, p. 83, line 2267.

## The Penalties of Rebellion

The primary task of a medieval king was to manage his aristocracy: to use patronage to encourage service and loyalty; to withhold it or, in some cases, show his disfavour, if he wished to punish or bring to heel enemies or opponents; to balance the very greatest men against each other or against groups of lesser men; to prevent the formations of factions, unless he could handle them to his own advantage; above all, to prevent the formation of an opposition faction of any size. Politics of this kind required skilful judgement. Sometimes it might be necessary to tolerate aristocratic greed or violence; sometimes the nettle had to be grasped and great noble families broken and dispossessed; there had to be ways for the king's enemies to become his friends or servants. A king's rule was made or unmade by his judgement in these matters.

Once rebellious barons had been defeated, the king could be presented with a choice between crushing them completely or winning them over. On several occasions under the Norman kings, great men or great dynasties were dispossessed. Odo of Bayeux, who had been the richest man in England after the king, was exiled and stripped of his estates in 1088. The Montgomery family was treated in a similar fashion in 1102. In this way deterrent lessons were given and the store of lands at the king's disposal increased. Yet it is clear that even loyal barons were made uneasy by so complete an uprooting of high-born men. Partly they were simply startled and intimidated but they also had a case to make: breaking one's enemies was not always and everywhere the most sensible policy.

After the defeat of the rebellion against William Rufus in 1088, his barons urged leniency on the king:

if you remit your anger against these men [the rebels] and benevolently retain them with you, or at least allow them to depart in peace, you will enjoy the benefits of their friendship and service on many future occasions. It may be that the man who harms you, later obeys you as a friend.[147]

William was shrewd enough to recognize both the truth of this statement and the importance of giving due weight to his followers' advice, but he was also sensible enough to make distinctions between those, like Odo, whom he needed to break, and those whom he could use. Hence 'he punished the disobedience of some men with harsh judgments but deliberately ignored the guilt of others.'[148] Similarly, Henry I could break men, but was also capable of reconciliation with his enemies. He dispossessed William de Warenne of the earldom of Surrey for opposing him in 1101, but restored him in 1102 or 1103 and thereafter the earl 'blossomed as one of his chief and closest friends'.[149]

---

[147] Orderic 8. 2 (4, p. 132).     [148] Ibid., p. 134.     [149] Orderic 11. 2 (6, p. 14).

After defeating and capturing the rebel Waleran of Meulan in 1124, Henry eventually freed him and restored his position; 'they then became as good friends as they were earlier enemies'.[150]

During the Angevin period, the complete dispossession of aristocratic rebels seems to have become a rare occurrence. Henry II's clemency in dealing with his enemies was remarked upon by his treasurer, Richard fitz Neal. After he captured those who rebelled against him in 1173–4, 'few lost their lands and none were degraded or suffered mutilation or death'.[151] Another member of Henry's court, Gerald of Wales, also praised Henry for his conduct on this occasion, for, 'when his enemies were defeated and overwhelmed on every side, he accorded them their life and honour'.[152] The earls of Chester and Leicester, two of the leading rebels of 1173–4, were indeed imprisoned and deprived of their lands but they were very soon set free and, at the Council of Northampton in January 1177, restored to their estates. Although his bearing to Henry II had been insulting and aggressive during the hostilities, the earl of Leicester found that submission on this occasion earned immediate rewards. He had been challenged by one of his tenants, who claimed to hold his land directly of the king. Rather than fighting the case in the law courts, the earl stated that

he did not wish to plead concerning this land or any other against the king's wishes, but conceded that this and all his other holdings were in the king's mercy. When the king heard him speaking so dutifully, he was moved by affection and restored him completely to all his holdings, as he had held them fifteen days before the war, although the king retained in his own hands the castle of Mountsorrel and the castle of Pacy, the only two of his castles still standing. The king also restored to him the whole of Leicester, and the forest that the entire county court had sworn to be royal demesne, for the king knew that this had been done through enmity, because the king bore hatred against the earl.[153]

A king who was unable or unwilling to stomach reconciliation of this kind was showing not strength but weakness. John is perhaps the most dramatic instance of a vindictive ruler, but Stephen too nursed grudges, and, in both cases, their implacability sowed dragons' teeth.

The master medievalist, F. W. Maitland, observed the remarkable clemency with which 'the frank, open rebellions of the great folk' were treated in the time of the Norman and Angevin kings, in contrast with the 'ages of blood' which followed in the later Middle Ages and Tudor period. He cites earl Waltheof, executed in 1075, and William of Eu, blinded and castrated after being convicted of involvement in the rebellion of 1095, as 'almost the only cases in which a high-born rebel loses either life or limb by

---

[150] *ASC*, p. 259 (1129).   [151] *Dial. scacc.*, p. 76.
[152] Gerald, *Exp.* 1. 45 (p. 124).   [153] *Gesta Hen. II* 1, p. 134.

judicial sentence'.[154] The dealings of Henry II with those who rebelled against him bear out the perception that the political system of twelfth-century England was indeed marked by 'the compassionate treatment of defeated high-status enemies'.[155] It was only a relative compassion, since imprisonment for life, as in the cases of Robert de Mowbray, Robert, brother of Henry I, and Robert de Bellême, was not unknown, and there were still such atrocities as John's murder of Arthur and starving to death of Matilda de Braose and her son, but there was no such post-battlefield slaughter as would occur during the Wars of the Roses.

Between the later eleventh and the early fourteenth century, defeated political opponents of high birth were rarely dispossessed and scarcely ever maimed or killed in cold blood. This situation seems to have been different not only from that in the later medieval period but also that in the early Middle Ages. These centuries thus stand out in the history of English political violence. Another contrast is not chronological but geographical. While the power struggles of Norman and Angevin England rarely ended in the deliberate slaughter of defeated aristocratic enemies, the older pattern seems to have lasted longer in the Celtic polities of the British Isles. The kings and princes of Wales, Ireland, and Gaelic Scotland continued to employ blinding, maiming, and killing in their conflicts with rivals from both within and without their families.

The contrast between the parts of the British Isles is brought out by a poignant juxtaposition in Roger of Howden's history. His report of the terms of settlement of 1174 between Henry II and his sons, which included a general pardon on both sides, is immediately followed in his text by the account of the quarrel within the ruling dynasty of Galloway, that culminated in the blinding and castration of Uhtred of Galloway by his nephew Malcolm, with fatal results.[156] While the routine employment of blinding and castration was far from unknown in Norman and Angevin England, it was not something that the high-born regularly inflicted on one another. As Henry the Young King and his brothers settled terms with their father, against whom they had fought for eighteen months, Uhtred of Galloway went blindly and bloodily to his death.

The distinctive customs and rhetoric of rebellion in our period were coloured by the fact that the great men were bound to each other by ties of homage or tenure. It was universally recognized that such ties entailed moral

---

[154] Frederick Pollock and Frederic William Maitland, *The History of English Law before the Time of Edward I* (2nd edn., 2 vols.; Cambridge, 1898, reissued 1968), vol. 2, p. 506 and n.

[155] John Gillingham, '1066 and the Introduction of Chivalry', in John Hudson and George Garnett (eds.), *Law and Government in Medieval England and Normandy: Essays in Honour of Sir James Holt* (Cambridge, 1994), pp. 31–55, at p. 32.

[156] *Gesta Hen. II* 1, pp. 79–80; R. Howd. 2, p. 69.

and legal obligations and it was not always clear that a vassal's duty to his lord should be subordinated to his duties as a subject to his king. One instance of this kind of thinking, although in very unusual circumstances, is provided by the rebellion of Baldwin de Redvers against Stephen in 1136. Baldwin had never accepted Stephen as king. When his garrison at Exeter sued for terms from the king, the party among Stephen's own forces who were eager that the rebels be treated mildly argued 'they have not sworn an oath to the king's majesty and have not taken up arms except out of fealty to their lord'.[157] Since they had never bound themselves to Stephen, their resistance could not be treason; in following their lord, they were indeed behaving honourably. Such thinking made rebellion more conceivable and more justifiable. It also provided a case for clemency towards defeated rebels.

The right of aristocrats to use force in the course of their quarrels was simply a given in most parts of medieval Europe. In England, the tradition of a powerful monarchy inhibiting such private warfare was strong, but, after 1066, the top ranks of the English aristocracy came from Normandy and continued to hold lands there. They thought as Norman lords, as well as subjects of the king of the English, and in Normandy the norms governing violent disputing were different and more lax. The chronicler Orderic Vitalis, writing in Normandy, explains that in England waging war and burning one's neighbours' farms was 'an unheard-of crime in that country and one that can be atoned for only by a heavy punishment'.[158] By implication such destructive vendettas were regarded as less of an enormity by the Normans. It is hard to believe that a great Anglo-Norman baron changed his attitudes immediately he crossed the Channel. Even the author of the law-book attributed to Glanville, who was clearly a royalist and a legal official of the Angevin kings, acknowledged that vassals might have a duty to participate in armed conflict between aristocrats: 'If anyone has done homage to different lords for different fiefs and those lords attack each other, he must obey his chief lord if he requires him to go with him in person against his other lord.'[159]

This tradition of justified aristocratic violence could invest resistance to the king with a kind of acceptability. The practice of 'defiance' (diffidatio), whereby those about to rebel publicly renounced their allegiance to their lord, shows thinking of the same type: bonds of subordination and obedience to the Crown were not irrevocable or innate, if a man had good cause he could proclaim that his lord was no longer his lord and then fight against him honourably. Two notable instances occurred in 1138. In that year Robert, earl of Gloucester, the illegitimate son of Henry I who was to be the main supporter of his half-sister Matilda in her fight for the Crown, sent his messengers to king Stephen and 'renounced friendship and fealty, detaching himself

---

[157] Gesta Stephani 20 (p. 42).    [158] Orderic 11. 2 (6, p. 18).    [159] Glanville 9. 1 (p. 104).

from his homage'. Now, 'with the king defied', he could fight openly for Matilda's cause.[160]

In the same year Robert Bruce (ancestor of the victor of Bannockburn), who was a great landholder in both the kingdom of England and the kingdom of Scotland, confronted the dilemma created by a Scottish invasion of England. Did his loyalty to Stephen, king of the English, or to David, king of Scots, take precedence? As the armies of the Scottish king and the northern barons confronted each other on what was soon to be the battlefield of the Standard, he made up his mind. With the consent of the other English barons, Robert went to see David, 'either to dissuade him from battle, or to break with him legitimately according to the custom of the land'. Robert counselled the king, as his 'faithful man' (*fidelis*), to agree terms, but was met with an accusation of treason from David's fiery nephew, William, son of Duncan. Bruce then 'released himself from the homage that he had performed to him for the barony he held from him' and returned to take up his position in the ranks of the northern barons.[161] At least in his own eyes, washing his hands of his lord freed him of the imputation of treason.

## Rebels with a Cause: Magna Carta

In 1215 the rebel barons observed the niceties of feudal custom. Just like Robert of Gloucester and Robert Bruce, 'they defied the king and renounced their homage' before beginning hostilities. They also, however, painted themselves in rather less mundane colours—for they were 'the army of God', their leader Robert fitz Walter 'marshal of the army of God and of Holy Church'.[162] The rising against John was the first baronial rebellion to depict itself as a just struggle for a political programme.

### Critics of the Angevin Kings

The opposition to the Angevin kings that resulted in Magna Carta can be characterized as a fusion of two traditions: the instinctual baronial insistence on aristocratic rights and the more elaborate and articulate stance of the clerical critics of Angevin government. The latter group included some ecclesiastics who were themselves in royal service. This did not prevent them from making caustic criticisms of the king and the royal government, especially if they felt that they had not received the rewards they deserved.

One of the more outspoken critics of Henry II was Ralph Niger, a learned clerk who had served in the household of Henry the Young King. In his

---

[160] W. Malm., *HN* 467 (p. 23).
[161] Ailr. Riev., *Rel. de Standardo*, pp. 192–5; J. Hexham, p. 293; R. Hexham, p. 162.
[162] R. Coggesh., p. 171.

*Chronicle*, written probably in the decade after the death of Henry II, he summarized his objections to the old king's methods:

Once he had obtained the kingdom of the English, he placed slaves, bastards and common soldiers in charge of the chamber, the household and the kingdom . . . all that his great men could expect from him was dishonour; he deprived them of their inherited estates or gradually whittled them down by trickery. By his own authority he appointed the triflers of his court as bishops and abbots and employed them as royal officials. . . . He forbade his chief men from marrying or giving their daughters in marriage without the king's knowledge . . . he abolished old laws and every year issued new ones, called assises. He revived the geld of his grandfather's day. . . . a plunderer of his own men, he crushed almost everyone with his scutages (military taxes), inquests and a flood of forced services . . . he undermined the written privileges of all, prepared traps for the liberties of all . . . he retained or sold off inheritances . . . he prevaricated in determining lawsuits and often sold justice . . .[163]

There is much more, but the basic charges are clear: heavy taxation, elevation of low-born officials, slow and venal justice, disregard for the property rights and dignities of the aristocracy. These are points echoed in the writings of Gerald of Wales, another Angevin curial clerk. Although he sought the favour and patronage of Henry II and his sons, he could also turn a poisoned pen against them. Henry, wrote Gerald, 'was, from beginning to end, an oppressor of the nobility, weighing equity and injustice, right and wrong, as it suited him. He sold and delayed justice, his word was changeable and deceitful . . .'[164]

Alongside these objections, directed against the king's creation of an official class and his manipulation of the system of justice, ecclesiastics of the Angevin period raised others, more specifically directed against the royal power over the Church. Episcopal appointments, in particular, were an issue, for it was a crucial matter whether the king could, in practice, appoint his own bishops, or whether the local clergy could exercise freedom of election. 'Freedom of the Church' was the slogan of the ecclesiastical party (see below, pp. 406–7). In their eyes the Angevin regime was simply a tyranny. 'In the realms of tyrants,' wrote Gerald of Wales, 'where the churches are oppressed and suffer from violent rulers, bishops are made at the king's command.'[165] The great crisis between king John and the Church arose over the election of the archbishop of Canterbury in 1206. The Canterbury monks, the bishops of the province of Canterbury, and the king himself all claimed a right in this election. When the monks and the bishops appealed to Rome, they brought the case to the attention of one of the most determined and adroit of the medieval popes, Innocent III. Innocent asserted that the monks had the right

---

[163] Ralph Niger, *Chronicle*, ed. R. Anstruther (Caxton Soc.; 1851), pp. 167–9.
[164] Gerald, *Prin.* 2. 3 (p. 160).     [165] Gerald, *Spec. eccl.* 4. 32 (p. 337).

to elect and, with a little encouragement, ensured that they chose his candidate, the Paris-trained theologian and cardinal, Stephen Langton. After 1206, John's opponents thus included a man trained in the most rigorous intellectual tradition that the age offered.

## Magna Carta

John's reconciliation with the Church in 1213 involved the installation of Stephen Langton as archbishop of Canterbury. In the following year, the collapse of the king's military enterprises on the continent left him vulnerable to the baronial opposition. By the end of 1214 his opponents were circulating copies of the Coronation Charter of Henry I, a document that had been issued over a century before, when Henry was seeking to win support from the baronage by promising a more predictable and less predatory regime. This ancient manifesto was to be the basis of their demands. Early in the New Year 'some of the barons who had demanded that charter assembled at London, with the support, it is said, of many of the bishops'. Negotiations with the king did not go well and the tone of confrontation sharpened. The supporters of the charter declared their unanimity in biblically inspired rhetoric: 'they were of one voice and one mind, that they would place themselves as a wall before the house of the Lord and take a stand for the liberty of Church and kingdom'. In response John demanded a renewal of the oath of fealty throughout England, ordering that those who took it should swear to support him, not only against all men but also 'against the charter'.[166]

A confrontation was now imminent, not simply between the supporters of one member of the ruling dynasty and the supporters of another, as in 1088 or 1173, but between a party of barons and bishops who had espoused a set of demands—'the charter'—and those who stood by the king. It soon became clear that John would only concede the baronial demands if he were threatened with force. Accordingly, the rebels assembled in arms, the northerners, who formed a substantial proportion of the opposition, meeting at Stamford, in April 1215, and then marching south, being joined by other opponents of John on the way. Negotiations between the rebels and the king went on, conducted by Stephen Langton and others, but were fruitless. Events were dramatically accelerated by the rebel seizure of London on 17 May, an operation made much easier by the support given to the barons by many of the citizens. Faced with the loss of his chief city, John decided to come to terms, although he had no expectation of a permanent settlement and was already planning for the war that he saw would follow. Nevertheless, after long discussions, in which Langton was again a central figure, Magna Carta was drawn up

---

[166] Barnwell Chron., p. 218.

and sealed with the royal seal at Runnymede. The surviving copies bear the date 15 June.

Some of the provisions of Magna Carta are aimed at dismantling John's machinery of control: the expulsion of foreign mercenaries, the return of hostages, the remission of the huge fines and financial obligations into which his barons had been lured. Yet it is much more than a political settlement and most of its clauses have a permanent and general character. The Charter is, indeed, in the form of a royal grant to all free men in perpetuity. In it the king promises to limit his authority and observe certain set procedures. Much of the detail concerns the regulation of the king's feudal rights, matters that were obviously of great importance to his barons. John pledged himself and his successors not to abuse the overlord's right to have custody of minor heirs, to levy inheritance payments, to arrange the marriages of minor heirs, heiresses, and widows. He also agreed to lighten the burden represented by the royal Forest, land under a special, and much resented, law. Moreover, in a clause pregnant with future significance, he promised not to levy the taxes known as 'scutage' and 'aid' without 'the common counsel of the kingdom'.

'The law of the land' is one of the great watchwords of Magna Carta, standing in opposition to the king's mere will. Yet, in a paradox that is perhaps only superficial, the rebels of 1215 did not want less royal justice but more. While the clauses dealing with the king's feudal rights seek to place clear limits on their exercise, the provisions regarding royal justice do not seek to limit it but to make it more regular, equitable, and accessible. The legal changes that had taken place under Henry II (discussed below) were irreversible. Royal justice was now the favoured first resort. All that was required was that it should obey its own rules. From this circumstance stem the great resounding clauses 39 and 40:

No free man shall be seized, imprisoned, dispossessed, outlawed, exiled or ruined in any way, nor shall we attack him or send men to attack him, except by the lawful judgment of his peers and the law of the land.

To no one will we sell, to no one will we deny or delay right or justice.

It is not at all anachronistic to see in Magna Carta the animating principles of consent to taxation, due process, and the rule of law.

In 1215, however, what was probably more remarkable was the arrangement outlined in clause 61, the so-called 'security clause' (by far the longest in the whole Charter). This established a committee of twenty-five barons. Any complaint that the king or any of his servants were infringing the terms of the Charter was to be brought before members of this committee and, if the king refused to rectify the matter, the twenty-five barons were then permitted to put pressure on the king by seizing his castles, lands, and other royal possessions. This is the perfectly normal medieval legal process called 'distraint', but it is here being applied, quite exceptionally, to the king by a baronial council. Distraint had customarily been exerted by superiors over inferiors; here it was envisaged being exercised against the monarch himself. Moreover, a general oath of obedience to the Twenty-five was to be exacted. Hence, when they apply force in order to defend the Charter, the barons are to be supported by 'the commune of the whole land' (*communa tocius terre*).

These revolutionary arrangements could not have been permanently acceptable to any medieval king who wished to remain a ruler in fact rather than in name only. John certainly planned to have Magna Carta invalidated as soon as possible. In this he could draw on powerful support, for, ever since his submission to the Church in 1213, he had enjoyed the backing of Innocent III. The pope did not desert him in his hour of need and not only annulled Magna Carta but also suspended Langton as archbishop for his refusal to take a stand against the rebels. After a few months in the summer of 1215 when the king and the Twenty-five made fitful attempts to cooperate or, at least, negotiate, open war began again.

The civil war of 1215–17 began as a war over the Charter. When rebels submitted to the king, they had to make an explicit renunciation of Magna Carta. It developed very quickly, however, into a dynastic war, for, faced with an intransigent and powerful king, the rebels decided to appeal for help to the Capetians, offering the throne to Louis, son of Philip Augustus of France. He landed in England on 21 May 1216 and marched to London, where he was received by the rebel barons and the citizens. 'The madness of slavery is over,' enthused Gerald of Wales, 'the time of liberty has been granted, English necks are free from the yoke.'[167] Many of John's supporters now went over to Louis. Alexander II, king of Scots, occupied the northern counties, that Louis, like Henry the Young King a generation earlier, had offered to the Scottish king as the price of support. The Angevins and Capetians, who had fought so long across the fields of northern France were now engaged in full-scale warfare in England itself.

In the midst of the war, John died. This transformed the situation. Barons who could never be reconciled to John, might find loyalty to his infant son, Henry III, more palatable. The child was swiftly crowned and then, two weeks later, on 12 November 1216, in a bold and startling move, a revised version of Magna Carta was issued in his name. Some of the clauses that restricted royal power, including of course the security clause, were omitted, but the bulk of the text is identical with that of 1215. Because the young king did not yet have his own seal, the revised Charter was sealed with the seals of William Marshal, the regent, and Guala, the papal legate. The legate thus approved what the pope had annulled the previous year. The royalists had

---

[167] Robert Bartlett, *Gerald of Wales 1146–1223* (Oxford, 1982), p. 222.

appropriated the rebels' cause. Hence the military defeat of Louis and the rebels in 1217 did not mean the rejection of the programme of 1215. Indeed, as soon as the treaty ending the war and securing Louis's withdrawal to France had been sealed, the Charter was reissued yet again, a symbol that the victory of John's son and the implementation of the rebels' proposals could go hand in hand.

The rebellion of 1215 was the first English revolt to have the goal of enforcing a complex, general, and written programme. Magna Carta was concerned, in its own words, with 'reform [*emendatio*] of the kingdom' (clause 61). Of course, personal motives intermingled with the programmatic. Two of the chief rebels of 1215, Eustace de Vescy and Robert fitz Walter, hated John and had conspired to kill him in 1212. Nevertheless, the barons of the 'army of God and of Holy Church' had a project of reform. Baronial rebels of later generations looked back to Magna Carta when they drafted their own blueprints for good government. Inspired by a sense that the powerful and unpredictable rule of the Angevins could not be left untrammelled, Magna Carta looked forward to the reform programmes and constitutions of the future. It also provided a theatre of reconciliation after the civil war. The (third) reissue of Magna Carta in 1225 has as witnesses not only men who had stood loyal to John, like Hubert de Burgh and Peter des Roches, but also Stephen Langton and eight of the committee of Twenty-five, among them the arch-rebel Robert fitz Walter. It is fitting that this version of 1225 remains the earliest statute on the English Statute Book.

# CHAPTER 2

# England and Beyond

## I. ENGLAND AND THE BRITISH ISLES

Although English people sometimes forget it, England is not an island. It occupies, in fact, somewhat less than 60 per cent of the land surface of the island of Britain. Both to the west and to the north the medieval kingdom of England had land boundaries. The western and northern regions thus faced the problems and opportunities of a territorial frontier in a way that no other parts of the realm did. There was a reputation for lawlessness in these parts. Orderic Vitalis, writing of William the Conqueror's determination to establish himself in his early years, says, 'In the northern and western extremities of the kingdom an unchecked savagery had ruled until now and, under Edward the Confessor and his predecessors, those areas had disdained to obey the king of England unless it suited them.'[1] A century later, in 1166, the lord of Wooler in Northumberland, only twelve miles south of the Tweed, explained to Henry II that he had established several military tenants on his lands 'because I dwell in your borderlands and often require brave men'.[2]

The English monarchy was the richest and most powerful in the British Isles, but not the only one and not the oldest. English kings had to have dealings with other kings and princes within the islands, who would be unlikely to acknowledge the superiority of the kings of England unless they were forced to. For centuries the stronger Anglo-Saxon rulers had sought to impose an overlordship on these other kings, not always destroying their regality but demanding that it be recognized as an inferior type, and the Norman and Angevin kings, with their wider resources and the favourable wind of migration and expansion, could demand recognition of their superiority all the more imperiously.

To the west, beyond Offa's Dyke, there were the princes of Wales, such as the rulers of Gwynedd, Powys, and Deheubarth, engaged in their own endless political and military competition, as well as warfare against—and alliances with—the English. To the north lay the realm of the kings of Scots,

---

[1] Orderic 4 (2, p. 210).     [2] *RBE* 1, p. 440.

securely established on the Tweed for the last century, and probably exercising suzerainty over most of Cumbria, including its most important centre, Carlisle. Further west were the independent or semi-independent kingdoms and principalities of Galloway, the Isles, Man, and, further still, Ireland.

## Wales

When the Normans seized power in England, they needed at once to secure the boundaries of the kingdom. William the Conqueror's response to the existence of a dangerous western frontier, which might be breached at any time by raiders from Wales, was to create a series of border earldoms—Hereford, Shrewsbury, and Chester—whose earls had greater autonomy than usual and these he entrusted to some of his chief followers. It appears that, very soon after the establishment of these earldoms, the Normans along the Welsh March transformed a defensive into an aggressive policy and began making inroads into Wales itself. Their main military tool, as in England itself, was the castle, and soon the river valleys and coastal plains of Wales were dotted with the mounds of motte-and-bailey castles, serving as safe refuges for bands of knights and followers and bases for further conquest. In 1081 king William himself marched across south Wales to St David's, freeing English captives, imposing tribute upon Rhys ap Tewdwr of Deheubarth, and, it seems likely, building a castle at Cardiff.[3]

The situation along the Anglo-Welsh frontier in 1086 is illuminated by the Domesday Survey (see Map 2). The border zone bore many marks of war. Domesday Book classifies several clusters of settlements along the frontier as 'waste', with reference either to their current state or that in the recent past.[4] The forty or so tiny settlements in the districts of Rhuddlan and Englefield (Tegeingl) that had been attached to the earldom of Chester 'were waste when earl Hugh received them' (in the 1070s).[5] The district of Archenfield or Erging in western Herefordshire had been devastated by Gruffudd ap Llywelyn, the Welsh king who was killed in 1063, while in the north-west corner of the same county fourteen places 'in the March of Wales' had lands that could have supported 54 plough-teams but were waste at the time of the survey. Some of these were held by Osbern fitz Richard and Domesday Book gives a stark picture of his life on the frontier: 'on these wastelands woods have grown up and here Osbern hunts and takes what he can get. Nothing else.'[6] The strip of land along the border between England and Wales was

---

[3] *ASC*, p. 214; *Brut (RBH)*, p. 31; C. J. Spurgeon, 'Mottes and Castle-Ringworks in Wales', in J. R. Kenyon and R. Avent (eds.), *Castles in Wales and the Marches: Essays in Honour of D. J. Cathcart King* (Cardiff, 1987), pp. 23–49, at pp. 38–41.

[4] Darby, *Domesday England*, pp. 252–9.    [5] *DB* 1, 269 (Chs. FT 1. 1).

[6] *DB* 1, 181, 183b, 186b (Hef. 1. 49, 9. 13, 24. 3, 5).

MAP 2. *Wales in the Norman period*

among the most thinly settled parts of the kingdom, with Domesday population densities under 12 per square mile, compared with a median figure for England of 31.[7]

By no means all the destruction in the border counties is to be attributed to Welsh raids. The Normans themselves were responsible for some in the years after the Conquest, either through punitive devastation or as a by-product of the building of castles—the earl's castle at Shrewsbury occupied the site of 51 dwellings.[8] The castle was indeed the most obvious symptom and symbol of the militarized nature of the border. Domesday Book mentions only

---

[7] Darby, *Domesday England*, pp. 91, 93 (using a multiplier of 5).
[8] *DB* 1, 252 (Shr. C. 14).

49 castles: 8 of them are on the Anglo-Welsh frontier. Rhuddlan, held by
Robert of Rhuddlan, the cousin of the earl of Chester, is described as 'newly
made', while Montgomery, the creation of Roger de Montgomery, earl of
Shrewsbury, haughtily brought the very place names of northern France to
the Welsh border.[9] Several of the castles in the southern section of the
frontier—Chepstow, Ewyas Harold, Clifford—were built or rebuilt by
William fitz Osbern, earl of Hereford (d. 1071), and his great stone hall-keep
at Chepstow, on the cliffs above the river Wye, is the most striking surviving
example of the military architecture of the Welsh frontier in Norman times
(Plate 2). Defences could also be more modest. Among the waste lands in the
north-west corner of Herefordshire lay Eardisley, where Domesday Book
records that the land 'does not pay land-tax or any other customary payment
and is not part of any hundred [a hundred was a subdivision of a county]. It
lies in the middle of a wood and there is a fortified house there.'[10] The
dangerous limbo of frontier life could not be better exemplified.

By 1086 the Norman earls and their followers had begun to push the limits
of their power further westwards, through forms of domination more or less
direct. Already before 1066 the Welsh district of Archenfield had been
incorporated into Herefordshire, although it retained its Welsh customs and
certain peculiar rights and duties, such as that of providing priests to carry the
king's messages to the Welsh.[11] Domesday Book records several of these areas
whose special features mark them out as recent conquests. Of Rhuddlan and
Englefield it is expressly recorded that they had never been assessed in hides,
the standard fiscal units of the Old English kingdom.[12] Elsewhere along the
border newly acquired land was also rated in the current practical measure of
the 'ploughland' rather than in the traditional hide. Many of the border castles were the foci of 'castleries', areas outside the usual territorial system and
rendering dues and services at the central fortress. Caerleon, for instance, on
the west bank of the river Usk, formed such a castlery. There the Norman lord
William of Ecouis, who took his name from a place seventeen miles south-east
of Rouen, had eight ploughlands. These he had granted out to his follower
Thurstan. The tenants and dependants there included 'three Welshmen living by Welsh law', two smallholders paying rent in honey, and three slaves.[13]
The nearby settlements of Nether Gwent, between the rivers Wye and Usk,
were grouped into units of thirteen or fourteen villages, each under a Welsh
reeve responsible for the rents of honey, pigs, cows, and hawks.[14]

Beyond the areas like Caerleon and Rhuddlan, where Norman lords had
settled their followers, or the villages of Nether Gwent, where a Welsh

---

[9] *DB* 1, 269, 254 (Chs. FT 2. 19; Shr. 4, 1. 35).    [10] *DB* 1, 184b (Hef. 10. 46).
[11] *DB* 1, 179 (Hef. A).    [12] *DB* 1, 269 (Chs. FT 2. 18).    [13] *DB* 1, 185b (Hef. 14. 1).
[14] *DB* 1, 162 (Gls. W. 2).

ministerial class answered to them directly, lay less closely subordinated regions that paid tribute. The cantref (administative division) of Arwystli was deemed to be 'appurtenant to the castle of Montgomery' and paid £6 per annum to the earls of Shrewsbury. They also received £4. 5s. from 'the Welshman Tewdwr, who holds a Welsh district from the earl', the district probably being Nanheudy in the Vale of Llangollen.[15] Reginald the Sheriff, a vassal of the earls of Shrewsbury who had built the castle at Oswestry, received 60s. from the district of Cynllaith and eight cows from the Welshmen of Edeyrnion, while to the north the cantrefs of Rhos and Rhufoniog were worth £12 to Robert of Rhuddlan, though the details of how he exploited them are not known.[16]

Clearly the levels of control exercised by the Normans in Wales varied according to the opportunities offered. In the years immediately following the compilation of Domesday Book, opportunities seem to have been great. From the bases already established along every stretch of the border, Norman knights and their followings penetrated deep into Wales. The year 1093 saw the death in battle of Rhys ap Tewdwr of Deheubarth, killed by 'the French who were inhabiting Brecon'.[17] At the same time, the earls of Shrewsbury led an advance from their base on the Middle March into Ceredigion (Cardiganshire) and Dyfed (Pembrokeshire), and, says the Welsh chronicle, the *Brut*, 'they fortified them with castles and they seized all the lands of the Britons'. The Welsh kingdoms of Morgannwg and Gwynllyg were occupied by Robert fitz Hamo, one of William Rufus's most favoured barons, and formed the basis of the Norman lordship of Glamorgan, centred on its chief castle of Cardiff.

In the north the earl of Chester and Robert of Rhuddlan pressed westwards along the coastal plain. Domesday Book records that Robert was paying the king £40 per annum for 'North Wales' and he clearly tried to make his tenure a reality, building a castle at Degannwy above the mouth of the Conwy. Here, however, early in the reign of William Rufus, he was killed by the Welsh, who stuck his severed head on the mast of one of their ships. Despite this, the Norman advance in the north continued. In 1098 the earls of Shrewsbury and Chester occupied Anglesey, although they had the misfortune to run into Magnus Barelegs, king of Norway, who was there with a Viking fleet, and the earl of Shrewsbury was killed in the ensuing fighting.

Thus, in the 1090s, from Cardiff to Pembroke to Anglesey, Norman invaders penetrated Wales, built their castles, and settled their followers. The king of England was not deeply involved in this process at a direct level. Rufus launched inconclusive expeditions in 1095 and 1097, but there was no

---

[15] *DB* 1, 253b (Shr. 4. 1. 13, 15); Darby, *Domesday England*, p. 329.
[16] *DB* 1, 253b, 255, 269 (Shr. 4, 1. 11, 4, 3. 42; Chs. G. 3).      [17] *Brut (RBH)*, p. 33.

attempt to build up royal demesne lands in Wales or the March. The great baronial families, like the Montgomery earls of Shrewsbury or the de Braose, who were established in Radnor by the 1090s and were to become dominant figures in the central part of the March in later generations, seized control of Welsh kingdoms or sub-kingdoms and stepped into the positions of their native predecessors. This is one of the reasons that the formal powers of these Marcher lords were so much greater than that of their counterparts within the kingdom of England proper. Welsh resistance was often fierce. In 1094, in the words of the *Brut*, 'the Britons threw off the rule of the French, being unable to suffer their tyranny'. The bloody end of Robert of Rhuddlan has already been mentioned and the northern extension of Norman power was indeed to falter and go into reverse, with the native princes of Gwynedd reestablishing their power in Anglesey, Snowdonia, and the surrounding region in the concluding years of the eleventh century.

By the year 1100, a pattern had been established that was, in its basic outlines, to last throughout the twelfth and early thirteenth centuries. The eastern and southern parts of Wales were occupied by Marcher lordships, Pembroke, Glamorgan, Brecon, and others, while northern and central parts remained largely under the control of the various Welsh princes, Gwynedd in the north, Deheubarth (deprived of some of its component parts) in the south, Powys in the north-central March. Wales had always been extremely politically decentralized and now that pattern was complicated by the existence of both native and intrusive lordships. The political and military history of Wales in the twelfth and thirteenth centuries is a story of perennial violent competition between a large number of Welsh and Anglo-Norman powers, in which fortunes rose and fell with dramatic suddenness, alliances were made and betrayed, and conflict was as often between Welsh and Welsh or Norman and Norman as it was between Norman and Welsh.

Sometimes English kings did become a presence on the Welsh scene. Henry I was a particularly dominant figure, making and breaking individuals and families. Very early in his reign he changed the political situation in the March of Wales fundamentally by dispossessing the house of Montgomery, after which the earldom of Shrewsbury lapsed. He acquired Robert fitz Hamo's inheritance for his own illegitimate son Robert, marrying him to fitz Hamo's heiress, Mabel, and making him earl of Gloucester in 1122. Thereafter the earldom, with its component lordship of Glamorgan, was one of the central political features of south Wales and the March. King Henry also brought to Wales the Clare family, a dynasty that was to be of central importance there for two centuries. Gilbert fitz Richard of Clare, the first of the family to acquire Welsh lands, was apparently eager to enjoy the fruits of this new frontier. Writing of the year 1110, the *Brut* records the king sent to Gilbert fitz Richard, who was brave, renowned and powerful, and a friend to the king—and he was a man eminent in all his actions—to ask him to come to him. And he came. And the king said to him: 'You were always,' said he, 'seeking of me a portion of the territory of the Britons. I will now give you the territory of Cadwgan [ap Bleddyn]. Go and take possession of it.' And then he gladly accepted it from the king. And then, gathering a host, along with his comrades he came to Ceredigion. And he took possession of it and built in it two castles . . .[18]

Eventually Gilbert constructed more than two castles, planting one in each of the *commotes*, the constituent administrative districts, of Ceredigion. His son was to be ambushed and killed by the Welsh in 1136, and Ceredigion did not stay in the family's possession, but various branches of the Clares were to be major forces in Wales in later generations, holding the lordships of Pembroke and of Glamorgan, the latter inherited from the family of Robert of Gloucester.

The activities of Henry I were not limited to manipulating the destinies of the Marcher families. He also established the first significant royal territorial holdings in Wales, including Carmarthen, where he had an important royal castle built, and Pembroke, which he retained in his hands after the fall of the Montgomeries and organized exactly as an English shire, with a royal sheriff rendering his accounts at the Exchequer. He strengthened the Anglo-Norman hold over Pembrokeshire by bringing to the area a colony of Flemings, immigrants who would have a vested interest in the new regime and who were, indeed, to be engaged in unremitting struggle with the native Welsh. 'They are a brave and sturdy people,' wrote one twelfth-century observer, 'mortal enemies of the Welsh, with whom they engage in endless conflict.'[19] Henry was, moreover, a master at exploiting the rivalries of the native Welsh princes to keep them dependent. In the last resort, if he deemed it necessary, the king led large-scale expeditions into Wales, as he did in 1114 and 1121, quickly securing the submission of Welsh princes whose behaviour had displeased him. The impression Henry made on the Welsh is summed up by the author of the *Brut*:

King Henry, the man who had tamed all the chieftains of the island of Britain through his might and power and who had subdued many lands beyond the sea to his rule, some by main strength and arms, others by innumerable gifts of gold and silver, the man against whom none can contend save God himself, He who bestowed such authority on him.[20]

Much of the structure that Henry had created in Wales collapsed on his death. There was a major resurgence of native Welsh power in 1136. Ceredigion was reconquered and, in the ensuing years, Anglo–Norman castles like Carmarthen, Oswestry, and Mold (Flintshire) fell into the hands of the native

---

[18] *Brut (RBH)*, pp. 71–3.     [19] Gerald, *Itin.* I. 11 (p. 83).     [20] *Brut (RBH)*, p. 91.

Welsh. King Stephen was no more able to control the Welsh than he was his own baronage, while his opponents, the Angevin party, although they included great Marcher lords like Robert of Gloucester, were more concerned with the civil war in England than with pursuing an aggressive policy in Wales. Indeed, alliances and understandings with native dynasts and the use of native Welsh troops against their English opponents were both more attractive and more feasible options.

In these middle decades of the twelfth century successful native leaders emerged in the person of Owain Gwynedd of Gwynedd and, rather later, Rhys ap Gruffudd ('the Lord Rhys', as he was known) of Deheubarth, grandson of the Rhys ap Tewdwr killed by the Anglo-Normans of Brecon in 1093. Owain and the Lord Rhys contained or destroyed rivals from within their own dynasties, led campaigns against their enemies among the other native princes and made considerable territorial gains at the expense of the Anglo-Normans. Even after the re-establishment of strong royal government in England following the accession of Henry II in 1154, these rulers were able to maintain a power more independent and more extensive than that of their forebears in the time of Henry I. Henry II's expeditions of 1157, 1163, and 1165, the first designed to bring the submission of Owain Gwynedd, the second directed against the Lord Rhys, and the third a notorious fiasco in which a large English army striking into north Wales from Shrewsbury was forced to withdraw by torrential rain, failure of supplies, and Welsh harassment, did not produce any lasting results. Eventually new accommodations were reached. Especially after the death of the hostile Owain in 1170, the English king was willing to recognize the rulers of Gwynedd and Deheubarth as subordinate kings and to confirm, or even augment, their territories and status. The Lord Rhys was actually appointed 'justiciar of all Deheubarth' by Henry. This new approach had its advantages—in the course of the great rebellion of 1173–4, Henry II could count on the support of the rulers of native Wales, the Lord Rhys leading his Welsh followers to besiege the castle of Tutbury in Staffordshire, which was held by the king's enemy, earl Ferrers.

The political geography of Wales thus continued to manifest the dualism that had characterized it ever since the Normans began to establish themselves in the country in the 1070s. Both native principalities and Anglo-Norman Marcher lordships existed and were recognized by the kings of England as legitimate, if inferior, powers. The dualism was replicated on a smaller scale within the Marcher lordships themselves, for many were divided between a relatively heavily colonized, feudalized, and Anglicized lowland section and upland areas that were left in the hands of the native Welsh, often under their own lords. This distinction between 'Englishry' and 'Welshry', as they were later termed, can be seen in the lordship of Glamorgan. The coastal strip between Newport and the Gower was heavily settled, with castles, boroughs, among them Cardiff, the largest urban settlement in medieval Wales, and many manors and knights' fees. Some of these, like Flemingston and Colwinston, probably bear the names of their Anglo-Norman lords. In contrast, in the upland valleys, the Welsh lords of Senghennydd, Meisgyn, Glynrhondda, and Afan ruled over a society much more like that of pre-conquest Wales. They gave nominal recognition to the overlordship of the earl of Gloucester but had considerable autonomy and could bite back when bitten, as in 1158 when Ifor Bach of Senghennydd, described by a contemporary as 'a man small of stature but of immense spirit, possessing some wooded hill country, in the manner of the Welsh', whose tenure of his lands was threatened, kidnapped the earl and countess from within Cardiff castle itself.[21]

Political life within the Welsh principalities and the Marcher lordships followed different patterns. The latter practised unitary inheritance with clear rules of succession and hence maintained their unity, unless partitioned among co-heiresses, over the generations. Within the Welsh principalities, on the other hand, it was recognized that all sons had rights, even if of different mothers or illegitimate by the standards of canon law. Conflicts over the partition of princely inheritances between brothers, between uncles and nephews, and between cousins were endemic. Between 1111 and 1160 seven members of the Powys dynasty were killed, blinded, or castrated by other members of the dynasty.[22] Only when there was a leader of quite exceptional authority and skill could a native Welsh principality transcend this internal violence and make a wider political mark.

At the very end of the twelfth century, while the dynasty of the Lord Rhys, who died in 1197, splintered into competing segments, it became clear that the northern Welsh principality of Gwynedd had acquired a new and powerful ruler of this stamp. Emerging at the top after a long struggle within his family, Llywelyn ap Iorwerth went on to acquire the lands of his rival Gwenwynwyn of South Powys and, although forced to submit temporarily to king John, who led two expeditions against him in 1211, he took advantage of John's internal difficulties to resume an independent and aggressive policy. Throughout the English civil war of 1215–17 he expanded his power, capturing the important royal centres of Carmarthen and Cardigan and, in 1218, as the war ended, securing most of his gains by making peace with the English royal government. He had to perform homage but was granted custody of Cardigan, Carmarthen, and the lands of Gwenwynwyn. He reigned until his death in 1240 and, though he faced many military and political upheavals,

---

[21] Gerald, *Itin.* 1. 6 (pp. 63–4).
[22] Rees Davies, *Conquest, Coexistence and Change: Wales 1063–1415* (Oxford, 1987) (reissued as *Age of Conquest: Wales 1063–1415*), diagram 1, p. 60.

Llywelyn was never decisively beaten back from the position of dominance he had acquired by 1218. The thirteenth century was to end with the complete destruction of the house of Gwynedd, but it is understandable that the Marcher lords of southern and eastern Wales about 1225 regarded Llywelyn's miniature state as an impressive and threatening presence.

## Scotland

The relationship between England and Scotland was quite different from that between England and Wales. The border itself was not the same kind of frontier. Whereas the boundary between England and Wales marked a sharp linguistic and cultural break, and had at one point in the eighth century even been marked by an earthwork ditch and bank running hundreds of miles from north coast to south, the Anglo-Scottish frontier was only gradually defined in the eleventh and twelfth centuries and, in any case, for much of its length separated two societies, those of Northumbria and Lothian, that were linguistically, socially, and economically indistinguishable and that had for centuries been part of the same political unit, the kingdom of Northumbria. It was only after the collapse of Northumbria at the end of the ninth century that something like a power vacuum in the region had enabled first the kings of Scots and then the Wessex monarchs to intrude, control, and compete. As they did so, they divided up a world that had long been one.

The language spoken between the Forth and the Tweed differed from that spoken south of the Tweed only as much as the dialect of one English district differed from that of another. A far sharper linguistic divide separated the Gaelic-speaking parts of the kingdom of Scotland from those parts of the kingdom where English/Scots was spoken. At the abbey of Melrose in the Tweed valley there were recitations of religious literature in English verse that would doubtless have been reasonably comprehensible to the monks of Durham, across the border, but quite alien to Gaelic-speakers from further north or west within the kingdom.[23]

This cultural unity is also shown in some aspects of religious life, such as the cult of the great cross-border saint Cuthbert. The major shrine of St Cuthbert was at Durham, where his incorrupt body lay, but he was revered widely in both kingdoms. Kirkcudbright, 'Cuthbert's church', in Galloway took its name from the saint and posthumous miracles performed by Cuthbert are recorded there and in Lothian in the 1160s. Cuthbert's servants and property also spanned the frontier. In the 1090s Edgar, king of Scots, granted to the monks of Durham the region around Coldingham in Berwickshire and by the 1130s there was a priory there, which continued as a dependency of

---

[23] Joc. Furn., *V. Waltheof*, p. 271.

Durham until the late Middle Ages, despite the Wars of Independence. The Durham monks were not finally forced to abandon their Scottish daughter house until 1462. Conversely, religious houses in the Scottish realm had lands and rights in England. Dryburgh abbey, not far from Coldingham, had claims on the church of Bozeat in Northamptonshire, which had been granted to it by the wife of Hugh de Morville, Constable of Scotland (d. 1162), and, despite some difficulties with this distant asset, the canons of Dryburgh managed to draw revenue from it until at least the mid-thirteenth century.[24]

The social and cultural unity of what we now regard as southern Scotland and northern England is brought out in the territorial nomenclature. The term 'Scotland' was reserved for the Gaelic-speaking area north of the Forth, while the region between the Forth and Tweed, known as Lothian, was often regarded as part of England, as it had once been politically. Thus, writing of events in 1091, the *Anglo-Saxon Chronicle* regards transit southwards across the Forth as a movement from 'Scotland' to 'Lothian in England'. Another author writing at roughly the same time could describe the Firth of Forth as 'the sea that separates Lothian from Scotland'.[25] The monk Adam of Dryburgh, writing in his Berwickshire abbey late in the twelfth century, described himself as being 'in the land of the English and in the kingdom of the Scots' (*in terra Anglorum et in regno Scotorum*).[26] The pattern of political lordship, it was well recognized at the time, did not involve a sharp line between two units called 'Scotland' and 'England'. Durham and Dunbar had different lords but were part of the same world.

Nevertheless, despite this unity spanning the political frontier, kings of Scots and kings of England might well find themselves at war. Large-scale Anglo-Scottish warfare in this period falls into four distinct phases: 1070–93, 1136–9, 1173–4, 1215–17.

The first phase was the most protracted. William the Conqueror had established his authority in the north of England by spectacular violence and was not hesitant about extending his mastery further when faced with the threat of the vigorous king of Scots, Malcolm Canmore. Malcolm raided Northumberland a total of five times in his reign (1058–93), on the last occasion meeting his death. William's response to the attack of 1070 was to invade Scotland in 1072 and secure the submission of Malcolm, who, according to the *Anglo-Saxon Chronicle*, 'gave hostages and became his man'. In 1080 the Conqueror's son, Robert, consolidated these steps by ravaging southern

---

[24] Stringer, *Earl David*, pp. 145–8; *idem* (ed.), *Essays on Nobility of Medieval Scotland* (Edinburgh, 1985), pp. 44–71.

[25] *ASC*, p. 226; Turgot, *V. Margaret*, p. 247.

[26] Adam of Dryburgh, *De tripartito tabernaculo* 2. 120 (*PL* 198, col. 723).

Scotland and by building a castle on the Tyne at the place thenceforth to be called Newcastle. Early in his reign, in response to a Scots invasion of northern England in 1091, William Rufus also took an army into Lothian and received Malcolm's renewed submission. Two years later, while raiding Northumberland, Malcolm and his son Edward were killed by Robert de Mowbray, the Norman earl of that region.

After these hostilities of 1070–93, however, there were only three other junctures in the whole Norman and Angevin period when kings led armies across the Border in either direction. On all three occasions the conflict took place at a time of civil strife in England when the kings of Scots were allied with opponents of the king of England. The first and most dramatic phase occurred after the death of Henry I in 1135 and Stephen's seizure of the throne. David I felt sincerely committed to the claims of Henry's daughter, Matilda, and could also pursue his own ends by pursuing hers. In the winter of 1135–6, immediately after Stephen's coronation, he led an army south and seized key points, including Carlisle. He again led plundering forces southwards twice during 1138. Despite the defeat he sustained at the Battle of the Standard in that year and Stephen's counter-raids of 1138 and 1139, he was eventually ceded Northumberland and Cumbria by Stephen. Scots kings were again seen in arms in the north of England in 1173 and 1174, as David's grandson, William the Lion, pursued his claim to Northumberland by co-operating with the great rebellion against Henry II. This effort came to a catastrophic end when William was captured by English forces before Alnwick. Finally, during the English civil war of 1215–17, William's son, Alexander II, intervened repeatedly, king John responding by capturing Berwick and plundering in the south of Scotland in 1216.

On each of these occasions armies of Scots, headed by their kings, ravaged Northumbria, and the chroniclers lament the atrocities, the looting, and enslavement that went on. The English kings repaid them in the same coin. Yet one must also remark how rare such campaigns were. In the century and a half from 1075 to 1225 only twelve years saw armies crossing the border in either direction. Obviously, there might be cross-border raiding and fighting on a lesser scale, but a comparison of the situation on the Anglo-Scottish border with that on the frontiers of Normandy, where the Norman and Angevin kings undertook campaigns in every decade of our period, or, indeed, with the much more violent Anglo-Scottish border of the later Middle Ages, shows how relatively calm the twelfth-century Border was. The two centuries between the death of Malcolm Canmore in 1093 and the ominous intervention of the ageing and demonic Edward I in the 1290s form the most peaceful period in the whole history of relations between Britain's two largest kingdoms.

One reason for this was that Malcolm Canmore's marriage to the royal

English exile, Margaret, eventually brought to the Scottish throne a series of kings who were as much at home in England as Scotland. In particular, Margaret's youngest son, David, who ruled from 1124 to 1153, was raised as a truly Anglo-Scottish figure and, as king, made major changes that furthered the cultural convergence and political interdependence of the two kingdoms. Brought up at the English court, he was a particular favourite of Henry I of England, who was married to his sister Matilda, and, in 1113, gave him the great estate and earldom of Northampton (also known as Huntingdon), along with Matilda, daughter of earl Waltheof, as his wife. David was thus an English earl before he was a Scottish king. When he succeeded to the throne in 1124, there was no reason to give up his earlier lands and status, and the honor of Huntingdon remained in the hands of members of the Scottish royal family (with some breaks) down to 1237.

As a prominent Anglo-Norman baron as well as king of Scots, David was well able to implement his policy of endowing and settling Anglo-Norman aristocrats in his kingdom. In 1094 the Scots had agreed to acknowledge Duncan, son of Malcolm Canmore, as king, 'on the condition that he no longer introduce into Scotland either English or Normans to serve him as soldiers',[27] so clearly the recruitment of Anglo-Norman knights by the kings of Scots was already in progress at that time, but David I and his grandsons made such recruitment one of their basic policies. Eventually a whole new section of the Scottish aristocracy was created, that was of French ancestry, held its lands by feudal tenure, and often had estates on both sides of the Anglo-Scottish border.

David I's grant of Annandale to Robert Bruce, ancestor of the later kings of Scots, is one of the best known cases of the establishment of an Anglo-Norman baron in Scotland. The Bruces had their origin in Brix, south of Cherbourg, and Robert, who served as a justice for Henry I, was endowed by that king with a large estate in Yorkshire. As a regular attender at Henry's court, he would have been familiar with the young Scottish prince, who likewise served as one of Henry's justices, and after 1114 he was also a tenant of David, as earl of Huntingdon, for lands in Rutland. These ties form the background to the grant of Annandale, which may have been one of David's earliest acts after he became king. Planting Bruce in Annandale was one way of checking and controlling the dangerous and semi-autonomous lordship of Galloway. The death of their common benefactor, Henry I, brought strains to the relationship between Bruce and king David, and at the Battle of the Standard in 1138 they fought against each other, Bruce's identity as a Yorkshire baron here being stronger than that as a vassal of king David. Yet Bruce's younger son and namesake fought with the Scots king on that

---

[27] Flor. Worcs. 2, p. 32; cf. *ASC*, p. 228.

occasion. It was this younger son who inherited Annandale and handed it on through four further generations of Robert Bruces to the eventual victor of Bannockburn. This line had its main holding in Scotland but continued in possession of English lands, at Hartness in county Durham, and in its patronage of the family monastery of Guisborough in Yorkshire.

The Bruces are but the most well-known of a whole catalogue of Anglo-Norman aristocratic families settling in the kingdom of Scotland in this period. Another, also with a distant regal destiny, was the Stewarts. Walter, founder of the family in Scotland, was the younger son of Alan fitz Flaald, a lord of Breton descent who held the shrievalty of Shropshire and the lordship of Oswestry under Henry I. He entered the service of king David about 1136, was made hereditary royal steward (hence the surname), and granted lands in Renfrewshire and elsewhere, while his elder brother remained based in Shropshire and was ancestor of the later medieval fitz Alans, earls of Arundel. The Scottish branch brought with them from their original base in the Welsh March a devotion to St Milburga, the local saint of Much Wenlock in Shropshire, who was one of the original dedicatees of the Stewart family house, Paisley abbey.[28] The cross-border aristocracy created and reinforced such religious and cultural linkages of every type. In the early thirteenth century Thomas de Colville, constable of Dumfries castle, granted land in Galloway, for the souls of kings David I, Malcolm IV, and William I, to Vaudey Abbey in Lincolnshire. The original site of Vaudey was at nearby Bytham, which was under the lordship of William de Colville, presumably Thomas's relative.[29] The fact that a Lincolnshire abbey thus received land in Galloway for the souls of Scottish kings is only explicable because of the existence of an aristocratic family with members in both kingdoms.

Despite the ever deeper strands binding the English and Scottish political classes together, there remained two major issues that brought recurrent tension between the kings of England and Scotland: the relative standing of the two monarchs and their competing claims in Cumbria and Northumberland.

The territorial issue would not be formally settled until the Treaty of York of 1237, when Alexander II renounced his claim to the counties of Northumberland, Cumberland, and Westmoreland, but the establishment of the border along much its present line had actually been effected in reality by the end of the eleventh century. Lothian passed under Scottish rule finally and definitively in the first quarter of the eleventh century and thereafter the Tweed was the usual and customary boundary between England and Scotland on the east. Earl Siward of Northumbria (d. 1055), for example, was described as

[28] Ian B. Cowan and D. E. Easson, *Medieval Religious Houses: Scotland* (2nd edn.; London, 1976), pp. 64–5.
[29] Geoffrey Barrow, *The Anglo-Norman Era in Scottish History* (Oxford, 1980), p. 177.

'governing the earldom of the whole province of the Northumbrians from Humber to Tweed'.[30] The situation in the west was complicated by Strathclyde or Cumbria, a region that had been an independent British kingdom, but became a Scottish client state in the eleventh century. The southern half, Cumberland, was specifically described as 'under the rule of king Malcolm' in 1070.[31] After that date there is no definite information about the status of the region until 1092. In that year William Rufus

went north to Carlisle with a great army and there he restored the town and then built a castle. He drove out Dolfin, the previous ruler of the land, and garrisoned the castle with his own men before returning south. He sent many peasants there with their wives and livestock to live there and cultivate the land.[32]

Even if the exact descent and standing of Dolfin is not clear, the general import of this activity is: the establishment of English rule through a fortified military settlement backed by rural colonization. It seems likely that Malcolm Canmore's visit to Rufus's court in 1093, when he was snubbed by the English king and the two rulers 'parted in great enmity', was connected with the English king's annexation of Cumbria.[33]

Immediately after this abortive meeting with William Rufus, Malcolm made his last and fatal raid into Northumberland. Thereafter the Scottish kings were in no position to adopt an aggressive policy. Disputes within the dynasty left Malcolm's sons as virtual clients of William Rufus. Twice, in 1094 and 1097, the English king gave military support to them in their struggle against their uncle, Donald Ban, and the eventually successful claimant, Edgar, unmistakably owed his throne to William. In these circumstances, the Scots kings could not press territorial claims. Edgar's brothers and successors, Alexander I and David I, likewise made no move. The English succession crisis of 1135 freed David's hand. His seizure of Cumbria early the following year must have realized long-nursed ambitions. Stephen was forced to recognize this reversal of Rufus's annexation and for the rest of his life David could regard Carlisle as one of the chief seats of his kingdom. He minted coins there, his court often met there and, in 1153, having possessed the city for seventeen years, he died there.

The incorporation of Northumberland was an even more impressive extension of the power of the king of Scots. It is evident from the negotiations of 1136 that David considered that he had some claim on the earldom of Northumberland, possibly through his wife, the daughter of earl Waltheof of Northumberland, and in 1139 he was able to realize this claim in the person of his son Henry, to whom king Stephen conceded the earldom. Although

---

[30] S. Durh., *HDE* 3. 9 (p. 91).       [31] S. Durh., *HR* 156 (p. 191).
[32] *ASC*, p. 227.       [33] *ASC*, p. 228.

Henry held the area as a vassal of the English king, he had in practice virtual autonomy, minting coins in his own name ('Earl Henry') at Corbridge, and ruling what was recognized as a distinctly peaceable and orderly principality throughout the anarchy of Stephen's reign. After earl Henry's death in 1152, the earldom passed to his younger son, William.

When Henry II came to the English throne in 1154, he therefore found Cumbria part of the Scottish kingdom and Northumberland in the hands of a member of the Scottish royal family. If he had been less insistent on his rights, perhaps Newcastle and Carlisle would today be north of the Border. As it was, he had both the power and the inclination to disregard the promise he had made to David I in 1149, when he needed him, that he would concede him Northumberland if he became king. Three years after his accession, in 1157, Henry secured from David's grandchildren and heirs, Malcolm IV and earl William (later himself king), the surrender of their lands south of the Solway and Tweed. As one chronicler noted, the young Scots king 'prudently recognized that in this matter the king of England overcame the merit of the case with the power of his force'.[34] The Border was thus restored to what it had been in the years 1092–1136 and was to remain so throughout the years until its formal recognition by treaty in 1237, despite the continued claims of the Scots kings, that led to military efforts by William the Lion (the dispossessed earl of 1157) in 1173–4 and his son Alexander II in 1215–17.

The problem of the homage that the kings of Scots performed was less concrete and less pressing than the territorial issue but still potentially explosive. Kings could certainly be vassals of other kings, as the king of England was of the king of France, but as feudal law crystallized and refined in the twelfth century the question arose of what they were doing homage *for*. The territorialization of the vassalic bond meant that when homage was performed, awkward or theoretical types might ask 'for what fief is this given?' Just as the kings of England were clear that they were the vassals of the kings of France for Normandy, not for the kingdom of England, so the kings of Scots tried to distinguish the homage they did for their English lands (Huntingdon etc.) from homage for the kingdom of Scotland. The kings of England might have another view.

Malcolm Canmore and his sons and successors did homage to the kings of England, sometimes because they were forced to, sometimes because they needed their help. After David's accession in 1124, it was obvious that possession of the earldom of Huntingdon by the Scottish kings would entail homage. Indeed, one of the reasons that David I did not accept the earldoms of Huntingdon and Northumberland from king Stephen, but allowed them to be bestowed on his son Henry was that he could thus avoid performing

---

[34] W. Newb. 2. 4 (1, p. 105).

homage to the English king. Henry II's imperious settlement of 1157 involved, alongside the Scottish surrender of Northumberland and Cumbria,
the performance of homage by Malcolm IV. Since he was given back the earldom of Huntingdon, lost during the Anarchy, as a consolation prize, and
since, according to one source, his homage was made 'reserving all his dignities', it may be that the Scottish king did not consider he was performing
homage for Scotland.[35]

William the Lion's bad luck or misjudgement at Alnwick meant that
Henry II could impose stricter control over the king of Scots than any previous English king. By the terms of the settlement confirmed at Falaise in 1174
William became the 'liege man' of the English king 'for Scotland and for all
his other lands' and swore fealty to him, also doing homage and swearing
fealty to the heir-presumptive Henry the Young King. The bishops and
abbots of Scotland recognized Henry II as their liege lord, although the exact
relationship between the English and Scottish churches was left carefully
vague. The earls and barons of Scotland were to do homage and swear fealty
to Henry II and his heirs as their liege lord. The political superiority of the
king of England over Scotland could not have been made more explicit. As
practical counterparts to these rituals and promises, five important Scottish
castles (Roxburgh, Berwick, Jedburgh, Edinburgh, and Stirling) were to be
handed over to the English king, along with twenty-one important hostages,
including William the Lion's brother, David.[36]

William's chance to shake off the restrictions and promises imposed upon
him at Falaise came in 1189, with the accession of an English king willing to
sell anything to finance his crusade. At Canterbury in that year, Richard I restored to the Scottish king the castles he still held and the allegiances of his
men. He cancelled 'all the agreements that our good father, Henry, king of the
English, extorted from him through his captivity in new charters'. William's
only promise was to be Richard's liege man 'for all the lands for which his
ancestors were liege men of our ancestors', a formula that could be interpreted happily by either side.[37] Not mentioned in the formal record of the
proceedings is the payment of 10,000 marks (over £6,500) made to Richard
for this agreement.[38]

William the Lion was never reconciled to the loss of his childhood lordship
of Northumberland, but his repeated attempts to secure it were fruitless. In
1209 he was even forced to a humiliating agreement with king John, whereby
he paid an enormous sum to the English king and handed over to him his two
daughters to be married. This treaty was made 'against the will of the
Scots'.[39] A few years later William's son, Alexander II, had the opportunity

---

[35] *Melrose Chron.*, p. 76.      [36] Stones, *Rels.*, pp. 2–10 [1–5].
[37] Stones, *Rels.*, pp. 12–16 [6–8].      [38] *Gesta Hen. II* 2, p. 98; *Melrose Chron.*, p. 98.
[39] *Melrose Chron.*, p. 108.

to pursue his father's life-long ambition, as John's reign collapsed in civil war. Many of the rebel barons were based in the north of England and Alexander received their homage, as well as besieging royal castles and seizing the city of Carlisle. In the summer of 1216 he marched the entire length of England, coming to Dover to do homage to Louis of France, whom the rebels had invited to take the throne. Alexander continued military activity in the north of England until the rebel cause was completely defeated and then made his peace, surrendering Carlisle and restoring the border as it had been. At Christmas 1217 he did homage to Henry III and the earldom of Huntingdon was restored to his uncle David. There was to be no further warfare between England and Scotland for as long as his dynasty lasted.

## Ireland

Although there is no such contiguous frontier as in the case of Wales and Scotland, the fortunes of England and Ireland have always been closely intertwined. It is only 122 nautical miles from the mouth of the Liffey to the mouth of the Mersey and the sea crossing to or from Ireland via Wales is half that distance. Ireland's geographical location meant that many of its contacts with the wider European scene were through England. Irish missionaries had helped to build the foundations of Anglo-Saxon Christian culture, while during the Viking period the bonds had been even stronger, for the ties between the various Scandinavian colonies in the British Isles ran across the seaways. There had even been briefly a kingdom that included both Dublin and York. In the eleventh century, Ireland was, from the English viewpoint, a market, buying slaves and selling furs, a threat, sending raiders to the coasts of Britain, and an ancient Christian community with close ties to England. In the twelfth century, for the first time, it became also a field of conquest and colonization.

It was political disputes within Ireland that led to the involvement of forces from across the Irish Sea. In the year 1166 Dermot MacMurrough (Diarmait Mac Murchada), king of Leinster, a vigorous and ruthless competitor in the endless struggle for supremacy among the Irish kings, had been worsted by his enemies, led by the High King, Rory O'Connor (Ruaidrí Ua Conchobair) of Connacht, and forced to go into exile. The exiled king came first to Bristol, a port with long established trading links with Ireland, and then sought out Henry II, finally finding him in Aquitaine, to ask permission to recruit from among his vassals. Norman knights had been recruited by the rulers of the British Isles ever since the middle of the eleventh century, when they had served in the retinues of Edward the Confessor and Macbeth, so Dermot's line of action is nothing surprising. If Scottish kings and Welsh princes found that a stiffening of Anglo-Norman horsemen and archers could be an asset in their conflicts with their rivals, then it was natural for a dispossessed Irish ruler to seek their services too.

Dermot had great success both in recruiting Anglo-Norman troops and in deploying them for his own interests. In particular, he was able to enrol a group of military leaders from among the lords and knights of the south Welsh March, men whose fathers or grandfathers had come to Wales to conquer and settle and who were familiar with the incessant small-scale warfare of a politically fragmented land. Notable in this group were the descendants of Nesta, daughter of Rhys ap Tewdwr of Deheubarth, by her various Anglo-Norman partners. Her grandchildren and great-grandchildren included Robert fitz Stephen, Meiler fitz Henry, and the fitz Gerald clan, all men endowed with lands and lordship in Pembrokeshire who agreed to participate in Dermot's restoration. The most important figure with whom the king of Leinster concluded terms was Richard of Clare ('Strongbow'), lord of Chepstow, and also dispossessed earl of Pembroke, to whom, according to contemporary Anglo-Norman sources, Dermot offered the hand of his daughter and succession to the kingdom of Leinster.

Dermot was soon back in his kingdom and, with the help of his new troops from south Wales, began an aggressive and expansionary policy. In the summer of 1169 Robert fitz Stephen landed near Wexford with 30 knights, 60 armoured sergeants, and 300 archers (south Wales was famous for its longbowmen). Over the next twelve months he was followed by his cousins Maurice fitz Gerald, ancestor of the Geraldines who were to dominate late medieval Ireland, and Raymond le Gros, who between them brought 20 more knights and 200 archers. Finally Strongbow himself landed near Waterford on 23 August 1170 with 200 knights and 1,000 other troops. With this support Dermot was able to capture the Norse-Irish towns of Waterford and Dublin. Yet although, in the words of one contemporary source, 'Through the English he was exalted, with great pride and haughtiness', his victories were soon over.[40] In May 1171 he died, leaving Strongbow and his Anglo-Normans with a difficult predicament.

The decision of the Anglo-Norman leaders in Ireland in 1171 neither to return across the Irish Sea nor to seek to enter the service of some other Irish king but to set up their own lordship over Leinster and Dublin was a critical development. It implied an attempt to create a political entity spanning the sea, with Chepstow and Kilkenny under the same master. It also provoked a swift and forceful reaction from the English king, who had no intention of seeing any of his barons assume an unchecked semi-regal position in Ireland. Henry II at once placed an embargo on trade with Ireland, commanded the Anglo-Normans there to return or face harsh penalties, confiscated

---

[40] *Song of Dermot and the Earl*, lines 1060–1, ed. and tr. Goddard H. Orpen (Oxford, 1892), p. 80.

Strongbow's English lands and began preparations for a royal expedition to Ireland. His suspicions were not absurd. There was a precedent for dangerous alliances between disaffected barons and Irish kings, for during the rebellion of the Montgomery family in 1102, Arnulf de Montgomery, lord of Pembroke, had negotiated a marriage alliance with Murchertach O'Brien (Muirchertach Ua Briain), king of Munster, from which he derived some military support. Strongbow, whose father had been created earl of Pembroke by king Stephen but who had been deprived of the earldom by Henry II, had good cause to resent the king.

Henry II's expedition to Ireland in 1171–2 laid the foundation of the subsequent Lordship of Ireland. As in Wales, there was to be dualistic arrangement, whereby both Anglo-Norman lords and native Irish kings were to recognize the authority of the English Crown. Strongbow submitted to the king even before he landed in Ireland, ceding Dublin and other areas to him and, in return, gaining royal recognition of his possession of a trimmed-down Leinster, held as a fief from the king. The other Anglo-Normans also submitted. Meath was handed over to one of Henry II's barons, Hugh de Lacy, possibly as a counterweight to Strongbow's Leinster, while the areas beyond Leinster, Meath and the royal demesne lands of Dublin and Waterford were to remain in the hands of the existing dynasties. The kings of Desmond and Thomond came to meet the English king as he made his progress from Waterford, where he had landed, to Dublin. They recognized Henry's superior lordship, promising tribute, and, in the case of the king of Desmond, delivering hostages. Many other Irish kings came to the king at Dublin and likewise made formal and ceremonial submission at the Christmas court there. The only major native Irish ruler who did not submit in 1171–2 was Rory O'Connor of Connacht (although the evidence on this subject is not completely unequivocal).[41]

The year 1169 has acquired something of the same fateful ring in the Irish historical imagination that 1066 has for the English and there is equally good reason for it. The arrival of Anglo-Norman forces in Ireland in that year had as a rapid and direct consequence the creation of an Anglo-Irish aristocracy and the submission of the rulers of Ireland to the English Crown. The formation of the Lordship of Ireland in the period after 1169 meant that a wholly new political structure had come into being in the British Isles. There had never previously been a settler community in Ireland owing allegiance to the king of England but henceforth such a creation was to be a significant and often central feature of British politics. English Ireland was meant to take its pattern from England: 'the laws of our land of Ireland and of England are and

---

[41] *Gesta Hen. II* 1, p. 25; R. Howd. 2, p. 30; R. Diceto, *Ymag.* 1, p. 348; Gerv. Cant., p. 235, report that he did not submit, Gerald, *Exp.* 1. 33 (pp. 94–6), that he did.

should be identical', wrote the English royal government in 1223.[42] A system of counties, with sheriffs and coroners, was gradually established and central institutions modelled on those of England, like the central courts and Exchequer, were developed. A royal deputy, the Justiciar, based in Dublin castle, headed the administration.

More important for the establishment and maintenance of Anglo-Norman power in Ireland than this replication of England's institutions was the settlement of a colonial aristocracy of men of English, French, Welsh, or Flemish descent, who expropriated previous Irish rulers and created new lordships secured by castles and envisaged as feudal tenures. The great tenants in chief of such lordships as Leinster and Meath would grant out fiefs to their own barons and knights. A charter recording an enfeoffment of this kind from the early days of the settlement is that granted by Hugh de Lacy, lord of Meath (1172–86), to Gilbert de Nugent:

Hugh de Lacy to all sons of Holy Mother Church and to his men and his friends, French, English and Irish, greeting. Know that I have given and confirmed by this present charter to Gilbert de Nugent and his heirs the whole of Delvin, which the O'Phelans held in the time of the Irish, with all its appurtenances and villages which are within Delvin . . . for his service of five knights to be performed by him and his heirs within my land of Meath, to be held from me and my heirs freely and honourably and fully.[43]

This is a hereditary grant by specified military service of lands held by a named Irish predecessor 'in the time of the Irish' (!) Parts of Ireland were thus being divided up into knights' fees and granted out to an immigrant aristocracy.

Some of the beneficiaries, like the fitz Geralds, belonged to that early group who had responded to the call of Dermot MacMurrough; others, and these were increasingly important over time, received lands in Ireland through royal favour. Angevin administrators, like Bertram de Verdon, one of Henry II's sheriffs and judges who was given Dundalk, or the relatives and protégés of Angevin administrators, like Theobald Walter, nephew of the head of the English administration, Ranulf de Glanville, who was endowed with lands in Munster, were not the free-lance adventurers of the early years. Ulster, or, rather, parts of it, came under Anglo-Norman rule in an unusual way. John de Courcy, member of a baronial family with interests in various parts of Normandy and England, especially in the north-west, was part of the Dublin garrison in the mid-1170s. Growing bored and restless during the winter of 1176–7, he led a group of 22 knights and 300 footmen up the east coast to Ulidia (eastern Ulster), where he managed to defeat the local Irish

[42] Rot. litt. claus. 1, p. 497.
[43] Richard Butler, Some Notices of the Castle . . . of Trim (Trim, 1835), pp. 252–3.

king and seize Downpatrick, which became the centre of his new lordship. He held it through several decades of constant warfare, building castles, erecting new monasteries, and settling his vassals, until in 1205 he was dispossessed by Anglo-Norman rivals with royal backing. Ulster, raised to the status of an earldom, was granted to Hugh de Lacy, younger brother of the lord of Meath.

Henry II's plans for Ireland changed several times between his expedition of 1171–2 and his death in 1189. One initiative is marked by the treaty of Windsor of 1175. This was an agreement drawn up between Henry II and Rory O'Connor. Whether or not the High King had subjected himself to Henry in Ireland in 1171–2, he certainly did so now. According to the terms of the treaty, 'the king of England has conceded to Rory, king of Connacht, his liege man, that he should be king under him, as long as he serves him loyally'. Rory was to arrange for the payment of one animal hide in ten to the king from the whole area still under native Irish rule and, in return, his authority was acknowledged over that whole area: 'he shall have all the rest of the land and its inhabitants under him'. The royal demesne lands of Dublin and Waterford were expressly excluded, as were Leinster, Meath, and other lands of the king's barons.[44] The arrangement envisaged has some similarities with that Henry had come to in Wales, with the Lord Rhys recognized as a superior native authority in south Wales in the areas outside the lands of the king and the Marcher lords.

The arrangements made in 1175 are of greater interest for the light they shed on the assumptions behind royal thinking than for their effect. The native Irish kings were no more ready to submit unanimously to Rory's over-lordship when required to do so by a document drawn up at Windsor than they had been when faced with his campaigns in the years prior to Henry's expedition to Ireland. The Anglo-Normans in Ireland were no happier about being limited to Leinster and Meath. Within two years of the treaty of Windsor, Henry II had made rather different arrangements concerning Ireland. His youngest son John was to be king of Ireland, while speculative grants of the kingdoms of Thomond and Desmond were made to Anglo-Norman vassals, their chief cities of Limerick and Cork being reserved for the Crown. John was only 9 years old at the time, but soon after he had been knighted, at the age of 17, he headed an expedition to Ireland, intended to assert his authority over both the Anglo-Norman barons there and the native Irish kings.

John's expedition of 1185 was a notorious fiasco. Complaints were made that the soldiery were left unpaid, that patronage was distributed tactlessly and that a general lethargy and self-seeking pervaded the whole operation. Gerald of Wales tells the famous story of how John's young companions alienated the first native Irish who came to make their submission by

---

[44] *Gesta Hen. II* 1, pp. 102–3; R. Howd. 2, pp. 84–5.

mocking them and pulling the long beards that they wore according to Irish custom. The important Irish kings of Thomond, Desmond, and Connacht kept their distance. John's first encounter with his new lordship was thus inauspicious; nor was he ever to obtain the Crown that his father had sought for him—he remained 'Lord' rather than 'King' of Ireland. In 1199, when John was crowned king of England he united the two titles, and the style 'King of England and Lord of Ireland' was to be borne by all English kings until Henry VIII adopted the title king of Ireland.

The direct and enduring association of the lordship of Ireland and the Crown of England was thus, in a sense, fortuitous. If Richard I had had a son to succeed him, Ireland could have become a political unit with its own dynasty, perhaps subordinate to the Crown in some way but not directly united in the person of the king. As it was, the king of England was the lord of Ireland. This is particularly obvious in the case of John. He maintained a close personal interest in Irish affairs and, in 1210, became the second reigning English monarch to lead an army into Ireland (and the last for 184 years). This campaign was a more efficient operation than his youthful expedition of 1185. Like his father forty years earlier, he was more concerned to control the Anglo-Norman baronage than to subdue the native Irish. One of his great barons, William de Braose, had fallen foul of John and taken refuge in Ireland, where he held the lordship of Limerick and where the lord of Meath, Walter de Lacy, was his son-in-law. John's campaign of 1210 secured the submission or expulsion of all the Anglo-Norman barons of Ireland, culminating in the successful siege of Carrickfergus castle and the flight of its lord, Walter de Lacy's brother Hugh, earl of Ulster, along with William de Braose's wife and son (soon captured). John received the submission of many native Irish kings, took the lordships of Limerick, Meath, and Ulster into his own hands, issued a declaration confirming that the Lordship of Ireland would follow English law and returned across the Irish Sea.

## English Overlordship in the British Isles

English kings had always had an interest in establishing their political authority over other parts of the British Isles, even if this was rarely a predominant or sustained interest. The Norman and Angevin kings attained an overlordship that was more effective, more closely defined and territorially greater than any of their predecessors. They were usually able to insist on formal recognition from the other kings and princes of the British Isles that they were subordinate rulers holding their territories from the king of England. Even in the case of Scotland, the largest and most autonomous political unit in the British Isles after England, political circumstances often permitted very clear demonstrations of English authority. A charter of Edgar, the Scots king put on the throne by English military aid in the 1090s, reads 'I, Edgar, son of Malcolm, king of Scots, possessing the land of Lothian and the kingdom of Scotland by the gift of my lord, William, king of the English, and as a paternal inheritance . . .', while the *Anglo-Saxon Chronicle* refers to the succession of his brother Alexander I in 1107 'as king Henry granted him'.[45]

English superiority was sometimes shown in a paternalistic fashion. It was usually English kings who knighted other rulers rather than vice-versa (Henry of Anjou's dubbing by king David in 1149 indicates how unusual political relationships were in the middle years of the twelfth century). William Rufus knighted Duncan II of Scotland, Henry I knighted Owain ap Cadwgan of Powys.[46] In 1209 king John made himself responsible for the marriages of William the Lion's daughters and, three years later, knighted William's son and heir, Alexander, in London. English kings expected Scots kings to come to their court, rather than vice-versa, and even had customary arrangements for supplying them and escorting them en route.[47]

Military service was another expression of this hierarchy. Scottish kings were, on occasion, found in the entourage of English kings on military expeditions. Alexander I accompanied Henry I during his invasion of Wales in 1114, Malcolm IV was with Henry II when he besieged Toulouse in 1159 (and was knighted by the king in France), while in the spring or summer of 1166 William the Lion crossed over to France at the expense of Henry II, who was then engaged in spasmodic military operations against his continental opponents, and 'attempted deeds of knightly prowess'.[48] The Welsh princes who submitted to the English kings also had on occasion to perform military service for them. So we find the tumultuous Owain ap Cadwgan in Henry I's entourage in France in 1114–15.[49]

Ceremonial homage was obviously the simplest and the most public form of recognition of subordination. On an occasion such as that at the royal palace of Woodstock on 1 August 1163, when Henry II and his son received the homage of Malcolm IV of Scotland, the Lord Rhys of Deheubarth, Owain Gwynedd of Gwynedd, and other Welsh leaders, the English king must have felt that his overlordship of Britain had been recognized in a quite satisfactory way.[50] In the single year 1177 Henry made new arrangements for Ireland, including the designation of his son John as king there, received the homage of all the leading princes of Wales, enhancing the territories of some of them, and placed his castellans in the southern Scottish castles of

---

[45] *Early Scottish Charters prior to 1153*, ed. Archibald C. Lawrie (Glasgow, 1905), no. XV; the genuineness of the charter is maintained by A. A. M. Duncan, 'The Earliest Scottish Charters', *Scottish Historical Review*, 37 (1958), pp. 103–35; *ASC*, p. 241.

[46] W. Malm., *GR* 5. 400 (2, p. 476); OMT edn., p. 724. *Brut (RBH)*, p. 83.

[47] Stones, *Rels.*, pp. 18–22 [9–11].

[48] *Melrose Chron.*, p. 80.      [49] *Brut (RBH)*, p. 83.      [50] R. Diceto, *Ymag.* 1, p. 311.

Roxburgh, Edinburgh, and Berwick, in accordance with the terms of the Treaty of Falaise. Like the other Norman and Angevin kings, Henry demanded that his superiority be recognized but had no intention of removing the local kings and princes of Scotland, Wales, or Ireland. Except in the rare patches of royal demesne, like Dublin and Carmarthen, he was to be an overlord not a direct lord.

## The English Church and the British Isles

The story of the extension and enforcement of English royal overlordship in the British Isles in the Norman and Angevin period is closely intertwined with that of the ambitions of the English Church to assert its superior authority in Wales, Scotland and Ireland. When Lanfranc came to Canterbury as its first Norman archbishop in 1070, he soon became embroiled in a dispute with the archbishop of York over the question of the ecclesiastical primacy. The polemics of the case drew from him a statement of his claim to ecclesiastical authority over the whole of the British Isles: 'my predecessors exercised the primacy over the church of York and the whole island called Britain and also Ireland.'[51] This was an assertion that subsequent archbishops were to maintain. In 1119 archbishop Ralph, writing to the pope, claimed that from its earliest days 'the church of Canterbury has not ceased to provide pastoral care for the whole of Britain and Ireland, both as a benevolence and from its rights of primacy'.[52]

In certain circumstances the archbishops were able to give these pretensions some reality. In the late eleventh and early twelfth centuries they consecrated half a dozen bishops from the Viking towns of Ireland, notably from Dublin itself, whose four incumbents between 1074 and 1121 were all consecrated at Canterbury or at the archbishop's manor of Lambeth and swore an oath of canonical obedience to the archbishops. In the profession of obedience that was given by bishop Patrick of Dublin in 1074 Lanfranc is referred to as 'primate of the Britains' (*primas Britanniarum*), probably meaning 'of the British Isles'.[53] Many of these bishops, although Irish, had been monks in English monasteries. Letters from archbishops Lanfranc and Anselm to various Irish rulers are respectful but also contain vigorous denunciation of the moral failings of the Irish and the inadequacies of Irish ecclesiastical institutions. At this time, then, Canterbury's ecclesiastical authority was certainly recognized in some parts of Ireland.

In Ireland Canterbury's claims were thus accepted voluntarily by some of the Viking towns and also by the native Irish overlords of those towns,

---

[51] Lanfranc, *Letters*, ed. and tr. Helen Clover and Margaret Gibson (OMT; 1979), no. 4, p. 50.
[52] *Historians of the Church of York*, ed. J. Raine (3 vols., RS; 1879–94), vol. 2, p. 236.
[53] *Canterbury Professions*, ed. Michael Richter (Canterbury and York Soc. 67; 1973), no. 36, p. 29.

especially the kings of the O'Brien (Ua Briain) dynasty. In Wales, in contrast, ecclesiastical subordination was largely a consequence of military and political subordination. The Welsh bishops had never been subordinate to the English church but, as the Anglo-Normans conquered parts of Wales, the conquerors appointed their own nominees to bishoprics under their control. The first was Hervey, a Breton, who became bishop of Bangor in 1092 in the wake of the subjection of the north Welsh coast. His Welsh flock did not suffer him long:

Since they did not show the respect and reverence due to a bishop, he wielded the sharp two-edged sword to subdue them, constraining them both with repeated excommunications and with the host of his kinsmen and other followers. They resisted him none the less and pressed him with such dangers that they killed his brother and intended to deal with him in the same way, if they could lay hands on him.[54]

Hervey followed the path of discretion, returning to England, where he was eventually given the less demanding see of Ely.

Despite this debacle, the continued Anglo-Norman conquest did allow the imposition of the authority of Canterbury in its wake. Urban, appointed bishop of Llandaff in 1107, is the first Welsh bishop whose profession of obedience to the archbishop of Canterbury has survived. Although of Welsh family, he had been a priest in the diocese of Worcester, so the authority of Canterbury was not completely alien to him, but it is perhaps more important that his cathedral see was in the immediate vicinity of Cardiff castle, centre of Anglo-Norman power in south-east Wales, and he would be well aware of the political realities. Some years later, in 1115, Bernard, chancellor to Henry I's queen, Matilda, was appointed to the see of St David's, 'against the will and in despite of all the clergy of the Britons [i.e. Welsh]'.[55] In 1120 a native Welsh successor to the exiled bishop Hervey was finally appointed in Bangor. With the agreement of the native prince of Gwynedd, Gruffudd ap Cynan, he took the oath of obedience to Canterbury, thus indicating that native opposition could be directed more strongly against alien appointees than against ecclesiastical subordination.

In a relatively short period the archbishopric of Canterbury had thus exerted its authority over the Welsh dioceses and was to continue to insist that every ecclesiastic elected to an episcopal see in Wales swear a public and formal oath of obedience to the archbishop. Many of the bishops of the twelfth and thirteenth centuries were themselves of English or Anglo-Norman origin. Of the five bishops of St David's in the years 1115–1229, only one, Iorwerth (1215–29), was of purely Welsh descent. Another, David fitz Gerald (1148–76), was the son of a Norman lord and the Welsh princess

[54] Lib. Eliensis 3. 1 (p. 245).     [55] Brut (RBH), p. 83.

Nesta, while the remaining three had no Welsh blood. Bishop Bernard (1115–48) was a royal clerk, Peter de Leia (1176–98) was described as 'a foreigner with not a single relative in the whole of Wales', while Geoffrey de Henlaw (nominated 1199, consecrated 1203, died 1214) was actually the personal physician to the archbishop of Canterbury.[56]

The relationship of the English Church with Scotland was cast in a different institutional mould from that with Ireland and Wales, since the archbishopric of Canterbury was not here the undisputed representative of the English Church. The claims of the archbishopric of York extended well north of the Anglo-Scottish border (wherever that might be at any time) and in 1072 even Canterbury had recognized York's claims to authority over the bishops from the Humber 'to the furthest limits of Scotland'.[57] The bishops of Whithorn in the south-western part of the kingdom of the Scots regularly made professions of obedience to York, while Michael, the first recorded bishop of the revived diocese of Glasgow, was consecrated by Thomas, archbishop of York (1109–14), and professed obedience to him as his metropolitan. Not all Scottish bishops were so responsive to York's demands, however. Michael's successor at Glasgow, John, fought a long and dogged fight against York's claims, and the bishops of St Andrews who were consecrated by archbishops of York in 1109 and 1127 made explicit reservations of their rights on those occasions.

One aspect of the Scottish ecclesiastical hierarchy that made it particularly vulnerable to York's claims was its lack of an archbishopric. The fact that the bishop of St Andrews was known as 'bishop of the Scots' suggests the traditional eminence of that see, but its status was quite undefined. Several attempts were made to convert St Andrews into an archbishopric of the kind recognizable to a twelfth-century canon lawyer, but, despite the support of the Scottish kings, they came to nothing. Nevertheless, the Scottish bishops generally sought to maintain their independence. At the council of Northampton in 1176 Henry II demanded of the Scottish clergy 'that they should make the submission to the English church that they had customarily owed in the time of his predecessors as kings of England'. Their answer was 'that their predecessors had never made any submission to the church of England and neither should they make any'. The archbishop of York, raising his expected claim, rather had the ground cut from under him when the archbishop of Canterbury claimed that the Scottish church should be subject to him, not York, and eventually the king let the Scottish prelates leave. They at once sent envoys to the pope, Alexander III, to secure his support in the face of these demands.[58]

---

[56] Gerald, *Symb. el.*, p. 314.    [57] *Councils and Synods* I/ii, p. 602.
[58] *Gesta Hen. II* 1, pp. 111–12.

It was indeed a shift in the attitude of the papacy that was of fundamental importance in freeing the Scottish church. Between 1100 and 1170 the popes issued no less than eighteen letters commanding Scottish bishops to obey the archbishop of York, but in the 1170s it seems that Alexander III, perhaps in the aftermath of Becket's murder and the subsequent shadow over the English king, became open to the idea of a Scottish church that did not obey any external archbishop.[59] A clear and explicit statement of the independence of the Scottish church is contained in the papal bull *Cum universi*, issued by Celestine III in 1192: 'the Scottish church should be directly subject to the apostolic see, whose special daughter she is'.[60] Thereafter the Scottish church remained in the unusual constitutional position of having no arch-bishopric and being immediately under the papacy. 'The fullness of papal power', sourly commented one English observer with reference to this case, 'casts down many worthy parties and raises up many unworthy ones.'[61]

The Irish church asserted its autonomy as an ecclesiastical unit much earlier than the Scottish. Although, as already mentioned, some Irish bishops were consecrated by archbishops of Canterbury in the early years of the twelfth century, in the Synods of Ráith Bressail in 1111 and Kells in 1152 the Irish church developed, and won papal recognition for, its own independent episcopal hierarchy. There were four archbishoprics (Armagh, Dublin, Cashel, and Tuam), corresponding roughly to the traditional division of Ireland into Ulster, Leinster, Munster, and Connacht, with the primacy of Armagh recognized, and some thirty-five bishoprics under them. Canter-bury was completely excluded. Crucial in securing this outcome, which was certainly not inevitable, was the existence of native reformers with ties to Rome. The Synod of Ráith Bressail was presided over by Gilbert, bishop of Limerick, as papal legate; Malachy of Armagh, the reforming hero of the second quarter of the twelfth century, was a friend of St Bernard and visited Rome twice in pursuit of the reorganization of the Irish episcopal structure. Because of the efforts of such men, native Irish ecclesiastics who were willing to reshape the structure and customs of the Irish church along lines that could be supported by papalist high churchmen and canonists, the Irish church was completely constitutionally independent of the English church at the time of the subordination of the island to Henry II in 1171. Although clergy of English descent were to occupy the episcopal sees and other clerical posts in the colonized parts of the country in increasing numbers,

---

[59] Robert Somerville, *Scotia Pontificia: Papal Letters to Scotland before the Pontificate of Innocent III* (Oxford, 1982), pp. 7–8, 76–7.
[60] Ibid., no. 156, pp. 142–4; *Gesta Ric. I* 2, pp. 234–5; R. Howd. 2, pp. 360–1 (attributed to Clement III); 3, pp. 173–4 (JL 16836).
[61] Gerv. Tilb. 2. 10 (p. 918).

there was never to be a question of Canterbury asserting its supremacy as it had done in Wales.

Partially inspired by developments in Ireland and Scotland, some of the Welsh bishops fought a rear-guard action against Canterbury's claims. Interestingly, these last struggles for Welsh ecclesiastical independence were conducted not by native Welsh churchmen but by men of French or mainly Anglo-Norman descent. The reason is that allegiance to and identification with one's own diocese was often a stronger impulse than any supposedly national loyalty. Bishop Bernard of St David's was, without a doubt, politically loyal to the new Anglo-Norman regime. He wished, nevertheless, to have a status and a freedom as great as that of the archbishop of Canterbury. In the 1120s, 1130s, and 1140s, Bernard and the cathedral chapter of St David's raised the issue repeatedly with the papacy, arguing that historically the Welsh church had been independent, that Wales was quite distinct from England and that Bernard was the heir to archiepiscopal status going back to the days of St David himself, or beyond. In 1147 both bishop Bernard and his antagonist Theobald, archbishop of Canterbury, were at the papal court arguing their case. The pope, Eugenius III, ruled that Bernard should be 'personally obedient' to Theobald 'as to his own metropolitan' but that the issue of principle—the status of the church of St David's—should be determined at a hearing in the following year.[62] Bernard's death intervened and Theobald ensured the election of a compliant successor.

Fifty years later the battle was resumed. It was to be a battle royal but also a final defeat for the cause of Welsh ecclesiastical autonomy. Gerald of Wales, elected to the see of St David's in 1199, was an ecclesiastic of mixed Anglo-Norman and Welsh descent and a man whose sense of bitter personal disappointment transformed him, late in his career, into an unexpected and extreme champion of an independent Welsh church. He wished to be not simply bishop but archbishop of St David's and from his fertile and plausible pen there poured forth all the arguments to be made: Canterbury had abused its authority in Wales, riding on the back of an intrusive and violent conquest, imposing unworthy alien bishops onto Welsh sees; Wales was distinct in language, law, and custom from England; the Welsh church was far older than the English church; St David's had had twenty-five archbishops in the past.

Argument was not everything. There was also power. And the kings of England and archbishops of Canterbury had no wish to see a separate Welsh church. Hubert Walter, at this time not only archbishop of Canterbury but also royal chancellor, supposedly argued,

if the rigour of ecclesiastical authority, exercised by Canterbury, to whose ecclesiastical province that people [i.e. the Welsh] are known to be subject, had not restrained

[62] Gerald, *Inv.* 2. 2 (pp. 135–6) (JL 9090).

the barbarity of that wild and untamed race, then they would have withdrawn their allegiance from the king in frequent and continual rebellion, bringing disorder to the whole of England.[63]

King John, a pragmatist and sceptic in ecclesiastical affairs, nevertheless also came to the conclusion that Gerald might be stirring up political trouble and eventually declared him 'an enemy of the king'. In 1203, after three long trips to Rome in pursuit of his case, Gerald had to make a final, comprehensive renunciation of his claims. The Welsh church was to remain part of the province of Canterbury until 1920.

The ecclesiastical politics of Ireland, Wales, and Scotland should not be seen in isolation from the secular politics. One of the reasons the Scottish church was able to resist the claims of York, even when these were given papal backing, was that the Scottish kings had an interest in keeping the Scottish bishops free of the authority of an English archbishop. When Henry I subdued Wales, 'he placed the Welsh church, that he had found free, under the church of his kingdom, just as he subjected the land to his realm'.[64] Yet secular politics did not simply dictate the pattern of ecclesiastical structures. An increasingly active papacy, applying increasingly refined canonical principles, had a central part to play. Although in the early twelfth century Anglo-Norman domination in Wales led to the subordination of the Welsh church to Canterbury, by the late twelfth century it was impossible for the subjection of Ireland to the king of England to lead to the subjection of the Irish church to the English church. The transformation of ecclesiastical structures in Wales, Ireland, and Scotland in the twelfth century took place alongside conquest, colonization, and Anglicization but was not always a simple direct consequence of it.

## Social Changes

The extension of the power of the English monarchy, aristocracy, and Church into other parts of the British Isles in the Norman and Angevin period was accompanied by urban and rural migration and the introduction of new social forms mediated via England. Castles and fiefs were imported into the rest of the British Isles from England and the new towns that were founded in great numbers in Wales, Scotland, and Ireland in the twelfth and thirteenth centuries often drew both their constitutional form and their population from England. The Scottish Law of the Four Boroughs, an urban code the core of which dates to the reign of David I, was based upon the customs of Newcastle upon Tyne, while the laws of Breteuil, a set of Norman customs brought to Hereford after the Norman Conquest by William fitz

---

[63] Ibid. 1. 1 (p. 85).     [64] Ibid. 4. 2 (p. 164).

Osbern, lord of Breteuil, spread to many urban foundations in Wales and Ireland. The settlers of the new towns were frequently of English or continental origin, as their names indicate, and the boroughs long remained the most resolutely Anglicized enclaves in Wales, Scotland, and Ireland. A document of the early twelfth century refers characteristically to 'all the burgesses, French, English and Flemish' of Kidwelly.[65] The Dublin guild merchant lists of about 1200 give the names of several thousand traders, a very large proportion of them of obviously English origin: 'Andrew of Worcester', 'Geoffrey of Winchester', 'John of Bristol', etc.[66]

English migration into rural districts was also important. In southern and eastern Ireland, tenant lists of about 1300 show large numbers of rural inhabitants with English names, most probably the descendants of immigrants from Britain who had come over in the late twelfth and early thirteenth centuries. The place names of southern Pembrokeshire are mainly English, indicating fairly heavy colonization in the wake of the establishment of Anglo-Norman political and military power there. One of the most noticeable results of this movement of conquest and settlement in the twelfth and thirteenth centuries was the territorial expansion of the English language, for the new settlers in both town and country would be predominantly English-speaking, even if there would also be some use of French in administrative documents and high culture. The personal names of burgesses and free tenants and the appearance in later documents of field names like 'Langley', 'Modhilfeld', 'Westmedes', 'Gretemedes', and so on, recorded at Gowran in county Kilkenny in 1306, suggest an Anglophone world at a quite local and lowly level in the more heavily colonized areas, like Leinster.[67]

The period 1075–1225 thus saw major and permanent changes in the relations between England and the other parts of the British Isles. Migration of people from England, usually under the leadership of aristocrats of French descent, changed the population map and, especially, the linguistic map of the British Isles. English was now spoken over a far wider area. With the immigrants came some new techniques, especially military, such as castle-building, and some new institutions, especially feudal and urban. The eventual outcome of this process of immigration and intrusion suggests that the incomers had sufficient advantages, in techniques, organization, or simply numbers, to establish themselves in the new environments in the face of opposition from those already in possession, but that they did not have the ability, or perhaps did not desire, to take over the whole of the territories into

[65] *Monasticon* 4, pp. 64–5.

[66] *The Dublin Guild Merchant Roll, c.1190–1265*, ed. Philomena Connolly and Geoffrey Martin (Dublin, 1992).

[67] *Red Book of Ormond*, ed. Newport B. White (Irish Manuscripts Commission; Dublin, 1932), p. 34.

which they moved. The result in Wales and Ireland was a division of the country into more heavily Anglicized and less heavily Anglicized zones. Because Wales and Ireland remained partly conquered lands, with settler and native societies living alongside each other, often in conflict, they were more militarized than the kingdom of England. Town walls were more common, castles had a more active military role, feudal knight service did not slide so quickly into being a simply financial arrangement. The native societies of Wales, Scotland, and Ireland were able to adopt some features of the incomers' society, such as castle-building and perhaps new structures of lordship, but only in the case of Scotland do we find a wholesale adoption of the new features, and an encouragement of immigration, under the firm control of the native dynasty. The result there was a powerful and enduring state, ruled by the ancestral dynasty, but one that was culturally Anglicized, especially in its lowland bases.

## English Attitudes

There is unambiguous evidence from our period that the educated classes of England already regarded the peoples of the other parts of the British Isles with a condescending or hostile eye. They expressed the opinion that, not only were these northern and western parts poorer and less developed than England or France, but that the inhabitants lacked both the cultural amenities and the moral standards of civilized peoples—in short, they were 'barbarians'.

They noticed first the preponderance of pastoral farming and the relative absence of urban and commercial life. In Ireland and Wales 'the fields are mainly used for pasture' and the Irish 'despise agriculture' and live 'a pastoral life'.[68] William of Malmesbury contrasted the half-starved rural Irish with 'the English and French, who have a more civilized style of life and inhabit trading towns'.[69] This lack of economic development was attributable not to a lack of natural resources but to the sloth and ignorance of the inhabitants. According to the author of the *Deeds of king Stephen* (*Gesta Stephani*), who was perhaps Robert, bishop of Bath (1136–66), Scotland was potentially a rich land, full of fertile woodland and flocks of animals and possessing good harbours and rich islands. The problem was the inhabitants: they were 'barbaric', 'filthy', and exceptionally brutal in war.[70] The chronicler William of Newburgh wrote that the soil of Ireland would be fertile if properly cultivated, 'but it has a population that is uncivilized and barbarous, almost entirely ignorant of law and discipline and lazy in agriculture'.[71]

[68] Gerald, *Top.* 3. 10 (p. 151); Gerald, *Descr.* 1. 17 (p. 201).
[69] W. Malm., *GR* 5. 409 (2, p. 485); OMT edn., p. 738.  [70] *Gesta Stephani* 26 (p. 54).
[71] W. Newb. 2. 26 (1, pp. 165–6).

The negative characterization of the 'barbarians' of Wales, Scotland, and Ireland that was developed by English and Anglo-Norman clerical writers, perhaps most notably by Gerald of Wales, who wrote four works on Welsh and Irish history, ethnography, and natural history in the years 1186–94, stressed the political decentralization, not to say chaos, of their societies, the brutality of their methods of waging war, and the improper forms of marriage and family life prevalent among them.

Sometimes an indictment of the Welsh, Scots, or Irish as barbarians was combined with censure of their specific failings as Christians. In this way divergences from ecclesiastical norms could be marshalled as part of an overall concept of ethnic inferiority. The English monk Turgot, writing his eulogy of queen Margaret of Scotland (d. 1093), herself of English descent, relates how she found among the Scots 'many things contrary to the rule of right faith and the holy custom of the universal church'. In particular, mass was often celebrated 'by some barbarous rite'. All these abuses were the targets of Margaret's reforming and Anglicizing zeal.[72] The same note is taken up, in a much more strident and violent vein, in the papal bull *Laudabiliter* of 1155–6, in which Hadrian IV (the only Englishman ever to be pope) authorized the king of England to invade Ireland 'in order to expand the boundaries of the Church, to declare the truth of the Christian faith to uninstructed and primitive peoples and to uproot the weeds of vice from the field of the Lord'.[73] It has been convincingly suggested that *Laudabiliter* was issued in response to representations from the church of Canterbury, worried about the recent completion of the new Irish ecclesiastical hierarchy at the Synod of Kells in 1152, which, according to one contemporary, had been 'accomplished against the custom of the ancients and the honour of the church of Canterbury'.[74] The papal rhetoric was presumably a simple recycling of the message of the Canterbury envoys. Ecclesiastical deviance could become a pretext for attempted conquest, as is brought home by the use Gerald of Wales later made of *Laudabiliter* to justify Henry II's exercise of domination in Ireland after 1171.

Amidst this glut of complacent disapproval, the exception that proves the rule is the attitude of the English to the Scots royal dynasty, which was given full marks for distancing itself from its barbarous past and enforcing new and more civilized norms. David I in particular was seen as the standard bearer of new ways. According to William of Malmesbury David was 'more courtly' than his predecessors and, 'had, from boyhood, been polished by contact and fellowship with our people, so that he had rubbed off all the

[72] Turgot, *V. Margaret*, pp. 243–5.    [73] Gerald, *Exp.* 2. 5 (p. 144).
[74] R. Torigni, p. 166; see Marie-Thérèse Flanagan, *Irish Society, Anglo-Norman Settlers, Angevin Kingship: Interactions in Ireland in the Late Twelfth Century* (Oxford, 1989), pp. 38–55.

rust of Scottish barbarism', while William of Newburgh called him 'a non-barbarous king of a barbarous people'.[75] Addressing a personified Scotland, Ailred of Rievaulx records his delight that David I had 'reformed your barbarous ways by means of the Christian religion'.[76] Starting with the marriage of Alexander I to Sibyl, illegitimate daughter of Henry I, in 1107, every king of Scots until the extinction of the native dynasty (with the obvious exception of the unmarried Malcolm IV) took his wife or wives from the French or Anglo-Norman aristocracy and by the early thirteenth century this 'Anglicization' or 'Gallicization' of the dynasty had gone so far that one English chronicler expressed the opinion that 'the more recent kings of Scots declare themselves rather French, as by descent, so also in manners, language and costume, and, now that the Scots have been pressed down into utter servitude, they admit only Frenchmen into their household and service'.[77] The Scottish kings could enter the civilized world only by stopping being Scots.

Gervase of Tilbury, who served both Henry II and his son Henry 'the Young King' before embarking upon a career in the service of continental potentates, supplies a good example of how an articulate yet uninformed Angevin courtier saw the British Isles beyond England. His remarks on Ireland and Scotland are as follows:

Ireland was inhabited continuously by the Scottic people until the time of the illustrious king Henry [II] . . . who, once the foul Irish race had been expelled, was the first to divide the country up among the English to be held as knights' fees, though not without the shedding of much blood of English and Britons. As a result, that land, that from ancient times had sustained itself from the milk of animals, neglected the Lenten fast, consumed raw meat, given itself up to foulness and despised religion, now sees a new religious fervour flourish among its inhabitants . . .

Likewise Scotland was once inhabited by the Scots, men of a foul way of life, but now that they have been expelled and knights have been summoned there and enfeoffed, the land has a succession of holy kings or kings doing holy work down to our own time.[78]

The melange of ideas and images here—the crude pastoral life, the slackness in the religious life, the 'foulness' of the original Scottic inhabitants, contrasted with the piety, feudalism, and holy kings of the new dispensation—gives us in concentrated essence the myth of how the English brought civilization to the lesser breeds of the surrounding lands. It is no surprise that

---

[75] W. Malm., *GR* 5. 400 (2, pp. 476–7); OMT edn., p. 726. W. Newb. 1. 23 (1, p. 72).
[76] Ailred of Rievaulx, *Eulogium Davidis* 9, in *Pinkerton's Lives of the Scottish Saints*, rev. W. M. Metcalfe (2 vols.; Paisley, 1889), vol. 2, p. 279.
[77] Barnwell Chron., p. 206.     [78] Gerv. Tilb. 2. 10 (pp. 916–17).

'The Beginnings of English Imperialism' have been seen not in the sixteenth century, but in the twelfth.[79]

## 2. ENGLAND AND THE WIDER WORLD

England's immediate ties and closest political connections were with northern France and with the other parts of the British Isles, but contacts with a wider world were also varied and important: trade, pilgrimage, diplomacy, dynastic marriage, crusade, and warfare all brought the English and their Anglo-French rulers into touch with the whole of Latin Christendom and beyond. The structure of the Church provided a trellis on which the exchange of personnel, ideas, and culture flourished. The first two post-Conquest archbishops of Canterbury were both Italians. It may even be true that England was more closely enmeshed with the European and Mediterranean world in this period than it had been at any time since the days of the Roman Empire.

### Scandinavia and Germany

The period saw a shift in England from a northern to a southern orientation. The Scandinavian world had been of central importance for later Anglo-Saxon England. As a consequence of the Viking attacks of the ninth, tenth, and eleventh centuries, the settlement of Danes and Norwegians throughout the eastern and northern parts of the country and finally the incorporation of the kingdom into Canute's North Sea empire, the ties binding England and Scandinavia were multiple and strong. The units of land assessment, the terms of local organization, and the patterns of personal names in the Danelaw, that part of England ceded to the Vikings under king Alfred, bore a recognizably Scandinavian imprint. The conquest of the country by Canute in 1016 meant that subsequent Danish and Norwegian kings could raise a claim to the English throne, as happened in 1066, when Harald Hardrada invaded, and 1086, when Canute IV of Denmark planned to do so before he was murdered.

One consequence of the new bond with France that followed from the Norman Conquest was a decline of the traditional importance of Scandinavia in English affairs. Traders continued to cross the North Sea, of course, but the dense intertwining of English and Scandinavian politics that had characterized the last centuries of the Anglo-Saxon kingdom ceased. The kings of England were now more concerned with the affairs of the Vexin and the Loire

[79] John Gillingham, 'The Beginnings of English Imperialism', *Jnl Historical Sociology*, 5 (1992), pp. 392–409.

valley than with the question of who ruled in Roskilde. The occasional Scandinavian king might still seek pickings in England, but the scale of such incidents only underlines their insignificance. In the early 1150s, for instance, during the troubles of Stephen's reign, Eystein II of Norway seized the chance to sail across the North Sea and ravage the English coastal regions. Landing on the island of Farne, where some Durham monks lived as hermits, the Norwegian soldiers roasted the monks' sheep for dinner and took their house-timbers to repair the ships.[80] This opportunistic piracy obviously bears no comparison with the empire-building of the previous century.

The diminishing centrality of Scandinavia was emphasized by the increasing importance of commercial ties between eastern England and the nearer parts of continental Europe. As the growth of the Flemish cloth industry created a market there for English wool, a deep interdependence arose that had political as well as economic ramifications. Disruption of Anglo-Flemish trade was one of the weapons with which English kings could threaten the counts of Flanders as they sought to draw them into their orbit and away from the Capetians. The Rhineland was also an important area for both English traders and English kings. German merchants came to take the place of the Scandinavians who had traded in London. Ties with Cologne were especially close. Henry II granted the citizens of Cologne permission to sell their wine in London and to have their own guildhall there. This was located on the present site of Cannon Street Station and close to the site where the Hanseatic merchants had their premises, the 'Steelyard', in the later Middle Ages. Richard and John confirmed and extended their father's protection of the men of Cologne.[81] The interest of the Angevin kings in Germany was intensified by their dynastic involvement with one of its most important princely houses, the Welfs.

## The Welf Alliance

The marriage of Henry II's daughter, Matilda, with Henry the Lion, duke of Saxony and Bavaria, in 1168 initiated an association between the Angevin and Welf dynasties that was to be of great political significance, culminating in the alliance between king John and Otto IV, the son of Henry the Lion, that was brought crashing down by the Capetians in 1214.[82] The Welfs were the greatest family in Germany after the Hohenstaufen emperors themselves.

---

[80] Reg., *Libellus* 29 (pp. 65–6); Snorre Sturlason, *Heimskringla*, ed. and tr. E. Monsen and A. H. Smith (Cambridge, 1932), pp. 678–9.

[81] *Hansisches Urkundenbuch* 1, ed. K. Höhlbaum (Halle, 1876), nos. 13–14, 25, 40, 84, pp. 8, 16, 22–3, 37; Mary Lobel (ed.), *The City of London* (British Atlas of Historic Towns 3; 1989), pp. 76, 94, and maps; M. Weinbaum, 'Stalhof und Deutsche Gildhalle zu London', *Hansische Geschichtsblätter*, 33 (1928), pp. 45–65.

[82] Jens Ahlers, *Die Welfen und die englischen Könige 1165–1235* (Hildesheim, 1987).

Frederick Barbarossa, the Holy Roman Emperor, had bought the support, or at least the acquiescence, of Henry the Lion only by giving him a free hand in his huge domains. Eventually, however, a crisis arose. Indeed one reason that ties were so close between Welfs and Angevins is that Henry the Lion spent much time at the Angevin court during periods of exile from Germany.

After a quarrel with Barbarossa, duke Henry was deprived of his fiefs in 1180 and sent into exile the following year. The length of this exile was to be at least three years and, even then, his return would require the emperor's approval. Henry II lobbied energetically on his son-in-law's behalf, obtaining several concessions regarding the conditions of his exile, and took him in when he left Germany: 'as the time came near when the duke had to leave his land and kindred, he and his wife, with his sons and daughters, and with the counts and barons and great men of his land, left their land and kindred and came to Normandy, to Henry, king of England, the duchess' father, who received them joyfully'.[83] Soon afterwards, the great men of Saxony returned, loaded with gifts from the king of England, while Henry the Lion set out on pilgrimage to Compostella, leaving his wife, who was pregnant, with her father in Normandy. The following Christmas, 1182, duke Henry and his family were at Henry II's festive court at Caen.

It seems that the Welfs spent the whole of 1183 in the Angevin lands in France. In 1184 the duchess of Saxony, again pregnant, accompanied her father, the king, to England, where she gave birth to a son in Winchester. Curiously, therefore, Henry the Lion's son, William, ancestor of the later dukes of Brunswick and of the Hanoverian kings of England, was born in the old Anglo-Saxon capital. Duke Henry soon crossed the Channel to join his wife and new child, and the whole family were again assembled at king Henry's Christmas court at Windsor in 1184. Immediately after that came the news that Henry II's attempts to secure the return of his son-in-law to Germany had been successful. An embassy sent to the pope had persuaded him to intervene with Frederick Barbarossa and allow duke Henry's exile to end. The Welf duke does not appear to have hurried his return, however, for there is mention of him hunting with the king at his palace of Clarendon in February or March 1185 and he did not cross to the continent until the very end of April and did not return to Germany until October.

The return of Henry the Lion to Germany in 1185 did not mark the end of intimate relations between the Angevins and Welfs, for he left two of his children, William 'of Winchester' and Matilda, in the care of their grandparents, while his older children, Henry and Otto, were again in England in 1188. The following year duke Henry himself was once more seeking refuge with Henry II, for before Frederick Barbarossa departed on crusade, the duke had

    [83] *Gesta Hen. II* 1, p. 288; R. Howd. 2, p. 269.

promised the emperor that he would leave Germany for three years. Henry the Lion was in the Angevin domains, perhaps even with the king, when Henry II died on 6 July at Chinon. He then went to England with the new king, his brother-in-law, Richard I, before again crossing the Channel, in ships provided by the king, in order, despite his promise, to return to Germany to re-establish his power.

Henry the Lion's sons Otto and William remained in England and Richard I proved as reliable a supporter of his Welf nephews as his father had been of their father. Apart from paying the costs of their household, he attempted to make permanent provision for them, especially for his favourite, Otto. In 1190 Richard endowed Otto with the *comitatus* (either 'county' or 'earldom') of York, although he found so much local opposition that he eventually gave him Poitou in exchange.[84] In 1195, the year that Henry the Lion died, the king negotiated an agreement with another leonine ruler, William the Lion, king of Scots. William had no son at that time. Otto was to be William's heir, marry his daughter and be endowed with a huge appanage comprising southern Scotland and northern England, although here again the king's plans were nullified by the hostility of the native aristocracy.[85] Eventually the English king was able to help secure his nephew a title grander than earl of York or king of Scots, for his support was essential in procuring Otto's election as 'king of the Romans' (the title borne by the Holy Roman Emperor before his imperial coronation).

From 1198, when Otto IV was elected king of the Romans, to 1214, the date of the battle of Bouvines, the political history of western Europe was dominated by the confrontation between the Angevin–Welf alliance and its opponents, the Capetian kings of France and the Hohenstaufen dynasty of Germany. The Hohenstaufen, the family to which Frederick Barbarossa had belonged, put up a rival king of the Romans in 1198, in the person of Frederick's son, Philip of Swabia, and a civil war followed in Germany that was to last for twenty years. Just as the Angevin kings supported their nephew Otto, so Philip Augustus of France backed his opponent, Philip of Swabia. The struggle between Angevin and Capetian thus intertwined with that between Welf and Hohenstaufen. When John made peace with Philip Augustus in the Treaty of Le Goulet of 1200, he had to promise to give no further help to Otto. When war between the two kings broke out again in 1202, John and Otto made a formal alliance. Over the following years Otto received financial support from the English king and, in return, made concrete proposals for an invasion of France from Germany. In 1207 Otto visited England and was received in great state.

The campaigns of 1214, in which John, Otto, and their allies launched a

---

[84] R. Howd. 3, p. 86.    [85] Ibid., pp. 298–9, 308.

concerted attack against the French king, were the most substantial result of the Angevin–Welf alliance. John led an army to Poitou, where he had considerable success, even being able to re-enter Angers, the ancient capital of his dynasty. Meanwhile a coalition of forces threatened France from the north. These included Otto, the count of Flanders, and the count of Boulogne, backed by English troops under the command of John's illegitimate half-brother, William Longsword, earl of Salisbury. The confrontation between these allies and Philip Augustus at Bouvines in Flanders on 27 July 1214 turned out to be a battle of long-term significance. Philip's victory was complete. The counts of Flanders and Boulogne were captured and sent off to imprisonment in Péronne and in the Louvre. The earl of Salisbury, after being clubbed on the head by the bishop of Beauvais, was also taken prisoner. Otto IV fled from Bouvines and into obscurity. The family ties between Angevin and Welf and the silver that Richard and John had poured unceasingly into the hands of the princes of the Low Countries and the Rhineland had not been able to prevent Philip Augustus establishing the Capetian monarchy as the chief power in north-west Europe.

## The Mediterranean World

Writing, cities, Latin culture, and Christianity had come to north-western Europe from the Mediterranean and, even after a thousand years, the people of the Atlantic and North Sea world remembered their paternity. The geography of the Bible was Levantine, the language of religion and learning was Italic, the imagery of empire Roman. The contemporary Mediterranean had some of this magic still. The wealth of the Mediterranean realms was legendary. Gerald of Wales, discussing the income of the various monarchs, estimated the current regular income of the kings of England at 12,000 marks, that of the German emperor at 300,000 marks. 'This is little or nothing', he comments, 'in comparison with the income and treasure of the Greek emperors, or even the Sicilian king, before the destruction of that empire and that kingdom by the Latins. For one city in Sicily, Palermo, provides a larger regular annual income to the king of Sicily than the whole of England now provides for the king of England.'[86] As this comment shows, there could be a provincial impressionableness in the remarks northerners made about the south.

    The Mediterranean was not, however, simply a dream landscape. Real contact between England and the region intensified throughout the period discussed here. One impetus was the rise of the papacy to a position of juridical supremacy within the western Church. Rome had always been

[86] Gerald, *Prin.* 3. 30 (pp. 316–17).

recognized as a repository of saints and a goal of pilgrimage—'the city that displays in their thousands the martyrs' trophies in imperial purple'[87]—but now it was also the supreme tribunal for a litigious society. At the same time, the boom in Italian commerce, with the opening up of the Mediterranean to western shipping, integrated western Europe and the shores of that sea more tightly than before. In the very same period, perhaps not coincidentally, the crusading movement brought thousands of men, and some women, from north-western Europe to the Levant.

The Mediterranean world thus became more familiar to the English and the English were increasingly present in the Mediterranean. Diplomatic, political, and commercial ties multiplied. London merchants settled in Genoa.[88] Henry II married a daughter to a king of Castile and was called in to act as arbitrator in a dispute between Castile and Navarre. Ties with the Norman kingdom of Sicily were especially close.[89] Contemporaries were aware of the similarities in the origins of the regimes of the two conquest states: a battle-speech addressed to 'the noble lords of England of Norman birth' before the battle of the Standard in 1138 declares that 'fierce England fell captive to you, rich Apulia flourished again in your possession'.[90] Contact between the Anglo-Normans of the north and the Normans of the south was frequent. Anselm spent some of his exile in southern Italy and clerks and scholars, like Adelard of Bath, Robert of Cricklade, and John of Salisbury, journeyed there. Some English clerics obtained high ecclesiastical office in the kingdom of Sicily; the Englishman Richard Palmer was bishop of Syracuse and then archbishop of Messina (1183–95). Others serving in the royal administration included Robert of Selby, chancellor to king Roger of Sicily, and Thomas Brown, who went out to Sicily, obtained high office under the Norman kings, and then returned to England to put his skills to work in Henry II's Exchequer. The bonds between the two realms were symbolized and strengthened by the marriage of Joanna, daughter of Henry II, with William II of Sicily in 1177.

## England and Byzantium

When educated or well-informed Englishmen of the twelfth century cast their mind's eye over the known world, they saw hovering at its edge the empire of Byzantium, ancient, wealthy, and exotic. Its capital, Constantinople, was by far the largest city in Europe and every English account of it

---

[87] Osbert, *Letters*, no. 21, p. 91.

[88] R. L. Reynolds, 'Some English Settlers in Genoa in the Late Twelfth Century', *Economic History Review*, 4 (1932–4), pp. 317–23.

[89] Evelyn Jamison, 'The Sicilian Norman Kingdom in the Mind of Anglo-Norman Contemporaries', *Proceedings of the British Academy*, 24 (1938), pp. 237–85.

[90] H. Hunt. 10. 8 (p. 714) (RS edn., p. 262).

exudes awe at its size and wealth. 'The city is surrounded by vast walls,' wrote William of Malmesbury, 'but is still crowded because of the influx of numberless people . . . the sea girds the city around and supplies it with commodities from all the world.'[91] One English chronicler expressed the opinion that the population of Constantinople was greater than that of the whole area between York and the Thames.[92]

It was not only for its physical resources that the city was renowned. Its precious store of relics was the wonder and envy of westerners:

There is in that city the cross of the Lord brought from Jerusalem by Helena; it is the resting place of the apostles Andrew, James, the brother of the Lord, and Matthias, the prophets Elijah, Samuel, Daniel and many others, Luke the evangelist, innumerable martyrs, the confessors John Chrysostom, Basil, Gregory of Nazianzus and Spyridion, the virgins Agatha and Lucy and all the saints whose bodies the emperors have been able to bring there from every part of the world.[93]

One of the earliest records in our period of an Englishman in Constantinople is of the monk Joseph, in the city in the early 1090s on the return journey from Jerusalem, trying to buy relics of St Andrew from the imperial chapel and finding useful intermediaries and interpreters among the resident English in the emperor's service.[94]

There were channels of communication across the 1,500 miles between England and Constantinople. English chroniclers were reasonably well informed about affairs within the Byzantine empire. William of Malmesbury lists the emperors from Constantine to his own day, while historians of the later twelfth century have full accounts of the dramatic reign and gory end of Andronicus I (1183–5).[95] Also, despite the distances involved and the linguistic problems, there were diplomatic exchanges between the Norman and Angevin kings and the emperors of Byzantium. At some point between 1100 and 1116 Alexius I Comnenus sent an embassy to Henry I, bearing letters and gifts. This was headed by an Englishman, Wulfric of Lincoln, who supposedly enjoyed great familiarity with the emperor. Perhaps he was one of the Anglo-Saxon refugees who had gone east in the wake of the Norman Conquest. Apart from the letters, about which we sadly have no information, Wulfric brought the special treasure of Constantinople, relics, including an arm of John Chrysostom that he deposited in the monastery of Abingdon.[96] It is clear that Alexius also transmitted pieces of the True Cross to the

[91] W. Malm., *GR* 4. 355 (2, p. 411); OMT edn., p. 624.      [92] R. Coggesh., p. 150.

[93] W. Malm., *GR* 4. 356 (2, p. 413); OMT edn., pp. 626–8.

[94] Charles Homer Haskins, 'A Canterbury Monk at Constantinople', *EHR* 25 (1910), pp. 293–4.

[95] W. Malm., *GR* 4. 356 (2, pp. 412–13); OMT edn., p. 626; *Gesta Hen. II* 1, pp. 251–61; R. Howd. 2, pp. 201–8; Map 2. 18 (pp. 174–8).

[96] *Abingdon Chron.* 2, pp. 46–7, 157.

English royal court, on this or other occasions, for Henry's foundation of Reading later possessed some of Christ's foreskin or umbilical cord (the monks were unsure which) 'with a cross of the wood of the Lord in a cloth that the emperor of Constantinople sent to Henry the first, king of the English', while Holy Trinity, Aldgate, founded by Henry's queen, Matilda, had a piece given to it by its foundress, obtained from her husband, the king, who had received it in turn from Alexius.[97]

Contact seems to have been particularly close in the reigns of Manuel Comnenus (1143–80) and Henry II (1154–89), who were connected by family ties, their wives, Maria of Antioch and Eleanor of Aquitaine, being first cousins.[98] Manuel sent a long letter to Henry describing the battle of Myriocephalon in 1176, an encounter usually classed as a major Byzantine defeat, but depicted by Manuel as a stand-off, and the emperor notes his pleasure in having 'certain magnates of your highness with us' on that occasion, also referring to Henry as 'our dear friend . . . bound to our imperial highness by the close consanguinity of our children'.[99] Manuel had a reputation for favouring westerners and being interested in the west, and it appears that he dispatched envoys specifically to ask Henry to furnish him with details about 'the site and nature of the island of Britain and its more notable features'.[100] It is not known whether one of the envoys was that 'Robert, envoy of the emperor of Constantinople' who was provided with rich clothes at king Henry's expense in 1179.[101] It should be noted that, as in the case of Wulfric of Lincoln, the envoy sent by the Byzantine emperor has a western name, and is presumably an Anglo-Norman who had spent time in the east.

These diplomatic exchanges had a friendly enough tone—Henry sent Manuel a gift of dogs—but a feeling of estrangement between Latins and Greeks was already ancient by the eleventh century, fuelled by the rival claims of western and eastern emperors to be true heirs of Rome and the divergence between the two churches. Gerald of Wales wrote that since the revival of the western empire under Charlemagne 'the Greeks resent the Latins and regard them as hateful, so much that they had withdrawn themselves from subjection and obedience to the Roman church, until in our own day they were partly brought back to subjection by the Latins occupying their city and empire'.[102] The crusading movement that began in 1095, although originally seen as a cooperative venture between the feudal princes of the west and the Byzantine empire, in reality poisoned relations further, through mutual suspicion and misunderstanding. It is not surprising that the Greeks

[97] BL MS Egerton 3031, fo. 6ᵛ; *Aldgate Cart.*, p. 230.
[98] A. A. Vasiliev, 'Manuel Comnenus and Henry Plantagenet', *Byzantische Zeitschrift*, 29 (1929–30), pp. 233–44.
[99] *Gesta Hen. II* 1, pp. 128–30; R. Howd. 2, pp. 102–4.      [100] Gerald, *Descr.* 1. 8 (p. 181).
[101] PR 25 HII, p. 125.      [102] Gerald, *Prin.* 1. 17 (p. 75).

were wary of the arrival in their capital of Norman troops from southern
Italy, when those same men had recently conquered Byzantine territory on
both sides of the Adriatic.

English writers of the later twelfth century shared the contemptuous attitude to the Greeks that had been elaborated by the Normans and other west
Europeans. Greeks were 'effeminate' and it was the utmost shame to be
beaten by them.[103] They were 'soft and woman-like, talkative and tricky, lacking loyalty or strength when faced with the enemy'.[104] The hostility and scorn
that westerners felt for the 'Griffons', as they termed the Greeks, came to a
climax in the Fourth Crusade, when western crusading armies turned on
their former allies, but events in the Third Crusade foreshadowed the crisis.
In 1190 the English crusaders under Richard I clashed with the Greek population of Sicily, the king building a fortification called 'Mategriffun', i.e. 'Kill
Griffon', while in the following spring he conquered Cyprus, placing its
Greek ruler, Isaac Comnenus, in chains of silver and gold, as he had promised
him he would not put him in irons![105] The loot from Cyprus was spectacular:
'golden cups, vessels and bowls, silver jars, huge cauldrons and urns, golden
saddles, bridles and spurs, precious stones with special powers . . . garments
of scarlet, silk cloth of wonderful patterns and great value'.[106] The imperial
standard of Isaac Comnenus, fashioned of cloth of gold, was sent as a trophy
and thank-offering to the abbey of Bury St Edmunds.[107] The sack of Constantinople in 1204 was to send a wave of such booty washing across western
Europe. Although there were few English participants on the Fourth Crusade, English churches were happy to benefit from the supernatural bounty
newly released into circulation. One of the most famous relics of the later
Middle Ages, the Holy Rood of Bromholm, was brought to Norfolk by an
English priest who had walked off with it from the imperial chapel in 1205.[108]

## England and the Crusades

The period covered by this book coincides with the first great age of the crusading movement, which was launched by pope Urban II at the Council of
Clermont in 1095. In the following year several huge expeditions made their
way from western Europe eastwards towards the Muslim world. All of these
suffered badly, some encountered disaster, but in the summer of 1099 a de-
pleted body of knights, footsoldiers, and followers stormed Jerusalem in a
bloody assault that returned it to Christian rule for the first time since the seventh century. Shortly afterwards it became the capital of a new Catholic

---

[103] R. Devizes, p. 20.        [104] Map 2. 18 (p. 174).
[105] *Itin. reg. Ric.* 2. 12, 20, 40 (pp. 154–5, 168, 203); Ambroise, *L'Estoire de la guerre sainte*, lines 937–40,
2034–55, ed. Gaston Paris (Paris, 1897), cols. 26, 55; *Gesta Ric. I* 2, pp. 138, 167; R. Howd. 3, pp. 67, 111.
[106] *Itin. reg. Ric.* 2. 41 (pp. 203–4).
[107] *Gesta Ric. I* 2, p. 164; R. Howd. 3, p. 108.        [108] R. Coggesh., pp. 201–3.

kingdom, while other crusading states—Tripoli, Antioch, Edessa—came to cover the entire Levantine coast and extend inland even beyond the Euphrates.

There is evidence for the participation in the First Crusade both of English crusaders, in the sense of men and women of Anglo-Saxon descent, and, more plentifully, of Norman crusaders who had acquired lands and connections in England. English sailors, perhaps in the service of the Byzantine emperor, seized the important Syrian port of Latakia (Laodicea) in the winter of 1097–8. The wife of Baldwin of Boulogne, one of the leaders of the crusade, who died at Marasch in Cilicia in October 1097, was described by the chronicler Albert of Aachen as 'Baldwin's most noble wife, whom he had brought from the kingdom of England'; he gives her name as Godwera.[109] William the Conqueror's eldest son, Robert, duke of Normandy, was one of the most important of the crusading commanders and he was accompanied by several members of great Anglo-Norman families. English involvement continued in the subsequent crusading expedition of 1102, when Edgar Atheling, the last male representative of the house of Wessex, went out to Palestine.

The English contribution to the earlier crusades was slight but specialized. Both in the First Crusade and in the Second Crusade of 1147, English shipping transported crusaders and initiated attacks on Muslim coastal areas. The capture of Lisbon by a fleet of English, Norman, and other western sailors was indeed the chief military success of the expedition of 1147. Contingents from London, East Anglia, Kent, Hastings, Southampton, and Bristol are mentioned among the 164 vessels that assembled at Dartmouth in the spring of that year. They sailed to Portugal, made an agreement with king Affonso about the attack on Lisbon, and initiated a four-month siege of the city that culminated in its capitulation on 22 October. The first bishop of the revived see of Lisbon was an Englishman, Gilbert of Hastings. In 1151 he visited his home country, urging his compatriots to join in the conquest of the Iberian peninsula from the Muslims.[110]

## English Kings and the Crusade
One of the striking features about the leadership of the First Crusade was the absence of kings. It was an expedition headed by the great dukes and counts, not by royal monarchs. The Second Crusade was quite different, in that the kings of both France and Germany led armies to the east. In neither case, however, did a king of England participate. This was not necessarily due to lack of interest. King Stephen, whose father had been one of the leaders of the First

---

[109] Albert of Aachen, *Historia Hierosolymitana* 3. 27, *Recueil des historiens des croisades, Historiens occidentaux* (5 vols.; Paris, 1844–95), vol. 4, p. 358; for discussion of her identity, William of Tyre, *A History of Deeds Done beyond the Sea*, tr. E. A. Babcock and A. C. Krey (2 vols.; New York, 1943), vol. 1, p. 178 n. 20.

[110] *De exp. Lyxb.*, *passim*; J. Hexham, p. 324.

Crusade, gave what support he could to the crusading enterprise, even though
he was clearly unable to leave his kingdom in the middle of civil war. His wife,
Matilda, who also had family ties to crusader Jerusalem, being the niece of its
first two rulers, Godfrey de Bouillon and king Baldwin I, was a major patroness of the crusading orders. The links of kinship between the kings of
England and the ruling dynasty of Jerusalem were not weakened when the
Angevins came to the throne. Henry II's grandfather, Fulk V, had relinquished the county of Anjou to his son in order to take up the offer of the
heiress and the throne of Jerusalem. His sons by this second wife and his
grandson ruled there until 1185. For most of the reign of Henry II, the ruler of
the kingdom of Jerusalem was thus either an uncle or a cousin (see Figure 2).

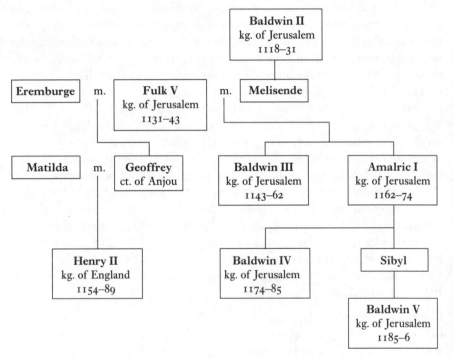

FIGURE 2. *The Angevin kings and the kings of Jerusalem*

This connection was not forgotten, especially during the succession crisis
of the 1180s, when the throne of Jerusalem was occupied by the leper king,
Baldwin IV, followed by the child king, Baldwin V, before the male line died
out completely. In 1184–5 Heraclius, patriarch of Jerusalem, led an embassy
'to the Christian princes in Europe' to seek for help. He came to Henry II
bearing a letter from Pope Lucius III, in which Lucius urged the king to

'follow in the footsteps of your predecessors'. The Canterbury chronicler, Gervase of Canterbury, wrote, implausibly but significantly, that in 1185 the men of the kingdom of Jerusalem had made 'a certain youth, a relative of the king of the English, king of Jerusalem, to win the goodwill of the king of the English'.[111] It is also revealing that Baldwin IV specified in his will that, should his young heir die, an electoral college of the Pope, the Emperor, and the kings of France and England should decide on the claims of his two sisters.[112] These four rulers were the leaders of western Christendom, as viewed from its furthest eastern outpost, and Henry II's place among them was unquestioned. Contemporaries presumed that, as one of the chief men of the West, he had a special duty to the Holy Land. Henry repeatedly promised that he would take the cross, but not until 1189, the last year of his life, did he do so, although he did provide financial support for the Holy Land. In the event, while Henry II, Richard (in 1188), and John (in 1215) all took the cross, Richard was the only English king in this period actually to go on crusade.

## The Military Orders

Among the most remarkable institutions to emerge from the crusading movement were the military orders, bodies of men committed both to the discipline, poverty, and celibacy of the monk and to the active violence of the knight. The earliest were the Templars, founded in the kingdom of Jerusalem in 1120 under the leadership of a knight from Champagne, Hugh de Payns, who envisaged a group of Christian knights dedicated to the protection of pilgrims to Jerusalem. Very soon the Order began to receive donations and support from the aristocrats and chief ecclesiastics of Europe. St Bernard himself wrote in praise of this 'New Knighthood'. In 1128 Hugh de Payns came to England, with the approval of Henry I, to raise revenue and recruits. 'He was received by all good men and everyone gave him treasure,' records the *Anglo-Saxon Chronicle*, 'and he bade the people go out to Jerusalem and so more folk went, either with him or after him, than ever had gone since the first expedition in pope Urban's day.'[113]

The enthusiastic response to the Templar call resulted in their endowment with estates throughout England. Royal patronage was important. The earliest dated grant of land in England to the Templars is the charter issued by Stephen's wife, queen Matilda, in 1137, whereby she endowed them with the manor and church of Cressing in Essex. This was the first of several donations made by Matilda from her inherited estate, the great honor of Boulogne. Essex, where the counts of Boulogne held large amounts of land, became one of the counties with the thickest scattering of Templar

[111] W. Newb. 3. 12 (1, p. 246); *Gesta Hen. II* 1, p. 333; Gerv. Cant., p. 325.
[112] *Chronique d'Ernoul et de Bernard le Trésorier* 10, ed. L. de Mas Lastrie (Paris, 1871), pp. 116–17.
[113] *ASC*, p. 259.

properties. Cowley, the only Oxfordshire manor of the counts of Boulogne at the time of the Domesday survey, was also given by queen Matilda to the Templars and became the site of a Templar house (preceptory).[114] Stephen backed his wife's patronage with confirmations and grants of special exemptions, while his barons and courtiers followed suit. The change of dynasty in 1154 made no difference to the pattern of royal support. In a charter probably dating to the first year of his reign, Henry II confirmed all the grants made to the Templars and extended to them judicial and fiscal privileges.[115] From the second year of his reign (1155–6), the Templars were granted a mark (13s. 4d.) per annum from each county in England. As this would not bring in much more than £20 a year, it was not a significant source of revenue, but it did serve as a permanent reminder, in every part of England, of the king's approval of the Order.

Royal donations were not the only ones. Landholders of every rank were willing to support the new knighthood. Great magnates, like the earls of Chester and Warwick, royal officials, like William of Hastings, Henry II's domestic steward, and lesser proprietors, like Geoffrey of Burnham (in Haxey, Lincs.), who gave a meadow 66 feet wide by the river Trent, all contributed to the growth of the Templars' estate.[116] By 1185, when they drew up a survey of their property, they had manors or revenues in thirty-two of England's thirty-nine counties, the only barren areas for them being the shires of the extreme north and north-west, plus (perhaps surprisingly) Norfolk. By 1225 there were between thirty and forty Templar houses in England. Some have left their mark in the place names: Temple in Cornwall, Temple Cowley, near Oxford, Temple Ewell, by Dover, and, of course, the Inner Temple, Middle Temple, and Temple Bar in London, marking the site of the Order's English headquarters, where their round church (dedicated by the patriarch of Jerusalem in 1185) can still be seen. Its distinctive shape was a permanent reminder to any passing between the City and Westminster of the Church of the Holy Sepulchre on which it was modelled. The presence of the Templars and the other military orders made it harder to forget Jerusalem.

## The Third Crusade

The crusade that involved England more than any other was the Third Crusade, in which Richard I eventually came to take on the role of leader of the western effort in Palestine. This Crusade was a direct response to the conquest of Jerusalem by the great Muslim leader, Saladin. After destroying the army of the kingdom of Jerusalem at the battle of Hattin in 1187, Saladin had occupied virtually every city and fortress of the kingdom. Only in Tyre was a foothold maintained, where Conrad of Montferrat, one of the

---

[114] *RRAN* 3, nos. 843–5, 850, pp. 310–12, 313.     [115] *Templar Records*, p. 138.
[116] *Templar Records*, pp. 16, 26–7, 31–2, 79, 81, 83, 107–8, 114, 166, 258–9.

contenders for the throne of Jerusalem, continued a stubborn defence. His rival for the kingship, Guy of Lusignan, husband of Sibyl, heiress to the kingdom, did not want to be outdone and had undertaken a spectacular military enterprise, the siege of Acre, the kingdom's most important port, which had been one of Saladin's conquests in 1187. The first task of the crusading armies that set out from western Europe in 1189–90 would be to bring this siege to a successful conclusion.

The siege of Acre, that lasted very nearly two whole years, from August 1189 to July 1191, became the focus of the energy and attention of the whole of Latin Christendom. Contingents came to join Guy's besieging army from Germany and the Low Countries, France, Italy, Hungary, and Denmark. Western chroniclers followed the fortunes of the besiegers, desperately situated as they were between the garrison of Acre and Saladin's surrounding forces. Even before the arrival of king Richard, the English presence was substantial. Ranulf de Glanville, formerly chief justiciar under Henry II, and Baldwin, archbishop of Canterbury, led an advance guard to Acre in 1190; both were to die there. With them was Hubert Walter, bishop of Salisbury, later himself to be archbishop of Canterbury, chief justiciar, and chancellor. Part of his training in administrative skills was the organization of a collection to relieve the poorer English crusaders in the siege.

Richard I had set out, with his lord, fellow crusader, and subsequent deadly enemy, Philip Augustus of France, from the Burgundian abbey of Vézelay on 4 July 1190, but did not expect to reach the Holy Land until after the winter, when shipping in the Mediterranean paused. He spent the intervening months in the kingdom of Sicily, where he embroiled himself in local politics and in disputes with king Philip. Finally setting out for the eastern Mediterranean in the spring of 1191, Richard encountered one more diversion before finally arriving in the Holy Land. As mentioned above, Cyprus had been ruled for some years by a breakaway Byzantine aristocrat, Isaac Comnenus. While the English fleet was en route from Sicily to Palestine, a storm separated the vessels and some were shipwrecked on the Cypriot shore. The local population mistreated the survivors, while Isaac tried to lure ashore Richard's sister, Joanna, and his fiancée, Berengaria, who were in a vessel at Limassol. When Richard himself arrived, his anger at their treatment led him to undertake the conquest of the island, that he effected within three weeks. On 12 May Richard I married Berengaria in Limassol.

Finally, on 8 June, Richard and his fleet reached Acre. Philip Augustus had already arrived. Contingents from 'the whole breadth of Christendom' were now assembled for a final attempt to take the city.[117] Night and day the stone-throwing machines of the two kings hurled giant rocks at the walls, one of

[117] *Itin. reg. Ric.*, p. 228.

them killing twelve defenders with a single impact. The besieged responded by setting some of the machines on fire with the inflammable substance called Greek Fire. The crusaders dug tunnels under the walls, in the attempt to undermine them. The Muslims dug counter-tunnels. Repeated assaults were launched on the city, while Saladin hovered in the vicinity with his relieving force. 'What can I say', asked one Christian participant admiringly, 'about that pagan people, that defended the city in such a manner?'[118] Eventually, however, the besieged Muslims decided they would have to surrender. Terms were agreed. In return for the life and liberty of the Muslims of Acre, the Christians were to be paid a huge sum of gold and 2,500 Christian prisoners were to be released. On 12 July, five weeks after Richard's arrival, Acre capitulated to the crusaders. Within three weeks, Philip Augustus was on his way back to France. Within six weeks, after a dispute about the terms of the capitulation, Richard ordered 2,700 of the Muslim prisoners to be executed before the walls of Acre.

Because of his wealth, military talent, and natural imperiousness, Richard now became the de facto commander of the Christian forces in Palestine. He remained in the country for sixteen months, winning a pitched battle at Arsuf in September 1191, and establishing Christian control of the narrow coastal strip that was henceforth to constitute the kingdom of Jerusalem. Twice he approached close to Jerusalem, but Richard was eventually forced to the conclusion that he would not be able to capture the Holy City in a reasonable period of time. On 9 October 1192 the king sailed from Acre on his return voyage.

## Holy War

Crusade was war of a very particular kind. Despite the sordid squabble over plunder with which it ended, the expedition against Lisbon in 1147 was conceived as a holy enterprise. Each ship had a priest; weekly confession and communion were prescribed. During the long months of the siege the Christians' morale was maintained by miraculous cures and apparitions. A speech put into the mouth of 'a certain priest' (perhaps the author of the account of the campaign), on the occasion of the blessing of the English siege-tower, captures the tone of this militant Christianity. Flourishing a piece of the True Cross, he incited his fellow crusaders with a powerful blend of admonition and encouragement:

Behold, brethren, behold the wood of the Lord's cross; kneel and prostrate yourselves on the ground; beat your sinful breasts; stand ready for the Lord's help; for it will come, it will come. You shall see the Lord's help upon you. Adore Christ the Lord, who stretched his hands and feet on the wood of this saving cross, for your salvation and glory. Under this banner— only do not hold back!—you will conquer.

---

[118]  *Itin. reg. Ric.*, p. 228.

The aristocracy was a military caste and always liable to become involved in a life of violence. The Crusade could be presented to them in terms they understood. It was, in the words of a song from the Second Crusade, 'a tournament between heaven and hell'.[119] It offered good violence that could cleanse the taint of the bad violence that was part of their lives. William Peverel of Dover, one of the more vicious of the military commanders in the civil war between Stephen and Matilda, was eventually moved to go off on the Second Crusade, in order to clear the burden on his soul: 'repenting of the evils he had mercilessly inflicted on the people, he sought out the holy place of Jerusalem, to expiate his sins and there, after doing many glorious deeds against the obstinate enemies of the Christian faith, he died a blessed death.'[120] Sin and remission of sin could come from the very same activity, armed violence; the difference was made by the enemy one fought.

Sometimes crusade offered an honourable and spiritually advantageous exit strategy for those defeated or ruined in political struggle. Ivo of Grandmesnil, who incurred the enmity of Henry I early in that king's reign, decided 'that he would never recover the king's friendship that he had lost, so he decided to go on crusade'.[121] Some of those who were dispossessed during the Anarchy of Stephen's reign took the cross.[122] An example is provided by Roger de Mowbray, an important baron who lost lands in both England and Normandy as a consequence of the civil war and who joined Louis VI on the Second Crusade, distinguishing himself in single combat against a Muslim emir. Roger eventually regained most of his lost estates but was again involved in conflict and dispossession after his participation in the great revolt of 1173–4. In the wake of this he seems once again to have sought solace by a prudent absence in the Holy Land. Roger must have felt the lure of the crusade deeply, for he again returned to the Holy Land in 1186, now in his mid-sixties, and was captured at the battle of Hattin in the following year. Ransomed from the Muslims, he died in Palestine in 1188. Three years later, his son and heir, Nigel de Mowbray, was one of the English crusaders who died during the siege of Acre.[123]

No crusade after the First can be called an unqualified military success. For contemporaries, such failures had to be accounted for within the logic of holy war. If true piety led to victory, then the explanation for defeat was obviously sin. The wretched outcome of the Second Crusade was, according to the

---

[119] J. Bedier and P. Aubrey (eds.), *Les Chansons de croisade* (Paris, 1909), p. 10 ('Chevalier, mult estes guariz', lines 49–50).

[120] *Gesta Stephani* 94 (p. 178). [121] Orderic 11. 2 (6, p. 18).

[122] S. Loewenfeld (ed.), *Epistolae pontificum Romanorum ineditae* (Leipzig, 1885), no. 199, p. 104 (JL 8959).

[123] J. Hexham, p. 319; *Mowbray Charters*, pp. xxvi-xxxii; *Gesta Hen. II* 1, p. 359; 2, pp. 22, 149; R. Howd. 2, pp. 316, 325.

chronicler Henry of Huntingdon, a consequence of the crusaders' pride, promiscuity, and plundering. God spurned them and their army dissolved like a spider's web.[124] The even more disastrous debacle of 1187, when the kingdom of Jerusalem was almost entirely lost after Hattin, similarly induced moralistic reflections in thoughtful men: 'no one should doubt that the cause of this wretched and notorious disaster was a more than usual abundance of sin'.[125] Perspectives of this kind explain the recurrent efforts to keep crusading armies pure, with restrictions on gambling, luxury, and the presence of women.

Unease about individual crusading efforts was relatively common. Criticism of the enterprise as a whole was much rarer, although not unknown. Peter of Blois, who wrote a great deal intended to stir up enthusiasm for the Third Crusade, at one point cites the counter-argument a sceptic might make: 'but you say, "whoever kills pagans commits homicide; I do not wish men to incur the crime of homicide, for the Lord abhors a man of blood"'. Peter is not impressed with this line of thought:

My friend, it is a matter of importance how someone kills, for, if he acts in obedience to the law, the law excuses him from the charge of homicide. And can he be excused by any greater law than the general institution of the Church, the command of the highest pontiff, zeal for the Lord and love of Christ? It is meritorious for Christians, fired by zealous love, manfully to attack those who blaspheme Christ, pollute the sanctuary of the Lord and humiliate the glory of our saviour in pride and derision.[126]

In this vigorous defence it is possible also to catch a glimpse of the doubts and reservations about the crusade that the noise of its protagonists often drowned out. The writer who left the fullest and most detailed record of such reservations is Ralph Niger, who was a theologian, a chronicler, and, at the end of his life, a canon of Lincoln cathedral. Writing at exactly the same time as Peter of Blois, Ralph produced a catalogue of arguments for not going on crusade: true piety required a journey to the spiritual Jerusalem, not the earthly one; there were many other appropriate ways to wipe out one's sins; the papal promise of a full remission of sins for crusaders would only be efficacious if they had made restitution for their sins; it was, in any case, wrong to kill Saracens—'for they are human beings, even if infidels'.[127]

The voice of Ralph Niger was an isolated one. The crusades had become rooted in England. English participation was significant, especially from the later twelfth century. English resources were channelled to support the Holy Land, via the endowment of the military orders, by crusade taxation,

---

[124] H. Hunt. 10. 27 (p. 752) (RS edn., pp. 280–1).
[125] W. Newb. 3. 15 (1, p. 250).    [126] P. Blois, *Letters*, no. 232 (cols. 552–3).
[127] Radulfus Niger, *De re militari et triplici via peregrinationis Ierosolimitane* 4. 12, ed. Ludwig Schmugge (Berlin, 1977), p. 205; George Flahiff, '*Deus non vult*: A Critic of the Third Crusade', *Medieval Studies*, 9 (1947), pp. 162–88.

initiated by Henry II, and by the funding of individual crusaders. Richard I supposedly said that he would sell London to finance his crusade, if he could find a buyer, and his outlay on the enterprise in the first year of his reign has been calculated at 70 per cent of his annual revenue.[128] At the other end of the financial scale, there are instances like that of Robert of Leaveland, hereditary keeper of the palace of Westminster and the Fleet prison, who was knighted by king John on New Year's day, 1202, and took the cross on the following day. Arrangements were made for the custody of the palace and the prison in his absence, along with the guardianship of Robert's son and heir. He was permitted by the king to mortgage any of his lands and revenues in England for three years, and a sum equivalent to three years' income from his office were advanced to him. This would total £54 15s. The new royal knight was now ready to join the Fourth Crusade.[129]

The crusades not only introduced English aristocrats and clerics to the Mediterranean world, they also brought them into contact with Christians from many other parts of western Europe. The crusading army that occupied Damietta in Egypt during the Fifth Crusade of 1217–21 contained, along with an English contingent that included the earls of Chester, Winchester, Salisbury, Arundel, and Derby, men from France, Italy, Germany, Hungary, and the crusading states. When the English knights John de Harcourt and Emeric de Sacy died there, with their last words bequeathing land in Leicestershire and Hampshire to the knights Templars, they were in the company of comrades from many lands. Crusading armies were far from immune from national squabbles, but they were nevertheless international bodies, pursuing a goal that was shared by the whole of western Christendom.

As a result of the emphasis on the crusade and the crusading arena, the mental geography of the English became curiously lopsided. The point can be illustrated by a short passage from Roger of Howden's chronicle. The author was a royal clerk who had actually been on the Third Crusade and later retired to the parsonage of Howden in Yorkshire. Writing of the year 1201, he identifies it by reference to the ruling monarchs at the time:

In the same year, when pope Innocent III ruled in the city of Rome; Saphadin the brother of Saladin in the holy city of Jerusalem; Alexius the fratricide in the city of Constantinople; Leo in Armenia; Aimery de Lusignan in the cities of Tyre and Sidon and Acre and the island of Cyprus; when Raymond was prince in the city of Antioch; Otto, emperor-elect of the Romans, brother [actually son] of Henry duke of Saxony, in Germany; Philip in France; John in England; Sverre Birkbain in Norway; Canute in Denmark; William in Scotland; Godred in the Isle of Man; and John de Courcy in Ulster . . .[130]

---

[128] R. Devizes, p. 9; Christopher Tyerman, *England and the Crusades, 1095–1588* (Chicago, 1988), p. 188.

[129] *Rot. lib.*, pp. 25–6; PR 4 John, p. 284.     [130] R. Howd. 4, p. 162.

This list is somewhat eccentric. The high profile of the North Sea world is not surprising, given that the author was located so near the Humber, but the complete omission of the Iberian peninsula or eastern Europe is remarkable. The most conspicuous thing, however, and this is a direct consequence of the crusading movement, is how large the eastern Mediterranean looms in the picture. Of fourteen rulers mentioned, five have their territories in that part of the world. The only non-Christian ruler, Saladin's brother, is obviously included because he held Jerusalem. Raymond of Antioch (which is what Howden systematically calls Bohemond III) is listed, while Alfonso VIII of Castile and Peter II of Aragon are not, although the distance from Yorkshire to Syria is almost three times that from Yorkshire to Spain. That dissonance indicates the spatial bias that the crusading movement had brought to the mental world of the English over the course of the twelfth century. It is appropriate that the oldest pub in England is called the Trip to Jerusalem.

# CHAPTER 3

# Lordship and Government

## I. KINGSHIP AND LORDSHIP

England in our period was a land in which ties of lordship and dependence were among the most essential and characteristic features of society. Reciprocal, but unequal, relationships of a personal kind tied lords and men in networks of mutual support. Lordship of this kind sharply marks off medieval from modern western societies. It involved a blend of powers and authorities usually kept distinct in the modern world, for all medieval lordship included elements that we would now distinguish as rights of property and rights of jurisdiction. In the nice formulation of Gierke, as translated by Maitland, 'in their concept of *dominium* (lordship) Rulership and Ownership were blent'.[1] The apparatus of power that great lords possessed—armed men, treasure, courts, lands, officials, secretariats—had much in common with that of the king. Lords had powers that look, by modern definitions, too 'public' to be in 'private' hands.

Conversely, the powers that kings exercised often had a curiously 'private' flavour. In 1167 king Henry II wanted to marry his eldest daughter to Henry the Lion, duke of Saxony and Bavaria. A marriage, then as now, was an expensive item on a father's budget. Fortunately, prevailing feudal custom allowed a lord to raise money in the form of an 'aid' (*auxilium*) for this purpose. Henry procured from his vassals, the barons, about £3,000 in this way, a figure representing about 10 per cent of the average annual royal revenue. No modern western leader is allowed to attempt to reduce the deficit by levying a tax on the occasion of a daughter's marriage. There was nothing specifically regal about the right Henry was exercising. All his barons and many of their vassals could act in a similar way when their daughters were married—these levies were a perquisite of being a lord, not of being a king. Relations between a king and his barons can thus be seen as but a sub-set of relations between lords and vassals in general. Magna Carta, after regulating the rights that the

---

[1] Otto Gierke, *Political Theories of the Middle Ages*, tr. F. W. Maitland (Cambridge, 1900), p. 88.

king could exercise over his barons, goes on to say: 'All the men of our kingdom, both cleric and lay, shall observe in regard to themselves and their men,
these customs and liberties which we have granted to be observed in our
kingdom in regard to us and our men.'[2]

What is the best way to describe such an aspect of medieval kingship? Both
the combination of 'Rulership' and 'Ownership' in medieval lordship and the
feudal and family elements in a kingship like Henry II's make it clear that the
application of the distinction between private and public customary in
nineteenth-century European law (or that present in Roman Law) to the very
different world of the High Middle Ages may lead to anachronism. We can, if
we wish, label a regime like that of the Norman and Angevin kings 'feudal
monarchy'. Since all the great magnates of twelfth-century England were
indeed vassals of the king and did homage to him, this is not, prima facie, a
ridiculous choice of term. Or we may prefer the concept popularized by the
sociologist Max Weber—'patrimonial state'. The patrimonial state is one
based not on the *imperium* of Roman public law, but on the *patrimonium* of
Roman private law. *Patrimonium* is not public or corporate but belongs to an
individual.[3] Clearly, the dynastic nature of regal rule means that kings did regard the kingdom as their patrimony, something they inherited by right and
owned, in the same way that a baron inherited and owned his estate.

However, although kings were lords, they were also more than lords. The
kingdom of England was not simply an aristocratic estate writ large. Henry II
could pay for his daughter's wedding with his vassals' money, but he was also
anointed, while his vassals were not. Kingship provided a foundation of
claims that were inherently wider and, given the right circumstances, capable
of greater expansion than those of any non-royal lord: the king had a recognized duty to protect the Church and maintain justice; he possessed a special
authority over the coinage and the main roads (the 'king's highway'); while
his barons did homage to him, he did not do homage to them; all adult males
took an oath of allegiance to him; he could not be sued; some offences fell only
under his jurisdiction; and he was hedged about with the distinctive symbolism of regality.

Any discussion of government—the apparatus and pattern of rule—in
England in this period must take account both of the lordship that was exercised by the king and others alike and also of the distinctive position of the
king.

---

[2] *Sel. Charters*, pp. 300–1 (cl. 60).
[3] 'Publicum ius est quod ad statum rei Romanae spectat, privatum quod ad singulorum utilitatem
pertinet', *Institutes* 1. 1. 4.

## 2. REGALITY

### The Crown

Kings were set apart by special rites and symbols, of which coronation and the crown had the greatest importance. The word 'Crown' indeed served as an abstraction designating the royal rights viewed collectively. From the time of Henry I, the king's reserved jurisdiction was described as extending over 'pleas that pertain to the king's Crown' or 'pleas of the Crown'.[4] Cases regarding advowsons (the right of nomination to ecclesiastical position), an Angevin king would assert, 'pertain to the Crown and my dignity'.[5] When, during the absence of Richard I on crusade, the castellan of the royal castle of Lincoln did homage to his brother John, this was deemed 'to be to the dishonour of the Crown'.[6] The physical object, the golden head-piece, thus served to express a conception of regality that was more than just the dues claimed by an individual Richard or Henry.

### The Interregnal Period

Physical crowning remained, nevertheless, essential. The Norman and Angevin kings did not claim to succeed to the royal title immediately upon the death of their predecessor, as was the case later in English history. It was coronation that made a king and kings dated their regnal years from the day of that ceremony. The period between the death of one king and the coronation of another was thus a dangerous interlude. Its atmosphere is suggested by the many payments to knights and soldiers 'to guard the country after the death of King Richard', mentioned in the royal financial records for 1199.[7] This interregnal period averaged a month during the epoch of the Norman and Angevin kings, but this average conceals a wide range. The interval between kings could be very short indeed if political circumstances demanded it. The briefest such period was three days in 1100, between William Rufus's death in the New Forest on Thursday 2 August and his brother Henry's coronation in Westminster on Sunday 5 August. Henry worked with speed, swiftly cutting the ground from under his older brother Robert, who might well be considered to have a better claim. Once anointed, Henry proved tenacious in his grip.

The longest interregnal periods, in 1154, 1189, and 1199, approached two months. The explanation for the lengthy intervals in those years varies. In 1154 Henry of Anjou was already recognized as his predecessor's heir by the Treaty of Winchester; nevertheless the chief men of England sent for Henry,

---

[4] PR 31 HI, p. 91; *Elenchus*, no. 30, p. 63.    [5] Glanville 4. 13–14 (pp. 52–3).
[6] R. Devizes, p. 30.    [7] PR 1 John, pp. 38, 71; cf. 79, 87.

who was then in France, 'to come and take the kingdom without delay'. Things did not go smoothly. Henry was delayed for weeks by contrary winds and weather. The peaceful state of the kingdom during that tense period was a source of wonder to the chronicler Henry of Huntingdon. 'England was without a king for about six weeks,' he wrote, 'but not, by God's grace, without peace, either because of love of the approaching king or because of fear of him.' The fact of peace in a prolonged interregnal period was so astonishing to the chronicler that he was moved to celebrate it in verse:

> The king was dead but kingless England did
>     not lack peace—
> You, Henry, are the first in the world to have
>     performed this wonder.
> Not yet king, not yet present, you
>     nevertheless can do
> What a king was unable to do when present
>     . . .[8]

In 1189 and 1199 likewise the new king was—characteristically—in France when his predecessor died. Both Richard and John had pressing political and military business to deal with on that side of the Channel before they were free to cross to England and both also underwent formal investiture as duke of Normandy prior to sailing to England for their coronation. John sent on an advance party, led by the archbishop of Canterbury and William Marshal, 'to secure the peace of England' by extracting an oath of fealty from all free men 'to John, duke of Normandy, son of king Henry'. Despite this, 'all who had castles fortified them with men and provisions and weapons'.[9] As the wording of this oath makes clear, John could not demand an oath as king until he had been crowned, although he did have the title duke of Normandy. Another title available to the king-apparent in the interregnal period was 'lord of England [or of the English]'. This was assumed, for example, in a charter of 'Richard, lord of England/the English', dating to August 1189, after the death of his father, Henry II, and before his coronation.[10] The assertive nature of the title is revealed particularly in the case of Matilda, daughter of Henry I, who styled herself 'lady of the English' from 1141 when, after the capture of Stephen, her coronation seemed imminent.[11]

The great rivals of the Norman and Angevin kings, the Capetian monarchs of France, had adopted a different practice regarding royal succession. They had their heirs crowned during their lifetime, so that there would not be even

---

[8] H. Hunt. 10. 40 (p. 776) (RS edn., p. 291).        [9] R. Howd. 4, p. 88.
[10] *Ancient Charters, Royal and Private, prior to 1200*, ed. J. H. Round (PRS 10; 1888), no. 55, pp. 91–2, with comment.
[11] *RRAN* 3, p. xxix.

a momentary interregnum. Thus Louis VII, whose reign is usually dated in the history books to 1137–80, had actually been anointed in Rheims cathedral in 1131, during the lifetime of his father, Louis VI, and Louis VII's own son, Philip Augustus, was crowned in 1179, the year before becoming sole king on the death of his father. There is only one instance of this practice in England, when Henry II had his son, Henry the Young King, crowned in 1170. 'He was scarcely of marriageable age,' wrote one of the Young King's courtiers, 'when he was anointed king, crowned with the paternal diadem and called "the Young King"'.[12] After his early death, his father did not repeat the tactic. But, if 1170 provides the only instance of the coronation of an heir during the lifetime of his father, it is clear that the advantages of such a potentially smooth succession were apparent. Stephen spent several years vainly trying to have his older son, Eustace, crowned. Another device aimed at ensuring the succession, although one far less effective than coronation in the lifetime of the preceding king, was the exaction of an oath to accept an heir-designate. Henry I had 'all the free men of England and Normandy' swear an oath to his 12-year-old son William.[13] After William's death he several times had his great men formally recognize Matilda as his heir.

## Coronation

It was naturally a cause for general relief when the kingless state was ended by coronation. The ceremony, which, by custom, took place in Westminster Abbey on a Sunday (except in the case of John, who was crowned on Ascension Day), consisted of an elaborate series of prayers and rites. The king-to-be was conducted into the church by the bishops and there prostrated himself before the altar, while prayers were chanted. After being raised to his feet, the king swore the threefold coronation oath, to preserve the peace of the Church and the Christian people, to prohibit looting and crime, and to maintain justice and mercy in his judgments. One of the bishops then asked the surrounding clergy and people if they wished to have such a ruler, to which they replied 'we wish it and grant it'.

The ceremony now continued with the anointing of the king, usually by the archbishop of Canterbury. He was anointed on his hands, breast, shoulders, and arms with holy oil and on his head with chrism, an especially sacred form of holy oil that could only be consecrated by a bishop and was used in baptism, confirmation, and ordination. Its employment hence stressed the sacramental nature of kingship. By contrast, the next stage of the rite was of a secular origin, even if its conduct was by now in the hands of ecclesiastics. The king was girded with a sword, to defend the Church and protect the weak, then

---

[12] Gerv. Tilb. 2. 20 (p. 946).    [13] W. Malm., *GR* 5. 419 (2, p. 495); OMT edn., p. 758.

crowned and invested with ring, sceptre, and rod. After giving the kiss of peace to the bishops, he was enthroned, while the 'Te Deum' was sung.[14]

The coronation liturgy stressed, naturally enough, God as ruler:

Almighty and eternal God, creator of everything, ruler of angels, king of kings and lord of lords, who made Abraham, your faithful servant, triumph over his enemies, who brought many victories to Moses and Joshua, the leaders of the people, who raised David, your serving-boy, to the height of the kingdom, and who endowed Solomon with wisdom and the ineffable gift of peace, heed our humble prayers, we beseech thee. Multiply the gift of your blessings on this your servant, whom we, in obedient devotion, have chosen as king, and surround him always and everywhere with the power of your right hand . . .[15]

This prayer, that was uttered between the acclamation by the people and the anointing, rehearses a roll-call of Old Testament judges, generals, and kings as predecessors and models for the new king of England. The God invoked here is the god of power who brings victory and exaltation. 'Make him blessed, O Lord,' another prayer calls, 'and victor over his enemies.'[16]

Crowned, girded with the sword, holding the rod and sceptre, the new king was presented as judge and war-leader. Similarly, the image of the king in majesty that appears on the royal seal (Plate 3) shows him sitting enthroned with crown, orb, and drawn sword, a vigorous depiction of majestic and coercive power. Moreover, raised to his office by anointing in a way no other layman was, he was now 'the Lord's anointed' (*Christus Domini*). There was a suitably triumphant special chant for the ruler, the *Laudes regiae*, as they are traditionally termed, beginning with the words 'Christ conquers, Christ reigns, Christ commands'. The *Laudes* were sung at the coronation and asked for 'peace, safety and victory for the king of the English, crowned by God', as well as seeking special help for him from the royal martyr saints Edmund, Hermengild, and Oswald.[17]

The most detailed surviving account of a coronation from this period is Roger of Howden's description of the crowning of Richard I. He lists the nineteen archbishops, bishops, and bishops-elect who were present, the thirteen abbots, two of whom had come from France, the eleven earls, including the king's brother, John, count of Mortain and earl of Gloucester, the seventeen great barons and officials. The procession to the church is described in detail, the clergy going first with candles and incense, then the barons and

---

[14] *Magd. Pont.*, pp. 89–95; despite doubts, it has generally been accepted that this, the so-called 'Third English Ordo' was the liturgy used in this period: J. Brückmann, 'The *Ordines* of the Third Recension of the Medieval Coronation Order', in T. A. Sandquist and M. R. Powicke (eds.), *Essays in Medieval History Presented to Bertie Wilkinson* (Toronto, 1969) pp. 99–115.

[15] *Magd. Pont.*, pp. 89–90.　　[16] Ibid., p. 92.

[17] Ibid., pp. 252–4; H. E. J. Cowdrey, 'The Anglo-Norman *Laudes Regiae*', *Viator*, 12 (1981), pp. 37–78, at pp. 72–3; in general E. H. Kantorowicz, *Laudes regiae* (Berkeley, 1946).

earls bearing the regalia, followed by Richard, led by two bishops and under a silk canopy, finally 'all the crowd of counts and barons and knights and others, clergy and laymen'. After the coronation service, a mass followed, then a banquet.[18] The coronation banquet would be a time for the exchange of gifts. While they were feasting together after he had been crowned, Richard I gave the archbishop of Canterbury a huge ivory horn, that the archbishop in turn dispatched to the shrine of Thomas Becket.[19]

Coronation elevated the king above all his subjects but it also involved him in solemn promises. These could be invoked in political discussion. Thus, during the course of the dispute between Henry II and Thomas Becket, the archbishop urged the king 'to be mindful of the promise you made, when you were consecrated and anointed king, to preserve the liberty of God's church'.[20] Some twenty years later, in the spring of 1185, when a great assembly debated whether the same monarch, Henry II, should lead an expedition to the Holy Land in person or should continue his task of governing the kingdom of England, 'some of those present mentioned the three things that the king had promised when he was about to be consecrated'—namely to preserve peace, order, and justice, in the terms of the coronation oath. The assembly concluded that it would be better if he remained to govern and defend his own kingdom than if he went to help the crusader states in person.[21] An appeal could be made to the coronation promises in this way a good thirty years after they had been given.

## Crown-Wearings

When Adeliza of Louvain was being consecrated queen in 1121, the archbishop of Canterbury, who was about to begin the ceremony, noticed that Henry I was already sitting crowned on his throne. Who had put the crown on the king, the archbishop wanted to know. This was his exclusive right. Henry sheepishly admitted he had forgotten this. The archbishop untied the chin strap that kept the crown in place, removed the crown, replaced it and then began the consecration service for Adeliza.[22] Kings were not expected to put on their crowns habitually or casually, like a businessman donning a bowler.

The fact that wearing the crown was a ritual formality helps clarify the practice of 'crown-wearings', special occasions when the king wore his crown and displayed himself crowned in public splendour. Although this was

---

[18] *Gesta Hen. II* 2, pp. 78–83.

[19] *Epistolae Cantuarienses* 324, ed. William Stubbs, *Chronicles and Memorials of the Reign of Richard I* (2 vols., RS; 1864–5), vol. 2, p. 308.

[20] *Becket Mats.* 5, p. 282 (Becket Letters 154).      [21] R. Diceto, *Ymag.* 2, pp. 33–4.

[22] Eadmer, *HN*, pp. 292–3.

traditional upon the continent, regular employment of the rite in England is associated with William the Conqueror. In his summary of William's reign, the author of the *Anglo-Saxon Chronicle* writes that the king 'had great dignity and wore his crown three times a year when he was in England. At Easter he wore it at Winchester, at Whitsun at Westminster and at Christmas at Gloucester, and on those occasions all the great men of the whole of England were with him, abbots and earls, thegns and knights.'[23] A generation later, William of Malmesbury explicitly attributed the origin of the custom to the king: 'king William introduced the custom, which his successors later allowed to fall into abeyance, that three times a year all the leading men came to his court to discuss the business of the realm and at the same time to see the glory of the king, as he went about exalted by his bejewelled diadem.'[24] The *Laudes* were sung on these occasions, as well as at inaugural coronations, and a royal document of 1100 refers to the customary payment of an ounce of gold that the singers of the *Laudes* received 'at all the feasts in which I wear my crown'.[25]

Both Stephen and, in his early years, Henry II continued the practice of crown-wearings, but several chroniclers mention that, after he had worn his crown at Worcester in 1158, Henry II 'placed his crown on the altar and was never crowned again'.[26] The motives for this are not clear and it is, in any event, certain that the great royal assemblies of the later part of the king's reign were still marked by high ceremony and formality. At Christmas 1186 the great barons did ceremonial service at Henry's table at Guildford, while in 1188 the clerks 'who sang *Christus vincit* before the king at Whitsun' were paid 25 shillings, a rather more generous sum than the earlier ounce of gold.[27]

Henry's son, Richard, was to find a special reason for reviving the ceremonial crown-wearing, a reason that links him with his less successful predecessor, king Stephen. Stephen and Richard were the only two kings of this period to suffer the indignity of being taken prisoner by their enemies, the former during the civil war with Matilda, the latter by a hostile German prince when returning from the crusade. Both underwent a kind of 're-coronation' after their release, clearly designed to emphasize their return to fully regal status. After his capture at the battle of Lincoln early in 1141, Stephen spent nine months as a prisoner of the Angevin party. The first Christmas after his release he and his queen were formally crowned in

---

[23] *ASC*, pp. 219–20, *s.a.* 1086 (*recte* 1087).     [24] W. Malm., *V. Wulfstan* 2. 12 (p. 34).

[25] J. A. Robinson, *Gilbert Crispin* (Cambridge, 1911), p. 141, no. 18; *RRAN* 2, no. 490, p. 2.

[26] R. Diceto, *Ymag.* 1, p. 302; R. Howd. 1, p. 216 (with wrong date); cf. PR 4 HII, p. 175; H. G. Richardson, 'The Coronation in Medieval England', *Traditio*, 16 (1960), pp. 111–202, at p. 127, doubts this.

[27] *Gesta Hen. II* 2, p. 3; PR 34 HII, p. 19.

Canterbury cathedral by the archbishop, who then celebrated mass. Afterwards the *Laudes* were sung. There could be no question of repeating the ceremony of anointing, for that was a unique and irreversible act, but a crowning of this type reasserted Stephen's regality in a bold and public manner.[28]

The ceremony of Christmas 1141 was taken as an explicit model when Richard I faced a similar situation half-a-century later. After his release from captivity in 1194, Richard was advised by the archbishop of Canterbury and other leading men to undergo a new crowning ceremony. This was planned for Easter but pressure of events forced it to be postponed to the following Sunday. On that day, 17 April 1194, at Winchester, the traditional site for the Easter crown-wearings of the Norman kings, the archbishop entered Richard's chamber and placed the rod and sceptre in the king's hands and the crown on his head. They then went in procession to church, accompanied by barons carrying lighted candles and a canopy over the king's head, while the king of Scots and two earls bore swords in golden sheaths. After various prayers and chants, the archbishop and the bishop of London led the king to his throne and mass was sung, including the special prayer for the king and the *Laudes*. After taking communion, Richard returned to the palace, changed into more comfortable robes and 'a lighter crown' and presided over a feast. In this way he sought to wipe away 'the disgrace of captivity'.[29]

His successor, John, also had several 'coronations' after his first in 1199. His 'second coronation', as it was termed, took place at Westminster on Sunday, 8 October 1200, and was combined with the anointing and coronation of his new wife, Isabella of Angoulême. Some stray entries in the royal financial records give a glimpse of the varied splendours of the occasion: two royal clerks, Eustace the chaplain and Ambrose, were paid 25s. for singing *Christus vincit* (the *Laudes*), while a sum of almost £75 was spent on robes for the ceremony.[30] John's 'third coronation' was at Canterbury on Easter Sunday (25 March 1201). This third coronation was not only a splendid public occasion but also served as an important legal terminus. Certain legal proceedings were subject to a limitation of time; after 1202 a plea of novel disseisin, i.e. recent unjust dispossession (see pp. 192–3 below), would only be allowed in the courts if the offence had taken place 'after the coronation of the lord king at Canterbury'. This limitation was in force throughout the rest of John's reign.[31]

---

[28] Gerv. Cant., pp. 123–4, 524, 527 (a date of 1141 is generally preferred to Gervase's 1142).
[29] Gerv. Cant., pp. 524–6; R. Howd. 3, pp. 247–8.  [30] *Rot. lib.*, pp. 1, 4–5.
[31] C. T. Flower, *Introduction to the Curia Regis Rolls* (Selden Soc. 62; 1944 for 1943), p. 159; the first mention of this limitation is *CRR* 2, p. 96.

## The King's Touch

The kings of England were not only made holy by anointing but also seem, at some point, to have acquired a miraculous ability to cure swelling of the throat glands, a disease later referred to as 'the king's evil'.[32] The first English king recorded as having power of this type is Edward the Confessor (d. 1066), who healed a woman with swollen throat glands.[33] When recounting this miracle many years later, in the 1120s, the chronicler William of Malmesbury expressed irritation with those of his contemporaries who claimed that 'power to cure this disease does not stem from sanctity but hereditarily from royal stock'.[34] He may have been taking a swipe at the contemporary Capetian kings of France, to whom this power was also attributed,[35] but perhaps a more natural reading is that he was referring to the Norman kings of his own day. Writing in the 1180s, Peter of Blois, a familiar figure at the court of Henry II, also referred to this healing power. 'The lord king is holy and the Lord's anointed,' he wrote, 'and he did not receive the sacrament of royal unction in vain. If anyone does not know, or doubts, its power, then it can be fully demonstrated by the diminution of groin disease and the cure of scrofula.'[36] The tradition, although seldom mentioned, is continuous and explicit. The kings of England had healing powers.

## 3. THE HOUSEHOLD AND HOUSEHOLD ADMINISTRATION

Although they were marked out from other lords by their splendour and sacrality, kings were still lords and exercised their power in many of the same ways as their great men, the barons and the bishops. The core of magnate authority and the main theatre of the life of a lord was the household—the family members, friends, followers, armed men, officials, chaplains, clerks, and servants around the central figure of king, earl, baron, or prelate. The dazzling impact of a great household is conveyed in the awestruck words of Henry of Huntingdon, who entered the household of Robert Bloet (bishop of Lincoln, 1093–1123) as a young boy: 'When I saw the glory of our bishop Robert, the handsome knights, noble youths, valuable horses, golden and gilded vessels, the number of dishes, the splendour of those who served them, the purple and satin garments, then I thought nothing could be more

---

[32] Marc Bloch, *Les Rois thaumaturges* (Strasbourg, 1924); Frank Barlow, 'The King's Evil', *EHR* 95 (1980), pp. 3–27.

[33] *V. Aedwardi regis* 2. 2, ed. Frank Barlow (2nd edn., OMT; 1992), pp. 92–4.

[34] W. Malm., *GR* 2. 222 (1, p. 273); OMT edn., pp. 406–8.

[35] Guibert of Nogent, *De pignoribus sanctorum* 1. 1 (*PL* 156, col. 616).

[36] P. Blois, *Letters*, no. 150 (col. 440).

blessed.'[37] The lordly household was not only a locus of power but also a centre of display and conspicuous consumption.

The number of people in a household varied, not only according to the rank of the lord, but also as it adjusted itself to different circumstances: war and peace, sedentary periods and travel, great festivals or routine time. One calculation is that, in the later thirteenth century, fifty years after the close of the period discussed here, the average size of a great lord's household was about 35, that of an ordinary knight a dozen or so.[38] The king's household was obviously the largest. A document from about 1135 entitled 'The Organization of the King's Household' (*Constitutio domus regis*), describing the payments made to the king's clerical and domestic officers, lists well over a hundred, excluding the hunting staff who were periodically present and numbered probably another fifty. This figure obviously does not include the subordinate households of other members of the royal family nor visiting dignitaries and their retinues.

The document groups the royal officers and servants into various departments: the chapel, pantry, larder, lord's kitchen, great kitchen, buttery, chamber, marshalsea, each responsible for running one specialized aspect of the household—the bread supply, cooking for the household, transport and security, etc. Positions were carefully specified. There was the cook of the lord's kitchen; the man of the cook of the lord's kitchen; the usher of the lord's kitchen; the man of the usher of the lord's kitchen; the scullion of the lord's kitchen; the man of the scullion of the lord's kitchen's, etc. There was even 'a servant who receives the venison'. Each officer and servant, from the great to the lowly, received a daily allowance in a mixture of cash, food and drink, and candles. The chancellor was given five shillings a day, plus one fine and two ordinary wheaten loaves, a sester (four gallons) of fine wine and a sester of ordinary wine, one large candle and forty candle ends. A chamberlain had two shillings, one ordinary wheaten loaf, a sester of ordinary wine, one small candle and twenty-four candle ends. The humblest attendants received only their daily food.

The household of a great lord was organized no differently from that of the king. A document of the early thirteenth century dealing with the following of the abbot of Westminster mentions seven officers, each in charge of a separate office: the seneschal had responsibility for the hall, the chamberlain for the chamber, the pantler for the pantry (the bread supply), the butler for the buttery (the drink), the usher for the door, the cook for the kitchen, and the marshal for the marshalsea, i.e. the horses and stables.[39] Each part of the

[37] H. Hunt., *De contemptu mundi* I (p. 586).
[38] Kate Mertes, *The English Noble Household, 1250–1600* (Oxford, 1988), p. 218.
[39] Stenton, *First Century*, pp. 71–3, 267–9.

residence—the public space of the hall, the more private space of the lord's chamber, the functional units of kitchen and stables, and the critical entry point, the door—as well as the basic requirements of bread and drink, was thus the special duty of one of the household officials.

The stewardship was one of the higher offices, sometimes held by aristocratic relatives of the lord, as in the case, coincidentally, of both the chief rebels of 1095, Robert, earl of Northumbria, and William of Eu, who employed their nephews as their stewards.[40] The steward was one of the most responsible baronial officials, enforcing his lord's judgements and representing him on important occasions. When, in 1107, the dying Milo Crispin of Wallingford wished to grant land to the monks of Abingdon, it was his steward and chaplain whom he sent to make the donation.[41] The Latin term for steward was either *dapifer* (literally, 'the man who brings in the dishes') or, later, *senescallus* (seneschal), but the word 'steward' was itself of Old English origin. According to the *Anglo-Saxon Chronicle*, when the White Ship went down in 1120, it took with it 'many of the king's retinue, stewards [*stiwardas*], chamberlains [*burthenas*, i.e. 'bower-thegns'] and cupbearers [*byrlas*], and men of various offices'.[42]

Some officers were not permanently present in the household but served in rotation. The dispensers of bread and the chamberlains of the royal household did this. It is clear that the butlers of the earls of Chester also took their turn at his court, otherwise living on their own lands. A charter of earl Ranulf II of Chester from about 1142 grants land to one of his butlers in return for his service. The butler's obligations include mewing a hawk, 'when he is in his own house, like a free man, after leaving my court'. While he is 'in my court . . . performing his service for me' [*in mysterio mihi*] he is free of all other obligations.[43] The grant of land in return for specified household service, as in this instance, was commonplace. It tended to be linked naturally with hereditary tenure of office. A famous example is the office of royal marshal, held by Gilbert Marshal under Henry I, his son John Marshal under Henry I and Stephen, and by his sons, John and William, under the Angevin kings.

What all the different levels of the household staff had in common was service and service could be menial but also led to power and position. Domesday Book, which mentions various stewards, chamberlains, butlers, constables, marshals, and cooks, shows how this ministerial class, of every rank, had embedded itself in the countryside through service of the great. Land in Bedfordshire was disputed between William, a royal chamberlain, and Aethelwulf, chamberlain of Odo of Bayeux; William fitz Osbern, earl of Hereford, had endowed one of his cooks with a small farm near Gloucester;

---

[40] *ASC*, pp. 231, 232 (1095, 1096).     [41] *Abingdon Chron.* 2, p. 97.
[42] *ASC*, p. 249.     [43] *Chester Charters*, no. 55, pp. 67–8.

Alfred, the butler of the count of Mortain, held scattered estates from his lord in the south-west and elsewhere.[44] The royal and aristocratic household was indeed one of the greatest channels of social mobility in the medieval world. It brought a small number of people of very varied social background into daily contact with the powerful. There they could display their talents. The household officers served to keep a large group supplied with the necessities of daily life and, in doing so, formed an embryonic administration. This was especially true of the royal court. It was a natural progression from counting the king's loaves to collecting his taxes, from writing his letters to drafting his laws, from buying his horses to leading his armies. The regal Stewarts of Scotland and the vice-regal Butlers of Ireland did not disdain to bear surnames originating in their ancestors' duties as stewards and butlers in this period.

## 4. ITINERATION

The households of great men were almost always on the move. Kings, bishops, and the higher aristocracy had properties in many places and would travel from one to another. Business, pleasure, or ceremony might also take them on the road: royal councils and ecclesiastical assemblies, hunting and tournament, church dedications, coronations and pilgrimage, all required the large and voracious aristocratic household to journey across the country. It has been calculated that king John's court moved, on average, thirteen or fourteen times a month. His retinue could thus expect to sleep in the same place for only two or three nights in a row.[45]

Such an itinerant household had to be portable. In the treatise on 'The Organization of the King's Household' there is mention of 'the bearer of the king's bed' and 'the tent-keeper', each with his servant and pack-horse. Pack-horses were assigned also to the napier (who was responsible for the linen), to the keeper of the tables, and to the scullions of the king's kitchen and of the great kitchen, who were responsible for the bowls and dishes. The chaplain and the sergeant of the buttery each had two pack-horses, while carters are mentioned for the great kitchen, larder, and buttery. Forward planning was essential: two of the king's four bakers were always sent ahead to prepare bread at the next destination. The Pipe Rolls that record the expenditure of the Angevin kings likewise mention the carts and cart horses that carried the king's kitchen and buttery and that transported his venison and detail the never-ending outlays on saddle-bags, saddle-cloths, panniers, and halters for

---

[44] *DB* 1, 216, 162b (Bdf. 40. 3; Gls. 1. 6); *RRAN* 1, p. xxvii.
[45] Brian Hindle, *Medieval Roads* (2nd edn.; Princes Risborough, 1989), p. 30, fig. 1.

the pack-horses and harness and cart-covers for the wagons. In 1207 the king instructed his bailiffs of Winchester to purchase 'a pack-horse saddle with girth, reins and halter, to transport our chapel'.[46]

The arrival of a great lord or lady with all his or her followers would be a major event in the communities through which they passed. The poem *Tristan* describes how Tristan and his companion climbed into a tree to watch the arrival of queen Isolde's retinue. First came the servants of various ranks, including message-boys, cooks, and grooms, along with the hunting dogs—trackers and hounds—under the care of the hunt-servants and beaters; then the *herberjurs*, who had the important task of finding billets for the night; next there were horses of different kinds, pack-horses, hunters, and palfreys, and falcons too; there followed washerwomen and chambermaids, whose tasks were 'to make beds and sew clothes'; then, finally, the 'knights and damsels' who were the queen's immediate companions, singing as they went along. Tristan's companion 'marvelled at the retinue which was so large'.[47] Every great aristocratic retinue would have this core of the well-born, surrounded by the servants who fulfilled the menial tasks and the animals who provided one of their most important recreations.

Such grand entries were not purely literary fiction. In 1158 Henry II's chancellor, Thomas Becket, was sent on an embassy to Paris which he undertook with all the extravagance he could command.[48] Two hundred horsemen—knights, clerks, stewards, squires, and the sons of nobles—accompanied him. There were eight wagons, each drawn by five great horses. Two of these wagons were loaded solely with barrels of top quality beer. The chapel, chamber, store, and kitchen each had its own wagon, while the remainder carried food, drink, tapestries, bedding, and other gear. Twelve pack-horses bore the chancellor's gold and silver plate, his money, clothes, and the sacred vessels and books for the chapel. Tied to each wagon was a fierce hunting dog, sitting on the back of each pack-horse a monkey. As the retinue entered the villages and fortresses of northern France, the 250 footmen in the van would begin singing English songs; then would follow the hounds and hunt-servants, the wagons, making the cobbles ring with their iron-bound wheels, the pack-horses, squires with their masters' shields, horses, and falcons, then the household officials, followed by knights and clerks, riding two by two, and finally Becket and his close friends. Such a retinue was a spectacle. 'It is no wonder', wrote the historian and moralist Henry of Huntingdon, 'that crowds of women and youths or men of the

---

[46] *Rot. litt. claus.* 1, p. 89.

[47] Thomas, *Tristan*, Strasburg fragment, ed. Bartina H. Wind, *Les Fragments du Roman de Tristan* (2nd edn.; Geneva and Paris, 1960), pp. 80–3.

[48] W. f. Stephen, *V. Thomas* 19–20 (*recte* 21) (pp. 29–33).

frivolous type rush out to see kings. But even wise and discreet men are driven to go and watch them . . .'[49]

The great household whose itinerary we know best is, unsurprisingly, the king's. There were some strong continuities in the travel patterns of the Norman and Angevin kings within England.[50] Like Henry I, Henry II is recorded most frequently at Westminster, Winchester, and Woodstock (near Oxford). Following fairly close behind as stopping places were Windsor and then, in the case of each king, a centre in the southern Midlands: the royal manor of Brampton (Hunts.) under Henry I, Northampton under Henry II— Henry I even assigned land at Brampton 'for the accommodation of his barons when they came to meet the king there'.[51] The Thames valley, Hampshire, and the immediately adjacent areas thus formed the, fairly limited, area in which the English kings were usually to be found. Northern England, East Anglia, the south-western peninsula and even the south-east outside London were much less visited.

The nature of the surviving sources means that John is the first king whose movements can be traced on an almost daily basis (see Map 3). As the map of his journeys in England shows, the bias towards the old Wessex region is still clear, and the relatively unvisited status of East Anglia and the south-west also emerges. Even though John is notorious for knowing the north of England better than any previous Norman or Angevin king, and for infuriating its aristocracy more fundamentally, there remain large areas beyond the Trent that saw him rarely. Even a manic and sometimes desperate king like John did not get to every corner of his kingdom. A typical few weeks in the endless journey that was the life of king John's court occurred in spring 1209, at the beginning of the king's eleventh regnal year, that commenced on 7 May 1209. On Friday 8 May the court was at Gloucester. That day it set off southwards and, over the next three weeks, it is recorded at the following places:

| | |
|---|---|
| Sunday 10 May | Bristol |
| Wednesday 13 May | Bath |
| Thursday 14 May | Bath |
| Saturday 16 May | Marlborough |
| Sunday 17 May (Whitsun) | Marlborough |

---

[49] H. Hunt., *De contemptu mundi* 12 (p. 604).

[50] Of course, it is artificial to limit attention solely to the king's travels in England, since most rulers were more likely to be in France. The needs of regular marine transportation were thus added to the other logistical problems facing the royal and some other great households. Useful maps of royal travel in France are in Thomas K. Keefe, 'Place–Date Distribution of Royal Charters and the Historical Geography of Patronage Strategies at the Court of King Henry II Plantagenet', *Haskins Society Jnl* 2 (1990), pp. 180–1 (Henry II); John Gillingham, *Richard Coeur de Lion: Kingship, Chivalry, and War in the Twelfth Century* (London, 1994), p. 55 (John, 1199–1202).

[51] *CRR* 7, pp. 349–50.

| | |
|---|---|
| Monday 18 May | Marlborough |
| | Ludgershall |
| Wednesday 20 May | Winchester |
| Friday 22 May | Winchester |
| | Southampton |
| Saturday 23 May | Southampton |
| Sunday 24 May (Trinity Sunday) | Portchester |
| Wednesday 27 May | Aldingbourne (Sussex) |
| Thursday 28 May | Arundel |
| | Bramber |
| | Knepp (Sussex) |
| Friday 29 May | Knepp |

The total distance the court travelled between Gloucester and Knepp, using as a simple measure the sum of the distances, as the crow flies, from each stopping place to the next, was 170 miles. This averages eight miles per day, but there would, of course, be some days with no travel. The distance covered each day by the whole court was limited by the speed of the carts carrying the kitchen equipment and supplies. It is unlikely that the court could travel more than twelve to fifteen miles in a day. This is comparable to the daily rate of travel that has been calculated for the German court of the eleventh and twelfth centuries.[52]

It is noticeable that of the ten different places that John's court stayed overnight in this period, nine had royal castles or houses—Knepp castle was in John's hands at this time after the confiscation of the lands of William de Braose in the previous year. On only one occasion, at the bishop of Chichester's palace of Aldingbourne, did the king draw on the hospitality of his subjects. The patterns of itineration were obviously deeply involved with the question of where a large and hungry household might stay. The Norman and Angevin kings were tough men used to the outdoor life and could easily face a night under canvas. In 1209 there is mention of 'eight cart-horses to draw the king's tents'.[53] A royal tent could indeed be an expensive item and the one manufactured for Henry II in 1177 cost £15. 17s. 1d., a sum that could buy 100 oxen at that time.[54] Yet it does not seem that tents were used generally or regularly. Kings and other lords preferred to stay under a roof, either their own or that of a subject, vassal, or tenant.

One goal that lords had in mind as they built up their estates was the creation of a network of places to stay. Roger de Mortimer (d. 1153) was tempted to assert his claims over the village of Snitton because 'the place was very con-

---

[52] Martina Reinke, 'Die Reisegeschwindigkeit des deutschen Königshofes im 11. und 12. Jahrhundert nördlich der Alpen', *Blätter für deutsche Landesgeschichte*, 123 (1987), pp. 225–51.
[53] PR 11 John, p. 27.  [54] PR 23 HII, p. 198.

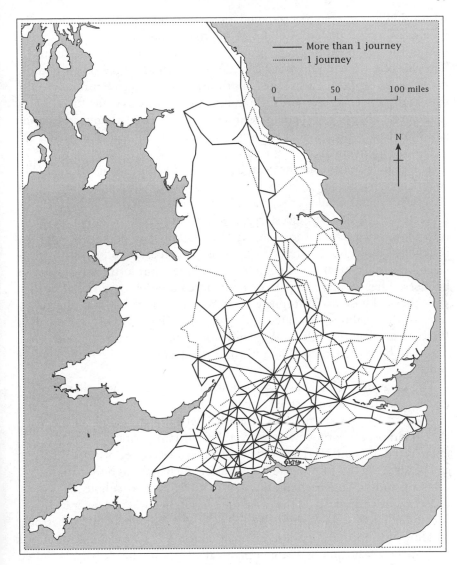

MAP 3. *King John's journeys in England*

venient to receive him en route from Wigmore to Cleobury', two of his most important estates (Snitton is about ten miles from the former and about seven miles from the latter).[55] The monks of Abingdon were delighted to obtain property at Colnbrook in the southern tip of Buckinghamshire in the reign of Henry I, because previously they had lacked a dwelling of their own

[55] *Wigmore Chron.*, p. 438.

where they could obtain accommodation when undertaking 'the many laborious miles to London'. Colnbrook, on the main road an easy day's travel west of the city, filled this gap, 'providing a very convenient place to stay'.[56] The role of a scattered manorial complex as a system of staging posts could not be more explicit. Town houses in the more important centres were also extremely convenient for lords who might have to attend court there. Many of the great abbeys had them. The abbot of Battle had lodgings in London and Winchester, the abbot of Ramsey a stone house with a cellar outside the walls of London north of Cripplegate.[57]

The grandest venue for the great household was the aristocratic hall. The twelfth century saw the creation of many large halls, in timber or stone, by the ecclesiastical and secular aristocracy. Those constructed by Robert, earl of Leicester (1118–68), at Leicester and William de Vere, bishop of Hereford (1186–98), at Hereford were aisled timber buildings of great size: approximately 80 feet by 60 feet in the former case, 100 feet by 50 feet, with an attached chamber-block, in the latter.[58] The kings outdid their magnates as builders. Their castles and palaces were more numerous and elaborate than any others. Those at Westminster and Winchester had, at varying times, some of the qualities associated with a capital. The surviving stone hall of Westminster Palace, built by William Rufus, who held court there in 1099, may have been the largest hall in Europe: 240 feet long and 67 feet 6 inches wide.

The kings of England possessed twenty or thirty residences that were not castles and have been termed variously 'palaces', 'hunting-lodges', and 'houses'. A famous example is Clarendon, set amid the woods of the Wiltshire–Hampshire borders, where several important political assemblies met in the reign of Henry II. Henry expended considerable effort on expanding and beautifying this hunting-lodge or palace. A chapel was built with marble columns and he constructed an aisled hall of flint and rubble, 82 feet by 52 feet, with a raised dais at the east end. The kitchen was in a separate building immediately west of the hall and there were chambers and other outbuildings grouped around a large open courtyard. Especial attention was paid to the excavation of a wine cellar, called 'La Roche', a barrel-vaulted structure reached by eighteen broad stone steps, that still survive under the mould of the Wiltshire countryside.[59]

John, by no choice of his own, spent more time in England than any of his predecessors except Stephen, and it is not surprising that he increased the

---

[56] *Abingdon Chron.* 2, p. 98.     [57] *Battle Chron.*, p. 72; *Ramsey Cart.* 1, p. 139, no. 61.

[58] John Blair, 'The Twelfth-Century Bishop's Palace at Hereford', *Medieval Archaeology*, 31 (1987), pp. 59–72; N. W. Alcock and R. J. Buckley, 'Leicester Castle: The Great Hall', ibid., pp. 73–9.

[59] T. B. James and A. M. Robinson, *Clarendon Palace* (Reports of the Research Committee of the Soc. of Antiquaries of London 45; 1988).

number of royal houses and spent large amounts on them—over £4,000 over the course of his reign.[60] Many do deserve the title 'hunting-lodge'. A clever map in the magisterial survey of royal building, *The King's Works*, shows the close relationship between royal houses and royal Forests.[61] A broken belt of Forest ran from the New Forest, near to Winchester and the royal embarkation points for France, northwards through the woods of Oxfordshire and Rockingham Forest, as far as Sherwood Forest. This belt was dotted with royal residences: Clarendon, Woodstock, Geddington, Clipstone. This last was constructed in the 1160s and enlarged in the following decade, when expenditure is recorded on a chamber, chapel, fishpond, and deer-park there. It was visited by all three Angevin kings, even Richard I, who came there in 1194 'to see Clipstone and the forests of Sherwood, which he had never seen before; and they pleased him greatly'.[62] Counties without royal Forest, like the south-eastern counties, East Anglia, or the south-west, had no royal residences. Kings loved to be where they could hunt.

In the absence of residences of one's own, it was possible to draw on the resources of one's tenants or vassals. Sometimes duties of hospitality were explicitly prescribed. In 1133, for instance, abbot Geoffrey of Burton granted land in Stretton in Dunsmore and Wolston in Warwickshire to 'Roger, the brother of the monk Gerald' on the condition that Roger build 'a fine house and a fine chamber and a fine privy' in Wolston and provide hospitality for the abbot there.[63] A formal agreement made in the year 1215, indicating the annual hospitality owed to the abbot of Westminster by his tenant Ivo of Deene (in Northamptonshire), specifies that Ivo must be given a fortnight's notice in writing of the abbot's visit, that the abbot's chief servants should take over the running of the household during his stay and that Ivo should provide food, drink, and 'everything else necessary for his honourable reception', including two candles, each a pound in weight, to burn before the abbot at night. If the visit lasted longer than twenty-four hours, the abbot then had to pay for what his household consumed.[64] The king himself might use the residences of ordinary subjects. We know that Henry II was staying at the house of Waldeve of Walton when the building was burned down because the king gave Waldeve 30 shillings worth of land in Chesterton, Staffs., in compensation.[65] Perhaps the fire had been started by the courtiers or servants.

Failing all else, there would be a frantic scramble for impromptu billets. The search for a bed at the end of a long day could lead to dissension and even violence. A midsummer council held at Oxford in 1139 saw street-fighting

[60] *King's Works* 1, p. 82.    [61] Ibid., p. 85 (fig. 15).    [62] R. Howd. 3, p. 240.

[63] BL Stowe Ch. 103; facsimile in G. F. Warner and H. J. Ellis, *Facsimiles of Royal and Other Charters in the British Museum* 1 (London, 1903), plate IX, no. 13; BL Loans 30, fos. 38–38ᵛ; Burton Cart., p. 33.

[64] Stenton, *First Century*, pp. 71–3, 267–9.    [65] PR 1 John, p. 165.

between the *herberjurs* of the count of Brittany and those of the episcopal family headed by Roger, bishop of Salisbury:

a quarrel broke out between the bishops' men and those of count Alan of Brittany over the lodgings they claimed. The sad outcome was that the bishop of Salisbury's men, who were sitting down to eat, left their meal half-eaten and jumped up to fight, starting with curses but soon drawing their swords. Alan's followers fled, his nephew narrowly avoiding death. The bishop's men did not obtain victory without shedding blood, for many were wounded and one knight killed.[66]

This quarrel over lodgings was to lead to the first major political crisis of Stephen's reign.

Such incidents were perennial given an itinerant court and a hot-tempered aristocracy. Seventy years after the row at Oxford, a similar quarrel over lodgings broke out as king John's court assembled at Marlborough. Geoffrey de Mandeville, son of the earl of Essex, sent his sergeants on ahead, and they found 'very fine lodgings' for him, but the servants of William Brewer, one of John's most untiring officials, arrived and expelled Geoffrey's men. When Geoffrey de Mandeville himself arrived, his servants reported, 'Sire, see how the servants of lord William Brewer have thrown us out of the lodgings that we took for your use.' Geoffrey then asked William Brewer's servants to clear out and, on their refusal, a brawl ensued, in which he killed one of them. Only energetic family support allowed him to get away with this.[67]

The discomfort and uncertainty of the itinerant court is the subject of a long and heartfelt letter by Peter of Blois, a man who knew the household of Henry II well.[68] 'The life of the court,' he reflected, 'is death to the soul.' The food and drink served there is unpalatable or even health-threatening. The marshals are insufferable, having to be bribed to provide lodgings and willing to eject less important courtiers from their accommodation in favour of more important ones. Likewise, the ushers refuse to admit anyone to the king's presence unless they are given regular gifts. At court every day is unpredictable. If the king announces that he will not be travelling on a certain day, he is sure to be off at first light, forcing his men to rush around like madmen, rousing the pack-horses and crashing the carts into one another. If he says he will be setting out to a certain destination, he is sure to sleep until noon. The loaded pack-horses and carts stand waiting, the outriders snooze, the merchants of the court worry, everyone mutters and ponders. At last an enquiry is sent to the court prostitutes to see about the king's travel plans, 'for that kind of court follower often knows the secrets of the palace'. When the king is finally on the road, there may be a last minute change of plan, taking the court

---

[66] W. Malm., *HN* 469 (pp. 26–7).     [67] *Hist. ducs Norm.*, pp. 116–18.
[68] P. Blois, *Letters*, no. 14 (cols. 42–51).

not to a well stocked town but to some desolate spot where there is a roof and dinner only for the king:

So, after wandering three or four miles through unfamiliar woodland, often in darkness, we believed we had fulfilled our desires if we found some foul and dirty hut. There was very frequently fierce and bitter struggle among the courtiers over a hovel. They sought with their swords for lodging that it would have been unworthy for pigs to quarrel over.

No wonder Peter of Blois refers to 'the lost years I spent in the trifles of the court'.

It is natural to ask why so much effort was spent on transporting households, some of them very large, endlessly across the country. There is some twelfth-century comment on this. The Canterbury monk, Eadmer, gives the reasons why his master, archbishop Anselm, was continually on the move between his manors, rather than staying in the attractive monastic ambience of Canterbury. He was partly compelled by custom and the demands of the large retinue that the archiepiscopal dignity demanded, but two practical considerations prevented his living continuously at Canterbury. One was the burden of bringing supplies to the town; another that, if he did not supervise his estates, the local villagers would have no redress against the oppressiveness of the archbishop's reeves.[69] So contemporaries themselves advanced both an economic and an administrative or social rationale for itineration.

The economic rationale for itineration is that lords needed to go from manor to manor eating up the local produce. Otherwise, in Eadmer's words, 'their men would be burdened by bringing provisions to town'. Apparent support for this practice seems to come from the custom of assessing lands and manors in units of 'one night's provisions' (*firma unius noctis*) or 'one day's provisions' (*firma unius diei*). Evidence for such assessment is particularly clear on royal manors. Thus the king's Hampshire manors of Basingstoke, Kingsclere, and Hurstbourne together rendered 'one day's provisions'.[70] The arrangement, as it appears in Domesday Book, was concentrated especially in the old Wessex area, and was already at that time well on the way to being replaced by a system of money payments, with a day's provision being reckoned at approximately £100. However, it would be wrong to see these provisions to support the court for the day or the night necessarily or even usually being consumed on the spot. The royal treasurer, Richard fitz Neal, writing about 1178, when the payments were entirely in cash, claims to have known men who saw the original practice of food rents in operation—but the provisions were brought from the manors to the court; the court did not go to the manors.[71]

---

[69] Eadmer, *V. Anselm*, p. 71.     [70] *DB* i, 39 (Ham. i. 44).     [71] *Dial. scacc.*, p. 41.

It is, in fact, clear, that itineration did not avoid but entailed moving provisions around the country. This was obviously true in the case of the imported wine that served as a distinguishing feature of aristocratic consumption. Wherever the royal court went, lumbering wagons full of barrels had to go. An audit of the king's wine in 1201 recorded over 700 tuns (casks containing 252 gallons) of wine, much of it stored in fifteen of the royal castles and houses, such as Clarendon, Ludgershall, and Marlborough.[72] Directing a wine lake of 180,000 gallons to where it was needed was a major logistical undertaking. It was not only such luxury imports that were carried across the country, however. In 1130 the sheriff of Oxford spent £2. 7s. 5½d. on transporting royal property and supplies from Woodstock to Clarendon. These included not only wine and the royal robes but also the simple staple grain.[73] The foodstuffs were going to court, not the court to the foodstuffs.

One of the earliest surviving household accounts, that of Hugh de Neville, the Chief Forester, from spring 1207, shows a highly itinerant retinue, moving from Geddington in Northamptonshire to Cambridge to Clarendon to Marlborough to Geddington again to Windsor to Marlborough again to Gloucester to Marlborough again to Portchester, all in the space of eight weeks.[74] Each day's expenses are recorded. Occasionally the needs of Hugh's household were supplied by others: 'On Sunday [4 March] we were at Kimbolton [Hunts.] at the justiciar's expense, on Monday at Southoe [Hunts.] at the expense of Saher de Quincy'. Hugh was one of John's most important officials and perhaps the king would expect his other ministers, like the chief justiciar, Geoffrey fitz Peter, or his barons, like Saher de Quincy, who was created earl of Winchester that very week, to offer him hospitality. The account records many others on whom the burden fell, such as the bishop of Salisbury, the abbot of Abingdon, and Ralph Musard, who entertained Hugh and his household at his manor of *Musardia* (Miserden, Glos.). Sometimes Hugh simply drew on the stocks of the royal castles of which he was custodian. By far the commonest way that he fed his men, however, was by buying their food: 'Wednesday [11 April] at Reading . . . for bread 3s. 1½d., for beer 1s. 6½d., for wine 1s. 3d., for herring 8d., for whiting 9d., for salmon 9d., for hay 1s. 1d., for litter 1s. 1½d., for oats 2s. 7½d., for firewood 2½d., for charcoal 3d., for shoeing the horses 9d.' Hugh's household was certainly not moving primarily in order to consume its own manorial stocks—his officials were pumping fifteen or sixteen shillings a day into local economies.

A sedentary court was not inconceivable and the development of towns, trade, and money eased the problems of governmental departments

---

[72] PR 4 John, pp. 82–4.     [73] PR 31 HI, p. 1.

[74] *Household Accounts from Medieval England*, ed. C. M. Woolgar (2 vols.; Oxford, 1992), vol. 1, pp. 110–16.

permanently fixed in a city. Gradually some of the main administrative offices went 'out of court', i.e. ceased to travel with the king. A permanent treasury at Winchester, where much of the king's money and his financial records were stored, already existed at the time of the Norman Conquest. By the reign of Henry II the Exchequer was fixed in London, where it had it own buildings. The chancery went out of court during the course of the thirteenth century. Itinerant households cannot be explained by the impossibility of fixed capitals and sedentary courts. Itineration was not forced on kings and lords, it was chosen by them. One reason was to seek out good hunting. Another purpose at the higher levels was political and administrative. Eadmer highlights how important it was to supervise local officials and hear the complaints of those subject to them. The coming of the king's court to a locality brought the local aristocracy and clergy into contact with their royal lord, impressed a glamorous and majestic image on the local population, enabled grievances and requests to be made more immediately, and stopped the king's local officers getting away with too much. It was lordship on the march.

## 5. ASSEMBLIES

An alternative to visiting every corner of the kingdom was to bring men from every corner of the kingdom to a great assembly. The Norman and Angevin kings periodically gathered their chief men, both ecclesiastical and lay, for purposes political, symbolic, and convivial. A typical description of such an occasion is the following, regarding a royal council of 1163: 'An assembly of bishops, abbots and magnates was gathered at London, to deal with royal business and confirm the peace of the kingdom.'[75] Such meetings were regular and not infrequent when the king was in the country. Henry I appears to have held two or three a year in the periods when he was in England. The great crown-wearings at Easter, Whitsun, and Christmas were obvious occasions not only for ritual and revelry but also for consultation and decision-making. Meetings could also be summoned at other times. In 1115 Henry I 'ordered all his bishops and the chief men of the whole kingdom to come together to his court . . . and so, as the king had commanded, an assembly of them all was held in the king's palace at Westminster on 16 September'.[76] In 1123, in the words of the *Anglo-Saxon Chronicle*, 'the king sent his writs throughout England and commanded all his bishops and his abbots and his thegns to come to his council [*to his gewitenen mot*] on Candlemas day [2 February] at Gloucester'. *Witenagemot*, meaning 'the meeting of the wise men', is the Old English word for such royally convened assemblies of the lay and clerical elite.

[75] Lambeth Anon. 12 (p. 95).   [76] Eadmer, *HN*, p. 231.

If all the bishops, abbots, and thegns—i.e. the chief lay aristocrats—did come to the royal court, they and their followers would constitute an enormous throng. No attendance lists survive, but it is clear that such meetings must have brought thousands of people together. The witnesses to the Constitutions of Clarendon, drawn up at a royal council at the king's palace of Clarendon in January 1164, include 14 bishops, 10 earls and counts, and 28 other important laymen, many of them great barons. Since these 52 magnates, and the 'many other great men of the kingdom' who are mentioned as present but not named, would each have a substantial retinue of companions, followers, and servants, the crowd assembled on those winter days must have been enormous.[77] The magnate retinues alone, if we take the average size as 35, as suggested above, would number over 1,800 individuals.

The business transacted at these meetings was often of the greatest political importance. Those of 1170 may be taken as an example. In that year Henry II arrived in England on 3 March, after having spent the last four years on the continent. He celebrated Easter (5 April) at Windsor, in the company of William the Lion, king of Scots, his brother, David, and 'almost all the nobles and great men of England, the bishops as well as the earls and barons'. He then went on to London 'and there he held a great council about the coronation of his eldest son, Henry, and about the laws of his kingdom and there he deposed almost all the sheriffs of England and their bailiffs for mistreating the men of his kingdom.' He instituted an inquiry into the sheriffs' conduct, that was to report back to him in London on 14 June. The same day was assigned for the coronation of the younger Henry. On the morning after the coronation the Young King received the homage of William the Lion and David and of 'all the earls and barons and free tenants of the kingdom'. Henry II then returned to Normandy to pursue his negotiations with Louis VII of France and his estranged archbishop, Thomas Becket.[78]

The king had been in England for only three and a half months, but during that time he had held three large assemblies, one at Windsor and two at London, at which the lay and ecclesiastical aristocracy had attended, along with the king of Scots. Important issues had been dealt with. The coronation of the Young King, as has been mentioned, is the only instance of the designation of a royal heir in this manner in the entire period. The crack of firm control over the sheriffs was what prevented English local officials drifting into autonomy or entrenched hereditary status. These meetings had obviously also been scenes of gargantuan consumption and ostentatious finery and their settings were grand and new—the king had spent hundreds of pounds on the residences within Windsor castle in the few years preceding the Easter court that met there in 1170.

---

[77] *Councils and Synods* 1/ii, pp. 877–8.      [78] *Gesta Hen. II* 1, pp. 3–6; Gerv. Cant., pp. 216–20.

Both dynastic and administrative issues were common matters for discussion at the great assemblies. The Domesday inquest was devised at William the Conqueror's court at Gloucester in 1085 after the king 'had great thought and deep speech with his wise men' [*witan*].[79] Most of Henry I's dynastic arrangements—recognition of his son William as his heir, his second marriage to Adeliza of Louvain, recognition of his daughter Matilda as his heir—were discussed or effected at large gatherings of the chief men. When he did not follow this course before marrying off Matilda to Geoffrey of Anjou, it was indeed a cause of great resentment. Henry II's arbitration between the kings of Castile and Navarre in 1177 was not a settlement that the king devised individually. He summoned 'the archbishops, bishops, earls and barons of the whole of England to be with him in London on Sunday 13 March, to have their counsel about a judgement to be made between the two Spanish kings'. On the appointed day fifteen bishops arrived and with them 'so many abbots, deans and archdeacons that they could not be counted; also there came innumerable earls and barons of the kingdom'. It was this assembly, not the king, that made the adjudication.[80]

The language in which the proceedings of such councils are recorded assumes the central role of advice and consent. 'Counsel' was one of the traditional duties that a vassal owed a lord. Like kings, barons had their councils, with whom they discussed important matters. It might well be wise to air large and permanent changes in the resources of the estate in council. In 1089 the earl of Chester wrote that he had discussed the grant of an estate to the monastery of Abingdon 'with my wife and with my barons, and I have concluded in my council that I shall grant it to God and the holy church'.[81] The provisioning of the household of the northern baron Roger de Mowbray was a matter raised 'when the lord discussed business in private with his council'.[82] Aristocratic society was imbued with these practices, for it was an assumption of the ideal of good lordship, which the king shared, that lords would seek advice from their men.

Even the most autocratic of rulers paid lip-service to the ideal. Henry I claimed to have been crowned 'by the common counsel of the barons of the whole kingdom of England' and John's biting taxation of 1207 was supposedly sanctioned by 'common counsel and the assent of our council at Oxford'.[83] It is hard to be sure what reality lay behind such formulae. It would probably be too cynical to regard them simply as an ideological coating. A chronicler as acute and dour as Roger of Howden is willing to attribute

[79] *ASC*, p. 216.     [80] *Gesta Hen. II* 1, pp. 138–54.     [81] *Chester Charters*, no. 2, p. 2.
[82] *Monasticon* 5, p. 350; Stenton, *First Century*, pp. 73–5. The source is not certainly dependable: *Mowbray Charters*, no. 37 n., p. 31.
[83] Liebermann, *Gesetze* 1, p. 521 (CHn cor); *Sel. Charters*, p. 117; Robertson, *Laws*, p. 276; *Rot. litt. pat.*, p. 72.

specific decisions of a powerful king like Henry II to the advice he received. In the single year 1177, in addition to the commission to hear the case of the kings of Castile and Navarre, we learn of a meeting of the bishops, earls, barons, and knights at Windsor that discussed 'the peace and security of the kingdom' and at whose advice the king placed the custody of certain of his castles into the hands of his household knights; the appointment of a Templar, Roger, as royal almoner 'by the counsel of his bishops and other wise men of his kingdom'; and an assembly of bishops, earls, barons, and knights at Winchester, at whose advice the king postponed his return across the Channel.[84] There were ways for the Norman and Angevin kings to learn what their great men thought and it appears that they often listened.

Those who attended these assemblies were primarily, or perhaps exclusively, tenants and vassals of the Crown. The king was their lord in a stronger sense than that in which he was lord of every English man and woman. The advice they offered was what they owed as vassals. They spoke for themselves and their peers; they did not represent others. Towards the end of our period, however, there is the hint of a concept of representation playing a part in these great assemblies. In 1212 and 1213 king John conceived a novel form of assembly that included representative knights from each county. Writing to the sheriff of each shire in 1212, he commanded 'you will come before us with all the speed you may and bring with you six of the more lawworthy and prudent knights of your county, to do what we shall tell them'.[85] The following year the sheriffs were ordered to arrange for 'four prudent knights' from their county to meet the king at Oxford on 15 November, 'to speak with us about the affairs of our kingdom'.[86] Little is known about these meetings and the tone of the first injunction suggests they were being assembled to receive orders rather than give advice, but it is clear that these knights were intended to be representative of their counties: six or four knights are to come from each county, there is no question of all tenants of the Crown being called, nor, indeed, any requirement that the representative knights be tenants of the Crown. It is exactly the same principle by which the later 'knights of the shire' were summoned to Parliament.

Another foretaste of the parliamentary regime is to be found in John's reign. Clauses 12 and 14 of Magna Carta of 1215 specified that certain taxes were to be levied only 'through the common counsel of our kingdom' and that this counsel was to be obtained at a meeting to which the bishops, earls, and greater barons were to be summoned by individual letter and others holding land directly from the Crown through the sheriffs. Forty days' notice of the meeting was required and the venue and purpose had to be announced.

---

[84] *Gesta Hen. II* 1, pp. 160, 169, 178.    [85] *Rot. litt. claus.* 1, p. 132.    [86] *Sel. Charters*, p. 282.

These provisions are famous as a distant ancestor of the principle of 'no taxation without representation' and also as foreshadowing the distinction of the aristocracy into peers (who in later centuries received individual summons to Parliament) and the remainder of the gentle class. The idea of representation, as seen in 1212 and 1213, is absent here. Yet it is obvious from these baronial demands that, not only did the landed class presume that some parts of royal government should be conducted only by consent, but that it might even be possible to prescribe a regular, institutional mechanism to obtain that consent.

## 6. TERRITORIAL ADMINISTRATION

### Counties

England was unique amongst western European kingdoms in being composed of a uniform and universal framework of smaller territorial units, the counties or shires. Some of the older ones, like Kent and Sussex, derived from ancient independent Anglo-Saxon kingdoms; others, such as the Mercian shires, which were almost invariably named after their county towns (Cambridgeshire, Oxfordshire, Buckinghamshire, etc.), were the conscious creation of the late Anglo-Saxon monarchy. By the time of Domesday Book the county network south of the Tees was very nearly complete. The ephemeral Winchcombeshire had disappeared into Gloucestershire, while Leicestershire is named for the first time in Domesday Book. Rutland was just assuming its tiny but tenacious separateness, though it was still regarded in the survey as an appendage of Nottinghamshire. Domesday Book deals with thirty-three counties (excluding Rutland), all of which lasted, with only minor boundary changes, until local government reorganization in 1974. The final total of English counties was thirty-nine, of which five were late-evolving northern counties. Durham was the special preserve of its bishop, while the other northern counties (Lancashire, Cumberland, Westmoreland, and Northumberland) came into existence very gradually over the course of the twelfth century. The amorphousness of the north, at least in southern eyes, is graphically reflected in the geographical description of England given by Gervase of Canterbury in the late twelfth century. He names the thirty-three Domesday counties, including Yorkshire, but then consigns most of the rest of England to a 'Richmondshire' stretching from the North Riding to Carlisle. He includes Durham and Northumberland in an unshired 'bishopric of Durham'.[87] This may simply be ignorance, however. Richard, prior of Hexham, writing in the 1150s, is quite precise, stating that the boundary

---

[87] Gerv. Cant., *Mappa mundi* (*Works* 2, pp. 417–41).

between the county of Northumberland and the 'land of St Cuthbert' (i.e.
Durham), lay along the Derwent and Tyne (as it still does) and that Northumberland was bordered on the west by Westmoreland and Cumberland.[88]

England was thus a kingdom composed of a uniform network of territorial units under the authority of royal officials, the sheriffs. To this generalization there are, however, two exceptions. First, kings occasionally gave away counties to their relatives and, though such arrangements were temporary, they were often quite long-term. Henry I endowed his queen, Adeliza, with the county of Shropshire in 1126 and she survived until 1151. One of Henry's illegitimate sons, Reginald, was given Cornwall, with the title of earl, by his half-sister Matilda in 1140 and the county did not account to the royal Exchequer until after his death in 1175. Here we see counties disappearing from the view of the royal financial administration for decades. Richard I's grant to his brother John of Derbyshire, Nottinghamshire, and the four southwestern counties, which could have resulted in the formation of a major princely territory, in fact lasted only from the king's accession in 1189 to John's forfeiture for rebellion in 1194, but during those years the six counties rendered no accounts to the royal government.

In addition to these temporary appanages, there were two counties where the king's standing came to be notably and permanently different from that elsewhere in the kingdom. Both Cheshire and Durham developed in a distinctive fashion, eventually attaining a kind of autonomy that was, in the later Middle Ages, to be termed 'palatine status'. Domesday Book records that all land in Cheshire was held of the earl of Chester, none directly of the king. Both the earl of Chester and bishop of Durham appointed their own sheriffs. Their chief tenants continued to be termed 'barons' long after other magnates had abandoned this practice. While the other counties of England accounted annually at the Exchequer, Cheshire and Durham did not (unless temporarily in the king's hands through minorities or episcopal vacancies) and neither were they visited by the king's itinerant justices on their periodic visitations of the kingdom. The bishop of Durham was also one of the few magnates in England allowed to have his own mint, although the coins were struck in the king's name from centrally issued dies. When Magna Carta was issued for England, a separate Magna Carta for Cheshire was issued by the earl. Just as the king had his 'pleas of the crown', judicial cases especially reserved to his authority, so the earl had his equivalent 'pleas of the sword'.

However, despite the temporary appanages and the exceptional position of Cheshire and Durham, it is the uniformity of the English shire system that is striking. The basic units, the counties, were not large. Their average size was about 1,250 square miles, though this figure reflects the existence of the giant

---

[88]  Richard of Hexham, *Historia Haugustaldensis ecclesiae*, pref. (*Priory Hexham*, p. 2).

county of Yorkshire, itself divided into subsidiary Ridings. Median size was 1,000 square miles and most counties (27 of the 39) were between 600 and 1,600 square miles. The majority of settlements were within a day's walk from the county town. Counties could thus really be the focus for local society and, although they were created and maintained for the king and his purposes, they did gradually come to form communities of interest and self-perception.

## The Sheriff

The shire was headed by the sheriff ('shire-reeve'), a royal official who held his position at the king's pleasure and fulfilled a range of duties, primarily judicial and financial. He presided over the county court and was responsible for the annual payment that each shire made to the king. Because many English counties were quite small, it was not uncommon for the same man to be sheriff of two adjoining counties. Enduring pairs of this kind were Derbyshire and Nottinghamshire, Norfolk and Suffolk, and Buckinghamshire and Bedfordshire. On occasion this meant that the county courts also met jointly: Derbyshire and Nottinghamshire had a common county court. Possession of more than two shrievalties was also not unknown, as in the remarkable case of Hugh of Buckland, who was sheriff of eight counties in the reign of Henry I.[89]

Sheriffs were usually laymen and were largely drawn from three overlapping groups: the barons, royal administrators, and local gentry. Many of William the Conqueror's sheriffs were substantial barons, like Geoffrey de Mandeville, sheriff of Middlesex and holder of a barony worth £800 a year, one of the dozen wealthiest men in the country. Others were of more modest landed wealth and some seem not to have been more than local landholders. Henry I was renowned for 'raising from the dust men of common stock', in the words of the chronicler Orderic Vitalis, and some of these 'new men' served as sheriffs: Orderic's list includes Hugh of Buckland, the great pluralist sheriff.[90] Many of Henry's household officers also served as sheriffs of counties. Others were drawn from the administrative staff of the magnates: Hugh of Leicester, sheriff of Northamptonshire, Warwickshire, and Leicestershire, was also the steward of Matilda de Senlis, heiress to the earldom of Huntingdon.[91] The mixture was not fundamentally different a century later. King John had 46 sheriffs in the first six years of his reign: 17 were barons, 12 were knights, 11 were professional royal officers, 7 are of unknown, and therefore presumably modest, origin and two were professional administrators who served both the king and other lords.[92]

---

[89] *Abingdon Chron.* 2, p. 117.    [90] Orderic 11. 2 (6, p. 16).
[91] *Monasticon* 5, p. 178.    [92] Painter, *John*, p. 92.

In choosing their sheriffs, kings had to strike a balance. They needed to appoint men with sufficient standing to exercise authority over the landed and military aristocracy of the county, yet they did not wish them to become entrenched and unaccountable. An especially sensitive issue was the inheritance of shrieval office. If the office became the property of an aristocratic family, the king's discretion and control would be weakened. There are such cases. Roger de Pîtres, sheriff of Gloucester and constable of Gloucester castle in the 1070s, was followed in his offices by his brother, son, and grandson. This last, Miles of Gloucester, obtained office also in the royal household, was given a rich heiress, and crowned his rise by becoming earl of Hereford in 1141.[93] It was in Stephen's reign that the danger of the king's losing control of his counties was at its height. The appointment of many more earls, indeed the possibility of there being an earl for every county, suggests that command in the localities was now to be exercised by aristocrats with hereditary title rather than by appointed royal officials. The rivals in the civil war had to make concessions. Matilda granted Geoffrey de Mandeville not only the earldom of Essex (that Stephen had already given him) but also, as hereditary possessions, the custody of the Tower of London, the shrievalty of Essex, and the position of chief justice of Essex. 'I give and grant to him and his heirs', her charter reads, 'in fee and heredity, to hold of me and my heirs, the shrievalty of Essex.'[94]

The restoration of royal authority under the Angevin kings ensured that such a trend was reversed. Henry II exercised firm control over his sheriffs, as the Inquest of Sheriffs of 1170 shows. This was the inquiry, ordered by the king, into how much the sheriffs and other local officers had taken from their counties 'to the burden of the land and the men'. As a consequence, twenty-two out of twenty-nine sheriffs or deputies were dismissed, their replacements often being officials of the royal Exchequer.[95] The sheriffs were not to drift from being royal appointees to being local grandees, as had happened with the counts and viscounts of France and Germany earlier in the Middle Ages. They remained dismissable and accountable. This is seen particularly clearly in the financial dealings between king and sheriffs.

Sheriffs were expected to make regular payments to the Crown, but it was also presumed that they would be taking in much more than they handed over. It is the profitability of shrieval office that explains why men were willing to pay for it. In 1130 Robert d'Oilly, sheriff of Oxford, owed the king 400 marks (£226. 13s. 4d.) 'for having the county', and in 1200 William de Stuteville

[93] D. G. Walker, 'The "Honours" of the Earls of Hereford in the Twelfth Century', *Transactions of the Bristol and Gloucestershire Archaeological Soc.* 79 (1960–1), pp. 174–211.

[94] *RRAN* 3, no. 274, pp. 99–101.

[95] *Gesta Hen. II* 1, pp. 4–5; 2, pp. lxvi–lxix; Gerv. Cant., pp. 216–19.

offered king John £1,000 to be sheriff of Yorkshire.[96] These payments were one way the king could get more from the sheriff than the traditional fixed amounts. Another was to impose an 'increment', an annual surcharge over and above the usual payment. On his return from captivity in 1194 and after having quelled the revolt of his brother John, Richard I auctioned off many of the shrievalties and imposed substantial increments on the sheriffs. Osbert de Longchamps obtained the shrievalty of Norfolk and Suffolk but had to promise an annual increment of 100 marks (£66. 13s. 4d.), while his brother Henry received Worcestershire, after offering a gift of 10 marks and agreeing to an increment of £40. He replaced a baronial sheriff, William de Beauchamp, whose family had held the office intermittently since the Norman Conquest. Only six sheriffs remained in office throughout the year.[97]

John's ingenuity devised a yet more certain method of tapping the sheriffs. Instead of agreeing to a fixed payment, of whatever size, he instituted in the year 1204 the practice of having custodian sheriffs. They had to account for everything they received from the county. The result, visible in the Exchequer accounts of Michaelmas, 1205, was a 30 per cent increase in payments from the counties. Salaried officials had proved more productive instruments of royal government than the old speculator-sheriffs. John was not able to continue his experiment, partly because of the political crises that gathered in the later part of his reign, but here, as in other areas of fiscal policy, he first instituted what were to be the main patterns of royal financial policy in the later medieval period.

## The County Court

One of the strongest forces shaping county identity was the county court. In the late Anglo-Saxon period this met twice a year, but meetings gradually became far more frequent. Henry I found it necessary to command that the county courts meet only at their customary sites and at the customary times, unless he himself summoned them.[98] The implication is that they were meeting more often and at more variable venues than in the past. His ruling was obviously in vain, for by the early thirteenth century some county courts were meeting as often as every three weeks. The 1217 reissue of Magna Carta ruled that county courts should not be held more frequently than once a month and three years later the sheriff of Surrey was fined 'because he allowed the county court to meet within three weeks'.[99] There were some traditional venues, but in some shires the court met at varying sites. The county town was an obvious meeting place, provided that a large enough

[96] *Rot. obl.*, p. 109.     [97] PR 6 RI, pp. xvii–xx.
[98] Liebermann, *Gesetze* 1, p. 524; *Sel. Charters*, pp. 121–2; Robertson, *Laws*, p. 286.
[99] *Sel. Charters*, p. 343; CRR 8, p. 223.

room could be found. Reginald, earl of Cornwall, noted that the prior of Launceston had, at some point in the 1140s, vindicated his claim to the borough status of Old Launceston 'in full county court before me at my castle of Launceston'.[100] In 1166 a Yorkshire land grant was confirmed 'before the county court in the crypt of St Peter's church' (i.e. York Minster).[101]

The court was presided over by the sheriff, who received all the fines and forfeitures imposed there, except in those counties that had an earl, when the earl customarily took a third of the court's profits. It was attended by the local landholders. The law treatise titled *The Laws of Henry I* (*Leges Henrici Primi*), dating to 1115 or thereabouts, specifies those who must attend as 'the bishops, earls, sheriffs, deputies, hundredmen, aldermen, stewards, reeves, barons, subtenants, village reeves and other lords of estates', but it is unlikely that such a full range came to all the meetings. If a baron's steward attended the county court, that discharged the obligation for all his lord's lands in the county.[102] Sometimes the duty of attending the shire court fell on particular tenants: there were four rent-paying tenants of the abbey of Burton in the time of Henry I whose duties explicitly included going to the shire court.[103]

A record of a meeting of the county courts of Norfolk and Suffolk in the reign of Stephen shows the vitality of the county court and the way it served as a reservoir of local knowledge and tradition.[104] The king had summoned a special meeting of the two counties at Norwich. The court met in the bishop's garden and was presided over, not by the sheriff, but by William Martel, the king's steward. The bishops of Norwich and Ely and the abbots of Bury St Edmunds and Holme (Norfolk) were present, along with 'very many of the barons of the province . . . and many other worthy and wise men and suitors of the court'. The first case they heard was a very unusual one, a charge of treason against two knights. Almost before proceedings had begun, however, the abbot of Bury interposed, claiming that as the knights were vassals of the abbey, he had the right to try them in his own court. He went off to the king with the charters that supported his case, and Stephen instructed him 'to take the privileges to my justice and to the county court and have them read out'. He would confirm whatever rights 'the barons of the counties' recognized Bury to have.

Returning to the assembled court, the abbot had the charters read out. Then followed a vigorous discussion. The decisive speech was made by an old man, Hervey de Glanville. Standing in the middle of the gathering, he addressed the court:

---

[100] George Oliver, *Monasticon diocesis Exoniensis* (Exeter, 1846), p. 23; Van Caen., *Lawsuits* 1, pp. 277–8, no. 322.

[101] *EYC* 2, no. 718, p. 64.      [102] *LHP* 7. 2, 7. 7b (pp. 98–100).

[103] *Burton Surveys*, pp. 216, 242, 245.

[104] Helen Cam, 'An East Anglian Shire-moot of Stephen's Reign, 1148–53', *EHR* (1924), pp. 568–71.

Worthy and most wise men, it is long since I first heard the charters of St Edmunds that have just been read out and they were always authoritative until today. I wish you to know that I am, as you can see, a very old man and I remember many things that happened in the time of king Henry and before, when justice and right, peace and loyalty flourished in England . . . I say to you truly, I attest and affirm, that it is now fifty years since I first began to attend the hundred courts and the county courts with my father, both before I had an estate and afterwards, to the present day. Whenever a case arose in the county courts concerning a man of the eight and a half hundreds (belonging to Bury), the abbot or his steward and servants claimed that case and transferred it to the court of St Edmunds.

Hervey de Glanville's self-admiring posture as the voice of tradition should not divert attention from the fact that he, and others like him, did indeed preserve the memory of the customs of the county. The author of the law-book, coincidentally but wrongly, attributed to Hervey's son, Ranulf de Glanville, says that he will not deal with the county court 'because of the diversity of customs in the counties'.[105] Local, orally transmitted procedures and practices formed the foundation of the activities of the county courts. Participation by the county landowners trained them to think in county terms.

### The Sense of County Community

Counties were treated as units by the royal government for its own purposes—tax assessment, inquisitions, and the like. When coroners were first appointed, in 1194, it was natural for them to operate on a county basis. The charters of kings or great lords with such addresses as 'to the bishop of Norwich and the justice and barons and all loyal men of Norfolk and Suffolk' or 'to all the barons of Oxfordshire' show how county communities operated as obvious collective recipients of instructions and information coming from above.[106] Yet the county was not merely the passive object of royal lordship. There is evidence for autonomous action on the part of the landholders of the county and for a sense of loyalty and identity focused on the shire.

One way that the sense of county community expressed itself was in the desire of the men of the shire to have a sheriff from their own county. In 1204–5 the men of Cornwall offered king John 2,200 marks (£1,466. 13s. 4d.) for a variety of privileges and exemptions, including the right 'to have a sheriff from among their own, in such a way that they would choose some of the best men of the county and present them to the king, who would choose whom he wished from those presented to him'; a few years later, in 1210–11, the men of Dorset and Somerset (two counties traditionally held by one sheriff) offered 1,200 marks (£800) 'so that the king would appoint for them a sheriff from among their own, a resident in those counties'.[107] The attempt to

---

[105] Glanville 12. 23 (p. 147).    [106] *RRAN* 3, no. 287, p. 108; *Chester Charters*, no. 6, pp. 12–13.
[107] PR 6 John, p. 40; 12 John, p. 75.

secure a sheriff from the county was both an expression of county solidarity and, if successful, a means of furthering it.

A lively dispute in the county court of Somerset, in the very year that the men of Cornwall made their offer to have a local sheriff, reveals the hostile feelings that a sheriff from outside the county could arouse.[108] Richard Revel had ejected William Dacus from his holding in the county and William had brought a suit against him. At a meeting of the county court William produced letters from the royal justices awarding him 60 marks (£40) damages and commanding the sheriff to ensure they were paid. At this Richard Revel's son, Richard Revel junior, protested and asserted that 'he and his father and his brothers were native and well born men of the county' (*naturales homines et gentiles . . . de patria*). The sheriff, Alan of Whitton, replied, reasonably enough, that he knew that, but this should not stop him from carrying out the orders of the royal judges. Richard answered that 'they were native and well born men of the county'—the dull inflexibility of his thinking appears to have matched the violence of his father. The sheriff again repeated his point, whereupon Richard was driven to elaborate his argument with insult: 'they were indeed native and well born men of the county but he was a carpetbagger' [*adventicius*]. Alan admitted he was from another county, but perhaps, he said, as native and well born in his county as Richard was in his. This slanging match eventually came to the attention of the king's central court and an inquiry was ordered. It brings out very vividly both the strength and parochialism of county sentiment.

An unusual insight into the antagonisms and loyalties that might focus on the county can be obtained from an exchange of poems between a monk of Peterborough and a Norfolk man that is found in thirteenth-century manuscripts and may date from our period.[109] The monk's poem is a denigration of the men of Norfolk, the reply is a defence. 'A decree went out from Caesar', begins the monk's poem, in a parody of Luke's gospel, 'commanding all the provinces to be described'. After the emperor's envoys had travelled throughout the world and returned with their reports, one of them addressed the emperor: 'hear me, lord, I have crossed the seas and traversed every land, but, to tell the truth, there is no province so detestable as Norfolk.' He then goes into details. The soil is sterile, the people deceitful. When Satan fell from heaven, Norfolk was the first place he blighted. The people of Norfolk are stupider than beasts. If you ask a Norfolk man for directions, he will tell you to 'go as the crow flies'; he will carry his own goods to market, to spare his donkey; if he finds a beetle in a pile of horse dung, he will think it a bird and take it home to eat. The men of Norfolk harbour grudges and are cunning in

---

[108] *CRR* 3, p. 129.
[109] *Early Mysteries and Other Latin Poems*, ed. T. Wright (London, 1838), pp. 93–106.

their revenge. 'I have told you,' concludes the poem, 'some of the ways and deeds of the people of Norfolk—a parchment the width of Norfolk could not contain them all. So, let us pray, with devout mind, that God correct the vices of these men, or destroy the people and the county together!'

The poem in response is a dogged, if pedestrian, rebuttal of these charges. The Peterborough monk is a liar. His stories are absurd. The people of Norfolk are not stupid—'there are no men with a greater reputation for good sense in the whole of England'. It was Christ, not Satan, who visited Norfolk and left a hereditary blessing on the inhabitants. The poet rises to eulogy:

Whoever once comes to Norfolk does not seek to leave as long as he lives, for when he sees such a good county, he believes he is living in paradise. It is a fertile land, full of riches, abounding in all kind of good things. There the people are without malice . . . there you will find warlike knights, noble barons, distinguished magnates . . .

And this eulogy is inspired by local patriotism:

God, grant that the people of Norfolk may live in peace and prosperity; destroy those who hate them and make them cease their detractions. I do not wish to stir up any man's hatred. I dare to say this openly only because I am of Norfolk stock and it is right that I defend my county.

The county was not a mere administrative unit; it could be an object of love.

### Counties and Regions

A final point worth making about the network of English shires is that the county, a relatively small unit, was the largest secular subdivision of the kingdom. This had not been true in the Anglo-Saxon period. Then the counties had been grouped into larger units headed by ealdormen or earls. Under Edward the Confessor, last of the Wessex line, earldoms like those of Wessex, Mercia, and Northumbria, whose names perpetuated the memory of earlier independent kingdoms, were far larger then any shire. These great earldoms disappeared soon after the Conquest. The Conqueror appointed a few earls, but they were associated only with a single county. In most of England there was no intermediate layer between king and county.

Some memory of the old provincial subdivisions survived. The *Laws of Henry I* state quite boldly, 'the kingdom of England is divided into three parts, Wessex, Mercia and the Danelaw'.[110] A list of the different counties making up the *Westsexenlaga, Denelaga,* and *Merchenelaga* was copied quite frequently long after the Conquest.[111] The *Laws of William I* (*Leis Willelme*), a compilation of legal learning from the twelfth century, records the different levels of fines due for the same offence in the 'Mercianlaw', 'Westsaxonlaw',

---

[110] *LHP* 6. 1 (p. 96).
[111] Simeon, *Op.* 2, p. 393; Thomas Gale, *Historiae Britannicae . . . scriptores XV* (Oxford, 1691), p. 560.

and 'Danelaw' (*Merchenlahe, Westsexenelahe*, and *Denelahe*),[112] but such legal distinctions soon disappeared. In incidental references in the writing of the twelfth century we can see how the old terms lingered on. From writers of the Norman period we have references to bishoprics 'of the East Angles' and 'of the South Saxons' and to an 'earl of the Mercians', where modern historians would tend to talk of the sees of Elmham and Selsey and of the earl of Shrewsbury.[113] A journey from Cirencester to Wallingford means going 'from the province of the Mercians to the West Saxons', a trip to Haselbury in Somerset can be described, in a work written about 1185, as going 'into the region of the West Saxons'.[114] Sometimes new labels of this kind emerged: John of Hexham writes of the king of Scots' journey 'into Southanglia' (*in Suthangliam*) in 1141.[115] But all this is not very significant. The great territorial subdivisions of England were ghosts not living creatures.

It is quite justifiable to stress two opposite points about England in this period: it was full of local diversity and it was, by contemporary standards, remarkably homogeneous. Variation in practice and custom was patent. A traveller across the kingdom would encounter many different standards of measurement. Early in the twelfth century the acre in Sussex was forty perches long and four wide, the perch containing sixteen feet.[116] At Snelland in Lincolnshire land was granted 'as measured by a perch of eighteen feet'.[117] In 1189 newly cleared ('assarted') land in Worcestershire was assessed in acres based on a perch of 25 and a half feet.[118] As in linear measurement, there was great variation in dialect, and this could give birth to a sense of regional identity. William of Malmesbury noted that the 'language of the Northumbrians' was incomprehensible to 'us southerners'.[119] A certain regional snobbery might ensue. It is not untypical when an author writing in the monastery of Bury St Edmunds refers to the inhabitants of Cumbria as a 'barbarous people'.[120]

Yet, despite the complexity of custom and the fragmentation of language, the kingdom of England was one of the most uniform political entities in medieval Europe. The network of shires is a partial explanation, and an embodiment, of that fact.

## Hundreds and Townships

The county was composed of smaller territorial units, called hundreds in the south and wapentakes in the old Danelaw area. Their history is more variable

---

[112] Liebermann, *Gesetze* 1, pp. 494–6 (Leis Wl. 3); Robertson, *Laws*, p. 254.
[113] Flor. Worcs. 2, p. 6; Orderic 8. 2 (4, p. 126).     [114] *Lib. Eliensis* 3. 60 (p. 307).
[115] J. Hexham, p. 309.     [116] *Battle Chron.*, p. 50.     [117] *Danelaw Docs.*, no. 229, pp. 160–1.
[118] *Worcester Cart.*, no. 325, p. 171.     [119] W. Malm., *GP* 99 (p. 209).
[120] *Mir. sancti Edmundi* 12 (attributed to abbot Samson), *Mem. Edm.* 1, p. 186.

than that of the counties and hundreds were reshaped and renamed to a greater degree. Domesday Book records about 730 hundreds and wapen-takes, but there were only 628 in the 1270s.[121] They varied considerably in size. At the time of the Domesday survey, Leicestershire comprised only four wapentakes, while Sussex had 59 hundreds. This meant that the Leicester wapentake averaged just over 200 square miles, the Sussex hundred not quite 25 square miles. Obviously, population density made a difference, and there is a clear correlation between the counties with smaller hundreds (in the south of England and East Anglia) and those with higher recorded populations.

Like the county, the hundred had its court, that met frequently (every two to four weeks) and was attended by local landowners who owed 'suit of court', the duty of attendance. Twice a year a specially large meeting of the hundred court was held, presided over by the sheriff, and at this an inquiry was made whether every free adult male was enrolled in a tithing or frankpledge, a group that was collectively responsible for its members' conduct. The frankpledge system was intended to supplement the tiny police organization of the period. The other members of a tithing had to bear the consequences of the criminal activity of one of their number. In 1170, for instance, the men of the frankpledge of Sunbury (Middx.) had to pay one mark (13s. 4d.) because 'they did not detain a man accused of homicide'.[122]

Hundreds came into the hands of barons and great churches much more often than counties. Kings were willing to give them away. 'Know', wrote William Rufus to the sheriff and barons of Huntingdonshire, 'that I have granted the hundred of Normancross to the monks and abbot of Thorney to be held for an annual rent of a hundred shillings'.[123] The 'eight and a half hundreds' of the abbey of Bury St Edmunds were mentioned above (p. 153). These, covering the whole of west Suffolk, had been granted to the monks by Edward the Confessor. They defended their rights in them vigorously. Abbot Samson (1182–1211) fought off the claim of the earl of Hertford to receive customary payments from the abbey's hundred of Risbridge in the hundred court itself, and refused to acknowledge the hereditary right asserted by Adam de Cockfield to hold the half-hundred of Cosford from him.[124] By the late thirteenth century over half the hundreds in the country were in the pos-session of bishops, abbeys, and barons. In these private hundreds, the lord's representative presided over the court and the lord took the profits. The Angevin kings had to keep a watchful eye not only on the doings of their sher-iffs but also on 'those who held the hundreds that the barons have in the shire, either at a fixed fee or as custodians'.[125]

---

[121] Helen Cam, *The Hundred and the Hundred Rolls* (London, 1930), p. 137.
[122] PR 16 HII, p. 18.   [123] *RRAN* I, app., no. lxxxi, p. 139.   [124] Joc. Brak., pp. 57–9.
[125] Gerv. Cant., p. 217; *Sel. Charters*, p. 175.

Something of the practicalities of hundred administration is revealed in a document of about 1208, in which the new lord of the wapentake of Langbargh in Yorkshire agreed to limit his officials to one chief sergeant with three horses and three mounted sergeants under him.[126] These four mounted sergeants had responsibility for an area of about 1,500 square miles between the Tees and the North York Moors. included in their beat was the coast between the mouth of the Tees and the vicinity of Ravenscar south of Whitby, a distance of thirty miles or so. No settlement for which they were responsible would be more than a day's ride away, even if they were at one extremity of the wapentake, but there can be little doubt that most places would regard the presence of the wapentake sergeants as exceptional rather than routine.

When Henry II ordered the Inquest of Sheriffs in 1170, he commanded that inquiry should be made of what had been extorted 'from each hundred and from each township and from each man'.[127] Between the individual and the hundred, therefore, he pictured the township (villata). This, like the county and the hundred, was a corporate body with definite duties and responsibilities. The Domesday inquest required the testimony of the priest, reeve, and six villagers from each township.[128] A similar delegation, of priest, reeve, and four 'of the better men of the township' might be required to attend the county court.[129] The township also had a central part to play in the system of public presentment of crime, as it is revealed in the legislation and court records of the Angevin period. This was based upon charges and suspicions reported not only by 'twelve of the more law-worthy men of the hundred', but also by 'four of the more law-worthy men of each township'.[130]

It is possible to see how complete and effective England's local territorial organization was from the procedure employed to raise a tax on movable property in 1225. The king appointed tax collectors for each shire. The sheriff summoned all the knights of the shire to meet them at an assembly where four knights would be chosen from each hundred or wapentake. These knights then had the duty of going through the hundred for which they were responsible (it could not be that in which they lived) and receiving from each inhabitant a sworn declaration of the value of his or her property. The tax was based on a percentage of this. The knights would receive the cash 'through the hands of four of the law-worthy men and of the reeves of each township' and transmit it to the shire collectors. A fragmentary record reveals the details of this process of assessment for the Lincolnshire wapentake of Aswardhurn. It consists of a roll of twenty-four parchment sheets, each containing the valuation for one or two of the townships in the wapentake. The names of

---

[126] Cartularium prioratus de Gyseburne, ed. W. Brown (2 vols., Surtees Soc. 86, 89; 1889–94), vol. 1, no. 213, pp. 92–4.

[127] Gerv. Cant., p. 216.      [128] ICC, p. 97.      [129] LHP 7. 7b (p. 100).

[130] Sel. Charters, p. 170.

the individuals and their property are recorded down to the last piglet, sheep-skin, and bushel of grain.[131] The villagers of twelfth- and thirteenth-century England could be located in an exact and comprehensive framework of tithing, township, hundred, and county. This was the organization by means of which law was applied and money extracted.

## 7. ROYAL FINANCES

English kings spent money on the grand scale, on war especially, but also on buildings, servants, food and drink, clothes and jewellery, horses and hounds. They had their followers to reward and their charity to bestow. This large expense required a large revenue. The four main components of this revenue were (1) the Crown lands (the royal demesne), (2) income derived from rights of feudal overlordship, (3) taxation, and (4) the profits of justice. In 1130, the total of the king's revenue audited at the Exchequer was £24,500. Of this approximately 40 per cent came from the royal demesne; 16 per cent from feudal overlordship; 14 per cent from tax; and 12 per cent from justice.

The royal Exchequer originated in the annual audit of the money owed by the sheriffs and some other debtors. It is first mentioned by name in 1110 and the earliest surviving record of its audit is the Pipe Roll of 1130. Initially it was an occasion rather than an institution and, indeed, began life as a physical object—a chequered cloth on which sums could be done. It retained this simple sense even after it had acquired other meanings. In 1166 the sheriff of Worcester paid 3s. 10d. for a 'chess-board' or 'exchequer' (the words are identical—*scaccarium*) at Worcester 'for doing the royal receipts'.[132] By the reign of Henry II, however, the Exchequer had its own premises in Westminster, which was its usual home. Its written records and the wooden tallies that served as receipts were stored there. Here the 'barons of the Exchequer' conducted the audit and also acted as a court of law. Here the officials of the lower Exchequer counted and tested pennies, cut tallies, and noted down what was paid in.

The relationship between the income recorded on the Pipe Rolls of the Exchequer and the total royal revenue is a hard subject to explore. The king received revenue from his lands outside England. He could take payments directly in his chamber and these might not necessarily go through the Exchequer accounting procedure. Most important, extraordinary taxation, that is, the special levies raised periodically, do not usually show up in the Pipe Rolls. It is only by luck that the figure raised by the tax on income and movable property in 1207—a staggering £60,000—is known. The huge sums

---

[131] *Rolls Fifteenth*, pp. v–vi, viii–ix, 4–45; *Sel. Charters*, pp. 351–3; *Pat. Rolls HIII* 1, pp. 560–1.
[132] PR 12 HII, p. 81.

raised for Richard's ransom have left virtually no documentary trace. Special accounting arrangements were obviously made on such occasions and their records are not preserved, with the exception of a few concerning the tallage of the Jews. In such circumstances, an estimate of the royal revenue can only be a guess. But it is not impossible to guess sensibly.

### The Royal Demesne, 1086–1225

The king was a great landowner, possessing over 18 per cent of the landed estates of the kingdom (by value) at the time of the Domesday survey in 1086. Royal lands of considerable extent were to be found in virtually every county. In 1086 there were four shires in which the king possessed over 30 per cent of the land (by value) and another eight in which he had between 20 and 30 per cent. Almost everywhere he had more than 10 per cent. This meant that the monarchy was drawing revenue from every part of the kingdom and that royal estates gave a local physical focus of royal power everywhere. Unlike his contemporaries in France or Germany, the king of England was not confronted with any large tract of the kingdom in which he was without landed property.

Of course, the geographical distribution of royal estates was not uniform. The old Wessex area was, unsurprisingly, thick with royal manors, but it is noteworthy that royal estates did not thin out significantly as one moved north. Certainly, as the historian William of Malmesbury noted, 'it is well known that the kings of the English and, after them, of the Normans, spend more time in the south than in the north',[133] but this was not reflected in the pattern of land-holding. Norfolk and Derbyshire, for example, counties in which the king was rarely seen, both numbered among the shires where royal estates constituted more than 20 per cent of the total (in both shires manors confiscated from the Anglo-Saxon earls were important constituents of the Conqueror's demesne). Indeed, the royal lands that clustered between the lower Tees and the Cleveland Hills and, on the other coast, those in Furness and the southern edges of the Lake District are among the most northerly estates recorded in Domesday Book.

Apart from Chester and Shropshire, which William the Conqueror had handed over completely to their earls, it was—perhaps unexpectedly—the south-east of England where royal property was thinnest. Royal land represented only 8 per cent of the value of Kent, 7 per cent of Hertfordshire, 1 per cent of Sussex, and less than 0.2 per cent of Middlesex. The paucity of royal land in Kent and Sussex is explained by the fact that the Conqueror had granted vast estates in those counties to his magnates, Odo of Bayeux in Kent

---

[133] W. Malm., *GP* 99 (p. 209).

and the lords of the rapes in Sussex, while in Middlesex and Hertfordshire royal land had not been extensive before the Conquest. Given the scarcity of royal lands in the south-east, it is not surprising that the Norman and Angevin kings had no palaces or hunting-lodges in this corner of their kingdom. Their usual route to their French dominions lay via Winchester through Hampshire, not via the ports of Kent or Sussex.

Because of his enormous estates, the king could draw on the revenues that all great landowners could expect, not only the produce of his farms but also money income from peasant rents and sales of crops and livestock. The usual way of exploiting the royal estates was not to manage them directly by minutely accountable officials but either to take a lump sum from the sheriffs, who would then deal with them, or to lease them out to middlemen or entrepreneurs who would pay a fixed sum and then make all they could from the estate in question. The process is termed 'farming' and the payment made by the sheriffs for the royal manors in their county is known as the county farm. This method of dealing with one's estates was common among all major landowners in the period and had the advantage of producing predictable income without the need for a large or complicated estate administration. The annual county farms for which sheriffs were accountable thus represented primarily a payment in lieu of the royal demesne revenue from a given county, although sheriffs did receive regular income other than that from the royal manors (notably profits from the county court).

The total annual payment due from county farms was somewhat over £10,000. Although there was a tendency for the level of payment to become fixed and customary, it was not impossible to increase farms. By 1160 county farms were almost 20 per cent higher than they had been in 1130.[134] The imposition of increments was another way to squeeze more from the shires. The county farm of Derbyshire and Nottinghamshire, which were treated as a pair, was supplemented from 1170 by an increment equal to about 5 per cent of the original farm. The selling of shrievalties and John's experiment in which custodian sheriffs accounted for their total income (see above, pp. 150–1) are other examples of the way the royal government struggled to rack up this side of its income.

Royal demesne fluctuated. Kings had to exercise patronage, to reward their family, friends, and servants. The gift of royal demesne was one of the most treasured rewards. In the reign of Henry II, the sheriff of Devon was allowed £122. 10s. against the farm of his county for 'lands given to earl Reginald from the manors that pertain to the farm of Devonshire'. Since the total farm of Devon was only £312. 7s. , no less than 40 per cent of the county farm

---

[134] Emilie Amt, *The Accession of Henry II in England: Royal Government Restored, 1149–1159* (Woodbridge, 1993), p. 156.

was going to support Reginald, who was earl of Cornwall and an illegitimate son of Henry I. Cornwall itself was so fully in Reginald's hands that the county did not even account at the Exchequer until after the earl's death in 1175. Alienation of royal demesne had a political purpose—to win support and to encourage service—but it could only serve that purpose by reducing regular royal income.

Land was also always coming into the king's hands, however, either permanently, through confiscation or default of heirs (escheat), or temporarily while the heir was under age or an unmarried woman. These forfeitures, escheats, and wardships represented a considerable source of income and patronage. Estates that came into the king's hands were frequently not farmed by the sheriff but by others, who were individually accountable for them, and might pay a substantial amount. Alternatively, they could be granted out as favours and rewards. The honor of Lancaster, held under the Norman kings by Roger the Poitevin, a member of the great and unruly house of Montgomery, was confiscated by Henry I in 1102 and given as part of his enormous endowment to his nephew Stephen of Blois. Stephen lost control of it during his reign as king, but it was passed on to his son, William of Blois, in 1154. After William's death, it was then in the hands of his widow until 1164. Thereafter it was in royal hands continuously, except for the years 1189–94 when John held it as part of his appanage. It was farmed out for an annual payment of £200 under the Angevins.[135] The honor of Lancaster therefore served alternately as a source of direct revenue for the king and as a component part of a great estate for one of his favoured relatives.

Like other lords, the king had the customary right to impose a tallage on the men of his demesne. This was an arbitrary payment demanded from his own serfs, his townsmen, and, in the case of the king, his Jews. Thus, in 1176, the sheriffs of Cambridgeshire and Huntingdonshire accounted not only for the county farm and other miscellaneous dues, but also for 'the assessment on the king's demesnes'.[136] The borough of Huntingdon made the substantial payment of £16, while £2. 7s. 8d. was levied on the borough of Cambridge. Six rural manors were also tallaged. Four of these are recorded as royal demesne in Domesday Book, so they had been in the king's hands for generations. They paid amounts between two and seven shillings. One manor, Linton, was tallaged three marks (£2), 'while it was in the king's hands'. Linton was a manor of the earldom of Richmond, which was in royal custody during this period. The last, Bottisham, which paid £4. 15s. 4d.—more than the borough of Cambridge—was part of the Giffard honor, that had escheated to the Crown in 1164 and remained in royal hands until Richard I divided it between William Marshal and the earl of Hertford. In all, the tallage of the boroughs,

[135] Sanders, *Baronies*, pp. 126–8.     [136] PR 22 HII, pp. 71–2.

ancient royal demesne manors, and escheats of the two counties brought in more than £26. Tallages provided modest but useful sums, especially if levied frequently. One of John's tallages brought in £8,276.[137]

## Feudal Aids and Incidents

The king of England was not only a landowner but also a lord of vassals and like all lords could expect certain payments from them. A lord had the customary right to seek a money payment ('aid') from his vassals when he knighted his son, married off his daughter, or needed to be ransomed. Thus the knightly tenants of Henry de Ryes, lord of the barony of Hockering in Norfolk, had to pay when his son, Hubert, was knighted, and his daughter married in the late 1160s. Richard, son of Radbod, holder of half a knights' fee, 'gave to Henry de Ryes one mark of silver for the marriage of his daughter'. Alexander of Drayton, holder of four knights' fees, 'gave six marks, three for the marriage of his lord's daughter, and three for his son, Hubert de Ryes'.[138] As a lord, the king was entitled to similar payments, so that the marriage of Henry II's daughter in 1167 could serve as the occasion for a levy of £3,000 on his barons (above, p. 121).

Moreover, a lord could derive financial benefit from incidents in the transmission of his vassal's fief. When a vassal died, the heir had to pay a sum to the lord for recognition of his right to inherit; this was known as a 'relief'. The lord had the rights of wardship (custody of minor heirs) and marriage (control of the marriage of heiresses and minor heirs). The king had the right of wardship in a peculiarly potent form. The custom of 'prerogative wardship' meant that the king claimed the custody of the whole inheritance of a minor heir if any of his land—'even one acre'—were held of the Crown directly.[139] If a man holding fifty knights' fees from some earl and one from the king left a minor heir, the wardship would go to the king, not the earl.

These feudal aids and incidents could be profitable and there was a permanent tension between the desire of the royal government to exploit them to the full and the wish of the king's vassals to render them less onerous, more regular, and better attuned to the interests of the baronial family. As soon as he seized the throne, Henry I sought to win support by offering his baronage 'just and lawful reliefs' and a free and consensual policy on wardship and on the marriage of the ladies of baronial families, especially heiresses.[140] The evidence from Henry's reign, however, does not suggest anything other than the

---

[137] Painter, *John*, p. 126.     [138] *RBE* 1, pp. 400–1; 2, pp. cclxxiii–cclxxv; Sanders, *Baronies*, p. 53.

[139] Glanvill 7. 10 (p. 84); Joc. Brak., p. 58; *Rot. dom.*, pp. 66–7; for an innovative view, S. F. C. Milson, 'The Origin of Prerogative Wardship', in John Hudson and George Garnett (eds.), *Law and Government in Medieval England and Normandy: Essays in Honour of Sir James Holt*, (Cambridge, 1994), pp. 223–44.

[140] Liebermann, *Gesetze* 1, pp. 521–2 (CHn cor); *Sel. Charters*, p. 118; Robertson, *Laws*, pp. 276–8.

usual exploitation of these rights for patronage and income. The Pipe Roll of 1130, the earliest surviving royal accounts, record thousands of pounds in reliefs and in payments to obtain wardships or marriages: Geoffrey de Mandeville owed a relief of £866. 13s. 4d.; the great royal administrator and social climber, Geoffrey de Clinton, paid 80 marks (£53. 6s. 8d.) for the wardship of the young Northamptonshire landowner William de Dive; Ranulf II, the new earl of Chester, was burdened with a debt of £1,000 owing from the relief his late father had promised.[141] Henry's Angevin descendants were just as ready to tap their powers as feudal lords, indeed, increasingly so. The average payment that aristocrats made for consent to marriage was 101 marks under Henry II, 174 marks under Richard I, and 314 marks under John. Altogether John collected over 40,000 marks (about £27,000) from payments for consent to marriage or the right not to marry.[142] Limitations and restrictions on the king's powers to levy reliefs and manipulate wardship and marriage form one of the main themes of Magna Carta.

Also stemming from the king's rights as a feudal lord was the levy known as scutage ('shield money'), a payment made in lieu of a vassal's military service and calculated on the knights' fee. Most major landholders holding their land directly from the king (tenants-in-chief) held their estates by military service, owing a certain number of knights. Thus the royal records of the later twelfth century indicate the earl of Essex owed 60 knights, the earl of Oxford 30, the lords of Wormegay in Norfolk 15, and so on. On occasion this service might be required or offered in what was presumably its original form, the dispatch of mounted warriors, but far more commonly the obligation was commuted to a monetary payment. Scutage was levied increasingly frequently over the course of the Angevin period. Henry II imposed one every four or five years, Richard one every three years, John one every eighteen months. Rates also increased. Most of Henry II's scutages were levied at two marks (£1. 6s. 8d.) per knights' fee, most of John's at twice that rate.

Once tenants-in-chief received a demand for scutage, they naturally raised the money from their own tenants. In due course the obligation to contribute to scutage became associated with the land itself, so that a plot of land could be granted on the terms that it 'pays to the chief lord two pence toward a scutage of twenty shillings [per fee] and proportionately more or less', or a tenement of forty acres be held 'for the service of a twentieth part of a knight's fee, namely paying twelve pence toward a scutage of twenty shillings and proportionately more or less'.[143] Scutage was not in principle a general land tax, but it came to resemble one in practice.

---

[141] PR 31 HI, pp. 55, 83, 110.          [142] Waugh, *Lordship*, pp. 157–60.
[143] *Feet of Fines of the Tenth Year of the Reign of King Richard I* (PRS 24; 1900), nos. 34, 102, pp. 24, 70.

## Taxation

The king's income was thus in part like that of any lord but in part it was also distinctively royal, for he took money from his subjects as their king as well as making demands upon his vassals as their lord or expropriating the property of his serfs, townsmen, and Jews as their master. England was unusual in Europe at this time in having a land tax that was in principle universal, falling not simply on the king's own estates but on all land in England. The geld, as it was called, had originally been created to supply tribute to the invading Danes, but showed the tendency that all emergency taxation has—to endure. 'England suffers this misfortune to this day,' wrote one cleric in the reign of Rufus. 'It would be a happy, rich and sweet country if it were not for these royal exactions.'[144]

The geld was assessed on the hide (or, in the northern Danelaw, its equivalent, the carucate). This was a unit of assessment dating back to the early days of Anglo-Saxon England. The first question in the Domesday inquest, after those asking the name of the manor and its tenant, was 'how many hides are there?'[145] Most entries in Domesday Book indeed begin with the name of the manor followed by the number of hides. Because the hide was a unit of fiscal assessment, rather than an area (although it is conventionally equated with 120 acres), manors that were exempt from taxation, such as some favoured royal estates, had no hides. It was also possible for the hidation to change: 'The monks [of Winchester] hold Havant from the bishopric of Winchester; they have always held it; in the time of king Edward it was assessed at ten hides, now at seven hides.'[146] Such exemptions and variations mean that the assessment of England in hides was not a perfect reflection of its wealth. On the other hand, it is fairly well established that hidation was not arbitrary. It did roughly correspond to wealth and population. A large, rich estate would thus tend to pay higher taxes.

In the Norman period geld was usually levied annually at a rate of two shillings per hide, bringing in £2,400 in 1130.[147] Exemptions could be granted by the king as a matter of favour and some, such as the barons of the Exchequer, claimed them as a right. These exemptions could be substantial—they amounted to over 40 per cent of the total amount due in 1130—and were a relatively painless way of exercising royal patronage. After 1162 the general land tax disappeared for a generation, but in 1194, as the royal government employed every expedient to raise money for king Richard's enormous ransom, it was revived under the name of hidage or carucage, at the customary rate of two shillings per hide. It was levied again in 1198, 1200,

---

[144] Hermann the Archdeacon, *Mir. sancti Edmundi* 3 (*Mem. Edm.* 1, p. 33).
[145] *ICC*, p. 97.     [146] *DB* 1, 43 (Ham. 3. 27).     [147] Green, *Govt.*, pp. 69, 223.

1217, 1220, and, with a more restricted liability, 1224, but this was the last occasion it was imposed. In 1220, at the familiar rate of two shillings per hide, it produced £3,400.[148] Inflation means that this represents less in real terms than the £2,400 of ninety years earlier, but it was still a useful tax that could be assessed simply.

Details of the assessment method of the carucage of 1198 are given by the chronicler Roger of Howden. A clerk and a knight were sent to each county and, sitting alongside the sheriff and a select group of local knights, they summoned three groups of representatives from the county: the seneschals of barons with lands in the county; the lord or bailiff, the reeve, and four 'legal men, free or villein' from each township; and two knights from each hundred. All swore to give a truthful record of how many carucates of cultivable land there were in each township, working with a carucate of 100 acres. They were also to specify how much was in the lord's demesne, how much held by villeins, how much had been granted to the church. All this information was to be written down in rolls, one copy of which was to be held by the clerk sent out by the king, one by the knight, one by the sheriff, while the barons' seneschals had a copy of the section relevant to their lands. The tax was to be levied at 5 shillings per carucate. The knights of the hundred and the hundred bailiffs were to be responsible for transmitting the money to the sheriff, who, in turn, would answer to the Exchequer.[149]

The procedure envisaged for collecting the 1198 carucage demonstrates the powerful impact of royal government, the central role of written records and the way that large numbers of local people, from knights to villeins, could be harnessed to the tasks of the central administration. Even in a small county, such as Bedfordshire, with about 150 townships and a dozen hundreds, the summons would bring in almost a thousand men. The rolls recording the local resources would be available at the Exchequer, so that the sheriff's payments could be monitored. Even though some counties negotiated the payment of a lump sum instead of the onerous inquisition, the central truth remains that a kingdom of 50,000 square miles was being effectively assessed and taxed at central command.[150]

A different form of tax, that required a complex mechanism of assessment but could produce very high returns, was the percentage levy on movable wealth and income. The principle was the same as that of the Church's tithe, and royal taxation of this type was indeed first introduced to pay for the pious enterprise of the crusade. This was in 1166, when Henry II instituted a tax on movables and revenues 'for the defence and help of the eastern church and

---

[148] *Rolls Fifteenth*, p. iii.      [149] R. Howd. 4, pp. 46–7.
[150] For payments 'to be free of the carucage inquisition', see PR 1 John, pp. 16, 29, 36, 58, 78, 84, 98, 113, 217, 227, 259, 288.

land', and similar levies were raised in 1185 and 1188.[151] A tax on movables and income at the astounding rate of 25 per cent was imposed as part of the funding of Richard's ransom, while John raised such taxes on several occasions. In 1207 a 'thirteenth', i.e. a tax of about 8 per cent, was levied on both income and movable property. Despite protests and evasion, it yielded £60,000, a huge amount when we consider that the annual ordinary royal income in John's reign averaged about £35,000.[152]

One of the earliest instances of this new sort of tax was the levy of 1188, the so-called 'Saladin Tithe', intended to support the crusade and comprising a tenth of all revenues and movable property. Certain goods were exempt, including a knight's horse and arms, the clergy's books and vestments, and gems, and a blanket exemption was granted to those going on crusade themselves. The bishops were to proclaim the tithe through the parishes and threaten defaulters with excommunication. The money was to be collected in each parish in the presence of the parish priest, the rural dean, a Templar, a Hospitaller, a servant of the king, a clerk of the king, a servant of the local baron, a clerk of the local baron, and a clerk of the bishop while 'if anyone gives less than he ought, according to their knowledge, four or six lawful men shall be chosen from the parish, who shall declare upon oath what amount he ought to have declared'. The chief men of London, York, and the other towns were summoned before the king in person to pay their tithe.[153] These details show both the difficulties in getting a reliable assessment and also the importance of the Church, in announcing the tax, providing the territorial framework, and much of the personnel for its collection and in enforcing it.

The assessment and collection of such taxes meant that the royal government became concerned with the everyday details of the lives of men and women at almost all social levels. The records of the assessment of the fifteenth of 1225, mentioned above (p. 158) show this minute scrutiny:

This is the value of the moveable property of Sir Philip of Kyme by the oath of four law-worthy men. He has 14 oxen worth 4s. each, 7 cows worth 3s. each, 4 heifers worth 2s. each and 2 two-year old bullocks worth 12d. each. The total of his moveable property is £4. 7s. The fifteenth of this is 5s. 9½d.

This is the value of the moveable property of the men of Kyme by the oath of four law-worthy men. Lina the widow has an ox worth 4s. and a cow worth 3s. The fifteenth of this is 5½d. Roger son of William Grant has 7s. 1d. The fifteenth of this is 5½d. . . . [154]

The list then goes on to give details of 56 peasant taxpayers.

[151] Gerv. Cant., p. 198.
[152] Rot. obl., p. 459; Mark Ormrod, 'Royal Finance in Thirteenth-Century England', *Thirteenth-Century England*, 5 (1993), pp. 141–64, at p. 148.
[153] *Gesta Hen. II* 2, pp. 31–3; R. Howd. 2, pp. 335–8.          [154] *Rolls Fifteenth*, p. 4.

Such powerfully intrusive royal taxation relied on the efforts of a cadre of administrators. One of them was Alexander of Pointon, who, with four colleagues, was appointed to gather the fifteenth of 1225 in Lincolnshire. He was a local landowner, but not a great one, and had plenty of experience of the workings of royal justice and administration. He had served as a judge regularly from 1202, taken part in various inquests during John's reign, and acted as custodian of lands in royal hands. He had already been collector of the thirteenth of 1207 and the carucage of 1220 in Lincolnshire. He thus combined long administrative experience in the royal service with an established but not predominant position in his local county. He was typical in this respect of the men who were to run England for the next 500 years.

One other fiscal innovation of the Angevin period, John's customs on imports and exports, imposed in 1202 and abandoned in 1207, are another example of his precocious ingenuity in administrative and financial matters—in the later Middle Ages customs were to be one of the mainstays of English royal finance. The levy consisted of a fifteenth of the value of all imports and exports and was collected by specially appointed commissioners. John probably got about £2,500 a year from customs duties while his experiment was in force.[155]

## Income from Justice

The king was the fount of justice but his waters did not run freely. There was no universal right of unimpeded access to royal justice. The royal writs that initiated many kinds of legal action had to be paid for. By the end of the twelfth century the routine judicial writs, 'writs of course', as they were called, could, indeed, be had for a relatively small fee—sometimes as little as half a mark (6s. 8d.)—but that fee had to be paid. Moreover, some writs 'of course' were much more costly than half a mark. The first Pipe Roll of John's reign (1199) lists eleven debts owed for having a 'writ of right', a writ that initiated a suit concerning the rightful possession of a piece of land. Griffin, son of Walter, had offered a mail-coat to have a writ concerning a fief in Devon. One debtor was paying off the last instalment of a forty shilling offer. The remaining nine had promised payments totalling £44, an average of nearly £5 each.[156] A dispute over one knight's fee (an estate supposed to support a knight, see below, pp. 222–4), which many of these cases were, thus required an initial outlay of the equivalent of half a year's income from that estate. It was doubtless worth it if you won. The king would profit in any event.

One litigant who recorded his wearisome path through the Angevin judicial machinery was Richard de Anstey, who claimed and won the right to

[155] Painter, *John*, pp. 136–9.
[156] PR 1 John, pp. 10, 41, 43, 46, 154, 170, 197, 224, 234, 248, 253.

inherit his uncle's lands in a suit that lasted from 1158 to 1163.[157] He began the case by sending a messenger to the king, who was then in Normandy, 'for a royal writ to bring my opponents to court'. Five years later, in the royal hunting-lodge of Woodstock, judgment was given in his favour. Much of the intervening litigation had taken place in the church courts, but the suit began and ended with the king—and with payments to the king. Richard made a detailed record of his expenses in pursuing the case, in court payments, travelling costs, and bribes. They totalled £344. 7s. 4d. The largest single item was an offering of 100 marks (£66. 13s. 4d.) to the king.

Some proffers could be even higher. Barons were willing to pay large amounts to have royal writs or to obtain royal inquests into their claims. A sum of 500 marks (£333. 6s. 8d.) was agreed between Roland of Galloway and the king for an inquest into his wife's rights to lands in the earldom of Huntingdon.[158] Richard of Clare, earl of Hertford, offered king John £100 for a writ to initiate proceedings about a manor he claimed as an inheritance.[159] Another of John's barons, William de Braose, also offered £100, 'to have the king's record and right judgment concerning the case between him and Henry de Nonant about Totnes'. The agreement in this instance was that the case would be heard before the king in person, on a specified date (17 April 1200) and that the sum of £100 would be payable even if William lost the case; if he won, however, he would pay the king 700 marks (£466. 13s. 4d.).[160]

These proffers of hundreds of pounds arose because the king's courts decided the descent of land, including the great estates of the aristocracy, in cases of dispute. They also exercised criminal jurisdiction and this too had its profits, although usually modest ones in comparison. A microcosmic example of the profitability of royal criminal justice is provided by the case of Walter, son of Robert, accused of killing his brother Andrew in 1202. Walter fled rather than face the charge. He was a member of the frankpledge of Withern (Lincs.), who consequently had to pay a fine of £1 for failing to detain him. Since he was a fugitive, Walter's chattels, valued at 13s. 8d., were forfeit to the Crown and were delivered to Ralph, the reeve of Brattleby. Ralph, however, failed to produce them when the royal justices arrived, and was himself fined 3s. 4d. for this default (although subsequently pardoned). Because the English descent of the victim, Andrew, was not demonstrated ('presentment of Englishry'), the whole wapentake was liable to the *murdrum* fine (see above, p. 1). This amounted to £5. This one violent crime thus produced a total of £6. 17s. in fines and forfeitures for the Crown—enough to buy a couple of fine war-horses.[161]

---

[157] Patricia Barnes, 'The Anstey Case', in Patricia Barnes and C. F. Slade (eds.), *A Medieval Miscellany for Doris May Stenton* (PRS n.s. 36; 1962 for 1960), pp. 1–24.

[158] *Rot. obl.*, p. 84.    [159] Ibid., p. 178.    [160] Ibid., p. 46.

[161] *Earliest Lincs. Ass. Rolls*, pp. 98, 171–2.

### 'The Forest'

A special place in the machinery of justice was occupied by the Forest. This did not mean 'woodland', but 'places under the Forest Law' (see below, pp. 673–4). Its primary purpose was to protect the king's hunting, but the courts and justices of the Forest did their job with a very broad interpretation of their task. Forest was an important source of cash as well as venison. Fines for such offences as killing deer, clearing woodland, or keeping hounds in the royal Forest were high. The Pipe Roll of 1130, the only one surviving from the reign of Henry I, records total debts for Forest pleas of over £1,400.[162] Forty-five years later, Henry II's Forest eyre of 1175 showed that Forest jurisdiction continued to be profitable: this special judicial visitation raised over £12,000 from fines for infringements and offences.[163]

The methods employed by Henry's Chief Forester, Alan de Neville, brought him a reputation for a harshness verging on extortion. Even the chief justiciar, Robert, earl of Leicester, complained of 'the pressing exactions of Alan's men [*Alaniorum*] of which the king was quite unaware'.[164] King Henry's reservations about his servant's conduct are also shown in a story recorded by the monks of Battle Abbey, who had themselves suffered from Alan's activities, but it is a story that also indicates that the king's distaste did not extend to refusing the profits that accrued. After Alan's death, according to the tale, some monks went to the king to request that his body be buried in their abbey, hoping, supposedly, to obtain some of the Forester's wealth this way. Henry replied: 'I will have his money, you can have his body, the demons of hell his soul.'[165] Alan's was a name that endured beyond the grave, for even in 1218 the local jurors of Huntingdonshire were complaining about the bad customs he had introduced fifty years before.[166]

One sign of the resentment that the Forest created is the willingness of county and local communities to pay for their area to be freed from Forest Law. Such disafforestation could be expensive. In 1190 the knights of Surrey paid 200 marks (£133. 6s. 8d.) to Richard I 'to be free of all that pertains to the Forest, from the river Wey to Kent and from the Guildford road southwards' and in 1201 the county had to offer John 300 marks (£200) for a confirmation of his brother's charter.[167] The continual pressure from the localities explains the appearance, in times of royal weakness, of concessions such as that of king Stephen—'I release and grant to the churches and the kingdom all the Forests that king Henry added'—or that conveyed in the brusque words of Magna Carta, clause 47: 'All Forests that have been created in our time shall

---

[162] PR 31 HI, pp. 32, 77, 106, 153; Green, *Govt.*, p. 225.
[163] Charles R. Young, *The Royal Forests of Medieval England* (Leicester, 1979), pp. 23–4, 39.
[164] *Dial. scacc.*, pp. 58–9.  [165] *Battle Chron.*, p. 222.  [166] King, *Peterborough*, p. 72.
[167] PR 2 RI, p. 155; *Rot. obl.*, p. 157.

be disafforested immediately.' In times of royal strength—that is, most of the time—the royal Forest was not only the theatre of royal recreation but also a significant source of royal income.

## A Case Study: Staffordshire

To illustrate the material resources and financial administration of the English kings in this period we may take the Pipe Roll accounts for a reasonably manageable county, Staffordshire, at two separate points in time.[168] The first, the fifth year of Henry II (1158–9), saw the sheriff, Robert of Stafford, paying to the treasury £55. 15s. 10d. as a contribution towards his county farm. This was in assayed money (i.e. its silver content had been tested and a discount made for light coin, etc.). Against the farm of his county he could also claim various allowances, either in payments made during the course of the year at the king's command or in the value of royal manors that had previously been his responsibility but were now in others' hands.

Under the first heading came the payment of one mark (13s. 4d.) to the Templars, a fixed charge on every English county under the Angevins; the wages of the keeper of the royal hunting-lodge at Cannock Chase, totalling £1. 10s. 5d., i.e. a penny a day; work on the king's new hunting-lodge at Radmore and its enclosures, costing £25. 2s. 4d.; and a gift of twenty marks (£13. 6s. 8d.) to Geoffrey Marmion. Under the latter heading, alienated royal lands, there were discounted £10 for lands in Tardebigge given to the Cistercians of Bordesley (although Tardebigge was in Worcestershire it had been the responsibility of the sheriff of Staffordshire since at least the reign of William I); £8 for lands in Penkridge held by Walter Hose; and £30 for lands in Trentham, which was being 'farmed' (leased) by the sheriff of Worcester. The total of these allowances came to £88. 12s. 9d. This, however, was not assayed money but simple coin, and the standard Exchequer procedure was to discount it at 5 per cent before crediting it to the sheriff. Once this had been done, the new total (£84. 4s. 2d.), added to the amount the sheriff had already paid in assayed money (£55. 15s. 10d.), amounted to exactly £140, the usual county farm of Staffordshire in this period.

The sheriff was also responsible for collecting taxes and 1158–9 saw the heavy burden of the royal *donum* ('gift'!) levied to pay for Henry II's campaign against Toulouse. Much of the weight of this fell on the church, as is reflected by the hundred marks (£66. 13s. 4d.) that the sheriff of Staffordshire paid in from the bishop of Chester's *donum*. The bishop's knights also had to pay, at the rate of two marks per knight's fee. Of the thirty marks (£20) they owed, £17 was paid, and the remaining amount due from three knights, Henry fitz

---

[168] For the following, PR 5 HII, pp. 28–9.

Gerald, Geoffrey Marmion, and Roger of Samford, was pardoned on the king's written instructions (Marmion was obviously in favour for some reason, perhaps because he had provided military service in the Toulouse campaign). The boroughs of Stafford and Tamworth contributed payments, also called *donum*, of £10 and £5, respectively, while the moneyers of Stafford paid a mark, probably connected with the recoinage of the previous year. The last item that Robert of Stafford accounted for was an unexplained debt of forty marks owed by Bertram de Verdon, a local landowner who was himself eventually to be an Angevin sheriff and administrator. Of his debt, eighteen marks (£12) was paid, twenty marks pardoned, and two marks owing.

This summary of the Staffordshire account for 1159 shows the way the English monarchy could draw on the local resources of the country to fund central political and military endeavours. If we wish to calculate the overall contribution made by the county to royal revenue in current coin, we know that the farm of £140 of assayed money represents £147. 7s. 4d. of coin at the usual rate of discount and of this £48 has to be deducted for alienated royal lands. If we add to the resulting sum of £99. 7s. 4d. the proceeds of the *donum* for Toulouse and the *donum* from the boroughs at £98. 13s. 4d. and the miscellaneous income from the moneyers and Bertram de Verdon at £12. 13s. 4d., we reach a total of £210. 14s. that the sheriff of Staffordshire extracted from his county for his royal master in 1159. This is not a very significant proportion of total royal income accounted for at the Exchequer, which amounted to over £19,000 in 1159, but the analysis demonstrates the meticulousness and thoroughness of the royal financial administration, which cast its eye on the penny a day for the keeper of the king's hunting-lodge just as it did on the hefty payment from the bishop of Chester. Revenue squeezed from the farmers and traders of Staffordshire was being used to pay for the activities of Henry II's mercenaries in the Toulousain, 700 miles away.

The 1159 Pipe Roll account also sheds some light on the fortunes of royal estates in this period. The three royal manors which the sheriff of Staffordshire could claim as deductions (Tardebigge, Trentham, and Penkridge) had passed out of his hands in different ways. All three had been recorded as royal estates in Domesday Book. Tardebigge was probably granted away by king Stephen, since it was the property of his favourite, Waleran de Meulan, by 1138, when Waleran gave it to his new abbey of Bordesley. Consequently the Angevin opponents of Stephen were in a slightly delicate position. They did not want the opprobrium of disendowing the Cistercians of Bordesley but nor were they willing to accept the validity of Stephen's acts. They found a solution by becoming patrons of Bordesley themselves, claiming it as their own foundation and recognizing the permanent loss of Tardebigge to the Cistercians. Henry II's mother, the empress Matilda, describes herself as foundress of the abbey in a charter of 1141. The lost estate was then recorded on the Pipe Rolls as an allowance against the sheriff's farm right through the Angevin period.[169]

Some of the revenue from Trentham had also been diverted to the Church. The estate had come into the hands of the earls of Chester at some point in the period 1086–1153, again in all likelihood during Stephen's reign, and earl Ranulf made a grant from it on his deathbed in 1153, giving a hundred shillings revenue there 'that king Henry [I] used to have' to the Augustinians of Trentham. Although Henry II succeeded in regaining the manor at the start of his reign, he acknowledged the grant that the canons had received from it, just as he did that to the monks of Bordesley. The hundred shillings represented one-sixth of the annual farm of the manor, and other alienations followed, so that by 1189 the money paid in from Trentham represented only half of the total farm. Trentham was farmed by a succession of farmers over the reign of Henry II but the hundred shillings for the canons of Trentham was regularly noted. As in the case of Tardebigge, a grant by an encroaching baron of Stephen's reign had resulted in the permanent transfer of royal demesne to a religious house.[170]

In contrast, Penkridge passed from the royal demesne into the possession of a lay aristocrat, Walter Hose. There is no evidence as to how he acquired it, but he had it at the beginning of Henry II's reign and kept it until 1172. Then, although Walter had a son, the manor returned into the king's hands and remained there, being regularly tallaged, until 1207, when Hugh Hose, Walter's son, offered the king 200 marks ($£133. 13s. 4d.$) and two palfreys to have his father's manor. Its value was now estimated at £10, an increase of 25 per cent since his father's time. Hugh was not to have Penkridge for long. It was taken from him during the year 1209–10 and by 1212 he was in the king's prison. Hugh was not only lord of Penkridge but also a baron of Meath and he seems to have been a victim of king John's punitive expedition to Ireland in 1210, a campaign that ended with the expulsion of the de Lacy lord of Meath, Hugh's feudal superior. Hugh Hose was eventually pardoned and restored to his Irish lands, but before that he was, we may presume, forced to grant away Penkridge to the archbishop of Dublin, one of John's most reliable officials.[171]

Of these three estates, recorded as royal in 1086, two (Tardebigge and Penkridge) had thus passed out of the king's hands by the end of our period, and one (Trentham) had been permanently diminished in value by grants made from it. The bulk of the losses occurred in Stephen's reign. The beneficiaries were religious houses and also, eventually, the family of a royal administrator. Yet the story is not simply of lands drifting out of royal control.

---

[169] *RRAN* 3, nos. 115–16, pp. 42–3; *Cal. Ch. Rolls* 2, pp. 63–5; *Monasticon* 5, pp. 409–10.

[170] *Chester Charters*, no. 117, p. 132; 'Chartulary of the Austin Priory of Trentham', ed. F. Parker, *CHS* 11 (1890), pp. 293–336, at pp. 300–1; *VCH Staffordshire* 3, pp. 255–6.

[171] *Bk. Fees* 1, p. 143; *Rot. obl.*, pp. 403, 471; *Rot. chart.*, p. 218; *Rot. litt. claus.* 1, p. 223.

We have been following three estates which we know left the hands of the local sheriff at some point and such alienations have to be balanced by the lands that came into royal possession, for there was an unending fluctuation in the royal estate, gains as well as losses.

Moreover, two additional points are worth making. First, we should note the tenacity with which the royal administration kept record of the originally royal nature of these lands. If we look at the Pipe Roll for the fourth year of Henry III (1219–20), for example, we find the sheriff of Staffordshire dutifully recording 'to the monks of Bordesley £10 in assayed money in Tardebigge, to the canons of Trentham one hundred shillings . . . in Penkridge £10 . . .'[172] Tardebigge had been lost to the Crown eighty years before and, in the 'undying hand' of a religious corporation, was unlikely to be recovered, but its ancient status as a royal manor was preserved in the records of the Exchequer. Second, although Penkridge did eventually cease to be a royal possession, the Angevin kings had had plenty from it: perhaps it had been a usurpation of Walter Hose's in the reign of Stephen, but perhaps it had been his reward as an Angevin follower. From 1172 to 1207, back in royal hands, it provided regular income to the Crown. Hugh Hose only recovered it by making substantial payments and his tenure was short. Eventually the estate ended up as part of the reward of an important royal administrator, a piece of patronage that was essential to maintain the Angevin administration as it was. Giving land away was not necessarily a sign of weakness.

It would be laborious to analyse another year in the same way as we have just done, but it is worth looking quickly at a later Pipe Roll account for Staffordshire to point out changes over the Angevin period. Forty years after Robert of Stafford rendered his account for 1158–9, another Staffordshire sheriff accounted at the Exchequer. The Pipe Roll for 1198–9 gives details of the traditional £140 farm, with allowances for Tardebigge and Trentham, and also for payments for work on the county jails and the castle at Newcastle under Lyme. The largest allowance was £22. 13s. that the sheriff had paid out to restock the royal manors with cattle, swine, and horses. The shire farm, however, was dwarfed by the other items of account. A total of £254. 7s. 6d. was paid in over and above the farm, and debts of £332. 19s. 3.5 d. were also recorded, these items altogether amounting to four times the county farm. This increase in the size of business is reflected in the size of the records: the Pipe Roll for 1159 consists of eighteen parchment sheets, that for 1199 of thirty-eight. Some of this non-farm income was made up of levies, such as the scutages that fell on the knights' fees and tallages of the royal manors; much of it came from the separate farms of the royal forests in Staffordshire; and a substantial proportion resulted from judicial fines and from money

172  PR 4 HIII, p. 171.

offered to have royal favour—ranging from fines of a mark or two for breach of the Assize of Wine to the £100 that Philip of Kinver had to promise (and £50 of which he paid) in order to have his tenure of the king's forest of Kinver renewed at John's accession.

This comparison of the accounts of 1159 and 1199 thus shows how the financial business of the Angevin administration increased in scale and diversified in scope, with miscellaneous proffers and agreements and judicial profits figuring more largely in the later than the early period. One of the Angevins' most observant, if also most opinionated, courtiers, Gerald of Wales, noticed that Henry II and his sons 'took care to make up in incidental payments what they lacked in regular income, relying more on casual than on established sources of revenue'.[173] At all times, however, the English monarchy rested on the twin foundations of great domainal wealth and the assured ability to tax its subjects.

## Total Royal Revenue

The royal demesne, feudal incidents, taxation, and justice—these formed the main sources of the king's revenue. Income from abbeys and bishoprics during vacancies between incumbents was also important. But a true balance sheet for the Norman or Angevin monarchs would include many things now unknown and imponderable: the value of the thousands of deer, boar, fowl, and other game they brought back from the hunt, meeting the protein needs of the court at no actual outlay; the gifts they received and did not order to be written down in their rolls; the profits of war. Treasure trove was the king's. Richard I died pursuing it. John had excavations undertaken at Corbridge in 1201, when he heard that treasure lay buried there, but turned up only ancient inscriptions.[174] If he had found something more valuable, it would doubtless have eluded the calculations of modern historians.

These unrecorded payments and passing windfalls cannot be measured, but the revenue accounted for at the Exchequer can. This was done for the whole of the reigns of Henry II and Richard and for sample years of John's reign by the historian J. H. Ramsay and the results published in 1925.[175] His efforts have been subject to numerous criticisms but perhaps unfairly. When his totals are compared with those of the most meticulous recent research, the difference in totals is never more than 9 per cent and often far less.[176] Thus, even if we assume that the errors are Ramsay's rather than the later

---

[173] Gerald, *Prin.* 3. 30 (p. 316).    [174] R. Howd. 4, p. 157.

[175] James Ramsay, *A History of the Revenues of the Kings of England 1066–1399* (2 vols.; Oxford, 1925).

[176] A comparison of Ramsay's sums 'paid in and accounted for' and 'payments and expenditure' in Emilie Amt, *The Accession of Henry II in England: Royal Government Restored, 1149–1159* (Woodbridge, 1993), pp. 194–7, reveals the following differences: 2 HII—4%; 3 HII—4%; 4 HII—9%; 5 HII—7%; Ramsay and Green, *Govt.*, p. 223–5 ('amount paid' and 'expenditure') disagree by only 0.028% for 31 HI!

historians', his figures offer a reasonable guide to trends and totals, with the advantage that they cover a long period (1155–1214). Ramsay sensibly defined revenue as 'money paid in' plus 'local payments allowed for', excluding debt, the value of alienated demesne, etc. His totals are shown in Figure 3.

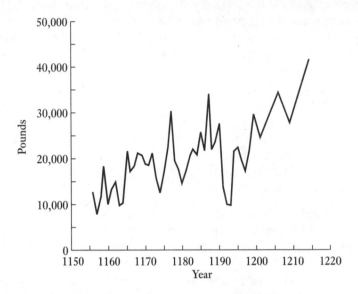

FIGURE 3. *Royal revenues accounted for at the Exchequer, 1155–1214*

The pattern is clear: a long-term increase with marked annual fluctuations. The average annual income for the decade 1165–74 is about £18,500, that for the five sample years of John's reign (1199, 1201, 1206, 1209, 1214) about £32,000, an increase of 73 per cent over 40 years. It is necessary, of course, to take account of inflation. Between the 1160s and the second decade of the thirteenth century the price of oxen increased by 128 per cent, the price of wheat by 138 per cent.[177] The swiftest price increases came in John's reign. It is clear that royal revenue from the sources that accounted at the Exchequer was completely failing to keep pace with inflation. John's Exchequer received an amount three-quarters again as high as his father's had in the earlier part of his reign, but food and livestock were costing well over twice as much.

The survival of the solitary Pipe Roll from 1130 and the work of David Carpenter on the Pipe Rolls of the minority of Henry III enable the picture to be extended. In 1130, £24,500 was paid in or accounted for at the Exchequer. Henry I therefore had a level of Exchequer income in that year that his grandson only matched in three years of his reign (1177, 1185, and 1187) and that

[177] Hallam, *Agrarian Hist.*, pp. 733–6, 747–55.

was only attained once in the reign of Richard (1190). It is only with John that the level of 1130 is regularly surpassed. The civil war of 1215–17 then resulted in a dramatic collapse of royal revenue. In the first six years of the 1220s (1220–5), the average amount accounted for at the Exchequer was about £12,700, about half that of a century earlier (and representing, of course, an even greater drop in purchasing power).[178] The ordinary income of the Crown not only swam against the stream of inflation but could also be sent swirling by the sudden eddies of political crisis.

Total royal revenue was obviously higher than the sums accounted for at the Exchequer. In John's reign, for instance, it has been estimated that the royal government had an average annual income, from England alone, of almost £60,000.[179] This enormous amount was mainly stimulated by, and spent on, the king's war with Philip Augustus. The pressure that the kings of England felt to defend their territories was transmitted to their subjects as a painstaking and unwearying pursuit of their silver pennies.

## 8. COURTS AND JUDGMENTS

In Norman England, as in Anglo-Saxon England, disputes could come for settlement and offenders for discipline to various kinds of forum: manor court, hundred court, county court, borough court, feudal court, church court, and the king's court. The local courts of hundred and shire had a varied jurisdiction. The hundred court was the place where, twice a year, the tithings—the collective surety-groups into which men were gathered—were checked for completeness. It also dealt with lesser cases, both disputes over property and minor wrongs, such as the charge brought, about 1110, against the miller Gamel of Sutton Courtenay, who allegedly had the trick of stealing turves at night from the manor of Culham, across the Thames in Oxfordshire. Culham belonged to the monks of Abingdon and they raised the issue in what must have been for them the obvious court of first instance. 'When he was accused of this outrage in the hundred court and was unable to deny it, he had to suffer the force of the law. The justices of the hundred court decreed that he should pay the abbot and the church 150 pence in compensation.' In the event, the abbot showed mercy and remitted most of the payment, 'as witnessed by all who were in the hundred court'.[180]

The county court originally had a wide jurisdiction in suits of many types. Henry I ruled that disputes over land between the vassals of two different

---

[178] David Carpenter, *The Minority of Henry III* (London, 1990), p. 413.

[179] Deduced from Mark Ormrod, 'Royal Finance in Thirteenth-Century England', *Thirteenth-Century England*, 5 (1993), pp. 155, 162 (gross).

[180] *Abingdon Chron.* 2, p. 118.

lords should be heard in the county court. The sentence of outlawry could only be proclaimed there. Before the reign of Henry II, who instituted important changes in legal procedure, the county court was one of the busiest courts, where most disputes over land and most serious criminal cases came. This was the regular local forum where men such as Hervey de Glanville (above, pp. 152–3) learned and transmitted the traditional legal customs of the county.

The lord's feudal court was the court for his men. 'Every lord', wrote the author of *The Laws of Henry I*, 'is allowed to summon his men, so that he may do justice upon them in his court.'[181] This right was recognized by the king, himself the greatest of lords. Henry I ruled that, in disputes between the vassals of his barons, 'the case shall be heard in the court of their lord'.[182] The lord was a master of a household and retinue and this position entailed jurisdictional authority. 'He was a member of the household of the earl of Gloucester', records the royal plea roll for Gloucestershire about one defendant in 1221, 'and hence under the jurisdiction of the earl'.[183] Not only did the aristocrats and great ecclesiastics possess an intrinsic judicial authority over their vassals, tenants, and retainers, they might also exercise wider rights over whole areas, like hundreds that had come under their control, and over men who were not their direct dependants. This so-called franchisal jurisdiction usually covered petty theft and affrays, as well as conveying the right to hang thieves who were caught red-handed, but it could be even more extensive. In his court for the 'eight and a half hundreds' of west Suffolk, the abbot of Bury St Edmunds dealt with every kind of case, including rape and (probably) homicide. His authority extended over all freeholders in those hundreds.

The king himself was the highest source of justice. He could pronounce judgment in person, with the advice of his counsellors, or through justices and commissioners specially delegated to try cases. Because he was frequently overseas, the practice arose of having a chief justiciar, who could stand in for him, in judicial as in other matters. Roger, bishop of Salisbury, the chief minister of Henry I, is a precursor. In the Angevin period there were formally appointed ministers with the title chief justiciar, men like Ranulf de Glanville, who held the office from 1179 to 1189, and is recorded issuing writs in his own name and presiding over sessions of the Exchequer and the king's chief court at Westminster.

Royal justices were equally active in the localities. In the time of Henry I there are references to justices who appear to have been based permanently in

<hr />

[181] *LHP* 55. 1 (p. 172).
[182] Liebermann, *Gesetze* 1, p. 524; *Sel. Charters*, p. 122; Robertson, *Laws*, p. 286.
[183] *Pleas of the Crown for the County of Gloucester . . . 1221*, ed. F. W. Maitland (London, 1884), no. 234, p. 56.

the counties. Others were sent out for special occasions. At some point between 1114 and 1126 a quarrel between the Benedictine monks of Burton upon Trent and their neighbour, the baron Robert de Ferrers, required such intervention. The document recording the settlement of the dispute begins, 'This is the agreement that was made, before many witnesses and great men, between Robert de Ferrers and Geoffrey, abbot of Burton. There was great discord between them over part of a wood that the monks of Burton claimed, so much so that word came to king Henry.' The witnesses to the document include two of the king's greatest men, Robert, bishop of Chester (the local diocesan), and William Peverel, lord of the Peak, 'whom the king sent to arrange this agreement'. The settlement had been concluded in Robert de Ferrers' chief castle at Tutbury and then ratified in the chapter house at Burton. Robert promised to be 'friend and guardian' of the monks, the monks promised to pray for him and his family; he admitted their right to the disputed wood, but they agreed to rent it to him. A dispute between two of the king's tenants-in-chief—for Henry I certainly regarded Burton abbey as held from him—had thus been resolved by an ad hoc commission of great men sent out to quieten the region.

The various courts, local, seignorial, and royal, were interlinked. Cases could be removed from a seignorial court to a county court through the process termed 'tolt'. Many cases that began in the county court could be transferred to the royal justices, by means of the writ known, from its opening word, as *pone* ('place'). Royal justices often sat in the county court, presiding over special sessions. In 1155 the earl of Hereford wrote to the newly crowned Henry II, informing him that he and the whole hundred of Upper Whitstone in Gloucestershire testified that a disputed stretch of land called 'The Ridge' lay in the abbot of Gloucester's township of Standish. Therefore, he concluded, 'it seems just that the abbot should have his court there, or else the case should come before your justice in the shire, where the truth of the matter may be examined by the county court.'[184] Here the right to hold a seignorial court was upheld by the hundred, while the prospect was envisaged of a further decision, made before the royal justice in the county court. The various courts neither operated as manifest rivals nor constituted an integrated system, but rather they comprised a network characterized by much cross-referencing, supervision, and overlap of function.

## Oath and Ordeal

Procedure in the various courts revolved around the pleadings of the parties, the information supplied by local juries, the evidence of documents, and the

---

[184] *Historia et cartularium monasterii sancti Petri Gloucestriae*, ed. William Henry Hart (3 vols., RS; 1863–7), vol. 2, p. 98.

statements of witnesses. Very often some kind of compromise could be reached. In the hard cases and those where a decisive result was sought, a conclusive form of proof was required. This was provided by oath and ordeal. Both invoked God. Both brought the supernatural into the courtroom.

Oaths were essential at many points in a lawsuit. An accusation would be backed up by an oath. Juries swore that what they were about to say would be true. Most significantly, an accusation could be refuted by an exculpatory oath, taken either alone or with 'oath-helpers' (compurgators). When Gilbert of Sempringham and his canons were accused of sending aid overseas to the banished archbishop, Thomas Becket, contrary to the king's command, the justices offered him the opportunity of clearing himself by swearing an oath.[185] When Philip of Sarnesfield claimed that he had no obligation to pay rent to the Reading abbey dependency of Leominster, the abbot's court adjudged that he should prove his claim 'twelve-handed', i.e. with eleven supporters swearing alongside him.[186] The Church courts and the urban courts were particularly disposed to employ procedures based on oath and compurgation.

Swearing an oath moved the case to a more intense, spiritual plane. One of the parties or the accused invoked God as his witness. Oaths were customarily sworn upon the Gospels or upon the relics of the saints. Exceptionally, when appealing against the decision of the court of his lord, the archbishop of Canterbury, John Marshal, swore the necessary oath upon a church service book known as a troper, but this provoked general disapproval and was used by the archbishop as an argument that John's proceedings were invalid. 'It is not the custom of the country to swear on a troper, but one must kneel before the four gospels', as one of his party wrote.[187] When the monks of Thorney were in dispute with a local landowner, they carried the relics of the saints that they kept in their church to the disputed land for him to swear upon.[188]

Ordeals likewise represented an appeal to God. They were of two types. In the unilateral form one of the parties underwent a test and the outcome determined the case, while in the bilateral the two parties or their champions fought it out in battle. The latter was deemed a kind of ordeal, rather than simply a clash of naked force, because the theory was that God would give victory to the innocent or righteous. There were two kind of unilateral ordeal current in Norman and Angevin England. The first was trial by hot iron. This involved the accused walking a set number of paces holding a heated iron, the hand then being bound and after three days inspected. Guilt or innocence was determined by whether the hand was healing cleanly. The other

---

[185] *Bk. Gilbert*, p. 72.     [186] Foliot, *Letters*, no. 119, p. 159.
[187] Guernes de Pont-Sainte-Maxence, *La Vie de Saint Thomas Becket*, ed. H. E. Walberg (Les Classiques français du Moyen Age; 1936), lines 1456–7, p. 45.
[188] Van Caen., *Lawsuits* 1, p. 161, no. 193.

kind of unilateral ordeal was trial by cold water, in which the accused was thrown into a pool or pit of water. If he sank, he was innocent, if he floated, guilty.

The rituals for the ordeal show how the sacred was mixed with the judicial. The ordeal iron was first exorcized. The priest placed it on the altar prior to celebrating mass. He invoked God's blessing on it: 'Bless, O Lord, through the strength of your power, this metal, removing every demonic falsehood and dispelling the magic and trickery of the unbelievers, so that in it the truth of a most truthful judgment may be made clear to believers, through your holy name.' Before the ordeal took place, the priest prayed again, asking God that 'the righteousness of justice should be manifested'. He again blessed the hot iron: 'deign to send your holy and true blessing on this iron, so that it should be a pleasing coolness to those who carry it with justice and fortitude but a burning fire to the wicked . . .' He concluded, 'May the blessing of God the Father and the Son and the Holy Spirit descend on this iron, to discern the true judgment of God.'[189] Similar prayers and blessings were uttered over the water employed in the ordeal of cold water and over the shield and staff used in ordeal by battle.[190]

Trial by battle was introduced to England by the Normans and originally the English were allowed to opt instead for trial by hot iron. It was a form of proof used extensively both in cases involving accusations of crime and in disputes over property. When an individual raised a serious accusation, such as a charge of homicide or theft, against another, the normal expectation was that the case would be determined by battle. The sacrist of Canterbury cathedral recalled such a case in the convent's own court, when 'two peasants fought a duel before me at Hollingbourne on account of a theft, and I had the vanquished party hanged, under the convent's powers of justice'.[191] A case from the 1170s illustrates some of the characteristics of the procedure. Two men at Richmond market were haggling over the price of a foal. The prospective buyer, who was 'tall, strong and brawny', attempted the stratagem of claiming that the foal was his—'the foal is mine,' he threatened, 'how come you have him? If you deny it, the strength of my body and the power of justice will be able to convict you as a liar and recover the stolen object, that I have long sought and now found in your possession.' As a result of the altercation, the townsmen seized the two and adjudged that the seller should 'either clear himself through battle or undergo the penalty for theft', while the buyer had to 'prosecute the charge of theft and convict him of guilt'. The accused was given leave first to return to his own locality and settle his business. He then

---

[189] *Magd. Pont.*, pp. 179–80.    [190] Ibid., pp. 181–5, 207–9.
[191] *Epistolae Cantuarienses* 324, ed. William Stubbs, *Chronicles and Memorials of the Reign of Richard I* (2 vols., RS; 1864–5), vol. 2, p. 309.

returned, accompanied by his brother, to the spot where the duel was to take place. For three days he practised, 'learning as much as he could of the business of duelling'. His brother encouraged him to call on St Thomas Becket for aid. Eventually,

the fight began. The accuser attacked and beat his opponent with a middle-sized staff. But he, safeguarded by the protection of the martyr [i.e. Becket] and the shield of faith, did not feel the impact of the blows and, just like an expert duellist, battered the accuser on the head and right arm, until he was overcome and, humbling himself at the feet of the judges, was forced to beg forgiveness for the false charge he had brought.[192]

The words put into the mouth of the accuser in this case—'the strength of my body and the power of justice will be able to convict you'—encapsulate the blend of physical and moral force upon which the duel was premissed. The horse-trader's plight illustrates well the handicap of the pacific man faced with a legal proof that gave the advantage to the 'expert duellist'. Although it was possible to employ a champion, instead of fighting on one's own behalf, this was allowed only in strictly specified circumstances. It was natural, too, to seek the aid of the saints in such a perilous and sanctified trial. The fate of the accuser shows, however, that trial by battle was perilous for both parties—a vanquished accuser was punished, usually by a fine.

Civil cases were also determined by battle, although the property concerned had to be of a certain value—over ten shillings, according to *The Laws of Henry I*.[193] A straightforward instance is recorded in the *Abingdon Chronicle*:

In the time of abbot Ingulph [d. 1158], a dispute arose between the bursar of Winchester and the abbot over a piece of pasture called Summerleas, lying between Uffington and Woolstone. The case continued for a long time, until it was settled by battle and the pasture adjudged to this monastery through the victory of the abbot's champion, according to the custom of the kingdom.[194]

Since success in battle depended on God's will, victors sometimes made a thank-offering from the lands they won. Thus Roger de Clere gave rights in the church of Fotherby, part of his Lincolnshire fief, to the Gilbertine canons, because, in his own words, 'I acquired the fief in the court of the lord king at London by battle through God's help, and thus I judged it necessary to give some part of the fief to the service of God.'[195] His words suggest some of the relief that would be felt by the victor in trial by battle. It was, indeed,

---

[192] W. Cant., *Mir. Thos.* 3. 40 (pp. 295–6).        [193] *LHP* 59. 16a (p. 188).

[194] *Abingdon Chron.* 2, p. 213.

[195] *Transcripts of Charters to the Gilbertine House etc.*, ed. F. M. Stenton (Lincoln Record Soc. 18; 1922), no. 9, p. 43; cf. no. 10, p. 43.

generally recognized that combat was 'a risky and uncertain business', with the chance of 'the disgrace of perpetual infamy' or even 'unexpected and untimely death'.[196] The clergy and townsmen sought and, to a large degree, obtained exemption from trial by battle. Eventually, as we shall see below, alternatives were devised. The only parties likely to embrace the prospect with any degree of enthusiasm were the 'approvers', convicted felons who were spared on the condition that they accused and fought their comrades or other criminals. It was a way to avoid punishment for men like Robert, son of Patrick, captured at Kidderminster in 1221 in company with thieves, who 'confessed that he is a thief . . . and turns approver to fight five battles'.[197]

Unlike trial by battle, the unilateral ordeals of iron and water were employed in England only in criminal cases (with the exception of a few volunteered at the time of the Domesday inquest). Henry II made widespread use of them in the drive against crime initiated by his Assize of Clarendon of 1166. According to this enactment, juries of twelve men of every hundred and four men of every township were to supply the names of anyone who, within the last twelve years, had been accused or was suspected of robbery, murder, or theft, or of harbouring robbers, murderers, or thieves. The sheriffs were to seize those accused or suspected and bring them before the royal justices. Unless they had been caught with stolen goods and were of bad repute, they could undergo trial by cold water. If they failed, they lost a foot (and, after 1176, their right hand too). If they passed the ordeal but had a bad reputation, they had to go into life-long exile from the kingdom.

The survival from the Angevin period of Pipe Rolls and plea rolls with details of judicial activities allows some rough statistical observations to be made about how trial by ordeal worked in practice. Of the recorded cases, 17 per cent involved the hot iron, 83 per cent cold water. If the observation in the law-book attributed to Glanville, that hot iron was the form of ordeal for free men and cold water for serfs, is reliable, then it was the unfree who were by far the most common targets of Angevin criminal justice.[198] Hot iron was also the only ordeal to which women were subject—probably on ground of sexual decorum, to avoid the display of soaking bodices and floating skirts. Perhaps the most striking conclusion, however, concerns the outcome of the ordeal test: just under two-thirds of those who underwent the ordeal passed. Since the majority of ordeals were of cold water, this statistic can be explained either by the way the human body behaves in water, or, more circuitously, by the way courts decided what it was to float or to sink. To place the case before

---

[196] Glanville 2. 7 (p. 28).

[197] *Rolls of the Justices in Eyre for Lincolnshire (1218–19) and Worcestershire (1221)*, ed. Doris Stenton (Selden Soc. 53; 1934), no. 1177, p. 578.

[198] Glanville 14. 2 (p. 173).

God was also to put it into the hands of a small body of men with opinions and feelings of their own.

## Punishment

As the provisions of the Assize of Clarendon demonstrate, harsh mutilatory justice was a feature of the criminal law of the time. It was only part of a wide range of chastisements and penalties. At one extreme was the ritual public humiliation that faced those who transgressed the norms of the local community. In Chester anyone brewing bad beer could be 'put in the shit-seat' [*cathedra stercoris*].[199] At the other extreme was the death penalty, usually inflicted in this period by hanging, although crimes that were viewed as particularly heinous might have special punishments. The mad cleric who killed the infant son of earl David of Huntingdon (later David I of Scotland) was tied to the tails of four wild horses and pulled apart.[200] Burning to death was particularly the fate of women, like Alice, the wife of Robert of Wheatley, who, early in the thirteenth century, was burned to death at Louth in Lincolnshire 'on account of felony in regard to the death of Robert her husband'.[201]

The balance between execution and mutilation was ever changing. William I supposedly ruled that capital punishment should be replaced by blinding and castration in all criminal cases.[202] If he did indeed do so, his son Henry I reinstated hanging for red-handed theft and robbery.[203] In 1124 the royal justice Ralph Basset held a court in Leicestershire and 'hanged there in a short time more thieves than ever before, forty-four men altogether, and six who were blinded and castrated.'[204] It was possession of the gallows that marked out those lords who claimed routine franchisal jurisdiction over thieves. When the abbot of Crowland lost a lawsuit in 1193, the bitterest consequence was the removal of 'the gallows on which were hanged the thieves caught in the township of Crowland, by the judgment of the abbot's court'.[205] The law-book attributed to Glanville, written in 1188, lists crimes punishable by execution or mutilation. These include: treason, homicide, arson, robbery, and rape.[206] The chronicler Ralph of Diceto distinguished the penal policy of Henry II's judges: fines or imprisonment for breach of the Forest Law, hanging for homicide, exile for treason, mutilation for lesser crimes.[207]

Execution, mutilation, confiscation of property, exile, and imprisonment were all, at various times, visited by the Norman and Angevin kings on rebels,

---

[199] *DB* 1, 262b (Chs. C. 18).      [200] Orderic 8. 22 (4, p. 276).      [201] *Rot. chart.*, p. 86.
[202] Liebermann, *Gesetze* 1, pp. 488, 491 (Wl art. 10; Wl art. Lond. retr. 17); Robertson, *Laws*, pp. 242, 250.
[203] Flor. Worcs. 2, p. 57.      [204] *ASC*, p. 254.
[205] Stenton, *Engl. Justice*, p. 172; Van Caen., *Lawsuits* 2, p. 679, no. 641.
[206] Glanvill 1. 2 (p. 3).      [207] R. Diceto, *Ymag.* 1, p. 434.

and traitors. After the rebellion of 1075, the high-ranking Breton and Norman participants were exiled, dispossessed, or imprisoned, but the chief native aristocrat implicated, earl Waltheof, was executed according to 'English law'.[208] Some Bretons were blinded, but these may have been non-noble.[209] In the aftermath of the rebellion of 1095, William of Eu was accused of treason and defeated in trial by battle. He was then blinded and castrated.[210] Tampering with the royal coinage, which bore the king's image and yielded him great profit, was a crime that aroused the king's particular anger. The twelve days of Christmas 1124-5 were a grim festivity for the moneyers who minted the coins of Henry I. Outraged by what he considered the deficiencies of the coins they had been issuing, the king had them rounded up and deprived of their testicles and right hands.[211] As late as 1130 Brand the Moneyer owed the king £20 'so that he might not be mutilated with the other moneyers'.[212] The king's court could claim that mutilation was a more merciful punishment than execution, as it did explicitly in cases in 1203 and 1220, but it was also a deterrent.[213] When offenders were 'punished by mutilation of their limbs, they offer a pitiable spectacle to the people and restrain the bold daring of men like them by their terrible example'.[214]

Those defeated after a private accusation were often punished by their accuser; 'he who prosecutes shall carry out the judgment', as the rule was phrased in the twelfth-century code for Preston.[215] One gory example is the case of Thomas of Eldersfield (Worcs.), who, in the year 1221, was defeated in combat by his adversary, George, who had accused Thomas of wounding him. The royal justices before whom the fight had taken place decided to be merciful: 'Although, according to the custom of the kingdom, he [Thomas] should have been hanged, the justices nevertheless mixed mercy with justice, and judged that he should be castrated and blinded. They directed the victor's relatives and kinsmen to carry out this sentence.' This they did with gusto, moved 'more by the pleasure of revenge than the love of justice'. The eyes were thrown to the ground, the testicles used as footballs, the local lads kicking them playfully at the girls. The savagery cannot have been tempered by the fact that George's wife had previously been Thomas's mistress.[216]

It is clear from the account of Thomas of Eldersfield's mutilation that ordeals and punishments could gather a crowd. Execution was likewise a

---

[208] Orderic 4 (2, pp. 316–18).     [209] *ASC*, p. 212.
[210] *ASC*, p. 232 (1096).     [211] *ASC*, p. 255 (1125).
[212] PR 31 HI, p. 42.     [213] *PBKJ* 3, no. 739, pp. 81–2; *CRR* 8, pp. 276–8.
[214] *Dial. scacc.*, p. 88.     [215] *Borough Charters*, p. 73.
[216] *Mir. Wulfstan* 2. 16 (pp. 169–71); *Pleas of the Crown for the County of Gloucester . . . 1221*, ed. F. W. Maitland (London, 1884), no. 87, pp. 21–2, 141–2.

public spectacle. The details of a hanging are sometimes revealed. When the knight Gilbert of Plumpton was about to be hanged at Worcester in 1184, his hands were tied behind his back, his eyes covered with green clay and an iron chain placed around his neck.[217] In the following decade the dissident urban leader, William fitz Osbern, was dragged from his place of judgment in the Tower of London to Tyburn before being hanged and his body was left in chains—treatment that was in later times the mark of punishment for treason.[218] Gerald of Wales complained of the contemporary practice of denying communion to thieves about to be hanged and of burying them, not in consecrated ground, but alongside the gallows.[219] Although sheriffs often claimed their expenses for hanging criminals, there seems to have been no regular hangman. According to the theologian Thomas of Chobham, writing early in the thirteenth century, the English custom was for there to be no official executioner, but 'when anyone is dragged to the gallows, someone who is met on the way is forced to hang the condemned man', in return receiving the dead man's clothes or a small payment.[220]

The prison was a greater rarity in medieval than in modern society, but was not unknown. The royal jail of the Fleet in London is recorded as early as 1130, while the Assize of Clarendon required that there be a jail in every county, situated in a borough or royal castle. The costs of building and maintaining county jails are a regular feature of sheriffs' accounts, along with the costs of ordeals and executions. Imprisonment could, of course, be used for many ends. Some of these, such as the incarceration of political enemies, were scarcely judicial. If Henry I kept his brother Robert and the rebel Robert de Bellême in captivity until their deaths, it was out of prudence rather than after judgment. Other uses of imprisonment, however, were more clearly part of a legal process. A case from Lincolnshire in 1202 shows its employment both to ensure safe custody while the accused awaited trial and as a coercive measure applied to a recalcitrant plaintiff. Cristiana, widow of William, son of John, accused the brothers Ralph and Richard of killing her husband. Ralph was seized and put in jail. The sheriff reported that he died there, although the jurors said they had seen him 'wandering through the county' after he had been in jail. The other defendant, Richard, claimed that Cristiana had already withdrawn her accusation in the presence of the chief justiciar, Geoffrey fitz Peter. The county bore record 'that she had been placed in jail because she was unwilling to prosecute the case and afterwards she agreed to pay a fine of one mark, which has been paid to the Exchequer.'[221]

[217] *Gesta Hen. II* 1, p. 315.     [218] R. Diceto, *Ymag.* 2, p. 143.
[219] Gerald, *Gemma* 1. 40 (p. 116).     [220] T. Chobham, *SC*, pp. 432–3.
[221] *Earliest Lincs. Ass. Rolls*, p. 152.

Cristiana's imprisonment could be viewed equally plausibly as a punishment for making a frivolous accusation or as a form of pressure to extort a fine for the same. The law-book attributed to Glanville notes that those who fail to pursue a criminal accusation 'should be put in prison and kept in custody until they are willing to pursue the accusation'.[222]

Imprisonment for debt likewise has a dual aspect, as punishment and pressure. Richard fitz Neal, in his *Dialogue on the Exchequer*, explained that those who failed to pay their debts to the Crown could be imprisoned. Stewards who had given a guarantee for their lord's debts could be chained and placed in a deep dungeon, but other debtors were kept in 'free custody', above the jail.[223] This was, again, more of an incentive to the debtor to arrange for the settlement of the debt than, strictly speaking, a punishment. Truly penal imprisonment did take place in some circumstances. In certain types of lawsuit, jurors who could be proved to have given a false verdict were punished by imprisonment for a year.[224] The Forest Charter of 1217 promises that no one will be executed or mutilated for Forest offences. Instead they will be fined, or, if they have no property with which to pay a fine, they will be imprisoned for a year and a day. Then they must either find sureties or go into exile.[225] These fixed-term confinements clearly imply that imprisonment was seen as a penalty for certain offences. Prisons, whether used to keep accused criminals, to compel litigants, or to punish offenders, were thus a part of the royal and seignorial machinery of justice.

For the lesser offences financial penalties were usual. These 'amercements', as they are termed, ranged from huge sums paid by the barons for infringement of the Forest Law to the odd mark levied on litigants who had committed some procedural irregularity. There was nothing new about the exaction of monetary penalties. In the Anglo-Saxon period there had been a scale of payments to be made, not only to an injured party or his kindred, but also to the king. The Normans and Angevins continued to expect that the exercise of justice would involve the extraction of pennies: offenders might 'ransom' themselves, those who brought unsuccessful pleas pay for their failure, jurors be fined for contradicting themselves.

## The Ritual of Lawsuits

Lawsuits were, in the twelfth century as today, dramas. Especially when the property involved was valuable or the participants important, the line between a judicial and a political process was hard to identify. Litigants would mobilize their friends, seek to influence the courts, perhaps negotiate

---

[222] Glanville 1. 32 (p. 21).
[223] *Dial. scacc.*, pp. 21, 116–17.
[224] Glanville 2. 19 (p. 36).
[225] *Sel. Charters*, pp. 346–7.

with their opponents. The exact details of the law were not always easy to ascertain and there could be argument about custom and precedent, as well as fact.

A splendid insight into the workings of a lawsuit in this period is provided by the poet Gaimar's account of the trial of earl Godwine.[226] It has two advantages as a source: it is in French and it is fictional. French was the vernacular tongue of upper-class laymen and of upper-class churchmen (when off duty), and Gaimar's text thus gives us the flavour, and indeed the terminology, of court procedure far more vividly than texts which transmute the oral pleadings, debates, and terms of art of Anglo-French litigation into formal Latin. Also, being an invented narrative, written about 1140 but purporting to give the detail of an event of a century earlier, the story must be based on the author's sense of what would be plausible and credible to a contemporary listener. We are fairly safe in concluding that the trial is thus a realistic imagined picture. Since it is fictional, however, the author was able to insert passages, speeches, and details that an austerely historical account would have to omit. Gaimar knows the private debates of the court members word for word. He is the omniscient narrator. For us, reading his text, this means we have a picture of a lawsuit as complete, informal, and vivid as any we can get. The fact that it never happened is actually an advantage.

The context is that earl Godwine has been implicated in the murder of Alfred, the brother of Edward the Confessor. The earl had wisely sought refuge abroad but now returns to England to seek to restore his position. The first thing he does is contact his friends, asking them to intercede with the king. He requests that he 'should have his right' (*sun dreit preïst*). The king allows him to be brought before him on the condition 'that he would follow the king's judgment' (*que jugement siwist le rei*). Godwine has to provide both pledges (*gage*), that is valuable objects that he may forfeit if he is in breach of conditions, and powerful men as his sureties, or guarantors. Permission to come to court in the first place thus has to be negotiated and a network of conditions and guarantees has been created.

King Edward opens proceedings with a formal appeal or accusation (*l'ad apelez*) that Godwine has betrayed and killed his brother 'as a felon' (*cum fel*). Specifying felony made the charge much more serious, for the term denoted a particularly heinous offence, often implying breach of faith to one's lord. If Godwine wished to clear himself of the charge, the king added, he must do so by offering proof (*il l'en ferat prover*). Edward is here notifying Godwine and the court that he is demanding formal refutation of some kind.

Godwine denied the charge formally:

---

[226] Gaimar, lines 4861–5028, pp. 154–60.

> ... I deny all
> That you have recounted [*cuntez*] here.
> I shall deny it word for word.
> I shall clear myself by trial [*jugement*]
> And I have given you my gage
> That trial shall be accepted.
> Of your appeal and my reply
> These barons here shall speak the right.

Formal denial, 'word for word', was the standard step as described in the later law-book (Glanville). Edward had made his appeal in the form of a *cunte*, a statement of his case, and Godwine claimed the right to refute it.

After the exchange of appeal and denial, matters were placed in the hands of the suitors of the court. Since this was a high political plea, the suitors were of high status, including twelve counts or earls, sitting on a bench. When the king commanded them to proceed to judgment, they withdrew to a private chamber and sat 'to judge the right' (*pur dreit jugier*). Here begins the most interesting part of Gaimar's account, for he puts into the mouths of four different magnates four different sets of legal arguments. The first speaker, Maerleswain, recapitulates the situation: you have heard the *cunte* appealed and completely denied, he says. The charge is felony. However, he goes on, here elaborating a specifically legal argument, there are no witnesses, which a charge of felony would require. He concludes hopefully that 'I think they can still be friends'. The second speaker, Siward, also addresses the status of felony: Godwine's simple denial would be acceptable, if the accusation were not one of felony. A charge of felony requires proof (*jugement*), namely ordeal of fire, water, or battle. He reflects sombrely, 'the appeal of a king is a big thing' (*Ço est grant chose, apel de rei*).

Frithugist, the next speaker, disagrees. An accusation without witnesses does not require proof of this kind. Such a 'blind appeal' (*orp apel*) can be refuted quite well by the oath of the accused. Finally, Leofric speaks. He too is stuck by the political realities: 'King Edward wears the crown, his appeal is a big thing' (*Edward li reis porte corone, | Grant chose afiert a sun apel*). On the other hand, Godwine has asked for mercy and has offered guarantees. He excludes ordeal and battle, because 'Someone who wants to bring another to the iron or have him float in the water ought by right to have witnesses who have seen or heard'. Let us, he suggests, make an arbitrated award (*un esguard*) rather than insist on a judicial proof (*jugement*), and let us make it unanimously (*en esgardum comunelment*). He then specifies what Godwine should offer to Edward: rich armour, homage, and hostages. The earl should fling himself on the king's mercy. This, concludes Leofric, would be an honourable settlement. So it turns out.

The interest of this account lies partly in the technicalities of trial procedure that are revealed. The details of appeal and denial, the debate over forms of proof and the status of the offence can all be tied to the non-fictional sources of the twelfth century, such as the law-books and narratives of historical pleas. It also, however, throws light on the non-legal pressures at work in trials. The status of the accuser, the desire to reconcile, the need to preserve face, are as important as the details of which accusations require the support of witnesses and whether simple exculpation through oath is acceptable. The suitors of the court are a group who have their own opinions about the laws and customs of England but they also recognize that the king's appeal is a 'big thing', even while harbouring the hope that friendship can be restored. Especially at its higher levels, this is probably how Norman justice worked.

## The Birth of the Common Law

As the debate invented by Gaimar shows, legal disputes stimulated reflection and argument, some of it of a general kind. One residue of this world of vigorous discussion about legal questions is the literature of law that survives from the period. The most influential was the law-book attributed to Glanville, but other material, some of it technical, like the texts of assizes and the registers of writs, some of it more theoretical, like the writings of the church lawyers, emerged into written form, often carrying the marks of the disagreements and doubts that lay behind it.

The law-books, assizes, and canon-law collections arose from debate that took place not only in the course of suits themselves but in the entourages of all great men. The biographer of Hugh, bishop of Lincoln (1185–1200), tells how the bishop was once engaged in conversation with learned men, when discussion turned to a certain biblical text with legal implications: 'if thy brother shall trespass against thee, go and tell him his fault between thee and him alone' (Matt. 18: 15). The experts in canon and civil law who were present could not agree on how this text should be applied to the usual legal requirements 'concerning bringing two or three witnesses or the form of proclaiming a brother's offence to the church'. Eventually the bishop himself told a story of how, as a young canon in charge of a parish in his native Burgundy, he had dealt with a notorious adulterer.[227] The elements here—a relaxed but learned discussion involving men who had been trained in the law and were accustomed to presiding over courts, the vexed issue of scriptural injunctions, the introduction of contemporary personal experience—are characteristic of the milieu in which law was made in the twelfth century. Book-learning and experience were both present; practical concerns were

---

[227] Ad. Eyns., *V. Hugh* 1. 6 (1, pp. 19–21).

central, but abstract rules drawn from the tradition channelled or challenged them. The bishop of Lincoln knew Jesus' commands, had lawyers in his train, but had also himself had to deal with the sexual life of lay people in his parish.

Undoubtedly the most important new developments to arise from this world of legal discussion and improvisation were those that took place in royal justice under Henry II. These concerned both the administration of justice and judicial procedure. In the latter half of his reign Henry instituted the so-called general eyres, which were to be the most important embodiment of local royal justice for the next century or so. Eyres were regular, country-wide visitations by royal judges with specific powers and duties. A body of justices, between two and nine in number, would be assigned a group of counties to visit. These groups or circuits were intended to cover the whole country, with the exception of the exempt counties of Chester and Durham. In the course of the visitation of 1188–9, for example, there were five circuits, each with seven, eight, or nine judges. The eyre justices would come to a county town or other important local centre and there, for the space of a week or several weeks, hear the cases within their jurisdiction, then move on to a neighbouring county. In 1201 the group of six justices assigned to the south-western counties, headed by the eminent legal expert Simon of Pattishall, sat at Sherbourne in Dorset 27 May–3 June, at Ilchester in Somerset 3–16 June, at Launceston in Cornwall 18–25 June, and, back in Somerset, at Taunton 3–6 July to deal with outstanding cases.

The business of the eyre was wide. The instructions to the itinerant justices in 1194 command them to inquire into and deal with the pleas of the Crown (those in which the king had special rights or interests), all pleas initiated by royal writs, the tenancies, wardships, and marriage-rights that had fallen into the king's hands, criminal cases, payments for the king's ransom, the recent rebellion headed by the king's brother, sale of wine against the regulations, cases regarding ownership of land below a certain value, the election of coroners, a tallage of the royal demesne, the loans of the Jews, and the exactions of local royal officials.[228] It was a heavy burden, and not an exclusively judicial one. In the course of time some of these duties became the responsibility of specialized officers, but the eyre business was always extensive.

At the same time as the general eyres were instituted, during the last decades of the twelfth century, a central court at Westminster evolved, hiving off from the Exchequer and sitting for four regular law terms from the 1190s. This Court of Common Pleas, or the Bench, heard civil cases of all kinds and was often referred to by the justices in eyre. Both eyre justices and justices of the Bench came to be increasingly professional, for, although a large number

[228] R. Howd. 3, pp. 262–7.

of men served as justices of the Angevin kings, there was nevertheless a core group of permanent expert judges serving both at Westminster and on eyre. The long judicial careers of men like Hugh Bardolf, who served as an itinerant justice and a judge of the Bench in the period 1185–1203, or Simon of Pattishall, who served on the Bench for twenty-five years (1190–1215), created continuity, routine, and a sense of professional cohesion.

This expansion and professionalization of royal justice was linked with the increased business that had been generated for the courts by Henry II's new legal procedures (assizes). In a world in which power and wealth were based fundamentally on landed property, the descent and transmission of estates was the central concern of civil litigation. In his possessory assizes (the most important of which are known by their French names of novel disseisin and mort d'ancestor), the king and his legal advisers developed quick and simple ways of resolving disputes over possession of land. Novel disseisin addressed itself to the situation in which one party claimed to have been recently expelled from a property of which he was in peaceful possession, mort d'ancestor with a case where the plaintiff sought to establish that he was the rightful heir. In both assizes, the procedure was initiated by the relatively inexpensive purchase of a writ from the royal Chancery, instructing the local sheriff to assemble a jury of twelve free men from the neighbourhood, and to have the jury and the parties before the royal justices on their next visit to the county. The jury would then be asked to answer clearly formulated questions. In the case of novel disseisin, 'Was the plaintiff evicted unjustly and without judgment from an estate of which he was in peaceful possession?' In the assize of mort d'ancestor, 'Was the plaintiff's father in peaceful possession of the estate in question when he died and is the plaintiff the heir?'

The jury—a body of men who take an oath to give a truthful answer (verdict) to a question put to them by an authority—was by no means an invention of the late twelfth century. The Norman and Angevin kings used juries extensively for discovering information of all kinds. It was Henry II's assizes, however, that initiated their routine judicial employment. The simple procedures of novel disseisin and mort d'ancestor, relying for determination not on battle, ordeal, or the oaths of the parties but on the verdict of a local jury, proved extremely popular. Soon the justices in eyre could expect to hear dozens of cases when they arrived in the counties. They could be dispatched speedily:

An assize was held to determine if Robert, son of Brictive, unjustly and without judgment dispossessed Richard of Swaby of his free holding in Swaby within the terms of the assize. The jurors say that he did so dispossess him. Judgment: Richard shall recover possession and Robert is liable to be fined. Damages, three shillings; fine, half a mark [6s. 8d.].

An assize was held to determine if Ralph de Normanville unjustly and without judgment dispossessed Juliana of Reasby of her free holding in Reasby within the terms of the assize. The jurors say that he did not so dispossess her. Judgment: Juliana is liable to be fined for a false claim.[229]

Novel disseisin and mort d'ancestor are termed possessory assizes because they dealt with the question of possession, not right. It was their great strength that they focused on single, specific issues. The question of right still had to be addressed, however, and yet another innovation of the second half of the reign of Henry II was a new assize—the Grand Assize—to deal with cases in which it was not peaceful possession but greater right that was claimed. As in the possessory assizes, a decision by jury now became available, although the procedure was not as streamlined as in novel disseisin and mort d'ancestor, and the jury had to be composed of knights rather than simply free men.

The Grand Assize and the possessory assizes made jury verdicts the standard procedure in civil litigation. In the criminal law, juries of presentment were already employed to identify those suspected of serious offences, although proof was usually by ordeal. In 1215, however, the Fourth Lateran Council prohibited clerical participation in ordeals. It was the climax of several generations of doubt and debate on the issue within ecclesiastical and academic circles. As a result, a new form of criminal procedure had to be adopted. With the jury already a regular and vital component of the English judicial system, it is not surprising that its use was now extended to fill the gap. After 1215 the criminal trial jury assumed the central role in deciding guilt or innocence that it still has. The unilateral ordeal disappeared from English courts forever; battle was available only in private accusations of treason or felony or in civil action under the writ of right, in both cases only if the defendant agreed.

Between 1160 and 1220 the administration of English law and justice had been transformed. Juries had replaced ordeal in all vital matters. Litigation over land was now primarily conducted in the royal courts. A body of professional justices administered technical, uniform legal procedures at Westminster and in the counties. The English Common Law had been born.

## 9. RECORDS AND RECORD-KEEPING

### Domesday Book

Lordship and government in no way depended upon writing but could make use of it, to issue commands, set down information, or record transactions. Monks and clerks, who were more familiar with writing than the rest of the population, preferred to obtain written confirmation of the grants made to

---

[229] *Earliest Lincs. Ass. Rolls*, p. 236.

them. Kings could send out instructions in writs as well as orally, by messenger. Lists of various kinds could be used to assess and check what was owed by subjects, vassals, or tenants. The use of such written instruments became increasingly common over the course of time.

There is an oddity, however, in the pattern of documentary evidence surviving from England in the period 1075–1225. Although, in general, written sources become more numerous, richer, and more varied in character as the period progresses, especially after the 'record revolution' about 1200, there is one great exception, standing alone and dominating the late eleventh century: Domesday Book. There is nothing comparable in scope and detail for any other part of Europe at this time or for long afterwards either in England or elsewhere. It is a survey carried out at the level of the kingdom, intended to cover every piece of productive land, every tenant, every plough, and, if it did not achieve complete success in that aim, it came so close as to induce subsequent generations to summon up the image of the Last Judgement when they wished to convey its searching and inescapable inquisitorial eye.

The Domesday survey was ordered by William I after he had celebrated Christmas at Gloucester in 1085:

After this the king had great thought and deep speech with his wise men about his land and how it was settled and with what men. Then he sent his men throughout England to every county and discovered how many hundred hides there were in the county and what land and stock the king himself had there and what rights he ought to have in the county over the year. He also caused to be written down how much land his archbishops, bishops and abbots and earls had and what and how much every landowner in England had in land and stock, and its value in money. His inquiry was so strict that there was not a hide nor a yard of land nor even an ox or cow or pig that was omitted from the record. All the records were then brought to him.[230]

The astonishment of contemporaries at the Domesday survey can be justly shared by modern observers of its product, Domesday Book. In two volumes (a detailed account of East Anglia and a rather more condensed survey of the rest of England), its 832 parchment folios contain a description of the places, people, and resources of eleventh-century England that is breathtaking in its detail and comprehensiveness. The East Anglia volume does indeed record even the oxen, cows, and pigs on the lords' farms.

It is certain that the survey was completed before William's death in September 1087 and it may even have been finished by the time he assembled the chief landholders of England to do him homage at Salisbury in August 1086. The accomplishment in such a short time of an inquiry that both spanned the kingdom and peeped into the farmyard is witness to the Conqueror's will and the fear he could inspire. It also shows the responsiveness of the inherited

[230] *ASC*, p. 216.

territorial framework of county and hundred. The commissioners sent out by the king could attend the county court and there hear the sworn evidence of representatives from each hundred in the shire regarding the information they sought: the name of each manor, its holder before the Conquest and its present holder, the number of hides, the number of ploughs on the lord's farm, the number of men, etc.

There was thus in existence an administrative structure, inherited from the Anglo-Saxon kingdom, that could provide a vast amount of information quickly and thoroughly. This information was then preserved by being written down. The existence of subordinate and ancillary records and the format of Domesday Book itself give some idea of the amount of sifting, collating, and copying that were involved. The information is listed county by county, but within counties it is ordered not hundred by hundred but by landowner. The record of each county starts with a list of the landholders in that shire: first the king, then the ecclesiastics, then the laymen in order of rank. This list is numbered and the same numbers are used for reference in the body of the text. Running headings are used to identify the county and capital letters and rubrication (headings in red ink) are employed to highlight the subdivisions of the text. As well as being a massive compendium of information, Domesday Book is a model of lay-out technique (see Plate 4).

The written records containing the information derived from the Domesday survey were preserved in the royal treasury at Winchester (it is not clear exactly when they were assembled into book form). Here the officials of the treasury had a convenient and accessible register of the estates of the king and his tenants-in-chief, along with their value, in each county. Soon landholders were appealing to this source to vindicate their claims to property. When the Conqueror's son, William Rufus, ordered the restitution of some land in Norfolk to the abbey of St Benet of Holme, he added 'and know that this land was registered in my records, that are in my treasury at Winchester, as belonging to the church of St Benet'.[231] In 1111 the abbot of Abingdon appeared before the Exchequer court at Winchester and 'proved his case through the Book of the Treasury [i.e. Domesday Book]'.[232] Yet Domesday Book was not a text it would be easy to keep up to date. Landownership might undergo many changes. Knowing the number of villeins and ploughs on an estate in 1086 would not help in assessing its resources in 1186. After the reign of Henry I it was not used to support claims, until revived in the mid-thirteenth century as a record of the ancient demesne of the Crown. Although it was a spectacular administrative achievement and a monument of record-making, Domesday Book stands isolated in its time.

[231] *Monasticon* 3, p. 86.     [232] *Abingdon Chron.* 2, p. 116.

## The Increase in Documents

The increase in surviving documentation over the course of our period can be illustrated by taking a representative bishopric and a representative earldom and calculating the number of extant documents per bishop and per earl from the late eleventh to the early thirteenth century. The following data relate to the bishopric of Chichester and the earldom of Chester.[233]

| Bishops of Chichester | Documents per year |
| --- | --- |
| Ralph Luffa, 1091–1123 | 0.22 |
| Seffrid I, 1125–45 | 0.35 |
| Hilary, 1147–69 | 1.6 |
| John Greenford, 1174–80 | 2.3 |
| Seffrid II, 1180–1204 | 3.0 |
| Simon, 1204–7 | 4.3 |

| Earls of Chester | Documents per year |
| --- | --- |
| Hugh I, 1071–1101 | 0.033 |
| Richard, 1101–20 | 0.158 |
| Ranulf I, 1120–9 | 0.444 |
| Ranulf II, 1129–53 | 3.333 |
| Hugh II, 1153–81 | 2.321 |
| Ranulf III, 1181–1232 | 3.824 |

Since the number of successive bishops and earls is identical and the chronological range very close, the figures can also be graphed for comparison (see Figure 4).

The trend is unmistakable. In every instance, bar one, later bishops and earls left a greater documentary imprint than their predecessors. More documents survive from the bishops than from their concurrent earls—again with one exception. The atypical prominence of Ranulf II's documentary output does not invalidate the conclusions as to general trends, but serves as a warning that particular individuals and particular political circumstances may create unusual knots in the grain.

Obviously a great deal has been lost. Of the several hundred writs authorizing expenditure that are mentioned in the Pipe Roll for 1130 not one survives in the archives. It is important to distinguish an increase in output from the greater likelihood of survival as we move forward in time. Yet the evidence makes it clear that both elements were at work. The king found it necessary to employ an increasing number of scribes and this implies that the royal Chancery was increasingly busy. The number of scribes regularly employed in the Chancery about 1100 was two. This figure doubled by 1130. It sank again during the disturbances of the 1140s, with perhaps a solitary scribe

[233] Source: *Chichester Acta*; *Chester Charters*.

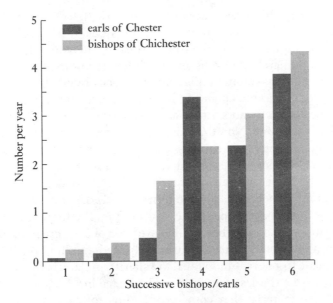

FIGURE 4. *Charters issued by the earls of Chester and the bishops of Chichester*

active at the end of Stephen's reign, but then increased once more when Henry II restored order. Under Henry and Richard there were four or five Chancery scribes working at any one time.[234]

The proliferation of documents was not simply a matter of more being produced, but also involved a diversification in the types of record. Surveys of various types, miniature Domesdays, multiplied. When abbot Geoffrey of Burton took up his office in 1114, one of his first acts was to commission a survey of the abbey's lands. The results were written down, and provide a full, precise record of the resources of the abbey's farms and the obligations of its peasant tenants. The abbot, or his steward, could find out at once how much land and how many plough teams there were on a given manor, ascertain the names and number of the serfs and free tenants and how much land each of them held and what they owed in rent. Some ten years after this survey, abbot Geoffrey had another made, with all the details updated.

Such surveys of lands and tenants' obligations became increasingly common. There are a few (from Peterborough, the English lands of the abbey of Caen, and, possibly, Shaftesbury) that date, like the Burton surveys, from the reign of Henry I. In the later years of Henry II they multiply. The manors of St Pauls, London, were surveyed at the command of Ralph of Diceto in 1181, the first year of his deanship of the cathedral. In 1183 Hugh de Puiset, bishop

[234] T. A. M. Bishop, *Scriptores regis* (Oxford, 1961), p. 30.

of Durham, 'had all the revenues of his bishopric, fixed rents and customs, written down' in what came to be called Boldon Book.[235] In 1185 the Templars organized an inquest into all their properties in England. The local results were sent in on parchment rolls and the information then transcribed into 65 folios of a handy volume measuring 10 inches by 6½ inches.[236] In 1189 Henry de Soilly became abbot of Glastonbury and immediately ordered a survey of the abbot's manors. Lords had always been eager to exact the utmost of what they were owed. Now they could use written means to help them do so.

The Angevin kings were equally keen to have written records of their resources. In 1166 Henry II commanded all his barons to send him, in writing, a notice of the names of their knights, how much they held, and when they had been granted their fiefs. The modern printed edition of the returns from this inquest is 260 pages long. If the returns from the Inquest of Sheriffs of 1170 had survived so well, they would have been of even greater bulk, for the information requested on that occasion required a written report on every payment made from every individual to a sheriff, prelate, baron, or their representatives over the last four years. The surviving fragments show how much detailed material they contained, listing, for example, the names of 39 burgesses of Castle Rising (Norfolk) and the payments each had made to the steward of their lord, the Earl of Arundel.[237] In 1185, the same year that the Templars carried out their inquest, Henry II had his justices-in-eyre inquire into the widows and wards who were in his custody. The results were recorded on rolls, twelve of which survive. They give details of the age of the widow or ward, whether he or she had brothers, sisters, or children, what their property was worth, with particulars of the livestock. The combination of travelling royal commissioners, local juries, and written record was exactly that which had produced Domesday Book. If the inquests of the Angevin period left no such immense monument, they are perhaps all the more significant for their frequency.

As is clear from the nature of these surveys, one of the purposes of having a written record was to enable checks to be made. The artificial memory of writing helped ensure nothing was lost sight of. This is nowhere clearer than in financial accounts and it is not surprising that the earliest complete series of royal records is the Pipe Rolls recording the annual audit of the sheriffs and other Crown debtors. After the first isolated survival, from 1130, the uninterrupted sequence begins in 1156 and runs until 1832. Debts that were not paid off were transferred to the roll for the succeeding year. In this way, the Exchequer maintained a tenacious grip on what it was owed. Others than the

---

[235] *Boldon Book, Northumberland and Durham*, ed. D. Austin (Chichester, 1982, supplementary vol. to Domesday Book, ed. John Morris), p. 10.

[236] *Templar Records*, pp. xvi n. 2, xxxi.     [237] *RBE* 2, p. cclxviii.

king found it useful or enlightening to keep a written record of their financial transactions. Richard de Anstey kept a record of his legal expenses from 1158 to 1163 (above, pp. 168–9). The earliest surviving daily accounts of household expenditure date from the last third of the twelfth century.[238] This would be an obvious area of a prudent lord's concern. Abbot Samson of Bury, who was responsible for drawing up a 'general description' of his abbey's rights and revenues, was notable for listening to the record of his household expenses in person.[239]

One sign of an increasing reliance upon written record is the copying of documents. A text derived from a text takes its users ever deeper into the textual world. Ecclesiastics were the first to engage in this kind of copying, for, as the great English churches accumulated charters recording their lands and rights, they found it convenient to devise easy ways of referring to them. One way was to copy out the texts of the charters, either in full or in abbreviated form, into a book. This could be arranged thematically (often topographically) or given a table of contents for easy consultation. Such cartularies, as they are termed, enabled the whole of the title deeds of a cathedral or abbey to be carried under the arm. The earliest surviving English examples come from Worcester, the first being produced in the first years of the eleventh century, the next in the 1090s. This was complied by a monk named Hemming, who explains his motives in the text itself:

I have compiled this little book of the possessions of our monastery so that it should be clear to those who come after us which landed properties should rightfully belong to this monastery, namely for the sustenance of the monks serving God, even if we do not possess them at the moment because of unjust force or deceitful spoliation.[240]

There are approaching thirty cartularies surviving from the twelfth century and their production increased greatly in the following century. To record in writing the written records of your rights seemed an increasingly prudent measure.

## The Record Revolution

Cartularies record documents granted to the body that drew up the cartulary—incoming documents. A yet more systematic bureaucratic practice is the recording of outgoing documents. This was taken up first by the royal government. From John's reign the Chancery adopted the system of

---

[238] *Household Accounts from Medieval England*, ed. C. M. Woolgar (2 vols.; Oxford, 1992), vol. 1, pp. 10, 107–10.
[239] Joc. Brak., pp. 29, 42.
[240] *Hemingi Chartularium Ecclesiae Wigorniensis*, ed. Thomas Hearne (2 vols.; Oxford, 1723), vol. 1, p. 282.

enrolling copies of the charters and letters that it issued. These were classified as charters (solemn grants), letters close (sent sealed and folded), and letters patent (sent sealed and open). Charter Rolls begin in 1199, Close Rolls (initially under the designation Liberate Rolls) in 1200, Patent Rolls in 1201. Because of the existence of these continuous detailed records of business done, the reign of John is the first period in English history when political history can be described on a daily basis. The Chancellor at the time of the innovation was Hubert Walter, archbishop of Canterbury, and there is every reason to assume that he was personally responsible.

The assumption is strengthened by Hubert's record in his earlier office as chief justiciar (1193–8). In a document of the year 1195 there is an unusually explicit record of bureaucratic innovation. It relates to the procedure for making 'final concords'. These were agreements between parties made before the king's justices. They were recorded in chirographs, i.e. sheets of parchment on which the text was written twice and which were then cut in two, each party retaining a copy. In 1195, at Hubert Walter's instigation, it was decided that a third copy should also be produced for record purposes. An agreement involving Theobald Walter, the archbishop's brother, as one of the parties, was drawn up and then endorsed:

This is the first chirograph that was made in the court of the lord king in the form of three chirographs according to the command of the archbishop of Canterbury and other barons of the lord king, so that by this form a record can be made to be transmitted to the treasurer to be preserved in the treasury.[241]

These third copies, or 'feet of fines' as they are termed, were henceforth filed away regularly. Hubert Walter was clearly an active proponent of the habit of keeping archive copies.

The beginning of Chancery enrolments under John is the culmination of a decade of documentary experimentation on the part of the royal government. The regular dating of royal documents began with the accession of Richard I. Royal charters and letters from before that time can only be dated inferentially, usually to a range of years. From Richard's reign, all such acts have day, year, and place of issue. The king's daily itinerary becomes clearly visible. The first surviving plea rolls, recording the cases that came before the royal justices, either on eyre or at Westminster, date from 1194. Thereafter they multiply rapidly and the workings of the judicial system are suddenly revealed in an entirely new way. In the same year, Hubert Walter ordered the appointment of coroners in each county, who were to keep a roll recording the pleas of the Crown. At every level lordship and government were leaving deeper and wider written traces.

---

[241] *Feet of Fines of the Reign of Henry II, etc.* (PRS 17; 1894), no. 21, p. 21.

The spate of new documentation was not confined to the king's administration, although his government was the pace-setter and model. In 1208 there begin the continuous series of Pipe Rolls of the bishopric of Winchester, the annual accounts of the manors belonging to the bishop. They are not the static, 'snapshot' surveys that ecclesiastics had often taken as they entered office, but a regular and repeated assessment of income, expenditure, and assets. They are detailed enough to enable a calculation to be made of the survival rate of lambs on the estate. The bishop of Winchester in 1208 was Peter des Roches, one of king John's most important administrators, with a special responsibility, and penchant, for financial affairs. A similar overlap between ecclesiastical and royal administration can be observed in the case of Hugh of Wells, who was keeper of the king's seal before becoming bishop of Lincoln in 1209. His is the earliest surviving bishop's register, giving details of the daily administration of the diocese. His Chancery background explains why the register is in the form of a roll rather than the more usual ecclesiastical format of a book.

Clerks had always had a part to play in lordship and government, but over the course of time their tasks became more numerous and diverse. Written instruments and written records multiplied. Particularly notably in the case of the royal government, increasing business, professionalization, and specialization marked the transition to new styles of administration. In 1075 English royal lordship had been, by contemporary standards, exceptionally powerful and unified. In 1225 it was still so, but, because of the elaboration of the specialized procedures and personnel of chancery and archive and the creation of the courts, actions and rules of the Common Law, it now also presided over a bureaucratic and judicial apparatus that had not been in existence a century and a half before.

CHAPTER 4

# The Aristocracy

## 1. THE STRUCTURE OF THE ARISTOCRACY

In common with most of pre-industrial Europe, England in this period was an aristocratic society: great wealth and power were in the hands of a few. The evidence of Domesday Book suggests that about half the income generated in the country was held by less than 200 barons, the rest going to the king or the Church. These 200 men and their families thus formed a small dominant group whose patronage shaped the fortunes of lesser families and whose feuds and friendships constituted politics. The range of wealth even in this baronial group was large—Domesday Book records that the lands of the count of Mortain comprised 793 manors, worth altogether over £2,500 per annum, while, at the other extreme, Robert of Aumale had 15, worth a total of £26.[1]

### The Feudal Hierarchy

The count of Mortain did not expect to keep his 793 manors under his own direct control. Although some of them were required to generate food for consumption or sale and to yield cash rents, many were granted out to tenants in return for various services. If the tenants held by military service, then they would be required to serve their lord in war, to garrison his castles, and to provide counsel and, in certain circumstances, monetary assistance. They would be enfeoffed by the lord, i.e. granted their fief, or dependent tenure, and the bond between them would be publicly manifested in the ceremony of homage, whereby the tenant became the lord's vassal or 'man' (*homme*).

The English aristocracy was structured both by a feudal hierarchy and an economic hierarchy. On the one hand, there was the simple question of how much land one had. By this yardstick the count of Mortain was a hundred times wealthier than Robert of Aumale. On the other hand, becoming a man's vassal meant recognizing his superiority, albeit often in ceremonial or formal terms. It did not take long for the two hierarchies to become irreversibly

[1] Sidney Painter, *Studies in the History of the English Feudal Barony* (Baltimore, 1943), pp. 17–18.

entangled. A vassal might hold one piece of land from a lord, but the lord might be his vassal for another. Vassals could be far richer and more powerful than their lords. A wealthy and powerful aristocrat might hold no lands directly from the Crown, thus not being a baron in the sense of 'direct tenant of the Crown', but might be far superior in wealth and authority to one of the poorer barons. The existence of such multiple lordship and vassalage explains the development of the idea of liege lordship: 'a liege lord, as he is popularly called, is the man to whom alone one is bound by lordship in such a way that against him one owes nothing to any other (except the king)'.[2]

The English aristocracy was, speaking strictly, a class of landholders rather than landowners. The basic assumption about landed property was that it was held of another, a lord, and only the king, the apex of the pyramid, had no one above him. A consequence was that several individuals might have rights, of different kinds, in the same piece of land. Domesday Book records many examples of the simplest form of tenurial chain, that is, the tenant of a manor holding his estate from a baron who held his lands in turn from the king. The entry for Idbury in Oxfordshire, for example, reads, 'Ralph de Mortimer holds Idbury from the king and Odelard holds it from him.' Ralph was one of the Conqueror's greater barons, holding land in twelve counties; Odelard was a fairly humble follower of his, with two estates held from Ralph in Berkshire in addition to Idbury. The immediate manorial lord, as far as the peasant tenants were concerned, was Odelard. But Ralph de Mortimer and the king would both regard Idbury as 'theirs' in some sense, and in certain circumstances, such as Odelard's death or the necessity of raising an army, they would have direct claims to make upon the property.

The complexities that arose from enfeoffment can be illustrated by the situation in the barony of Stafford, as described in the survey of knights' fees of 1166.[3] A knight's fee was a fief owing the full service of one knight. Baronies were assessed as owing a certain number of knights to the king. The lord of the honor of Stafford, Robert of Stafford, recognized that his barony was answerable for sixty fees. Fifty-one of these had already been granted out as fiefs before 1135. Figure 5 shows the pattern of enfeoffment: the 51 fees had been granted out in 26 parcels that ranged in size from two-thirds of a fee to six fees. In nine cases the recipients had kept all their fees in their own hands, in thirteen cases they had kept some in their own hands but had granted out others as sub-fiefs, and in four cases they had granted out all the fiefs they had received. In the diagram fees granted out are shown to the right of the box indicating the tenant's total holding. Hence the first box represents

[2] *Dial. scacc.*, p. 83.

[3] *RBE* 1, pp. 264–8; G. Wrottesley and R. W. Eyton, 'The Liber Niger Scaccarii or the Black Book of the Exchequer (A.D. 1166)', *Collections for a History of Staffordshire* 1 (1880), pp. 145–240, at pp. 148–50 (text), 159–88 (commentary); the seven fees attributed to Robert fitz Ralph appear to be an error for six.

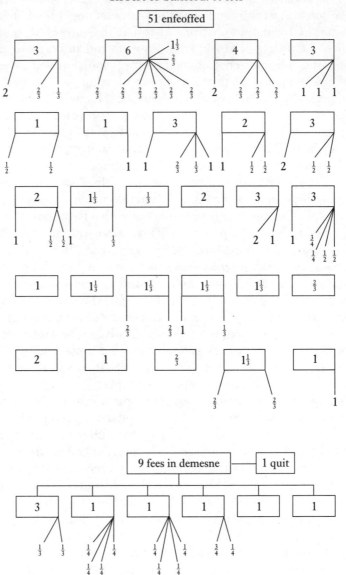

FIGURE 5. *The barony of Robert of Stafford, 1166*

a fee of three knights' fees granted to William fitz Gilbert, who had retained two in his own hands and enfeoffed Geoffrey Peron with two-thirds of a fee and Ralph of Milwich with one-third. Sometime the process of enfeoffment continued to a further level, as in the case of William de Chainai, who held a fee from Robert of Stafford and had granted half of it to Baldwin, who had in turn enfeoffed his brother Payn on a quarter-fee (the fifth box on the chart; only the first level of sub-enfeoffment is shown). Most of the nine fees that Robert of Stafford kept in demesne had also been filled with tenants, holding fees or fractions of fees. When one takes into account these sub-enfeoffments, another fee that was deemed 'quit', i.e. had been written off in the accounting, and a fee that, according to Robert, was being occupied unjustly, the lord of the barony of Stafford had in his own hands two and one-third fees of the sixty he answered for. He did not so much control a great estate as preside over a network of tenants and clients.

In all, 78 tenants and sub-tenants of the Stafford estate are listed in the 1166 survey. Some were related to each other, like the brothers Baldwin and Payn just mentioned, and others were kinsmen of the lord himself. The barony of Stafford eventually passed, in 1194, to Robert's daughter Millicent, whose husband, Hervey Bagot, was either the same man who held three knights' fees of Robert in 1166 or his son. One ecclesiastic was involved in this network, the abbot of Evesham, holding one fee (Wrottesley, Staffs.), held from him in turn by Adam of Wrottesley. Some of the Stafford tenants were themselves great lords. Henry d'Oilly, who held three fees from Robert of Stafford, also answered for more than thirty fees held 'in chief', i.e. directly from the king. Others had no more than the half-fee or third of a fee they are recorded as possessing in 1166. This is probably especially true of those who bore surnames derived from their local estate, like the four sub-tenants of Osbert Basewin: William of Greatford (Lincs., three-quarters of a fee), Cadiou of Cheadle (Staffs., a quarter-fee), Alexander of Denton (Lincs., half a fee), and Roger of Creeton (Lincs., half a fee). Osbert Basewin himself, holding three fees from Robert of Stafford, exemplifies the longevity of lord–vassal ties, for Domesday Book records a 'Basewin, Robert of Stafford's man' holding land at Creeton in Lincolnshire from Robert, grandfather and namesake of the baron of 1166. We see here three generations of links between a baronial family and its local vassals and tenants.

Feudal hierarchies might gradually come to be formal, purely legal arrangements, but they were not fictions. A hierarchy of authority of this type meant that even an apparently simple grant of land might have ramifications at every level. When Drogo de Andely made a grant of a hide of land to the monks of Abingdon, this was confirmed by each of his superiors in the tenurial chain, first by his immediate lord, Nigel d'Oilly, then by the superior lord, the earl of Chester, finally by king Henry I himself. The language of feudal dependence used to describe this transaction is very explicit: Drogo is 'a certain noble knight holding in fee from Nigel d'Oilly'; the property 'is reckoned part of the fee of the earl of Chester, from whom Nigel d'Oilly holds it and, through Nigel, Drogo'. For the grant to be as full and free as possible, a series of acts of consent and exemption are required, the earl freeing the land from the service due to him, the king releasing it from the obligation to pay geld, etc. The multiple layers of lordship bearing upon one small plot could not be better exemplified. As the Abingdon chronicler himself observes, 'different lordships lay on the land in different respects'.[4]

## Social Semantics

Lord and man, lord and tenant, lord and vassal, are terms that describe a relationship. They do not imply any particular level of wealth or any specific place in the social hierarchy as a whole. A vassal could be a wealthy man, a lord a relatively poor one. There were other categories current in twelfth-century England, however, that grouped people in a different way, into large classes that were arranged one above the other in terms of prestige and standing. Two examples of such hierarchies emerge from Angevin administrative documents. The first is that employed in the Assize of Arms of 1181 to estimate the quality of arms and armour that was appropriate for each group.[5] In descending order the categories are:

(1) those with a knight's fee; also free laymen with 16 marks (£10. 13s. 4d.) chattels or income;
(2) free laymen with 10 marks (£6. 6s. 8d.) chattels or income;
(3) burgesses and the whole body of free men.

In the following decade Richard I's government drew up a tariff of charges for those participating in tournaments.[6] They are as follows:

(1) count/earl          20 marks
(2) baron               10 marks
(3) knight with land     4 marks
(4) knight without land  2 marks

Such hierarchies are hybrid, based in part upon title or rank, in part upon wealth. The former consisted of discrete named categories ('earl', 'baron', 'free man'), the latter was a continuous scale, upon which the legislator had to mark an arbitrary point ('16 marks', '10 marks'). One could expect that the hierarchies of status and wealth would show considerable parallelism, so that barons would tend to be richer than knights, knights than free men, etc., but

---

[4] *Abingdon Chron.* 2, pp. 67–70.
[5] *Gesta Hen. II* 1, p. 278; R. Howd. 2, p. 261; *Sel. Charters*, p. 183.
[6] R. Howd. 3, p. 268.

there was also, of course, the possibility of discrepancies, the poor knight and the rich merchant being perhaps classic instances.

Other class and status-group terms and categories are found in the literature of the period. Describing the crowds flocking to the shrine of Edmund king and martyr, the poet Denis Piramus wrote how people of all orders came: bishops, abbots, counts or earls, barons, knights, bachelors, squires, citizens, burgesses, and peasants. Here is a neat social ladder, in which high clergy, various grades of high and low aristocrats, townsmen, and peasantry are ranged in descending order.[7]

What emerges from both official documentation and literary sources is that there was technically no noble class in England in this period. Although there were earls, barons, and knights—all of whom it is certainly sensible to regard as aristocrats—there was no unified group of nobles with privileges that marked them off from the rest of the population. The sharpest line, and one that was etched more deeply and clearly as a consequence of the changes in the judicial system under the Angevins, was that between freeman and villein (see below, pp. 321–5). But there was no distinct and significant line between noble and freeman.

There was indeed a vocabulary of nobility and gentility, but it was a loose and non-technical one. Terms such as 'noble' (*nobilis*), 'well-born' (*generosus, gentilis*), 'affluent' (*dives homo*), 'powerful' (*potens*), and 'magnate' (*magnas, procer*) are found in the Latin sources of the period, but their usage does not support the idea that there was a distinct class of aristocrats who were so labelled. Walter Map, for instance, writes on one occasion as if society were divided simply into two classes, the well-born (*generosi*) and the serfs or rustics (*servi/rustici*).[8] There is also some evidence for contemporary perceptions of society as divided fairly exhaustively into the knightly (*milites*) and the (unfree) rustics (*rustici*).[9] Such an opposition would class a poor free man with the knights and barons, as opposed to the unfree. In fact, this is precisely what the English Common Law did—it was the law of all free men, regardless of economic standing.

Indeed, formal titles of status were used rarely in this period compared with later times. Few donors or witnesses in charters have honorifics or titles. A charter of William, earl of Gloucester (1147–83), granting land in Essex was witnessed by ten men, only two of them bearing a title: Hamo fitz Geoffrey, the constable, and William fitz Nicholas, the marshal. Apart from these two, identified by their household office, the witnesses are simply

---

[7] Denis Piramus, *La Vie seint Edmund le rey*, lines 2869–81 (*Mem. Edm.* 2, p. 217).

[8] Map 1. 10 (p. 12).

[9] e.g. O. Cheriton, *Parabolae* 113 (p. 308) (said to archbishop Baldwin): 'bishops treat their subjects as cruelly as knights their peasants' (*non tantum milites in rusticos sed episcopi in subditos gravissime seviunt*).

named: Richard de St Quentin, Ranulf fitz Gerold, etc. Yet some of these
men, possibly all of them, were knights. Richard de St Quentin held a large
fief of ten knights' fees from the earl, another witness, Adam de Sumery, held
seven knights' fees from him.[10] A hundred years later, a charter witnessed by
such men would most likely title them 'sir' (*dominus*) and explicitly refer to
them as knights. For the aristocracy of the twelfth century, formal title, even
in such public contexts as the witnessing of charters, seems to have been of
less importance.

## Earls

During this period there was, in fact, only one formal honorific title held by
the English aristocracy, that of earl. The word was of Anglo-Scandinavian
origin and scribes writing in Latin rendered it as *comes*, equivalent to the
French 'count' (*cuens*). Those who bore the title formed a small elite within
the aristocracy. During the reign of William the Conqueror there were only
seven earldoms in existence at one time or another: the joint earldom of
Huntingdon/Northampton, the border earldoms of Kent, Northumberland, Chester, Shrewsbury, and Hereford, and the earldom of East Anglia.
The last two were suppressed after the rebellion of 1075. Under William
Rufus two new earldoms were created but two also lapsed and under Henry I
three were created and one destroyed, so that by the time of Stephen's accession in 1135 there were still only seven earldoms: Huntingdon/Northamp-
ton, Buckingham, Chester, Gloucester, Leicester, Surrey, and Warwick.

    Stephen had a quite different attitude to earldoms and created them liber-
ally in the first years of his reign. Once the civil war began in 1139, his
Angevin rivals followed his example. Hence the number of earls more than
tripled between 1135 and 1141. It has indeed been suggested that Stephen's
intention was to have an earl for virtually every English county, of which
there were thirty-nine. After the explosion of Stephen's reign, however, there
was a long period with no further creations (although sometimes earldoms
were renewed after long vacancies). The first new earldom after Stephen's
reign was that of Winchester, created by king John in 1207 for Saher de
Quincy, and this was John's only creation. No further earldoms were created
until 1227. Hence, there was under the Angevins a return to the parsimo-
nious policy of the first Norman kings in the matter of conferring such titles.

    Although Henry II created no new earldoms, he did not systematically
suppress those granted in his predecessor's reign. Moreover, in contrast to
what happened in the time of the Conqueror and his sons, no earls were
deprived of their titles after 1157 and female descent of earldoms was

---

[10] *Gloucester Charters*, no. 158, pp. 147–8, facsimile plate XV; *RBE* 1, p. 288.

increasingly recognized. Hence the situation established about 1140, namely that there should be about twenty earls rather than half-a-dozen, continued throughout the Angevin period. Even so, the earls continued to form a very small group amongst the major tenants of the Crown and the comital title was obviously deemed the highest social distinction that a lay magnate could attain. In the year 1200, for instance, there were only sixteen earldoms in England.

The honor of an earl was contained in the title. Creation, at least by the late twelfth century, was through the girding on of a ceremonial sword. In 1191 there is an explicit reference to 'Robert de Breteuil, the son of Robert, the deceased earl of Leicester, to whom the king had recently given his father's earldom and whom he had girded with the sword of the earldom of Leicester'.[11] Earls took their title from a county and even those who were normally known by their family name had a county associated with the title: the earls Warenne or earls Ferrers were termed so much more frequently than they were styled earls of Surrey or earls of Derby, but there was no doubt that Surrey and Derby were their titular counties. In contemporary Latin the very word for 'county' and 'earldom' was identical, so that the passage about Robert, earl of Leicester, cited above, could equally well be translated 'girded with the sword of the county of Leicester' as 'girded with the sword of the earldom of Leicester'.

The main tie between earl and county was the so-called 'third penny', that is, the third of the profits of the county court and the royal boroughs that went to the earl. As the royal treasurer, Richard fitz Neal, writing in the late 1170s, explained,

An earl is the one who receives a third part of the income from pleas in each county . . . only those receive it whom the generosity of kings, in consideration of their distinguished service or outstanding merit, creates earls, and decrees are to receive it by virtue of this dignity, either hereditarily or personally.[12]

After Henry de Bohun's designation as earl of Hereford in 1200, the king instructed the sheriff of Hereford to pay him £20 per annum 'on account of the earldom'.[13]

Although there were great barons who did not hold the comital title, there was clearly a link between the size of a magnate's estate and his chance of being an earl—all those laymen with more than 100 knights' fees on their estates in 1166 held the title of earl.[14] Earls were thus among the wealthiest and most powerful lay aristocrats. One family that was distinguished by holding, for a time, two comital titles, was the house of Clare (see Figure 6).

---

[11] *Gesta Ric. I*, p. 156; R. Howd. 3, p. 94.    [12] *Dial. scacc.*, pp. 64–5.
[13] *Rot. lib.*, p. 5.    [14] Keefe, *Assessments*, app. II.

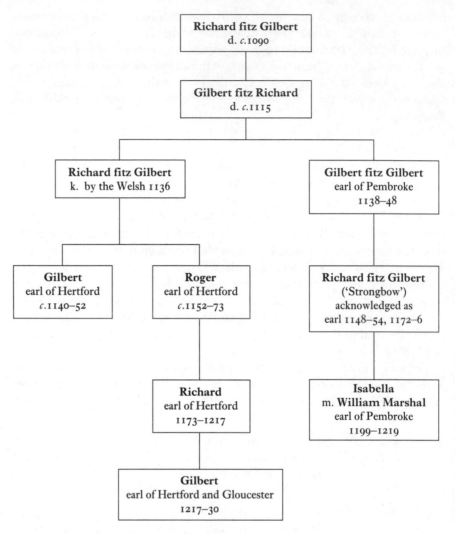

FIGURE 6.  *The earls of the house of Clare, 1138–1230*

The Clares descended from Gilbert de Brionne, guardian of the young
William the Conqueror, who had been assassinated in 1040 during the feuds
that characterized the young duke's minority. Gilbert's son, Richard fitz
Gilbert, had benefited enormously from William's generosity after the
conquest of England, acquiring an estate that included Tonbridge in Kent,
where he had an important castle, Clare in Suffolk, from which the
family borrowed its name, and, clustering around them, estates worth, in
total, £873 p.a., making him among the half-dozen wealthiest men in

England.[15] His son, Gilbert fitz Richard, was involved in the rising of 1088 against Rufus, being captured in his own castle at Tonbridge, and, although not dispossessed or exiled, was never trusted by the king again. The family returned to favour in the reign of Henry I. The younger members were given lordships and abbacies, while the association of the Clares with the Anglo-Norman expansion westwards into Wales and Ireland began in 1110, when Henry offered Gilbert of Clare the Welsh region of Ceredigion (Cardiganshire), if he could 'take possession of it' (see above, pp. 73–4). The Clares were to be among the main agents of Anglo-Norman power in south Wales for the next two hundred years.

Until the reign of Stephen, the Clares possessed enormous wealth and exercised great power without bearing any distinctive title of rank. With Stephen's new policy of distributing the comital title more freely, they were obvious candidates for an earldom, and, in fact, acquired two in (or shortly after) 1138. Gilbert fitz Richard, head of the family since the death of his father during the Welsh uprising of 1136, was made earl of Hertford, while his uncle Gilbert fitz Gilbert became earl of Pembroke. Both titles were new. The two earls were generally loyal to Stephen, although Gilbert of Hertford deserted him during the battle of Lincoln in 1141, and both were in rebellion in 1147, before being subsequently reconciled. Gilbert, earl of Pembroke, died in 1148 and was succeeded by his son, Richard fitz Gilbert ('Strongbow'). In 1153 he witnessed the treaty of Westminster between Stephen and Henry of Anjou as earl of Pembroke, but after Henry succeeded to the throne in the following year, it was an honor that was denied to him. It is not clear why the Hertford line were allowed to retain their dignity, which was equally a creation of Henry's enemy, Stephen.

The story of Richard fitz Gilbert's adventure in Ireland, his acquisition of the lordship of Leinster in 1171 and his reconciliation with Henry II, has been told earlier (pp. 86–7). One consequence was that the royal government now allowed him to be styled 'earl' again. He did not enjoy his restored dignity long and, when he died in 1176, his children were infants. A son was long in royal custody, but died before coming of age, and Strongbow's inheritance came to his daughter, Isabella, a valuable heiress who was married off to the Angevin stalwart, William Marshal. Eventually, in 1199, at his coronation, John girded William with the comital sword, thus initiating the Marshal line of earls of Pembroke.

The Clare hold on the title of Hertford was far more secure. Indeed, it was continuous from its creation about 1138 to the death of the young Gilbert of Clare at Bannockburn in 1314. The earls of Clare, as they were usually known, were among the greatest aristocrats in England. The inquest into

---

[15] Richard Mortimer, 'The Beginnings of the Honour of Clare', *ANS* 3 (1980), pp. 119–41, at p. 119.

knight's fees of 1166 shows them holding a total of 150 fees, which places them comfortably among the ten wealthiest and most powerful men in the kingdom. Earl Roger was frequently in attendance at the king's court, was one of the commissioners entrusted with the Inquest of Sheriffs in 1170, and struggled to maintain his position in Wales. Despite his great wealth, he was never highly prominent in the political or military affairs of his time. His son and successor, Richard, did eventually play a part in the high politics of the kingdom, but only at the end of his life, during the rebellion of 1215 against John, when both he and his son and heir, Gilbert, were among the leaders of the baronial rebellion. Father and son were likewise both captured by the royalists at the battle of Lincoln in 1217. When earl Richard died, later that year, there was, despite the family's recent record of resistance, no doubt that his son would succeed him, both as earl of Hertford and, through his mother, one of the Gloucester heiresses, earl of Gloucester. By the early thirteenth century a relatively settled transmission of comital titles had been established.

The Clare earls of this period were rarely prominent, as military leaders, crusaders, officials of the royal government, or even rebels. They did not need to be. They had extensive lands, a large body of vassals and retainers, and an assurance of high descent. They were, moreover, the centre of an enormous kin-network. As one contemporary observed, 'Almost all the nobles of England were related to the earl of Clare'.[16] Earl Richard of Clare may, indeed, have been stirred to rebellion partly by the fact that one of the victims of John's cruelty, William de Braose junior, was his son-in-law. His engagement in dramatic political conflict was atypical. The Clares were a family established at the highest level of the aristocracy. Most of their lives was presumably spent in enjoying that position.

## Barons

In the sense of 'substantial tenant holding directly from a lord', the term 'baron' was not limited to those holding of the Crown. A great lord would have his own major tenants holding in chief from him and these could also be styled 'barons'. The earl of Gloucester would routinely address his charters to 'all my barons'.[17] The great churches also had their barons. In the 1120s a land transaction involving the abbey of Ramsey, which had been first agreed in the monastic chapter in the abbey church, was later confirmed at one of the abbey's manors 'in the presence of the barons of the church of Ramsey'.[18]

Yet the term was used especially and increasingly exclusively to describe the greater tenants-in-chief of the Crown. Obviously the word 'greater' does

[16] W. f. Stephen, *V. Thomas* 32, p. 43.     [17] *Gloucester Charters*, index, s.v. 'baron'.
[18] *Ramsey Chron.*, p. 254; *Ramsey Cart.* 1, p. 142, no. 68.

not provide an exact measure and there may be some doubt as to where the line should be drawn between barons and non-baronial tenants-in-chief. Magna Carta prescribed that the relief, i.e. inheritance duty, payable on an earldom or barony should be £100, and thereafter, if it is possible to find out the relief paid, this should make possible a clear categorization of lordships into baronial and non-baronial. Before 1215 the situation is less clear-cut. Writing in the late 1170s, Richard fitz Neal explicitly states that there is no fixed level of relief for 'those who hold directly from the Crown in chief, i.e. greater and lesser baronies'. He does, however, claim that entries in the Pipe Rolls will be in different form for estates that are 'honors' or baronies and those 'estates that are smaller, consisting of one, two or three manors'.[19] According to Richard, the king's treasurer, therefore, a few manors did not constitute a barony.

Working with a retrospective and practical perspective, historians have categorized as baronies estates with a certain level of income or comprising a certain number of knights' fees (the two criteria are by no means precisely equivalent). The survey of feudal service initiated by Henry II in 1166 enables fairly exact figures to be given for the number of tenants-in-chief and the size of their holdings in knights' fees at that time. The 270 lay tenant-in-chiefs can be grouped according to size as follows:[20]

| Number of knights' fees | Number of estates |
|---|---|
| 0–9 | 136 |
| 10–19 | 46 |
| 20–39 | 41 |
| 40+ | 47 |

There were thus 134 lay lords whose estates comprised ten or more knights' fees. It would be uncontentious to call these men barons. A case could be made for including those with smaller estates, with perhaps as few as five knights' fees. If this is done, men of baronial rank would number 164. In any event, the approximate size of the baronial class was in the range 100–200 families. These families enjoyed incomes that varied as much as the number of fees they held. In the Angevin period the average annual income of a baron was about £200. While many had incomes below £100 p.a., the annual income of the wealthiest non-comital baron, Roger de Lacy, constable of Chester (d. 1211), reached £800.[21] This made him richer than several earls. At the other end of the scale, it becomes an arbitrary matter to differentiate minor barons from the wealthier knights.

---

[19] *Dial. scacc.*, pp. 94–6.    [20] Keefe, *Assessments*, p. 45, table 5.
[21] Sidney Painter, *Studies in the History of the English Feudal Barony* (Baltimore, 1943), pp. 170–1.

## Knights

'Knight' (French *chevalier*, Latin *miles*) is a complex term because historians dealing with the eleventh and twelfth centuries have used it in at least three main senses: it can have a functional military meaning—the knight is a heavy cavalryman, with the full mail-coat and war-horse, as depicted on the Bayeux Tapestry (see Plate 5); it can have a ceremonial meaning—the knight is a man who has been 'knighted', undergoing the rituals (discussed below) that mark him out from others; and it can have a social or economic meaning, referring to the landed stratum somewhat lower than the barons and somewhat higher than the ordinary freemen. It is evident that the potential for confusion is great. Not only is there the possibility, indeed probability, that a man may be a knight in one sense and not in another, there is also, in the case of the first, functional, sense and the third, social, sense, the difficulty of inexact boundaries. Where do we stop talking of poor knights and start talking of rich freemen or yeomen; where is the line between the knight and the non-knightly 'man-at-arms' with armour and horse?

As is explicit in Richard I's fees for tournaments (above, p. 206), a knight could be without land. Such landless men would attach themselves to the household of great lords, temporarily or permanently, making themselves useful and dreaming of the landed estate they hoped one day to receive. In 1166 Hugh de Lacy, a great baron on the Welsh Marches, listed his knights in response to Henry II's inquest into knights' fees. At the end he names a group of eight who each held land worth £5 or £6 p.a. from him and had no fixed service. 'Some live with me and I find their necessities,' reported Hugh, 'some are in my castles in Wales and I find their necessities.'[22] These men had landed estates that were less valuable than those customarily viewed as capable of supporting a knight and they lived either in their lord's household or in his castles. They were more fortunate than some household knights, in that they did have a separate source of income, albeit small, but their lives would centre around the lord's hall and the lord's requirements.

Once they had been granted fiefs—'housed' (*chassez*) or 'enfeoffed' (*fiufé*) in the aristocratic vernacular[23]—knights could put down territorial roots. They would transmit their estates to their children, creating 'county families'. In this way a local knightly class arose, men with a manor or two who might attend the county court, serve as coroners or tax collectors in their shire, perhaps act as stewards for a regional magnate. On the honor (great estate) of Huntingdon there were some eighty families of knightly rank or above in the time of earl David (1185–1219). These included some of baronial status but also many holding simply a few knights' fees. Reginald of Oakley

---

[22] *RBE* 1, p. 283.
[23] e.g. Marie de France, *Le Fresne*, line 314, *Bisclavret*, line 188 (*Lais*, pp. 43, 53).

represented the fourth generation of his family to hold a knightly tenancy from the earldom, consisting of the manors of Great Oakley in Northamptonshire and Childerley in Cambridgeshire. He served as the earl's estate steward about 1190. His contemporary, Ralph Morin, held the manor of Harrold in Bedfordshire from the earl, but also small tenancies elsewhere from other lords. He made his way in the Angevin local administration, serving as deputy sheriff of Northamptonshire in 1184 and being attached to the household of John, son of Henry II. His involvement with John's rebellion in 1194 meant that he was deprived of his lands, but he was restored when the rebel prince became king in 1199 and was made sheriff of Devon in 1201. He was typical of his class, with a modest landed base that he increased through useful service, sharing in the vicissitudes of his lords, patronizing local religious houses, entangled to some degree in Jewish debt, but able to perpetuate and augment his family's fortunes.[24]

The existence of lineages like the Oakleys and Morins encouraged the idea that knighthood was a dignity inhering in particular families. When the Cistercian Jocelin of Furness criticized monks 'born of knightly stock' who were obsessed with their aristocratic relatives, he is not simply using the phrase as a synonym for 'with fathers who were knights'.[25] The implication is that some families were of knightly status, whether or not individual members of those families actually served as heavy cavalry or underwent the rituals of dubbing. In this sense women could be of knightly stock, like the widow of Peter de Pelleville, who had held a knight's fee in Norfolk and died in 1184, who is herself described as 'born from knights'.[26] The context of this reference, a list of widows whom the king had the right to give in marriage, suggests that her knightly descent is recorded as an attractive and prestigious attribute. It is this development that enables us to talk of a knightly class.

The judicial changes introduced during the Angevin period placed a new emphasis on knighthood. Certain roles in the new procedures could only be taken by knights. The Grand Assize required a jury composed entirely of knights. If a litigant claimed that he could not attend court because of serious illness, four knights from the county had to visit him to ascertain that his claim was true. The record of cases being transferred from the county court to Westminster had to be brought by knights. County coroners were knights. In all these ways, heavy judicial and administrative duties fell on knights. As a consequence, it became important to be quite clear who was and who was not a knight.

This new clarity, coupled with the proliferation of records about the year

---

[24] William Farrer, *Honors and Knights' Fees* (3 vols.; London, 1923–5), vol. 2, pp. 327–9, 351–4; Stringer, *Earl David*, pp. 132, 157, 165, 258, 303 n. 34.
[25] Joc. Furn., *V. Waltheof*, p. 259.          [26] *Rot. dom.*, p. 53.

1200, enables an informed estimate to be made of the number of knights in England. The inquest of 1166, supplemented by other related evidence, shows that at that time there were about 7,500 knights' fees in England.[27] This is not the number of knights, however, for not every knight held a knight's fee—some had more, some less, and knights' fees could be fragmented into smaller holdings, often held by tenants who were not knights. The figure from 1166 thus simply provides an initial order of magnitude for discussion. Analysis of the judicial records of John's reign yields lists of knights serving on the Grand Assize and in other capacities reserved to men of their status. The most careful estimate of the total number of knights in England at this period based on these sources suggests a figure of 4,500–5,000 knights.[28]

Knights may have had heavy duties under the Angevins, but they also enjoyed recognized rights and privileges, even when down on their luck. Henry II decreed that a knight who was imprisoned for debt should not be placed in the body of the jail but kept in 'free custody' above it. Although his property could be sold to pay off his debts, his horse was immune, 'lest he who has been raised to the dignity of knight [eques] be forced to go on foot'.[29] Over the course of the twelfth and thirteenth centuries knighthood becomes ever more clearly a social rank. From the 1220s the term 'knight' (miles) occurs with increasing frequency as an honorific title after the name of men witnessing charters. It does not seem to be the case that more knights are witnessing, but rather that those that do so wish to assert their knightly status more explicitly and formally.[30]

### The Margins of the Aristocracy

If the English aristocracy towards the end of our period included no more than 20 earls, 200 barons, and 5,000 knights, then how many families below the level of the knights considered themselves or were considered aristocrats—'well-born', living off rents and the labour of others rather than putting their hands to the plough? Was there indeed a category of gentle or noble that included more than earls, barons, and knights? The Assize of Arms of 1181 placed free laymen with 16 marks (£10. 13s. 4d.) chattels or income on a par with holders of a knight's fee. The most natural conclusion to draw from this is that there was a class of people with 'knightly' incomes who

---

[27] Keefe, *Assessments*, p. 154.

[28] Kathryn Faulkner, 'The Transformation of Knighthood in Early Thirteenth-Century England', *EHR* 111 (1996), pp. 1–23.

[29] *Dial. scacc.*, pp. 117, 111.

[30] Donald F. Fleming, '*Milites* as Attestors to Charters in England, 1101–1300', *Albion*, 22 (1990), pp. 185–98.

were not knights. The Assize then goes on to distinguish free laymen with 10 marks (£6. 6s. 8d.) chattels or income from the remaining free men. Here is a pointer to a class that was not of 'knightly' income, but still marked out from the mass of freeholders.

Such men might not hold by military tenure (i.e. knights' fees or fractions of knights' fees). There were other forms of free tenure. One was sergeanty, the holding of land in return for a specified service other than knightly. These services were very varied, as is revealed by the survey of the honor of Lancaster in 1210–12, which lists the sergeanty tenures of the honor (then in the king's hands). Men held in return for serving as 'chief sergeant' of the hundred; guarding the king's ship; escorting the king's treasure; supplying or keeping goshawks or hounds; serving as crossbowman, carpenter, or local lawman. Clearly these are very varied and disparate services. Although sergeants were free men, some of their duties did involve physical labour and some of their tenements were small—Robert son of John had 12 acres of land for shoeing the king's cart-horses.[31] They cannot be regarded as a social group, but those of them with reasonable amounts of land and honourable services may reasonably be classed as minor aristocrats. The regulations issued before the Third Crusade classified 'clerks, knights and sergeants' together and distinguished them from 'burgesses and rustics'.[32]

Other men held land by a tenure termed 'fee-farm', a kind of hereditary leasehold involving a fixed annual rent, often together with other honourable services. When, sometime in the late 1120s, the abbot of Burton granted a lease of some of his abbey's lands at Leigh in Staffordshire to 'his liegeman Andrew', he specified the following services that Andrew would owe:

He has sworn full fidelity to the monks as their liegeman; he owes them, as a free man, the service of going in his own person where the abbot commands, either with or without the abbot. He should give the abbot honourable hospitality when he comes to the area and should make a suitable payment from his own property when the abbot requires it. If there is need he should, like the other men of the abbey, lend his carts and those of his men to bring timber from the wood for the building work on the monastery. He should moreover pay 60 shillings per annum. When he dies, the church will receive all his portion of his movable property, and his body will be interred honourably in the church.[33]

A virtually identical set of services was specified in the charter in which the abbot granted the estate at Darlaston (Staffs.) to Orm of Darlaston and his

---

[31] *RBE* 2, pp. 570–1.
[32] *Gesta Hen. II* 2, p. 32; Gerv. Cant., p. 409; W. Newb. 3. 23 (1, p. 273).
[33] Burton Cart., p. 34.

son Robert.[34] The fact that Robert's mother was the daughter of a sheriff of Staffordshire gives some idea of the social status of the lessees, while Orm's name indicates his origin in the Anglo-Scandinavian landholding class of the Danelaw. Sometimes specifically legal services were also required from such tenants. The family that held Okeover in Dovedale from Burton abbey was expected 'to go to the king's court with the abbot on the monastery's business, at the abbot's expense . . . and to come to the abbot's court to judge thieves who have been apprehended or to judge cases involving trial by battle'.[35] Ralph fitz Urvoi, who held Hampton from the abbey, was obliged 'to attend the abbot's lawsuits in Staffordshire whenever summoned with due notice'.[36]

The advantages to Burton abbey of having a group of tenants of this standing are clear. Apart from the regular cash income they supplied—of the range of £1 to £3 per annum each—they provided honourable company for the abbot on his travels and in court, they could be asked for advice and they had their own world of lay connections that could be useful. They were often tenants of more than one lord and might form a bridge between them. The Okeovers held land of the priory of Tutbury and the Ferrers earls as well as of Burton, and an agreement between Burton and one of its lessees specifically exempted him from attendance at court 'if he was on the service of his lord Robert de Ferrers'.[37] Such men were, moreover, a reservoir of simple physical force: when the monks went to market in Chester or Nantwich, they could rely on the protection of Robert of Darlaston, who would accompany them there and back; and Robert had also promised 'to defend the monks' land from evildoers'. In this way the abbot could call on a circle of laymen tied to the abbey by tenure, service, and sometimes, as in the case of 'Herbert the abbot's nephew', family relationship.

Men like Andrew of Leigh, Orm and Robert of Darlaston, and the other lessees formed a class intermediate between knights and peasants. They did not hold by military tenure but neither is it likely that they engaged in much manual work on their estates; they attended the royal courts and the court of their lord; they had peasant tenants, whose rents and services supported them; and they mingled with and intermarried with the class of aristocrats above them. Andrew of Leigh's service was that of 'a free man' (*liber homo*) and the link between lessee and the church was to culminate in 'honourable' burial. This free and honourable class can perhaps be seen as the equivalent of the lesser gentry of later times.

---

[34] Burton Cart., pp. 35–6.
[35] G. Wrottesley, 'The Okeovers of Okeover', *Collections for a History of Staffordshire*, n.s. 7 (1904), pp. 130–1.
[36] Burton Surveys, p. 224; Burton Cart., p. 32.        [37] Burton Cart., p. 34.

## 2. THE ARISTOCRATIC ESTATE

### The Honor

The largest aristocratic estates, held by the earls and barons, were termed 'honors': assemblages of estates held by military tenure. They consisted not of unbroken stretches of magnate territory but of dozens of manors or holdings scattered across counties and intermingled with the lands of other lords. However they had been created, honors had an inertial tendency to be treated as a unit even if the line of the original holders died out. Thus, the honor of Wallingford, a great accumulation of 100 knights' fees created soon after the Norman Conquest and held by the Angevin loyalist Brian fitz Count during Stephen's reign, passed to the Crown in the middle of the twelfth century. Thereafter it recurs in the Pipe Rolls, the records of the annual royal audit, as a separate accounting and administrative unit. It could be granted out as an entity, as it was in 1189 to form part of John's appanage. Neither when held by the king nor when held by John was it merged with the other lands of its holder. The honor of Wallingford even won an enduring place in administrative history when, in the Assize of Clarendon of 1166, it was prescribed that 'no one should prevent sheriffs entering their court or land, be they within a castle or outside a castle or even in the honor of Wallingford'. These great honors thus formed a recognizable feature in the tenurial and administrative landscape of twelfth-century England.

The honor represented a principle of territorial administration different from that of the county. Rather than comprising a homogenous and continuous unit of land under the authority of one royal official, the honor was given whatever coherence it had by common tenure. While all the inhabitants of Gloucestershire were subject to the sheriff and county court of Gloucester, it was the vassals and tenants of the earl of Gloucester, wherever they were situated, who owed service to the earl and could be summoned to his court. Much of England's history depended on which bonds were to be more significant.

The real importance of the honor as a social and political unit is difficult to assess. In general, historians have tended to believe that it was a central focus for the magnates and knights of the Norman period, but became of diminishing importance under the Angevins, especially as royal justice impinged upon some of its activities. It was obviously always necessary for a vassal or tenant to know to whom he owed the services that formed a condition of his tenure, but this relationship could be formal or purely financial. On the other hand, a vassal or tenant might provide his lord with personal military service, act as his household or estate official, and attend him frequently in person. Another factor influencing the strength of the bond was whether the tenant held land from many lords or had one, or one main, lord. An honor where the tenants held land only from one lord and attended him personally would clearly be very different from an honor that was little more than an accounting device.

Just as the county court was one of the main vehicles for county identity, so the court of the honor, presided over by the lord or his representative, was one of the central institutions of the great feudal estate. Evidence for the honor court is not extensive, but there is enough to allow us to see gatherings of a lord and his vassals and tenants, adjudicating disputes among their number and witnessing property transactions. Thus, when, in the 1120s or 1130s, William de Anisy, a tenant of Henry de Port, wished to transfer some of his lands to a younger son, Richard de Anisy, he did this at Basingstoke, Henry de Port's chief manor, and the transaction was witnessed by more than thirty of the tenants and vassals of the honor.[38] In 1174 William de Audri, a tenant of the earldom of Huntingdon, granted land in Draughton (Northants) to Stephen of Ecton and his son, and received their homage in the court of earl David of Huntingdon.[39] Courts like those of Henry de Port and earl David were public venues, where tenants would meet to engage in both formal and informal business, reinforcing a sense that they were associates and fellows.

It was not only simple conveyances that came before the honorial courts. Henry I recognized that 'cases concerning the demarcation or seizure of land . . . between the vassals of any baron . . . should be heard in the court of their lord'.[40] Such land disputes were taken to lord's courts even after the expansion of royal justice under Henry II. The records of the eyre of the south-west counties in 1201 have many references to such cases. One tenant 'had recovered possession of the land in the court of the prior of Bodmin, and the prior's sergeant had put him in possession'; two disputants had taken their case over a parcel of land to the 'court of Judhael de Mohun' in Somerset and there made an agreement.[41]

Yet the honorial court was not simply and always an agency that promoted solidarity between lord and vassals. It could also be the forum for conflict between them, for the most delicate cases that came before the honorial court were disputes between the lord and one of his men. In actions of this kind there might be reasonable fears of partiality. During Stephen's reign a dispute broke out between the Marcher baron Hugh de Mortimer and his vassal and steward, Oliver de Merlemond. Hugh 'had him summoned three times

---

[38] *Bk. Seals*, no. 301, pp. 207–8 and plate V; Stenton, *First Century*, p. 55.
[39] Stringer, *Earl David*, pp. 232–3 (David was in temporary possession at this time).
[40] Liebermann, *Gesetze* 1, p. 524; *Sel. Charters*, p. 122; Robertson, *Laws*, p. 286.
[41] *PBKJ* 2, nos. 478, 522, 634, pp. 124, 142, 182–3.

in his court to answer the complaints he had against him. Because Oliver feared the malice and cruelty of his lord, he did not dare to appear in his court.'[42] One of the most serious complaints a vassal could make about a lord was denial of justice, refusal to deal with legitimate grievances. After his release from captivity in 1141, king Stephen complained that he had been seized by his own men even though 'he had never denied justice to them'.[43] Presumably the implication of his words is that denial of justice would have constituted at least an extenuating circumstance for even such a drastic step as imprisoning one's lord.

The ties that bound lords and men in the honorial framework could thus obviously be a source of conflict as well as cohesion. In such conflicts it was not always the lord who had the advantage. Ecclesiastical lords of lay vassals were particularly vulnerable and this vulnerability was increased in times of weak government, like Stephen's reign. The bishop of Salisbury, for instance, listing his knights in 1166, twelve years after Stephen's death, complained of one of his tenants: 'Walter Walerand holds one knight's fee, for which he performed service to my predecessor, and for me he does only the service of half a knight, because he dispossessed me of the service of half a knight in the time of war.'[44] Walerand, who was a baron in his own right, was obviously powerful enough to seize the opportunity to halve his obligations for this tenancy. The disorders of Stephen's reign had given him the necessary cover. Disputes over services of this type were a common and perennial feature of lord–vassal relations.

The author of the legal treatise that goes under the name of Glanville, writing in the last years of Henry II's reign, noted that the customs and practices of lords' courts 'were so many and so various that they cannot easily be put down in writing'.[45] Yet he did not dispute their authority: lords can hold their court wherever they wish within their fee; they can force their men to come to their court to answer charges of disloyalty or default of service.[46] The tone of this voice from the heart of the Angevin legal establishment is not hostile to seignorial justice. Nevertheless, the effect of many of the changes that Henry II initiated was to diminish the importance of seignorial jurisdiction in land cases. No one need answer a plea concerning a free tenement unless a royal writ was served. Some, highly attractive, procedures were only available in the king's court. The transfer of a case from a lord's court to the king's court was relatively simple. Because of this, it became rare for land disputes to be terminated by judgment in seignorial courts. One force that gave a focus to the honor had been weakened.

---

[42] *Wigmore Chron.*, p. 424.   [43] W. Malm., *HN* 501 (p. 62).   [44] *RBE* 1, p. 237.
[45] Glanville 12. 6 (p. 139).   [46] Ibid. 12. 7, 9. 1 (pp. 140, 105).

In some cases, it appears that tenants were witnessing their lord's charters less frequently in the early thirteenth century than they had done in the previous century. Professional administrators replaced the great honorial tenants as seignorial officials. Yet it is too simple to see this simply as a withering of the lord–vassal relationship. Any lord, from great semi-regal magnate to country gentleman, had to recruit and reward men in order to maintain his position as a lord. The ties that bound them to him were of many different types. He could expect to have kin, vassals, retainers, tenants, and friends: the legal, social, and moral obligations and connections would vary according to the nature of these bonds, as well as individual personality and circumstance. The Norman Conquest had given the chief Norman lords an unparalleled opportunity to reward followers with land. As this garrison aristocracy became a county society, one consequence was that the immediacy of links between lord and tenant diminished. Tenants still had their obligations: to attend their lord's court, pay him scutage, recognize his rights of wardship, etc. The relationship might be no more than that. Yet knightly tenants remained one of the most obvious groups from whom magnates would recruit their active following.

## Resources

### Knights' Fees

The records of the Norman and Angevin period frequently mention the term 'knight's fee'. It is used to specify the amount of service due from a landholding and must originally have implied that such a holding was deemed adequate to support one knight. An early example comes from Westminster: 'We, Gilbert the abbot and the convent of Westminster, have given to William Baynard a certain farm in the township of Westminster . . . to house him and to be held by him for the whole of his life by the service of one knight'.[47] In reality, the range of knights' fees in both area and value was great.

In 1135 the important royal official Richard Basset held 184¼ carucates of land, which were assessed as fifteen knights' fees, equating a fee with just over 12¼ carucates. At the conventional rate of 120 acres to the carucate, this would make a knight's fee about 1,500 acres.[48] In 1166 the Lincolnshire baron Lambert de Scoteny held 16¼ carucates for the service of ten knights, hence a knight's fee of 195 acres, about an eighth the size of Richard Basset's fees.[49] Some allowance in such cases must be made for the possibility that the carucate might vary regionally, but the key influence was probably favourable assessment for political or other reasons. Fees are recorded that range from

---

[47] *Westminster Charters*, no. 236, p. 109.
[48] *RBE* I, p. 329.        [49] *RBE* I, p. 385.

half a carucate to sixty carucates.[50] The monetary value of a knight's fee also varied. The average fee on the estates of the archbishop of Canterbury in the late eleventh century was worth £6 per annum, but the individual fees range from £1 to £20.[51] The eight and a half fees of the knights of Shaftesbury about the year 1130 ranged in value from 10 shillings to £4. 5s., but these seem to have been poor or small fees.[52] There is twelfth-century evidence that the proper, appropriate or reasonable income from a knight's fee was reckoned to be £10 or £20 per annum and this would harmonize quite well with the provision of the Assize of Arms, quoted above, equating knights and 'free laymen with 16 marks [£10. 13s. 4d.] chattels or income'.[53]

If we wish to form a concrete picture of what a knight's fee actually involved in physical resources, an example is provided by the estate of Hugh de Candos at Burnham in Norfolk, which was divided between his two daughters in 1209, leaving each of them and their husbands with one fee. Hence the share of one of the sisters, which is described in detail in a document from that year, represents one fee. It was made up of various components: the rents due from free tenants; the villeins and their lands; the arable and other lands of the lord's demesne; and rights over mills, markets, and churches. In the first category were 15 free tenements, one of them assessed at a fifth of a knight's fee and 14 others that paid a total of 14 shillings per year. Eight of these contributed to the payment of scutage when it was levied, at rates varying from a farthing per pound (i.e. 1/960) to four and a half pence per mark (i.e. 1/35.5). There were 34 villein tenements, some held jointly by groups of brothers or sisters.

The demesne lands—those worked directly by the lord  are described in the document in minute detail: 57 individual pieces of land are mentioned, including pasture, meadow, and moorland as well as arable, and are identified in a variety of ways, by name (Oldesties, Blacchille, Tuncroft), previous tenants ('the land that was Hervey the priest's', 'the croft that was Ralph Hulloc's') and sometimes by measurement and location ('fifteen acres lying near to the village of Docking to the north', 'half a rood and four feet of land at *Harnesho* toward the west'). Finally, there were the lucrative miscellaneous rights and resources, including two mills, the advowsons (i.e. right to present the rector) of two churches, St Margaret's and All Saints, and a share in the market at Burnham.[54] Clearly this was a substantial estate and its holders

---

[50] Keefe, *Assessments*, pp. 21–2.      [51] Ibid., p. 23.

[52] Ann Williams, 'The Knights of Shaftesbury Abbey', *ANS* 8 (1985), pp. 214–42, at p. 240, table 3.

[53] Stenton, *First Century*, pp. 166–9; Keefe, *Assessments*, pp. 23–4.

[54] *Feet of Fines for the County of Norfolk . . . 1201–1215, for the County of Suffolk . . . 1199–1214*, ed. Barbara Dodwell (PRS n.s. 32; 1958 for 1956), no. 210, pp. 100–3.

would be important local figures. It was not, however, composed of a uniform and continuous piece of landed property—the 57 pieces of demesne land would be intermingled with the lands of others, and they formed only one aspect of the lord's resources: rents, contributions to taxation, shares in market profits, and the patronage of the local church were all important too. The estate exemplifies well both the concrete realities and the complexity that lie behind the formula, 'one knight's fee'.

## Baronies

The components of baronial income were, in many respects, the same as those of knightly income: rents, the sale of agricultural produce, rights in churches and mills, scutage due from sub-tenants holding by military service. Big or small, the aristocratic estate was a rent-collecting machine, an agricultural enterprise, and a set of lordly claims. A few of the greater lords might have a town from which they drew revenue. Tewkesbury was a borough of the earls of Gloucester and rendered them somewhat over £10 per annum, mostly in rents, but also in revenue from the fair and from judicial profits.[55] The only major town held by a baron, however, was Leicester, under the lordship of the earls of Leicester.

A characteristic mixture of types of income is revealed in the accounts for the honor of Christchurch (Hants.) for 1224–5.[56] This was one of the component parts of the estates of the earl of Devon, who also held the honor of Plympton in Devon and the whole of the Isle of Wight. The honor of Christchurch consisted of the borough of Christchurch, with its two subsidiary estates of Burton and Holdenhurst, the borough and manor of Lymington and the manors of Ibberton (Dorset), Breamore, and Rumbridge. Rents brought in about £58. Revenues from the borough of Christchurch included court profits, a tax or 'aid', and income from the fisheries and markets. These totalled almost £27. Court profits, miscellaneous rights, and the sale of grain from the other manors and Lymington brought in another £28. In addition, the military tenants had to pay scutage, unless excused. The fees of the honor were scattered over Hampshire, Dorset, Wiltshire, Oxfordshire, and Gloucestershire. There were almost 32 of them and they should have rendered 64 marks (£42. 13s. 4d.) at the current rate of scutage, but a large number were exempt, notably those in the powerful hands of the earl Marshal. The core of directly exploited boroughs and manors, centred on Christchurch, the location of one of the earl's castles and his favourite

---

[55] PR 2 John, p. 127.
[56] *Roll of Divers Accounts for the Early Years of the Reign of Henry III, etc.*, ed. F. A. Cazel (PRS n.s. 44; 1982 for 1974–5), pp. 27–32.

religious house, shaded off into a network of financial and legal claims over holdings in distant counties.

A small and unusually compact barony was that centred on Berkeley in southern Gloucestershire. In 1191 it was inherited by Robert fitz Maurice, who was charged an inheritance tax (relief) of £1,000 for it. This was an exceptionally high amount, ten times the sum that would be prescribed for a baronial relief in Magna Carta, and would obviously diminish Robert's income for years to come. The barony was assessed at five knights' fees and thus paid £5 for each of the scutages levied in the 1190s at the rate of £1 per fee. Since no estates had been granted out in knight's fees, this must have been paid from Robert's own income. The annual income of Robert's estate was about £90, drawn from a cluster of manors between the lower Severn and the Cotswolds. There is record of their annual 'farm' or fixed annual leasehold value in 1195 and these are plotted on Map 4.[57]

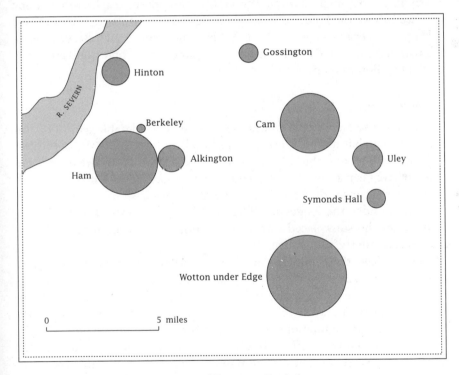

MAP 4. *A small barony: Berkeley, 1195*

---

[57] PR 3 RI, p. 98; PR 6 RI, p. 3; PR 7 RI, pp. 55–6. There was also some income from the unidentified *Dena*.

*Value of the Berkeley manors per annum*

| | |
|---|---|
| Alkington | £7 |
| Berkeley | £2. 14s. |
| Cam | £16 |
| Gossington | £5 |
| Ham | £17 |
| Hinton | £7. 3s. 6d. |
| Symonds Hall | £5 |
| Uley | £8 |
| Wotton under Edge | £21 |

The honors of Christchurch and Berkeley both provided about £100 a year for their lords, from rents, farm produce, court rights, and other sources. Quite apart from the fact that the earl of Devon had two other honors in his hands as well as Christchurch, revenues of this order placed their holders clearly in the baronial stratum, although in the poorer reaches of it. They were well above the holder of a knight's fee or two, with a revenue perhaps only one-fifth or one-tenth as great. Yet in some respects all aristocrats were comparable: they held their land on the same legal conditions and they sought to follow a common style of life.

## Legal Status

In principle, the aristocratic landholder enjoyed considerable security in his estate. Although it was recognized that a lord had the right, in the last resort, to dispossess a tenant who failed to perform the service he owed, this does not seem to have been a common occurrence. Kings like Henry I might, indeed, break their barons if they rebelled, but even dispossession for rebellion became rare under the Angevins. The land law that was elaborated under Henry II and his sons placed a strong presumption in favour of peaceful possession and orderly inheritance.

Nevertheless, there were no outright proprietors in medieval England, other than the king. Lords claimed, and usually enforced, their superior rights. Among the most significant of these were the levying of a relief or inheritance payment and the custody of minor and unmarried female heirs. Both presupposed limitations on the rights of the immediate holder of the land. His heir could not succeed freely. Nor did custody of his minor heirs fall to his family. Moreover, the common practice of lords confirming their tenants' grants and gifts implies that the tenants did not have untrammelled disposition of their property.

The rules of inheritance that were developed and made ever more explicit in the course of the twelfth century were strongly biased in favour of transmission of land within the immediate family. The Assize of Northampton of

1176 makes a quite clear statement: 'if any free tenant dies, let his heirs remain in such seisin [possession] of his fee as their father had on the day on which he was alive and dead'. Military tenures, i.e. land held by knight service, descended by primogeniture. In families holding estates of this kind, as the law-book attributed to Glanville puts it, 'according to the law of the kingdom of England, the first-born son succeeds his father in everything'.[58] Other forms of freehold land might be subject to different rules of inheritance. Land held in socage—an ancient form of non-military free tenure—was sometimes partible, i.e. divided among all surviving sons, but sometimes went to the eldest son and sometimes to the youngest.[59] Court cases might turn on 'whether the socage land were partible'.[60]

Father–son inheritance was the simplest kind, but hereditary claims were recognized far beyond this. If a man died without children, then his brother could succeed, and, if he lacked brothers or nephews, his uncle or cousin had a right. When the young Robert de Stuteville, heir to a great Yorkshire barony, died in 1205, he was succeeded by his uncle Nicholas. Collateral inheritance of this type increased the chances of a bond between a family and particular estates continuing over generations. A study of the descent of 192 baronies over the period 1200–1327 has shown that only 17 per cent of them descended exclusively from father to son over that period. Another 13 per cent, however, descended on occasion through other male heirs, such as brothers, uncles, and cousins.[61] In this way the paternal lineage retained possession of ancestral lands.

One of the more fraught questions in the inheritance law of this period was the question whether the son of a deceased second brother had a greater right than a third brother to succeed a childless oldest brother. It mattered so much because the Angevin succession in 1199 turned on it. Richard had died leaving two possible heirs: Arthur, the son of his deceased brother, Geoffrey, and John, his youngest brother (see Figure 1). Significantly, the succession of king John to the throne in 1199, passing over the son of his elder brother, shackled all considerations of cases between uncles and nephews in the English law courts for more than a generation. The 'king's case', as it was called, brings out the fact that the kingdom of England itself could be seen as an 'honor'. If the land law could be shaped (albeit temporarily) by the royal succession, presumably royal succession was seen as a kind of inheritance of landed property.

An important distinction was eventually established between the rules of inheritance governing property and those applied to transmission of office. All the evidence is that landed estates held by military or socage tenure were

---

[58] Glanville 7. 3 (p. 75).     [59] Ibid.     [60] *CRR* i, pp. 314–15.
[61] Waugh, *Lordship*, p. 19.

usually deemed heritable and the growth of the Common Law over the
course of the twelfth century made the rules of inheritance quite explicit.
Office, however, was not usually inherited. Indeed, one difference between
the earldom of a county and the shrievalty of a county is that the former was
conceived of far more as heritable property than the latter. If sheriffs had
usually been succeeded by their sons in life tenures (as happened in exceptional cases—see above, pp. 150–1), we would eventually have to regard the
shrievalty as property rather than office.

This is not to say that hereditary office was unknown, at various levels of
society. At some point in the 1140s, for instance, the Earl of Chester rendered
the office of cook in the comital kitchen to Wimund, son of Hamo the cook,
giving him 'all the land that was his father's and his office [*misterium*] in my
kitchen, so that he should be a cook there with the others, as his right and inheritance'.[62] The office is hereditary; the land goes with the office. More exalted positions, such as the great offices of the royal household were also
transmitted hereditarily. Yet, overall, it is clear that the large majority of positions that brought power and authority—such as those of estate steward,
castellan, sheriff, justice—were not hereditary, nor, indeed, life tenures.

The rights of daughters were greater than those of collateral male kin. It
was established early that, in the case of a military tenant who died leaving
only daughters, those daughters would inherit. In the thirteenth century a
barony descended in the female line on average once a year.[63] If there were
more than one daughter, the estate would be divided equally between them.
Hence feudal estates faced a genetic lottery of particular anxiety. A lord
with four daughters and no sons faced the prospect not only of his land leaving the male line but also of its fragmentation into the hands of numerous
sons-in-law.

However unhappy a patriarch in this situation might be, strict inheritance
rules meant that, not only were lords inhibited from interfering in their tenants' estates, but also individual aristocrats had limited control over the
transmission and distribution of their property. Since the right of testament-
ary disposition of landed property was severely limited, landholders could
not determine who would inherit the bulk of their estate. Even their ability to
make gifts and grants during their lifetime, for instance for religious donations, was constrained by lords and potential heirs who would feel that their
voice should be heard. Careful landholders sought their consent. Robert
Gernon, conveying one of his tenancies to Abingdon abbey in 1104, secured
the assent not only of his two sons but also of three named nephews.[64]

A distinction was made between inherited land and acquisitions, and the

---

[62] *Chester Charters*, no. 80, pp. 92–3.     [63] Waugh, *Lordship*, tables 1.1 and 1.2, pp. 19, 21.
[64] *Abingdon Chron.* 2, p. 98.

sentiment was that the claims of the family on the latter were less weighty. The enormous booty of the Norman Conquest created an aristocracy that had large amounts of acquired land to distribute, but as the generations passed this situation naturally changed. The distinction endured, however. Property could be specified as 'that land which I can give freely, from my own purchase and acquisition'.[65] The separate nature of acquired land also emerges from the dealings following the death of Hugh Bigod, earl of Norfolk, in 1177. His son, Roger, came to the king seeking his entire inheritance; at the same time Roger's stepmother, earl Hugh's second wife, 'offered the king many great gifts that he should grant to her son the earl's purchases and acquisitions'.[66] However stable and explicit the land law was, there were always areas for negotiation and bargaining—and it was always worthwhile paying for the king's favour.

## 3. THE LIFE OF THE ARISTOCRACY

### Birth and Bearing

One of the most commonly held assumptions of the Middle Ages was that social class was in the blood. The very terms of social classification implied this: unfree peasants were *nativi*—the word means simply 'born', but implies 'born unfree'; the upper classes were *generosi*, a word related to 'genetic', and again meaning 'born', but, in this case 'high born'. It was impossible to escape your birth status. The twelfth-century English poem, *The Owl and the Nightingale*, expresses this conventional view: 'a wicked man | from a foul brood [*fule brode*] | who mingles with free men [*fro monne*] | always knows his origins | and that he comes from an addled egg, | even though he lies in a free nest.'[67]

The aristocrats of Anglo-Norman and Angevin England believed that they were superior to others in blood and birth. They were noble not only 'by nature' but also 'by blood'.[68] Those who flattered and praised them stressed their descent and pedigree. When the monk William of Malmesbury sent an adulatory letter to Robert, earl of Gloucester, the illegitimate son of Henry I, he wrote, 'If anyone were ever noble, you surpass them all; you trace your descent from outstanding kings and counts and your character emulates their ways.'[69]

Christian moralists never tired of distinguishing nobility of descent from true nobility of soul, but their need to do so points to the prevalence and importance of the concept of blood nobility. Adam of Eynsham, the chaplain

[65] *Monasticon* 6/ii, p. 895.     [66] *Gesta Hen. II* 1, pp. 143–4.
[67] *The Owl and the Nightingale*, lines 129–34, ed. E. G. Stanley (London, 1960), p. 53.
[68] *Wigmore Chron.*, p. 420.     [69] W. Malm., *GR* 5. 446 (2, p. 519); OMT edn., p. 798.

and biographer of Hugh, bishop of Lincoln (1186–1200), begins his *Life* of
the saintly bishop by reflections on this point: 'Distinguished parents of
noble stock adorn the honour of their eminent children all the more brightly
and justly if they are the source, not only of a lineage of noble descent, but also
of the material of virtue and the incentive to goodness.' Hugh was 'a man
noble in blood but even more noble in his holiness'.[70] Adam's point is clear;
but so are his assumptions—that there is such a thing as nobility of blood
transmitted through noble stock.

Family pride was a natural consequence of nobility of blood. The centrality of such family pride and family solidarity is manifest in the remarks an Ely
monk made about Richard, abbot of Ely (1100–1107). Abbot Richard's father
was Richard fitz Gilbert, head of the great house of Clare, and his mother the
high-born Rohese Giffard:

When he went to the king's court, he was feared second only to the king, for he was
walled around by a great crowd of relatives, who, as the whole of England knew and
recognized, were of Clare [*Ricardi*] and Giffard [*Gifardi*] descent. The Clares and the
Giffards are two kindreds from the same region, who have made their lineage illustrious by their reputation for power and the size of their family. They dominate every
assembly of nobles by their magnificence and numbers.[71]

The aristocratic nuclear family was not particularly large. An analysis of
the royal register of wards and widows of 1185 allows the composition of 112
land-holding families of baronial and knightly status to be ascertained and
this evidence suggests an average family size among the aristocracy of 5.4—
two parents and three or four children.[72] Yet the nuclear family was lodged in
a mesh of related families, tied together through blood or marriage in a complex of interests and esteem. The *Ricardi* and the *Gifardi* were aristocratic
clans; as noted above (p. 212), contemporaries remarked how 'Almost all the
nobles of England were related to the earl of Clare'.

But if your birth made you an aristocrat, it was your bearing that demonstrated it. The moralists asked, 'What of those who assume supercilious gestures and bellow out words full of pride, in order to be taken for noblemen
[*generosi*]?'[73] The implication is that an overbearing manner and an arrogant
tone mark out the aristocrat. Haughtiness was indeed built in to the very vocabulary of the period. Contempt for social inferiors is shown in the way that
the terms used to describe the peasantry, like *vilain*, came to imply moral opprobrium. The aristocracy labelled what they did not approve 'peasant-like'.

---

[70] Ad. Eyns., *V. Hugh* 1. 1 (1, p. 5).
[71] *Lib. Eliensis*, p. 226; the recurrent baptismal name of the Clares was Richard, hence the *Ricardi*.
[72] John S. Moore, 'The Anglo-Norman Family: Size and Structure', *ANS* 14 (1991), pp. 153–96, at
pp. 167–9. This figure is computed by excluding the 'freemen's families'.
[73] Alex. Nequam, *DNR* 2. 175 (p. 312).

Aristocratic values were not limited to a blind sense of superiority. Aristocrats were expected to be brave. Writing in the middle years of the twelfth
century, the chronicler Henry of Huntingdon told the story of earl Siward, a
heroic figure of the Anglo-Saxon past. When informed that his son had been
killed in battle against the Scots, the earl asked if his son's wounds were on the
front or the back of his body. Being told they were on the front, he replied, 'I
rejoice, for I would not deem any other death worthy for myself or my son.'[74]
Stoic acceptance of death—one's own or that of cherished kin—was part of
the noble ideal.

This courage was to be displayed and invoked. During the campaign of
1174 a small body of English knights, advancing through the fog, suspected
that the Scottish army must be near. The more cautious of them suggested
retreat but Bernard de Balliol, 'a noble and large-spirited man, replied, "Let
he who wishes retreat, but I will advance, even if no one follows. I will not
mark myself with a blot of eternal blame."' When the king of the Scots real-
izes the enemy is upon him, he prepares to attack them, saying to his retainers, 'Now we shall see who knows how to be a knight!'[75] These passages
(recorded by an Augustinian canon) make clear not only that boldness is ad-
mirable, but also that bold men might be expected to draw attention to their
boldness. In this lack of reticence, the knights of the twelfth century were
heirs of the boastful thanes of the Germanic past rather than ancestors of the
understated British officer of modern tradition.

Aristocratic courage was ideally, whatever the realities, to be matched by
loyalty. Men had lords and lords had men and the link between them was supposed to be a firm and trustworthy one. Kings addressed their charters to 'all
my faithful men'. It was legal lore that 'Every man owes fidelity to his lord, in
life and limb, earthly honour and observance of his counsel'.[76] The bond was
meant to be mutual: 'the bond of loyalty applies to both lordship and homage,
so that what the man owes to the lord because of his homage is also owed by
the lord to his man because of lordship, except for deference alone.'[77]

One limited but very practical obligation that arose from this mutual bond
was the duty to ransom one's lord or one's man. The most spectacular case in
this period was that of Richard I, when the whole kingdom was drained of its
silver to ransom the king, but warfare of all kinds produced a crop of prisoners whose freedom was up for sale. Magna Carta explicitly recognized the
right of the king to levy an 'aid' to pay his ransom and also the right of a lord
to raise money from his free tenants in the same circumstance (clauses 12 and
15). Lords might also help ransom their men. King John lent £1,000 marks
to help pay the ransom of Roger de Lacy, constable of Chester, after Roger

[74] H. Hunt. 6. 22 (pp. 376–8).        [75] W. Newb. 2. 33 (1, pp. 184–5).
[76] LHP 55. 3 (p. 172).        [77] Glanville 9. 4 (p. 107).

had been captured by Philip Augustus when Château Gaillard fell in 1204.[78]
The king then pardoned him the debt. On a humbler level, there were men
like Stephen de Lawa, who, probably during the civil war of 1215–17, was
'held in heavy chains and forced by elaborate tortures to pay a ransom' and
whose lords, the prior and convent of Worcester, made a large payment to restore him 'to life and liberty'.[79]

To help ransom one's lord or vassal was also a way of expressing the supposedly aristocratic virtue of largesse or generosity. The very word derives
from the Latin *generositas*, the quality of being well born. To give freely indicated a noble spirit. Nor was it without practical benefits, for generosity attracted followers and followers brought power. The young king Arthur, as
portrayed in the 1130s in the *History of the Kings of Britain* (*Historia regum
Britannie*) of Geoffrey of Monmouth, is a leader who instinctively knew this:

Arthur was a young man of fifteen years of age, endowed with unheard-of spirit and
generosity.... Once he had been inaugurated as king, he showed his generosity in the
accustomed way. So great a crowd of knights thronged to him that he exhausted what
he had to grant. But if someone has innate generosity, along with courage, even if he
is lacking for a time, he will never suffer continual poverty.[80]

To be like Arthur, brave, lavish, spirited, was to be the ideal aristocrat, to
win honour and esteem. This was not an easy task. Esteem was won in a competitive world and could be lost if not defended. Honour was gained at others'
expense. Here are the reflections of the fictional knight Milun, hearing of the
exploits of a young newcomer who had been making his name in France:

He grieved and lamented that this knight was held in such esteem when, as long as he
himself could journey to tournaments and bear arms, no one else in the land should
be valued or praised. He thought only of one thing: he would quickly cross the sea
and joust with the knight, to do him harm and injury. Because of his anger, he wanted
to fight him and try to unhorse him: then he would be dishonoured.[81]

The caste pride of the aristocracy did not undermine its fierce individualism.

## Knighting

The male members of the upper ranks of the English aristocracy would customarily be knighted. Knighting took place in the late teens or soon after.
William the Conqueror knighted his son Henry in 1086 when the boy was 17
or 18.[82] Stephen's son Eustace was about 16 or 17 years of age when he was

---

[78] PR 5 John, p. 214.        [79] *Worcester Cart.*, no. 276, p. 146.
[80] Geoff. Monm., *HRB* 9. 1 (143), p. 101.
[81] Marie de France, *Milun*, lines 345–57 (*Lais*, pp. 110–11).
[82] *ASC*, pp. 216–17, *s.a.* 1085 (*recte* 1086); he was born May 1068–May 1069 and the ceremony took
place at Whitsun.

knighted in 1147.[83] Henry of Anjou, the future Henry II, was knighted in 1149, aged 16. Geoffrey of Brittany, his son, was knighted by his father at the age of 19 or 20.[84] Henry knighted his youngest son, John, prior to sending him to his new lordship in Ireland in 1185; he was then 17.[85] The author of the law-book attributed to Glanville suggests a slightly later age, saying that the son of a knight comes of age at 21.[86] Since coming of age and knighting were customarily equated, his statement does not fit perfectly with the actual cases mentioned above. Since, however, as is clear, most of the detailed information available concerns the very highest level, the sons of kings, it is possible that they were knighted earlier than ordinary aristocrats.

The ritual involved in knighting is not described at any length in the sources of this period, though several clerical sources mention the practice of the aspirant knight offering his sword on the altar.[87] The *Anglo-Saxon Chronicle* uses the phrase 'dubbed as knight' (*dubbade . . . to ridere*) for the knighting of Henry in 1086—notably using the rare *ridere* (i.e. 'rider') instead of the eventually more common English *cniht* ('servant, retainer, knight'). The chronicler Roger of Howden, describing the ceremony of 1178, when Henry II dubbed his son Geoffrey, simply tells how the king 'made Geoffrey a knight' (*fecit Gaufridum . . . militem*) and describes the ceremony as 'reception of knightly office' (*susceptio militaris officii*). Another contemporary chronicler is equally laconic but gives the crucial physical detail: 'The king of England endowed his son, Geoffrey, duke of Brittany, with the knightly belt at Woodstock on 6 August.'[88] The essence of knighting was girding with a swordbelt. In 1147 Stephen 'honoured his son by girding him with the belt of knighthood in the presence of the barons'. During a lawsuit in the 1190s, the abbot of Crowland complained of the status of those who had been commissioned to inspect the land at issue, since 'they are not of the knightly order nor girded with the sword'.[89] A disgraced knight would be 'deprived of his belt'.[90]

An account of the deeds of Hereward the Wake, written probably in the reign of Henry I, has some interesting things to say about knighthood. The hero, Hereward, goes to abbot Brand of Peterborough 'so that he could gird him with the knightly sword and belt in the English fashion. He did this lest the local people upbraid him, ruler and leader of many as he was, with not being a knight.' The French, according to the author of the account, apparently considered knighting by a monk an inferior form of the ritual; Hereward thought quite the opposite—

[83] *Gesta Stephani* 109 (p. 208); H. Hunt. 10. 29 (p. 754) (RS edn., p. 282) dates Eustace's knighting to 1149.
[84] *Gesta Hen. II* 1, p. 207; R. Howd. 2, p. 166.        [85] *Gesta Hen. II* 1, p. 336; R. Howd. 2, p. 303.
[86] Glanville 7. 9 (p. 82).        [87] J. Salisb., *Policr.* 6. 10 (2, p. 24); P. Blois, *Letters*, no. 94 (col. 294).
[88] R. Diceto, *Ymag.* 1, p. 426.        [89] Stenton, *Engl. Justice*, p. 170.        [90] R. Devizes, p. 22.

Hence the custom has arisen at Ely that if anyone is to be made a knight, he must on that day offer a naked sword on the altar during high mass. After the gospel, the monk singing the mass touches him with the sword on his naked neck, giving him a blessing. The young warrior receives the sword from him and is thus duly made a knight.[91]

Here we have a bold assertion that girding with sword and belt was 'the English fashion'; clear evidence that there was a presumption that those who ruled and led soldiers should be knights; an intriguing distinction between French and English attitudes to knighting by monks; and a good contemporary description of one local variant of dubbing. There is an echo of these issues in the contemporary ruling of the Council of Westminster, an assembly dominated by French and foreign-born prelates: 'abbots should not make knights'.[92]

The belting of a knight was a ceremonial moment like the belting of an earl, bringing those who underwent it to a new status—'order' or 'office' are among the terms used for knighthood. It was also in a very ancient tradition of the arming of the new warrior. When David, king of Scots, knighted his great-nephew, Henry of Anjou, the ritual is described in the following words: 'he gave him the weapons of manhood'.[93] Just as, when a serf was made a freeman, he was handed the lance or sword of a freeman, so entry into the military order was signified by the arming of the new knight.[94] Harold's knighting by William of Normandy, as depicted on the Bayeux Tapestry, is a ritual of just this type.

Often the ceremony would take place after the young aristocrats had spent time in the household of some great man. When Thomas Becket was chancellor, for example, 'the great men of the kingdom of England and of neighbouring kingdoms sent their children into his service, and he would raise them honourably and train them and then send them back to their parents endowed with the belt of knighthood'.[95] In the late twelfth-century romance, *Ipomedon*, by Hue de Rotelande, the son of the king of Ireland, who had been brought up at the court of Meleager, king of Sicily, is introduced into the story just after he has been knighted: 'he was newly dubbed. He had served Meleager, who had brought him up from childhood and had then made him a knight . . . the king, who had brought him up as a squire, had given him arms.'[96] This transition from the rank of squire (*vadlez*) to knight is described also in the poet Gaimar's account of William Rufus: 'He dubbed many nobles . . . he dubbed thirty squires . . . he dubbed them richly.' According to Gaimar this chivalric note followed Rufus to the grave, for 'he was buried in

[91] *Gesta Herw.*, pp. 368–9.      [92] *Councils and Synods* 1/ii, p. 676.
[93] H. Hunt. 10. 29 (p. 754) (RS edn., p. 282).
[94] *LHP* 78. 1 (p. 242); Liebermann, *Gesetze* 1, p. 491 (Wl. art. Lon. retr. 15); Robertson, *Laws*, p. 248.
[95] W. f. Stephen, *V. Thomas* 12 (p. 22).      [96] Hue, *Ipom.*, lines 3331–5, 4621–3, pp. 214, 271.

the rich cloak in which the day before William de Munfichet had been dubbed.'[97]

Rich cloaks for the ceremony of knighting were still being purchased a century later, as the accounts for king John's expenses make clear. In 1204 £33 was spent on 'three robes of scarlet, three of green cloth, two brocades, one mattress [or cushion] and other things necessary for making one knight', while another £6. 18s. was laid out on clothes and armour for the knighting of the king's squire, Thomas Sturmy. A few years later, in 1209, over £21 was spent on 'three silk robes and three robes of green cloth with deerskin and three coverlets and three mattresses [or cushions] and three saddles with reins and three pairs of linen sheets and three pairs of shirts and breeches and the other small trappings for making knights'.[98] Sadly, there are no detailed descriptions of what was done with all these cloths and mattresses (or cushions). Perhaps there was a ceremonial dressing of the new knight. At any rate, he was certainly supplied with all the ostentatious finery that his new status required.

## Display

Aristocratic culture was a culture of display. The description of Hugh of Avranches, earl of Chester (d. 1101), given by Orderic Vitalis, exemplifies the hedonistic, materialistic, athletic, public, and noisy nature of the great aristocratic household:

He loved the world and worldly pomp and thought that they were the highest blessing that human beings could attain. He was always the first in battle, lavish in his giving, took great pleasure in games and luxuries, in actors, horses, dogs and other vanities of this kind. He was surrounded by a huge household, in which there were crowds of boys, both nobles and commoners, making a great noise, as well as honourable clerks and knights with whom he shared his labours and his wealth.[99]

A similar note is struck by the poet Gaimar, writing about 1140, when he sketches out what, in his opinion, are the most important features of the court life of Henry I. A proper portrayal would give a sense 'of the feasts which the king held, of the woods, of the jokes, of the gallantry, and of the love which the best king showed, who ever was or ever will be'. It would tell 'about the fairest deeds, that is about love and gallantry, and woodland sports and jokes, and of feasts and splendour, of largesse and riches, and of the barons whom he led and the great gifts he gave; of this a man might well sing'.[100] Feasting, hunting, joking, love, gifts—that is the ideal picture of the aristocratic court.

---

[97] Gaimar, lines 6076, 6079, 6099, 6392–5, pp. 192–3, 202.
[98] PR 6 John, pp. 213, 120; PR 11 John, p. 10.
[99] Orderic 6. 2 (3, p. 216).     [100] Gaimar, lines 6495–9, p. 205.

As is usually the case, the rich not only consumed more, they consumed differently—they were wine drinkers rather than beer drinkers, their food would be highly spiced, they might run to silk and fur for their clothes. The purchases made for the feasts held by king John in 1211 can be taken as representative, differing only in scale from that of his barons: 90 lbs. of pepper, 28 lbs. of cumin, half a pound of galingale, 3 lbs. of cinnamon, one pound of cloves, half a pound of nutmeg, 2 lbs. of ginger, wine of Auxerre, white wine, French wine, Gascon wine, Angevin wine, 1,450 lbs. of almonds, 1,500 dates, five baskets of figs, 153 lbs. of cotton, 60 silken cloths from Spain, 1,250 yards of ruby scarlet cloth, etc., etc.[101] An English peasant entering this world of exotic glamour would have felt himself in a fantasy.

Entertainment in the aristocratic hall would be provided by minstrels and jesters. As one sour monastic critic put it, 'The great men of the land, sons of the kingdom of vanity, are accustomed to retain men of this kind, who have the ability to arouse those lords and their household into joking and laughter with their silly words and gestures.'[102] Such entertainers can be found mentioned in Domesday Book, where there is record of Berdic 'the king's jester' (*joculator regis*) and of Adelina, a female jester (*joculatrix*), who had been given a small plot of land in Hampshire by Roger, earl of Hereford.[103] Both Berdic and Adelina were among the lucky members of their class who obtained property as a reward for their skills as entertainers. It was a recognized mark of aristocratic generosity 'to give clothes to the minstrels' [*jugleürs*], but gifts of land were more precious.[104]

The jocular note of some of these grants still rings through. About 1180 the earl of Gloucester gave a plot of land in Bristol to his harper, 'in return for a dish full of beans, to be rendered annually at my Exchequer in Bristol'.[105] Miles, earl of Hereford, granted land to his jester who bore the indicative name *Folebarba*, 'crazy beard'.[106] Herbert, son of Roland, held thirty acres in Suffolk from Henry II in return for serving the king as a jester.[107] Records from the thirteenth century show what this service consisted of, for in them the land is referred to as 'the sergeanty that used to belong to Roland the Farter . . . for which every Christmas he used to leap, whistle and fart before the king'.[108] It is hard to avoid agreeing with the eminent historian J. H. Round in his comment that this 'throws light on the royal sense of

---

[101] PR 13 John, p. xxii.
[102] Jocelin of Furness, *V. Kentigerni* 45, ed. and tr. A. P. Forbes, *Lives of St Ninian and St Kentigern* (The Historians of Scotland 5; Edinburgh, 1874), p. 241.
[103] *DB* 1, 162, 38 (Gls. W. 4; Ham. 1. 25).        [104] Marie de France, *Lanval*, line 211 (*Lais* p. 63).
[105] *Gloucester Charters*, no. 188, pp. 166–7.
[106] 'Charters of the Earldom of Hereford', ed. David Walker, *Camden Miscellany* 22 (Camden, 4th ser., 1; 1964), pp. 1–75, no. 7, at p. 15.
[107] *Rot. dom.*, p. 62.        [108] *Bk. Fees* 2, p. 1174.

humour'.[109] Aristocratic courts may have been more like rugby clubs than like Camelot.

The indoor games that the aristocrats themselves engaged in were primarily chess and dice. Chess was a game that spread to the Christian west from the Islamic world in the late tenth century and its eastern origin is witnessed by its name, deriving ultimately from the Persian *shah*, 'king', although some of its more unfamiliar features were modified to conform to its new environment: queen and bishop replaced their earlier equivalents, vizier and elephant.[110] It was an aristocratic game and was listed among the seven skills of a good knight by Petrus Alfonsi, Henry I's physician.[111] The poems of Marie de France, who was connected with the Angevin court, contain vignettes of 'two knights, sitting at a big table, where they amused themselves with a game of chess' and of a king, sitting in his daughter's chamber and playing chess with a knight who was one of her tutors.[112] Chess allusions came naturally to the twelfth-century aristocrat. Marie's contemporary, Alexander Nequam, recounts a tale of how Louis VI of France, in flight before the forces of Henry I, found that one of the English king's knights had seized his reins. 'Fie upon you!' he cried, 'Don't you know that a king may not be taken even in chess?'[113]

Yet, although the aristocratic hall or chamber was the natural venue for the game, chess was not a diversion for eggheads, but, just like dice, a game on which money was staked. Hence both forms of gaming could lead to quarrels. It was thought necessary to advise the aristocracy, 'If you lose money playing at dice or chess, do not let anger plant savage rage in your heart.'[114] Nequam refers not only to the desperate ploys of gamesters at dice but also to the way that, during a chess game, 'insults are frequently uttered and the game does not maintain the dignity of a serious occupation but degenerates into a brawl'.[115] One tale explains the hostility between king John and the dissident aristocrat Fulk fitz Warin by a childhood quarrel between the two over a game of chess, during which John 'took the chess board and struck Fulk a great blow with it'.[116] Such disputes could be fatal. A robber knight in Stephen's reign was ambushed and run through by a lance by 'his enemy, who had previously been his companion at dice'.[117]

---

[109] *Rot. dom.*, p. 62 n. 3.

[110] Richard Eales, 'The Game of Chess: An Aspect of Medieval Knightly Culture', in C. Harper-Bill and Ruth Harvey (eds.), *The Ideals and Practice of Medieval Knighthood* (1) (Woodbridge, 1986), pp. 12–34.

[111] Petrus Alfonsi, *Disciplina clericalis* 4, ed. A. Hilka and W. Söderhjelm (Acta Societatis Scientiarum Fennicae 38/iv; Helsinki, 1911), p. 10.

[112] *Milun*, lines 198–200, *Eliduc*, lines 483–8 (*Lais*, pp. 107, 139).

[113] Alex. Nequam, *DNR* 2. 184 (p. 325).        [114] D. Beccles, lines 1419–20, p. 49.

[115] Alex. Nequam, *DNR* 2. 183–4 (pp. 323–4, 326).

[116] *Fouke le Fitz Waryn*, ed. E. J. Hathaway (ANTS 26–8; 1975), p. 22.

[117] Reg., *Libellus* 67 (p. 137).

The general tenor of aristocratic life is revealed indirectly in the rules about how crusaders should behave. As participants in holy war, they were to leave behind the ostentation of their ordinary existence. Hence, there is a kind of inverse evidence of aristocratic style in the list of prohibitions issued prior to such expeditions as the Third Crusade. Crusaders were not to swear, to play at dice, to wear sable or squirrel fur, or scarlet cloth, or decoratively slashed clothing, not to buy more than two courses for their meal, nor was any crusader to take a woman with him on the expedition, except for a respectable washerwoman.[118] This penitential regime immediately summons up its opposite, the ordinary aristocratic life, with its swearing, gambling, rich clothes, feasting, and the company of women other than respectable washerwomen.

## Horse and Hound

'He who has stayed at school till the age of 12 and never ridden a horse is fit only to be a priest', ran a well-known saying of the twelfth century,[119] and the first of Petrus Alfonsi's seven knightly skills was riding. Training began with childhood games. When Simon de Senlis, earl of Huntingdon (d. 1153), was a little boy, he 'used to collect branches and brushwood to build a castle and, mounting a toy-horse as his steed and brandishing a branch like a lance, would, with other boys of his own age, undertake the guard and defence of this imaginary play-castle, imitating the ways of knights'.[120] As aristocratic boys grew older, they replaced toy horses with real. The account of the education of the young hero Horn in the late twelfth-century *Romance of Horn* gives horsemanship a central place in his training:

There was no musical instrument under heaven known to mortal man in which the majestic lord Horn did not surpass everyone. Likewise he mastered hunting of the beast of the wood and the waterfowl. No one was his match in swordsmanship. . . . No one, compared to him, could handle a horse well, nor carry shield or crystal buckler.[121]

Horses had a social stratification as definite as that of those who rode them. There was the destrier, the great war horse, that was not ridden on ordinary journeys: 'The destrier is spared while travelling to be reserved for a greater labour. . . . When it goes armoured into battle, it shows the greatness of its noble heart and its boldness through its joyful limbs and swift and happy movement.'[122] There was the hunter (*chascurus*). There was the palfrey,

---

[118] *Gesta Hen. II* 2, p. 32; Gerv. Cant., p. 409; W. Newb. 3. 23 (1, p. 274).

[119] Marc Bloch, *Feudal Society* (Eng. tr.; London, 1961), pp. 293–4.

[120] Joc. Furn., *V. Waltheof*, p. 251.

[121] Thomas, *The Romance of Horn* 18, lines 375–81, ed. Mildred K. Pope (2 vols., ANTS 9/10, 12/13; 1955–64), vol. 1, pp. 12–13.

[122] Alex. Nequam, *DNR* 2. 158 (pp. 259–60).

ridden by ladies or knights at their ease and 'decorated with handsome trappings, little bells jingling sweetly at its breast'.[123] There was the rouncey, 'suited to servants and robbers'.[124] In 1196 a royal messenger sent to Ireland was given ten marks (£6. 6s. 8d.) 'to buy a rouncey and for a robe and for his expenses going and returning'.[125]

The world of hunting—of horse, hound, and hawk—was pre-eminently an aristocratic world. 'In our days,' complained the moralist John of Salisbury, 'the scholarship of the aristocracy consists in hunting jargon.'[126] Legal restrictions hemmed around the right of lesser men to seek out birds and beasts for food or pleasure. The tone was set by the king himself, who claimed far-reaching monopolies in the chase and enforced them with a special and notoriously fierce judicial regime, 'Forest Law'. He reserved for himself the deer and the boar. Although one of the concessions of the Charter of the Forest of 1217 was that bishops and barons obeying a summons to the royal court could take 'a beast or two from the royal Forest' en route, this was a rare privilege.[127] Grants to hunt foxes, hares, and wildcats with dogs were more common. The otter was also regarded as fair game. In 1200 William fitz Wakelin gave the king 60 marks (£40) to have the right to hunt hare, fox, cat, and otter with dogs in his woods in Derbyshire and Nottinghamshire, while John, bishop of Ely (1220–5), granted one of his tenants permission to have otter-hounds on his lands and agreed that they need not be 'lawed', i.e. have their claws removed, as was standard with dogs in protected woodland.[128]

Like horses, dogs were bred to distinct types. Those that tracked by scent were distinguished from the other hounds. When Richard I sent presents of dogs to Saladin, they were differentiated as 'greyhounds and brachets, that is trackers' [*odorisequos*].[129] There were usually only one or two on the hunt, as in the case of the pack that the bishop of Ely had to give to the king in 1202, consisting of 'twelve hounds and one lyam-hound'—a kind of bloodhound held on a leash and trained to hunt by scent.[130] Some royal sergeants held their lands by the service of keeping and training such a tracker.[131] This specialization of dogs can be seen in the references in the description of the royal household from 1136 of greyhounds (*leporarii* or 'hare hounds'); the lyam-hound; and the undifferentiated hounds of the pack.[132] The Pipe Rolls that record royal income and expenditure under the Angevin kings refer to these same types, as well as to fox hounds, *valtri* (probably boarhounds), spaniels (*espanielli*), 'bercelets', which are lyam-hounds under a new name, and setters. The Pipe Roll of 1218–19 gives us an incidental picture of a noisy hunt,

[123] Ibid., p. 260.     [124] Alex. Nequam, *Ut.*, p. 103.     [125] PR 8 RI (Chancellor's Roll), p. 20.
[126] J. Salisb., *Policr.* 1. 4 (1, p. 23).     [127] *Sel. Charters*, p. 347.
[128] *Rot. obl.*, p. 57; *Cal. Ch. Rolls* 1, p. 55.     [129] *Gesta Hen. II* 2, p. 180.
[130] PR 4 John, p. 136.     [131] Round, *King's Sergeants*, pp. 279–84.
[132] *Const. domus regis*, p. 135; a guide to terminology in Round, *King's Sergeants*, pp. 268–303.

when it mentions the expenses of two royal huntsmen 'with their four horses and two grooms and the two boarhounds, along with eight of the king's greyhounds and two kennel-men with eighteen hounds for hunting the boar in the royal forest of Dean'.[133]

The Bayeux Tapestry provides a vivid portrait of the aristocrat on the move: Harold of Wessex riding on his stallion, his hounds running ahead, his hawk on his wrist (see Plate 6). Hunting with birds of prey was another of the aristocratic sports that marked off the upper levels of society. It was indeed the sport of kings, for all the evidence is that the Angevins were fanatical devotees of the sport. Every time Henry II or his sons crossed the Channel, the king's hawks and falcons in their cages went with them. Falcons from Ireland, Spain, Norway, and Iceland were especially prized and could be offered to win the king's goodwill.[134] Outlays on the birds and offers of hawks and falcons recur continually in the Pipe Rolls. In the year 1179, for instance, the king was given, offered, or claimed a total of 96 hawks and 6 gerfalcons (the great northern falcon), as well as spending £35. 6s. 8d. on purchasing birds.[135] The big Scandinavian birds could be bought at Boston market, others were found within the king's domains. In the later twelfth century, there is mention of falcons being captured for the king in south Wales and Devon.[136]

Hunting was a vigorous outdoor activity and was not without its risks. Hunting with bows and arrows in woodland was particularly dangerous. Visibility was limited and the range of the weapons great. The perils are clear from the details of William Rufus's death. The king was hunting deer in the New Forest and had just shot, but only wounded, a stag. While he followed its progress, shading his eyes against the rays of the setting sun, his companion Walter Tirel took aim at another stag and accidentally shot the king in the chest.[137] Rufus was the best known but not the only victim of a hunting accident. Both his elder brother Richard and his nephew, also Richard (son of Robert of Normandy), were killed in the New Forest while hunting, the former apparently colliding with a branch while cantering through the woods, the latter either in the same way or, according to some accounts, accidentally shot through the neck by one of his companions.[138] This was obviously a common hazard. In 1143 'Miles, earl of Hereford, was slain by the arrow of a certain knight of his own who was aiming at a stag, while hunting along with him.'[139]

---

[133] PR 3 HIII, p. 13.     [134] e.g. *Dial. scacc.*, p. 121; PR 15 HII, p. 16.

[135] PR 25 HII, index s.v. *accipiter.*     [136] Gerald, *Exp.* 1. 29 (p. 90); PR 1 John, p. 188.

[137] W. Malm., *GR* 4. 333 (2, p. 378); OMT edn., p. 574.

[138] Ibid. 3. 275 (2, pp. 332–3); OMT edn., p. 504; Orderic 5. 11; 10. 14 (3, p. 114; 5, p. 282); Flor. Worcs. 2, p. 45.

[139] *Brut (RBH)*, p. 119.

The aristocratic fondness for hunting helped shape rural society by foster-ing a corps of lower-class huntsmen and falconers whose activities would bring them into close and regular contact with their lords. Hugh of Avranches, earl of Chester, was famous for 'thinking more highly of falconers and huntsmen than of those who cultivated the land or prayed to heaven'.[140] Such men might receive beneficial treatment. Domesday Book records the exemptions granted by earl Ralph of East Anglia (1069–75) to a Norfolk free-holder called Judichael 'because he was the earl's falconer'.[141] A century later the lord of Copeland granted out a quarter of Crosthwaite in Cumbria 'for the service of tending his goshawks'.[142] Royal service tenures of this type were es-pecially numerous. From the time of Henry II, in virtue of their office, royal otter-hunters held land at Aylesbury that was still known as 'Otterarsfee' as late as the Tudor period.[143] The taste for the hunt and the penumbra of rural service it generates have been among the most enduring features of the Eng-lish aristocracy.

## The New Cultural Style

A landed and martial aristocracy, proud of its birth and living a life of outdoor sport, indoor display, and conspicuous consumption was no new thing in the Europe of the year 1100. Over the course of the twelfth century, however, this immemorial aristocratic stratum acquired a highly distinctive cultural tint. New styles and fashions emerged, that were to be important, and in some cases, defining features of the aristocracy for the rest of the Middle Ages and beyond.

### Tournament

The tournament, a war-game involving large numbers of mounted knights who attempted to overthrow their opponents, developed in northern France in the course of the eleventh century. It was not only a spectacular display of cavalry skirmishing, but could be profitable. The victors were able to claim the horse and armour of the losers. The most famous jouster of the later twelfth century, William Marshal, alleged that he had acquired the horses, arms, and armour of five hundred knights in tournaments in northern France.[144] It was a sport for the aristocracy and one that became an obsession of the European upper class.

The tournament was slow in coming to England. The earliest mention of tournaments from an English source dates to the time of Henry I and reveals unmistakably that the custom had not yet established itself in the country. It

---

[140] Orderic 4 (2, p. 262).     [141] *DB* 2, 125b (Nfk. 1. 131).
[142] *Monasticon* 3, p. 584.     [143] Round, *King's Sergeants*, pp. 299–301.
[144] *Hist. Guill. Mar.* 2, p. 305, lines 18483–5.

is a grant of land in Warwickshire, to be held by the recipient, Turchill Fundus, from the donor, Osbert of Arden, in return for carrying Osbert's painted lances from London or Northampton to his house at Kingsbury (War.) and for attending Osbert when he wished 'to go overseas to tournaments'.[145] Clearly the kind of duty to which Turchill was obliged would have included attendance at tournaments in England, if there had been any.

The first recorded tournament in England coincides with the disturbances of Stephen's reign. In 1142, as part of his attempt 'to restore the kingdom to its former dignity and unity', the king broke up the tourneying at York between the men of earl William of Aumale and earl Alan of Richmond.[146] Although there had been no tournaments in England during the reign of Henry I, the Anglo-Norman aristocracy would be familiar with them from France, and Stephen's own troops are described as 'expert in the art of jousting'.[147] This surge of enthusiasm for the chivalric hobby during the relaxed conditions of the reign was commented on, many years later, by the historian and Augustinian canon, William of Newburgh:

Military contests of this type, arising not from animosities but solely for training and the display of prowess, were never known in England, except in the days of king Stephen, when, on account of the king's undue softness, public discipline had no force. In the time of the kings before him and in the reign of Henry II, who succeeded him, these exercises for young knights were strictly prohibited and whoever, from a desire for martial glory, wished to undertake such exercises, had to go to neighbouring countries to do so.[148]

His views fit perfectly with the evidence from Osbert of Arden's charter.

The Church was opposed to tournaments on moral and spiritual grounds. Condemnations were issued at several of the important councils of the twelfth century, including the Third Lateran Council in 1179. To place one's life in danger either for gain or for pride was a sin, not to mention the stimulus to vice of all kinds that such occasions represented. Writing in 1187, the theologian and critic Ralph Niger expressed his disapproval of and contempt for tournaments:

In tournaments, knights waste away their patrimony, their efforts and even their life and soul, simply out of greed for empty praise and popular reputation. Even if there is no cause for enmity, the exercise becomes a battle, and vanity, avarice and folly compound together into pure wickedness.[149]

---

[145] G. F. Warner and H. J. Ellis, *Facsimiles of Royal and Other Charters in the British Museum* i (London, 1903), no. 12, plate IX (BL Cotton Charter XXII. 3).

[146] J. Hexham, p. 312.          [147] W. Malm., *HN* 489 (p. 49).

[148] W. Newb. 5. 4 (2, p. 422).

[149] Radulfus Niger, *De re militari et triplici via peregrinationis Ierosolimitane* 1. 36, ed. Ludwig Schmugge (Berlin, 1977), p. 114.

English kings seem to have been more concerned with public order than with vice. Gatherings of aristocrats in arms were not something they wished to encourage. As a result of the strict controls they imposed, England had a reputation among the international Anglo-French aristocracy as a tame land, no place for 'those who put all their hearts into wandering and fighting in tournaments'. Northern France was the land of real knighthood (*chevalerie*).[150] The first king to relax England's strict regime was, appropriately, the great chivalric hero, Richard I. In 1194 he authorized a licensing system for tournaments in England. Henceforth they could take place in five designated localities on payment of a licensing fee plus a charge for each participant. Safeguards were put in place to ensure that the fees were paid and to prevent random pillaging by knights on their way to and from tournaments.[151] The royal records sometimes allow a glimpse of the system at work: in 1198 the chief justiciar, Geoffrey fitz Peter, accounted for 100 marks (£66. 13s. 4d.) 'from tournaments'; in 1201 earl David of Huntingdon was pardoned 25 marks (£16. 13s. 4d.) that he owed 'for tournaments and for the pledges of those tourneying'.[152]

Despite the royal licensing procedure, tournaments still had the potential to generate disorder and focus opposition to the king. The danger was especially conspicuous in the aftermath of the civil war of 1215–17. Even after Louis of France withdrew from England at the end of 1217, some of his French knights were permitted to stay on to engage in tournaments, but these occasions came to be seen as 'a danger to the kingdom and spoliation of the poor' and were prohibited under pain of excommunication.[153] The use of such a sanction makes it clear that the ecclesiastical hostility to the tournament could be usefully harnessed to opposition based on political prudence. Such bans were reiterated during Henry III's minority, when papal influence was strong. William of Aumale, grandson of the man whose tournaments had been broken up by king Stephen and one of the most notable dissidents of the early years of Henry's reign, actually suffered the penalty of excommunication.[154] The prohibitions of the first years of the minority were issued under the authority of William Marshal, the most famous knight-errant and tournament champion of the twelfth century. It is piquant to envisage him, now an aged and responsible regent of England, banning tournaments on the grounds of security.[155]

Tournaments could indeed be unruly places. Richard I's prohibition of

[150] *Hist. Guill. Mar.* 1, pp. 56–7, lines 1531–50.
[151] *Foedera, conventiones, litterae et . . . acta publica . . .*, ed. Thomas Rymer (new edn., 4 vols. in 7 parts, Record Commission; 1816–69), vol. 1/i, p. 65.
[152] PR 10 RI, p. 64; PR 3 John, p. 178.     [153] *Ann. Dunst.*, p. 51.
[154] *CRR* 8, p. 158.     [155] *Rot. litt. pat.*, pp. 116, 174.

pillaging by those attending them speaks for itself. They were places where horse thieves might ply their trade.[156] They had some of the aspects of fairs and were occasionally termed so, but they were lethal fairs. Participants did face the risk of death. Geoffrey de Mandeville, earl of Essex, was killed in tournament in 1216, fought in London during Louis of France's occupation. One chronicler describes the event in revealing words: 'he died from a wound received when, in the French manner, the knights attacked each other with spears and lances, galloping their horses towards each other'.[157] Even in 1216 tournaments still had a French flavour.

Tournaments were simultaneously a source of glory, a training exercise, and a commercial business. In a passage criticizing tournaments written by Alexander Nequam, theologian and canon of Cirencester, about the year 1200, he first refers to knights 'who desire to barter their lives for praise and, careless of their own souls, expose themselves to mortal danger in pursuit of vainglorious reputation'. Here is the ancient heroic ideal of renown sought through peril, and also the ancient clerical distaste for such recklessness. Then Nequam makes explicit the second aspect of tournaments: 'they engage seriously in war games and occupy themselves in the image of war, in order to become more adept in military conflict.' As Nequam's contemporary, Roger of Howden, pointed out, training for war made the participant ready for war: 'he who has seen his own blood, whose teeth have cracked under a blow, he who has been thrown to the ground and felt the full weight of his adversary's body—such a man goes into battle with greater hope.'[158] Yet more material things were at stake than honour and expertise. Knights defeated in tournaments had to pay ransoms. Nequam reveals a sordid side to the undertaking when he criticizes those knights who made underhand deals with their opponents, agreeing to let them capture the young and inexperienced knights on their own side in return for a share of the ransom.[159]

During the twelfth century, the tournament became one of the main features of aristocratic life, in reality and in literature. To undertake a tournament was, by definition, 'to practice knighthood' [*faire chevalerie*].[160] The public display of one's ability and spirit as a mounted warrior with lance and shield was proof of one's worth as a member of the knightly order. Neither the sight of one's own blood, nor the cracking of one's teeth, nor the wordy moralizing of the clergy, nor the interference of royal administrators could check the 'beautiful horror' of the tournament.[161]

---

[156] *CRR* 1, p. 50.      [157] R. Coggesh., p. 179; cf. *Hist. ducs Norm.*, pp. 164–5.
[158] R. Howd. 2, pp. 166–7, citing Seneca, ep. 13.      [159] Alex. Nequam, *DNR* 2. 175 (p. 312).
[160] *Hist. Guill. Mar.* 1, p. 7, line 176.      [161] Alex. Nequam, *DNR* 2. 175 (p. 312).

## New Emblems

### Seals

The use of impressions on wax to authenticate written instructions or commands was widespread in medieval Europe. By the last years of Anglo-Saxon rule, English royal charters were being authenticated by appending impressions of the king's great seal that showed the monarch on his throne with the symbols of regal authority. After the Norman Conquest, William the Conqueror continued the practice but introduced a significant innovation by depicting himself enthroned in majesty on one side of his seal and armed on horseback on the other, thus economically invoking both his claims as ruler and the force that backed those claims. Large seals with equestrian images were soon imitated by members of the Anglo-Norman aristocracy. A charter of Ilbert de Lacy, granting the manor of Tingewick in Buckinghamshire to an abbey in Rouen, has a seal showing Ilbert as a mounted warrior. This dates to *c*.1090.[162] The practice soon became customary among the upper levels of the aristocracy.

The seals of male lay aristocrats were round, unlike the oval forms used by women and churches. Those of the Norman and Angevin baronage bear an image of the aristocrat as mounted warrior: with lance and long shield in the early twelfth century, with shorter shield and sword from the middle of the century. Around the image are impressed the words identifying the sender to the literate: 'William de Mandeville, earl of Essex' etc. The formal grants of lands, rights, or revenues that the magnates issued would now carry with them these strikingly assertive militaristic images. An armed man on horseback symbolized the great aristocrat.

The use of seals spread downwards through the aristocracy. This was a process that was not always welcomed. During one court case, Henry II's chief justiciar, Richard de Lucy, was confronted by a knight who questioned the authenticity of some charters supposedly issued by his ancestors on the ground that the documents bore no seal. The justiciar inquired whether the knight himself had a seal and, when told that he did, 'said mockingly, "It was not the custom of old for every petty knight to have a seal, for it is only kings and great men who should use them."'[163] The knightly class won the day, however. Nor did the dissemination of seals cease with them. By the early thirteenth century, the use of seals had spread to boroughs and to most free landholders. During the course of the thirteenth century, artisans and even villeins began to use them.

---

[162] Michael Clanchy, *From Memory to Written Record: England 1066–1307* (2nd edn.; Oxford, 1993), plate I, with refs.

[163] *Battle Chron.*, p. 214.

In order to serve its purpose, the seal design had to be fairly stable. A lord who used half-a-dozen different emblems would only be creating confusion. Yet there were occasions when seals were changed. Sometimes kings made a deliberate—and closely datable—decision to introduce a new seal. Richard I changed the design of his Great Seal in 1194 after his release from captivity, perhaps marking his resumption of undiminished regality. Lesser lords also varied their emblems. In 1190 or thereabouts Henry de Percy promised to Reading Abbey that, should he change his seal, he would freely and without payment seal again the charter which the abbey had received from him.[164] The implication is that there might be reasonable doubt about the validity of a grant made under one seal if the donor was known to use another.

The twelfth-century aristocratic seal represents a novel medium of noble self-presentation; it also provides the most important surviving evidence for the development of another new style of aristocratic display, heraldic arms.

## Heraldry

The tradition of warriors bearing symbols and emblems into battle was ancient. The legions had followed their eagles; boar-crested helmets are mentioned in the Old English epic *Beowulf*. These practices continued in the Norman and Angevin period. The Bayeux Tapestry shows commanders carrying banners, while some of the shields depicted there bear both abstract and figural images that would have been easily identifiable. The roughly contemporary poem, *The Song of Roland*, tells of knights who have shields with 'many cognizances' [*multes cunoisances*]—i.e. identifying markings.[165]

Military standards were a regular part of the ordering and the psychology of war. Just like Harold, the last Anglo–Saxon king, Richard I bore 'a terrible dragon banner' into battle.[166] At the battle of Arsuf in 1191 'the Normans and English rode behind the man carrying the dragon banner'.[167] Indeed, on that occasion the privilege of carrying the banner was a controversial matter. King Richard handed it to Peter de Praeres, despite the claim of the Yorkshire baron Robert Trussebut that the duty of bearing the standard was his hereditary right.[168] To bear a banner was a duty and a privilege. Earls disputed the right to carry the banner of St Edmund into battle at the head of the knights of Bury St Edmunds.[169] By the later twelfth century, knights of high status were marked out by their right to carry a banner: the account of the tournament adventures of William Marshal in France distinguishes 'those who carry a banner'—knights banneret—from the ordinary body of knights.[170]

[164] *EYC* 11, no. 292, p. 361.
[165] *Chanson de Roland*, line 3090, ed. F. Whitehead (Oxford, 1942), p. 90.
[166] R. Devizes, p. 23; Gerv. Tilb. 2. 17 (p. 935).
[167] Ambroise, *L'Estoire de la guerre sainte*, lines 6153–4, ed. Gaston Paris (Paris, 1897), col. 164.
[168] R. Howd. 3, p. 129.        [169] Joc. Brak, p. 57.
[170] e.g. *Hist. Guill. Mar.* 1, pp. 162, 163, 164, lines 4485, 4504, 4537.

Martial symbols and emblems were thus not new, but the elaborate, rule-governed heraldry that emerged in the twelfth century was. The bearing of hereditary symbols—some abstract, others representing stylized animals or objects—on the shield or the seal or on surcoats and horse trappings was a novel way for barons and knights to proclaim their family identity and their high birth. Although decorative designs had been used on shields and elsewhere from time immemorial, the heraldic arms that emerged in the twelfth century were distinguished by being the mark of a family and by the increasingly well-defined rules that applied both to their form and to their use.

The earliest examples of heraldic arms among the Anglo-Norman baronage are the 'checky' (chequerboard) design of Waleran, count of Meulan and earl of Worcester (d. 1166), and the chevrons of Gilbert of Clare, earl of Hertford (d. 1152).[171] Both these earls' seals depict a mounted warrior, who, in the former case, bears a checky design on his shield, surcoat, and banner, and, in the latter case, chevrons on his shield. Both emblems were carried by later family members. Down to the extinction of their line, the Clare earls bore three gold chevrons on a red shield. Gilbert of Clare's sister, Rohese, also had chevrons on her seal.[172] Two of Waleran of Meulan's great nephews, Robert, earl of Leicester, and William, earl Warenne, had the checky coat-of-arms.[173]

It may not be coincidental that English heraldry begins in the same years as the English tournament, about 1140. The need to identify a knight whose face was partially covered by helmet, nose guard, and mail coif was especially acute in the confusion of the tournament. The contestants would be divided into two sides and it was important to know at once who one faced and whether he were a proper target for capture and ransom. A clear geometrical or symbolic design upon a shield could serve this purpose, for, in tournament, unlike battle, contest was customarily between mounted knights spurring at each other face to face. It was even more important, perhaps, that the spectators could tell who was who, in order to follow the fortunes of their favourites and give the coveted praise where it was due. This identifying function of coats of arms is explicit in the French romances of the late twelfth century: 'Do you see the one with the gold band across a red shield? That is Governal de Roberdic. And do you see the one behind him, who has a dragon and an eagle placed side by side on his shield? That's the king of Aragon's son . . .'[174]

---

[171] J. H. Round, 'The Introduction of Armorial Bearings into England', *Archaeological Jnl* 51 (1894), pp. 43–8; R. H. Ellis, *Catalogue of Seals in the Public Record Office: Personal Seals* (2 vols.; London, 1978–81), no. 1200; *Bk. Seals*, no. 84, pp. 58–9; C. H. Hunter Blair, 'Armorials upon English Seals', *Archaeologia*, 89 (1943), pp. 1–26, pl. IIg.

[172] Birch, *Seals*, no. 13048; C. H. Hunter Blair, 'Armorials upon English Seals', *Archaeologia*, 89 (1943), pp. 1–26, pl. XVIk; R. Marks and A. Payne (eds.), *British Heraldry* (London, 1978), p. 16.

[173] David Crouch, *The Image of Aristocracy in Britain, 1000–1300* (London, 1992), p. 231.

[174] Chrétien de Troyes, *Le Chevalier de la charrette*, lines 5773–80, ed. Mario Roques (Paris, 1958), p. 176.

Over the course of the second half of the twelfth century evidence for armorial bearings multiplies. By the end of that century, aristocratic seals began to depict the coat of arms—i.e. the shield with its heraldic devices—only, as an alternative to the figure of a mounted knight. Families of lesser standing than the great earls took up the practice of heraldry. Just as the knights and gentry adopted seals, so they imitated the magnates in displaying armorial bearings. Although no rolls-of-arms survive from this period (the earliest dates to about 1255), surviving imprints of coats-of-arms on seals show that members of the knightly aristocracy had hereditary heraldic arms by the end of the twelfth century.

A special technical vocabulary, based on French, developed to describe the colours and images of heraldry. Rules were devised, prescribing, for example, that the heraldic metals *or* (gold) and *argent* (silver) could not be placed on each other but on one of the heraldic 'colours'. The positions that the heraldic beasts could adopt were limited, stylized, and given technical appellations. Thus, the royal arms of England, as adopted by Richard I in 1194, are, in the language of heraldry (blazon) 'gules, three lions passant guardant or', i.e. on a red field, three golden lions, facing outwards, with their right foreleg raised. John of Salisbury had ironically called the technical terms used in hunting 'the scholarship of the aristocracy' (above, p. 239). The terms of heraldry offered a new elitist pastime of the same stamp.

The choice of symbols in heraldry reflects partly a need for clear, bright shapes and colours, partly an ancient tradition of the invocation of animal power. The lion is easily the most common creature represented on aristocratic shields in north-western Europe, despite not being indigenous to the region. It appears on over 15 per cent of arms, easily outstripping the next most popular beast, the eagle, which figures on less than 3 per cent. By the twelfth century, this exotic animal had virtually displaced the earlier Germanic warrior totemism of wolf, bear, or boar.[175] It is quite clear what it meant to carry an image of a lion into battle. Gerald of Wales, in eulogizing the French kings, contrasted the peaceful fleur-de-lys that they bore as their arms with the practice of 'other princes, who display savage and predatory beasts, such as bears, leopards and lions, on their arms and banners as an emblem of ferocity'.[176]

Another source of heraldic designs was the pun, a play on the name of the bearer. One of Becket's murderers, the knight Reginald fitz Urse, is depicted in a contemporary manuscript bearing a shield with a bear (*urse*) upon it (Plate 9). The 'luce', or pike, appears on the seal of Richard de Lucy in

---

[175] Michel Pastoureau, 'Quel est le roi des animaux?', in *Le Monde animal et ses representations au Moyen Age* (Toulouse, 1985), pp. 133–42.
[176] Gerald, *Prin.* 3. 30 (p. 320).

Stephen's reign.[177] These so-called 'canting' arms reduplicate the link between the hereditary names that aristocrats bore and their hereditary armorial bearings. The arms summon up the name not simply by association but
also by the punning reference.

Heraldic arms never lost a military edge—they were, after all, 'arms'. Yet
their importance as tokens of good family came to be far more central. Arms
were associated with families; women could bear them; related families
might have related arms. A new means had been created of placing on public
display those family values on which aristocracy was predicated. Moreover,
although the employment of heraldic devices, like that of seals, did percolate
down through society, armorial bearings were always more exclusive. Indeed,
eventually the bearing of arms came to be a test of gentility.

The bearing of heraldic arms and the use of seals, often marked with those
arms, introduced among the aristocracy the use of visual symbols that simultaneously enabled the user to be identified as (a) an aristocrat in general and
(b) a member of a specific aristocratic family. Armorial bearings neatly indi-
viduated the bearer at the same time as they stated his class, and they did so
by public and, primarily, non-verbal means.

*Arthurian Legend and Literature*

Amongst the elements of the new aristocratic culture of the twelfth century,
along with tournaments, armorial bearings, and equestrian seals, was a new
literature. This literature consisted of vernacular narratives that mirrored
and idealized the lives of the aristocracy. Of all these stories and story-cycles,
the tales of Arthur and his court were the most popular and widespread.

It is certain that stories about Arthur were being told in the Celtic-
speaking regions in the early twelfth century. An incident from the very early
years of that century shows the strength of attachment to the legend of 'the
once and future king' in the Celtic parts of Britain. In 1113 canons from the
French cathedral of Laon arrived in England to raise funds for the rebuilding
of their church. Upon reaching Cornwall they were informed that this was
the land of Arthur and were shown Arthur's seat and oven. At Bodmin the attachment to the local hero manifested itself in a more aggressive form. 'Just as
the Bretons dispute with the French on account of king Arthur,' recorded one
of the canons of Laon, 'so a man began to quarrel with one of our servants,
saying that Arthur was still alive'. Only narrowly was bloodshed avoided.[178]

Arthur's transformation from the returning king of Cornish or Breton
legend to a hero of the aristocracy of the Anglo-French world was effected by
the work of Geoffrey of Monmouth, whose Latin *History of the Kings of
Britain* took up, refashioned, and relaunched the figure of Arthur. Arthur is

[177] Birch, *Seals*, nos. 11439, 2245.          [178] Hermann, *Mir. Laud.* 2. 15–16 (col. 983).

presented as a great conqueror, who subdued the British Isles and the whole of France. Bearing a golden dragon as his banner, he routed the Saxons, annexed Ireland, and vanquished the Romans. His court was the international model for refined behaviour. The noblest men of Europe sought 'to conduct themselves, in matters of dress and the bearing of arms, in the manner of Arthur's knights'. At his great Whitsun court at Caerleon, he wore his crown ceremonially in the cathedral church before the kings and magnates subject to him, who had poured in from every part with their trains of horses and mules. After the service there was feasting in the palace, the steward leading a thousand ermine-clad nobles, who served the food, while the butler presided over the distribution of drink of every kind. Next followed the tournament, the knights engaging in mounted warfare, while the ladies watched from the walls and incited them.

In those days Britain held such a place of honour that it surpassed all other kingdoms in wealth, luxurious adornments and the courtliness of its inhabitants. Any of its knights who obtained a reputation for courage wore clothes and arms of one colour. Fashionable women, who wore clothes matching them, would disdain to have as a lover anyone who had not proved himself three times in battle. In this way they were made more chaste and better and the knights became more courageous for love of them.[179]

This powerful fantasy of riches, love, and knightly prowess launched a craze. Many copies of Geoffrey's *History* circulated in twelfth-century England and a French version of it was produced by the poet Gaimar, to serve as the first part of his own *History of the English* (*Estoire des Engleis*). This was composed about 1140. Around this same time the Cistercian Ailred of Rievaulx had a conversation with one of the novices under his care as novice-master. The novice confessed that he had often been moved to tears, 'by the stories that are made up everywhere about this Arthur—whoever he was'.[180] Ailred's monastery, Rievaulx, had been founded by the Yorkshire baron, Walter Espec, who is known to have owned a copy of Geoffrey of Monmouth's *History*. Not far from Rievaulx and from Walter Espec's castle of Helmsley was Beverley, whose sacrist at this time, Alfred, noted the popularity and fashionability of Arthurian stories: 'if you did not know those stories, you risked being branded an ignorant clod'.[181] Arthur had conquered not only Saxons and Romans but also the fashion-conscious aristocracy of Norman England.

Arthur's tale was taken up by the Norman poet Wace, whose *Romance of Brutus* (*Roman de Brut*), dealing with the legendary history of Britain from the time of Brutus, its founder, was completed in 1155. He is the first to mention

---

[179] Geoff. Monm., *HRB*, books 9–10 (143–76), esp. 9. 11–14 (154, 156–7), pp. 107, 109–12.
[180] Ailr. Riev., *Speculum caritatis* 2. 17 (*Op. asc.*, p. 90).
[181] *Aluredi Beverlacensis Annales*, ed. Thomas Hearne (Oxford, 1716), pp. 2–3.

the Round Table, Arthur's ingenious device for seating his knights without provoking quarrels over precedence. A copy of Wace's work was presented to Eleanor of Aquitaine. Other Arthurian tales circulated in Angevin circles. One of the Anglo-Norman lords who served as a hostage in Germany for king Richard's ransom had with him a French verse *Lancelot*. He lent it to a German poet, Ulrich von Zatzikhoven, who produced a German version.[182]

Henry II was supposedly one of the forces behind excavations at Glastonbury that revealed the tombs of Arthur and Guinevere there, simultaneously creating a new Arthurian shrine and undermining the prospect of Arthur as returning Celtic hero. Henry was happy enough to see Arthur's conquest of Ireland used to justify his own rule there, but also seems to have wanted to pluck the sting from the myth of the once and future king. He must have been aware of the dangers, for his own grandson, the posthumous son of Geoffrey of Brittany, was christened Arthur at his birth in 1187 as a mark of defiance by the Breton nobility.[183]

Not everyone had confidence in the historicity of Arthur. Indeed, by the early thirteenth century to call something 'a story of Arthur' meant that you thought it a pack of lies.[184] Nevertheless, a particular coloration borrowed from the legends and literature of Arthur and his knights had begun to tint the life of the English aristocracy and was to continue to do so. Some of this was expressed in their pageantry and emblems. Richard I possessed Arthur's sword Excalibur (*Caliburne*).[185] The dragon banner he had carried at Arsuf was in the tradition not only of Harold of Wessex but also of Arthur of Britain. Tristan's sword was among king John's regalia.[186] By the middle of the thirteenth century, tournaments were held with Arthurian motifs. They were known as 'Round Tables'. The names of the aristocracy began to reflect the tales that moved them so. Isolde was one of the more common female names in early thirteenth-century England. It was a name that occurs among the Anglo-Norman landholding class as early as Domesday Book, but it is hard to believe it had not been promoted by the tales of Tristan, Mark, and Isolde that were being composed and circulated in England from the time of Henry II. At the end of our period the foundations of aristocratic life continued to be landed wealth and military power, as they had ever been, but the cultural image the aristocracy projected and absorbed was now more elaborate, more ceremonious, and more romantic than in the past.

---

[182] Ulrich von Zatzikhoven, *Lanzelet*, ed. K. A. Hahn (Frankfurt, 1845; repr. Berlin, 1965), lines 9330–49.
[183] W. Newb. 3. 7 (1, p. 235).  [184] Gerald, *Inv.* 4. 2 (p. 167).
[185] *Gesta Ric. I*, p. 159; R. Howd. 3, p. 97.  [186] *Rot. litt. pat.*, p. 77.

# CHAPTER 5

# Warfare

Although England was dominated by an aristocracy trained in armed combat, it was, by the standards of the time, a relatively peaceful country. Large-scale warfare was rare. The endemic violence of Wales, to which the Anglo-Normans contributed so much, occasionally spilled over into the counties of the Welsh March, and the Scots did make incursions across the Border, but such incidents were uncommon. Invasion from overseas was sometimes threatened but never materialized, except by invitation in 1216. England suffered more from war taxation than from war. The king of England's wars were fought in France. Organized armed violence within England took the form of spasmodic rebellions, such as those of 1088 and 1173–4 discussed above (pp. 52–7), but only on two occasions within our period did these conflicts last long or threaten the fundamental order: first during the so-called Anarchy of Stephen's reign, between the outbreak of full-scale hostilities in 1139 and the Treaty of Winchester in 1153, and then again during the civil war that followed Magna Carta, a war that was settled politically by treaty in 1217 but still required several further years of pacification.

Nevertheless, the military aristocracy had not lost its function. Decades in which there was no fighting in England were still the exception, while war in France was virtually continuous. The young men of the aristocracy were trained fighters; the king's major expense was the conduct of war; England was covered with hundreds of fortifications.

## 1. WAGING WAR

### Arms and Armour

Very little survives of the arms and armour of the Norman and Angevin period. Knowledge of the subject depends primarily on the images depicted in contemporary manuscripts, sculpture, and, in one magnificent case, embroidery, supplemented with the occasional documentary or narrative reference. Fortunately the Bayeux Tapestry provides a unique starting-point, with dozens of detailed scenes of combat.

The Assize of Arms of 1181 prescribed the following arms and armour for the various classes. Those who held a knight's fee or had over 16 marks (£10. 13s. 4d.) in chattels or income should possess a mail-coat, helmet, shield, and lance. Free men with over 10 marks (£6. 13s. 4d.) in chattels or income were required to own a mail-shirt (*albergellum*), iron cap, and lance, while burgesses and the remaining free men had to have a padded coat, iron cap, and lance.[1] As these provisions make clear, the full-length mail-coat was the rarest and most expensive type of body armour. Shirts of mails and padded doublets were more common forms of protection. It was the obligation of the borough of Dunstable in the early thirteenth century to provide one mail-coat, nine short coats of mail, and twelve doublets for the royal levy and this ratio expresses the relative frequency of the different types of body protection.[2] Difference in size was reflected in difference in cost. In 1194 a mail-coat was valued at £2, a mail-shirt at £1.[3] At the same time a leather hat and doublet for the king's sailors cost only 6s.[4]

The Norman knights on the Bayeux Tapestry have the complete mail-coat, reaching to their knees. It was made of interlinked rings of metal and is likely to have weighed about 25–30 lbs. A coif of mail protected the neck and went up over the head, underneath the helmet. The Tapestry shows leggings of mail only on William the Conqueror and count Eustace of Boulogne, suggesting that this refinement was for the very great. The knights' helmets are conical, with the nose-piece that has become a popular emblem of the Normans, even though the Anglo-Saxon warriors are depicted with it too. Their shields are the large, kite-shaped type that was well suited to protect the left side of a mounted fighter. The main knightly offensive weapons are the lance and sword. The former was perhaps ten feet long and could be used overarm, underarm, or couched, while the larger swords of the time (some of which have survived) might have a blade of 34 inches. This all represented an immense amount of metalwork. As the contemporary abbot of Westminster put it, 'There are scarcely black-smiths enough and there is scarcely iron enough to make all the weapons of war.'[5]

A depiction of the murder of archbishop Thomas Becket from a century later than the Tapestry (Plate 9) shows little change in knightly gear. The two murderers illustrated here in the foreground have precisely the same mail-coats and coifs as those on the Bayeux Tapestry. One, identifiable as Reginald fitz Urse from his heraldic bearings, has mail leggings, laced behind the calf. He also wears a simple round helmet, without nose-piece, while his companion

[1] *Gesta Hen. II* 1, p. 278; R. Howd. 2, p. 261; *Sel. Charters*, p. 183.     [2] *Ann. Dunst.*, p. 35.
[3] *Rotuli curiae regis* (1194–1200), ed. Francis Palgrave (2 vols., Rec. Comm.; 1835), vol. 1, p. 51.
[4] PR 7 RI, p. 113.
[5] Gilbert Crispin, *Disputatio Iudei et Christiani* 44, ed. Anna Sapir Abulafia and G. R. Evans, *The Works of Gilbert Crispin* (*Auctores Britannici Medii Aevi* 8; 1986), p. 17.

has the flat-topped style that had come into use in the second half of the twelfth century. Both wield long swords and carry triangular shields, curved to the body. There are no essential differences from the knights of Hastings. The only development that eventually gave the knight of the thirteenth century a different look from that of the eleventh was the rise of the great helm, a cylindrical helmet that covered the whole face, with eye-slits for vision and perforations for breathing, but this appeared late and was by no means universal.

The image of king Harold struck in the eye by a Norman arrow is a reminder of the importance of bows at Hastings. Throughout the period archers were valuable troops, having a major part in the defeat of the Scottish army at the battle of the Standard in 1138 as well as forming the bulk of the army that Henry II took to Ireland in 1171. Their bows of yew were not expensive to produce and hence great numbers of archers could be armed relatively easily. In the summer of 1216, after the landing of Louis of France, a thousand archers carried on a guerrilla warfare against the French amidst the trees of the Sussex Weald.[6] By contrast, crossbows, often made of horn, were more elaborate and more expensive. Crossbowmen were highly prized experts and many are named individually in the Pipe Rolls of the Angevin kings. One of John's master crossbowmen was paid 9d. a day throughout the whole of the latter part of the king's reign, as well as being given robes for himself, his companions, and their wives.[7] Maintaining a powerful force of crossbowman was a matter of importance to the king and one he was prepared to pay for. In 1215 John ordered 10,000 quarrels (crossbow missiles) of various sizes for his castle of Marlborough.[8]

The crossbow, with its slow rate of fire, was particularly suited to use from fixed and protected positions. Hence crossbowmen were an especial danger for those besieging castles and towns. Robert fitz Walter, one of the leaders of the baronial revolt against John, saw his standard bearer shot in the head by a crossbow bolt while the barons were besieging Northampton. Eustace de Vescy, Robert's fellow in the rebel leadership, was killed by a crossbow bolt fired by the besieged garrison of Barnard Castle. The 250 crossbowmen in the royalist army at the battle of Lincoln in 1217, who were stationed on the walls of Lincoln castle, caused great destruction among their opponents.[9] The besiegers could also deploy crossbowmen if they had a secure site. When the royal army besieged Bedford in 1224, the king's engineers built a tall wooden structure from which the crossbowmen could dominate the besieged castle.[10]

[6]   R. Wend. 2, p. 182 (Paris, *CM* 2, p. 655).
[7]   PR 11 John, p. 58; PR 12 John, p. 111; PR 13 John, p. 176; PR 14 John, p. 146.
[8]   *Memoranda Roll* 10 John etc., ed. R. Allen Brown (PRS n.s. 31; 1957 for 1955), p. 130.
[9]   R. Wend. 2, pp. 116, 194, 212, 215–16 (Paris, *CM* 2, pp. 586–7, 666; 3, pp. 18, 21).
[10]   R. Wend. 2, p. 280 (Paris, *CM* 3, p. 86).

## Wasting

When, at the end of his life, William the Conqueror lay sick at his Norman capital of Rouen, his enemy, king Philip of France, joked 'the king of England lies at Rouen like a woman in labour'. Word of this remark reached the ailing king. 'When I go to mass after the birth,' he remarked grimly, 'I will offer him a hundred thousand candles.'[11] Fire was the simple and universal herald of war. Wooden houses and barns, crops in the fields, even the timber palisades and towers of castles could be annihilated with relatively little effort and no complex equipment.

The usual form that warfare took, apart from the siege of the enemy's strong places, was the deliberate devastation of his land. 'Destroy your enemies and waste their country; let everything be set alight by flame and burning; leave nothing for them . . . on which they could have dinner . . . this is how war should be begun.'[12] Such is the advice given by Philip, count of Flanders, at the beginning of the great war of 1173–4 between Henry II and his enemies. It was followed with a will. Systematic devastation and plundering had strategic purposes in addition to the fun it obviously provided for the perpetrators. There are cases where it was part of a scorched earth policy, designed to deny invaders any possibility of living off the land. In 1085 William I had the coastal areas of England laid waste, so that invaders from overseas would have no supplies to seize when they landed.[13] Stephen burned all the villages around Dunster castle in 1139 'leaving nothing that his enemies could eat'.[14] Removing one's enemy's corn and cattle not only starved him but also supplied one's own forces. While he was besieging the barons in Rochester castle in 1215, John 'sent plunderers in every direction, who brought in food to maintain the army'. The following year the royalist garrison of Dover seized the chance offered by the departure of the besieging forces 'to make hostile incursions through the county and secure their castle with everything they needed'.[15]

In the civil war of 1215–17 plundering was indeed one of the primary activities of the forces in arms. John's campaigns in the winter of 1215–16 were particularly notorious for the burning of houses and other buildings, the kidnapping and torture of men to extract ransoms, the cutting down of orchards, and the seizure of booty. The king's death brought no respite. On one occasion in the following winter, the royalist mercenary commander Fawkes de Bréauté assembled a force of knights and mercenaries from various garrisons and came to St Albans, which he plundered, taking many captives and extorting a payment of £100 from the abbot to save the abbey from being burned. Fawkes then went off to his castle of Bedford with his

---

[11] W. Malm., *GR* 3. 281 (2, p. 336); OMT edn., p. 510.
[12] Fantosme, lines 443–6, 449, pp. 32–4.      [13] *ASC*, p. 216.
[14] W. Malm., *HN* 480 (pp. 36–7).      [15] R. Wend. 2, pp. 149, 199 (Paris, *CM* 2, p. 624; 3, p. 5).

booty.[16] After the battle of Lincoln in 1217 the victorious royalist army plundered the cathedral, where the women and children had taken refuge during the street-fighting and the burgesses and others had stored their property for safe-keeping.[17]

Even after the war had been formally settled by treaty in September 1217, some of the combatants found it impossible to return to the habits of peacetime: 'there were in these days many people in England who had found it very sweet to live by plunder in the time of the war just ended, so that, after peace had been made and granted to all, they could not hold back their hands from booty.'[18] A particularly turbulent figure was William, earl of Aumale. In 1221 he collected troops at his castle of Bytham (Lincs.), plundered the surrounding villages, and carried off many men for ransom. Eventually a royal army had to be mustered to repress him.[19] To wage war was to ransack barns, drive off livestock, and imprison the local population.

## Battle

Sieges, ravaging, the occasional skirmish—these were the usual incidents of warfare in our period. Battles were rare and risky, although a few decisive ones did take place. Since many of the king's wars were fought overseas, several of the more dramatic encounters occurred abroad. All the important battles in the wars of succession that followed the death of William the Conqueror were fought in France. Henry I acquired Normandy at Tinchebray in 1106 and held on to it with victories at Brémule in 1119 and Bourgtheroulde in 1124. Richard fought only two battles as king, both of them in Palestine. Battles within England, with the exception of the defeat of the invading Scots in 1138, were limited to a few occasions during civil wars and rebellions. Two of the battles with the greatest immediate political consequences were fought at Lincoln, one in 1141 when king Stephen was defeated and captured, another in 1217 when the forces of the young Henry III inflicted a heavy defeat on the troops of Louis of France and the rebel barons.

Almost all these battles involved dismounted as well as mounted knights. Indeed, a decisive cavalry charge was a rarity. The heavily armoured dismounted knight could strengthen a battle line of less well protected infantry. Moreover, if knights dismounted, they expressed a deeper commitment to the outcome of the battle, since they had no easy exit by mounted flight. When one of the rebel leaders at Bourgtheroulde saw one of the royalist commanders, Odo Borleng, getting ready to fight on foot, he commented to his companions: 'Look, Odo Borleng and his men have dismounted. Know that he will strive tenaciously for victory. A warlike knight who fights on foot with

[16] R. Wend. 2, p. 205 (Paris, *CM* 3, p. 12).  [17] Barnwell Chron., p. 238.
[18] R. Wend. 2, pp. 226–7 (Paris, *CM* 3, p. 33).  [19] R. Wend. 2, pp. 255–6 (Paris, *CM* 3, pp. 60–1).

his men does not flee but either dies or conquers.'[20] This was a judgement that king Stephen would have fully endorsed, as he made a desperate last stand at Lincoln, dismounted among his footsoldiers, while his earls and mercenaries galloped off.

An important encounter in the great rebellion against Henry II in 1173-4 was the battle of Fornham on 17 October 1173, when royalist forces defeated the rebel earl of Leicester (for the political background, see pp. 54-5 above).[21] Less than three weeks earlier the earl had landed at Walton, in the south-eastern tip of Suffolk, with a force he had brought over from Flanders. After failing to capture the royal castle at Walton, he made his base at the castle at Framlingham. This belonged to Hugh Bigod, earl of Norfolk, another rebel. Local attacks and ravaging were undertaken. On 13 October Leicester captured the castle of Haughley, sixteen miles from Framlingham. This was in royal hands and had been entrusted to Ranulf de Broc, who was the doorkeeper of the royal chamber as well as the organizing spirit behind Becket's murder. The rebels burned the castle and forced the garrison of thirty knights to pay a ransom. The earl now determined to march across country to his own main centre at Leicester. This had come under attack from royalist forces, so it required support. Some sources also mention tension between Leicester and his hosts at Framlingham, the earl and countess of Norfolk. Another records the supposed words of the earl of Derby, also a rebel, encouraging the earl: 'if you could ride as far as Leicester, before Easter you would be able to get to the Tower of London without trouble.'

The earl of Leicester's forces were intercepted well before they left Suffolk. Royalist troops had mustered at Bury St Edmunds under the command of Richard de Lucy, the chief justiciar, Humphrey de Bohun, the constable, and the earls of Cornwall, Gloucester, and Arundel. Among them were three hundred knights of the king serving for wages, as well as Roger Bigod, son of the rebel earl of Norfolk. The royalists marched out under the banner of St Edmund, whose shrine was nearby in the abbey at Bury, and encountered their opponents at Fornham. Facing them were Flemish mercenaries, estimated by one source at three thousand in number. The fighting spirit of both sides is conveyed in Jordan Fantosme's vernacular account of the battle. 'We have not come here to pass the time of day,' say the Flemings, 'but to destroy king Henry, that old warrior, and have the wool we desire'—Flanders was famous for its cloth trade. The earl of Arundel, on seeing the enemy, cries out to Roger Bigod, 'Let us attack them for the honour of God and St Edmund!', to which Roger replies 'As you please! I have never desired anything more in my life than to destroy those Flemings I see coming on here!'

[20] Orderic 12. 39 (6, p. 350).
[21] For the following, see Fantosme, lines 833–1095, pp. 62–80; R. Diceto, *Ymag.* 1, pp. 377–8; *Gesta Hen. II* 1, pp. 61–2; R. Howd. 2, pp. 54–5; W. Newb. 2. 30 (1, pp. 178–9).

So 'terrible battle was joined'. An initial royalist attack was repulsed, but soon the balance tilted. The Flemings were cut down in the marshy field: 'They gathered the wool of England very late; crows and buzzards descend on their bodies . . .' The earl of Leicester, his wife, his kinsman from France, Hugh del Chastel, and the mounted troops were taken prisoner. The Flemings were hunted down. The local rural population could now take its revenge on the predators: 'in all the countryside there was no peasant nor serf who did not go after the Flemings to destroy them with fork and flail'. In just this way the defeated at the battle of the Standard and the battle of Lincoln in 1217 felt the savage anger of those who were otherwise always the victims of armed men, 'the men of the villages'.[22]

### Naval Warfare

In the eleventh century both Anglo–Saxons and Normans could draw on the long Scandinavian tradition of naval expertise. Fleets of hundreds of ships were built and deployed with skill. The Bayeux Tapestry provides an incomparable pictorial record of the construction, provisioning, and launching of such an armada. We are taken from the felling of the trees to the invasion itself. The ships depicted in the Tapestry have life-like masts, sails, rigging, tillers, and anchors. They are of the Viking longship type, often with striped sails, oar-holes, and figureheads of dragons and other beasts. The Viking world continued to echo in the naval traditions of the twelfth century too— the king's great ship in which he and members of the royal family crossed the Channel was termed a *snecca*, a poetic word for a longship deriving from the Old Norse for 'serpent' (modern Norwegian *snekke*).

Once the events of 1066 had created the cross-Channel state, the strategic role of the Channel became even more vital. William the Conqueror crossed the Channel probably seventeen times in the twenty-one years of his reign.[23] On every occasion he would have been accompanied by an armed retinue and sometimes by larger forces. The armada of 1066 has left a unique visual image in the Bayeux Tapestry, but it was not the only invasion fleet to traverse the Channel in this period. In 1101 Robert, duke of Normandy, crossed the Channel with 200 ships and landed his army of knights, archers, and infantry at Portsmouth. His brother and rival, Henry I, had earlier sent out naval forces to harass his brother's ships in their Norman berths, but these had gone over to Robert.[24] In 1142, during a later civil war, Robert of Gloucester crossed from Normandy to England with over 300 knights in 52 ships.[25] John's expedition to Poitou in 1206 was carried in 200 ships.[26] Perhaps the

---

[22] R. Hexham, p. 164; R. Wend. 2, p. 219 (Paris, *CM* 3, p. 24).
[23] Le Patourel, *Norman Empire*, p. 164.     [24] *Ann. Wint.*, p. 41, for the size of the fleet.
[25] W. Malm., *HN* 521 (p. 74).     [26] PR 8 John, p. 148.

largest maritime expedition in the Channel since 1066 was that of Louis of France, who landed at Thanet in 1216 with 600 ordinary ships and 80 capacious merchant ships (cogs).[27]

The *snecca* had a permanent highly paid skipper, but the English kings usually relied on ships and men raised from the ports for short periods of service. Such duties went back to Anglo-Saxon times. The entry for Dover in *Domesday Book* records that it was ancient custom that 'the burgesses gave twenty ships to the king once a year for fifteen days, with twenty-one men in each ship'.[28] Exactly the same duty lay on Hastings, according to a charter issued by Henry II, probably in 1158. If the vessels were required for more than fifteen days, this would be at the king's cost.[29] Both Dover and Hastings were members of the group of maritime towns known as the Cinque Ports (first mentioned by this name in 1161), that enjoyed special privileges in return for their naval duties.[30] In 1196, for instance, during his expedition to Brittany, Richard engaged the experienced naval commander Alan Trenchemer to head a force consisting of the ships of the Cinque Ports as well as three longships with twice the normal complement of crew. These latter were paid for a month at 2*d*. per day and the expenditure on the Cinque Ports contingent would suggest that they supplied their customary 57 ships for fifteen days at their own expense and fifteen days at the king's.[31]

Another occasion on which the Cinque Ports supplied ships was the assembly of king Richard's crusading fleet in 1190. The accounts of Henry of Cornhill, who was the administrator responsible for that fleet, reveal something of the scope and costs of a major naval expedition.[32] Henry had purchased 40 ships, or shares in them, and paid out a year's wages for over a thousand sailors. There were 20 to 24 crewmen per ship and they received 2*d*. per day, with the skippers getting twice that. The value of the ships purchased ranged from £50 to £66. Outlay on ships and wages, along with miscellaneous expenses such as work on the *snecca*, approached £5,000. It was obviously highly unusual to send a large fleet on a campaign that would take it on a voyage of 4,000 miles, to encounter enemies far from the shores of England, but it was evidently within the capabilities, both technical and organizational, of the Angevin kingdom.

Naval activity intensified during the war between the Angevins and Philip Augustus. This was virtually continuous in the thirty years between Philip's invasion of Normandy in 1193, while Richard was held captive in Germany, and the French king's death in 1223. Immediately upon his release from captivity, Richard planned and developed Portsmouth as a naval base for

[27] R. Wend. 2, p. 180 (Paris, *CM* 2, p. 653).    [28] *DB* 1, 1 (Ken. D. 2).
[29] Katharine Murray, *Constitutional History of the Cinque Ports* (Manchester, 1935), pp. 232–3; *Cal. Ch. Rolls* 3, pp. 219–20.
[30] PR 7 HII, pp. 56, 59.    [31] PR 8 RI (Chancellor's Roll), p. 20.    [32] PR 2 RI, pp. 8–9.

operations in the Channel. A town was established on the site, settlers brought there and privileges granted. The king himself had a house in the town and in John's reign a wall was constructed around the dock where the royal galleys berthed.[33] These galleys, large, oar-powered vessels that are first mentioned in English sources at the time of Richard's crusade, were being constructed for the king's use in large numbers at this time. Over £360 was spent on their construction at London in 1205. A list dating to the same year gives the location of fifty of the royal galleys stationed around the English and Irish coasts. In the period 1210–12 a concerted building campaign took place, under the direction of William of Wrotham, archdeacon of Taunton, who was one of the king's more important administrators and had special responsibility for ports, customs, and the navy. Twenty new galleys and thirty-four other ships were constructed at Winchelsea and Romney, while a great deal of repair work and furnishing and equipping also went on. Work was done on the king's great boat, *Deulabeneie* ('God bless her') and his barge *Portejoie* ('Bring joy'). Timber and a thousand yards of canvas were sent down to Winchelsea.[34]

The fleets that William of Wrotham had built were large and dangerous. One flotilla for which he was the paymaster consisted of 20 galleys and 40 other ships, crewed by a total of 1,291 seamen, another of 6 galleys, 91 other ships, and 1,202 sailors. They swept the seas around England, capturing enemy ships and taking their cargoes. The chance survival of an Exchequer document tells us that between 25 April and 8 September 1212 the galleys under the command of Geoffrey de Lucy seized thirteen Norman ships and plundered another five. The vessels were brought back to Portsmouth and those that were serviceable were redeployed in the king's wars, many going to Wales, where John planned a summer campaign against the Welsh, although some, like the 'old and damaged' *Countess*, were left to rot in Portsmouth harbour. The plunder included 666 tuns (casks containing 252 gallons) of wine, 756½ quarters of grain, and 3,140 quarters of salt. Some of this was sent off to provision the king's forces, some sold, and some stored in Portsmouth. Not only were the merchants of the whole northern French coast being terrorized—men from Morlaix (Finisterre), St Malo, Guernsey, Varaville (Calvados), Dieppe, and Gravelines were among the victims—but John was feeding his ravenous regime for free.[35]

This large-scale official piracy was obviously an important part of the task of the Angevin navy—as late as 1227 the royal government was still trying to sort out what had happened to all the ships that had passed through the hands

---

[33] *CRR* 6, p. 305; PR 6 RI, pp. 6–7, 10: PR 7 RI, p. 36; PR 8 RI, pp. 197–8; PR 9 RI, p. 24: PR 10 RI, p. 24; charter in *Foedera, conventiones, litterae et . . . acta publica . . .*, ed. Thomas Rymer (new edn., 4 vols. in 7 parts, Record Commission; 1816–69), vol. 1, p. 63; *Rot. litt. claus.* 1, p. 117; PR 14 John, pp. 75–6.

[34] PR 7 John, p. 10; *Rot. litt. claus.* 1, pp. 33, 55; *Rot. litt. pat.*, p. 52; PR 14 John, pp. 75–6.

[35] Beryl Formoy, 'A Maritime Indenture of 1212', *EHR* 41 (1926), pp. 556–9.

of William of Wrotham[36]—but a more momentous duty was the prevention of invasion. After expelling John from northern France, Philip Augustus intended to keep on going and land in England. John's newly strengthened navy was one of the main obstacles to the French king's plans. In 1213 a large naval force was sent across the Channel to Flanders to attack Philip's invasion fleet, which had assembled at the mouth of the river Zwijn. The French vessels were found at anchor and unprotected and large numbers of them were burned or plundered. King Philip abandoned the project for the time being. Even after his son Louis had made a successful landing in 1216, English naval power had an important part to play, for after Louis's defeat at Lincoln in May 1217 his cause depended on reinforcement from France. That summer the issue was decided at sea. A French fleet of 80 ships, commanded by the infamous Eustace the Monk, was sailing across the Channel to Louis's aid when it encountered a hostile English fleet that had sailed from Sandwich, one of the Cinque Ports. Although the English fleet was only half the size of the opposition, the English were 'aggressive and well skilled in naval warfare'. The English crossbowmen and archers caused many casualties, while their iron-prowed galleys crashed into and sank several French vessels. Since they had manoeuvred so that the wind was behind them, they were also able to throw quicklime into the eyes of the French forces, blinding them. A large number of French ships were captured and Eustace the Monk killed.[37] Within three weeks Louis had agreed to end the war and leave England.

## 2. RECRUITMENT

Troops could be raised in a variety of ways. There were local and urban militias, while in times of emergency, a general summons might be issued to all free and able men. To meet the Scottish invasion of 1138, for example, the archbishop of York commanded throughout his diocese that 'all who could go to war' should join the muster, with their parish priests at their head, bearing crosses, banners, and relics of the saints.[38] During such crises kings might invoke their subjects' sense of shame to stir them to arms. Facing rebellion in 1088, William Rufus 'sent all over England and commanded that every man who was not *nithing* should come to him, be they French or English, from town or from country'.[39] *Nithing* was an English term and meant 'man without honour'—it was applied, for example, to the treacherous earl Swein, who had seized and killed his unsuspecting kinsman and fellow earl, Beorn,

[36] *Rot. litt. claus.* 2, p. 213.
[37] R. Wend. 2, pp. 221–2 (Paris, *CM* 3, pp. 26–7); *Hist. Guill. Mar.* 2, pp. 259–68, lines 17262–500; *Hist. ducs Norm.*, pp. 200–2.
[38] Ailr. Riev., *Rel. de Standardo*, p. 182.          [39] *ASC*, p. 224, *s.a.* 1087.

in 1049.[40] Rufus was thus saying, 'come to arms, if you are a man'. Similarly, in 1213, fearing a French invasion, king John summoned the 'earls, barons, knights and all free men and servants, whoever they may be and from whoever they hold, who ought or are able to possess arms . . . to defend the land of England. No one who can bear arms shall remain behind, unless he wishes to be called *culvert*.'[41] The *culvert* was a kind of servile peasant and the insult of being so labelled corresponds to the disgrace of being a *nithing* in the older English terminology. Such general calls to arms might, however, produce troops of uncertain quality. When Henry I's brother, Robert, invaded from Normandy in 1101, the army that the king assembled included many Englishmen and countryfolk, whom Henry had to encourage and instruct in the use of their weapons.[42]

## Feudal Levies

A much more selective principle of recruitment lay behind the feudal levy. In the Angevin period the obligations of tenants-in-chief to the king were assessed in terms of knight service. This is the case not only with the barons but also with most of the bishops and some of the older monasteries. Thus, the survey of knights' fees undertaken in 1166 reveals that 'the abbey of Chertsey owes three knights' for the royal service; Gervase Paynel refers, in his reply to the king's questionnaire, to 'the knights for whom my predecessors did service to your predecessors, and I to you, namely fifty'; Peter de la Mare wrote, 'Know that I hold Lavington (Wilts.) in demesne for the service of two knights'.[43] The service owed was thus expressed as a certain number of knights. Of course this obligation was often met by providing cash rather than tangible knights (see the discussion of scutage, above, p. 164), but throughout the period real physical military service was also rendered. In 1217, for instance, the royal government ordered a muster of 'the whole service that the archbishops, bishops, abbots and monks, earls, barons and others owe to us'.[44] The following year an army was raised to besiege Newark and details of the forces summoned are recorded in a surviving Chancery document. A total of 115 named tenants-in-chief was expected to produce 470 knights. In addition John, lord of Monmouth, was required to send 60 miners (important in siege operations), while eight sheriffs, representing twelve counties, had to come 'with the knights and sergeants of their counties who owe service in the army'.[45]

One of the earliest pieces of evidence for fixed service quotas is a writ sent by William the Conqueror to Aethelwig, abbot of Evesham, in 1072:

---

[40] *ASC*, p. 171 (C text).    [41] R. Wend. 2, p. 66 (Paris, *CM* 2, pp. 538–9).
[42] W. Malm., *GR* 5. 395 (2, p. 472); OMT edn., p. 716.    [43] *RBE* 1, pp. 198, 270, 246.
[44] *Sel. Charters*, p. 340.
[45] I. J. Sanders, *Feudal Military Service in England* (Oxford, 1956), app. 2, pp. 108–14.

I command you to summon all those within your jurisdiction to bring to my presence all the knights they owe me, in a state of readiness, at Clarendon a week after Whitsun. You too should come before me on that day and bring with you those five knights that you owe me from your abbey, likewise in a state of readiness.[46]

Evesham's obligation in later times was indeed five (or sometimes four and a half) knights.

The tenants-in-chief could meet their military obligation to the king in various ways. One was to grant out land to tenants who would have the duty of serving as knights. At some point between 1088 and 1106 John de Villula, bishop of Bath, granted two hides of land in Cold Aston (Glos.) to Hubert Hose 'as a fief . . . on condition that he provide military service, with arms and horse . . . and he has become the bishop's own liegeman on these terms'.[47] Thenceforth the bishop could have relied on Hubert to fulfil part of his own military obligation to the king (the see was liable to provide twenty knights) and, indeed, members of the Hose family occur as knights of the bishop for many subsequent generations. There were other variants in the way tenants supported the military obligations of their lords. On the estates of Ramsey abbey 22 tenants, some of them 'franklins' holding fifty acres or so, combined their efforts to support four knights, the abbey's quota.[48] The number of knights' fees that a lord granted out did not always correspond exactly to the number of knights he owed to the king. Indeed, one of the purposes of the inquest into knights' fees of 1166 was to explore the discrepancy.

Sometimes the king requested a force smaller than the total knight service he was owed and required the knights who did not serve to support those who did, presumably for a longer term of service. Thus, when Henry II invaded Wales in 1157, he 'prepared a great expedition, in such a way that, throughout England, every two knights equipped a third'.[49] His son, Richard, followed a similar practice in 1194: 'he ordered that everyone should perform the third part of the knight service that lay on each fief, to cross with him into Normandy'.[50] He also hoped to raise an elite force of knights who would be supported by his vassals in England for a continuous year's service and paid 3s. a day, three times as much as the average knightly wage.[51] King John once ordered every nine knights to support a fully equipped tenth.[52] Eventually permanently reduced quotas of service were negotiated. The earls of Derby, who owed 60 knights in the twelfth century, faced a summons for only five in 1218. Hervey Bagot, lord of Stafford in 1218, was also summoned at that time to provide five knights, although the barony had been assessed at sixty in the

[46] Sel. Charters, p. 97; for the debate on the authenticity of this writ, see Regesta regum Anglo-Normannorum: The Acta of William I, 1066–1087, ed. David Bates (Oxford, 1998), no. 131, pp. 449–52.
[47] EEA, 10. Bath and Wells 1061–1205, ed. Frances Ramsey (1995), no. 2, pp. 1–2.
[48] RBE i, pp. 370–1.    [49] R. Torigni, p. 193.    [50] R. Howd. 3, p. 242.
[51] R. Howd. 4, p. 40.    [52] Rot. litt. pat., p. 55.

previous generation (see above, pp. 203–5). The abbot of Bury St Edmunds owed 40 knights in the twelfth century but was called on to supply only ten in 1218. These reductions were not universal—the abbot of Evesham had to lead his five knights in 1218 just as he had done in 1072—nor were they fixed by the end of our period, but the evidence is clear that personal military service was exacted at a much lower rate in the thirteenth than in the twelfth century, even though scutage continued to be levied on the old, higher assessment. The explanation for this development is not obvious.

The precise terms of service of the feudal levies are not always clear. Even the duration of their service in the army is not known with certainty, although it is likely to have been forty days. It can also be presumed that they were expected to be of a certain standard. This would explain Rufus's complaint that the knights sent by the archbishop of Canterbury for the Welsh campaign of 1097 were 'not properly trained nor suitable for war'.[53] The fact that the kings of England were also great feudal princes in France meant that the issue of overseas service was especially significant. In 1094 William Rufus summoned a large force to join him in France, although in the event he simply took the ten shillings that each man had brought with him for his expenses and sent them home.[54] In the reign of Henry I, a fief of half a knight's fee was held from the abbey of Abingdon for services that included 'expeditions both this side of the sea and beyond it'.[55] At the close of the twelfth century, the obligation to serve abroad became contentious. During a debate on military service at an assembly at Oxford in 1197, Hugh, bishop of Lincoln, asserted, 'I know that the church of Lincoln owes military service to the king, but only within this country; she has no obligations beyond the borders of England.'[56] This was exactly the claim raised by the rebel barons in John's reign.

Feudal obligation was not limited to service in the army. It extended also to garrison duty at castles ('castle-guard'). The knights of Abingdon abbey owed garrison service at Windsor castle from the time of William I, while the service of more than 170 knights' fees was assigned to the great castle of Dover. Castle-guard was generally commuted to a money-payment, but even as late as 1215 Magna Carta specified that the king could not refuse personal service for castle-guard and insist on a money-payment instead (clause 29).

In addition to knight service, there existed also other military tenures, such as that of the *muntatores* of the Welsh March, who served as light horsemen, and military sergeanty. Men holding by this tenure had such duties as serving as or providing sergeants (men-at-arms less well equipped than knights), archers, or crossbowmen. Surveys from very early in the thirteenth century describe such duties:

---

[53] Eadmer, *HN*, p. 79.     [54] *ASC*, p. 229.     [55] *Abingdon Chron.* 2, p. 135.
[56] Ad. Eyns., *V. Hugh* 5. 5 (2, p. 99).

Samson of Molesey holds half of Molesey [Surrey] through service as a crossbow-man.

Ralph de Tosny holds Walthamstow for the sergeanty of going on campaign in person with the king.

William, son of John, holds in Layer [Essex] by the sergeanty of going to Wales with the lord king, with a horse, sack and fastenings, at the king's expense.[57]

These tenures in the south-eastern counties were thus able to help equip a royal campaign in Wales with its fighting force and supply train. At every level, from the earl of Derby with his quota of sixty knights, to William, son of John, with his horse and sack, territorial holdings entailed military service.

## Household Troops

The simplest way of meeting the need for troops was to maintain knights and other trained warriors in one's own household. Having such a permanent body of fighting men at hand had both advantages and disadvantages. They were always there; but then again, they were always there. They must be fed and housed; they needed to be kept in good heart during dismal winters; they had to be restrained from getting out of hand. Several monastic writers describe the awkwardness and turmoil caused by using resident knights to meet their abbey's service quotas. At Worcester bishop Wulfstan responded obediently to the command that William the Conqueror issued, on the advice of archbishop Lanfranc, 'that the courts of the great men should be defended by knights'. One of the problems that arose was the drinking. At first the knights found their tongues loosed, then they succumbed to laughter, next descended to threats and insults, and finally almost came to blows.[58]

A writer at Ely in the twelfth century expressed disapproval of the way William the Conqueror had imposed feudal service on the monasteries and bishoprics of England. For his Scottish campaign of 1072 the king 'had commanded all the abbots and bishops of the whole of England to send the military service they owed and he established that henceforth, as a permanent obligation, they should provide contingents to the kings of the English for his military campaigns'. The abbot of Ely at the time had begged in vain to be excused from these 'intolerable and novel exactions'. King William had ignored him and demanded that the abbey maintain a garrison of forty knights in the Isle of Ely.

The abbot came sadly away. He assembled knights from among his well-born dependants, gave arms to many of them and, as the king had commanded, kept the

---

[57] *RBE* 2, pp. 456–7, 561, 506; cf. entry s.v. *broca* (2), in *Dict. Med. Latin*, p. 218.
[58] W. Malm., *V. Wulfstan* 3. 16 (pp. 55–6).

specified number of knights within the hall of the church. They received daily wages and provisions from the cellarer, which placed an intolerable and excessive burden on the place.

It is not stated whether drunken brawling was one of the problems. The response of the abbot to this situation was to grant the knights dependent estates from the abbey lands in return for their providing the service required:

he did not do this of his own free will, nor was he seeking the favour of the wealthy nor was he moved by affection for his relatives, when he allowed intruders to hold some of the lands of St Etheldreda [Ely's saint] as fiefs . . . so that they should serve the king in his campaigns and the church remain forever undisturbed.[59]

A very similar report survives from Abingdon. There it was recorded that abbot Adelelm (1071–83), the first Norman incumbent, had originally met the king's demands for knights by keeping a paid body around him but had then settled them on the abbey's manors, specifying how much service each owed. William the Conqueror's policy is described by the Abingdon chronicler in the following words: 'by the king's command it was noted in the annual records how many knights were to be demanded from the bishops, how many from the abbots, to defend the state [*ad publicam rem tuendam*].'[60] These are the fixed quotas that emerge from the government documents of the Angevin period.

These cases show household knights as a temporary solution, soon replaced by the permanent one of enfeoffed knights, but the examples all concern religious houses. Secular lords, including the king, had a greater interest in maintaining standing troops of household knights. The royal military household played a central part in the king's wars. Before the battle of Tinchebray Henry I 'assembled the commanders of his household and gave them their instructions for combat'.[61] During the revolt of 1123–4 in Normandy he 'stationed his household troops in the castles under picked leaders'. In the spring these garrisons concentrated to give battle at Bourgtheroulde. Prior to the engagement, one of the king's knights encouraged his fellows: if they did not fight bravely, 'how shall we dare to face the king? We should justly lose our wages as well as our reputation and ought no longer feed on the king's bread.'[62] A paid and permanent force of household followers was the core of the royal armies throughout the period.

## Mercenaries

Many knights and other fighting men fought for pay. To call them 'mercenaries' may perhaps evoke a misleading note of glamour or depravity, but wandering professional soldiers were certainly of importance in the endless

---

[59] *Lib. Eliensis* 2. 134 (pp. 216–17).   [60] *Abingdon Chron.* 2, p. 3.
[61] Orderic 11. 20 (6, p. 88).   [62] Ibid. 12. 39 (6, pp. 346–50).

warfare of Europe's rulers. They scented conflict and flocked to open-handed rulers like William Rufus. His liberality to his knights was legendary: 'knights came to him from every region this side of the Alps and he bestowed funds on them lavishly'. It was the 'paid knights' who had most cause to grieve his death.[63] Stephen likewise relied on 'great retinues of paid knights'.[64]

Certain areas were especially suitable recruiting grounds for paid soldiers. Many came from the poorer, pastoral peripheries of the Norman-Angevin empire, such as Wales and Brittany, but urban and overcrowded Flanders and Brabant also provided troops of mercenaries for hire. Henry I employed many Breton fighting men in his wars. 'Because that people is so poverty-stricken in its own homeland,' noted William of Malmesbury, 'they earn their pay in foreign gold by service abroad . . . whenever the king required paid soldiers, he poured out large sums to the Bretons.'[65] Bretons, and also Flemings, quickly saw the opportunities that the civil war of Stephen's reign offered: 'many men from Flanders and Brittany, who were accustomed to live off plunder, fell upon England in the hope of great booty'.[66] Flemings were employed by the rebels of 1173–4, while in the winter of 1215–16 king John ravaged the north of England 'with his Flemings and his crossbowmen', although after the landing of Louis of France many of the Flemings went over to him.[67]

In the late twelfth century, the armies of the competing princes of western Europe were often fortified with troops of fearsome mercenaries known as 'Brabanters' or '*Bragmanni*'. In 1174 Henry II crossed from France to England to confront the rebels 'with a mounted retinue and a crowd of Brabanters'.[68] The forces sent by the chancellor, William de Longchamps, to arrest Geoffrey Plantagenet, illegitimate son of Henry II, during the factional struggles of 1191, included '*Bragmanni* and hired Flemish mercenaries'.[69] These mobile professional fighters even earned the distinction of condemnation by name at the Third Lateran Council of 1179. Such troops of professional mercenaries were also termed 'routiers'. Walter Map writes of them, 'armoured from head to foot in iron and leather, armed with clubs and with steel, they reduce monasteries, villages and towns to ashes, commit violent and joyless adultery, saying in the fullness of their heart, "There is no God".'[70] During the rebellion of 1173–4, just as the rebels recruited from Flanders, Henry II had 'bands of mercenary Brabanters, that they call routiers' in his pay.[71] One of Richard I's most important and terrifying commanders was Mercader, 'prince of the Brabanters' or 'prince of the

[63] W. Malm., *GR* 4. 314, 333 (2, pp. 368, 379); OMT edn., pp. 558, 576.
[64] R. Hexham, p. 145.     [65] W. Malm., *GR* 5. 402 (2, p. 478); OMT edn., p. 728.
[66] W. Malm., *HN* 483 (p. 41); cf. W. Newb. 2. 1 (1, p. 101).
[67] R. Wend. 2, pp. 162, 182 (Paris, *CM* 2, pp. 636, 655).     [68] W. Newb. 2. 32 (1, p. 181).
[69] Gerald, *V. Geoffrey* 2. 1 (p. 391).
[70] Map 1. 29 (p. 118).     [71] W. Newb. 2. 27 (1, p. 172).

routiers.'[72] In 1215 John's barons demanded that he dismiss 'foreign mercenary soldiers, the crossbowmen, routiers and sergeants who came with horses and arms to the damage of the kingdom'.[73]

The Welsh were tough soldiers from a poor land and could be hired by the hundred to fight in the king of England's wars. When, in 1174, Henry II marched to relieve Rouen, which was being besieged by the king of France and Henry's own rebellious son, he brought with him not only his notorious 'Brabanter' mercenaries but also a thousand Welshmen. In the first assault 'the king sent his Welshmen over the Seine and they forced their way without loss through the king of France's camp to the big wood on the other side, killing more than a hundred of the king of France's men.'[74] Henry's son, Richard, also appreciated the value of Welsh infantry. The army he assembled at Portsmouth in the spring of 1194 was full of them, although on this occasion savage fighting broke out between the Welsh and the Brabanters in the camp while the king was out hunting and was not quelled until his return.[75] During the last days of Angevin rule in Normandy (1202–4) Welsh troops were transported to France in large numbers. In 1202 the sheriff of Sussex paid out 100 shillings in hiring two ships to convey 540 Welsh footmen and twenty mounted men-at-arms, each with two horses, across the Channel and the same year Geoffrey fitz Peter, John's chief justiciar, disbursed £74 to Cadwallon ab Ifor 'crossing the sea in the king's service with 200 footmen'. This Cadwallon was a younger brother of the lord of Senghennydd, an upland fief in Glamorgan dependent on the earldom of Gloucester, which was in John's possession, so that, in this case, recruitment of Welsh troops both depended upon and strengthened a bond between the Angevin house and a native dynast. The employment of large numbers of Welsh foot soldiers by the kings of England and their use in foreign war continued throughout the medieval period. The stage Welshman Fluellen in Shakespeare's *Henry V* had a basis in reality.

The different kinds of recruits—feudal and other levies, household troops, mercenaries—should not be classified too emphatically into separate categories. William of Ypres, for example, an illegitimate cadet of the Flemish comital family, is frequently and reasonably described as the leader of king Stephen's Flemish mercenaries, but after the king's capture in 1141, command of his household troops was taken by William, along with Faramus of Boulogne, nephew of the queen, Matilda.[76] Mercenary and household service were not mutually exclusive. One of the household knights of Henry I who fought at Bourgtheroulde was Henry de La Pommeraye. Later he

---

[72] R. Howd. 4, p. 16; R. Diceto, *Ymag.* 2, p. 152; Ad. Eyns., *V. Hugh* 5. 7 (2, p. 114).
[73] *Sel. Charters*, p. 289 (Articles of the Barons c. 41).
[74] *Gesta Hen. II* 1, p. 74; R. Howd. 2, p. 65.        [75] R. Howd. 3, p. 251.        [76] J. Hexham, p. 310.

became assistant constable and his daily allowance of two shillings, bread, wine, and candles is mentioned in the text of about 1136 that describes the arrangement of the royal household. He was also by this time, however, the holder of a barony in Devon assessed at 32 knights' fees.[77] When he fought for Henry I or Stephen, it is doubtful if he distinguished sharply in his own mind between his household and his feudal obligations. Anselm pictured knights serving in the lord's court, some 'for the lands that they hold of him', others 'for pay'.[78] The forces that fought in the endemic warfare of the Norman and Angevin period did so for various rewards and from more than one type of obligation.

## 3. CASTLES

The Norman period saw a revolution in the nature of fortification in England and, as a consequence, deep changes not only in methods of waging war but also in the patterns of aristocratic power. The castle was an innovation, brought by the Normans from their French homeland, where it had been of fundamental importance in restructuring French society in the eleventh century. 'The fortifications that the French call "castles",' wrote Orderic Vitalis, 'were very rare in the English regions and hence, although the English were warlike and bold, they were weaker in resisting their enemies'.[79] William the Conqueror's army built two castles in the fortnight between their landing and the battle of Hastings and, in this respect, they started as they meant to go on. Hundreds of fortifications of the new type were built in the generations after the Conquest. For the rest of the Middle Ages castles were to be the building blocks of royal and magnate military and political power—'the bones of the kingdom', in the words of William of Newburgh.[80]

The innovation that the castle represented can be best considered by comparing it with the fortifications existing in the earlier Middle Ages. Put simply, these consisted either of large communal earthwork perimeters, such as the *burhs* constructed by the Wessex kings in their conflict with the Danes, or of aristocratic halls, built of wood and perhaps surrounded by a timber stockade with a gatehouse. The function of the former, to defend whole communities, is reflected in their size. *Burhs* vary considerably in extent, but have a median area of 25 acres.[81] Many of them went on to become boroughs. There were a few very small *burhs*, of five or ten acres, but not many of them. In contrast, castles were usually only a couple of acres. Even the great bailey of

---

[77] Orderic 12. 38–9 (6, pp. 346–8); *Const. domus regis*, p. 134; *RBE* 1, pp. 260–1; Sanders, *Baronies*, pp. 106–7; Green, *Govt.*, pp. 266–7.

[78] Eadmer, *V. Anselm*, p. 94.

[79] Orderic 4 (2, p. 218).      [80] W. Newb. 4. 14 (1, p. 331).      [81] Hill, *Atlas*, fig. 235, p. 143.

Berkhamstead, one of the largest Norman fortifications, covers less than four acres.

Moreover, the concentration of defence that the castle represented was not simply a matter of a smaller perimeter, for the crucial feature of the new castle was its central defensive structure, the tower. Here it contrasted sharply with the old aristocratic timber hall. As far as one can tell, the main vulnerability of the Germanic hall was that it could be easily surrounded and set on fire. Feuds often ended with the desperate defenders fleeing out onto the swords of their attackers. Like the bishop of Durham and his men in 1080, who were trapped by their enemies in a wooden church at Gateshead, they faced a choice between death by burning or at the hands of their enemies: 'the fire forced them to flee onto the weapons of their foes, the weapons drove them back into the fire'.[82] Now castles were by no means immune to fire, but the central tower had first to be reached and in the common motte-and-bailey form of castle this was rendered difficult by placing it on an artificial mound (the 'motte'). From the height of the tower on the motte the defenders had a fine viewing- and shooting-platform above the heads of their attackers. This central core of the castle, the motte, was about half-an-acre or so at its base and less than one tenth of an acre at the top. In the rare event of the central feature being a stone tower rather than a wooden tower on a mound, the area covered would be even less—the central keep of the Tower of London is only about 100 feet square. Castles were meant to offer a defensive circuit but also to have a hard core, so that loss of the outer works need not be critical. In his campaign of 1116 in south Wales Gruffudd ap Rhys found that he could take the 'outer castles' of the new Norman fortifications but that the 'tower' or 'keep' would hold out.[83]

The new castles were thus smaller, designed to protect leaders and their retinues, not communities, and they relied on height as much as on the creation of barriers. The simple motte-and-bailey did not demand very much technically, the bulk of the labour involved in its construction being earthmoving and rough carpentry. Such labour could be had from a subject population, which was thus forced to construct the instruments of its own subjection.

### The Castles of Hertfordshire

A manageable and not atypical sample of castles is provided by those in the county of Hertfordshire (see Table 1 and Map 5).[84] There are sixteen castles

---

[82] S. Durh., *HDE* 3. 24 (p. 117).      [83] *Brut (RBH)*, pp. 87–8.

[84] Derek Renn, *Medieval Castles in Hertfordshire* (Chichester, 1971); D. J. Cathcart King, *Castellarium Anglicanum* (2 vols.; Millwood, NJ, 1983), vol. 1, pp. 218–23; South Mimms is not included in the analysis below, being in Middlesex in this period.

that can plausibly be thought to have existed in this period, although only six of them are explicitly mentioned in written sources. It is reasonable to assign mottes to the years 1066–1225, since they were a Norman introduction and, if they had been constructed after 1225, they would show up in the richer sources of the thirteenth century. Some of the mottes also have associated twelfth-century churches and pottery finds.

TABLE 1. *Hertfordshire castles, 1075–1225*

|  | Holder | Motte | First mention |
|---|---|---|---|
| Anstey | Baron | √ | 1218 |
| Anstey 2 |  | √ |  |
| Barkway |  | √ |  |
| Benington | Baron |  | 1177 |
| Berkhamstead | Baron/King | √ | 1086 (implied) |
| Bishop's Stortford | Bishop | √ | 1085–7 |
| Brent Pelham |  | √ |  |
| Great Wymondley |  | √ |  |
| Hertford | King | √ | 1171 |
| Little Hadham |  | √ |  |
| Pirton (Toot Hill) |  | √ |  |
| Sandon |  | √ |  |
| St Albans | King |  | 1151×1154 |
| Standon |  | √ |  |
| Therfield |  | √ |  |
| Walkern | Baron | √ |  |

Two of the castles, Hertford and Berkhamstead, were royal either continuously or for most of the period. Although there is no early written mention of it, it is probable that a castle was built at Hertford, the county town, soon after the Conquest. King William passed this way and had a habit of erecting castles in the county towns. Hertford castle consists of a small motte beside the river Lea and a large bailey, enclosed within a stone perimeter wall, perhaps the result of the expenditure of £191 in 1171–4. Costs of repairs and maintenance recur in the royal records thereafter, including expenditure on the hall within the bailey in the 1190s. Berkhamstead, with its huge bailey, is, as mentioned, one of the largest Norman castles in the country. At the time of the Domesday survey the manor was held by Robert, count of Mortain, the Conqueror's half-brother, and mention in Domesday Book of a ditcher or dyke-builder ( *fossarius*) with a substantial holding on the estate might imply that the castle already existed. The counts of Mortain lost their lands through rebellion early in the reign of Henry I and by 1123 Berkhamstead castle was in the possession of the king's chancellor, Ranulf, who died that year from a

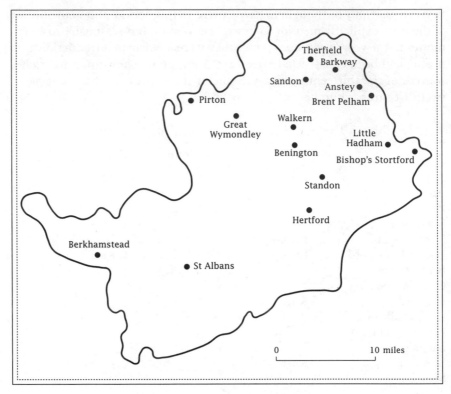

MAP 5. *Castles of Hertfordshire*

fall from his horse within sight of the castle.[85] For the rest of the period the castle was either directly in the king's hands, or administered on his behalf by custodians or, on two occasions, the dower property of queens.

Another castle that was, at least nominally, royal, was the 'defence or little fortification' erected at St Albans within the earthworks of the old Anglo-Saxon royal fortress called Kingsbury. The custodians of this place had built the new castle during Stephen's reign and then, according to the hostile report of the neighbouring monks, 'had claimed that they were loyal servants of the king and guardians of the peace and of the country, but in fact disturbed the peace and country and went after their own gain and illicit profits . . .' In response to the request of the abbot of St Albans, king Stephen had the place destroyed. To be on the safe side, the abbot then had the site of 'the robbers' lair' ploughed and sowed.[86]

---

[85] H. Hunt. 7. 34 (pp. 468–70).      [86] *Gesta S. Alb.* 1, p. 122.

As its name suggests, the castle at Bishop's Stortford was an episcopal fortification. It was granted to Maurice, bishop of London, by William the Conqueror, either when he appointed him bishop at Christmas 1085 or very soon thereafter.[87] It remained in episcopal hands. In 1137, when Anselm, abbot of Bury, was attempting to assert his claim to the bishopric, it was a natural step for him to occupy the castle.[88] Bishop's Stortford castle was a strong fortification, with a motte forty feet high, its summit surrounded by flint walls. The bailey is about 100 yards in diameter and was protected by a moat.

Three castles, Anstey, Benington, and Walkern, were situated in the chief manors of baronial families. Benington, an important barony of thirty knights' fees, was in the hands of the family of de Valoynes from the time of Domesday Book.[89] Walkern, held by Eudo, one of Henry I's stewards, passed to his sub-tenant, Hamo de St Clair, on his death in 1120, and then through the de St Clair and de Lanvaley families. They were substantial figures. More than one member of the family served as custodian of the royal castle of Colchester in Essex and the William de Lanvaley of John's reign had land in ten counties.[90] Anstey was different from the other two, in being a mesne barony, i.e. it was not held directly from the king, but from an intermediate lord, in this case the count of Boulogne. Domesday Book gives the count of Boulogne as the holder of Anstey but from Stephen's reign there is evidence of a family which took its name from the manor. Its earliest known member is Hubert, chamberlain to Stephen's queen, Matilda. His son and heir was that Richard de Anstey who kept the detailed record of the expenses of his lawsuit early in the reign of Henry II (above, pp. 168–9). Richard's son Hubert de Anstey, who died in 1210, held five knights' fees of the honor of Boulogne, as well as various other estates.[91]

The majority of the Hertfordshire castles left no trace in the written record and cannot be assigned to individual builders or holders with certainty. Sometimes, however, it is possible to make a guess about their origins. Pirton, where the motte and a twelfth-century church stand inside a large bailey, was one of the most important holdings of the de Limesy family. Ralph de Limesy, the lord of Pirton at the time of Domesday Book, was of baronial standing, holding lands in eleven counties valued at well over £150. He had been closely involved with the earls of Hereford, who were dispossessed for rebellion in 1075, and he himself lost some lands at about that time. Perhaps it is significant that the motte at Pirton, his most valuable manor, 'seems unfinished'.[92] The incomplete castle could conceivably be a monument to the

[87] *Early Charters St Paul's*, nos. 5, 12, pp. 11–12, 14–15.
[88] R. Diceto, *Abbrev.*, p. 250.     [89] Sanders, *Baronies*, pp. 12–13.
[90] Ibid., pp. 92–3; *Rot. litt. claus.* 1, p. 265.
[91] Paul Brand, 'New Light on the Anstey Case', *Essex Archaeology and History*, 15 (1983), pp. 68–83.
[92] Derek Renn, *Medieval Castles in Hertfordshire* (Chichester, 1971), p. 22.

clipping of the wings of a Conquest baron. The motte at Therfield, nine miles north-east of Pirton, was under construction in the middle of the twelfth century, was never finished and was destroyed forcibly. Such a sequence suggests a fortification of Stephen's reign that was demolished upon the restoration of order. Therfield was a property of the abbey of Ramsey, a monastic house that suffered badly from the incursions and depredations of the Anarchy. In the later years of Stephen's reign the abbot of Ramsey was paying out protection money to the garrisons of twenty-four castles on and around his estates.[93] Perhaps Therfield was one of them.

Although most of the Hertfordshire castles are mere grassy mounds without a story, a few can be glimpsed in action. In 1173–4, during the great rebellion against Henry II, the royal castle of Hertford was garrisoned and strengthened, perhaps in response to the threat of Benington castle, five miles to the north, for that seems to have been a rebel centre. In the course of the pacification following the rebellion the sheriff of Hertfordshire purchased '100 picks to cast down the keep at Benington'.[94] The destruction of Benington cannot have been complete, since twenty years later both Hertford and Benington castles were again on a war footing during John's rebellion (it is not clear why Benington was in royal hands at this time). Richard I's government paid for ten knights, twenty mounted sergeants, and twenty foot sergeants to serve as a garrison for the two castles for fifty days. In addition, building work was done at Hertford.[95]

All the Hertfordshire castles of which written record survives were caught up in the troubles of the last years of John's reign. Bishop's Stortford was destroyed, probably in 1211, as retaliation for the part played by the bishop of London in John's excommunication during his dispute with the papacy.[96] In the following year, when Robert fitz Walter fled the kingdom after an abortive plot to assassinate the king, his two castles were likewise destroyed. These were Baynard's Castle within the City of London and Benington, which he had acquired by marriage to Gunnora, heiress of the Valoynes barons.[97] This seems to have been the end of Benington's career as a castle, but Bishop's Stortford was restored to the bishop and rebuilt after John's settlement with the Church in 1213.[98]

The civil war of 1215–17 re-emphasized the importance of these castles. New work was done on Anstey castle by Nicholas de Anstey, who joined the rebel cause. The removal of these new defences was a condition of his reconciliation with the royal government after the war.[99] The royal castles of

---

[93] *Ramsey Chron.*, p. 328; for a suggested alternative reading, see Edmund King, 'The Anarchy of King Stephen's Reign', *Transactions of the Royal Historical Soc.*, 5th ser., 34 (1984), pp. 133–53, at p. 136 n. 14.

[94] PR 19 HII, p. 13; PR 20 HII, pp. 67, 73; PR 23 HII, p. 144.        [95] PR 5 RI, p. 2.

[96] Thomas Walsingham, *Ypodigma Neustriae*, ed. H. T. Riley (RS; 1876), p. 129.

[97] *Ann. Dunst.*, p. 35.        [98] *Rot. litt. pat.*, pp. 101, 124.        [99] *Rot. litt. claus.* 1, p. 350.

Berkhamstead and Hertford were both besieged by Louis of France in 1216.[100] The French prince and his army of Frenchmen and English rebels arrived before Hertford castle on 12 November and surrounded it. Siege engines were erected in a great circle around the castle and an attempt made to destroy the walls. The garrison was headed by Walter de Godardville, a knight of the household of Fawkes de Bréauté, one of king John's leading military captains who continued to be indispensable to the royalist cause during the minority government of Henry III. Walter and his men inflicted many casualties on the French besiegers but eventually, on 6 December, after a siege of 25 days, they surrendered to Louis, being allowed to depart with their horse and weapons.

The French and the rebels moved on at once to Berkhamstead. Here the defence was in the hands of Waleran the German, another of John's military commanders from overseas. In 1215 Berkhamstead had been strengthened and repaired with timbers taken from Berkhamstead forest. Now, in the winter of 1216, the same forest sheltered the tents of the besieging army. A sortie of knights and sergeants from the castle succeeded in plundering the rebel baggage and supply-carts and in carrying off the banner of one of the leaders, William de Mandeville, but, despite the vigour of the defence, Louis's siege machines were relentless, ranged in a circle around the castle and hurling stones at its walls (the earthen banks on which the machines were placed can still be seen). Eventually, after two weeks of battering, the royal garrison, with the king's consent, surrendered, being, like their fellows at Hertford, allowed to withdraw honourably, with their horses and weapons. Louis placed his own garrison in the castle and moved on.

The events of November and December 1216 show that the castles that had originally been raised to secure Norman control over a conquered England were still of central military importance a century and a half later. Control of the land required control of the castles. This was as true in the war between Louis of France and the government of Henry III as it was in the days of Robert of Mortain. The motte-and-baileys of the Conquest, suitably strengthened with stone walls in the twelfth century, were still the main pivots of the Hertfordshire campaign of 1216. The civil war was predominantly a castle war: over 200 were certainly used during 1215–17.[101]

## Form and Function

Hertfordshire is a county of about 640 square miles. Sixteen castles within such an area represents one every 40 square miles. Generalized over the country as a whole, this level of density would imply that the total number of

[100] R. Wend. 2, pp. 200–1 (Paris, *CM* 3, pp. 5–6, 8–9), for the following.
[101] Painter, *John*, p. 352.

castles in the kingdom was 1,250. This is a higher figure than is generally cited but is not inconceivable. There were never, of course, this number of castles in use at any one time, but the sum total of castles ever constructed in the period could well be of such an order of magnitude. The number of documented castles is much smaller. Domesday Book mentions only 49 castles. Less than a hundred occur in written sources prior to 1100. A meticulous study of castles mentioned in the reigns of Henry II and his sons (1154–1216) found 327 that existed at some point in those years.[102] Clearly, there is a great difference between well-documented, permanent, and extensive castles like Dover or the Tower of London and temporary mottes with no recorded history. Taken as a whole, however, the construction and maintenance of a thousand new fortifications was one of the most marked features of the history of England in this period.

Archaeological excavation has revealed the details of the construction of some motte-and-bailey castles. At South Mimms and Abinger traces were found of the wooden structures that surmounted the motte. The top of the motte at Abinger was surrounded by a wooden palisade, within which there was a kind of look-out tower—'a box on stilts'.[103] A raised platform of this kind, on a mound that was already twenty feet high, would have given the occupants (whoever they were) the possibility of surveying their surroundings and, if they faced enemies, of occupying a commanding position. The place did not, however, offer any comforts or amenities and the archaeological record shows that Abinger was a short-lived fortification of the Anarchy. South Mimms was more substantial. Earthen banks enclose an area over 300 feet in diameter, within which is a motte with a diameter of 100 feet at its base. Excavation has shown that a wooden tower rose up through the motte and this, unlike the platform at Abinger, had clear signs of occupation. It was about 35 feet square, had a lead roof, and was probably plastered internally. Candlesticks, arrowheads, buckles, and pottery were found. It was perhaps a defence built by Geoffrey de Mandeville, earl of Essex, one of the more notorious of the barons of Stephen's reign.[104]

At the other end of the spectrum are the great stone keeps that were first built in the Conqueror's reign and some of which still stand, dominating their surroundings. The most famous is the Tower of London, constructed under the supervision of Gundulf, bishop of Rochester, in the last years of

---

[102] R. Allen Brown, 'A List of Castles, 1154–1216', *EHR* 74 (1959), pp. 249–80; see also Richard Eales, 'Royal Power and Castles in Norman England', in C. Harper-Bill and Ruth Harvey (eds.), *The Ideals and Practice of Medieval Knighthood* 3 (Woodbridge, 1990), pp. 49–78, at pp. 54–7.

[103] Brian Hope-Taylor, 'The Excavation of a Motte at Abinger, Surrey', *Archaeological Jnl* 107 (1950), pp. 15–43; see also John Blair, 'William Fitz Ansculf and the Abinger Motte', ibid. 138 (1981), pp. 146–8.

[104] J. P. C. Kent, 'Excavations at the Motte and Bailey Castle of South Mimms, Herts., 1960–7', *Barnet and District Historical Soc. Bulletin*, 15 (1968).

William I.[105] Located in the south-east corner of the city of London, it rises three storeys high, with walls that are 15 feet thick at the base. Access, as in most keeps, was at first floor level. Within is a hall and chapel. Ninety feet in height and a hundred feet square, it was the largest secular stone building raised in England since Roman times. It was soon outstripped, however, by another great stone keep of the Conquest, that at Colchester: 110 feet by 150 feet and originally three storeys tall. Stone keeps of this style were expensive and rare, but a few continued to be built throughout the period. That at Rochester was constructed by William of Corbeil, archbishop of Canterbury (1123–36), who placed his 'remarkable tower' within the stone walls built earlier by bishop Gundulf, the mastermind behind the Tower of London.[106] A few years later the de Veres raised their huge and elegant keep at Heding-ham in Essex. A large internal arch spans the entire hall and bears the weight of the stories above, while the doors and fireplace have finely carved arches. Henry II was especially active in the construction of strong stone keeps, such as those at Scarborough, Newcastle, and Dover, the last built at a cost of about £4,000.

Building in stone was more expensive than timber construction, but brought prestige and offered greater security, especially against fire, and durability: the wooden palisades and towers of the motte-and-bailey castle must have rotted within a generation. Hence, in many cases, stone walls re-placed earlier timber ones in the course of the twelfth century. Sometimes a stone perimeter wall was built around the summit of the motte, creating a so-called 'shell keep'. Windsor, Berkhamstead, and Trematon in Cornwall are notable surviving examples. A continuous stone wall around the bailey or baileys—a 'curtain wall'—was also a common elaboration of the period. Eventually castles were built that consisted only of such walls, strengthened by projecting towers. An early example is Framlingham in Suffolk, built by earl Roger Bigod about 1190, on the site of the earlier castle that had been des-troyed as a consequence of his father's rebellion in 1173–4. It consists of a curtain wall with thirteen projecting rectangular towers, open at the back. The area enclosed within the wall is a little over an acre. The high stone wall of Framlingham serves instead of motte or keep.

At the very end of the period considered here a new architectural develop-ment is discernible. Round towers began to be built in place of the square or rectangular ones of the previous period. A particular forcing ground for castle design was the Welsh Marches and here the round towers and round keeps of William Marshal's castles of Pembroke and Chepstow, dating

---

[105] *Text Roff.* 201, p. 212, fo. 210ᵛ.
[106] Gerv. Cant., *Actus pontificum Cantuarensis ecclesiae* (*Works* 2, p. 382); *Text Roff.* 88, pp. 145–8, fos. 173–174ᵛ.

probably from the first decade of the thirteenth century, and those of Hubert de Burgh's castles of Skenfrith and Grosmont, dating from the 1220s, are early representatives of the new style. Round towers offered no corners to be attacked by hostile sappers. A row of projecting round towers could provide mutual supporting fire, whereas square towers left uncovered ground at their outer base. As a consequence of these advantages, the curtain wall with projecting round towers became a standard model for thirteenth-century castles. When the square corner tower of the keep of Rochester castle was rebuilt after being damaged in the Civil War of 1215–17, it was reconstructed as a round tower. This left the keep with three square corner towers and one round corner tower, a permanent vivid reminder of the development of military architecture in the twelfth and thirteenth centuries.

Control of castles was an essential element in the exercise of power. The balance of royal and baronial authority was affected by how many castles were in the king's hands and how many in those of his magnates. It has been calculated that at the beginning of the reign of Henry II the barons had five times as many castles as the king but that by 1214, sixty years later, the ratio was less than two to one.[107] By the latter date fewer than half of the baronies of England had a castle or castles.[108] The Angevin kings thus clearly pursued a policy, or habit of action consistent enough to be called a policy, that reduced the imbalance in castle-power between them and their great men. At the same time as they took the opportunity to seize or demolish the castles of baronial opponents, they poured money into strengthening and enlarging their own. The Angevins spent at least £780 per year on building work at their castles. Dover absorbed over £8,000 during the reigns of Henry II and his sons, the Tower of London £4,000.[109] This is to take no account of the huge sums they expended on castle-building in France.

A revealing and remarkable example of royal castle construction is Orford in Suffolk, built by Henry II between 1165 and 1173 at a cost of over £1,400.[110] It is significant that work began in 1165. In that year the king restored to Hugh Bigod, earl of Norfolk, the two Suffolk castles of Framlingham and Bungay that he had confiscated early in his reign, when attempting to restore royal authority in the aftermath of the Anarchy. Bigod was an ambitious and disgruntled man, who had served as steward to Henry I, been instrumental in Stephen's accession, and then gone over to the Angevins,

---

[107] R. Allen Brown, 'A List of Castles, 1154–1216', *EHR* 74 (1959), pp. 249–80, at pp. 249, 256–7.

[108] Painter, *John*, p. 19, estimates: 197 lay and 39 ecclesiastical baronies in England *c.*1200; 127 castles on 89 lay baronies, 13 on 6 ecclesiastical ones; 15 of the lay baronies, with 12 castles, were escheated; John had earldom of Gloucester with three castles. So 73 lay barons had 112 castles.

[109] R. Allen Brown, 'Royal Castle Building in England', *EHR* 70 (1955), pp. 353–98; *King's Works* 1, pp. 64–7; 2, p. 1023; N. J. G. Pounds, *The Medieval Castle in England and Wales* (Cambridge, 1990), pp. 76–80.

[110] *King's Works* 2, pp. 769–70; T. A. Heslop, 'Orford Castle, Nostalgia and Sophisticated Living', *Architectural History*, 34 (1991), pp. 36–58.

acquiring the comital title on the way. In 1173 he was to be one of the leaders of the great revolt against Henry II. The king naturally felt that, if Bigod was to have two important castles in east Suffolk, he should have one too.[111] Orford is of a very unusual, perhaps unique, design (see Plate 10). The keep is cylindrical inside, polygonal outside, and has three projecting rectangular towers, one with a forebuilding attached. Accommodation within is extensive and varied—spacious halls with large fireplaces, chambers, carefully sited toilets, kitchens. There is a chapel, a well, a cistern. Some features of Orford, such as the circular hall, radiating window niches, and (no longer extant) conical roof, may have been intended to evoke the ancient palaces of the Orient. Henry II was making a loud statement of his regal authority in this uncertain part of east Suffolk. Orford was, however, more than a symbol. During the revolt of 1173–4, it proved an effective impediment to Bigod. He did not besiege it but could not leave the area while it stood threateningly in the heart of the region where his power was based.

Once they had constructed their castles, kings had to retain control of them. Royal castellans might well develop proprietary feelings for the fortifications in their charge. In some cases the king even acknowledged hereditary claims to castellanships. William de Lanvaley, lord of the Hertfordshire barony of Walkern (above, p. 273), vindicated his right to the hereditary custodianship of Colchester castle in 1215.[112] The Beauchamps held Worcester castle as an adjunct to their hereditary shrievalty of Worcestershire. Such cases were, however, rare. Of more general significance were the rights of the king to authorize or prohibit the construction of non-royal castles and to take them into his own hands at need.

A general right of royal supervision of castle-building is mentioned in the private legal compilation of about 1115, *The Laws of Henry I*. This lists 'building a castle without permission' (*castellatio sine licentia*) as one of the offences that place the offender in the king's mercy and also asserts the royal monopoly of 'fortifications with threefold defences' (*castellatio trium scannorum*).[113] A concrete instance of the enforcement of such a right appears about this same time, when, during the rebellion of Robert de Bellême in 1102, Henry I besieged his castle of Bridgnorth (Salop), 'which he had established against the command of the king'.[114] After periods of civil war in the reigns of Stephen and John, the reassertion of royal power entailed the destruction of so-called 'adulterine' castles. In 1217 these were defined as 'those that were constructed or rebuilt since the beginning of the war'.[115] Hugh de Puiset,

---

[111] R. Allen Brown, 'Framlingham Castle and Bigod 1154–1216', *Procs. Suffolk Institute of Archaeology*, 25 (1952), pp. 127–48.
[112] Barnwell Chron., p. 221; *Rot. litt. pat.*, p. 151.
[113] *LHP* 10. 1, 13. 1 (pp. 108, 116).   [114] *Brut (RBH)*, p. 43.
[115] *Sel. Charters*, p. 344 (Magna Carta of 1217).

bishop of Durham (1153–95), won a special dispensation from Henry II for the episcopal castle of Northallerton, that had been erected during Stephen's reign: 'of all the adulterine castles that were ordered to be destroyed throughout England at that time, it alone could remain intact.' Hugh abused his privilege, however, by joining the rebellion of 1173–4 and fortifying the castle against the king. After the suppression of the rebellion Henry ordered Northallerton to be razed to the ground.[116] An 'adulterine' castle was one constructed without the king's assent, as is made clear in a letter of Richard de Umfraville of 1220 appealing against the command to destroy his castle of Harbottle (Northumberland). The castle, he wrote, 'is not adulterine, since it was constructed with the assent and at the command of the lord king'.[117]

Kings might also claim the right to take possession even of authorized private castles when circumstances required it. After Stephen's seizure of the bishops' castles in 1139, his actions were justified by the archbishop of Rouen: 'because these are uncertain times, all the chief men should hand over the keys of their castles to the king, to do with as he will, for he works for the peace of all; this is the custom of other peoples'.[118] Perhaps the reference to 'the custom of other peoples' suggests that the claim was an innovation, presumably of French origin, but, if so, it seems to have been maintained by Stephen's successor, Henry II. In 1157 Henry took possession of the castles of both William, count of Boulogne, son of king Stephen, and Hugh Bigod.[119] According to some accounts, in 1176 the king 'took into his own hands all the castles of England'.[120] If he did so, the seizure was temporary or symbolic or both, but, in any event, it represents a striking assertion of a royal right of entry.

The location of the thousand or so castles that existed in England in this period was determined partly by feudal and partly by natural geography. Barons who had a castle usually sited it at their most important manor, termed the 'head' (*caput*) of the barony. For great lords, a network of such castles would be both convenient and prestigious. The Clare estates were clustered in two large groups, one in western Kent and eastern Surrey, the other on the borders of Suffolk and Essex (see above, pp. 210–11). Each had a focal castle, at Tonbridge and Clare, respectively. The demesne manors of Roger de Mowbray about 1170 numbered seven, and five of these possessed

[116] Geoffrey of Coldingham, *Liber de statu ecclesiae Dunhelmensis* 7, ed. James Raine, *Historiae Dunhelmensis scriptores tres* (Surtees Soc. 9; 1839), p. 12; S. Durh., *HDE*, p. 148; *Gesta Hen. II* 1, pp. 67, 73, 160; R. Howd. 2, pp. 57, 65.

[117] *Royal and Other Historical Letters Illustrative of the Reign of Henry III*, ed. W. W. Shirley (2 vols., RS; 1862–6), vol. 1, pp. 140–1 (1220).

[118] W. Malm., *HN* 475 (p. 33).

[119] R. Torigni, pp. 192–3; R. Allen Brown, 'Framlingham Castle and Bigod 1154–1216', *Procs. Suffolk Institute of Archaeology*, 25 (1952), pp. 127–48, at pp. 130–2.

[120] *Gesta Hen. II* 1, p. 124; R. Howd. 2, p. 105; R. Diceto, *Ymag.* 1, p. 414.

castles: Burton in Lonsdale, Kirkby Malzeard and Thirsk in Yorkshire, Kinnard in Lincolnshire, and Brinklow in Warwickshire.[121] The rationale for the distribution of his castles was the distribution of demesne manors and this most likely had no strategic significance whatever.

Geography was not, of course, irrelevant. At the level of local considerations, castles needed a water supply. They might be sited to control a river crossing or command a pass or gap. At the level of the kingdom, there were strategic points that castles could secure. The huge, expensive, and elaborate fortress at Dover was placed there because it was 'the key of England'.[122] The density of castles in the Welsh Marches was a response to the insecurity of that border, while some of the castles of the north of England were certainly built as a defence against Scottish raids. The purpose of Norham, constructed on a promontory above the Tweed by Ranulf Flambard, bishop of Durham (1099–1128), was 'to inhibit the raids of brigands and the incursions of the Scots'.[123] Carlisle, fortified by William Rufus after his seizure of Cumbria in 1092, must have been intended to secure the region against its former Scottish overlords. In the case of many of the fortifications raised in the North in the later eleventh century, however, it is hard to say whether the primary purpose was protection against the northern kingdom or against dissident locals. The castles at Newcastle and Durham date from the time when the Normans were as much concerned to secure their control of the north of England as to protect it from incursions by the Scots.

Many castles, including some of the most important, were located in towns. One of William the Conqueror's more drastic policies was the demolition of whole quarters of English towns in order to accommodate his new, intrusive castles. In the city of York, which had been divided into seven 'shires' in the late Anglo-Saxon period, one shire was recorded in Domesday Book as 'laid waste for the castles' (there were two castles at York). At Lincoln, similarly, about one in seven of the city properties was 'destroyed on account of the castle'. Domesday Book mentions such destruction in nine other boroughs.[124] In some places where there is no explicit contemporary evidence of this type, the town plan demonstrates to this day how the castle was stamped onto the pre-existing topography. The motte at Oxford rises from a castle precinct that clearly overlays and obliterates one end of the Anglo-Saxon *burh*. Eventually most of the county towns of England had a castle, which served as the sheriff's administrative centre, repository, and gaol.

England was thus covered with a network of castles, ranging in scale and style from the tall stone keep of the Tower overlooking London to the hundreds of short-lived motte-and-baileys in every corner of the countryside. Not

---

[121] *Mowbray Charters*, p. xliv.     [122] Paris, *CM* 3, p. 28.     [123] S. Durh., *HDE*, p. 140.
[124] *DB* 1, 298, 336, 336b (Yks. C. 1a; Lin. C. 19, 26); Darby, *Domesday England*, p. 295.

all were permanently on a war footing. Some might have only a skeleton staff.
When the bishop of London's castle at Bishop's Stortford was in royal hands in
1189 it had only a watchman and a porter.[125] Once hostilities threatened, castles
needed to be repaired, restocked, and garrisoned. They were not always in a
state of readiness. Yet, once garrisoned, the wide, deep pattern of castles meant
that warfare was shaped by their presence. A campaign in an encastellated
landscape was fundamentally different from one in unencastellated terrain.

Garrisoned castles could be ignored only at peril. Garrisons could sally
out to harass passing forces. The rebel earl Ralph of East Anglia was unable
to pursue the aggressive campaign he intended in 1075 because he was
attacked by local levies and castle garrisons ('*castel menn*').[126] Knights from
Wark castle seized David I's supply train during the Scottish invasion of
1138.[127] Garrisons could also form the components of an army. In 1216, in
order to relieve pressure on Windsor, king John 'gathered together a large
army from the garrisons of his castles'.[128] Even simply as a centre of plundering and stronghold for booty, an active hostile castle was an irritant, a drain,
and an insult.

Hence most military activity in England in this period revolved around the
seizure and defence of castles. The balance between attacker and defender
depended, obviously, on a host of local considerations, but even a small garrison could delay large forces. A frontal assault by besiegers was rarely their
first preference. Castles could be blockaded and starved out, though this was
a lengthy task, or they could be subjected to the pounding and probing of a
variety of siege weapons. For the siege of Marlborough, during John's unsuccessful rebellion of 1194, a petrary and a mangonel were sent from Reading, the former on carts provided by the monks of Reading abbey, and another
petrary and mangonel, plus mattocks, large shields, and scaling ladders, were
dispatched from Winchester. Both petraries and mangonels were stone-
throwing machines, the former larger and capable of throwing heavier pro-
jectiles than the latter. They could also be used to launch missiles other than
rocks and the employment of incendiaries at Marlborough is suggested by
the record of pitch and sulphur sent there.[129] Later in the same year 'Greek
Fire', a combustible substance much used in Mediterranean warfare, was
dispatched to Nottingham for the siege of John's castle there.[130]

The development of sophisticated siege-machines went hand-in-hand
with the elaboration of castle defences—indeed the royal 'engineers' were responsible both for building castles and for constructing mangonels and the
like.[131] The first mention of the trebuchet in England occurs in a description

[125] PR 1 RI, p. 12.     [126] *ASC*, p. 211.     [127] R. Hexham, p. 157; J. Hexham, p. 291.
[128] R. Wend. 2, p. 192 (Paris, *CM* 2, p. 665).
[129] PR 6 RI, p. xv.     [130] PR 6 RI, p. 175.     [131] *King's Works* 1, pp. 57–61.

of the siege of Dover by Louis of France in 1217.[132] This was a siege engine that operated by a counterweight, a heavy mass that shot a projectile upwards as it swung downwards. It could achieve a high elevation and it has been calculated that it was able to cast a missile weighing 200 lbs. a distance of 300 yards. Despite the presence of trebuchets, however, Henry II's building work at Dover stood the test and the castle held out. The previous year, during John's siege of Rochester castle, he had sent miners to undermine first the outer wall, then the corner of the keep. This had been successful. At the siege of Bedford in 1224, the royal army had employed stone-throwing machines, a tall wooden tower to overlook the castle, and 'tortoises', mobile sheds to protect the attackers. An array of elaborate devices was thus essential for the endemic siege warfare of the castle age.

Castles could also be confronted with castles—'siege-castles' or 'counter-castles', erected in the immediate vicinity to protect a harassing and besieging force. William Rufus built one called *Malvesin*—'Bad Neighbour'—in front of Bamburgh castle when he besieged it in 1095. Likewise, when his successor, Henry I, besieged Arundel castle in 1102 and realized that a quick outcome was unlikely, 'he had castles made in front of it and filled them with his men'. The counter-castles of Stephen's reign are especially numerous, no fewer than five being erected, at one time or another, around the Angevin stronghold of Wallingford.[133]

## Castle-Based Warfare: Stephen's Reign

Castles were associated with oppression from their earliest days. In the words of the *Anglo-Saxon Chronicle*, William the Conqueror 'had castles constructed and poor men oppressed'.[134] The longest and most notorious period in which a castle-based terror was imposed on the country was Stephen's reign. Again the *Anglo-Saxon Chronicle* gives a memorable description:

every powerful man built his castles and held them against him [Stephen] and filled the land full of castles. They grievously oppressed the wretched people of the land with the building work on the castles. When the castles were built, they filled them with devils and evil men. Then they seized anyone they thought had any property, by night and by day, both men and women, and imprisoned them and tortured them for their gold and silver. . . . They levied payments from the villages . . . and when the wretched people had no more to give, they plundered and burned all the villages. . . . If two or three men came riding into a village, all the villagers would flee, for they thought they were robbers . . .[135]

---

132 *Ann. Dunst.*, p. 49, *s.a.* 1215.
133 *ASC*, pp. 231, 237; *Gesta Stephani* 42, 94, 117 (pp. 92, 184, 226).
134 *ASC*, p. 220, *s.a.* 1086.
135 *ASC*, pp. 264–5, *s.a.* 1137.

William of Malmesbury tells a similar story:

There were many castles throughout England, each defending its territory or, to tell
the truth, plundering it. The knights from the castles carried off flocks and herds
from the fields, sparing neither churches nor churchyards. They seized landholders,
peasants, anyone they thought had money, and forced them by great tortures to
promise anything. After they had plundered the houses of the wretched country folk
to the very straw, they imprisoned them in fetters and did not let them go until they
had given everything they possessed in ransom.[136]

A predatory regime thus came into existence, of lords based in castles, extorting ransoms and protection money from the surroundings and rustling
livestock to feed their followers. In one sense they represented simply a more
rapacious and unpredictable version to the seigneurial regime under which
the rural inhabitants of medieval England lived at the best of times. However,
the cruelty of these castle-lords, their greediness, and, especially their disregard for ecclesiastical property, ensured that their names would ring down
the years in the pages of monastic chroniclers as embodiments of feudal
anarchy.

Twenty years after Stephen's death, a monk of Selby in Yorkshire set down
in writing some of the troubles that had afflicted the inhabitants of his part of
the country during the Anarchy.[137] The horrors had begun with the building
of a castle. Henry de Lacy, member of a northern baronial family that exploited the disturbed conditions of the time to recover lost lands and position, raised a castle at Selby. Within a week of its completion his enemy, earl
William of Aumale, grandfather of the man of the same name whose garrison
had terrorized Lincolnshire in 1221 (above, p. 256), attacked it. First, the
earl's forces stormed into the town, impelling the townsfolk to seek refuge in
the abbey and its grounds. The 'troops of enemies and plunderers' followed
the refugees there, breaking down the gates of the church, seizing horses that
had been led into the churchyard for safety and pulling people out of the
church itself to be held for ransom. Once earl William's men had reassembled, they began their assault on the castle. The first day's attacks were fruitless and, to vent their frustration, they burned down the town. After a few
days, however, they were able to capture the castle. Henry de Lacy's knights
were ejected and the earl placed his own men there. Now the suffering truly
began.

The members of the garrison 'applied themselves to robbery, spending
their time plundering the area, oppressing everyone weaker than they'. They
had a special predilection for kidnapping, seizing those they thought might

[136] W. Malm., *HN* 483 (pp. 40–1).
[137] *Historia monasterii Selebiensis* 2. 5–20, in *The Coucher Book of Selby*, ed. J. T. Fowler, (2 vols., Yorkshire Archaeological and Topographical Association, Record series, 10, 13; 1981–3), vol. 1, pp. [33]–[44].

have cash and holding them in chains in Selby castle until relatives bought their freedom. One victim was a skinner from Pontefract, who, when not being tortured in order to extort money, was kept with his hands chained behind his back and his legs in wooden stocks. Another was a little boy, left as a hostage by his father, and kept in chains. A woman was likewise held as a surety for her husband's ransom of nine marks (£6). When he was only able to send nine pence, the knight who held her captive, after threatening to cut off her breasts or hands, left her chained outside, half-naked, throughout the winter night. Others who suffered from the attentions of the 'castle men' included a young cleric, seven well-off men all from the same locality, and a certain William, who was kept in a house at the top of the castle with a chain around his neck fastened to the roof above. One peasant was tormented by 'the tyrants' in many devious ways: suspended by his feet or his hands, with mail-coats used to weigh him down; held above smoky fires (both forms of torture also mentioned in the *Anglo-Saxon Chronicle*); plunged beneath icy waters in winter. Nor was there honour among thieves. Once, when two knights of the garrison found that fifteen marks had been stolen from them during the hours of darkness, they blamed their squire, Martin, and tortured him so unbearably that, seizing a pair of scissors from a nearby seamstress, he plunged them into his own heart to escape the suffering.

The monk of Selby tells these stories to show how those who suffered could count on the help of the local saint, Germanus, whose relics were to be found in Selby abbey. St Germanus freed those who prayed to him and even helped restore the squire Martin to health. Yet reading this account, one is less impressed by the powers of Germanus than by the heartlessness of the petty powers who dominated and terrorized this district of Yorkshire from their new castle.

In many regions the civil war between Stephen and Matilda dissolved very early into localized gangsterism of the Selby type. Neither the king nor his rival were able to exert control of their supposed followers. That is indeed why the period is customarily termed 'the Anarchy' rather than 'the Civil War'. One of the deep causes for this was the power that castles gave even to small-scale lords. Possession of castles gave their masters the option, even if a temporary one, of biding their time. In 1139, when the civil war had hardly begun in earnest, 'Some of the castellans shut themselves up in the safety of their fortresses and watched for the outcome of events'.[138] The reassertion of royal, or any central power, required a daunting and seemingly endless campaign of siege and seizure of castles. In the radical decentralization of political power that took place in England in the middle years of the twelfth century the castle was a basic instrument. In Stephen's reign, wrote the

[138] W. Malm., *HN* 480 (p. 36).

Durham monk, Reginald, 'Virtually every fresh young knight was given command of some castle. In those days no one had the slightest reputation unless he was master of a castle garrison. Hence each of them, on the basis of his usurpations, became a petty king.'[139] This was an opinion shared by the Augustinian canon, William of Newburgh: 'There were as many kings, or rather tyrants, as there were lords of castles.'[140] Less than a day's ride from William's priory of Newburgh, the garrison of Selby had demonstrated what that meant.

[139] Reg., *Libellus* 67 (pp. 134–5).      [140] W. Newb. 1. 22 (1, pp. 69–70).

# CHAPTER 6

# The Rural Foundations

## I. THE PHYSICAL FRAMEWORK

Writing at the very end of the eleventh century, the Flemish monk Goscelin was struck by England's physical resources:

There stretch before you the most fertile fields, flourishing meadows, broad swathes of arable land, rich pastures, flocks dripping with milk, spirited horses and flocks. It is watered by fountains of leaping spray, bubbling streams, notable and excellent rivers, lakes and pools crowded with fish and birds and the coming and going of boats, all well suited for cities and people. Groves and woods are in leaf, field and hill full of acorns and woodland fruit, rich in game of all kinds.[1]

Geology, topography, and climate are among the more constant aspects of any country's history. They are not unchanging. One has only to think of changes in coastline, the deposit of alluvium, gradual alterations in the upper layers of the earth through drainage or the addition of chemicals, deforestation, shifts towards warmer or colder, or wetter or drier weather to recognize that the physical England of one epoch is different from that of another. Nevertheless, the fundamental framework still exhibits continuities of a general nature. England constitutes the larger part of a very large island, it has a coastline of over 1,800 miles in length, with no great rivers but many good harbours. Although lying above 50° north latitude, its climate is warmed by the Gulf Stream and moderated by the sea. An important distinction exists between the north and the west, on the one hand, and the south and the east, on the other, based both on physical geography, the older, harder rocks and hillier terrain being in the north and west, and a climatic difference, with the north and west cooler in summer and wetter throughout the year. All these basic features, with their implications for human settlement and land use, were the same in the twelfth century as they are today and, given that human beings at that time had far less power to control their physical environment, their influence must have been even more significant.

---

[1] Goscelin, *Hist. Augustine*, col. 51.

Alongside these fundamental similarities, there are also important differences between the geography of England in the twelfth and the twentieth centuries. The first to be considered is the climate itself, for in recent generations historians and scientists have been able to demonstrate that climatic change takes place not only over millennia but also over centuries. For the years covered in this book the most significant discovery is the existence of a so-called 'Medieval Warm Period'. Scientists have assigned this period somewhat differing chronological ranges but in most interpretations the epoch 1075–1225 falls squarely within it. The hypothesis of a period when temperatures were higher than both the succeeding 'Little Ice Age' and the twentieth century was originally elaborated by the meteorologist H. H. Lamb, mainly, it seems, on the basis of an analysis of the chroniclers' reports of weather. It might seem remarkable that such a subjective and imperfect type of source would yield a reliable account of long-term climatic trends, but the work of subsequent scientists, using the techniques of physical science rather than relying on the sour comments of monastic weather-watchers, has vindicated the hypothesis. Analysis has been undertaken of variations over time in the height of the tree-line, the upper limits of tillage, the pollen deposited in peat bogs and other receptive sites, the wetness of such bogs and the width of tree-rings from trees and timber. These results can be compared with the patterns revealed by the chemical investigation of the material obtained from deep bores into the earth, ice-caps, and sediments. It is not certain that the Medieval Warm Period was a global phenomenon, but the relative warmth of England in the period discussed here seems to have been established with some degree of certainty.[2]

Average summer temperatures were probably about 1° C higher than those of the twentieth century. Annual rainfall may not have been much lower than today, but the higher temperatures encouraged evaporation from the soil. In comparison with the Little Ice Age that was to follow in the later Middle Ages and early modern period, overall rainfall was lower, summers warmer, and winters milder. One consequence was that crops like the grape vine were able to flourish in England. Domesday Book lists about forty-five places with vineyards, the most northerly at Ely. Some are explicitly stated to be recent, so it seems that Norman taste as well as warm summers may be

---

[2] H. H. Lamb, *Climate, Present, Past and Future*, 2. *Climatic History and the Future* (London, 1977), esp. pp. 435–49, 'The Medieval Warm Epoch or Little Optimum', and the tables on pp. 561–5; for some recent scientific evidence, see *Climate History*, 26, nos. 2–3 (1994); on the Little Ice Age, J. M. Grove, *The Little Ice Age* (London, 1988). Pierre Alexandre, *Le Climat en Europe au Moyen Age* (Paris, 1987), undertakes a Lamb-like review of all narrative sources for the French, German, and north Italian lands in the period 1000–1425 and concludes: (1) that such sources can only be used with confidence after 1160 and (2) that the medieval optimum was around 1300, later than many have suggested.

relevant to the spread of the vine in England.[3] Writing forty years after the Domesday survey, William of Malmesbury described a vineyard that a Greek monk had planted at Malmesbury in the previous century, also noted the practice of staking of vines on the estates of Thorney abbey, somewhat north of Ely, and was enthusiastic in his description of the wine produced in the Vale of Gloucester: 'In this region the vines are thicker, the grapes more plentiful and their flavour more delightful than in any other part of England. Those who drink this wine do not have to contort their lips because of the sharp and unpleasant taste, indeed it is little inferior to French wine in sweetness.'[4] Of more fundamental importance than the availability of good English wine was the fact that arable cultivation could be carried on at higher altitudes than in subsequent centuries, as witnessed by medieval farmsteads around the 1,000 foot contour on the moors and dales.

If the contours of cultivation were different, so too was the outline of the country itself, for the coastline had not yet assumed its familiar modern shape in every detail. In particular, silting has filled out the coastline of Kent and Sussex, while erosion has carried away sites along the shores of Yorkshire and East Anglia. Wilsthorpe (Yorks., ER), recorded as a berewick or outlier of Bridlington in Domesday Book, is today an abandoned site slipping slowly into the sea, and nearby Auburn, where in 1086 the northern landowner Karli had half a carucate, is now beneath the waves.[5] Domesday Book records that Dunwich in Suffolk used to contain two carucates in the time of Edward the Confessor, but now only one since 'the sea has carried off the other one'.[6]

The largest divergence from the modern map is in the Fenland area. Only minor drainage works had taken place by the twelfth century and the Wash extended several miles beyond the modern coastline, while the marshes of the Fens made hundreds of square miles uninhabitable. The great Fenland monasteries, such as Crowland, Thorney, and Ely, were literal islands. The pattern of settlements recorded in Domesday Book clearly shows the great unsettled swathe in what is now rich black farmland.[7] The narrow habitable strip between the waters of the Wash and the peat bogs of the Fens was

[3] Darby, *Domesday England*, pp. 275–7, 362–3; Hill, *Atlas*, map 196, p. 113.

[4] W. Malm., *GP* 260, 186, 153 (pp. 415, 326, 292).

[5] *DB* 1, 299b, 301 (Yks. 1. Y. 11, 1. E. 13); M. W. Beresford, 'The Lost Villages of Yorkshire', pt. 1, *Yorkshire Archaeological Jnl* 38 (1955), pp. 44–70, at pp. 70 and 57; map in J. A. Steers, *The Coastline of England and Wales* (2nd edn.; Cambridge, 1964), fig. 89, p. 410, from T. Sheppard, *The Lost Towns of the Yorkshire Coast* (London, 1912), frontispiece; Darby, *Domesday Gazetteer*, map 57; H. C. Darby and I. S. Maxwell, *The Domesday Geography of Northern England* (Cambridge, 1962), p. 174.

[6] *DB* 2, 311b (Sfk. 6. 84).

[7] Good maps and discussion in Hill, *Atlas*, maps 15, 17, 19–22, pp. 10–15; H. C. Darby, *The Domesday Geography of Eastern England* (3rd edn.; Cambridge, 1971); *idem, The Medieval Fenland* (2nd edn.; Newton Abbot, 1974).

particularly vulnerable. In 1086 Wrangle in southern Lincolnshire, situated in that strip of land, was 'waste on account of flooding by the sea'.[8] Neverthe-less, the Fens were being nibbled at, and sometimes more than that. In 1166 the bishop of Ely reported that, within the last thirty years, he had established 2½ knights' fees 'on encroachments from the marsh, that had never pre-viously yielded any profit'.[9]

## 2. POPULATION

It is not possible to do more than guess at the size of the English population in this period, but we have, in Domesday Book, a piece of evidence that makes our guesses far more plausible than they would otherwise be. Domesday Book was not intended as a population census. It lists a rural population of 268,863 individuals, but that is certainly not the population of England in 1086 and, in order to obtain that figure we have to make some assumptions about what Domesday Book leaves out. Accidental oversights in a project of this kind are, of course, to be expected, but there are other omissions of a more systematic type. The most straightforward are geographical, for some parts of the kingdom, such as most of the northern counties and the import-ant cities of London and Winchester, are not covered by Domesday Book. Then there are certain categories of person which seem to be incompletely recorded, notably ecclesiastics. The monastic population is not mentioned and the figures for priests cannot be comprehensive—there must have been more than one priest in Devon! Such omissions are, however, either relatively easily compensated for in our calculations, or statistically unimportant. The problem comes with the peasant tenants and slaves, who together constitute the vast majority (99 per cent) of the individuals enumerated in Domesday Book.

There are two uncertainties. First, since not all family members are listed, only tenants, we have to make an assumption about the average family size. Do the fifty-nine tenants in a village like Bermondsey (Surrey) imply an actual population of 180, 240, or 300 people? Second, was there a village population of sub-tenants or landless people not recorded in Domesday?

The first issue is the less difficult. Evidence from thirteenth-century Eng-land, which must have had a demographic regime very similar to that of the late eleventh century, points to a peasant household of an average size of 4.7 persons.[10] If this figure holds good for two centuries earlier, the recorded Domesday rural population of 268,863 represents a total rural population of

---

[8] *DB* 1, 367b (Lin. 57. 36).     [9] *RBE* 1, p. 364.

[10] H. E. Hallam, 'Some Thirteenth-Century Censuses', *Economic History Review*, 2nd ser., 10 (1957–8), pp. 340–61, at p. 340; Hallam, *Agrarian Hist.*, p. 536.

somewhat over 1.26 million. To this must be added an estimate for the north-ernmost counties, for the urban population, for ecclesiastics and their house-holds, and for the secular aristocrats and their households. In his great study of the geography of Domesday England, H. C. Darby reckoned the unre-corded population of northern England at about 33,000 and the total urban population at 120,000 (although that may be rather high, it is probably bal-anced out by general omissions in the survey).[11] If the ecclesiastical hierarchy was numerically insignificant—maybe a thousand monks and 10,000 cler-ics—then we must add their servants and dependants, possibly bringing the total to 50,000. The secular aristocracy, the tenants-in-chief, and sub-tenants of Domesday Book, were perhaps 7,000 in number, but they had families (7,000 multiplied by 4.7 gives almost 33,000, although it should be remem-bered that aristocratic family size may have been as high as 5.4)[12] and their household dependants were perhaps as numerous again. We should then, to take account of the northern counties, the urban population, and the ecclesi-astical and secular upper-class network, add a further 269,000 people to our calculations, giving a total estimated population of a little over 1.5 million. Few historians would argue that the population of England in the later eleventh century was lower than that.

The real imponderable is the unrecorded rural population of sub-tenants and landless people. Since medieval surveys were drawn up not out of general demographic curiosity but in order to ensure that peasant rents and dues were not slipping through the landlord's grasp, the peasant who paid no rent or dues to the lord was of little interest. It seems likely that Domesday Book worked on the same principle—what mattered was the resources of the manor, including tenants, but not sub-tenants or the landless. The size of this hypothetical unrecorded population is obviously crucial. It has been argued that it could be as large as 50 per cent of the total figure of recorded tenants,[13] and, indeed, evidence from one manor in the middle of the thirteenth century shows a landless population about half the size of the tenant population.[14] If indeed about one-third of the population was landless and this ratio is applied to the 1,500,000 postulated above for the Domesday population, the eventual total population would be 2,250,000. There is nothing at all improb-able in this figure, but it should be remembered that it is based on a

---

[11] Darby, *Domesday England*, p. 89; the figure of 33,000 is derived from his 25,000 for the four north-ern counties plus his estimate of 1,800 omitted tenants from Lancashire, to which the multiplier of 4.7 has been applied.

[12] Above, p. 230.

[13] M. M. Postan (ed.), *The Cambridge Economic History of Europe* 1 (2nd edn.; Cambridge, 1966), p. 562; *idem*, *The Medieval Economy and Society* (London, 1972), p. 31.

[14] J. Z. Titow, 'Some Evidence of the Thirteenth Century Population Increase', *Economic History Review*, 2nd ser., 14 (1961–2), pp. 218–24.

hypothetical assumption about the proportion of non-tenants and that the population growth of the twelfth and thirteenth centuries probably implies that this proportion was smaller in 1086 than 150 years later.

## Demographic Trends

If the population of England in 1086 was indeed two and a quarter million, then all the evidence suggests that it was considerably more by 1225. Direct evidence about population trends in this period is very rare. One exception, from late in the period, is provided by the lists of those paying the 'hundred-penny' on the bishop of Winchester's manor of Taunton (Somerset). Since the hundredpenny was levied on all adult males, not simply on tenants, it does not need to be adjusted to take account of a hypothetical hidden population. The figures carry on far beyond our period and reveal a long-term rising trend, an average annual increase of 0.85 per cent between 1209 and 1311. For the decade and a half when the figures overlap with the period dealt with in this book (1209–1225), they show a population increase averaging 1.22 per cent per annum, which is a rate very much higher than any general figure recorded for England between 1500 and 1800.[15] Not every year saw an increase and in particular there is a fall between 1214 and 1219, coinciding with the troubled years of civil war in England, but the trend is clear.

### Evidence of Holdings

The Taunton evidence comes from very late in our period and is limited to one manor. There is other evidence of demographic trends, but it is more indirect. One indication is the number of peasant holdings recorded for manors about which we have information at different times. Take, for example, the estates of the abbey of Ramsey, scattered from Norfolk and Lincolnshire to Bedfordshire and Hertfordshire, but with a dense nucleus around the monastery itself in Huntingdonshire. Manorial surveys drawn up in the second half of the twelfth century give lists of the peasant tenants which can be compared with the number of tenants given in Domesday Book. In every case where comparison is possible, there is a rise in numbers, sometimes of as little as 8 per cent, but more frequently of 50 or 100 per cent or more. On one manor, Cranfield in Bedfordshire, there were very nearly three times as many tenants when the estate was surveyed about the middle of the twelfth century as there had been in 1086. The median growth rate for the Ramsey manors is 64 per cent.[16]

---

[15] J. Z. Titow, 'Some Evidence of the Thirteenth Century Population Increase', *Economic History Review*, 2nd ser., 14 (1961–2), pp. 218–24.

[16] Calculated from J. A. Raftis, *The Estates of Ramsey Abbey* (Toronto, 1957), p. 67, table X.

This kind of evidence presents some problems of interpretation, which can be illustrated by the manorial survey of Warboys in Huntingdonshire from about 1200.[17] It lists 114 tenants of the abbey: thirteen of them had a full peasant holding or virgate, of thirty acres; fifty of them had a half-virgate; there were fourteen cotlands, that is, small holdings of perhaps five acres or so, seven of them held by individual tenants, while two were in the hands of one of the virgate-holders, two were held by another tenant, and three were in the possession of Geoffrey of Winchester, an important freehold tenant of the abbey. Similar to the cotlands were the ploughmen's holdings (*acreman-lands*), which numbered six, although four of them had been gathered into the hands of one tenant. There was thus a total of thirteen tenants with small-holdings, although one of them was also a virgate-holder (and has been counted under that category in the following table). The manor also contained thirty-eight tofts, that is, small enclosed plots. Most of those holding a toft held one only, although a few had more than one and a few had a half-toft or shared one. Altogether there were in fact thirty-eight tenants holding tofts, one of them being the freeholder Geoffrey of Winchester, mentioned above. Finally, there is record of two tenants holding unspecified 'land' in the fields. Table 2 compares this picture with that presented by Domesday Book.

TABLE 2. *Tenants and tenures on the manor of Warboys*
*1086 and about 1200*

| Category of tenant/tenure | Domesday Book tenants | Tenants about 1200 | Tenures about 1200 |
|---|---|---|---|
| Villeins/virgates | 34 | 63 | 38 |
| Small-holders/-ings | 13 | 13 | 20 |
| Toft-holders/Tofts | | 38 | 38 |
| TOTALS | 47 | 114 | 96 |

If we simply compare Domesday tenants and those listed in the later survey, we would conclude that there had been a population increase of 143 per cent over the century between the two snapshots of the estate. If we were more sceptical, we might note that there is actually a closer correspondence between the number of *tenures* listed in the late twelfth century and the Domesday *tenants* than there is between tenants at each date. It is not impossible that (1) the 34 villeins of 1086 conceal shared or sub-let virgates and (2) there were toft-holders in 1086 but Domesday Book was not concerned to list them.

---

[17] *Ramsey Cart.* 3, pp. 253–7, no. 647.

Another problem is of being sure that the estate described in Domesday Book and that of the twelfth-century survey are identical. There are plenty of instances of Domesday descriptions covering more than one later manor and, even when this is not so, land transfers did not cease in 1086: land might have been granted to or removed from the estate at some time. In the case of Warboys there is documentary evidence of some land in the manor being 'restored' to the abbey at the command of Henry I in 1121.[18] Here the language suggests the return of property that had previously been part of the estate, so the comparison between the Domesday and the later figures would still hold, but it would be reassuring if this were known definitely.

It would be wrong to be unyieldingly sceptical about the possibility of using this evidence. If we consider how the number of peasant holdings might multiply in fact, and not only in appearance, there are three possible ways, and there is definite evidence for each of them in the period we are studying.

## 1. Subdivision of Holdings

In some parts of the country inheritance customs prescribed the division of a free peasant holding among all sons on the father's death. Naturally this tended over the generations to result in numerous small properties, although, of course, sometimes there was only one son and sometimes land could be reintegrated or built up by purchase. The regions where such partible inheritance was most common lay in the east of the country, notably in East Anglia and in Kent, where the custom was termed *gavelkind*. Unfree holdings might also be divided. Although this was not a general inheritance custom, the proliferation of half- or quarter-virgate holdings where evidence suggests that earlier tenements had been full virgates, implies that division had taken place, perhaps by sale as well as by inheritance.

## 2. New Tenures on the Lord's Demesne

There are instances of land that had been 'in demesne', that is, in the lord's hand, being leased to tenants. This did not always mean that there would be more tenants, since it is, of course, possible that existing tenants would simply take on the newly available land, but there do seem to be many cases of new tenancies carved out of the demesne. The survey of Brancaster (Norfolk), one of the Ramsey abbey manors, has entries of the kind: 'Habbe holds one acre of demesne for four pence. . . . Liveva holds one acre and a croft of demesne for four pence'.[19] This shows smallholdings being formed from the demesne lands about the middle of the twelfth century. Sometimes

---

[18] *Ramsey Chron.*, pp. 231, 281–2; *Ramsey Cart.* 1, p. 248, no. 178; *RRAN* 2, nos. 1262, 1262a, 1293, pp. 158, 165.

[19] *Ramsey Cart.* 3, p. 264, no. 649.

demesnes were rented out wholesale. In 1212–13 the Oxfordshire baron Robert Arsic leased out his demesne lands at Cogges to twenty-three free peasants in parcels of an acre or two, at a rent of a shilling an acre and with the requirement that they should build a house on each acre they held.[20]

## 3. Clearing of New Land

'When forest groves or thickets that could provide pasture for livestock or cover for wild animals are cut down and, after they have been cut down and rooted up, the land is turned over and cultivated, then we call that an assart.'[21] So the king's treasurer, Richard fitz Neal, defines one of the most common features of the landscape of his day—newly cleared land. Everywhere in the twelfth century we come across mention of these 'assarts'. They are usually small plots of land cleared from woodland by individual peasant tenants, who held them at money rent. As the bishop of Worcester was advised in the 1150s or 1160s, 'the lands that have been carved out of the woods and converted to arable land may be handed over to those whose labour cleared them, in hereditary tenure at an annual money rent'.[22] The advice was well directed, for the bishops of Worcester were familiar with the process of assarting: in 1189 Richard I granted them freedom from Forest jurisdiction for 614 acres of assarts on their estates.[23]

The manor of Cranfield, belonging to Ramsey abbey, has already been mentioned as an example of an estate where the number of tenants had apparently almost tripled in the seventy or eighty years after Domesday Book. Fortunately, the survey of Cranfield is detailed and explicit on one aspect of this expansion: tenants had been clearing new lands. After an account of the demesne livestock and a statement of the duties of the free and servile tenants, there is a heading, 'The assarts that were never burdened with labour services'. Then follows a long list of tenants, with the amounts of land and the rent they paid.[24] It is not quite clear whether the heading with its reference to assarts applies to all the remaining entries in the survey, but in any event the overall total of cleared land must be more than 300 acres and could be twice that amount. Plots ranged in size from half an acre to forty-eight acres and were being let for rents about one or two pence per acre for land burdened with the royal tax (geld), and 3d., 4d., or even 8d., for land exempt from it.

The nature of such enclosures is indicated by the detailed description of the boundaries of the assart at West Bromwich (Staffs.) given by Guy de Offeny to the monks of Worcester in the early 1140s:

the boundary begins at the small twisted oak tree on the Alton road and follows the road almost to the stream and then turns towards the big oak tree and from there goes

---

[20] *Bk. Seals*, no. 114, pp. 76–8 (BL Harley Charter 45 D 18).    [21] *Dial. scacc.*, p. 60.

[22] *Decretals* 3. 13. 7 (col. 514) (JL 14132).    [23] *Worcester Cart.*, no. 325, p. 171.

[24] *Ramsey Cart.* 3, pp. 301–4, no. 671.

above Simon's marsh to the tree, called in English 'birch', that is cut on the east side and from that tree it follows the road opposite the hill to the twisted oak where it began.[25]

Bounded by trees, roads, and a marsh, this small and irregular piece of land is not described as lying in any of the great open fields, nor indeed measured in any standard unit.

Much of the new land brought into cultivation in this period was taken from the woodland. One calculation is that about 15 per cent of England was woodland in 1086 and that this had fallen to about 10 per cent by the middle of the fourteenth century.[26] Reflecting on this estimate, we can choose either to stress the amount of clearance that had taken place by the time of Domesday Book or to emphasize the amount continuing in the following centuries, at the rate of 17 acres a day for every day between 1086 and 1350. The implied attrition rate of woodland in the twelfth and thirteenth centuries would be 0.15 per cent per annum.

The scale of the clearances should not be exaggerated. A study of the clearances undertaken on the estates of the bishopric of Worcester in the twelfth and thirteenth centuries concludes that, of the total cultivated area of between 40,000 and 50,000 acres that existed by 1300, only 2,000 acres or so had been brought under the plough in the previous century and a half.[27] Expansion over the period 1150–1300 at this rate represents an annual average increase of the cultivated area of between 0.02 per cent and 0.04 per cent, rather lower than the estimate for woodland disappearance quoted above for England as a whole.

In these ways, by the division of peasant holdings, the leasing out of the demesne and the clearance of new land, new tenancies arose in the course of time. The most ambitious study of the number of peasant holdings on English manors in this period concludes that between 1086 and 1230 they increased by 256 per cent.[28] Taking this as a surrogate measure for the population, it indicates an annual rate of growth of 0.65 per cent, which is higher than that of the English population in the period 1541–1871.[29] If we apply this rate of increase to the hypothetical figure of 2,250,000 for the Domesday population, we get a total population of 5,760,000 for 1230.

The overall picture of the demographic situation in England in our period is thus of a growing population and an increase in the cultivated area, but with the former growing faster than the latter. Guesses for rates of

---

[25] *Worcester Cart.*, no. 190, pp. 101–2.

[26] Oliver Rackham, *The History of the Countryside* (London, 1986), p. 88.

[27] Christopher Dyer, *Lords and Peasants in a Changing Society: The Estates of the Bishopric of Worcester, 680–1540* (Cambridge, 1980), p. 96.

[28] Hallam, *Agrarian Hist.*, p. 588.

[29] E. A. Wrigley and R. S. Schofield, *The Population History of England 1541–1871* (Cambridge, Mass., 1981).

population growth per annum are of such orders as 0.65 per cent and 1.22 per cent, while rates of land clearance have been estimated at 0.02 per cent and 0.15 per cent. We can only conclude that individual living standards were declining, unless there were productivity increases of a scale for which there is no evidence.

Population grows by fertility outrunning mortality. There is no statistical evidence for either subject in the twelfth century, but a few reasonable assumptions can be made. In the absence of effective contraception, the number of births per woman would be high. The instance recorded in the royal records in 1185 of a young woman of thirty, who was already twice widowed and had seven children under ten years of age, is an extreme, but not a bizarre, instance.[30] Given the medical, sanitary, and dietary situation, we can assume most of these children would not reach adulthood. Life expectancy must have been very low by modern standards. Figures from the bishop of Winchester's estates a generation after our period (1244–9) indicate a death rate among adult unfree tenants of 27 per thousand, which, because of the much higher death rates that must be presumed for babies and young children, implies an overall rate perhaps as high as 40 per thousand.[31] This is a very high level, comparable with nineteenth-century India and Russia. If population was indeed growing, then obviously the birth rate would have to be even higher, in the range 46–52 per thousand. This again is extremely high in historical terms and suggests that the so-called 'European marriage pattern', characterized by late marriage and the existence of many unmarried people, could not have applied at this time.

We do not have to assume, nor is it likely, that the population growth of our period was anything new. It is more probable that it simply continued a long-term trend that had been filling up English peasant society for centuries. Hence we do not have to postulate major changes in the components of mortality and fertility at this time: age at marriage, diet, epidemiology were, one can guess, relatively constant. Year by year the population expanded, as it had done throughout the later Anglo-Saxon period.

## 3. SETTLEMENT PATTERNS

Domesday Book names about 13,400 places. If we divide the hypothetical population total of 2,250,000 by that number, we obtain an average of 168 people per named place. This is not a sophisticated procedure, but it gives an order of magnitude to work with. Obviously there was great regional variation.

[30] *Rot. dom.*, p. 10.
[31] M. M. Postan and J. Z. Titow, 'Heriots and Prices on Winchester Manors', repr. in Postan's *Essays on Medieval Agriculture* (Cambridge, 1973), pp. 150–85, esp. pp. 159–61, 175, 182.

Average recorded population ranges from three, four, or five per place in the northern counties and eight or so in Derbyshire and Staffordshire, to a group of counties in which an average of over thirty recorded inhabitants per place suggests total actual numbers of 250 or more. These latter counties—Essex, Berkshire, Kent, Cambridgeshire, Middlesex, and Norfolk—are all located in the wealthy south-east and there is a clear correlation between the value of a county per acre and the population size of its individual places.

However, the jump from a name in Domesday Book to a 'village' in the late eleventh-century landscape is more hazardous than might at first appear. The listing in Domesday Book of the various tenants under the heading of a named manor does not imply that they all lived in a single settlement. The name might refer to the largest settlement on the estate, but there could also be many smaller outlying settlements with their own names, unrecorded in Domesday Book. The name might apply to an estate containing small and scattered hamlets and farmsteads but no village at all. The total number of named settlements in England in 1086 was therefore far higher than the 13,400 listed in Domesday Book. In the case of Kent, where the landscape was dominated by hamlets rather than villages, it can be demonstrated that, in addition to the 347 settlements named in Domesday Book, there were at least another 167 in the eleventh century, representing one-third of the total.[32]

The nucleated village, that is, a rural settlement with a large number of houses grouped together, is by no means the only type in England today, and the same was true in the eleventh and twelfth centuries. In many parts of the country, such as Kent, the south-west, or the Welsh Marches, a dispersed settlement pattern of hamlets and scattered farmsteads was more common. This can sometimes be related to terrain or land-use, as in the north and the west, where dispersed settlement can be associated with the predominance of pastoralism, a form of farming that both requires and supports a lower density of population. The figures in Domesday Book show that the areas of the country where arable was least important, as measured by the density of plough-teams, were also the areas where population density was low. Cornwall and the northern counties, including Cheshire, Staffordshire, and Derbyshire, represented the extreme of this non-arable and thinly populated world. Dispersed settlement did not always mean pastoralism, however. Intense arable farming could take place in areas of dispersed settlement. It seems that in East Anglia, the most densely populated region of England in this period, the large nucleated village was not the most common form of settlement.

One surprising hypothesis that has been advanced by the last generation or

[32] Darby, *Domesday England*, p. 24.

two of archaeologists and landscape historians is that, even in parts of the country where it is now common, the nucleated village is not, in fact, a constant and unchanging feature of the rural scene. The evidence has accumulated that many villages began only in the late Anglo-Saxon period or the immediately following 150 years. Sometimes the regularity of their plan suggests that a conscious act of foundation took place, perhaps initiated by manorial lords, who, it is often presumed, were the only ones with sufficient power to make such a fundamental change in settlement patterns.[33]

It is too early to say if this theory about the development of English villages will become firmly established. Excavation is the only technique that can fully demonstrate the occupation history of a village site and excavation is expensive and time-consuming. Alternative forms of analysis, based on the survey of pottery fragments found on the surface or on working backwards in time from nineteenth-century maps, although important, are obviously less conclusive. Nevertheless, the number of villages that can be shown to be newly established in the late Anglo-Saxon period or in the twelfth century continues to grow. Work at sites such as West Whelpington, Northumberland, and Thrislington in County Durham suggests that these villages were first laid out regularly in rows of tofts and crofts in the twelfth century.[34] Using quite a different approach, attempts have been made to explain the regular lay-out of house-plots that nineteenth-century maps reveal in some villages by a conscious process of planning in the medieval period.[35] It may well be the case, then, that a continuing process of nucleation, of reorganization of rural settlement into large, planned villages, was a characteristic of the period covered in this book.

From those villages that have been excavated we can obtain some idea of at least the external features of peasant life. Two good examples are Goltho in Lincolnshire and Barton Blount in Derbyshire, where some of the peasant crofts were excavated in 1968–70. Since these villages were abandoned at the end of the Middle Ages, the sites were not disturbed by modern constructions. The medieval village of Goltho contained a manor house, a chapel, and thirty-seven crofts, that of Barton Blount a hall, church, and forty-three crofts (see Map 6).[36] If every one of these was occupied, we might expect a village population of something like 200 people.

---

[33] e.g. Christopher Taylor, *Village and Farmstead: A History of Rural Settlement in England* (London, 1983), cap. 8, 'The Making of Villages'; Carenza Lewis *et al.*, *Village, Hamlet and Field: Changing Medieval Settlements in Central England* (Manchester, 1996).

[34] Michael Aston *et al.* (eds.), *The Rural Settlements of Medieval England* (Oxford, 1989), p. 267.

[35] P. Allerston, 'English Village Development: Findings from the Pickering District of North Yorkshire', *Trans. Institute of British Geographers*, 51 (1970), pp. 95–109; J. A. Sheppard, 'Metrological Analysis of Regular Village Plans in Yorkshire', *Agricultural History Review*, 22 (1974), pp. 118–35.

[36] Guy Beresford, *The Medieval Clay-Land Village: Excavations at Goltho and Barton Blount* (London, 1975), pp. 7, 9.

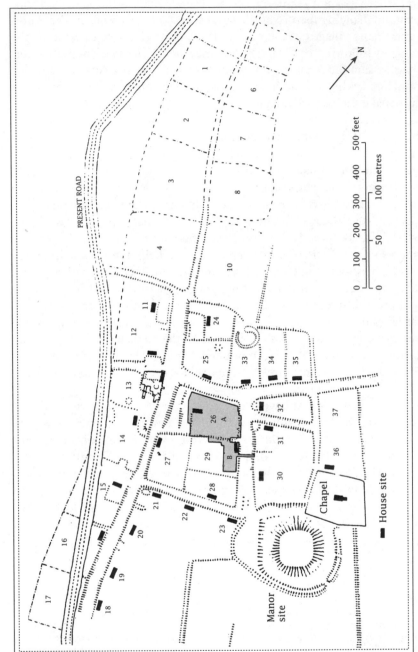

MAP 6. *The village of Goltho*

The houses that existed during the period 1075–1225 were constructed of timber, with clay floors and probably clay walls. One of those at Goltho, dating to the late eleventh century, was 9 feet by 24 feet and divided between a living area with a central hearth and a byre where animals were kept. Access to the house was through the byre. On the same croft another house was constructed in the late twelfth century. This was larger, 14½ feet by 30 feet, and was divided into two rooms by a passage.[37]

The average life of a wooden peasant house in this period could not have been more than a generation. The timbers of the walls rested either in or on the ground and would rot over the course of time. The impermanence of peasant houses is underlined by the fact that they were considered movable. In 1180 some of the peasant tenants of Witham, who were being relocated, 'moved their houses elsewhere, to live in them again', even though they consisted only of 'ancient huts with rotten timbers and old, fallen-down walls'.[38] The houses at Goltho, with their unjointed timbers resting on the surface of the ground, would have been just such constructions, movable, prone to decay, and short-lived.

The general shift from wood to stone in peasant buildings does not occur until after our period, but there are, as would be expected, some examples of stone building in areas where the material was easily available. The twelfth-century long-house at Gomeldon (Wilts.) had a low flint wall for part of its perimeter, while the farmstead at Beere, North Tawton (Devon), which dates to the late twelfth or thirteenth century, had a long-house, barn, and corn-drying kiln, all with low stone walls. The living area of the long-house, with a central hearth and a partitioned sleeping section, was approximately 23 feet by 14 feet.[39] The roofing of peasant houses of this time does not survive and cannot be reconstructed from excavation, but the natural assumption is that the buildings were thatched.

If we want to picture a peasant family of the twelfth century at home as best we can from the available evidence, then we should see a group of five people in a living space perhaps 24 feet by 12 feet, with a clay floor, unglazed but shuttered windows and an open hearth in the middle of the room. It is a scene that seems to offer more intimacy than privacy.

The crofts on which the peasant house stood were usually surrounded by a ditch and bank and this ensured their relative stability. House site might change every generation, as the easily perishable timber constructions were replaced or relocated, but the crofts themselves were more enduring. They

[37] Beresford, *The Medieval Clay-Land Village*, pp. 23, 32 (fig. 14).

[38] Ad. Eyns., *V. Hugh* 2. 5 (1, pp. 62–3).

[39] David Algar and John Musty, 'Gomeldon', *Current Archaeology*, 14 (1969), pp. 87–91; E. M. Jope and R. I. Threlfall, 'Excavation of a Medieval Settlement at Beere, North Tawton, Devon', *Medieval Archaeology*, 2 (1958), pp. 112–40.

offered more than a site for a house. The dimensions of those at Goltho varied considerably, but almost all were over a quarter acre and many approached an acre in size, providing ample room for a garden, chickens, outbuildings, and space for livestock. Documents from other villages in twelfth-century Lincolnshire mention crofts of half or three-quarters of an acre.[40] In some villages there are surviving marks of ridge-and-furrow in the crofts, indicating that they might even be cultivated with the plough.[41]

## 4. LAND USE AND AGRICULTURAL TECHNIQUE

### The Plough and Plough-Team

The predominant form of farming in medieval England was arable cultivation, with the plough as its main implement and cereal crops its product. Domesday Book lists over 80,000 plough-teams at work in England in 1086, one for every 400 acres of land in the kingdom, and, given the amount of land that was either uncultivated or pastoral, this means that over most of the country the plough-team at work must have been one of the most common and familiar sights. In the thirteenth century it was reckoned that a plough-team could work 180 acres, and assuming this applied in the earlier period too, then 80,000 teams could manage very close to half the total area of England.[42] It has indeed been suggested that as much land was under the plough in England in the twelfth century as in the nineteenth.[43]

The plough was clearly the fundamental implement upon which human subsistence depended in this period: 'a divine piece of work, discovered by some lofty genius, whose utility transcends the power of writing to express'.[44] Although there are not many contemporary descriptions or depictions of the plough, it is possible to attempt a visualization. Upon a wooden framework were mounted the coulter, that cut through the soil, and the asymmetrical share and mould-board that turned the furrow over, while curving handles were provided for the ploughman to guide it and wheels to make its passage easier. Oxen were harnessed singly or in pairs in line ahead and a 'driver' with a goad prodded them on. In some depictions, like that in the early twelfth-century manuscript of *The City of God* from Canterbury, birds follow the plough, waiting for the delicacies that would be turned up (see Plate 7).

[40] *Danelaw Docs.*, nos. 18, 336, pp. 13–14, 252.

[41] Grenville Astill and Annie Grant (eds.), *The Countryside of Medieval England* (Oxford, 1988), p. 50.

[42] *Seneschauchy* 1. 6, ed. Dorothea Oschinsky, *Walter of Henley and Other Treatises on Estate Management and Accounting* (Oxford, 1971), p. 264.

[43] F. M. Maitland, *Domesday Book and Beyond* (Cambridge, 1897), pp. 435–6; M. M. Postan, *The Medieval Economy and Society* (London, 1972), p. 18.

[44] Alex. Nequam, *DNR* 2. 169 (p. 280).

The usual plough-team employed on the lords' home farms or demesnes was made up of eight oxen, although the teams of the peasant tenants would be smaller. Horses were rarely used for traction, although their importance increased over the course of time. It has been calculated that at the time of the Domesday survey horses formed a mere 5 per cent of traction animals, but by the early twelfth century they reached 8 per cent and by the late twelfth century they had climbed to 15 per cent.[45] This still means, of course, that oxen formed 85 per cent of all draught animals and in some regions they might be even more dominant. On the bishop of Winchester's lands the accounts from 1210–11 show that 87.4 per cent of draught animals were oxen. The first explicit mention of the use of horses for ploughing occurs in the records of Ramsey abbey from the time of Henry I (1100–35). At Ringstead in Norfolk, for instance, the abbey had three plough-teams, each consisting of four oxen and three horses. Such mixed teams were not uncommon, blending, to some extent, the power of the ox and the speed of the horse, which could serve as a pace-maker. The relative values of the two kinds of animal—32 pence for oxen, 48 pence for horses—shows that horse traction at this time represented a high investment, although evidence from the later twelfth and thirteenth century suggests that oxen were by then slightly more valuable than plough-horses.[46]

The metal components of the plough, the coulter and share, required a rarer material and skill than the wooden parts and lords sometimes specified that their tenants should provide a supply of them. The four manorial dependants of Much Marcle in Herefordshire who had become burgesses of Hereford were required to pay an annual levy of eighteen ploughshares to their home manor, while one of the tenants of the Templars at Sharnbrook in Bedfordshire paid 'one ploughshare or two pence'.[47] Indeed the metal parts were so essential to the plough that it could even be equated with them, as in the levy that was assessed 'on each plough, that is, on the coulter and share'.[48] Lords were careful over details when it came to the plough. The tenants of Temple Ewell, for instance, had the explicit obligation of fetching plough wheels from Canterbury.[49]

Because plough-teams were long and awkward to manage, it was desirable to turn them around as seldom as possible when ploughing. Hence the arable tended to be cultivated in long strips, with turning places (headlands) at the extremities—the modern English word 'furlong', i.e. 220 yards, originally meaning 'one furrow length', gives a rough idea of the scale involved. Later

---

[45] For the following, see John Langdon, *Horses, Oxen and Technological Innovation: The Use of Draught Animals in English Farming from 1066 to 1500* (Cambridge, 1986).

[46] *Ramsey Cart.* 3, p. 266, no. 651.  [47] *DB* 1, 179b (Hef. 1. 7); *Templar Records*, p. 76.

[48] *Mir. John Bev.*, p. 298.  [49] *Templar Records*, p. 23.

thirteenth-century recommended practice was that the individual furrow should be about one foot wide.[50] The asymmetrical plough pushed the soil to one side and, as the plough-team went up and down the strip, ploughing the soil in towards the centre, a characteristic undulating 'ridge-and-furrow' terrain was produced, with a distance of roughly 13 to 15 feet between the crests of the ridges.[51] Ridge-and-furrow provided both a simple drainage system and a way of marking out individual holdings in the fields, since holdings were formed of groups of ridges ('selions'). The ghost of this pattern can still be seen in areas that were subsequently converted to pasture (Plate 11).

## Crops

The main grains grown by the arable farmers of England were wheat, rye, barley, and oats. The two former were sown in the autumn and allowed to stand the winter and hence were termed 'winter corn', while the faster grow-ing oats and barley were sown in the spring.[52] They were also sown more densely than wheat. Often the arable was divided equally between winter and spring grains, as is implied by the duties of the villagers of Castor (Northants), who had to plough 27 acres at the winter sowing (*hivernage*) and the same amount at the spring sowing (*tremeis*) or is stated explicitly at Felsted (Essex), where, in the time of Henry I, the demesne had 300 acres under crop, half of it wheat and half oats.[53] Sometimes the balance was less even. In the 1150s the demesne at Leighton (Beds.) had 243 acres sown 'at the winter sowing' and 116 at the spring sowing (*tremeis*).[54]

For most of the period covered by this book there is no evidence for the level of agricultural productivity, but from the year 1208 onwards records survive—although they are incomplete—that allow us to form a detailed pic-ture of the agrarian economy on the estates of the bishop of Winchester. From the Winchester accounts it is possible to calculate crop yields on some thirty or so manors in southern England for six years in our period: 1211, 1218, 1219, 1220, 1224, and 1225. The results are shown in Table 3.[55]

---

[50] Walter of Henley, *Husbandry* 28–9, ed. Dorothea Oschinsky, *Walter of Henley and Other Treatises on Estate Management and Accounting* (Oxford, 1971), pp. 314–15.

[51] On dimensions, Grenville Astill and Annie Grant (eds.), *The Countryside of Medieval England* (Oxford, 1988), p. 74.

[52] Burton Surveys, p. 239.          [53] *Petr. Chron.*, p. 163; *Caen Custumals*, p. 33.

[54] Robert Richmond, 'Three Records of the Alien Priory of Grove and the Manor of Leighton Buzzard', *Bedfordshire Historical Record Soc.* 8 (1924), pp. 15–46, at p. 23.

[55] J. Z. Titow, *Winchester Yields: A Study in Agricultural Productivity* (Cambridge, 1972), pp. 43, 53, 63. The figures represent the average of each year and crop adjusted to restore the tithe that was deducted in the field.

TABLE 3. *Yield per seed sown on the Winchester estates, 1211–1225*

| Year | Wheat | Barley | Oats |
|---|---|---|---|
| 1211 | 3.51 | 4.29 | 2.84 |
| 1218 | 3.3 | 3.89 | 2.9 |
| 1219 | 3.91 | 4.48 | 2.66 |
| 1220 | 3.52 | 4.29 | 2.67 |
| 1224 | 3.34 | 4.42 | 3.09 |
| 1225 | 4.28 | 5.3 | 3.07 |
| AVERAGE FOR SIX YEARS | 3.64 | 4.45 | 2.87 |

Obviously yields were very low by modern standards. An acre of wheat, sown at the rate recommended by contemporaries of 3.2 bushels per acre,[56] would produce, on average, 11.65 bushels of wheat, equivalent to about one-quarter a ton of grain. Modern farmers can expect 3 to 3.5 tons of wheat per acre, even in the less clement parts of Britain. Even the highest average yield—for barley in the good year of 1225—was only 5.3 to one.

One-tenth of the harvest was gathered up in the fields for the church; deducting the seed corn for next year's crop immediately reduced the remainder by one-third or one-quarter. Hence, in the early thirteenth century, each grain of wheat sown was only producing two and a quarter grains for sale or consumption, each grain of barley three, and each grain of oats a miserable one and a half. These are average figures and bad years, like 1218, might see yields of wheat and oats on some unlucky manors, like Bitterne in Hampshire or Morton in Buckinghamshire, so low as to make it impossible to supply seed-corn from the local harvest. It is generally recognized that the yields on the Winchester estates were low even by the standards of thirteenth-century England, but these figures make clear how close to the edge the farmers of the period were living.

There was little that could be done to increase the productivity of the soil beyond fallowing and manuring. Marling—mixing in chalk or lime to heavy soils, or 'cheering the fields with chalk', in the words of one twelfth-century writer—was practised;[57] the prior of Earl's Colne (Essex) was praised for purchasing a worthless and infertile piece of land and then 'making it good and fruitful by the admixture of the earth commonly called *marl*'.[58] It was possible to improve drainage; to plant nitrogen-fixing legumes; to plough more

---

[56] Robert Richmond, 'Three Records of the Alien Priory of Grove and the Manor of Leighton Buzzard', *Bedfordshire Historical Record Soc.* 8 (1924), pp. 15–46, at p. 23.

[57] Alex. Nequam, *Ut.*, p. 113.     [58] *Abingdon Chron.* 2, p. 294.

frequently. Yet all this was of limited effect. The overall impression that one receives of farming practice in England in this period is that the contribution of human effort was poignantly dwarfed by the imponderables of weather, pests, and diseases. Contemporary scientific knowledge and technology offered little. When English peasants hung dead crows above newly sown fields to scare off the other birds, perhaps they were doing the best they could.[59]

## Livestock

Domesday Book does not usually give detailed figures for livestock, although the number of plough oxen can be deduced from the standard information about plough-teams, but the chance survival of fuller Domesday records for two regions, East Anglia and the South-west, makes it possible to say something about the relative proportions of different kinds of farm animals, other than the draught oxen, in late eleventh-century England (see Figure 7).[60]

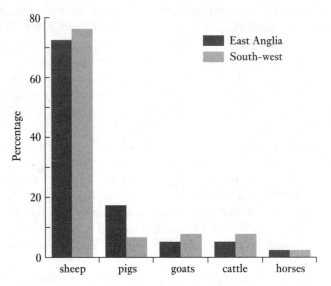

FIGURE 7. *Proportions of Domesday livestock*

These figures relate only to demesne animals, that is, stock on the lord's own home farm, not that possessed by the peasant tenantry, and it is possible that the proportions of peasant animals would have been different, but the overall pattern is unlikely to be very misleading. The preponderance of sheep is obvious. About three-quarters of the stock listed were sheep, which were grazed in large numbers on marshes in both regions, in the East Anglian

[59] Map 1. 10 (p. 14).     [60] Based on Darby, *Domesday England*, pp. 162–70.

Breckland and on the chalk downs of Dorset. Very much less significant were the demesne pigs, although in East Anglia they formed 17 per cent of the total. Goats and non-draught cattle were minority animals, 5 per cent each in East Anglia, 8 per cent each in the South-west. Finally, horses made up about 1 per cent of recorded demesne farm animals. They were used for harrowing and carting.

This is the picture excluding the draught oxen. It is hard to build them into our calculations, but if we assume that demesne plough-teams formed between one-fifth and one-third of the total number of plough-teams and that each team consisted of eight oxen, then we must adjust our figures to allow for draught oxen making up something like 10 to 15 per cent of the total. Even after this modification, it is clearly the case that the most common farm animal to be seen in the English countryside of this period was the sheep (forming 63 per cent of all demesne animals if we assume that draught oxen formed 15 per cent).

The evidence from the end of our period, the early thirteenth century, suggests that little had changed in the composition of English livestock. Tax returns from south Wiltshire in 1225 show that 75 per cent of the animals owned by the peasantry were sheep and the records of the bishop of Winchester's estates in 1208–9 show a similar pattern, although this information relates only to demesne animals.[61] On the bishop's estates, sheep formed over 81 per cent of the total livestock, cattle only 10 per cent—although it should be noted that both south Wiltshire and the Winchester estates included a large amount of land specially suited to sheep-rearing (see Figure 8).

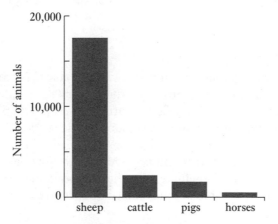

FIGURE 8. *Livestock on the Winchester estates, 1208–1209*

[61] M. M. Postan, *Essays on Medieval Agriculture* (Cambridge, 1973), table 11.1, p. 227 (the tax returns have been published since Postan wrote: *Rolls Fifteenth*, pp. 46–106); *The Pipe Roll of the Bishopric of Winchester 1208–1209*, ed. Hubert Hall (London, 1903), p. xlviii.

The archaeological evidence, in the form of bone fragments, harmonizes with this picture only to a certain extent. While the minority status of horses and goats is confirmed (although the bones of the latter are hard to distinguish from those of sheep), and the relative place of the pig is similar, the predominance of sheep over cattle does not appear so strikingly in the archaeological record. One survey based on analysis of animal bones suggests that something like 45 per cent of animals in a village setting were sheep, just over 30 per cent cattle, and just over 20 per cent pigs, while in towns and castles cattle bones were as common or more common than those from sheep.[62] Obviously eating patterns as well as the actual number of livestock are relevant here—excavation of the remains of beef-eating communities will produce more cattle bones than a random survey of the countryside. Another survey, concentrating on the South-west, one of the regions for which Domesday Book figures exist, suggests that, over the whole medieval period, cattle were usually between 40 and 50 per cent of the total, sheep between 30 and 50 per cent and pigs a distant third, usually less than 20 per cent.[63]

The discrepancies between the Domesday Book figures and other survey evidence and the archaeological record are significant but do not constitute a paradox. It is clearly the case that sheep and cattle were the predominant animals, although their relative importance has not yet been established unambiguously. Pigs were important suppliers of meat, even though they rarely formed more than one-fifth of the total stock. Other quadrupeds were rarer. There is the prospect of much more information coming from archaeological investigation and careful differentiation of period, type of site, and nature of the deposits being excavated may remove some of the apparent surviving discrepancies.

## Open Fields

The pressure of population meant that it was desirable to have as much arable as possible, yet this presented problems: the animals also needed pasture and, in the absence of artificial fertiliser, continually cropped land would soon become exhausted. One solution was found in the so-called 'open-field' or 'Midland' system, in which one-half or one-third of the arable was left uncropped (fallow) each year and provided rough grazing, on stubble and weeds, at the same time benefiting from the droppings of the animals pasturing on it. In this way arable was maximized but pasture was still available for

---

[62] Annie Grant, 'Animal Resources', in Grenvill Astill and Annie Grant (eds.), *The Countryside of Medieval England* (Oxford, 1988), pp. 149–87, at 152 (fig. 8.2).
[63] Bruce Levitan, 'Medieval Animal Husbandry in South West England', in N. D. Balaam *et al.* (eds.), *Studies in the Palaeoeconomy and Environment of South West England* (BAR, British Series 181; 1987), pp. 51–80.

draft oxen and other livestock. Because application of animal manure was the main way of nourishing the soil, the right to control animals' droppings was a jealously guarded one. Lords often insisted that tenants' livestock should be grazed on the demesne fallow and this 'right of fold', a monopoly on dung, was a valuable asset. At Mickleover in Derbyshire the peasantry even had to work a day on the lord's demesne in order to have the right to bring their cows back to their homesteads for milking.[64]

In the open-field system, the arable land was divided into two or three fields, one of which would be fallow at any given time. Holdings were divided roughly equally between the fields. In 1199, when the manor of Preston (Northants) was divided, one party received 95 acres of arable land and some meadow of the demesne and this was specified as consisting of 44 acres and some meadow in one field and 51 acres and some meadow in the other.[65] When the men of Hutthorpe (Northants) endowed their local chapel with land about the middle of the twelfth century, they gave 'from each virgate one acre on one side of the village and one acre on the other'.[66] There is also good evidence for existence of the three-field system. At Waterbeach in Cambridgeshire there was certainly a three-field system by the middle years of the twelfth century, for at that time holdings are mentioned consisting of, respectively, 'a curtillage and nine acres, three in each field' and 'a curtillage and six acres, namely two in each field' (the 'curtillage' is the toft and croft containing the house, garden, etc.).[67] There are cases of a village going over from a two-field to a three-field system and thus increasing the total acreage under crop at any one time, but they are not numerous: ten definite and five probable in the whole period up to 1350.[68] The primary component of a holding in the open-field or Midland system was thus a group of strips of arable located in two or three fields. The strips in any one field might all be adjacent but were often not.

The lord's own land, the demesne, was often scattered among the holdings of the tenantry. A late twelfth-century description of the demesne lands of the lord of Great Limber (Lincs.) lists 28 separate plots of arable, of widely varying size: 'on the Searby road, two furlongs of 6 selions (strips) . . . at *Sablones*, one furlong of 4 selions . . . at *Steyneberg*, 2 selions . . . under *Langhuil*, two furlongs of 6 selions in the west field . . . at *Claxhou*, one furlong of 24 selions'.[69] Although this scattering of strips might have its

[64] Burton Surveys, p. 230.

[65] *Feet of Fines of the Tenth Year of the Reign of King Richard I* (PRS 24; 1900), no. 225, pp. 151–2.

[66] *Danelaw Docs.*, no. 465, pp. 342–3.

[67] *Monasticon* i, p. 484; *Rec. actes Hen. II* 2, no. 546, pp. 123–4.

[68] H. S. A. Fox, 'The Alleged Transformation from Two-field to Three-field Systems in Medieval England', *Economic History Review*, 2nd ser., 39 (1986), pp. 526–48.

[69] *Danelaw Docs.*, pp. lviii–lix, n. 2.

rationale, in distributing the risk of crop failure, flooding, and other hazards, lords had the power to redistribute and concentrate their demesne lands. This was done by Hugh fitz Odo, lord of Great Sturton (Lincs.), when, granting half his demesne to Kirkstead abbey, he explained,

since the furlongs of my demesne lie intermingled with the lands of my men and the monks wish to live remote from others, I have combined the lands of my demesne and the lands of my men at the far end of the fields towards Minting and given the whole of it to the monks and in exchange I have given to my men of Sturton land from my demesne.[70]

Because of the two- or three-year rotation and because the animals were let loose on the fallow at a specific time, this system of cultivation imposed a form of communal discipline: everyone with a share in the arable fields had to follow the same crop rotation and farming rhythms. It combined individual-istic and communal aspects: the land was held and worked by the individual tenant, but he could not do with it just as he wished, and during the fallow period everyone's animals would roam over every individual's holdings.

A holding in the arable field carried with it appurtenances, especially the right to share in local pasture and common land. A full peasant holding in an open-field village would consist of a homestead on an enclosure in the village, portions of arable in each of the fields, plus meadow and grazing rights. An example is the property in Snelland (Lincs.) described in a document of the later twelfth century.[71] It consisted of a toft, surrounded by a ditch, situated between two other tofts, and stretching from the road back to a water-course and a marsh, on the other side of which was the arable land. Belonging to the toft was a bovate of 20 acres of land (the acre being measured by the long northern perch of 18 feet). This was in two equal parts, one on each side of the village. In addition the holding contained 'as much meadow as belongs to 20 acres' and pasture for 100 sheep. The holding was thus a complex and inte-grated ecological and economic unit. It provided room for a dwelling, garden, cereal production, meadow, and pasture. The animals to plough the arable would be fed from the stubble of the fallow, the hay from the meadow, and some of the oats from the field. Milk, cheese, and wool came from the sheep pastured. The marsh might offer reeds and various small food sources.

The low productivity of arable farming makes the place of such non-arable resources as the marsh and pasture at Snelland even more vital. Any commu-nity that had access to lakes, large pools, fens, estuaries, or reasonably sized rivers would treat them as a rich source of food—fish, fowl, eggs—while peat could be dug for fuel, as in Lincolnshire, for example,[72] and suitable reeds

[70] *Danelaw Docs.*, no. 202, pp. 140–1.          [71] Ibid., no. 229, pp. 160–1.
[72] *Bury Docs.*, no. 205, p. 173.

might provide roofing material. To collect these resources, boats with poles or paddles would be used. Nine such have been found in the mud of the river Mersey.[73] They date from the eleventh and twelfth centuries and were made by splitting an oaken log lengthways and hollowing it out and shaping it to create a canoe shape. They were between nine and twelve feet in length and about three feet wide. Such vessels would have been ideal for negotiating reedy lakes or the fringes of water courses.

These non-arable resources were under pressure from cereal hunger. Clearance of new land was never a matter of simply opening up unused wilderness. It often meant the conversion of pasture to arable and the pastoralists might have something to say on the subject. When the hermit Godric began to clear land and grow crops at Finchale in Durham, the local peasantry became enraged, 'for the place he was cultivating had previously been the peasants' common pasture'. They tried to drive him off by harassing him, eventually loosing their flocks among his growing crops, but Godric had miraculous protection.[74] Even in relatively sparsely populated areas, there were individuals and communities who had claims on wasteland, marsh, woodland, and rough pasture, while in more densely occupied landscapes watchful neighbours and tenants would be willing to fight for their invaluable grazing rights. Until the Statute of Merton of 1236, free tenants with grazing rights could prevent their lord from assarting the land on which they grazed their stock.[75] Even when the freeholders were themselves willing to engage in clearance, the precious resource needed to be guarded, as in the Soke of Peterborough in 1215, when the freeholders purchased the right to clear and enclose their woodland but also carefully specified that they should retain their rights of common pasture in the fen.[76]

## Food and Famine

In a world of low productivity with no techniques for the large-scale storage of food, the state of each year's harvest was the crucial determinant of how well the bulk of the population would live and how many of the infants, aged, and sick would die. Monastic chroniclers were in some ways extremely privileged consumers, but they were also members of communities that possessed agricultural estates and hence aware of harvest prospects and results. The authors of the so-called 'E' version of the *Anglo-Saxon Chronicle*, which

---

[73] Sean McGrail and Roy Switsur, 'Medieval Logboats of the River Mersey: A Classification Study', in McGrail (ed.), *The Archaeology of Medieval Ships and Harbours in Northern Europe* (BAR, International Ser. 66; 1979), pp. 93–115.

[74] Reg., *V. Godric* 26 (pp. 74–5).

[75] Frederick Pollock and Frederic William Maitland, *The History of English Law before the Time of Edward I* (2nd edn., 2 vols.; Cambridge, 1898, reissued 1968), vol. 1, p. 622; *CRR* 10, p. 259.

[76] King, *Peterborough*, pp. 75, 175–6.

reflects observations made first at Canterbury and then at Peterborough, have a lot to say about weather, disease, and crops. In 1105 'the crops were ruined'; in 1110 bad weather meant that 'the crops in the fields were spoiled and the fruit ruined'; the following year bad weather again meant that 'the crops in the fields were spoiled' and the situation was made worse by a disease among the livestock (*orfcwealm*); next year disease hit the human population (*mancwealm*); in 1115 there was another outbreak of disease among livestock; the following year there was rain at harvest-time and a shortage of mast to feed the pigs; in 1117 there was a dearth of corn because of the rainy weather.

Now, the *Anglo-Saxon Chronicle* in its post-Conquest incarnation has a notoriously gloomy tone. The concluding comment for the year 1086—'and always things got worse and worse'—expresses the *Chronicle*'s outlook well. Yet it is doubtless only reflecting reality in its sensitivity to weather, especially to heavy rains at seedtime and harvest, and to the recurrence of both human and animal disease. Poor harvests and sudden illness could not be guarded against and had to be expected. They constituted the fundamental precariousness of life in pre-industrial society. Nevertheless, the impression that the *Chronicle* and other narrative sources leave is that it was not common for people in twelfth-century England to starve to death. This happened. The chronicler William of Newburgh, writing of the year 1196, says that 'in many places the mass of the poor perished through hunger'.[77] Yet the real killer in famine years seems to have been disease striking a weakened population. In the disastrous year 1087, according to the *Chronicle*,

such a disease struck the people that nearly every other man was in dreadful straits with fever, so that many men died of that affliction. Then, because of bad weather, such a famine befell the whole of England that many hundred men died a wretched death through hunger . . . the wretched people lay at death's door and then came sharp hunger and destroyed them.

Many other chronicle references link famine and disease in this way. In 1175, for example, 'there was lethal disease in England and the surrounding regions so that often seven or eight corpses were buried in a day. Immediately after this disease there followed serious famine.'[78] The general impression given is that it was unusual for large numbers to die through shortage of food alone. Indeed, the way that chroniclers record famines reflects this, since when they wish to convey the severity of a famine, they usually do so by saying how expensive grain became. The very bad year of 1125 was described as 'the dearest year of our time, when a horse-load of grain was sold for six shillings'; in 1203 'there was a great famine, so that a quarter of grain was sold

---

[77] W. Newb. 5. 26 (2, p. 484).        [78] *Gesta Hen. II* 1, p. 104; R. Howd. 2, p. 85.

for fourteen shillings'.[79] The outcome of a poor harvest usually seems to have been hunger and impoverishment rather than deaths on a large scale.

## 5. THE MANORIAL ECONOMY

A common feature of the medieval English manor was the existence of two elements, the peasant tenantry and the demesne farm. On most estates the lord kept some land to be farmed directly for his own produce or profit, while renting out the rest in peasant holdings. The tenants had to pay rent, which could be in the form of cash, labour, or produce, while the demesne, the lord's own holding, was cultivated by estate servants, by tenants performing labour services, by hired labour, or by a combination of the three. Most manorial lords thus expected to receive income both from the direct exploitation of their demesne and from the tenantry.

Let the bishop of Winchester's manor at Hambledon in Hampshire provide us with a concrete instance of the workings of the demesne economy. Detailed accounts survive for the bishop's estates from 1208 until the end of the Middle Ages, and those for the financial year 1210–11 have been edited (see Figure 9).[80] In Hambledon that year Matthew the sergeant and the reeves Everard and Serlo collected £28. 18s. 11½d. in rent from the peasant tenants. The total rent due from the manor was actually slightly higher, but the estate officials, such as the reeve, ploughmen, blacksmith, etc. occupied their holdings rent-free. In addition to the rents, the peasantry paid £4. 14s. 8d. in dues for the right to graze their animals on the lord's land and obtain some exemptions from manorial obligations. A fairly substantial amount (£5. 7s. 0d.) came from court fines, that is, the income from the bishop's manorial court. Some of these items from the court are clearly judicial in the twentieth-century use of the term: there are fines for breach of the peace and trespass, for example. Others are on the borderline between the judicial and the private disciplinary act: several tenants are fined 'for having grain', presumably for filching produce from the demesne. Other court profits came from matters that would now be deemed purely economic—payments to take up a holding, for example—while yet others relate to lords' rights that are being exercised over unfree dependants, such as payments to give one's daughter in marriage. The medieval lord was a landlord but he was also a judge and a master and nothing could better illustrate the involved mixture than this record of apparently miscellaneous fines. The men of Hambledon had to pay their lord for their land but they also had to pay him for permission to arrange the marriage of their daughters.

[79] H. Hunt. 7. 36 (p. 474); *Annals of Tewkesbury, Ann. Mon.* 1, p. 57.
[80] *The Pipe Roll of the Bishopric of Winchester 1210–1211*, ed. N. R. Holt (Manchester, 1964).

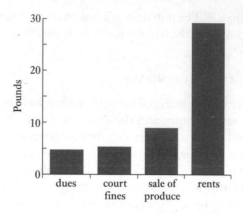

FIGURE 9. *Cash income at Hambledon, 1210–1211*

Sale of the produce of the demesne made up a relatively small proportion of the total cash income at Hambledon that year: £8. 16s. 10d. out of £47. 17s. 5½d., or just under 18.5 per cent. The most valuable item in these cash sales was grain, followed by livestock, sheep's milk and wool and wool-fells. The relative unimportance of sales of demesne produce does not indicate a small demesne at Hambledon, however. Four hundred acres were sown in 1210–11, with wheat, mancorn (mixed wheat and rye), barley, and oats. The demesne flock started the year with 460 sheep and ended it with 494. Clearly this was a busy home farm. It is equally clear that the manor was not geared predominantly to production for the market.

What then, was the destination of the produce? Since yields were low, the bulk of the cereal crop (45 per cent) had to be saved for the following year's seed corn. Then a large portion went to the estate servants as part of their wage and a considerable amount, in the form of beer and barley bread, was consumed by the peasant tenants when they did 'boon works', that is obligatory services on the lord's demesne for which they were nevertheless provided with food and drink. A small proportion (12.5 per cent) was sold, and minor amounts went to fatten the pigs, feed the oxen in winter, and provide 'prebends' (regular allowances in kind) for the bishop's officials, such as the estate steward Roger Wacelin, who received 7 bushels of oats from Hambledon. With the exception of these prebends and the small amount sold, the grain produced in Hambledon was consumed in Hambledon (see Figure 10).

The story is slightly different for animals. The draught teams, mainly oxen, seem to have been numerous enough for six superfluous oxen to have been sold, and there was clearly also a limited market in live sheep—thirty-five were bought and twenty-two were sold in the year. The sheep flock was, however, expected mainly to reproduce and increase naturally, although the

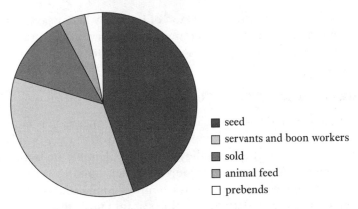

■ seed
□ servants and boon workers
■ sold
■ animal feed
□ prebends

FIGURE 10.  *Use of the grain crop at Hambledon, 1210–1211*

very high mortality among lambs (70 out of 154 died before being weaned) limited the rate of increase. Apart from their milk, the sheep were kept primarily for their wool, but the sale of this commodity was not principally dealt with at the level of the local manor. The 364 fleeces that the flock produced (after deduction of tithes) were sent off to Southwark, where the bishop had a palace and the busy market of London lay across the bridge. At prices then current, they would have fetched about £3. 17s. 0d. This would not, however, be accounted as part of the cash income of Hambledon, because the lord had the right to take what he wanted in kind from his estates and consume or sell it as he thought fit. Likewise, of the 72 pigs at Hambledon, 20 were sent to the kitchens of the episcopal manor house at Bishops Waltham, while the 36 chickens received in customary payments were all forwarded to Lovington in Somerset, presumably for the bishop's use when he was en route to his great manor at Taunton.

Looked at from the lord's point of view, the manorial economy of Hambledon involved a large cash income from peasant rents, a smaller cash income from the sale of produce from the demesne and his court profits and a useful supply of pigs and chickens for his kitchen. The cost of working the manor was partly paid for from remission of rent and food allowances for reeves and estate servants, although Matthew the sergeant received a salary of £3, the largest single item in the expenses. The tenantry had to work on the lord's land, although they were sometimes fed when they did so, and they had to provide a cash rent. It is probably therefore the case that they were more deeply enmeshed in the market economy than the manorial officials.

Hambledon is a specimen example of the composite nature of the manorial economy, showing the mixture of cash, kind, and labour in peasant rent, the levels of self-sufficiency and the role of the market. Manors varied according to a host of considerations: soil, climate, and terrain; demography;

nearness to markets and towns; the kind of lord they had; peasant standing; inheritance practices and other customs. The history of the rural regime of medieval England is, at the detailed local level, the story of these things.


## 6. RURAL SOCIAL STRUCTURE

England in our period was a peasant society. That means that most people were rural small-holders, working plots of land through their own labour. If they had relatively large holdings they might supplement the labour of their own family by that of servants or labourers; if their holding were very small, they might themselves have to work as labourers on the lands of others, or as craftsmen. Unlike the modern family, the peasant family drew the bulk of its sustenance from the produce of its own holdings—the calories that were consumed usually had their origin from an area within sight, or at least easy reach. Since production and consumption were so intimately linked within the peasant family and holding, it is misleading to distinguish a specifically 'economic' aspect of peasant life. Agricultural work, domestic labour, child-rearing, marketing—all were part of a continuous web of activity that is not susceptible to a clear division into 'economic' and 'social' and can often not be given straightforward economic quantification.

Peasants' fortunes were determined partly by the amount of land they possessed and partly by their status, free or servile. Both had to be considered. It is clear that the limitations of servitude were resented, but also that freedom without an adequate acreage was an empty thing. When the royal serfs on the manor of Witham in Somerset were given the choice between being relocated to another royal manor with holdings of the same size or of being granted their freedom and going where they would, 'some chose land and others freedom'.[81] More remarkably, when 38 peasants (*rustici*) who were being cleared off their holdings for the foundation of Revesby abbey were offered the same choice, 31 preferred 'to be landless but lordless'.[82] They obviously shared the view of the fable-writer Walter Anglicus: 'a free beggar is richer than a rich slave'.[83]

Any analysis of the peasant population in our period must begin with the data of Domesday Book. Table 4 shows, in simplified form, the various groups of the rural population as recorded there. The Domesday categories seem to reflect a mixture of status and wealth. The *villani*, who form the

---

[81] Ad. Eyns., *V. Hugh* 2. 5 (1, p. 62).

[82] *Facsimiles of Early Charters from Northamptonshire Collections*, ed. F. M. Stenton (Northamptonshire Record Soc. 4; 1930), pp. 1–7; John Hatcher, 'English Serfdom and Villeinage: Towards a Reassessment', *Past and Present*, 90 (1981), pp. 3–39, at pp. 31–2.

[83] Walter Anglicus, *Fable* 51, line 17, ed. Kenneth McKenzie and William A. Oldfather, *Ysopet-Avionnet: The Latin and French Texts* (Univ. of Illinois Studies in Language and Literature 5/4; 1919), p. 158.

largest group, are those holding full-size plots of land, sufficient to support them and their families. The cottagers ('bordars', 'cottars', and 'coscets') were probably of the same legal standing as the *villani* but had small-holdings—they were not holders of full plots in the fields. The existence of a group of 'free peasants' ('freemen' and 'sokemen') obviously implies that there was some sense in which the *villani* and cottagers were less than fully free and this is a subject to which we shall return. It is simply worth noting here that while some free peasants held plots as large as or larger than those of the *villani*, others had small-holdings comparable to the cottagers—they were distinguished by status not by wealth. The lowest group in terms of status was the slaves (*servi*).

TABLE 4. *Categories of the rural population in Domesday Book*

| Category | Number | Per cent |
|----------|--------|----------|
| *Villani* | 109,000 | 40 |
| Cottagers | 89,000 | 30 |
| Free peasants | 37,000 | 15 |
| Slaves | 28,000 | 10 |
| Miscellaneous | 6,000 | 5 |

## Slaves

Eleventh-century England was familiar with slave-trading and slave-raiding, particularly geared to supplying slaves for Ireland. Every summer Irish pirates descended on the north Devon coast 'carrying the inhabitants off into captivity, to sell them elsewhere as slaves and maidservants'.[84] The men of Bristol had a regular trade, buying up youngsters of both sexes throughout England and bringing them to their port for shipment to Ireland. Wulfstan, bishop of Worcester (1062–95), denounced the trade and, with the backing of Archbishop Lanfranc, was eventually able to stop it.[85] The Council of Westminster assembled by Anselm in 1102 reiterated the prohibition: 'Henceforth let no one dare to engage in that wicked trade, which has until now been customary in England, namely the selling of human beings as if they were brute beasts.'[86] Some contemporaries saw the abolition of the slave trade as one of the civilizing influences following in the aftermath of the Norman Conquest. The monk Lawrence of Durham, writing in the early 1130s, thought that the slave trade was one of the ancient distinguishing customs of

---

[84] *Mir. Nectan*, p. 408.
[85] W. Malm., *V. Wulfstan* 2. 20 (pp. 43–4); W. Malm., *GR* 3. 269 (2, p. 329); OMT edn., pp. 496–8.
[86] *Councils and Synods* 1/ii, p. 678.

the English, Irish, and Scots, characterized by the especially wicked prac-tice—'crueller than the savagery of the beasts'—of selling one's own family members. The Normans had introduced a far more kindly regime in this respect, claimed Lawrence, while Scotland and Ireland, 'still having rulers of their own race', maintained the practice, albeit at a reduced level.[87]

There was thus a category of person in eleventh-century England that cor-responds to the popular image of propertyless and abused human chattels conjured up by the word 'slave'. Such were the Bristol slaves intended for Ire-land—chained together, the girls among them raped before they were sold. The *servi* recorded in their thousands in Domesday Book, however, were not universally of this type. Although the 'maidservants' (*ancillae*) listed under the manorial resources were probably landless single women bound to the estate, it is likely that the majority of these 'slaves' were the equivalent of those later called *famuli*, unfree estate servants with their own plots, families, and even servants. They seem to have been particularly responsible for work-ing the ploughs on the demesne, the home farm. Their status did not make them non-persons. Within a generation or so of Domesday Book, in the time of Henry I, a document describing the rights and duties of the *servi* on the manor of Felsted in Essex even envisages the possibility that they might have free-born wives and free-born servants.[88]

Domesday Book indicates that the 10 per cent of the rural population clas-sified as slaves were distributed unevenly across the country, being much more numerous proportionally in the western counties, where they formed over 19 per cent of the population in Cornwall, Devon, Gloucestershire, and Shropshire.[89] Domesday Book also shows that the number of slaves was declining in the later eleventh century. In the entries for Essex, details are given not only of the number of slaves at the time of the Domesday survey, but also of their number 'in King Edward's day', i.e. during the reign of the last king of the Wessex line, who died in 1066. The figure for 1086 is 25 per cent lower than that for the earlier period.[90]

Slaves could be freed by a formal process known as manumission. The Church accounted it a pious act to free one's slaves (though not to free the Church's slaves) and many Anglo-Saxon wills contained a clause releasing slaves from their servitude. The release of slaves continued after the Con-quest. Domesday Book records that the landowner William Leofric had owned twelve slaves on his estate of Hailes in Gloucestershire, but 'he has

---

[87] Lawrence of Durham, *V. sanctae Brigidae*, ed. W. W. Heist, *Vitae sanctorum Hiberniae ex codice olim Salmanticensi nunc Bruxellensi* (*Subsidia hagiographica* 28; Brussels, 1965), p. 1.

[88] *Caen Custumals*, p. 33.

[89] Darby, *Domesday England*, pp. 72–4, 76–7; John Moore, 'Domesday Slavery', *ANS* 11 (1988), pp. 191–220, has argued that the total slave population in 1086 was more like 12 per cent.

[90] David A. E. Pelteret, *Slavery in Early Medieval England* (Woodbridge, 1995), p. 205.

made them free'.[91] Such manumissions would obviously result in a slow decline in the number of slaves, unless it were counterbalanced either by a large natural increase in their numbers or a replenishment from sources outside England by slave-raiding or purchase, neither of which seems to have happened.

The apparent disappearance of slavery between the time of Domesday Book and approximately 1120 is partly also a matter of relabelling. The unfree ploughman attached to the estate was now called by other names than *servus*, 'slave'. He might be termed *bovarius*, 'ox-man', or simply *famulus*, 'household servant'. On the estates of Shaftesbury abbey in the first half of the twelfth century about one-third of the small-holders were *famuli*, paying no rent but sometimes receiving a stipend and serving as ploughmen, shepherds, woodwards, etc.[92] In 1086 they might well have been listed under the 'slaves' and their conditions, both social and economic, were probably no different from the Domesday *servus*.

## The Size of Peasant Holdings

Medieval England was a land of small farms. The number of the entirely landless was probably not large and hence property-holding, even if of a modest scale, was widespread. For an individual peasant, the amount of land he or she possessed was the main determinant of standard of living, status, and prospects.

The 'standard' large peasant holding or virgate might vary in size from 12 to 80 customary acres but was usually about 30 or 40. It was a substantial holding by the standards of twelfth-century rural society and could be expected to support a peasant family. Virgate-holders were, however, a minority amongst the peasant tenantry. On the manors of the abbey of Burton upon Trent, surveyed in 1114–15, villeins with holdings of this size formed only one in three of the tenants.[93] The other two-thirds held less. A half-virgate of 15 to 20 acres was still a reasonably sized holding that might support a family and such a tenure was also common. The Domesday Book *villanus* was typically a holder of a virgate or half-virgate. Small-holders, the bordars and cottars of Domesday Book, would hold something like 5 acres. About 40 per cent of the rural population listed in 1086 were *villani*, about 40 per cent unfree small-holders (counting cottagers and slaves). The free peasantry, who made up 15 per cent of the population, had holdings of very

[91] *DB* 1, 167b (Gls. 38. 2).

[92] Kathleen Cooke, 'Shaftesbury Abbey in the Eleventh and Twelfth Centuries', M. Litt. thesis (Oxford, 1982), p. 121, on the basis of BL Harley 61, fos. 38ᵛ–52ᵛ (the dating of this survey is uncertain).

[93] J. F. R. Walmsley, 'The Estates of Burton Abbey from the Eleventh to the Fourteenth Centuries', Ph.D. thesis (Birmingham, 1972), cap. 3.

varied size, some being small-holders, some having properties far above the virgate-size of the villeins. Hence it would not be too inaccurate to view the peasant tenantry at the end of the eleventh century as divided roughly equally between the holders of a virgate or a half-virgate, on the one hand, and those who held less, on the other.

TABLE 5.  *Size of tenant holdings on some twelfth-century estates*

| Estate | Virgate or more (%) | Half-virgate (%) | Less than half a virgate (%) |
|---|---|---|---|
| Shaftesbury about 1130 | 39 | 22 | 39 |
| Worcester about 1170 | 25 | 30 | 45 |
| Shaftesbury about 1180 | 40 | 24 | 36 |
| Durham 1183 | 59 | 25 | 16 |
| Glastonbury 1189 | 44 | 30 | 26 |

Surveys of various estates were undertaken in the twelfth century and from the information preserved in these it is sometimes possible to calculate the distribution of peasant tenures by size. Some such patterns are shown in Table 5.[94] As the chart reveals, on these estates half-virgate holders constituted, fairly consistently, about one-quarter of the tenantry. The average proportion of holders of full virgates on the five estates was 40 per cent, although the range—from 25 to 59 per cent—was great. Small-holders usually made up between one-quarter and one-half of the tenants, except for the exceptional case of Durham, where they formed only one in six of the tenants. The difference between the Domesday situation, where small-holders constituted about half the population, and these estates, where they were less numerous, is probably to be explained by the fact that the twelfth-century surveys come from heavily manorialized ecclesiastical estates, where large standard holdings were more common and survived longer. Nor do any of the surveys relate to East Anglia, an area that had a very numerous small-holding peasantry.

[94] Christopher Dyer, *Lords and Peasants in a Changing Society: The Estates of the Bishopric of Worcester, 680–1540* (Cambridge, 1980), p. 89, table 8; Kathleen Cooke, 'Shaftesbury Abbey in the Eleventh and Twelfth Centuries', M.Litt. thesis (Oxford, 1982), p. 131, table 8, p. 149, table 11; Hallam, *Agrarian Hist.*, p. 687, table 6.39, p. 654, table 6.30 (taking '10–20' acres as a half-virgate).

## Freedom and Villeinage

During the course of the twelfth century, the English Common Law developed a complex and detailed set of concepts and procedures relating to unfree status (villeinage). Indeed, one of the distinguishing features of the new procedures introduced into the land law during the reign of Henry II was that they excluded villeins. The Common Law protected freehold and was the law of free men and, as it evolved, it drew a sharper line between the free and the unfree. Before the time of the Angevin reforms, however, distinctions were not so stark. It is misleading to translate the term *villanus* as 'villein' when it occurs in the eleventh or first half of the twelfth century, since villeinage implies that particular lack of freedom defined by the Angevin lawyers and we cannot say simply and unequivocally that the Domesday Book *villanus* was unfree. In the twelfth century, the author of the *Annals of Waverley*, large parts of which is simply a translation of the *Anglo-Saxon Chronicle*, rendered the *Chronicle*'s 'many ceorls' (*mycele maenige cyrlisces folces*) in the entry for the year 1092 as 'many *villani*'.[95] If *villanus* could thus be seen as an equivalent of the Anglo-Saxon ceorl, then it is worth noting that the ceorl was deemed free.

Over the course of the twelfth century the unfreedom of the majority of the rural population came to be stressed and defined in a way that it had not been before. Symptomatic is the development of the word *rusticus*—'country-dweller', 'peasant'—into a term that implied that those it described were not free. By 1190 the monks of Worcester were making a systematic distinction between bequests from 'free men' (*liberi homines*) and from *rustici*.[96] *Villanus* itself, a term that meant originally simply 'villager' and applied to 40 per cent of the rural population in Domesday Book, assumed the newly precise meaning of *villein*, accompanied by the abstract noun 'villeinage'. A charter of the 1190s refers to 'the whole lordship that I and my predecessors had in that land, i.e. in demesne and in the free tenements and in the villeinage'.[97] Alongside these labels of serfdom there was also the term *nativus*—the word means literally 'born' and refers to people who were 'born unfree'. 'Rustics', 'villeins', 'neifs' (*nativi*)—these were the newly classified unfree of England in 1200.

One fundamental freedom that was denied to many peasant tenants was the freedom to leave. In a world where labour was often scarce, tying one's tenants to the manor was one way of ensuring that rents and labour services would be provided regularly. It is evident from rules about runaways (*fugitivi*) that many country dwellers were considered by their lords to be bound

---

[95] *Ann. Wav.*, p. 202.  [96] *Worcester Cart.*, no. 334, pp. 178–9.
[97] Thomas Madox, *Formulare Anglicanum* (London, 1702), p. 274.

permanently to the estate. The so-called *Laws of William I* rule that 'serfs [*nativi, naifs*] shall not leave their lands nor seek devices to defraud their lord of the service they owe'.[98] The Norman and Angevin kings issued writs requiring their officials to secure the return of runaway peasants to their lords. A writ of William Rufus for the abbey of Ramsey orders his officials 'to ensure the return of the fugitives who have fled the lands of the abbey of Ramsey unjustly and without permission and to see that no one retains them unjustly', a mandate of Henry I instructs 'all his sheriffs and officials throughout England in whose areas of jurisdiction the runaways of the abbey of Abingdon should happen to be found' to restore them to the abbey and specifies a fine of ten pounds for anyone retaining them unjustly, while eventually such instructions became a matter of course, enshrined in Glanville's formulaic writ 'for having your serf'.[99] Careful estate administrators would keep lists of 'runaways' in their records.[100]

A story that puts a little flesh on the dry bones of these laws and writs is told by the monk Reginald of Durham in his account of the wonders performed by St Cuthbert. It concerns a poor man of Middleton in Northumbria (possibly Middleton near Belford). 'His lord had frequently burdened him and other poor men with heavy and wrongful claims,' writes Reginald, 'extorting from his poor tenants many other things over and above their yearly rent.' This man had been singled out because he was slightly better off than the others. He eventually decided on flight. 'He gathered together all he had and tied it all up in bundles, and, arising at night, he set out with his wife and sons, his oxen, sheep and lambs.' They headed for Lindisfarne, but the lord and his men pursued them. His wife and companions suggested flight to Lothian, but the man persevered and got through with all his paraphernalia. 'The cart creaked across the hissing sands, the feet of the animals rang on the pebbles and the cries of the herdsmen struck the ear. Oxen mooed, sheep baaed, horses neighed and men shouted at the animals so that the air resounded with the din.' The mobility of this relatively well-provided pastoralist was obviously critical in enabling him to escape with his resources; it was his lord's unremitting demands that had driven him to it.[101]

A sure and chilling sign of unfreedom was that one could be given away or sold. When the pious baron Arnulf de Hesdin made a donation of the tithes of his Kentish manor of Chelsfield to the church of Rochester about the year 1090, for the sake of the souls of his father, his mother, and himself, he threw in, lastly if not least, 'a *villanus* with five acres of land'.[102] About the year 1170

---

[98] Liebermann, *Gesetze* 1, pp. 512–13 (Leis Wl 30); Robertson, *Laws*, p. 268 n. 4.

[99] *Chronicon Abbatiae Ramesiensis*, ed. W. Dunn Macray (Rolls Series; 1886), p. 212; *Abingdon Chron.* 2, pp. 81–2; Glanvill 12. 11 (p. 153); Van Caen., *Writs*, pp. 467–77, nos. 103–24, 'writ of naifty'.

[100] e.g. BL Harley 61, fos. 62ᵛ–63, 59 (Shaftesbury abbey).

[101] Reg., *Libellus* 105 (pp. 234–6).     [102] *Text Roff.* 107, p. 163, fo. 184.

the knight Gilbert fitz Ralph announced, 'I have sold to Robert, prior of Bury St Edmunds, and the convent there, for 24 shillings, Aluric son of Stannard the fuller, who was my man, with all the progeny that has descended from him or will descend from him forever.'[103] It is not customary for historians to use the term 'slavery' when referring to late twelfth-century England, but here we have as clear an example as there could be of a human being treated as a commodity and as breeding stock.

As the Common Law concept of villeinage developed, it became important to be able to distinguish free people and villeins. This was not a simple task, for the criteria of freedom and servitude were not self-evident. Some burdens that lay heavily on the Norman *villanus*, such as 'heriot', the payment of 'the best beast he has, horse or ox or cow' as a death duty, were owed by free men too. In essence there was no difference between the heriot paid by many peasants and the feudal relief owed by knights and barons upon inheritance. Indeed heriot could be called 'the relief of the *villanus*'.[104] The lawyers of the thirteenth century eventually came to lay special stress on three tests of villeinage: merchet, tallage, and uncertain labour services. Merchet was a payment made for permission to give a daughter in marriage, tallage an arbitrary levy taken either annually or at longer intervals, and uncertainty of labour service implied that the villeins had to turn up to perform service on the demesne several days a week without knowing beforehand exactly what their tasks would be.

Payment of merchet often did mark the distinction between free and unfree. The survey of peasant obligations on the manor of Minchinhampton (Glos.) about 1200 records the distinction as follows: 'a free man will give his daughter in marriage after obtaining our permission but will not pay for it; the unfree will pay'.[105] Yet it was not an absolutely sure criterion of servitude, for there are cases of free men paying for permission to marry off their daughters. The levy called *gersum* on the estates of Bury St Edmunds was of this nature. It was clearly recognized as a mark of relative unfreedom even there, however, for some privileged tenants were exempt, like John Ralph of Livermere (Suffolk): 'this John holds more freely than the others, he gives his daughters without *gersum*'.[106] Moreover, the fact that merchet had been paid in some boroughs, which were otherwise havens of personal freedom, shows that the association of exemption from merchet and liberty was not exact.[107] Neither was tallage entirely easy to distinguish from numerous other kinds of payments that dependants and tenants made to their lords.

[103] *Bury Docs.*, no. 203, p. 172.
[104] Liebermann, *Gesetze* 1, p. 506 (Leis Wl 20. 3); Robertson, *Laws*, p. 262.
[105] *Caen Custumals*, p. 75.
[106] *The Kalendar of Abbot Samson*, ed. R. H. C. Davis (Camden, 3rd ser., 84; 1954), p. 6.
[107] e.g. *DB* 1, 252 (Shr. C. 5).

One of the most obvious distinctions amongst the peasant tenantry was between those who had to march off to work on the lord's farm for two or three days a week and those who did not. Although labour services in themselves, particularly the obligation to help with the ploughing and harvesting, did not imply servile status, the heavy burden of weekly work, and in particular the uncertainty of services required, could be taken as a defining feature of villeinage. It was thus important whether a peasant tenant faced this obligation at the time when villeinage was being defined. Earlier, in the first half of the twelfth century, it is clear that there was movement between labour services and money rent. It has indeed been argued that the twelfth century sees a general shift towards money rent and away from labour services, a tendency that was then reversed about 1200 as landlords saw the profits that could be made from sale of demesne produce. Although the evidence for this general tendency towards commutation to cash rent is not unequivocal, the possibility of such movement is certain and again points to the fluidity of social categories before the freezing effects of the law were felt: in the early twelfth century a *villanus* could stop being a *villanus* by paying money rent, in the thirteenth a villein was indelibly inscribed with his status.

The right to bear arms was the mark of a free man. When a master freed one of his unfree dependants, he 'should place in his hands a lance and a sword or whatever the arms of free men are'; once this is done 'then he is made a free man'.[108] In a case that occurred in 1198, the abbot of Evesham claimed that Roger son of Hubert, who lived on the abbey's Northamptonshire lands, was 'his villein who owed him servile work and servile customs' and produced Roger's three brothers and four of his cousins to testify that the family was unfree. Roger defended himself vigorously. He was no villein, he said, nor a serf nor born in villeinage and had never performed servile work or rendered servile customs to the abbot. He was a free man and bore arms according to the Assize of Arms as a free man should. Of his brothers, two had become villeins voluntarily, as they had a perfect right to do, and the third had been subject to coercion by the abbot. These four cousins were not who they claimed to be—he could produce cousins who were free men. Let a jury determine whether he were a free man or not.[109]

The case of Roger son of Hubert shows both the ambiguities of unfree status and the vigour with which personal liberty could be claimed and defended. The uncertainties about the criteria of villeinage and the line between free and unfree stem from the fact that the lawyers of the Angevin period were seeking to impose a new and inappropriate clarity on a social reality that was vast and complex. Everybody in England had limitations on

---

[108] *LHP* 78. 1 (p. 242); Liebermann, *Gesetze* 1, p. 491 (Wl. art. Lon. retr. 15); Robertson, *Laws*, p. 248.
[109] *CRR* 1, pp. 45–6, 67.

their freedom, of a sort, everybody had a superior, of a sort. The enormous expansion of royal justice under Henry II and his sons made it a newly pressing issue whether a tenant could or could not sue his lord in the king's courts. Free men could, villeins could not. That was why the question was pressed home in a way that would not have made sense a few generations earlier. The confusion stemming from Common Law villeinage has many faces: the distinction between status and tenure, so that a free man might hold villein land and hence be bound to villein services; the problems of intermarriage and the status of children of mixed marriages; the delicacy of the position eventually reached, that the villein was unfree only in relation to his master.

That there was harshness and humiliation in the lives of unfree peasants cannot be denied. In 1201 a Cornish lord 'held his serf in chains because he wished to run away'.[110] A few years later Ralph Priest, a defendant in a case that turned on villeinage status, heard William de Pinkenny, the opposing party, claim, as proof of Ralph's unfree status, that 'he had once sold one of Ralph's sisters for four shillings'.[111] To be chained, to have one's sister sold for cash, these were the legally permitted and sometimes actual consequences of villeinage. Thoughtful Christian opinion sought to distinguish serfs from true chattels: 'a Christian should not own a serf in the same way that he owns a horse or silver'.[112] Yet their chattel status was endorsed by the lawyers and must have sometimes informed the behaviour of lords and bailiffs. In an illuminating simile, the *Anchoresses' Guide* (*Ancrene Riwle*) compares the flatterer who encourages a wicked man in his evil deeds to 'one who says to the knight who robs his poor men, "Ah, sir, how well you do! The peasant [*cheorl*] ought always to be well plucked and shorn, for he is like the willow that sprouts the better the oftener it is pollarded".'[113]

If all this suggests that class relations were highly antagonistic, then it is also worth pointing out that, although magnate rebellion was recurrent in Norman and Angevin England, lower-class risings were virtually unknown. Indeed, one of the most remarkable differences between the period under discussion in this book and the later medieval period, especially the fourteenth and fifteenth centuries, is the absence of any large-scale armed peasant insurrection. Nor has collective peasant resistance of a local kind left any trace in the record. There was indeed a special place in hell for 'hired ploughmen and oxherds who plough their lords' land badly on purpose', but this implies a resistance only of the most sullen and individual kind.[114] Roger son of Hubert claimed to be a free man and he valued that freedom, but he did not seek to overthrow his lords in association with others of his class.

---

[110] *PBKJ* 2, no. 284, p. 60.    [111] *CRR* 5, p. 94.

[112] Robert of Bridlington, *The Bridlington Dialogue: An Exposition of the Rule of St Augustine for the Life of the Clergy*, ed. and tr. a religious of C.S.M.V. (London, 1960), p. 87.

[113] *Ancr. Wisse*, p. 46.    [114] *Vis. Thurkill*, p. 26.

## Peasant Rent: Three Case Studies

In the twelfth century a few enterprising landlords commissioned estate surveys that reveal in some detail the external features of English rural society: numbers of tenants, size of holdings, level of rent, etc. Three manors, from Staffordshire, Kent, and Durham, will be analysed to show both the common characteristics and the variety of peasant conditions.

Among the estates of Burton abbey surveyed in 1115 was that at Stapenhill (Staffs., formerly Derbys.), just across the Trent from the abbey. Here there was demesne arable worked by three plough-teams as well as thirty peasant tenants holding various amounts of land on diverse terms. The *villani* numbered twelve and fell into two groups, seven of them holding two bovates (something in the range of 16–33 acres) and five of them one bovate (8–16½ acres).[115] Godric the smith had the same size holding and performed the same duties as the two-bovate holders but is listed separately. Those with the larger holdings had to work on the lord's demesne for two days a week, those with the smaller holdings for one day only, but their other services were identical: to fetch salt and fish and provide a horse for the abbot's journey to court, or pay cash in lieu of these duties; to plough[116] one acre in order to be free of the obligation of fold; to plough half an acre in spring; to pay pannage, the charge the lord made for letting the tenants pasture their pigs in the woods; to render two hens at Christmas; to bring one cart-load of wood to the manor house; to go wherever sent; to make a sester (8 bushels) of malt; to plough twice a year when required to by the lord, over and above the other ploughing duties. The obligations of the *villani* thus involved a large amount of agricultural labour, in which the task of ploughing was especially emphasized, and onerous carrying duties. Renders in cash and kind were far less important.

The next tenants listed at Stapenhill are the oxherds (*bovarii*). There were four of them, each holding a bovate and working one day a week on the demesne. Their name implies that their main duty was ploughing. Alongside them were four cottagers (*cotseti*), one holding five acres carved out of the demesne and another three possessing only a house and garden. These cottagers also worked one day a week on the demesne. The last group is formed of rent-paying tenants (*censarii*), who did not have to provide weekly labour on the demesne but paid a money rent and were bound to occasional services. The largest tenant was Leving the goldsmith, holding four bovates, a croft, and a mill for 6s. 3d. and the duty of exercising his craft for the monastery without pay (but with his food provided). Here is a classic instance of a

---

[115] Burton Surveys, p. 281, gives evidence for the size of the bovate on the Burton estates.

[116] Taking *warectat* as an error for *arat*.

consumer demand that could have been met commercially, by the purchase of gold ornaments and vessels or the hiring of independent craftsmen, being provided for within the manorial system itself: the craftsman the lord employed was remunerated by a land-holding, the tenure of the holding entailed the obligation of working his craft.

In addition to Leving the goldsmith, another nine *censarii* are named. One of them is Godric the smith, who, unless he was a namesake, which seems unlikely, was the same man who held two bovates on *villanus*-terms. Clearly it was possible to hold different portions of land on different terms, although the fact that Godric was listed separately from the other *villani* may reflect ambivalence about his exact status on the part of those conducting the survey. The *censarii* rented plots of one, two, or four bovates mostly at a standard rate of 1s. 6d. per bovate, plus assorted services. Godric the smith had to maintain two ploughs. Ailwin Bishop, in addition to paying 6s. for his four bovates, had to fence four perches (40–100 feet, depending on the size of the perch) at the manor house and four perches at the wood, lend his plough twice a year, come mowing three times in August with all his household and provide a man for the hunt when required.

Another survey of Stapenhill, conducted a decade or so later, shows some of the minor changes that must always have been at work, altering the detail of the tenurial pattern. Several of the same tenants occur. Leving the goldsmith had increased his holding slightly, while Ulnod, listed under the *villani* in the earlier survey, was now holding his two bovates as a rent-payer. The oxherds are named in this second survey and their duty of tending the demesne ploughs is made explicit. The interplay of tenure and status emerges sharply in the entry for Ailwin Fretecorn, who 'in addition to the two bovates that he holds in return for labour services as a *villanus*, has a house and three acres of demesne as a cottager and for this he works one day a week.' Rent levels are unchanged in the later survey but the overall number of tenants is 10 per cent lower, with fewer one-bovate holders. This drop is found in all the Burton manors for which evidence is available and there seems no obvious explanation for it.[117]

Judged simply by the property distribution, the peasantry of Stapenhill were relatively well off by contemporary standards. Table 5 (above) shows that only on the Durham estates did small-holders (those with less than a half-virgate) form under one-quarter of the total tenantry. At Stapenhill this class formed just under 17 per cent in 1115 and just over 22 per cent in the later survey. The stratification was therefore similar to that of the reasonably well-endowed northern peasantry, with small-holders in a clear minority.

---

[117] J. F. R. Walmsley, 'The Estates of Burton Abbey from the Eleventh to the Fourteenth Centuries', Ph.D. thesis (Birmingham, 1972), p. 61.

But the material circumstances of the peasant tenants at Stapenhill were determined by their conditions of tenure as well as the amount of land they
held. Was it better to be a rent-payer with one bovate or a *villanus* with two?
By a purely economic calculation, the *villanus* holding one bovate would be
better off than the rent-payer with the same amount if his services were
actually worth less than 1s. 6d., the rent for a bovate. This is a difficult calculation to make and it is moreover clear that the dependency and subordination represented by the obligation to perform labour services, especially
regular week-work, were resented intrinsically, regardless of the value of
their wage equivalent.

If tenants might have opinions on whether they preferred to work on the
lord's farm or pay him cash, so too lords made calculations about whether
money rent or labour rent suited their interests better. In 1115 the abbot and
monks of Burton could count on 113 man-days of labour per week on their
demesne at Stapenhill, excluding the specified extra services, and also received £1. 6s. 3d. per annum in money rent from the *censarii*, again not to
mention their other services. A host of factors might influence the abbot's
decision as to whether this was the best mixture of the two elements. Our
other examples show some of these.

The Templar estate of Temple Ewell (Kent), not far from Dover, surveyed
in 1185, shows marked differences from Stapenhill.[118] The number of tenants
was larger, probably 49 (judgement has to be exercised about how many tenants with the same name were in fact identical), but their holdings were
smaller. Apart from two exceptional cases of tenures of 30 and 25 acres, none
of the tenants held more than 20 acres and the vast majority held less than 10.
A holding of a few acres was typical and many had just a garden. Special
labour services were attached to two groups of holdings: (1) a group of 49
acres, whose tenants enjoyed the very low rent of 3d. per acre but in return
faced a range of duties—heaping and transporting grain, harrowing, making
malt, salting and drying herring, making fences and sheep-folds, repairing
the barns, and fetching and carrying a variety of things, grain, salt, plough-
gear, to and from Canterbury or Dover; (2) the holdings of a small group of
seven tenants were charged with special services in the Wealden woodland
that was attached to the manor; they had to act as swineherds, summon the
special Wealden manor court, and transport the sheep-folds from place to
place when these were moved to ensure that the dung was spread evenly over
the fields. The remaining tenants paid only money rent. Rents ranged from
5d. to 16d. per acre, although the latter was quite exceptional and otherwise
12d. per acre was the highest rent. This is a much higher level than the rent-
payers of Stapenhill faced; their 1s. 6d. per bovate represents 1d.–2¼d. per

---

[118] *Templar Records*, pp. 21–4.

acre, depending on the size of the bovate, although, of course, this is 70 years earlier than the Ewell survey. The Templars drew a total rental income of £7. 1s. 6½d. from their manor.

The Stapenhill tenantry had holdings that were relatively substantial arable farms, for which about half of them had to pay money rent and about half were burdened with onerous weekly work on the demesne. At Temple Ewell the typical figure was a small-holder with a few acres or a garden, paying money rent but owing few or no labour services. The contrast may indeed be partly chronological, between the early and late twelfth century, but it is also regional—between the corn-fields of the Midlands and the enclosures, orchards, and gardens of Kent, legal—between impartible and partible inheritance practices, and institutional—between the preferences of a hungry Benedictine abbey and those of an international crusading order, eager for cash.

The final example is Boldon in County Durham, a manor of the bishop of Durham covered in the great survey of the bishop's lands undertaken in 1183.[119] Here we have a simple structure: 22 *villani*, 12 cottagers, and 2 other tenants, one a substantial freeholder paying money rent, the other holding 12 acres for the specialized duty of keeping the village pound. Each of the *villani* held 30 acres and, in return, paid a heavy rent made up of labour, cash, and kind: working three days a week on the demesne, in addition to many other specified ploughing, harrowing, and reaping duties, paying 3s. 10d. in dues and rendering oats, timber, and eggs. When St Cuthbert's Fair was held at Durham, every two of the *villani* had to construct a stall there and they might also be required to build a house 40 feet long and 15 feet wide (compare the dimensions of the peasant houses discussed above, p. 301). The cottagers each had 12 acres, for which they worked on the demesne two days a week and rendered 12 hens and 60 eggs. In addition, the whole village had to provide a customary payment of 17s., the equivalent of 6d. for each of the *villani* and cottagers. Boldon, which formed the model for many other episcopal manors, was thus an estate virtually without rent-payers, although the money payments of the Boldon *villani* were heavier than those of their namesakes at Stapenhill. The fundamental distinction in the village was between holders of 30 acres who worked three days a week on the demesne and holders of 12 acres who worked two. It would be of great interest to know what social relations between members of the two categories were, but our sources—lists of rents, holdings, and service drawn up by landlords—do not touch on such things.

---

[119] *Boldon Book, Northumberland and Durham*, ed. D. Austin (Chichester, 1982, supplementary vol. to Domesday Book, ed. John Morris), pp. 12–14.

It was the permutations of rent-level, rent-type, and size of holdings that shaped the political economy of the twelfth-century manor and village. Stapenhill, Temple Ewell, and Boldon are simply three concrete patterns from the hundreds that could be drawn. Everywhere and throughout our period lords drew on the unfree and unremunerated labour of their tenants, but also demanded of them silver pennies and Christmas chickens. There seems little doubt that the peasantry preferred to pay cash rents rather than to perform labour services, but were also willing to take on land burdened with such services if that were the only way of increasing their holdings when they had the capacity to do so. Lords might have their own reasons for demanding cash, produce, or labour. Obviously labour was only relevant when there was a functioning demesne and sometimes demesnes were small or non-existent. It is often the case that smaller or more distant manors were mainly occupied by rent-payers. The structure of the aristocratic estate, like local inheritance practices, demography, and geography, created the setting in which the majority of the English population laboured and lived their lives.

# CHAPTER 7

# Towns and Trade

## 1. URBANIZATION

Norman and Angevin England shared in the general revival of urban life that took place throughout Europe in the eleventh, twelfth, and thirteenth centuries. Urban growth meant, on the one hand, the multiplication of places where clusters of population made a living from non-agricultural activities—trading, artisanal production, and the urban services such as law, tavern-keeping, and prostitution. It also meant the creation and dissemination of new kinds of legal status and corporate identity, as the European chartered town slowly took shape. The new economic life demanded new constitutional forms.

Domesday Book lists 112 boroughs.[1] The term 'borough' itself and the allied term for those who dwelt within boroughs, 'burgesses', were new coinages in the Latin of the eleventh century. Some of these sites were older than the word used to describe them, for several were within the walls of old Roman towns, while others had their origin in the fortified towns of Anglo-Saxon England, known as *burhs*. A few had grown up around important abbeys, such as Bury St Edmunds, or were primarily coastal trading places like Southampton. Despite these diverse roots, those responsible for the Domesday survey obviously felt that they had something in common that could be summarized by the label 'borough'.

Occasionally information is given in Domesday Book that allows an estimate of town size. Derby had 100 burgesses and 40 'lesser folk'; at Cambridge there is mention of 324 occupied tenements.[2] If one assumes an average household size of 4.5, then Derby would have a population of 630, Cambridge almost 1,500. These are the smaller towns. Guesses have been made as to the number of inhabitants of the larger towns at the time of the Domesday survey, although the absence of two of the most important cities, London and Winchester, from Domesday Book makes the exercise difficult. London may

---

[1] Darby, *Domesday England*, p. 289; note also his reservations, pp. 290–1.
[2] *DB* 1, 280, 189 (Ntt. B; Cam. B).

have had 12,000 inhabitants; Winchester 6,000 or more; York, Lincoln, and Norwich 5,000 each.[3] These are tiny settlements by the standards of the modern world and even by the standards of some other eleventh-century societies—contemporary Constantinople may have had a population of 400,000—but it is clear that the boroughs of eleventh-century England were distinct from other settlements both in the relative size of their population and in their functions. Some were also clearly marked out physically. Town walls are mentioned at seven boroughs and town ditches at three others.

The growth of towns in the eleventh, twelfth, and thirteenth centuries meant both an increase in the size of existing towns and the proliferation of new ones. Between the Norman Conquest and the 1220s more than 125 planned towns were founded in England.[4] Domesday Book itself reveals new towns recently formed. The first appearance in history of Rye in Sussex is there, under the name of the manor from which it grew, *Ramesleie*: 'the abbot of Fécamp holds *Ramesleie* from the king . . . in this manor there is a new borough with 64 burgesses paying £7. 18s.' (approx. 30d. each).[5] At Bury St Edmunds Domesday Book records 'There are now 342 houses on the abbey's lands which used to be arable in the time of King Edward.'[6] This number of houses might imply an additional population of 1,500, clearly a trading and artisanal community serving both the monks of Bury and the surrounding countryside.

Forty-four years after the Domesday survey, the survival of the solitary Pipe Roll from the reign of Henry I enables another snapshot to be taken of the English urban scene. Table 6 ranks the chief cities of England according to the amount they contributed to the aid (tax) from cities and boroughs in 1130.[7] Only towns paying £15 or more are included. London dominates, paying £120, half as much again as the next most important contributor, Winchester. Below the level of Gloucester and Wallingford were another fifteen individual towns contributing smaller amounts, as well as the small boroughs of Wiltshire and Dorset, that were treated as a group. Winchcombe in Gloucestershire was assessed at £3, one-fortieth of the amount levied on London.

Most of these major towns are ports (although none is situated directly on the sea coast) or they are at important river crossings—London, of course, was both. The more important of them are episcopal sees and many are

---

[3] Darby, *Domesday England*, pp. 302–8.

[4] Maurice Beresford, *New Towns of the Middle Ages* (London, 1967), p. 328.

[5] *DB* 1, 17 (Ssx. 5. 1).    [6] *DB* 2, 372 (Sfk. 14. 167).

[7] Calculated from PR 31 HI; F. M. Maitland, *Domesday Book and Beyond* (Cambridge, 1897), p. 175; Carl Stephenson, *Borough and Town* (Cambridge, Mass., 1933), pp. 222–5.

TABLE 6.  *Towns ranked by contribution to the urban aid of 1130*

| Town | Aid paid (£) | Origin | Bishop's seat |
|---|---|---|---|
| London | 120 | Roman | √ |
| Winchester | 80 | Roman | √ |
| Lincoln | 60 | Roman | √ |
| York | 40 | Roman | √ |
| Norwich | 30 | Tenth century | √ |
| Canterbury | 20 | Roman | √ |
| Colchester | 20 | Roman | |
| Oxford | 20 | Tenth century | |
| Gloucester | 15 | Roman | |
| Wallingford | 15 | Ninth century | |

within the perimeter of an old Roman city, even if their street plans show that continuity of settlement had been broken in the Dark Ages. Places like Winchester, Colchester, and Gloucester indeed bear the mark of Roman origin in their very names—the Anglo-Saxons called a Roman city a *ceaster*. The town that drew its name most simply from *ceaster*—i.e. Chester—is, however, absent from this list, since it was part of the privileged earldom of Chester and not subject to the aid. It would doubtless otherwise have appeared. In 1086, at the time of the Domesday survey, Chester was the ninth town in England as measured by the size of the annual payment it made to the king, contributing more than either Oxford or Gloucester. Bristol and Leicester were likewise in baronial hands and do not appear on the list. Worcester, too, which was a royal town, should probably be added; the Pipe Roll account for Worcestershire in 1130 is missing.

Map 7 shows Winchester, the second city of the kingdom as measured by its taxable capacity in 1130, and one which has left richer documentation than many and been explored more rigorously archaeologically than any.[8] The Roman walls enclosed an area of 145 acres, most of which was densely covered with houses and shops. The street plan did not date back to Roman times, but had been laid out in the ninth century. Beyond the walls, along the main roads, were growing suburbs that eventually covered about 275 acres. One part of the walled city, the south-east quarter, was reserved not for townsmen and traders but for the royal and ecclesiastical establishment and its huge stone buildings—three monastic communities (one of them also the cathedral), the bishop's palace, the king's palace. Norman building programmes had marked the city. In the south-west corner a castle was built, destroying houses and lanes, while the palaces and the cathedral were extended

---

[8] For the following, see Biddle, *Winchester*.

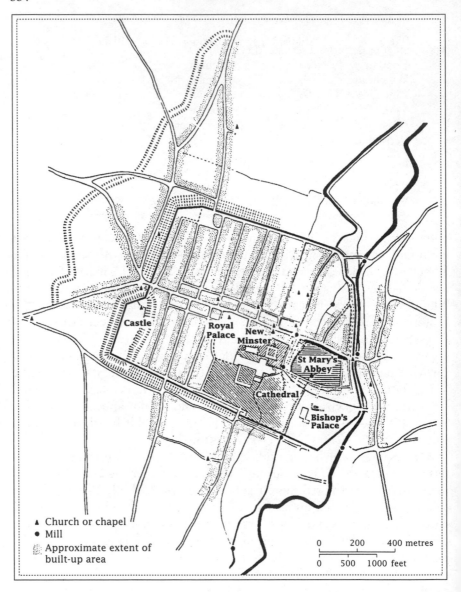

MAP 7. *Winchester around 1110*

or reconstructed. In the castle the king kept his treasure and his archives, including Domesday Book (the 'Book of Winchester' as it was also known). The new Norman cathedral, which was begun in 1079 and completed in 1093, was one of the largest buildings in western Europe. From 1110 onwards building went on at Hyde Abbey in the suburbs, where one of the city monasteries was relocated, and on the bishop's grand new palace. Outside of the town, on the adjoining down, St Giles' Fair was held annually.

Because of its importance as a royal and ecclesiastical centre, there were many royal officials, priests, and clerks who either resided in Winchester or held property there. The city was also one of the more important centres of minting in Norman England and the moneyers formed a small, specialized, and wealthy group. Their names suggest that they were of English descent and it was probably their expertise that had secured their position despite the Norman Conquest. Men like Cheping the Rich and his son Hugh, who succeeded him as a moneyer, produced their coins in small forges located in the central part of the High Street, north of the cathedral, and accumulated urban property from the profits.

Below this elite group came a wide and varied body of craftsmen: goldsmiths; tailors and dyers, weavers and fullers; blacksmiths; tanners and leather-workers; and a host of tradesmen providing food and drink—butchers, bakers, brewers, cooks, vintners, etc. As is understandable in a city with a great ecclesiastical establishment and major building programmes, there were masons, carpenters, and painters. Dozens of burgesses, like Richard of Bayeux, Geoffrey of St-Lô, and Ralph of Fougères, bore names indicating that they or their parents had come to Winchester from Normandy or other parts of northern France. These townsmen lived in the crowded streets running off the High Street, which itself formed the city's market-place, a broad thoroughfare extending half a mile across the city from the West Gate to the East Gate. The richer of them might have two-storied houses of stone, others simply shacks in the yards of the city or the sprawling suburbs. On Sundays they could worship in one of the city's fifty-seven parish churches. As a human environment and as an economic structure Winchester was distinctively urban.

## 2. TOWN LAW

The burgesses of England's boroughs had rights and duties different from those of the surrounding rural population. An early and simple example is provided by a document relating to the burgesses of Bury St Edmunds and dating to about 1135.[9] Burgesses had to pay a halfpenny for each urban plot (burgage) they occupied, guard the town, and repair the town-ditch. They need not plead at the ordinary local courts of shire or hundred but only at their own 'portemannemox'—the word means 'the court of the men of the town'. Burgage property was secure after a year and a day, i.e. no lawsuit could be raised about a burgage if it had been in someone's peaceful

---

[9] *Elenchus*, no. 25, pp. 57–8.

possession for that period, and a burgess without heirs could sell to anyone. The right and duty of self-defence, jurisdictional autonomy, streamlined property law—these formed the essence of Bury's urban regime.

These same features, but elaborated and augmented, are also to be seen in the customs of Newcastle upon Tyne that date originally from the time of Henry I.[10] Lawsuits are to be determined within the borough and burgage property is secure after a year and a day. There is to be free alienability of land. Moreover, any peasant (*rusticus*) living in the borough is free after a year and a day—a provision encapsulated in the later proverb 'town air makes you free'. Burgesses are to be immune from trial by battle, are not to be fined more than six *oras* (8s.) for any offence and need not pay merchet, heriot, nor the other encumbrances of serfdom, nor are they subject to the seigneurial monopolies—each burgess may have an oven and handmill. Finally, and this is the solitary commercial provision in the code, only burgesses are to buy merchandise within the town.

The essence of the town law that developed in England as in other parts of Europe was freedom. The urban plot that the burgess possessed was a 'free burgage', with a low, fixed cash rent and liberal provisions for sale and inheritance. This freedom was also personal: town air could make a villein free. Certain commercial freedoms were also included, notably exemption from tolls. Tolls were internal customs duties that were levied on goods in transit at all the obvious bottlenecks—town-gates, bridges, harbours—and at fairs and markets. Exemption from toll thus gave an immediate commercial advantage by lessening the seller's costs and increasing his potential profit. A lord could only free burgesses from the obligation to pay toll within his own lands and hence the most valued and wide-reaching exemption was that offered by the king. In 1190 Richard I granted the merchants of Winchester comprehensive exemption 'from toll and lastage [a due charged per load] and pontage [bridge-toll], within fairs and outside them, and through all the ports of the sea of all our lands, this side of the sea and beyond'.[11]

Within this general framework of urban law, individual towns might develop a distinctive pattern of rights and duties that marked them out. The customs of a particular town could then serve as the model for newly created boroughs. In the early 1140s, for example, the burgesses of Coventry were granted the laws and customs of citizens of Lincoln.[12] When the prospering port of Lynn (King's Lynn) was granted borough status in 1204, its burgesses were given free choice of a model: 'the lord king granted that we should chose a borough in England, whichever we willed, and then that our town of Lynn should have the same liberties as that town has, and we have

---

[10] *Elenchus*, no. 22, pp. 53–4.      [11] Ibid., no. 57, p. 96.
[12] *The Early Records of Medieval Coventry*, ed. Peter Coss (London, 1986), no. 11, pp. 18–19.

chosen Oxford.'[13] It was not always important centres like Lincoln and Oxford that served this function, however. Many towns on the Welsh Marches, as well as in Wales and Ireland itself, based their juridical arrangements on the obscure Norman town of Breteuil. Brought to Hereford by William fitz Osbern, who was both lord of Breteuil and earl of Hereford, the laws of Breteuil spread west with the Anglo-Normans. There are even cases of urban law being bestowed on non-burgesses. Henry II granted 'the canons of St Paul's, Bedford, and their men all the liberties that the burgesses of Bedford have' (Bedford's burgesses in turn having the customs of Oxford).[14]

## 3. URBAN SELF-GOVERNMENT

There was no original conflict of interest between townsmen and feudal lords. Lords were willing to foster urban growth on their land because of the profits it brought. Even at the outset, the charter establishing the new town's rights would have to be paid for. The Angevin kings did not issue their charters for free and nor did their barons. In 1194 Roger de Lacy granted a generous charter to his burgesses of Pontefract, but they paid him £200 for doing so.[15] Once established, towns would produce a revenue, in the form of burgage rents, tolls, and the profits of justice, far higher than the same area could generate from purely agricultural profits. It was the opinion of the monks of Bury at the end of the twelfth century that 'the revenues and returns of all the good towns and boroughs of England were growing and increasing, to the profit of their owners and the enrichment of their lords' and their opinion was well founded.[16]

An example of how towns could enrich lords is provided by Stratford-upon-Avon. In the twelfth century it was a rural manor belonging to the bishop of Worcester, inhabited by 42 villeins and a few small-holders, who paid money rent and provided labour services. There was a smithy and a very profitable mill. In 1196, by an act of lordly *fiat*, a borough was created at Stratford. There was to be a weekly market and standard burgage holdings paying a shilling per annum as rent. The burgesses were freed from toll. This set of privileges proved sufficient to generate an entirely new type of settlement on the site. Within fifty years Stratford was a market town of about 1,000 inhabitants, mainly artisans and others offering specialized services for the surrounding countryside. Burgage rents alone brought in about £12 a year. Since a comparable area of farmland would provide a rent of only 16*s*., the bishop's income merely from rental had been increased fifteen fold.[17]

---

[13] *Borough Charters*, p. 32.    [14] *Rec. actes Hen. II* 2, no. 706, p. 330; *Borough Charters*, p. 8.
[15] *EYC* 3, no. 1523, pp. 209–11.    [16] Joc. Brak., p. 77.
[17] E. M. Carus-Wilson, 'The First Half-Century of the Borough of Stratford-upon-Avon', *Economic History Review*, 2nd ser., 18 (1965), pp. 46–63.

As a town belonging to a bishop, Stratford was among the minority of English boroughs that had an ecclesiastical lord. In the mid-thirteenth century 40 per cent of boroughs were royal, 35 per cent baronial, and only 25 per cent ecclesiastical.[18] Moreover, not only did the king have more boroughs than other lords but he was lord of virtually all the major towns, the only notable exceptions being Leicester, in the hands of the earl of Leicester, Chester, held by the earl of Chester, and Durham, under its bishop. Bristol was the most valuable property of the earls of Gloucester in the first half of the twelfth century, but the king was not willing to concede it completely. By garrisoning Bristol castle and granting the citizens of Bristol a royal charter, Henry II ensured that this important trading town did not drift completely into the earls' control.[19] The marriage of his son John to the heiress of the earldom brought the town into royal hands, where it remained.

The royal hand was heavy and English towns never achieved the level of autonomy that some of the cities of continental Europe attained. They did, however, evolve the institutions and offices of a more limited urban self-government. From Anglo-Saxon times boroughs had possessed courts separate from those of the counties in which they lay and this juridical autonomy continued and developed in the Norman and Angevin period. Although cases of serious crime were reserved to royal justices, the borough courts had extensive civil jurisdiction. Sometimes forms of procedure in the towns differed from those of the nascent Common Law. In many circumstances, for instance, burgesses continued to be able to clear themselves by swearing an oath, rather than through juries.

Alongside this jurisdictional autonomy there developed an equally important financial autonomy. This was often the decisive spur to urban self-government. Towns owed their lords payments from burgage rents, tolls, the profits of justice, etc. and it was common practice for these various and fluctuating sums to be compounded by one fixed payment, 'the farm of the borough'. If the townsmen themselves took responsibility for ensuring the payment of the borough farm, then they simultaneously entered into a collective relationship with their lord and had perforce to make arrangements for the money to be raised and paid, thus stimulating institutional development. If the lord granted the burgesses the right to deal in this way perpetually or heritably ('in fee farm'), then he was permanently forswearing the right to control the everyday details of urban finances and indeed forcing the townsmen to manage an important aspect of town life themselves.

Lincoln was an important city that was willing to pay for the right to run

[18] Maurice Beresford and H. P. R. Finberg, *English Medieval Boroughs: A Handlist* (Newton Abbot, 1973), pp. 40–6.
[19] *Gloucester Charters*, p. 4.

its own affairs. In 1130 the burgesses of Lincoln offered the king 20 marks of silver and four marks of gold 'so that they might hold their city of the king in chief'—i.e. directly of the Crown, like a baron.[20] The annual farm of the borough was £180 and this payment to the king in 1130 is the approximate equivalent of one-quarter of the annual payment. The arrangement was confirmed early in his reign by Henry II, who issued a charter announcing that 'I have delivered my city of Lincoln to the citizens of that city for the "farm" that was customary in the time of king Henry my grandfather', and his son, Richard I, made this situation hereditary.[21] Similarly, Alan, earl of Richmond (1136–46), granted to his burgesses of Richmond the borough of Richmond 'perpetually . . . in fee farm, paying me each year £29'.[22] Permanent arrangements of this kind made it inevitable that the burgesses would develop a collective organization. It is not surprising that the earliest English municipal seal dates to 1191, for a municipal seal was a visible sign of the new corporate identity that towns were creating.[23]

Urban corporations developed all the more naturally because town dwellers were familiar with collective organization for a variety of purposes. There had been guilds, associations formed for mutual aid, religious acts, and drinking, in the towns of Anglo-Saxon England. The Cambridge guild statutes of about 1000 provide for the funeral expenses of members, religious duties, and aid when a member was ill or the victim of fire.[24] Such guilds had common property. The very first folio of Domesday Book mentions that Dover had its 'guildhall of the burgesses', while Winchester had its hall 'where the good men of Winchester used to drink their guild'.[25]

Guilds were originally 'assemblies of drinkers' and continued to be so.[26] They developed many other facets too, however, including the pursuit of economic interests. The craft guilds, associations of those practising a given trade in a particular town, were not only friendly societies but also coalitions dedicated to the exclusion of outsiders. If town law was marked by freedom, urban organizations insisted that this freedom was for members only. The weavers' guild at London, which existed at least from the time of Henry I, paid the king for the right to have a guild and enjoyed a local monopoly of practising the trade.[27] Weavers seem to have organized particularly early and the Pipe Roll of 1130 mentions weavers' guilds at Oxford, Winchester, Huntingdon, and Lincoln, as well as London, in addition to a guild of cordwainers

[20] PR 31 HI, p. 114.     [21] *Elenchus*, no. 41, p. 74; *Borough Charters*, p. 221.
[22] *EYC* 4, no. 20, p. 22.
[23] James Tait, *The Medieval English Borough* (Manchester, 1936), p. 235.
[24] B. Thorpe (ed.), *Diplomatarium Anglicum Aevi Saxonici* (London, 1865), pp. 610–13.
[25] *Winton Domesday* 2. 712, ed. Frank Barlow, in Biddle, *Winchester*, p. 120; cf. ibid. 1. 10, p. 34.
[26] Gerald, *V. Geoffrey* 2. 8 (p. 404).     [27] *Elenchus*, no. 42, pp. 74–5.

at Oxford and (by implication) a guild of fullers at Winchester.[28] Craft guilds had their own officials and revenues. The guild of bakers that was authorized at Bury St Edmunds by the abbot, the lord of the town, in the 1170s had an alderman at its head and took a share in the fines paid by those who breached its monopoly or by members who baked poor bread.[29]

The guild that was to have the most formative role in shaping the self-governing town of the twelfth and thirteenth centuries was the guild merchant, an association of the town's merchants and chief burgesses that was often indistinguishable from the governing body of the town. There was one at Leicester as early as the reign of William I and one at Oxford before 1107.[30] The first mention of a guild merchant at Winchester is in a charter of Henry II dating to the first years of his reign.[31] By then they were common in English towns. Grants of trading privileges were sometimes made to the members of the guild merchant rather than to the burgesses, although the distinction was not an easy one to make, as is illustrated by the fact that, in 1147, a charter could be issued by 'the citizens of Oxford of the community of the city and the guild merchant'.[32] The phrasing does not encourage townsmen and guildsmen to be differentiated. Membership of the guild could indeed be viewed as a sign of the right to full participation in the privileges of the town. The serf did not become free simply by living in a town for a year and a day; he had to live there 'in such a way that he is received into their commune, i.e. guild, as a citizen'.[33]

A particularly full account of the formation of a self-governing town happens to survive for Ipswich.[34] On 25 May 1200, in return for a payment of 100 marks (£66. 13s. 4d.), king John issued a charter granting the borough of Ipswich to the burgesses of Ipswich hereditarily for the annual farm.[35] They were exempted from toll, given juridical autonomy, allowed to form a guild merchant, and, in general, granted 'all the free customs' enjoyed by 'the other burgesses of our free boroughs of England'. The king also permitted the burgesses to elect, from among their own number and 'by the common counsel of the town', two town bailiffs and four coroners.

The month after the charter was issued, on Thursday, 29 June, the whole body of townsmen assembled in the churchyard of the church of St Mary-le-Tower and chose John, son of Norman, and William de Belines as bailiffs of

---

[28] PR 31 HI, pp. 2, 5, 37, 48, 109, 144.     [29] Bury Docs., no. 166, p. 149.
[30] Records of the Borough of Leicester 1, ed. Mary Bateson (London, 1899), no. 1, p. 1; Elenchus, no. 21, pp. 52–3.
[31] Sel. Charters, p. 196.     [32] Elenchus, no. 34, pp. 66–7.
[33] Glanvill 5. 5 (p. 58).
[34] Elenchus, no. 62, pp. 103–7; the reference to 'the feast of the translation of St Thomas the Martyr' proves that the text must have been composed after 1220, but this does not invalidate its account.
[35] PR 2 John, p. 148; Elenchus, no. 61, pp. 101–2.

Ipswich. The two men swore to undertake their office dutifully and to treat both rich and poor well and honestly. The same two, along with two others, were then chosen as coroners. So far the assembly had simply followed the requirements of John's charter. Now, however, it was decided that there should also be twelve 'chief portmen' (*capitales portmanni*) 'as there are in other free boroughs of England, and they should have full power to govern and defend the borough and the liberties of the borough, to render judgment in the town and to ordain and do in the borough everything that might be for the good state and honour of the town'. The meeting was then adjourned until the following Sunday, when the election of the 'chief portmen' would take place.

On that day, 2 July 1200, the whole body of townsmen gathered in the churchyard again and it was agreed that the bailiffs and coroners would chose four honest men from each parish in the town (there were more than a dozen parishes in Ipswich) and this electoral college would then chose the twelve portmen. The portmen who were then elected included all the recently selected bailiffs and coroners as well as eight others, and they all swore to govern well and fairly, while the townsmen swore to obey the new town government and protect the town's liberties. Arrangements were made for the safe keeping of the royal charter and a day assigned for the first meeting of the bailiffs, coroners, and portmen. This took place on Thursday, 13 July. There the details of the new administration were planned. Four men were to assist the bailiffs in collecting the dues from the town and paying the farm to the royal Exchequer. Two beadles were to be sworn in, with the power to make arrests and enforce the orders of the town officials. A town seal was to be made and entrusted to a group of leading burgesses. A schedule was agreed for the election of an alderman to head the guild merchant and a group of four burgesses to help him. The new charter was to be read out in the county courts of Norfolk and Suffolk to ensure the widest possible publicity for the new rights of the men of Ipswich.

This busy programme was completed by two further meetings of the townsmen. At the first, on Sunday, 10 September, all the new ordinances and arrangements were read out and approved, the bailiffs were re-elected and the four collectors of dues and the two beadles were chosen. At the second, on Thursday, 12 October, the bailiffs showed the new seal to the community. It was entrusted to a group of three (including John, son of Norman, and William de Belines), who were also given charge of the charter. They swore not to abuse the seal. Then the alderman of the guild merchant and his four associates were elected. They announced that 'all who had the liberty of the town' should come on a certain day to place themselves in the guild and pay the entry fee. Events concluded with the grant of a meadow to the portmen, as recompense for their efforts, and the drawing up of two rolls, one containing the laws and customs of the town, the other the statutes of the guild merchant, the former to be kept by the bailiffs, the latter by the alderman of the guild.

In this way, over the course of the summer months of the year 1200, a new urban government was created. It had revenues, specialized officials, coercive power, and legal identity. Its charter and the roll containing its laws (nick-named *le Domesday*) were the nucleus of an archive and the foundations of its authority. A characteristic dualism between town and guild merchant created parallel institutions, but ones that were in the same hands—the alderman and four councillors of the guild merchant were all also portmen. Officials, councillors, and townsmen were bound together by oaths. A small group ran both town and guild. Talk of 'the good state and honour of the town' suggests a note of urban pride; promises to treat both rich and poor alike are a re-minder that 'free boroughs' were more free for some than others.

## 4. LONDON

When he granted his charter to the burgesses of Ipswich, king John explicitly protected the 'liberties and free customs of the citizens of London'. London was special, in its size, significance, and self-conceit. 'Among the noble cities of the world that are celebrated by fame,' wrote William fitz Stephen at the beginning of his laudation of the city, 'the city of London, the seat of the king-dom of England, is one that spreads its name more widely, sends its wealth and merchandise further afield and raises its head more high.' London's pre-eminence was indisputable. Its citizens were termed 'barons'. Even the Welsh chronicle, the *Brut y Tywysogyon*, called it 'the head and crown of all the kingdom of England'.[36]

The core of London was the area of 330 acres enclosed within the Roman walls, but housing beyond the walls and the existence of adjacent or nearby settlements at Southwark, Westminster, and elsewhere created a population cluster that had no parallel in the British Isles. A central role was played by London Bridge, the lowest crossing point of the Thames. Along the river, be-tween the Tower on the east and St Paul's on the west, were the quays and moorings that made London a major seaport. In the streets behind lay busy markets, workshops, and a hundred parish churches. Although the walls were Roman, the street plan dated from the Anglo-Saxon period and centred on the two main market areas of West Cheap (Cheapside) and East Cheap, the names representing the Old English *ceape*, 'market'.

The chief authorities in London in the twelfth century were the sheriffs and aldermen. The office of sheriff of London, which was amalgamated with

---

[36] *Brut (RBH)*, p. 41.

that of Middlesex, was usually held by more than one person: in 1129–30 there were four sheriffs, for most of the 1160s two. Moreover, in the first half of the century there were, alongside the sheriffs, local justices. These men represented royal authority over the city and had important judicial and financial responsibilities, such as presiding over meetings of the weekly hustings court and arranging payment of the annual farm. At a more local level, as early as the reign of Henry I, and probably earlier, there was also a network of wards under the aldermen. Eventually there were to be twenty-four wards, each with an alderman, and it is likely that this arrangement dated from early times. These aldermen were members of the city elite but then so too were most of the sheriffs and justices of London. The city was not ruled by outsiders, foisted on to London by a suspicious royal government, but by local grandees. Their horizons were, however, wide. The London elite of wealth and power comprised families that were associated with both the city and the royal administration and that accumulated property both within and outside the city. The Cornhills, Blunds, and Bucuintes ('Oily Mouths'), who each provided at least three sheriffs of London in this period, were not only money-lenders, landlords, and sometimes aldermen within the city, but also frequently officials of the royal household and lords of manors.

In 1130 the Londoners offered 100 marks (£66. 13s. 4d.) 'to have sheriffs of their own choice' and, although it is not clear how long the arrangement lasted, it is good evidence that they, like the men of Lincoln or Ipswich, were interested in, and willing to pay for, guaranteed self-government.[37] They were assisted in winning this goal by their political importance. The largest and wealthiest town in the country could obviously take advantage of factionalism or royal weakness to bargain for its terms. It seems to have done so in Stephen's reign, accepting him as king and providing vital financial and military support for him in return for recognition of its corporate autonomy. In 1191, after a long period of reduced expectations, the citizens of London again took the opportunity offered by political disputes, on this occasion those stimulated by king Richard's absence, and established a commune, that is, a corporate body whose members were bound together by a solemn oath. Urban communes were common in parts of continental Europe and these sometimes developed into powerful semi-autonomous city-states, but their formation in England had hitherto been repressed by the Angevin kings. Henry II's justices fined the burgesses who tried to form communes at Gloucester and York in the 1170s.[38]

Conservative ecclesiastical observers were aghast at this development in London: 'a commune means commotion of the common people, consternation of the kingdom, contempt of the priesthood'.[39] Achieved in a moment of

[37] PR 31 HI, p. 148.    [38] PR 16 HII, p. 79; PR 22 HII, p. 106.    [39] R. Devizes, p. 49.

monarchical weakness, the corporate identity of London was to endure nevertheless. It was symbolized by the new office of mayor. The first holder, Henry fitz Ailwin, was an experienced city alderman and the son and grandson of aldermen whose English names proclaimed their membership of the old native city elite. Henry held office from 1191 until his death in 1212. It was probably during this time that the first city seal was made.[40] Soon after Henry fitz Ailwin's death, king John was induced to grant his 'barons of the city of London' all their ancient liberties and the right to elect a mayor annually.[41] This privilege was negotiated during the troubles of 1215 and the special weight of London emerges yet again in the provisions of Magna Carta in that year: no 'aid' was to be levied from London without common consent; the city was to have 'all its ancient liberties and its free customs'; the destruction of fish-weirs on the Thames, specified in clause 33, reiterated an ancient concern of the Londoners that river traffic not be impeded; the mayor of London, fitz Ailwin's successor, Serlo the Mercer, was the only non-baronial figure among the group of Twenty-five who were to supervise the proper execution of Magna Carta. The pursuit of London's autonomy and the programme of liberties for the kingdom as a whole had become entwined.

## 5. URBAN UNREST

Urban riots were infrequent under the Norman and Angevin kings and rarely of political significance. One of the more dramatic urban disturbances of the period was that associated with the name of William fitz Osbern, a citizen of London who took up the role of 'the advocate of the poor'.[42] The rich citizens of London, he argued, had managed to evade the heavy taxation of the 1190s and to impose the burden instead on the impoverished. 'I am the saviour of the poor,' he preached. 'You poor people have felt the heavy hand of the rich; now draw from my fountain the waters of saving doctrine . . . for the time of your visitation is coming . . . I shall divide the humble and faithful people from the proud and faithless . . .' Fitz Osbern was clearly a demagogue of great talent. A striking figure, with the long beard he cultivated and that gave him the nickname 'the Bearded', he had received a formal education, been on crusade, and attained civic office in London.[43] Even in the eyes of a critic he was 'sharp-witted, lettered to a degree, extraordinarily eloquent, with a kind of inborn heedlessness of mind and manners that made him eager to make a great name for himself'.

---

[40] James Tait, *The Medieval English Borough* (Manchester, 1936), p. 236.

[41] *Elenchus*, no. 68, p. 115.

[42] The fullest source is W. Newb. 5. 20–1 (2, pp. 466–73); see also R. Howd. 4, pp. 5–6; R. Diceto, *Ymag.* 2, pp. 143–4.

[43] *Gesta Hen. II* 2, p. 116, establishes that he was on the Third Crusade.

In the spring of 1196 Fitz Osbern became the acknowledged leader of the poor Londoners. He addressed meetings with his stirring rhetoric, travelled with a great crowd to protect him, and initiated, according to one source, 'a powerful conspiracy, inspired by the zeal of the poor against the insolence of the rich'. Rumours spread that he had 52,000 supporters, that stocks of house-breaking equipment had been prepared, to break into the houses of the wealthy citizens. Fitz Osbern was careful not to direct his actions against the king and made a point of going to Normandy to put his case before Richard and assert his loyalty. On his return, the chief justiciar, Hubert Walter, arch-bishop of Canterbury, decided that, whatever the king's personal views, Fitz Osbern had to be suppressed. First, he secured hostages from the Londoners. Then two well-born citizens of London were commissioned to seize Fitz Os-bern when the crowds that usually surrounded him were absent. In the strug-gle that followed Fitz Osbern killed one of those sent to arrest him and then took refuge in Bow Church. Hubert Walter was obviously not interested in half-measures. He surrounded the church with armed men and ordered it set on fire. As he rushed out from the flames and smoke, Fitz Osbern was stabbed and wounded. Swiftly condemned by the royal court, he was dragged by horses to the gallows at Tyburn and hanged with nine of his companions.

Even after these drastic coercive measures, Fitz Osbern enjoyed a posthu-mous popularity. His followers called him a martyr, while a priest who was re-lated to him took around the chain in which his body had been hanged, performing miraculous cures. The gallows itself was secretly taken away to be venerated, while the number of those seeking earth from the spot where he died—'as if it had been consecrated by the hanged man's blood'—was so great that their excavations eventually created a deep pit. Again, Hubert Wal-ter took decisive action. An armed force was sent to disperse the crowd that habitually gathered at the site of Fitz Osbern's execution and soldiers were left on guard there, while the priest with the miraculous chain was subjected to ecclesiastical discipline. Only now, in the words of the hostile commenta-tor, William of Newburgh, 'did the edifice of superstition collapse and the popular movement subside'.

The events of spring 1196 show that urban popular unrest could reach such threatening proportions that the royal government would have recourse to immediate and ruthless repression. Yet incidents of this kind were un-usual. Whatever the social tensions in the profoundly unequal and hierarch-ical world of twelfth-century England, they scarcely ever found expression in coordinated lower-class rebellion. Kings needed to be careful of their aristo-crats, but king and aristocracy as a class faced no armed challenge of a kind to be found in other periods of history. English towns were unruly and un-healthy places, but they offered no fundamental challenge to the distribution of political and social power.

## 6. THE JEWS

### Numbers and Distribution

One distinctive feature of the larger towns of Norman and Angevin England was the presence of Jews. This was new. At the time of the Norman Conquest in 1066 there was no resident Jewish community in England, and there had not been one since the days of the Roman Empire. Rouen, however, chief city of the Norman dukes, had a significant and active Jewish population and, during the reign of William I, these Norman Jews came to London, establishing a Jewish presence that would last until 1290, when all Jews were expelled from England. Throughout the two centuries of its existence English medieval Jewry remained Francophone and was closely linked with northern French Jewry.

There is no evidence for Jewish settlement outside London before the 1140s, but in the second half of the twelfth century Jewish communities, even if perhaps small ones, are recorded at more than twenty sites in England. The contribution they made to royal taxes is probably an indication of their relative size and wealth and Figure 11 charts the amount that was levied on each community in 1194 (York, which would otherwise be expected to occupy second place, does not appear in the list because of the pogrom of 1190).[44]

The 21 places in this list of 1194 can be compared with the 17 mentioned in a comparable tax document of 1221.[45] The towns that recur among the top ten communities on the two lists (if we reinstate York) are London, York, Lincoln, Canterbury, Northampton, Winchester, and Norwich. Significant Jewish settlement could thus be found in all the more important urban centres, including both ancient royal and ecclesiastical cities, like Winchester and Canterbury, and the more recent and more purely mercantile towns, such as Norwich. By the later twelfth century, Jews were settled in English towns as far north as York and as far west as Exeter.

Numbers were low. It is impossible to establish an exact figure for the size of the Jewish population of medieval England, but an informed guess is that it was probably less than 5,000 at its maximum about the year 1200.[46] Since Jewish communities in any given town were small, they tended to keep in close contact with those in other towns and there seems to have been considerable geographical mobility, Jews moving from one town to another, either

---

[44] 'The Northampton "Donum" of 1194', ed. Israel Abrahams, JHSE, *Miscellanies* 1 (1925), pp. lix–lxxiv.

[45] Helena M. Chew, 'A Jewish Aid to Marry A.D. 1221', *Trans. JHSE* 11 (1928, for 1924–7), pp. 92–111.

[46] Vivian D. Lipman, 'Anatomy of Medieval Anglo-Jewry', *Trans. JHSE* 21 (1968), pp. 64–77, at pp. 64–5.

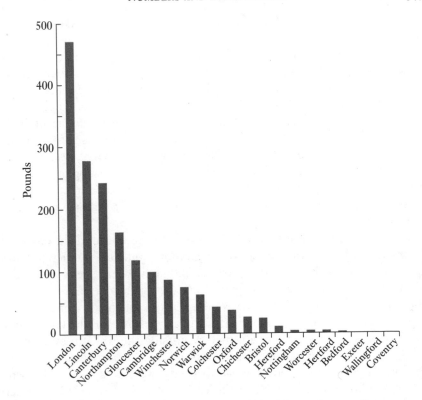

FIGURE 11. *Contributions of Jewish communities to the tax of 1194*

temporarily or permanently. During this period there were no ghettos, in the sense of circumscribed or walled areas within which Jews were forced to live, but Jewish settlement in any given town tended to cluster naturally in certain areas, called Jewries. That in London lay in the heart of the city between Cheapside and Catte Street (now Gresham Street). The existence in this area of a series of neighbouring properties, each owned by Jews, is shown in a document of 1226, whereby Samson, the son of Isaac, granted to Abraham his son a plot 'in the parish of St Lawrence in Jewry . . . lying between the land that belonged to Abraham, the son of Avigai, to the east, and the land of Judah of Warwick, to the west, and stretching from the king's highway to the synagogue'.[47] As is also clear from this passage, not only was the chief Jewish synagogue located in this area, as one would expect, but even the local Christian church had adopted the identifying tag 'in Jewry'. The modern street name Old Jewry perpetuates the memory of this long lost Jewish community settled within earshot of the busiest market in England.

[47] Richardson, *Jewry*, p. 241.

Jewish communities had some degree of autonomy. Lawsuits between Jews could be decided without reference to outsiders. The Jews were considered a 'commune' or corporate entity and dealings with the authorities could be channelled through their leaders. There is even reference to a 'chapter of the Jews', a body that could apparently define Jewish law.[48] The essential physical adjuncts of Jewish community life were the synagogue and the cemetery. The earliest written evidence for the existence of Jewish synagogues in England is the reference by the monk Gervase of Canterbury to the Jews in Canterbury in 1188 'praying in synagogues', but it is inconceivable that the London Jews had not had a synagogue very much earlier.[49] The document of 1226 cited above refers to the Great Synagogue of the London Jewry, situated at that time in Ironmonger Lane off Cheapside.

Jews were buried in their own cemeteries, located beyond the city-walls. At first the only burying ground was in London, outside Cripplegate, and all English Jews were brought there for burial, like Eleazar ('Deus-adiuvet') of Norwich, whose corpse was carried from Norwich to London for burial about 1146 or the son of Moses of Wallingford, transported from Oxford to London on a wheeled cart about 1180.[50] In 1177, however, the king granted permission for Jews 'to have a cemetery outside the walls in every city in England'.[51] The Jews of York quickly took advantage of this and established their burial ground just north-west of the city-walls, at a site still known as Jewbury. This was excavated in the early 1980s and revealed an orderly array of what were probably in total a thousand burials, in plain coffins of pine or oak. No tombstones were found, but wooden markers may have been used. Examination of the skeletons resulted in some interesting conclusions about the Jewish population. Its total size at any one time was about 250. When compared with human remains from contemporary non-Jewish cemeteries in York, the Jews showed some distinctive genetic features— Jewish men tended to be shorter than Christian men and the skull shape of the Jews tended to be different. Given that they were both immigrant and endogamous, it is not surprising that there were identifiable physical differences of this kind. Moreover, Jewish women seemed to have lived longer than their Christian counterparts—a phenomenon perhaps to be explained by the reasonably well established fact that the Jewish family tended to be smaller and consequently the dangers of childbirth were encountered less often.

---

[48] PR 3 RI, p. 98.     [49] Gerv. Cant., p. 405.
[50] T. Monm., *V. William* 2. 13 (p. 98); Philip, *Mir. Fridesw.* 39 (p. 577).
[51] *Gesta Hen. II* 1, p. 182; R. Howd. 2, p. 137.

## Economic Activities

The primary economic activity of the Jewish community in medieval England was moneylending. It is possible to find stray references to Jews engaged in other activities—selling wine, acting as doctors, serving as crossbowmen, like 'the Jew Abraham the Crossbowman', to whom king John granted a house (formerly occupied by another Jewish family) in Canterbury in 1215.[52] Nevertheless, because they were debarred, *de facto* or *de jure*, from many other occupations, it was financial dealings that proved the main means of livelihood for the medieval English Jewish community. The Rouen Jews who came to England in the Conqueror's reign presumably brought their capital with them.

There were plenty of customers. At every social level, from the king down, the ready supply of cash that could be obtained from Jewish lenders was welcome, to supplement or anticipate revenue, to increase consumption, or to fend off disaster. The earliest available documentation, in the Pipe Roll of 1130, shows the Jews of London as creditors of the earl of Chester and of Richard fitz Gilbert, head of the great baronial family of Clare, and there is evidence throughout the period that the highest ranks of the aristocracy might need or wish to borrow.[53] While he was royal chancellor, Thomas Becket borrowed 500 marks ($£333. 6s. 8d.$) from a Jewish lender to help him pay for his expenses in the campaign against Toulouse in 1159.[54] As might be expected from the nature of the sources, there is very little surviving evidence for borrowing at the humblest level, although the general indications are that there were poor Jews engaged in pawnbroking and lending of small amounts. The loans that were recorded are primarily to landowners, including lesser landowners and religious houses.

Jews were permitted to take movable property as a gage or surety for their loans, with the exception of certain types of object. According to the Assize of Arms of 1181, mail-coats that came into their possession could not be retained but must be sold or otherwise disposed of, 'so that they may continue to be in the king's service'.[55] Blood-stained clothing could not be accepted as a pledge—for obvious reasons. Nor, in principle, could church property.[56] Hard pressed ecclesiastics might choose to ignore this restriction, however. When bishop Nigel of Ely had difficulty in raising money in the 1140s, he pawned a bejewelled gold cross and an ancient gospel book to the Jews of Cambridge.[57] Nigel's indebtedness was, in fact, chronic, for it was not until the last year of his life (he died in 1169) that he extricated himself from debt to Jewish moneylenders, with the help of his son, then royal treasurer.[58]

---

[52] Richardson, *Jewry*, pp. 26–7; *Rot. litt. claus.* 1, p. 220.     [53] PR 31 HI, pp. 53, 148–9.
[54] W. f. Stephen, *V. Thomas* 42 (pp. 53–4).     [55] *Gesta Hen. II* 1, p. 279; R. Howd. 2, p. 261.
[56] *Rot. chart.*, p. 93.     [57] *Lib. Eliensis* 3. 50, 92 (pp. 290, 339).     [58] PR 14 HII, p. 222.

Jewish rights over land are a more complicated issue. There is no doubt that urban property was being conveyed to Jews 'in fee and heredity', to hold perpetually in return for rent, from the first half of the twelfth century. About 1140 the canons of St Paul's, London, granted the land in the city that had previously been held from them by the Christians Alric Parole and Osbert the Smith to two Jews, Benedict and Abraham, son of Simon, to be held by them and their heirs 'as freely and peaceably and honourably as any of their other tenants in the city'.[59] Town houses can be found in Jewish possession right down to the time of the expulsion. Rural land was apparently treated differently, for, although Jewish lenders could accept manors and arable holdings as a surety for loans, and, if the debtor defaulted, could enter into lawful possession of them and let them or sell them to other Christians, they could not apparently hold them themselves 'in fee and heredity'. One law case of 1220 turned on the plea that 'Isaac is a Jew and does not have land in fee'.[60] Jews thus controlled the fortunes of many manors but did not themselves reside in the manor houses as lords.

The best attested effect of Jewish moneylending on the land market was thus not the direct occupation of land by Jews, but the stimulus it gave to the circulation of land from deeply indebted borrowers to other Christians who would clear their debts in return for their land. Those with cash could thus take advantage of the difficulties of those without. In 1223 Peter fitz Alulf granted to Eustace, bishop of London, 40 acres in Acton at a nominal rent, in return for which the bishop settled Peter's debt of 10 marks ($£6. 13s. 4d.$) to Aaron, son of Abraham. A Hebrew quittance is attached to the Latin document recording this transaction.[61] Religious houses were often able to invest in encumbered estates. The abbey of Meaux in Yorkshire acquired property from the heavily indebted baron, William Fossard, in this way. 'He owed more than 1,800 marks ($£1,200$) to the Jews,' records the abbey chronicle, 'and had gaged lands to them. Because of this the total of his debts increased daily and put in jeopardy everything he had. William therefore asked Philip, our abbot, to accept a portion of his lands and undertake to clear his debts.' The chronicler goes on to complain of the various legal entanglements that came in the wake of this arrangement, but there is no doubt that Fossard property ended up in the monks' possession.[62]

Jewish business and judicial documents, known as 'starrs' (ultimately from the Hebrew 'sheṭar', plural 'sheṭaroth'), survive in some quantity from

---

[59] Michael Adler, 'Medieval Jewish Manuscripts in the Library of St Paul's Cathedral, London', JHSE, *Miscellanies* 3 (1937), pp. 15–33, at pp. 17–20.

[60] *CRR* 9, p. 24.

[61] Adler, 'Medieval Jewish Manuscripts', pp. 15–33, at pp. 25–8.

[62] *Chronica monasterii de Melsa*, ed. E. A. Bond (3 vols., RS; 1866–8), vol. 1, pp. 173–8; Richardson, *Jewry*, pp. 89–90.

twelfth- and thirteenth-century England and deal with a variety of matters, especially acquittance of debt. The records of the Exchequer of the Jews, discussed below, show such starrs in use. In 1218, for example, Thomas de Mara claimed that he was discharged of all his debts that the Jew Copin of Oxford had taken over from Isaac, son of Moses, producing a 'starr of quittance' that stated he was free of all obligations.[63] Such starrs indicate that the ability to write was relatively widespread among the Jewish population and that French, Latin, and Hebrew were all acceptable to Jews for drafting documents.

One of the wealthiest Jewish moneylenders was Aaron of Lincoln, who died in 1186. For some reason his sons did not inherit his business and all his debts fell into the king's hands. Custom did not allow the royal government to continue to exact interest, but Aaron's debtors were still liable to repay the capital. The business generated by the acquisition of Aaron's loans was so enormous that a separate exchequer, the 'Exchequer of Aaron', had to be created and a register was drawn up of all Aaron's bonds. Only a fragment of this record survives, cataloguing what was due from the tiny county of Rutland, but even this is enough to show the extent and the range of Aaron's business.[64] Eleven debts are enumerated, the largest being £115 borrowed by Aubrey de Dammartin, the smallest a mere 6s. 8d. (one mark) owed by a certain Truve. Some of the bonds are for loans borrowed from Jews other than Aaron, and these had presumably come into his hands through the workings of a market in bonds. Interest rates were 22%, 44%, or, in one case, 66% per annum (i.e. one, two, or three pence per week per pound). There are four parsons, one religious house, and a royal chamberlain among the debtors and their obligations are guaranteed either by gages of land or by personal sureties. The debts of one parson are guaranteed by two other parsons, both themselves indebted to the Jews, while the guarantors of Herbert, parson of Whissendine, are twenty in number. The net of indebtedness was wide and deep.

## Kings and Jews

'Jews and all their property are the king's.' So reads a clause from one of the law-books compiled in England in the first half of the twelfth century.[65] This special relationship to ruling princes was a feature of Jewish history dating well back into the early Middle Ages. Because of their status as a non-Christian minority, the Jews did not fit into the usual communal and seigneurial mechanisms of protection and security. They needed special protection. This the ruler was prepared to offer—for a price. The Carolingian emperors of the ninth century had established a precedent, taking the Jews under their wing, and the holy Roman emperors of the twelfth century

---

[63] Cole, *Docs.*, p. 286.   [64] Richardson, *Jewry*, pp. 247–53.
[65] Liebermann, *Gesetze* 1, p. 650 (E Cf. 25).

continued to offer the same kind of protection. The obverse was that the Jews were the emperor's property—'they pertained to the [imperial] chamber', as the phrase had it.[66] The situation in England seems to have been identical. Jews were peculiarly the king's and that meant, on the one hand, that he would try to protect them from being harmed by anyone else, and, on the other, that he would feel free to fleece them when he deemed it necessary. The king's outrage when Jews were injured was not humanitarianism but fury that his assets had been damaged and his rights infringed. As king John put it in 1203, reproving the Londoners for molesting his Jews, 'If we had given our peace to a dog, it ought to be inviolably observed.'[67]

Kings thus offered protection at a price. The general legal rights of the Jews of England, as they were enjoyed under the Norman and Angevin kings, are recorded in a royal charter of confirmation that was issued in 1201.[68] They were permitted to reside in the king's lands, to travel where they would and have secure possession of their 'lands, fiefs, pledges and escheats [reverted estates]'. Lawsuits between Christians and Jews were carefully regulated. Jews need appear only before the royal judges or the local royal castellans; the plaintiff (whether Christian or Jew) required witnesses of both religions; in the absence of witnesses, an accused Jew could clear himself by an oath on the roll of the Law; when a Christian brought a case against a Jew and it was not a plea of the Crown, it was 'to be judged by the Jew's fellows'. Jewish inheritance rights in chattels and debts were guaranteed and Jews were allowed freedom from tolls and customs. In principle, these constituted a substantial set of safeguards and privileges.

The price that the Jews paid for being 'our own property', as the charter of 1201 put it, was to be the king's milch-cow. Because Jews were the king's own property, they could be tallaged at will—that is, subjected to periodic financial exactions. These impositions could be heavy. Between 1186 and 1194 the Jews of England paid several tallages and levies, one of a large but unknown amount, others amounting to a minimum of 20,000 marks ($£13,333. 6s. 8d.$), while the London Jews had to surrender a quarter of their movable property.[69] King John charged the Jews of England 4,000 marks ($£2,666. 13s. 4d.$) for the charter confirming their privileges and imposed a tallage of the same amount in 1207, plus one-tenth of the value of their debts. In 1210 he had the Jews of England, or perhaps their leaders, imprisoned and subjected to another enormous tallage. In that year several of the richer Jews were accused of tax evasion and either fined or hanged, while many of the poorer Jews fled overseas.[70]

---

[66] *MGH, Diplomata Frederici I* 1, ed. H. Appelt (Hanover, 1975), no. 166, p. 285.
[67] *Rot. litt. pat.*, p. 33.          [68] *Rot. chart.*, p. 93.
[69] Richardson, *Jewry*, p. 165.          [70] Ibid., pp. 166–72.

Because of their special relationship to the king, it was the business of the Crown to regulate moneylending undertaken by Jews. The enforcement of debts, either during the lifetime of the Jewish lender or if he died intestate and his debts fell into royal hands, was a recurrent concern of royal officials. The Pipe Roll of 1130 records that two Jews, Abraham and Deuslesalt, had offered the king one gold mark for his help in recovering their debts from Osbert of Leicester, and the rolls of the reign of Henry II and his sons continue to be full of similar references.[71] The creation of a separate office to deal with the debts of Aaron of Lincoln has already been mentioned. In 1194, the year that the Exchequer of Aaron was finally wound up, the royal government introduced a new level of regulation, perhaps building on the experience acquired from dealing with Aaron's business. Henceforth all loans that Jews made, and the gages on which they were secured, were to be registered. Documents were to be drawn up in duplicate, one copy being retained by the Jewish lender, the other being deposited in an official chest (*archa*). Access to this chest, which had three locks, was only possible when two designated Jews, two designated Christians, and the two royal clerks with special responsibilities for Jewish affairs acted in concert. The royal clerks were to keep a roll on which all transactions were recorded. These official chests were to be located at several centres of Jewish moneylending activity.[72]

The system instituted in 1194 was to endure and to develop. By 1221 there were seventeen recognized centres where Jewish loans could be registered. The royal clerks of 1194 were succeeded by a regular series of keepers or justices of the Jews. In 1198, for instance, the keepers were Simon of Pattishall, Henry of Whiston, Benedict de Talmont, and Joseph Aaron, and they were dealing with such matters as whether the knight Richard of Bisbrooke was quit of his debt and could reclaim his manor of Bisbrooke (Rutland); what the exact terms were of the arrangement between Richard of Sanford and the Jewish moneylender Benedict Pernaz, whereby Richard assumed responsibility for the debts of his deceased father-in-law, Hugh de Bayeux; and how good was the claim of St Augustine's abbey, Canterbury, to be free of all Jewish debts.[73] The Justices of the Jews, or, as they were sometimes called, the Exchequer of Jews, kept rolls recording business before the court and these survive from 1218, giving a good idea of the wide and varied activities into which these special commissioners for Jewish affairs might become involved. Given the close entanglement of Jewish and royal finance, it is not surprising that the Jews were seen as ugly tools of greedy kings. 'Jews are the sponges of kings', wrote the theologian William de Montibus, chancellor of Lincoln

---

[71] PR 31 HI, p. 147.    [72] R. Howd. 3, pp. 266–7.    [73] PR 10 RI, pp. 125, 165, 210.

1194–1213. 'They are bloodsuckers of Christian purses, by whose robbery kings despoil and deprive poor men of their goods.'[74]

Because kings regarded the Jews as useful 'sponges', they wanted to keep them under their own monopolistic control. This meant that the Jewish policies of the king and the Church did not always coincide. In 1215 the Fourth Lateran Council ruled that Jews and Muslims 'shall be publicly distinguished from other people by their dress'. Discrimination of this visible type was necessary, the church leaders of Europe argued, in order to prevent unwitting sexual contact between members of the different faiths. Rules about Muslim dress were not a pressing issue in England, but in 1218 the regency government, that included the papal legate, Guala, ordered that the provision for distinctive clothing for Jews be enforced. The sheriffs of six counties and the mayor of London were commanded to ensure that 'all Jews, wherever they may walk or ride, within the town or outside it, should wear on the upper part of their clothing two strips on their breast made of white linen or parchment, so that Jews may be distinguished from Christians by this visible sign'.[75] Like most rules of the English royal government, however, this one could be circumvented for a price and the royal financial records of 1221 show both individual and communal payments for permission to dispense with the Jewish badge.[76] It is indicative that this widespread exemption was being granted at virtually the same time that the English bishops were solemnly reinforcing the requirement in their council at Oxford in 1222.[77] The friction between royal and ecclesiastical interests was low-key but constant. In 1219 the papal legate Pandulf, successor to Guala, tried to suspend the action of Isaac of Norwich, who was attempting to recover his debts from the monks of Westminster before the Justices of the Jews.[78] The previous year the royal government insisted that no cases of debt should go before the ecclesiastical courts, while affirming that the Jews had the king's protection, 'whatever prohibitions may have been issued by the bishop of Hereford, for he has nothing to do with our Jews'. The phrase echoes that of an order of king John, summing up the royal view on the matter: 'the bishops have nothing to do with our Jews'.[79]

## Anti-Semitism

It is perhaps not surprising that a small, exclusive, and culturally distinctive group, deeply involved in moneylending, would stir up hostility on the part of the majority community. Attacks on Flemings and Italians in England

---

[74] *Similitudinarius*, MS Peterhouse 255, fo. 112ᵛ.      [75] *Rot. litt. claus.* 1, p. 378.

[76] Richardson, *Jewry*, p. 179.      [77] *Councils and Synods* 2/i, p. 121.

[78] *Royal and Other Historical Letters Illustrative of the Reign of Henry III*, ed. W. W. Shirley (2 vols., RS; 1862–6), vol. 1, pp. 35–6, no. 28.

[79] *Pat. Rolls HIII* 1, p. 157.

in the later Middle Ages show that a vicious blend of xenophobia and eco-nomic resentment need not focus exclusively on Jews. Yet the Jews were unique, as the only group of non-Christians legally tolerated in England, and a group with over a thousand years of a difficult history of relations with Christians.

In the fourth century, when the Christian Church first attained legal status and began to integrate itself with the state, its leaders had determined both that the practice of the Jewish religion was to be tolerated and also that Jews were to suffer many forms of official discrimination. They were barred from the civil service and the legal profession and mixed marriages and conversion to Judaism were banned, even though, in the words of the Theodosian Code of 438 'it is universally acknowledged that the Jewish sect is not prohibited by law'.[80] The popes of the twelfth century maintained this ambivalence. While reiterating and expanding the legal restrictions and constraints on Jews, they also issued a series of bulls specifying that there should be no compulsory baptism of Jews, no extra-judicial violence or deprivation of property, no change in their approved customs, no attacks on them with sticks and stones during their holy days, no forced labour, no desecration of their cemeteries, no digging up of their dead to look for money. Of course, this kind of legisla-tion must, as always, be regarded not only as evidence of papal intentions, but also as a catalogue of what was likely to be inflicted on Jews.

The official policy of the Church was to tolerate the Jews but also to expose their errors and work for their conversion. The twelfth century sees a spate of polemical literature, in which the Christian–Jewish argument was pursued. The usual form was a dialogue, with representatives of the two religions tak-ing turns to make their case. Some of these texts were extremely popular. The *Dispute between a Jew and a Christian* of abbot Gilbert Crispin of Westmin-ster, written about 1090, survives in twenty twelfth-century manuscripts.[81] In it a learned Jew, who had been educated at Mainz, and abbot Gilbert argue about the status of Old Testament Law, the necessity of the Incarnation, and the legitimacy of making images of the deity, as well as engaging in detailed and recondite discussion of biblical translation and exegesis. Abbot Gilbert could apparently be convincing, for there is record of a monk of Westminster in his time who was a convert from Judaism.

The pressures upon the Jewish population were indeed sometimes great enough to lead individual Jews to the path of conversion. Yet, though they thus freed themselves from relentless harassment, they did so only by

---

[80] *Codex Theodosianus* 16. 8. 9 (393 AD), ed. T. Mommsen and Paul Meyer, *Theodosiani libri XVI* (2 vols.; Berlin, 1905), vol. 1, p. 889.

[81] Anna Sapir Abulafia and G. R. Evans (eds.), *The Works of Gilbert Crispin* (*Auctores Britannici Medii Aevi* 8; 1986), p. xxvii.

becoming pariahs to their former community and often insecure members of
their new one. It was natural for Jews to show hostility to converts and sometimes they sought to use force to prevent what they saw as apostasy, as appears
to be the case with Jeremiah the Jew, fined one mark (6s. 8d.) in 1180 'because
of Isabella the convert, whom he imprisoned'.[82] The situation of the converted Jew was a difficult one financially as well as psychologically. In 1199
pope Innocent III commanded the Augustinian canons of Leicester to take
under their care an impoverished convert from Judaism, who 'at the instigation of a certain nobleman, had spurned and abandoned all the wealth that he
had, preferring to follow Christ rather than rot in the mire of riches, and had
received the sacrament of baptism'. After his patron's death, the convert had
fallen on hard times and had obviously gone to the pope and suggested to Innocent that he should ensure there was no relapse simply because he was des-
titute.[83] Judging by later evidence, although it might seem a powerful
disincentive, it was the rule that converted Jews sacrificed all their property.
Hence, as the pope observed in his letter, 'after they have received baptism,
many fall into distress on account of their indigence'. Henry III was to found
a House for Converts in London in 1232, but in our period there was no such
institutional support. Conversion in the opposite direction, from Christianity to Judaism, was naturally not common, although one spectacular case in
1222 attracted the attention of the chroniclers. A deacon who had 'circum-
cized himself for love of a Jewish woman' was degraded from his clerical
orders and then handed over to the king's officers, who burned him outside
the walls of Oxford.[84]

The general tone of anti-Semitism in Christian culture grew sharper in the
twelfth and thirteenth centuries. Among the vehicles of this new bigotry was
the accusation of ritual murder raised against the Jews. England has the sad
distinction of being the site of the first such case. In the week before Easter in
1144, according to the fantasy fabricated by the Norwich monk, Thomas of
Monmouth, the Jews of Norwich seized a young apprentice called William,
tortured him and killed him, then dumped the body in a nearby wood. The
murder was not a piece of random savagery, but part of an international Jewish conspiracy:

their ancient writings said that the Jews would never obtain their freedom nor return
to the land of their fathers, without the shedding of human blood. Hence it was an ancient custom of theirs that every year they must sacrifice a Christian in some part of
the world to the most high God in scorn and contempt of Christ.[85]

---

[82]  PR 26 HII, p. 129.

[83]  Innocent III, ep. 2. 225 (234), ed. Othmar Hageneder et al., Die Register Innocenz' III. 2 (Vienna,
1979), pp. 431–2.

[84]  R. Coggesh., pp. 190–1; Barnwell Chron., p. 251; Ann. Dunst., p. 76.

[85]  T. Monm., V. William 2. 9 (p. 93).

William's family sought to raise charges against the Jews and witnesses came forward, including a Christian maidservant of the Jews, but the Norwich Jews, according to Thomas of Monmouth, were able to call on the protection of the royal sheriff and the compliance of the king to evade the accusation.

Although William's status as a martyr was, in fact, not established without some signs of scepticism, a tradition was born. The Norwich case was the first involving an accusation of ritual murder directed against the Jews but it was not the last. The charge became a staple of anti-Semitism both in England and abroad. An incident at Winchester in 1192 has many similarities to the case of William of Norwich. A poor orphan French boy came to England and was apprenticed as a cobbler. He worked for a Winchester Jew but disappeared on Good Friday. His companion charged the Jews with crucifying him, while a Christian maidservant of the Jews asserted that she had seen the boy enter the Jews' storeroom but had not seen him come out again. The case went to trial but did not result in a conviction, partly because the witnesses were of insufficient weight, the apprentice's companion being under age and the maidservant 'disreputable' (*infamis*) because she served Jews, and partly, according to a hostile chronicler, because the judges succumbed to bribery.[86] The urban and artisanal milieu, the role of poor Christians in Jewish service, and the occasional resistance of judicial authorities to the more violent and fantastic forms of anti-Semitism are all reminiscent of the Norwich case.

One reverie of the anti-Semite was the expulsion of the Jews from the land. Members of the knightly class who fell into debt to the Jews might consider such a dramatic solution to their problems—how it would simplify their affairs if the Jews simply disappeared! Roger of Asterby, a Lincolnshire knight indebted to Aaron of Lincoln, to whom he had even pawned his mail-coat, received visionary instructions from St Peter and the archangel Gabriel, telling him to instruct king Henry II to fulfil seven commands. The longest of them concerned the Jews: 'he should expel the Jews from his land, leaving them a portion of their wealth to enable them to make the journey and to support their family, but not letting them retain any of their pledges or bonds, which should be returned to those who gave them.'[87] Henry II, who, like other Norman and Angevin kings was criticized for the favour he showed to the Jews, paid no attention, though his great-grandson, Edward I, would have been a more receptive audience.

More unrestrained than the antagonistic tactics of libel and judicial accusation and the hostile plan for expulsion was simple physical violence. Although official ecclesiastical policy frowned on it, non-judicial violence directed against Jews was not uncommon in Europe at this period.

---

[86] R. Devizes, pp. 64–9.      [87] Gerald, *Prin.* 2. 13 (pp. 183–6).

Large-scale pogroms began with the crusading movement. The First Crusade, launched by pope Urban II in 1095, had as one of its earliest consequences a series of attacks upon the Jews of northern France and the Rhineland, and in 1146, during the preparations for the Second Crusade, the Rhineland again saw massacres and forced conversions. England was only peripherally involved in the first two crusades and was not the scene of similar violence until the time of the Third Crusade, the most 'English' of all the expeditions to the Holy Land. With the accession of Richard I, the crusader king, massacres began. The chronicler Richard of Devizes, writing of the killings of Jews that took place after the coronation of Richard I on 3 September 1189, shows a gleeful savagery:

on the day of the coronation, about the time when the Son is sacrificed to the Father [in the mass], the Jews in the city of London began to be sacrificed to their father, the devil... the other towns and cities of the region emulated the faithful Londoners and with a like devotion sent those bloodsuckers bloodily to hell.

Only Winchester, where Richard himself lived, 'spared its worms', but merely because it awaited a time when it could expel this 'diseased matter' more completely.[88]

Early in 1190 attacks on Jews took place in several English towns. At the trading port of Lynn the Jews were massacred and their houses burned, the pogrom supposedly being a reaction to an assault by the Jews on one of their own number who had converted. Young sailors and merchants from overseas were particularly zealous participants in the killing and looting, sailing off quickly with their plunder, while the local burgesses were a little more cautious 'through fear of the king'. Forty miles away, at Stamford, anti-Jewish violence was initiated by a group of young crusaders, 'indignant that the enemies of the cross of Christ had such great possessions'. Some Jews were killed, others took refuge in the castle, while their houses were plundered.[89] Massacres also occurred at Norwich and Bury St Edmunds.[90] A planned assault on the Jews of Lincoln was forestalled by the courageous opposition of bishop Hugh and, perhaps even more, by their swift removal into the castle.[91]

The violence was at its most horrible in York.[92] Here 'neither fear of a most ferocious king, nor the force of law, nor reason, nor humanity' restrained a savage attack, led by a group of nobles who were deeply burdened by debts to the Jews. Joined by bands of crusaders, they began the assault by forcing their way into the house of the recently deceased Jewish moneylender Benedict,

---

[88] R. Devizes, pp. 3–4.     [89] W. Newb. 4. 7–8 (1, pp. 309–11).
[90] R. Diceto, *Ymag.* 2, pp. 75–6.
[91] W. Newb. 4. 9 (1, p. 312); Ad. Eyns., *V. Hugh* 4. 4 (2, p. 17 and n. 1).
[92] The fullest account is W. Newb. 4. 9–11 (1, pp. 312–24), from which quotations in the following paragraphs are taken; see also *Gesta Ric. I* 2, p. 107; R. Howd. 3, pp. 33–4.

killing everyone in it, including Benedict's widow and children, and then setting it on fire. Most of the York Jews, like their fellows in Stamford and Lincoln, now took refuge in the royal castle (Clifford's Tower). Meanwhile,
attackers continued to plunder Jewish property. Any Jew found outside the
castle was offered the choice of baptism or death.

At this point there occurred a fatal breakdown of confidence between the
Jews inside the castle and the royal castellan. He had gone out on business,
but on his return the Jews, doubtful of his integrity, refused to re-admit him.
Irate at what he saw as Jewish trickery, the castellan immediately sought the
help of the sheriff of Yorkshire, who arrived with a band of local knights and
ordered an attack on the castle. A huge force of Christians now assembled
outside the castle—artisans and apprentices from York, knights and others
from the surrounding countryside, many clerics, including a rabid hermit
dressed in white, 'who strove to convince the others that they were doing
godly work'. The sheriff was aghast at what he had stirred up, but 'once
spirits are aroused, neither reason nor authority has any weight to stop them'.

The Jews in the castle had neither sufficient food nor weapons to undertake an effective defence. They did what they could, hurling down stones on
the attackers, one of which killed the fanatical hermit, but, as the Christians
brought up siege machines, they realized that there was no hope. One of their
leaders, a learned Jew from overseas (possibly Rabbi Yomtob of Joigny), now
addressed them: 'God, whom you ought not ask "Why do you do this?", commands us now to die for His law. . . . So, since the creator now requires back
the life that He gave us, let us render it to Him voluntarily with our own
hands'. Not every Jew was convinced by this appeal to the ancient Jewish tradition of self-martyrdom, but the majority preferred to die at the hands of
their own family and fellows than to trust to the good intentions of the Christians. After setting fire to their property and to the castle itself, the Jewish
men slit the throats of their wives and children before undertaking their own
suicide. Those who remained, now caught between the fire and the besiegers,
promised to accept baptism: 'receive us as brothers, who once were enemies,
and let us live with you in peace and in the faith of Christ'. One of the leaders
of the Christian attackers, the indebted Yorkshire knight Richard Malebisse,
swore that they would not be harmed. As soon as they descended from the
castle, they were all killed.

The events at York show the double jeopardy in which Jews were placed, as
non-Christians and as moneylenders. The crusaders and clerics who participated in the looting and slaughter could reassure themselves that they were
engaged in 'godly work'. Those who were indebted to the Jews could take advantage of the opportunity offered to clear their debts in the most direct and
brutal way—as soon as the last Jew had been killed, the Christian crowd
rushed off to the cathedral, where the Jewish bonds were stored for safe

keeping, and made a bonfire of them in the nave of the church. Naturally, the royal government was incensed at the treatment the Jews of York had received. The sheriff and castellan were dismissed, while confiscation, fines, and imprisonment were inflicted on those of the perpetrators who could be identified or apprehended. Under the shadow of royal protection, Jews returned to York. Within thirty years of the massacre, the Jewish community there was again one of the richest and most significant in England.

It is clear from such incidents as the pogrom of 1190 that the Jews were an exposed and vulnerable minority in the English towns of the twelfth and thirteenth century. Despite, or because of, this precarious situation, their hold on their cultural identity was tenacious. The words of the Jewish moneylender Benedict of York bear witness to this. During the anti-Jewish riot at the coronation of Richard I in 1189, Benedict was beaten and forced to undergo baptism. After order had been restored, he was brought before the king, who asked him whether he was a Christian. 'He replied that he had been forcibly baptized by the Christians but that he had always been a Jew in spirit and wished to die as one.'[93]

## 7. TRADE: THE FRAMEWORK

People do not trade purely for pleasure. They trade because a profit can be made, and this profit arises from the gap between the value a purchaser places upon an object and the costs the seller has incurred in putting it before the purchaser. The purchaser's evaluation is influenced both by needs and resources: a starving man will pay whatever he must for food, because his need is great, a wealthy lady may purchase a luxury for a very high price because that price represents only an insignificant portion of her income. When looking at patterns of trade in Norman and Angevin England, we can begin our analysis with this gap between purchaser's evaluation and trader's costs.

Items that were universally required but only locally available would inevitably be traded: metal and salt are prominent examples. There must also have been constant and expert dealing in livestock. Household requirements that could, in theory, have been produced at home, but were available at a reasonable price and of far higher standard from professional craftsmen, were also bought and sold: pottery, implements of horn or bone, leather goods, such as shoes and saddles. Cloth and clothing are perhaps the most important commodities in this category. Most families had a member who could spin, but weaving and dyeing were specialist crafts, and clothing that was prettier, more uniform, or more comfortable than homespun was a desirable purchase.

[93] W. Newb. 4. 1 (1, p. 299).

Transport costs are also important. Since land transport was much more expensive than water transport, it is likely that the purchaser would find cheaper products at places with good access by sea or river. In fact, England, being part of an island with an indented coast and slow-flowing rivers, was ideally suited to water-borne trade. Cities like York, Lincoln, and Exeter, considered inland towns in modern terms, were important ports in the twelfth century. Sea-borne trade took place along the coast as well as across the seas, as exemplified by the twenty-four ships from Hastings that paid tolls at Saltfleet in Lincolnshire some time in the reign of William the Conqueror.[94] The costs even of water transport, however, were not negligible. In 1200 it cost £1. 3s. 6d. to transport £10 worth of lead down the coast from Boston to Sandwich, transport thus representing 11.75 per cent of the purchase price.[95]

Aristocrats obviously had a greater income than the rest of the population and were willing to spend it on luxuries, this conspicuous consumption not only gratifying their appetites and desires but also serving to mark them out from the rest of humanity. In 1194 Richard I provided the young German noble, Otto of Brunswick, with three hoods of Lindsey and two dyed robes of Stamford (Lindseys and Stamfords were types of high-quality cloth, named after their place of production). The total cost of these items was fifty shillings (£2. 10s.).[96] This was the equivalent of ten months' wages for a skilled sailor. Even if this sailor were able to save a quarter of his wages, it would take him well over three years of full-time employment to accumulate enough for these hoods and robes, so easily given by one great prince to another. Many of the more exotic imports into England, such as silk and spices, were drawn there by the attraction of this aristocratic spending power.

The circulation of goods was not limited to commercial transactions. There were non-market solutions to the problems of supply. Salt, for instance, did not have to be purchased at market. Domesday Book records many manors in the west Midlands that possessed a salt pan or pans in the great salt-producing centre of Droitwich in Worcestershire. One of these, Princes Risborough (Bucks.), was seventy miles from Droitwich. Attached to the manor was 'a salt-worker in Droitwich who renders packloads of salt'.[97] The manor house at Princes Risborough thus did not have to budget for the purchase of this essential item—a manorial rather than a market solution had been found. Equally significant were goods transferred as gifts rather than through exchange. Gift-giving at all levels was important symbolically and among the aristocracy and royalty could well involve items of enormous value. Vessels of precious metal, costly clothes, jewellery, and animals

---

[94] *DB* 1, 375b (Lin. CS. 39).    [95] PR 2 John, p. 89.
[96] PR 6 RI, p. 221.    [97] *DB* 1, 143b (Bkm. 1. 3).

circulated among the upper class, both lay and ecclesiastical, to win favour and to mark the high dignity of recipient and donor.

However, even allowing for this considerable amount of non-commercial circulation, it is clear that trading was important and increasingly so. One sign is the existence of specialized commercial venues. Obviously a great deal of buying and selling must have gone on informally between neighbours, friends, and family, but authorized public markets and fairs offered wider choices and certain guarantees for buyers and sellers. The predictability of venue meant that buyers could be sure to find a range of commodities available and sellers could be sure to find buyers. The multiplication of markets and fairs over the period is an index of the growth and diversification of trade. Already in Domesday Book there is mention of 'new markets', like that at Bolingbroke (Lincs.). The market at Tewkesbury had been established by queen Matilda (1066–83) and was bringing in a revenue of 11s. 8d. per annum, primarily from tolls and rents.[98] This growth continued throughout the period. At the time of the Domesday survey of 1086 Oxfordshire had two markets, at Oxford and Bampton, but over the course of the next 140 years another ten were established, dotted regularly across the county.[99] A network of such density, with one market for every 60 square miles, would give almost everybody in the county the chance to walk to market, while the fact that these markets were held on different days would permit professional traders to establish a circuit of permanent business.

The markets of Oxfordshire were located in small towns or villages and served the needs of the craftsmen, farmers, and minor landlords of the locality. On a grander scale there were the annual fairs, some of which were important centres of international trade. Four of these, Boston, Stamford, St Ives, and Lynn, ringed the Fens and were familiar destinations for merchants sailing from the continent to the Wash and the waterways that drained into it. The Scandinavians and Flemings were frequent visitors there, as were the Germans, like the merchant from Cologne who was given permission in 1213 to go to the fairs of Boston 'with his cog and return thence to his own region with the merchandise he has bought'.[100] The 'cog' was the biggest trading vessel of the day and would probably have arrived at Boston with a cargo of wine, cloth, or luxury items and returned loaded with wool, hides, and grain. Of the same standing as these eastern fairs was St Giles' Fair, Winchester, held every September outside the city. Like them, it was usually worth £100 or more per annum to its lord—the equivalent of the income of a small barony.

---

[98] *DB* 1, 351, 163b (Lin. 14. 66; Gls. 1. 24).

[99] David Postles, 'Markets for Rural Produce in Oxfordshire, 1086–1350', *Midland History*, 12 (1987), pp. 14–26.

[100] *Rot. litt. claus.* 1, p. 137.

Fairs were distinctive, not only in terms of the activity taking place but also judicially. When Henry I granted the bishop and monks of Norwich permission to hold, or to extend the length of, fairs in Norwich, Lynn, and Hoxne, he included a series of judicial privileges 'and all the customs that pertain to the rights of fairs'.[101] Special rules applied to large gatherings of strangers where plenty of money (and plenty of drink) were at hand. It was not a formality when the king granted his special protection to those going to or coming from fairs, as he did in 1110 when authorizing the fair at St Ives.[102]

The four great long-distance roads that twelfth-century England inherited from the distant past were Ermine Street, the Foss Way, Icknield Street, and Watling Street. The first is the Great North Road, the second ran from Lincoln to the south-west peninsula, the third traversed the country from East Anglia to Wiltshire, while Watling Street ran from Dover to Chester via London. According to some writers these roads were constructed by the ancient (and legendary) king Belinus, who issued special laws to enforce peace and security on them, but, in any event, they were certainly under the king's special protection in the twelfth century.[103] These four roads were, of course, only the few that had a widespread or fabulous reputation. The whole country was covered by tracks, droveways, and paths of a variety of types. Rates of travel would depend upon the condition of road and the weather.

Fastest speeds were reached by unimpeded horsemen. It was considered remarkable that a group of knights could travel 24 miles between dawn and 'the fifth hour' of a summer's day.[104] By medieval reckoning, the 'hour' was one-twelfth of the time between sunrise and sunset and hence variable (see below, p. 634). If one postulates a 16-hour day for this incident, which took place in Northumberland in July, the knights would have covered the distance in 6 hours 40 minutes, a speed of just over 3½ miles per hour. A daily rate of 25 miles was not at all unthinkable. It apparently took seven or eight days for news of Becket's death on 29 December 1170 to reach Devon, a distance of at least 200 miles.[105] This rate of dissemination, twenty-five miles a day or more, suggests that messengers were sent expressly for the purpose of conveying the news. Pack-horses and carts travelled at a much slower pace, but could perhaps manage half that distance. As suggested above (p. 136), the royal court, that certainly had both carts and pack-horses, might cover

---

[101] *The Charters of Norwich Cathedral Priory*, ed. Barbara Dodwell (2 vols., PRS n.s. 40 and 46; 1974 for 1965–6, 1985 for 1978–80), vol. 1, no. 17, pp. 11–12; *RRAN* 2, no. 762, p. 55.

[102] *Ramsey Cart.* 1, p. 240, no. 162; 2, p. 101, no. 240; *RRAN* 2, no. 953, pp. 94–5 (cf. no. 1916, p. 292).

[103] H. Hunt. 1. 7 (pp. 22–4); Geoff. Monm., *HRB* 3. 5 (39), pp. 26–7; A. Bell (ed.), 'The Anglo-Norman *Description of England*: An Edition', lines 230–56, in Ian Short (ed.), *Anglo-Norman Anniversary Essays* (ANTS; 1993), pp. 31–47, at pp. 43–4; Liebermann, *Gesetze* 1, pp. 510, 637 (Leis Wl 26; E Cf. 12); Robertson, *Laws*, p. 266.

[104] W. Newb. 2. 33 (1, p. 184).     [105] Gerald, *V. Remigius* 27 (p. 55).

12 miles per day. Although water transport was cheaper and usually quicker, the roads and tracks of the twelfth century could bear heavy wheeled transport, at least in the summer months.

The network of roads depended upon hundreds of fords and bridges, that allowed individual travellers, pack-horses, and carts to make their way across the rivers and streams that could otherwise check or defeat them. The twelfth century saw an efflorescence of bridge-building. At Durham, where the fact that the windings of the Wear almost made the city an island gave bridges a special significance, the first bridge was built about 1120, when bishop Ranulf Flambard 'joined the two banks of the river Wear by constructing an arching stone bridge of wonderful workmanship'.[106] A second bridge, the Elvet or New Bridge, was constructed by a later bishop, Hugh de Puiset (1153–95).[107] Bridges had commercial implications and it is significant that both Durham's Old Bridge and New Bridge led directly to the market area. At St Ives a stimulus to the development of the fair must have been the bridge that was constructed across the Ouse shortly before the fair was authorized by the king. It debouches directly into the market place where the fair was held.[108] The most famous of the new stone bridges constructed in this period was London Bridge. There was already a wooden bridge, of course, as there had been since Roman times, and money was spent on its upkeep. In 1130, for instance, the sum of £25 was spent 'in making two arches of London Bridge'.[109] The rebuilding in stone began in 1176, under the auspices of Peter, chaplain of St Mary Colechurch. When he died in 1205 the work was sufficiently complete for him to be buried, appropriately, in the chapel on the bridge.[110] Almost a thousand feet long, it was to be a central feature of London, both economically and symbolically, for centuries to come.

The roads and rivers of England could take a variety of commodities down to the seaports to be exported and carry back the goods that came from abroad. The volume of this overseas trade is hard to estimate, although some customs figures do survive from John's reign. He imposed a duty of one-fifteenth on most imports and exports. This produced about £3,750 per annum, suggesting that the value of the trade on which it was levied was £56,250.[111] Allowing for the exempt commodities and the exclusion of the important port of Bristol, it is not unreasonable to see English overseas trade in the early years of the thirteenth century as worth well over £60,000 per annum (which was the annual royal income at the time).

[106] S. Durh., *HDE*, p. 140.

[107] Geoffrey of Coldingham, *Liber de statu ecclesiae Dunhelmensis* 7, ed. James Raine, *Historiae Dunhelmensis scriptores tres* (Surtees Soc. 9; 1839), p. 12.

[108] *Ramsey Cart.* 3, p. 214, no. 332.    [109] PR 31 HI, p. 144.

[110] *Ann. Wav.*, pp. 240, 256–7.    [111] PR 6 John, p. 218.

The most important ports for export and import were, with the exception of Southampton, along the east coast, some of these, like Boston, Lynn, and Newcastle, being new creations of our period. The economic growth taking place in north-west Europe at this time, with the intensification of manufacturing in Flanders, the rise of the great international exchanges of the Champagne fairs and urban development in the Rhineland, drew England into its field; as wool went out, wine came in and a host of other commodities were traded in busy ports and markets. At the same time the maritime links between the south-west of England and western France, and the trade from Chester and Bristol to Ireland, continued and intensified.

## 8. COMMODITIES

### Foodstuffs

The highest evaluation is put upon food that can stop you starving. When harvests are bad, grain has to be bought. William of Malmesbury noticed that the flood of foreign merchants in London meant that food could be obtained there more cheaply than elsewhere, even when harvests were poor.[112] In this world of bread and beer the import and export of grain were basic issues. There is evidence that grain was sometimes imported into England,[113] but the country was usually spared famine and grain was more often exported, although the king demanded that his permission be given (and paid for). Thus in 1180 Aernaldus, son of Mabel, offered the king two gerfalcons to be allowed to export grain to Norway from an East Anglian port and in 1199 similarly William Pepper offered £1 'to have permission to export 200 quarters of corn to Norway'.[114] Those who flouted the requirement were fined. In 1179 Simon, son of Peter of Wiggenhall, Roger Passlew of Wiggenhall, Alured of Lynn, and Siward of Lynn were each fined half a mark 'for grain exported without licence'. This group of Lynn merchants (Wiggenhall is a village about five miles from the port) had, however, disappeared to Norway.[115] Trading with the king's enemies was punished more severely. In 1197 heavy fines were laid on those merchants of the southern and eastern coasts who had ignored the ban on trading with Flanders and sent corn there. Amongst these audacious offenders Lynn again figures prominently, the town receiving an enormous collective fine of 1,000 marks (£666. 13s. 4d.).[116]

---

[112] W. Malm., *GP* 73 (p. 140).

[113] A. Thierry (ed.), *Recueil des monuments inédits de l'histoire du Tiers Etat* 1 (Paris, 1850), no. 306, p. 801, for a case of grain imported by Amiens merchants during the minority of Henry III.

[114] PR 26 HII, p. 23; PR 1 John, p. 289.     [115] PR 25 HII, p. 6.

[116] PR 10 RI, pp. 92–3, 137–8, 209; for date, intro., pp. xiv–xv.

The grain export from eastern England to Scandinavia and Flanders was obviously substantial enough to merit risks.

Herring was abundant off the east coast of England and could be caught by the thousand. Salted and transported, it made a cheap source of protein. It was often found in the meals given to villeins working on the lord's demesne and, as a cheap mainstay for the lower classes, may be regarded as the medieval equivalent of the potato. Religious communities had a special need for large and regular supplies of fish because their dietary regime excluded meat on certain days and in certain seasons. The canons of Waltham in Essex sent twenty-four carts each year to Norwich to purchase herrings, the round trip approaching two hundred miles.[117] Salt was also essential, not merely as a condiment but also as the primary means of preserving meat and fish. In the absence of refrigeration or other forms of preservation, salting was the way that the life of perishable food could be extended. Naturally, most of the salt came from coastal production. Domesday Book lists hundreds of salt workings along the eastern and southern coasts, as well as the salt centre of Droitwich discussed earlier.

The requirements of the liturgy and the tastes of the Frenchified aristocracy meant that wine was among the more important imports into England. There were English vineyards but neither their number nor the quality of wine they produced satisfied demand. Wine was brought in by the Cologne merchants from Germany, but the bulk of the imports came from France. In this period English kings were also lords of extensive lands in France, where wine production was large-scale and the quality high, and this influenced the pattern of importation. Merchants from Rouen were bringing wine into London in the twelfth century, but after 1154 the Angevin connection entailed a shift southwards in trade as well as politics. In 1201 king John's stock of wine at Southampton included 105 tuns of Poitevin wine, 143 tuns of Angevin, and 150 tuns of wine from Le Blanc (Indre), also in the Loire basin.[118] By the end of the period, about 1225, with the loss of the territories outside the south-west of France, Gascon wine had assumed the importance that it was to retain throughout the rest of the Middle Ages and beyond. A Norman, Angevin, and Gascon period are to be found in the history of the wine-trade as in that of the territorial links.

## Metals

Metal was vitally important for tools and weapons but metallic ores are not found everywhere. Commerce in metal and metal products was thus one of the most ancient forms of trade and had been going on since the Bronze Age.

---

[117] *Early Waltham Charters*, no. 600, pp. 412–13.        [118] PR 4 John, p. 82.

England had a reasonable, although not extremely rich, supply of metallic ores. Iron is found widely in small quantities, but the special importance of certain areas emerges in Domesday Book and in later records. The iron ore of north-eastern Northamptonshire was certainly exploited, while the Forest of Dean was presumably the source of the renders of iron from Gloucestershire. Smelting needed charcoal and the woods were the place to find it. The royal accounts of the later twelfth century mention large quantities of iron implements from the Forest of Dean, such as the 2,000 pickaxes, 1,000 mattocks, 3,000 spades, 100 axes, and 60,000 nails supplied to the royal army in Ireland in 1171–2.[119] It is an area that seems to have dominated English iron production.

Lead was important for roofs, gutters, and vessels of various types. Domesday Book refers to lead mining in Derbyshire and 'Peak lead' is mentioned in a late eleventh-century document.[120] The Mendip Hills in Somerset and the 'mines of Carlisle' also produced lead. The latter were actually located near Alston on the South Tyne, a river that provided a natural route for transportation. In 1179 Henry II gave two hundred cartloads of lead from the mines of Carlisle to the abbey of Clairvaux in Burgundy. This bulky gift was transported to Newcastle and then shipped to Rouen, for forwarding onwards.[121] A few years later 25 cartloads of lead from the same source were loaded at Jarrow and transported down the east coast to Stratford, east of London, for work on the abbey of Waltham.[122] These mines of Carlisle provide a classic example of mining boom-and-bust, being leased out by the Crown for ever increasing amounts from 1130 to 1180 and then shrinking rapidly in value to one-thirtieth of their peak level by 1230.

At the end of the eleventh century, the Flemish monk Goscelin wrote in praise of his adopted country of England. Many of his words are borrowed from the opening chapter of Bede's *Ecclesiastical History*, but when he comes to Bede's inventory of metals to be found in the country, he makes a significant addition to the list: tin.[123] To this foreigner, English tin required a special mention. It came exclusively from the tin mines of Cornwall and Devon and was probably the heaviest, if not the most valuable, of English exports. Estimates of production based on the tax paid under the Angevin kings suggest a dramatic rise, from about 120,000 lbs. in 1160, to 700,000 lbs. by 1194 and then a spectacular 1,200,000 lbs. in 1214, ten times the level of 1160.[124] It was exported down the Atlantic coast of France by men like 'Oger and William, merchants of Bayonne', who shipped 260,000 lbs. of tin in 1198.[125]

[119] PR 17 HII, p. 84; PR 18 HII, p. 122.
[120] Darby, *Domesday England*, pp. 268–9; *ICC*, p. 191.     [121] PR 25 HII, pp. 27, 30.
[122] PR 29 HII, p. 57.       [123] Goscelin, *Hist. Augustine*, col. 52.
[124] John Hatcher, *English Tin Production and Trade before 1550* (Oxford, 1973), pp. 18–20, 152–4.
[125] PR 10 RI, p. 182.

It provided a useful return cargo for wine importers, supplied the king of England with a regular source of income and supported a specialized way of life in the south-west peninsula that lasted until the end of the twentieth century.

## Wool and Cloth

Sheep were by far the most common domestic animals in the English countryside (above, pp. 306–8). They supplied not only meat, milk, and cheese but also wool for both domestic and foreign manufacture. The growth of the textile industry in Flanders, just across the narrow seas from England, provided an insatiable market for English wool. An account survives of the vicissitudes of a group of Flemish merchants who went to England to buy wool in the spring of 1113.[126] They sailed from Wissant, an important maritime town located between Calais and Boulogne, carrying with them over three hundred marks of silver in purses and pouches. After a narrow escape from pirates, they landed in England and went all over the country purchasing wool. This was stored in a warehouse in Dover, but, before it could be exported, both the building and its contents were destroyed by fire. These merchants were obviously not typical in their luck, but the picture of traders from the Low Countries bringing bullion to England to purchase wool in large quantities is entirely characteristic of the cross-Channel commerce of the period.

Writing in the 1130s, Henry of Huntingdon commented upon the flow of silver from the Low Countries into England, drawn there by 'the wonderful richness of fish and meat, precious wool and milk, and flocks without number'.[127] England was a supplier of food and raw materials for northern Europe's most urbanized and industrial region. By the later part of the twelfth century some of the monastic orders began to specialize in wool production. The wool crop of both the Cistercians and the Gilbertines for 1193 was requisitioned to help pay for the ransom of Richard I and it was demanded of the Cistercians also in 1194 but a financial composition was agreed instead.[128] In the regulations for John's customs, special provision was made for 'the wool of the abbeys'.[129] The growth of medieval Europe's first large-scale manufacturing industry just across the Narrow Seas was stimulating equally large-scale production for export.

By no means all English wool ended up on the looms of Ghent or Bruges. Textile production also took place at home. Some of this output comprised the luxury hangings and vestments for which England was already famous in the eleventh century—'the golden embroideries of the English maidens', as

---

[126] Hermann, *Mir. Laud.* 2. 4–5 (cols. 975–7).     [127] H. Hunt. 1. 1 (p. 10).
[128] R. Howd. 3, pp. 210–11, 242.     [129] *Rot. litt. pat.*, pp. 42–3.

one admiring foreign observer put it.[130] Much of it was also dyed woollen cloth of a variety of types. 'Burel' was a coarse cloth that could be useful for mass provisioning: 2,000 ells of burel were sent to the king's army in Ireland in 1172.[131] 'Hauberget'—apparently so called because its weave resembled a mail-coat or hauberk—was more expensive and was sometimes dyed with 'grain', a costly imported scarlet dye made from the dried bodies of a species of Mediterranean insect. It was being exported from England by the early thirteenth century, for in 1208 permission was given to three merchants from Boulogne to buy 820 marks (£546. 13s. 4d.) worth of 'hauberget of Stamford' and carry it freely out of England.[132] 'Scarlet' was one of the most expensive cloths. The term originally denoted not a colour but a type of cloth—hence it is no paradox to refer to 'two robes of green scarlet'—and its price reached eight shillings an ell (45 inches).[133] These are only a few of the varieties being produced within England and sold either for home use or export.

Textile production involved several stages, each of which was undertaken by different types of worker in different locations. The initial task of producing yarn from wool by spinning was 'women's work'. During the war fever that preceded the launching of the Third Crusade, those who did not take the cross were sometimes sent a distaff and weights, an equivalent of the white feather of the First World War, as a sign that 'whoever did not participate in this expedition should betake himself with shame to women's work'.[134] Spinning could take place almost anywhere, especially at home. Once the wool had been spun it was taken out of women's hands and issued to male weavers. They needed slightly more complex equipment, in the form of a loom, and were, as mentioned above, amongst the earliest groups of artisans to form craft guilds.

When the cloth was woven, it was 'fulled', that is, immersed in water with the astringent mineral called fuller's earth and beaten. This removed oil and grease and felted the material. The work was heavy, done either by hand or by trampling the cloth in long vats (hence the surnames 'Walker' and 'Fuller' are actually synonyms). The fullers who did the work seem to have been a tough lot and rather looked down upon: those at Winchester had been given the task of mutilating outlaws, while several towns barred fullers from citizenship.[135] Fulling is one of the few tasks that underwent a revolutionary mechanization during the Middle Ages. Instead of relying on human hands or feet, fulling mills harnessed water power to raise and lower wooden hammers to beat the

---

[130] Goscelin, *Hist. Augustine*, cols. 51–2.    [131] PR 18 HII, p. 84.

[132] *Rot. litt. pat.*, p. 86.    [133] PR 7 John, p. 112; *Rot. litt. claus.* 1, p. 104.

[134] *Itin. reg. Ric.* 1. 17 (p. 33).

[135] PR 31 HI, p. 37; *CRR* 1, p. 259; *Beverley Town Documents*, ed. Arthur Leach (Selden Soc. 14; 1900), pp. 134–5; *Munimenta Gildhallae Londoniensis*, ed. H. T. Riley (3 vols., RS; 1859–62), vol. 2, p. 130.

cloth. References to fulling mills in England begin in the second half of the twelfth century. The Templars had constructed one on their estate at Barton in Gloucestershire by 1185.[136] The bishop of Winchester's accounts from 1208–9 list fulling-mills at Alresford, Bishop's Sutton, and Bishop Waltham in Hampshire and Brightwell in Berkshire. They grew increasingly common throughout the thirteenth century.

Dyeing was the final stage in cloth production and it required a variety of substances, some of which had to be brought from abroad. Alum, a mineral used to fix the colour of the dyed cloth, originated in the Mediterranean. This was imported to England by Flemish merchants.[137] Even when the raw materials for dyes could be grown in England, as in the case of the woad plant, which produced a much valued blue shade, demand was such that overseas supplies were also required. The import of woad was a major business. In 1194 merchants were willing to pay almost £100 to have permission to bring woad into England and the tax on woad imports levied late in John's reign was producing about £250 per annum.[138] The implication of the latter figure is that thousands of pounds' worth of the dye was coming in, reaching all the ports of the east and south coasts, especially those of Kent and Sussex. Since the main production area was the Somme valley, this pattern is understandable. The dyers needed considerable capital and seem to have assumed a dominant and entrepreneurial position in the textile industry, employing fullers and weavers and trying to keep them in a subordinate position.

Textile manufacture was one of the most industrialized branches of production and exhibited many of the features of later industry: specialized processes carried out by different groups in different venues; mechanization; struggle between associations of merchant capitalists and manual workers. Even if England was primarily a rural country, providing raw materials and food to more urbanized neighbours, it now had, for the first time, a manufacturing industry of some scale. That industry would continue to shape the English economy until the twentieth century.

## 9. COINAGE AND MONETIZATION

The English coinage was notable for its high silver content and its stability. Henry of Huntingdon attributed this to the steady flow of silver from Germany, as merchants purchased England's foodstuffs and raw materials— 'whence all her currency is made of pure silver'.[139] His estimate was not far off. The English silver penny, or 'sterling', was maintained throughout most

---

[136] *Templar Records*, p. 50.    [137] e.g. PR 6 RI, p. 118.
[138] PR 8 RI (Chancellor's Roll), p. 17; PR 13 John, pp. 186–7 (the figures are for 17 months).
[139] H. Hunt. 1. 1. (p. 10).

of the Norman and Angevin period at a weight of about 1.45 grammes and a fineness of 92.5 per cent. Although the shilling (12*d*.), mark (13*s*. 4*d*.), and pound were used as accounting units, the penny was the only coin, and half and quarter pennies were made simply by cutting the penny along its axis.

One emblem of public power is the issuing of money and a sign of the authority of the English kings was the high degree of royal centralization in matters of the coinage. Except in Stephen's reign, their mastery was uncontested. A few great ecclesiastics, such as the archbishops of York and Canterbury, the bishop of Durham and the abbot of Bury, had the right to have a mint, but their moneyers struck coin in the king's name from centrally issued dies. Normally, therefore, the general imagery of the English penny was as uniform as its weight. On one side would be a representation of the king, showing his head and shoulders and often depicting him holding a sceptre, together with his name. On the reverse there was an abstract design, usually based on the cross; this side also bore the name of the moneyer who had produced the coin and the place of issue.

Despite this basic iconographic continuity, the monetary policy of the Norman period was marked by periodic remodelling of the coinage. Every two or three years pennies with a slightly different style of design would be introduced and the old type taken out of circulation. Just as foreign coin coming into the country had to be exchanged for sterling and was not acceptable as currency, so the new pennies had to be bought with the old. One purpose of this operation was to make a profit for the king, for the moneyers had to pay him for the new dies. In the early years of Henry II a different policy was introduced. After 1158, when a coinage of a new design, the so-called 'Cross and Crosslets' type, was adopted, the periodic recoinages were abandoned. Cross and crosslets coins continued to circulate for a generation or more. Then, in 1180, another new design, the so-called 'Short Cross' type, was inaugurated and this style continued to the end of our period and beyond. Its success was so great that no one was willing to tamper even with its inscription, so that English pennies bore the legend 'King Henry' throughout the reigns of Richard I and John.

Because the coinage was a source of royal profit and a symbol of royal power, kings enforced fierce rules and inflicted savage punishments designed to maintain its standard. Those using the old money after the new had been instituted were liable to fines. Henry I promised in his coronation charter that 'if anyone—a moneyer or anyone else—is seized with false money, full justice will be done'.[140] Later in his reign he had the chance to show how seriously he took his promise. In 1124 the silver pennies shipped over to Normandy to pay

---

[140] Liebermann, *Gesetze* 1, p. 522 (CHn cor); *Sel. Charters*, p. 118; Robertson, *Laws*, p. 278.

Henry's troops turned out to be well below the standard required. The king's response was grim:

he sent to England and commanded that all the moneyers there were in England should be deprived of their right hands and their testicles, because a pound would not buy a penny's worth at market. Bishop Roger of Salisbury sent all over England and commanded them all to come to Winchester at Christmas. There they came and they took them, one by one, and deprived them of their right hands and testicles.[141]

The moneyers did not always have such an unpleasant Christmas. They formed a closely interrelated elite in the boroughs and could, like Cheping the Rich of Winchester (above, p. 335) do well and found dynasties of urban oligarchs. They were, however, an oligarchy gradually contracting in numbers. Minting in the Norman period took place at many different centres— 65 at the time of Domesday survey—but the long-term trend was for concentration of minting in fewer and fewer locations. In the years immediately after 1158, when the 'Cross and Crosslets' type of penny was introduced, some thirty mints were in operation. By the 1170s this was reduced to twelve. In 1220 only six mints were in operation—London, Canterbury, Durham, Bury, York, and Winchester—with the two former absolutely preponderant in terms of production.[142]

Gold coins were not minted in England but they did circulate there. The Mediterranean region was a gold-minting zone throughout our period and Islamic and Byzantine gold coins arrived in England and were highly prized. Wulfstan, bishop of Worcester, 'had one of those gold coins that they call bezants, after the city once known as Byzantium, now as Constantinople'.[143] These bezants circulated widely and were worth two shillings sterling (the gold–silver ratio was 1:9 at this time).[144] They were used particularly for payments in which an element of ritual deference or respect was involved, such as the premium payment made by the new tenant when a rental was agreed or an offering at a saint's shrine. When a dispute between the nuns of Godstow and the canons of Norton (Ches.) was settled by the canons' complete renunciation of their claims, the nuns offered them 'one bezant annually at Michaelmas for the sake of good peace'.[145] It was a gesture made to allow the canons to save face and the exotic gold coin was the right medium for it.

---

[141] *ASC*, p. 255 (1125).

[142] J. J. North, *English Hammered Coinage*, 1. *Early Anglo-Saxon–Henry III, c.600–1272* (3rd edn.; London, 1994).

[143] W. Malm., *V. Wulfstan* 2. 9 (p. 33).

[144] e.g. PR 31 HI, p. 147; Peter Spufford, *Money and its Use in Medieval Europe* (Cambridge, 1987), p. 272.

[145] *EEA*, 4. *Lincoln 1186–1206*, ed. David Smith (1986), no. 243, p. 160.

The scale of minting and the amount of money in circulation can sometimes be deduced from indirect indicators, although the only direct evidence comes from very late in our period, in the form of accounts from the mints of London and Canterbury in the years 1220–2. These, the two most active mints in the country, were producing about four million pennies per annum at this time.[146] For the earlier period, one estimate is that the total output of the 'Cross and Crosslets' type in the years 1158–80 was between twenty and thirty million pennies, assuming an initial recoinage of ten million pennies in 1158, followed by an annual output of 500,000–750,000 pennies. The scale of minting increased dramatically with the recoinage of 1180. Between that date and 1204 it is likely that pennies were being produced at the rate of four million per annum.[147] In 1205 concern over the quality of the penny stimulated a large-scale recoinage. Coins that were less than seven-eighths the proper weight were withdrawn from circulation and reminted. The new coins were to have a clear border to prevent 'clipping', that is, the shaving of a slice of silver from the edge. Penalties were prescribed for those with light-weight coin in their possession. Sixteen mints were activated to handle this major recoinage.[148] It has been estimated that at this point there were about sixty million pennies in circulation.[149]

These figures convey some idea of the enormous numbers of silver pennies in England. Given the relative absence of credit arrangements and 'paper banking', there was a need to transport large amounts of coin. For example, the city reeves of Lincoln bringing the 'farm' (fixed payment) of the city to London in John's reign faced the task of transporting £180, i.e. 43,200 pennies, a distance of 200 miles; this number of pennies would weigh 139 lbs. Some of the farm was spent locally, at the king's command and for his purposes, and sometimes part could be discharged in kind—in 1201 cloth of 'Lincoln green' formed an element of the payment—and, moreover, the sum was discharged in two payments per year, but, on the other hand, there might be payment of arrears. At any event, the reeves faced the annual problem of transporting over 100 lbs. weight of pennies.[150] This must have been a main concern of all sheriffs and towns. The cost of bags and other gear for transporting pennies is a recurrent cost in the Pipe Rolls, like the three shillings that the royal servant Ralph of Cornhill paid to buy six casks 'to bring pennies to the lord king' in 1194.[151]

Transporting money was not just an issue for the king. When, in the late

[146] C. E. Blunt and J. D. Brand, 'Mint Output of Henry III', *British Numismatic Jnl* 39 (1970), pp. 61–6.
[147] Peter Spufford, *Money and its Use in Medieval Europe* (Cambridge, 1987), pp. 196–7.
[148] PR 7 John, pp. xxvii–xxxii; Painter, *John*, pp. 145–8.
[149] N. J. Mayhew, 'Money and Prices in England from Henry II to Edward III', *Agricultural History Review*, 35 (1987), pp. 121–31, at p. 125.
[150] *Earliest Lincs. Ass. Rolls*, p. 166; PR 3 John, p. 2.        [151] PR 6 RI, p. 175.

twelfth century, the abbot of Malmesbury granted various properties in Winchester to Hugh Camberlane, he obliged Hugh to send the annual rent of twelve shillings to Malmesbury at his own expense at the two terms of Easter and Michaelmas (29 Sept.).[152] Hugh thus faced the task of arranging the transport of 72 pennies over 55 miles every spring and autumn. A different arrangement was made when Michael de Wanchy granted half of his manor of Stanstead to the canons of Waltham abbey for a rent of £12 per annum. He specified that 'the canons shall render [the money] to me and my heirs at Waltham, £6 at Easter and £6 at Michaelmas, and the person who comes for the rent at those times shall be at Waltham at the expense of the canons until he receives it.'[153] This is not only a neat device to encourage prompt payment but also throws a little light on what must have been a major traffic of emissaries collecting and transporting silver pennies across the English countryside.

The early decades of the thirteenth century saw a sharp rise in many prices. Wheat was selling at a mean price of less than 2 shillings a quarter in the 1160s but almost 6 shillings in the first decade of the thirteenth century, although it then settled at 4 or 5 shillings for the next half-century. The sharp increase was in the years about 1200.[154] Livestock purchase prices between 1160 and 1230 are shown in Figure 12.[155] Clearly the turning point again occurs about 1200, when the price of oxen and plough-horses, that had been reasonably constant, begins a steep climb. Between the 1190s and the 1220s the price of oxen increased by 125 per cent, that of plough-horses by slightly more.

Explanations of inflation tend to fall into two types, those stressing the pattern of supply and demand and those concentrating on monetary factors, although in reality both are usually linked and intermingled. The silver supply of western Europe in the later twelfth century certainly did increase greatly, as new mines in the margraviate of Meissen were opened up. England would suck in this silver through Cologne and Flanders. Even though much of it would be spent on Angevin projects on the continent, there would still be the classic inflationary situation of too much money chasing too few goods. One possible explanation of the rather more gradual rise in sheep prices is that the demands of the Flemish cloth industry had stimulated a concentration on sheep rearing and a consequent flattening of prices. There was more silver, there were more sheep, but the same number of oxen and horses.

The increasing amount of money in circulation was a cause, a consequence, and a symbol of the increasing commercialization of England in

[152] *Registrum Malmesburiense*, ed. J. S. Brewer (2 vols., RS; 1879–80), vol. 2, pp. 35–6.
[153] Richardson, *Jewry*, pp. 244–5.    [154] Hallam, *Agrarian Hist.*, pp. 734–6, 747–55.
[155] Ibid., p. 748.

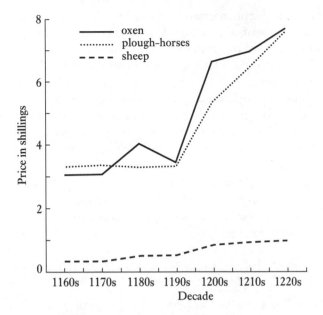

FIGURE 12. *Livestock prices, 1160–1230*

these years. More transactions were accomplished through the medium of cash than in the past. Peasant rents were increasingly in money rather than labour or produce. Large-scale moneylending, by the Jews and by foreign merchants, extended credit and created debt. One consequence of the increasing scale and extent of trade was the emergence of a group of people who were engaged in exchange full-time as their only occupation, like the forty-two men listed in Domesday Book in the borough of Tutbury, 'living from their trading alone'.[156] Large-scale warfare was another instrument of monetization. One of the impulses behind the shift from food rents to money rents on the royal manors was supposedly Henry I's continental wars. Because of these, in the words of his grandson's treasurer, 'coined money became absolutely essential to him'.[157] Soldiers did not want perishable treasure.

One small sign of 'monetary thinking' is the existence of terms that designated land by the revenue that could be obtained from it: the 'librate' (*librata*) was a piece of property that could be expected to bring in a pound a year, the 'solidate' (*solidata*) and the 'denariate' (*denariata*) similarly producing a shilling and a penny. Thus, when Nigel d'Aubigny made an exchange of lands in Essex with the abbey of Bec during the reign of Henry I, he specified the property he was giving as '20 librates of land in Dunton in

[156] *DB* 1, 248b (Sts. 10. 1).     [157] *Dial. scacc.*, p. 41.

Essex'; when king Stephen granted property in Hertfordshire to the Templars in 1142, he described it as '40 solidates of land in the manor of Dinsley'; while a document from the priory of Lewes about 1095 mentions '20 denariates of land in Binham'.[158] This is a very precise and very monetary way of conceptualizing land.

Not everyone was enchanted by commercialization. The values that trading seemed to encourage could be viewed negatively. 'Very few people engage in business who do not make their money from another's loss', opined one Canterbury monk, while the haughty Norman princess in the Anglo-Norman poem *Waldef* expresses utter contempt for the dirty business in her disdainful utterance—'I am not a burgess' daughter, to change my love from man to man, for their gold and silver'.[159] All the evidence is, however, that both monks and princesses had to face an increasingly monetized and increasingly commercial world.

[158] *Mowbray Charters*, no. 11, p. 15; *Templar Records*, pp. 212–13; *RRAN* 3, no. 858, p. 315; *The Cartulary of the Priory of St Pancras of Lewes*, ed. L. F. Salzman (2 vols., Sussex Rec. Soc. 38, 40; 1932–4), vol. 1, p. 12.

[159] W. Cant, *Mir. Thos.* 4. 13 (p. 326); *Le Roman de Waldef*, lines 1310–12, ed. A. J. Holden (Geneva, 1984), p. 66.

# CHAPTER 8

# The Institutional Church

From the seventh century, when it was established, to the sixteenth, when it underwent fundamental transformation, the English Church was one of the most dominant, visible, and pervasive forces in English society. In the period covered here, Christian baptism and Christian burial were virtually universal, while, to an ever-increasing extent, those who married did so through the forms of Christian matrimony. All these rites of passage were handled by ritual specialists, the priests and other clergy, whose legal standing, dress, and appearance set them off from others. Ethics and theology were in their hands. Writing and formal education were largely the monopoly of clerks or of the religious (monks and canons regular). The Church was rich. At the time of the Domesday inquest in 1086 it owned one-fifth of the wealth of the country. It laid claim to one-tenth of the income of all Christians. Such a combination of economic power, ubiquity, and psychological intrusion made the Church a fundamental and formative institution.

## 1. THE HIERARCHY

### Clerks

'Clerk and lay' was a contemporary verbal tag conveying a basic distinction. Certain men would be marked out, initially simply by their haircut, the tonsure, as members of a different order of society from their lay brothers. Once the ceremony of shaving the crown of their head had been performed, they would enjoy the privileges and face the obligations of clerks. Clerks were a minority—perhaps 5 per cent of the adult male population—but they were to be found everywhere, serving not only as parish priests and cathedral clergy but also as chaplains, secretaries, and teachers. They were meant to wear monochrome clothing, avoid taverns and tournaments, and renounce the carrying of weapons.

These clerks constituted the secular clergy—as distinct from the monks and regular canons of the religious orders—and were organized into a hierarchy. It was a hierarchy partly of office and partly of 'order' or clerical status.

At the bottom were mere clerks, men who had received the tonsure, the distinctive outward sign of clerical status, but were not in orders. Above them were the clerks who had been ordained to one of the minor orders (psalmist or cantor, doorkeeper, lector, exorcist, and acolyte), but who had not reached one of the major orders of subdeacon, deacon, or priest. Clerks in minor orders might be married. They often attained important ecclesiastical office and could hold churches as long as they provided a priest to undertake services in them. Certain offices did require the higher orders: an archdeacon had to be a deacon, a bishop had to be a priest. A clerk could do quite well without such status, however, and it was not at all uncommon for a newly elected bishop to have to be ordained priest before he could be consecrated as bishop. In 1096 two royal chaplains, Gerard and Samson, had to be ordained both deacon and priest before they could take up their offices as bishop of Hereford and Worcester, respectively.[1] The two hierarchies of office and order were thus linked, but not completely integrated. Mere tonsured clerics might well be poor, or married with children, or of no fixed abode, but they might also enjoy the profits of rich ecclesiastical benefices and hold positions of some power.

### The Parish and the Parish Priest

The local representative of the Church was the parish priest. Except where subordinate chapels had acquired these rights (see below), baptism and burial took place at the parish church with the rector or vicar officiating. These rites took place in physical settings only to be found in certain churches. Statutes prescribed that 'Every baptismal church should have a font made of stone or some other suitable material and it should be covered properly and treated reverently and not used for any other purpose.'[2] A parish church always had a cemetery. The font and the graveyard represented entry into and departure from the earthly community and these gateways were in the keeping of the parish.

Parish churches received income of three kinds: offerings, endowments, and tithes. Although it was insisted that there should be no official charges for baptism, marriage, or burial, the custom of making offerings to the priest on such occasions was deeply ingrained. Even the rigorists conceded that it was permissible to accept 'something offered voluntarily *at* these ceremonies but not *in return for* them'.[3] In addition, there were collections made at services and various customary annual payments, such as the 'church-scot' in produce paid at Martinmas (11 Nov.). Besides these offerings, the parish had a

---

[1] Eadmer, *HN*, p. 74.     [2] *Councils and Synods* 2/i, pp. 31, 68–9.
[3] Gerald, *Gemma* 1. 13 (p. 46).

regular source of income in its landed endowment, which could be large. When the church of East Carlton (Northants) was raised to parochial status between 1109 and 1120, it was on condition that the local landholders provide it with an endowment. Three named freeholders had to provide a total of two and a half bovates and the villeins of Carlton had to give another fifteen acres; in addition a dwelling for the priest was to be provided.[4] The area of a bovate varied from place to place, so it is not possible to be precise about the total size of this endowment, but it was probably over fifty acres, a very substantial farm by contemporary standards.

The most contentious source of income was tithe, the tenth levied on agricultural produce. The Council of Westminster of 1175 listed the things that were tithable: 'grain, wine, fruit, new-born livestock, wool, lambs, cheese, flax, hemp, and other things that are replenished each year'.[5] Small-scale agricultural producers, the typical parishioners of medieval England, naturally resented seeing a tenth of their crop carted off and resistance and evasion were commonplace. Just as perennial were clerical attempts to enforce the payment of tithes. When Gilbert of Sempringham was rector of Sempringham he discovered that one of his parishioners had evaded the tithe-collectors and taken his whole harvest to his barn:

When the rector discovered this, he immediately compelled the peasant to throw all his grain out of the barn and to count it out, handful by handful, in front of him. He then had a tenth part of it, that belonged to him and the church, heaped up in the village street and set fire to it, burning it as mark of his detestation of this offence and as a deterrent to others, judging it unworthy that what was secretly stolen from God and Holy Church should come into the use of men.[6]

The smouldering bonfire in the street at Sempringham is a good symbol of the church's intransigence in its claim for tithe—better for the contested corn to be consumed in a kind of burnt offering that to go to secular use.

Comprising a tenth of the agricultural produce of the parish, the rents or harvest from a possibly large farm, and the flow of diverse offerings, parochial income could thus be considerable. It is not surprising that attempts were made to divert it from the local priest. Frequently the rector, who took the income, was not resident in the parish and might not even be a priest. Successful pluralists might hold many parishes. They then had to provide for a priest to perform services in the parish church. Links between rector and parish could thus be purely financial. One pluralist of the late twelfth century confessed that he scarcely knew the name of the vicar who performed the services in the parish of which he was rector.[7]

---

[4] Avrom Saltman, *Theobald, Archbishop of Canterbury* (London, 1956), p. 422; date from *EEA*, 1. *Lincoln 1067–1185*, ed. David Smith (1980), p. 7.

[5] *Councils and Synods* 1/ii, pp. 988–9.    [6] *Bk. Gilbert*, pp. 18–20.    [7] Gerald, *Symb. el.*, p. 259.

Because churches were sources of income as well as centres of religious worship, they were eagerly acquired by monastic communities, who made various arrangements to secure revenue from them. One way was to institute a parson who agreed to make an annual payment or 'pension'. Another, more interventionist, tactic was to take all the revenues of the church and then pay a stipend, often quite modest, to a priest who would serve as 'vicar' (i.e. substitute or deputy). The trend seems to have been towards this more direct form of management, just as it was in the administration of manors. The author of the *Chronicle of Battle Abbey*, writing late in the reign of Henry II, says that some 'moderns' criticized the former abbot, Walter de Lucy (1139–71), for not instituting vicars in all the abbey's churches: 'for it is said that he could have transferred those churches and all the profits arising from them to his monastery, instituting vicars to serve in them for a decent annual stipend'. Instead of 'this modern plan', the abbot had granted the churches to clerks in return for a pension, thus being content with a portion of the income when he could have had all.[8]

Besides the parish churches, there were chapels of various types, some attached to a monastic or collegiate church, some the private chapels of great men, but also chapels erected to serve the religious needs of communities within large parishes. Some of these even acquired baptismal and burial rights, although they remained dependent in some ways on the mother church. In the early thirteenth century the large Surrey parish of Godalming had five chapels. That at Chiddingfold was over five miles from the mother church, and the chapel at Haslemere was almost another four miles beyond that at Chiddingfold, on which it was dependent. Before these chapels were built the difficulties of travelling to and from the mother church, especially in winter, must have been great.[9] Like parish churches, chapels required resources and could have their own endowments. The men of Hutthorpe (Northants), for example, endowed their local chapel with two acres from each virgate (full peasant holding).[10]

Parochial churches viewed burial as a lucrative right that they were not prepared to yield easily. The words of one of the provisions of the Council of Westminster in 1102 make this clear: 'The bodies of the dead are not to be taken out of the parish for burial, lest the parish priest lose what he should rightly receive from that.'[11] It was not unknown for the body of a parishioner buried wrongfully elsewhere to be dug up and reburied in the proper churchyard.[12] The large and ancient church of Christchurch in Hampshire claimed

---

[8]  *Battle Chron.*, pp. 250–2.

[9]  John Blair, *Early Medieval Surrey* (Surrey Archaeological Soc.; 1991), pp. 157–8, based on *Reg. Osm.* 1, pp. 296–8.

[10]  *Danelaw Docs.*, no. 465, pp. 342–3.     [11]  *Councils and Synods* 1/ii, p. 678.

[12]  e.g. *Abingdon Chron.* 2, pp. 121–2.

a huge parish and kept a jealous eye on its rights: regarding the church in the village of Boldre, almost nine miles from Christchurch, the clergy of Christchurch insisted

no-one should be buried at Boldre except cottars and slaves of the manor on which the church is founded, who were so poor they did not have the wherewithal to allow them to be carried to Christchurch; both free men and villeins ought, one and all, to go to Christchurch on all feasts and pay there their tithes and church-scot and alms, and to carry their dead there for burial.[13]

If the parish church were indeed eight or nine miles distant, a funeral would involve a sixteen-mile journey, half of it with the burden of the corpse. In winter such an effort would be hard for all and perhaps completely beyond the strength of a widow or mourning mother.

The convenience of having a church nearby was a common stimulus to new foundations. An account of the foundation of the chapel at Whistley (Berks.), which belonged to the abbey of Abingdon, explains that in the early days of Abbot Adelelm (1071–83), there was no church there

for it appertained to the priest of the parish of Sonning. But because it was difficult in winter for the inhabitants to cross the ford to Sonning to hear church service, and also because when the abbot stayed in the area there was nowhere to celebrate mass, a wooden chapel was built there, dedicated to St Nicholas, and it was consecrated by Osmund, bishop of Salisbury.

A subsequent dispute led to the recording of the exact rights of the chapel and the mother church in writing in a document of 1089.[14] In this case the avowed motives for creating a new centre of worship were both the needs of the local inhabitants and the requirements of the lord of the place.

The local lord could indeed be a major protagonist in the formation of new ecclesiastical units. In 1147 the parson of the great Wiltshire church of St Lawrence, Downton, had to concede to the new church of St Mary, Standlynch, within his parish, the right to undertake baptisms and burials and to receive tithes from the fief of Robert de Bayeux. A house and four acres had been provided for the new priest by Robert de Bayeux and the incumbent would be chosen by the parson of Downton 'with the just and lawful counsel of Robert and his heirs'. Some tokens of subordination were retained: the priest of Standlynch had to pay half a mark of silver each Whitsun to the parson of Downton and 'place it on the altar of the mother church of St Lawrence', while Robert de Bayeux and his successors 'must come each year to the mother church of St Lawrence, if they are in Standlynch at

[13] P. H. Hase, 'The Mother Churches of Hampshire', in John Blair (ed.), *Minsters and Parish Churches: The Local Church in Transition, 950–1200* (Oxford, 1988), pp. 45–66, at p. 60.

[14] *Abingdon Chron.* 2, pp. 18–19.

Whitsun or on St Lawrence's day.'[15] The importance of the initiative of the local lord, Robert de Bayeux, is clear.

Rough calculations suggest that the average parish size in pre-industrial England was about 2,500 acres.[16] Of the 39 English counties, the majority (nineteen) had an average parish size of between 2,000 and 3,000 acres, while in a further seven the average parish was slightly smaller—between 1,500 and 2,000 acres in extent. In only a dozen shires were parishes usually more than 3,000 acres (Middlesex was quite exceptional because the multiplicity of small London parishes gave it a very diminutive average parish size). The twelve counties with large parishes were, apart from one instance on the Welsh Marches (Shropshire), either in the south-west peninsula (Cornwall, Devon) or in the north and north-west of the country.[17] In Northumberland, a county of almost 1,300,000 acres and only approximately 115 parishes, the average size of the parish was thus over 11,000 acres, but this was the extreme case. People living in the usual English parish of the fully developed parochial system would normally not have to walk more than a mile or so to their parish church. A network of this density was the product of centuries, and it seems that in the period 1075–1225 it was still developing.

*A Case Study: Brixton Hundred*

Brixton Hundred, forming the extreme north-eastern part of the county of Surrey, may serve as a case study (see Map 8). The great ecclesiastical tax survey of 1291 names sixteen churches within the boundaries of the Hundred, although a seventeenth that certainly existed (Newington) was omitted. Of these seventeen churches only seven are recorded in the Domesday Survey of 1086, one of them (Streatham) as a chapel rather than a church. Of the ten churches that emerge into written record between 1086 and 1291, six receive their earliest mention in the twelfth century, although the church of Barnes, first recorded in 1181, seems to have remained dependent on its mother church of Wimbledon. Four more churches are first referred to in the thirteenth century. Of course, the first mention of a church in writing and its actual origin are by no means the same thing. However, we know that churches were being founded in this period and the fact that the earliest

---

[15] *EEA*, 8. *Winchester 1070–1204*, ed. M. J. Franklin (1993), no. 108, pp. 73–5.

[16] The following figures are based on the lists of pre-1832 parishes in Cecil Humphrey–Smith, *The Phillimore Atlas and Index of Parish Registers* (2nd edn.; Chichester, 1995). If the figure of 9,500 parishes for the whole of England in the late thirteenth century, as suggested by J. R. H. Moorman, *Church Life in England in the Thirteenth Century* (Cambridge, 1945), p. 5, is correct, the average parish size at that time would be around 3,350 acres—cf. his statement, 'The average English parish in the thirteenth century covered about four thousand acres' (p. 12).

[17] Cheshire, Cumberland, Derbyshire, Durham, Lancashire, Northumberland, Staffordshire, Westmoreland, Yorkshire.

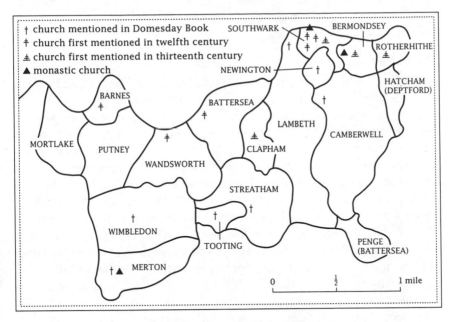

† church mentioned in Domesday Book
‡ church first mentioned in twelfth century
± church first mentioned in thirteenth century
▲ monastic church

MAP 8. *Parishes of Brixton Hundred*

recorded churches are found on the larger and richer estates is some reassurance that the pattern is not a mere illusion arising from increasing written evidence.

New churches sprang up in various parts of the Hundred. Southwark, at the southern end of London Bridge, was in effect a suburb of London and shared in that city's prodigious growth. Apart from the minster recorded there in 1086—which later became the priory of St Mary's and is now Southwark Cathedral—three parishes (St Olave's, St George's, and St Margaret's) emerged in the first half of the twelfth century, to be joined by a fourth (St Mary Magdalene's) in the early thirteenth century. Battersea and Wandsworth were not far away and their churches are first mentioned in the year 1157. The huge archiepiscopal estate at Wimbledon, covering Mortlake, Barnes, and Putney, was served by only one church in 1086, but saw new chapels at those locations in the following centuries. Barnes has already been mentioned; the chapel at Putney is recorded only in 1291 (not in the papal taxation records but elsewhere); while the chapel at Mortlake was founded as late as 1348 expressly 'for the rest of the bodies and the saving of the souls of the tenants of East Sheen and Mortlake, who are very far distant from their parish church'.[18] The formation of a parochial network might thus be a process taking centuries. Even in 1658 it was still being argued that Putney

---

[18] *Calendar of the Patent Rolls (1348–50)* (London, 1905), p. 88.

should be a separate parish, since it was 'situated from the said parish church of Wimbledon about two miles'.[19]

## Clerical Marriage

One of the most bitter struggles of the period was the attempt to outlaw clerical, especially priestly, marriage and the associated practice of the inheritance of benefices. Reformers of an austere bent, some of monastic background, demanded that priests be celibate and chaste. This went against long tradition and ingrained custom. Respected priestly dynasties were to be found in possession of many English churches. One of the most notable examples was the family that held the church of Hexham for over a century. The last member to do so was Eilaf, the father of Ailred of Rievaulx, who died in 1138. Much later than this the transmission of ecclesiastical benefices from father to son was still a familiar transaction. Abbot Joseph of Reading (1173–86) granted to Osbert, son of Osbert, the chapel of Eye in Herefordshire 'just as his father held it in the year and on the day that he departed from this world', for an annual payment of £2.[20] Priests with sons had a natural inclination to look after them and often considered that the best way to do this was by having them succeed to their office and income. Such men were responsible parents, like the priest Withgar, parson of Mendlesham in Suffolk, who 'wished to provide for his own after him' and approached the patron of the church, the abbot of Battle, to persuade him to present his son Nicholas to the bishop as the next incumbent. This the abbot did, although only after negotiating a 400 per cent increase in the payment the parson had to make to the abbot.[21]

If the custom of married and hereditary priests was deep-rooted, then the assault on the custom was also sustained and vigorous. Official pronouncements throughout the period reiterate the theme. Lanfranc's Council of Winchester of 1076 ruled that, although married priests were not to be forced to give up the wives they had, in future no priests could marry nor could married men be ordained.[22] In 1102 the Council of Westminster, presided over by archbishop Anselm, ruled that priests and deacons could not marry or keep their wives if they had them; that priests who maintained 'illicit relations with a woman' could not celebrate mass; that henceforth clerks should take a vow of chastity before they were ordained as subdeacons or higher; and that 'sons of priests should not inherit their fathers' churches'.[23] A generation later, in 1129, another council ordered that all archdeacons and priests should

---

[19] *VCH Surrey* 4, p. 83.

[20] Brian Kemp, 'Hereditary Benefices in the Medieval English Church: A Herefordshire Example', *Bulletin of the Institute of Historical Research*, 43 (1970), pp. 1–15, at pp. 11–12.

[21] *Battle Chron.*, p. 240.     [22] *Councils and Synods* 1/ii, p. 619.

[23] Ibid., p. 675.

give up their wives within two months, but was undercut by the king's willingness to take a cash sum from the priests instead.[24]

The campaign continued throughout the Angevin period, with strong backing from popes like Alexander III (1159–81). The attack on the married clergy had two aspects. On the one hand was the practical matter that married clergy would naturally hope that their sons would inherit their benefices. Transmission of ecclesiastical office by inheritance might seem inappropriate. In the words of pope Alexander, 'it is not consonant with reason that sons should succeed their fathers in churches, since the sanctuary of God cannot be possessed by hereditary right'.[25] The reform movement of the eleventh and twelfth century aimed to ensure that the western clergy should not be a caste, distinguished by blood and birth, but a vocational group recruited by selection and training. A parish priest should be chosen because he was suitable, not because he was the son of the previous parish priest. On the other hand, there was also the issue of pollution: sex was contaminating and priests should be pure. 'It is commanded that from the time of his reception of holy orders a priest should always practice sexual continence and keep his vessel clean in all holiness', wrote one high principled cleric.[26] The reformers wanted the Catholic priest to be like a monk, not like a family man.

The reformers won a partial victory. By the middle of the twelfth century it was uncommon for the higher clergy to be married or transmit their benefices to sons. By the thirteenth century married priests were far less usual than they had been. Yet it would be false to picture the parsonages of England in 1200 as peopled with solitary celibates. On the contrary, one acerbic critic, writing about that time, asserted that 'the houses and huts of our parish priests are lorded over by their mistresses and full of creaking cradles, new-born babies and squalling children'.[27]

In one area, the English Common Law, reform had a success. From the viewpoint of the rigorist, priests could not have wives; if they lived with women and had children by them, then these women must, by definition, be 'concubines' (*focaria* was the Latin term used, meaning literally 'companion of the hearth'). This was not the only point of view even in the early thirteenth century, for critics at that time still railed against priests 'who dare to get married in front of the church, saying that no one can prohibit priests from getting married like other men'.[28] The king's justices, however, agreed with the reformers. English Common Law accepted that the son of a priest was *ipso facto* illegitimate. Thus in the Lincolnshire hearings of 1202 Luke, son of Abraham, lost his claim to the land of his deceased uncle Benedict

---

[24] *ASC*, pp. 259–60; H. Hunt. 7. 40 (pp. 482–4).
[25] Duggan, 'Equity' (p. 67).      [26] Gerald, *Gemma* 2. 5 (pp. 185–6).
[27] Gerald, *Spec. eccl.* 4. 22 (p. 313).      [28] T. Chobham, *SC*, p. 384.

because Benedict 'was the son of a priest and hence a bastard', and bastards did not pass on an inheritance except through their direct descendants. Since Benedict was not only a priest but also the son of a priest this evidence not only demonstrates the way the secular law buttressed the prejudice of the canon law against priests having children but also shows how deep-seated these priestly families were in the English countryside.[29]

### Parish Churches

In 1075 there were thousands of parish churches in England. By 1225 there were many more. The intense building activity of the period was remarked upon by contemporaries. Active bishops like Wulfstan of Worcester (1062–95) were praised for promoting the building of new churches: 'in every part of his diocese he constructed churches on his own estates and pressed for them to be constructed on others'.[30] William of Malmesbury wrote that, after the Norman Conquest, 'everywhere you could see churches rising up in the villages and minsters in the towns and cities, built in a style of a new kind'.[31] The most powerful reminders of the building programmes of the Norman and Angevin epoch are the hundreds of churches, great and small, that still survive, in whole or in part, from that time. A church like Iffley (Oxon.), built in the 1170s, is a perfect example (Plate 12).[32] Despite subsequent remodelling and restoration, the plan and most of the features visible today are those of a particularly beautiful church of the Angevin period. The church has a nave, central tower, and chancel that together form a building almost 100 feet long and varying from 16 to 20 feet in width. The large font is from the same period as the church itself. There are south, north, and west doorways, each consisting of a recessed round-headed arch decorated with carving. The west front is especially grand, with a top row of three round-headed windows, a central circular window (a Victorian restoration based on the traces of the twelfth-century original), and the great west door, all lavishly carved with geometric designs and the curious 'beak-head' motif—rows of glaring-eyed and sharp-beaked birds' heads that appear to grip the mouldings of the arch, a design very popular in twelfth-century English churches.[33] In scale, solidity, and form it would have been unequalled in its local world.

Naturally, not all churches were as large and elaborate as Iffley. A late

---

[29] *Earliest Lincs. Ass. Rolls*, pp. 69–70.

[30] W. Malm., *V. Wulfstan* 3. 10 (p. 52).    [31] W. Malm., *GR* 3. 246 (2, p. 306); OMT edn., p. 460.

[32] Jennifer Sherwood and Nikolaus Pevsner, *Oxfordshire* (The Buildings of England; 1974), pp. 658–61 and plate 11; *VCH Oxfordshire* 5, pp. 201–4; Royal Commission on . . . Historical Monuments, *City of Oxford* (London, 1939), pp. 151–4.

[33] Françoise Henry and George Zarnecki, 'Romanesque Arches Decorated with Human and Animal Heads', *Jnl British Archaeological Association*, 3rd ser., 20–1 (1957–8), pp. 1–34, with plates.

eleventh-century church that has been excavated at Hatch on the Hampshire Downs was a simple two-celled building of chalk and flint. The nave was 34 feet long, the chancel less than 13 feet (although later enlarged).[34] Some urban churches in towns with many parishes were yet smaller: in the twelfth century the parish church of St Mary Tanner Street in Winchester had a nave about 12 feet by 15 feet.[35] Yet the investigation of church building in this period suggests a definite trend towards expansion. Wooden buildings were replaced by stone and existing churches were extended, through lengthening the chancel or nave or the addition of porches or aisles. The physical setting of parish worship, of baptism and burial tended to become more imposing over the course of time.[36]

## Bishops

The chief office in the English church hierarchy was that of bishop. Light is cast on some of the everyday duties of a bishop by the very first surviving bishop's register, that of Hugh of Wells, bishop of Lincoln (1209–35).[37] The majority of the entries concern institutions to benefices, that is, the formal appointment by the bishop of a cleric to be parson or vicar of a church. The choice of parson lay not with the bishop but with the patron of the church, who 'presented' the candidate to the bishop, who alone could actually institute him. The patron could be a layman or a monastic community. It was the bishop's duty to ensure that the benefice was in fact vacant and to decide on competing claims to present. In most cases he had also to consider existing interests in the benefice, either in the form of 'pensions' payable to third parties or because a vicar had been installed to perform the actual parochial duties.

The following entry, concerning Chesterton in Oxfordshire, is not atypical:

William of Paris, clerk, is presented to the church of Chesterton by William, archdeacon of London, because he has custody of the land and heir of Robert of Chesterton, and, after an inquiry made by the archdeacon of Oxford and certification to the lord bishop by letters patent of the dean of Hereford of the death of Gerald de Barri, the last rector of the church, he is admitted to it and canonically instituted parson in it. Reservation is made of the perpetual vicarage that Master Ranulf de

---

[34] P. J. Fasham and G. Keevil, *Brighton Hill South (Hatch Warren): An Iron Age Farmstead and Deserted Medieval Village in Hampshire* (Wessex Archaeology Report 7; Salisbury, 1995), pp. 77–9.

[35] Biddle, *Winchester*, p. 334.

[36] e.g., Richard Morris, *The Church in British Archaeology* (Council for British Archaeology Research Report 47; 1983), p. 83, fig. 24.

[37] *Rot. Hug. Welles*; for a detailed analysis of the rolls, David Smith, 'The Rolls of Hugh of Wells, Bishop of Lincoln 1209–35', *Bulletin of the Institute of Historical Research*, 45 (1972), pp. 155–95.

Besaciis has in the church. He will hold the whole church with its appurtenances as vicar for as long as he lives, paying five and a half marks to William of Paris as rector.[38]

In this situation there were four parties to consider: the patron, the patron's guardian (who happened to be an archdeacon in a different diocese), the new rector, and the incumbent vicar. An inquiry had to be undertaken by the local archdeacon and correspondence entered into with the dean of Hereford to ensure that the rectory was in fact vacant. It was evidently a complex piece of business to appoint a new rector—and the diocese of Lincoln comprised 1,600 parishes.

Also in bishop Hugh's register are details of other kinds of business: grants of revenues, lands, churches, and wardship, relaxation of penance for those who contribute to bridge construction or a leper hospital, a licence for a private chapel, notification of a verdict in a matrimonial case, letters of protection for a crusader, permission for the bishop of Salisbury to send preachers into the diocese to collect for the building of Salisbury cathedral. This material, varied as it is, still does not by any means illustrate all the work of a bishop. His liturgical, judicial, and political duties, not to mention his role as feudal lord and landlord, meant that the bishop had heavy obligations, as well as great powers. Only a bishop could ordain priests, consecrate churches, and confirm the faithful; he had a busy court; he was a lord of lands and men, and servant and adviser of the king.

## Bishop and Diocese
### Archdeacons

The average size of the English bishopric was about 3,000 square miles. In a geometrically symmetrical world this would mean that no settlement was more than one day's ride from its bishop's seat. Reality was messier. At one extreme the tiny bishopric of Rochester was no more than thirty-five miles across at its widest, while the huge diocese of Lincoln required at least five days hard riding to go from its southern tip near Reading to its northern extremity on the Humber. The response to the demands of such distances, coupled with the growing amount of ecclesiastical business, was territorial subdivision. The primary subordinate unit of the bishopric was the archdeaconry.

A uniform system of territorial archdeaconries seems to have been the creation of the generation after the Norman Conquest. An ecclesiastical council held at Windsor in 1070 ordered 'that bishops should appoint archdeacons in their churches' and Remigius, bishop of Lincoln (1067–92), who was probably present, is known to have followed this injunction. 'He placed seven

---

[38] *Rot. Hug. Welles* 2, pp. 9–10.

archdeacons over the seven regions under his rule', wrote Henry of Huntingdon, a later incumbent of one of these archdeaconries.[39] The diocese of Lincoln even acquired an eighth archdeaconry in the course of the twelfth century, but, as the largest see in England, it was not representative. London, with four archdeaconries, was more typical, while some small dioceses had only a single archdeacon. The archdeacon acted as the bishop's deputy and representative and had the duty of supervising the parish churches of his archdeaconry, ensuring, for example, that they had proper vessels and that the priest knew how to celebrate Mass. He was also responsible for enforcing moral standards among both clergy and laity.

Archdeacons acquired a bad reputation. They were accused of exercising a local tyranny, 'burdening the laity with their allegations and the clergy with undue exactions'.[40] Gilbert of Sempringham declined the offer of an archdeaconry in the diocese of Lincoln, calling it 'the quickest path to damnation'.[41] Some individuals fitted this unfriendly characterization. Complaints were raised that the archdeacon of Chester in the later twelfth century was squeezing money out of those who were accused of some offence or had been commanded to undergo trial by ordeal and that he was travelling from church to church with a large mounted retinue demanding hospitality.[42]

The complaints raised against archdeacons reflect the fact that the Church was exercising an ever more intrusive and effective government. By the early thirteenth century there existed a hierarchy of ecclesiastical courts and officials that covered the country in a relatively dense network. The bishop himself, his 'Official' (a deputy whose position emerged in the late twelfth century), the archdeacons, and the rural deans below them all exercised judicial and administrative authority at different levels. The personnel of the ecclesiastical hierarchy were more numerous than ever before. They controlled great resources and ran a complex legal and bureaucratic machine. It is not surprising that contact between the Church and the secular world sometimes led to chafing.

## Cathedral Chapters

The group of clergy with whom the bishop had most constant, and sometimes difficult, relations were those of his cathedral chapter. In secular cathedrals he had a delicate path to tread with his canons, a body of well-paid, educated, supposedly celibate men like himself, who had a strong sense of their dignity and rights. Monastic chapters could be even more prickly. The main tendencies in the organization of secular cathedral chapters in this period were (1) division of the property and revenues of the diocese between the bishop

---

[39] *Councils and Synods* 1/ii, p. 580; H. Hunt. *De contemptu mundi* 4, p. 590.
[40] Lambeth Anon. 12 (pp. 95–6).    [41] *Bk. Gilbert*, p. 28.
[42] *Decretals* 1. 23. 6, col. 151 (JL 13857).

and chapter; (2) allocation of most of the chapter property to individual canons as prebends; (3) elaboration within the body of canons of a group of dignitaries with special roles, usually dean, chancellor, precentor, and treasurer. These trends created a relatively wealthy body of canons and strengthened the independence and standing of the chapter. Since cathedral prebends were attractive to royal clerks and other pluralists, it became common for canons to be frequently non-resident, employing vicars in their place to perform the cathedral services.

At York prebends were introduced by archbishop Thomas I (1070–1100):

For many years the canons lived together in common, but the archbishop then decided, upon advice, to give to each one a prebend from the lands of St Peter [York Minster], much of which lay desolate. The purpose was to increase the number of canons and to encourage each one, as it were for his own sake, to build up and cultivate his share with greater zeal.[43]

Developments at Chichester can be traced from the time of Domesday Book.[44] This lists sixteen hides held by the canons 'in common', but also two hides at Treyford (Sussex) held by Robert 'as a prebend of the church of Chichester'.[45] The number of separate prebends increased steadily, so that by the end of the twelfth century there were 23, excluding those of the archdeacons and dignitaries. First mention of a dean dates to 1108, of a precentor to about 1122, while the treasurership and chancellorship were founded by bishop Hilary (1147–69). Statutes of 1197 regulate the common fund of the chapter, i.e. that part of the chapter endowment that had not been allocated to individual prebends. Apart from a daily distribution of bread, 12d. per week was to be paid to resident canons from this source, while vicars were to receive 3d. a week, in addition to their stipend from the canon employing them.[46]

Each of the secular cathedrals eventually had between 25 to 50 prebends, giving a total of more than 300 in the English church as a whole. These 300 positions varied greatly in value but many of them provided a large and steady income for royal clerks, younger sons of the aristocracy, and other clerical careerists. The statute regulating residence adopted by the chapter of St Paul's in 1192 gives the names of the holders of the thirty prebends of the diocese of London.[47] These include the four dignitaries of dean, master of the schools (as the chancellor was termed at this time in London), precentor, and treasurer, and the four archdeacons of the diocese (London, Essex, Middlesex, and Colchester). Four canons are expressly titled 'Master', indicating that they had pursued higher study, while others not so titled certainly were

[43] Hugh Chanter, p. 18.    [44] *Chichester Acta*, pp. 41–8.
[45] *DB* 1, 17, 23 (Ssx. 3. 10, 11. 8).    [46] *Chichester Acta*, no. 101, pp. 157–9.
[47] R. Diceto, *Op.* 2, pp. lxix–lxxiii; *Fasti*, 1. St Paul's, London, passim.

Masters, such as the historian, Ralph of Diceto, who served as dean, and the courtier and literary man, Walter Map.

The webs of family influence are apparent in the London chapter. One canon mentioned in 1192 was 'Henry, son of the bishop'; he was not son of the current incumbent but of a predecessor, Robert de Sigillo, bishop of London (1141–50), who had been a royal clerk before becoming a monk and hence could legitimately have been married. Relatives of other bishops, such as Richard de Belmeis I (1108–27), his nephew Richard de Belmeis II (1152–62), and Gilbert Foliot (1163–87), were also represented. Robert Banastre, archdeacon of Essex and prebendary of Islington, was Gilbert Foliot's nephew and it is natural to assume that Henry Banastre, treasurer and prebendary of Wilsden, and Gilbert Banastre, prebendary of Consumpta-per-Mare, were also family members.[48] The bishop at the time of the statute, 1192, was Richard fitz Neal, the royal treasurer, who was the son of bishop Nigel of Ely. It was presumably at his initiative that his relative, William of Ely, was appointed prebendary of Caddington Minor.[49] William of Ely succeeded bishop Richard as royal treasurer in 1196 and served until the breakdown of government in 1215, receiving lands and office under king John in addition to his London prebend. The echo of another great voice of patronage is heard in the reference in the document of 1192 to 'Lawrence, nephew of pope Celestine' (Celestine III, pope at this time), who held the prebend of Ealdland.

This profile of the London chapter thus reveals a large group of propertied and educated men, who engaged in literary activity, participated in both royal and ecclesiastical government, and were deeply imbedded in ties of family patronage. Some of them were responsible for running the diocese, many of them bought and sold London property, each had his solid economic foundation in his prebend—a relationship symbolized by the naming of some of the prebends after their incumbents (e.g. Mapesbury from Walter Map, Reculversland from Hugh of Reculver). Several held prebends or posts in other dioceses. The cathedral clergy, and their counterparts in other collegiate churches, formed a small interlocking elite of wealth, learning, and authority.

## Cathedral Churches

The construction and enlargement of parish churches in this period was paralleled by building activity on the cathedrals. Great new cathedral churches

---

[48] Foliot, *Letters*, index, s.v. 'Banastre'; Adrian Morey and Christopher Brooke, *Gilbert Foliot and his Letters* (Cambridge, 1965), index, s.v. 'Banastre'.

[49] William's name was omitted by oversight from the printed text: H. G. Richardson, review of *Early Charters St Pauls*, EHR 57 (1942), p. 132 n. 1.

rose above the bishops' cities, eclipsing in scale and elegance those that had gone before. At Durham the foundation stone of the present enormous cathedral was laid on 11 August 1093. The eastern end was completed by 1099 and work continued on the nave as money allowed, until it was finished at some point between 1128 and 1133. Bishop Hugh de Puiset (1153–95) enlarged and beautified the cathedral, embellishing the interior with marble and stained glass windows, having a shrine of gold and silver made for the bones of the Venerable Bede, and instigating the building of the Galilee chapel at the west end of the church. After this had been constructed the total length of the cathedral must have been close to its present 500 feet.[50] The slender columns and lightness of the Galilee contrast with the enormous pillars and monumental solidity of the earlier nave, but both together constitute one of the most awe-inspiring Romanesque interiors in England. The stone ribbed vaults, with which the whole building is roofed, mark a major new development in church construction and were soon imitated in other great churches.

Canterbury cathedral was also completely rebuilt in the later eleventh century, although, in contrast to Durham, virtually nothing of that period remains. When Lanfranc, the first Norman archbishop, was appointed in 1070, he found his cathedral in ruins, destroyed by a recent fire. He rebuilt it completely and quickly, creating a church whose beauty and splendour were commented upon by contemporaries. Under his successor, Anselm, further extensive building work was undertaken, notably a remodelling and extension of the eastern end of the church. This was completed by 1130, when the new building was dedicated. The crypt from this period, with its carved capitals and wall paintings, survives to the present day. Most of the eastern part of the Norman church was, however, destroyed by fire in 1174, just over a century after the Saxon cathedral had burned down.

The rebuilding that took place at Canterbury after the fire of 1174 is notable for three things. It marks the introduction of the Gothic style into England; it transformed the east end of the church to accommodate Canterbury's new saint, Thomas Becket; and it was described in detail by a contemporary, Gervase of Canterbury. He tells how, on 5 September 1174, some huts outside the churchyard caught fire. The high wind blew sparks onto the roof of the cathedral and, unnoticed by anyone, they fell through gaps in the lead onto the roof-beams below. The whole roof area was aflame and the roof lead melting before the fire was noticed—'Woe! Woe! The church is burning!' The roof fell in, crashing down onto the monks' choir-stalls. Flames rose more than twenty feet high. Between them ran monks seeking to retrieve the

---

[50] S. Durh., *HDE*, pp. 129, 139–40, 141, 168.

relics of the saints that lay scattered on the ground and looters eager for valuable plunder.

In the aftermath of the fire, architects were called in for consultation from all over England and France. The rebuilding was eventually entrusted to William of Sens, 'on account of his genius and good reputation'. He advised that the old pillars of the choir had to be completely removed. The first twelve months after the fire were taken up with this demolition work, as well as the importation of stone and the making of cranes and wooden templates for the masons. Finally, in September 1175, rebuilding of the choir started. William was able to make good progress, erecting four columns in 1175, two in 1176, four again in 1177 and no less than ten in 1178, vaulting them as he proceeded. Then, in the summer of that year, as he stood on the scaffolding fifty feet above the ground, it suddenly collapsed and he crashed down in a pile of wood and stone. Completely disabled, he bravely attempted to continue directing the work from his bed, but, finally giving up hope of recovery, he returned home crippled to France.

William's successor was another William, an Englishman, 'small in body, but very skilful and capable in many kinds of work'. He carried on the project through 1179, continuing the task of vaulting and also preparing a new eastern extension of the cathedral to serve as a chapel for Becket's shrine. Foundations were dug in the churchyard adjoining the cathedral to the east and walls were begun. By the autumn of 1179 the monks were getting impatient to use their new choir, and William pressed on with the work so quickly that they were able to celebrate Easter 1180 there, sheltered by a temporary wooden wall at the east end of the church. Over the next few years the east end was completed. Although nothing could be done in 1183 'because of lack of funds', the following year saw the work brought to an end. When the new archbishop, Baldwin of Ford, was enthroned on 19 May 1185, he could look around him at an architectural setting that was 'unparalleled and worthy of all praise'.

The end product of the ten years' labour of William of Sens, William the Englishman, and their masons and labourers can still be seen. The east end of Canterbury cathedral is one of the great works of English Gothic, its pointed arches, slender columns, and diffused light giving an immediate visual impression quite different from Durham, built eighty years earlier. Gervase of Canterbury remarked on the contrast between the new choir at Canterbury, with its tall columns, gracefully carved capitals and the glint of marble, and its plain Norman predecessor. The Trinity Chapel east of the choir, the work of William the Englishman, was to receive Becket's bones in 1220 and became the most popular pilgrimage destination in England. The liturgy of the monks could unfold and the devotion of pilgrims declare itself on an exquisite stage.

## The Two Archbishops

Bishops were deeply interested in their position in the hierarchy. The first business before the council that Lanfranc convened at London in 1075 was the seating arrangements. It was established 'that the archbishop of York should sit at the right of the archbishop of Canterbury, the bishop of London at his left and the bishop of Winchester next to the archbishop of York, but if the archbishop of York were absent then the bishop of London should sit at his right and the bishop of Winchester at his left'.[51] The fact that this question of seating precedence mattered to the bishops more than their personal dignity is demonstrated by the squabble at the Council of Westminster in 1102. The archbishop of York, noticing that the archbishop of Canterbury had a seat higher than all the rest, cursed the man who had set it up, kicked the seat over, and refused to be take his place until he himself had a seat as high as the other archbishop's.[52]

The most time-consuming and dreary of these contests was indeed that between Canterbury and York. As the only two English archbishoprics, their relationship required definition. The York position was that the two prelates were equal, but, from the time of Lanfranc, the archbishops of Canterbury claimed to be, not simply archbishops, but primates, with authority over the other archbishopric. Archbishops of Canterbury demanded, and sometimes managed to get, professions of obedience from archbishops of York, and they sought, but never obtained, definitive and unequivocal rulings in their favour from the papacy. The controversy generated a great deal of polemic, such as Hugh the Chanter's *History of the Church of York*, and a collection of forged papal letters, produced at Canterbury.

The Canterbury–York dispute disrupted the English church repeatedly during the Norman period. Thurstan, nominated by Henry I as archbishop of York in 1114, refused to make the profession of obedience to Canterbury and was only able to be consecrated five years later, after seeking out the pope, who was then in France, and being consecrated by him. Long months of negotiation were then necessary before the king would be reconciled with the archbishop and allow him to return to York. The battle between Canterbury and York subsided in intensity in the Angevin period, when it was clear that the papacy would not grant a formal primacy, but its rumblings continued. In 1163 the papal council summoned to Tours to deal with schism in the church was distracted for three days while the archbishop of York advanced his claims and rehearsed the whole history of the dispute.[53]

---

[51] *Councils and Synods* 1/ii, pp. 612–13.
[52] Hugh Chanter, p. 22.
[53] S. Rouen, *Draco* 3. 13, lines 1007–70 (pp. 744–6).

*1. Henry I threatened by peasants and knights in his dreams*

The chronicler John of Worcester describes how Henry I had three nightmares, in which he was threatened in turn by each of the three orders of medieval society—the peasants, the knights, and the ecclesiastics. His source for this story was the king's own physician, who had consequently suggested to the king that he should give alms to redeem his sins.

*2. William fitz Osbern's hall-keep at Chepstow*

This is one of the earliest surviving stone hall-keeps, built by William fitz Osbern, earl of Hereford, in the late 1060s. It is on the Welsh side of the river Wye and formed the base for Anglo–Norman incursions into Wales.

*3. The royal seals of Henry II and Richard I*

Documents issued by the royal chancery could be authenticated by appending the royal seal, that served also to convey an image of the king in majesty, enthroned and crowned with the orb and sword of his office. The reverse shows the king mounted and armed.

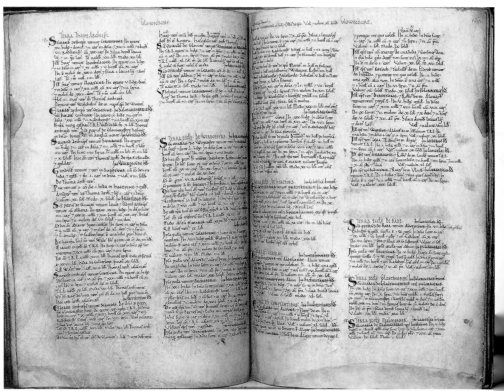

*4. A page of Domesday Book*

Domesday Book is not only a unique source of information on the resources of virtually every corner of England, but is also remarkable for its skilful lay-out and presentation, with running headings and carefully indicated sub-divisions.

5. *Armoured horseman from the Bayeux Tapestry*
This unusual visual record from the late eleventh century recounts the story of the Norman Conquest and is a rich source for military history. Here are depicted the elite heavy cavalrymen (*milites* or 'knights') with their full-length mail coats, spears or lances, swords and shields, mounted on their large ungelded war-horses (*destriers*).

6. *Riding with hawk and hounds from the Bayeux Tapestry*
A late-eleventh-century image of English and French noblemen with horses, hawks, and hounds. Hunting was an upper-class obsession.

*7. Wheeled plough at work*

The fundamental tool of agricultural labour was the plough. Domesday Book lists 80,000 plough-teams at work in England in 1086. This illustration comes from a copy of St Augustine's *City of God*, produced in Canterbury in the early twelfth century.

*8. The tombs of the Angevins at Fontevrault*

Henry II, Eleanor of Aquitaine, and Richard I are all interred in the abbey of Fontevrault in Anjou, underlining through their last resting place the centrality that France had for the Angevin dynasty. These are early examples of life-size recumbent tomb effigies.

*9. Depiction of the murder of archbishop Thomas Becket*
Becket's murder in Canterbury cathedral on 29 December 1170 was a traumatic and dramatic event that shocked contemporaries. This illustration from a late-twelfth-century Psalter shows the weapons and armour of the period, and also contains an early depiction of heraldic arms (the bear of Reginald fitz Urse).

*10. Orford Castle*
Orford castle is unusual in its design. The keep is cylindrical inside, polygonal outside, and has three projecting rectangular towers. It was built by Henry II between 1165 and 1173 at a cost of over £1,400 and was intended primarily as a check on Hugh Bigod, earl of Norfolk.

*11. Pattern of open-fields surviving as ridge and furrow at Padbury, Bucks.* The ridges and furrows created by medieval ploughing practices sometimes survive to the present day if the land was subsequently turned over to pasture. They often cut through the boundaries of the smaller fields of the enclosure period.

*12. Iffley church, west front*
An impressive example of a parish church in the Romanesque style. The period saw a great deal of church building, the enlargement of existing churches, and the replacement of wooden by stone constructions.

*13. Virgin and Child from a twelfth-century copy of St Augustine's Commentary on the Psalms from Eynsham Abbey*
This image from the Benedictine abbey of Eynsham, which was dedicated to the Virgin Mary, conveys the hieratic majesty of the Queen of Heaven, who was a major focus of contemporary devotion.

*14. Crocodiles from the bestiary*
Bestiary illustrations were not based on observations of animals but transmitted a tradition in which animals were seen as moral or allegorical symbols. Here we see the crocodile devouring a man and the hydrus (a water-snake) entering the crocodile's body.

## The Composition of the Episcopate

There were never many holders of the episcopal dignity—two archbishops and a maximum of fifteen bishops—and appointments to the office were major political decisions.[54] An episcopal election took place, on average, only once a year. The new incumbent would immediately become a major land-lord, a local, perhaps regional, and possibly national potentate, and a master of knights, castles, and money as well as religious director of his see. He could expect to preside over his diocese for well over a decade and might survive much longer—Henry of Blois, brother of king Stephen and bishop of the richest English diocese, Winchester, and Hugh de Puiset, bishop of Durham, an important northern diocese with exceptionally independent powers, both ruled their sees for forty-two years (1129–71 and 1153–95, respectively). It was obviously important to make the right choice as bishoprics became vacant. It was possible, however, for there to be more than one opinion about what constituted the 'right choice'.

Canon lawyers and ecclesiastical idealists had worked out several defin-itions of what was required of a good bishop. 'Before a bishop is ordained,' prescribed the standard twelfth-century canon law text, 'he should be exam-ined to see if he is by nature wise, peaceable, temperate, chaste, sober, careful in his business, humble, friendly, merciful, lettered, learned in God's law, skilful in interpreting scripture, well-versed in church teaching.'[55] These demanding criteria were needed because the bishop's function was so important. In the words of pope Paschal II, establishing the diocese of Ely in 1108, 'A bishop's task is to teach God's people through his words and influ-ence them through his life and to win for the true shepherd the souls entrusted to him.'[56] Ecclesiastical appointments were, by their very nature, always encrusted with a moralistic rhetoric of this kind. If one turns to the actual composition of the episcopate in Norman and Angevin England, other qualities than wisdom, chastity, and humility emerge.

In the Anglo-Saxon kingdom that William I acquired in 1066 a symbiosis of royal and episcopal power was ancient. The interpenetration of the royal government and the ecclesiastical hierarchy, represented by the large number of royal clerks who became bishops, had a long history. The rapprochement of Church and secular power that took place under Constantine, the first Christian emperor of Rome, had been continued by the Germanic kings of western Europe as they converted to the Mediterranean religion. Christian bishops offered the early barbarian kings the skills of literacy, wide horizons, ideology, and moral advice. They were more than willing to give a royalist

---

[54] The figure fifteen excludes the bishops of the four Welsh sees that were eventually subordinated to Canterbury.

[55] Gratian 1. 23. 2 (col. 79).  [56] Anselm, *Op.* 5, ep. 457, pp. 405–6 (JL 6212).

tinge to their thinking and to accept the gifts of lands and authority that kings bestowed upon them. In the following centuries clerks and bishops continued to offer various kinds of specialist expertise, especially administrative. The English church was indeed organized according to principles that made it look more like a modern state than the English monarchy did: hierarchy, clear territorial circumscriptions, concepts of office and election, formalized routines and procedure, and the cherishing of written record. Men with experience of this world could be useful in maintaining efficient schemes of fiscal expropriation or military recruitment. Domesday Book, the Exchequer, the Chancery, and plea rolls—all the main monuments of Norman and Angevin bureaucracy—are associated with leading ecclesiastics.

Bishops were recruited from three main groups, the most important being the clerks in the royal administration, for whom a bishopric was the richest and most desirable reward. The king's chancellors usually received one almost of right, but lesser figures in the Chancery and other royal officials were also rewarded in this way. Another type of clerk was also appointed to bishoprics, namely those who had attained some prominence in the Church but had not been involved in royal government. These might have qualified themselves by administrative service in a bishop's household or as archdeacon or cathedral dignitary, occasionally by intellectual eminence or learning, sometimes even by spiritual or moral distinction. The line between these two groups of clerks was not always clear. A talented clerk might move from royal to episcopal service or vice-versa, and royal clerks might well be rewarded with archdeaconries or other ecclesiastical offices before becoming bishops. In general, however, one can make out a group of bishops who were clearly royal administrators and another group who received their office without significant prior involvement in royal government. Finally there were the monks and regular canons who provided over one-fifth of all bishops in the period covered here. Not everyone saw monks as a spiritual elite who gave distinction to the episcopate. The secular clerk Gerald of Wales wrote of 'the great problems that have arisen in our time for the English Church through the election of monks and, conversely, the great profit and honour derived from the clerks who have been elected'.[57] At the end of the twelfth century there was something of a movement to replace monks with secular canons in some sees, a movement that was successful in Coventry for a limited period (1190–7) and generated a lengthy and noisy controversy at Canterbury.

The relative importance of the three groups in providing bishops changed over time and these changes are shown in Table 7 and Figure 13, which summarize appointments to the episcopate in the period 1070 to 1224. The three groups are labelled 'royal clerks' (it includes a few figures of higher

---

[57] Gerald, *Spec. eccl.* 2. 25 (p. 75).

standing promoted because of their ties with the king), 'monks', and 'ecclesi-astical clerks'.

TABLE 7. *Appointments to the English episcopate, 1070–1224*

| Reign | Royal clerks | Monks | Ecclesiastical clerks | Total |
|---|---|---|---|---|
| William I | 10 | 4 | 1 | 15 |
| William II | 6 | 2 | 0 | 8 |
| Henry I | 16 | 8 | 4 | 28 |
| Stephen | 1 | 8 | 10 | 19 |
| Henry II | 10 | 5 | 13 | 28 |
| Richard I | 8 | 1 | 7 | 16 |
| John | 11 | 1 | 7 | 19 |
| Henry III (to 1224) | 4 | 3 | 5 | 12 |
| TOTAL | 66 | 32 | 47 | 145[a] |

[a] Five bishops are of unknown background (three under William I and one each under William II and Henry I).

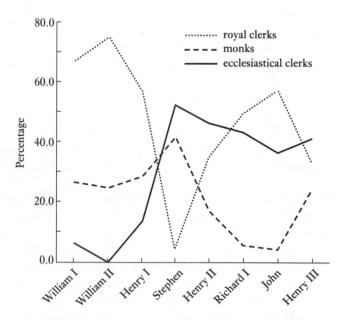

FIGURE 13. *Appointments to the episcopate, 1066–1224*

As one can see, the long-term trends are a persistently significant role for the royal clerks and officials, who form 45 per cent of all episcopal appointees; a decline in the number of monks appointed as bishops (from almost one-third in the period 1070–1149 to less than 13 per cent in the period 1150–1224); and the impact and expansion of the new category of ecclesiastical clerks, who were quite insignificant under the first three Norman kings but formed 45 per cent of all appointments in the following period (1135–1224).

In 1070 William I appointed five new bishops. One of them, created archbishop of Canterbury, was the famous scholar Lanfranc, an Italian who had become successively prior of Bec and abbot of Caen and was clearly a trusted servant of the duke-king. The other four new bishops were all chaplains or clerks of William. One, Herfast, had served as his chancellor; another, Thomas, had already received ecclesiastical promotion as canon and treasurer of the cathedral of Bayeux. These four ex-chaplains ruled the dioceses of Thetford, Chichester, Winchester, and York for 14, 17, 28, and 30 years, respectively. In 1085, towards the end of his life, king William made appointments to the bishoprics of Thetford (again vacant), London, and Chester; again all three new bishops were royal chaplains. They held their sees for 6, 22, and 32 years, respectively. William's son and successor, William Rufus, continued the practice, 'bestowing ecclesiastical honours on the clerks and monks of his court like a paymaster paying his troops'.[58] The result of such appointments was that at any one time under the first three Norman kings a majority of bishops in office would have risen through the royal chancery or chapel. Kings could use bishoprics to reward their clerical servants and the episcopal bench had a definite pro-monarchical tinge.

The second largest group among the bishops of William I and his sons was formed by monks. A peculiarity of the episcopal structure of England was the existence of a number of cathedrals served not by bodies of canons but by monks. This association of bishop's see and monastic community went back to the tenth-century monastic revival, when Canterbury, Worcester, and Winchester, centres of the movement, had been reorganized in this way. The Normans were not only happy to accept these arrangements but also extended them. Rochester and Durham were transformed from secular to monastic churches in 1083, as was Norwich slightly later. In two dioceses (Bath and Wells in 1088 and Coventry and Lichfield in 1102) bishops adopted monastic houses as second sees along with their inherited centres served by canons. Moreover, both of the entirely new dioceses created in the early twelfth century (Ely, 1109, and Carlisle, 1133) were monastic, Carlisle being rather unusual in that it housed an Augustinian rather than a Benedictine

---

[58] Orderic 10. 2 (5, p. 202).

community. Thus, by 1133 ten of England's seventeen dioceses had monastic sees.

In some of the monastic sees, it became fairly common to appoint monks as bishops. Canterbury, for example, had a succession of monks, at first drawn from the prestigious Norman abbey of Bec, where archbishops Lanfranc, Anselm, and Theobald had been monks and served as either prior or abbot. The Canterbury community clearly became used to the idea of a monastic archbishop, for in 1123, when William of Corbeil was appointed, there were uneasy feelings among the monks. Even though the new archbishop was a canon regular (indistinguishable in the eyes of most contemporaries from a monk), 'the monks were alarmed at the appointment, since he was a clerk'. There was even a rumour that the non-monastic bishops had determined to have a clerical primate, since 'it seemed to them no small diminution of their glory to have a single monk rule over so many clerks'.[59] Of the ten archbishops of Canterbury appointed in the period 1070–1224, seven were monks or canons regular. Another diocese dominated by monks at this time was the small, poor see of Rochester, which was virtually dependent on Canterbury. The first four Norman bishops were all French monks, two of them from Bec. Later in the twelfth century, however, the archbishops tended to bestow the see of Rochester either on relatives or on favoured clerks of their household, reflecting in miniature the shift from monastic to 'ecclesiastical' promotions mentioned above.

Monks were very rarely appointed to episcopal office in their own cathedral priory. Monastic bishops were recruited from other religious houses for their talents and were quite likely to be appointed to non-monastic dioceses: the Carthusian Hugh, bishop of Lincoln (canonized in 1220), or the Cluniac Gilbert Foliot, successively prior of Cluny, abbot of Gloucester, bishop of Hereford, and bishop of London (d. 1187), are well-known examples. Despite the large number of monastic cathedrals, the English episcopate was not particularly monastic by comparative standards. In eleventh- and twelfth-century France 40 per cent of bishops were monastic.[60] This is a higher figure even than that for the years 1070–1149 in England (33 per cent), although there were no monastic cathedrals in France. The existence of numerous monastic cathedrals in England thus did not lead to a distinctively monastic episcopate. Nevertheless, except during John's reign, there were usually a couple of monastic bishops and at times, such as the 1080s or 1140s, they might form one-third of the episcopate.

---

[59] W. Malm., *GP* 73 (p. 146 and n. 4).

[60] Bernard Guillemain, 'Les Origines des évêques en France aux XIe.–XIIe. siècles', in *Le istituzioni ecclesiastiche della 'Societas Christiana' dei secoli XI–XII*, I. *Papato, cardinalato ed episcopato* (Atti della quinta Settimana internazionale di studio; Mendola, 1971; Milan, 1974); pp. 374–402.

Ecclesiastical clerks, those who rose through the hierarchy of the Church without prior connection with the royal administration, began to emerge in the later years of Henry I. Alexander, bishop of Lincoln, who was appointed in 1123, had been educated at the important French scholastic centre of Laon and held the archdeaconry of Salisbury at the time of his promotion. He was nephew or son of Roger, bishop of Salisbury, the king's chief minister, and this clearly explains his appointment, but there is no evidence that Alexander was a clerk of the king or served in the royal administration. Similarly, Roger de Clinton, archdeacon of Lincoln, who was appointed to Chester in 1129, was nephew of the royal official Geoffrey de Clinton, but is not recorded as in royal service himself. There is a distinction between royal officials securing the promotion of their relatives, who already held positions in the Church hierarchy, and who might have to pay for the favour (as was rumoured in the case of the Clintons) and the king rewarding his own clerks with bishoprics.

Also in the 1120s we see the emergence of two other kinds of ecclesiastical clerks: episcopal clerks, like John, bishop of Rochester, nephew and clerk of the archbishop of Canterbury, and archdeacon of Canterbury at the time of his promotion, and famous scholars, such as Gilbert the Universal, a renowned French theologian, made bishop of London in 1127. These appointments of the 1120s set the pattern for the new type of episcopal appointees: relatives and clerks of bishops, or relatives of important figures at court, archdeacons, with a smattering of those chosen for scholarly or other ecclesiastical prominence.

Almost all bishops appointed in the generations after the Norman Conquest were foreign or of foreign descent. The English episcopate was very quickly and thoroughly Normanized after 1066. Within ten years of the battle of Hastings the only surviving bishops of the pre-Conquest period were three Lotharingians—Giso of Wells, Walter of Hereford, and Hereman of Ramsbury—and the solitary bishop of English birth, Wulfstan of Worcester. All the new appointments were of foreigners. Not all were Norman, but most, like archbishops Lanfranc and Anselm, Italians by birth, had served in the Norman Church. This foreign complexion of the church leadership in England continued for generations. It was not until the 1130s that there is any appointment to a bishopric of a man clearly either of English ancestry or born in England. In 1133 the newly created see of Carlisle was filled by Aethelwulf, whose name and Yorkshire lands strongly suggest that he was of English descent, while a few years later, in 1136, Robert, described as 'Flemish by descent but born in England', became bishop of Bath and Wells.[61] As the twelfth century progressed, appointments of men born in England became more common, though most tended to be of French

---

[61] Flor. Worcs. 2, p. 95; cf. Le Patourel, *Norman Empire*, pp. 49–51.

descent, and there also continued to be a substantial number of bishops of foreign birth. At the very beginning of the thirteenth century Italian clerics promoted with papal backing made their appearance, although only in tiny numbers. Throughout this period the episcopate thus had a foreign colouring—one English priest complained that, since he knew no French, he was 'forced to remain dumb in the presence of the bishop and archdeacon'.[62]

Stephen's reign exhibits in the field of episcopal appointments, as in so much else, a distinct anomaly in the overall pattern of episcopal recruitment. Throughout the entire reign the only figure promoted to the episcopate who remotely resembles the royal clerks and officials of the earlier Norman kings is William fitz Herbert, archbishop of York (he once occurs in a charter of Stephen described as 'my chaplain').[63] Otherwise all those promoted were either monks or ecclesiastical clerks. The influence of Stephen's brother, Henry of Blois, bishop of Winchester, and of Theobald, archbishop of Canterbury, both of them monks, made itself felt strongly. The Flemish-descended Robert of Bath and Wells was a Cluniac monk like Henry of Blois and received the see after serving as administrator of bishop Henry's own abbey of Glastonbury; Hilary, appointed bishop of Chichester in 1147, had been a clerk of Henry of Blois; Walter, promoted to Rochester in the following year, was archbishop Theobald's brother and had served as archdeacon of Canterbury since soon after his brother became archbishop; while John of Pagham, bishop of Worcester from 1151, was a clerk of the archbishop. Clearly control of episcopal appointments had slipped from royal hands into those of the great ecclesiastical potentates, even if the political consequences were modified by the fact that one of these powers was the king's brother. By the end of Stephen's reign only Nigel of Ely remained of the old-style royal clerks among the bishops.

Henry II began the return to his grandfather's early policy soon after he came to the throne, giving Worcester to the royal clerk Alfred in 1158 and Canterbury to his chancellor Thomas Becket in 1162. The Becket conflict then disrupted English ecclesiastical life for a decade, so that between 1163 and 1173 no new appointments were made to the episcopal bench. When Henry was finally able to resume appointments, he filled seven vacant sees within a few months. Canterbury received a monk again, Richard, prior of Dover, a former chaplain of archbishop Theobald, but the remaining bishops were all either local diocesan clergy or royal clerks. These latter were Richard of Ilchester, Geoffrey Ridel, and John of Oxford, all of whom had been in royal service for a decade or more and who had served Henry loyally during the conflict with Becket. They were very much in the tradition of William Warelwast, a royal clerk under William Rufus and Henry I, who had been

---

[62] J. Ford, *V. Wulfric* 1. 14 (pp. 28–9).     [63] *RRAN* 3, no. 979, p. 362.

employed in harassing Anselm during his struggle with those kings and had been rewarded with the bishopric of Exeter in 1107—Angevin kingship took up where that of the first two generations of Norman kings had left off. Yet not quite: ecclesiastical clerks were a permanent addition to the scene. The Church had developed its own hierarchy, with its own ramifications and ladders of promotion. Men who worked hard in their dioceses or served their bishop well, plus the occasional scholar, were now common candidates for episcopal office. Under Henry II they outnumbered royal clerks and other curial appointments.

Richard and John took their father's preferences to a further extreme. The promotion of such men as Eustace, keeper of the king's seal, to the bishopric of Ely in 1197 or that of Simon of Wells, receiving money in king John's chamber in 1201 and bishop of Chichester in 1204, are indicative of a return to the highly curial episcopate of early Norman days. Yet many of these civil servant bishops were now passing through a much more elaborate system of higher education than had previously been the case, earning the title 'Master' (*magister*) as they did so. Thirty per cent of the bishops elected in the period 1180–1223 were Masters.[64] Education, administrative skills, and conspicuous piety might always raise aspiring clerics to the highest rank in the Church. There were indeed magnate bishops, like Giles de Braose of Hereford (1200–1215), son of the great baron, William de Braose, and episcopal dynasties, such as Roger of Salisbury and his sons, nephews, and grandsons, holders of four dioceses over 94 years, but the episcopacy always held out the prospect of social mobility and promotion through individual talent.

## Kingly Power and Priestly Power

### Three Conflicts

Although friction between kings and ecclesiastics was not usually intense, there were three dramatic episodes in the period during which confrontations between archbishops of Canterbury and kings led to exile, anathema, and, in one instance, murder: the conflicts between Anselm and both William Rufus and Henry I, between Becket and Henry II, and between Stephen Langton and John.

After William Rufus had unwillingly appointed Anselm archbishop in 1093 and Anselm had, as unwillingly, accepted the position, there followed a constant series of discordant incidents between king and archbishop, some trivial, some of greater significance. The amount that the archbishopric should contribute to the royal tax of 1094, which of two rival popes to recognize, whether a council of the English Church could be held, the quality of

[64] Baldwin, *Masters*, 1, p. 154.

the troops that the archbishop contributed to the Welsh campaign of 1097—all these issues created an atmosphere of frustration and exasperation that eventually induced Anselm to seek permission to visit the pope for guidance. In October 1097 he went into voluntary exile. Anselm spent three years away from England, during which time the revenues of the archbishopric went to the king, and in those years he made contact with the leaders of the reforming movement of the day, Urban II and Hugh, archbishop of Lyon.

During his exile Anselm absorbed the more radical demands of the reformers, including their objection to the practice of ecclesiastics doing homage to lay people, even kings. Hence it was that when Rufus's successor, Henry I, invited the archbishop to return to England in 1100, there was, instead of the anticipated settlement and reconciliation, a dispute in which much deeper issues of principle were raised. After Anselm refused to do homage to Henry (although he had done homage to Rufus), there was a period of prolonged negotiations, which led eventually, in 1103, to a joint mission to Rome, where both Anselm and the king's emissary pleaded their case. Afterwards, Anselm was refused permission to return to England and began another period of exile, to which even his friends considered he adapted far too easily. He spent eighteen months at Lyon 'in the greatest peace and quiet'.[65] Eventually resolving that the king's occupation of the lands of his archbishopric could no longer be tolerated, he set out for Normandy, intent upon excommunicating Henry. Thanks to the mediation of Adela, countess of Blois, Henry's sister, this was avoided. King and archbishop met at Laigle and a start was made on resolving their differences. The crucial development was the willingness of the flexible pope, Paschal II, to give way on the issue of homage. In 1106 Anselm returned to England and the following year, on 3 August, compromise terms were made public: henceforth the king would not invest ecclesiastics with the symbols of their spiritual authority, the ring and crozier, but he would continue to expect them to do homage.

Anselm's experience was one of the shaping forces in the mind of a later archbishop, Thomas Becket, who similarly sought out the pope and embraced exile when he found difficulties in his dealings with Henry II. Although Becket had been Henry's chancellor and the two men had been friends, as soon as he became archbishop in 1162 a series of disputes began, reminiscent in their mixture of the petty and the principled of those between Anselm and Rufus. There were quarrels over the property of the church of Canterbury, the details of royal taxation and the extent that clerks could be treated differently from lay people in the law courts. In this age of increasing literacy and increasing legal definition, an attempt was made to put the king's view of the situation in writing, in a document to which the bishops would

[65] Eadmer, *HN*, p. 158.

then subscribe. These Constitutions of Clarendon of 1164 were, in the eyes of Henry II, 'a record and acknowledgement of some of the customs and liberties and rights of his ancestors'. Becket vacillated but eventually accepted the Constitutions. He was to regret this.

Despite Becket's consent to the Constitutions, disputes continued throughout 1164 and reached a culmination in a state trial at Northampton in October of that year. The king threw every charge he could at the archbishop, including asking for accounts of his term as chancellor, and eventually forced Becket into desperate measures. The archbishop appealed to the pope, fled Northampton, and made his way in disguise to the Channel, where, at Sandwich on 2 November, he embarked for France. His next six years were spent in exile. He had the consistent backing of Louis VII of France, the less certain support of pope Alexander III and the shelter of the Cistercians of Pontigny. Nevertheless, Henry II controlled the English church throughout this period and it was only with difficulty and after long negotiations that a formal reconciliation was effected in 1170. It was paper-thin. At the beginning of December Becket re-entered his cathedral city of Canterbury; on 29 December he was murdered in the cathedral there by four knights of Henry II, convinced they were fulfilling his deepest will.

Neither Henry II nor the Norman kings in dispute with Anselm ever suffered the ultimate ecclesiastical sanctions: excommunication, that is, exclusion from the body of faithful Christians, or interdict, the suspension of the sacraments in the land. The clash between John and the Church was to see both. The starting point of the dispute was a complex struggle over the right to appoint a successor to Hubert Walter, archbishop of Canterbury, who died in 1205. The monks of Canterbury had their candidate, the bishops of the province felt they should have a say, appeals were made to Rome. While John went ahead with his own appointment in the time-honoured way of the Norman and Angevin kings, the confident and energetic pope, Innocent III, decided that he himself should have the last word and secured the election of Stephen Langton, a theologian, cardinal, and reformer. Langton was consecrated by the pope on 17 June 1207.

John did not accept this appropriation of one of his most important rights with equanimity. He drove the Canterbury monks out of England and seized the lands of the archbishopric, commanding that they should not even be cultivated. Langton was denied entry to the kingdom. Negotiations between king and pope dragged on and Innocent authorized an interdict, which was proclaimed on 24 March 1208. The doors of the churches were shut, divine service suspended, and all the sacraments, except baptism and extreme unction, withdrawn. This situation was to endure for over six years. In the autumn of 1209 John was excommunicated. Bishops fled abroad and, since many bishoprics were already vacant, by the end of that year there was only one bishop left in England. John was enjoying the huge revenues from confiscated ecclesiastical property. It was the pressure of internal opposition, the threat of deposition, and the fear of an invasion of Philip Augustus of France that eventually brought him to terms in 1213. Langton took up his see, John dramatically surrendered the kingdom to the pope, receiving it back as a papal vassal, and was absolved from excommunication. In the summer of 1214 the Interdict was lifted and normal church services resumed.

These three dramas, that took place over 120 years, had many common features but also some differences that illustrate the general course of development in the Church in this period. On every occasion kings were able to tolerate long periods in which their senior archbishop was in exile: Becket indeed spent far more of his pontificate in exile than in England. During these years the revenues of the archbishopric, and sometimes other bishoprics, went to the king. In the later 1160s Henry II was receiving £1,500 a year from Canterbury. John's profit from bishoprics taken into his hands during the Interdict was enormous—£9,275 in the year 1212 alone. It is unsurprising in such circumstances that the pressure for a settlement had to be great before kings bowed to it. Just as the king was happy to keep bishoprics vacant after the death of their incumbent, receiving the revenue until a new appointment was made, so he was ready to pocket the windfalls of such disputes.

Nor did the royal intransigence lead to loss of control of episcopal appointments. In every instance of a long exile of an archbishop of Canterbury, the backlog of appointments was dealt with by the wholesale installation of royal servants in the vacant sees. After the pronouncement of the compromise on investiture and homage in 1107, the king 'made appointments to those bishoprics and abbacies which in England or in Normandy were without head or shepherd. There were so many of them that there was nobody who remembered so many being given together ever before.'[66] Amongst those appointed in 1107 and 1108 were many royal clerks, including William Warelwast, the man who had searched Anselm's baggage when he left England on his first exile in 1097 and informed him that he could not return in 1103. Similarly in 1173, after the settlement of the Becket dispute, and in 1214, after the ending of the Interdict, bishoprics were filled with royal servants.

### Vexed Issues

The recurring issues in the disputes between the king and the Church were control of church appointments, the nature of ecclesiastical property, and the demarcation of judicial powers.

[66] *ASC*, p. 241.

## The Appointment of Bishops

Most of the Norman and Angevin kings simply took it for granted that they could appoint bishops. The selection of a candidate usually took place in the royal chapel; the newly elected bishop had to do homage to the king; the king would announce his choice in words like those of Henry I appointing Richard de Belmeis to London: 'King Henry, to all his faithful men, French and English, greeting. Know that I have granted to Richard de Belmeis the bishopric of London . . .'[67] Yet there were dissentient voices. Hugh, bishop of Lincoln, whose saintly reputation allowed him a free tongue with the Angevin kings, upbraided Henry II for leaving bishoprics and monasteries vacant, so that he could take their revenues, and for 'abusing the power that his predecessors had usurped of appointing bishops and abbots'. How much better it would be, said Hugh, if the king were to permit 'free elections according to the rules of canon law'.[68]

'Free election' as defined by canon law placed the selection of the new bishop in the hands of the local cathedral clergy. It was unlikely that the king would be willing to concede such a crucial political power to these assemblies of ecclesiastical careerists, younger sons of local landowners and royal clerks. He allowed forms of election, but usually made his own wishes clear. In 1215, for example, when the see of York was vacant and the canons sought permission from king John to make an election, he gave it, along with the request that they elect Walter de Grey, bishop of Worcester, who had served as John's chancellor from 1205 until 1214. Spurning the former chancellor as 'uneducated', the canons of York elected instead Simon Langton, brother of the archbishop of Canterbury. John immediately wrote to Innocent III, who had become an ally since his submission to the papacy in 1213, complaining of this. When the canons of York arrived before the pope, requesting that he confirm the election, Innocent refused, quashed the election and demanded a fresh one. Getting the message, the canons elected Walter de Grey, citing his virginity as a good recommendation for him. 'By St Peter!' replied the pope, 'Virginity is a great virtue; we give the bishopric to him.' Walter de Grey, who was present, could be invested immediately and returned to England as archbishop, although supposedly some £10,000 poorer because of what he had had to spend on oiling the machinery of the papal court.[69] The king had got his way, although to do so he had had to enlist papal support and his candidate had to spend freely.

Walter de Grey's £10,000 was a remarkable, perhaps apocryphal, amount, but the exchange of large sums of money on the occasion of episcopal elec-

---

[67] *Early Charters St Paul's*, no. 31, p. 25; *RRAN* 2, no. 881, p. 80.
[68] Ad. Eyns., *V. Hugh* 2. 7 (1, pp. 71–2).
[69] R. Wend. 2, pp. 153–4, 160–1 (Paris, *CM* 2, pp. 628–9, 634–5).

tions was commonplace. Since high ecclesiastical office brought power and wealth, men were willing to pay for it. 'Simony', the buying and selling of positions in the Church, was condemned with horror by the reformers, who viewed it as a kind of heresy, but was understandably common. Whenever an election was impending horse-trading would start. For instance, when the archbishopric of York was vacant in 1140, the earl of Aumale offered his support for a potential candidate in return for a life-tenancy of one of the archbishop's richest estates.[70] Ranulf Flambard, chief minister of William Rufus, was supposed to have paid £1,000 for the bishopric of Durham.[71] 'Free election' was a powerful reforming slogan, but a slogan is all it was.

## Ecclesiastical Property

Since the fourth century the Christian Church had been accumulating property. Churches were not only 'cures of souls' but also 'benefices'. As a cure of souls they were the focus for the sacraments, for preaching and instruction, for prayer and ritual and belief. As a benefice—significantly a word that could also mean 'fief'—they were a piece of property. This dualism was fundamental.

When Anselm urged William Rufus to make appointments to vacant abbeys, the king replied, 'What concern is that of yours? Aren't the abbeys mine? You do what you like with your estates and can't I do what I like with my abbeys?'[72] It is doubtless the case that Rufus's proprietorial sense was particularly strong, but even more moderate kings and lords had a firm opinion that lands held by the Church had originally been given by laymen. In their eyes this meant that lay lords, and especially kings, continued to have moral and perhaps legal rights over them. The Angevin law-book attributed to Glanville put it in measured but unambiguous terms. The reason bishops and abbots cannot permanently alienate any part of their demesne is that 'their baronies come from the charitable gift of the king and his predecessors'.[73] Henry II gave a sharp demonstration of this way of thinking when the Gilbertine Order was in inner turmoil: 'If the Order were to be altered, he would take back all the demesnes and possessions that he had conferred . . .'[74]

The Constitutions of Clarendon of 1164 refer to 'the archbishops, bishops and all ecclesiastical persons who hold from the king in chief and have their possessions from the lord king as a barony'. It is clear that, in the eyes of those who drafted the Constitutions, the greater ecclesiastics held baronies from the king. This is exactly what was argued during the trial of William of St Calais, bishop of Durham, in 1088. Because Rufus suspected him of involvement in the rebellion of that year, he seized the bishop's lands and

---

[70] Joc. Furn., *V. Waltheof*, p. 256.     [71] W. Malm., *GP* 134 (p. 274 n. 3).
[72] Eadmer, *HN*, pp. 49–50.     [73] Glanville 7. 1 (p. 74).     [74] *Bk. Gilbert*, p. 82.

brought him to trial at Salisbury. William demanded restitution of his bishopric before trial, but the court told him 'you must justify yourself to the king before he restores your fief [*feudum*]'. The bishop countered by saying 'I want restitution of my bishopric [*episcopatus*]—no one is talking about fiefs.' He complained that he had not been summoned 'canonically' and had been forced to answer in a lay court. Archbishop Lanfranc, who was presiding over the court, responded: 'We are sitting in judgment on you regarding your fief, not your bishopric.' Bishop William countered, 'I have not mentioned my fief, nor even said I had one, but I am complaining about dispossession of my bishopric.' To this Lanfranc replied: 'I may not have heard you mention your fief, but I know you have a great fief . . .' In the event the outcome depended on the king's will rather than legal technicalities, but the debate brings out very dramatically the amphibious nature of the bishops of Norman England—they were barons as well as pastors. To high churchmen the king's practice of taking possession of a dead bishop's chattels and drawing the revenue of the bishopric as long as it was vacant was a tyrannous outrage, but from the royal viewpoint he was simply exercising his lordship over a rather unusual kind of barony.

## Law

Clerks claimed they were subject to a different law from other men. To some extent, kings conceded the point. In 1202 two Lincolnshire men, William and Robert, were accused of burglary before the royal justices. William was tried and convicted by the ordeal of water, but Robert's fate was different: 'Robert is a clerk and a deacon and hence is handed over to the Official to clear himself in Court Christian.'[75] Since the method of clearing oneself in the church courts was by taking an oath, Robert's clerical status had given him a valuable privilege. The special treatment of clerks accused of crimes was one of the few permanent ecclesiastical gains from the Becket dispute.

The Church had its own substantive law, its own courts, and its own procedures and all three underwent important development in this period. New law-books became available. Gratian's *Decretum*, composed about 1140, offered a full, systematically organized compendium of canon law, while a stream of papal letters (decretals), eventually to be codified in Gregory IX's *Decretals* of 1234, clarified and innovated in all areas. Increasing numbers of ecclesiastics acquired specialized training in law. Ecclesiastical courts proliferated and became busier. Much the same could also be said of royal justice and it is this parallel development of the two legal and judicial systems that made it especially important to demarcate their spheres. By 1200 most of the outstanding issues had been resolved. The exact procedure for dealing with

---

[75] *Earliest Lincs. Ass. Rolls*, p. 104.

clerks accused of crimes had been clarified. It was recognized that marriage was a matter for the Church but advowson—the right to present to a church benefice—a matter for the royal courts. The Church had jurisdiction over wills. An acceptable delimitation of ecclesiastical and secular authority had been established.

One further issue was the degree to which ecclesiastics might be involved in the administration of secular justice. Canon law was quite explicit about the limits of clerical involvement: 'The exercise of blood justice is not permitted to those who perform the Lord's sacraments.'[76] Just as the reformers wanted to keep the clergy free from the pollution of sex, so the canonists wanted to ensure there was no blood on their hands. On the other hand, the bishops and other prelates were powerful, learned men and many of them had long experience of the working of the royal administration. Neither they nor the king himself wished to see them debarred from judicial activity. Of the thirteen justices who served most frequently in the last years of Henry II, seven were laymen and six clerks. These six included three bishops, one archdeacon, and two canons of London. Both of these canons became bishops under Richard I and continued to serve as justices.[77]

Gradually, during the thirteenth century, the involvement of the clergy in the administration of royal justice dwindled. The awkwardness of a bishop in priestly orders presiding over a visitation by the king's itinerant justices seems to have become less tolerable. Even under Henry II there is evident discomfort in the views expressed by Ralph of Diceto on the subject. He tells how the king experimented with various classes of person as judges and finally resolved on appointing bishops, since they would do justice to the poor and not be susceptible to bribery by the rich. Yet Ralph is uneasy: 'If it is objected that these prelates mixed themselves up in secular business against the rules of canon law, they can counter the rigour of the canons with the king's insistence, the king's pious intention, his action pleasing to God and praiseworthy among men.'[78] Ralph was dean of St Paul's and both his bishop and several of his fellow canons were royal justices. It is not known if his arguments soothed their consciences. A more severe view is that of his contemporary, William of Newburgh. Criticizing the assumption of the office of chief justiciar by Hugh de Puiset, bishop of Durham, he thunders that God will not accept the divided loyalties of 'a bishop who wishes to please both the heavenly and the earthly king'.[79] The voice of the critics seems finally to have won the argument.

---

[76] Gratian 2. 23. 8. 30 (col. 964).

[77] Ralph V. Turner, *The English Judiciary in the Age of Glanvill and Bracton, c.1176–1239* (Cambridge, 1985), pp. 19, 32, 299–302.

[78] R. Diceto, *Ymag.* 1, pp. 434–5.        [79] W. Newb. 4. 4 (1, p. 303).

## England and the Papacy

Over the course of the 150 years between 1075 and 1225, the involvement of England with the papacy became ever more regular and important. Two moments that symbolize the difference between the situation at the beginning and the end of the period are the demand for fealty made by pope Gregory VII of William the Conqueror in 1080, to which the king replied simply 'I do not wish to perform fealty', and John's subjection to the papacy in 1213, making England a papal fief.[80] In the interim kings had occasionally written of their subjection to the papacy in feudal terms. Henry II, for instance, told Alexander III in 1173: 'the kingdom of England is under your jurisdiction and, as far as the obligation of feudal law is concerned, I am held and bound to you as a subject.'[81] This was written, however, in a letter appealing for the pope's help against Henry's rebellious sons. In 1213 John was quite explicit: 'we offer and freely grant to God and his holy apostles Peter and Paul and to our mother, the holy Roman Church, and to our lord pope Innocent and his catholic successors the whole kingdom of England'.[82]

A century of deepening ties lay behind this dramatic moment. One great motor was judicial. The pope was universally recognized as the ultimate court of appeal and, as canon law was clarified, monastic houses multiplied, and ecclesiastical organization grew more sophisticated, the number of cases that ended up at Rome increased. The popes of the twelfth century included many specialists in canon law, such as Alexander III and Innocent III, and they were capable of devoting meticulous attention to legal issues. In one letter to the bishop of Ely, Innocent III gave a detailed opinion on nineteen distinct legal queries that the bishop had raised. To cite only two: is it permissible to deduct necessary expenses for operating a mill or a fishery before paying tithes from them? If a clerk is presented to a church by a lay patron and the bishop rules that he should not be admitted to it and the clerk then appeals to the pope and the patron then presents a second candidate who is admitted, can the first clerk be excluded from the church? The intricacy of the situations and the interweaving of lay and clerical, ecclesiastical authority and property rights, fed an ever-swelling legal system, centred on the papacy.

The links between England and the papacy involved, on the one hand, travel to Rome by English ecclesiastics and, on the other, representatives and delegates of the papacy exercising authority in England. The general councils that were held at the Lateran between 1123 and 1215 were attended by bishops and abbots from England. Nine bishops and eleven heads of religious houses were present at the great Fourth Lateran Council of 1215. In addition litigants were

---

[80] William's letter in *Councils and Synods* 1/ii, pp. 628–9.
[81] *Rec. actes Hen. II* 2, no. 460, p. 9.          [82] *Sel. Charters*, p. 279.

constantly crossing the Alps. The attempt by Gerald of Wales to establish an independent archbishopric of St David's involved him in three trips to Rome, in 1199–1200, 1201, and 1202–3. He returned as a pilgrim in 1206.

Coming in the other direction were papal legates, who exercised full delegated authority during the period of their commission, and nuncios, with limited powers. Sometimes legatine powers were granted to local bishops, as in the notable case of Henry of Blois, bishop of Winchester, who was papal legate from 1139 to 1143 and during that period dominated the English Church far more effectively than the archbishop of Canterbury did. On other occasions Italian or French churchmen were sent as legates. In 1138, for instance, the French Cluniac, Alberic, cardinal bishop of Ostia, came to England as papal legate. He undertook negotiations between the English and the Scots, who were at war at that time, relying especially on the guidance of Stephen's queen, Matilda; he held a council of the English church at Westminster, which issued seventeen canons regulating on such issues as the administration of sacraments, ordination, investiture, simony, clerical marriage and the inheritance of benefices, violence against clerics, and the clothing and hairstyles of nuns; he organized the election of a new archbishop of Canterbury, Theobald, whom he consecrated on 8 January 1139; and he invited the bishops and chief abbots to attend the forthcoming Second Lateran Council.[83]

Stephen's reception of Alberic had at first been very cool and in this respect he was typical of the Norman kings, but their lack of enthusiasm rarely deepened into outright hostility. More outspoken opposition came from the archbishops of Canterbury, who thought legatine powers belonged properly to them and were wary of active papal emissaries, like Alberic, 'plucking up what needed to be plucked up, destroying what needed to be destroyed, building up what needed to be built up, planting what needed to be planted'.[84] For long periods the archbishops did secure legatine powers: Theobald was legate from 1150 to 1161, Hubert Walter from 1195 to 1198. Powerful foreign ecclesiastics continued to be sent, however, and the culmination of legatine authority in England was the period 1216–21, when two successive Italian legates, Guala and Pandulf, helped steer the kingdom through a time of civil war and minority government.

The pope had other means besides legations to exercise control over English affairs. The practice of empowering English ecclesiastics to hear lawsuits locally as representatives of the pope (judges-delegate) became common in the twelfth century. Since he did not have a central bureaucracy large enough to hear every case himself, it was sensible for the pope to delegate in this way. He could choose and guide his local judges, shaping the canon law as he did so. The large number of collections of decretals, papal letters enunciating

<hr />

[83] *Councils and Synods* 1/ii, pp. 766–79.    [84] J. Worcs., p. 49.

legal rules, that were made in England in the decades after 1180 testify to the close attention English ecclesiastics paid to papally formulated canon law. Papal provisions represented yet a further means of influence. The pope could always request that a certain appointment to a church benefice be made and, in an increasing number of situations, he might himself claim the right to appoint. This is what happened in the case of Stephen Langton in 1207. Lesser positions were also being filled by papal nominees and papal nephews. By 1221 the number of English ecclesiastical benefices being held by non-resident Italians caused such alarm that a ruling was sought from the pope to alleviate the situation. He promised that when these non-resident clerks died, the next appointment would lie with the local patron and would not be claimed by the pope.[85]

Appeals to Rome, papal councils, legations, judges-delegate, provisions—by such means and instruments England and the papacy became more deeply enmeshed over the course of the period covered here. Kings of the thirteenth century did not expect to control 'their' church in quite the way that William the Conqueror had done. Yet they retained many powers, formal and informal, and, given a cooperative pope, need not regret the developments of the previous century and a half. In some ways the English bishops were greater losers, subject to papal authority and, intermittently from 1199, papal taxation. Their judicial autonomy and control over ecclesiastical appointments diminished as papal power grew. In the 1220s it was not the king, but the archbishop of Canterbury, Stephen Langton, who was negotiating with the pope to secure that no legate would be sent to England.[86]

## 2. THE RELIGIOUS

### Inherited Ideals

The period 1075–1225 saw the foundation of English monastic houses at a rate faster than in any other comparable period in history—nine a year in the middle of the twelfth century. From its early centuries Christianity had been familiar with the idea of communities permanently dedicated to celibacy and the religious life. In the eleventh-century West such communities usually modelled themselves on the Benedictine Rule, which had been drawn up in sixth-century Italy and was adopted throughout western Europe in the Carolingian period and after. The Benedictine monk or nun was committed in principle to a series of ideals: stability—the intention to spend one's life in the monastery where one took monastic vows; individual poverty; chastity; obedience to superiors in the monastery; and a willingness to submit to

---

[85] *Councils and Synods* 2/i, pp. 96–8; Po. 6569.    [86] *Ann. Dunst.* p. 74.

discipline, including corporal punishment. According to the Rule, the human will was the enemy to be targeted and broken: 'My message is addressed to all those who renounce their own wishes . . . None of those in the monastery follow the desire of their own hearts . . . neither their bodies not their desires are theirs to do with as they will'.[87]

Monks renounced the things that ordinary human life is made of: property, family, sex, greed, violence, self-will. No monk was meant to possess personal property. If a monk died and it was found that he had kept some secret private possessions, he could not be buried in the monks' cemetery, no mass could be said for him, no bell tolled.[88] Monks could not inherit property. They could not marry. Their sexuality was to be controlled and shackled. The bodily desires (concupiscence) that lead to lust and gluttony had to be tamed: 'concupiscence, which is innate and inherent in us, can be weakened and subdued by long discipline and continual spiritual training, so that it does not prevail; it cannot be completely rooted out.'[89] The monastic life was devised to fetter the individual desire and will.

The utterances of monks, like all other aspects of their lives, were subject to discipline, a discipline that paradoxically demanded both that they raise their voices more than other men and that they maintain greater silence. Monasteries were 'God's castles, in which the knights of Christ the King keep watch against spiritual wickedness'.[90] Monks 'kept watch' by doing 'God's work' (opus Dei), that is, engaging in the continual round of services. In the choir their duty was to maintain the flow of chant in the psalms, hymns, and prayers of the Office and Mass. Yet outside the choir their voices could be heard only in tightly confined contexts. In the highly elaborated liturgy of the Benedictine houses, a monk would spend hours in church services, living a life dedicated to communal chant. Contrasting with these hours of vocal music would be the silence of refectory, dormitory, or study area, where monks could only communicate by manual signs. This, at least, was the ideal. In reality these enclosed communities of celibates tended to generate gossip and reformers and rigorists frequently complained of the 'malicious remarks and worldly talk' in monastic conversation.[91] 'Young monks of our own day,' grumbled one Carthusian writer about 1215, 'have the tendency to relax in idle sloth and laziness, trifling signs and empty chatter.'[92]

---

[87] Rule of Benedict, prol., caps. 3, 33, ed. Adalbert de Vogüé and Jean Neufville, La Règle de Saint Benoît (2 vols., Sources chrétiennes 181–2; 1972), vol. 1, pp. 412, 454; vol. 2, p. 562.

[88] Councils and Synods 1/ii, pp. 613, 1070.

[89] Baldwin, Sermo 3. 40 (Tractatus 11), Op., p. 57 (PL 204, col. 525).

[90] W. Newb. 1. 15 (1, p. 53), with a biblical reference to Eph. 6: 12.

[91] Ailred, V. Niniani, c. 9, ed. A. P. Forbes, Lives of St Ninian and St Kentigern (Edinburgh, 1874), p. 150.

[92] Wilmart, 'Maître Adam', p. 216.

The poverty, sexlessness, and silence of the monk and nun make sense of the legal maxim that the professed religious was legally dead. According to English royal law in the late twelfth century, the appropriate writ for an heir to take out to gain a father's property if the father had become a monk was a version of 'mort d'ancestor'—'death of an ancestor'.[93] To become a monk was to die.

## Recruitment

Monks were recruited either as children, who were given to the monastery by their parents and hence called *oblati* or oblates, 'offerings', or from adults turning to the monastic life and hence called *conversi*, 'those who have turned [from the world]'. The balance of oblates and adult recruits varied over time and between religious orders. Traditional Benedictine monasticism presumed that large numbers would begin the monastic life as child oblates. A notable example was Orderic Vitalis. Orderic was born in Shropshire in 1075 of an English mother and a Norman father. At the age of ten his father sent him off to the Norman monastery of St-Évroul. Writing of this forty-two years later, Orderic still has the taste of bitterness and pain in his mouth:

I did not see my father from the time he drove me into exile, like a hated stepson, for love of the Creator. Since then forty-two years have passed, during which time the world has gone through many changes. I often think of these things . . .[94]

For the monk, now in his fifties, the memory of being sent away from mother and father at the age of 10 was still green. Orderic's was a particularly harsh experience, since he was not only sent into a strange community but one whose native language he did not speak—he adopted the second name Vitalis, in fact, because 'Orderic' sounded too English and uncouth for the Norman monks of St-Évroul.[95]

The boys given to a monastery, like the young Orderic, were subject to the physical discipline of their master and Anselm evokes a picture of them 'trembling under the master's rod'.[96] They were to be silent, to sit still, to be separated from the rest of the community, to be under constant supervision. Monks were even forbidden to smile at the young boy novices.[97]

Child oblation belonged to a world in which it was deemed not merely imaginable but meritorious to give a young boy or girl as a gift to God. In the twelfth century a more demanding view of individual intention made such an institution questionable. Some of the new orders, such as the Cistercians, refused to accept child oblates at all and their example slowly influenced the practice of the older houses. Popes insisted that boys under 14 and girls under 12 could make no binding commitment to the monastic life. After the middle

[93]  Glanvill 13. 6 (p. 151).      [94]  Orderic 5. 14 (3, p. 150).      [95]  Ibid. 13. 45 (6, p. 554).
[96]  Eadmer, *V. Anselm*, p. 71.      [97]  Lanfr., *Const.*, pp. 115–18.

of the twelfth century it was far less common for children to be offered to monasteries in the traditional way.

Orderic Vitalis describes not only his own oblation but also several cases of adult conversion. He tells how five noble members of the household of the earl of Chester were moved by the preaching of the earl's chaplain, Gerold, to become Benedictine monks. Gerold had cleverly appealed to these military aristocrats by reciting stories of the soldier saints such as George and Maurice. Of these five converts, who entered Orderic's own monastery of St-Évroul in Normandy, the first was a nephew of the earl of Surrey, the second and third were a nephew of the sheriff of Leicester and his squire, the fourth a brother of the lord of Brecon, and the fifth a well-born chaplain. The plunge of these high aristocrats into the cloister was obviously meant to be a shock and a transformation. Once in St-Évroul the nephew of the earl of Surrey made his speciality the cleaning of the monks' shoes. Yet they maintained contact with their families and substantial landed endowments came to the monastery from their brothers and nephews.[98]

Adult entry to the monastic life had immediate repercussions in the world of family and property that surrounded the monastic compound. There is record of one Northamptonshire landowner, Gilbert de Monte, who became a monk of the Benedictine house of Eynsham (Oxon.) about 1177. He left a wife, four daughters, and an 8-year-old son. Since Gilbert held his land directly from the king, the property came into royal custody and his wife and children became royal wards. The profits of the land now went to the royal sheriff, who also had the right to marry off the children to suitors of his choosing. When Gilbert joined the Benedictines, he was thus not only making a personal decision to embrace poverty and obedience but also abandoning his family and his property to the will of a stranger. It is hard to say whether the apparent strength of his religious convictions or the coolness of his family feelings is the more striking.[99]

Laymen who joined a monastic community as adults, especially in relatively advanced years, would be far less familiar with books and the liturgy than those who had been brought up as oblates. Elias Paynell, who eventually became abbot of Selby (1143–54), was an adult convert to monasticism. He was described as 'completely unlettered [laicus], except for knowledge of the psalms, as you would expect from a convert knight'.[100] Another case concerns Robert de Saint Martin, who had entered the convent at Durham as an adult, also having previously been a knight. As a monk, he saw his former power and worldly savoir faire evaporate. 'As he had been wealthy and witty in the

[98] Orderic 5. 12; 6. 2, 4 (3, pp. 118, 216, 226–32).      [99] Rot. dom., p. 29.

[100] Historia monasterii Selebiensis 2. 4, in The Coucher Book of Selby, ed. J. T. Fowler (2 vols., Yorkshire Archaeological and Topographical Association, Record series, 10, 13; 1981–3), vol. 1, p. 33.

secular world, so now, transferred to the monastery, he appeared uninstructed and ignorant of ecclesiastical matters.' He tried fruitlessly to learn
the seven penitential psalms, the Lord's Prayer, and the Creed. Each night he
forgot what he had learned the day before and the text just seemed to him *bar-
barismum totum*—'double Dutch'. His vexation and embarrassment increased to the point that he eventually began to rail at the local saints,
Cuthbert and Bede, whose bones lay buried in Durham: 'So, Cuthbert, have
you called me from the secular world because you wanted to make me a laughing stock in your church?' Then, with a final outraged, 'You, Cuthbert, you
and your Bede!', he threw his psalter at the shrine. The outburst did not provoke the saint's anger but stirred him to help. When the convert knight went
to reclaim his psalter, he found that he could read it with ease, and thereafter
he could scarcely ever be separated from his book. He recorded his devotion
to St Cuthbert by having an image of the saint painted on the margin of the
first folio.[101]

Entry to a monastery, either as child or adult, was not free. It was customary for the parents of an oblate or the convert himself to make a gift on entry
to the monastery. This principle of bringing a 'dowry' was sometimes given
official sanction. Any canon of York cathedral who wished 'to change his life
and his habit' and enter the religious life was allowed by archbishop Thurstan
to give two-thirds of his prebendal revenue for a year to the monastery he
entered.[102] A church was an especially appropriate gift at the time a son or
daughter was enrolled in a monastery. When Ralph, the son of Guy de
Offeny, became a monk at Worcester in the early 1140s, his father granted to
the monks the church of West Bromwich (Staffs.) with appurtenant land.[103]

Attempts were made to stop this practice, which could be viewed by the
more rigorous as a kind of simony. The Council of Westminster in 1127 ruled
'We condemn fixed money payments for reception as canons, monks or nuns',
and a similar canon was issued by the Council of Westminster of 1175.[104] In
the early years of the thirteenth century the saintly Edmund Rich, who was
entrusted by his dying mother with a sum of money to buy places in a nunnery
for his two little sisters, regarded such a transaction as against his conscience.
He eventually found a house, Catesby in Northamptonshire, that was willing
to accept them for free. Once they were nuns, Edmund and his brother could
make gifts to Catesby with a clear conscience.[105] As in the case of other targets
of clerical reformers, the gift at entry may have been less blatant in the thirteenth century than in the eleventh, but it lived on in various forms and would
do so as long as the social realities that generated it did not change.

[101] Reg., *Libellus* 76 (pp. 158–60).      [102] *EYC* I, no. 150, pp. 130–1.
[103] *Worcester Cart.*, no. 190, pp. 101–2.      [104] *Councils and Synods* I/ii, pp. 747, 987.
[105] Mathew Paris, *V. sancti Edmundi* I, 25, ed. C. H. Lawrence, *St Edmund of Abingdon* (Oxford, 1960),
pp. 222, 250 (cf. p. 107).

One of the most convincing indications of the esteem in which the religious life was held was the practice of assuming the monastic habit *ad succurrendum*, that is, on the deathbed. This was such a common occurrence that the monks of Worcester made special arrangements for bequests from free men 'if they are made monks *ad succurrendum*'.[106] Even mockers and worldings might pay this ultimate tribute: 'they disparage monasticism during their life, but do not presume to feel safe when faced with death unless they have the monk's habit and cowl *ad succurrendum*'.[107] A notable instance of a death-bed convert is Ralph Basset, one of the most important of Henry I's justices and founder of a dynasty of royal servants. He had a close relationship with the black monks of Abingdon and had indicated that, if he ever became a monk, he wished to do so in that house and that he wished to be buried there. In the year 1130 he suddenly fell dangerously ill at Northampton and, 'suspecting that he was dying, he asked to be dressed in the monk's habit'. After bequeathing a large amount of money and a landed estate to the monks of Abingdon, he died and his body was carried in state to the abbey, there to be received by the community 'as one of their brethren' and to be buried in the chapter house.[108] This is how it was meant to work. A harder case was the tragi-comic situation of a man becoming a monk because he thought he was going to die and then recovering to find himself bound by his vows.[109]

## The Variety of Religious Orders

At the time of the Norman Conquest, there were thirty-seven Benedictine religious houses for men in England, most of them dating effectively from the great monastic revival of the tenth century. They were found only in certain parts of the country, there being none west of the Tamar and Severn or north of the Trent (except Burton, on its left bank). In wealth they ranged from a value of £828 per annum to £12 per annum. Nunneries were fewer still and poorer—ten houses, only two of them worth more than £150.

Soon after the Norman Conquest this monastic map began to be extended and deepened by waves of new monastic orders, mostly of French origin, establishing religious houses in the country (see Table 8). What is meant by a 'new order' can vary. Sometimes it signifies a new set of monastic customs and practices, sometimes also a whole new organizational structure. The reformed Benedictine orders, such as the Cistercians, continued to revere the Benedictine Rule, but supplemented it with customs and statutes of their own. The Augustinian canons are so called because they did not follow the

---

[106] *Worcester Cart.*, no. 334, p. 178.
[107] Odo of Canterbury, *Epistola ad Adam*, ed. J. Mabillon, *Vetera analecta* (4 vols., Paris, 1675–85), vol. 1, p. 477.
[108] *Abingdon Chron.* 2, pp. 170–1.      [109] Anselm, ep. 335 (*Op.* 5, pp. 271–2).

Benedictine rule but that attributed to St Augustine. The Arrouaisians, Victorines, Premonstratensians, and Canons of the Holy Sepulchre were all Augustinian canons who had formed separate congregations. Only one religious order originated in England, the Gilbertines, founded in the early 1130s by Gilbert of Sempringham, son of a Lincolnshire knightly family. They were unusual in being an order that comprised both nuns and regular canons on the same site, the nuns following the Benedictine Rule, the canons the Augustinian.

TABLE 8. *The introduction of the religious orders into England*

| Order | First house in England |
| --- | --- |
| Cluniac | 1077 |
| Augustinian canons | c.1100 |
| Tironensian | c.1120 |
| Canons of the Holy Sepulchre | c.1120 |
| Savigniac | 1124 |
| Cistercian | 1128 |
| Gilbertine | c.1131 |
| Arrouaisian | 1133 |
| Victorine | c.1133 |
| Premonstratensian | 1143 |
| Fontevrault | c.1154 |
| Carthusian | 1178–9 |
| Grandmont | c.1204 |

Probably the most obvious difference between members of the various orders would be the colour of their clothes. A secondary distinction, important to the ecclesiastically informed observer, would be that between monks and regular canons (although many contemporaries were unsure of the difference). Writing in the later twelfth century, the Canterbury monk Gervase drew up a list of the religious houses of England, categorizing them by order. The underlying categories are quite simple: black monks (Benedictines), white monks (Cistercians), black canons (Augustinians), white canons (Premonstratensians), black nuns (Benedictines), white nuns (Cistercians and others). He sometimes adds 'of Cluny' or 'of Tiron' but not systematically. Even for this informed Benedictine, the complexity of the religious orders could be reduced to black and white, to monk, canon, and nun.

*A Case Study: Devon*

The basic line of development in the number and nature of religious houses in England in this period can be exemplified by the case of Devon (see Map 9). Here there were two ancient Benedictine abbeys, Tavistock, founded

MAP 9. *Religious houses in Devon, 1075–1225*

in the late tenth century during the Benedictine revival of that period, and Buckfast, whose early history is obscure, but which may well date from the same period. At the time of the Domesday survey in 1086 these were the only two religious houses in Devon. Neither was rich by the standards of contemporary English monasticism. Tavistock, with estates valued at less than £80 per annum, was only about one-tenth as well endowed as the great houses like Glastonbury or Ely, and came twenty-eighth out of forty-seven houses in economic rank. Buckfast, with less than £18, was forty-fourth in rank, and may even have died out in the period after Domesday Book.

These old abbeys were joined, from 1087 onwards, by a number of Benedictine priories, dependent on other English or French abbeys. Eventually there were nine of them. Totnes and Barnstaple were founded by an important local baron, Judhael of Totnes, who made the former dependent on St Sergius at Angers and the latter (one of three Cluniac houses in Devon) on St Martin-des-Champs at Paris. Exeter had two priories, St Nicholas, a dependency of Battle abbey founded in 1087, and St James, another dependency of St Martin-des-Champs. Kerswell was the other Cluniac priory, dependent on Montacute in Somerset. Cowick was a priory of Bec in Normandy, Modbury of St Pierre-sur-Dives, Otterton of Mont-St-Michel, and Pilton of Malmesbury. These nine Benedictine priories were all founded in a relatively short period between 1087 and 1144 and they filled out the monastic map of Devon to a considerable degree, though none of them contained a large number of monks. Six were dependencies of French monasteries and presumably reflect the religious loyalties of their founders among the French-descended landholding class of Norman England. In addition to these Benedictine priories for men, one solitary priory for women was founded. This was Polsloe, established by 1160 and located just outside the city of Exeter. It was Devon's only female religious house in this period.

From the 1120s and 1130s new types of religious house began to appear in Devon. The Augustinian canons, committed to a slightly more self-consciously evangelical and outward-looking form of the monastic life, arrived in 1121, when the old Anglo-Saxon collegiate church of Plympton was refounded as an Augustinian priory. Four more Augustinian houses were established in the following half-century: at Marsh Barton, where a dependency of Plympton was set up; at Ipplepen, where a small cell of St Pierre de Rillé was established in the 1140s; at Leigh near the Somerset border, which then acquired its present name of Canonsleigh; and at Hartland, where the old community of hereditary clerks guarding St Nechtan's bones was replaced by canons of the Arrouaisian obedience probably in the 1160s. One of the Hartland canons described the impact of the new community in unqualified terms: 'Once they had arrived, they illuminated the region with their exemplary way of life, gave peace to the nations, preaching brotherly love in the fear of God, and freeing God's people from the vices and errors into which they had been lured.'[110] A further Arrouaisian house was established at Frithelstock about 1220, bringing the total number of Augustinian houses in Devon at that time to six.

The last wave of monastic foundation to reach Devon in the period discussed here was that of the reformed Benedictines of the early twelfth century, the Cistercians, Savigniacs, and Premonstratensians. In 1136 Cistercians from Waverley, the first house of the Order in England, arrived at Brightley, but moved after only a few years to Forde (which was at this period part of Devon), establishing a flourishing Cistercian house where, in the later twelfth century, important religious literature was written.[111] One of its abbots,

[110] *Mir. Nectan*, p. 412.
[111] See Christopher Holdsworth, 'The Cistercians in Devon', in C. Harper-Bill *et al.* (eds.), *Studies in Medieval History Presented to R. Allen Brown* (Woodbridge, 1989), pp. 179–91.

Baldwin, became archbishop of Canterbury and died in Palestine during the Third Crusade. In the same year that Brightley began, monks from Savigny in Normandy came to Buckfast, the ancient impoverished Benedictine site, and there either refounded or transformed the house, creating a Savigniac abbey which joined the Cistercian Order when the two Orders merged in 1147. Further houses of the new orders were not again founded until much later in the century. The Premonstratensian abbey founded at Torre in 1196, which was to become one of the largest and richest of the houses of white canons, and Dunkeswell, a daughter house of Forde abbey founded in 1201, brought to four the total number of houses of the new orders in Devon. These last two were both the creations of William Brewer, one of the most talented and ambitious of the administrators in the service of the Angevin kings.[112]

The monastic map of Devon about 1220, before the arrival of the friars in England, thus shows groups of different age and type. Of the twenty-one communities, only one had an unbroken history going back to the Anglo-Saxon period. Of the others, half were Benedictine priories founded in the years 1087–1144, just over a quarter were Augustinian houses dating to after 1121, and just under a quarter were reformed Benedictine communities established after 1136. The period of most activity was clearly 1087–1160, which saw three-quarters of the new foundations. Thereafter new monastic houses were established much less frequently: two Augustinian houses date to the 1160s, then Torre is founded in 1196, Dunkeswell in 1201, and Frithelstock about 1220.

The basic pattern of monastic history in Devon—both as concerns types of community and chronology—would be true of England as a whole. One informed estimate would see a tenfold increase in the number of religious houses in England between 1086 and 1150, followed by a more gradual rate of increase, bringing the total up by a further 25 per cent over the period 1150–1220.[113] The successive waves of Benedictine priories, Augustinian houses, and reformed Benedictines can be clearly identified. By the 1220s there were well over 700 religious houses of various types in England.

## Benedictines

The autonomous Benedictine houses were the oldest and richest in England and included such giants as Glastonbury, Ely, Bury, the two male monasteries in the royal city of Winchester, the two rival communities at Canterbury, and also Westminster abbey, setting for the coronation. They were ruled by

---

[112] Ralph V. Turner, *Men Raised from the Dust: Administrative Service and Upward Mobility in Angevin England* (Philadelphia, 1988), pp. 87–8.

[113] David Knowles and R. Neville Hadcock, *Medieval Religious Houses: England and Wales* (rev. edn.; London, 1971), app.

their abbots, some of whom were figures of political importance in the kingdom. Most of them had dependencies (priories), that could themselves be
large and important houses. Great Malvern, for example, was a priory dependent on Westminster abbey, yet it had 26 monks, a substantial number,
supported a hospital for 30 poor people, and had dependent priories of its
own, such as Alvecote in Warwickshire, founded in 1159 for four monks.[114]

A sub-group of the Benedictines was formed by the Cluniac houses. Cluny
in Burgundy had, since its origin in the early tenth century, become one of the
most important abbeys in western Christendom and the head of a huge congregation of dependencies. Between 1077, when the monastery of Lewes was
founded, and the middle of the twelfth century, some twenty to twenty-five
members of the Order were established in England. They were all technically
priories, dependent on other houses of the Order, some, like Lewes, directly
on the mother house of Cluny, others on French Cluniac houses such as
St Martin-des-Champs in Paris or La Charité on the Loire, and some, of
course, as the number of English houses multiplied, on other priories within
the kingdom. Thetford priory in Norfolk, for instance, was a dependency of
Lewes. In addition to these Cluniac priories, which were legally dependent
on Cluny, there were other, less formal streams of Cluniac influence. Reading,
the great new foundation of Henry I, was in no way subordinate to Cluny but
it had Cluniac customs and its first monks came from Cluny.

A large house of black monks, whether independent or Cluniac, formed a
major economic centre as well as being a focus of religious life. At Peterborough in the 1120s there were, in addition to sixty monks, also the full array of
support mechanisms, including a bakery with a staff of nine, a brewery with
a staff of six, two cooks, and five other staff working in the kitchen, two servants responsible for the church, and a tailor's workshop with two tailors, a
laundryman, a servant who fetched wood, and a cordwainer to make shoes.
The basic needs of the monks, for bread, beer, hot food, and clothing, could
thus be met in the monastic compound itself. The mention of two carters
'who bring stones for work on the church' and of a mason recalls the building
work that was going on at Peterborough throughout the twelfth century, producing the great chancel and nave that stand today. A leper house, with thirteen lepers and three servants, was also supported from the monastic
revenues.[115] A network of twenty-five manors, centred around the abbey but
extending as far as northern Lincolnshire and central Northamptonshire,
provided an income of almost £400 per annum to support this large-scale
consumption and expenditure at the monastic site.[116]

One of the most vivid pictures of the life of a great old Benedictine

---

[114] *Monasticon* 3, p. 442; *VCH Worcestershire* 2, p. 142; *VCH Warwickshire* 2, p. 62.
[115] *Petr. Chron.*, pp. 167–8.      [116] Ibid., pp. 157–68; King, *Peterborough*, pp. 140–4.

monastery is presented in the *Chronicle* of Jocelin of Brakelond, a monk of
Bury St Edmunds writing at the very end of the twelfth century. Jocelin, who
held several important positions in the abbey and was close to abbot Samson
(1182–1210), whom he portrays with energy and sympathy but not without
occasional criticism, was deeply involved in the running of the community.
He brings us as close as it is possible to get to the habits and concerns of a body
of twelfth-century English monks.

If we read Jocelin's *Chronicle* asking what it was that most stirred the feelings of the average monk, the subjects that emerge from his pages are three in
number: promotion within the monastery, relations between the abbot and
the other monks, and threats from bodies outside the monastery. All three
were major topics of monastic gossip, all three raised strong feelings, all three
might lead to the law-courts or even physical violence.

Promotion, in the form of appointment to one of the monastic offices—
prior, sub-prior, sacrist, cellarer, and so on—or even, at the highest level,
election as abbot, raised passions and consumed time and energy. These occasions were memorable events in the life of the monastery, so that it makes
sense for Jocelin to date the beginning of his record 'from the year in which
prior Hugh was deposed and replaced by prior Robert'. His justly famous account of the election of Samson occupies over one-tenth of the entire *Chronicle* and is full of lively dialogue in which the monks express their opinions on
the merits of different candidates:

That brother is a learned man, eloquent and prudent, strict in his observance; he has
loved our community very much and has endured many evils for the possessions of
the church; he is worthy to be made abbot.

That brother is a good manager, as is shown by his good stewardship and by the offices he has filled so well and by the buildings and repairs that he has made. He can
work hard and defend our house and he is something of a clerk, though 'much learning maketh him not mad'. He is worthy to be abbot.[117]

This kind of lobbying and sounding out will be very familiar to anyone who
has been involved in making an appointment. A high point was reached during the periodic bleedings that the monks underwent on medical grounds.
Sitting comfortably recuperating after this procedure 'the monks are accustomed to reveal the secrets of their hearts to each other and to confer with one
another'.[118]

The politics of electing an abbot divided the monks when it came to deciding who was the best candidate from among their midst but united them on
one issue: they wanted one of their own, not an outsider. The crucial question
was 'whether the king would grant us a free election'.[119] Despite their different

[117] Joc. Brak., p. 12.     [118] Ibid., p. 14.     [119] Ibid., p. 17.

preferences, the Bury monks determined that 'anyone the lord the king wanted should be accepted, provided that he were a son of our church'.[120] The tensions of an abbatial election were thus peculiarly intense, since the jealousies and rivalries within the monastery were compounded by a desperate underlying urge to exclude anyone from outside. The result was prolonged negotiations among the monks and complex procedures to reach their goal. In the election of 1182 the convent chose six monks whose task was to select three possible candidates. These three names were then written in a sealed document, which was taken to the king by a delegation of thirteen monks. The delegation had authority to accept any Bury monk as abbot, but no outsider without the consent of the entire convent. Even this system of checks and balances did not, of course, give a result that pleased everyone.

Just as the opening pages of Jocelin's *Chronicle* are dominated by the problem of the election of an abbot in 1182, so the chief issue of the closing pages is the appointment of a prior in 1200. The debate started even before the former prior was dead. It rapidly became clear that abbot Samson had his own favoured candidate and monks who wished to win the abbot's favour began to lobby for him. Others, 'few, indeed, in number, but more commendable in counsel', thought the abbot's candidate inexperienced and put forward the sub-prior, 'a mature, learned and eloquent man . . . who had proved himself and become known to us as sub-prior'.[121] The factions were quite unequal and the abbot was able to manipulate the situation with ease. His candidate was quickly appointed, giving Jocelin food for thought: 'Turning over in my mind what I had seen and heard, I began to think deeply about why and for what merits a man of that type should be promoted to such a great position.'[122] This question, and the politics surrounding it, must have been consuming passions for any body of monks in the twelfth century.

Elections and promotions were peculiarly dramatic, since they had a clear focus and goal that isolated a judgement about an individual monk and involved a process of decision-making that elevated him above his fellows, but the interplay of power continued within the monastery all the time, even when no such decision had to be taken. In particular, abbot and monks continually eyed each other with suspicion and manoeuvred around each other with cunning.

The tension between abbot and convent was not only a matter of clashing personalities or the normal problems of discipline and hierarchy. Abbots became increasingly distant from the other monks, as they moved into their own quarters, eating and sleeping separately from the body of monks. Divergent material interests were also involved. The property of the abbey was split between a portion assigned to the abbot and a portion assigned to the

---

[120] Joc. Brak., p. 18.    [121] Ibid., p. 125.    [122] Ibid., p. 129.

convent. This had a beneficial side for the convent because, when the king took control of the abbatial lands during vacancies between abbots, the convent's lands were immune. The division of abbatial and conventual revenues took place at Bury during the abbacy of abbot Robert (1102–7), and Jocelin, writing a century later, praises him for it, referring to 'the noble deed of abbot Robert, who separated our property and income from that of the abbot'.[123]

The separation of their property did not mean that the convent was exempt from the abbot's authority. A story told by Jocelin about a disagreement that blew up between abbot and convent in 1199 underlines this essential fact.[124] The lay doorkeeper of the monastery, Ralph, had become involved in litigation against some of the monastic officials. The convent, under the leadership of the prior, decided to retaliate. They could not rightfully deprive him of his corrody, the regular allowance for his maintenance that had been granted to him by charter, but they took away certain extra allowances that the cellarer and sub-cellarer had given him on their own initiative. The doorkeeper now gathered together as supporters 'some of the men who ate at the abbot's table', presumably Samson's relatives and close friends, and complained to the abbot that he had been wrongfully deprived of his corrody, without the abbot's being consulted. At the next chapter meeting, when the whole convent assembled to discuss business, Samson complained about this. Upon hearing that the action had been taken with the consent of the whole body of monks, he cried out, in the opening words of the book of Isaiah, 'I have nourished and brought up children and they have rebelled against me!' The cellarer was commanded to return Ralph's allowance and, when he proved stubborn, Samson forbade him to eat or drink until he had obeyed.

While the abbot was away from the monastery, the monks assembled in chapter and debated the matter. The cellarer said he would rather resign his office than obey. The younger monks and the novices gave him noisy support, but the 'older and wiser members of the community' thought it more prudent to yield to the abbot. Samson returned to the monastery but refused to mix with the monks because of their 'conspiracies' and kept himself apart in his own chamber. One of the ringleaders of the opposition was excommunicated and placed in fetters, others given light sentences. Next day the monks decided to submit. At an emotional chapter meeting a reconciliation was celebrated, the excommunications lifted. Samson ordered that Ralph the doorkeeper should receive his full allowances as before. 'We disguised our feeling about this,' writes Jocelin, 'since we had at last learned that there is no lord who does not wish to lord it over others.'

---

[123] Ibid., p. 90.
[124] Ibid., pp. 117–20; *The Kalendar of Abbot Samson*, ed. R. H. C. Davis (Camden, 3rd ser., 84; 1954), pp. 90–1, throws light on Ralph the doorkeeper's corrody and other allowances.

The abbot was a lord. Samson knew this well, for he himself had, when younger, been disciplined by the previous abbot of Bury. On that occasion he feared so much that he might be imprisoned by the abbot that he had hidden beneath St Edmund's shrine in the abbey church. In the event he was sent into a temporary exile at the Cluniac priory at Castle Acre in Norfolk.[125] Incidents like this, and the quarrel over Ralph the doorkeeper, demonstrate how monarchical a position the abbot possessed in the autonomous Benedictine monastery. Bury's extensive jurisdiction in West Suffolk made Samson's position even prouder—'I serve the barony of St Edmund and his realm', he asserted.[126]

However deeply divided the abbot and convent might be on occasion, they united immediately in the face of threats from bodies outside the monastery. Bishops were a constant irritant. In the eleventh century the local bishop, Herfast of Thetford, had actually tried to take over the abbey as his diocesan see—an ambition shared by many other bishops with poor dioceses and rich abbeys in them. This outcome had been avoided, but the local bishop (whose seat was now in Norwich) was still an object of suspicion in Samson's time. When the church of Woolpit came into the abbot's hands, he allowed the convent an annual payment of 10 marks (£6. 13s. 4d.) from it. 'I would willingly give it to you entirely, if I could,' he said to the monks, 'but I know that the bishop of Norwich would oppose me, or, if he allowed it, would seize the opportunity to claim subjection and obedience from you, which would be unwise and improper.'[127]

Archbishops were also troublesome. Under Samson's predecessor, abbot Hugh, a delegation had to be sent to Rome to obtain exemption from a threatened legatine visit of archbishop Richard of Canterbury.[128] Samson himself obtained a papal grant conveying 'a general exemption for himself and his successors from all archbishops of Canterbury'.[129] The manor of Eleigh, that belonged to Canterbury but was in the jurisdiction of Bury, proved a source of contention. After a murder there, the archbishop's men refused to allow those accused of the crime to appear in the abbey's court. Samson complained to the king, Henry II, but also took more direct action: 'at dawn about eighty armed men were sent to the village of Eleigh and took the three murderers by surprise, binding them and carrying them off to Bury, where they were thrown into the deepest dungeon.'[130] The case dragged on inconclusively, but Samson had certainly shown a willingness to use both law and force to uphold the rights he claimed for his monastery. His bold assertion rings true: 'he was the kind of man who would never allow the liberty of his church to be shaken, not for lack of knowledge nor for lack of money, even if he had to die or be condemned to perpetual exile'.[131]

[125] Joc. Brak., pp. 4, 49.      [126] Ibid., p. 54.      [127] Ibid., pp. 49–50.
[128] Ibid., p. 5.      [129] Ibid., p. 56.      [130] Ibid., pp. 50–2.      [131] Ibid., p. 84.

## Augustinians

The Augustinian Rule was short and general, hence adaptable. Harmony, chastity, and the absence of private property were the things it stressed. It could be combined with other models, as in the case of the Premonstratensians, who followed the Augustinian Rule but were organized along the same lines as the Cistercians, and it served both for independent houses and for congregations of associated houses, like the Arrouaisians and Victorines. This flexibility partly explains the enormous popularity of Augustinian houses. Another explanation is the fact that Augustinian abbeys and priories tended to be smaller and less well endowed than the old Benedictine monasteries. It was less costly to establish them. Moreover, many Augustinian houses were not entirely new foundations but came into existence through the transformation of earlier minsters and collegiate churches into regular religious communities. The secular canons who had previously served the church were usually allowed to keep their prebends for their lifetime, although there are some instances where they themselves joined the new community as regular canons. Waltham, one of the wealthiest Augustinian houses in England, had been a collegiate church before Henry II brought regular canons there in 1177.

The reign of Henry I saw the first blossoming of the order. Holy Trinity, Aldgate, founded by queen Matilda in 1108, was one of the more important houses and a centre of further plantations. It had close contacts with the royal family. Priors of Holy Trinity acted as confessors both to the founder, Henry I's queen Matilda, and to Stephen's queen, another Matilda. Stephen's infant son, Baldwin, and daughter, Matilda, were buried beside the altar of the Holy Trinity there, while the first two of Henry II's children born after his accession were baptized in the church.[132] Henry I himself founded five Augustinian houses and his officials, such as Gilbert the Sheriff, founder of Merton, many more. Yet what is notable about the regular canons is the fact that, especially as time went on, most of their patrons were drawn not from royalty or magnates but from local landholders of middling rank.

Moderate means supported moderate men. The characteristic temperance and discretion of the canons was remarked upon by Gerald of Wales, himself a secular clerk:

The order of canons is more content with moderation and temperance than the other orders and, for the most part, keeps ambition in check. The canons are placed in the world but, to the best of their ability, avoid contagion by the world, keeping free of gluttony and drunkenness and being ashamed to incur public disgrace through luxury or lust.[133]

---

[132] *Aldgate Cart.*, pp. 230, 232.      [133] Gerald, *Itin.* 1. 3 (pp. 46–7).

The Augustinians formed the comfortable, respectable, and learned mass of the religious orders in England.

## Cistercians

The first Cistercian monks to enter England established the monastery of Waverley in Surrey in 1128. A few years later, in 1131, a second house, Tintern abbey, was founded in Monmouthshire and the following spring the Cistercians settled at Rievaulx in Yorkshire. After the creation of these pioneering communities, monasteries of the white monks were established in England at an average rate of one or two per year until 1153, when a temporary prohibition on the founding of new houses enacted by the Cistercian Chapter-General came into effect. The single year 1147 saw no fewer than seven new Cistercian foundations, ranging geographically from Buckinghamshire to Yorkshire and from Lincolnshire to Herefordshire.

The remarkable growth of the new order depended on recruits and patronage and both were available in abundance. The Cistercians appeared to be the champions of a more demanding and authentic kind of monasticism and hence attracted those who took the pursuit of Christian perfection seriously. Many who became Cistercians were already members of religious orders and were drawn by the Cistercians' close adherence to the monastic rule and their pure and austere life. The name that the white monks won for themselves is vividly evidenced in Walter Daniel's *Life of Ailred*. Ailred, later to become abbot of Rievaulx, started his career as a high-ranking official of the king of Scots. While engaged in some business in the neighbourhood of York, he heard tell from a friend

how some wonderful monks had come from overseas to England. They were remarkable for their monastic life and were white in dress and in name . . . they embrace poverty . . . and are bound together by such strong bonds of love that their community seems as 'terrible as an army with banners' [*Song of Songs* 6. 3] . . . they have no private property, do not talk together, never undertake anything by their own will . . .[134]

Inspired by this heroic account, Ailred went to seek out these 'angelic men' and, accompanied by the founder of Rievaulx, the Yorkshire baron Walter Espec, visited the monastery. The prior, guestmaster, and gatekeeper took him in to prayers and then preached to him. Ailred was overcome and burst into tears. He spent that night at Walter Espec's castle and then intended to return north to the Scottish court but, on the way, travelling on a road overlooking Rievaulx, he determined to go down to the monastery and learn more. The monks there received him with honour and, seeing his seriousness, were aroused 'to make their way into his mind with sharper

[134] W. Dan., *V. Ailred* 5 (pp. 10–11).

suggestions'. Eventually he agreed to become a monk. 'All rejoice, all are happy . . . he divided up and gave away all that he had' and, after a four-day period in the guesthouse, he was accepted among the novices.[135]

Ailred's conversion must have been paralleled in the lives of hundreds of other aspirant monks in the middle decades of the twelfth century. Once inside the order, of course, doubts and second thoughts might arise. Waltheof, the brother of the earl of Huntingdon, was prior of the Augustinian house of Kirkham in Yorkshire, but, about the year 1145, felt moved 'to seek the path of a more austere form of monasticism'. After taking advice from Ailred, whom he knew, he entered the Cistercian order. He immediately began to think he might have made a mistake:

The food and drink seemed to him tasteless, the clothes rough and contemptible, the manual labour hard, the drawing out of vigils and psalms burdensome, and the whole tenor of the order too austere. He looked back to his earlier years as a canon and began to think that the institutions of the canons, although less demanding, were more sensible and hence more likely to save souls . . . he considered leaving the Cistercian order and returning to the canons.[136]

Waltheof persevered through this period of doubt and eventually became abbot of one of Rievaulx's daughter houses, Melrose, but such doubt and revulsion were not uncommon.

The distinctive features of the Cistercians included not only their ideology of harsh austerity but also a new kind of organizational structure that was integrated in an entirely original way: every monastery was part of a chain of command that stretched back to Cîteaux (see Map 10). Every Cistercian abbey had a mother house, whose abbot was responsible for the daughter house, conducting an annual visitation and having custody during vacancies. This mother house would have a mother house of its own, and so on. The abbey of Flaxley in Gloucestershire, for example, founded in 1151, was a daughter house of Bordesley in Worcestershire, that had supplied Flaxley with its first monks. Bordesley had been founded in 1138 as a daughter of Garendon in Leicestershire, itself founded in 1133 as a daughter of Waverley, the first Cistercian house in England, which was a daughter of L'Aumône in the county of Blois. L'Aumône was itself founded, as a daughter of Cîteaux, in 1121. The chain of supervision thus involved six abbeys and stretched from Burgundy to Gloucestershire. It was an articulated organization of a new type, unlike the simpler monarchical structure of the Cluniacs. Affiliation—this system of mother and daughter houses—and the annual Chapter-General held at Cîteaux, which abbots were meant to attend, gave the Order a unity that had not hitherto existed within the monastic world.

[135] Ibid. 6–8 (pp. 13–16).
[136] Joc. Furn., *V. Waltheof*, pp. 257–8; the correct reading is 'vigiliarum et psalmodiae *protelatio* gravis'.

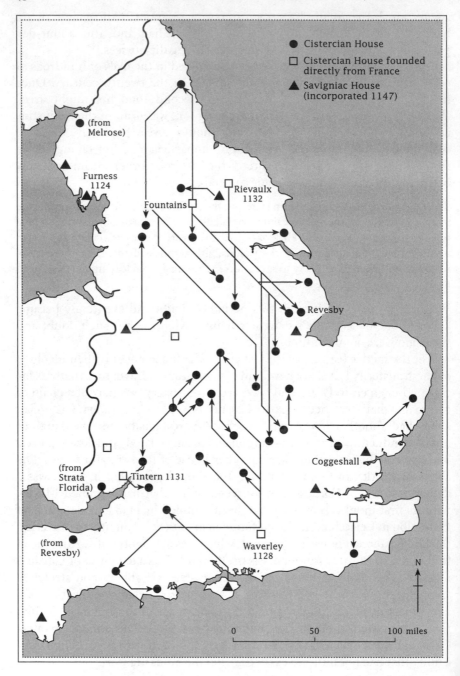

● Cistercian House

□ Cistercian House founded
   directly from France

▲ Savigniac House
   (incorporated 1147)

(from
Melrose)

Furness
1124

Rievaulx
1132

Fountains

Revesby

(from
Strata
Florida)

Tintern 1131

Coggeshall

(from
Revesby)

Waverley
1128

N

0        50        100 miles

MAP 10.  *Cistercian houses in England (to 1200)*

   This novel unity was expressed also in the uniformity of the design and dedication of the Cistercian abbey churches. Every Cistercian abbey was dedicated to the Virgin Mary. This universal saint, who had left no earthly sepulchre (being assumed directly into heaven), suited an order that tried as much as possible to transcend local conditions and to eschew the cult of holy tombs that distinguished so many of the churches of the black monks. Church plan was likewise as similar as possible, from Burgundy to the farthest reaches of the Order. Cistercian churches were usually cruciform in shape, with a square east end, and characterized by relative simplicity of design and detail. Elaborate painting and carving were frowned upon. The plain white interiors of the early churches of the white monks must have made a strikingly puritanical impression in contrast with the painting, gilding, and intricate sculpture of the buildings of the older orders.

   Although he never came to England, Bernard of Clairvaux, the leading figure of the Cistercian movement, had an impact in the country, both during his life, through personal contacts and his involvement with English ecclesiastical politics, and after his death, through his writings and reputation. The establishment of Rievaulx was the result of a mission he sent from Clairvaux. It was Bernard's relentless opposition to William fitz Herbert, who had been elected archbishop of York in 1141, that cleared the way for the election of the first Cistercian bishop in England. This was Henry Murdac, who replaced William as archbishop in 1147, with the backing of the new Cistercian pope, Eugenius III. Ailred of Rievaulx's *Mirror of Charity* (*Speculum caritatis*), one of the most important pieces of English monastic writing in this period, was composed at Bernard's command. Bernard's enormous but unfinished *Sermons on the Song of Songs* were taken up and continued by two English Cistercians, Gilbert of Hoyland and John of Ford. The great Cistercian leader thus left his mark in England as he did throughout western Christendom.

   For those who did not themselves envisage becoming Cistercian monks there were other ways of showing support for the new order and winning merit by association with it. Patrons, like Walter Espec, founder of Rievaulx, provided the material resources that sustained the intricate network of abbeys. Fountains, another Yorkshire Cistercian house, quickly built up a complex of land in the Yorkshire Dales, given by or bought from local magnates, gentry, and even peasantry, and soon became one of the main producers in the English wool trade.[137] Initially the Cistercians were extremists on the question of what they could accept as property. Their statutes forbade them to own 'churches, tithes, manors, serfs or rents'. Entanglement with the secular world of this type was to be avoided. Such strict self-denial was, in the long term, impossible to sustain, but, in their early generations, there is no

----

[137] Joan Wardrop, *Fountains Abbey and its Benefactors 1132–1300* (Kalamazoo, Mich., 1987).

doubt that the endowments of the Cistercians were of a different type from those of the older Benedictine houses. They intended to work their lands directly. This had an important consequence. Because they were not prepared to live off the profits of peasant tenants, the Cistercians created a labour force of their own, in the form of the lay brethren, second-class monks who shared all the restrictions of the monastic life but were debarred from full participation in it (see below, pp. 434–5). Even this harsh condition must have had its attractions, for there seems to have been no problem recruiting large numbers of lay brothers. Some of the Cistercian abbeys had huge populations. One euphoric account credits Rievaulx under Ailred with 140 monks and 500 lay brothers.[138] This may be an exaggeration, but a more sober source suggests that there were 70 monks and 120 lay brothers at Waverley in 1187.[139]

## Carthusians

The Carthusians had the reputation of a strict elite. Their houses were small and they recruited selectively. No Carthusian house had more than thirteen monks and there were never very many houses. A distinctive feature of the order was its attempt to combine the individualism of the hermit life with the community-based monasticism traditional in the west. Monks lived in separate quarters and spent most of their time there, coming together only for services. The Carthusian led a life of solitary prayer, contemplation, and work, marked by physical austerities, such as the wearing of the hair shirt. 'Each lived by himself, but had nothing of his own and did not act for himself.'[140]

The mother house of the order was the monastery of La Grande Chartreuse in the Alps, founded in the late eleventh century, and from which the order took its name. Only one English Carthusian house was established in this period in England, Witham in Somerset, instituted by Henry II in 1178–9. Soon afterwards he recruited Hugh of Avalon, who was at that time a monk of La Grande Chartreuse, as prior of the house. Hugh (later canonized as St Hugh of Lincoln) combined the practical energy needed to make Witham a secure and stable establishment and the spiritual confidence to lead and inspire a group of monks committed to uncompromising standards. 'He built up the house of Witham from the foundations, he ordered it, he filled it with the very best of men.'[141]

The Carthusians were legendarily austere. Later their proud motto was to be 'Never reformed because never deformed' and at the Reformation the intransigent Catholic loyalty of the priors and monks of the Order won for them particularly barbaric treatment from Henry VIII. In the twelfth

---

[138] W. Dan., *V. Ailred* 30 (p. 38). Powicke thinks this figure includes lay servants.
[139] *Ann. Wav.*, p. 244.        [140] Ad. Eyns., *V. Hugh* 1. 7 (1, p. 23).
[141] Ad. Eyns., *V. Hugh* 2. prol. (1, p. 45).

century, however, there were critics as well as admirers of the lonely austerity of their way of life. Richard of Devizes, a Benedictine monk of St Swithun's, Winchester, writing in the 1190s, dedicated his *Chronicle* to the Carthusian Robert, who had previously been prior of Winchester. Mockingly, Richard suggests that he had himself considered following Robert in transferring to the Carthusians, 'in order to see how much more lofty and closer to heaven is the Carthusian cell than the cloister at Winchester'. He comments cattily how remarkable it is that the Carthusians, 'living alone and apart and outside the world', can still have such good knowledge of all the news.[142]

Richard of Devizes is also the probable author of the *Annals of Winchester* and in this composition too we find hints of his urge to cut the Carthusians down to size. He tells the story of Walter, who was successively sub-prior of Hyde abbey, outside the walls of Winchester, and prior of the cathedral priory of Bath. Both houses were independent Benedictine communities. Walter was, according to Richard of Devizes, rigorous in maintaining the standards of monastic life. However, moved by inner reflections on the transitoriness of worldly reputation, Walter decided to become a Carthusian at Witham:

This prelate, preferring to benefit himself alone rather than to preside over others, became a Carthusian. A monk of Hyde abbey came to visit him and saw him—a man who shortly before had given such efforts to saving souls—busy with his pots and vegetables. The monk laughed and said 'Father, what you are doing is *kere*, your business is *kirewiwere*.' Walter returned to himself, understanding that it is holier to save many souls than one alone, and resumed his office of prior.[143]

The strange expressions that the monk uses cannot be easily explained, but their contemptuous tone is self-evident. Here the imputation of spiritual selfishness, which was, on occasion, applied to monks of any order, is being raised as a criticism of the eremetical style of the Carthusians. The ancient English Benedictine houses, which sometimes housed scores of monks and had a strongly communal and corporate way of life, are voicing through Richard their disdain for the religious individualism and fussy domestic preoccupations of these newcomers.

It was not only the Benedictines who resented poaching of their numbers by the new order. Another figure who entered Witham at this time was Adam, abbot of the Scottish Premonstratensian house of Dryburgh. While in France, ironically enough on a visit to the mother house of Prémontré, his imagination had been fired by the Carthusians he had encountered, and, 'burning with flaming desire for the solitary way of life', he entered Witham rather than return to his position as abbot of Dryburgh. The Premonstratensians did not give him up easily and made serious efforts to compel him to

---

[142] R. Devizes, pp. 1–2.    [143] *Ann. Wint.*, p. 68.

rejoin their order. Eventually, it was only the intercession of Hugh of Avalon, now bishop of Lincoln, that secured a letter from the abbot of Prémontré releasing Adam from his obedience. Hugh had argued that 'anyone is allowed to change to a stricter way of life' and had himself had the experience of freeing himself from one order (in his case the Augustinian canons) in order to become a Carthusian.[144] Within the monastic world itself there was gradation of austerity and commitment.

## Lay Brothers

Although monks often termed themselves 'servants', this conceit did not usually extend to cleaning their own shoes or doing their own washing. They expected to be served by their social inferiors. In the Benedictine houses there were as many servants as monks. It was indeed an oddity that the Carthusians engaged in some menial chores, but even they did not expect to undertake the back-breaking labour of cultivating the fields. For this role they had, in emulation of the Cistercians, recruited lay brothers.

The institution of lay brethren, as developed by the Cistercians and others, enabled the monks to continue their endless cycle of prayer and chant while a shadow brotherhood did the manual work. Recruited from a lower class, forbidden to learn to read, bearded (unlike the shaven monks), the Cistercian lay brothers lived in a parallel universe to the choir monks, having their own refectory, dormitory, and section of the church. The Carthusians even had an entirely separate church for them. At Witham the 'upper church', for the monks, was stone, while the 'lower church', for the lay brothers, was of wood. The traditional medieval image of society depicted 'those who work' maintaining 'those who pray'—peasant labour supporting an ecclesiastical establishment. The Cistercians and Carthusians had brought 'those who work' into the monastery, but in the process deprived them of sex, family, and property. The lay brothers were a kind of gelded peasantry.

It is not surprising that resentment arose between two groups of men in such close proximity, with so many shared fortunes but with permanently segregated functions. A particularly remarkable demonstration of this friction is the so-called revolt of the lay brothers of the Gilbertine order. The Gilbertines had their origin in a community of seven nuns founded by Gilbert of Sempringham about 1131. These were served by lay sisters. Then, 'because women's efforts are of little effect without the help of men', Gilbert assigned lay brothers to perform the heavier work for them. The author of the *Life of Gilbert* describes their social origins: 'some of these he had raised from childhood at his own expense, some had run away from their lords, although the monastic name made them free, and others were poor beggars'. All were

---

[144] Wilmart, 'Maître Adam'.

driven to take the habit 'both by the poverty of their human life and the desire for a heavenly life'.[145] Finally, the complex Gilbertine constitution was completed by the inclusion of male canons.

The full Gilbertine house thus included four elements: nuns, lay sisters, canons, and lay brothers. Dissatisfaction among this last group blew up in the 1160s. Most intransigent of Gilbert's opponents was a lay brother called Ogger, a smith, whom Gilbert had brought up from boyhood. He and his allies complained that sexual misbehaviour occurred between canons and nuns, that Gilbert had tried to change the constitution of the order and that, when the lay brothers had obtained a papal letter in response to their charges, Gilbert had decried it as forged. The accusations that the lay brothers raised in the dispute are not all entirely clear and some seem hardly to merit the fury and tenacity that was shown. Yet this is perhaps in itself significant. An underlying bitterness was being expressed and specific issues were secondary. On the one hand was the resentment of the lay brothers at their subordinate position and the harshness of their way of life, on the other the social arrogance of the well born and educated canons. In their view, the difficult lay brothers were 'servants presuming to attack their lord, despicable men assailing an important figure, obscure men setting themselves against a noble'. These illiterate, lower-class workers had brought Gilbert's name into disrepute, yet they were, in words taken from the book of Job, men 'whose fathers he would have disdained to have set with the dogs of his flock'. Ogger was a member of a penniless family saved by Gilbert's charity, but he persevered in his enmity to his death, earning the title 'hammer of the saint'.[146] Those monastic orders that adopted the institution of lay brethren had sown organized social division in the monastery and sometimes reaped the harvest.

## Female Religious

There were far fewer opportunities for women to pursue the religious life than there were for men. The ratio of male to female religious communities at the time of the Norman Conquest—37:10—remained exactly the same over the course of the monastic boom of the following two centuries. By the middle of the thirteenth century there were something like 550 male communities and 150 female. Hence, just as there were three to four times as many male monasteries as female in the time of William the Conqueror, so there were in the England of Henry III. Nor could women attain the full autonomy that male houses sometimes approached. Only priests could celebrate mass and only men could be priests. Some forms of manual labour were also

---

[145] *Bk. Gilbert*, pp. 36–8.

[146] Ibid., pp. lv–lxii, 76–82, 116–18, 134–66, 343–4, 346–9; Brian Golding, *Gilbert of Sempringham and the Gilbertine Order c.1130–c.1300* (Oxford, 1995), pp. 40–51, 458–62.

deemed inappropriate for women. For these two very different reasons, communities of female religious could not be self-sufficient.

It seems likely that most nuns entered the religious life as a consequence of a decision taken by their families rather than from a powerful individual vocation. Benedictine nunneries, like Benedictine monasteries, expected many of their recruits to be donated as children by their parents. A document from the great nunnery of Shaftesbury dating to the later eleventh century gives details of 'the lands that men gave to the church of St Edward at Shaftesbury with their daughters'.[147] There are thirteen names, mainly of the lesser Norman baronage, and the donations made with the girls are usually of about £2 annual value. In one unusual case the evidence survives to show how this compares with the cost of marrying off a daughter, for Domesday Book records that Serlo de Burci had given an estate worth £5 to William de Falaise 'with his daughter' and another estate, worth £2, to Shaftesbury abbey 'for his daughter who is there'.[148] It was thus not cheap to send one's daughter to a prestigious nunnery like Shaftesbury, but it was cheaper than endowing her for marriage.

It was not always daughters who were provided for in this way. A charter of the Essex landholder Roger fitz Reinfrid, dating to the late 1170s or 1180s, conveys one-twelfth of a knight's fee to the nuns of Clerkenwell on the condition that 'the nuns shall receive Alice my wife and Margaret her mother as nuns in their chapter whenever it please Alice and Margaret'. If the women died away from Clerkenwell, the nuns were to arrange for them to be buried in the nunnery and to perform the same obsequies for them as for one of their own nuns, even if they had not yet taken the habit; Roger himself was to be commemorated in this same way.[149] Nunneries could thus offer a quiet berth for a widow and mother-in-law as well as being a cheaper alternative to a dowry for a daughter. There is also occasional evidence that the religious life was seen as a respectable option for those who were unable to manage, one way or another, in the outside world. The role of nunneries as refuges for the unmarriageable is shown by the sad story of the daughter of a wealthy citizen of London whose potential suitors rejected her on account of her limp and whose parents eventually decided to make her a nun at Barking.[150] A few thousand ladies could live a sheltered and comfortable communal life, on condition it was a celibate life.

The nunneries in existence at the time of the Norman Conquest were, for

[147] BL Harley 61, fo. 54.

[148] *DB* 1, 96b, 98 (Som. 27. 3, 37. 7); see Kathleen Cooke, 'Donors and Daughters: Shaftesbury Abbey's Benefactors, Endowments and Nuns *c*.1086–1130', *ANS* 12 (1990), pp. 29–45.

[149] *The Cartulary of St Mary Clerkenwell*, ed. W. O. Hassall (Camden, 3rd ser., 71; 1949), no. 105, pp. 70–1.

[150] *Mir. Erkenwald* 18 (p. 160).

the most part, creations of the tenth-century monastic revival, although Shaftesbury and Wilton, the largest and richest, claimed to go back to king Alfred's days. These houses had enjoyed the patronage of the West Saxon royal dynasty and their abbesses and nuns were often of royal or high aristocratic birth. The aristocratic character of these old Benedictine nunneries was not changed by the Conquest and the new regime. In the 1080s Christina, sister of Edgar Atheling, the last of the Wessex line, was a nun of Romsey, a nunnery that was later, between 1155 and 1160, under the rule of Mary, daughter of king Stephen, while, somewhat later still, Shaftesbury was governed by abbess Mary, half-sister of Henry II.

Benedictine nunneries of this type, with royal and episcopal backing and high-born ladies as foundresses or abbesses, continued to be founded in the Norman period. Malling in Kent was the project of Gundulf, bishop of Rochester (1077–1108), himself a Benedictine monk. With the advice of archbishop Anselm—another monk—he arranged for the construction of a church dedicated to St Mary and the other buildings necessary for the convent and assembled a group of nuns, recruiting the first prioresses from other nunneries. His concern for the proper physical endowment influenced the kind of recruits he could get: 'he acquired rents and lands for them from wherever he could and took pains to embellish their church with many adornments, and hence many woman, including even nobles, were happy to submit to his rule'.[151] Aristocratic ladies might be willing to forgo the mixed pleasures of marriage and childbed if their surroundings were appropriate to their status.

Godstow near Oxford was founded by 'the worthy matron Edith, devoted to God', who 'built the church there from the first stone at her own cost'. This well-born widow then assumed the position of abbess. The dedication ceremony in January 1139 was attended by a great crowd of bishops and barons, headed by king Stephen and his queen, Matilda, and the recently consecrated archbishop of Canterbury, Theobald. All made suitable gifts. The bishop in whose diocese the new nunnery lay and who performed the dedication ceremony, Alexander of Lincoln, granted the nuns a hundred shillings a year from his market at Banbury.[152] Eventually Godstow was to be one of the richer nunneries of England and won the favour of Henry II, whose mistress, Fair Rosamund, was buried there (until St Hugh of Lincoln insisted that she be dug up). The scene on the day of dedication shows the forces that supported female religious life: the initiative of an English lady, the approval of the king and queen, the baronage and the bishops, and the diversion of

[151] V. Gundulfi 34, ed. Rodney Thomson, The Life of Gundulf (Toronto, 1977), p. 58.
[152] EEA, 1. Lincoln 1067–1185, ed. David Smith (1980), no. 33, pp. 20–2; The English Register of Godstow Nunnery, ed. Andrew Clark (EETS 129, 130, 142; 1905–11), pp. 26–30.

even the most recent and commercial revenues, such as the profits of urban markets, to sustain a life of celibacy and prayer.

Malling and Godstow were relatively wealthy and well supported Benedictine abbeys about whose foundation there is clear evidence. Much more common were the numerous priories for women established in this period with smaller endowments, about whose foundation, monastic affiliation, and sometimes even existence there is less certainty. In Yorkshire, for instance, there were no nunneries at the beginning of the twelfth century. By the reign of John twenty-four had come into existence, plus one Gilbertine double house, for nuns and canons. The first Yorkshire nunnery, St Clement's, York, was founded between 1125 and 1133 by archbishop Thurstan. The middle decades of the century then saw a boom in foundations, followed by a much more gradual increase in numbers over the rest of the century. These nunneries were poor, their landed property was concentrated in the locality and their patrons were the local Yorkshire gentry, many of whom placed female members of the family in the house which received their gifts. They formed small communities of girls and women of the gentry, living off rents and the profits of sheep farming.[153]

Communities of unmarried high-born ladies naturally attracted sexual attention and sexual rumour. Abbess Beatrice of Amesbury was deposed in 1177 after being convicted of having given birth to three children since she had become a nun, although it is perhaps suspicious that this charge coincided with the king's desire to replace the convent at Amesbury with nuns from his favoured house of Fontevrault.[154] A more spectacular case was that of a nun at Watton, a Gilbertine house for both men and women.[155] The report goes that a nun, who had been placed in the house, quite exceptionally, as a child oblate, was, when older, made pregnant by one of the lay brothers. When this became apparent, the brother fled and the nun was left exposed to the fury of her fellow nuns. Controlling their urge to burn her or flay her, they simply tore off her veil, whipped her and then chained her in a prison on a diet of bread and water. Finding out from her by trickery where her lover might be found, they informed the canons, who arranged an ambush for the man, using as a lure one of their number disguised as the nun. Once the lay brother was captured, the nuns, 'eager to revenge the insult to virginity', asked the canons 'if the young man might be sent to them for a little while'. Once he was in their hands, they forced the pregnant nun to castrate him.

---

[153] Janet Burton, *The Yorkshire Nunneries in the Twelfth and Thirteenth Centuries* (Borthwick Papers 56; 1979).

[154] *Gesta Hen. II* 1, pp. 135, 354.

[155] Ailred, *De sanctimoniali de Wattun* (*PL* 195, cols. 789–96); Giles Constable, 'Aelred of Rievaulx and the Nun of Watton', in Derek Baker (ed.), *Medieval Women* (Studies in Church History, Subsidia 1; 1978), pp. 205–26.

One of the senior nuns then stuffed the man's testicles into the girl's mouth. 'See,' commented Ailred of Rievaulx, who recounts the story, 'what zeal was burning in these champions of chastity, these persecutors of uncleanness, who loved Christ above all things!'

Events such as these cannot have been common. The nuns of Watton were so fierce because their security, indeed their existence as a community, depended on continued prestige among the lay population and the clergy. That prestige was earned, fundamentally, by their chastity, preferably their virginity. Their savagery towards the errant nun and lay brother expressed not only the repressed energy of their own sexuality but also their outrage at the threat this behaviour raised to the fundamental rules of their lives.

## Hermits and Solitaries

Not all of those who felt the desire to live a full-time religious life entered communities of monks, canons, or nuns. There were still chances for an individual to strike out alone and dedicate himself or herself to a life of prayer and contemplation, supported by a minimal economic base. Enclosed solitaries (anchorites and anchoresses) and hermits, while they cannot have been numerous overall, were to be found everywhere in England. Anchorites and anchoresses were shut up for life in small chambers attached to churches; hermits had freedom of movement but lived a solitary life dedicated to prayer and good works. Wulfric of Haselbury, a Somerset priest, was enclosed in a cell on the side of the church at Haselbury in 1125 and remained there for thirty years; Christina of Markyate, a well-born English girl from Huntingdon, escaped the marriage her parents planned for her and spent two years enclosed with the anchoress Alfwen at Flamstead and four years in a tiny chamber off the hermitage of Roger at Markyate, before taking over the hermitage herself after Roger's death; Godric of Finchale, born of lowly but pious parents in Norfolk, had a long and adventurous career as a merchant prior to establishing his hermitage at Finchale near Durham.[156]

These are but the best recorded cases. The financial records of the Angevin kings show them supporting up to ten or eleven enclosed anchorites per year, usually at a rate of a penny a day.[157] In 1197, for example, the royal government made payments to four anchoresses and four anchorites at this rate and to two other anchoresses at the rate of a halfpenny a day, in addition to a payment of seven shillings to a hermit in the woods of Aston Clinton (Bucks.).[158] Some of the enclosed solitaries were attached to urban churches, such as the anchoresses of St Owen's, Hereford, or St James, Colchester. A few can be

[156] J. Ford, *V. Wulfric*; *V. Christina*; Reg., *V. Godric*.
[157] Ann K. Warren, *Anchorites and their Patrons in Medieval England* (Berkeley, 1985), pp. 136–7.
[158] PR 9 RI, index s.v. 'anachorita', 'heremita', 'inclusa/us'.

identified by name and traced over several years, like Geldwin the priest, anchorite of Winchester, who is mentioned in the accounts from 1187 to 1215.

Anchorites and anchoresses were common enough to warrant the elaboration of a special liturgical ceremony for their enclosure. The ritual specified that the candidate for enclosure should lie prostrate in the church: if a woman, at the west end, if a lay man at the entrance to the choir, if a priest in the choir. Two clerks would recite the litany, a series of invocations to the saints, to which the choir would respond, 'Pray for him [or her]'. The bishop, if he were present, or priest would then scatter blessed water and dispense the perfume of incense over the postulant. Then two priests would raise up the candidate and place burning candles in his or her hands. A series of appropriate readings followed, such as 'Come, my people, enter thou into thy chambers, and shut thy doors about thee' (Isaiah 26: 20), followed by further chants. The postulant then offered the candles on the altar and, after mass had been celebrated, was led into the enclosed chamber while the attendant clergy chanted, 'May angels lead you into paradise . . .' The chamber was then sprinkled with holy water and perfumed with incense. Then part of the Office of the Dead was celebrated and the bishop or priest scattered dust on the head of the new anchorite or anchoress. Finally all withdrew, singing a chant from the Office of the Dead, sealing the door as they did so.[159]

Despite the graveyard finality of this ritual, there is every evidence that recluses had contact with the world around them. Their cells had windows. The early thirteenth-century *Anchoresses' Guide* describes three: a window into the church, to enable the recluse to witness the celebration of mass, a 'house-window', for contact with the servants, and a 'parlour window', for conversation with visitors.[160] Counsellors of recluses warned against the dangers of gossip and over-talkativeness. 'Be as little fond of your windows as you can . . .,' urged the *Anchoresses' Guide*, 'an anchoress should be as silent as possible and not be like a hen, cackling after she has laid.'[161] Ailred of Rievaulx gives a vivid picture of gossip at the parlour window: 'you will scarcely find any solitary anchoress these days without a talkative old dame or scandalmongering woman at her window, who fills her time with stories, feeding her with rumour and slander.'[162]

Hermits and enclosed solitaries had servants and were in constant conversation with visitors. They gave advice, sometimes made prophecies, or effected miraculous cures, and they kept a careful eye on their food supply. Wulfric of Haselbury customarily received food from the monks of the neighbouring Cluniac house of Montacute. For some reason the cellarer began sending the anchorite's servant away empty. 'May God today take away from

---

[159] *Magd. Pont.*, pp. 243–4.     [160] *Ancr. Wisse*, p. 37.     [161] Ibid., pp. 30, 35–6.
[162] Ailr. Riev., *De institutione inclusarum* 2 (*Op. asc.*, p. 638).

him his sustenance, as he has taken away mine', proclaimed Wulfric, and that very day the cellarer drowned on a journey.[163] Christina of Markyate was less drastic with those who denied her food. A story told to illustrate her clairvoyance recounts how she once refused to eat a dish placed before her and her guests, because she knew that the ingredients had come from the garden of a neighbour who had once refused her some herbs.[164] These holy solitaries, dotted about England in their cells and hermitages, could be awkward neighbours.

## The First Friars in England

In the early 1220s, at the very end of the period considered here, a revolutionary new religious movement reached England. Orders of friars, inspired by the charisma of St Francis and given shape by the strategic thinking of St Dominic, were born in the first decades of the thirteenth century. A conscious proselytising mission brought the Dominicans to England in 1221. Making straight for Oxford, the intellectual centre of the country, they established the first friary there. The Franciscans followed shortly afterwards, in 1224. When they landed they were kept in custody in Dover castle until they could prove they were orthodox, but, having passed this test, they went on immediately to establish houses at Canterbury, London, and Oxford.[165]

The friars differed radically from the earlier monastic orders. They did not expect to stay cloistered in the same monastery all their lives, but moved from place to place. They were supposed to live from donations rather than endowments. They had an active missionary role. Early on, they infiltrated the universities and occupied a dominant position in the intellectual world. They were preachers and teachers, based in the growing towns. Their success was immediate: by the middle of the thirteenth century England had fifty Franciscan houses alone, based in each of the major towns of England. They made a deep impact on English religious life, but their story lies beyond the chronological limits of this volume.

[163] J. Ford, *V. Wulfric* 2. 45 (pp. 61–3).
[164] *V. Christina*, p. 190.
[165] *Chronicon de Lanercost*, ed. Joseph Stevenson (Bannatyne Club; 1839), p. 30.

# CHAPTER 9

---

# Religious Life

## I. CONCEPTS OF THE HOLY

### Hallowing

Like most religions, medieval Christianity designated certain persons, places, objects, and times as holy. They were to be treated with special reverence and were exempt from many of the normal rules that applied to the mundane. The Church possessed an extensive repertoire of rituals designed to set aside people, buildings, and objects in this way. In his service book a twelfth-century bishop had directions not only for ordaining clerics and dedicating churches but also for consecrating bells, candles, church ornaments, branches for distribution on Palm Sunday, salt for use in baptism, a pilgrim's staff, a knight's sword, and the fire and water used for trial by ordeal.[1] If they were blessed in the proper ritual way all these things could be given a special and sanctified status. They became officially holy.

A good example of the ritual designation of a site in this way is the episcopal dedication of a church. When a bishop dedicated a church, he marked out the circuit of the sacred place by leading a procession around the building six times before entering it. Inside, he traced with his staff on the floor of the church a great 'X' made up of the letters of the Greek and Latin alphabets, and then mixed a holy concoction of salt, ashes, water, wine, and chrism (holy oil), with which he sprayed the interior and exterior walls three times. This was to drive away phantasms and demons. He then drew the sign of the cross on the inner and outer walls in chrism in twelve places before proceeding to enclose relics in the altar, bless the altar-cloth, and then, in fresh vestments, celebrate mass and preach a sermon.[2]

The elements used in the ceremony themselves needed to be exorcized before they were safe to use in blessings:

I exorcize you, creature of water, in the name of God the Father omnipotent and in the name of Jesus Christ his son and the Holy Spirit, so that every strength of our adversary, every assault of the devil, every phantasm and all powers of the enemy be

---

[1] *Magd. Pont., passim.*    [2] Ibid., pp. 98–124.

uprooted and expelled from this creature of water. Hence I exorcize you, creature of water, through the living God, through the true God, through the holy God and through our lord Jesus Christ, so that you become holy water, blessed water, and wherever you are poured out or sprinkled, in house or in field, you will drive away every phantasm and every power of the Enemy and you will be consecrated holy water fit for the dedication of this church.[3]

As is clear from this formula, one could expect natural substances to harbour evil spirits. Only after the elements had been freed from demonic taint, could they be used to mark out the sacred boundaries of the church.

Holiness was imparted primarily by uttering words—the invocation of God, the exorcism of the elements—but other techniques were also employed. Special gestures and substances formed part of the rites. As is evident from the passage just quoted, holy water was a powerful instrument of sanctification. It was created every Sunday by blessing water in the church and dispensed from a special sprinkler (aspersorium). It was used in a great variety of rituals. The corpse on the bier was sprinkled with holy water.[4] The order of service from Salisbury describes the blessing of the water on Advent Sunday (the first day of Advent) by the priest, who then sprinkled it over the altars, the other clerics, and the lay people present.[5] When monks received an important visitor the abbot would sprinkle him with holy water from a sprinkler.[6]

Apart from its use in these regular rituals, sprinkling with holy water could also serve in emergencies. It could drive away demons, like the one who tried to enter the chancel of the church at Stisted in Essex disguised as a woman, but was sent spinning into a meadow two furlongs away when sprinkled with holy water by the deacon.[7] When a lightening bolt struck the monastery of Winchcombe in 1091, the foul smell that followed convinced the monks that this was not a natural event but a diabolic attack: 'with happy daring they escaped the delusions of the Enemy by sprinkling holy water.'[8] The occult powers of blessed water were widely recognized. The reason that it was recommended that fonts be sealed and locked was to avoid magicians stealing and using the water in them.[9]

As important as water was oil. There were three types used for ritual purposes: holy oil, the oil of the sick, and chrism. The first had various functions, including the primary unction at baptism, the second, as its name suggests, was used to anoint the sick, while chrism—oil mixed with balsam—was employed for a variety of important rites, such as ordination and confirmation. These oils were hallowed by the bishop's blessing on Maundy Thursday (the Thursday before Easter), the bishop himself supplying the expensive

---

[3] *Magd. Pont.*, pp. 106–7.    [4] e.g. ibid., p. 195.    [5] *Reg. Osm.* 1, pp. 116–18.
[6] Lanfr., *Const.*, p. 71.    [7] *Vis. Thurkill*, pp. 18–19.
[8] W. Malm., *GR* 4. 323 (2, p. 375); OMT edn., p. 568.    [9] *Councils and Synods* 2/i, p. 68.

imported balsam. The oils were then stored or transmitted as required. Extreme unction, the anointing of those in danger of death, was a ritual that the laity seem to have taken seriously. There even seems to have been a belief, shared by lay people and less educated priests, that once the sick had received this unction, it could never be repeated, nor, even if they recovered, could they resume ordinary sexual relations.[10]

Another exotic foreign ingredient, besides the balsam used in chrism, was incense. Both were sweet-smelling substances procured from trees or plants of the Mediterranean. Incense was burned in a special container (the thurible) and used to perfume the air around a large variety of holy places and persons. The scent drove off evil spirits, as is clear from the ceremony for the blessing of the incense: 'wherever this incense may be, there you shall not dare approach nor presume to do anything evil, but, whoever you are, you unclean spirit, you will flee far away with all your cunning tricks.'[11] Like much of the ritual apparatus of medieval Christianity, the diffusion of the fumes from incense was a line of defence against demons.

Alongside this repertoire of words and hallowed substances were the ritual gestures that also effected the change from the secular to the spiritual. Breathing was one form, signing with the cross another. In the ceremony of baptism both were used. After the triple renunciation of the devil, his works, and all his pomp, the priest blew in the face of the candidate for baptism, commanding Satan to come out, and then made the sign of the cross on his or her forehead. Similarly, during the consecration of holy oil and chrism, the bishop made the sign of the cross upon the vessels containing the oil and blew on them.[12]

Making the sign of the cross was indeed one of the most widespread of Christian observances, used as a safeguard and blessing in a thousand circumstances. It was customary, for instance, to make the sign of the cross over food or drink before consuming it and there is even the case of a devil entering a woman's body through a lettuce over which she had failed to make the sign.[13] Baldwin of Ford noted that 'priests are accustomed to give blessings by uttering words and making the sign of the cross' and the gesture was indeed a commonplace in the idiom of ritual, employed during the consecration of the eucharistic host, made over the eyes of a sick person by the visiting priest, and in other ceremonial moments.[14] Like holy water, it could be relied on to avert danger encountered outside the world of ecclesiastical ritual: Anselm once quelled a fire in the city of Winchester simply by 'raising his right hand and making the sign of the cross'.[15]

---

[10] *Councils and Synods* 2/i, pp. 90–1; Alex. Ashby, *De modo pred.*, p. 933.    [11] *Magd. Pont.*, p. 139.
[12] Ibid., pp. 170, 163, 165.    [13] O. Cheriton, *Parabolae* 100 (p. 303).
[14] Baldwin of Ford, *De sacramento altaris*, ed. J. Morson (2 vols., *Sources chrétiennes* 93–4; 1963), vol. 1, p. 118 (*PL* 204, col. 654).
[15] Eadmer, *V. Anselm*, p. 66.

Sanctified persons, places, and things could thus be marked out by rituals that were generally understood. To sign with the cross, sprinkle with holy water, anoint with chrism, was to move something from one category to another. A new classification followed from the ceremonial act. Clerics asserted, and lay people usually concurred, that ecclesiastical rites created holiness, a special status that the ordinary did not possess. Not all space was ordinary and uniform. Not everybody was familiar and commonplace. Some locations, people, and things were sharply distinguished by their heightened, distinct, and designated holiness.

## Sanctuary

Because churches were publicly recognized as holy places, they could offer asylum. Once he had reached a church, a criminal could no longer be seized for execution or mutilation: 'whatever crime a man has committed, if he can come to holy church he shall have immunity for life and limb.'[16] The dash to asylum must have been an anxious race, as it was for the savage pirate chief known as Barabas, escaping his captors, who 'took the road to Canterbury, knowing that he would lose neither life nor limb if he could reach the asylum of Christchurch'.[17] Once within sanctuary, a criminal need not come to court but had the choice of 'abjuring the realm', that is, of promising to leave the kingdom, never to return. He lost his land and his chattels, but his neck, hands, and testicles would be safe.

All churches offered sanctuary but some provided a stronger asylum than others. A group of important northern churches had especially solid and carefully defined rights. One was Hexham. Here the sanctity of the church extended into its surroundings, although in a diluted form. Richard, prior of Hexham, described the concentric circles around the relics in his church. Breach of sanctuary, that is, assault upon a person who had sought asylum, was punished by a fine of £16 if it took place within a mile of the church, in the area marked out by four crosses; the fine increased to £32 if the offence occurred within the town itself; to £48 if within the church precincts; to £96 if within the church; to a staggering £144 if within the choir of the church; while a breach of sanctuary at the shrine of the saints or by the stone chair 'that the English call the "stool of peace" [*fridstol*]' was beyond recompense.[18] The protective power, the supernatural aura and the effrontery involved in breaking it were thus not distributed evenly, but had a hot core and a cooler periphery.

---

[16] Liebermann, *Gesetze* 1, p. 492 (Leis Wl 1); Robertson, *Laws*, p. 252.

[17] Osbern of Canterbury, *Mir. sancti Dunstani*, ed. William Stubbs, *Memorials of St Dunstan* (RS; 1874), p. 154.

[18] Richard of Hexham, *Historia Haugustaldensis ecclesiae* 14 (*Priory Hexham*, p. 61); cf. Van Caen., *Lawsuits* 1, pp. 140–2, no. 172; Liebermann, *Gesetze* 1, pp. 630–1 (E Cf. 5–6).

Another of these northern churches was Durham. Anyone seeking refuge at the shrine of St Cuthbert there was immune for thirty-seven days; the fine for breach of this sanctuary was £96, as for an infraction within the church at Hexham.[19] A case that illustrates the workings—and the limitations—of sanctuary is related by the monk, Reginald of Durham. A young official of the bishop of Durham was murdered and the killer sought refuge in Durham cathedral, pursued by the young man's friends and relatives. They surrounded the church. The killer was unable to go out, even to the toilet. At first the pursuers were inhibited by the holiness of the church, but eventually six of them entered it, caught the killer at the altar of the Holy Cross, south of St Cuthbert's tomb, where one of them slit his throat. The avenger fled Durham, but was unable to get far, impeded by Cuthbert's protective power, and was captured and placed in chains in an underground dungeon. The cathedral church meanwhile was being reconciled after its pollution with blood. The original killer, although his wounds had appeared mortal, recovered 'with St Cuthbert as his doctor', and was forgiven by the bishop. Reginald, who tells the story, has no doubt that the man was guilty of the initial murder, but it is the violation of sanctuary that shocks him.[20] The great sanctuary door-knocker at Durham, in the shape of a lion's head survives to this day as a reminder of the shelter that holy space offered.

## Pollution

Durham cathedral, splattered in blood from the assault mentioned by Reginald of Durham, required formal 'reconciliation'. The sacredness imparted by consecration could be tainted. Holy places like churches and cemeteries could be polluted by the shedding of blood or other violations and they would then require a special service to restore their integral holiness. This service was similar to the dedication ceremony but stressed the restoring and cleansing power of God:

O God, whose goodness has no beginning and no limit . . . whose benevolence prefers to purify by grace rather than strike in anger anything that has been polluted by negligence, committed in wrath, stimulated by drunkenness or overturned by lust, we humbly pray you to sanctify this place and to purify, through your blessing, poured from above, whatever was polluted by the guile of the Enemy who pursues us . . .[21]

The most notorious case of pollution by blood in this period was the murder of archbishop Thomas Becket in Canterbury cathedral in 1170. He was killed on 29 December and church services in the cathedral were then suspended until 21 December 1171: 'the monks whispered the day and night

---

[19] S. Durh., *HDE* 2. 13 (pp. 69–70); *Historia de sancto Cuthberto* 13, in Simeon, *Op.* 1, p. 203.
[20] Reg., *Libellus* 60–1 (pp. 119–22).     [21] *Magd. Pont.*, p. 130.

services in their chapter-house, without chant; the crosses in the church were covered and the altars empty, as in Passion Week'.[22] Finally the bishops of Exeter and Chester reconciled the church, the monks could re-enter it and masses could again be celebrated there. Ironically, the blood that had soiled the monks' cathedral church was also the foundation of the cult that brought them fame and wealth. Small bottles of the (enormously diluted) blood of the martyred archbishop were one of the main attractions at Canterbury.

Blood was not the only contaminating agent. Birth and death could also pollute. In a monastery, the monastic priest who was delegated to perform mass that week could not wash a corpse.[23] The hands that consecrated the host were not to be contaminated by touching a dead body. The custom of the churching of women implied that after childbirth mothers needed to undergo a rite of purification. Official church teaching was that a woman could enter church to thank God even on the day she had given birth. However, the existence of rituals for the formal admission of a woman into the church by a priest after childbirth and the terminology of purification used to describe this ceremony suggest that the idea of a taint or uncleanness derived from giving birth was not absent.

One twelfth-century author tells of a woman going to church 'on the day of her purification, there to offer in solemn rites a sacrifice for her expiation'.[24] 'Expiation' quite clearly means 'making amends' or 'cleansing'. The statutes of the diocese of Salisbury issued about 1218 show a similar sense of the imperfection of the new mother in their ruling that 'When women come to purification after childbirth, the priests should give them only blessed bread and not communion'.[25] The 'sacrifice' that the woman should offer on these occasions was quite concrete. There is a touching story of a poor Northumbrian woman who had given birth but was not able to go to church 'because she did not have a suitable offering, as was customary on these occasions'; a kindly hermit provided a little wax that met the need.[26]

## Cursing

If holy power could be contaminated by contact with impure substances, it could also, in all its full force, be directed to negative as well as positive ends. The obverse of blessing was cursing. Sometimes this was merely a casual malediction. The holy anchorite Wulfric of Haselbury killed a mouse that had gnawed his cape by cursing it. 'Perish the mouse that has damaged my cape!' he said and the mouse fell dead at his feet, 'so great was the force of his

---

[22] Gerv. Cant., p. 229.     [23] Lanfr., *Const.*, p. 124.
[24] Gerald of Wales (Giraldus Cambrensis), *V. Ethelberti*, ed. M. J. James, 'Two Lives of St Ethelbert, King and Martyr', *EHR* 32 (1917), pp. 214–44, at p. 235.
[25] *Councils and Synods* 2/i, p. 80.     [26] Reg., *Libellus* 78 (p. 163).

word'. 'By its death', comments Wulfric's Cistercian biographer, 'it gave glory to God and peace to the holy man.'[27] As noted above (pp. 440–1), Wulfric's curses could harm men as well as beasts and such mortal outcomes were effected by other saints too. When St Hugh of Lincoln was attempting to reconcile an estranged husband and wife, the irate woman spat in his face. He said to her, 'Since you have not wanted my blessing but have desired my curse, lo! a curse shall take hold of you.' He excommunicated her and within a few days the woman was dead.[28]

Excommunication, segregating an individual from the Christian community, was a regulated and legal form of the curse. It was intended to be an awesome act, pronounced publicly, with lighted candles and church bells sounding. Its effects on its victims were grave:

God's grace and protection are withdrawn from them; they are left to their own devices, free to fall into the death of sin; greater power is given to the devil to rage furiously against the body and soul of the excommunicate, since God's grace is withdrawn from them; the sacraments of the church, prayers and blessings do not help them . . .[29]

There is ample evidence for disregard of excommunication, including the notable case of king John, who was excommunicate for almost four years, but also many signs that lay people could be impressed and intimidated by it. The day after the sheriff of Pembroke was excommunicated with the full ritual of bells and lighted candles, he submitted to corporal punishment, submission, and reconciliation. The normal spiritual props and supports were no longer available to the excommunicate and most took this seriously.

Another weapon in the ecclesiastical arsenal, alongside the carefully aimed dart of excommunication, was a more general withdrawal of divine service. This was a kind of spiritual strike or boycott, in which the ritual specialists simply refused to cooperate and fulfil the role expected of them. During a quarrel with Henry I over royal financial demands on his clergy, Ralph Luffa, bishop of Chichester, suspended divine office in his diocese and ordered the doors of the churches to be blocked with thorns.[30] This was a traditional practice. Robert de Béthune, bishop of Hereford, in dispute with Miles of Gloucester, earl of Hereford, about 1142, not only excommunicated the earl and 'the whole city of Hereford', but also 'had the doors of the church blocked with thorns and the crosses taken down and placed on the ground'.[31] The dramatic touch of placing the revered emblem of the cross in such a lowly position was designed to shock, to make the offenders think again and to bring them to their senses. It was intended to rub their noses in the

[27] J. Ford, V. Wulfric 1. 30 (p. 46).
[28] Ad. Eyns., V. Hugh 2, pp. 31–2.          [29] Gerald, Gemma 1. 53 (pp. 158–9).
[30] W. Malm., GP 96 (p. 206).          [31] Wigmore Chron., p. 424.

reversal of right order that they had brought about. As specialists in the holy, the clergy were well placed to manipulate it to make their point.

## 2. DEVOTION

### Liturgy

Medieval Christianity was a religion of ritual. The ritual pattern consisted of the daily chant of Divine Office, punctuated by the less frequent but universal rite of Mass. Both the year and the individual human life were ritually structured, from Easter to Whitsun to Christmas, from baptism to burial. High points of ceremony were the seven sacraments of baptism, confirmation, penance, communion, extreme unction, marriage, and ordination. Whatever else the clergy might be, they were meant to be skilled practitioners of ritual.

The Office consisted of a series of services ('hours') that ranged from the night office of Matins, through Lauds, Prime, Terce, Sext, None, and Vespers to the office of Compline, recited before bed. Each of these services consisted primarily of prayers, Psalms, and hymns, with readings from the Bible or other material appropriate to the occasion—on a saint's day there might be readings from the Life of that saint. The full cycle of the Office was celebrated in monasteries and collegiate churches and versions of it were recommended to parish priests, anchorites, etc. The Mass was a ritual of a different form. It centred upon the consecration of bread and wine by the priest and the subsequent consumption of these sanctified elements.

The only religious service most English people were likely to attend was the Sunday mass at their local parish church. It is impossible to be sure how widespread or frequent attendance was. Reference is made to the ordinary Sunday mass only when something unusual took place, as at Leverton (Lincs.), when the parishioners on their way to Sunday morning service were disturbed by a group of drunken rowdies who had supposedly been in the village tavern since Saturday afternoon. They violently hauled off their more dutiful neighbours and the service was eventually abandoned.[32] Even if they made it to church, parishioners still might not behave with the reverence that the ecclesiastical authorities deemed appropriate. 'Let every priest exhort his parishioners to turn their attention in church to prayer, not to shouting or vacuous story-telling', enjoined one archbishop.[33] The English-born theologian Robert of Courson referred to the practice of going to church to see one's

---

[32] C. R. Cheney, *From Becket to Langton: English Church Government 1170–1213* (Manchester, 1956), pp. 196–8.
[33] *Councils and Synods* 2/i, p. 31.

mistress.[34] The solemn moment when the priest fell into silent prayer before the consecration of the eucharist seems to have called forth a riot of chatting and joking: 'at that point some people have the habit of exchanging gossip, turning the silence that is ordained for religious reverence into an occasion for empty frivolity'.[35]

Perhaps one reason that the congregation was so prone to lapse into chatter and gossip was that attendance at mass did not usually involve participation in holy communion. The lay people were spectators not participants. Even conscientious clerics aimed only to persuade lay people to take communion three times a year, at Easter, Whitsun, and Christmas, or, failing that, at least at Easter. It is possible there was a paradoxical process here: clerical insistence on the extraordinary nature of the eucharist led to infrequent lay communion and lack of lay participation led to casual behaviour during the ritual.

Stress on the wondrousness of the eucharist there certainly was. 'The value of this sacrament,' wrote the Cistercian Baldwin of Ford, 'is great and beyond estimation . . . before consecration the true substance of bread is there, but during consecration it is transformed and changed by the power of the words into the true flesh of Christ . . .'[36] The doctrine of transubstantiation meant that Christ's body and blood were literally present on the altar, were literally consumed in communion. The consecrated host should thus be treated with reverence. It was 'the food of angels'. When the priest carried it through the street to the sick, he should be preceded by a light and a cross.[37] There was obsessive concern that no drops of the consecrated wine or crumbs of the consecrated bread should fall to the ground through negligence. If wine were spilled after consecration, the surface where it fell had to be scraped up and dropped into the piscina, the recess especially designated for receiving the sacred by-products of ritual processes.[38]

The abstruse doctrine of transubstantiation was given a concrete and vivid aspect through stories of eucharistic miracles, when Christ's blood and body were revealed without the cloak of wine and bread. On one occasion St Hugh of Lincoln was celebrating mass in the church at his manor of Buckden (Hunts.), when, as he consecrated the host, he found he was holding Christ 'in the form of a little baby'.[39] Gerald of Wales tells of an incident that occurred in Arras at some point in the 1160s or 1170s. A priest carelessly left the consecrated host with a sick woman, who tied it in a silk robe and left it in

---

[34] John Baldwin, 'Five Discourse on Desire: Sexuality and Gender in Northern France around 1200', *Speculum*, 66 (1991), pp. 797–819, at p. 802.

[35] Alex. Ashby, *De modo pred.*, p. 910.

[36] Baldwin, *Sermo* 4. 1–3 (*Tractatus* 1), *Op.*, p. 67 (*PL* 204, col. 403).

[37] *Councils and Synods* 1/ii, pp. 1048, 1061; 2/i, p. 28; Gerald, *Gemma* 1. 6 (p. 20).

[38] Lanfr., *Const.*, p. 90.          [39] Ad. Eyns., *V. Hugh* 5. 3 (2, p. 86).

a chest. One night the chest glowed with supernatural light. On opening the chest, the woman and her husband found that the knot enclosing the host seemed to be stained with fresh blood. They took it to the priest who untied it to find a host, half in the form of bleeding flesh, half in the form of bread, with the letters that were imprinted on the host being visible in both parts. According to Gerald, the whole region, which had been infested by heretics, was now brought back 'to the certainty of faith and the true way'. He himself, passing through the town a week later, had his faith strengthened: 'I had always been a firm believer in this article of faith, but, by the certainty of what I learned from eye-witnesses and what I ascertained in person, I was made firmer and more confident.'[40] Even this complacently orthodox cleric could find miraculous support for the doctrine of transubstantiation reassuring.

## Preaching

Sermons were given in many different circumstances and to various audiences. Monastic communities were accustomed to hear their superiors preach to them, scholars might assemble to listen to learned preachers, church councils usually allowed time for a sermon. Sometimes issues of the day could be discussed in sermons, as when archbishop Stephen Langton used a sermon he was preaching at St Paul's to explain why the Interdict had not yet been raised from England. The lengthy sermon Langton preached on the first anniversary of the translation of Becket's relics in 1220 also survives, an expert example of extended, learned Latin preaching.[41] Langton took the duty of preaching seriously and enjoined parish priests 'to instruct the congregations that have been entrusted to them with the food of the word of God, lest they be rightly judged dumb dogs'.[42]

The Sunday sermon at the parish church was considered crucial for the religious formation of the mass of the population. Priests were encouraged to instruct their parishioners in the elementary beliefs and practices of the Christian faith. They should teach them the Lord's Prayer, the Creed, and the formula of confession, and also the necessity of faith, hope, and charity.[43] They should propound to them their moral duties towards their neighbours, as enshrined in the seven works of mercy: visiting the sick, giving drink to the thirsty, feeding the hungry, ransoming captives, clothing the naked, giving hospitality to strangers, and burying the dead.[44] The sermon was also the time to hold out the joys of heaven and the horrors of hell: 'In every sermon there should be a reminder of the rewards of the saved and the sufferings of

---

[40] Gerald, *Gemma* 1. 11 (pp. 40–1).
[41] Stephen Langton, *Selected Sermons*, ed. Phyllis Roberts (Toronto, 1980), pp. 37–51, 67–94.
[42] *Councils and Synods* 2/i, p. 110.
[43] Ibid. 1/ii, pp. 1070–1; cf. 2/i, p. 31.     [44] T. Chobham, *SP*, p. 28.

the damned, so that the congregation may be moved to fulfil what they have been commanded to do both by love and fear.'[45]

The frequency of preaching is difficult to establish. Ralph Luffa, bishop of Chichester (1091–1123) was praised for going on preaching tours of his diocese three times a year.[46] This suggests that a sermon from a bishop was a rarity, but throws little light on the activities of the average parish priest. Again, it is clear that some heads of religious houses were willing and able to preach in English to local people. Abbot Samson of Bury had a pulpit set up in the abbey church from which he preached to the people in his own Norfolk dialect.[47] Odo, abbot of Battle (1175–1200), composed commentaries on scripture and other treatises that he set down in written form but also delivered orally 'for the edification of his hearers, sometimes speaking French, sometimes Latin, and frequently in the mother tongue for the edification of the uneducated ordinary people'.[48] Those within reach of such conscientious abbots could thus hear skilful sermons in a language they understood, but again this says nothing about the standards of the parish priest.

Those priests who had no natural aptitude for the sermon could seek help in various ways. The practice of preachers learning other people's sermons by heart is referred to and defended.[49] There is also occasionally mention of a 'Book of Sermons' among the service books of a church, such as that in the inventory of the books and ornaments of the minor collegiate church of Heytesbury (Wilts.) in 1220.[50] By the early years of the thirteenth century, guides to preaching were being written in England, some, like that by Alexander of Ashby, with model sermons attached. Thomas of Chobham's *Outline of the Art of Preaching* (*Summa de arte praedicandi*), composed about 1220, is a particularly substantial example of a preacher's manual. Thomas was himself a highly educated man, having spent several years studying in Paris, but he was clear that a sermon should not be a lecture. 'We can teach knowledge but not preach it', he remarks. Preaching should be concerned solely with what makes us better human beings.[51]

Thomas shows an awareness of the needs of different audiences, explaining that 'different forms of preaching are required for great men and knights, for burgesses, for freemen, for serfs, for women, for clerics', and he has a large amount of practical and technical advice: it is not necessary to give

[45] Alex. Ashby, *De modo pred.*, p. 907.

[46] W. Malm., *GP* 96 (pp. 206–7); for a collection of bishop's sermons from this period, see Herbert de Losinga, *Sermons*, ed. E. M. Goulburn and H. Symonds, *Life, Letters and Sermons of Herbert de Losinga* (2 vols.; London, 1878), vol. 1.

[47] Joc. Brak., p. 40.

[48] *Battle Chron.*, pp. 306–8; for his writing, see Richard Sharpe, *A Handlist of the Latin Writers of Great Britain and Ireland before 1540* (Turnhout, 1997), pp. 402–3.

[49] Joc. Brak., p. 128.      [50] *Reg. Osm.* 1, p. 294.      [51] T. Chobham, *SP*, p. 143.

exact citations for authorities that are quoted; the preacher should suit his voice to his subject; when dealing with frightening things he should 'have a slightly trembling voice, like one who is afraid'; he should not, however, have inflamed eyes or wildly gesticulating hands, 'more like an actor than a preacher'.[52] In all such questions of expression and style, the work draws heavily on ancient Roman handbooks of rhetoric.

Yet, although Thomas of Chobham devotes much attention to the construction and delivery of the sermon, he spends even more time discussing the content. The first things to stress are the pains of hell and the joys of heaven, since human beings would not care whether they were good or wicked 'unless they expected punishment or reward after death'. The preacher should convey the 'good news' of the Gospel: the promise of beatitude, the remission of sins, adoption as sons of God, the resurrection of the dead, the eternal inheritance, the company of angels. He should assail 'the lust of the flesh', including gluttony and sexual desire, 'the lust of the eye', those self-regarding vices like avarice and ambition, and 'the pride of life', especially since 'no vice is more natural to human beings'. He should expound the four cardinal virtues, prudence, justice, fortitude, and temperance, and the three supernatural or theological virtues of faith, hope, and charity.[53]

A sermon in English recorded in a twelfth-century collection illustrates the actual practice of preaching. This was designed for delivery on the second Sunday in Lent and begins, in a way Thomas of Chobham would have approved, with 'the three things that all men need to know and have, faith, hope and charity'. Faith means belief in the Trinity of Father, Son, and Holy Ghost, one God, who created all things. Hope is directed to eternal life and the rewards of heaven. Charity is love of God and one's neighbour. God dwells in those who have charity and, to make themselves worthy to become the dwelling-place of God, all Christians should cleanse themselves through six methods: confession, repentance, vigils, fasting, prayer, and alms-giving. The main part of the sermon deals with these six methods, especially repentance. Those who are ashamed to repent now will repent later—in hell. 'Men,' cries the preacher, 'let us beware the intense terrors of those unending torments of hell.' Fasting is especially commended 'at this holy season' (i.e. Lent). All should pray and reflect on God's law; 'and he who can read, should read, and he who cannot, should listen to him who reads'. Scattered within the sermon are a few passages from the Bible and the Fathers, sometimes in Latin, but in that case immediately translated into 'our language'. The closing formula presents the joys of the life to come 'with the Father and with the Son and with the Holy Ghost, world without end. Amen.' The whole thing must have

---

[52] T. Chobham, pp. 276, 286, 302–3.    [53] Ibid., pp. 89–136 *passim*; cf. pp. 143–259 *passim*.

taken less than twelve minutes to deliver but provided a concentrated draught of Christian theology and ethics for those willing to swallow it.[54]

## Six Ways to Cleanse the Soul

### Confession and Repentance

Of the six methods to cleanse the soul propounded in the sermon just discussed, confession and repentance were the first. Medieval Christianity taught that all human beings had sinned and needed to be cleansed of sin. The rite of baptism removed 'original sin', the guilt that was innate to all humans, but subsequent actual sins need to be cleared by confession and penance. These formed, in an image which writers of the twelfth century borrowed from St Jerome, 'the second plank after the shipwreck'. Baptism offered the first plank to which drowning human souls might cling, confession and penance the second.[55]

Over the course of our period the importance of confession was stressed ever more earnestly. Lay people were urged to confess at least once a year, just as they were encouraged to receive annual communion. This annual confession usually took place on Maundy Thursday (the day before Good Friday), which was known as 'the day of absolution'.[56] Ecclesiastics underlined the power of confession to wipe away sins. At the Last Judgement all vices and sins would be made public unless, during the sinner's lifetime, they had been 'covered over' by confession.[57] 'Confession', it was said, 'destroys sins so completely that even the devil has no recollection of them.'[58] Handbooks for confessors were produced, paralleling the guides to preaching—Thomas of Chobham wrote treatises of both kinds. These guides dealt with the practical and psychological task of the priest hearing confession and included some discussion of the theological issues involved. There had been a large penitential literature in the early Middle Ages, but this tended to concern itself mainly with a set of elaborate tariffs: how many days, or years, should one perform penance for homicide, for theft, for adultery, etc. The confessors' manuals of about 1200 and later focused much more intimately upon the relationship between the priest and the lay people for whom he was responsible.

The confessors' handbooks and the diocesan statutes show attentive concern for the details of procedure. Confessors had to show tact when dealing with women. They were to hear their confessions in public view, although

[54] *Twelfth-Century Homilies in MS Bodley* 343, ed. A. O. Belfour (EETS 137; 1909), pp. 51–9.

[55] P. Blois, *Confess.*, col. 1078; Bart. Ex., p. 178; *Councils and Synods* 1/ii, p. 1062; Jerome, ep. 130 (*PL* 22, col. 1115).

[56] T. Monm., *V. William* 1. 6 (p. 26).

[57] Ailred of Rievaulx, *Sermo* 1. 7, ed. Gaetano Raciti, *Sermones I–XLVI* (CCCM 2A; 1989), p. 4 (*PL* 195, col. 210).

[58] Gerald, *Gemma* 1. 17 (p. 53).

not, of course, within earshot of bystanders. They should not impose on a
married woman such a penance that her husband suspect her of 'some enormous secret offence'.[59] When penitents confessed to a sin such as theft or
fraud, then they must be commanded to restore the property they had taken
unjustly; saying masses or giving alms was not a sufficient penance for them.[60]
Priests required confessors of their own. The Statutes issued by archbishop
Stephen Langton in 1213 or 1214 prescribe that every priest have a confessor,
that two members of each chapter undertake this task for their fellow canons
and that in cases of doubt or difficulty recourse be had to the archbishop's
'chief penitentiaries'.[61]

The proliferation of priests with specialist duties as confessors, such as
those mentioned in Langton's statutes, is another sign of the new emphasis
being placed upon this aspect of Christian practice. Although it was held that
in certain circumstances absolution could only be granted by the bishop, it
became common for him to delegate this authority. In the 1140s the bishop of
Norwich 'appointed the monk Wichmann as his representative to advise penitents', while the canons of the legatine council of York of 1195 mention a 'general confessor of the diocese', who was to impose penance and grant absolution
for certain cases in the bishop's absence.[62] A few years later, in 1198, Hugh of
Lincoln sent a local sorceress to the prior of Huntingdon, 'penitentiary of the
region', for confession and penance.[63] In addition to such district commissioners, high-born members of royal and noble families would have their own personal confessors. Queen Matilda, first wife of Henry I, and her namesake,
Stephen's queen, both had the services of priors of Holy Trinity, Aldgate, as
confessors (above, p. 427). A grant made by Euphemia, countess of Oxford, in
the mid-1150s was witnessed by her confessor, Robert the chaplain.[64]

The full process of penitence required three steps: 'contrition of the heart,
confession of the mouth, affliction of the flesh'.[65] After the sorrow and the
avowal of guilt came some form of penance, some routine of self-denial or
devotion prescribed by the priest as a fitting amends for the sinner. The
greater the sin, the heavier the penance. One of the confessor's chief skills was
weighing out penance according to the nature of the sinner and the sin.

Attention should be paid to whether the penitent is free or servile, clerk or lay or
monk; and, if a clerk, of what order or rank; if a lay person, whether married or not;
also, whether the penitent is rich or poor, a child, youth, adult or elderly, wise or
stupid, healthy or sick, a man or a woman, virgin or debauched, chaste or unchaste,

[59] *Councils and Synods* 1/ii, p. 1062; 2/i, pp. 32, 71–2.      [60] Ibid. 2/i, p. 74.
[61] Ibid., pp. 27, 113.
[62] T. Monm., *V. William* 1. 8, 2. 7 (pp. 30, 84); *Councils and Synods* 1/ii, p. 1051.
[63] Ad. Eyns., *V. Hugh* 5. 8 (2, p. 118).
[64] *Cartularium prioratus de Colne* (Essex Arch. Soc.; 1946), no. 56, pp. 29–30.
[65] P. Blois, *Confess.*, col. 1086.

if they have a position whose duties can be performed without sin or not . . . consideration must be paid as to whether the sin is venial or mortal, public or secret, done knowingly or in ignorance, voluntarily or not, with forethought or not, if solely in thought or word or also in deed . . .[66]

This delicate calculus would then result in the imposition of a penance ranging from the slight, such as recitation of prayers, to the severe, including, perhaps, a pilgrimage to a distant shrine. One unusually dramatic and visible form of penance for grave sins was the wearing of iron bands around the arms or body. A man from Reepham in Lincolnshire, for instance, who had quarrelled with his brother over their lands and in a fit of rage had killed him and his sons with a pitchfork, was condemned to banishment, wearing the iron of the fork in a ring around his arm.[67]

The visit to Becket's tomb undertaken by Henry II in 1174 is a famous example of public expiation. The king dismounted outside Canterbury and entered the city barefoot, in plain woollen garments. Prostrate and weeping before the tomb of the murdered archbishop, he received physical punishment from the monks and other clerics, then spent the night there in prayer and fasting. In the morning he heard mass and then went on his way to London.[68] Bare feet, plain clothes, tears, physical chastisement, prayer, and fasting—every aspect of this ritual performance followed the rules of the penitential code. One of the signs of king Henry's sincerity was his disregard not only for 'the harshness of the way and the tenderness of his feet' as he entered Canterbury but also for 'the spectacle he displayed to the common crowd' [*spectaculum vulgi*]. This shaming function gave public penance its merit but it also made it hard to stomach for a proud aristocracy, highly sensitive to its honour. 'Many of our contemporaries,' commented Peter of Blois, archdeacon of Bath, 'and especially knights, are ashamed to undergo penance before others, for to some of them it appears that this stems either from hypocrisy or from weakness and feebleness of spirit.'[69]

Peter of Blois's analysis of the psychological obstacles to confession and penance identifies four main types: shame, fear, hope, desperation. Some are ashamed to confess their sins; they should remember how 'the book of their conscience will be opened before all on the Day of Judgement'; they should not be ashamed to acknowledge what they have not been ashamed to do. Some are afraid of the burden of penance; let them think how much more insufferable are the pains of hell. Others hope they will have a long life and

---

[66] Bart. Ex., pp. 194–5.         [67] T. Monm., *V. William* 6. 10 (pp. 236–9).

[68] Gerv. Cant., pp. 248–9; *Gesta Hen. II* 1, p. 72; R. Howd. 2, pp. 61–2; Edward Grim, *V. sancti Thomae* 91–3 (*Becket Mats.* 2, pp. 445–7).

[69] Peter of Blois, *Dialogus inter regem Henricum II et abbatem Bonevallis*, ed. R. B. C. Huygens, *Revue Bénédictine* 68 (1958), pp. 87–112, at p. 110 (*PL* 207, col. 986).

can defer action—but life is brief and uncertain. Those who despair of for-giveness should remember God's mercy towards sinners like David, the thief on the cross, or those who crucified him.[70]

The penitential system spanned this world and the next. Although there was no hope for those who died unrepentant in a state of mortal sin, those who died repentant, but with their penances incomplete, had a remedy. The fires of Purgatory would cleanse them and render them fit for heaven. More-over, some paths guaranteed salvation. A repentant crusader had the assur-ance that 'whoever begins and completes so holy a journey with devotion or dies on it will obtain absolution from all his sins which he has confessed with a contrite and humble heart and he will receive the fruit of eternal reward from him who repays all'.[71]

## Vigils, Fasting, Prayer, and Alms-Giving

'Every man that thinks to obtain heavenly bliss, must earn it here on earth, through fasting and through alms-giving, through continual prayer and bod-ily abstinence.'[72] This typical formula of Christian asceticism equates three things: deliberate physical self-denial and austerity, such as fasting and sleep-deprivation; prayer; and charitable giving, to the poor or to the Church. All three counted as 'good works', bringing merit and helping to win heaven. All three could be undertaken voluntarily, but might also be prescribed as a penance. All three could be undertaken vicariously, for the benefit of others, as well as for oneself.

Asceticism, the denial of bodily pleasure and the infliction of physical pain and discomfort, was a deep-rooted Christian practice, going back to biblical precedents and institutionalized in monasticism. A spiritual athlete like the anchorite Wulfric of Haselbury followed a regime that included an abstemious diet of oaten bread and porridge, frequent fasting and overnight vigils, the wearing of a hair shirt and a heavy mail coat, and baths in cold water; he was praised as 'a butcher of his own flesh'.[73] Devout behaviour of a less extreme kind still involved regular fasting. Special times of the year were set aside for fasts, including the Ember Days, groups of three days at the beginning of each of the four seasons, and Lent. Physical restraint won spiritual merit.

It was recognized that this tendency to equate harsh treatment of the body and religious devotion could lead to excess. The author of the *Anchoresses' Guide* warns the female recluse that she needs her confessor's permission for such austerities as 'wearing iron, hair or hedgehog skin, or beating herself

---

[70] P. Blois, *Confess.*, col. 1080.      [71] Eugenius III, ep. 48 (*PL* 180, col. 1066).
[72] *Twelfth-Century Homilies in MS Bodley* 343, ed. A. O. Belfour (EETS 137; 1909), p. 96.
[73] J. Ford, *V. Wulfric*, esp. 1. 3–5 (pp. 17–19).

with them, or with a scourge weighted with lead, or with holly or briars, or drawing blood . . . she should not sting herself with nettles, beat herself in front or cut herself . . .'[74] The world conjured up by this passage, of discomfort, abrasions, and self-mutilation inflicted in private in the pursuit of a spiritual goal, is not a psychotic aberration but a natural corollary of medieval Christian spirituality.

Prayer was a way of communicating with God and the saints, but also a kind of ascetic exercise. Perpetual prayer was part of the austere discipline that trained the mind and body. The full-time ascetics, the monks, nuns, anchorites, and hermits, were committed to a life of prayer and the larger monasteries, in particular, represented an enormous investment, of land, wealth, buildings, personnel, and time, in continual prayer. The common liturgical prayers and the Psalms went up from thousands of voices every day. Alongside the growth of institutions committed to this incessant communal prayer, there was a movement to make prayer more familiar to lay people. Prayer was recommended when getting up in the morning and going to bed at night: 'at those times we begin a new battle, as it were'.[75] The simpler prayers, especially the Lord's Prayer, were supposed to be taught by a parish priest to his flock. There is evidence of the practice of rote prayer by laity. William of Malmesbury refers to an early form of rosary that Lady Godiva had bequeathed to her foundation of Coventry. It was 'a circle of precious stones that she had strung on a thread, so that by touching each of them as she began each prayer she would not leave any out'.[76]

The third way of obtaining heavenly bliss was alms-giving. Charity was valued as much for the benefit it brought to the soul of the giver as for the alleviation of the earthly suffering of the poor or sick. Like prayer and self-denial, it was part of the programme of redemption. To give alms was to create 'a bridge to paradise'.[77] On Maundy Thursday, when monks washed the feet of poor men and gave them drink and money, the brethren who had died during the preceding year 'ought to have their poor', that is, the ceremony should be performed on behalf of the dead monks, so that they might still have the spiritual benefit that accrued from it.[78]

Whatever the professional theologians might say, the religion of the twelfth century was one in which salvation was interpreted to mean 'deserving heaven'. Eternal bliss could be attained and eternal pain avoided by confessing one's sins and following a penitential discipline of self-denial, ritual observance, and alms-giving. There was a clearly formulated list of the sins that one might commit, and indeed be expected to commit: pride, vanity, envy, anger, despair, greed, gluttony, lechery. There was also, however, a

---

[74] *Ancr. Wisse*, p. 214.     [75] Alex. Ashby, *De modo pred.*, p. 910.
[76] W. Malm., *GP* 175 (p. 311).     [77] Stenton, *First Century*, p. 261.     [78] Lanfr., *Const.*, p. 32.

clearly formulated list of ways to restore and redress the situation. Human beings were not expected to be perfect, but they could escape the full consequences of their imperfection.

## Christianity and the Bible

There is a sense in which English people of this period were familiar with the Bible and a sense in which they were not. The story of the nativity, crucifixion, and resurrection, and many of the Old Testament stories too, would be communicated in many different forms—pictures, carvings, drama, vernacular sermons. Paintings and sculptures in the churches could serve as 'the books of the laity'.[79] An everyday episode from the very early years of the thirteenth century shows at least two of these media in operation. During the performance of a Resurrection play in the churchyard in Beverley Minster, some people entered the church in order to look at Beverley's famous pictures.[80] Both the drama and the paintings would convey some of the Bible story. The names of Jesus and Mary, the image of Samson, the tale of paradise and the Fall—these would be generally well known. Yet the general standard of literacy meant that first-hand acquaintance with scripture was unusual and even the literate would not be accustomed to handling, let alone studying, a complete Bible.

Hence, although the Bible was full of stories, the fact that most lay people were illiterate meant that the easiest and most direct access they had to religious doctrine was through visual symbols. These tended to embody a fixed or timeless image for contemplation. The cross and the crucified Christ were amongst the most powerful of these icons. Lanfranc, when planning the choreography of Holy Week, specifically prescribed that laymen and clerks should be allowed into the monastic church to venerate the crucifix on Good Friday.[81] The image of the Virgin Mary was another focus of devotion that had become distant and distinct from its biblical and narrative roots (see below, p. 469).

Lists of the property of parish churches surviving from the early thirteenth century show that they might include a Psalter among their service books, but did not have complete Bibles. The great illustrated Bibles produced in this period suggest rather that complete Bibles were rare and precious than that they were commonly available texts. The Winchester Bible, which is 23 inches by 14½ inches, required the skins of 250 calves and is filled with illustrations and rich decoration that took over 20 years to execute

[79] William de Montibus, *Distinctiones theologicae*, quoted by Joseph Goering, *William de Montibus (c.1140–1213): The Schools and the Literature of Pastoral Care* (Toronto, 1992), p. 261 n. 2.
[80] J. Raine (ed.), *Historians of the Church of York* (3 vols., RS; 1879–94), vol. 1, pp. 327–47.
[81] Lanfr., *Const.*, p. 41.

(and even then were never completed), or the Le Puiset Bible, measuring over 18 inches by 12 inches, in four volumes, with a surviving original binding of elaborately tooled brown hide and silver inlaid clasps, were great treasures, not works of easy reference. The scriptural nature of Christianity could be expressed in the fetishization of books as numinous objects as well as in stress on the need to know the Word of God.

Biblical texts could themselves become charms. The opening words of St John's Gospel—'In the beginning was the Word'—were particularly favoured, perhaps because of a combination of their mystery, their prominent position in the gospel, and their seeming stress on the creative and fundamental power of language. Ailred of Rievaulx, one of the leading English Cistercian spiritual writers, carried 'a text of John's Gospel' around with him for many years.[82] Similarly Richard the Engineer, the bishop of Durham's architect, had a little silk bag in which he kept writings with 'the names of the Saviour and the beginnings of the gospels':

He believed that by this means it would not be difficult for God to bestow on him the gift of grace and the splendour of glory through the merit of his faith, so that from this solace he could have help against the storms of this wretched and tempestuous life and against the hostile powers of wickedness and perfidy on high.[83]

Scriptural texts were chanted by monks and canons and studied by theologians, but their wider dissemination was as verbal amulets: 'They are powerful medicine and chase away phantasms, especially the beginning of John's gospel.'[84]


## 3. SAINTS AND THEIR CULTS

Since the early centuries of Christianity, certain dead members of the Christian community had been acknowledged for their holiness and their special powers of intercession with the deity. These were the saints, whose tombs received veneration and whose memory was recalled on the anniversary of their death—or their birthday (*dies natalis*), as it was known. Originally the cult of the saints centred around the tombs of the martyrs, but, with the official acceptance of Christianity in the fourth century, sanctity began to be ascribed to those who had lived exemplary lives, even if they had not died for the faith. Over the following centuries the fragmentation of holy bodies and the removal of remains from one shrine to another had resulted in a dense saturation of the Christian world with holy bones. A list drawn up in the

---

[82] W. Dan., *V. Ailred* 36 (p. 44). It is unclear whether the whole text or simply the opening verses are meant.

[83] Reg., *Libellus* 47 (pp. 94–8); cf. 54 (pp. 111–12).     [84] Gerald, *Gemma* 1. 48 (p. 129).

twelfth century listing only those English shrines containing the whole body of a saint names 129.[85]

## Contemporary Saints

This catalogue of saints was augmented by new recruits, men and women who came to be recognized as saints and revered as such. Recognition as a saint can mean more than one thing. The modern Catholic definition, posthumous canonization by the pope, was not the only form of such recognition in the twelfth century and was indeed exceptional at that time. Only five English candidates received official papal canonization in the period covered by this book: Edward the Confessor in 1161, Thomas Becket in 1173, Gilbert of Sempringham in 1202, Wulfstan of Worcester in 1203, and Hugh of Lincoln in 1220, although William of York's case was far enough advanced for him to be canonized in 1226. It was only under popes Alexander III (1159–81) and Innocent III (1198–1216) that the papal claim to a monopoly of official canonization was established, and even after Innocent's pontificate the vast majority of Christians continued to treat as saints those whom they regarded as such, whatever papal views on the matter might be. Basically a saint was someone to whom cult was paid—and that involved invocation, veneration at the tomb, and special liturgical commemoration, such as celebration of a feast day.

Even with this wider definition of saint, it appears that there were barely twenty people who lived in England in the period 1075–1225 and were acknowledged as saints during that time, as Table 9 shows. For some of them, the evidence of cult is, in fact, very thin. Ailred of Rievaulx (d. 1167) was depicted, in the *Life* written by his monk Walter Daniel, as a great monastic leader with miraculous and prophetic powers, yet Walter's text survives only in a solitary manuscript and there is no solid evidence of a cult of Ailred until late in the Middle Ages. Similarly the *Life* of Robert de Béthune, bishop of Hereford (1131–48), written by William of Wycombe, describes miraculous cures at Robert's tomb in Hereford cathedral, but there are no other traces of a cult. In these cases the evidence for contemporary veneration as a saint rests basically on the literary activities of a single protagonist. Fully fledged cults with clear evidence of enduring pilgrimage, numerous miracles, and liturgical commemoration number less than ten.

The figures who were the subject of contemporary veneration reveal certain patterns. First, all the saints living and venerated in this period were men. (The evidence for the cult of Christina of Markyate is so fragile as to be best ignored.) This male coloration to English saints is indeed a striking feature for the whole medieval period, the only exception being the Anglo-Saxon

---

[85] *The Peterborough Chronicle of Hugh Candidus*, ed. William T. Mellows (London, 1949), p. 62.

TABLE 9. *Saints living and commemorated, 1075–1225*

| Name | Died | Feast | Canonized | Status |
|---|---|---|---|---|
| Ailred of Rievaulx | 1167 | 12 Jan. | | Cistercian abbot |
| Anselm | 1109 | 21 Apr. | 1720 | Benedictine abbot; archbishop |
| Bartholomew of Farne | 1193 | 24 June | | Benedictine monk; hermit |
| Christina of Markyate | c.1160 | 5 Dec. | | Hermit; prioress |
| Faricius of Abingdon | 1117 | 23 Feb. | | Benedictine abbot |
| Gilbert of Sempringham | 1189 | 4 Feb. | 1202 | Gilbertine abbot |
| Godric of Finchale | 1170 | 21 May | | Hermit |
| Henry of Coquet | 1120 | 16 Jan. | | Hermit |
| Hugh of Lincoln | 1200 | 17 Nov. | 1220 | Carthusian prior; bishop |
| Osmund of Salisbury | 1099 | 4 Dec. | 1457 | Bishop |
| Remigius of Lincoln | 1092 | 7 May | | Bishop |
| Robert de Béthune | 1148 | 16 Apr. | | Austin prior; bishop |
| Robert of Bury | 1181 | 10 June | | 'Martyr' |
| Robert of Knaresborough | 1218 | 24 Sept. | | Hermit |
| Robert of Newminster | 1159 | 7 June | | Cistercian abbot |
| Thomas Becket | 1170 | 29 Dec. | 1173 | Archbishop |
| William of Norwich | 1144 | 26 Mar. | | 'Martyr' |
| William of Rievaulx | 1145 | 2 Aug. | | Cistercian abbot |
| William of York | 1154 | 8 June | 1226 | Archbishop |
| Wulfric of Haselbury | 1154 | 20 Feb. | | Priest; hermit |
| Wulfstan of Worcester | 1095 | 19 Jan. | 1203 | Benedictine prior; bishop |

abbess saints, mainly of the seventh and eighth centuries. Of course, English devotees could find many female saints, including the greatest focus of veneration after God himself, the Virgin Mary, but there was no cult of contemporary native holy women, as existed in other countries, such as Italy. This male dominance is linked to the fact that the majority of contemporary English saints were either bishops or heads of male religious houses or both. The pattern of sanctity thus reinforced the claims of the official church hierarchy rather than modified it.

After prelates, the next largest category among the contemporary saints is formed by the hermits. There were five of these (Bartholomew of Farne, Godric of Finchale, Henry of Coquet, Robert of Knaresborough, and Wulfric of Haselbury) and they constitute a remarkably uniform group: four were from a small section of the north of England (Northumberland, Durham, and the West Riding), while all five of them were of native English or Anglo-Scandinavian descent. In this they contrast with the prelate-saints, the large majority of whom were either foreign-born or, if born in England, of foreign descent. A final small group of saints is formed by William of Norwich and Robert of Bury, two boys supposedly martyred by the Jews. The legend of such boy martyrs has its origins in England in this period (see above, pp. 356–7).

Not all of these figures were recognized as particularly holy during their lifetimes. In some cases, there seems to have been many years between the death of the individual and the cry that he was a saint. The most striking example is that of Osmund, bishop of Salisbury, who died in 1099 but whose canonization proceedings began only in 1228. Miracles reported before a panel of investigators in that year included some dating back seventy years or so.[86] In a case such as this, there can be little doubt that a group of clerics decided at some point that they wished to further the claims of their group by championing the body enshrined in their church. The actual activities and personality of the living figure were relatively unimportant. In other cases, however, good contemporary evidence survives to show certain prelates and hermits being regarded as holy men during their lifetimes and being reverenced as such immediately after their deaths. In these cases, we can observe contemporary conceptions of the holy man, be it the powerful prelate or the prophetic and unpredicatable hermit.

## Shrines and Relics

The activities of the saint did not end with his or her death, indeed dead saints were far more common and often more helpful than living ones. Located in their tombs or in specially constructed shrines, the dead bodies, or parts of bodies, of the saints offered supernatural power for those who came to seek their help. The shrine of a famous saint, like Etheldreda of Ely, towered above the east end of the church in a glittering glory:

The virgin body of St Etheldreda is enclosed in a marble vessel within her shrine. . . . The part of the shrine facing the altar is of silver, with raised images of gold . . . the left hand side of the shrine consists of a wall of silver, with sixteen raised gilded images, ninety-four great crystals and 149 smaller stones of crystal and glass. The

---

[86] *Can. Osmund.*

eastern part of the shrine is of silver with gilded raised images. There are two crystal lions with thirty-two crystals and three stones of glass and eight enamels and seven small ornaments . . . in the southern part are sixteen ungilded images of silver and a border of gilded silver . . .[87]

This dazzling construction, permanently lit by the light of gleaming candles, must have both attracted and awed those seeking the shrine. In this it conveyed an accurate impression of the nature of holy relics: their power was sought out but they could also be dangerous. Tolinus, sacrist of Bury St Edmunds, although a good and pious man, suffered because he touched the body of St Edmund incautiously. Soon after he did so, he died in an accident. The three men who had been present when he inspected the saint's body also died within the year. Tolinus appeared to his friends in dreams, explaining that he was being punished in the afterlife for having presumptuously handled the saint's relics.[88]

People went to the shrines of the saints for many reasons: to pray, to seek miraculous healing, to gain spiritual merit, to thank the saint for a benefit, to have a short holiday away from prying neighbours. A Newcastle merchant went regularly to the shrine of St Oswin at Tynemouth before embarking on a voyage, offering a candle there and 'commending himself and his goods to the protection of the saint'.[89] A vow to visit a shrine might be provoked by some dramatic cure or deliverance. Henry I promised to undertake a pilgrimage to Bury St Edmunds (as well as a seven-year moratorium on levying geld) during a storm at sea and 'as soon as he had made his vow, there was a great calm.'[90]

Relations between followers and saints were modelled on the bond between lord and dependant. Saints were addressed in a language of lordship partly inherited from the ancient world, partly adapted from that of contemporary earthly lordship and strongly coloured by legal terminology. The saint was patron, protector, defender, advocate; he or she offered patronage, protection, defence, advocacy. The term *patrocinium*—what a patron offers—recurs in all the Latin texts dealing with the saints, and suggests the advocacy and aid provided by a superior who can represent an inferior. The saints had power that could be exerted on behalf of others, if those others knew how to tap it. As the Canterbury monk Eadmer put it, 'God has provided for us patrons, through whom we may obtain what we would not be able to obtain through ourselves alone.'[91]

---

[87] *Lib. Eliensis* 3. 50 (p. 289).
[88] *Mir. sancti Edmundi* 5 (attributed to abbot Samson), *Mem. Edm.* 1, pp. 168–73.
[89] *V. Oswini* 29, ed. James Raine, in *Miscellanea Biographica* (Surtess Soc. 8; 1838), pp. 1–59, at p. 42.
[90] J. Worcs., p. 34.
[91] Eadmer, *Sententia de memoria sanctorum quos veneraris*, ed. A. Wilmart, *Revue des sciences religieuses*, 15 (1935), p. 191.

The specifically legal aspect of *patrocinium* sometimes comes out clearly, for instance in the following story about St Cuthbert. Early in the reign of Henry II the monks of the Cistercian monastery of Furness in Cumbria were in dispute with a local magnate, who had taken land they claimed as their own and who seemed to enjoy the king's favour. Neither the hearing before the royal judges nor the appeal to Rome were going well. At length the abbot turned to his monks with the following advice: 'Since human power must give way to divine commands, let us appeal to the patronage of a protector whose power no violent plundering predator can withstand; let us entrust the prosecution of our suit to the blessed confessor Cuthbert.' The monks then built an altar to Cuthbert and found that the next time they went to the royal court, everyone was in their favour.[92]

Representation in the courtroom was only one small part of saintly patronage. The situations in which saints could be invoked were manifold. They could offer their support during the fearful and public task of mustering an army for battle, as in 1138, when the Scots invaded the north of England and the archbishop of York, Thurstan, summoned all able-bodied men to resist the invaders. They were to march out 'from every parish, with their priests before them bearing the cross and banners and relics of the saints'.[93] Thurstan thus not only envisaged mobilization by parish but also saw the holy remains of the saints playing somewhat the part of regimental colours.

In face of natural dangers and disasters the precarious communities of the period could often only fall back on saintly aid. When fire caught hold in the thatch and timber towns, a common response was to bring out saints' relics. At Durham the monks would rush St Cuthbert's relics out of the cathedral to the threatened area. 'We have frequently seen the greedy balls of fire stay their step as the relics arrived,' wrote one Durham monk, 'giving way as they approached and no longer touching the places, roofs and dwellings that they hallowed by their presence.' During one particularly violent fire, the monk bearing St Cuthbert's standard and another carrying a pyx with the host entered the flames unharmed.[94]

Weather was as unpredictable as fire and here too the saints played their part, calming storms, bringing rain or fending it off. The account of the miracles of St Modwenna of Burton upon Trent, a text written in the 1120s or 1130s, tells of a foreman engaged in organizing work for the abbey church who when 'he realized from the movement of the air that impending rain might hinder the task, called out secretly within his heart many times to the name of the Lord and the name of Modwenna and immediately through God's grace procured weather good for work and clear skies.'

[92] Reg., *Libellus* 55 (pp. 112–14).
[93] Ailr. Riev., *Rel. de Standardo*, p. 182.    [94] Reg., *Libellus* 39 (pp. 82–3).

Saintly patronage offered help not only in the face of the elements, but also against the threat of human enemies. The Miracles of St Modwenna contain a characteristic sample of vindictive miracles directed primarily at local aristocrats and officials who had infringed the abbey's property rights—seigneurial foresters who impound Burton's animals, local lords who threaten to poach Burton's peasantry, royal officials who bring suits against tenants of the abbey. Most of the victims of Modwenna's anger suffered the extreme penalty, death, though a few were merely blinded or driven mad by the saint.

The commonest miraculous activity of the saints, however, was healing. Of the miracles recorded at saints' shrines in England in this period, 90 per cent are cures. An absolutely typical example is the following, a cure effected at the shrine of St Frideswide in Oxford in 1180, the year the relics of that virgin saint were ceremonially translated (i.e. moved):

There was in the same city [i.e. Oxford] a certain young girl called Adelitia, living outside the walls of the city, who, for some time before the translation of the blessed virgin [i.e. Frideswide], had been afflicted with the following misfortune: her eyelids were so weighed down with swellings that she could not open her eyes on account of the weight of her lids and was unable to see anything. The girl's mother, full of maternal sympathy, consulted doctors about her daughter's health and spent on them the little that she had, but without success. The illness continued to grow worse and her condition deteriorated from day to day. At length the mother sought the refuge of divine mercy and led her daughter every day to the church of the blessed virgin, praying devoutly for her cure . . .

On Maundy Thursday [17 April 1180], before mass was celebrated, as the young girl lay prostrate in prayer on the tomb of the blessed virgin, suddenly the weight on her eyelids was rubbed away, as if a hand had scraped it off, the swelling gradually subsided and she recovered perfect sight. A bloody discharge flowed from her eyes for a long time. Soon afterwards, she was cured by the goodness of God's hand, so that not a trace of her former illness remained.[95]

This was only one of St Frideswide's numerous cures. A poor woman from Exeter coming to her shrine was cured from dropsy; a 4-year-old boy from Lincoln, who suffered from curvature of the spine and legs of unequal length, made his painful way to Oxford on crutches and there 'he received the power of walking properly and standing straight'; a woman named Richildis carried her crippled infant daughter on her shoulders from Winchester to receive 'from the divine hand the straightness that nature had denied'.[96] In total, there are records of about a hundred cures at Frideswide's shrine, and hers was only one of dozens that offered supernatural healing in this period.

---

[95] Philip, *Mir. Fridesw.* 9 (pp. 569–70).    [96] Ibid. 22–4 (pp. 572–3).

The burial place of a saint was indeed a *medicabile sepulcrum*—'a healing tomb'.[97]

The saints had, of course, demands to make in return for their help. The first gift they demanded was reverence. Reverence involved addressing the saint, either in the elaborate specialized liturgy of monk and cleric or in the simpler invocations of the individual devotee. Intense speech with invisible beings is, of course, common religious behaviour but medieval Christianity was especially centred on it. Hence the name of the saint was vital. Indeed, one of the things that defined a saint was the special treatment given to his or her name—invoked, written down in ecclesiastical calendars, the object of dedicated buildings, or other items. And as the altar or the eucharistic host might provide a physical focus for speech with the invisible deity, so relics of the saints or their images gave the possibility of spatial direction for utterances addressed to the invisible patrons.

The reverence that living human followers gave to the saints was mirrored in the worship the saints in heaven paid to God. The monk Eadmer pictured two groups engaged in intercessory prayer: the faithful before the relics of the saints and the saints before God: 'They [the faithful on earth] prostrate their entire bodies before their relics, go down on the ground on bended knees, make their entreaties with downcast faces—and do the saints stand before God unmoving, refusing to hear, caring nothing for them—who would say that?'[98] The saints could thus be moved to make reverent entreaty to God by receiving it from human followers. The more reverent the earthly attention, the swifter the intercession. The Gilbertine canon who composed *The Book of St Gilbert* knew this about the saints: 'if we ever need their help, the more devoted we have been as their worshippers, the quicker they will be to bring us aid.'[99] 'Be mindful', the saint could be entreated, 'of those who have been mindful of you.'[100]

Saints also had more concrete demands than the singing of their praises. Candles and money were the most common. In theory voluntary, the free-will offerings made to the saints in fact resembled those 'gifts' or *dona* that the kings of England demanded. The exact nature of the freedom involved is nicely illustrated by the case of a cleric who sought help for his illness from St Edmund at Bury but was told by a lady who appeared to him in a vision to go instead to the shrine of St Modwenna at Burton. He did so, 'bringing with him a voluntary offering *as he had been commanded*'.

Saints could make quite explicit demands of their followers. St William of Norwich, for example, the boy supposedly martyred by Jews in 1144, drove

[97] T. Monm., *V. William* 3. 13 (p. 146).
[98] Eadmer, *Sententia de memoria sanctorum quos veneraris*, ed. A. Wilmart, *Revue des sciences religieuses*, 15 (1935), p. 190.
[99] *Bk. Gilbert*, p. 314.    [100] Orderic 7. 13 (4, p. 74).

hard bargains. When the Norwich monk Richard of Lynn came to his tomb suffering from a fever, William appeared to him in a vision. 'Why have you come, Richard,' he asked, 'and what do you want?' 'Lord,' replied the monk, 'I am sick and desire to be healed.' 'You've brought nothing, you've offered nothing, brother,' complained the saint. 'But if I do cure you, what will you give in return?' Brother Richard tactfully asked what the saint would like. 'I love candles,' responded St William, 'and so I want the candles that you have.' At this the sick monk claimed to have no candles. 'Yes you do, brother,' contradicted the saint, 'and some of them are very big and beautiful . . . I want to have them all, and especially those beautiful ones you are intending to give to your sister-in-law.'

Fear of his sister-in-law apparently loomed larger in the monk's mind than fear of the saint, for he expressed unwillingness to give those particular candles. ' "So," ' said St William, 'moved to anger, "you love her more than me? . . . Why have you come to me for a cure when you do not love me in your heart? . . . I suggest you bring those candles here tomorrow for, if you refuse, know without a doubt that I shall have them whether you will or no." ' Despite the threats, brother Richard prevaricated. Soon thereafter the saint again appeared to him in a vision, struck him on the head and, within twenty-four hours, he was dead. His sister-in-law arrived in Norwich as the death bell knelled, but the candles had already been taken and placed on the saint's tomb.[101]

Not all saints killed suppliants in order to get their candles, but all felt they had legitimate demands to make of their followers. Monetary payments were also important, either in the form of a single offering, often of a penny bent in two as an indication of its votive nature, or as an annual payment. Shrines were often covered with coins and it was indeed a common trick for thieves to approach a shrine as if to kiss it and to sneak a penny off in their mouths. In the year 1198 the shrine of St Cuthbert at Durham had on it 107 bezants (the imported gold coins worth two shillings sterling) and 45 rings—the coins alone represent the contemporary value of more than fifty oxen.[102]

Along with coins, shrines would be crowded with ex-votos—images, models, and objects associated with the miraculous cure. At the shrine of St Erkenwald in St Paul's, London, these included a wax hand, given by a woman cured of a shrivelled hand, and a pair of wax eyes, recalling the recovery of a young man's sight.[103] Chains from prisoners who had been miraculously freed would be hung in the church of the appropriate saint, 'for people to see as a memorial of the miracle'.[104] The crowded altars and shrines, with

[101] T. Monm., *V. William* 3. 12 (pp. 136–45).
[102] David Rollason *et al.* (eds.), *Anglo-Norman Durham 1093–1193* (Woodbridge, 1994), p. 15 n. 63.
[103] *Mir. Erkenwald* 5, 7 (pp. 132, 138).        [104] e.g. Orderic 6. 10 (3, p. 358).

their broken chains, wax models, candles, and coins, were a permanent indication of the supernatural power dispensed by the saint's bones.

## The Marian Cult

The Virgin Mary had a special place in the religious affections of medieval Christians. She was the mother of God, ever virgin, queen of heaven, with a central role in salvation: 'Through Adam human beings lost all the good for which they were created, through Mary human nature recovered all that good and more.'[105] St Mary's was by far the most common dedication of parish churches. All Cistercian abbeys were dedicated to her. Perhaps because she left no bodily remains on earth, images of Mary were especially important. In the church of Ely in the eleventh century there was an altar to Mary and on it a life-sized image of the saint, sitting on a throne and holding the Christ child on her lap, all decorated with silver, gold, and jewels.[106] This fell victim to William the Conqueror's predations, but similar images were common. The church of St Mary at Monks Kirby in Warwickshire had 'an image of the blessed virgin, carved in wood and finely decorated with gold and silver', with the Christ child also on his mother's lap.[107] There was even a special ritual for blessing the image of the Virgin Mary, which was expected to keep off thunder and lightening, fire, flood, war, and disease and bring peace and abundance.[108]

The destruction of images at the Reformation and afterwards means that few medieval sculptures of Mary survive, but their impact can be imagined from manuscript paintings like that in a twelfth-century copy of St Augustine's *Commentary on the Psalms* from Eynsham Abbey (Plate 13). Eynsham had a special cult of the Virgin Mary and the image in the book is suitably magnificent. Virtually filling a large page 18 inches high by 12 inches wide, the figure of Mary sits, crowned and enthroned, with a sceptre in her right hand and the Christ Child cradled in her left. She looks out directly at the observer with an unsmiling, exalted gaze, brought dramatically into the foreground by twin mandorlas of green and red behind her. Queen of heaven she certainly appears.

The earliest anthologies of miracles attributed to the Virgin Mary were composed in England in the early twelfth century. Three authors, Anselm, abbot of Bury, nephew of his namesake the famous archbishop, Dominic, prior of Evesham, and the monastic chronicler William of Malmesbury produced collections that proved extremely popular. They circulated widely, were continually augmented, and later translated into Old French. Their message was simple and reassuring. They told how Mary's intercession could

---

[105] Eadmer, *Tractatus*, p. 18 (*PL* 159, col. 307).   [106] *Lib. Eliensis*, pp. 132, 194–5.
[107] Gerald, *Gemma* 1. 33 (p. 105).   [108] *Magd. Pont.*, pp. 144–5.

help in even the most desperate cases. Mary was also distinguished by the number of days in the year especially dedicated to her. Feasts of the Purification, Annunciation, Assumption, and Nativity had long been celebrated in England. These marked important moments in her life. The Purification (2 February) was her 'churching', when she resumed attendance at the Temple after childbirth and presented her son there. In English it was termed Candlemas and was marked by a procession with lighted candles. The Annunciation, celebrating the announcement to Mary by the angel Gabriel that she was to be the mother of Christ, fell on 25 March, 'Lady Day'. In some reckonings this was the first day of the new year, adding another layer of significance to the Marian feast. The Assumption (15 August) commemorated the day when Mary was taken bodily into heaven, leaving no physical remains for worshippers, except such fragments as hair, milk, or clothing. The Nativity of Mary (8 September) was also an important liturgical feast.

A new celebration, the Feast of the Conception, marking Mary's conception, had been introduced in a few churches in eleventh-century England. For some reason it faded away about the 1050s but was revived early in the following century by such champions of Mary as Osbert of Clare, prior of Westminster, and Anselm, abbot of Bury. Abbot Anselm gave the monks of Bury lands and revenues to support this and other Marian celebrations: not only the Feast of the Conception, but also an otherwise extremely rare celebration, the Expectation of the Virgin Mary, on 18 December, as well as a daily mass of the Virgin Mary for the health of king Henry I 'and the prosperity of his realm'.[109] Both the doctrine of the Immaculate Conception—the idea that Mary had been born free from original sin—and the feast of the Conception itself were controversial. Eadmer, St Anselm's chaplain and biographer, wrote a treatise defending the doctrine, dealing with such tricky problems as, 'if the Virgin Mary had died before Jesus was born, would she still have been free of original sin?'[110] In 1129 those who believed that the feast was an absurd innovation won the backing of two great curial bishops, Roger of Salisbury and Bernard of St David's, who tried to ban the celebration. The king himself, however, seems to have leaned in the opposite direction. According to Osbert of Clare, abbot Hugh of Reading, head of king Henry's own most important religious foundation, celebrated this feast 'at the request of king Henry'. A council decided in favour of the new Marian ceremony.[111]

The polemic continued throughout the century. St Bernard, who, despite his devotion to Mary, did not accept the doctrine of the Immaculate Conception, was attacked for this in a treatise by an English monk, Nicholas of St Albans. A counter-attack was then launched on Nicholas by the Cistercian

---

[109] *Bury Docs.*, no. 112, pp. 112–13.     [110] Eadmer, *Tractatus*, p. 23 (*PL* 159, col. 309).
[111] Osbert, *Letters*, no. 7, pp. 65–8; cf. J. Worcs., p. 29 n. 5; *Councils and Synods* 1/ii, p. 751.

writer, Walter Daniel, a monk of Rievaulx.[112] The tide was, however, in favour of the protagonists of the feast. By 1150 it was observed in many of the great Benedictine abbeys.[113] An incident from the end of the century shows both the continued doubts that many had and the growing body of opinion in favour of the feast. The Oxford theologian Alexander Nequam was so sure that it was wrong to celebrate the feast, that he always planned to lecture on that day like any other. The curious circumstance that every year he fell ill and could not teach on that day finally convinced him that the Conception should be solemnly celebrated.[114] The views of Eadmer, Osbert, and abbot Anselm were winning the battle. England was in the vanguard of the new practice. Writing about 1178, the French abbot Peter of Celle thought that English sponsorship of the Feast of the Immaculate Conception could only be explained by the moist English climate, which made the English prone to dreams and visions.[115] There was perhaps a touch of romanticism in this championing of the idea of Mary's immaculate conception by these adult, male prelates.

In addition to her importance in the annual cycle of the liturgy, Mary had a weekly commemoration. Saturday was her special day, with a votive mass and Office. Going even further than this weekly commemoration, abbot Benedict of Tewkesbury (1124–37) and prior Warin of Worcester (d. about 1141) both ensured that the Hours of the Virgin Mary or her Mass were celebrated daily in their churches and she, in return, revealed to Warin in a vision that he and Benedict enjoyed the special honour of being 'Saint Mary's chaplains'.[116] There are signs that Marian devotion continued to increase in the early thirteenth century. It was abbot William of St Albans (1214–35) who introduced into the abbey the custom of singing the Mass of the Virgin Mary daily.[117] The Statutes of the diocese of Salisbury issued about 1218 instructed priests to teach their parishioners not only the Lord's Prayer and Creed but also the *Ave Maria*, the angel's salutation to Mary.[118] Eadmer's effusive words to the Virgin obviously expressed the views of many: 'you are, after God, our highest and most particular consolation; you are our happy and blessed glorification; you lead us and carry us to the kingdom of heaven.'[119]

## Control of Cult

There was throughout this period an uneasiness on the part of the official religious authorities about the boundaries of the holy. It was very difficult to

---

[112] Nicholas of St Albans, *De celebranda conceptione beatae Mariae*, ed. C. H. Talbot, *Revue Bénédictine*, 64 (1954), pp. 92–117; W. Dan., *V. Ailred*, pp. xviii–xix.

[113] Edmund Bishop, *Liturgica historica* (Oxford, 1918), p. 247.

[114] Hunt, *Nequam*, p. 8 and n. 36.   [115] Peter of Celle, ep. 171 (*PL* 202, col. 614).

[116] J. Worcs., pp. 41–2.   [117] *Gesta S. Alb.* 1, pp. 284–5.

[118] *Councils and Synods* 2/i, p. 61.   [119] Eadmer, *Tractatus*, p. 43 (*PL* 159, col. 315).

prevent people treating as sacred some persons, places, or times that had not
been sanctioned by the Church. The Council of Westminster of 1102 ruled,
'Let no one, through unheard-of boldness, treat as holy any bodies of the
dead, or springs, or other things (as we have known has happened), without
permission of the bishop.'[120] As is clear from this ruling, it was not only unau-
thorized saints' cults that were a cause for concern. The widespread veneration of holy wells was common and not all could be Christianized by
association with some saint. St Hugh of Lincoln, who died in 1200, had 'a bitter struggle' to stop the veneration of springs at Berkhamstead in Hertfordshire, High Wycombe in Buckinghamshire, and other places in his diocese.[121]

   Cults sprang up spontaneously and not all won the approval of ecclesiastical authorities. Violent death seems to have been particularly likely to stimu-
late a cult, even if other signs of saintliness were absent. In 1190 one of the
men who had plundered the Jews in the heated atmosphere of the Third Crusade was killed by an accomplice; his body was thrown outside the walls of
Northampton, where the murder had occurred. Within a short while
rumours of miracles spread, pilgrims began to congregate and the local
clergy were won over by the profits to be made. 'The more perceptive' supposedly laughed at the cult but it needed the forceful intervention of the local
bishop to suppress 'the superstitious veneration of the dead man'.[122] A few
years later another victim of violent death was also the focus of an incipient
cult. This was the London demagogue William fitz Osbern ('Longbeard'),
executed in 1196 (above, pp. 344–5). Soon after the execution miracles were
attributed to him as a martyr. A priest related to him furthered his cult. The
gallows where he was hanged and the soil below it were treated as holy.
Hubert Walter had to send soldiers to break up the crowds and guard the
spot.[123] It is clear that the leaders of the church had to undertake vigorous
action if they wished to police the growth of cults.


## 4. OVERSEAS PILGRIMAGE

In addition to the scores of saintly shrines dotted about England, there were
more distant goals of pilgrimage. Several important Christian holy places
were located on the edges of the Christian world or on remote rocky headlands where sea and land formed a foamy perimeter. A journey to one of
these sites would win extra merit through its difficulty and danger. The religious worth of a pilgrimage could indeed be measured by a careful calculation of its arduousness: pope Calixtus II declared that, for English pilgrims,

---

[120] *Councils and Synods* 1/ii, p. 678.        [121] Ad. Eyns., *V. Hugh* 5. 17 (2, p. 201).
[122] W. Newb. 4. 8 (1, pp. 310–12); cf. Ad. Eyns., *V. Hugh* 5. 17 (2, p. 201).
[123] W. Newb. 5. 21 (2, pp. 471–3).

two visits to St David's in Wales were the spiritual equivalent of one trip to Rome.[124]

Of all overseas pilgrim goals in this period, there were three that stood out: Jerusalem, Rome, and Santiago. The first was the site of Jesus' life and death and the supposed scene of his resurrection; the Church of the Holy Sepulchre could be viewed as the very birthplace of Christianity. Rome housed the tombs of the great founding figures of the Church, Peter and Paul, as well as those of thousands of other martyrs. It was the seat of the papacy and also rich in imperial traditions. Santiago, the latecomer to the ranks of major pilgrimage sites, claimed the bones of the apostle James and, by the later eleventh century, had become one of the most important shrines in western Europe, with a pilgrim trail leading across northern Spain and France and then on into the rest of the continent. The first recorded pilgrims from England occur about 1100.[125]

People of all social levels were attracted to long-distance pilgrimage. In his early life Godric of Finchale visited both Jerusalem and Compostela, cannily combining the roles of 'merchant and pilgrim'.[126] Waleran de Meulan, earl of Worcester, made a pilgrimage to Compostela in the 1140s, issuing a charter in Normandy 'on my way to St James'.[127] A few years after this great magnate had made his journey, Botilda, the wife of the cook at Norwich priory, travelled with a party of pilgrims to St Gilles, Arles, and Santiago.[128] Bishops as well as cooks' wives could be found at the great Spanish shrine. Gilbert Glanvill, bishop of Rochester (1185–1214),[129] went to Santiago and his contemporary and colleague Philip, bishop of Durham, made a pilgrimage there in 1201. Bishop Philip crossed from Dover to Wissant in early February, and by Easter (25 March) had travelled 360 miles south, reaching St Jean d'Angély where the head of John the Baptist was on display. He completed the whole trip within the calendar year, but must have got into financial difficulties at some point, since he had to borrow 200 marks (£133. 6s. 8d.) during the return leg. His creditor was the king himself, then at Chinon in Anjou, and the repayment of his debt is recorded in the royal accounts for Michaelmas 1201.[130]

A pilgrimage to one of these distant shrines was an extraordinary and significant event in an individual's life. When Ranulf, earl of Chester, granted the fief of Wheatley (Notts.) to his half-brother, William, earl of Lincoln, he

---

[124] W. Malm., *GR* 5. 435 (2, pp. 507–8); OMT edn., pp. 778–80.
[125] Derek W. Lomax, 'The First English Pilgrims to Santiago de Compostela', in Henry Mayr-Harting and R. I. Moore (eds.), *Studies in Medieval History Presented to R. H. C. Davis* (London, 1985), pp. 165–75.
[126] Reg., *V. Godric* 5 (p. 31).
[127] *Rec. actes Hen. II, Introduction*, p. 466 n. 6; cf. HMC, *Fifth Report* (London, 1876), appendix, p. 301.
[128] T. Monm., *V. William* 4. 10 (p. 178).     [129] *Canterbury Cases*, no. A. 15, p. 46.
[130] R. Howd. 4, pp. 157, 161, 174; PR 3 John, p. 246.

carefully dated the transaction 'on the day after the feast of the Holy Cross that is celebrated in September, in the year that William, earl of Lincoln, returned from the journey to St James the apostle'. One consequence of this dating is that modern scholars can be certain of the day on which this grant was made, namely 15 September, the day after the feast of the Exaltation of the Holy Cross, but are uncertain of the year (1144 has been suggested). For the participants the highly charged and personally memorable pilgrimage was a more significant dating tool than the abstract year of grace.[131]

Pilgrims faced the same difficulties that any long-distance traveller of this period encountered. The departure of a family member or property-holder entailed a throng of potential problems. In 1200 Matilda of Wolseley (Staffs.) had to go to court to obtain her dower when her husband died en route to Compostella.[132] Such situations explain why a church council in that very same year ruled that a spouse needed to get the consent of his or her partner before going on a distant pilgrimage.[133] Money problems, like those of bishop Philip of Durham mentioned above, must also have been common. Accommodation was necessary. English pilgrims arriving in Rome in the Norman period could find lodgings at the 'English School' (*Scola Anglorum*), 'the great hospice where the English dwell'.[134] This was between the Tiber and St Peter's, by the church of Santa Maria 'of the Saxons'. During the second half of the twelfth century, however, this institution fell into financial difficulties. About 1163 Peter, cardinal deacon of San Eustachio, wrote to archbishop Thomas Becket asking for help in a fund-raising campaign for 'the church of Santa Maria of the Saxons, which receives the English who come on pilgrimage to the threshold of the apostles'.[135] These efforts do not seem to have been successful. Early in his pontificate Innocent III took over the site and constructed the Hospital of the Holy Spirit on it. The association of the place with the English was not at once forgotten, and king John was gratefully remembered by the Hospital for his donations, but it seems that its function as a hostel specifically for English pilgrims ceased about 1200.[136]

## Saewulf in Jerusalem

One English pilgrim to the Holy Land who left an account of his travels, and the difficulties he encountered along the way, was Saewulf, who visited

---

[131] *Chester Charters*, no. 70, pp. 82–4; the identification of Wheatley is tentative.
[132] *CRR* 1, p. 151.     [133] *Councils and Synods* 1/ii, p. 1068.
[134] Geoffrey of Burton, *V. sanctae Modwennae* 34 (BL Add. 57533, fo. 102).
[135] *Becket Mats.* 5, pp. 64–5 (Becket Letters 39).
[136] Innocent III, ep. 7. 95, ed. Othmar Hageneder *et al.*, *Die Register Innocenz' III.* 7 (Vienna, 1997), pp. 151–5; Gerald, *Inv.* 5. 12 (p. 192); *Rot. chart.*, p. 123; C. R. Cheney, *Pope Innocent III and England* (Stuttgart, 1976), pp. 237–8.

Jerusalem 'in order to pray at the Lord's tomb' in 1102, at a time when the crusaders were still in the early stages of establishing their control of Palestine and Syria.[137] He sailed from Apulia on 13 July, going via Corfu and Cephalonia to the Gulf of Corinth. Then he went on foot to Negroponte (Euboea), where he took another ship, which carried him via the Greek islands of the Aegean and Cyprus to Jaffa. He arrived there on 12 October, the trip from Italy to Palestine having taken exactly thirteen weeks. Saewulf now spent over seven months in the Holy Land, visiting as many biblical sites as he was able. He gives an elaborate description of Jerusalem and its holy places—the church of the Holy Sepulchre, the Temple of the Lord, the Mount of Olives, the room where the Last Supper took place. Every spot was rich with historical and religious meaning:

Afterwards one goes up to the mount of Calvary, where the patriarch Abraham, at God's command, made an altar and prepared to sacrifice his son to him. Afterwards, in that same place, the Son of God, whom he prefigured, was sacrificed as a victim to God the Father for the redemption of the world. . . . Below is the place called Golgotha, where Adam is said to have been resurrected from the dead by the stream of the Lord's blood flowing over him.

Saewulf also visited Bethlehem, Jericho, and the Jordan and the holy sites in Galilee before he boarded ship again at Jaffa on 17 May 1103. He was not, however, returning to England by the same route he had come, for he intended to visit Constantinople 'in order to pray there'. He describes his travels via Cyprus, Rhodes, and Smyrna, then, passing near the remains of 'the most ancient and famous city of Troy', into the Sea of Marmara about Michaelmas (29 September 1103). Here, at the city of Heraclea (modern Eregli), 'whence, according to the Greeks, Helen was abducted by Paris', his account unfortunately breaks off.

Even the part of Saewulf's itinerary that we know about, from Apulia to Heraclea, took him over fourteen months, so his entire round trip (presuming that he did reach home) was probably at least two years in duration. The dangers that he faced come vividly to life in his account. On the very first day out at sea, the ship he was travelling on was damaged and had to turn back for repairs. After he disembarked at Jaffa, a storm blew up, swamping the ship he had just left and many others—'we saw innumerable corpses of drowned men and women lying miserably on the shore . . . of the thirty big ships, all of them laden with pilgrims and merchandise, scarcely seven remained unharmed.' On the hard and rocky climb from Jaffa to Jerusalem, Saewulf saw by the side of the road the corpses of stragglers who had fallen victim to brigands; in the background bands of Muslims appeared and disappeared in the hills. When

---

[137] Saewulf, *Relatio de peregrinatione*, ed. R. B. C. Huygens, *Peregrinationes tres* (CCCM 139; 1994), pp. 59–77.

finally back on ship again, sailing along the Palestinian coast north of Jaffa, Saewulf experienced a threatening encounter with Muslim ships from Tyre and Sidon. The ship's company and the passengers on the Christian ship 'snatched up their weapons and defended the castle of our ship with armed men'. Eventually the Muslim vessel moved off, but other Christian ships were not so lucky and were seized and plundered. The length and the dangers of the Jerusalem pilgrimage are very clear in Saewulf's account, as also, implicitly, is the strength of his desire to make the journey.

## 5. DISSENT

### Anti-clericalism

The clerical order consisted of a small group of privileged men who avoided manual work if they could, specialized in moralizing, and were supposed to maintain higher standards than the bulk of the population. It is natural that they were hated as much as they were admired. One London labourer, reproved by a canon of St Paul's for working on a holy day, supposedly replied:

Clerics have so much leisure that they can leave their own business to interfere in that of others. You are indeed free to celebrate every day as a holiday, growing slack in idleness and eating other people's food. Since no necessity forces you to work, you can happily chant all day and all night. Your life is to be reckoned more a game than a real occupation . . . you clerics are noisy drones, yet you look down on our life . . . keep your feast days and your chanting and leave the work of strong men to us . . .[138]

The contempt for clerical parasitism is biting—clerical activity is useless and hollow, not the work of real men.

A different aspect of anti-clerical feeling comes out in a comment supposedly made by king Henry II at his hunting-lodge at Clarendon, after his most voluble and self-righteous clerk, Gerald of Wales, had urged him to go on crusade. 'These clerks,' said the king, 'can summon us boldly to arms and dangers since they themselves will not suffer a blow in battle nor will they undertake any burdens they can avoid.'[139] The militant clergy of the crusading epoch had certainly created the possibility of such a lay response: on the one hand, they preached to the military aristocracy the spiritual value of properly directed armed violence, on the other, they insisted that clerics should not bear arms or shed blood. They sought to direct bloodshed but not participate in it. Occasional impatient dismissiveness, like that reported of king Henry, is entirely understandable.

---

[138] *Mir. Erkenwald* 2 (p. 112).     [139] Gerald, *Prin.* 2. 26 (p. 207).

It was not only exasperated labourers or angry kings who uttered contemptuous language of this type. Ecclesiastics themselves did not form a united front. Antagonism between clerks and monks was often deep and fierce, so that clerks could express a hostility to monks that rivalled that of lay people. Hugh de Nonant, bishop of Coventry (1185–98), who expelled the monks from Coventry and replaced them with secular clerics, supposedly said, 'I call my clerks gods and the monks demons.'[140] Writers like Walter Map and Gerald of Wales, both secular clerics, were unrestrained in their comments on the vices of the monks of their day. The black monks had a reputation for gluttony, the Cistercians for avarice. Gerald tells the story of Ranulf de Glanville, chief justiciar under Henry II, pondering which monastic order he should patronize; 'when he thought of the black monks, they seemed to him too devoted to their bellies, when he considered the Cistercians, he had to reject them as too grasping and self-seeking.' His opinion of the Cistercians was based in part on his experience in the law courts, for 'he used to say that he had never seen monks of any other order convicted so often of forging charters or seals and fraudulently moving boundary markers'. Ranulf eventually determined to found houses of Augustinian and Premonstratensian canons.[141]

The Cistercian reputation as 'grasping and self-seeking' derived partly from their policy of acquiring property around their monasteries and then evicting the local tenants, in order to create the 'desert places' that they saw as the ideal monastic site. 'Their statutes instruct them,' wrote Walter Map, 'to inhabit desert places, and if they cannot find them, they create them. Wherever they are summoned, they hunt down the habitations of men and quickly and forcibly reduce them to wilderness . . . they root up villages and churches and evict the parishioners . . . their rule does not permit them to preserve but commands them to destroy.'[142] Map's language may be exaggerated but his charges can be supported by documentary evidence.[143] The Cistercians were not, in fact, the only order that sought a clean slate for its model communities. When the Carthusians came to Witham in Somerset in the late 1170s the local people 'feared that the monks would not be satisfied with their own property but would desire to take possession of their acres too'.[144] The fear was not groundless. The unfree tenants living in the immediate vicinity of the new monastery were evicted 'lest the deep silence of the monks' solitude be disturbed by any noise or by people going to and fro'. It was only the special consideration shown by St Hugh, the prior of Witham, that ensured for these unfortunate serfs a reasonable compensation.[145]

[140] R. Devizes, pp. 69–73.     [141] Gerald, *Spec. eccl.* 3. 16 (pp. 244–5).     [142] Map 1. 25 (p. 92).
[143] R. A. Donkin, 'Settlement and Depopulation on Cistercian Estates during the Twelfth and Thirteenth Centuries', *Bulletin of the Institute of Historical Research*, 33 (1960), pp. 141–65.
[144] Ad. Eyns., *V. Hugh* 2. 1 (1, p. 47).     [145] Ibid. 2. 5 (1, pp. 61–3).

Some criticisms of monks came from within their own ranks and were highly partisan, like the views of the Cistercian abbot Serlo of Wilton, who asserted, 'I would rather die as a black dog than a black monk'.[146] Yet others stemmed from a laity whose irreverence is perhaps not fully represented in the surviving written records. On the morning of William Rufus's death, a monk's prophetic and ominous dream was related to him. The tone of contempt in the king's response may have been more common among the lay aristocracy than credulous respect: 'he is a monk and dreams like a monk— for money; give him a hundred shillings'.[147]

## Scepticism and Heresy

Rejection of the official and public face of religion could be unthinking and spontaneous. It would probably be fruitless to ask for a reasoned critique of the cult of the saints from the man who lowered his breeches and broke wind in the direction of St Aldhelm's shrine as it was carried past.[148] Yet critical reflection there certainly was. English men and women of this period thought about religious matters and not all of them came to conclusions that agreed with the authorized teaching of the Church.

There are many people who do not believe that God exists. They consider that the universe has always been as it is now and is ruled by chance rather than by Providence. Many people consider only what they can see and do not believe in good or bad angels, nor do they think that the human soul lives on after the death of the body.[149]

So wrote the prior of Holy Trinity, Aldgate, about 1200. Although it is a story from just north of the Border, the tale of one of the lay brothers of the Cistercian monastery of Melrose in the late twelfth century may not be irrelevant to the experience of the religious of England too: his study of the Old Testament convinced him that Judaism was preferable to Christianity, so that 'eventually his disbelief grew to such an extent that he came to believe that there is no other life than this present one and that what the Bible says about the punishment of the wicked and the joys of the saved is empty nothing.'[150] Simple materialism and disbelief in the afterlife were probably widespread, although they leave little trace in the sources written by clerics and monks.

Among the most frequent doubts mentioned by contemporaries is hesitancy about the literal transformation of bread and wine into the body and blood of Christ in the eucharist. Priests were urged 'to instruct lay people,

---

[146] Gerald, *Spec. eccl.* 2. 33 (p. 105).  [147] W. Malm., *GR* 4. 333 (2, p. 378); OMT edn., p. 572.
[148] W. Malm., *GP* 275 (p. 438).  [149] Peter Cornw., *Liber rev.*, fo. 2.
[150] Joc. Furn., *V. Waltheof*, p. 270.

whenever they take communion, that they should have no doubt that it is truly the body and blood of Christ'.[151] In one of his model sermons Alexander of Ashby exhorted his listeners: 'Do not believe that this does not take place, do not doubt whether it takes place, do not inquire how it takes place.'[152] Herbert of Bosham, confidant and biographer of archbishop Thomas Becket, explained the saint's briskness in celebrating mass by his desire to avoid the sceptical thoughts that the devil tends to place in the mind at that time. Because the sacrifice of the mass is so acceptable to God, it is just then, 'at the hour of this sacrifice, that the exterminating angel sends out his sharpest and most subtle suggestions'.[153]

Organized movements of sceptics, critics, or disbelievers were, however, unknown. In some ways this is surprising. The period covered by this book saw the rise of large-scale heresy in western Europe for the first time for centuries. By the later twelfth century, the ecclesiastical authorities were in dismay at the scale of organized and systematic religious dissent. In 1208 pope Innocent III turned the weapon of the crusade against southern French heretics, the Cathars or Albigensians, and within a generation thereafter the papal inquisition was founded, to root out and destroy heresy. The English were well aware of these developments. The contacts between church leaders at an international level made details of the spread of and campaign against heresy common knowledge. The Albigensian Crusade, in particular, drew the attention of observers throughout Europe.

Given this situation, it is striking that heretical beliefs and movements were virtually absent from England. Indeed, not until the late fourteenth century did such a movement emerge. The absence of heresy from England is perhaps made comprehensible by the fate of the solitary heretical group recorded in the country in this period. This consisted of a number of men and women, 'German by nation and language', headed by a certain Gerard, who arrived in the country in the mid-1160s. The group was not large; sixteen or thirty are alternative estimates of its size. According to hostile observers Gerard was the only one with any education. They were soon arrested and brought before Henry II and the bishops at a Council in Oxford early in 1166. Asked about their beliefs, they denied the sacraments of baptism, mass, and marriage, and expressed themselves willing to suffer persecution for the truth they recognized. The authorities obliged. Branded, beaten, and half-naked, they were cast out into the countryside and strict commands were issued that no one should help them. If they found refuge in anyone's house, the structure of that house was to be carried out of the village or town and burned, thus symbolically cleansing it of the pollution that the presence of

---

[151] *Councils and Synods* 2/i, p. 77.    [152] Alex. Ashby, *De modo pred.*, p. 932.
[153] Herbert of Bosham, *V. sancti Thomae* 3. 13 (*Becket Mats.* 3, p. 215).

heretics represented. The members of the group died wretchedly and their solitary English convert recanted. 'The pious harshness of these severe measures', commented one chronicler, 'not only purged the kingdom of England of the sickness that had crept into it, but also, by striking fear into the heretics, guarded against any future outbreak.'[154]

Ailred, abbot of Rievaulx, was writing his dialogue *On the Soul* (*De anima*) at exactly this time and mentions these heretics. He describes them as 'some ridiculous bumpkins, weavers, both men and women, who are trying to revive a wicked heresy that the holy fathers long ago condemned and buried.' His interlocutor in the dialogue comments, 'I have heard that many of them are held in chains while the king has assembled a council of wise men to decide what to do with such creatures. They disparage marriage, reject the sacrament of the altar, deny the resurrection of the body and deem as nothing the power of baptism.'[155] Here again, the denial of the sacraments figures largely in this account of their beliefs, while their lowly origin, now made more specific, figures in the characterization of their social status. The association of weavers with heresy eventually became commonplace and this is an early conspicuous example of it. One annalist simply says, of the year 1166, 'King Henry held a council at Oxford, in which the heresy of the weavers was condemned.'[156] The bishop of Worcester wrote worriedly seeking advice as to what he should do when these 'weavers' turned up in his diocese.[157]

With the destruction of this foreign group the story of heresy in England ends for two hundred years, excepting a solitary and otherwise unexplained reference to the burning of an 'Albigensian' at London in 1210.[158] The swift and decisive action of the secular power in a small, heavily governed kingdom like England was enough to suppress religious dissent. Although the penalties that Henry inflicted at Oxford were in accordance with those prescribed by the ecclesiastical authorities, for the Council of Rheims a few years earlier in 1157 had specified branding and expulsion as the proper punishment for heretics, it was the king's vigorous enforcement of them through the secular arm and in secular legislation that made them effective.

It may also be true, however, that English social structure did not foster the growth of heresy. Heretical activity tended to thrive in Europe's urban belt, that zone of relatively intense urbanization stretching from central Italy to the Low Countries. London could conceivably be included as a northern outpost of this area, but in general England was not one of the most urbanized parts of Europe. If the large artisanal populations of the towns of politically decentralized northern Italy and the Rhineland had a special affinity for

---

[154] W. Newb. 2. 13 (1, pp. 131–4) (the main source); *Sel. Charters*, p. 173 (Assize of Clarendon c. 21).
[155] Ailr. Riev., *De anima* 1. 59–60 (*Op. asc.*, pp. 703–4).
[156] *Annals of Tewkesbury*, *Ann. Mon.* 1, p. 49.     [157] Foliot, *Letters*, nos. 157–8, pp. 207–10.
[158] Arnolf fitz Thedmar, *De antiquis legibus liber*, ed. Thomas Stapleton (Camden Soc. 34; 1846), p. 3.

heretical beliefs and attitudes, it may be that the insignificance of England's urban population was as important as harsh royal action in keeping England 'immune from heretical plagues'.[159] As in the case of the suppression of the fitz Osbern disturbances in London in 1196 (above, pp. 344–5), the relatively slightly urbanized nature of English society meant that sharp repression of urban dissent could be effective. Be that as it may, in the early thirteenth-century it was a self-congratulatory commonplace that 'heresy, thank God, is not prevalent in England'.[160]

[159] W. Newb. 2. 13 (1, p. 132).        [160] *Ancr. Wisse*, p. 44.

# CHAPTER 10

# Cultural Patterns

## I. LANGUAGES AND LITERATURES

### Spoken Languages

*Introduction*

Apart from the Hebrew that had limited oral use among the tiny Jewish community, and the Cornish and Welsh spoken in parts of the south-west and along the Welsh borders, there were three main languages used for oral communication in England in the period covered here: English, French, and Latin. Although there is little direct evidence about the use of spoken language, some natural assumptions can be made. There is no doubt about the character of Latin: it was a language that was learned by an educated minority and was spoken in very restricted but prestigious spheres—the Church, law and administration, education. There is, moreover, no question that English was the 'mother tongue'—the first language acquired naturally in infancy—of the vast majority of people in England. The status of spoken French in Norman and Angevin England is a more controversial matter.

The coexistence of a learned language, Latin, and the local vernacular was a common feature of medieval European society. Such dualism can indeed be found elsewhere in the world: in India the sacred language, Sanskrit, existed alongside many languages actually spoken in everyday life by the local populations, and in the Islamic world today the classical Arabic of the Koran is taught as a special skill to those whose native language may be a very colloquial form of Arabic or a non-Arabic tongue. Such a linguistic regime has two fundamental consequences: those who master the learned tongue have access to an international educated community and to the inherited cultural stock of the prestige language, and every local community is divided horizontally between the cultural elite who command that language and the majority who do not. This was precisely the situation in twelfth-century England, where the literate—which meant 'literate in Latin'—or 'clerks' (*clerici*) could communicate with fellow clerks in every part of Europe and penetrate the Latin texts of the Bible, the Roman Law, or the classical poets, while they were surrounded at home by a large majority for whom these things were a closed book.

Those who were educated in Latin sometimes spoke contemptuously of the English vernacular, deeming it 'barbaric'. Benedict of Peterborough, the monk who wrote down the miracles that occurred at Thomas Becket's shrine, often omitted the names of the places of origin of those healed because of their vernacular uncouthness: 'he was called Robert, the son of a Surrey knight— the barbarous name of the village has not stuck firmly in my memory'; 'we were overjoyed by the case of a girl called Letitia, born of a noble father and a common mother, from a region and estate the names of which I omit because of their barbarity'.[1] The chronicler of Ramsey abbey speaks of translating into Latin documents 'written in the barbarism of English' and likewise when Gerald of Wales said that, in cases of dire necessity, laymen could baptize children, uttering the baptismal formula either in Latin or their own vernacular, the term he employed for the latter was 'barbarian' (*barbara*).[2]

The existence of a condescending elite educated in Latin and a majority employing the vernacular was thus nothing unusual. What made England after the Norman Conquest a special case was the coexistence of two vernaculars, English and French. Whatever the exact status and dissemination of French (a subject to be discussed below), there can be little doubt that English society was more broadly and truly multilingual in the period from the Conquest down to the fourteenth century than it has ever been since.

In discussing this multilingual world, it is important to distinguish different types of language use and levels of linguistic competence. Everyone has a mother tongue and some people have two, but the mother tongue may not be the language that an adult actually uses most often—acquired languages can be current coin. One must obviously distinguish not only different levels of competence in a language, but also between the ability to understand it, speak it, read it, and write it. Most important of all is the point that language choice in a multilingual situation is contextual: it is necessary to ask not only which language is spoken, but by whom, in which milieu, for what purpose. As the emperor Charles V is reputed to have said in the sixteenth century, 'I speak Spanish to God, Italian to women, French to men and German to my horse.'

## Spoken Latin

Although Latin was a learned language, it was also a spoken one. Monks and clerics who used Latin constantly in church would be familiar with the utterance of the language and there is evidence that is was used colloquially as well as for business or ceremony. Formal ecclesiastical occasions often called for it,

---

[1] Benedict of Peterborough, *Mir. sancti Thomae* 1. 15; 4. 31 (*Becket Mats.* 2, pp. 47, 205).
[2] *Ramsey Chron.*, p. 176; Gerald, *Gemma* 1. 12 (p. 43).

of course. At the Council of Winchester in 1139, for instance, it is explicitly reported that Henry of Blois, bishop of Winchester, the papal legate presiding, 'delivered his speech, which was addressed to the literate, in Latin'.[3] Sermons were certainly preached in Latin, when the audience was appropriate, for example a body of monks or canons, or a local synod. Latin was also the usual language of the church courts. There was also a limited oral use of Latin beyond ecclesiastical circles. Kings might need to use it on some public occasions, even if only in brief phases.[4]

William of Malmesbury, writing of the good things that happened at his monastery in the 1090s during the abbacy of abbot Godfrey, claims that during that time 'the monks, who used to babble only with vernacular letters, became fully educated'.[5] William himself could read Old English, but his derisive tone suggests that he did not have a high opinion of his brethren whose linguistic attainments were limited to the vernacular. It is possible that there was a rise in the quality of the Latinity of monks in the generations after the Norman Conquest. There were certainly many more monks, and they needed at least some familiarity with oral Latin. Developments in higher education also created new Latin-speaking milieux. The practice of sending potential clerks to Paris or other places overseas to be educated in the schools and the emergence in England of the University of Oxford (see below, pp. 508–14) placed many English teenagers in an environment where the language of instruction and examination was Latin.

Latin provided an international language for clerks and monks. Ecclesiastics from overseas could make themselves understood easily enough in ecclesiastical circles. When two canons from Spain came to the abbey of St Albans in the first half of the twelfth century, their spokesman explained himself in Latin 'since he knew no English'.[6] Conversely, English clerics overseas had a common means of communication with the ecclesiastics they encountered. Latin was the language of international ecclesiastical assemblies or councils. Becket was reputed by his friends to have spoken 'eloquently and skilfully in Latin' to the papal legates at the conference held near Gisors in 1167, although a hostile observer claimed that, on another formal public occasion, the papal council of Tours in 1163, the archbishop had to keep silent 'because he was insufficiently educated in speaking Latin'.[7] The constant traffic between the English Church and Rome was both an indication of and a stimulus to the everyday use of spoken Latin.

Command of Latin opened up the world for those who knew it, but it could also be used to exclude. There is an indirect indication of this in an incident

---

[3] W. Malm., *HN* 471 (p. 29).    [4] Gerald, *Inv.* 1. 5 (pp. 100–1).
[5] W. Malm., *GP* 271 (pp. 431–2).    [6] *Gesta S. Alb.* 1, p. 88.
[7] J. Salisb., *Letters* 231 (2, p. 418); S. Rouen, *Draco* 3. 13, line 998 (p. 744).

in the life of the famous English hermit Godric of Finchale. On one occasion four Durham monks came to visit him. The conversation between them was in English and Godric discussed the Bible and ethical questions 'just as if he were a *litteratus* [i.e. literate in Latin]'. After a while, writes one of the monks, 'we turned to each other and began to talk amongst ourselves in Latin'. Much to their amazement, Godric was able to understand what they were saying.[8] Here the point is Godric's miraculous ability and the monks had no malicious intent in excluding him, but the situation makes clear that the *litterati*, the Latin-literate, usually did have the option of excluding the laity by use of their own private language.

Latin was a language that had to be learned and not every monk or cleric did so to the same degree of proficiency. Stories of inadequate Latin abound. Gerald of Wales gives a chain of such tales, directed especially against his own personal enemies, like Hubert Walter, archbishop of Canterbury (1193–1205), who even his friends admitted was only 'moderately literate'.[9] On one occasion the archbishop was presiding at a law court in Oxford and asked the parties *Vultis stare isto compromisso?* ('Do you wish to stand by this compromise?'), giving the dative of *iste* ('this') wrongly as *isto* instead of *isti*. One of his advisers murmured *isti*, whereupon the archbishop corrected both *isto* and the noun that he had actually got right, producing *Vultis stare isti compromissi?* Eventually the clerks in the courtroom could not restrain their laughter.

Another story of Gerald's tells of a parish priest preaching on the text of the parable of the two debtors in Luke's gospel (7: 40–3). One of the debtors owed five-hundred pence (*denarios quingentos*) the other fifty (*quinquaginta*). The priest was, however, unable to distinguish these two numerals and translated them both as 'fifty'. The village reeve then objected 'But neither of them got more than the other, then, since they both had fifty and no more.' Whereupon the priest, 'feeling that he had been caught out', explained that one sum was in the currency of Anjou and the other in English sterling.[10]

Coming from the pen of so talented a Latin stylist and so irritable a temperament as Gerald's, these anecdotes could not reasonably be viewed as the whole story, but there are, from the early thirteenth century, records of inspections of local clergy that bear out the picture of uneasy Latinity. In 1222 William, dean of Salisbury, held a chapter at Sonning in Berkshire and there examined the chaplains who served in the numerous chapels in that parish. One of them, Vitalis, had a rough time:

He was examined on the gospel for the first Sunday in Advent and it was found that he had no capacity or understanding. Next he was tested on the phrase from the canon of the mass *Te igitur, clementissime Pater* ['You, therefore, most merciful

---

[8] Reg., *V. Godric* 79 (pp. 179–80).     [9] Wilmart, 'Maître Adam', p. 227.
[10] Gerald, *Gemma* 2. 35–6 (pp. 342, 345); Gerald, *Inv.* 1. 5 (p. 100).

Father']. He did not know what case *Te* was, nor what governed it. And when it was suggested to him that he should think carefully what might most appropriately govern *Te*, he said '*Pater*, for he governs everything'. Asked what *clementissime* was, what its case was and how it is declined, he did not know. Asked what *clemens* ['merciful'] was, he did not know.[11]

Anyone who has undergone an oral examination may feel a touch of sympathy with the besieged Vitalis, but he certainly could not have been a competent interpreter of a Latin-based scripture and liturgy to a vernacular congregation. Even among clerks, proficiency in Latin could not be presumed.

## Spoken French

Vernacular French—termed in contemporary sources French, Norman, Romance, or Gallic[12]—was obviously the mother tongue of the rulers of England in the first generation after the Norman Conquest. King, barons, great churchmen, and most of the lower aristocracy had been born and brought up in northern France. At the start of our period, then, in the year 1075, there can be no doubt that at the top level of society French was the native vernacular.

Throughout the Norman and Angevin period the royal court remained the great Francophone centre. William I made an effort to learn English, in order to participate in court hearings without an interpreter, but had no success.[13] There is no definite evidence for the amount of English commanded by his sons William Rufus and Henry I, but French was certainly their mother tongue. Both Stephen and Henry II were great French princes before they became kings of England. Richard I and John grew up as the children of French-speaking parents and Richard spent virtually no time in England. French-speaking queens reinforced the Francophone nature of the court. For 108 years out of the 150 in the period 1075–1225 there was a queen consort who had been born and raised in France or a French-speaking environment. Some, like Eleanor of Aquitaine, continued to be politically important after their husband's death, and hence continued to make French the language of central power and patronage. Even in 1192, forty years after her marriage to Henry of Anjou and thirty-eight after her coronation as queen of England, she still needed an interpreter when dealing with the local English population.[14]

Her husband's command of English was not much stronger. A story told by Gerald of Wales and dating to the year 1172 recounts how a mysterious figure came to bring a warning to Henry II. He spoke in English, greeting the

---

[11] *Reg. Osm.* 1, p. 304.

[12] e.g. W. Malm., *GP* 143 (p. 285) (*Normannica lingua*); *Gesta Herw.*, p. 385 (*Romana lingua*); *Mir. John Bev.*, p. 299 (*Francice*); Councils and Synods 2/i, pp. 68–9 (*Gallico = Romano*).

[13] Orderic 4 (2, p. 256).      [14] R. Devizes, p. 59.

king with the words '*God holde thee, cuning*' ('God keep you, king!'), before giving his message. The king then turned to his equerry, the knight Philip of Marcross, and said to him in French, 'Ask that peasant whether he has dreamed all this.' The knight put the question and received the reply in English.[15] If there is any truth in the story (and Gerald claimed to have heard it from Philip of Marcross himself) it seems to show that Henry II had enough knowledge of English to understand what was being said to him, but needed a bilingual intermediary to be understood by monoglot Englishmen (unless, of course, he speaks through the knight simply as a mark of social distance). This would fit in well with Walter Map's comment that the king 'had some knowledge of every language from the Channel to the river Jordan, but himself employed only Latin and French'.[16] Like his mother Matilda, daughter of Henry I, he could probably grasp a passage of Latin but would be happier when it could then be expounded in French.[17]

The nature of spoken French beyond the court circle is a more controversial issue. Some have regarded it as widespread, others as the practice of a tiny minority. For some it is the mother tongue of the aristocracy well into the twelfth century, for others it lost the status of being anyone's mother tongue in England within a generation of the Norman Conquest. Evidence for the use of French in England in this period is not rich—but explicit evidence for the use of any particular spoken language is unusual. Sermons were certainly preached in French. Abbot Samson of Bury (1182–1211) said that 'in many churches sermons are preached before the community in French or English', referring here not to preaching before lay congregations but to preaching *within* the religious community.[18] The implication is that bodies of monks in late twelfth-century England might well be able to follow a French sermon. On his crusade preaching tour of 1188 Gerald of Wales preached in French, though he then required an interpreter to convey his meaning.[19] This obviously tells us more about Gerald's linguistic skill (and pretensions) than his hearers', but again it points to oral fluency in French in higher ecclesiastical circles.

Other anecdotes support the idea that French was not uncommon among the higher members of the ecclesiastical hierarchy. When Thomas Becket appeared in a vision after his death to Benedict of Peterborough, a Canterbury monk, Benedict thought it natural to address the archbishop in French (though the reply was in Latin).[20] Because the local priest of Haselbury in Somerset knew no French, he was 'forced to remain dumb in the presence of

---

[15] Gerald, *Itin.* 1. 6 (pp. 64–5), repeated in Gerald, *Exp.* 1. 40 (pp. 108–10), and Gerald, *Prin.* 2. 12 pp. 180–2.

[16] Map 5. 6 (p. 476).   [17] *Becket Mats.* 5, pp. 148–9 (Becket Letters 76).

[18] Joc. Brak., p. 128.   [19] Gerald, *De reb.* 2. 18 (p. 76); Gerald, *Itin.* 1. 11 (p. 83).

[20] Benedict of Peterborough, *Mir. sancti Thomae* 1. 1 (*Becket Mats.* 2, p. 27).

the bishop and archdeacon', suggesting here a real practical and symbolic linguistic fissure in the administration of the diocese.[21] Nor did the French-speaking kings of England have any hesitation in appointing ecclesiastics from France or Francophone parts of the continent to English bishoprics and hence, throughout the twelfth century and beyond, there were in England French-speaking bishops ignorant of English. Hugh, bishop of Lincoln (1186–1200), who was recruited to England from La Grande Chartreuse, the mother house of the Carthusians, by Henry II in person, made a deep impression on his contemporaries and was canonized twenty years after his death, but he required an interpreter to deal with his English flock. The Norman William de Longchamps, bishop of Ely (1189–97), not only had a low opinion of the English, holding the theory that they had declined in both literary and military pre-eminence through lechery and drunkenness, but 'was completely ignorant of the English language'. This was a disadvantage to him when in 1191, disguised as a woman, he was attempting to escape from his enemies and found himself unable to reply to questions put to him by the local people.[22]

French was clearly a language with prestige, used more by the wealthy and powerful than by the poor and weak. The legend of Hereward the Wake, composed in the early twelfth century, tells how he overheard the plans of the Normans because 'since they thought he was a peasant, they presumed he would not know their language'.[23] Abbot Henry de Longchamps of Crowland objected to viewers in a lawsuit in the 1190s 'because they were not of knightly rank nor girded with the sword and the third of them could not speak French'.[24] It is probable that his remark was intended to point out the low social standing of the third viewer rather than to raise any specific practical problem that lack of knowledge of French might entail.

A more ambiguous story comes from the pen of Jocelin of Brakelond, biographer of abbot Samson of Bury. Jocelin praises the abbot for his unwillingness to lease out the abbey manors. One exception was the manor of Thorpe, 'which he confirmed to a certain man of English descent, who was bound to the soil, and whom he trusted because he was a good farmer and could not speak French'.[25] Even if this is a joke, it must have a meaning. Perhaps the man's linguistic limitations reflect his lack of social pretensions and hence he could be trusted not to cause trouble by claiming more than the abbot was willing to concede. Perhaps it meant that he would be handicapped if he tried to pursue a lawsuit to gain greater security for his tenure. In any

[21] J. Ford, V. Wulfric 1. 14 (pp. 28–9).

[22] Ad. Eyns., V. Hugh 4. 2, 5. 8 (2, pp. 7, 118); Gerald, V. Geoffrey 2. 12, 19 (pp. 411, 424); Gesta Ric. I 2, p. 219; R. Howd. 3, p. 146.

[23] Gesta Herw., p. 385; cf. Lib. Eliensis 2. 106 (p. 183).          [24] Stenton, Engl. Justice, p. 170.

[25] Joc. Brak., p. 33.

case the image of the bluff, rural, lower-class Englishman who knows no French, tells us that the ability to speak French had the opposite resonances. Evidence from a later period, the early fourteenth century, confirms this pattern of association: French was more upper-class and urban than English.[26]

This did not mean that men from the English villages were unable to acquire fluent French. William Paternoster, for instance, almoner of the hospital at Beverley in the second half of the twelfth century and a native of the Yorkshire village of Beilby, was able to speak both French and English, and it seems probable that he acquired his spoken French in Beverley rather than in France.[27] The statutes of the diocese of Salisbury of about 1218 envisaged laymen baptizing children in emergencies 'either in French or in English' and ordered the words of the wedding service to be taught to the bride and groom in either language.[28] Nor would the burgesses of English towns have been given or adopted French nicknames—Richard Bonemfant, William Mauveisin, etc.—unless French had been a current vernacular in the twelfth-century urban environment.[29]

From the fact that French was spoken in England and acquired in England by people who had never been to France, it followed that English French came to diverge from continental French. By the second half of the twelfth century there was a perception in England that the French spoken there was not only different from but also inferior to that spoken in France, especially around Paris. There was even a current term for badly spoken French— 'Marlborough French'.[30] The anonymous nun of Barking who wrote a *Life* of Edward the Confessor in French and dedicated it to the Francophone monarchs, Henry II and Eleanor of Aquitaine, apologized for her French: 'I know the faulty French of England, which is where I acquired it; you who learned it elsewhere, correct it when necessary.'[31] At the end of the twelfth century John Blund learned good French in England from his uncles, one a canon of Lincoln, who had themselves studied in France; their accent was described as 'elegant and pure and very different from the rough, corrupt French of the English'.[32] A norm had grown up, by which English French was found wanting. The line is direct from the Marlborough French of the twelfth century to Chaucer's prioress of the fourteenth, who spoke French 'after the scole of Stratford atte Bowe, | For French of Paris was to her unknowe.'

One way to maintain fluency in the kind of French spoken on the continent was to send children to France to learn the language there. Throughout our

---

[26] Michael Richter, *Sprache und Gesellschaft im Mittelalter* (Stuttgart, 1979), p. 190.

[27] *Mir. John Bev.*, p. 312.    [28] *Councils and Synods* 2/i, pp. 68–9, 87.

[29] Cecily Clark, 'People and Languages in Post-Conquest Canterbury', *Jnl Medieval History*, 2 (1976), pp. 1–33, at pp. 20–1.

[30] Map 5. 6 (p. 496).

[31] *La Vie d'Edouard le Confesseur*, ed. Östen Södergård (Uppsala, 1948), lines 7–10, p. 109.

[32] Gerald, *Spec. duorum*, p. 56.

period there was a high aristocracy with lands and connections in France (see above, pp. 13–17). Gervase of Tilbury writes that 'it is the custom among the greatest nobles of England to send their sons to be brought up in France in order to be trained in arms and have the barbarity of their native language removed'.[33] Although this observation occurs in a passage in which Gervase is discussing the reign of Edward the Confessor, it seems likely that it is based on practice in Gervase's own time, the late twelfth and early thirteenth century. Another method of attaining the same end was to employ tutors from France, like Simon, son of Durand, a Norman of teenage years who was sent by his father to England 'to teach his language to the son of a certain knight'. Simon's days as a language teacher must date to the 1170s.[34] Knowledge of 'correct' French was thus, by the later part of the twelfth century (if not before), a prestigious ability that the children of the aristocracy had to work hard to acquire.

Evidence from place names supports this picture of French as always a minority language and soon a learned one. Unlike earlier Anglo-Saxon and Scandinavian settlement, the arrival of the Normans left virtually no imprint on place names. There were a few castles, monasteries, and manors with French names of fashion like Richmond, Pontefract, Beaulieu, and Beaumont, and a scattering of so called feudal suffixes indicating a family's or abbey's ownership, like Stoke Mandeville or Tooting Bec, but the overall impact was slight. A language with so restricted a social basis as French could not change something as widespread and habitual as the pattern of place names.

### Spoken English

It can be taken for granted that English was both the mother tongue and the usual tongue of the vast majority of people in England, even though explicit evidence to demonstrate this is rare. The practice of giving sermons in English 'for the edification of the uneducated ordinary people', discussed above (p. 452), is well attested. English was not only a plebeian tongue, however. It is recorded that Waltheof, abbot of Melrose, spoke both French and English 'eloquently and fluently'.[35] Since he was the brother of Simon de Senlis, earl of Huntingdon, and was born in the first decade of the twelfth century, we have unequivocal evidence that children of the highest aristocracy were acquiring fluency in English within forty years of the Conquest. This is not intrinsically surprising.

Occasionally the Latin texts of the time offer a window through which the world of oral English can be glimpsed. The Cistercian biographer of Ailred of Rievaulx lapses from the learned to the vernacular to give the very words

---

[33] Gerv. Tilb. 2. 20 (p. 945).     [34] W. Cant., *Mir. Thos.* 4. 36 (pp. 347–8).
[35] Joc. Furn., *V. Waltheof*, p. 260.

that Ailred called out in his death agony: *for crist luve* ('for the love of Christ!').[36] Not all life is lived *in extremis*, but the language one turns to as death approaches has some claim to be the one used most spontaneously—though Ailred's biographer explained it by saying that the English monosyllable *crist* was easier to utter and more sweet.

Lyrics in English are also sometimes recorded. Gerald of Wales tells the story of a priest who could not get the chorus of a love song out of his mind and, instead of chanting *Dominus vobiscum* ('the Lord be with you') at mass, sang out *Swete lamman dhin are* ('Sweet love, have mercy').[37] At Ely the tradition was preserved that king Canute had once been rowed past the monastery and, being enchanted by the sound of the monks' singing, had composed the following lines:

> Merie sungen the muneches binnen Ely
> Tha Cnut ching rue ther by.
> Roweth cnites noer the lant
> and here we thes muneches sæng.

('Sweetly sang the monks in Ely | as King Canute rowed by. | Row, men, nearer the land | and hear we these monks sing.')

According to the Ely monk who recorded this in the twelfth century, 'This is sung in chorus among the people to this day.'[38] Such snippets are witness to a vast lost world of English song.

Recent scholarship of great energy and sophistication has mapped the complex pattern of English dialects in the later Middle Ages.[39] It makes sense to assume that a pattern of similar complexity existed earlier, though the scarcity of sources in English makes it impossible to know the situation in the twelfth century in any detail. Occasionally dialect differences were mentioned by contemporary authors. The biographer of abbot Samson noted that, when preaching in English, the abbot used his native Norfolk dialect (which, if later patterns held, would be rather different from that of Suffolk, where Bury was located), while the imp Malekin, who appeared in Suffolk in the reign of Richard I 'spoke English after the dialect of that region'.[40] The perennial southern complaint about the incomprehensibility of northerners first emerges in this period with William of Malmesbury's plangent comment, 'The whole language of the Northumbrians, especially in York, is so grating and uncouth that we southerners cannot understand a word of it.'[41]

---

[36] W. Dan., *V. Ailred* 54 (p. 60).      [37] Gerald, *Gemma* 1. 43 (p. 120).
[38] *Lib. Eliensis* 2. 85 (pp. 153–4).
[39] *A Linguistic Atlas of Late Medieval English*, ed. A. McIntosh *et al.* (4 vols.; Aberdeen, 1986).
[40] Joc. Brak., p. 40; R. Coggesh., p. 121.      [41] W. Malm., *GP* 99 (p. 209).

## Written Languages

At all times the spoken world of the pre-electronic past has to be recovered through the very different medium of the written word. For twelfth-century English that written word is also almost invariably in a different language. During this period the main developments in the fortunes of the different written languages were the demise and partial recovery of English, the birth of French, and the efflorescence of Latin.

In the general development of written texts in the Middle Ages, England was distinctive in two ways. The first was that there existed a large and early body of writing in the Old English vernacular. While, in many parts of western Europe, vernacular languages only began to generate a substantial body of literature in the twelfth century and this only surpassed literature in Latin in volume in the fourteenth century, Anglo-Saxon England was distinguished by the largest and most impressive bodies of vernacular literature in the whole of the early medieval West. Partly stimulated by King Alfred's programme of cultural reform, a large number of both translations from Latin into Old English and original works in the vernacular were produced. By the early eleventh century, poetry, historical writing, religious literature, laws, writs, and wills in English formed a vernacular written corpus far larger than any other in western Europe. This was the world to which the Normans came in 1066. Their arrival doomed it to extinction.

The Norman Conquest also marked the emergence of the second distinctive trait in medieval English linguistic and literary history: the long coexistence of two written vernaculars, English and French. The history of 'the vernacular' in Norman and Angevin England is more involved than that in a country with a single vernacular. These two features, the early extensive use of Old English and the co-existence of English and French after the Conquest, mean that questions about when the vernacular began to be used, to what extent, and for what purpose, may be answered in more than one way. In France or Germany a relatively simple story of Latin gradually being supplemented or replaced by the vernacular can be told. In England, the early use of Old English for a wide variety of purposes means that development did not correspond to such a linear evolution.

The language of documentation illustrates this point. When the Normans conquered England, they found many documents, such as writs, that would be written in Latin in their homeland, but were written in English in England. Unaccustomed as they were to this custom, as to the language, they soon abandoned it. A few documents either in Old English or in both Latin and Old English were issued by the Norman kings, but they are rare. Soon Latin assumed a monopoly in official documentation. The period 1050–1100 thus sees an extension of Latin at the expense of the vernacular.

French made a late, gradual, and hesitant appearance as a language of documentation. An unofficial compilation of legal material, termed the *Laws of William I* (*Leis Willelme*), was produced around the middle of the twelfth century; one of the returns to the Inquest of Sheriffs of 1170 is a scrappy piece of Anglo-Norman; while the first piece of French on the royal Chancery rolls is a charter of Stephen Langton from 1215.[42] Only in the middle of the thirteenth century does the vernacular begin to appear regularly alongside, although always less frequently than, Latin. French and English then jostle together for the rest of the Middle Ages, both becoming increasingly common in official record and documentation. Between the eleventh and fourteenth centuries the language of official writing therefore changed from mixed Latin and vernacular, to purely Latin, to Latin and two vernaculars.

## Written English

The century and a half covered by this book was a low point in the production of literature in English. Very soon after the Conquest the tradition of issuing writs and laws in English dried up and the composition of poetry and religious works also soon came to a virtual end. This does not mean that no manuscripts in English were being copied in the monasteries of the time, however, for there seems to have been, in some centres particularly, an interest in copying Old English texts, even if little new composition was being undertaken. Neil Ker surveyed all manuscripts prior to 1200 that contain substantial amounts of Old English: out of a total of 189 manuscripts, 27 (14 per cent) were produced in the twelfth century.[43]

The monastic communities of Canterbury, Rochester, and Worcester all had an active interest in the Anglo-Saxon past, which was expressed in the copying of old texts. About the year 1120 the manuscript called the *Textus Roffensis* ('Rochester Text') was written at that centre. It is mainly in Old English, with portions in Latin, and contains Anglo-Saxon law codes, genealogies of kings, lists of bishops, and a collection of Rochester charters. The work probably had a practical rather than (or as well as) a purely antiquarian purpose and includes a text of Henry I's coronation charter (in Latin) as well as the older laws.[44]

Another relatively flourishing part of the Old English literary heritage was the homiletic tradition. A manuscript produced around the middle of the

[42] Liebermann, *Gesetze* 1, pp. 492–520; Robertson, *Laws*, pp. 252–74; Helen Richardson, 'A Twelfth Century Anglo-Norman Charter', *Bulletin of the John Rylands Library*, 24 (1940), pp. 168–72; *eadem* (as Helen Suggett), 'An Anglo-Norman Return to the Inquest of Sheriffs', ibid. 27 (1942), pp. 179–81; *Rot. chart.*, p. 209 and plate at p. xli; Michael Clanchy, *From Memory to Written Record: England 1066–1307* (2nd edn., Oxford, 1993), pp. 218–19.

[43] N. R. Ker, *Catalogue of Manuscripts containing Anglo-Saxon* (Oxford, 1957), pp. xv–xix.

[44] *Text Roff.*

twelfth century in either Rochester or Canterbury contains sermons and theological tracts, mainly by the late Anglo-Saxon abbot Ælfric, but with such contemporary texts as an English translation of a sermon by Ralph d'Escures, archbishop of Canterbury (d. 1122).[45] Such a collection shows both the interest in pre-Conquest religious and literary culture and the active survival of that culture. Library catalogues of the twelfth century, like that from the monastery of Burton, which lists seven books in English, including an English version of the classical romance *Apollonius of Tyre*, as well as a Psalter, Hymnal, etc., show that a stock, albeit a small one, was available if there was demand.[46]

Gradually, however, Old English texts became the preserve of antiquarians. By the early thirteenth century, even at a place like Worcester, where numerous Old English manuscripts could be found, they were the object of study by eccentric individuals rather than a standard part of every monk's reading. The anonymous Worcester monk known, rather charmingly, from his handwriting as 'the Tremulous Hand', went through these texts, jotting down Latin or Middle English equivalents to the words he found unfamiliar, sometimes getting them wrong, drawing up vocabulary lists. Old English had crossed the threshold to being a dead language.[47]

A particularly interesting light is shed on the linguistic and literary development of English by the *Anglo-Saxon Chronicle*. This had begun as a kind of official history in the reign of king Alfred and had been continued at various monasteries over the following centuries. The *Chronicle* did not stop dead at the Conquest. At Peterborough a text was indeed continued into the reign of Henry II, with its last entry describing the appointment of a new abbot of Peterborough early in 1155. This *Peterborough Chronicle* was written up at various times. It seems that, after Peterborough's own copy of the *Anglo-Saxon Chronicle* was destroyed by fire, a fresh start was made by copying out a version borrowed from Canterbury. This was done in 1121. Then the local Peterborough historian added entries as events occurred between 1122 and 1131. Finally, after a period in which no entries were made, someone in 1155 gave an account of the intervening years up to his own time. The changes in the kind of English employed by the copyist of 1121, the First Continuator, and the Second Continuator are important as guides to the changing nature of the language.[48]

The dating of other English works of the period is very difficult, relying on

---

[45] R. D.-N. Warner, *Early English Homilies from the Twelfth-Century Manuscript Vespasian D. xiv* (EETS 152; 1917).

[46] *Engl. Ben. Libr.*, pp. 33–42.

[47] Christine Franzen, *The Tremulous Hand of Worcester: A Study of Old English in the Thirteenth Century* (Oxford, 1991).

[48] *The Peterborough Chronicle, 1070–1154*, ed. Cecily Clark (2nd edn.; Oxford, 1970), pp. xv–xvii, xxxvii–lxxiv.

such uncertain criteria as handwriting or language. There seems, however, to be a hiatus between the last gasps of the *Peterborough Chronicle* and the years around 1200, to which several works are assigned. This would make the half-century 1150–1200 the very lowest point in the history of literary composition in English. From the last years of the twelfth century, however, there are signs of renewed activity in several different genres.

One of the striking things about the new work is that its language is unlike the standard literary West Saxon in which the productions of the eleventh century or the main section of the *Peterborough Chronicle* were composed. Historians of the English language indeed draw the line between Old English and Early Middle English in the twelfth century. Early Middle English is different in a number of ways: the complex inflectional system of Old English, in which endings marked the cases, numbers, and genders of nouns and adjectives and the persons, numbers, tenses, and moods of verbs, was dramatically simplified; partly as a consequence, word order was standardized, the modern English sequence subject–verb–object becoming dominant over other variants; various phonological and orthographic changes took place; and the beginnings of the influx of French vocabulary can be noticed. These were the first steps of a process that was eventually to make English one of the least Germanic of the Germanic languages.

An example will illustrate the point. With reference to Christmas 1122, the First Continuator of the *Peterborough Chronicle* notes:

On þyssum geare wæs se king Henri on Cristestyde æt Dunestaple ond þær comen þes eorles sandermen of Angeow to him ond þeonen he ferde to Wudestoke ond his biscopes ond his hird eal mid him.[49]

(þ corresponds to modern 'th'.) A literal translation is: 'In this year was the king Henry at Christmas at Dunstable and there came the earl's messengers of Anjou to him and thence he went to Woodstock and his bishops and retinue all with him.'

Both the first two clauses have the word order verb–subject rather than the modern subject–verb. There are several examples of now obsolete inflectional endings: *þyssum geare* is the dative of *þis gear* after the preposition *on*; in the phrase 'the earl's messengers' not only is the noun 'earl' inflected, as in modern English, but the article 'the' is also in the genitive. The vocabulary, apart from proper names and the long naturalized 'biscop', is exclusively Germanic.

If we turn to a sentence from the *Anchoresses' Guide*, written about a century later, we read (on the subject of the different kinds of flatterer):

þe forme, yef a mon is god, preiseð him biuoren him seolf, and makeð him, inohreaðe,

---

[49] Ibid., p. 42; *ASC*, p. 251, *s.a.* 1123.

yet betere ðen he beo, and, yef he seið wel oðer deð wel, heueð hit to hehe up wið ouerherunge.[50]

(ð is another form of 'th'.) 'The first, if a man is good, praises him before himself [to his face] and makes him, readily enough, yet better than he is, and, if he says well or does well, raises it too high up with excessive praise.' Here the word order is virtually that of modern English, inflections are, except in the case of the pronoun, unimportant and we have a trace of French in the verbs 'preise', from Old French *preisier*.

Such developments are only partly a result of actual changes in the language over the period 1050–1200; they also represent the emergence into writing of various types of spoken English that had previously been submerged under the standard literary form. The disappearance of this standard signified the end of one phase of literature in English and the beginning of another, which is continuous to the present.

The English works attributed to the years around 1200 and marking the birth of writing in Middle English vary very much in their kind. One group of texts consists of religious and devotional prose, some of it written specifically for women, and localizable to the West Midlands. Amongst these texts are the so called 'Katherine Group' consisting of *Lives* of saints Katherine, Margaret, and Juliana, a homily entitled *The Custody of the Soul* (*Sawles Ward*), and a treatise on the virtues of virginity; the collection of short religious works associated with *The Wooing of Our Lord*; and the long piece of advice to women living as recluses, the *Anchoresses' Guide* mentioned above. Very different from these works are the satirical debate-poem *The Owl and the Nightingale*, hard to date but probably from this period and composed by the Surrey clerk Nicholas of Guildford; and the historical epic, the *Brut*, by the Worcestershire priest Layamon, who employed English alliterative verse in some ways reminiscent of Old English heroic poetry.

Some of the difficulties encountered by those writing in English after the death of standard West Saxon come out in the poem called the *Ormulum*.[51] This was written possibly around 1200 by an Augustinian canon named Orm, at the instance of his brother and fellow Augustinian Walter. It is an English versification of the gospel readings for the year, 10,000 lines of which survive. The manuscript of the *Ormulum* was probably written out by the author himself and uses a distinctive spelling system he had himself devised. Doubling of consonants is employed to indicate the length of the preceding syllable, thus producing such remarkable looking lines as:

*Nu brotherr Wallterr, brotherr min, affterr the flaeshess kinde* (Now, brother Walter, my brother after the flesh).

---

[50] *Ancr. Wisse*, p. 46.     [51] Ed. R. M. White and R. Holt (2 vols.; Oxford, 1878).

Nobody has ever been very kind about the literary merit of the *Ormulum*, but it represents a bold and unusual attempt to face the problem of putting sounds on parchment, a problem that was particularly acute for a language like English that had, in the twelfth century, come close to ceasing to be a written language.

## Written French

Written works produced in French were far more numerous and varied than those produced in English, partly because of the patronage of the Franco-phone royal court but also because there existed in England an aristocratic class interested in hearing history, romance, and hagiography recited in French and, indeed, in owning books in French. The Yorkshire baron Walter Espec, one of the great exponents of Norman pride, thought that 'reading history or listening to the recital of the deeds of our ancestors' were appropriate pas-times for an elderly aristocrat.[52] Constance, wife of Ralph fitz Gilbert, a Lin-colnshire landowner, commissioned Gaimar's *History of the English* (*Estoire des Engleis*), owned a French Life of king Henry I, and was also a borrower of Latin texts, while Gilbert fitz Baderon, lord of Monmouth, who died around 1191, had 'many books in Latin and French in his castle'.[53]

The claim that French literature was invented in England is a little extreme, but only a little. A remarkably large and diverse body of writing in French emerged from the Anglo-Norman world in a period when French literary composition was only beginning in continental France. The earliest manuscript of the great French epic, the *Song of Roland*, is English. Henry I's court was an early focus of literary composition in French. Benedict's *Voyage of St Brendan* was dedicated in succession to Henry I's wives Matilda and Adeliza, Philip de Thaon's *Bestiary* to Adeliza and, many years later, to Eleanor of Aquitaine, while another work of Philip's, *The Computus* (*Li cumpoz*), a calendrical guide which has been called the earliest technical trea-tise in French, was addressed to Philip's uncle Humphrey de Thaon, chap-lain of the high court official Eudo Dapifer (d. 1120). In the following generations historical writing, such as Gaimar's and Jordan Fantosme's *Chronicle*, translations of parts of the Bible, and a spate of saints' lives and romances show the continued liveliness of French literary activity in England.

The French language was thus used in England for a wide variety of types of writing. Sometimes a single author was versatile in different genres, like the poet Denis Piramus, who, at some time during the reign of Henry II, com-posed 4,000 lines in French about St Edmund, king and martyr, the saint

---

[52] Ailr. Riev., *Rel. de Standardo*, p. 185.
[53] Gaimar, lines 6428–52, 6487–92, pp. 203–5; Hue, *Proth.*, lines 12708–10, 2, p. 174.

whose bones were enshrined at Bury St Edmunds. 'I am called Denis Piramus,' he announces, 'and the joyful days of my youth are gone. I am drawing
towards old age and it is right that I should repent.' As part of his penance he
turned his poetical skills to religious ends, for, as he says, his earlier poetical
themes had been more worldly:

I have spent my life as a sinner in a very foolish way; I have spent my life in sin and
folly. When I frequented the court with the courtiers, I made *sirventes*, *chansons*, *rimes*
and *saluts* [types of secular lyric], among the lovers and their mistresses.

Denis's *Life of St Edmund* was written for the monks of Bury, some of whom
were certainly speakers of French, either as mother tongue or acquired language. His skills as a poet seem to have transferred smoothly from the world
of the court and courtly love to that of monastic devotion to the saints.[54]

One French writer who can be assigned to a particular time and place with
unusual exactness is Hue de Rotelande, author of two romances, *Ipomedon*
and *Protheselaus*.[55] The former, which is the earlier, mentions the siege of
Rouen by Louis VII in 1174, and hence must be later than that date, while the
latter is dedicated to Gilbert fitz Baderon of Monmouth, just mentioned,
who was dead by 1191. The composition of the two works can thus be
assigned to the period 1175–90. Hue himself tells us where he lives, in the
envoi to the *Ipomedon*:

> At Credenhill in my house
> I have a charter of absolution.
> If there is any lady or maiden
> Or rich widow or young woman
> Who does not believe that I have it,
> Come there, I will show it to her.
> Before she returns from there
> The charter will be registered for her
> And it will not be too great a wrong
> If the seal hangs from her behind.[56]

Apart from the obscure sexual reference, wholly in keeping with the poem,
which has passages of remarkable obscenity, we learn here that Hue lived in
Credenhill, about four miles north-west of Hereford.

*Ipomedon* is a romance of about 10,000 lines, written in octosyllabic coup-
lets, dealing with the military and amorous adventures of Ipomedon, prince
of Apulia, a wholly imaginary figure needless to say. He falls in love with La
Fiere ('the Proud Lady'), princess of Calabria, distinguishes himself at a
great three-day tournament and marries La Fiere after saving her from a

---

[54] Denis Piramus. *La Vie seint Edmund le rey*, lines 1–8, 16–19 (*Mem. Edm.* 2, p. 137).
[55] Hue, *Ipom.*; *Proth.*     [56] Hue, *Ipom.*, lines 10571–80, p. 517.

pagan Indian prince. On the way the plot takes a hundred turns and by-ways, including episodes where Ipomedon disguises himself as a fool, participates in numerous wars, and comes across his long-lost half-brother.

Much of the action is concerned with military combat, either in earnest or in the dangerous play of the tournament and the amount of space devoted to these topics and the detailed technical language used in their description suggest an audience of connoisseurs. In the following passage Ipomedon, disguised in armour all of white, confronts Antenor, duke of Spain, in the tournament:

Duke Antenor comes towards him, like a man afraid of nothing. He has a scarlet pennon fastened to his lance by a ribbon. He covers himself with his shield and points his lance. . . . Ipomedon sees him coming, shows not the slightest trace of flinching, spurs his war-horse, lowers his lance and rushes headlong towards him. They throw themselves on each other with fury as their shields clash. . . . Duke Antenor was valorous, bold and proud. . . . He struck him on the shield, hit it below the boss and his lance passed through, pennant and all, breaking off many links from his fine coat of mail. The sharp steel glanced just by his breast but it did not touch his body. Great was the blow he gave; the lance flew into splinters.[57]

Then follows a description of Ipomedon's devastating counter-stroke, that unhorses the duke. These long and literally blow-by-blow accounts of the joust are marked by vigorous action and simple but vivid description. The vocabulary of military equipment is precise: in the passage just cited, Ipomedon's horse is termed a *destrer*, that is, the 'destrier' or heavy war-horse, and the mail coat is a *hauberc jazerant*, literally 'a mail-coat of Algiers'—*jazerant* is from the Arabic *ǧazā'irī*, 'Algiers' (perhaps because that city was famous for the quality of its mail) and was a common epithet for mail-coats in medieval French literature.[58] Each stage of the physical conflict is described with attention. Here are the interests and activities of a military aristocracy seen through the dramatizing and idealizing lens of literature.

Next in importance to this absorption in the violent physical combats of male aristocrats is the theme of romantic love. In *Ipomedon* this love is the conventional courtly love (*amur fine*) of twelfth-century literature, an extreme and aristocratic sentiment often expressed in terms of psychological turmoil. Hue de Rotelande emphasizes the agitation and pain of love. In describing the feelings of Ismeine, a friend of La Fiere who has fallen in love with Ipomedon, even though he is in disguise as a fool, he writes:

Time and again she thinks, time and again she turns; she gets ready to rise from her bed. She rises, sweet and beautiful, and puts on her cloak. She reflects much before she rises; time and again she rises, time and again she sits. 'O God,' she says, 'I am so

---

[57] Hue, *Ipom.*, lines 3635–64, pp. 228–9.
[58] Tobler-Lommatzsch, *Altfranzosisches Worterbuch* 4 (Berlin, 1960), cols. 1608–9; Walther von Wartburg, *Französisches etymologisches Worterbuch* 19 (Basel, 1967), pp. 56–7.

mad, like a fool who has studied in a school of fools. Folly is my master, I am a fool, as a fool I throw myself at this fool . . .'[59]

At the conclusion of the poem Hue sums up his theme:

Hue de Rotelande tells and shows you in this writing that no-one from that time, neither knight nor lettered clerk, loved like Ipomedon . . . the god of love commands you to love faithfully, without guile or falsehood . . .[60]

There is enough facetiousness and coarseness in the poem to make it possible to see irony here, but that, of course, must always be in the eye of the beholder. Given its length, a recitation of the whole poem might take six or seven hours and can thus be imagined as giving entertainment in a baronial hall for three or four successive nights. The cadences of Norman-French romance were quite at home in the Welsh Marches.

### Written Latin

By far the largest body of written material produced in the period covered here was in Latin. This is true of literary works as well as documentary and religious material, for Latin was a living language of story-telling, love poetry, and satire as well as the official medium of education, law, and the Church. The great best-seller, Geoffrey of Monmouth's Latin *History of the Kings of Britain*, survives in two hundred medieval manuscripts—the whole body of works produced in English and French during our period is contained in fewer. Latin texts had a freedom in time and space that the vernaculars lacked. A good library might contain poems written in Rome in the first century BC, doctrinal works from fourth-century Africa, and the latest productions of Paris theologians, all in a linguistic standard comprehensible to anyone with a good Latin education. This inherited, and continually augmented, store of Latin literature stimulated response, criticism, and imitation. Learned men of the period were in dialogue with those of the ancient world and the Christian past as well as with each other.

Latin was the language of writing in both secular and ecclesiastical government. Charters, writs, letters, accounts, and surveys would all be in Latin. Such material was produced and used by a body of clerks literate in Latin. They were also required to translate it into a language accessible to the majority of the population. There were cases when a writ would turn up and no one would be able to read it, as happened in the court of the Oxfordshire knight Alan fitz Roland in 1198, when a writ of the chief justiciar, Hubert Walter, was delivered but 'there was no clerk there at the time to read it' and one had to be sent for.[61] Most of the time, however, the transmission of

---

[59] Hue, *Ipom.*, lines 9117–26, pp. 458–9.
[60] Ibid., lines 10553–64, p. 516.  [61] *CRR* i, p. 46.

instructions phrased in the learned language to the ordinary vernaculars seems to have taken place efficiently.

Epistolary communication was also in Latin and every great man needed clerks to draft his letters and perhaps to read out incoming correspondence. Some of these letters were of enduring interest either for their content or their style and were formed into letter collections. The Becket controversy generated an enormous number of polemical letters and hundreds of these were assembled into a collection by Alan of Tewkesbury, a Canterbury monk, a few years after the archbishop's death. In its earliest form the collection had 535 texts. A generation or so later these were used to create a composite 'Life and Letters', a biography of Becket with the correspondence inserted at appropriate points in the narrative.[62] Becket's clerk and adviser, John of Salisbury, made two collections of his own letters. The first, containing 135 items, dates to his years in the service of Becket's predecessor, archbishop Theobald, and many of the letters were composed by John in Theobald's name. The later collection deals with the Becket years and consists of almost 200 letters.[63]

Another man proud of his Latin letters was Peter of Blois, archdeacon of Bath (and later of London). He put together a collection of a hundred or so letters in the 1180s, claiming that he did so at the command of the king, Henry II: 'You asked me to collect the letters that I had sent at different times to various people and to assemble this diverse material in one fascicle.'[64] Peter's letters are not focused on one major issue, like the Becket collections, but they serve to illustrate style and contain moral advice and general reflections. There are letters of advice, exhortation, warning, occasionally of encouragement or commiseration. A few concern political issues or are written to or on behalf of princes and prelates, but others are to family or friends. They are highly rhetorical, filled with both biblical and classical allusions, and are pervaded with the flavour of the lively, learned, and often prickly world of educated Anglo-French clerks. They were also a great literary success. Peter revised and reissued them at least once and possibly twice, and they survive in some 200 manuscript copies.

Latin was thus the normal medium of formal written communication. It was also the language of liturgy. The texts to be found in the thousands of service books possessed by churches great and small were in Latin. Moreover, almost all works of law, theology, or natural science and the vast majority of histories, saints' lives, and sermons were also written in Latin. Indeed, the

[62] A. Duggan, *Thomas Becket: A Textual History of his Letters* (Oxford, 1980).

[63] J. Salisb., *Letters*.

[64] P. Blois, *Letters*, no. 1 (col. 1); Lena Wahlgren, *The Letter Collections of Peter of Blois* (Gothenburg, 1993).

richness and diversity of the Latin literature produced in England in this period gives it a claim to be the greatest epoch of English Latin. Many authors were eloquent in several genres. John of Salisbury's output included, alongside the hundreds of letters just mentioned, the *Metalogicon*, which surveys the contemporary intellectual scene and weighs the relative merits of literary and logical studies, the *Policraticus*, a blend of political theory and moral satire on the vices of court life, and a long philosophical poem, the *Entheticus*, as well as a history of events at the papal court and lives of archbishops Anselm and Becket. The surviving works of Gerald of Wales number sixteen, excluding letters, poems, and short pieces, and range from a description of the natural history and customs of Ireland to a long account of his own attempts to become archbishop of St David's.

A remarkable example of the fresh, current Latin of the twelfth century is provided by Walter Map's *Courtiers' Trifles*. This is an assemblage of anecdotes, legends, and sometimes barbed comments on contemporary life, especially the court and the monks. Such light and miscellaneous literature was popular in Angevin royal circles—Henry II's son, Henry 'the Young King', had requested a 'book of amusing tales' (*liber facetiarum*) from Gervase of Tilbury, a clerical raconteur of much the same stamp as Map.[65] *Courtiers' Trifles* makes up in vivacity for what it lacks in organization. The first section of the book contains a comparison of the court with hell, complaints on the difficulties of running a household, a story about king Herla, supposed leader of the Wild Hunt that roams endlessly through the world, a piece of gossip about the Portuguese court, a long survey of the monastic orders, an account of the interview of pope Alexander III with the Waldensian heretics, and concludes with a story told to Map by a Neapolitan nobleman about three hermits living in the wild woods. Although it is a rag-bag, Map's book is never dull. Its versatile and colourful language is a perfect example of the everyday clerical Latin of educated, but non-academic, culture in the twelfth century.

### The Interplay of Languages

The coexistence of three languages, in spoken and written form, led to continual linguistic interaction and exchange. There were many who could speak, read, and write more than one language. Alexander, prior of Ely in the 1150s, was described as 'eloquent in the Latin, French and English languages', and abbot Samson of Bury was 'eloquent in French and Latin' as well as in his own English dialect.[66] Gilbert Foliot (d. 1187), successively abbot of Gloucester, bishop of Hereford, and bishop of London, was praised

---

[65] Gerv. Tilb., pref., p. 883.     [66] *Lib. Eliensis* 3. 64 (p. 316); Joc. Brak., p. 40.

as 'a man most accomplished in the three languages, Latin, French and English, and eloquent and clear in each of them'.[67]

Not everyone, of course, was trilingually fluent. Those who were not often depended on the services of those who were. Interpreters and translators were indispensable guides in the elaborate linguistic landscape of twelfth-century England. In 1106 an inquiry was held into the rights and privileges of the church of York. Five royal justices presided, all of them of French birth or ancestry. They convened the county court and charged the twelve heredi-tary 'lawmen' of York, the local wise men, to make a true statement of the Church's customs. The lawmen, with one exception, bore Anglo-Scandinavian names. The linguistic gap between the Norman judges and the York assembly was bridged by Ansketel of Bulmer, reeve of the North Riding, who served as interpreter.[68] Here, forty years after the Norman Conquest, royal justices and the leaders of the local community could still not speak to each other directly. The role of an interpreter like Ansketel was vital.

The new Norman bishops and abbots appointed after the Conquest found they had subordinates and subjects who spoke an alien tongue and took meas-ures to deal with that linguistic gap. The abbots of Ramsey, for instance, retained an interpreter in their entourage in the first half of the twelfth cen-tury. Indeed, it seems as if the position was hereditary, for Hugh the inter-preter was followed by his son Gocelin the interpreter, and it is not likely at this date that this simply represents an inherited surname. Gocelin is styled both 'interpreter' in Latin (*interpres*) and 'latimer' in French (*le Latimer*) and it is probable that his task involved triliniguality. The surname Latimer goes back to this period when someone was often needed as a simultaneous trans-lator to and from Latin—a 'latiner'.[69]

A similar kind of linguistic aid was offered by the numerous glossaries or glossed texts from this period. Word-lists of terms in the different languages had an obvious function for learning and reference. An Anglo-Norman glossary of Old English legal terms is attributed to Alexander, archdeacon of Salisbury, later bishop of Lincoln (1123–48).[70] This gives the technical terms of Old English law with simple French explanations:

| | |
|---|---|
| *Ferdwite* | 'Fine for failing to go on a military expedition' |
| *Hamsokne* | 'Fine for forcible entry' · |
| *Infangenðef* | 'Thief caught on your land' |

Some glossaries are trilingual. One, in a manuscript of the second half of the

---

[67] Map 1. 13 (p. 36).    [68] Van Caen., *Lawsuits* 1, p. 139, no. 172.

[69] *Ramsey Chron.* pp. 236, 245, 253, 260, 295; *Ramsey Cart.* 1, pp. 129, 137, 253, nos. 40, 57, 187; 2, p. 259, no. 370.

[70] HMC, *Ninth Report* (London, 1883), appendix, p. 60.

twelfth century from Peterborough, deals with the names of animals.[71] The following entry is characteristic. It gives two alternative Latin terms for horse (one a pure Ciceronian form, the other absorbed from Celtic), then the English ('horse or steed'), followed by the French terms for three different types of horse (destrier or war-horse, palfrey, rouncey):

*equus sive caballus: 'hors' scilicet 'stede' id est destrer aut palefrei aut runci*

Such tools are simple but glossing could be carried to a high state, as exemplified most notably in the Eadwine Psalter. This huge Psalter, produced at Canterbury in the middle decades of the twelfth century, contains three variant Latin texts of the Psalms in parallel columns, each of them with a gloss. One gloss comprises a Latin explanatory commentary, the two other are interlinear translations, into Old English and French, although the Old English apparently shows signs of having been copied by a scribe who was not fully conversant with that language. It is a telling monument to the hierarchy of languages in an age of particular linguistic complexity.[72]

The multilingual cultural world of twelfth-century England naturally witnessed the active borrowing of vocabulary from one language into another. The most striking long-term result was an enormous infusion of Romance words into English. This was a process that continued long beyond the period covered in this book, but we can see its early phases then. Already the *Peterborough Chronicle* has a smattering of words borrowed from French, some of them of major significance, like 'war', 'peace', 'justice', 'court', and 'treasure'. It is not accidental that these words are all nouns, because these are the elements that pass most easily from one language to another; more than 70 per cent of English borrowing from Romance is of nouns.[73]

The word 'homage', for example, referring to the ceremony by which one free man became the vassal of another, has a complex trilingual life. Its ultimate root is the Latin *homo*, meaning 'man' (for a vassal was the 'man' of another), and from this a late Latin abstract noun *hominaticum* seems to have developed. By the twelfth century this had produced a French word *homage*—in Hue de Rotelande's *Ipomedon* the hero 'received the homages' (*les homages*) of his new subjects when he became king.[74] French *homage* in turn generated a new Latin term *homagium*, that was used not only by educated foreign ecclesiastics like Anselm but also in twelfth-century English law-books such as the *Laws of Henry I* and Glanville and by twelfth-century

[71] BL Stowe 57, fos. 155ᵛ–165; Tony Hunt, *Teaching and Learning Latin in Thirteenth-Century England* (3 vols.; Cambridge, 1991), vol. 1, pp. 22–3.

[72] M. R. James, *The Canterbury Psalter* (London, 1935) (facsimile); Margaret Gibson *et al.* (eds.), *The Eadwine Psalter: Text, Image, and Monastic Culture in Twelfth-Century Canterbury* (London, 1992).

[73] *The Cambridge History of the English Language* 2, ed. Norman Blake (Cambridge, 1992), pp. 429, 431.

[74] Hue, *Ipom.*, line 7217, p. 381.

Latin chroniclers writing in England. It can be found in Latin charters of the reign of Henry I.[75] It was a naturalized piece of the Latin used in England.

Alongside *homagium*, however, there existed a word of purely Germanic descent meaning exactly the same thing: this was *manræden* (from 'man', just like 'homage' itself). It occurs in Old English before the Conquest and is used in the *Peterborough Chronicle*, where, for instance, it is recorded how in 1115–16 Henry I 'had all the chief men of Normandy do homage [*dydon manræden*] to his son'. The word can be found in Layamon around 1200, but in the thirteenth century was replaced in English by the French loan word 'homage'. The existence of a technical feudal term in each of the three main languages of twelfth-century England shows the linguistic flexibility of this complex society: baron, clerk, and freeholder could each name this important ritual in their own words. The eventual disappearance of the Germanic terms and its replacement by a Romance/Latin one is entirely characteristic of the long-term linguistic trend.

Like 'homage', 'jail' was a word that spanned the languages. The classical Latin *cavea*, which meant a cavity or a cage, had produced the diminutive *caveola*, which had then been worn down in French to *gaiole*. Hue de Rotelande uses the word when describing characters 'thrown into jail' (*en la gaole*).[76] In the twelfth century the word was 'latinized', first occurring in Latin in English sources from the 1150s, in forms such as *gaiola* or *gaolia*. As might be expected, given the scarcity of written sources in English, its first English appearance was not until late in the thirteenth century—*in helle is a deop gayhol* ('in hell is a deep jail').[77] Words like 'homage' and 'jail' show the lexical common ground that existed between the three languages of twelfth-century England, a common ground that made it relatively easy for words to become naturalized in a language other than the one in which they had arisen.

It was not only individual words that migrated from one language to another. Whole literary texts were translated, taking on the characteristics of the new idiom in the process. There was passage both from vernacular to Latin and from Latin to vernacular. Saints' lives were translated from Latin into French. Clemence of Barking's *Life of St Katherine* and the anonymous nun of Barking's *Life of Edward the Confessor* are two examples that we happen to know were the work of nuns from the great Benedictine nunnery east of London. Hagiographic texts were also adapted from Old English into Latin. William of Malmesbury's Latin version of Coleman's *Life of St Wulfstan* is a noteworthy instance, since William's translation into the learned language survives, while the vernacular original has disappeared.

---

[75] Burton Cart., pp. 31, 33.     [76] Hue, *Proth.*, line 2650, I, p. 74.
[77] *Dict. Med. Latin*, p. 1044, s.v. 'gaiola'; 'The XI Pains of Hell', line 219, ed. Richard Morris, in *An Old English Miscellany* (EETS 49; 1872), p. 153.

The *Laws of Henry I* consist mainly of Latin versions of Old English law codes. There was also translation from one vernacular into another. Parts of Gaimar's *History of the English*, for example, comprise a French rendering of passages from the *Anglo-Saxon Chronicle*.

One of the more remarkable trilingual trajectories of the twelfth- and thirteenth-century literary world was that leading to Layamon's *Brut*. Geoffrey of Monmouth wrote his Latin *History of the Kings of Britain* in the 1130s, claiming to draw on 'a very old book in the British tongue' and launching King Arthur on his path to world fame. Very soon a French translation was produced by the Norman poet Wace. This *Romance of Brutus* (*Le Roman de Brut*)—so called from Brutus, supposed founder of Britain—was then used, some half-century or so later, by the Worcestershire priest Layamon as the basis of his own work. Layamon's *Brut* is the first telling of the story of King Arthur in English. It is also remarkable for its many echoes of Old English poetic style, especially its use of alliteration, and, most surprisingly, given its genesis, for the almost complete absence of words of French origin. We thus go from a pseudo-historical classic in Latin prose via a twelfth-century French verse adaptation to something that has been compared with *Beowulf* or the *Battle of Maldon*, the great heroic poems of Old English literature.

The remarkable linguistic complexity and cultural vivacity of England in this period can be summoned up by reflecting that Walter Map, author of the Latin miscellany *Courtiers' Trifles*, Hue de Rotelande, author of the French romances *Ipomedon* and *Protheselaus*, and Layamon, author of the English historical epic *Brut*, all lived within thirty miles of each other and wrote perhaps within a generation, certainly within two. At the end of the twelfth century the small rural world of Herefordshire and Worcestershire was thus producing a trilingual literature of substance and verve, in which Old English traditions, the new French romance, and the Latin of the clerks were all represented.

## 2. EDUCATION AND HIGH LEARNING

### Elementary Schools in England

The education of the literate began with the acquisition of Latin. This could be obtained from the local parish priest or some other cleric. Orderic Vitalis, the historian, learned to read and write between the ages of 5 and 10 under the instruction of Siward, priest of St Peter's, Shrewsbury.[78] More than thirty places are mentioned as having schools in the period covered here and,

---

[78] Orderic 13. 45 (6, p. 552).

although it is not always certain what their scope or level was, there is no doubt that elementary education was available in every region of England and even in some small places, like Yarm, on the Yorkshire bank of the Tees, where a clerk ran a school in the 1130s.[79] The comments of the Durham monk, Reginald, writing around 1170, show that the drone of boys learning Latin and the thwack of corporal punishment were everyday sounds. In Norham, he writes, 'there is an ancient church dedicated to St Cuthbert, in which, according to the custom now quite common and familiar, boys would at times devote themselves to study, stirred by the love of learning as well as sometimes driven by fear of the blows of the fierce schoolmaster.' One of the pupils was so intimidated by the prospect of these blows that he threw the key of the church door into the river Tweed.[80]

These parish schools probably depended very much on the interest and initiative of the individual priest or clerk. Rather more enduring were the schools attached to corporate religious foundations, such as the song schools and grammar schools of the cathedrals or schools like those of Huntingdon and Dunstable that were owned by local monasteries. A school could be a source of profit, a fact that itself demonstrates the existence of a demand for this kind of education, and contemporary records reveal competition over the right to run a school—between two clerks of the bishop of Winchester in that city or between the parson and the vicar of Ludlow.[81] In London, St Paul's had a near monopoly: the canons were instructed to excommunicate anyone 'who presumes to teach in the city of London without the permission of Henry, Master of the Schools, with the exception of those who run the schools of St Mary le Bow ['of the Arches'] and St Martin le Grand.'[82] The Master of the Schools was a cathedral canon with his own endowment and the keys of the cathedral book-cupboard.[83]

William fitz Stephen's account of the schools of London, written in 1173–4, confirms this situation, as well as giving a vivid description of the public display of Latin virtuosity that schoolboys and schoolmasters could undertake:

In London there are three principal churches that have famous schools as the ancient privilege of their rank, but there are also many schools that are allowed as a personal favour to teachers renowned for philosophy. On feast days the masters assemble in the churches to celebrate. The scholars debate. . . . The boys of the different schools

---

[79] Reg., *Libellus* 17 (p. 34).    [80] Reg., *Libellus* 73 (pp. 148–51).

[81] J. Salisb., *Letters* 56 (1, pp. 95–6); C. R. Cheney, *English Bishops' Chanceries, 1100–1250* (Manchester, 1950), pp. 157–8.

[82] *Early Charters St Paul's*, no. 275, p. 217; *EEA*, 8. *Winchester 1070–1204*, ed. M. J. Franklin (1993), no. 79, p. 55.

[83] *Early Charters St Paul's*, nos. 273–4, 276, pp. 215–19.

compete with each other in verse composition and contend concerning the principles
of the art of grammar or the rules of the past tense and the supine.[84]

Boys who had reached the dexterity in Latin suggested here were ready to
proceed to higher education. If they did so, they entered a world in the midst
of a great transformation.

## Higher Education

### Study Abroad

During the 150 years covered by this book, the structure of higher education
in western Europe underwent a deep and permanent change that put in place
many of the features we recognize today: universities, students, academics,
exams, degrees, graduates. In the forefront of these developments were the
great centres of Paris and Bologna, the former with a special reputation for
logic and theology, the latter famous for its legal studies, but there were many
lesser foci, including some in England. Because the European university
emerged from a long and gradual process of institutionalization rather than
being planned and executed in one self-conscious act, it has become customary to distinguish the twelfth-century centres of higher education in northern France and elsewhere prior to the crystallization of formal university
features in the first decades of the thirteenth century as 'the Schools'. Of
course, once people knew what a university was, it became possible to found
one, and this happened from the 1220s.

Boys who had learned their Latin and were willing and able to go on to
higher education received instruction in 'the arts', a term referring to the so-
called seven liberal arts, grouped into the *trivium* (grammar, rhetoric, and
logic) and *quadrivium* (arithmetic, geometry, music, astronomy). The former,
dealing with 'the power of language' rather than 'the secrets of Nature',[85] had
far greater prominence in the Schools. Logic eventually came to be the main
constituent of the arts course. Most students would go no further than this
stage, but ambitious, determined, and well-funded ones could proceed to the
higher studies of law, medicine, or theology. Theology was, by common consent, 'the queen of the sciences', though the attractions of law and medicine,
are clear from their nickname—'the lucrative sciences'.

The expansion of higher education in the twelfth century produced a class
of graduates ('Masters') seeking employment in the Church or in the service
of lay rulers. A schooling in the arts provided fluency in Latin, a patina of
culture, and familiarity with the rules of formal logical reasoning, while those
who had progressed to the study of law could offer knowledge of canon law

---

[84]   W. f. Stephen, *V. Thomas* 9 (pp. 4–5).
[85]   John of Salisbury, *Metalogicon* 1. 12, ed. C. C. J. Webb (Oxford, 1929), p. 30.

(the law of the Church) or Roman Law. By the year 1200 government and administration included many men trained in the Schools, who had gone through a common educational syllabus stressing Latin literacy, logic, and law. Everywhere these young graduates contributed to the dynamism and style of growing bureaucracies. The top ranks of the Church were increasingly occupied by such men—at the end of our period half of the canons of an important cathedral like Salisbury bore the title 'Master'.[86]

England's position in these developments was far from central, but neither was it unimportant. As well as producing two small indigenous universities at Oxford and Cambridge, it contributed disproportionately to the activity of the Schools overseas. From around 1100 English students poured into the Schools. Those at Bologna were not a negligible group. Peter of Blois and, perhaps, Baldwin, archbishop of Canterbury (1184–90), attended the school of Hubert Crivelli (later to be pope Urban III) in Bologna in the early 1150s.[87] Gilbert Foliot, bishop of London (1163–87), sent his nephew, Richard Foliot, to study at Bologna in the late 1160s, although he worried about his health there.[88] The letters of another English student at Bologna in those same years reveal some of the other uncertainties of university life: although Master David of London was a canon of St Paul's, London, he had recurrent financial problems and he vividly sketches his accumulating debts and vigilant creditors.[89] Bologna offered the best training in Roman and canon law, but northern France was the main destination for aspiring English clerks. Partly for geographical reasons but partly too because England's predominantly agrarian social structure and system of customary law had less use for Bolognese Roman Law, more bright students from England went to northern France, especially Paris, than to northern Italy. Indeed, they came to have a significant presence there. Some 38 per cent of the Masters at Paris in the period 1179–1215 whose origins are known came from England.[90]

Students and scholars from England were present in the schools of northern France throughout our period. At the beginning, in the reigns of William the Conqueror and his sons, it was simply a customary Norman habit. Roger of Salisbury, Henry I's chief minister, sent his nephews Nigel and Alexander to study in Laon, a school at the height of its reputation in the early twelfth century, and for Roger, who was originally from Caen in Normandy, the

---

[86] *Fasti*, 4. *Salisbury*, pp. xxxv–xxxvi, 139–41.

[87] E. Revell, *The Later Letters of Peter of Blois* (Auctores Britannici Medii Aevi 13; Oxford, 1993), no. 10, p. 56 and nn.

[88] Foliot, *Letters*, nos. 191–2, pp. 263–4.

[89] *Spicilegium Liberianum*, ed. F. Liverani (Florence, 1864), pp. 603–5; Z. N. Brooke, 'Master David of London and the Part He Played in the Becket Crisis', in H. W. C. Davis (ed.), *Essays in History Presented to R. L. Poole* (Oxford, 1927), pp. 27–45.

[90] Baldwin, *Masters*, 1, p. 149.

choice of a northern French school was entirely natural.[91] Nigel went on to become royal treasurer (1126–33) and bishop of Ely (1133–69), and, though it can only be a matter of speculation how his theological training as a young man influenced his later administrative and episcopal career, we have here nevertheless the important new phenomenon of a twelfth-century Fenland diocese being governed by a man with French scholarly training. Bishops with such a background were to become increasingly common.

The roll-call of those from England who studied in Paris or other centres in northern France is long and ranges from such notable figures as Robert of Courson, a Paris master of theology who ended up as a cardinal and enacted the first statutes for the nascent University of Paris in 1215, through middle-ranking ecclesiastics like Walter Map, a student in the 1150s and subsequently archdeacon of Oxford and author of the *Courtiers' Trifles* mentioned above, to obscure figures like Gervase, a cleric of Durham, who 'went to Paris to acquire secular or scholastic learning' and spent several years there in the 1170s or 1180s.[92] The first Parisian college, the Collège de Dix-huit, was founded, in the year 1180, by an Englishman, Jocius of London.[93]

Sometimes it is possible to catch a glimpse of the young expatriate students in the streets and lodging-houses of Paris. Gerald of Wales was there at the time of birth of the future Philip II (21 August 1165) and tells how he was roused from his bed by the clanging of bells and the noise of people running through the streets with lighted candles. As he stuck his head out of his window, two old ladies were gambolling about in the square. Catching sight of Gerald, one of them called up, 'We now have a king given us by God and a powerful heir to the kingdom by God's gift, who will bring shame and destruction to your king.'[94] Twenty-eight years later another English student was sitting at his books in Paris, when he heard news of Philip's wars. He jotted in the margin of the manuscript he was studying (a commentary on the Psalms by the Paris theologian Peter the Chanter), 'Gisors was surrendered through treachery to Philip, the French king, in the year 1193.' We know he was English, because the jotting is written in English, and we know where he was because at some later point the anonymous student added a further note: 'I wrote this sitting at my books in Paris on the day Gisors was captured.'[95]

One of the more detailed first-hand accounts of the activities of an English student in the Schools of northern France is that written by John of Salisbury.[96] After receiving his grounding in Latin from a local priest, John went to

---

[91] Hermann, *Mir. Laud.* 2. 13 (col. 983).     [92] Reg., *V. Godric* 201 (pp. 452–3).

[93] *Chartularium Universitatis Parisiensis* 1, ed. H. Denifle (Paris, 1889), no. 50, pp. 49–50.

[94] Gerald, *Prin.* 3. 25 (pp. 292–3).

[95] N. R. Ker, *Catalogue of Manuscripts Containing Anglo-Saxon* (Oxford, 1957), p. 331, from BL Royal 10 C v.

[96] John of Salisbury, *Metalogicon* 2. 10, ed. C. C. J. Webb (Oxford, 1929), pp. 77–83.

Paris in 1136, probably in his late teens, and studied the rudiments of logic under one of the most famous teachers of the century, Peter Abelard. His instruction took place on the Mont Sainte-Geneviève, on the Left Bank, one of several centres of scholarly activity in and around Paris at this time. Almost two years were spent in studying logic under Abelard and two other masters, Alberic and the Englishman Robert of Melun (later bishop of Hereford). John then spent three years under William of Conches, a Norman scholar who was well known for his writings on natural science and who sometimes faced criticism as a materialist. John saw him, however, primarily as a grammarian. After this the chronology and location of John's studies is not absolutely certain, but there is no doubt that he studied or revised the *quadrivium* and rhetoric under various masters, himself took up teaching in order to have an income and then went on to pursue theology under Gilbert de la Porée, Robert Pullen (another English master), and Simon of Poissy. 'So', he says, 'I spent almost twelve years in study of various kinds.' In 1147, at the end of this period, he entered the service of the archbishop of Canterbury.

In his description of these years, John gives thoughtful characterizations of the abilities and limitations of the different scholars he encountered. Alberic 'was very exacting, finding a subject for enquiry everywhere, so that, however smooth the surface, he could see a flaw, and, in the words of the proverb, he would find a knot in a bulrush.' John described Robert of Melun as 'quick in his replies, never avoiding the issue in question, but willing to take up each side of a contradictory position or, after advancing many different arguments, to teach that there was no single answer.' If the questing mind of Alberic had been joined to the precision and clarity of Robert, then, John thought, there would be no disputant their equal—and it is significant that it is their qualities as disputants that John considers, for the logic that formed the foundation of the arts course made it second nature for these students and masters to think of scholarship and learning in terms of debate.

John's twelve years of study were not without financial difficulties, as he himself admits, but the investment paid off. After he was taken into the service of Theobald, archbishop of Canterbury in 1147, he continued to serve the archbishops, as adviser, emissary, and secretary, for the next three decades, picking up canonries at Salisbury and Exeter—though also having to share in Becket's long exile from England. Eventually, in 1176, John won the ultimate prize, appointment as bishop, returning to the land of his student years to hold the see of Chartres until his death in 1180. The training in logic and literature that John had acquired so laboriously bore fruit in official correspondence, eloquent advocacy at the papal court, and also in his own literary works (listed above, p. 502), major monuments of twelfth-century humanist scholarship.

John names eleven masters who taught him and five fields of study he pursued—logic, grammar, rhetoric, theology, and, 'to a certain extent', the *quadrivium*. There were few places in the Catholic world where such a diversity of instruction was available. Paris, the thriving capital of the Capetian monarchs, was by the 1130s beginning to be also the intellectual capital of north-west Europe. Yet, especially by the latter part of the twelfth century, it was not absolutely necessary to go abroad to obtain higher education. England had several centres where teenage clerics could advance beyond elementary Latin.

## The Emergence of English Universities

Around 1200 Alexander, prior of Canon's Ashby, looked back on the changes in education since his own childhood. 'When I was a schoolboy,' he remarked, 'you could scarcely find any teacher who was not driven by ambition to earn money by teaching. But now, by the grace of God, there are many who teach for free . . .' He singled out masters at Northampton, Oxford, and Exeter for special mention.[97] It is not clear what level of instruction Alexander is referring to, but the towns in his list are known, from other evidence, to have been centres of advanced teaching. The royal accounts reveal that a clerk of the king's daughter, Eleanor, was being supported 'in the schools at Northampton' for five years in the later 1170s, at a cost of two shillings per week. He was obviously not engaged in elementary studies.[98] A reference from the last quarter of the twelfth century shows that Northampton had a reputation for the study of liberal arts and natural philosophy.[99] The availability of legal education at Exeter is attested by the fact that, before he became a monk at Evesham in 1200, Thomas of Marlborough taught canon and Roman law at Exeter and Oxford.[100]

Other centres could be added to the list. The existence of 'Master Ralph, canon of London and a distinguished teacher of theology'[101] suggests that theology was being taught in London during the reign of Henry II. Lincoln had a particularly prominent place. William de Montibus (d. 1213), a Lincoln man, taught theology at Paris in the 1170s before returning to his native city, where he continued to give instruction and attract scholars, such as Gerald of Wales, who spent several years at Lincoln in the 1190s, composing theological and hagiographical works. Lincoln continued to be a centre of higher study after William's death. In 1221 Master John of Berwick was given permission to absent himself from his church of Molesworth (Hunts.) for two

---

[97] Alex. Ashby, *De modo pred.*, p. 922.
[98] PR 22 HII, p. 47; PR 23 HII, p. 89: PR 24 HII, p. 49; PR 25 HII, p. 61; PR 26 HII, p. 81; PR 27 HII, p. 67.
[99] D. Morley 1. 3 (p. 212).
[100] *Chronicon abbatiae de Evesham*, ed. W. D. Macray (RS· 1863), p. 267.
[101] W. f. Stephen, *V. Thomas* 144 (p. 143); *Fasti*, 1. *St Paul's, London*, p. 49.

years to attend the schools of Lincoln.[102] Since he already had the title Master, he must have completed the initial stages of his higher education before he went to Lincoln.

By the later twelfth century it was clear that Oxford was emerging as the most important of the English schools. It drew scholars from other parts of the country, like the young Yorkshire clerk Stephen, 'at Oxford for the sake of his studies' around the year 1180.[103] In 1187 Gerald of Wales gave a public reading of his newly composed *Topography of Ireland* (*Topographia Hibernica*) in Oxford. He chose Oxford because 'that was the place in England where the clergy had flourished most'. He read the work on three successive days, entertaining different groups on each occasion, first the poor of the town, next 'all the teachers of different subjects and the students of greater reputation and standing', finally 'the remaining students, along with the knights of the town and many burgesses'.[104] Clearly by this time Oxford was a town with a substantial scholarly community.

Gerald names neither the teachers whom he feasted nor their subjects, but the picture of academic activity at Oxford emerges more clearly in the decades after he gave his reading. In the period 1190–1209 the names of more than twenty teachers of arts and ten or so teachers of the higher studies of law and theology are known.[105] Masters John of Tynemouth, Simon of Sywell, and Honorius are known to have taught law at Oxford in the 1190s.[106] The two former became canons of Lincoln, the diocese in which Oxford was situated. Already by this time the reputation of Oxford as a centre of legal study was wide enough to draw students from overseas. Two brothers from Frisia, Emo and Addo, studied law at Oxford in the 1190s, assiduously copying out the essential texts like the papal decretal collections and the *Poor Man's Book* (*Liber pauperum*), an introduction to Roman Law composed by Master Vacarius, an Italian lawyer who made his career in England.[107] It was from this work that the academic lawyers received their nickname of *pauperiste*.[108] Oxford offered theology as well as law. Alexander Nequam, who had studied at Paris, 'lectured publicly in theology' at Oxford in the 1190s, before he became an Augustinian canon in 1197.[109] Two Oxford theology teachers are

---

[102] *Rot. Hug. Welles* 3, p. 35.    [103] Philip, *Mir. Fridesw.* 51 (p. 579).

[104] Gerald, *De reb.* 2. 16 (pp. 72–3).

[105] *The History of the University of Oxford*, 1. *The Early Oxford Schools*, ed. J. I. Catto (Oxford, 1984), p. 37 n. 1.

[106] *Chronicon abbatiae de Evesham*, ed. W. D. Macray (RS; 1863), p. 126.

[107] *Emonis et Menkonis Chronica*, ed. L. Weiland, *MGH*, *Scriptores* 23 (Hanover, 1874), pp. 467, 524, 551; on Vacarius and the *Liber pauperum*, Francis De Zulueta and Peter Stein, *The Teaching of Roman Law in England around 1200* (Selden Soc.; 1990), pp. xxii–xxxvii.

[108] Gerald, *Spec. eccl.*, pref., ed. R. W. Hunt, 'The Preface to the *Speculum Ecclesiae* of Gerald of Wales', *Viator*, 8 (1977), p. 205.

[109] Hunt, *Nequam*, p. 8 and n. 36.

mentioned in a document of around 1202.[110] One of them is elsewhere termed 'master of the scholars of Oxford'.[111]

Oxford's shift from the informal structures characteristic of its first period of spontaneous growth to the officially regulated institution of the thirteenth century was stimulated by murder. In 1209 a student killed a woman and fled. His room-mates were arrested by the town authorities and hanged. In protest, almost the entire body of teachers and students left Oxford, some for Paris, some for Reading, some for Cambridge, where they formed the nucleus of England's second university. Because this incident occurred in the middle of the Interdict, it took some years to be finally settled and it was not until 1214 that an agreement was drawn up to regulate relations between the scholars and the town. This was issued under the aegis of the papal legate, Nicholas of Tusculum, and not only imposed penance on those responsible for the hangings and ordered the town to make an annual payment towards poor students, but also provided for more everyday matters, such as the level of student rents and the cost of food. Blackleg teachers who had continued to give lectures during the years 1209–14 were forbidden to teach for three years.[112]

The document setting out the legate's terms contains the first mention of a chancellor at Oxford. The distribution of the town payment to the poor students was to be arranged by the bishop, the archdeacon, the archdeacon's official, 'or the chancellor whom the bishop of Lincoln will put in charge of the scholars there'. This is an explicit indication that a more clearly defined organization was to be created for the teachers and students at Oxford—the earlier 'master of the scholars of Oxford' seems to have been either informal or ephemeral. The creation of the chancellorship was the first step towards corporate identity. By the end of our period both Oxford and Cambridge had come into existence as recognized and regulated centres of study. The chancellor of Cambridge is first mentioned in 1225.[113] Royal writs of 1231 give the chancellor and masters of both places the power to have disobedient clerks imprisoned, insist that every student should have an acknowledged teacher and require the townsmen to charge reasonable rents.[114] A new institution, the university, had come into being.

[110] *Eynsham Cartulary* 2, ed. H. E. Salter (Oxford Hist. Soc. 51; 1908), pp. 45–7.

[111] C. R. Cheney and Mary Cheney (eds.), *The Letters of Innocent III (1198–1216) Concerning England and Wales* (Oxford, 1967), no. 279, pp. 220–1.

[112] R. Wend. 2, p. 51 (Paris, *CM* 2, pp. 525–6); *Melrose Chron.*, p. 107; *Medieval Archives of the University of Oxford* 1, ed. H. E. Salter (Oxford Hist. Soc. 70; 1917), pp. 2–10.

[113] *CRR* 12, pp. 129–30.

[114] *Close Rolls of the Reign of Henry III: 1227–31* (London, 1902), pp. 586–7.

*Academic Society*

The expansion of higher education in the twelfth and thirteenth centuries meant that academic centres now housed relatively large numbers of teenage boys living away from home. Such groups had never previously existed except during the temporary emancipation of an armed expedition or in the discipline and enclosure of the monastery. It is understandable that 'student culture' came to mean rowdiness, drinking, and the pursuit of girls. When Burnel the Ass, the main character in the satirical fable written by Nigel, a monk of Canterbury, at the end of the twelfth century, comes to Paris to study, he decides to join the English students there:

Because he considered the English to be the most discerning, he decided to join with them. They are outstanding for their manners, elegant in speech and in appearance, strong in intelligence and wise in their advice. They pour gifts on the people, hate misers, multiply the courses at dinner and drink without limit. They have only three failings: 'Weisheil' and 'Drincheil' and 'Kind Lady' . . .[115]

'Weisheil' and 'Drincheil' were the traditional English toasts, evidently familiar even in the streets of Paris, thronged as they were by English students. Throughout the medieval period tavern-keepers and prostitutes could make a fair living in university towns.

Academic training created new social types and new forms of consciousness. In some ways they sat uneasily with the old. On the one hand, pragmatic administrators, who had worked out quite adequate ways of counting taxes or recording agreements in court and debts to the king, might find the learning of the fresh-faced graduates over-complex and abstruse. A man like Hubert Walter, archbishop of Canterbury, chief justiciar and Chancellor (d. 1205), was mocked for the clumsiness of his Latin by the Paris-trained clerk Gerald of Wales and the legal expert Martin, although he was perhaps the greatest administrator of the whole Norman and Angevin period.[116] On the other hand, the smart clerics with training in logic and law were also the objects of suspicion, envy, and distrust on the part of those who thought that the purpose of clerical training was the care of souls. Great monastic theologians like St Bernard attacked the fatuousness and self-centredness of the scholastic cleric, while a series of satirists and critics mocked the sterility and worldly ambition of the arts student.

The ideologies of asceticism, contemplation, and pastoral care were powerful. In the case of a scholar like Gerald of Wales, we can see how a highly educated man, with a love of literature almost as great as his regard for himself, and a Latin style of power and verve, was continually seeking to defend himself against the charges—generated within as well as from others—that

---

[115] Nigel, *Spec. Stult.*, lines 1515–21, pp. 64–5.     [116] Gerald, *Gemma* 2. 36 (p. 345).

he had neglected the true purpose of Christian learning. William de Montibus, the Lincoln theologian, was of the opinion that Gerald should write theological works, not histories and the like, that were unbecoming to his mature years.[117] Gerald was sensitive to the criticism, to such a degree that he passed it on to Walter Map. 'Your mouth,' he wrote, 'has been witty and eloquent in charming human ears; now let it be constant and fertile in divine praises.'[118] The steady flow of academics into monastic life shows that some took this advice literally and profoundly.

Yet, if men like Alexander Nequam abandoned his teaching career at Oxford to join the Augustinians of Cirencester, deeming 'the life of the cloistered' one step nearer heaven than 'the life of scholars', there were many who continued to enter the Schools.[119] For some, an academic training and the title of Master were steps on the ladder of advancement. Planning his course of studies, Burnel the Ass lets himself daydream of the final accolade: 'a title shall precede my name and I'll be "Master Burnel" in name and fact. If anyone forgets to call me "Master", he'll be my mortal enemy . . . the crowds will rush up shouting, "Here comes the Master!" '[120] Burnel's academic career was not a success, but the influx of men titled 'Master' into secular and ecclesiastical government in the later twelfth and thirteenth centuries shows that others achieved his goal.

The Church not only supervised and attempted to control the new academic world but was also willing to provide some funding for it. Alexander of Ashby has already been quoted on the increasing availability of free teaching in his own times. The statutes of the diocese of Salisbury issued around 1218 show that it was deemed desirable that an ecclesiastical benefice should be reserved for a Master to teach grammar to poor scholars free of charge.[121] Advanced study could also be supported financially from the revenues of an ecclesiastical benefice. Thus in 1218 Walter, the parson of Stoke in Oxfordshire, was permitted to attend the Schools 'overseas' and yet retain full control of his living.[122] The canons of St Paul's were allowed to draw forty shillings a year from the common funds, as well as their own prebendal income, while studying at the Schools for as long as three years.[123]

Education offered a few people a path to positions of power and wealth that was independent of inherited status. Henry II's chief justiciar, Ranulf de Glanville, was of the opinion that although well-born people (*generosi*) disdained to have their children learn their letters, serfs and peasants (*servi* and *rustici*) had their children educated in the liberal arts so that they might

[117] Gerald, *Spec. duorum*, p. 168.        [118] Gerald, *Symb. el.*, p. 284.
[119] Hunt, *Nequam*, p. 9 n. 43, citing Nequam's *Commentary on the Song of Songs* 2. 16.
[120] Nigel, *Spec. Stult.*, lines 1205–8, 1212, p. 58.        [121] *Councils and Synods* 2/i, p. 94.
[122] *Rot. Hug. Welles* 1, p. 108.        [123] R. Diceto, *Op.* 2, p. lxxi.

become rich.[124] Whatever the class bias so patent in this view, there is no doubt that education offered one limited avenue whereby the low born could attain positions of authority and power, and the wealth that went with them. In a world where ascribed status, the rank people were born to, was so crucial, here was a small area where achieved status, what they made of themselves, could be important.

## The Heritage of the Ancient World

The high learning of the twelfth century drew on two deep roots, classical and Christian. The classical authors most familiar in our period were the Latin poets and prose writers of the first century BC and the first century AD, such as Cicero, Sallust, Virgil, Horace, and Ovid. They were valued not only as stylistic models but also for their ethics and moral philosophy, even if pagan Roman sources sometimes required adaptation for an ecclesiastical audience. As the treatise on *Spiritual Friendship* (*De spiritali amicitia*) by Ailred of Rievaulx demonstrates, it was not impossible to marry Roman ethics and monastic theology. Ailred's work, while assuming that 'the purpose of value of friendship should be referred to Christ', is in the direct tradition of Cicero's own treatise *On Friendship* (*De amicitia*), which it cites or alludes to more than seventy times.[125]

Indeed, ancient Latin learning and Christianity had fused long before the twelfth century. In the fourth and fifth centuries, as the Roman Empire adopted the new religion, Latin authors schooled in rhetoric and philosophy had assimilated the scriptural doctrine of Judaeo-Christian revelation. The first great master of this new synthesis, Augustine, was the godfather of the Middle Ages and by far the most common author found in the libraries of England in the Norman and Angevin period. In his *Christian Learning* (*De doctrina christiana*) Augustine had set out the justification for Christians studying history, natural science, logic, and rhetoric: these things helped in the understanding of the revealed truths of Scripture. Moreover, pagan writers often contained 'teaching in the liberal arts of use to the truth and some very valuable moral precepts'. Just as the Children of Israel had taken precious items from the Egyptians as they left Egypt, so Christians could plunder pagan literature and learning for their own purposes.[126]

The debate on the proper attitude to ancient pagan learning was certainly not dead in the twelfth century. There were those who thought that 'it is not seemly for the same mouth to preach Christ and recite

---

[124] Map 1. 10 (p. 12).
[125] Ailr. Riev., *De spiritali amicitia* 1. 8 (*Op. asc.*, p. 290); citations listed in *Aelred of Rievaulx's Spiritual Friendship*, tr. Mark Williams (Scranton, Pa., 1994), pp. 130–1.
[126] Augustine, *De doctrina christiana* 2. 40 (*PL* 34, col. 63).

Ovid'.[127] William of Malmesbury, whose classical learning was immense, had to defend himself against the charge of 'reading and copying so many pagan books'. He argued that 'he who reads them because he despises divine scripture and finds it wearisome commits a grave sin and should be punished . . . but he who reads them in order to employ their ornament and eloquence to the glory of God and his saints in his own writings . . . has, I believe, sinned in no way by taking pleasure in pagan books.'[128] Later in the century Peter of Blois faced a similar charge of saying things 'that smacked more of the pagan philosopher than of one who professes the Christian faith'. Peter defended the use of ancient learning, and also Roman Law, by Christians. It was not absurd 'that statements of philosophy or Roman Law should be admitted as part of Christian learning . . . when you have healing herbs, you do not ask where they come from or which gardener grew them, as long as they have healing power'.[129] Early the next century Alexander of Ashby, in his treatise on preaching, still had to excuse his use of 'precepts of the pagans' concerning rhetoric by the old image of 'despoiling the Egyptians'.[130]

Perhaps one of the reasons that controversy over the ancient authors was so animated in this period was that their works were becoming increasingly familiar to educated clerics. Not only was there an enormous efflorescence of the texts of Roman Law and a wave of translations of ancient Greek science and philosophy, but texts of the already standard Latin poets and prose writers became far more common. In the decades around 1100 the canons of Salisbury acquired from overseas copies of works by Plautus, Cicero, and other Roman authors and had copies made.[131] During the course of the twelfth-century the library at Rochester cathedral priory obtained copies of Cicero, Sallust, Suetonius, Terence, Virgil, Ovid, Persius, and Lucan. The early twelfth-century collection at Rochester, that was dominated by the works of Augustine and other patristic writers, was thus supplemented by more diverse material, allowing a greater familiarity with classical authors for those who wanted it.[132] The multiplication of anthologies of classical passages and the development of classicizing literary styles are other signs of this expanding interest in the authors of pagan Rome.

## Biblical Scholarship

However important and alluring Cicero, Ovid, and Virgil might be, the beginning and the end of learning was the Bible. The foundations of Latin

[127] Herbert Losinga, ep. 28, ed. Robert Anstruther (London, 1846) p. 54; cf. ep. 32, pp. 65–7.
[128] Rodney Thomson, *William of Malmesbury* (Woodbridge, 1987), pp. 51–2, from Cambr. UL Dd. 13. 2, a copy of William's collection of the works of Cicero.
[129] P. Blois, *Letters*, no. 8 (cols. 22–4).       [130] Alex. Ashby, *De modo pred.*, p. 903.
[131] Teresa Webber, *Scribes and Scholars at Salisbury Cathedral c.1075–c.1125* (Oxford, 1992), pp. 63–5.
[132] *Engl. Ben. Libr.*, pp. 469–526.

literacy were laid through learning the Psalms by heart, while the branch of study that stood highest in esteem was theology, that is 'study of the holy page'. Novices and experts alike pondered the text of scripture. It was an activity that led in myriad directions. Fully to grasp the meaning of the Bible required a knowledge of languages, rhetoric, history, science, and more. It was a text so huge, varied in genre, and miscellaneous in origin that exploring it became a branch of study in itself.

There were very few who could study scripture in the original languages. It is perhaps, at first sight, surprising that knowledge of Hebrew was easier to acquire than knowledge of Greek, but the existence of the Jewish community that had arrived with the Norman Conquest meant that all moderately sized towns had Hebrew texts and people who understood them. Hence a tiny number of enthusiasts were able to undertake serious Hebrew study. Maurice, prior of Kirkham, spent three years studying Hebrew as a young man, and copied out forty Psalms with his own hand from a Hebrew Psalter that had been owned by Gerard, archbishop of York (1100–1108).[133] His contemporary, Herbert of Bosham, friend and biographer of Thomas Becket, showed some knowledge of Hebrew in his commentary on Jerome's translation of the Hebrew Psalter.

For most students, however, the Bible meant the Latin Bible in the Vulgate translation of St Jerome. This was studied increasingly systematically. In the early twelfth century, scholars in northern France put together the Ordinary Gloss, a huge assemblage of passages commenting on every part of the Bible. This Gloss was often to be found as an accessory in Bible texts of the period, entered in the margins or, in the case of short passages, between the lines. Theologians like William de Montibus produced lists of biblical terms, arranged alphabetically. The present division of the books of the Bible into chapters, which provides a simple and universally recognized system of reference, was introduced by Stephen Langton, teacher at Paris and subsequently archbishop of Canterbury (1206–28).[134]

The traditional and common technique of biblical study was based on analysis of four senses of scripture. The first was the historical or literal—the Bible story of the Chosen People and the life of Jesus. The other three senses were all symbolic, in different ways. The tropological dealt with the moral lesson that might be learned; the allegorical with the symbolic meaning as far as it concerned the Church and its members here and now; anagogical with the symbolic meaning as far as it concerned God and the Last Things. Thus when the word 'Jerusalem' occurs in the Bible it could mean, according to the

---

[133] R. B. Dobson, *The Jews of Medieval York and the Massacre of March 1190* (Borthwick Papers 45; 1974), p. 4 n. 13.
[134] Beryl Smalley, *The Study of the Bible in the Middle Ages* (Oxford, 1952), pp. 222–4.

four different senses, (1) the city in Judaea; (2) the soul; (3) the Church Militant on earth; (4) the Church Triumphant in heaven.[135]

The method gave endless scope: 'a symbolic interpretation can be based on any property of any thing, whatever it may be, that can be applied either to the soul and its conduct, or to the head and members of the Church at present, or to God and heavenly things'. Rachel and Leah represent the contemplative and the active life; the angel sitting on the tomb of the risen Christ whose 'countenance was like lightning and his raiment white as snow' signifies that Christ's first coming was gentle but his second will be a terrible judgement; the fact that the priest Eli chastised his sons lightly indicates 'that prelates who do not correct those subject to them in a proper way will be punished'. The etymologies of words were significant, numerological patterns needed to be teased out, the habits of animals and other creatures could be brought into the system—the lion signifies fortitude, winter the frost of unbelief.

Biblical study epitomizes the book-based, moralistic culture of the time. Wisdom was to be sought by immersion in a text and that text could be elucidated by drawing on other texts. The world itself was a book, which could be read by those skilled in symbolic interpretation. It was a book with a lesson and that lesson was how to live. Written text, physical universe, and human behaviour were interlinked.

## Physical Science

One of the most important intellectual developments of the period was the influx of texts and techniques from the Islamic world. In the early Middle Ages the Islamic world was larger, richer, and more educated than the Christian world. When, in the period we are discussing, the West had advanced far enough to learn from it, that Islamic scholarship poured into Latin Christendom. The use of the astrolabe to measure the angular height of planets and stars, the compilation of astronomical tables, the revival of astrology, the introduction of so-called 'Arabic numerals'—all testify to the stream of scientific knowledge flowing into Christendom from Islam at this time. The traces are still visible in the initial syllable, the *al* ('the' in Arabic), found in the names of some mathematical disciplines and the very stars themselves. Algebra and Aldebaran pay homage to the Islamic bequest to western science.

The Islamic world was not only a direct source of scientific and philosophical learning but also a conduit for the science and natural philosophy of the ancient Greeks. Indeed, one of the most important intellectual developments of the twelfth and thirteenth centuries was the acquisition by the scholars of

---

[135] T. Chobham, *SP*, pp. 4–11, gives a clear summary of traditional techniques of exegesis; examples and quotations in the following paragraph are drawn from this source.

Latin Christendom of the corpus of ancient Greek science and philosophy, supplemented by the work of the Arabic masters who had studied and commented upon it. The first task was one of translation. In the twelfth century, most of the ancient material was translated not directly from the Greek, but from Arabic versions. Many parts of the Mediterranean world had the necessary bi- or tri-lingualism that made such activity possible, but Spain, with its large and literate populations of Jews, Muslims, and Arabic-speaking Christians, increasingly under Catholic rule, formed an especially favourable habitat for the transmission of Greco-Arabic learning.

English scholars who were interested in science and natural philosophy recognized the potential of the Spanish cultural environment. One of them was the Norfolk man, Daniel of Morley. He wrote scathingly of the 'infantile' scholars of Paris who devoted themselves to minute annotations of the Roman Law texts and contrasted this sterile world with the enticing vistas of Spain: 'Since the learning of the Arabs, that consists almost entirely in the *quadrivium* (scientific subjects), was celebrated at that time especially in Toledo, I hastened there to learn from the world's wiser philosophers.'[136] On his return to England, 'with a valuable load of books', he enjoyed the patronage of John, bishop of Norwich (1175–1200).

The work that Daniel of Morley composed on his return home brought some of 'the learning of the Arabs' to the Schools of England. His book, *The Nature of Earthly and Heavenly Bodies* (*Liber de naturis inferiorum et superiorum*), deals with the composition of the physical elements and the character of the stars and planets. He surveys the theories of the ancient Greek scientists: Thales held that the principle of all things was water, Heraclitus that everything was made of fire, Epicurus that the universe consisted of atoms and void. Daniel, following the main tradition in ancient and medieval physics, explains that the world is made up of four elements, earth, air, fire, and water. Each of these is constituted by blending the four qualities—hot and cold, dry and wet. Above the moon are the heavens, a finite but unchanging space in perpetual rotation.

Much of Daniel's science consists of theoretical deduction. Since the stars are not composed of different elements, he argues, they cannot have a colour, since it is axiomatic that 'every colour derives from the four qualities'. Hence the apparent coloration of the stars, including the planets, which were regarded as stars, has to be explained away. Vapours rising from the earth deceive the human eye, giving the impression that stars and planets have colour. Such illusions, points out Daniel, are common: a stick placed in water will appear to be bent; a white object casts a black shadow but is not itself black. None of this argumentation is based on conclusions drawn from

[136] D. Morley 1. pref. (p. 212).

observation of the stars and planets. It was simply part of the doctrine that the realm of the elements, and hence composite bodies and hence colour, did not extend above the moon.

The written sources that Daniel relies upon include many that had only just become available to western scholars, translations from the Arabic made in recent years by teams working in Toledo and elsewhere. These include several scientific works by Aristotle, that had long existed in Arabic versions but were only now being translated into Latin, as well as the works of Arabic authors like Abu Ma'shar, the great ninth-century writer on astronomy and astrology. In the thirteenth century, such Aristotelian and Arabic texts were to form the basis of western science and philosophy. English scholars like Daniel seem to have been interested in them especially early and intensely.

A predecessor of Daniel's in the search for 'the studies of the Arabs' was Adelard of Bath, who journeyed in the Mediterranean region in the early part of the twelfth century seeking scientific texts and instruction. He learned enough Arabic to make translations of works on astronomy and geometry, as well as producing several scientific compositions of his own. One of these, the *Natural Questions* (*Quaestiones naturales*), draws on the traditions of Salerno, a place where interest in the physical world was deep-rooted and where Latin, Greek, and Arabic texts could be found, to explore a host of scientific issues: 'the cause of the ebb and flow of the tides'; 'why the fingers are of unequal length'; 'whether the stars are animate'; 'why the living are afraid of the bodies of the dead'. Adelard strikes the posture of a rational, unbiased enquirer: 'I have learned from the Arab masters, guided by reason . . .' He contrasts the learning of the Arabs with that available in the schools of France, of which he had no higher opinion than did Daniel of Morley. Western scholarship relied upon the invocation of authorities. 'But what', asks Adelard, 'is authority but a halter? . . . mere authority cannot convince a philosopher.'[137]

Within a hundred years of the time Adelard wrote, Aristotelian and Arabic science and philosophy had conquered the newly created universities. At Oxford they formed the basis of the arts curriculum. English scholars continued to contribute to the transmission of this new learning. Alfred of Shareshill, a contemporary of Daniel of Morley, translated geological and botanical works from Arabic, wrote commentaries on newly translated works of Aristotle, and was the author of a composition of his own on the movement of the heart. This last is full of citations from Aristotle's scientific works and was itself a set text in the Arts Faculty at Paris in the thirteenth century. It is dedicated to Alexander Nequam, who taught at Oxford in the 1190s.[138]

---

[137] Adelard, *Quaestiones naturales*, pref., caps. 52, 36, 74, 46, 6, ed. Martin Müller (Beiträge zur Geschichte der Philosophie des Mittelalters 31/ii; Münster, 1934), pp. 1–4, 11.

[138] James K. Otte, 'The Life and Writings of Alfredus Anglicus', *Viator*, 3 (1972), pp. 275–91.

Because the science of the period was not based on the experimental method, it was branches of natural philosophy such as astronomy and geometry, depending upon observation or deductive reasoning, that developed most remarkably. Explanations in physics, chemistry, and biology tended to become exercises in untrammelled ingenuity. It cannot be denied that the scholarly and scientific world of the twelfth century was fundamentally different from that of the present day. Neither knowledge of the general patterns and composition of the material universe nor observations of individual flora and fauna had anything like the precision, complexity, reality, and depth to which later centuries have attained. Here we can only speak of human progress in knowledge. But the urge to know was present at all times. Lacking exact instruments, the ability to make precise measurements, a supporting set of beliefs or money, 'natural philosophy', as science was called in the period, could only be an episodic, peripheral, and eccentric pursuit. Yet it was pursued.

## Libraries

Because the English Reformation was so thorough in its destructiveness, it is not easy to picture or to reconstruct the libraries on which medieval learning was founded. It was the monasteries and large collegiate churches that had the institutional continuity to support a library. The personal collections of individual scholars, even of princes, were subject to the chances of sudden death and heedless heirs. Universities stimulated book production and exchange, but at this time they had no significant capital or property, let alone university or college libraries. Large and enduring collections of books were only to be found in the big churches, especially the old Benedictine monasteries.

It was one of the duties of a Benedictine abbot to foster the monastic library. Faricius, abbot of Abingdon (1100–17), employed full-time scribes to copy out the works of the Church Fathers, such as Augustine, Gregory the Great, and John Chrysostom, as well as medical treatises.[139] Gervase, abbot of Westminster (1138–57), allocated tithe income 'to the repair of books in the book-cupboard and for the other business pertaining to our cantor's office' (the cantor was in charge of the library as well as the chanting).[140] Simon, abbot of St Albans (1167–83), was praised for repairing the abbey's writing room (*scriptorium*) and permanently maintaining two or three scribes, who produced magnificent copies of the books of the Bible.[141] Not all monks were able to read and write, but it was the usual assumption that they would all take a book each Lent, to be read over the course of the forthcoming year.[142]

---

[139] *Abingdon Chron.* 2, p. 289.   [140] *Westminster Charters*, no. 251, p. 120.
[141] *Gesta S. Alb.* 1, pp. 184, 192.   [142] Lanfr., *Const.*, p. 19.

The library at Rochester cathedral priory was catalogued in 1122–3 and again in 1202.[143] The earlier list of books records 100 volumes, the later 241. Over the course of eighty years the library had not only doubled in size but also become more varied. As well as acquiring the classical texts already mentioned (p. 518), it obtained new works of many types: the standard canon law text, Gratian's *Decretum*, and the standard theological text, Peter Lombard's *Sentences*; William of Malmesbury's *Deeds of the Kings*; a *Life* of St Bernard and a collection of the miracles of Thomas Becket; and a great deal of biblical exegesis. Fifteen of the items in the list of 1202 formed 'the library of Master Hamo', who was presumably a teacher at Rochester. He had copies of Peter Lombard and Gratian, along with commentaries on the latter, several glossed books of the Bible, works of the classical authors Cicero, Suetonius, Ovid, and Claudian, books on rhetoric and grammar and a small collection of Aristotle. Although his collection was not enormous, it included texts representing each of the main branches of medieval study—the arts, law, and theology.

It was hard to build up a library. Books were expensive and laborious to produce. Every manuscript book had to be copied out by hand and scribal skills were rare. Apart from in the case of entirely new compositions, book production depended on borrowing manuscripts for copying. Although some clerics asserted that there was a moral duty to lend books—Stephen Langton even maintaining that 'not to lend your books is a kind of homicide'—possessors of precious manuscripts might feel differently.[144] Around 1110 Herbert Losinga, bishop of Norwich, was pestering an abbot called Richard to lend him copies of the letters of Augustine and Jerome, a lectionary (a book containing the Bible readings to be used in church services), and a volume of the ancient Jewish historian Josephus. This last had apparently caused the most difficulty: 'Send me the Josephus. You have often made the excuse that the book is falling to bits, but now that it has been corrected and rebound, no pretext is left to you'.[145]

The to-ing and fro-ing of manuscripts was important for keeping texts correct and up to date. Gerald of Wales sent a copy of his *Mirror of the Church* (*Speculum Ecclesie*) to the canons of Hereford, but asked for it back within a year to make corrections and additions. He also sent a copy of his works on Ireland, promising to send an enlarged version later and asking the canons then to return the other copy.[146] A different kind of revision occurred when

---

[143] *Engl. Ben. Libr.*, pp. 469–526; Mary P. Richards, *Texts and their Traditions in the Medieval Library of Rochester Cathedral Priory* (Trans. American Philosophical Soc. 78/3; 1988), cap. 1.

[144] Lesley Smith, 'Lending Books: The Growth of a Medieval Question from Langton to Bonaventure', in *eadem* and Benedicta Ward (eds.), *Intellectual Life in the Middle Ages: Essays Presented to Margaret Gibson* (London, 1992), p. 268 n. 16.

[145] Herbert Losinga, epp. 10, 60, ed. Robert Anstruther (London, 1846), pp. 16, 107.

[146] Gerald, *Op.* 1, p. 409 (*Epistola . . . de libris a se scriptis*).

the Cistercians of Fountains borrowed a manuscript of the *Life of St Godric* from the monks of Durham in order to make a copy. Since the original was not illuminated, they separated out the leaves and 'for love and honour of the saint' decorated it with colours.[147] The hand-copying of manuscripts, which was the only way a text could be reproduced, was a process that invited both error and embellishment.

Manuscripts not only circulated within England, but also crossed the sea. After the Norman Conquest there are many cases of French texts coming into England. For instance, all seventeen surviving English manuscripts of the first book of Cassiodorus' *Institutiones*, a programme of Christian learning written in the sixth century, derive from one continental manuscript. This was brought to England by the 1090s, when the canons of Salisbury made a copy of it. Another copy of the continental manuscript came to St Augustine's abbey, Canterbury, where it was copied and this copy then served as the exemplar for the other English manuscripts.[148] In the right circumstances, manuscripts could multiply quickly.

## 3. THE VISUAL ARTS

Painting, carving, sculpture, and fine metalwork were produced primarily for ecclesiastics or aristocrats. It is inconceivable that peasants and townspeople did not adorn their homes, but little is known of this. Nor, in fact, does very much survive from the world of the lay aristocracy. Hence the surviving culture of the Norman and Angevin period has a marked ecclesiastical bias that may be misleading. Nevertheless, it is doubtless the case that the most highly wrought, ornate, and elaborate human environments were to be found in the great church complexes.

They were themselves works of art. A monastery, with its church, cloister, chapter house, refectory, dormitory, infirmary, library, abbot's quarters, guesthouse, and kitchen, was a piece of ingenious design that manifested notable skills of planning and construction. The great stone churches and monasteries that could be found throughout the country were objects of admiration. Abbots, like the one depicted in Marie de France's tale of *Yonec*, might invite aristocratic visitors on a guided tour—'He would show them his dormitory, chapter-house and dining-hall.'[149] Surviving examples, like Ely, the interior of Tewkesbury abbey, or St Bartholomew the Great, a rare Romanesque London church, convey immediately the majesty of the huge stone buildings that rose above the fields and huts around them.

---

[147] Reg., *V. Godric* 212 (p. 466).
[148] Teresa Webber, *Scribes and Scholars at Salisbury Cathedral c.1075–c.1125* (Oxford, 1992), p. 46.
[149] Marie de France, *Yonec*, lines 491–2 (*Lais*, p. 94).

Not only were the buildings themselves huge investments, they housed treasures. They contained the greatest concentrations of precious metal, bright colour, and soft material in the country. When, around 1100, robbers broke into the abbey church of Peterborough, they found 'a great jewelled golden cross of twenty marks [almost 10 lbs] that was on the altar, two large chalices, a paten and the candlesticks given by archbishop Ælfric, all of gold'.[150] In the inventory of the treasures at Ramsey abbey that were lost during the civil war of Stephen's reign, we find listed images of Christ in majesty, of St Benedict, and of St John the Evangelist, all decorated with gold and jewels; of St Ivo and of St Mary, decorated with gold and silver, the latter 'the work of Ralph the Sacristan'; an image of the Saviour and another of St Mary, each weighing five marks (2.4 lbs); and silver images of the four evangelists and the twelve apostles.[151] Two chaplains of Henry I, Bernard and Nicholas, gave to the Augustinian church of St Stephen's, Launceston, 'a deep-blue banner, embroidered in gold, with a lamb stitched of gold in the centre and below it the stoning of St Stephen and the images of the four evangelists at the four corners'.[152]

A rare surviving example of the exquisite decorative art of the period is the Gloucester candlestick, now in the Victoria and Albert Museum in London. Commissioned by abbot Peter of Gloucester (1107–13), this masterpiece of metalwork is made of an alloy of copper and silver and stands twenty inches high. It is alive with human and monstrous animal figures, intertwined with each other and with foliage. Room is found for the symbols of the evangelists and inscriptions, one on a curling scroll. This complex and fantastic object reveals the astonishing skill in metal casting to be found in England in this period and gives a hint of a lost world of glittering beauty.[153]

Occasionally some of the images produced by craftsmen and artists of the period survive in the churches for which they were created. A walk around Canterbury cathedral today allows the observer not only to admire the surviving Romanesque and Early Gothic parts of the building but also to gaze at images from that time: the carved grotesques on the capitals in the early twelfth-century crypt, the wall painting of St Paul in the Anselm chapel, painted around 1160, and the glowing stained glass of the eastern part of the cathedral, in the choir and Trinity Chapel. This was produced and installed between the beginning of rebuilding after the fire of 1174 and the solemn translation of Becket's remains into the Trinity Chapel in 1220. The windows of the Trinity Chapel contain an unusual sequence depicting Becket's posthumous miracles. They form a consciously designed and executed artistic programme, one of the few to have survived the centuries.[154]

[150] *The Peterborough Chronicle of Hugh Candidus*, ed. William T. Mellows (London, 1949), p. 87.
[151] *Ramsey Cart.* 2, pp. 273–4, no. 391.    [152] Peter Cornw., *Liber rev.*, fo. 25ᵛ.
[153] *Engl. Rom. Art*, pp. 41, 73, 249.
[154] Madeline Caviness, *The Windows of Christ Church Cathedral, Canterbury* (London, 1981).

It is generally agreed that the twelfth century marks one of the high points of medieval English book illustration and the most arresting extant painted images from the period are those of the great illuminated manuscripts. Elaborate painted designs can be found both in the many decorated and historiated initials (the latter having figures and scenes within the letter) and in remarkable full-page pictures. The Psalter was the book most often illustrated but other texts—complete Bibles, saints' Lives, medical treatises, bestiaries (discussed below, pp. 674–81)—also contain large and beautiful pictures.

The St Albans Psalter, produced at St Albans around 1120 for Christina of Markyate, anchoress and later prioress, is one of the earliest examples of a Psalter with a preceding picture-cycle of the life of Christ.[155] This comprises forty full-page illustrations, each strongly framed within a decorative rectangular border. The first two pictures depict the Fall and Expulsion from Eden, the last represents King David playing a stringed instrument and one, inexplicably, is dedicated to an incident from the life of St Martin, but the remainder deal with New Testament scenes, from the Annunciation to Pentecost. They show richly coloured and clearly delineated figures in dramatic action.

These forty pictures are by no means all the illustration in the Psalter. The Calendar with which the book opens contains depictions of the zodiacal sign and the appropriate activity for each of the twelve months—June, for instance, shows a figure with a scythe, December a man killing a pig. Then, in addition to the full-page pictures already mentioned, there are other miscellaneous full-page illustrations, depicting Christ at Emmaus, the martyrdom of St Alban and King David (again). The *Life of St Alexius*, also included in the book, starts with a tinted drawing showing scenes from the saint's life. A tract on spiritual battle is illustrated by two knights fighting. Moreover, each of the Psalms, canticles, hymns, and prayers in the volume has an elaborate historiated initial—there are 212 in all. The first, the 'B' of *Beatus vir* (the opening words of the Psalms), is especially notable, showing King David (yet again) harping. The St Albans Psalter thus contains almost 300 painted images, some of them intricate and large. It is a masterpiece of the pictorial religious art of the period.

Later in the twelfth century, around 1150, another remarkable illustrated Psalter was produced at Canterbury. This, the Eadwine Psalter, has already been mentioned for the light it throws on the languages being used in England at this time (above, pp. 503–4). Its illustrations contrast notably with those of the St Albans Psalter. They are based on the picture-cycle in the ninth-century Utrecht Psalter, itself derived from classical models. The pictures

155 O. Pächt *et al.*, *The St Albans Psalter* (London, 1960).

are tinted drawings, showing many small figures in vivid action, set in lightly sketched and highly stylized landscapes. The Psalter also has two large illustrations of a quite different and highly exceptional kind: a full-page portrait of the scribe, Eadwine, at work, and, added slightly later, a large plan of the waterworks at Canterbury cathedral priory.

The main cycles of images in the St Albans and Eadwine Psalters show that a range of styles was available to English illuminators of the twelfth century. The tinted drawings with an open compositional arrangement on the page, such as are found in the Eadwine Psalter, go back to an Anglo-Saxon tradition. The St Albans pictures are of a very different type, with clear thick outlines defining areas of heavy rich colour. Solid hierarchical figures are set against backgrounds that are often abstract or simply fields of colour. The influence of the art of Byzantium and Germany has been seen in this style. Both styles co-existed in early twelfth-century England, but gradually the tradition of tinted line drawing declined in significance in comparison with the heavier 'Romanesque' technique. The contrast between the stylistic preferences of 1100 and 1200 are well exemplified by the picture-cycles in two illustrated Lives of St Cuthbert produced at Durham. The first, from around 1100, is in the open linear style of Anglo-Saxon tradition, the latter in the solid block style of English Romanesque.[156]

Many of the largest and most beautiful illuminated manuscripts were produced in the old Benedictine monasteries. St Albans, Canterbury, and Durham have already been mentioned. Winchester and Bury were also important centres. The Bury Bible is one of the great illuminated Bibles that were created at this time. It is large (20 inches by 14 or 515 × 350 mm.) and consumed so much parchment that calf-skins had to be imported from Scotland. The artist, working in the 1130s, was a Master Hugo, who was also a skilled sculptor who created other images and ornaments for Bury.[157] His painting is rather like that in the St Albans Psalter, with clear outlines, rich colours, and images placed in well-defined spaces, surrounded by decorated borders. Backgrounds are stylized landscapes or flat areas of colour. The emphasis is on the figures, whose tall, carefully modelled forms, vivid gestures and expressive eyes create an atmosphere of dramatic intensity.

In the Anglo-Saxon period artistic work had often been undertaken by leading ecclesiastics in person. This became much less common in the twelfth century. Abbots and bishops employed skilled artisans and artists, they did not themselves expect to be artisans and artists. Clearly some artisans, especially goldsmiths, had a high status, and men like Master Hugo of

---

[156] Malcolm Baker, 'Medieval Illustrations of Bede's Life of St Cuthbert', *Jnl Warburg and Courtauld Institute*, 41 (1978), pp. 16–40.

[157] *Gesta sacristarum monasterii sancti Edmundi*, *Mem. Edm.* 2, pp. 289–90.

Bury enjoyed a great reputation, but they were unmistakably answerable to patrons and customers. Artists were employees. The fact that the hand of the painter of the St Albans Psalter has also been seen in manuscripts produced for other churches suggests he may have been a full-time professional artist working on different commissions for various clients. It is not anachronistic to talk of an art market in the period. In the first decade of the thirteenth century it is likely that a workshop at Oxford was producing illustrated Psalters for a variety of customers.[158] A case such as that of the sculptor and painter who was hawking his wares at Durham fair in the middle years of the twelfth century shows that artistic work was even undertaken speculatively for sale on the open market.[159]

## 4. PERFORMANCE: SONG AND MUSIC, DANCE AND DRAMA

### Song and Music

There is nothing of a past culture that is lost so irretrievably as its performances—the singing and dancing that must have loomed so large for so many but has left no trace. We have the texts of some of the epics and romances, but cannot hear their oral delivery. The twelfth-century Exchequer is a hundred times better understood than any festivity, concert, or play of the period. This silence is deepened by the fact that very little written music or drama survives. In the case of secular song, this is perhaps understandable, but it is more surprising that so little liturgical music survives from the period. The main activity of the monasteries, cathedrals, and great minsters was chant.

Parts of both the Office and the Mass were sung. They could be chanted in single-line melody (plainsong) but might be elaborated into complex polyphonic performances. The music in the Winchester Troper of the early eleventh century shows that such chants were sung in Anglo-Saxon England.[160] Entirely new liturgical compositions were also created, like those in the Cambridge Songbook of the late twelfth century.[161] This contains 22 monodic and 13 polyphonic pieces, mainly *conductus*, that is Latin songs in stanzas.[162] They might be sung at moments in the service when there was a pause in liturgical chant, for example while the reader proceeded to the lectern to read the lesson.

---

[158] H. B. Graham, 'The Munich Psalter', in *The Year 1200: A Symposium* (New York, 1975), pp. 301–12.

[159] Reg., *V. Godric* 42 (pp. 101–2).

[160] *Winchester Troper*, ed. W. H. Frere (Henry Bradshaw Soc.; 1894).

[161] Cambr. UL Ff. i. 17 (1).

[162] John Caldwell, *The Oxford History of English Music* i (Oxford, 1991), pp. 19–23; facs. in *Early English Harmony*, ed. H. E. Wooldridge (London, 1897), plates 25–30, there dated to the thirteenth century.

Slight traces of vernacular song also survive, some in Norman French, like the crusading song *Parti de mal*, found, with music, in a manuscript of around 1200.[163] The only songs in English from this period with accompanying music are three short pieces by the hermit Godric of Finchale (d. 1170). One (*'Sainte Marie Virgine'*) was supposedly taught to him by the Virgin Mary herself. Another is a hymn to St Nicholas. The third records the song that was sung by Godric's deceased sister, Burgwen, when she appeared to him in a vision. Burgwen and two angels sang in turn the liturgical *Kyrie eleison*, *Christe eleison*, she then adding the vernacular lines 'Christ and St Mary have led me to the footstool, so that I need tread the earth with my bare feet no more'.[164]

Virtually nothing remains of the non-religious songs and music of the period, although occasional references convey a distant echo of that lost world of song. Stringed instruments, some plucked, some played with a bow, are depicted in contemporary carvings and pictures, as are various kinds of horn. There is mention of girls and women singing the songs of the hero Hereward.[165] It is known that the inhabitants of northern England had a tradition of part-singing, with a rumbling bass line and a sweet and playful descant.[166] Although some prelates, like the saintly bishop Robert of Hereford (1131–48), spurned 'singers and actors', there need be no impenetrable barrier between secular and ecclesiastical melodies.[167] Thomas, archbishop of York (1070–1100), was adept at bridging these worlds: 'he was powerful in voice and chant and composed many religious songs. If a minstrel sang in his hearing, he would immediately transform what he 'heard into divine praise.'[168]

## Dance and Drama

Christianity and dancing had never been easy partners. Other religions might have sacred dance, but the Judaeo-Christian tradition avoided it. Dancing was associated with paganism. In twelfth-century England it was also associated with the eleven ladies who danced at night. Yet it was not inconceivable that dance could be Christianized. It was the custom for young people to

---

[163] BL Harley 1717; facs. in *Early English Harmony*, ed. H. E. Wooldridge (London, 1897), Plate 8; J. Bedier and P. Aubrey (eds.), *Les Chansons de croisade* (Paris, 1909), pp. 69–73.

[164] BL Royal 5 F vii, fo. 85; facs. in G. Saintsbury, *A History of English Prosody* (3 vols.; 1906–10), vol. 1, frontispiece; ed., with music and discussion, E. J. Dobson and F. Ll. Harrison, *Medieval English Songs* (London, 1979), pp. 75–6, 103–9, 228–9, 295–6; J. Zupitza, 'Cantus Beati Godrici', *Englische Studien*, 11 (1888), pp. 401–32.

[165] *Gesta Herw.*, p. 344.         [166] Gerald, *Descr.* 1. 13 (pp. 189–90).

[167] William of Wycombe, *V. Roberti de Betune*, ed. Henry Wharton, *Anglia sacra* (2 vols.; London, 1691), vol. 2, pp. 293–321, at p. 309.

[168] W. Malm., *GP* 116 (p. 258).

dance in the churchyard on the eve of the local saint's feast day. Reginald of Durham tells of a chapel dedicated to Cuthbert, where the population gathered on St Cuthbert's day, the older folk praying inside the church, the younger, 'as is the custom of youth', singing and dancing outside.[169] At the church of North Burton (Burton Fleming), in the East Riding of Yorkshire, similar annual celebrations took place. After the service, 'when the clergy and congregation had left the church and locked the door, the young men, girls and boys played and joked and danced in the green space of the church-yard'.[170] This association of dancing and Christian festival was not, however, one that the church authorities chose to foster. In the early thirteenth century, ecclesiastical prohibitions were issued against dancing and 'lascivious games' in churches and churchyards.[171] These gatherings of 'loose women and fool-ish youths' on the saint's festival were 'to be prohibited with diligence'.[172]

Leading churchmen had a more tolerant attitude to drama. Liturgy and drama overlapped in a way that liturgy and dance did not. Indeed, amongst the earliest surviving dramatic texts from the Middle Ages are those describ-ing the Easter drama, when clergy dressed as the three Maries approached the model of the sepulchre that had been built in the church. This perform-ance had taken place in English churches since Anglo-Saxon times and was continued, and sometimes elaborated, in our period. An account of the Easter spectacle at the abbey of Eynsham in the 1190s tells how

in that church it is the custom on that day every year that, after matins have been sung, there is a dramatic representation of the Lord's resurrection. First there is the revelation by the angel, addressing the women at the sepulchre, who tells them of the triumph of their king and how they must inform the disciples. Then there is an enactment of Christ's appearance in the form of a gardener to his beloved Mary [Magdalene].[173]

Religious drama extended beyond such liturgically involved performances to rather more free-standing plays, based on saints' lives. Geoffrey, a school-teacher at Dunstable in the time of Henry I, organized a 'play of St Kather-ine' (*ludus de Sancta Katerina*), for which he borrowed copes from the monks of St Albans. This is an early instance of a miracle play (expressly so called) based on the life of a saint and involving special costume.[174] In his account of London written in 1173–4, William fitz Stephen, himself a Londoner, declares that, instead of theatrical displays, London has 'holier plays' repre-senting the lives of the confessors and the deaths of the martyrs.[175]

A surviving twelfth-century drama that was probably written in England

---

[169] Reg., *Libellus* 136 (p. 284).     [170] *Mir. John Bev.*, p. 323.
[171] *Councils and Synods* 2/i, pp. 35, 93.      [172] T. Chobham, *SC*, p. 260.
[173] *Vis. Eynsham*, p. 294.      [174] *Gesta S. Alb.* 1, p. 73.
[175] W. f. Stephen, *V. Thomas* 13 (p. 9).

is the *Play of Adam* (*Jeu d'Adam*). This deals with the Fall and the story of
Cain and Abel, concluding with a procession of prophets.[176] Stage directions
are in Latin, the text itself in French verse. It was designed to be performed
outside a church with a choir to sing passages from the Bible at appropriate
points. The set envisaged was quite elaborate:

Paradise should be constructed in an elevated position, surrounded by curtains and
silk hangings to such a height that people in paradise will be visible down to their
shoulders. There should be sweet-smelling flowers, intertwined with leaves, and
various types of tree with fruit hanging down, to give the effect of a lovely place.

It is possible to hear a true director's voice in the stage directions: 'Adam
should be dressed in a red tunic, Eve in a woman's dress of white, with a white
silk veil. Both should stand before the figure of God, Adam closer and with a
steady gaze, Eve with her eyes cast down.'

The dialogue involves a great deal of quick exchange:

DEVIL.    What are you doing, Adam?
ADAM.     I am living here with great pleasure.
DEVIL.    Is all well with you?
ADAM.     I know of nothing that troubles me.
DEVIL.    You could be even better.
ADAM.     I don't know how.
DEVIL.    Do you want to know?

Adam declines the Devil's suggestions but Eve is less firm. With its mechanical snake, devils running in and out of the audience and great dramatic dialogue, like the Devil's flattery of Eve or the hot words between Cain and Abel,
the *Play of Adam* must have been fun.


## 5. THE VALUE OF THE ARTS

The Church was the great generator of music and of images, mental,
pictorial, and sculptured. It also fostered their critics. The rhetoric of the
Cistercians, especially, often veered towards denunciation of what they
considered superfluous or distracting representations of the natural world.

Bernard, the great Cistercian leader, made a famous attack on the
gargoyles and monsters depicted in the exuberant carvings of some Benedictine churches, like those in Canterbury cathedral crypt. His disciple, Ailred
of Rievaulx, echoed his theme. Writing to his sister, an anchoress, he advised,
'Do not, on the pretext of devotion, glory in pictures or sculptures, the feathers

---

[176] Ed. David Bevington (as 'The Service for Representing Adam'), in *Medieval Drama* (Boston, 1975),
pp. 78–121, with facing translation.

of birds or varied images of animals or flowers.'[177] He elaborated the theme in his *Speculum caritatis* (*Mirror of Love*). 'Empty pleasure of the ears' and 'sensual pleasure of the eyes' were equally to be condemned. From Ailred's point of view, organ music and elaborate polyphony made churches more like theatres than places of worship. He attacked complex part-singing, embellished melodies, and soprano singing: 'Now the voice is constrained, now it breaks . . . sometimes it is forced to whinny like a horse, sometimes abandons manly force and sharpens into the high pitch of the female voice.' He gives a powerful depiction of an open-mouthed singer straining like one in agony— 'and they call all this religion!'

Visual delight was an equal distraction and 'superfluous beauty' to be condemned wherever it was found—'in bright, sweet colours, in pieces of craftsmanship, in clothes, shoes, vessels, pictures and sculptures'. Ailred imagines a disappointed visitor to a plain church (clearly Cistercian), where he finds no paintings, carvings, marble, or hangings decorated with scenes. If this hypothetical aesthete had pursued the religious life with understanding, he would not have become attached to 'these petty external glories'.[178]

As Ailred's words show, the proper place of music and visual art was controversial. It is significant that one of the texts copied into the St Albans Psalter, with its hundreds of beautiful and complex images, is a letter of pope Gregory I (590–604) that constitutes a classic defence of Christian images. 'It is one thing to adore a picture, another to learn from the subject of the picture what should be adored,' Gregory had written. 'Pictures convey to the illiterate what scripture conveys to those who can read . . .'[179] The fact that the Latin text of Gregory's letter is immediately followed in the Psalter by a French translation shows how powerful was the desire of the compiler to get this message across.

Ailred's suspicions of the pleasures of eye and ear were not uncommon in the religious culture of his time, but nor were they the only response to be found to art and music. Gerald of Wales, who could be as dogmatic as any Cistercian, melted when describing the joys of music: 'The sweet sound of music not only delights with its melodies but is also very profitable. It greatly cheers downcast spirits, clears clouded countenances, sets aside sternness and rigour and restores joy. Among all the joys nothing cheers and delights the human emotions more than music.' Gerald exemplifies the cheering effect of music by noting the way that workmen sing while they work. He is also aware of the pleasures of the trained ear, the satisfaction of 'those who perceive

---

[177] Ailr. Riev., *De institutione inclusarum* 24 (*Op. asc.*, p. 657).

[178] Ailr. Riev., *Speculum caritatis* 2. 23–4 (*Op. asc.*, pp. 97–101).

[179] Gregory the Great, *Registrum* 11. 10, ed. L. M. Hartmann, *MGH*, *Epistolae* 2 (Hanover, 1899), p. 270.

more subtly and discern the secrets of the technique more acutely' when listening to complex music.[180]

Enthusiasm like Gerald's must be set alongside Ailred's theoretical austerity. It was an enthusiasm felt by the laity as well as by ecclesiastics. There is record of a woman at the end of the eleventh century who heard of the kaleidoscopic beauties of the church ornaments at Durham and 'was set on fire by desire to see these new things'.[181] It is patent, and can be no surprise, that the mighty aesthetic creativity of the period was fed by, and inspired, avid appreciation of beauty.

---

[180] Gerald, *Top.* 3. 11–12 (pp. 154–7).     [181] S. Durh., *HDE* 2. 9 (pp. 60–1).

# CHAPTER 11

# The Course of Life

## I. CHILDHOOD

Although there were no effective artificial restraints on fertility in this period, the standard of nutrition and health probably meant that more women were naturally infertile than today. The desire for a child was as deeply felt then as now. The risks of childbirth and childhood were far greater. It was strongly suggested that women who expected to give birth should have water at hand, not for medicinal purposes, but to baptize the child if it seemed about to die. Unbaptized children went to hell. Pregnant women were urged to make their confession in good time, 'lest they be suddenly taken by surprise and have no access to a priest when they would'.[1]

The saints were invoked to bring fertility and aid in childbirth, just as in illness. The wife of one of William Rufus's barons, Robert fitz Hamo, grieving over her childlessness, came to pray at the shrine of St Benignus in Glastonbury, begged the monks in full chapter 'to appeal to the ears of their familiar patron', promising land worth £5 in the event of success, and was then wrapped by the abbot in the linen cloth from the saint's shrine. This combination of financial incentive and ritual was effective, although, to fitz Hamo's regret, only daughters were born. A similarly direct approach was taken by Hawisa, countess of Gloucester in the later twelfth century, who 'put her faith in the merits of St James and the prayers of his monks while in labour' and induced her husband to offer St James', Bristol, 100 acres of arable land, 'so that she should be freed from the pains of labour by the help of the holy patron of that church'.[2]

After the perils of birth, came those of childhood. Abandonment of infants was common enough to require special rules about whether exposed babies needed to be baptized or not. Their mothers, or whoever abandoned them, sometimes left with them a little salt, as a sign that they should be baptized (salt was placed in an infant's mouth during the baptismal ceremony).[3] If the

---

[1] *Councils and Synods* 2/i, p. 35; cf. Alex. Ashby, *De modo pred.*, p. 932.
[2] BL Add. 36985, fos. 2ᵛ, 4.    [3] *Councils and Synods* 1/ii, pp. 1049, 1061; 2/i, p. 31.

child were kept, it then faced a host of dangers. Whatever the wealth and status of the parents, infant mortality was high. William, earl of Gloucester (d. 1183), made an annual grant to St Nicholas, Exeter, for the health of his only son. He regarded it as a 'head payment', similar to those made by serfs to their lord: 'twelve pence as head-payment [*pro capitagio*] for Robert my son, that God conserve and protect him'.[4] Poignantly, the boy died in his teens.

Those who could afford it sent their children out to be breastfed by others. A woman whose milk dried up and was then miraculously restored, explained that she was breastfeeding her infant daughter herself, 'since she was poor and did not keep a nurse in her house'. The beer that she had given to the baby in the interval seems to have done it no harm, for she survived at least until her teens.[5] Adelard of Bath draws a pleasant picture of nurses calming crying babies with their crooning, and, as might be expected, affection grew up between child and nurse—Richard I gave his old nurse a large pension as soon as he ascended the throne.[6] Obviously many mothers did keep their babies with them and concern was frequently expressed that women should not overlie and smother the babies they had with them in bed.[7]

The first and most critical rite that the baby underwent was baptism. This entailed not only the public entry of the child into the Christian community but also its reception into a new family, that of the godparents. Each male child was required to have two male godparents and one female godparent, each female child two female and one male. Sometimes, as in the case of Godric of Finchale, the child took the name of a godparent.[8] The weaning of the child was also apparently marked publicly. The priest Wenstan of Norwich gave a banquet for his relatives on the day of the weaning (*ablactatio*) of his son William, about 1135.[9]

Childhood is not a phase of life that emerges with much sharpness or vivid detail in the sources of the period, although there are occasional vignettes: the boy playing with the top mentioned in the Life of Gilbert of Sempringham, the brothers of Gerald of Wales building sand castles on the sea shore, or, less idyllically, the boy observed by Anselm who had a bird on a string that he pulled whenever the poor creature tried to fly away.[10] Boys and girls were soon socialized into different paths. When Alexander Nequam paints a word-picture of an upper-class chamber, he pictures a group of young girls there, sewing and embroidering, with leather thimbles on their thumbs and the tips

---

[4] *Gloucester Charters*, no. 69, p. 74.      [5] *Can. Osmund*, p. 39.

[6] Adelard of Bath, *De eodem et diverso*, ed. Hans Wilner (Beiträge zur Geschichte der Philosophie des Mittelalters 4/i; Münster, 1903), p. 25; Hunt, *Nequam*, pp. 1–2.

[7] e.g. *Councils and Synods* 2/i, p. 32.      [8] Reg., *V. Godric* 10 (p. 23).

[9] T. Monm., *V. William* 1.2 (pp. 12–13).

[10] *Bk. Gilbert*, p. 74; Gerald, *De reb.* 1. 1 (p. 21); Eadmer, *V. Anselm*, p. 90.

of the fingers of their gloves open, so that they can do this delicate work.[11] Their brothers would be already training for the hunt or for war. When they went out riding the boys would ride astride, the girls side-saddle. Lower down the social scale certain kinds of labour, such as work in the laundry or the dairy, were deemed 'women's work'.[12]

There were several different ways of categorizing people into age groups. One version appears in the diagrams produced around 1100 at one of the Fenland monasteries to illustrate the eleventh-century scientific treatise of Byrhtferth.[13] This gives four 'Ages of Man', that are equated with the four seasons:

| | | |
|---|---|---|
| Boyhood | Spring | until 14 years of age |
| Young Manhood | Summer | until 28 years of age |
| Manhood | Autumn | until 48 years of age |
| Old Age | Winter | until 70 or 80 years of age |

More common was a division of human life into six ages. This had the authority of St Augustine and of Isidore of Seville, whose encyclopaedia was the chief reference book of the Middle Ages. Isidore distinguished infancy, boyhood, young manhood, manhood, middle age, and old age. The Six Ages theory had the aesthetic attraction that it could be harnessed to the Six Ages of human history (see below, p. 655). One of the windows in Canterbury cathedral depicts just such a parallelism.[14] Whatever age one was, or eventually attained, the resurrected body would be 33—the age of Christ at death.[15]

Of more immediate concern than the age at resurrection was the age of majority. This differed according to status and tenure. The law-book attributed to Glanville asserts that knights come of age at 21, sokeman at 15, and burgesses 'when they can count money and measure cloth'.[16] This last point could be interpreted simply as a piece of aristocratic disdain if it were not for the existence of later medieval borough customs with just such provisions. For instance, in the fourteenth century a burgess of Shrewsbury was of age 'when he knows how to measure ells of cloth and to tell a good penny from a bad one.[17]

The difference in the age of majority between those holding land by military tenure and by socage had important practical consequences. There were many situations where a minor could not plead in a court of law, be impleaded, or vouch to warranty (guarantee a grant when required). In some cases the

---

[11] Alex. Nequam, *Ut.*, p. 101.        [12] Map 1. 25 (p. 86).

[13] C. M. Kauffmann, *Romanesque Manuscripts, 1066–1190* (*A Survey of Manuscripts Illuminated in the British Isles* 3; London, 1975), plate 21.

[14] Madeline Caviness, *The Windows of Christ Church Cathedral, Canterbury* (London, 1981), pp. 110–11, figs. 186–7.

[15] Alex. Nequam, *DNR* 1. 4 (p. 30).        [16] Glanvill 7. 9 (p. 82).

[17] Mary Bateson (ed.), *Borough Customs* (2 vols., Selden Soc. 18 and 21; 1904–6), vol. 2, p. 158.

excuses for non-attendance in court that were usually permitted were not admitted in lawsuits involving a minor. In a case heard at Warwick in 1222 one
of the parties was initially denied permission to make an excuse for non-
attendance because the defendant was a minor. Subsequently, however, it was
established that the land in dispute was socage, not a military tenure. With the
relevant age of majority now 15 instead of 21, the defendant was not a minor
and the other party's excuse was allowed.[18]

For those of military status being knighted and coming of age were deemed
equivalent. In 1217 the royal government wrote to the Justiciar of Ireland, informing him that Maurice fitz Gerald had been 'girded with the belt of
knighthood' and hence he should be given the land 'that Gerald his father
had on the day he died . . . that has been in our hands through wardship since
he was not of full age'.[19] A wardship was granted until the boy 'is of such age
that he can hold land and be made a knight'.[20] The rules of majority came to
have intense political significance during the long minority of Henry III. In
1221 representatives of the regency government were arguing that it was the
common custom of England that no minor could make a binding transaction
concerning his father's possessions until he was aged 21, the age that wardship ended.[21] The long gap in the royal Charter Rolls, from 1216 to 1226,
reflects that belief about coming of age.

## 2. NAMING PATTERNS

One of the first and most basic decisions to be taken about a child was what its
name should be. Names were a serious matter. One newly converted regular
canon, who had been called Henry when a layman but had taken the name in
religion of Augustine, was worried that prayers for him under that new name
would not help him after death, since he was really Henry. The matter even
came to the attention of the pope, who was reassuring—after all, he himself
had taken a new name on promotion.[22]

### Choice of Name

With the Norman Conquest, a small alien group took over the kingdom of
England. Their names marked them out from the subject population just as
clearly as their language. In the first generation or two after 1066 a name

[18] Rolls of the Justices in Eyre for Gloucestershire, Warwickshire and Shropshire, 1221–2, ed. Doris
Stenton (Selden Soc. 59; 1940), nos. 1411, 1456, pp. 592, 610.
[19] Rot. litt. claus. 1, p. 314.        [20] RRAN 3, no. 482, p. 180.
[21] M. P. Sheehy, Pontificia Hibernica 1 (Dublin, 1962), no. 144, p. 229; see David Carpenter, The
Minority of Henry III (London, 1990), pp. 123–4, 240–1, 389.
[22] Innocent III, ep. 9. 136, ed. C. R. Cheney, Selected Letters of Pope Innocent III Concerning England
(NMC; 1953), no. 27, p. 83.

would be an almost certain indication of ethnic identity. Contemporaries were not unaware of this sharp disjunction. The twelfth-century poet Denis Piramus, writing of the Anglo-Saxon period, has the following to say when he tells of the four northern barons whom Ethelred the Unready hated:

> These four barons, that the king
> Hated so, were English.
> They were not called Richer,
> William, Robert, nor Walter.
> But one of them had the name Leofwine,
> And the next was called Aelfwine,
> The third Siward, the fourth Morcar.

Aptly summoning up these common Norman and English aristocratic names, the poet underlines the ethnic or national connotation of name choice: the barons were not called William, Robert, etc., *because* they were English.[23]

There is no doubt that the traditional Anglo-Saxon names sounded outlandish and comical to at least the first generations of Norman conquerors and settlers. The barons supporting Robert as king in 1101 called Henry I and his new Anglo-Scottish queen, who had the barbaric name of Edith, 'Godric' and 'Godgiva' in contemptuous derision. One consequence of this attitude was the cosmetic adoption of new names: when he arrived in Normandy in 1085 as a child oblate, Orderic Vitalis remembered that 'the name of Vitalis was given me in place of my English name, which sounded harsh to the Normans'; Henry I's wife attempted to avoid the derisive 'Godgiva' by becoming 'Matilda, who had previously been called Edith'; while one young boy, born in the Anglo-Scandinavian milieu of Whitby about 1110, was initially called Tostig, but, 'when his youthful companions mocked the name', changed it to the Norman William.[24]

This process of cultural constraint was powerful enough to lead to the wholesale adoption of Norman names by the native population. Three-quarters of the burgesses of Canterbury had these continental names within a century of the Conquest. By the early thirteenth century, the English peasantry had assimilated the names of the Norman aristocracy. Although there were places where the old Anglo-Scandinavian names were still to be found and although women's names tended to be slightly more conservative and traditional than men's, the general trend is unmistakable. The names of the Norman dynasty and the Domesday barons, such as William, Robert,

---

[23] Denis Piramus, *La Vie seint Edmund le rey*, lines 3885–91 (*Mem. Edm.* 2, p. 246). The names are unlikely to have a precise and informed reference.

[24] W. Malm., *GR* 5. 394 (2, p. 471); OMT edn., p. 716; Orderic 13. 45; 8. 22 (6, p. 554; 4, p. 272); Geoffrey of Durham, *V. Bartholomaei Farnensis* 1, in Simeon, *Op.* 1, pp. 295–325, at p. 296.

Richard, Roger, and Hugh, were the most common names in every stratum of English society by 1225. This shift to the Norman names seems to have been accompanied by a decline in the variety of available names. 'William', for instance, came to be a preponderant name for the rest of the Middle Ages. The popularity of the name was already apparent in the twelfth century. When Henry the Young King held court in Normandy at Christmas 1171, the guests supposedly included 110 knights named 'William'. They got together in one room and refused to let anyone in to eat with them unless he were called William![25]

Another force working to erode a distinctively Anglo–Scandinavian repertoire of names was the growing popularity of the names of the saints. The names of both biblical and non-biblical saints, like Thomas, John, Nicholas, Bartholomew, Katherine, and Margaret, were increasing in popularity throughout western Europe at this time. This is exemplified, in the case of England, by the two surveys of Winchester burgesses dating from 1115 and 1148. In the first, the percentage of these biblical and saints' names is 6 per cent, by the second, only a generation or so later, it had risen to 16 per cent.[26] By the early thirteenth century, the commonest English names after those brought by the Normans were those of the popular saints. Tostig, Siward, and Godric were fading stars.

The transformation of naming patterns in the period 1075–1225 highlights a central fact about names: they can be chosen. Each generation makes new choices and in these choices they are influenced by ever-changing fashions and interests. One tradition was obviously to name a child after someone of personal importance to the family. Orderic Vitalis was called Orderic after the priest who baptized him and who was his godfather.[27] More common was a family tradition of names, visible especially among the aristocracy. When the first son of Henry of Anjou (later Henry II) and Eleanor of Aquitaine was born on 17 August 1153, 'he was called William, a name that is almost the distinctive attribute of the counts of Poitou and dukes of Aquitaine'.[28] Since Eleanor's father bore the title William X, the point is a fair one. It is worth noting that the name also featured in the new prince's Norman ancestry and hence gave weight to both sides of his descent.

Parents might even try to ensure that an important family name was transmitted to the next generation by giving the same name to more than one child, as in the case of Ralph son of Thorald, whose charter was witnessed by 'lady Inga my wife with my son Roger and my other son Roger'.[29] This was a

---

[25] R. Torigni, p. 253.
[26] Cecily Clark, 'Battle *c.*1110: An Anthroponomist Looks at an Anglo–Norman New Town', *ANS* 2 (1980), pp. 21–41, at p. 28; cf. Biddle, *Winchester*, cap. 2.
[27] Orderic 13. 45 (6, p. 552).        [28] R. Torigni, p. 176.
[29] *Bury Docs.*, pp. lxxxv–lxxxvi, n. 6.

form of insurance policy quite understandable in an age of high mortality, though its psychological effects on the offspring themselves are hard to calculate. When we encounter the same practice among female children, like the Emma, daughter of Wimund, and 'her sister Emma', who held land at Stoke Newington in the late twelfth century, it may be that the same desire to perpetuate a family name is at work, but there is also the possibility that less care was taken in the individuation of girls, as seems to have been the case with women's names in ancient Rome.[30]

A special case of choice of name was the adoption of a new name by a mature individual. Instances of changes to avoid barbaric outlandishness have already been cited. More common was the selection of a name in religion by a convert to the religious life. This frequently involved replacement of vernacular Norman or Anglo-Scandinavian names by biblical ones. Augustine, formerly Henry, who was worried about the benefits of prayers said for him, is an instance. An intriguing case concerns William of Corbeil, prior of Chich in Essex and then archbishop of Canterbury (1123–36), who had a companion called Siward, 'whom the archbishop afterwards called Simon'.[31] Perhaps this French ecclesiastic welcomed the chance to drop the embarrassing 'Siward' under the pious cover of choosing a bible name.

Events in an individual's life might also be reflected in a name change. Although there is no way of being certain, it is possible that Romfare of Lincoln, whose name means 'Rome-farer', may be recalling a pilgrimage, like a modern Muslim called al-Hajj.[32] Those who were cured at the shrines of the saints sometimes adopted the name of their benefactor. Thus when a small boy was healed at the tomb of Godric of Finchale, 'his mother, on account of this miracle, had her son called no longer William but, as the Lord commanded in a vision, Godric.'[33] Here, through the influence of this English hermit-saint, we have a small counter-eddy to the rage for Norman names.

## Surnames

In our period it was unusual for men or women to be distinguished by a surname that had been borne by their parents and would be handed down to their children. Hereditary surnames were not common before the fourteenth century. It was, however, customary for people of this time to have a byname or *cognomen*, in the form of a nickname, toponym, occupational tag, or patronymic that distinguished them from others of the same baptismal name. There are dozens of Rogers recorded in Domesday Book but only one Roger

---

[30] *The Cartulary of St Mary Clerkenwell*, ed. W. O. Hassall (Camden, 3rd ser., 71; 1949), no. 65, p. 45; M. I. Finley, *Aspects of Antiquity* (London, 1968), p. 131.
[31] *Aldgate Cart.*, p. 228.      [32] *RRAN* 2, nos. 1043, 1120, 1253, and nn., pp. 114, 131, 156.
[33] Reg., *V. Godric* 176 (p. 434); cf. ibid. 143, 177 (pp. 418–19).

'God-Save-the-Ladies' (*Deus salvet dominas*), an Essex landholder whose gallantry rolls down the centuries. The urge to mark a special feature or attribute, physical or otherwise, explains the habit of giving nicknames even to members of the royal dynasty—surely men who needed little in the way of additional identification. It was their subjects who turned William II, Henry II, and John into William Rufus, Henry Courtmantle, and John Lackland. Toponyms were identifying tags drawn from a place of origin or residence. The principle emerges with charming simplicity in a document from the reign of Henry I: Wulnoth de Walbrook sells a plot of land he has on Walbrook, 'from which he is called Wulnoth of Walbrook'.[34] Occupational *cognomina*, like William (the) Cook, and patronymics, like Robert, son of Leonard, were also very common.

Aristocrats showed a distinctive naming pattern, in that they used surnames earlier and had heritable surnames earlier than other classes. This can be illustrated by analysis of the secondary name (*cognomen*) borne, in addition to the baptismal name, by the 398 important French tenants-in-chief listed at the beginning of the county entries in Domesday Book (see Table 10).

TABLE 10. *Cognomina among French tenants-in-chief, 1086*

| Type of name | Number | Per cent |
|---|---|---|
| French toponym | 107 | 27 |
| Patronymic | 72 | 18 |
| Office or occupation | 67 | 17 |
| Nickname | 55 | 14 |
| No *cognomen* | 50 | 13 |
| English toponym | 23 | 6 |
| Locative (Brito—'Breton' etc.) | 14 | 4 |
| Earldom or county | 10 | 3 |

Two features are striking: the low percentage of those aristocrats identified only by a baptismal name and the high proportion (one-third) bearing toponymics.[35] This is at least in part because aristocratic toponyms identified not simply, or even, place of origin but property. Richer de Laigle was not a man from Laigle but lord of Laigle. As he passed on his estates, so he passed on his name—hence the early hereditary tendency in aristocratic surnames.

Because aristocratic names were so closely entwined with aristocratic lands, there are several cases where the tenure of certain estates led to the adoption of the surname that was thought to go with them, even when no

---

[34] *Ramsey Cart.* 1, p. 139, no. 61: 'unde et ipse Wlnothus de Walebroc vocatus fuit'.

[35] J. C. Holt, *What's in a Name? Family Nomenclature and the Norman Conquest* (Stenton Lecture for 1981; Reading, 1982), p. 20.

direct descent in the male line was involved. Robert de Muschamps, lord of Wooler in Northumberland, was eventually succeeded by his daughter Cecily, who is referred to in the Pipe Roll of 1179–80 as 'Cecily de Muschamps'. She married Stephen de Bulmer, who answered for the Muschamps estates in the survey of knights' fees of 1166. Their son Thomas occurs as 'Thomas, son of Stephen de Bulmer', but also as 'Thomas de Muschamps' and his son, Robert, succeeding in 1190, is known as 'Robert de Muschamps'. Thomas thus assumed the surname not of the paternal but of the maternal line, the ancestors who had provided the bulk of the estates.[36]

This pattern is not unusual. Some of the famous families of later medieval England, like the Percy and Mowbray dynasties, did not descend in the unbroken male line from ancestors who bore those names at the time of the Domesday Survey. The Percy family of later medieval and modern times has as its direct male ancestor not the Domesday baron William de Percy but Jocelin of Louvain, opportunist brother of queen Adeliza (above, p. 44), who married William's great-granddaughter, Agnes de Percy. The Mowbrays provide a particularly remarkable case of the transmission of a surname via the transmission of property (see Figure 14). The name derives from the lordship of Montbray in Normandy. This was held by two generations of aristocrats, Roger and Robert de Mowbray. The latter was earl of Northumberland, rebelled in 1095 and was dispossessed and imprisoned for life. Shortly before his rebellion he had married Maud de Laigle, who lived on after her husband's imprisonment for many years in an ambiguous state, with a living husband she scarcely knew, before arrangements were made for her divorce and remarriage. In 1107 or 1108 she married Nigel d'Aubigny, one of Henry I's chief men. Her misfortunes were not over. Unable to bear Nigel a child, she was herself divorced. In 1118 Nigel married as his second wife Gundreda de Gournay, by whom he had a son, Roger. When this boy came of age in 1138, he enters the record as 'Roger de Mowbray'. He drew his name from his father's former wife's former husband. The reason why the name was transmitted through such an indirect chain was that the Norman estate of Montbray had passed from earl Robert to Maud to Nigel to Roger.

The aristocratic patronymic was constructed with the Old French word for son, *fiz*, and is conventionally rendered into modern English using 'fitz'. The Anglo-Norman adventurer in Ireland who occurs in narratives of the time as 'Robert le fiz Estevene', or, in Latin guise, as 'Robertus filius Stephani' is the 'Robert fitz Stephen' of modern history books. These patronymics cast a particularly sharp light on the process whereby surnames

---

[36] PR 26 HII, p. 142; *RBE* 1, p. 439; PR 18 HII, p. 67; PR 2 RI, p. 21; Sanders, *Baronies*, p. 100; *EYC* 2, pp. 127–9; *Cartularium abbathiae de Rievalle*, ed. J. C. Atkinson (Surtees Soc. 83; 1889 for 1887), no. 315, p. 221.

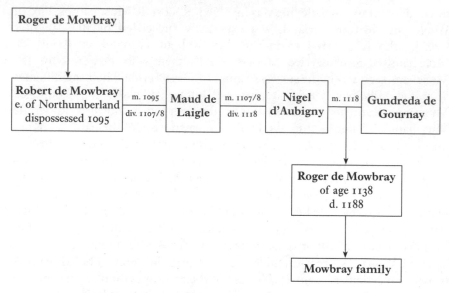

FIGURE 14.  *The transmission of the surname Mowbray*

became hereditary. Robert fitz Stephen was in fact the son of a man named
Stephen. If he had not been, then we could be sure that the 'fitz Stephen' had
become a hereditary surname. For some families we can trace the process of
the fossilization of the patronymic surname in detail.

Alan fitz Flaald, hereditary steward of the bishops of Dol in Brittany, was
close to Henry I. He witnessed ten of Henry's charters and had the king confirm his pious donations. He was given lands in England, notably in Shropshire, and was succeeded by his son, William fitz Alan, who was sheriff of
Shropshire and died in 1160. Until this point the family patronymics were
simple indicators of the father's name: Alan *was* the son of Flaald, William
*was* the son of Alan. The case of William fitz Alan's son, also called William,
is different. He came of age in 1175 and died in 1210 and left numerous traces
in the documentary record, being, like his father both an important baron and
sheriff of Shropshire. The monastic annalist who recorded his death calls
him 'William fitz Alan'.[37] Although he was the son of William, he is now 'a fitz
Alan', at least in the discourse of the annals.

If we look at his appellation in the documentary sources, for instance the
records of the royal government or the cartulary of Haughmond abbey, a
Shropshire monastery under the patronage of the family, two patterns
emerge. First, he is called 'William fitz Alan', and nothing else, in judicial
and financial records or when he is being referred to by others. Thus an

---

[37] *Ann. Dunst.*, p. 33.

agreement in the county court of Shropshire in 1190 was made 'when William fitz Alan was sheriff' and this is also how he is designated in the Pipe Rolls, when mention is made of his scutage obligations, activities as sheriff, etc.[38] Secondly, however, it is clear that he did sometimes still refer to himself, in charters that he himself issued or witnessed, not as 'William fitz Alan', but as 'William fitz William fitz Alan', i.e. 'William, son of William, son of Alan'. Moreover, the evidence of the Haughmond charters seems to suggest that this genuine patronymic was his early choice of style and that it was replaced, over the course of his lifetime, by the patronymic surname. Most of the charters in which he appears as 'William, son of William, son of Alan' are early, from the 1170s or 1180s. By contrast, only one of the, very numerous, charters in which he appears as 'William fitz Alan' are so early. Virtually all of them date to the 1190s or the first decade of the thirteenth century.

It is not implausible, therefore, to see William slowly adapting his own usage to the usage of those around him. What we call ourselves is subject to the pressure of what others call us. It is thus perhaps significant that one late example of William's use of the designation 'William, son of William, son of Alan' occurs in the document in which he made arrangements for his own burial. At that point who you thought you were was more important than what others thought about you.[39] The descendants of Henry I's courtier thus eventually became 'the Fitz Alans', but in the process, during the career of William, son of William, there was a time of hesitation between a true patronymic and a hereditary surname derived from a patronymic. The shift from the one to the other can be dated, in this instance, quite precisely to the years 1175–1210, with official practice leading the way.

Although hereditary surnames emerged earlier and were more widespread among the aristocracy than among other classes, the practice of having an additional tag, beyond the bare baptismal name, was common throughout society. About 1225, at the very end of the period covered in this book, the earl of Chester made a series of agreements with the free tenants who had rights in the West Fen of Bolingbroke (Lincs.), whereby they surrendered their rights to him, so that he could enclose it.[40] Apart from the interest these documents have as evidence for the enclosure of the fens and the pressure on the free peasantry, they also reveal the naming patterns of that social class at this time, since they record 102 names, all bar two of men. Of these 100 men, every one, without exception bears both a baptismal name and a further identifying element. The frequency of different types of *cognomen* is shown in Table 11.

---

[38] *Cartulary of Haughmond Abbey*, ed. Una Rees (Cardiff, 1985), no. 986, p. 190.

[39] Ibid., no. 290, pp. 73–4.     [40] *Chester Charters*, nos. 417–21, pp. 415–18.

TABLE 11. *Cognomina of Bolingbroke tenants about 1225*

| Form of cognomen | Number (and percentage) |
|---|---|
| Patronymic | 57 |
| Locative | 21 |
| Nickname | 13 |
| Occupational | 4 |
| Matronymic | 3 |
| 'Nephew of' | 2 |
| TOTAL | 100 |

As can be seen, patronymic identification was by far the commonest form: 'William son of Hervey, Alan son of Robert, Richard son of William', etc. Only three individuals are identified by their mother: 'John son of Emma, Robert son of Matilda, Geoffrey son of Isabella'. The significance of a matronym is unclear. It might suggest that the father had died early and the individual had always been identified by reference to the surviving parent; it might conceivably imply bastardy; or possibly the mothers so singled out were heiresses. The existence of two individuals called 'nephew of X' shows that there was some flexibility in the family member chosen as the relevant relative for identification.

After identification by relationship to another family member, the next most common form is identification by place, with the Latin *de* ('of') linking the forename either to a settlement ('of Huntingfield' (Suffolk), 'of Pinchbeck' (Lincs.)) or to a landscape feature ('of the rock', 'of the bridge'). Nicknames form the next most frequent group. Some refer to physical features ('black [haired]'), some to less obvious qualities ('kite', 'lamb'—although this might also be a reference to occupation or a contraction of Lambert). Surprisingly few *cognomina* are occupational: 'carpenter', 'smith', and 'cook' occur, as well as *cambrarius*, perhaps 'chamberlain'.

Beneath the Latin garb of the official documentation, these Lincolnshire villagers of the early thirteenth century were thus identified by such familiar tags as Harvey ('son of Hervey'), Robertson, Williamson, Black, Lamb, Smith, and Cook. Whether any of these were becoming hereditary is hard to say, although the existence of four different individuals with the name 'de rupe' ('of the rock') might suggest various branches of a family with this name rather than four relatives living in the same location or four unrelated men who had all acquired the same locative identification. In any event, it is clear that a second identifying element alongside the baptismal name was a universal practice and that in 60 per cent of cases this second element was 'son of X'.

## 3. LOVE, SEX, AND MARRIAGE

### Freedom to Marry and its Limitations

Of that conventional trio, birth, marriage, and death, the middle member of the group is distinguished by the fact that there is a certain amount of choice involved. During our period that element of choice came to be a central and defining feature of marriage, as two things became clear about marriage as a legal institution: first, that the ordinary secular courts would let the Church define what constituted a valid marriage; secondly, that the Church would see the essence of a valid marriage as the consent of the two parties. In this way many other considerations were relegated to secondary status: the interests of the families, the importance of public acknowledgement, the transmission of property, actual physical consummation. Naturally, these factors continued to exert their influence, but they had to do so in a world where marriage was defined in canon law as an agreement between two individuals.

It was during the pontificate of Alexander III (1159–81) that the canonical doctrine on marriage assumed its final form. For a marriage to be valid all that was required was that two parties who could legitimately marry each other either exchange words of consent in the present tense (*de praesenti*)—'I take you as my wife/husband'—or use the future tense (*de futuro*)—'I will marry you'—but follow this by physical consummation. Prior to this time there had been some debate on the exact constituents of a marriage, but now the ecclesiastical authorities had a clear guiding principle: the consent of the parties made a valid marriage. The lay courts were quite happy to concede decisions about the legitimacy of any given marriage to the Church. Glanville is unequivocal that, as soon as the issue of 'legitimate marriage' is broached, 'the case shall proceed no further in the court of the lord king but the archbishop or bishop shall be commanded to inform the lord king or his justices what he knows about that marriage and what his judgment is concerning it.'[41]

### Lords

The consent of a lord or parents or other family members was thus not required for a marriage to be legally valid. Customary obligations and the social realities, however, meant that they continued to exercise a great deal of control. Lords were simply not willing to let their dependants, of whatever status, make important decisions which often concerned the transmission of property without having their own say and in this they had the support of feudal and manorial custom.

[41] Glanville 7. 13 (p. 87).

A feudal lord had a recognized right to control the marriage of his tenants' daughters if they were heiresses. This right operated both during the lifetime of the tenant and also after his death, when the lord would become guardian of the daughter or daughters, even if of full age. It was a major offence to marry off one's daughter, if she could be expected to inherit, without the consent of one's lord. Even when Henry I was wooing his baronage by the promise of a liberal policy on marriages, he insisted on prior consultation.[42] In Glanville's summation, 'according to the custom of the kingdom, no woman who is the heir to land can be rightfully given in marriage without the direction and assent of the lord'.[43] Like most medieval rights, this one was for sale, and lords, especially the ultimate superior lord, the king, would sell 'marriages', i.e. the right to control the marriage of an heiress, to those who could pay for them, either to marry them themselves, give them to a relative, or resell them at profit. The accounts of the royal government under Henry II and his sons record sixty payments for permission to marry heiresses, in addition to thirty-one cases of punishment for those who had done so without permission. King John collected over £9,000 from payments to marry heiresses.[44] In addition, the lord exercised over his vassals a similar control over the marriage of male heirs who were under age and of widows. Eventually some limits were established to the king's right to specify a marriage partner, for the aristocracy felt strongly that marriages should not be 'disparaging', i.e. that heirs and heiresses should be married off only to their social equals. The English-born theologian Robert of Courson complained about disparagement and in 1215 the rebel barons insisted in Magna Carta that 'heirs shall be married without disparagement and the close relatives shall be informed of the match before it takes place', a point reiterated in later re-issues of the Charter.[45]

It was natural for a twelfth-century king to wish to control the descent of a major barony, but authority over subordinates' marriage extended throughout the social scale, down to the level of the unfree peasant. As the legal theory of villeinage crystallized in the early thirteenth century, it was indeed argued that it was a defining mark of unfreedom that one could not marry off one's daughter without making a payment (*merchet*) to the lord (see above, p. 323). Theory was too simple. It was certainly the case that the unfree were subject to this burden, but free peasants too often had to make such a payment.[46]

---

[42] Liebermann, *Gesetze* 1, pp. 521–2 (CHn cor); *Sel. Charters*, p. 118; Robertson, *Laws*, pp. 276–8.

[43] Glanvill 7. 12 (p. 85).      [44] Waugh, *Lordship*, tables 4.3 and 4.4, pp. 157, 159.

[45] Baldwin, *Masters* 2, p. 178 n. 133; *Sel. Charters*, p. 294 (Magna Carta c. 6).

[46] Paul Hyams, *Kings, Lords and Peasants in Medieval England: The Common Law of Villeinage in the Twelfth and Thirteenth Centuries* (Oxford, 1980), pp. 189–90.

Thus the daughter of the highest baron and the unfree serf alike could marry only after gaining the lord's approval and satisfying his exactions. There was no doubt that marriages contracted according to the rules of the Church but against the lord's will were licit—especially after the papal ruling under Hadrian IV (1154–9) that marriages of the unfree were valid—but violation of the lord's right to consent might provoke a strong reaction. Feudal tenants like Walter of Everington 'who married his wife without the king's permission, although she was in the king's gift' or Richard of Warwick, 'who married off his daughter without the lord king's permission', faced fines and the amounts might be high. Under Henry II the average fine was £75, roughly equivalent to five years' income for a knight.[47] In some cases offenders might have their property confiscated.[48]

Between lord and peasant manners could be rougher: one night early in 1220 Henry de Vere broke into the house of his tenant Roger of Kirkele at Mutford (Suffolk) in search of Roger's daughter, who was the wife of Thomas of Braddele. The girl escaped through the window, but, while searching through the premises, Henry set fire to the grain stored in the barn and barn and house burned down. Roger and his son-in-law brought a charge of arson. Henry de Vere's reply was that, indeed, the house had unfortunately burnt down, but that was an accident and, more significantly, 'Roger is his villein . . . and Thomas of Braddele married Roger's daughter against his will, whereas he could not marry her off without his agreement.'[49] We do not know the outcome of this case, but Henry de Vere clearly considered that the lord's customary rights could be sanctioned by violence. Of course, powerful lords did not require the sanction of custom for their violence and could resort to simple coercion to get their way, as apparently in the case of William de Roumare, earl of Lincoln (d. about 1161), who, for unknown reasons, was trying to put pressure on the Lincolnshire knight, Oliver the Angevin, to marry a certain woman and to do so 'seized him and held him in prison in fetters until he had forced him to swear that he would marry the woman.'[50]

## Kindred

Marriage was not only a bond between two individuals but between two families. Indeed, one purpose of marriage that was acknowledged in the twelfth century was to create 'new friends and relatives' (the Latin *amici* could mean either).[51] A marriage could mark the settlement of a dispute, constituting a new bond between rival kindreds. When Henry II gave Aubrey de Lisours in marriage to William fitz Godric it was explicitly 'so that the discord that had

---

[47] PR 26 HII, p. 41; PR 6 RI, p. 162; Waugh, *Lordship*, table 4. 4, p. 159.
[48] Waugh, *Lordship*, p. 88.  [49] *CRR* 9, pp. 336–7.
[50] Holtzmann and Kemp, pp. 20–1, no. 8 (JL 13937).  [51] Map 3. 4 (p. 262).

arisen between his relatives and hers should be laid to rest'.[52] This was a social function that the Church was sometimes forced to recognize. At the Council of Westminster in 1175, the ecclesiastical authorities prohibited the marriage of minors, 'except by special dispensation to achieve peace and reconciliation between princes and great men'.[53]

Because marriage was a bond between families, family members expected to have their say in the choice of marriage partner. This family pressure made itself felt most strongly when parents sought to exercise authority over their daughters. The quasi-autobiographical account of Christina of Markyate's long resistance to her parents' marriage plans shows the difficulties a young girl could have.[54] She was born into the old English urban aristocracy of Huntingdon and a young man of her own class, Burthred, sought her in marriage. He gained her parents' consent to the match, 'whether Christina agreed or not' (*vellet nollet Christina*). When he came to the house to discuss the wedding, however, Christina refused to listen, saying that she had vowed to live a virgin all her life. They laughed at her, but she remained unmoved. The family then began a campaign of pressure and persuasion: 'they offered gifts, promised great things . . . flattered her, threatened her'. A close cousin told her of the pleasures of being mistress of her own house. Eventually, when they were all assembled at the church, Christina yielded and gave her verbal consent to the marriage.

Burthred now began to build a new and bigger house for his bride and in the meantime Christina remained in her parents' house. She made it clear, however, that she would not be willing to have intercourse with Burthred. This unleashed an even more intense campaign of persuasion on the part of her family, especially her parents. They tried keeping her from going to church and taking her to parties instead. They let Burthred into her bedroom at night but Christina sat up with him, telling him exemplary stories of chaste marriages. She promised to live with him, 'so that the other townsmen will not taunt you for having been rejected by me', but chastely. On this occasion Burthred left her without having had intercourse, but his reception by his comrades, who called him 'a useless young fellow, lacking in spirit', impelled him to try again on two other occasions. Once he burst into her bedroom, determined to have her 'either through entreaty or by force', but she hid from him. His friends surged in looking for her, while she trembled behind the hangings, imagining herself 'dragged into their midst, surrounded by the

[52] *Decretals* 4. 2. 5, cols. 673–4 (JL 13887); for the case, see C. R. Cheney, *From Becket to Langton: English Church Government 1170–1213* (Manchester, 1956), pp. 58–9; Duggan, 'Equity', pp. 69–70; *Decretales ineditae saeculi XII*, ed. Stanley Chodorow and Charles Duggan (Monumenta iuris canonici, series collectionum 4; Vatican City, 1982), no. 71, p. 123, and comment on pp. 124–5.
[53] *Councils and Synods* I/ii, p. 981 (cf. p. 991).          [54] *V. Christina*, pp. 34–96.

threatening crowd who watched as she was given to the sport of the man who wished to corrupt her'. Miraculously, she avoided discovery.

Because Christina had in fact formally agreed to marry Burthred, it was possible for her parents to make a good case before the ecclesiastical authorities. Both the prior of Huntingdon and the bishop of Lincoln (Robert Bloet, 1093–1123) gave rulings in their favour. At one point her father conceded that there had been an element of coercion involved, but argued that 'if she rejects the marriage and spurns our authority, we shall be a laughing-stock in the eyes of our neighbours'. Christina's continued intransigence was punished by intimidation, constraint, and violence. Her father threatened to throw her out of the house, her mother grabbed her by the hair and beat her. Eventually, after careful secret planning and the generous use of bribes, Christina made her escape, disguised as a man, and was able to begin her chosen life as a religious solitary.

The story shows both the stifling inertia of social expectations—it was simply presumed that Christina would marry and create her own ostentatious domestic world as well-born wife and mother—and the fierce repression that followed any opposition to those patterns. One's standing in the eyes of one's neighbours was a constant obsession. It was unbearable to be rejected or made to look foolish. For a girl to deny the authority of her parents and her husband was a rebellion that must be crushed, lest the family's credibility founder in this competitive world of wagging and malicious tongues. The effectiveness of this pressure is best shown by the remarkable fact that Christina did indeed consent to the marriage. How many weddings in this period required coercion is not something we can know but cases like Christina's demonstrate the readiness of parents and other kin to use it.

*Church Rules*

Although the ecclesiastical authorities had determined that free consent between the parties was the essence of a marriage, canon law certainly did not allow unlimited choice of marriage partner. The most important restriction was the ban on marriages within the prohibited degrees. In accordance with the universal law of the Catholic Church, English ecclesiastical legislation of the eleventh and twelfth centuries reiterated the point that there was to be no marriage with relatives or relatives of one's dead wife 'to the seventh degree'.[55] This was interpreted to mean as far as sixth cousins and hence constituted a severe restriction on choice of marriage partner. The prohibition was extended even further by the concept of spiritual kinship: one was not allowed to marry a godparent or a godparent's child. A marriage that broke these rules could be stigmatized as 'incestuous'. Eventually the Church

---

[55] *Councils and Synods* 1/ii, pp. 614, 678, 741,

authorities themselves came to feel that this system was too restrictive and at the Fourth Lateran Council of 1215 the rules were changed. Marriage was now prohibited only to the fourth degree (i.e. as far as third cousins). Even then, it cannot always have been easy to find an approved partner, either in the intermarried world of the aristocracy or that of the village.

Age at marriage was also regulated by canon law. In some ecclesiastical rulings the age of discretion in matrimonial matters was fixed at 7. In a letter to the archbishop of York, pope Alexander III decreed that 'there can be no espousal or marriage before the age of seven', and in another case, dealing with a man from the diocese of Hereford who had been betrothed to a girl who was 'in the cradle', but had later married the girl's mother, the same pope ruled that the marriage should stand if the earlier betrothal had taken place when the girl was under 7.[56] There was, however, some variability of judgement about what constituted full age, as emerges from a case of the 1170s heard by the papal judges-delegate Roger, bishop of Worcester, and Adam, abbot of Evesham. The woman in the case alleged that she was espoused when only 5 years of age to the son of her guardian. As soon as she reached the age of discretion, she claimed, she left and married another. Her fiancé, however, asserted that she was 14 when the betrothal took place and that she lived with him uncomplainingly for a year before she was taken away furtively. The pope, in his commission to the judges, made 12 the critical age: if the girl was less than 12 at the time of the first engagement and did not consent to it, she should stay with her present husband, but if she had been 12 or over and gave her consent, she must go back to the guardian's son.[57]

## Rituals of Betrothal and Marriage

Since the Church had determined that the crucial component in a valid marriage was the consent of the parties, it was of course possible for marriage to be entered into secretly. Attempts were made to stop this, but were inhibited by the fundamental canon law principle 'marriage is contracted by consent alone'. A degree of publicity was a good thing in the eyes of the ecclesiastical authorities and perhaps also in the eyes of the female spouse, since it ensured that the man's responsibilities were widely recognized, and a marriage 'in front of the church' was the common and usual way of achieving this.[58] The insistence on the presence of witnesses, a public ceremony, and priestly blessing can be found throughout our period. At the Council of Winchester

---

[56] *Decretals* 4. 2. 4–5, cols. 673–4 (JL 13947 and 13887).

[57] Duggan, 'Equity', p. 82; Mary Cheney, *Roger, Bishop of Worcester 1164–1179* (Oxford, 1980), p. 355, no. 74.

[58] Michael M. Sheehan, 'Marriage Theory and Practice in the Conciliar Legislation and Diocesan Statutes of Medieval England', *Mediaeval Studies*, 40 (1978), pp. 408–60.

in 1076 it was ruled that 'no one should give his daughter or other relative to anyone without priestly blessing, otherwise it will be judged not a legitimate marriage but a fornicators' marriage' and the Council of Westminster of 1200 re-echoed the call: 'no-one may be joined in matrimony except publicly in front of the church and in the presence of a priest'.[59] The Church designed its rituals to secure the twin goals of public acknowledgement and ecclesiastical supervision of the marriage.

An innovative way of controlling marriage was introduced into England in 1200, when the first ecclesiastical legislation was issued relating to banns: 'No marriage should be contracted without a public announcement in church on three occasions'.[60] Gerald of Wales makes it clear that these three occasions should be the three Sundays preceding the wedding.[61] The idea of such a formal announcement is also found in the legislation of Odo de Sully, bishop of Paris (1197–1208) and became a universal requirement at the Fourth Lateran Council of 1215.[62] It was later elaborated, so that if strangers to the parish sought to be wed they required testimonial letters stating that the banns had been read in their own parish.[63]

The wedding service in our period had many similarities with that in the Church of England's Book of Common Prayer.[64] The priest began by asking if there were any reason why the bride and groom could not be legitimately married. The core of the ceremony was the interrogation of the couple: 'Do you take this woman . . . to keep in sickness and in health?' If both bride and groom said, 'I do' (*Volo*), the priest and the man giving the woman away then handed her to the groom, who placed a ring on her hand, saying, 'With this ring I honour you . . . with my body I wed you.' There were also less familiar features. The wedding ceremony itself took place at the church door and only afterwards did the wedding party go into the church to hear mass. The husband was expected to give his new wife her dower at the church door and might do so by handing over a symbolic object, such as a knife. During the mass the newly married couple would lie prostrate before the altar and the altar cloth would be held over them. The husband would kiss the bride but would do so after giving the kiss of peace to the priest during communion.

Lawsuits sometimes turned on whether a particular marriage had taken place or not and records of such cases supply details of actual ceremonies. Thus, about the year 1200, Agnes Parage was attempting to prove that she

[59] *Councils and Synods* 1/ii, pp. 620, 1067.     [60] Ibid., p. 1067.

[61] Gerald, *Gemma* 1. 13 (p. 46).

[62] *Les Statuts synodaux français du XIIe. s.*, 1. *Les Statuts de Paris et le synodal de l'Ouest (XIIIe. s.)*, ed. Odette Pontal (Coll. des documents inédits sur l'histoire de la France, Section de philologie et d'histoire jusqu'à 1610, série in-8o, 9; Paris, 1971), p. 66; Lateran IV c. 51, *Conciliorum oecumenicorum decreta*, ed. J. Alberigo *et al.* (3rd edn., Bologna, 1973), p. 258.

[63] *Councils and Synods* 2/i, p. 88.     [64] *Magd. Pont.*, pp. 202–5, 222–6.

had been legitimately married to Arnold of Thorley, while Arnold's brother denied this.[65] Substantial property was involved. Agnes produced witnesses who claimed to have been present at her marriage at Thremhall priory in Essex. They describe the proceedings at the west door of the church on a summer morning, with the prior in his vestments. Arnold had placed a ring on Agnes's hand with the words, 'With this ring I wed you and with my body I honour you'. A penny was put on a book, 'as is the custom in contracting marriages'. After Arnold had endowed Agnes with a third of his lands as dower, the group entered the church and heard mass, which the prior celebrated in a low voice without chanting, two canons holding the altar cloth over the couple. Agnes's father, brother, and stepbrother were present, but none of Arnold's family and Arnold had been heard to say 'that he did not want any of his relatives there by his side, since they hated Agnes, who had lived with Arnold for a long time before the marriage and borne him children'. Presumably one of these hostile relations was that brother who later brought the lawsuit against Agnes.

Less property was at stake in the case of the Londoners John the Blacksmith and Alice, niece of Ralph the baker, who were in dispute at about this same time.[66] John and Alice had lived together as man and wife but John had apparently then repudiated Alice. She produced witnesses who asserted that the couple had not only plighted their troth before lay people but had also proceeded, 'for greater security', to have a ceremony with a priest in the church of St Mary, Fenchurch Street. The priest there knew John the Blacksmith and thought that certain warnings and safeguards might be appropriate. He told the blacksmith to give proper consideration to the matter, to take the advice of his friends and relatives and perhaps to provide for a financial penalty, in case he broke his word. John replied that 'as long as he lived, he would not put her away in favour of another, prettier or uglier'. The priest then performed the ceremony, John and Alice accepting each other as man and wife 'by words of the present tense', giving each other their faith by their hands and making an offering on the altar. We also hear that the ceremony took place, unusually, in the chancel of the church, that John wore a blue cloak and Alice a blue cape and that, although there was no mass, there was a party after the wedding.

The tension between a solemn, ecclesiastically inspired idea of marriage and a continuing tradition of casual, secular marriage is evident in the statutes of the diocese of Salisbury issued about 1218. One of the statutes insists that marriage is a sacrament, indeed the first of the sacraments, since it had been instituted by God in paradise. An entirely different view is conjured up by the requirement that marriages be celebrated

---

[65] *Canterbury Cases*, no. A. 6, pp. 18–24.          [66] Ibid., no. A. 7, pp. 25–8.

with reverence and honour and not with laughing and joking, in taverns or at public feasts or drinking parties. Nor should anyone put a ring made of rushes or some other material, cheap or precious, on some girl's hand in fun, to be able to fornicate with her more freely, for he may find that, although he thinks he is joking, he has in fact bound himself to the obligations of matrimony.[67]

Informal and boisterous observances of this kind are also apparent in the custom of blessing the marriage bed, when an obliging cleric would enter the bridal room where the couple lay in bed 'to bless them and sign them with the cross'.[68] A story was told of the visit of John of Crema, the papal legate, to England in 1125. He was investigating various charges against Ranulf Flambard, bishop of Durham, and while at Durham was very much taken by a beautiful girl, the bishop's niece. Following her uncle's instructions, the girl went to bed with the legate 'to be instructed in Roman ways':

As soon as she got into his bed, the bishop entered the bedchamber, with his clerks and servants, carrying drinking cups and lanterns that dispelled the shades of night with their brightness. Standing around the legate's bed, they called in clear voices: 'Blessing! Blessing!' He was amazed and asked 'What in the name of St Peter are you doing?' 'Sir,' replied the bishop, 'it is the custom of our country that when a nobleman marries, this honour is owed him by his friends. Rise therefore and drink what is in this goblet I am carrying. If you refuse, you will certainly drink of the goblet after which there is no thirst.' Willy-nilly he arose and, naked to the groin, drank to the new bride half of what was in the bishop's goblet. The bishop left, now not worried about losing his see.[69]

Whatever the truth of this story (probably not much), the picture of nuptial customs it presents is likely to be accurate.

## Dower and Marriage-Portions

Marriage was a property transaction as well as a personal one. Two kinds of exchange were involved, dower and marriage-portion. Dower was provided for the wife from the husband's estate, while the marriage-portion was property given with the woman, usually by her father, on the occasion of the marriage. English Common Law provided that the wife had the right to expect a dower from her husband's property. In the case of those holding by military tenure, this was defined as a third, or specified property up to a third, of the husband's estate, conventionally given to the wife at the church door on the

[67] *Councils and Synods* 2/i, pp. 86–7; the opening words of the latter canon are based on those of a canon of Odo de Sully, bishop of Paris, but the details that follow are not and thus indubitably refer to English customs; *Les Statuts synodaux français du XIIe. s.*, 1. *Les Statuts de Paris et le synodal de l'Ouest (XIIIe. s.)*, ed. Odette Pontal (Coll. des documents inédits sur l'histoire de la France, Section de philologie et d'histoire jusqu'à 1610, série in–80, 9; Paris, 1971), p. 66.

[68] Marie de France, *Le Fresne*, line 407 (*Lais*, p. 45).

[69] *Ann. Wint.*, pp. 47–8; cf. H. Hunt. 7. 36 (pp. 472–4).

wedding day. The wife had no actual control over her dower during her husband's lifetime but, after the husband's death, a widow was entitled to enjoy her dower during her own lifetime. Tenants of non-military freeholds, such as socage and some burgage land, customarily provided a larger dower of half their property.

The marriage portion was the property the woman brought with her to the marriage. The common size of the marriage portion among the Yorkshire gentry in the Angevin period was half to one and a half carucates.[70] These knightly husbands could thus expect to increase their estates by 100 acres or so through marriage. Higher up the aristocratic ladder amounts were naturally greater. When Ansfrid of Cormeilles, a minor baron in Gloucestershire and Herefordshire in the time of William the Conqueror, married the niece of Walter de Lacy, his neighbour and lord, the marriage portion he received increased the value of his estates by 15 per cent, from about £60 to about £75.[71] Ranulf III, earl of Chester (1181–1232), provided for each of his sisters on their marriage, endowing them in accordance with their seniority and the status of their husbands. Matilda, who married earl David of Huntingdon, brother of the king of Scots, in 1190, received 60 librates of land (i.e. land estimated to render £60 a year) and the service of 15 knights, Agnes, marrying earl William de Ferrers in 1192, was given 10 librates of land and 5 knights' fees, while Hawisa, who became the wife of Robert de Quincy, an untitled and less wealthy landowner, in 1199–1200, had 10 librates of land and 3 knights' fees as her marriage portion.[72]

Because marriage connections between the propertied were so significant for their economic situation, the terms agreed between the families on these occasions were sometimes put into writing. The settlement between Roger, earl of Warwick, and Geoffrey de Clinton, when the earl gave him his daughter Agnes and remitted the service that Geoffrey owed from ten of the knights' fees that he held from him, was written down and attested by numerous witnesses representing both parties.[73] The marriage contract between William Marshal and Baldwin, count of Aumale, specified that William's eldest son should marry Baldwin's elder daughter, or, if she died before the marriage could take place, his younger daughter. Conversely, if William's eldest son died, Baldwin's daughter would marry his second son. Baldwin promised all his English lands as his daughter's marriage portion. Terms were put down in writing and confirmed in writing by the king. Since

---

[70] Hugh M. Thomas, *Vassals, Heiresses, Crusaders and Thugs: The Gentry of Angevin Yorkshire, 1154–1216* (Philadelphia, 1993), p. 121.

[71] *DB* 1, 169b–170, 186–186b (Gls. 68; Hef. 21).

[72] *Chester Charters*, nos. 220, 263, 308, pp. 220–1, 262, 305–7.

[73] *The Beauchamp Cartulary*, ed. Emma Mason (PRS, n.s. 43; 1980 for 1971–3), no. 285, pp. 162–3.

at the time of the contract the parties to the marriage were only 12 and 7 years old, respectively, it was nearly eleven years before the wedding was actually celebrated.[74] It is very clear from this contract that the marriage was a piece of business between two aristocratic families and had nothing whatever to do with the personal preferences of the young bride and groom.

## Divorce and Separation

In our period there was no divorce in the sense of the dissolution of a valid marriage. The conjugal partnership could only be legally broken up in two ways. There might be legal separation, after which the spouses lived separately but were still considered married, or there might be nullification, which was a statement that they had never been married, even if they had considered themselves married and had lived together and had children. The commonest ground for nullification was consanguinity, relationship within the prohibited degrees, and it was clearly used as a ploy to secure the effects of divorce.

An example is provided by the only instance of a royal divorce in this period. King John married Isabella, daughter of the earl of Gloucester, in 1189, receiving with her the huge Gloucester estates, but after his accession to the throne in 1199 he was 'seized by the hope of a more lofty marriage' and decided to invoke the grounds of consanguinity. Since John and Isabella had a common great-grandfather in Henry I, they were related in the third degree, a relationship certainly sufficient for annulment. What makes the exercise quite clearly a piece of cynical manipulation is the fact that at the time of his marriage, in response to opposition to the match from Baldwin, archbishop of Canterbury, John had apparently promised to seek papal dispensation. This had not been obtained, probably with a conscious intention of keeping the consanguinity weapon in reserve. Had he received a papal dispensation for the marriage, in 1199 John would have been in the same situation that faced Henry VIII when he wished to replace Catherine of Aragon. As it was, he could put her aside (though keeping her lands) with ease.[75]

Aristocratic life abounded in such cases, inspired by a variety of motives. Earl William de Roumare (d. about 1198) confessed that his wife had been secretly instigated by others to suggest that their marriage was suspect on the grounds of consanguinity and to seek an annulment. Although the earl did not believe the marriage was within the prohibited degrees, he was so incensed by his wife's contempt of him that he did not contest the action and

---

[74] *Hist. Guill. Mar.* 3, p. 208 n. 2; G. E. C(okayne), *The Complete Peerage* (rev. edn., 12 vols.; London, 1910–59), vol. 1, pp. 354 n. c, 10, 367; *Rot. chart.*, pp. 112–13; Waugh, *Lordship*, pp. 55–6.

[75] H. G. Richardson, 'The Marriage and Coronation of Isabelle of Angoulême', *EHR* 61 (1946), pp. 289–314, esp. pp. 289–95; quotation from R. Diceto, *Ymag.* 2, pp. 166–7.

the marriage was annulled in the Church courts.[76] The case of Maud de
Laigle has been referred to above (p. 543). Married to Robert de Mowbray,
earl of Northumberland, shortly before he was imprisoned for life, she eventually obtained a nullification on the grounds of consanguinity. Her second
husband, Nigel d'Aubigny, later divorced her, probably because she bore him
no children. The excuse, however, was 'that she had been the wife of one of
his relatives'.[77] A woman who was separated from her husband on the
grounds of consanguinity (or for sexual misconduct) did not have her dower,
and the fate of Maud de Laigle was obviously not a happy one. The Church
insisted that separation should only follow an ecclesiastical judgment and
could not be a matter of agreement between the parties.[78] The cases mentioned above, however, suggest that aristocrats were adept at using the rules
of consanguinity to get something like divorce on demand.

## Love and Sex

When thinking about the private or intimate emotions of the men and women
of the twelfth century, we cannot draw on sources such as diaries or personal
letters which are so important for our mental picture of later centuries. Probably very few were written in our period; none survive. It is indeed possible to
deduce emotions from anecdotes in chronicles and references in public
records—legal proceedings for example—but the fullest and most explicit
writing about the emotions is found in imaginative or fictional literature.
There are obvious problems of interpretation here. It would be naive to presume that the poems and romances are a mirror of life: they may be selective,
idealized, exaggerated, conventional, or burlesque. Yet it is equally naive to
believe that they shed no light on the inner lives of the people who lived at the
time. Writers make assumptions about human behaviour that are more likely
to be drawn from their own experience of the people around them than from
any other source. Conversely, what one reads or (more common in twelfth-
century circumstances) hears, can be a major force shaping one's presup-
positions and behaviour. A generation brought up on a literature of romantic
love is likely to find romantic love.

### In Marie de France

One writer who made love a central theme in one of her works was Marie de
France. Her *Lais* cannot be dated precisely, although they have usually been
seen as a product of the reign of Henry II (1154–89), but their connection
with England is reasonably certain: the earliest manuscript containing the

---

[76] Holtzmann and Kemp, pp. 56–7, no. 23 (JL 16611); Duggan, 'Equity', p. 71.
[77] Anselm, ep. 423 (*Op.* 5, p. 369); Orderic 8. 23 (4, pp. 282–4).
[78] *Councils and Synods* 2/i, p. 135.

*Lais* and the only one with a complete text is a mid-thirteenth-century book from Reading abbey; the contemporary success of Marie's *Lais* is mentioned by the twelfth-century poet Denis Piramus, who was writing, in all likelihood, at Bury St Edmunds; and the *Lais* themselves sometimes give the English equivalents for words—'this bird is *rossignol* in French and *nightingale* in proper English'.[79] The hypothesis that Marie was a French woman writing at least some of the time in England seems plausible.

The *Lais* consist of twelve short poetic narratives and their main topic is love—the passionate, romantic love (*druerie*) that can surprise and torment those who feel it. 'How my heart is taken by surprise!' exclaims one young girl as she falls in love and her lover is equally 'taken by surprise by love'.[80] This unexpected and overpowering passion is not pleasant. It is indeed a form of suffering: 'love is a wound within the body'.[81] The theme of *Yonec* is 'the grief and sorrow they [the lovers] suffered for love' and the *lai* of *Chaitivel* concludes by dwelling on 'The great suffering they [the lady's lovers] endured because of the love they had for you'.[82] When love strikes, the first symptom is often sleepless nights in which the lover is obsessed by images of the beloved and tormented by doubts about the outcome. The extremes of passion are expressed by the language of death. One lover says to his beloved 'lady, I am dying for you'; another exclaims 'You are my life and death!'[83]

Passionate romantic love can exist between unmarried people and can have a happy outcome in marriage but it more often involves adultery. Indeed, of the twelve *Lais*, eight involve adulterous relations (one apparently non-consummated) and a ninth centres on a rejected adulterous invitation. In almost every case the adultery is between an unmarried man and a married woman. The exception is the story of *Eliduc*, in which the eponymous hero, happily married in his native Brittany, falls in love with a noble girl in Devon, but this is the exceptional Platonic affair (he marries the girl after his wife has entered the convent). Unmarried women do have sexual relations but with unmarried men, not with other people's husbands: Gurun keeps the beautiful Le Fresne as his concubine (*suinant*), 'the Two Lovers' fulfil their love before they are married and indeed die before they can marry, and the unmarried knight Milun loves his unmarried lady 'so much that she became pregnant'.[84]

The moral dilemma of adultery was sometimes felt. The knight Lanval, in king Arthur's service, rejects the advances of Arthur's queen with the words, 'I do not want your love; I have served the king for a long time; I do not wish

[79] *Laüstic*, lines, 5–6 (*Lais*, p. 97).     [80] *Eliduc*, lines 387, 712 (*Lais*, pp. 137, 145).

[81] *Guigemar*, line 483 (*Lais*, p. 15).

[82] *Yonec*, lines 553–4, *Chaitivel*, lines 213–14 (*Lais*, pp. 96, 121).

[83] *Guigemar*, line 501 (cf. *Equitan*, line 114), *Eliduc*, line 671 (*Lais*, pp. 15, 29, 144).

[84] *Le Fresne*, line 323, *Milun*, lines 53–4 (*Lais*, pp. 43, 103).

to betray my faith; I will not wrong my lord for you or your love.'[85] In the mirror image of this situation, King Equitan reflects on the breach of trust involved in loving his seneschal's wife, although in the end his desires overcome him. Overall sympathy, however, lies with the passionate lovers, even if one partner is married to another. Husbands are sometimes seen as annoying impedimenta: in the story of *Milun*, when Milun's illegitimate son offers to kill the (quite blameless) man who has married his mother, in order to let Milun marry her, there is no hint of reproach for his action and it is only the convenient death of the husband that allows a less bloody happy ending for the lovers.[86] Even more striking is an incident in the *lai* of *Eliduc*. When Eliduc is returning by sea from Devon with Guilliadun, the noble girl he loves, one of the sailors reveals the fact that he is already married: 'Sire, you have a loyal wife; with this other one you are going against God and the law, against right and fidelity.' Eliduc responds by calling the sailor the son of a whore, knocking him down with an oar and kicking him overboard.[87] That is the last we hear of the sailor. The story goes on to describe how Eliduc is eventually enabled to marry his love.

Special understanding is expressed for the predicament of young wives with jealous older husbands. In the *lai* of *Guigemar*, the hero's lover is married to an exceptionally jealous old man who had constructed for her an enclosure with only one entrance. The keys are kept by a priest 'who had lost his lower members—otherwise he would not have been trusted'. She explains her predicament to Guigemar, who reaches her by sea: 'My husband is a powerful man of great lineage but he is very old and sorely jealous . . . he has locked me in this enclosure which has only one exit. An old priest guards the door—may God burn him in hellfire! I am enclosed here night and day.'[88] A similar defiant lack of reconciliation with her fate is displayed by the lady in *Yonec*, likewise married to a jealous older man and locked up with his sister as sole companion: 'Alas that I was ever born', she laments, 'My fate is hard. I am imprisoned in this tower and will leave it only through death. This jealous old man, what does he fear, to keep me in this prison? . . . Cursed be my family and the others who gave me to this jealous man!'[89] Unhappily for the elderly husbands, but happily for the plots of the *lais*, 'No one can be enclosed or guarded so strictly that they cannot find an opportunity.'[90]

Since so much love is adulterous, it is not surprising that secrecy was its necessary condition. In *Laüstic* the knight's wife and her neighbour, who are lovers, 'loved each other wisely and well, concealing their love and taking care

[85] *Lanval*, lines 270–4 (*Lais*, p. 65).    [86] *Milun*, lines 501–2 (*Lais*, p. 114).
[87] *Eliduc*, lines 830–64 (*Lais*, pp. 148–9).
[88] *Guigemar*, lines 209–60, 341–9 (*Lais*, pp. 8–9, 11–12).
[89] *Yonec*, lines 67–72, 81–4 (*Lais*, pp. 83–4).    [90] *Milun*, lines 288–90 (*Lais*, p. 109).

that they should not be seen or disturbed or suspected.'[91] The lovers who penetrate the enclosures where young wives pine seek to keep their secret. The discovery of the lovers is a frequent dramatic crisis in the tales, sometimes forebodingly foreseen. This secret love is a mutual relationship between equals: 'Love is not honourable unless it is equal.' Powerful men who rely on their status to keep their lovers are no better than the calculating and contemptible bourgeois.[92] *Druerie* was one of the few realms where equality between the sexes was the acknowledged ideal.

Intensity, loyalty, and reciprocity are the marks of true love. They may be found between husband and wife, but may not. Marriage itself did not secure them. When king Arthur gives out 'women and lands' to his retinue, it is property he is dispensing and the dynastic and territorial side of marriage might make it an enemy of passion. The knight Gurun is happy with his concubine, the beautiful foundling Le Fresne, but his landed knightly tenants (*li chevaler fiufé*) force him to take a wife in order to have a legitimate heir. The landless knights of Gurun's household (*li chevaler de la meisun*) join with the servants in their sorrow at this displacement of the charming Le Fresne by the demands of lineage and property. Happily the intricacies of the plot reveal that the concubine is in fact a great heiress and hence allow Gurun both to marry Le Fresne and satisfy the apprehensions of his propertied vassals.

Love was clearly, in part, a game. The beautiful Breton lady who had four gallants and saw no reason 'to lose three for the sake of one' sent all of them love-tokens—rings, sleeves (detachable), pennants. Each of the four bore these with pride and regarded himself as her lover. Yet even here the passion is not ludicrous. In trying to be worthy of her and by demonstrating their prowess in a bloody tournament, three of the lovers are killed and one maimed. Love was seen as a spur to achievement, especially military, an idea expressed in the image of the lady looking on while her lover or lovers seek to outdo all others to win her esteem. Love (*druerie*) was an incentive to chivalry (*chevalerie*).[93]

Marie de France was not alone in her portrayal of the power of romantic love. Thomas of Chobham, in his manual for confessors, noted the symptoms, though less sympathetically than Marie: 'Many fall into mad love, so that they can hardly be called back from their error. This kind of love is a sickness not only of the mind but also of the body, for the marrow swells, the veins are disturbed and all the body's senses are weakened.'[94] Others stressed the irresistible nature of romantic passion. Marie's contemporary, Hue de Rotelande, wrote, in his tale of love and knighthood, *Ipomedon*, that 'Courtly love [*fine amur*] has great power and can subdue even kings and queens,

---

[91] *Laüstic*, lines 29–32 (*Lais*, p. 97).     [92] *Equitan*, lines 137, 146–8, 151–2 (*Lais*, p. 29).
[93] *Equitan*, lines 15–16 (*Lais*, p. 26).     [94] T. Chobham, *SC*, p. 389.

princes and dukes, counts and barons. Neither sense nor reason has any power against love . . . what can avail against love? Certainly, in the end, nothing.'[95]

## Sexual Ideals

It is hard to go beyond the images of literature and find out anything about the actual sexual behaviour of people in England in our period, partly for the obvious reason that this is intrinsically the most private kind of activity, but also because of the very slanted nature of the sources. Since literacy was in the hands of men who generally acknowledged celibacy as a requirement and virginity as an ideal, it is not surprising that accounts of sexual activity and positive evaluations of it are scarce. More common is the heated denunciation of sexuality, often in very general terms that allow us to use the material as evidence only of the preoccupations of the writers themselves. The dominant sexual discourse in twelfth-century England was one that disparaged sexual desire and sexual activity.

The positive counterpart to this hostility to sex was the exaltation of virginity, especially female virginity. Here the ancient association between female virginity and the sacred, an association that was not original with Christianity but was espoused and embraced by it, coincided with male ideals about how women should keep themselves before marriage. The glorification of perpetual virginity was, naturally, a common theme in ascetic devotional writing. Virginity was seen as 'the highest virtue, a glorious beauty, the source of life, a matchless song, the crown of faith, the prop of hope, the ornament of the virtues, the mirror of purity, kindred of the angels, friend of health, the nourishment and support of most enduring love.'[96] Although it was not official theological doctrine that sexuality was a consequence of the Fall, it was held that Eve had been a virgin before she yielded to the devil's temptations. She had torn the white garment of her innocence and only the Virgin Mary, who was 'splendid above all the daughters of Eve' because she was 'the first of all women to take a vow of virginity to God', could sew up that rent. 'Wholeness' (*integritas*) was the special blessing of the virgin.[97]

Since virginity was so highly prized, its loss was one of the great irreversible experiences. Once the 'flower of virginity' had gone, a woman 'could never again attain the prize of virginity'.[98] It was ' a treasure that, once lost, is never found again, a blossom that, once cut, never grows again'.[99] As Anselm put it in his lament for his own lost virginity, once he had wallowed in filth and

[95] Hue, *Ipom.*, lines 9095–9110, p. 458.

[96] Geoffrey of Burton, *V. sanctae Modwennae* 2, BL Add. 57533, fo. 82.

[97] Osbert, *Letters*, nos. 40–1, pp. 135–48.    [98] T. Chobham, *SC*, p. 356.

[99] *Hale Meiðhad*, ed. Bella Millett and Jocelyn Wogan-Browne, in *Medieval English Prose for Women* (Oxford, 1990), pp. 8–10.

descended into the whirlpool of foul pleasures, virginity was no longer his beloved but his lost love. It was a grief to lose irrecoverably what should have been preserved unceasingly. The prize of virginity was forever beyond him.[100] In some convents the nuns who were virgins would carry lighted candles in festal processions, while those who were not would bear snuffed out candles, making a public visual statement of their loss, their past, their irremediable state.[101]

Hugh, bishop of Lincoln, had to insist that married people who were faithful to their spouses could attain heavenly glory, and he would not have had to do this unless people believed the opposite.[102] Official Church doctrine did not condemn marriage and responsible ecclesiastics sought to stress that virginity was not in itself a spiritual virtue.[103] Yet there were clearly strong countervailing views. The sexual rhetoric of religious writers was always more likely to veer into outright denunciation of sexual activity than into vindication of its licit married form.

A treatise like *Sacred Virginity* (*Hale Meiðhad*), written in English in the early thirteenth century to encourage girls to live a celibate life, seeks to persuade not only by describing the privileges and dignity of virginity in the sacred order but also by summoning up a hideous picture of the frustrations, anxieties, and disgustingness of married life.[104] The life of a virgin is an angelic and heavenly life. She will be like Jesus and the Virgin Mary. She should say to herself, 'I shall keep myself whole, as Nature made me', and will enter heaven physically intact as Eve was before the Fall. Of the three orders that will inhabit heaven, virgins, the continent, and the married, the virgins are clearly the highest in esteem and dignity. They will sing a clearer song in the company of the angels, their crowns will be brighter. Marriage wins a thirtyfold reward, widowhood a sixtyfold, but virginity a hundredfold.

All this glory is contrasted with the situation of the woman who enters the 'servitude' of marriage: dominated by a man, worn down by domestic cares, her body made a burden to her by pregnancy and a rack of pain by childbirth, but, above all, 'a slave of the flesh'. It is 'carnal thoughts that incite you and draw you with their goadings to carnal filth and physical pleasure, and egg you on to marriage and a husband's embrace'. The sexual act itself is shameful: 'that sinful act that begat you of your mother, that indecent burning of the flesh, the fiery itch of physical desire before that disgusting act, that bestial coupling, that shameless union, that filthy, stinking and wayward deed.' The pleasures of marriage are few in comparison to its vexations—married people 'are licking honey off thorns'. 'Now you are married and descend into

---

[100] Anselm, *Meditatio* 2 (*Op.* 3, pp. 80–3).    [101] T. Chobham, *SC*, pp. 392–3.
[102] Ad. Eyns., *V. Hugh* 4. 9 (2, pp. 46–7).    [103] e.g. T. Chobham, *SC*, p. 393.
[104] *Hale Meiðhad*, ed. Bella Millett and Jocelyn Wogan-Browne, in *Medieval English Prose for Women* (Oxford, 1990), pp. 2–43.

the foulness of the flesh, the life of an animal, servitude to a man and the world's misery.'

The tone of such writing often suggests that it is motivated by a hatred of the body rather than the simple concern for moral rules about sexual conduct. When archbishop Anselm wrote to Gunnhilda, daughter of Harold, the last Saxon king, upbraiding her for having abandoned the nunnery in pursuit of marriage to count Alan Rufus, lord of Richmond, who had subsequently died, he summoned up a macabre scene:

You loved count Alan and he loved you. Where is he now? Where has he gone, this lover you loved so much? Go now, my sister, place yourself with him in the bed where he now lies. Gather his worms to your breast. Embrace his corpse. Kiss closely his naked teeth, for the lips have now rotted away. Certainly he cares no more for your love, that used to delight him when he was alive. . . . This is what you loved in him.[105]

This necrophiliac fantasy is paralleled by the advice of Gerald of Wales, writing about a century later, who encourages the clergy to resist sexual temptation by summoning up to the mind's eye the picture of the woman they desire after she is dead: if you love her, don't you love decay and the stench of rotting flesh?[106]

Some of the vehemence of this language and imagery is probably fuelled by the harsh self-discipline that clerics and monks had to embrace. They were not sexless but aspired to sexual control, in the face of feelings that were tempestuous and deeply ingrained:

There is one evil above all others that has torn and tortured my mind ever since I was in the cradle, that grew with me in infancy and adolescence, clung to me in my young manhood and does not leave my weak old limbs even now: this evil is the desire for physical pleasure, the delight of the flesh, the tempest of lust.[107]

Real conquest of sexual impulses was an almost miraculous virtue. St Hugh of Lincoln was cured of sexual desire by a visionary experience of having a dead prior cut open his belly with a knife and remove a fiery tumour; another version of the story says it was a visionary castration.[108]

An alternative to such radical amputation was the avoidance of contagion. Careful seclusion of the sexes and avoidance of familiar contact between them might even go as far as the imposition of supernaturally sanctioned

---

[105] Anselm, ep. 169 (*Op.* 4, pp. 47–8); see R. W. Southern, *Saint Anselm: A Portrait in a Landscape* (Cambridge, 1990), pp. 262–4.

[106] Gerald, *Gemma* 2. 4 (p. 184).

[107] *Oratio* 4 (*PL* 158, col. 870), there attributed to St Anselm; the true author seems to have been Ralph, prior of Rochester and abbot of Battle (1107–24): R. W. Southern, *Saint Anselm: A Portrait in a Landscape* (Cambridge, 1990), pp. 372–6.

[108] Ad. Eyns., *V. Hugh* 2. 2 (1, pp. 50–2); Gerald, *Symb. el.*, p. 247; Gerald, *V. Remigius* 29 (pp. 76–7).

zones of exclusion. St Cuthbert of Durham was the saint with the most pronounced views on women's presence. In the year 1113, after her marriage to David, the future King of Scots, the countess Matilda passed through Durham on her way to Scotland. She came to the cathedral and arrived at the boundary in the churchyard beyond which women were not permitted. Her chamber-woman, Helisend, wished to test the strength of this prohibition and, disguising herself as a man, went into the church. Saint Cuthbert immediately appeared to his sacristan, uttering the following words: 'Go as quick as you can and throw out that bitch who has sullied the threshold of my church by entering it. . . . I can have no peace and quiet in this place of my repose as long as I smell that foul bitch . . .'[109] The sacristan obeyed his orders; Helisend eventually became a nun. The writer who tells this story thought it important to add that the saint 'did not persecute that sex through dislike but sought to remove occasion for sin by cutting out opportunity.'

If the explicit rationale presented here is that it is morally prudent to keep women out since their presence may constitute occasion for sexual sin by men, then there are also clear signs in the thinking of the period that sexuality may be intrinsically polluting. The idea of non-culpable pollution was explicitly espoused by those who argued that, although nocturnal emissions of semen during sleep were not sinful, those who experienced them 'incur some kind of uncleanness and on account of this they should purify themselves before they go to the altar or receive communion'.[110] Sexual activity was meant to be regulated by the rituals of sacred time. Advent and Lent were periods for sexual abstinence when marriages too were not to be celebrated. No advances were to be made to women who were menstruating or in childbed. Intercourse before communion was frowned on.

That some ordinary lay people did try to observe these rules is brought out by an intriguing story from the *Life* of Henry of Coquet, a Northumbrian hermit who died in 1120. This tells how a man decided to refrain from sexual intercourse with his wife during Lent. Far from praising him, however, the holy hermit rebuked him for presumption, because he had undertaken such a course 'without the counsel of your spiritual father'. The man was in fact punished by being transported naked into a stable by evil spirits.[111] It is a curious tale but important for showing the way earnest laymen might try to shape their own sexual lives by rules that had been devised by a celibate clergy. Monks and clerics generated a discourse that was body-hating, hostile to sexual activity, and suspicious of women. Its influence could be powerful beyond the cloister.

[109] Reg., *Libellus* 74 (pp. 151–4).   [110] T. Chobham, *SC*, p. 333.
[111] *V. sancti Henrici heremitae* 16 (*AASS*, 2 Jan, p. 426).

## Sexual Realities

It is sometimes possible to glimpse beyond the clerical moralizing to ordinary assumptions about sexual behaviour. Do not listen to those, writes Gerald of Wales, who say that simple fornication (i.e. ordinary heterosexual intercourse between two unmarried lay people) is natural and not a mortal sin. The statutes of the synod of Salisbury of about 1218 echo the point: 'It should be drilled into lay people in confessional and sermon that all sexual intercourse, unless it has the excuse of marriage, is a mortal sin.' Clearly someone thought otherwise. About the same time the theologian and sub-dean of Salisbury, Thomas of Chobham, described simple fornication as 'the common vice of almost everybody that seems quite excusable to many'.[112]

This picture of reasonably relaxed sexual behaviour can be given more detail from the cases that came before the ecclesiastical authorities. Records from English church courts only begin about the year 1200, but they can be supplemented before that time by papal letters to English ecclesiastics dealing with cases that required special advice or authority.[113] From such sources we hear of men sleeping with the mother or sister of their young fiancées, of men who abandoned wife and children to set up with other women, of long-term non-marital sexual partnerships, like that of John and Maxilla, of the diocese of Lincoln, who lived together for ten years, both before and after the death of John's legal wife, Alice, and had ten children. Despite the length of time they had cohabited and the number of their children, the pope ruled, they must separate.[114] In Hastings a burgess had lived with a woman for some years and she had borne him children. He then determined to marry, put away his lover, and wed a girl of 12. His previous partner made life so difficult for him that not only did he find it impossible to continue to live with his child bride, but eventually he set off for Jerusalem, never to be heard of again.[115] Such messy situations and loose ends are the reality of sexual life in twelfth-century England.

Sexual activity outside marriage was a common occurrence at every level. In the royal court it was even institutionalized. Henry de Mara held his estate in Oxfordshire 'for the service of being the lord king's doorkeeper and looking after the whores'.[116] Prostitutes could also be found following the courts of bishops.[117] Aristocratic courts were no different. Hugh of Avranches, earl of Chester (d. 1101), 'pursued the lusts of the flesh quite immoderately and fathered a large progeny of both sexes from his mistresses'.[118] Lower down

---

[112] Gerald, *Gemma* 2. 2 (p. 174); *Councils and Synods* 2/i, p. 72; T. Chobham, *SC*, p. 344; cf. Bart. Ex., pp. 236–7.

[113] See esp. Duggan, 'Equity'.    [114] Holtzmann and Kemp, pp. 60–1, no. 25 (JL 17678).

[115] Duggan, 'Equity', pp. 81–2.    [116] *Bk. Fees* 1, p. 103.

[117] T. Chobham, *SC*, p. 348.    [118] Orderic 4 (2, p. 262).

the social scale there is the case of Reginald of Bramton in Northampton-shire, holding a virgate and four acres, and thus being a substantial peasant farmer. After his death his daughter Hawisa claimed to be his heir. She re-pudiated the counter-claims of a certain Agnes and her son Robert by as-serting that 'Agnes had no right of entry to the property except from the fact that her father took Agnes into his house and, while Emma his wife, her [i.e. Hawisa's] mother, was still alive, fathered a son with her'.[119] At the low-est level of peasant society, servile women who engaged in sexual activity out-side marriage could be summoned before the manorial court and fined.[120]

Some of the non-marital relationships involved were relatively stable. The Statutes of Winchester 1224 initiated a drive against notorious fornicators and those with mistresses: they should marry them or promise to marry them if they slept with them again or at least pay a fine.[121] These mistresses were not necessarily casual and curtly discarded lovers. When he was chief minis-ter under William Rufus, Ranulf Flambard had an English mistress called Alveva, who bore him several sons. After he was appointed bishop of Durham in 1099, he married her off to a burgess of Huntingdon. Relations between Ranulf and Alveva remained good: he gave help to her relatives and often stayed with her when travelling between his diocese and London.[122] The marrying off of a great man's mistress occurs also in fictional form in the lay of Le Fresne, where it is suggested that when the lord seeks a proper wife his concubine be married off to 'some worthy man'.[123]

A natural consequence of the number of men and women living together outside wedlock and the frequency of casual extramarital sex was a large number of illegitimate births. There were bastards in every social class and group. Henry I fathered many, including the great earl of Gloucester. Henry II's illegitimate son, Geoffrey, became archbishop of York. When the canons of Salisbury assembled in 1228 to elect a bishop, several of them were deemed ineligible as candidates because of their illegitimacy.[124] Lower down the social scale, illegitimate birth is mainly recorded in the course of legal dis-putes over property. Since bastards could not inherit, it was a common tactic for one party to raise a charge of illegitimacy against the other. When this happened, it was the task of the Church to determine the issue of legitimacy and then the job of the secular courts, with this judgment available to them, to decide the property case.

A major difference between the law of bastardy in canon law and in the English Common law was that the latter refused to recognize the legitimacy

---

[119] *CRR* 1, pp. 310, 313.    [120] e.g. *Caen Custumals*, pp. 61, 73, 75.
[121] *Councils and Synods* 2/i, pp. 134–5.    [122] *V. Christina*, p. 40.
[123] Marie de France, *Le Fresne*, lines 371–2 (*Lais*, p. 44).    [124] *Reg. Osm.* 2, pp. 104–5.

of those whose parents subsequently married. The great lawyer-pope Alexander III put the position of the Church quite clearly in a letter to Bartholomew, bishop of Exeter: 'The power of marriage is so great that those who were born before marriage are deemed to be legitimate after it.'[125] The clash between the Common Law position—subsequent marriage did not legitimize bastards—and the canon law reached a famous culmination just after our period, at the Council of Merton in 1236, when, confronted with ecclesiastical pressure, 'the earls and barons replied with one voice that they did not wish to change the laws of England'.[126] The thousands of children born before or outside wedlock remained illegitimate.

Making love with someone else's wife or husband was a much more divisive and dangerous act than simple fornication. It involved issues of property, inheritance, and male honour as well as sexual ethics. Aristocratic men guarded their women vigilantly. Osbert of Clare noted how 'rich men guard their wives very carefully and appoint loyal followers as custodians of their womenfolk, so that the weaker sex should not give way to temptation'. Young aristocratic wives could find themselves in a regime of constant surveillance. 'What can be said about these custodians who exercise an unbridled tyranny over the wives of noblemen? If by chance she glances at anyone, if she should laugh, straightaway she is deemed to be false and is condemned as an adulteress, to be punished with blows as much as with words'.[127]

According to Thomas of Chobham, writing about 1215, a husband who found his wife in adultery was permitted to castrate her lover, even if the lover were a clerk.[128] A legal case from almost exactly this same time (1212) demonstrates the accuracy of his statement. Robert Butler of Candover in Hampshire suspected William Wake of adultery with his wife and banned him from entering his house. William allegedly ignored the prohibition and entered Robert's house and slept with his wife, whereupon Robert and his men castrated him. The king ordered that if this were a true account of events, then Robert and his men should have their lands and movable property, that had been seized, restored and should be in the king's peace. Clearly adultery was more than an extenuating circumstance in an assault of this kind, it was an exculpation.[129]

The main danger adulterers faced was from the aggrieved husband, but both secular and ecclesiastical punishments were also imposed. Domesday Book gives some instances of secular fines to be paid for adultery. In the

---

[125] *Decretals* 4. 17. 6 (col. 712) (JL 13917).
[126] Bracton, *De legibus et consuetudinibus Angliae*, fo. 417, ed. George E. Woodbine, rev. with tr. Samuel E. Thorne (4 vols.; Cambridge, Mass., 1968–77), vol. 4, p. 296.
[127] Osbert, *Letters*, nos. 22, 40, pp. 93, 137.          [128] T. Chobham, *SC*, pp. 192–3.
[129] *Rot. litt. claus.* 1, p. 126.

south-east of England the king and the archbishop of Canterbury divided the fines for adultery between them, the king taking the man's payment and the archbishop the woman's. Sometimes the right to the fine could be held by the local land-holders, as in Wallingford where ten privileged householders had the fine for adultery in their own houses.[130] The ecclesiastical penance for adultery recorded in the early thirteenth century was to be whipped naked through the streets of the town.[131]

Confronted with the rich variety of sexual practices in the world, the Church constructed a hierarchy of condemnation. The system propounded by Thomas of Chobham divided conjugal sex into the licit, the venially sinful, and the mortally sinful. Intercourse between spouses for the purpose of procreation and to pay the conjugal debt was licit. So too was intercourse for the purpose of avoiding fornication, 'as when someone is going to be in the company of lecherous women and fears he may fall and so cools himself off beforehand with his own wife'. It is a venial sin if a man sleeps with his wife solely out of sexual desire. Some circumstances make sexual intercourse between spouses a mortal sin: if there is excessive sexual pleasure—for 'a fervent lover of his own wife is an adulterer'; if the intercourse occurs 'in a part of the body not appointed for it'; if it takes place at a time when it is prohibited; if the woman is pregnant or menstruating—in the latter case any offspring are likely to be leprous; or if intercourse is in public with many watching.[132] As well as a hierarchy of sexual acts within marriage, there was a scale of sinful behaviour outside it: 'unnatural' heterosexual sex was bad; masturbation was worse; homosexuality even worse; and bestiality worst of all.[133]

The most common religious community in medieval England consisted of a body of celibate men, in close and uninterrrupted contact, accompanied by a group of boys or youths. It is not surprising that the issue of homosexuality was a live one for ecclesiastical leaders. A notable example is Anselm, archbishop of Canterbury. At least as he emerges from the pen of his biographer Eadmer, he seems to have had a particular antipathy to the sin of sodomy. As early as 1094, just after his consecration as archbishop, Anselm appealed to William Rufus to collaborate with him in a joint campaign against the vice, employing both ecclesiastical and secular sanctions. The crime, that had recently spread over England, he said, would end by turning the whole country into a Sodom.[134]

Rufus was not responsive, but Anselm was persistent. Early in the next reign he was able to summon a council of the whole English church. This met

---

[130] *DB* 1, 1, 26, 56b (Ken. D. 19; Ssx. 12. 1; Brk. B. 7).
[131] T. Chobham, *SC*, p. 368.        [132] Ibid., pp. 333–9.
[133] Ibid., p. 400.        [134] Eadmer, *HN*, p. 49.

at Westminster in 1102 and its longest ruling was concerned with sodomy: all who engaged in 'sodomitical vice' and all who helped them were to be excommunicated; if they were in orders they were to be degraded, if laymen to be deprived of their legal standing in the kingdom; while it was ruled that only bishops could give absolution for this grave sin.[135] Like most of Anselm's practical efforts, his campaign against sodomy came to little. The public excommunication of offenders, that was supposed to be issued in every church every Sunday, soon lapsed, giving 'fuel to the audacity of wicked minds to sin more freely henceforth'.[136] Although there is no later campaign as determined as Anselm's, ecclesiastical legislation a century later still listed 'the sin against nature' as one of the great offences, comparable to homicide, sacrilege, and incest.[137]

Anselm himself clearly perceived sodomy as widespread in England. Writing in the period just after the Council of Westminster, he expressed the opinion that 'until now this sin has been so common that scarcely anyone is ashamed of it, and many fall into it not knowing its enormity'.[138] It is hard to say how accurate his perception was. An accusation of homosexuality was meant to be derisive. In the *lai* of *Lanval*, when Arthur's queen has been rejected as a lover by the knight Lanval, she spits back: 'I have often been told that you have no desire for women and that you have well-trained young men with whom you take your pleasure.'[139] Hence many of the reports of homosexuality, attributed either to individuals or to groups, may represent slander or gossip rather then accurate reflections of the prevalence of homosexual relations. What does seem to emerge is that homosexuality was often attributed to court circles and to highly placed ecclesiastics and that, after the Council of Westminster, there was little in the way of determined effort to combat it.

This does not mean that monastic moralists softened their views. A monk of Eynsham, visiting the afterworld in a vision (discussed more fully below, pp. 603–12), saw a place of special horror reserved for those who had engaged in 'the sin that should not be named'. Hideous demons tortured them incessantly in a place of fire and stench. 'I had not hitherto suspected', confesses the monk, 'that the lesser sex had also sometimes been perverted by such foul acts.' He encounters a famous canon lawyer whose shame had prevented him from confessing on his deathbed. 'What we read about the wickedness of Sodom', reflects the monk, 'is still strong in the sons of Sodom. Their pride and wealth drag them into wicked ways, they do what is not proper, abusing their own bodies. They should not by right be called human beings, for their

---

[135] *Councils and Synods* 1/ii, pp. 678–9.       [136] W. Malm., *GP* 64 (p. 121 n. 1).
[137] *Councils and Synods* 2/i, p. 73.
[138] Anselm, ep. 257 (*Op*. 4, p. 170); *Councils and Synods* 1/ii, p. 687.
[139] Marie de France, *Lanval*, lines 279–82 (*Lais*, p. 65).

sin shows that they have degenerated from human nature into a bestial, or rather demonic, insanity . . .'[140]

Ecclesiastical indignation was aroused far more by the supposed perversion of homosexuality than by the violation of women, although the latter was regarded as an offence in secular law and the former was not. In early medieval law, many of the rules about 'rape' refer to abduction, that is, the forcible taking of a wife, rather than to casual violent sexual intercourse. The fear that lay behind the rules was not the woman's dread of violation but the worry of the kindred, that they might find themselves involved in ties with an unwanted man and his kin. There was also, however, a specific crime of forcible sexual intercourse, punishable, according to some sources of the Norman period, by castration, although others mention only a fine.[141]

An accusation of rape in this sense was one of the two criminal charges that a woman was allowed to bring on her own behalf (the other was the murder of her husband), but it involved a formidable procedure.[142] She had first to go immediately after the incident to the nearest village and show the signs of the assault, such as blood or torn clothes, to the 'responsible men' (*probi homines*) of the place, then bring her complaint before the hundred-reeve and finally make a public accusation at the next meeting of the county court. One can imagine a victim's reluctance to undergo such a process. Nevertheless, some women faced the potential humiliations in order to pursue justice, as in the following case, heard at York in 1208: 'Sibba, daughter of William, accuses William, son of Hugh of Bolton, of taking her outside the village of Wheldrake and having intercourse with her by force and beating her and making her bloody. She immediately went to Wheldrake and showed this fact to Alan Malecake and Walter de Beauvair, who bear witness to it.'[143]

Analysis of the judicial records that survive from late in our period (after 1194) shows that rape was not the subject of public prosecution (presentment) and that of the hundred or so recorded private prosecutions, like Sibba's, not one resulted in a conviction.[144] The reasons for this are not entirely clear. Obviously some accusations of rape were malicious or irrational. In one case in Lincolnshire in 1202 a woman supposedly accused her lover when he became betrothed to another woman. In Warwickshire in 1221 the jury in a rape trial said that the plaintiff had in fact been the accused's lover

---

[140] *Vis. Eynsham* 24–6 (pp. 323–30).

[141] *ASC*, p. 220, *s.a.* 1086; Liebermann, *Gesetze* 1, p. 504 (Leis Wl 18); Robertson, *Laws*, p. 262; *DB* 1, 26, 262b, 269b (Ssx. 12. 1; Chs. C. 8, R1. 40c).

[142] Glanvill 14. 1, 3, 6 (pp. 173, 174, 176); *Earliest Lincs. Ass. Rolls*, pp. 120–1; *PBKJ* 2, no. 730, p. 211; *Sel. Charters*, p. 299 (Magna Carta c. 54).

[143] *PBKJ* 4, no. 3491, p. 114.

[144] Roger D. Groot, 'The Crime of Rape temp. Richard I and John', *Jnl Legal History*, 9 (1988), pp. 323–34.

for a long time and that she had subsequently gone on living in her father's house for two years without raising any complaint.[145]

It is unlikely that most prosecutions for rape were of this type, yet nevertheless they did not result in convictions. Many, and possibly most, accusations were settled by a money payment (Sibba got twenty shillings from her violator). There are hints in the records that the female victims were often young, poor, and fatherless, the male perpetrators more powerful, at least on the local scale. Pressure to accept a cash settlement in such circumstances can easily be imagined.

Sometimes accusations of rape concluded with a marriage between plaintiff and accused. The author of the law tract attributed to Glanville thought that this should not be an automatic option for a convicted rapist, since otherwise 'men of servile condition would join themselves permanently to noble women through one moment of pollution or noble men would be united with common women'.[146] Presumably he is picturing a situation where there was a strong social expectation that the rapist would 'do the right thing' by the woman he had raped and his fears of social miscegenation make him think that an automatic rule of this kind is undesirable. It is hard to assess how realistic his picture is. He allowed such marriages, however, when they were made before judgment was given and with the consent of the royal justices and the relatives. There are indeed cases of rape victims and rapists marrying. The judges insisted that such agreements required their consent and even fined those who negotiated such reconciliations without official permission.[147]

Thomas of Chobham noted that pressure was often brought to bear on the perpetrators of rape to marry their victims. He thought the crucial issue was that they should be prepared to pay 'the price of the woman's shame'. In general, a man who slept with a woman without marrying her did her great wrong, 'because afterwards it will be difficult for her to find someone willing to marry her'.[148] There is other evidence for this requirement that a first-time bride be a virgin. The fact that the victim of a rape was a virgin is sometimes mentioned as an aggravating circumstance in the court records. In Marie de France's lai *Milun*, Milun's lover cries: 'Have a husband? How can I? I am no longer a virgin.'[149] There is a convergence here between the high estimation of virginity advanced by clerical and monastic ideologues and the simpler equation of honour and virginity assumed by lay society.

---

[145] *Earliest Lincs. Ass. Rolls*, p. 150; *Rolls of the Justices in Eyre for Gloucestershire, Warwickshire and Shropshire, 1221–2*, ed. Doris Stenton (Selden Soc. 59; 1940), no. 966, p. 410.
[146] Glanvill 14. 6 (p. 176).      [147] e.g. *Earliest Lincs. Ass. Rolls*, p. 140.
[148] T. Chobham, *SC*, pp. 190, 345, 394.      [149] Marie de France, *Milun*, lines 135–6 (*Lais*, p. 105).

## 4. MANNERS

### Presentation of the Body

*Hair and Dress*

One early twelfth-century account of the threatened invasion of Canute of Denmark in 1086 claims that among the numerous precautions taken by William the Conqueror was the injunction that the English, whose loyalty he distrusted, should 'shave their beards, adopt weapons and clothes of the Norman style and become completely like Frenchmen, in order to delude the eyes of the invaders'.[150] The picture of a Viking fleet approaching the English coast and becoming confused and disheartened by the sight of thousands of clean-shaven, stylishly dressed, and hence demonstrably Norman inhabitants may have a ludicrous ring, but the tale only makes sense if the assumption is that Norman and English identity could be clearly marked by hair and clothes.

Treatment of hair and choice of clothes are indeed the most important methods of giving a visible statement of identity. The fact that contemporaries distinguished ethnic groups by their hair styles is attested in every image of the Bayeux Tapestry, which depicts clean-shaven Normans, with their hair cut high on the back of their heads, and longer-haired, moustachioed Anglo-Saxons. The story of how king Harold's scouts returned with the report that the Norman army consisted almost entirely of priests is probably legendary, but makes the point that one of the first things to strike the Anglo-Saxons was that their opponents were clean-shaven.[151] Even a century later wearing beards could be viewed as an assertion of English identity and hostility to the Normans.[152] By this time other ethnic fissures were being expressed in the language of hair, for when the Anglo-Normans came into contact with the Irish, one of the most obvious differences between native and newcomer was in the treatment of hair and beard. When John was sent as Lord of Ireland in 1185, the young men in his retinue outraged the Irish chiefs by derisively pulling their long beards.

It was not just ethnicity that was indicated in this fashion, however. Hair codes also helped to mark class, order, age, and sex. Women wore their hair longer than men, unmarried women wore it loose, married women bound.

---

[150] Aelnoth of Canterbury, *Gesta Swenomagni regis et filiorum eius et passio gloriossimi Canuti regis et martyris* 12, ed. M. C. Gertz, *Vitae sanctorum Danorum* (Copenhagen, 1908–12), p. 99.

[151] W. Malm., *GR* 3. 239 (2, p. 301); OMT edn., p. 450; the passage was borrowed by Pseudo-Alanus, *Prophetia Anglicana Merlini . . . una cum septem libris explanationum . . . Alani de Insulis* (Frankfurt, 1603), p. 62.

[152] Paris, *CM* 2, p. 418.

Clerics were visibly distinguished from other men by their tonsure and their shaven face. Becoming a cleric involved 'cutting off the hair of the head for love of Jesus Christ', receiving an image of Christ's crown and shaving off the beard, 'that first-fruit of youth'.[153] Ecclesiastical rulings of the period constantly reiterated the requirement that the clerk's tonsure or 'crown' should be clear and visible.

Hair could express temporary emotional states as well as permanent identities. Loosing and tearing hair, for instance, was a sign of grief and distress: When the Scots raided the north of England in 1079 the women of Hexham 'uncovered their heads and tore their hair with their hands';[154] during the siege of Exeter in 1136, when king Stephen was starving out the rebel baron Baldwin de Redvers, Baldwin's wife came to the king to plead for mercy. She was 'barefoot, with her hair loosed over her shoulders and shedding showers of tears'.[155] Knights grieving over deaths in a tournament are described as 'unlacing the mail around their necks and tearing at their hair and beards'.[156]

Hair styles change with the times. Although the Norman followers of William the Conqueror are depicted on the Bayeux Tapestry with hair cropped very short at the back, the young men at the court of the Conqueror's sons, William Rufus and Henry I, adopted the fashion of long and luxuriant hair. Monastic observers were outraged. 'You all wear your hair like women,' declared the Benedictine, Serlo, bishop of Sées, to Henry I's courtiers, producing a pair of scissors from his bag and getting to work.[157] Anselm, who pushed a condemnation of the new fashion into the canons of the Council of Westminster in 1102, also made his views clear: 'Those who are unwilling to have a hair-cut may not enter church; if they do enter, the priest does not have to stop the service, but should announce to them that they enter against God's will and to their own damnation.'[158]

Here we have all the characteristic marks of a new fashion: a craze among the young and elegant; a sharp contrast with the style of the previous generation; the disapproving tones of the elders. It was at the court that such fads in hair and dress would be most evident and lively. Sometimes they would originate with a new regime. The reason Henry II was nicknamed Curtmantle ('short cloak') was that he had introduced the short cloak from Anjou, while at the time of Henry I the cloak in England trailed to the ground.[159] Court styles would often have an air of the outlandish and impractical. A courtier of William Rufus set the fashion for shoes with long curving toes like

---

[153] *Magd. Pont.*, pp. 57–8.

[154] Ailred of Rievaulx, *De sanctis ecclesiae Haugustaldensis* (*Priory Hexham*, p. 179).

[155] *Gesta Stephani* 19 (p. 40).          [156] Marie de France, *Chaitivel*, lines 137–8 (*Lais*, p. 119).

[157] Orderic 11. 11 (6, pp. 64–6).          [158] Anselm, ep. 257 (*Op.* 4, p. 170).

[159] Gerald, *Prin.* 3. 28 (p. 304).

rams' horns.[160] Throughout most of the period aristocratic ladies wore sleeves that dangled down to the level of their knees.

The status of the luxury class was commonly expressed in rich and exotic materials. Fur was a mark of opulence, but there was a hierarchy even for this expensive commodity. Sable and ermine were by far the most expensive types, used for the king's robes and bedspread. Northern furs were naturally more highly prized. The better squirrel skin was that of the 'northern squirrel', while exotica like polar-bear pelts made a suitable gift from Henry II to his favoured monks of Grandmont. Nuns were forbidden to wear the more luxurious furs, such as sable, marten, and ermine and restricted to 'lamb or black cat'.[161]

Contemporaries were sharply aware of this hierarchy of furs, as is wryly illustrated in a story concerning Wulfstan, the saintly bishop of Worcester, who died in 1095 as the last representative of the native English episcopate. The humble Wulfstan wore only lambskin. The great Norman magnate bishop, Geoffrey of Coutances, reprehended him for this, 'when he could and should wear sable, beaver or fox'. Wulfstan replied that men of worldly wisdom could wear the skins of cunning animals, but that he himself was an innocent soul and content with the innocent lamb. At least, insisted Geoffrey, wear cat. To this Wulfstan had a decisive counter-argument: he had often heard 'the Lamb of God' sung in church, but never 'the Cat of God'![162]

Concern over the luxuriousness of clothes was not matched by attention to bodily cleanliness. England was not part of the bath culture that could be found in the Mediterranean and elsewhere. Lanfranc's *Constitutions* envisage the monks bathing three times a year, at Christmas, Easter, and Whitsun, but their right not to bathe was recognized. Strict controls were in place to prevent a hint of sexuality—a curtain was placed around the bath, the bath attendants were not to be young, silence was to be observed. The experience was not meant to be pleasurable.[163] The records of payments made to king John's bath attendant, William Aquarius, reveal that the king took a bath, on average, once every three weeks.[164] Since each of these baths cost the considerable sum of 5*d*. or 6*d*., they were obviously elaborate and probably ceremonial affairs. They reinforce the impression that the royal and aristocratic courts of the medieval world combined what, to modern eyes and noses, would seem great luxury and great squalor: unwashed kings in robes of sable.

---

[160] Orderic 8. 10 (4, pp. 186–8).
[161] *Councils and Synods* 1/ii; pp. 749, 778; 2/ii, pp. 118–19.
[162] W. Malm., *V. Wulfstan* 3. 1 (p. 46); W. Malm., *GP* 141 (pp. 282–3).
[163] Lanfr., *Const.*, pp. 9–10.    [164] *Rot. lib.*, pp. 115, 137, 170.

*Gesture*

Ideals of etiquette and decorum extended to physical deportment. One monastic author, praising 'decent gait and bearing of the body', contrasted it with the ostentatious behaviour he had sometimes observed:

I blush to mention some men, who walk along as if they were rowing the air with their arms and shoulders, or have a haughty gait, like turtle-doves or peacocks or cranes. Some spread out their fingers while they talk, shake their heads, lift their eyebrows, seeming, by these gestures of the eyes, to shout out the words of Elihu [in the book of Job], 'Behold, my belly is as wine which hath no vent; it is ready to burst like new bottles.'[165]

It is always easy for the reserved to make the expressive appear ridiculous, but there is also a moralizing tone to these remarks. Similarly, proud bearing could be criticized and caricatured:

With neck raised up, his face elevated, his eyes cast up sidelong with arched eyebrows, the proud man thunders out imperious and puffed-up words, his shoulders play, almost too proud to bear the arms, his eyes glow and he threatens with his countenance, rising up on his toes, standing with legs crossed, puffing out his chest, bending back his neck, glowing in his face and with fiery eyes intimating anger and, touching his nose with his finger, threatening great things.[166]

The cult of restrained body-language seems to have been rooted in England as early as the twelfth century. Richard I's arrogant and unpopular minister, William de Longchamps, was blamed for introducing the French custom of serving on bended knee.[167] Servility, foreignness, and exaggerated gesture were already being associated.

One way in which bodily contact was freer in the twelfth century than in modern England was in the custom of the kiss. This was a conventional greeting between men, as well as between men and women in prescribed circumstances. A godmother could expect always to be greeted with a kiss by her godson, but a son would also kiss his father on meeting.[168] A bishop or abbot visiting a monastery would kiss all the monks in turn. When monks kissed a bishop, abbot, or secular prince, they genuflected as they did so.[169]

A specialized use of the kiss was in the kiss of peace. This was exchanged among the congregation at mass and was also used to symbolize formal reconciliation. After Henry II had spoken some harsh words to the prior and monks of Canterbury during discussion about the election of a new archbishop in 1184, 'he sought pardon with a kiss of peace and sent them all away

---

[165] Joc. Furn., *V. Waltheof*, p. 259; the biblical reference is Job 32: 19.

[166] *Vis. Thurkill*, p. 20 (partly drawn from John de Hauvilla's *Architrenius*).

[167] R. Devizes, p. 32.

[168] *Canterbury Cases*, no. A.8, p. 29; Marie de France, *Milun*, line 478 (*Lais*, p. 114).

[169] Lanfr., *Const.*, pp. 71–2.

in peace'.[170] When the bishop of Rochester was forced to concede that certain manors belonged to the monks of Rochester, not to him, he had to promise to give them peaceable possession and, 'as a sign of this, he received the monks in the kiss of peace'.[171]

Giving the kiss of peace was a significant act. It had its part in the political disputes of the period. A description of the meeting between Becket and Henry II at Northampton tells how the archbishop was 'ready to receive the grace of the kiss customary among the English, if the king anticipated it. He was not received to the kiss.'[172] The issue of whether the king would give the archbishop the kiss of peace was indeed one of the things that prolonged the Becket dispute. Relations of a personal kind were also expressed by giving or refusing the kiss. One way that the women of a parish could snub the priest's wife—or concubine as they might call her—was to refuse her the kiss of peace.[173] A very specific obligation that the kiss of peace entailed is revealed by the story of Richard of Clare, who controlled his desire to sleep with a wife of a certain knight, even though the opportunity arose, because he had given the knight the kiss of peace in church the previous Sunday and was 'unwilling to break the peace he had given'.[174] Bonds of duty could be created by public gesture.

## Drinking, Swearing, and Violence

The English had an international reputation as drinkers. John of Salisbury wrote that 'the English are noted among foreigners for their persistent drinking', the royal treasurer, Richard fitz Neal, believed that the high levels of crime in England were partly to be explained by 'the drunkenness, which is inborn in the inhabitants', while the haughty countess of Leicester judged the English better at boasting and drinking than fighting.[175] Geoffrey de Vinsauf, himself English, writes of 'that drinker, England' (*Anglia potatrix*).[176] It was noticed that the English on the Third Crusade gave priority to their drinking: 'even in the very midst of the blare of the war trumpets, they kept up the old English custom and opened their mouths wide with proper devotion to drain their goblets to the dregs'.[177]

Drinking and public sociability went together. Walter Map noted that 'in each parish the English have a house for drinking, called the guildhouse in English' and the word guild itself—the key term of medieval community

---

[170] Gerv. Cant., p. 318.     [171] *Councils and Synods* 1/ii, p. 813.

[172] W. f. Stephen, *V. Thomas* 38 (p. 50).     [173] T. Chobham, *SC*, p. 385.

[174] Gerald, *Gemma* 2. 12 (p. 228).

[175] J. Salisb., *Letters* 33 (1, pp. 56–7); *Dial. scacc.*, p. 87; Fantosme, lines 978–9, p. 72.

[176] Geoffrey de Vinsauf, *Poetria nova*, line 1003, ed. Edmond Faral, *Les Arts poétiques du XIIe. et du XIIIe. siècle* (Paris, 1924), p. 228.

[177] R. Devizes, pp. 73–4.

association—could be defined by contemporaries as 'an assembly of drinkers'.[178] Next to the churchyard in the village of Stoke near Hartland in north Devon 'was situated a house called the *hubernum* where the local people were accustomed to celebrate drinking parties together every year, in a kind of brotherhood'.[179] Communal drinking parties in specially assigned and named buildings were thus an essential feature of English life.

An 'ale' was a party. If it took place at a wedding it was a 'bride-ale' or bridal. The conspiracy of the earls against William I in 1075 was hatched at a wedding party. 'There was the bride-ale', comments the *Anglo-Saxon Chronicle*, slipping into rhyme, 'Many men's bale [doom]'. Another kind of 'ale' was the 'scotale'. 'Scot' means 'payment' and scotales were festivities at which attendance was compulsory and a levy was taken from the drinkers. Lords and officials might insist on them as a right. One of the tenants of the nunnery of Shaftesbury in the 1170s had to go 'to the scotale of the lady [abbess] as also to the scotale of the neighbours'.[180] Exemption from scotales was one of the privileges that might be granted to favoured towns, such as London and Winchester.[181] In the Charter of the Forest of 1217 the royal government promised that 'no forester or beadle shall make a scotale'.[182] The ecclesiastical authorities sometimes added their disapproval.[183]

Toasting was an integral part of these 'ales'. It was a competitive and provocative ritual, designed to make your drinking companion drink more and more. Gerald of Wales tells how Henry II, turning up at a Cistercian monastery bedraggled and unrecognizable after a day's hunting and being hospitably received there, was invited to drink by the abbot. 'He caused him to be brought many goblets of fine drink, in the English manner.' In order to encourage him to drink all the more, the abbot gave him, instead of the usual toast of 'Wesheil', the unusual toast 'Pril'. Henry, at first mystified, was instructed by the abbot that the appropriate response was not 'Drincheil', but 'Wril'. 'And so, challenging each other and drinking by turns, with the monks and lay brethren attending and serving them, they did not cease from repeating "Pril" and "Wril", egging each other on into the depths of the night.' When the abbot later came to visit the royal court, he was deeply embarrassed to have Henry greet him with the toast 'Pril': 'just as we were good comrades the other day,' insisted the king, 'eating and drinking and urging each other on through challenges to drink well, so we shall be now', and extracted a reluctant 'Wril' from the abbot.[184]

At the tables of the upper classes drinking was clearly not a continuous casual activity but a formalized ceremony. Some of the rules of drinking

---

[178] Map 2. 12 (p. 154); Gerald, *V. Geoffrey* 2. 8 (p. 404).
[179] *Mir. Nectan*, pp. 408–9.     [180] BL Harley 61, fo. 63.     [181] *Elenchus*, nos. 36, 57, pp. 70, 97.
[182] *Sel. Charters*, p. 346.     [183] *Councils and Synods* 2/i, pp. 36, 64, 93.
[184] Gerald, *Spec. eccl.* 3. 13 (pp. 213–15).

etiquette are mentioned in the tract by Daniel of Beccles, discussed below: if you are the lord's dining companion, drink when he commands you, then pass on the drink to others; only return the goblet to the lord if he says 'you drink first'; do not say 'you drink first' when the butler offers you drink; if he say 'Wesheil', you should answer 'Drincheil'; if the butler happens to be a young woman, you may say to her 'share the drink with me, drink first'; let no one else drink when the lord is drinking.[185]

The practice of a young woman serving the drink on formal occasions was common, perhaps customary. Christina of Markyate passed round the drink at the guild in Huntingdon.[186] Geoffrey of Monmouth recounts the story of the fifth-century British king Vortigern, confronted with a beautiful Saxon maiden, who brought to him a golden goblet full of wine and, kneeling before him, said 'Lord king, Waesseil!'. Advised by an interpreter of the proper response, Vortigern replied 'Drincheil' and, after ordering the girl to drink, 'took the goblet from her hand and kissed her and drank'.[187]

Beer was the most common drink in England, although wine was deemed to be of greater prestige. There was a tradition of debate over the virtues of the two drinks that even produced poems championing each of the beverages. 'Happy is the place made sweet by the sweetness of wine', wrote Peter of Blois. 'Grain joined with water cheers the mind and makes for joyful gatherings,' responded Robert of Beaufeu, a canon of Salisbury, in his 'Commendation of Beer'.[188] Wine had the high status of an import, for, although there were English vineyards, their product was reckoned inferior. Old native drinks from fruit and honey continued to be drunk. The abbot of Ely had an officer in charge of the mead (*medarius*), while one of the tenants of the abbey of Burton upon Trent had the duty of providing sweet-gale for mead-making.[189] Cider is described as 'the English drink'.[190]

William of Malmesbury noted how the customary heavy drinking at the court of great men could lead from cheerfulness, to talkativeness, to quarrels, to the threat of violence.[191] Swearing was the most obvious form of verbal violence. Societies seem to favour either the scatological or the sexual or the blasphemous in their style of oaths and exclamations, and England in this period was certainly of the third type. A long list of things not to swear by, written in the later twelfth century, makes this clear: 'Do not swear by Christ's advent, birth, passion, body, brain, bowels, beard, tomb, ears, feet, arms, legs, back . . . by God's temple, voice, stomach, tongue . . .'[192] An oath

---

[185] D. Beccles, lines 1066–76, p. 38.
[186] *V. Christina*, p. 48.     [187] Geoff. Monm., *HRB* 6. 12 (100), p. 67.
[188] E. Braunholtz, 'Die Streigedichte Peters von Blois und Roberts von Beaufeu über den Wert des Weines und Bieres', *Zeitschrift für romanische Philologie*, 47 (1927), pp. 30–8.
[189] *ICC*, p. 115; Burton Cart., p. 35.     [190] W. Dan., *V. Ailred*, p. 73 (Letter to Maurice).
[191] W. Malm., *V. Wulfstan* 3. 16 (p. 56).     [192] D. Beccles, lines 1421–37, pp. 49–50.

'by God's stomach' may strike us as unusual, but such dramatically corporeal language applied to the deity seems to have been a predilection of the Angevin kings. Henry II customarily swore 'by God's eyes', Richard I is recorded as swearing 'by God's throat!', and John 'by God's teeth!'[193] According to the sour moralist Gerald of Wales, it was one of the virtues of the kings of France that they swore simply, by the saints of France, and not 'by God's death, eyes, feet, teeth, throat or tumours'.[194] Such exclamations were not the monopoly of irreligious princes. During a dispute with his monks, the abbot Samson of Bury St Edmunds exclaimed 'By God's face!'[195] The Norman kings contented themselves with a more theologically orthodox range of profanity, William I customarily swearing 'by the resurrection and splendour of God' and Henry I 'by God's death'.[196]

As William of Malmesbury noted, drinking not only loosed tongues but sometimes led to violence. Stray but recurrent references to men killed returning from 'an ale' or on their way back from the tavern may simply suggest that those who had drunk too much were easy targets, but could also imply enmities that had blown up in an evening's drinking.[197] Ready recourse to violence was, in any case, a characteristic of this world. Everyone carried a knife, military training was a usual part of the upbringing of the aristocracy, policing was virtually absent. It was a touchy world, in which offence could be taken easily. Precedence was an important matter. When the poet Gaimar is describing the period of Danish rule in England under Canute and his sons, the image he chooses of English subordination is that of a spatial reticence, with the inferior hanging back to let the superior pass:

> And if they [the English] came upon a bridge
> They waited; it was ill if they moved
> Before the Dane had passed.[198]

In a story in the ancestral legend of the earls of Huntingdon it is exactly this case of jostling on a bridge that ignites violence. The tale, that was probably composed in the late eleventh or twelfth century, tells of Siward, ancestor of the comital house, coming to London:

Siward and his companions made their way towards London on foot. On a bridge not far from Westminster, he met Tostig, earl of Huntingdon, a Dane by birth. . . . He came so close to Siward on that little bridge that he dirtied his cloak with his muddy

---

[193] Gerald, *Gemma* 1. 54 (pp. 161–2); Gerald, *Spec. eccl.* 3. 13, 14 (pp. 215, 222); R. Devizes, p. 47; *Hist. ducs Norm.*, p. 117.

[194] Gerald, *Prin.* 3. 30 (pp. 318–19).        [195] Joc. Brak., p. 111.

[196] W. Malm., *GR* 3. 281, 5. 401 (2, pp. 336, 478); OMT edn., pp. 510, 728; Orderic 4 (2, p. 318); Gerald, *Gemma* 1. 54 (p. 162).

[197] *CRR* 1, p. 214; *Select Pleas of the Crown*, ed. F. W. Maitland (Selden Soc. 1; 1888 for 1887), no. 62, p. 28; *PBKJ* 2, no. 751, p. 223.

[198] Gaimar, lines 4765–7, p. 151.

feet. . . . Because of this Siward's blood ignited in his heart and kindled in him great anger. He controlled himself, however, and did not rush to take revenge immediately, because the man who had inflicted that disgrace on him was on the way to his lord's court. He waited on the bridge, however, remaining there motionless with his companions, until Tostig returned from court, when Siward pulled out his sword and cut off his head.[199]

The brush on the bridge enrages Siward. He restrains himself only because the man who has insulted him is en route to the king's court and hence enjoys special protection. When he returns, however, Siward is waiting. Decapitation may seem a drastic requital for muddying one's cloak, but the issue was who was to give way, and that was fundamental.

'Blood ignited' in Siward's heart because he had been put in a situation where he might lose face. This was a central concern. The triumph of rivals was insufferable. To be insulted or mocked by enemies was a mortification. When Odo of Bayeux surrendered Rochester castle to the forces of his nephew William Rufus he tried to negotiate the concession that, as the vanquished came out, the victors would not sound their trumpets 'as is customary when enemies are overcome or castles captured by force'. Rufus was absolutely unwilling to give way and as they left the garrison had to run the gauntlet of the sounds of jubilation and abuse.[200] In contrast, Roger de Stuteville, constable of Wark, forbade his garrison to jeer at the retreating Scots in 1174: 'Say nothing disrespectful, leave it be, for God's sake! Don't shout or hoot at these men of Scotland.'[201] His motive was presumably to stop them being spurred to return. The wisdom of his action can be judged by an incident in an earlier Scottish invasion, in 1138, when the insults hurled by the young men of Bamburgh at the passing Scottish troops had stirred the invaders to storm the defences and kill whoever they could catch.[202]

An insult or injury would not be settled until it had been avenged. The habitual implacability of the time is revealed in the story of Wimund, a curious adventurer of the 1130s and 1140s, who started as a monk of Furness, became bishop of Man, and ended up as a kind of war-lord of the Irish Sea. He was eventually captured, blinded, and castrated by his enemies and spent the rest of his life in the monastery of Byland telling his story to those who would listen. Although physically mutilated, his vindictiveness was unimpaired: 'if he had even a sparrow's eye, he said, his enemies would not be exulting in their deeds against him'.[203]

It required saintly intervention or extreme action to turn aside revenge. One of the achievements of Wulfstan, bishop of Worcester, was to reconcile 'those who had previously been implacable'. His hardest case was that of

---

[199] *Gesta antecess. Waldevi*, pp. 107–8.     [200] Orderic 8. 2 (4, pp. 132–4).
[201] Fantosme, lines 1293–4, p. 96.     [202] J. Hexham, p. 292.     [203] W. Newb. 1. 24 (1, p. 76).

William the Bald, who had killed a man by accident. The dead man's five brothers refused any amends and rejected Wulfstan's mediation, saying 'they would rather be excommunicated than fail to avenge the death of their brother'. The bishop pleaded with them, but 'the grief of their brother's death had so inflamed them that it had robbed them of any humanity'. It took Wulfstan's curse and the hand of divine vengeance to change their mind. The toughest of the brothers was suddenly struck with a fit, the insolence and arrogance of the others dissolved, and Wulfstan was able to offer 'health to the sufferer, safeguards to the others, peace to all'.[204]

There were other ways out of the cycle of revenge. A knight who accidentally shot Robert Curthose's son Richard, while they were hunting in the New Forest, became a monk, not only 'to expiate the guilt of homicide by turning his back on the world' but also 'to deflect the malevolent anger of the relatives and friends of the noble young man'.[205] He was no longer a target in the violent world of aristocratic feud because the self-abnegation of becoming a monk had removed him from that world. Some knights, who had killed two other knights, nephews of Scotland, abbot of St Augustine's, Canterbury (1070–87), 'feared that the deaths of those they had killed would be paid for by their own deaths' and took refuge at the shrine of St Dunstan in Canterbury cathedral. Here they stayed, unwilling to leave and unwilling, also, to let the monks of Canterbury undertake the solemn transfer of Dunstan's shrine that they had planned. In these difficult circumstances, the monks negotiated with abbot Scotland and with 'all those to whom it pertained to take vengeance'. However, these refused to forswear vengeance. It took a terrible vision of St Dunstan to bring round the abbot and his relatives.[206] No one in this story is thinking about judicial remedies. A killing was expected to provoke a counter-killing by the kindred of the dead men. This could be avoided only by the intervention by mediators and the protective and directive power of the supernatural.

### The 'Civilized Man'

Many of the details of everyday personal behaviour in our period are illuminated by what is probably the earliest English courtesy book, the *Urbanus* ('Civilized Man') of Daniel of Beccles.[207] In some 3,000 lines of Latin verse it gives advice on proper conduct in a dizzying range of situations: 'if you wish to belch, remember to look up at the ceiling'; 'do not attack your enemy while he is squatting to defecate'; 'if there is something you don't want people to

---

[204] W. Malm., *V. Wulfstan* 2. 15 (pp. 38–9).          [205] Orderic 10. 14 (5, p. 282).
[206] Osbern of Canterbury, *Mir. sancti Dunstani*, ed. William Stubbs, *Memorials of St Dunstan* (RS; 1874), p. 143.
[207] D. Beccles.

know, do not tell it to your wife'. Within the space of a mere twenty lines or so the poem goes from 'say thank you to your host', 'don't mount your horse in the hall', through 'if visitors have already eaten, give them a drink anyway', 'loosen your reins when riding over a bridge', and 'receive gifts from great men with gratitude' to 'if you are a judge, be just'. It is indeed possible that this highly episodic structure is a consequence of the fact that the treatise as it now stands was created by combining several earlier separate texts.

The poem ends with the lines 'Old King Henry first gave to the uncourtly the teaching written in this book. Here ends the *Book of the Civilized Man* by Daniel of Beccles'. The Tudor bibliographer John Bale says he had seen 'a certain old chronicle' that reported that Daniel was in the household of Henry II 'for over 30 years' and, although this reference is of the vaguest, the mention of king Henry in the text and the fact that some of the manuscripts of the work are as early as the thirteenth century, make it plausible that the poem was produced at the Angevin court.[208] It would thus come from the same milieu that was at this very time generating other manuals and hand-books, such as Glanville's treatise on the laws of England or Richard fitz Neal's guide to the workings of the Exchequer.

The tradition of courtesy books was an ancient one and guides to etiquette, some quite elaborate, can be found in most phases of European history. Petrus Alfonsi, the converted Spanish Jew who supposedly served as phys-ician to king Henry I, included a short section on table manners in his highly successful *Disciplina clericalis*, possibly drawing on the Islamic genre of *adab* literature, in which such topics figure. In the later Middle Ages and early modern times dozens of such guides were produced, including one by Eras-mus, and the tradition has continued to the present. It appears to be the case that Daniel of Beccles's treatise is the first English courtesy book and the fact that there are no obvious earlier direct sources might suggest that it marks a new self-consciousness about etiquette and decorum.

Despite the abrupt jumps of subject, there are recurrent themes in the poem. The first is the issue of hierarchy, for one of the primary concerns of the treatise is to give instruction in how to behave to superiors and inferiors. The basic expectation is that those addressed in the poem will have both a lord and servants, will have to look both up and down the social scale. It is sometimes clear from the advice given that a specific group and its particular duties are in the poet's mind. Thus 'if you are the clerk of some lord', you should be skilful at drafting letters, charters, rentals, records of scutage, etc., if you are a teacher, you should not hit your students on the head. Advice, often of a fairly banal kind, is given to knights, sailors, doctors, etc. The

---

[208] John Bale, *Scriptorum illustrium maioris Brytanniae . . . catalogus* (2 pts.; Basel, 1557–9), pt. 1, p. 221 (*centuria tertia* xvii).

assumption, however, is that the person addressed will be 'an honourable householder' (the Latin term is *herus* or *erus*), someone probably with a hall of his own but also with superiors upon whom he is in some sense dependent. We might call people of this type 'gentry' or, more debateably 'middle class', as long as we remember that they were located in the top 5 per cent of the population. The *herus* is introduced in the very first lines: 'Reader, if you wish to be adorned with good manners, if you wish to be respected and to lead a civilized life as a noble householder . . .'

The basic principle of a hierarchical society is that 'everywhere and always the lesser must give way to the greater' and this is shown in a host of ways, especially by physical gestures of deference. In church the kiss of peace, the holy water, and the blessed bread are to be given first to 'the more noble' (*nobilior*); at the door of church and house 'the greater' (*maior*) has precedence; at dinner, dishes should be presented first 'to the greater person' (*maiori persone*). When dining, it is important to have your face towards superiors, your back to inferiors. You should not talk too much when eating at the table of a *dives* (literally 'rich man', but probably with a specific meaning of 'noble'). If a *dives* offers you a kiss or speaks to you, you should uncover your head; if he is sitting when he offers the kiss, kneel. You should not sit with your legs crossed unless you are the lord, as this gesture is a mark of haughty pride (twelfth-century illustrations show only such figures as kings and judges sitting with their legs crossed).

The hierarchical world is structured by patronage. Seek out 'the patronage of a great man' (*patrocinium magnatis*), Daniel advises; 'let every rich *herus* set one lord over him'. The relationship is meant to bring mutual benefits, for, although 'it is a great source of security to have a powerful patron', 'you make your requests in vain if you are slow with gifts'. A constant circulation of favours and presents is what keeps the system of patronage turning over. 'Be his sworn retainer and give him gifts, if you wish to pluck sweet fruit from a lord'. Patrons are needed because this is a dangerous and competitive world and Daniel gives full advice on how to deal with various enemies, ranging from simple suggestions about travelling armed to subtler psychological proposals, such as concealing your difficulties from your enemies. Perhaps the injunction 'not to stare at strangers' was intended to stop strangers becoming enemies. Care must be taken to guard against actual or potential enemies, just as deference must be manifested visually to superiors.

The 'honourable householder' also has dealings with inferiors. Daniel is capable of sentimentalizing the master-servant relationship: 'A lord can have no more worthy treasure than a fitting multitude of trustworthy servants.' He is indeed empathetically aware of the servants' situation and warns masters against berating or beating their servants; 'it is better to live on bread and water in peace than to be bound in perpetual care to a haughty master'.

Servants should be paid the agreed wages; they need not kneel when handing their master the wisps of straw or hay with which he wipes his bottom. Yet alongside this moral concern, it is also possible to detect the posture of self-pity that masters of households have often slipped into. There is the 'servant problem': 'you rarely find anyone faithful in his duty as a servant; everyone puts love of his own gain first.' There are the burdens of the householder: 'the name of householder [*herus*] gives to the master endless cares . . . it is he who will be the slave; he will live and die a slave.' Daniel's paradox here is echoed exactly by his contemporary and fellow courtier, Walter Map: 'how is the king to control thousands of thousands and govern them peaceably when we poor lords [*patres*] are unable to control a few? . . . Every household has one slave and many lords, for the one in charge is the servant of all, while those who serve appear to be the lords'.[209]

A very striking feature of the regimen of manners advocated in the *Urbanus* is the importance of bodily restraint and self-control. The civilized man is clearly one who holds himself in. This applies to speech, to behaviour at table, and to bodily emissions. Talking should be a carefully regulated activity. When one is being spoken to, it is important to keep silent, keep the mouth shut, and look at the person speaking; when you speak, keep your head, fingers, and feet still. In any case, avoid too much talking: 'Be careful to whom, what, why and when you speak'; it is often better to keep your thoughts to yourself. The same reserve is to be observed in laughter. Do not laugh too loudly—'It is the sign of a level-headed man to laugh moderately, the mark of a brainless man to guffaw loudly.'

Table manners are, of course, a major topic in any book of etiquette. Whereas most activities that involve things entering or leaving the body took place privately, eating, especially in the big households, was a public activity. Moreover, medieval practice involved two partners sharing a setting and eating together. Decorum was thus an unavoidable issue. Daniel of Beccles has ample advice on the subject: do not put too big a piece of food in your mouth, talk with your mouth full, overload your spoon, play with your knife and spoon, blow on hot pottage, lick your fingers, clean out bowls with your fingers. He offers rules on giving toasts, cutting food, etiquette regarding your dining companion, and so on and so on.

The issue of what comes out of the body is particularly acute when people are putting things into their bodies. When you are dining, Daniel advises, do not blow your nose, spit, or sneeze in a boorish fashion; 'if you wish to belch, remember to look up at the ceiling'; if you clean out your nose into your hand (in this age before handkerchiefs), do not let people see what comes out; do not spit over the table; if you are unable to spit behind you, then spit into a

---

[209] Map i. 10 (p. 24).

cloth; in fact it is a good idea to have a seat that can be turned around, so that the diners can spit behind them. Guests and servants should not urinate in the hall, although the master may.

Delicacy requires that certain unavoidable things be done in private. You should break wind in quiet places and avoid picking off your fleas 'in the presence of the lord [*patronus*], in the presence of the servants in the hall'. You should not snap your fingers, take off your shoes, wash your feet or head, cut your hair or nails or shave 'in the presence of great men [*magnificis*], in the presence of ladies in the hall'. Clearly the hall was a public place, where certain private functions were out of place. Moreover, the fact that some bodily functions and physical grooming are not to be done before the great suggests the link between the bodily restraint that Daniel recommends and the physical gestures of deference he also prescribes—the bowing and doffing are the positive response to the presence of superiors, the inhibitions on picking off fleas the negative.

The *Urbanus* is clearly a tract addressed to men rather than women, as is shown, for instance, in its cheerless advice on visiting prostitutes: 'if you are overcome by erotic desire when you are young and your penis drives you to go to a prostitute, do not go to a common whore; empty your testicles quickly and depart (or withdraw) quickly.' There is advice on choice of wife, in which personal qualities and property are both considered, but no advice on choice of a husband. Most telling is the author's virtual equation of the subjects of women and sexuality. He shares the common medieval view that women were naturally sexually voracious.

When he opines that a woman's 'no' is not really a 'no', he does not offer this as advice for seducers or a justification for force, but rather as the resigned acceptance of a husband who knows no woman is faithful: 'when tempted by sweet words, even a chaste, good, dutiful, devout and kindly woman will resist scarcely anyone.' Daniel's picture of the promiscuity and lustfulness of women reaches an unusual pitch in what can only be called his cuckoldry fantasies. He pictures a woman in bed with her husband, the man already aroused, but the wife putting him off and thinking only of her lover. She obtains sexual satisfaction only with her lover: 'the lascivious woman throws herself around the neck of her lover, her fingers give him those secret touches that she denies to her husband in bed; one wicked act with her lover pleases the lascivious adulteress more than a hundred with her husband; women's minds always burn for the forbidden.' Daniel pictures her ready to fornicate 'whenever she has time and place' with anyone—'a cook or a half-wit, a peasant or a ploughman, or a chaplain with his fancy words . . . what she longs for is a thick, leaping, robust piece of equipment [*supellex*], long, smooth and stiff . . . such are the things that charm and delight women.'

Despite this inflamed and semi-pathological image of female promiscuity,

Daniel stresses also the importance of putting up with one's wife. Feelings of jealousy should be hidden: 'if you are jealous, do not whisper a word about it . . . when you are jealous, learn to look up at the ceiling'—here making a recommendation identical with that for concealing belching. Although he recognizes the husband's right to punish the adulterer, Daniel also insists that a husband is bound to keep his wife, even if she is guilty of adultery. 'Whatever your wife does, do not damage your marriage', he asserts. Even if your wife is a witch, a whore, proud, gluttonous, a drinker, deaf, blind, a sterile old woman or has leprosy, the scab, or bad breath, 'a man is bound to keep her—the ox bears the yoke unwillingly, but he bears it nevertheless'.

The combination of the vivid sense of women's sexual looseness with a strict insistence on not breaking the marriage is partly to be understood through the need to avoid public shame. It is better to look up at the ceiling and conceal your jealousy than to face the shame of acknowledging your wife's adultery: 'it is better to bury your shame as a husband than to disclose the evil that brings a blush to your face and produces ever renewed grief for your heart'. This is one of the troubles you should certainly conceal from your enemies.

A key dilemma that the *Urbanus* discusses is the sexual proposition from the wife of one's lord. Such advances combine the problems of hierarchical relations, control of bodily emissions, and sexual morality. Accepting the offer would result in an inversion of hierarchy, rejecting it would make an enemy of a powerful and appetitive woman. Daniel's solution, to pretend to be ill, does not cast the 'civilized man' in a heroic light, but it does highlight the problem of the 'man in the middle', faced with dangerous demands of 'women with balls' (*matrone testiculate*).

There is no doubt that Daniel of Beccles's tract stands as a very early written monument to the centuries-long attempt to inculcate reserve and restraint, to produce an 'expanding threshold of aversion'.[210] The fight against fidgeting, the effort to control bodily emissions and maintain correct posture, form the initial discipline of an individual who is to seek control and regulation in every branch of life. The household needs to be controlled, the finances of the estate need to be regulated. Daniel of Beccles seems to be thinking of the country gentleman who wishes to make it clear that the stress is on the 'gentleman' rather than the 'country'. Rusticity is to be avoided: handling food in front of your companion might lead to you being 'pointed out as a rustic'; you should not spit 'like a rustic' or eat 'like a ploughman'. Your hall should be as free as possible from menial activities: there should be no pigs or cats in your hall (although riding horses, hunting dogs, and hawks may be there), there should be no one carding wool, spinning, or retting flax

[210] Norbert Elias, *The Civilizing Process*, tr. Edmund Jephcott (Oxford, 1994), p. 67.

there and your shepherds and ploughmen should not double up as table servants. A major preoccupation is the continuous and difficult attempt to segregate the working life of an agrarian economy from the civilized enclave of the semi-public household space.

It is hard to say if anyone took all these directives to heart, but the genre was to flourish. It was in the late twelfth century that this system of advice was first given systematic written form. The imagined or intended audience was not a carefree aristocrat but someone who was both a lord and a dependant, fully aware of the complexity of relations in a hierarchical society. Hence the *Urbanus* is not a guide to self-assurance but a monument to anxiety. Women are inconstant, enemies are all around, there is endless need for carefulness over deference, the master is the slave. The 'civilized man' is a careful, controlled, and worried individual.

## 5. MEDICINE AND HEALING

Faced with sickness, the inhabitants of twelfth-century England could turn to two different medical traditions, a practical one, based on herbs and charms, and a learned one, inherited from the Greco-Roman world. It is probable that the former killed fewer people than the latter. Most of the charms would be harmless, or psychologically beneficial, while many of the herbs could have genuine positive effects. In contrast, learned doctors, as well as elaborating a large amount of abstruse, if innocuous, theory, employed some techniques, like blood-letting and cauterization, that were clearly physically disruptive. Lady Hawisa of Anwick (Lincs.) had 'a red and swollen arm' for over a month after a blood-letting and eventually sought the help of the saints, the doctors having been so disastrous.[211] Edelina, wife of Richard the saddler of Coleshill (War.) lost the use of her hand after a doctor had drawn blood from her thumb.[212]

Despite the very limited effectiveness of contemporary medicine, there were many doctors and they were eagerly sought out. Local empirical healers, with their ligatures, herbs, and incantations, are mainly anonymous, but they are frequently referred to, especially in the accounts of saints' miracles, where their failures serve to emphasize the power of the healing shrine. Even this role, of course, suggests that for most people doctors were the natural first recourse in time of sickness. Such accounts also throw light on the world of folk remedies, such as the sad attempt of a mother to heal her son, who was paralysed from the waist down and whose legs were curved back upon themselves. She placed him in a tub of hot water and then jumped on his knees.

---

[211] *Bk. Gilbert*, p. 270.     [212] *Mir. Wulfstan* 2. 7 (p. 153).

This 'popular, old woman's' remedy almost killed him.[213] The priest who recommended as a cure for the bite of a posionous spider the chewing of rue and
its application to the wound was less harmful: 'he experienced no good from
any of this'.[214]

The more successful physicians, with an upper-class clientele, are less
anonymous. John de Villula, bishop of Bath (d. 1122), made his fortune from
his medical practice, even before the royal contacts he enjoyed led him to a
bishopric. William of Malmesbury estimated him as 'a very skilled doctor,
not in theoretical knowledge, but in practice'.[215] His contemporary, the
Italian, Faricius, abbot of Abingdon (1100–17), became the most trusted
physician of Henry I. Along with his fellow-countryman, Grimbald, he attended queen Matilda's childbed in 1101. His medical skill did not bring him
universal esteem, however. When he was proposed as archbishop of Canterbury after Anselm's death, several bishops objected that they did not want an
archbishop who inspected women's urine—one of the standard diagnostic
techniques.[216]

During the twelfth century learned medicine was transformed by the influx of new material from the Muslim world. As in the fields of science and
philosophy (see above, pp. 520–2), translations from the Arabic were made in
regions where Islam and western Christendom touched, and then circulated
throughout the centres of learning in western Europe. Mediterranean
schools, like Salerno and Montpellier, acquired a reputation as centres of
learned medicine. This material came to England, as it did to every other part
of the Latin west. A good example of the circulation of the new medical
literature is provided by the books donated to Durham cathedral by 'Master
Herbert the doctor' some time in the twelfth century. Twenty-six items given
by Herbert are listed in the contemporary catalogue of Durham cathedral
library and several of these survive, bound together in two manuscript books
now in Cambridge and Edinburgh.[217]

Herbert's medical library included books on herbs, diseases, medicines,
works by contemporary physicians, such as the Case-studies (Consilia) of
Master Reginald of Montpellier and the Surgery of Master Roger of Salerno,
as well as many texts that had only become available in Latin during the previous century. Notable among these were the translations made by Constantine the African. Constantine, who was born in north Africa but ended his life
as a monk of Monte Cassino, was the perfect bridge between the world of

[213] W. Cant., Mir. Thos. 2. 33 (p. 188).    [214] Mir. Wulfstan 1. 18 (p. 125).
[215] W. Malm., GP 90 (p. 195).    [216] Abingdon Chron. 2, pp. 45, 50, 287.
[217] Cambridge, Jesus Coll. 44; National Library of Scotland, Advocates 18. 6. 11; Catalogues of the
Library of Durham Cathedral (Surtees Soc. 7; 1838), pp. 7–8; R. A. B. Mynors, Durham Cathedral Manuscripts (Oxford, 1939), p. 62, no. 92; M. R. James, A Descriptive Catalogue of the Manuscripts in the Library
of Jesus College, Cambridge (Cambridge, 1895), pp. 67–9.

Arabic science and medicine and the schools of the Latin west. Working in the last two decades of the eleventh century, Constantine translated from Arabic into Latin a large number of texts, that became central to western medicine. Herbert's collection thus included works that, only a century before, had been available only in the Islamic world and were accessible only to readers of Arabic. Now any educated man in Durham could read them.

Typical of these new medical texts were the two works by Isaac Judaeus that Herbert possessed, in Constantine's Latin version. Isaac (Ishak ben Sulayman al Isra'ili) was a Jewish physician who had worked in north Africa in the ninth century. Herbert had his treatises on fevers and on urine. The latter was a classic guide to the analysis of urine and went into print in the sixteenth century as current medical teaching.[218] It was based on the idea that useful diagnosis and prognosis could follow from consideration of the quantity, consistency, and colour of the patient's urine, along with the nature of any sediment it yielded. Isaac's teaching was premissed on the standard learned physiology of the Greco-Roman world, that the human body was composed of four humours; blood, phlegm, red choler (bile), and black bile. Each was composed of two of the contrasting qualities, dry/wet and hot/cold. Diversity of the colour of urine was in part to be explained by the predominance in the patient's body of one of the humours (this constituted their 'complexion'), along with other features, such as age, diet, and exercise. Thus 'in young people urine is reddish, pink or yellow, because red choler naturally dominates their complexion . . . in older people the urine is lemon-coloured and watery, since their natural heat has diminished . . . the urine of women is naturally white and thin on account of the coldness of their complexion'. The interlocking concepts of Isaac's theory formed a complete, naturalistic explanatory system: 'A warm, wet complexion produces urine that is reddish in colour and thick in consistency, for heat warms the blood, stimulates active heating and gives a reddish tincture to the urine, while wetness makes liquid denser . . .'

Doctors expected to be paid and, as we have seen, some became rich. Their clients had to have the money to pay. If they were poor, the chronic sick could have a miserable fate. One paralysed man in Salisbury about the year 1210 at first enjoyed the charity of a local householder, but when this ran out he was carried to 'the gate of Salisbury castle, where the ill are accustomed to lie'. For more than a year he lay there, at 'the gate of the sick' (*ad portam languidorum*), receiving alms from such passers-by as Thomas of Chobham, the sub-dean. One kindly canon, Philip of Saint Edward, had a shelter of sticks made for him, 'so that the pigs and dogs should not harm him'. Eventually he was cured by the

---

[218] *Omnia opera Ysaac* (Lyons, 1515), fos. 156–203, with the commentary of Petrus Hispanus.

miraculous intervention of St Osmund, whose tomb was in the nearby cathedral, but most in his situation would have died of exposure or exhaustion.[219]

Individual charity provided some relief. Bishop Hermann of Sherborne (d. 1078) had the custom 'that wherever he travelled in his daily journeys he took with him many infirm and sick people, who were restored by the sustenance he provided'.[220] More enduring provision was offered by hospitals. Hundreds were established during this period. Not all, however, were concerned with medical treatment. The term 'hospital' also applied to almshouses, which offered a sheltered home for the poor and elderly, and to hostels providing accommodation for pilgrims and poor travellers. Of those actually dedicated to the sick, a large number were leper hospitals, for this is the great age of the foundation of that particular institution, offering secluded and segregated housing for lepers on the outskirts of towns. Four of the five medieval hospitals in the Chichester area, for instance, were leper hospitals. One of them, St James and St Mary Magdalene, received an endowment at the end of the twelfth century from the bishop of Chichester, who also promised to give eight woollen tunics at Christmas and eight linen garments at Easter, implying that this was the number of inmates. The cemetery of this hospital has been excavated, revealing many skeletons with clear evidence of leprosy, such as loss of nasal bones.[221]

The period 1075–1225 thus saw the foundation of hundreds of hospitals, the elaboration of complex theories of the body and medicine, and the continued employment of traditional herbal and incantatory remedies. The effort put into healing was commensurate with the amount of suffering that was endured. It is probably sadly true that the results attained were quite incommensurate with the effort.

## 6. DEATH AND THE DEAD

### A Good Death

It was best to face death prepared. Sudden death was feared and a range of apprehensive practices were carried out to guard against it. Some believed that signing the forehead and breast with the words 'Jesus of Nazareth' was a guarantee against it.[222] It was also claimed that whoever fasted on 4 August, the vigil of the feast of St Oswald, king and martyr, would be granted

---

[219] *Can. Osmund*, pp. 36–9.

[220] *Passio sancti Eadwardi*, ed. Christine Fell, *Edward, King and Martyr* (Leeds, 1971), p. 14.

[221] *Chichester Acta*, no. 107, pp. 162–3; J. Magilton and F. Lee, 'The Leper Hospital of St James and St Mary Magdalene, Chichester', in Charlotte A. Roberts *et al.* (eds.), *Burial Archaeology* (BAR, British Ser. 211; 1989), pp. 249–65.

[222] *Vis. Eynsham*, p. 319.

foreknowledge of the day of his or her death. For every year that this pious duty was fulfilled, another day's foreknowledge would be given. Thus, bishop Maurice of Paris (d. 1196), knew the time of his death fifty days in advance, since he had fasted on that day for fifty years.[223]

Serious illness with its threat of death was one of the most common stimuli to pious reflection and self-reproach. The pain must be deserved. What had the sufferer done to merit punishment? How could things be rectified? The northern baron Nigel d'Aubigny, lying sick in his bed about the year 1110, was stirred in this way and wrote to the bishop and monks of Durham:

I beg God's mercy and ask for the intercession of St Mary, the holy confessor Cuthbert and of you, that you should have pity on me, because almighty God in his justice has struck me with severe bodily illness. Here I lie, in deep distress, not knowing what will become of me. Therefore I ask you to do for me what you would do for one of your brethren or a friend.

To back up his plea, Nigel returned two manors that he had earlier taken from the church of Durham. This was part of a general restoration of church and lay property that he undertook at this time, spurred by desire to avoid 'damnation of his soul' and 'hell everlasting'.[224]

The urge to buy salvation for one's soul by last minute grants to churches was so strong that, in order to protect lay estates, twelfth-century English law did not recognize the simple validity of gifts of land made while the giver was on his deathbed.[225] This was a necessary safeguard. Clerics were eager to seize the opportunity that the deathbed offered. As Robert de Beaumont, count of Meulan and earl of Leicester, lay dying in 1118, he was asked by the clergy around him, to whom he was making his confession, 'to return penitently the lands that he had taken from many by force and guile and to wash away the fault with his tears.' The dying magnate replied that he did not wish to disinherit his sons. 'The ministers of the Lord replied: "Your original inheritance and the lands you acquired justly should suffice for your sons. Give back the other properties or you have given up your soul to hell." '[226]

A century later, the *Life* of William Marshal depicts the dying baron facing much the same kind of pressure.[227] One of his old companions was concerned: 'Sire . . . the clerks tell us and have us understand that no one has any chance of salvation unless he returns what he has taken.' William was robustly confident: 'The clerks are too hard on us. They want to shave us too

[223] Gerv. Tilb. 2. 17 (p. 938).

[224] *Mowbray Charters*, no. 4, pp. 10–11; cf. nos. 2–3, 5–10, pp. 6–10, 11–15.

[225] Glanvill 7. 1 (p. 70); for discussion of this point, Michael Sheehan, *The Will in Medieval England* (Toronto, 1963), pp. 270–4.

[226] H. Hunt., *De contemptu mundi* 7–8, pp. 596–600.

[227] *Hist. Guill. Mar.*, 2, pp. 282–327, lines 17882–19106, describes at length the last sickness, death, and burial of William Marshal.

closely. I have captured 500 knights and taken their arms, armour and horses. If the kingdom of heaven is denied to me for that, there is nothing I can do, for I cannot return them.' He contented himself with the thought that he had committed himself to God and repented of his sins.

Whatever his views about the demands of the clergy, the Marshal's end was the model of a good death. When he grew ill he had himself taken to his own manor of Caversham—'if he was going to die, he would rather be on his own property than anywhere else'. Having surrendered the regency, he took thought for his own affairs: 'It would be well for me to finish my last will and to take great care for my soul, since the body is beyond hope. It would be well for me to free my thoughts from all earthly things and turn them to heavenly things, for my need of them is great.' He made provision for his younger sons and his remaining unmarried daughter. His last days were a family affair. As he lay on his deathbed he was surrounded by his family and household. Among the most poignant moments of this last scene is that in which his daughters sing to him.

His last words to his wife were 'Fair love, kiss me now, for you will never kiss me again.' This moment saw the married couple in the encircling embrace of their wide following: 'She came to him; he kissed her; he cried and she cried; from love and pity all the good people around them cried.' He planned the details of his burial with the same care and authority he had shown in ruling the kingdom. Two precious silk cloths that he had saved to cover him on the bier were fetched. He made it clear that he wished to be buried among the Templars. The Master of the English Templars himself came to visit him. He donned the Templar habit. Soon afterwards he was on the point of death. Calling to his faithful follower, John of Erley, he told him to open the windows and call his family and knights. As they came, he cried, 'I am dying. I commend you to God. I can stay with you no longer. I cannot defend myself against death.' Nor could he. His body was taken in state to the Temple Church in London, where the archbishop of Canterbury praised 'the best knight in the world'. His tomb can be seen there to this day.

## Burial

Proper burial of the dead was deemed the desirable and fitting end. Inability to recover a body was a painful thing. After the sinking of the White Ship in 1120, with the loss of the king's son and half the high Anglo-Norman aristocracy, 'the difficulty of recovering the bodies added to the calamity'.[228] As the *Anglo-Saxon Chronicle* puts it, 'to their friends this was a double grief: first, that they lost their lives so swiftly; second, that few of their bodies were found afterwards'.[229]

---

[228] W. Malm., *GR* 5. 419 (2, p. 497); OMT edn., p. 762.    [229] *ASC*, p. 249.

Disposal of the dead in medieval Christian societies involved burial of the whole body, usually stretched out flat in the earth. Cremation was viewed as a pagan and intolerable custom, nor, with some exceptions to be discussed below, was dismemberment permitted. After corpses had been washed, they were wrapped in a shroud, as shown on the Bayeux tapestry, where Edward the Confessor's corpse is carried on a bier and appears to be completely wrapped in a shroud. It is recorded that Carthusian monks were sewn into a cloth before being placed in the tomb.[230] There is also evidence that coffins were commonly used. Burial in wooden coffins is described as an ancient English custom by an Italian observer, writing about 1100.[231] Excavations of cemeteries often reveal the nails that were used to secure them.

The ruling that bodies of excommunicates were to not to be buried 'within churchyards either in stone or wood' reveals quite clearly the assumption that normally burial would be in wooden coffins or stone sarcophagi.[232] Interment in stone was considered superior to interment in wood. When the body of the young apprentice and potential saint William of Norwich was being brought for burial in the monks' cemetery at Norwich, the corpse was 'washed, dressed in a white garment, then wrapped in linen and laid back on the bier . . . a grave was dug in the cemetery by the wall of the chapter-house, where a coffin might be placed and the body interred within.' The digging, however, turned up an unused stone sarcophagus—a miracle in the eyes of the narrator.[233]

Most people were buried in the graveyard of their parish church. Burial in an abbey churchyard was a favour extended to respected patrons and friends of the monastery. Burial within the church itself was a special privilege and a sign of high status. When Geoffrey fitz Peter, the son of a forester, climbed to the summit of the English aristocracy through his service in the Angevin administration, one of his concerns was to remove the body of his father, which had been buried in the cemetery of Winchester cathedral, and have it reinterred inside the cathedral church.[234] It was both an act of filial piety and a public demonstration of Geoffrey's new status.

Aristocratic patrons could expect to find a place of even more distinguished interment in the abbey churches they had supported. Hugh de Mortimer, on his deathbed at Cleobury in 1181, was invested with the habit of an Augustinian canon by Ranulf, abbot of Wigmore, the Augustinian house that Hugh had fostered and favoured. Then 'the body was carried to his abbey of Wigmore and interred honourably before the high altar'. 'His soul,' added

---

[230] Wilmart, 'Maître Adam', p. 229.
[231] A. J. M. Edwards, 'An Early Twelfth Century Account of the Translation of St Milburga of Much Wenlock', *Transactions of the Shropshire Archaeological Society*, 57 (1961–4), pp. 134–51, at p. 145.
[232] *Councils and Synods* 1/ii, p. 801.       [233] T. Monm., *V. William* 1. 17 (p. 53).
[234] *Ann. Wint.*, p. 67

the canon of Wigmore who reported this, 'as we believe, rests with God's chosen ones.'[235] Burial before the high altar was a mark of special respect. Henry de Ferrers, founder of the Ferrers family monastery at Tutbury, at the door of the family's chief castle, was reinterred on the prestigious right side of the high altar in the priory church by his great-grandson, William, earl Ferrers, around 1165.[236]

Bishops and abbots were also buried within the churches they had ruled. Bishop Remigius of Lincoln was buried 'within sight of the altar of the Holy Cross' in his own cathedral of Lincoln.[237] Interment such as this, before the Rood that stood at the east end of the nave, was a sign of respect and honour. The body of archbishop Lanfranc was placed in the corresponding situation in Canterbury cathedral, although the rebuilding of the church meant that his body had later to be moved. The archbishops were buried in the cathedral, while the priors were interred in the chapter house. Archbishop Theobald's lead coffin was found in 1787.[238]

A particularly striking tomb, that still survives, is that of archbishop Hubert Walter (d. 1205). Unusually, rather than being a stone coffin sunk into the ground, it consists of a rectangular box-shaped sarcophagus of Purbeck marble above ground. It is decorated with six carved heads, perhaps in imitation of ancient Roman sarcophagi. Situated on the south side of the new Trinity Chapel created for Becket's shrine, Hubert Walter's bones were the only ones to keep company with the great Canterbury saint for 200 years.[239]

Of the kings of England who died in the period 1075–1225, four were buried in England, three in France. Apart from William II, who was buried hastily after his violent death in the nearest great church, Winchester cathedral, these kings were interred in religious houses which they had founded or patronized. William the Conqueror's body was transported from Rouen to St Stephen's, Caen, the abbey he himself had established in 1063. Henry I was brought to Reading, likewise his own foundation, and his troubled successor, Stephen, lay in his own church of Faversham in Kent. The Angevins Henry II and Richard I were entombed in Fontevrault, not an abbey of their own creation, but one with which they and their dynasty had strong links. Lastly, in accordance with his own express wishes, John was buried before the shrine of St Wulfstan in Worcester.

There are several points worth noting about this pattern. First, only two of

---

[235] *Wigmore Chron.*, p. 436.

[236] *The Cartulary of Tutbury Priory*, ed. Avrom Saltman (HMC, JP2; 1962), no. 53, pp. 66–7.

[237] Gerald, *V. Remigius* 5 (p. 22).

[238] Henry Boys, 'Observations on the Monument in Canterbury Cathedral called the Tomb of Theobald . . .', *Archaeologia*, 15 (1806), pp. 291–9.

[239] Christopher Wilson, 'The Medieval Monuments', in Patrick Collinson *et al.* (eds.), *A History of Canterbury Cathedral* (Oxford, 1995), pp. 451–510.

these kings were buried in the same place. There was no dynastic mausoleum of the enduring kind that the French royal family created in St Denis, where thirteen of the fifteen Capetian kings came to rest. The instability of the burial sites reflects the political instability of the royal line of England. William I and his sons did not create a St Denis in either Normandy or England, while Stephen's Faversham was a royal centre for his reign only. The new Angevin focus of the period after 1154 is reflected in the burials of Henry II and Richard I in Anjou, but it was a link that John was unable to maintain. Unlike the coronation, which was firmly connected to Westminster, royal interments reflected the shifting dynastic fortunes and geographical range of the English monarchy.

A second fact about royal burials is that, with one exception, kings were buried on the side of the Channel where they happened to die. This is not surprising on practical grounds and therefore concentrates attention on the one case where a royal corpse was shipped across the sea, that of Henry I. He died in the hunting-lodge at Lyons-la-Forêt, about fifteen miles or so from Rouen, on 1 December 1135 and was interred in Reading abbey on 5 January 1136.[240] Transporting the corpse was an elaborate business. In Rouen shortly after his death the king's entrails were removed for separate burial and embalming fluid applied. The body then had to rest for four wintry weeks at Caen waiting for a favourable wind before it could be taken across the Channel. Reading was very much Henry's own foundation. He had established it as a priory in 1121, bringing monks from Cluny, and then secured its elevation to an abbey and its rich endowment, avowedly 'for the salvation of my soul and that of king William my father and king William my brother and William my son and queen Matilda my mother and queen Matilda my wife and of all my predecessors and successors'.[241] Reading was thus a house founded specifically with the commemoration of the royal dynasty in mind. It is fitting that on his deathbed Henry I received 'spiritual counsel' from Hugh, archbishop of Rouen, for Hugh had previously been the first abbot of Reading. The abbey never became the royal mausoleum it was probably intended to be, although Henry I's widow was laid beside her husband in 1151, Henry II's infant son, William, was buried there in 1156, and an illegitimate son of Henry I, earl Reginald of Cornwall, was interred there in 1175. The new dynastic paths that royal history took under the houses of Blois and Anjou meant that Reading, while remaining rich and privileged, did not assume the role of a funerary equivalent of Westminster.

It was not often that items were buried with the dead. Christianity had tried to spiritualize the afterlife and it was not deemed necessary to send a

---

[240] For the date of 5 Jan. rather than 4 Jan., *Reading Cart.* 1, p. 14 n. 1.
[241] *Reading Cart.* 1., no. 1, p. 33.

dead person to the next world with the indispensable accoutrements of their status in this one—swords, spindles, horses, or slaves. The only exceptions were the vestments in which some great men, such as bishops, were buried, the chalice and paten placed in the tomb with priests, and a few items expressive of the Christian doctrine of penance: according to Lanfranc's *Constitutions* a written absolution of sins would be placed on the chest of a dead monk in his tomb, while inscribed lead crosses served a similar purpose for prelates.[242] A lead cross with papal absolution for bishop Godfrey of Chichester (d. 1088) was found in Chichester burial ground in the nineteenth century, while the pectoral cross found in the grave of bishop Giso of Wells, who died in the very same year, was inscribed with passages from the Mass for the Dead.[243] Sometimes lead plaques with the names and dates of the dead serving simply as identifying devices were placed on the breasts of prelates.

The practice of interring different parts of the body in different places developed gradually. Removing the intestines of a corpse that was not to be buried immediately, as in the case of Henry I, was simply precautionary. The intestines would then have separate burial. Robert Bloet, bishop of Lincoln, died at the royal palace of Woodstock, near Oxford, in 1123. His intestines were removed and interred at the nearby abbey of Eynsham, while the rest of his body was taken the hundred miles to his cathedral city for burial.[244] A subsequent incumbent of the same see was treated similarly three-quarters of a century later. Hugh of Lincoln's bowels were buried near the altar steps in the Temple Church in London, while his body was taken to Lincoln.[245] After king John's death, his intestines were removed and taken for burial at Croxden abbey, while his body was interred at Worcester cathedral, according to his own last wishes.[246]

Removing the heart for separate interment was much rarer and obviously an action with quite a different meaning. This special part of the body was placed in a location that was either dear to the dead person or had a significance to those responsible for the burial arrangements. It was not a hygienic or aesthetic measure but a symbolic one. After the death of Richard I in Poitou in 1199, his intestines were extracted and his body salted for preservation and taken for interment alongside his father at Fontevrault in Anjou. His heart—'of great size'—was buried at Rouen, capital of the Norman duchy.[247] Even possession of the heart of the lion-hearted king, however, did not prevent Rouen's falling to Philip Augustus five years after Richard's death.

---

[242] Lanfr., *Const.*, p. 130.

[243] Henry Mayr-Harting, *The Bishops of Chichester 1075–1207: Biographical Notes and Problems* (Chichester Papers 40; Chichester, 1963), plate IV; W. Rodwell, 'Lead Plaques from the Tombs of the Saxon Bishops of Wells', *Antiquaries Jnl* 59 (1979), pp. 407–10.

[244] W. Malm., *GP* 177 (p. 314). [245] Ad. Eyns., *V. Hugh* 5. 19 (2, p. 218).

[246] *Melrose Chron.*, p. 124; Barnwell Chron., p. 232. [247] Gerv. Cant., p. 593.

The high aristocracy might be buried with elaborate tombs. Mary, daughter of Malcolm Canmore of Scotland, sister of queen Matilda of England and wife of the count of Boulogne, died on 31 May 1116 and was buried in Bermondsey abbey, a wealthy Cluniac house not far from London. Her tomb was an elaborate record of her ancestry:

The marble tomb, carved with images of kings and queens, proclaims the dead woman's descent. An inscription engraved in golden letters on the surface of the tomb indicates briefly her name, life and ancestry: 'Here lies buried the noble countess Mary'.[248]

The message of the tomb, which is in both visual and verbal language, is the family descent of the individual within it.

Similarly, when the body of her sister Matilda, queen of Henry I, was moved to a new site within Westminster abbey during the reign of her grandson Henry II, it was marked by an inscription reading:

Here lies the lady Matilda II, the good queen of the English, once wife of king Henry I, mother of the empress Matilda, daughter of the lord Malcolm, once king of Scotland, and St Margaret, wife of that Malcolm. She died 1st May in the year of grace 1118. If we wished to tell everything about her goodness and uprightness of character, the day would not suffice. May the All High have mercy on her soul. Amen.[249]

This not only stresses Matilda's ancestry, which was both royal and saintly, but also her own virtues.

A surviving example from this period of a tomb of a high-born Norman lady is that of Gundrada, wife of William de Warenne, who died in childbirth in 1085 and was buried in the family foundation of Lewes. Her tombstone, however, is later, dating to the reconstruction of the priory in the 1140s. It is made of black limestone, is over six feet long and varies between eighteen inches and two feet in width. The decoration consists of a series of sixteen leaf-like designs, separated by lions' heads. Between them and around the edge of the tombstone runs an inscription recalling Gundrada's ancestry, praising her virtues, and appealing to the local saint, Pancras, to be benevolent to the dead noblewoman. Gundrada was 'offspring of dukes, ornament of her age, a noble seed' as well as the pious patroness of the poor. The day of her death (27 May) is also recorded.[250]

These examples thus show the practice of recording the ancestry and the date of death (but not of birth) of the deceased, along with a brief eulogy. Decoration might be abstract, as in the case of Gundrada, or figurative, like the 'images of kings and queens' on the tomb of the countess Mary.

---

[248] Marjorie Anderson, *Kings and Kingship in Early Scotland* (rev. edn.; Edinburgh, 1980), p. 255.
[249] *Aldgate Cart.*, p. 230; *Hyde Chron.*, p. 312, for the inscription on her original tomb.
[250] *Engl. Rom. Art*, no. 145, pp. 181–2.

Effigies of the dead were not common. The surviving recumbent effigies of Henry II, Eleanor of Aquitaine, and Richard I at Fontevrault form a rare and extraordinary group (Plate 8). Within England itself the earliest effigies are those of the bishops. An effigy in light relief at Exeter has been identified as that of bishop Bartholomew (d. 1184) and a similar tomb-slab at Salisbury probably commemorates bishop Jocelin, who died that same year. At Wells a series of carved episcopal effigies was created in the early decades of the thirteenth century and placed on the tombs of the Anglo-Saxon bishops of Wells. At around the same time the tomb of Henry Marshall, bishop of Exeter (d. 1206), was crowned with an effigy of the prelate. These episcopal effigies, mostly of Purbeck marble, are the earliest in a long and impressive series of late medieval tomb effigies, which came to commemorate lay people too in the course of the thirteenth century.

## Commemoration

One of the surest ways of securing a proper commemoration after death was to enter into confraternity with a monastery. Usually in return for a grant of land, the monks would promise to treat an outsider as one of their own, sometimes entering his or her name in a special 'Book of Life' that would be placed on the altar. Remembrance involved writing. Confraternity was conveyed by a ritual transmission of the Gospel text and enrolment in the earthly 'Book of Life' was seen as anticipation of entry in 'the page of the Book of Heaven'.[251] When Hugh, earl of Chester, granted an estate to the monks of Abingdon in 1090, he expected in return not only the sum of £30, but also spiritual benefits: 'and I shall be as one of your brethren, and my wife and my father and my mother shall be in your prayers, and we shall all be written in the book of commemoration and a funeral service shall be held for us, just as it is for one of the brethren of the church, wherever we may happen to die.'[252]

The twelfth-century confraternity list of Thorney abbey gives the names of about 2,300 men and women, mainly lay people, who enjoyed the privileges of confraternity with the abbey in the eleventh and twelfth centuries.[253] They range from kings and queens through barons and bishops to quite unidentifiable Roberts and Heloises, presumably local landowners who had perhaps made modest donations to the monastery. The benefits they could expect were sometimes spelt out in individual agreements, such as the

---

[251] Lanfr., *Const.*, p. 114; *Liber Vitae: Register and Martyrology of New Minster and Hyde Abbey*, ed. W. de Gray Birch (Hants. Rec. Soc.; 1892), pp. 11–12; *The Liber Vitae of the New Minster and Hyde Abbey Winchester*, ed. Simon Keynes (Early English Manuscripts in Facsimile 26; 1996), fo. 13.

[252] *Chester Charters*, no. 2, p. 2.

[253] BL Add. 40000, fos. 1ᵛ–12; discussed by Cecily Clark, 'British Library Additional MS. 40,000 ff. 1ᵛ–12r', *ANS* 7 (1984), pp. 50–68; for a good example of the analysis of such material, John Moore, 'Family-Entries in English *Libri Vitae*', *Nomina*, 16 (1992–3), pp. 99–128 and 18 (1995), pp. 77–117.

following, dating from 1085–1112, in which Geoffrey de Trelly made a land-grant to Thorney and received in return the right that

if I am inspired by merciful God to become a monk, I shall be received there as a monk, bringing with me a portion of my property. But if—God forbid—I pay the debt to nature as a layman, my men may carry me there to be buried. If I should die abroad and the monks are informed for certain that I am dead, they shall faithfully perform the obsequies for me just as for one of the monks. And then every year on the anniversary of my death let there be commemoration of my soul by the brethren.

Very similar terms were granted to Geoffrey's wife, while all his offspring were to have the right to be buried in the monks' cemetery.[254]

The names in the Thorney confraternity list were entered in groups and these groups represent both social units in this world and units of remembrance after death. Family ties and other bonds connected those who were commemorated. A clear, if not elaborate, example is the entry for William d'Aubigny Brito, an important baron active in the reigns of Henry I and Stephen: 'William d'Aubigny; Cecilia, his wife; William, Robert, Roger, his sons; Matilda, Basilia, his daughters; Roger, his clerk; Godfrey and Ralph, his knights.'[255] This is simplicity itself—a list of names to commemorate, each defined by relationship to the lord and patriarch, a core formed by the nuclear family and an outer circle of clerical and military followers.

More complex is the list of twenty-four names headed by Ralph Cheneduit.[256] These include Ralph's son William Cheneduit, his nephew William, his wife Matilda de Port, his two daughters both bearing the name Matilda, and three others with the surname Cheneduit. In addition this group contains seven men with the surname 'de Blacqueville', headed by Warin de Blacqueville, who is explicitly described in the fraternity list as 'a witness to our charter concerning the sixty acres at Charwelton [Northants]'. Since this charter survives, we can turn to it to find out that Warin was Ralph's knight (*miles meus*) and that he was only one of the witnesses to this grant by Ralph Cheneduit also to occur in the confraternity list alongside Ralph. The charter was granted to Thorney explicitly in return for confraternity with the monastery.[257] We do not always know the link between Ralph and the men and women alongside him on the list, but we can assume with confidence that 'Guy, king Henry's cook, and Hodeard his wife', who appear there, were tenants, vassals, friends, or relatives of the Cheneduits and expected to travel with them not only in a retinue jingling through the English Midland countryside but also into the afterlife.

[254] Cambridge, UL Add. 3021 (Red Book of Thorney), fo. 414ᵛ, printed Cecily Clark, 'British Library Additional MS. 40,000 ff. 1ᵛ–12ʳ', *ANS* 7 (1984), pp. 50–68, at p. 62; see also p. 58 and n. 37.

[255] BL Add. 40000, fo. 2.     [256] Ibid., fol. 2ᵛ.

[257] Cambridge UL Add. 3021, fo. 206; it can be dated to 1150–61.

It is a remarkable fact that the ratios of the sexes in the family names recorded in the 'Books of Life' of the Norman and Angevin periods are not even. Men outnumber women by far. In the Durham 'Book of Life' there are 151 men for every hundred women, in that from Winchester 163, while at Thorney the male: female ratio is a remarkable 182:100.[258] Such an imbalance is obviously not a demographic fact but a psychological and social one. It is not that these families had more men than women, but that they thought it more important that the men should be commemorated. A family chaplain or knightly retainer was included in the prayer fellowship more readily than a female relative and sons must have been recorded more systematically than daughters.

As is clear from the agreement between the monks of Thorney and Geoffrey de Trelly, mentioned above, commemoration of the day of death was far more important than any remembrance of the year. An observance on the anniversary of the death required some investment. Around 1170 it cost 30 shillings for the monks of Bath to celebrate the annual anniversary of John of Bath (1088–1122), the bishop who had moved his episcopal seat to Bath and was buried in their abbey.[259] On the first anniversary of the death of Henry I, his widow Adeliza gave to the abbey of Reading, where the king was buried, the manor of Aston (Herts.), granted the monks an annual payment of a hundred shillings to celebrate his anniversary, and also endowed them with lands 'to provide for the convent and other religious persons coming to the abbey on the occasion of the anniversary of my lord king Henry'. Some years later she added the gift of a church, the revenue from which was to pay for perpetual lights to burn before the consecrated host and before the king's tomb.[260]

So little is known about the thoughts and feelings of queen Adeliza that it is impossible to say what her emotions were when she ordered that perpetual light before her late husband's tomb. We do know that Henry I had commanded that a light should burn before the tomb of his first wife, Matilda, 'for ever'. A fixed charge of one halfpenny a day was placed on the king's London revenues to pay for the oil for the lamp, a sum that had increased to a penny a day by the reign of Henry II. It was still being paid at that rate in the reign of queen Matilda's great-great-grandson, Henry III, more than a century after 'the good queen's' death.[261] Perpetuity may be beyond human grasp, but a candle had been lit at her tomb every day for a hundred years.

The religious orders had their own arrangements for ensuring the fullest possible commemoration of their members. Sometimes, on the death of the

[258] John S. Moore, 'The Anglo-Norman Family: Size and Structure', *ANS* 14 (1991), pp. 153–96, at p. 173.
[259] PR 14 HII, p. 168; PR 15 HII, p. 23; PR 16 HII, p. 64; PR 17 HII, p. 23; PR 18 HII, p. 128.
[260] *Reading Cart.* 1, nos. 370, 459, 534–5, pp. 301, 353, 403–5.
[261] *RRAN* 2, no. 1377, p. 182; Pipe Rolls, *passim*.

head of the house, an itinerant embassy would be sent out with a mortuary roll. Coming to monasteries on the way, the bearers of the roll would request the prayers of its inmates and ask them to make an inscription on the roll. Mortuary rolls thus have some of the characteristics of an autograph book— a multiplicity of different hands, with entries of greatly varying length and type. That for Amphelisa, prioress of Lillechurch in Kent, begins with an emotional description of the sorrows felt by her nuns, goes on to praise her virtues, and concludes by asking for the prayers of the houses visited. Then, on the 37 feet of parchment that makes up the roll, come 372 entries, from religious houses in every part of England, from Cornwall to Northumberland, and beyond—St Andrews and Dunfermline dutifully made their inscriptions, alongside eight other Scottish houses.[262]

It is likely that Amphelisa's grieving sisters followed no particular system in their journeys and sought the prayers of any monasteries they happened to encounter. A more fixed and formal arrangement existed between those monastic congregations which had undertaken to commemorate deceased members of each other's communities. The monks of Rochester, for example, had by 1120 entered into mutual agreements with 28 English and Norman monasteries, specifying what form of commemoration was due when they were informed that a member of their sister house had died. The level of liturgical observance reflected the nature of the ties. Thus Rochester had close links with Canterbury cathedral priory and, when a monk of that house died, seven full Offices of the Dead were to be recited at Rochester, the *verba mea* (Psalm 5, associated with the service for the dead) was to be said every day for a month, each Rochester monk in priest's orders should celebrate seven masses, while monks who were not should recite Psalms. Exactly the same would be done for a deceased nun of Malling, a nunnery founded by the bishop of Rochester. The monks of Battle abbey were commemorated in a slightly less extensive way, with three Offices, without the *verba mea*, although the seven masses and psalmody were also required, and three poor people would be fed for a day—alms-giving for the dead was just as effective as prayer for the dead. Relations with St Augustine's, Canterbury, an old rival of Canterbury cathedral, were not so warm: three Offices only, with no other commemoration, was the due of a dead monk from St Augustine's.[263]

Friends and relatives of the dead were often intensely concerned to learn their fate after death. When one of the Gilbertine nuns of Watton died, the

---

[262] Cambridge, St John's College 271; M. R. James, *A Descriptive Catalogue of the Manuscripts in the Library of St John's College, Cambridge* (Cambridge, 1913), no. 271, pp. 317–18, prints the preface; C. E. Sayle, 'The Mortuary Roll of the Abbess of Lillechurch, Kent', *Procs. Cambridge Antiquarian Soc.*, n.s. 4 (1898–1903), pp. 383–409, describes the roll and lists the houses contributing; Sally Thompson, *Women Religious: The Founding of English Nunneries after the Norman Conquest* (Oxford, 1991), p. 11 n. 26, convincingly argues for an early rather than late thirteenth-century date.

[263] *Text Roff.* 214, pp. 231–4, fos. 222–223ᵛ.

others were accustomed to pray until the dead nun appeared to them in a dream or a vision 'to disclose the pain or the glory she had earned'.[264] Enormous efforts might be expended to secure a happy fate for the dead soul. At some point before his departure on the First Crusade, Arnulf de Hesdin endowed daily masses to be said for a year for his deceased parents, to be celebrated by the monks of Rochester.[265] After the death of Matilda, wife of Henry I, the following were supposedly offered for her soul: 47,000 masses, 9,000 recitals of the Psalter, 80 trentals, and the feeding of 67,820 poor.[266] Since the belief that the damned in hell could attain absolution by the intervention of any saint had to be decried as a heretical delusion, clearly some people thought that even the damned could be saved if sufficient spiritual power were enlisted on their behalf.[267]

The most enduring way of ensuring a perpetual prayer of intercession was the endowment of a chantry, that is, the special funding of a priest to say masses for one's own soul or the soul of any other specified beneficiary. Richard, bishop of London (1189–98), for example, arranged that the annual revenue of eight marks (£5. 6s. 8d.) received by St Paul's from the church of Cheshunt (Herts.) should be used to support two priests in the cathedral. One was to celebrate a daily mass for the present king, bishop, canons, and faithful people of the diocese, while the other did the same for the deceased kings, bishops, canons, and faithful people. Two altars were built for these services, dedicated to St Thomas Becket and St Denis.[268] Both the living and the dead needed the support of the eucharistic service and the saints. The most enduring memorial was indeed an undying foundation. The leper hospital of St Giles, Holborn, founded by Henry I's queen, Matilda, was referred to a century or more after her death as 'Queen Matilda's Memorial' (*memoriale Matildis regine*).[269]

## Visions of the Afterlife

Orderic Vitalis tells the story of an Anglo-Norman priest's encounter with his dead brother, who as a punishment for his life of fighting and plundering had to travel with a troop of the dead, bearing red-hot weapons and wearing spurs of fire. The suffering knight explains how his brother's priestly vocation had been of help to him and to their father:

when you were ordained in England and sang your first mass for the faithful departed, Ralph your father was delivered from his torments and my shield, which was

---

[264] Ailred of Rievaulx, *De sanctimoniali de Wattun* (PL 195, col. 790).
[265] *Text Roff.* 107, p. 163, fo. 184.    [266] *Hyde Chron.*, p. 312.
[267] Ad. Eyns., *V. Hugh* 1. 10 (1, p. 33).    [268] *Early Charters St Paul's*, no. 186, pp. 145–6.
[269] Paris, *CM* 2, p. 144; Suzanne Lewis, *The Art of Matthew Paris in the Chronica majora* (Berkeley, 1986), fig. 47, p. 90.

a great burden to me, fell away. . . . Remember me, I beg you, and help me with your pious prayers and alms: in one year from next Palm Sunday, I hope to be saved and, by the mercy of the Creator, freed from all punishment.[270]

Such encounters with the suffering dead were not uncommon, nor was it unusual to find them explaining the help they had received from the good deeds of their living relatives.

Indeed, there are accounts far more systematic than Orderic's anecdote of encounters with the dead and discussions of their fate. Such are the reports of visionary journeys to the afterlife, several of which survive from this period. In 1125 a 13-year old boy called Orm, from Howden in Yorkshire, lay in a coma for thirteen days, before returning to consciousness with an account of his experiences in heaven and hell. The monk Edmund, of the abbey of Eynsham in Oxfordshire, was likewise unconscious, for two days, 19–20 April 1196, undergoing a visionary journey through the purgatorial regions. Ten years later, in 1206, the Essex peasant Thurkill was insensible for a similar period, 28–29 October, and after his awakening gave a full description of what he had encountered in the afterlife. All these accounts were written down and circulated, along with other similar reports that had either been transmitted from earlier times, like the Vision of St Paul, or been imported from outside England, like the vision of the Irishman Tundal. One popular text that, although it describes a visionary experience in Ireland, was actually composed in England during this period is the tract on St Patrick's Purgatory. Written by a monk of the Cistercian abbot of Sawtry (Hunts.), this tells how the knight Eoghan entered the cave in an island in Lough Derg that was reputed to be the entrance to St Patrick's Purgatory and then passed through the purgatorial regions to the terrestrial paradise. This account and many others were copied into a vast anthology of visionary narratives compiled between 1200 and 1206 by Peter, prior of Holy Trinity, Aldgate, who includes a vision of the afterlife experienced by his own grandfather, the Cornish landowner Ailsi.[271]

With the exception of the knight Eoghan, who undergoes his experiences in the flesh, the visionaries leave their bodies behind when they are taken to the other world. Indeed, the first reaction of their family and friends to their state is to think that they have died. Orm is being wrapped for burial before it is noticed that he is still alive.[272] When Thurkill is taken away in the spirit, it

---

[270] Orderic 8. 17 (4, p. 248).

[271] *Vis. Orm*; *Vis. Eynsham*; *Vis. Thurkill*; *Purgatorium sancti Patricii*, ed. Karl Warnke, *Das Buch vom Espurgatoire S. Patrice de Marie de France und seine Quellen* (Bibliotheca Normannica 9; Halle, 1938), pp. 2–168 (even pages); Peter Cornw., *Liber rev.*; there is a synopsis of the last work in M. R. James, *A Descriptive Catalogue of the Manuscripts in the Library of Lambeth Palace: The Medieval Manuscripts* (Cambridge, 1932), pp. 71–85.

[272] *Vis. Orm*, p. 77.

is necessary for his saintly guide to blow into the mouth of the vacated body 'so that your body should not be deemed to be dead'.[273] The monks of Eynsham find brother Edmund sprawled on the floor and 'many proclaimed that he had already died', before they notice that he is breathing lightly.[274] The body is thus left in a comatose state while the soul goes on its journey, although there may still be some kind of link between the experiences of the soul of the visionary in the other world and those of his body in this—when Thurkill's soul coughs at the fumes from hell, his body coughs at exactly the same time.[275]

To protect them and guide them, the visionaries have saintly companions. Orm is accompanied by St Michael, Edmund of Eynsham by St Nicholas. Thurkill has several guides. He first encounters St Julian the Hospitaller (Thurkill is renowned for his hospitality), who has been sent to bring him to St James, whose shrine Thurkill had visited. In the other world St James commissions St Julian and the somewhat obscure St Dompninus 'to show his pilgrim the purgatorial places and the dwellings of the just'.[276] Later St Michael accompanies Thurkill into the higher reaches of the afterworld. These saintly guides not only fend off demons from the visionary but also provide for him a running commentary on the landscape of the afterlife and sometimes prompt him to action—when St Nicholas learns that the monk Edmund knows one of the souls in purgatory, he urges him, 'So, if you know him, speak to him.'[277]

The picture of the afterlife presented in the visionary literature of the period is one in which souls are subject to pain or bliss in accordance with the virtues they had exhibited while alive and the religious services performed for them after their death. Hell is characterized by flames, smoke, and stench, heaven by jewels, gold, and the company of the saints. The torments inflicted on those in hell or purgatory are described with great imaginative gusto. There is not often detailed physical description of the devils, although they are usually portrayed as black, but their glee at having humans souls as their prey and the delight they take in torturing them is a major theme. In the vision of Thurkill, a demon is seen galloping along on a black horse, 'while many evil spirits came leaping to meet him, cackling to one another about the prey he had brought'. The black horse turns out to be the soul of one of king John's barons, who had died the previous evening unshriven and without the benefit of the viaticum after a life of hard and ruthless injustice. 'His soul', explains the demon, 'has now been justly placed completely in my power, to torture incessantly in the torments of the pit. Do not be surprised that I have

---

[273] *Vis. Thurkill*, p. 6.    [274] *Vis. Eynsham*, p. 290.
[275] *Vis. Thurkill*, p. 12.    [276] Ibid., p. 11.    [277] *Vis. Eynsham*, p. 314.

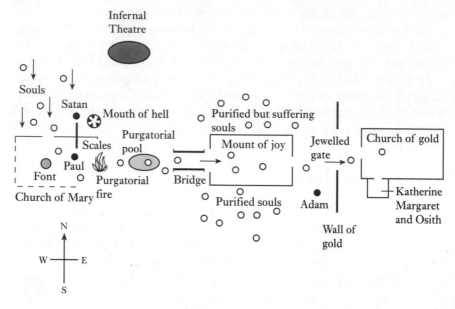

FIGURE 15.  *The geography of the afterlife*

transformed him into the shape of a horse, so that I can ride him, for we are allowed to change the souls of the damned into any shape or form we wish.'[278]

The geography of the afterlife is often concrete and elaborate. The vision of Thurkill is detailed enough to allow us to construct a map of the world beyond (Figure 15). He comes first to the church of St Mary, which is of open construction, like a monastic cloister, except to the north, where there is a wall about six feet high. In the middle of the church is a font, from which a bright flame emerges, fed by the tithes given by the righteous. The souls of the departed make for the north wall of the church and, if they are only moderately sinful, enter and proceed eastwards. The very sinful must be weighed on the scales between St Paul and Satan, and, if they fall to Satan's lot, are then cast down into the mouth of hell, that is nearby. To the north of this is the Infernal Theatre, where, every Saturday night, the devils force the souls of the damned to re-enact the sins for which they were condemned.

The souls that have deserved to undergo purgatorial cleansing pass eastwards first through fire, then through a pool, finally over a bridge bristling with nails and spikes. On the other side is the Mount of Joy, surmounted by a church. On the north and south sides are the purified souls awaiting final release through the help of their living friends and relatives. Beyond the church is a fountain where Adam awaits the final consummation of salvation.

[278]  *Vis. Thurkill*, pp. 18–19.

Further east still is a jewelled gate in a wall of gold and, on the other side, a church of gold. Inside is a chapel where the three virgin martyrs, Katherine, Margaret, and Osith reside in glory (there is a touch of Essex pride here, for Osith was venerated in Essex at St Osith's abbey, only 20 miles from Thurkill's home at Stisted). At this point in his journey Thurkill's saintly guides become aware that his friends on earth are attempting to drip-feed him holy water and have to rush his soul back into his body in order to avoid his drowning.

Thurkill's other-world geography has many particularities of detail. Indeed, it does not seem to be the case that there was a fixed and agreed picture of the dispositions of the afterlife. Orm's vision places heaven above the stars—the heavenly bodies appear much bigger to him, when he is transported past them, than they usually seem—while the entrance to hell is in a gloomy valley 'under the world'. Paradise, with its crowds of saints, is a separate place from heaven, where God sits enthroned with Mary and the Apostles. The monk of Eynsham deals with purgatorial places in an ascending (or descending) order of severity: 'the first place of torment', 'the second place of torment', and 'the third place of torment', the last reserved for those guilty of sodomy, but the physical description is vague. The first is a muddy swamp, the second a gloomy valley, the third a wide field overshadowed by foul smoke. Further on, according to the monk, one comes to the pleasant fields where those who have passed through the torments of purgatory stroll eastwards, becoming ever whiter as the air grows sweeter and the light brighter. Passing a crystalline wall, the monk and his guide St Nicholas enter paradise, where he sees God on his throne. This is not yet, however, 'the heaven of heavens, where the just rejoice in the sight of God, seeing him in his majesty'.[279]

It seems that every soul has some stain that needs to be burned off by purgatorial pain. Even those who are revered—rightly—as wonder-working saints may still be undergoing such a cleansing. The monk of Eynsham felt the need to cite authority at this point: 'whoever does not believe that sometimes a miracle takes place through the merits of those who are troubled in purgatory should refer to the fourth book of the Dialogues of St Gregory'. The case in point is that of Reginald, bishop of Bath and Wells (1174–91) and archbishop-elect of Canterbury (1191). 'I have heard,' reports the monk of Eynsham, 'that after his death he performed miraculous cures for certain weak and sick people.' Reginald had been a secret ascetic, keeping up the bearing and outward manner of a great bishop, but wearing a hair shirt and undergoing physical discipline to atone for the sins of his youth and those he committed in the bustling course of his duties.[280]

[279] *Vis. Eynsham*, p. 368.     [280] Ibid., pp. 350–1.

The 'merits' that ensured an easier passage through purgatory after death might be moral, such as charity and justice, but might also spring from asceticism, as in the case of bishop Reginald, or from ritual practice. Among those weighed in the scales between Satan and St Paul was a priest whose soul was so completely black that it brought a fierce glare from St Paul. The saint nevertheless sought to save him by placing all his weights in the scale. The beam still tilted towards Satan, until the apostle threw in the holy-water sprinkler, a sign of the priest's ceremonial role. The scale immediately sank down on St Paul's side, so violently that the weight on Satan's side fell out onto the devil's foot. Satan complained of unfairness and produced a written catalogue of the priest's sins, but 'the devil's writings were as nothing, being outweighed by the merits of good works'.[281] The 'good works' here must be equated, not with any moral virtues exhibited by the priest, but simply with his priestly function. The fact that he had the authority to sprinkle holy water made the difference between an eternity in hell and the prospect of heaven.

A similar ritual emphasis occurs in the case of the goldsmith whom the monk of Eynsham encounters. The monk had known this man during his life and, because he was a notorious drunkard and had died suddenly in a drunken stupor, the monk and all his other acquaintances had presumed that he must be 'lost and damned'. However, despite his ever-losing fight with drink, the goldsmith had always maintained a special devotion to St Nicholas, in whose parish he lived. He visited St Nicholas's chapel regularly, kept a lamp burning there, and, as far as possible, fulfilled his religious obligations, confessing twice a year, fasting at the proper season, and taking communion at Christmas. This stood him in good stead, for, as soon as he died and a crowd of demons appeared to snatch him off to hell, 'Lo! there came the most holy St Nicholas, my lord and advocate, whom I had invoked in my heart as I lay dying and whom I had always revered during my lifetime, although I was a sinner, and he tore me forcefully from their hands and brought me to this place of purgatory.'[282] Devotion to a saint can outweigh moral failings.

The living can help the dead. In all these accounts stress is placed on the importance of the assistance of those still on earth in freeing their loved ones from purgatorial pain and allowing them to progress to heaven. Debts must be settled, masses said. The details can be highly concrete, even mathematical. St Michael informs Thurkill of how many masses are required to enable each of the souls to progress into the church on the Mount of Joy, while the soul of his former lord, Roger Picot, tells him that he remains waiting because he still owes 40 pence to his workers and did not send an annual payment he owed to the canons of St Osith's. He instructs Thurkill to tell his son, William

[281] *Vis. Thurkill*, pp. 14–15.     [282] *Vis. Eynsham*, pp. 312–18.

Picot, to clear these obligations.[283] The monk of Eynsham is equally explicit that the amount of suffering that souls undergo in the afterlife is determined by 'the quality of their virtues and the quantity of relief offered for them after their death'.[284]

As any reader of Dante knows, the afterlife vision is a powerful way of expressing a view on one's own contemporaries. By making it clear who is saved and who not, it is possible to act as a judge on one's times, one's neighbours, or one's masters. Indeed, the allocation of individuals to hell or purgatory or heaven by the visionary is tantamount to a usurpation of the task of the Supreme Judge. The vision can be the vehicle for a general moralism, identifying specific vices and flaws, such as the scene witnessed by Thurkill where 'a proud man', 'a neglectful priest', 'a predatory knight', etc., are tormented, but it can also carry more precise messages. It is, indeed, not too much to say that visions of heaven and hell are contemporary social criticism. Again and again, the point is made that the rich and powerful on earth get no special treatment in the afterlife and may indeed fare worse. This is true too of those who have any pretensions to holiness, like monks and clerics. They can anticipate a judgment as harsh as that inflicted on any sinful layman, even if, like the priest weighed in the scales between Satan and St Paul, they just scrape through in the end. Orm describes the chosen saints who are within the walls of paradise, and then observes that 'outside the wall were some monks and many priests and they were not as happy as those within the walls.'[285] The monk of Eynsham reports that 'I saw that all those who had been judges or prelates on earth were harassed by a torture more bitter than the rest'.[286] In a sense, then, these texts promote a visionary levelling of society, suggesting that the privileges of neither the upper classes nor the ecclesiastics will last for ever.

This levelling and retributory urge is expressed most strongly in those passages where individual potentates or prelates are depicted in suffering. Indeed, the ardour with which the tortures are described suggest that the visionaries were not unfamiliar with the sadistic delight that they attribute to the demons. The gloating tone shows in the following passage, in which the monk of Eynsham encounters the soul of Henry II:

Who can conceive with what tortures he was afflicted, in his whole body and in every limb? He sat on a horse that continually breathed out pitch-black flame from its mouth and nostrils, with smoke and a hellish stench, as a torment to its rider. He was dressed as if for war in complete armour, and that was an unspeakable torment to him. For the armour he wore flashed out a fiery rain, like white-hot iron when it is

---

[283] *Vis. Thurkill*, p. 30.    [284] *Vis. Eynsham*, p. 308.
[285] *Vis. Orm*, p. 81.    [286] *Vis. Eynsham*, p. 306.

struck by hammers, and this burned him to the quick. . . .The saddle he sat upon was studded all over with fiery nails and spikes, so that it filled with horror anyone who beheld it from afar, but, as for the rider, those points pierced his liver and entrails.[287]

This is how an English monk of the year 1196 saw his recently deceased monarch. The charges against king Henry were his adultery, his unjust spilling of human blood, as, for instance, in his harsh enforcement of the Forest laws, and his heavy taxation. There might be little hope of resisting the Angevin kings while alive, but a fantasy revenge could be exacted in purgatory.

The pursuit of the very highest in this way was not at all uncommon in twelfth-century England. Henry I had likewise been seen in pain in the year 1141, six years after his death, by a monk of Bec who had been one of the king's knights:

the king appeared to him in a vision and said 'Do you know who I am?' He replied he did not know and the king said, 'I am he who was once called king Henry, your earthly lord, now wretched and unhappy.' Because the monk was so afraid, he said, 'Have no fear of me or of the things you are about to see.' Suddenly a horrible crowd of demons appeared, armed with swords and lances. They tore the king limb from limb and chopped him into pieces so that it seemed to the monk that nothing was left, and then the demons disappeared. After a little while the monk seemed to see a crowd of monks, with crosses and candles, begging the divine mercy on bended knees for the king's soul. Soon, by their prayers, the king returned to his earlier shape, then the monks in their turn disappeared. The king said to the monk who had been watching all this, 'Do you see, brother, what I am suffering for my sins and what I will suffer until the Day of Judgement? And behold what great good the monks bring me, in return for the slight benefits I offered to them.'[288]

The pursuit of the powerful reached lower down the scale than this. King's servants as well as kings might face the torments imposed upon them by demons and visionaries. One of the damned that Thurkill recognized was 'a man famous throughout England for his eloquence and knowledge of the law' but who 'had subverted many judgments by accepting bribes'. He had to act out his sins in the Infernal Theatre, 'turning first to the right then to the left, as if speaking with each of the parties in the lawsuit in turn, now advising one side about how to make their case, now protecting the other side by telling them how to reply and offer refutation, his hands in ceaseless action, taking money now from this party, now from that, and counting it'.[289] Although he is not named in the vision, the details that Thurkill gives enable this judge to be identified. He is Osbert fitz Hervey, the brother of Hubert Walter,

---

[287] *Vis. Eynsham*, pp. 347–8.     [288] Cambridge UL Ff. I. 27, p. 219.
[289] *Vis. Thurkill*, pp. 23–4.

archbishop of Canterbury, who served as a royal judge from 1191 until his death in 1206 and did well out of the royal service.[290]

More personal and more disturbing than these encounters with the rich and famous is an incident in Thurkill's vision involving the visionary's own family. When Thurkill and St Michael, his guide at that point, reach the church on the Mount of Joy, the Essex man expresses a desire to see his dead parents. Michael instructs him to search for them on the south side of the church. Here are those souls who are purified and feel no pain, except longing for their final goal. Thurkill cannot see his parents among them, so Michael leads him around to the north side of the church. Here is 'a great multitude lying face downwards on sharp flints and suffering from the savage blast of a cold north wind'. Of course, he cannot recognize anyone until St Michael commands them to stand up. 'Among the other faces he saw there, he discerned his father, horribly emaciated and wasted away in every limb. His appearance was so terrifying and deformed that, as Thurkill himself testified, it would strike fear and horror into thousands if they saw it face to face.' The father recognizes his son and explains that he is suffering still because of the sharp business practice he had engaged in during his life. St Michael adds that thirty masses would free him, but settles for ten on the grounds of Thurkill's poverty. Once these have been promised, Thurkill can accompany his father into the church on the Mount of Glory. 'But', adds the text, 'he was never able to find his mother or learn anything for certain about her state.'[291]

It would not be entirely extravagant to deduce something of Thurkill's feelings about his parents from this passage. His freely roving visionary mind chose to make his father suffer and yet also to liberate him, through his own good offices, while he consigns his mother to a shadowy oblivion. Perhaps Thurkill's fears as well as his wishes were at work to produce this chilling scenario, but it is hard to deny that the vision of the afterlife is one arena where scores can be settled and the unsatisfactory arrangements of this world be transformed.

These other-world journeys and visionary travels were frequently experienced by laymen (there are no records of women having such experiences) and not unusually by lower-class people, for instance the poor peasant Thurkill, but the final written account was always produced by a cleric. Orm's vision was recorded by Sigar, priest of a neighbouring parish, Thurkill's probably by the Cistercian Ralph of Coggeshall, while that of Ailsi the Cornishman found permanent record in the pen of his grandson, prior Peter. This means that there is a problem disentangling what the English laity

---

[290] Ralph V. Turner, *The English Judiciary in the Age of Glanvill and Bracton, c.1176–1239* (Cambridge, 1985), pp. 7, 73, 80, 90, 92, 113, 116–17, 123, 172, 296–7.

[291] *Vis. Thurkill*, pp. 31–2.

thought of the afterlife from the interpretations and additions introduced by the educated monks and priests who recorded their visions. It is clear that some of the authors had read earlier narratives and might well be tempted to shape their record accordingly. The author of the Vision of Thurkill, for instance, mentions in his preface Eoghan's journey through St Patrick's purgatory and the vision of the monk of Eynsham, as well as other visions of the afterlife. It is hard to distinguish literary commonplaces from generally held beliefs. For instance, the bridge that souls have to cross to reach heaven occurs in many of these texts. Is this best seen as part of a long literate Christian tradition or as a widespread and unreflective belief of twelfth-century English folk? One extreme position would be to argue that the clerical writers simply copied earlier texts, without regard to what the visionaries told them—and there is an example, albeit not from England, of a twelfth-century visionary complaining that the monk who wrote down his account had completely falsified it.[292] Another, more nuanced position, might be that the clerical amanuensis encouraged his illiterate informant, perhaps unconsciously, to shape his vision according to clerical expectations. A third position would be that this was unnecessary, for the unconscious minds of the laity had already been Christianized through the teaching of the church in sermons, plays, and pictures. It is an unanswerable question whether the English laity would have had a bridge in their afterlife if England had not been converted to Christianity.

Setting aside such cavils, there can be little doubt that the visions of the afterlife recorded in this period do contain representations of the fate of the soul beyond death that, even if composed of an amalgam of expressly theological teaching and less learned and less specifically Christian thinking, were current and powerful in the minds of men and women of the time. Most people would suffer pain after death; they could be helped by the prayers and alms of the living; they could expect to progress slowly towards paradise through the suffrages of the Church and the help of the saints.

## Revenants

It was painful, of course, to think of the souls of the dead suffering in purgatory or in hell, but more frightening was the possibility that they might return to earth in their physical form to haunt the living and do harm. Such revenants were not uncommon in this period. As the chronicler William of Newburgh, who wrote in the 1190s, put it, 'one would not easily believe that corpses come out of their graves and wander around, animated by I don't know what spirit, to terrorize or harm the living, unless there were many

[292] *Vis. Thurkill*, p. 51.

cases in our times, supported by ample testimony.'[293] He gives recent examples from Buckinghamshire and southern Scotland. The archdeacon and raconteur Walter Map, writing slightly earlier in the twelfth century, tells of a wicked man in the diocese of Hereford who returned from the dead and wandered at night through his village, calling out the names of villagers, who would then sicken and die within three days. The response of the bishop, Gilbert Foliot, to the problem was, 'Dig up the body and cut off the head with a spade, sprinkle it with holy water and re-inter it.'[294] An account written by the abbot of Burton tells of two runaway peasants about 1090, who died suddenly and were buried in wooden coffins, but

that very same day on which they were interred they appeared at evening, while the sun was still up, carrying on their shoulders the wooden coffins in which they had been buried. The whole following night they walked through the paths and fields of the village, now in the shape of men carrying wooden coffins on their shoulders, now in the likeness of bears or dogs or other animals. They spoke to the other peasants, banging on the walls of their houses and shouting, 'Move, quickly, move! Get going! Come!'

The villagers began to sicken and die. Eventually the bodies of two revenants were disinterred and decapitated while their hearts were torn out and burned.

These stories have some common features. Those who return from the dead in this way are described as having been wrongdoers in their lifetime. The chaplain who was buried at Melrose but returned to wander at night, and whose story is told by William of Newburgh, had been 'too secular and so addicted to the vanity of hunting that he was called Houndpriest'. The revenant from the diocese of Hereford was 'a wicked Welshman', while in another story from the pen of Walter Map it is 'a man who they say died as an unbeliever' who 'wandered around in his shroud'. The Burton peasants had run away from their lord.

In many cases there is an association of the walking dead with disease. In two of William of Newburgh's stories the hauntings are accompanied or followed by the spread of disease, and in one of them the revenant actually sucks blood in the traditional vampiric way: 'they wounded the lifeless corpse and immediately so much blood flowed from it that they realized it had sucked many people's blood.' In the cases from the diocese of Hereford and from Burton, the dead call on the living, who then sicken and die. Sometimes they wander with dogs or other animals, and are usually active at night, though in certain cases in daylight too. One of the stories told by William of Newburgh involves a dead man returning to his wife's bedroom, and the 'Houndpriest'

[293] W. Newb. 5. 24 (2, p. 477).    [294] Map 2. 27 (pp. 202–4).

also sought out the bedroom of his former lady, but there is not otherwise a strong sexual connotation in these accounts.

In every case the appropriate response is considered to be exhumation, followed by some combination of decapitation, tearing out of the heart and burning. There was obviously local lore about this. When the pyre was constructed to burn the revenant at Annan, 'one of the men said that a plague-bringing corpse would not burn unless the heart was extracted', while the English courtiers of bishop Hugh of Lincoln, confronted with the Buckinghamshire revenant, told him 'that such things often happened in England and it is perfectly clear by experience that the people can have no rest until the body of the wretched man is dug up and burned'. The evidence overall, which comes from many regions and periods, suggests a widespread acceptance of the idea that the dead, especially the wicked dead, could return to do harm and must be dealt with by being dug up and burned or dismembered.

The relationship of such beliefs and practices to the official Christianity that was preached by pastors and elaborated by theologians was not an easy one. Nevertheless, it was often to their local clergy and bishops that people disturbed by such phenomena turned in the first instance, and these prelates were not unwilling to give advice on how to deal with the walking dead. The Buckinghamshire case was taken to the archdeacon's synod and referred by him to bishop Hugh. The Burton case also went to the local bishop. Gilbert Foliot, who suggested disinterment and decapitation as an appropriate response to a revenant in his diocese, was a Cluniac monk, a scholar and one of the dominant prelates of the mid-twelfth century. There was certainly not a simple opposition between popular belief and practice and the views of the educated clergy.

Nevertheless, the explanation of the phenonomen had to be made in some way to fit Christian tenets. William of Newburgh manages a neat combination of Christian metaphysics and naturalism by describing the reanimation of the corpses as 'the work of Satan' but by attributing the spread of disease to the contaminated air that the corpses created. Indeed, describing a case at Berwick, he writes that 'the simpler folk feared that they might be attacked and beaten by the lifeless monster, while the more thoughtful were concerned that the air might be infected and corrupted from the wanderings of the plague-bringing corpse, with subsequent sickness and death'. Gilbert Foliot agreed that the actual agency behind the revenant was Satanic— 'perhaps', he said, 'the Lord has given to the evil angel of that lost soul the power to move about in that dead body'.

The return of the dead obviously raised central questions about salvation, damnation, and the power of penitence. The failings of the revenant in his lifetime could be interpreted in Christian terms. In some cases an insistence on the sacrament of penance shows a Christianization of the presumably pre- or non-Christian world of belief and practice about revenants. It is characteristic that it was Hugh, bishop of Lincoln, a foreigner and a member of strict monastic order, who refused to go along with his English advisers. Instead of having the Buckinghamshire revenant burned, a practice he considered 'unseemly and unworthy', he simply commanded that, when the corpse was dug up, a letter of absolution that he had sent should be placed on the dead man's chest before he was reinterred. The haunting promptly ceased.

This more explicitly Christian solution is paralleled in another story from Walter Map, who tells how a Northumbrian knight was sitting alone in his house one summer evening after dinner when he was visited by his long-dead father, wrapped in his shroud. The father reassured the son that he was no demon and intended no harm, insisting that the priest be called. The priest came, along with many others, and the revenant threw himself at his feet, proclaiming that he was one of those whom the priest had struck with a general anathema as withholders of tithes. 'But,' he added, 'through God's grace, the common prayers of the Church and the alms of the faithful have helped me so much that I may seek absolution.' He was forthwith absolved and returned in the company of the crowd to his grave, which closed over him. 'This novel case,' adds Map, 'has introduced a new topic for debate among the theologians.'[295] It well might.

[295] Map 2. 30 (p. 206).

# CHAPTER 12

# Cosmologies

## 1. TIME

### Past

The period 1075–1225 is one of the great ages of historical writing in England. History was not an academic subject, pursued by the masters of the emerging schools, but it was read and written by thoughtful and literate men in the monasteries and in the courts of kings, bishops, and barons. Because it did not form part of the syllabus of higher education, history was not subjected to the process of systematization and explication for pedagogic purposes that can be observed in the development of rhetoric, logic, theology, law, and natural science. It remained a branch of belles-lettres, something for the generally educated mind, not a discipline, not the preserve of a profession. Because of this, its products, the histories and chronicles of the time, are particularly fresh, direct, and appealing.

The quantity, quality, and variety are all alike impressive. Writers such as William of Malmesbury, William of Newburgh, and Roger of Howden combined an insatiably inquisitive mind, a well-developed critical sense, and the gift of writing lucid Latin prose. The twelfth century is often seen as the period when a new subjective individualism emerged in European culture, and one reason for this is that the fuller and more thoughtful texts of the contemporary historians allow us to form more complex pictures of the individual personalities that the historians write about and indeed of the historians themselves.

Contemporaries gave some explicit thought to the classification of historical writing. In the preface to his own *Chronicle*, the Canterbury monk Gervase of Canterbury distinguishes between historians and chroniclers. Their subject matter is identical, as is their intention—to attain the truth—but they differ in the form they adopt and the way they treat their material. A historian writes at length and with elegance, while a chronicler produces a brief and simple account. A historian attempts to charm his readers or hearers by presenting an attractive account of the deeds, ways, and life of the people he has chosen to describe, telling the truth but also keeping to the subject. A chronicler has fewer literary ambitions: he gives the years AD, records the deeds of kings and rulers that occurred in each year, and reports events, portents, and miracles. The distinction Gervase draws is a broad one, but can be of some use in categorizing the various kinds of historical writing undertaken in our period. Writers who follow an annalistic form, dealing with each year in turn, obviously differ from those who allow the twists and turns of their story to lead them away from the simple succession of the years.

The least polished historical records are the simple annals produced at many monastic centres. A good example of a modest annalistic compilation from an English monastery of the twelfth century is the *Winchcombe Annals*.[1] These run from the Incarnation to 1181 and in their earlier part, down to the year 1138, are drawn from the Worcester chronicle. The sources of the entries for the subsequent years have not all been identified with certainty and some must have been composed by the compiler, a monk of the ancient Benedictine house of Winchcombe (Glos.). Their nature and scale can be indicated by the entries for a few sample years:

*1149* Reinald, abbot of Evesham, departed from this life and was succeeded by William, a monk of the church of Canterbury.

*1155* The castles built throughout England in the days of king Stephen were cast down. Queen Eleanor gave birth to Henry. Pope Anastasius died and was succeeded by Hadrian, bishop of Albano.

*1177* An agreement was made between the lord pope Alexander III and the emperor Frederick, while that schismatic was at Monte Albano. On the eve of St Andrew's day there was seen, at the very same time on this side of the sea and beyond, a great brightness that glittered in a wonderful way and passed by the edge of the land, not swiftly like lightning but slowly, so that it could be seen by observers.

These annalistic entries conform exactly to Gervase's prescription: a brief and simple account giving the year AD and the deeds of rulers, events, and portents of that year. There is the local interest in the succession of abbots at nearby Evesham, but also concern over the politics of the kingdom, especially the establishment of firm rule after Stephen's reign and the birth of a son to the queen, and an eye, too, for the wider world of Christendom, with notes of papal affairs. It is striking, however, that the Winchcombe monk gives more space to the strange atmospheric phenomenon of 1177 than to the peace between the pope and the emperor in the same year. Although there are certain recurrent topics of interest, it would be too much to claim that there is a theme to these annals and items of very miscellaneous nature follow one another in disjointed succession.

---

[1] Ed. R. R. Darlington, in Patricia Barnes and C. F. Slade (eds.), *A Medieval Miscellany for Doris May Stenton* (PRS n.s. 36; 1962 for 1960), pp. 111–37.

Very different in kind are the great literary narratives that deal at length with the political affairs of England as a whole. Table 12 shows some of the more important histories of this type, with an indication of the years they cover and whether the author was a monk or a secular cleric. They are listed chronologically, by the date at which they conclude.

TABLE 12. *Selected histories of the period*

| Chronicle | Starts | Ends | Monk or cleric |
| --- | --- | --- | --- |
| Eadmer, *History of Recent Events* (*Historia novorum*) | 960 | 1109/22 | m |
| William of Malmesbury, *Deeds of the Kings* (*Gesta regum*) | 449 | 1120 | m |
| Symeon of Durham, *History of the Kings* (*Historia regum*) | 616 | 1129 | m |
| Henry of Huntingdon, *History of the English* (*Historia Anglorum*) | 55 BC | 1129/54 | c |
| Orderic Vitalis, *Ecclesiastical History* | 1 | 1141 | m |
| *Anglo-Saxon Chronicle* | 1 | 1154 | m |
| *Deeds of King Stephen* (*Gesta Stephani*) | 1135 | 1154 | c |
| William of Newburgh, *History of English Affairs* (*Historia rerum Anglicarum*) | 1066 | 1198 | m |
| Gervase of Canterbury, *Chronicle* (*Chronicon*) | 1135 | 1199 | m |
| Ralph of Diceto, *Images of History* (*Ymagines Historiarum*) | 1148 | 1199 | c |
| Roger of Howden, *Chronicle* (*Chronicon*) | 732 | 1201 | c |
| Ralph of Coggeshall, *Chronicle* (*Chronicon*) | 1066 | 1224 | m |

This is neither a comprehensive list nor a random sample, but the pattern it indicates, of monastic dominance in the first part of the period and the increasing role of clerical historians in the second, reflects reality. Of the first six authors on the list, five are Benedictines, while of the following six, only one, Gervase, is a Benedictine. As in other areas of cultural and religious life, the monopoly that the black monks possessed around 1100 was eroded over the course of the twelfth century both by secular clerics and by other orders.

Another striking feature of the pattern concerns the ethnic origins and identities of the authors. Of the first six, one, Eadmer, was certainly English, while the authors of the *Anglo-Saxon Chronicle* can also safely be assumed to be English monks. William of Malmesbury and Orderic Vitalis we know, from their own explicit statements, to be of mixed descent, with one French and one English parent, and a similar parentage has been suggested for

Henry of Huntingdon.[2] Symeon of Durham is likely to have been of English birth. Hence it is probable that every one of these authors of the late eleventh and first half of the twelfth century had English blood. All could read or speak English. They did not constitute an alien clerical presence in the manner of the French and Italian prelates who occupied the bishoprics and great abbacies of England in the generations after the Conquest. England's history was thus not colonized in the way that the upper reaches of the English church were.

It has indeed been suggested that the apparent boom in English historical (and hagiographical) writing after the Norman Conquest was partly inspired by a desire to salvage the English past from the great debacle of 1066. Monks of wholly or partly English descent in the older English monasteries, like Canterbury and Malmesbury, were seeking, according to this view, to salve the pain of the rupture of 1066 by evoking and nursing a sense of continuity with the English past. In contrast, the writers of the later twelfth century, whether they were of French or English descent (and by that period it is usually hard to say), had no such pressing compulsion. Born into a world where, as Richard fitz Neal observed, 'nowadays one can scarcely tell—as far as free men are concerned—who is of English and who of Norman descent',[3] they were now heirs to a magical transformation whereby both the Anglo-Saxons and the Normans could be 'us'. Disregarding the odd Anglophobic utterance, it is clear that by the later twelfth century an integrated English history could be hawked to even the most Francophone aristocrats and prelates.

The different temporal starting points adopted by the different historians are usually significant, since they imply different conceptions of *which* story is being told: the history of the Christian people, the English, the kingdom, a specific church. Henry of Huntingdon's decision to begin with the first Roman expedition to Britain is unusual but accords with his general schema of British/English history, which he saw as structured by the five great ruptures of invasions by the Romans, Picts and Scots, Anglo-Saxons, Vikings, and Normans. The original version of his history consisted of seven books dealing with the following topics: 'The Rule of the Romans in Britain', 'The Coming of the English', 'The Conversion of the English', 'The Rule of the English', 'The Danish Wars', 'The Coming of the Normans', 'The Rule of the Normans'. Such a narrative, structured around a sequence of invasions, is a common enough historical device, employed also, for instance, by the native chroniclers of medieval Ireland, who enshrined it in the aptly named *Book of Invasions of Ireland* (*Lebor Gabála Eireann*).

Other perspectives are also found. Orderic Vitalis and the *Anglo-Saxon*

[2] H. Hunt., p. xxvi.    [3] *Dial. scacc.*, p. 53.

*Chronicle* both start with the Incarnation, although this was seemingly an afterthought for Orderic, since in his original plan the first book begins with Norman history of the tenth and eleventh centuries, while the scheme of the *Anglo-Saxon Chronicle* had simply been inherited from its original compilers of the time of Alfred. William of Newburgh adds an unusual personal touch to his choice of starting point. Since, he says, historians have already covered the period to the death of Henry I (1135), he begins his detailed account with that event, although, in order to give some background, his chronicle actually commences with 'the coming of the Normans to England'. He will go quickly, he writes, through the period to the reign of Stephen, 'in whose first year I, William, was born'.[4] His history thus coincides with his own lifetime.

The Norman Conquest or the start of a new king's reign were obvious starting points. Eadmer's 960, Symeon's 616, and Howden's 732 require more explanation. Eadmer expressly states that his history will focus on the disputes between archbishop Anselm and the Norman kings, but that, in order to understand those quarrels fully, he must begin 'with the planting of the root from which grew the offshoot of those things that are my subject'.[5] His opening pages thus deal with the golden age of concord between the great tenth-century archbishop Dunstan and 'the most glorious king Edgar'. Symeon's *History of the Kings* begins in the seventh century, with the English kings of the conversion period, although the specific date 616 is more or less an accident of compilation, since it refers to some miscellaneous material prefaced to the main chronological thread. Howden sees his work as a continuation of Bede and hence begins where Bede leaves off.

With the exception of the author of the *Deeds of King Stephen*, who gives not a single date throughout his work, historical writers of this period usually aimed at chronological precision. Indeed Ralph of Diceto even went so far as to quote with approval the stern judgement that 'events that cannot be ascribed to specific reigns or periods cannot be regarded as historical'.[6] Most authors used the Christian era as their primary chronological framework, dating by the Incarnation. Bede had adopted and popularized the system of dating by years AD and BC first devised by the sixth-century monk, Dionysius Exiguus, and by the twelfth century it was a commonly available means of reckoning time. The most casual use of incarnational dating is in Henry of Huntingdon, who gives only a dozen dates in this form in his entire history and much prefers to date by regnal years.[7]

There are some traces in English historical writing of an alternative calculation of the date of the Incarnation, advanced by Marianus Scotus, an Irish monk living in Germany who composed a chronicle from the Creation to

---

[4] W. Newb. 1, pref. (1, p. 19).     [5] Eadmer, *HN*, p. 2
[6] R. Diceto, *Abbrev.*, p. 15.     [7] H. Hunt., p. lxiv.

1082. He believed that the system of Dionysius, that Bede used, was 22 years out and hence (our) 1082 was rightly 1104. Marianus' chronicle was brought to England by Robert de Losinga, bishop of Hereford (1079–95), a Lotharingian with a reputation for an interest in calculation, chronology, and astronomy, but had only a limited impact. The chronicle of John of Worcester gives the years according to Marianus' reckoning, so that 1125 is '1147', etc., and the historians William of Malmesbury and Gervase of Canterbury mention the system, but it never became widespread.[8]

When describing the period before their own time, the historians of the twelfth century had to rely on earlier written sources, sometimes supplemented with oral traditions. Medieval authors were bold about borrowing the words of earlier writers and the historians are no exception. It has been calculated, for instance, that about 75 per cent of Henry of Huntingdon's *History of the English* is drawn by direct quotation, summary, or translation from other writers.[9] Ralph of Diceto prefaced his own contemporary chronicle, *Images of History*, with a long selection of abstracts from earlier historians, entitled *Abbreviations of Chronicles* (*Abbreviationes Chronicorum*), that cover the years from the Creation to 1147. He names 47 illustrious writers in his preface to this anthology and he can be shown to have indeed used the great majority of them. Thus, he draws stories about the ancient Greek philosophers from the Roman writer Aulus Gellius, gives a short account of the views and life of the third-century theologian Origen based on passages from Augustine and Jerome, retails Byzantine legends about the building of Hagia Sophia via a Latin translation, while his account of Charlemagne rests mainly upon the world history of Sigebert of Gembloux (d. 1112).[10] All historians are compilers as well as composers, but the trait is particularly strongly marked in the historical writers of the Middle Ages.

The compilatory process can be illustrated by one of many possible examples, the early parts of Roger of Howden's *Chronicle*. For the period prior to 1148, which was beyond the limits of his own memory, Roger used a source called the *History since Bede* (*Historia post Bedam*), that had been put together at Durham in the middle of the twelfth century by interweaving passages from Symeon of Durham's *History of the Kings* and Henry of Huntingdon's *History of the English*. Each of these works was, in turn, a compilation. Symeon's history, for instance, incorporates Northumbrian annals of the eighth century, extracts from Asser's *Life of Alfred*, passages drawn from the

[8] W. Malm., *GP* 164 (pp. 300–1); W. Malm., *GR* 3. 292 (2, p. 345); OMT edn., pp. 524–6; Flor. Worcs., *passim*.

[9] H. Hunt., p. lxxxv.

[10] R. Diceto, *Abbrev.*, pp. 20–4, 37–43, 46, 68–9, 91–4, 124–33; *Op.* 2, pp. xvi–xxii; on the Hagia Sophia account, see also Krijnie N. Ciggaar, *Western Travellers to Constantinople: The West and Byzantium, 962–1204* (Leiden, 1996), pp. 50, 154.

*Anglo-Saxon Chronicle* and from John of Worcester, as well as original entries from the 1120s. Hence, when Roger of Howden writes that in 1089 'there was a great earthquake throughout England on Saturday 11 August, around about the third hour of the day', these exact words can be traced back, through the *History since Bede* and Symeon of Durham, to the Chronicle of John of Worcester.[11]

Several consequences follow from the fact that medieval historical writing often consists of strata of this type. First, we cannot assume that any particular passage in the works of a historian will be in his own words. Hence it is necessary when assessing the quality of a writer to be aware that much of what we read is simply direct quotation from other writers. Secondly, from the point of view of the modern historian seeking factual data, it is important that a chronicler of the twelfth century might have in front of him a far earlier work, that is now no longer extant. It may then be possible to reconstruct that earlier work and use its information (the value of Symeon of Durham and William of Malmesbury for Anglo-Saxon history is of this type). Of course, if, as here, we are interested primarily in the working methods of the twelfth-century historians, it is largely irrelevant whether they are transmitting otherwise unattainable material. What is of interest is what sources they had and what they did with them—their principles of selection, stylistic changes, and focus of interest.

Chroniclers with a wide perspective did deal with biblical, Roman, and papal history, if sometimes only in summary form, but most historians were consciously writing the history of the English. William of Malmesbury entitled his work *The Deeds of the Kings of the English* and the opening words of the preface are 'The deeds of the English . . .'. The main body of the text opens with the sentence: 'In the year 449 after the incarnation of the Lord, the Angles and Saxons came to England'.[12] Henry of Huntingdon entitled his work *History of the English* and described its subject as 'the affairs of this kingdom and the origins of our people'.[13]

Written materials for earlier English history varied considerably in scope and quality. For the formative period of the English church, the age of conversion of the seventh century, there was the extensive, authoritative, and influential account in Bede's *Ecclesiastical History of the English People*. This was highly valued. The twelfth century was the age most active in making copies of Bede's great history, as Figure 16 demonstrates.[14] It served not only

---

[11] R. Howd. 1, p. 142; S. Durh., *HR* 171 (p. 217); Flor. Worcs. 2, p. 26.

[12] W. Malm., *GR* prol., 1.1 (1, pp. 1, 5); OMT edn., pp. 14, 16.

[13] H. Hunt. prol., p. 4.

[14] R. H. C. Davis, 'Bede after Bede', in Christopher Harper-Bill *et al.* (eds.), *Studies in Medieval History Presented to R. Allen Brown* (Woodbridge, 1989), pp. 103–16; see also Antonia Gransden, 'Bede's Reputation as a Historian in Medieval England', *Jnl Ecclesiastical History*, 32 (1981), pp. 397–425.

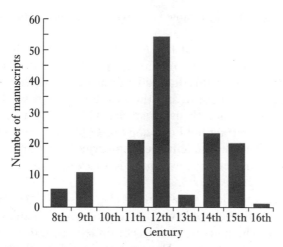

FIGURE 16. *Manuscripts of Bede's* Ecclesiastical History

as a guide to the deeds of the past but also as a stimulus to deeds in the present, notably of the monastic pioneers of the late eleventh century who re-established religious houses in the north of England on the sites of the monasteries mentioned by Bede. It is hard not to picture them with trowel in one hand and the *Ecclesiastical History* in the other.

Bede's high reputation is shown both by the explicit praise he received from twelfth-century historians and by their heavy dependence on him for the period he covers. Henry of Huntingdon, for example, refers to Bede as 'that holy and venerable man, a man of brilliant mind, a philosopher of Christ' and draws on 132 of the 140 chapters of the *Ecclesiastical History*.[15] The opening words of William of Malmesbury's *Deeds of the Kings* are 'Bede, a man of great learning and humility, made clear the course of English affairs from the arrival of the English in Britain to his own time, in plain, sweet lan-guage.'[16] Perhaps the author most familiar with Bede's *Ecclesiastical History* was Orderic Vitalis, an Anglo-Norman working in Normandy, who had copied out the entire work in his own hand.[17] The dominating position of the *Ecclesiastical History* reinforced the twelfth-century writers' focus upon England, for Bede had expressly concerned himself mainly with 'the famous men of *our* people' and this phrase was taken up and made their own by historians of the Norman and Angevin period. William of Newburgh's

[15] H. Hunt. 4. 11 (pp. 230, lxxxvi).       [16] W. Malm., *GR* prol. (1, p. 1); OMT edn., p. 14.
[17] Orderic 1 (pp. 56, 203).

opening words are, 'the venerable Bede wrote the history of our people, that is, the English'.[18]

Because of the existence of the *Ecclesiastical History*, historians of the twelfth century were far better informed about the seventh century than any other. The period prior to this time had only a vague and fleeting reality. Bede had something to say about it, and the assiduous might be able to obtain a copy of the sixth-century British historian Gildas. William of Newburgh prided himself on getting hold of a copy of Gildas and remarked how rare copies were.[19] Otherwise, the centuries before the Augustinian mission of 597 were relatively colourless, at least until Geoffrey of Monmouth revolutionized British history (see below).

The centuries after Bede's death in 735 also presented the historians of the twelfth century with the problem of inadequate source material. The *Anglo-Saxon Chronicle*, which in one version continued down to 1154, gave a basic annalistic narrative for the period between Bede and the Normans, but it was uneven in its coverage, often starkly expressed and written in a difficult vernacular. It was commonplace for writers of the Norman and Angevin period to lament the lack of successors to Bede: 'after him you will not easily find men who turned their minds to the composition of Latin histories of their own people'; 'after Bede there were those who have transmitted to us the sequences of events in our island, but they cannot be compared to him'.[20] William of Malmesbury saw it as one of his primary tasks to bridge the hiatus of 223 years between Bede and the reign of Edgar, where Eadmer's *History of Recent Events* takes up the story.[21] Because of this imbalance of sources, it was the kings and the saints of the conversion period who dominated the picture of the Anglo-Saxon past.

The *Anglo-Saxon Chronicle* was indispensable, but not always easy to use. About 40 per cent of Henry of Huntingdon's text is drawn from the *Chronicle*. His translations from Old English into Latin are usually accurate, although sometimes he mistakes rarer words for proper names, so that a non-existent warrior 'Froda' is conjured up out of the lines 'likewise the aged [*froda*] Constantine fled to his country in the north, that grey-haired warrior had no reason to exult', words that Henry renders 'Likewise Froda, the leader of the Northmen, and the chieftain Constantine could not exult'.[22] Henry admired Old English poetry and, when translating the verse sections of the *Chronicle*, used alliteration and other devices in his Latin renderings in

---

[18] Bede, *Ecclesiastical History*, pref., ed. Bertram Colgrave and R. A. B. Mynors (OMT; 1969), p. 2; W. Newb. 1, pref. (1, p. 11); cf. *Lib. Eliensis* 1. prol. (p. 6).

[19] W. Newb. 1, pref. (1, p. 11).

[20] W. Malm., *GR* prol. (1, p. 1); OMT edn., p. 14; W. Newb. 1, pref. (1, p. 18).

[21] W. Malm., *GR* prol. (1, p. 2); OMT edn., p. 14.

[22] H. Hunt., pp. lxxxv, xci–xcviii, 312 (5. 19).

an attempt to communicate 'the solemn dignity of the deeds and spirit of that people'.[23]

It was not uncommon for historians of the Norman period, looking back over the English past, to blame the Vikings for the paucity of sources that could tell them about the Anglo-Saxon past. This theory of a 'Viking hiatus' became almost a commonplace, a topos to be invoked whenever there were gaps in historical knowledge, resorted to especially when twelfth-century authors were unable to find reliable records of Anglo-Saxon saints. William of Malmesbury used the Viking lacuna in this way, to explain the lack of written evidence about the obscure St Rumon at Tavistock, whose 'reputation is not buttressed by the credibility of written report'. 'You find,' explains William, 'not only there but in many places in England that knowledge of the deeds of the saints has been wiped out, in my opinion by the violence of enemies, and that only their bare names and a few miracles claimed for them are known.'[24] His opinion was shared by the Cistercian spiritual writer and historian Ailred of Rievaulx. During the Danish invasions, he writes, the church of Hexham, along with its library, was completely ruined, and one of the worst blows was that 'In this devastation the records of the life and miracles of the saints that the holy fathers had transmitted in writing to the knowledge of posterity were destroyed.'[25] Looking back on their predecessors, the historical writers of the post-Conquest period thus saw a dismal expanse of mediocrity and loss, towered over by the glorious but isolated form of Bede.

Twelfth-century English chroniclers usually bring the story down to their own time. Indeed, the cessation of a chronicler's entries is often taken as an indication that the writer died at that point, since the assumption is that these historians wrote until they dropped ('As William's chronicle ends abruptly in 1198, he probably died in that year').[26] In some cases it is clear that historians chose a 'natural' stopping point, such as Eadmer's closing his *History of Recent Events* with Anselm's death in 1109, but were then unable to resist the temptation to update their work, adding supplementary material, like the two books that Eadmer added to the *History of Recent Events* giving an account of the fortunes of the church of Canterbury between 1109 and 1122. These historians were thus contemporary commentators as well as excavators of the past, often adding a year-by-year account as time went by. Henry

[23] H. Hunt. 5. 18 (p. 310); see A. G. Rigg, 'Henry of Huntingdon's Metrical Experiments', *Jnl Medieval Latin*, 1 (1991), pp. 60–72.

[24] W. Malm., *GP* 95 (p. 202).

[25] Ailred of Rievaulx, *De sanctis ecclesiae Haugustaldensis* (*Priory Hexham*, p. 190).

[26] Antonia Gransden, *Historical Writing in England*, 1. *c.550–c.1307* (London, 1974), p. 263, on William of Newburgh; for an alternative view, Kate Norgate, 'The Date of Composition of William of Newburgh's History', *EHR* 19 (1904), pp. 288–97.

of Huntingdon, for example, originally ended his history in 1129, but subsequently produced new versions ending in 1138, 1146, 1149, and 1154.

For this contemporary history, chroniclers could draw on their own eye-witness, the reports of those they met, and also written sources in the form of documents, letters, etc. The exact amount of contemporaneity even in 'contemporary' history varied. Orderic, for instance, wrote about the years 1137–41 year by year as they occurred, but his account of the Norman Conquest, which contains some independent and original information, was written fifty years after the battle of Hastings. Of course, stories from half a century ago can be accurate, but, because of their long passage through the channels of oral transmission and creative memory, they are not contemporary in the same sense as Orderic's annual record of the 1130s. Oral memory could be long. Henry of Huntingdon, who was probably born shortly before 1088, claimed to have heard details about the St Brice's Day massacre of 1002 (when an attempt was made to kill all the Danes in England) 'in my childhood from very old men'.[27] It is scarcely chronologically conceivable that these men were themselves conscious observers of the events of 1002, but the transmission need only have involved their fathers' telling them stories in their childhood.

For good contemporary history, contacts were essential. Those historians who were monks needed either to obtain information from travellers visiting their monastery or themselves to have the opportunity to travel more than the ideal monk was expected to. Eadmer, for instance, as chaplain to the archbishop of Canterbury, shared his master's journeyings to court and council, and was thus able to give vivid accounts of such episodes as Anselm's confrontation with William Rufus or the events of the Council of Bari in 1098. William of Malmesbury had less direct access to the scenes of power. Although he is believed to have travelled widely within England seeking materials for his histories, he was aware of these limitations, explaining the incompleteness of his picture of Henry I's reign by the fact that he is 'a private person, far from the secrets of the court'.[28] Clerical authors, of course, like Henry of Huntingdon and Roger of Howden (a royal justice), faced no such restrictions. Roger's mobility is brought out most strikingly in his account of the Third Crusade, in which he was a participant. The section of his history written between his arrival at Marseilles in 1191 and his return from Palestine in 1192 is virtually a travel diary.

The Cistercian monasteries formed a particularly extensive and active network for transmitting information. The *Chronicle of Melrose*, a Cistercian house in the southern part of the kingdom of Scotland, gives an account of the

---

[27] H. Hunt., pp. xxvi–xxvii, 340 (6. 2).
[28] W. Malm., *GR* 5, prol. (2, p. 465) OMT edn., p. 708.

naval battle that took place on 24 August 1217 off Sandwich, listing all the great men captured there and giving the number of less important captives. 'This total and the names of the great men,' the chronicler tells us, 'the lord abbot Roger of Warden wrote to the lord abbot William of Rievaulx.' Both Warden (in Bedfordshire) and Melrose were daughter-houses of Rievaulx, and abbot William had been abbot of the Scottish house before moving to Rievaulx. Hence the detailed news of a battle off the Kentish coast could pass easily via the pen of a Bedfordshire abbot to a Yorkshire abbot to a Scottish chronicler.

It is sometimes possible to glimpse the cloistered monastic historians chatting with their informants, picking up stories of distant places. William of Newburgh learned of some peculiar practices of the men of Ulster 'from a certain venerable bishop of that people'.[29] The tale of how Godfrey de Bouillon, one of the leaders of the First Crusade, killed a lion during the siege of Antioch was told to William of Malmesbury by 'a truthful man who said he had seen what I record here'.[30] Ralph of Coggeshall included in his history a story about an encounter between a heretic in Rheims and master Gervase of Tilbury, 'as we afterwards heard it from his own mouth'.[31] The theoretical seclusion and silence of the monastic life was in practice swamped by a world of hospitality, story-telling, and gossip.

Some historians were keen to include official documentation, such as diplomatic letters, the decrees of councils, and other administrative material in their chronicles, and, given the very ad hoc nature of archival preservation at this time, they are often very important for the transmission of these documents. Much of the legislation of Henry II, for instance, survives only because it was transcribed into the historical writings of the royal clerk and justice Roger of Howden. Chroniclers with a polemical purpose were particularly inclined to incorporate documentation, almost as a dossier for their case. Eadmer, who concentrated upon the clash between archbishop Anselm and the Crown, included in his *History of Recent Events* the texts of thirty letters, from popes, archbishop, and king, as well as the decrees of the Council of Westminster of 1102.

There is at least one case of a historian actually being sent a copy of official correspondence because he was known to be composing a chronicle. In 1192 Conrad of Montferrat, claimant to the kingdom of Jerusalem, was murdered, and suspicion for the act fell on Richard I. Soon afterwards a letter was in circulation that had supposedly been drawn up by the leaders of the Islamic sect of Assassins, clearing Richard of guilt. Ralph of Diceto, dean of London, received a copy of this letter from the chancellor of England, William de Longchamp, explicitly 'so that you can deal with it in your chronicle'.[32] This

---

[29] W. Newb. 3. 9 (1, p. 239).      [30] W. Malm., *GR* 4. 373 (2, p. 433); OMT edn., p. 658.
[31] R. Coggesh., p. 122.      [32] R. Diceto, *Ymag.* 2, p. 128.

is not only a conspicuous case of the manipulation of historical writing for the purpose of political propaganda, but also shows how a historian might be known by his contemporaries to be engaged upon historical composition.

Not all histories were general histories of the political affairs of the kingdom. Much historical effort was inspired by local loyalties and attachments, especially to the writer's own church. Many of the great monasteries, such as Abingdon, Peterborough, and Ramsey, produced their own chronicles in this period, focusing on the affairs of the monastery, albeit often with information on wider political or ecclesiastical events. In some the backbone is given to the narrative by a sequence of charters recording donations to the monks. Historical writing was one aspect of the general monastic impulse to further the prestige and property of one's own religious house. The *Chronicle of Battle Abbey*, for instance, is little more than a record of the abbey's lawsuits, written down 'as a warning to those who come after us or for their advantage'.[33]

The north of England had a particularly rich tradition of local history inspired by this kind of loyalty and litigiousness. Hexham, York, and Durham all produced historical writing. From Durham comes Symeon of Durham's *History of the Church of Durham*, which describes the fortunes of the community of St Cuthbert from the foundation of Lindisfarne down to the death of William of St Calais, bishop of Durham, in 1096. A continuation of this history was composed by another Durham monk and brings the record of events down to the year 1144. The story was then taken up by Geoffrey, sacrist of the Durham priory of Coldingham, who wrote his account of Durham affairs around 1214, covering the period from the end of the continuator's work in 1144 to that date. This accretive, multi-authored history is a common form of these 'house chronicles' that spring from an individual religious community. Geoffrey's blend of local and more general focus can be illustrated by some of his early chapter titles: 'the death of William, bishop of Durham, and the election of Hugh, bishop of Durham', 'the consecration of Hugh, bishop of Durham', 'Germanus is made prior of Durham', 'the death of Saint Godric and the passion of St Thomas, archbishop of Canterbury', 'the war between king Henry II and his sons', 'the ornaments that bishop Hugh gave to the church of Durham'.

As well as these local historians, there are writers of contemporary history who take a narrower focus than the affairs of the whole kingdom. One common form was the history of a specific military campaign. Ailred of Rievaulx wrote a short account of the Battle of the Standard of 1137; there is an anonymous description of the capture of Lisbon in 1147, in which many English participated; and Jordan Fantosme composed 2,000 lines of French verse on the great rebellion of 1173–4, ending neatly with the phrase 'the war is

---

[33] *Battle Chron.*, p. 32.

now over' ('La guerre est ore fenie'). Gerald of Wales's *Conquest of Ireland* (*Expugnatio Hibernica*) has a similarly military focus, although it continues the story of the English conquest over almost twenty years.

It is hard to say exactly where the genre 'history' ends and other forms begin. There was a great deal of biographical writing in the twelfth century, mainly, but not entirely, lives of saints. Gerald of Wales wrote an account of the tangled career of Geoffrey, archbishop of York, the illegitimate son of Henry II. A French verse biography of William Marshal, earl of Pembroke, was composed around 1225. Many of the lives of saints consist of a detailed factual record and are just as 'historical' in that sense as the chronicles. With the vernacular verse histories, like Jordan Fantosme's or the *History of William the Marshal*, we move close in form to the verse romances that were being written in the late twelfth century. Since history was a branch of literature, it would indeed be misleading to create two distinct categories of 'history' and 'literature'. Even the most earnest historian recognized that no good battle scene was complete without long, and necessarily invented, speeches from the leaders. History, biography, hagiography, and romance thus form a complex whole, not a range of easily distinguishable genres. Entertainment was recognized as a legitimate function of history.

It was also a commonplace that one of the purposes of historical writing was moral—to set out good and bad examples to be followed or shunned. A concrete pattern to be emulated or avoided was deemed to be more persuasive than mere abstract moralizing. As Gervase of Canterbury put it, 'There are many people whose minds are induced to avoid evil and do good more easily by examples than by prohibitions or precepts.'[34] History was a sermon of particular liveliness: 'To keep in mind the deeds and words and ways of our ancestors, records and chronicles and histories ought to be read out at festivals, the crimes of the wicked and the good deeds of the noble.'[35]

Because many of the historians writing at this time were members of monastic communities, they enjoyed the economic independence that comes from total personal poverty. They were not seeking to win the favour of a great lord or powerful bishop in order to obtain monetary reward or office and hence the role of the patron was a limited one. Not many of the histories written in this period were commissioned or were given dedications. Henry of Huntingdon wrote at the request of Alexander, bishop of Lincoln, and, not surprisingly, refers to the bishop's arrest by king Stephen as 'an infamous deed', but such direct links between patron and viewpoint are rare.[36]

---

[34] Gerv. Cant., p. 86.
[35] Wace, *Le Roman de Rou*, appendice, lines 1–6, ed. A. J. Holden (3 vols., Société des Anciens Textes Français; Paris, 1970–3), vol. 2, p. 309.
[36] H. Hunt. 10. 10 (p. 718) (RS edn., p. 265).

The relative independence of the main historians writing in this period is clear when we consider their attitude to the Crown. Scarcely any of them can be called 'royalist' in a strong sense. Although they take it for granted that England is a kingdom and they have opinions about how a king should rule, there is little in the way of obsequiousness and a great deal of sometimes strident criticism. As monks and clerics, these writers were more inclined to identify with the cause of their church or the Church or the religious life than to follow the star of a particular dynast. The tone of their outlook on kings is conveyed by the remarks that William of Newburgh made on the death of Henry II. In his chronicle the final chapter of Book Three, that concludes with Henry's death, is entitled 'the character of king Henry' and gives a summary, in about 800 words, of William's view of the dead monarch.[37] Although Henry was 'endowed with many virtues that are an adornment to the royal person', he was also 'given to certain vices that shame the Christian prince'. Among his failings were lust and an excessive addiction to the hunt, although in neither case was he as bad as his grandfather, Henry I. He was also too favourable to the Jews and kept bishoprics vacant in order to enjoy their revenues. His unhappy family life was a natural consequence of his wrongful marriage with the divorced Eleanor of Aquitaine. On the other hand, he kept public order, defended the poor and weak, and, in general, honoured the privileges of the church. His taxation was not too heavy and he preferred to resolve conflicts peacefully. Many people criticized him during his lifetime, but, in comparison with what came afterwards, under his son Richard, he emerges as 'an excellent and beneficial ruler'. The balance of William's remarks is, therefore, favourable, but the balance emerges only after a genuine scrutiny of the old king's ways. There is no toadying or glorification. Henry is assessed candidly as a Christian prince. His fate is, barely, satisfactory: 'while the Lord, in his holy severity, did not spare him in this life, we may piously believe that he prepared mercy for him in the other life'.

It might be expected that a stance more favourable to the Crown would be shown in the writings of historians who were themselves in royal service. In fact there are few examples. One royal administrator who produced historical writing, although unfortunately it does not survive, is Richard fitz Neal, Henry II's treasurer and author of the *Dialogue on the Exchequer* (*Dialogus de Scaccario*). Apart from this handbook to the workings of the royal audit machinery, Richard is known to have written a work called the *Tricolumnis*. It dealt, in three parallel columns, with 'the affairs of the English church', 'the remarkable deeds of king Henry II', and 'various public and private affairs and court judgments'. Richard believed the *Tricolumnis* 'might be of use to future ages and welcome to those with an interest in the state of the kingdom

[37] W. Newb. 3. 26 (1, pp. 280–3).

under that king'.[38] Written by a royal bureaucrat and focused on 'the state of the kingdom', the lost work would surely have stood at the head of the long tradition of English histories written by administrators.

The loss of the *Tricolumnis* makes Roger of Howden the first civil-service historian in English history whose work survives. He was a royal clerk and a royal judge in the 1170s and 1180s, being last recorded in an official capacity in the Pipe Roll of the first year of Richard's reign (1189–90) serving as a justice of the Forest in the north of England. He then went on the Third Crusade before, it can be presumed, retiring to his Yorkshire parsonage to continue work on his historical writing. He is a source of the first importance for political and administrative history. For the single year 1198, for example, he gives full accounts of the disputed election of a holy Roman emperor, the papal succession, quarrels within the English church, the progress of the war between Richard I and Philip Augustus of France, and intricate details of the assessment and collection of taxes. He gives the full texts of several papal letters, lists by name the prisoners Richard captured in battle, and incorporates in his narrative the terms of reference of the royal itinerant justices and the assize of the Forest, subjects of natural interest to him.

Howden's history is thus administrator's history. It is not, however, royalist history. The chronicler's lack of warm feeling for the Angevin kings he served has been rightly remarked upon. This is no panegyric of exaltation, in the style of the *Philippidos*, written by William the Breton, clerk of Philip Augustus of France, to celebrate 'the battles and famous deeds of greatspirited Philip'.[39] Howden portrays the pattern of politics and the workings of the royal administration but he does not write primarily to praise or justify the deeds of Henry II or Richard (although he approves of Richard the crusader). Indeed, rather than generating royalist historiography, the royal court seems to have hatched some hard and sometimes vicious critics of kings. Walter Map, who served at the court of Henry II, described the king not only as 'resplendent with many virtues' but also as 'darkened by some vices'. He singled out particularly Henry's tendency to procrastinate and draw business out.[40] Much more violent in his criticisms was Map's friend and fellow court clerk, Gerald of Wales, who, although he dedicated several of his historical and topographical writings to the Angevins, came to consider that the dynasty had blocked his preferment. Writing his late works in the reign of John, Gerald poured out his accumulated bile. Henry's reign had ended in 'vengeance, disaster and ignominy' that he brought upon himself,

---

[38] *Dial. scacc.*, p. 27.

[39] William the Breton, *Philippidos* 1, line 1, ed. H.-F. Delaborde, *Oeuvres de Rigord et de Guillaume le Breton* (2 vols., Société de l'histoire de France 210, 224; 1882–5), vol. 2, p. 6.

[40] Map 5. 6 (p. 484).

Richard I had 'raged against the Church with harsh exactions', indeed, the very family descent of the Angevins was 'completely corrupt'.[41]

Historians were meant to tell the truth. Both Gerald of Wales and William of Newburgh praised Gildas for his true historical impartiality, meaning by that phrase that he was willing to discuss both the good points and the bad points of his own people. This was to act 'like a historian'.[42] The consensus on this ideal of what history should be can be found even among authors who are apparently breaching it. William of Malmesbury's historical activity is more closely bound up with the royal family than is usual. The initial impetus to the composition of his *Deeds of the Kings* was given by Henry I's queen, Matilda, and, when completed after her death, it was dedicated to the king's illegitimate son, Robert, earl of Gloucester.[43] Earl Robert was the leader of the Angevin cause in the civil war that began in 1139, and William wrote his *Recent History* (*Historia novella*) at the earl's request. Its purpose was avowedly didactic: 'what can tend more to the increase of honour and what is more advantageous to justice than to learn about God's tender love towards the good and his punishment of perjurers?'[44] The perjurers are, of course, all those who swore the oath to accept the empress Matilda as Henry I's heir but then recognized Stephen in 1135–6. Understandably, William feels he has to defend himself against the charge of partiality. After a passage in which he gives lavish praise to earl Robert's unswerving loyalty, he adds, 'Let not the suspicion of flattery cause anyone to think that I do not write these things impartially, for I will not say anything from favour. The pure historical truth will be set out for the attention of posterity, without a trace of lying deceit.'[45] William was himself willing to lay the charge of bias, for in his *Deeds of the Kings* he referred to David the Scot, bishop of Bangor, who had written an account of the expedition into Italy of the emperor Henry V in 1110–11 'showing more favour to the king than befits an historian'. The only extenuating circumstance, in William's eyes, was that 'he was writing not history, but panegyric'.[46]

Given the unanimity of opinion that history should be true and impartial, it is singular that the most successful historical work produced in twelfth-century England was, without a doubt, Geoffrey of Monmouth's *History of the Kings of Britain*. It is almost entirely legendary, tracing the kings of Britain from the first king, Brutus, grandson of Aeneas, who gave his name to the

---

[41] Gerald, *Exp.* 2. 27 (p. 204); Gerald, *Prin.* 2. 29; 3. 27 (pp. 212, 301–2); Gerald, *V. sancti Hugonis*, in Gerald, *Op.* 7, p. 103.

[42] Gerald, *Descr.* 2. 2 (p. 207); W. Newb. 1, pref. (1, p. 11).

[43] Ewald Könsgen, 'Zwei unbekannte Briefe zu den *Gesta Regum Anglorum* des Wilhelm von Malmesbury', *Deutches Archiv*, 31 (1975), pp. 204–14; W. Malm., *GR* 5. 446 (2, pp. 518–21); OMT edn., pp. 8, 798.

[44] W. Malm., *HN*, pref. (p. 1).        [45] W. Malm., *HN* 503 (pp. 64–5).

[46] W. Malm., *GR* 5. 420 (2, pp. 498–9); OMT edn., p. 764.

island, down to Cadwallader, son of Cadwallo, who died in 698. One of its heroes is king Arthur, whose conquests on the continent of Europe, defeat by Mordred, and departure to the Isle of Avalon are described. A few contemporaries were sceptical of this newly discovered history. William of Newburgh decried it as nonsense, blaming Geoffrey for 'making up absurd fictions' and asserting that 'only a person ignorant of ancient history would have any doubt about how shamelessly and impudently he lies in almost everything'.[47] Gerald of Wales embodied his views of Geoffrey in an unusual story about a man vexed with evil spirits. When St John's Gospel was placed on his breast, the demons immediately flew off, but when it was replaced by Geoffrey's *History of the Kings of Britain*, they returned, 'settling thickly not only all over his body, but also on the book placed on him'.[48]

Most readers, however, were, captivated—and even Gerald was willing to draw on Geoffrey as well as lampoon him. The typical reaction seems to have been that of the chronicler Henry of Huntingdon, coming across a copy of Geoffrey's *History* while at the Norman monastery of Bec, and reporting, 'I was astonished to find writings about these things.' He immediately sent a summary of the book to one of his learned friends.[49] The work was enormously popular. Translations into the vernacular were made very early. The first part of Gaimar's *History of the English* (*Estoire des Engleis*), written about 1140, was based on Geoffrey of Monmouth's work, as was the *Romance of Brutus* (*Roman de Brut*) of the Norman poet Wace of about 1155. The stories of Brutus, Arthur, and Merlin thus made the transition from Latin prose to the wider world of French verse. When king John entertained himself at Windsor with 'a romance [i.e. French text] of the history of England', it may well have been Geoffrey's vision of early history that he absorbed.[50]

## Present

The rhythm of present time was established primarily by the revolution of the heavens: sunrise and sunset and the alternation of day and night; the crescendo of summer and the long nights of winter; and the varying phases of the moon, that never fitted exactly into the solar year but provided a convenient practical measure intermediate between day and year. Amongst people who spent much time out of doors and did not face the distraction of artificial lighting, knowledge of the movement of the stars and planets would be intimate. Imposed inexactly upon these natural patterns was the purely conventional but ancient seven-day week, that gave the framework for weekly market and day of rest.

The complexity of time measurement and its importance for the liturgical

---

[47] W. Newb. 1, pref. (1, pp. 11–19).    [48] Gerald, *Itin.* 1. 5 (p. 58).
[49] H. Hunt., pp. 558–82 (*Epistola Warino*).    [50] *Rot. litt. claus.* 1, p. 29.

life of monks and clerics stimulated the production of a large body of learned discussion and calculation of time and its computation. Less learned people would also need practical means of determining and communicating time. While the Church created and fostered a complex liturgical year, its official teaching also condemned 'observation of days', that is, the practice of those 'who are willing or unwilling to undertake things on certain days or certain months or certain years because they deem some times to be auspicious and others inauspicious',[51] and it is clear that non-Christian associations still marked some of the temporal rhythms by which people lived.

### The Rhythm of the Day

The day was divided into hours, but these were of two kinds: the 'natural hour', of which twenty-four made a day, and the 'conventional hour', which comprised one-twelfth of the time between sunrise and sunset. While the former was of invariable length, the latter varied, being longer in summer and shorter in winter. The end of the sixth (conventional) hour always signified midday, but the other points would vary in relation to the natural hour as the length of daylight increased or decreased. At midwinter the 'third hour', for instance, would be around forty minutes long and last from approximately 9.20 a.m. to 10.00 a.m. In summer it would be twice that length.

Several of the services of the Divine Office took their name from the hour at which they were supposed to be celebrated: 'terce', at the third hour, 'sext' at the sixth hour, 'none' at the ninth hour, although the correspondence was not always exact. Particularly remarkable is the shift of the word 'none', meaning the ninth hour, or mid-afternoon, to the meaning midday (noon in the modern sense). This occurred in English by 1300 but is scarcely visible by our period. Even as late as the last quarter of the thirteenth century it still made sense to talk of Christ's three hours on the cross extending from 'mid-day' to 'noon'.[52]

Hours could be registered by the sundial and also by water-clocks, in which a controlled flow of water measured out the day. These were particularly useful in monasteries, where a complex communal timetable was in force. One is recorded at Bury in 1198, when its large reservoir of liquid was helpful in efforts to put out a fire in the abbey church.[53] The mechanical clock was a tool of the future.

Alongside the two different systems of hours, there were also variations in the calculation of when the day was deemed to commence. One writer mentions four different systems: morning to morning, sunset to sunset,

[51] Gratian 2. 26. 7. 17, col. 1046, citing Augustine, *Enchiridion* 79 (*PL* 40, col. 270).

[52] 'The Passion of our Lord', lines 477–8, ed. Richard Morris, in *An Old English Miscellany* (EETS 49; 1872), p. 50; dated *c.*1275 in *The Oxford English Dictionary* (2nd edn., 1989), vol. 10, pp. 508–9, s.v. 'noon'.

[53] Joc. Brak., p. 107.

midday to midday, midnight to midnight.[54] The preceding evening exerted a considerable liturgical pull on the following day, with 'vigils' being celebrated before the major feasts (this probably explains why some saints' days are recorded as being celebrated on adjacent days in various calendars). Strict sabbatarians even thought that Sunday observance should start at none on Saturday, although another opinion was that it lasted from vespers to vespers.[55]

Sleep and eating are the great markers of the daily round. There is good evidence for the practice of a siesta in certain circles. Monks had an afternoon nap in summer. One story about the saintly Waltheof, abbot of Melrose (1149–59), begins with his turning up at the mother house of Rievaulx one summer's day to find all the monks asleep.[56] The English summer heat is not as draining as that of Italy, where Benedict had first devised his Rule, but the monks still had a very long day in summer. They were not the only ones to enjoy a snooze. In his idealized portrait of the court of Henry I, Walter Map tells how the king took counsel with his wise men in the morning, but that, after a midday meal and a sleep, the court gave itself over to pleasure and entertainment.[57]

The implication of Map's statement is that a major meal was taken around midday. Anyone who has read a novel by Jane Austen knows that the choice of meal-times can change radically over the course of time. We are not very well informed about meal-times in the Norman and Angevin period, but have some snippets of information. The monastic routine involved one main meal in winter and two in summer, although gradually it became more common for two meals to be taken in winter too. Dinner (*prandium*) would be about 2.30 p.m. in winter, around midday in summer.[58]

There was also variation between a one-meal and a two-meal model in the secular world, for Robert, count of Meulan and earl of Leicester (d. 1118), reportedly 'completely changed the ancient ways in dress and eating through his example, so that through him the practice of eating only once a day gradually came to prevail in the courts of all great men'.[59] Henry of Huntingdon also remarked on this custom but did not think favourably of it: 'it is the practice of our own time for great men to set food before their followers only once a day, either from meanness or, as they claim, fastidiousness'.[60] The perception here is of a more lavish and generous tradition that prevailed prior

[54] Adam of Balsham, *Ars Disserendi* 176, ed. L. Minio-Paluello, *Twelfth Century Logic: Texts and Studies* 1 (Rome, 1956), pp. 109–10.

[55] Robertson, *Laws*, pp. 22, 144, 166; Liebermann, *Gesetze* 1, pp. 199, 295 (*Quadripartitus*; *Instituta Cnuti*); R. Howd. 4, pp. 168–9; T. Chobham, *SC*, p. 267.

[56] Joc. Furn., *V. Waltheof*, p. 264.     [57] Map 5. 5 (p. 438).

[58] David Knowles, *The Monastic Order in England* (rev. edn.; Cambridge, 1963), pp. 456–8.

[59] W. Malm., *GR* 5. 407 (2, p. 483); OMT edn., p. 736.     [60] H. Hunt. 6. 20 (p. 370).

to 1100 being replaced by a more austere regime of aristocratic hospitality, based on a one-meal day.

Incidental references can usually be harmonized with the idea of a main meal in the early or mid-afternoon. When the English crusaders arriving at Lisbon in the summer of 1147 are described as landing 'around the tenth hour' and also 'around dinner time', this creates no problems.[61] One of the days about which we know most in the period, that of Becket's murder on 29 December 1170, can also be fitted into a comprehensible timetable. The assassins arrived after the main meal, when Becket was engaged in 'afternoon conversation' before vespers.[62] Rather more puzzling is mention of a Bristol sailor sitting down to eat 'around the third hour'.[63] Perhaps this was a light snack, perhaps routine at sea was different—or perhaps the sailor was very hungry.

A twelfth-century meal that can, curiously enough, be assigned to an exact time is that of 20 March 1140. On that day a solar eclipse took place and this was remarked by two independent monastic chroniclers. Both pointed out that the sun darkened at the ninth hour 'when men eat'. Because the pattern of solar eclipses can be established by objective scientific criteria quite independent of the remarks of contemporaries, this event can be timed precisely: it took place at 1.45 p.m. Since this was Lent, it is likely that this was the first and only meal of the day. Whatever other uncertainties surround the rhythm of the day in this period, we do know that 'almost everywhere it happened that men were sitting down at the dining table' at 1. 45 p. m. on 20 March 1140.[64]

## The Rhythm of the Week

Unlike the day, month, and year, the week has no sanction from the natural world. It is a purely conventional division—'that intruder the week'.[65] Nevertheless, it is convenient. A day free of work every seven, a market every seven, is not the only pattern into which human activity can be shaped, but such a rhythm is surely tolerable.

The medieval week derived partly from the Judaic tradition of a Sabbath day of rest but also from the pagan Roman astronomical week, in which each day was linked to a planetary body and its associated deity. The Germanic peoples had equated these deities with their own gods and goddesses and both in Latin and in the vernaculars the names of the days of the week witnessed their pagan ancestry. Thursday was 'the day of Jupiter' (dies Jovis)

---

[61] De exp. Lyxb., pp. 90, 96.

[62] Lambeth Anon. 46 (p. 129); Frank Barlow, Thomas Becket (London, 1986), p. 316 n. 22.

[63] Gerv. Tilb. 1. 13 (p. 894).

[64] W. Malm., HN 484 (pp. 42–3); ASC, p. 266; Hermann Mucke and Jean Meuss, Canon of Solar Eclipses (Vienna, 1992), p. 208, with correction from p. xxviii.

[65] F. H. Colson, The Week (Cambridge, 1926), p. 2.

in Latin, 'the day of Thor' in English. It is not surprising that Christian liturgies and many ecclesiastical authors employed the neutral terminology 'day two', 'day three' (*feria secunda, feria tertia*) rather than constantly recall the pagan gods.

Different days of the week had different associations and features, both ecclesiastical and secular. Some small-holders had the duty of working on their lord's demesnes on Mondays. They were known as 'Mondaymen' (*homines lunares*) and, later in the Middle Ages, their holdings had the name 'Monday lands'.[66] Friday was a day to abstain from meat. Domesday Book records fisheries producing 'fish for Fridays'.[67] Saturdays were dedicated to the Virgin Mary and her Office and Mass were recited on that day. According to Thomas of Chobham she was revered particularly on that day because she alone had kept the faith on the Saturday after the crucifixion, when all the other followers of Christ had despaired.[68]

Sunday was the day marked out as especially sacred. Sometimes fines for an offence committed then were higher than for the same offence at a less highly charged time, as at Chester in the late eleventh century, when the fines for bloodshed and killings between none on Saturday and Monday morning were twice those during the rest of the week. Commercial activity was similarly circumscribed, with the bishop of Chester levying a fine of four shillings from any merchant who opened up a bale of goods in that same period.[69]

The campaign against the holding of markets on Sundays intensified in the later twelfth century. In the year 1172, king Henry II was supposedly warned by a tall emaciated figure that evil would befall him unless 'you proclaim firmly through all the lands subject to you that markets should not be held on Sundays'.[70] Eleven years after evil had indeed fallen on Henry II, Eustace, abbot of Flaye in Normandy, a famous preacher, came to England and 'admonished and persuaded everyone that on Sundays they should desist from public markets and buying and selling and that after none on Saturday they should engage in no manual work; he induced many of both sexes to promise these things'.[71] His sabbatarian campaign was coupled with crusade preaching, exhortations to give up usury, and encouragement of alms-giving.

---

[66] *The Red Book of Worcester*, ed. Marjory Hollings (Worcestershire Historical Soc.; 1934–50), pp. 277, 407; see also index, p. 603, s.v. 'Tenants, customary—Monday men'; *Extenta Manerii de Hagleghe* (1305), *Procs. Suffolk Institute of Archaeology*, 3 (1863), p. 244.

[67] *DB* 1, 149 (Bkm. 19. 1).          [68] T. Chobham, *SC*, p. 124.

[69] *DB* 1, 262b, 263 (Chs. C. 5, B. 2).

[70] Gerald, *Itin.* 1. 6 (pp. 64–5), repeated in Gerald, *Exp.* 1. 40 (pp. 108–10), and Gerald, *Prin.* 2. 12 (pp. 180–2).

[71] For the preaching activities of Eustace of Flay, see R. Howd. 4, pp. 123–4, 167–72; Gerald of Wales, *V. sancti Hugonis* (*Op.* 7, pp. 121–2); Joc. Brak., p. 132; R. Coggesh., pp. 133–4; J. L. Cate, 'The English Mission of Eustace of Flay (1200–1201)', in *Etudes d'histoire dédiées à la mémoire de Henri Pirenne* (Brussels, 1937), pp. 67–89.

This activist social programme also had a liturgical side, for another practice he fostered was that of keeping a permanent light before the consecrated host. His efforts had some success but also met with opposition and the following year, 1201, he came back to England with the impressive backing of a letter from God. This had been found in the Holy Land and contained a long series of threats directed towards breakers of the sabbath:

It is my wish that no one shall engage in any work, except good works, from none on Saturday until sunrise on Monday and, if you do not obey this command, I swear to you by my Seat and my Throne that I will open the heavens and instead of rain I will rain on you rocks and timbers and hot water by night. . . . Hear my voice, lest you perish in the land on account of the Lord's holy day.

During this second visit abbot Eustace successfully induced the abbey of Bury St Edmunds to move its market from Sunday to Monday but he directed his attention particularly to the north of England and reportedly had a substantial amount of success here. Honourably received at York by archbishop Geoffrey (Henry II's illegitimate son), he preached to some effect. People promised to give up Sunday trading, except sale of food and drink to travellers, and to set aside some of their income to provide lights for churches and burial of the poor. The abbot prescribed the establishment of alms-boxes in churches and alms-dishes in the houses of the rich and he forbade the use of churches or churchyards for markets or court hearings. Altogether his activities constituted a wide-ranging revivalist campaign, in which care for the poor and sanctification of the holy were twin goals.

This sabbatarian campaign faced two main obstacles. One was the indifference or hostility of a large number of ordinary lay people. These otherwise obscure figures emerge from the contemporary account of punishments that befell those who failed to observe the abbot's (and God's) instructions. The list of those punished in various ways for working on a Saturday afternoon includes a carpenter in Beverley, working 'despite his wife's salutary warnings'; a female weaver and a man baking bread in Yorkshire villages; a miller at Wakefield and a woman in Lincolnshire who took her dough to the oven during the proscribed period. Two of these miracles of punishment involve blood flowing from the bread that has been baked or the grain that is being ground and here we can perhaps see a link of association with the eucharistic side of abbot Eustace's programme. In contrast, of course, there are the obedient ones: the woman who prepares dough but whose husband then tells her, 'It is Saturday and past none, leave it until Monday'. Checking her dough on the Sunday, to see how it is rising, the woman finds that it is now, 'at God's command', baked bread. The obedient few seem, however, to have been outnumbered by the indifferent many.

A second obstacle faced by the campaign against Sunday trading was the royal government. Angevin administration was interventionist and auto-cratic. Changes in such things as the time of markets did not pass it by. Hence the command 'that all who observed these teachings, especially those who had cast down Sunday markets, should be brought before the royal tribunal to answer concerning the Lord's day.' The records of the king's itinerant justices show exactly what was involved: Lichfield market had been moved from Sunday to Thursday 'and hence the town must pay a fine', records the eyre roll of 1203.[72] One of the pleas of the Crown dealt with by the justices in Northamptonshire in 1202 was that 'the market of Peterborough has been moved from Sunday to Saturday; it belongs to the abbot of Peterborough'.[73] The Pipe Roll for 1202–3 records a debt of two marks ($£1. 6s. 8d.$) due from the townsmen of Basingstoke 'that their market, which was on a Sunday, may be on a Monday'.[74]

Despite these difficulties, the Church continued its campaign. In 1213 or 1214 Stephen Langton, archbishop of Canterbury, instructed his clergy to prohibit their parishioners from attending Sunday markets under pain of ex-communication.[75] The minority government of Henry III, perhaps inspired by the convictions of one of its most important members, Peter des Roches, bishop of Winchester, actively encouraged the move of markets away from Sundays.[76] It would be naive to expect Sunday observance to be quickly and easily enforceable but equally naive not to be struck by the strength and tenacity of the campaign. The fight for the Christian week is an epic of Euro-pean history.

## The Rhythm of the Year

The year was both a natural and a conventional unit. The seasons of botan-ical growth, maturity, decline, and quiescence were influenced by a thousand things: rainfall, temperature, wind, and war. The calendar year was expected to be a fixed schedule. A complication was that there were two conventional schemes available. One was the Roman calendar whose basic outline is still familiar at the present day: twelve months running from January to Decem-ber, with months of a variable number of days. The other was the liturgical calendar, setting out the festivals of the Christian year, often commencing on St Andrews day (30 November) with the Advent season. Dates were commonly

---

[72] Ed. G. Wrottesley, 'Curia Regis Rolls of the Reigns of Richard I and John', *CHS* 3/i (1882), p. 93.

[73] *The Earliest Northamptonshire Assize Rolls*, ed. D. M. Stenton (Northamptonshire Record Soc. 5; 1930), p. 9, no. 43.

[74] PR 5 John, p. 148.　　[75] *Councils and Synods* 2/i, p. 35.

[76] J. L. Cate, 'The Church and Market Reform in England during the Reign of Henry III', in J. L. Cate and E. N. Anderson (eds.), *Medieval and Historiographical Essays in Honor of J. W. Thompson* (Chicago, 1938), pp. 27–65; Nicholas Vincent, *Peter des Roches: An Alien in English Politics, 1205–1238* (Cambridge, 1996), pp. 172–3.

given by reference to the liturgical year, making it important to know when such arcane festivals as Laetare Sunday or the octave of St Andrew fell.

Christian religious festivals are of two types, those that fall on the same day every year and those that do not—the 'movable feasts'. Medieval monastic calendars usually set out the Roman calendar year with the fixed festivals of the liturgical year noted at the appropriate point. The Roman dating system did not, however, identify a day of the month by its place in the succession of 28, 29, 30, or 31 days as we do (e.g. 27 November), but by how long it was before one of three fixed points in the month: the nones, the ides, and the kalends. The nones were on either the fifth or the seventh of the month, the ides on either the thirteenth or the fifteenth, the kalends always on the first (the origin of the word 'calendar'). Every day after the ides was described as being so many days before the kalends of the following month. The counting system was inclusive, reckoning both the first and last day involved. Thus the 27 November was 'V. kal. Dec.', i.e. five days (counting inclusively) before 1 December.

The liturgical year was a complex dance between the fixed dates, mainly saints' days, and the deep moving rhythm line of the major festivals, especially Easter, the centre of the church's year. The chief fixed feast was Christmas, which always fell on 25 December. Easter, the celebration of Christ's resurrection, was calculated by a complex formula, depending on the spring equinox and the lunar month, and, in the Middle Ages, could fall any time between 23 March and 26 April. Lent, Pentecost (Whitsun), and Ascension Day were determined by the date of Easter. While every year in the Roman calendar was thus identical (with the minor exception of leap years), the Christian liturgical year varied from year to year.

The beginning of the year was a matter of deep confusion. As Gervase of Canterbury, himself interested in chronological matters, observed, 'Some people begin the year at the Annunciation (25 March), some at the Passion (Easter), some at the Circumcision (1 Jan.) . . . but most, whom I shall follow, begin the year of grace at Christmas. For it is our custom to count men's years and age not from conception but from birth.'[77] There were thus four possible starting dates for the year—25 March (Annunciation), Easter, 1 January (Circumcision), and 25 December. The first of January, the old Roman New Year's Day, was the starting date for monastic calendars. Again, as Gervase of Canterbury notes, 'the solar year, according to Roman tradition and the custom of the church, begins on 1 January'.[78] Easter was not a common starting date in England, although the French royal chancery adopted it during the reign of Philip Augustus (1180–1223). General English practice shifted over the course of the period covered in this book from a year starting at Christmas towards one starting at the Annunciation (Lady Day). Christmas

---

[77] Gerv. Cant., pp. 231–2; cf. p. 88–91.      [78] Ibid., p. 88.

dating is the reason many contemporary chroniclers ascribe the murder of Becket, which modern historians date 29 December 1170, to AD 1171.[79]

Thomas of Chobham, writing in the early decades of the thirteenth century, gives a list of those Christian festivals which should be observed.[80] He divides them into feasts that are absolutely obligatory and those that 'are almost universally celebrated'. Table 13 shows his list, adapted for the year 1200, with the second category of feasts marked with an asterisk.

TABLE 13. *Feast days for the year 1200*

| | |
|---|---|
| 25 Dec. 1199 | Christmas Day |
| 26 Dec. | St Stephen |
| 27 Dec. | St John the Evangelist |
| 28 Dec. | Innocents |
| 29 Dec. | St Thomas Becket* |
| 31 Dec. | St Silvester |
| 1 Jan. 1200 | Octave of Christmas |
| 6 Jan. | Epiphany |
| 20 Jan. | Sts Fabian and Sebastian* |
| 21 Jan. | St Agnes* |
| 22 Jan. | St Vincent* |
| 2 Feb. | Purification of Virgin Mary (Candlemas) |
| 5 Feb. | St Agatha* |
| 25 Feb. | St Matthias (24 Feb. in non-leap years) |
| 12 Mar. | St Gregory* |
| 21 Mar. | St Benedict* |
| 25 Mar. | Annunciation |
| 9 Apr. | Easter (and following week) |
| 23 Apr. | St George* |
| 1 May | Sts Philip and James |
| 15–17 May | Rogation days |
| 18 May | Ascension |
| 28 May | Pentecost |
| 11 June | St Barnabas |
| 24 June | St John the Baptist |
| 29 June | Sts Peter and Paul |
| 20 July | St Margaret* |
| 22 July | St Mary Magdalene* |
| 25 July | St James |

[79] Gerald, *Exp.* 1. 20 (p. 74); Gerv. Cant., p. 231.

[80] T. Chobham, *SC*, pp. 266–7, with earlier sources identified; in the chart only the feast of Peter and Paul is listed; other Petrine feasts may also have been celebrated.

| | |
|---|---|
| 10 Aug. | St Lawrence |
| 15 Aug. | Assumption of Virgin Mary |
| 24 Aug. | St Bartholomew |
| 29 Aug. | Beheading of John the Baptist* |
| 8 Sept. | Nativity of Virgin Mary |
| 14 Sept. | Exaltation of the Cross |
| 21 Sept. | St Matthew |
| 29 Sept. | Michaelmas |
| 9 Oct. | St Denis* |
| 28 Oct. | Sts Simon and Jude |
| 1 Nov. | All Saints |
| 11 Nov. | Martinmas |
| 22 Nov. | St Cecilia* |
| 30 Nov. | St Andrew |
| 6 Dec. | St Nicholas |
| 13 Dec. | St Lucy* |
| 21 Dec. | St Thomas the apostle |

This general pattern was subject to hundreds of local variations. Every church celebrated the feast of the saint to whom it was dedicated, while there might be other local saints who were commemorated (often it is even possible to attribute a liturgical book to a specific church from the saints who are commemorated in it). Thomas of Chobham's list, which is a typical one, gives at least two and usually three or more festivals a month. The Christmas season had many more. If one adds Sundays and local feasts, the number of days that had to be observed as feasts might approach a hundred a year.

The Christian year and the natural year were not quite in step but had elements in common: a midwinter feast, to cheer the heart in dark days and bring the sun back, and a major spring festival, celebrating rebirth. St John's day was also Midsummer Day, the winter solstice approximately coincided with Christmas. The long holiday of the twelve days of Christmas was marked by gift-giving. Robes and presents were handed out by the king to his retainers at Christmas. Jocelin of Brakelond notes that it was 'the custom of the English' to give a present to their lord on New Year's day.[81] Epiphany marked the end of this festive season.

The Lenten season of penance and fasting began on Ash Wednesday, when the congregation were marked with ashes. The last Sunday in Lent was Palm Sunday, commemorating Christ's entry into Jerusalem. This was solemnized with processions. Lanfranc's *Constitutions* describe how palms, flowers, and foliage are blessed and distributed before the monks set out with banners,

---

[81] Joc. Brak., p. 62.

holy water, crosses, lighted candles, and incense, going outside the walls of the city and then returning.[82] The following week saw the great festival of Easter, with its complex and lengthy liturgy.

Easter coincided with spring and the renewal of natural growth. It was a favourite season for medieval rhapsody: 'this renewal of all things, this splendour and beauty, the very state of things, calls for a new song.'[83] For everyone working the land it was the time to sow. For the military aristocracy the return of good weather had another meaning : 'Easter, when tournaments, wars and fighting recommence.'[84] It was hard to fight in the mud, cold, and early evenings of winter. Spring meant the resumption of the campaigning season. Summer was even better. There is reference to 'the month of June, when kings are accustomed to go to war'.[85] Practical issues were involved. Richmond castle was garrisoned by 43 knights during June and July but only 26 during December and January.[86]

Pentecost or Whitsun, which fell seven weeks after Easter, well into springtime, was the last of the great movable feasts and was followed by a long period in which the liturgical pattern was relatively calm and regular. Mid-summer day was celebrated on 24 June. High summer had two important Marian feasts—the Assumption and the Nativity of the Blessed Virgin Mary on 15 August and 8 September. In this central part of the year most people would be preoccupied with haymaking and harvesting. Then, after harvest, rents would be paid and preparations made for the winter. Pigs could be fed in the woods in the autumn but there was not enough food to keep large numbers of them over the winter. The Anglo-Saxon name for November was 'blood month', because that was when the animals that could not be fed were slaughtered. A common medieval illustration of the labours appropriate to November shows a man about to brain a pig with an axe. After winter-ploughing and the slaughtering and salting of pigs, the nights would draw in towards Christmas again.

One important way that the agricultural year was patterned was by the fixed dates when rent was due. As an example of such dates we can take the rent terms mentioned in the Norfolk Feet of Fines for 1198.[87] Feet of Fines are legal documents recording agreements about property and many of them specify conditions of tenure. Seventy of the Norfolk Feet of Fines mention rent terms: in 21 cases, rent was paid in four instalments, in 17 in three, in 19

---

[82] Lanfr., *Const.*, pp. 22–6.

[83] Lawrence of Durham, *Dialogi*, ed. James Raine (Surtees Soc. 70; 1880 for 1878), lines 1–2, p. 1.

[84] Marie de France, *Milun*, lines 384–6 (*Lais*, p. 111).     [85] W. Newb. 2. 28 (1, p. 172).

[86] *Calendar of Inquisitions Miscellaneous* 1 (London, 1916), no. 519, pp. 167–8.

[87] *Feet of Fines for the County of Norfolk* (1198–1202), ed. Barbara Dodwell (PRS n.s. 27; 1952 for 1950), pp. 1–92; Reginald Lennard, *Rural England, 1086–1135: A Study of Social and Agrarian Conditions* (Oxford, 1959), pp. 185–9, for an earlier set of examples.

in two, and in 13 in one. As can be seen, there is a fairly even distribution between one, two, three, and four terms. By far the commonest term-day was Michaelmas (29 September), which occurs 60 times. This is not fortuitous, for the logical time to levy rent in an agricultural world would be after the autumn harvest. St Andrew's Day (30 November), which occurs 21 times, was also post-harvest and followed closely the time when much stock was slaughtered. To pay rent at Easter, however, which was the second most common term after Michaelmas, occurring 36 times, must obviously have involved some forward planning and saving.

Two things are noticeable about the pattern of the year revealed in these rent-terms: first, the enormous variation, with a total of 29 different patterns in the 70 instances, the very commonest scheme (two payments at Michaelmas and Easter) occurring only 11 times; secondly, the fact that all the terms are ecclesiastical feasts, several of them movable, and that even those which might have a secular tradition, such as Midsummer Day, are described in ecclesiastical terms (as St John's Day, 24 June). Even the annual rhythm of agricultural rents, therefore, had a Christian or Christianized pattern. A nice example comes from a Westminster charter of 1204, when the period of the year in which the swine could be fed from the fruits of beech, oak, etc., is described as the time 'when the mast lasts, namely between Michaelmas and Martinmas'.[88] A purely natural season is here described and defined by the feasts of the saints.

Throughout our period, although less decisively at its end than at its beginning, the dating of documents is a rarity. While it was important that a grant of land be witnessed by as many and as important people as possible, there was no strong reason why it should be dated precisely. One can imagine circumstances where it might be necessary to establish that one grant was earlier than another, and perhaps this was a consideration that led eventually to the general adoption of dating clauses in the later Middle Ages, but a public and well-witnessed transaction did not usually require such a clause in our period. It was otherwise with documents that specified repayment terms for loans or lengths of leases. In these it was crucial to make explicit the date at which the agreement came into force. Hence financial bonds and fixed-term leases bear precise dates, either of the drawing up of the deed or of the commencement of the arrangement.

Financial bonds, specifying when a loan was received or when interest became payable, are particularly explicit. Among the dates employed in the transactions of the great Jewish moneylender Aaron of Lincoln are 'Easter after Geoffrey, count of Brittany, the son of the king of England, was knighted' (1 April 1179), 'the octave of St Michael's day following the death

---

[88] *Westminster Charters*, no. 330, pp. 178–9.

of Richard de Lucy' (6 October 1179), 'St Lucy's day after Walter of Coutances was consecrated bishop of Lincoln' (18 October 1183), and 'St Andrew's day following the death of Richard, archbishop of Canterbury' (30 November 1184). The system of reference was thus to take a day from the liturgical year and to identify the year in relation to a public event, such as the death of a great man (Richard de Lucy was royal justiciar), the knighting of the king's son, the consecration of a bishop. Sometimes such events would have been familiar to contemporaries but are no longer precisely identifiable by modern historians. The dating of a loan to 'fifteen days before the feast of the Purification of St Mary following the death of Master Peter de Melida', with its specification of the year by the death of a well known canon of Lincoln cathedral, would have been adequate for Aaron of Lincoln and his debtor, Simon fitz Payn of Ryhall in Rutland (less than forty miles south of Lincoln and in the diocese), but all the resources of modern scholarship cannot now determine whether this document dates to 1180 or 1181.[89]

Other forms of dating were available. Days could be identified by the Roman dating system ('*V. kal. Dec.*') or by day and month ('the twenty-seventh day of November'). The year AD would be quite generally known. It was, for instance, inscribed on the Paschal candle that was kindled in churches each Easter.[90] Alternatively, a common and practical way of counting time was by the years of the reign of a king, the pontificate of a bishop, etc. Regnal years started with the coronation. Thus, the first year of Henry II runs from 19 December 1154 to 18 December 1155, the second year from 19 December 1155 to 18 December 1156, and so on. The most confusing regnal years are those of John. Since he was crowned on Ascension Day 1199, he decided to date his regnal years from Ascension Day to Ascension Day—and Ascension Day is a movable feast. Hence each of his regnal years begins on a different day and none would be exactly a year long. Regardless of such abstruse issues, however, by the early thirteenth century it was increasingly common for documents to be dated, in a variety of ways, clearly anchoring them in a well-defined present time, which could be fitted into the long series of past and future times.

## Future

The future was uncertain, but many thought that there were ways to discover it. Techniques and methods of prediction and prognostication flourished, despite a continuous rumble of ecclesiastical disapproval. Some of these keys to the future were simple, everyday occurrences that were read as signs and given good or bad significance. To encounter a leaping hare, a woman with

[89] Richardson, *Jewry*, pp. 248–50; *Fasti, 3. Lincoln*, pp. 133–4.     [90] Lanfr., *Const.*, p. 43.

her locks unbound, a blind man, a lame man, or a monk was bad luck; conversely, it boded well when a wolf or a dove approached, if water-birds flew from left to right, if one heard distant thunder on setting out or met a hunchback or a leper. The number of times one sneezed was highly significant. Some sought prognostications from the howling of dogs.[91]

In addition to these omens from the natural world or from chance encounters, there existed specialized techniques of fortune-telling. John of Salisbury describes how he himself was almost drawn into the world of crystal-gazers when he was a young boy learning Latin with a local priest. As well as teaching grammar, the priest practised divination and wished to use his pupils, John and another boy, in the course of his magic. Placing them on seats before him, he uttered some spells and then asked them to look at some fingernails smeared with holy oil and a smooth, scrubbed basin and tell him what they saw. John's fellow-pupil said that he saw some indistinct shapes, but John replied he saw only fingernails and a basin. His obtuse reaction meant that he was excluded from future sessions. 'So God had mercy on me at that young age', reflected John.[92]

Other forms of fortune-telling included palmistry, opening the Psalter at random, dream analysis, and 'inspection of swords'. This last was a divinatory practice used, amongst other things, for revealing the identity of thieves. It is not clear exactly what it involved but was evidently quite common. When a young novice at Pontefract priory was tormented by evil spirits, the prior speculated, 'perhaps he was involved in some kind of sorcery before he joined the convent, writing magical characters or inspecting swords'.[93] One particularly gruesome technique for obtaining foreknowledge is recorded in an allegation of 1222: 'A Jewish necromancer hired a boy and placed him in the skin of one who had recently died, in order that through this means and by necromantic incantations, he should be able to foresee the future. Future events appeared to the boy as if they were present and he answered questions put to him about them.'[94]

John of Salisbury reports that the fortune-gazing priest preceded his work by invoking names, 'which from their horror seemed to me, although I was only a boy, to be those of demons', and demons did indeed provide one important channel through which knowledge of the future was sought. A man, who, after a bout of insanity, had acquired the power to see and speak with demons, 'predicted many future events with their help'. He was almost always right about occurrences within the forthcoming year but became less

[91] P. Blois, *Letters*, no. 65 (cols. 190–5); J. Salisb., *Policr.* 2. 1 (1, pp. 65–6); T. Chobham, *SC*, pp. 477–8.

[92] J. Salisb., *Policr.* 2. 28 (1, pp. 164–5).          [93] W. Cant., *Mir. Thos.* 5. 8 (p. 381).

[94] R. Coggesh., p. 191.

accurate when he predicted the more distant future.[95] This reflected the nature of demonic foreknowledge. Learned men since the time of Augustine had insisted that demons did not actually have real knowledge of the future, they simply had greater evidence on which to base their claims. 'They make conjectures about future events from signs that are more evident to them than to us.' 'Relying on long experience of things and the subtlety of his nature, the devil makes conjectures about future things by reasoning inferentially from things that have already happened.'[96]

The devil is, of course, a liar, and those who relied on his predictions might well come to grief. This befell the monk of Ramsey, Daniel, who schemed and plotted to secure the resignation of his own abbot, Walter, and be appointed in his place. After a campaign of persuasion against the simple Walter and generous bribery of both the monks and the royal court, Daniel attained his goal. Walter resigned and he became abbot of Ramsey. Within eighteen days, however, the troops of Geoffrey de Mandeville, the violent and ambitious earl of Essex, occupied the monastery and dispersed the monks. 'Then was fulfilled the response that he had received from the demons through his witches and sorceresses. For, when they had asked them how long Daniel would be abbot, the demons answered "Eighteen", saying no more. The witches understood this to be a reference to years, when it meant days.'[97]

One form of prognostication that was, quite exceptionally, approved and even integrated into an official ecclesiastical ceremony involved the opening at random of the Gospels during the consecration of a bishop. Whatever phrase first came to the eye was then taken as foretelling the bishop's future career or character. Thus when Herbert Losinga, who had paid a large sum of money to be made bishop of Thetford (later Norwich), was consecrated in 1091, his prognostic was 'Friend, wherefore art thou come?'—Christ's words to Judas. Herbert burst into tears, promised to reform, and went off to Rome to seek reconciliation.[98] Others were more fortunate. The charitable Lanfranc turned up 'Give alms and all things are clean unto you'.[99] These prognostics could become generally known. A list compiled in the 1120s records the prognostics of forty-two contemporary or recently deceased bishops.[100] The Bible itself could thus provide a kind of fortune-telling.

The most elaborate and self-consciously scientific form of prediction was based upon examination of the stars and planets. Astrology had been a major

---

[95] Gerald, *Itin.* 1. 5 (pp. 57–8).     [96] W. Newb. 1, pref. (1, p. 12); Gerald, *Itin.* 1. 5 (pp. 59–60).

[97] *Ramsey Chron.*, pp. 329–30.

[98] W. Malm., *GP* 74 (pp. 151–2); the biblical verse is Matthew 26: 50.

[99] W. Malm., *GP* 43 (p. 68); the biblical verse is Luke 11: 41.

[100] George Henderson, '*Sortes Biblicae* in Twelfth-Century England: The List of Episcopal Prognostics in Cambridge, Trinity College MS R. 7. 5', in Daniel Williams (ed.), *England in the Twelfth Century* (Woodbridge, 1990), pp. 113–35.

activity in the ancient world and some of its terms, techniques, and texts remained current in the early Middle Ages, but it was the influx of Arabic science that fuelled a full revival of astrology in the twelfth century. Among the texts translated into Latin were many astrological works, including central texts like Abu Ma'shar's *Introduction to Astrology*, while tools such as the astrolabe and astronomical tables brought new precision and accuracy to observation and calculation of the movements of the heavens.

Astrological interests could be found among the episcopate of Norman England. Robert, bishop of Hereford, did not bother to go to Lincoln for the planned dedication of the new cathedral in 1092 because his 'precise investigation of the stars' had revealed that the ceremony would not in fact take place.[101] Robert was from Lotharingia, an area where the new astronomical and astrological learning was studied intensely. His successor, Gerard (bishop of Hereford 1096–1100, archbishop of York 1100–8), was another prelate with interest in astronomy. Supposedly he took guidance from one of the ancient Roman textbooks of astrology, the *Mathesis* of Julius Firmicus Maternus, and when he died, his head was found to be resting on 'a book of strange arts'.[102]

It is possible to know a little about some of the specific predictions made by practising astronomers in twelfth-century England. A group of four horoscopes for the year 1151 concerns the complex politics of the later years of Stephen's reign. They deal with such enigmatic issues as 'the arrival of a certain person in England' and 'the question concerning the army of Normandy'. Whoever cast these horoscopes had a high opinion of his art: 'we judge that the king will force his barons to do homage to his son, and that what is planned will not be accomplished without the astrologer'.[103] A generation later, the very unusual conjunction of all the planets on 16 September 1186, stimulated a great deal of astrological activity. Roger of Howden devotes pages of his chronicle to predictions by various astrologers, including such Arab masters as 'Corumphiza' and 'Pharamella of Cordoba'. He also gives a home-grown prediction from William the astrologer, clerk of John de Lacy, constable of Chester.[104]

William's astrological predictions combine scientific precision in the analysis of the positions of the planets with carefully vague applications to human affairs. 'The conjunction', he writes, 'will take place on the Tuesday, 16 September, at the first hour, with Mars in the ascendant, the sun in the east and the planets in the following positions . . . the sun at 30 degrees in the sign

---

[101] W. Malm., *GP* 177 (p. 313).      [102] W. Malm., *GP* 118 (pp. 259 n. 6, 260 n. 1).
[103] John North, 'Some Norman Horoscopes', in Charles Burnett (ed.), *Adelard of Bath: An English Scientist and Arabist of the Early Twelfth Century* (London, 1987), pp. 147–61.
[104] *Gesta Hen. II* 1, pp. 324–8; R. Howd. 2, pp. 290–8.

of Virgo, Jupiter at 2 degrees, 3 minutes, Venus at 3 degrees, 49 minutes . . .'
etc. Saturn signifies the pagans, the sun the Christian princes. 'Because the
sun is powerful in this configuration,' reasons William, 'a Christian man will
arise among us of great fame, whose name will be proclaimed as far as Arin'—
Arin was a legendary city, supposedly situated on the equator, that Arabic
astronomers used as a baseline. He goes on, 'because Mars is burned in the
sphere of the sun, blocked and surrounded by two bad things, Saturn and the
descending node of the lunar orbit, and absorbing their nature, its properties
signify sorrows, quarrels, fears, horror, killing and loss of property.' He cites
Abu Ma'shar's opinion that a configuration with Mars at the extremity and
Scorpio ascending is unfortunate and concludes with the uplifting advice
that 'the chief men should consult together, serve God and shun the devil, so
that the Lord may turn away the dangers that threaten'.

The use of astrology, like other forms of prediction and prognostication,
was controversial. Among its uncritical partisans was such an avid proponent
of Arabic learning as Daniel of Morley. 'Those who deny that the movements
of the stars have any power or effect', he spluttered, 'are so unabashedly
brainless that, before they have any knowledge of a subject, they begin to
decry its theories.'[105] Many Christian intellectuals had their reservations,
however. The idea of a future written in the stars seemed to challenge human
autonomy and individual responsibility. Alexander Nequam, while conced-
ing that the heavenly bodies do exert some influence, insisted that their
movements did not produce inevitable results. He criticized those who
asserted, for instance, that everyone born under Mercury was bound to
become a thief. 'The heavenly bodies do not diminish free will', he concluded.[106]

John of Salisbury, whose experience with the crystal-gazing priest had obviously left a mark, composed one of the longest and most intricate discussions
of foreknowledge and divination from this period.[107] He did not deny that it
was possible to deduce the future from signs in the present. First, God
reveals some future events by such natural but unusual incidents as the passage of comets. Secondly, there are regular natural signs, such as the patterns
of weather revealed in the evening sky that enable sailors and farmers to predict the forthcoming day. To observe the movements of birds was not absurd,
since their light bodies made them more aware of the movements of the air.

On the other hand, it is clear that 'omens are meaningless'. 'What does it
signify for the future', John asks, 'if someone sneezes once or more than
once?' The interpretation of dreams yields nonsense. The special enemy is
astrology, because it is so strong. It is more dangerous to ground your error
'in the solidity of nature and the power of reason', than in sneezes, birds, or

[105] D. Morley 10. 158 (p. 239).     [106] Alex. Nequam, *DNR* 1. 7 (pp. 39–41).
[107] J. Salisb., *Policr.* bk. 2 (1, pp. 65–169).

random encounters with wolves, lepers, or monks. Astrologers should not ascribe too great power to the planets and constellations. They must not disparage God's power or criticize the idea of free will. In any case, John argues, if the future can be changed, why create a science to understand it, and if it cannot, what is the point of such a science?

Less extensive, but equally reflective, are the remarks of Peter of Blois on this issue.[108] He had had an unusual experience. His brother, William of Blois, was a monk. One day a certain Master G. (his full name is not recorded) encountered William of Blois while setting out on a journey. It was bad luck to meet a monk. William of Blois made no effort to dispel this impression. He suggested that it would be unfortunate for Master G. to undertake his journey that day. Master G., was, however, a strict evangelical Christian: 'perfect in Christ, deeming that anything not rooted in the Christian faith was empty talk, he set out on his journey with complete confidence'. Sadly his confidence was misplaced. Master G. and his horse plunged into a flooded ravine, from which he only just escaped.

This striking incident inspired a vigorous discussion about omens. Peter of Blois, as the most learned man in the circle, was asked for his opinion on 'omens, dreams, spirits, bird-flight and sneezing'. He was clear that belief in prognostication and magic was inspired by the devil. Satan 'sends fantastical illusions into the minds of men, promising knowledge of the future from the flight of birds, encounters with men or beasts, dreams and so on. Thus he labels the course of events as auspicious or inauspicious, in order to trouble the quiet of our hearts with empty curiosity and besmirch the simplicity of our faith.' A range of practices and beliefs—image-magic, the evil eye, augury, astrology—are suggestions of the devil. Foreknowledge is not itself a lawful goal. 'Let it be the judgment of a Christian, to inquire nothing about the future but to humbly obey the disposition of Him who disposes everything agreeably . . . to seek knowledge of the future through auguries or other illicit means is a temptation of the devil and can lead to eternal damnation.' What then explains the accident that befell Master G.? 'My opinion', writes Peter, 'is that Master G. would have been in danger of drowning even if he had not met a monk.'

Peter's position is a rather unusual one for the period. The accident was just that, an accident, something that happened without preceding signs or special meaning. A similar viewpoint was expressed by Peter's contemporary, the chronicler Richard of Devizes. Writing of an eclipse of the sun that took place on 23 June 1191, he commented that 'those ignorant of the causes of things were amazed but those who are concerned with the workings of the universe say that such failures of sun and moon do not signify any future event'.[109] This is a very radically naturalistic viewpoint for his day. Usually a

[108]  P. Blois, *Letters*, no. 65 (cols. 190–5).       [109]  R. Devizes, p. 35.

dramatic variation in the natural patterns of the world suggested that a sign was being given. It is worth stressing both the prevalence of the majority view, that the world was full of signs if only one can read them, and the existence of this contrary minority opinion.

Although prediction and fortune-telling dealt with a wide range of affairs, such as good fortune on a journey or the identity of a thief, it throve especially when applied to political events. In a dynastic world so much hung on the fortune of individuals that a hunting accident or sudden illness could transform the political scene. Then as now uncertainty about critical issues was hard to bear. Since official Christianity offered no formal rituals for political divination, such as the pagan religions of the ancient world had supplied, unofficial forms of prediction, prognostication, and prophecy about the political future had fertile ground. They supplied the appearance of knowledge and predictability where there was none, offering pseudo-explanation and genuine consolation in a perplexing and often frightening world.

The uncertainties of war naturally fostered recourse to the diviners. Thomas Becket, royal chancellor at the time, consulted a soothsayer and a palm-reader before going on the Welsh expedition of 1157.[110] The fate of kings was another unpredictable eventuality that people sought to predict. During Henry II's long absence of four and a half years from England (1158–63), it was foretold that the king would never return. These predictions were spread—understandably—by the Welsh, but also apparently believed by one of the king's trusted barons, John Marshal.[111]

A particularly fully recorded case of political prophecy dates to the later years of John's reign, when the king's paranoia was increasing at much the same rate as he was making enemies. An uneducated ascetic visionary called Peter of Wakefield predicted that the king's reign would end by Ascension Day 1212. When this came to John's notice, he at first dismissed Peter as unlettered and insane. Some of the king's men became alarmed, however, as Peter wandered the country recounting his vision, and they eventually decided to imprison him. This turned out to be a tactical error: 'because of this his reputation grew enormously and his name became well-known; the man who was shortly before deemed spurious and despicable was now, because of his arrest, viewed as remarkable and spoken about everywhere.' After the predicted end of his reign had passed, John celebrated by having Peter of Wakefield hanged, along with his son.[112]

The Barnwell Chronicler, who tells this story, is not only acute enough to notice the counter-productive effect that repression of visionaries can have,

---

[110] J. Salisb., *Policr.* 2. 27 (1, p. 144).    [111] R. Diceto, *Ymag.* 1, p. 308.

[112] Barnwell Chron., pp. 208, 212; *Hist. ducs Norm.*, pp. 122–3; *Ann. Dunst.*, p. 34; R. Coggesh., p. 167; R. Wend. 2, pp. 62–3, 76–7 (Paris, *CM* 2, pp. 535, 546–7). The visionary is also called Peter of Pontefract.

but makes two other observations that are of general importance in analysing the dynamics of prophecy. Once Peter had been imprisoned, he writes, 'every day lies were added to lies, as is the way with the common people; every day new things were attributed to him and everyone, producing lies from his own head, asserted that Peter had said them.' Setting aside the author's haughty bias against the common people, we can nevertheless see the importance of the process he describes. Once a visionary or prophet had become well known by name, he (or, much more rarely, she) was henceforth a natural magnet for many kinds of unattributed or anonymous predictions. The great manuscript collections of miscellaneous written prophecies show this agglutinative and amalgamating tendency.

A second point emerges from the chronicler's account of how Peter's prophecies were disproved. The obvious way was to sit out Ascension Day, which John did with a cheerful face in the company of his bishops and magnates. Peter's prophecy had focused on Ascension Day 1212, because John had been crowned on Ascension Day 1199. However, since Ascension Day is a movable feast, in 1199 it fell on 27 May, but in 1212 on 23 May. This offered hope to those who had believed in Peter's prophecies. Once Ascension Day 1212 had passed, they argued that the vision had obviously not referred to Ascension Day literally, but to the anniversary of John's coronation. John had to wait a few more days to disprove this revised version of the prophecy. At this point, notes the chronicler, those who credited Peter 'turned to allegorical interpretations'. The three positions—a definite prophecy with a determinate date, a reinterpreted version with a revised date in the face of disappointment, and final recourse to allegory—indicate neatly the inventive resistance of prophecy to being proved wrong. There was no way a prophecy could fail, given agile defenders—and the Barnwell Chronicler explicitly notes that Peter's adherents included 'men who were great by the standards of this secular life and wise according to the world'.

Prophecies about political affairs circulated not only orally, in the utterances of men like Peter of Wakefield, but also in writing. A large corpus of written prophecy existed in manuscript and was studied, copied, and cited in monasteries and courts. The most extensive and successful piece of political prophecy of this type produced in England in this period was that composed by Geoffrey of Monmouth in the 1130s and inserted into his *History of the Kings of Britain* as the declaration of the mage Merlin. Its flavour can best be conveyed by quotation:

Meanwhile the fox will descend from the mountains and transform himself into a wolf. He will pretend to be going to parley with the boar, but will attack him by trickery and consume him totally. Then he will change himself into a boar and wait for his brothers, as if he had no limbs. But after they come, he will suddenly kill them with his teeth and be crowned with the head of a lion. In his days a serpent will be born that will threaten death to mortals. It will encircle London with its length and devour all who pass by.[113]

The animal symbolism, abrupt and unmotivated action, and lack of specific reference are characteristic of the genre.

Geoffrey's prophecies were a wild success. They were copied, imitated, commented upon, and applied to contemporary affairs. As well as being included in the *History of the Kings of Britain*, which survives in over 200 manuscript copies, the *Prophecies of Merlin* circulated separately in 85 manuscripts.[114] The first historian to use them—and he may even have had a text of the prophecies before Geoffrey had finished writing the *History*—was the half-English, half-Norman monk, Orderic Vitalis. He inserts a whole chapter on the subject into his own *Ecclesiastical History*.[115] 'That prophet', he writes, 'predicted in due order the events that were to come to pass in the northern islands and had them written down in figurative language.' Orderic has confidence in these dark sayings: 'The prophecies of Merlin have been manifestly fulfilled in many things over the course of the last six hundred years.' Since Geoffrey of Monmouth placed Merlin in the fifth century, much of his prophecy actually relates to the period between that time and the twelfth century, i.e. the past for Geoffrey and Orderic. It is not surprising that many of Merlin's predictions closely matched the events.

After giving a long extract from the prophecies, Orderic distinguishes between those that have already been fulfilled and those that refer to events 'that will be experienced by those yet to be born'. He thus locates his own time in the midst of the prophetic discourse. Anyone who knows history can interpret the passages relating to the past, while, in contrast, the present generation 'awaits in uncertainty the future that is ordained for them by the incalculable ordinance of God'. Orderic gives a few examples of interpretation from recent history—the dragon killed by the dart of envy is William Rufus, the 'Lion of Justice' is Henry I—but he expressly disclaims the project of writing a full commentary on the prophecies.

The interpretation of contemporary political events through the lens of the prophecies of Merlin became a prevalent habit among those involved in them and those recording them. The prophecies were bandied about during the Becket controversy and one of John of Salisbury's letters to Becket is an attempt to apply Merlin's dark utterances to the political events of summer 1166.[116] The chronicler Ralph of Diceto describes how William the Lion, king of Scots, was captured in 1174 and taken to the castle of Richmond, a

---

[113] Geoff. Monm., *HRB* 7. 4 (116. 44–5), p. 80.

[114] Julia Crick, 'Geoffrey of Monmouth, Prophecy and History', *Jnl Medieval History*, 18 (1992), p. 360 n. 13.

[115] Orderic, 12. 47 (6, pp. 380–8).     [116] J. Salisb., *Letters* 173 (2, pp. 134–6).

possession of the counts of Brittany. 'This happened', he comments, 'as a fulfilment of the prophecy', and then cites part of a passage from the *Prophecies of Merlin*. The full text of the prophecy reads, 'Scotland will become angry and, summoning her neighbours, will give herself over to bloodshed. A bit will be placed in her mouth that will be made in the Breton bay.' 'The Breton bay', explains Ralph, 'refers to the castle of Richmond, a possession of the counts of Brittany now and from ancient times by hereditary right.'[117]

The obscurity of prophetic language meant that constant reinterpretation was possible. One of the passages from the *Prophecies of Merlin* runs, 'the sixth will cast down the walls of Ireland'.[118] A learned Flemish monk, composing a commentary on the prophecies in seven books in the years 1168–70, thought this might apply to Henry II's sixth, illegitimate son, Geoffrey: 'they say he is of great character, for his age'.[119] Soon afterwards, the involvement of the Anglo-Normans in Ireland gave the prophecy a more natural referent. For Gerald of Wales, writing in 1189, it clearly applied to the submission of the Irish kings to Henry II in 1171.[120] Yet other applications were still viable. An annalist writing at Canterbury a generation later than Gerald interpreted the words as a reference to the expedition that king John ('the sixth' since the Norman Conquest) sent into Wales ('the walls of Ireland') in 1210.[121]

Prophecies such as those that Geoffrey of Monmouth fathered on Merlin claimed the authority of ancient sages and offered a coded key to past, present, and future. Their chief subject matter was political: battles and conquests, dynasties and succession. Written prophecy of a different kind also existed. This was concerned not with the doings of kings and outcome of battles, but with the great cosmic themes, especially the coming of the Last Days and the end of the world.

The physical universe had had a beginning and would certainly have an end. Learned men of the twelfth century knew that the world was about five or six thousand years old. This chronology had been established from the information given in the Bible about the life-spans of the patriarchs. By adding the age of Adam at the birth of his son, Seth, the age of Seth at the birth of his son, Enos, etc., and then calculating the length of the rule of the various Judges, it was possible to build a bridge between the Creation and the datable events of Middle Eastern and Greco-Roman history. Because of some variations in the texts and ambiguities in the biblical data, however, more than one precise date for Creation had been determined. Although it was known that the physical universe had been created on 18 March and

---

[117] R. Diceto, *Ymag.* 1, p. 384; Geoff. Monm., *HRB* 7. 3 (114. 14), p. 76.

[118] Geoff. Monm., *HRB* 7. 3 (114. 17), p. 76.

[119] *Prophetia Anglicana Merlini . . . una cum septem libris explanationum . . . Alani de Insulis* (Frankfurt, 1603), p. 91.

[120] Gerald, *Exp.* 1. 33 (p. 96).      [121] Gerv. Cant., *Gesta regum* (*Works* 2, p. 106).

Adam on 23 March, there was disagreement about how long ago this spring-time of the world had been. Twelfth-century authors, drawing on patristic and other sources, give the number of years between the Creation and the birth of Christ variously as 3,948, 3,952, 4,182, 5,154, and 5,199.[122]

Whatever their view of the exact date of Creation, most people presumed that the future would be shorter than the past. A common image was of 'the world growing old', and the elaborate theory of Six Ages always described the present time as being in the Sixth and final Age. The first five ages ran from the Creation to the time of Christ, when the Sixth Age began. This was the present age, and the last before the End: 'The Sixth Age of the world will end when the world ends, and then the Seventh Age will begin, which will have no end.'[123] In the *Vision of Orm*, discussed above, St Michael has a book in his hand and two-thirds of the pages have been turned over, while God and the Apostles have swords that are two-thirds out of their sheaths. The implication seems to be that time is two-thirds done. This would not contradict Orm's statement that there is still 'a good space of time' before the coming of Antichrist at the end of the Sixth Age.[124]

An alternative view did exist. The historian Henry of Huntingdon was somewhat unusual and disputed the idea that the end of the world was nigh, relying on the opinion of Herbert Losinga, bishop of Norwich, who argued that the period after the Incarnation must be longer than the period prior to it, 'the light longer than the shadow'. Since Henry makes this point in a discussion of whether his history would still be read a thousand years hence (the time is approaching when we can answer in the affirmative), clearly he believed that the physical world and human society would continue at least into the third millennium AD and perhaps into the fourth or fifth.[125] Henry's eye to posterity was not uncommon among authors and suggests a more hopeful and positive attitude to the future than the common view of an age-ing and decaying world. William of Malmesbury closed the preface to his *Deeds of the Kings* with the following direct glance at posterity: 'I do not esteem the judgement of my contemporaries very highly but I hope that among posterity, when favour and envy have both died, even if I shall not have a reputation for eloquence, at least I shall leave evidence of my industrious-ness.'[126] Contemplating the future had its consolations.

Christian doctrine about the end of the world was that the resurrection of the dead at the sound of the last trumpet would be followed by Christ's

---

[122] Orderic 1. 1 (1, pp. 134–5); R. Diceto, *Abbrev.*, p. 55; H. Hunt., p. 494; *Capitula de miraculis et trans-lationibus sancti Cuthberti*, in Simeon, *Op.* 1, p. 261.

[123] Lawrence of Durham, *Hypognosticon* 9, lines 539–40, cited by A. G. Rigg, *A History of Anglo-Latin Literature 1066–1422* (Cambridge, 1992), p. 56.

[124] *Vis. Orm*, pp. 78, 81, 82.      [125] H. Hunt., pp. 496–8.

[126] W. Malm., *GR*, prol. (1, p. 3); OMT edn., p. 16.

Second Coming and the Last Judgement. The signs that would indicate the imminence of Judgement Day had been tabulated in a short text attributed to St Jerome: in the fifteen days before the end, the sea would rise and then sink, the fish would gather and groan, the sea would level and burn, trees and plants would bleed, buildings collapse, rocks implode; there would be a great earthquake, mountain and valley would become level and people would lose the power to communicate; the stars would fall, the bones of the dead come together, the living die, the earth burn—'and after this will be the Judgement'. This text was known in twelfth-century England, being found, for instance, in a twelfth-century manuscript from Canterbury cathedral.[127]

The same manuscript contains another well-known vision of the end, the *Prophecy of the Tiburtine Sibyl*. This ancient, much reworked text, told the story of the Roman emperors, including, in its revised form, their medieval successors, down to the time of the last emperor. He would reign for 112 prosperous years, during which time the pagans and Jews would be converted to Christianity. Then the emperor would lay down his crown in Jerusalem. Next would follow the reign of Antichrist, who would eventually be killed by the archangel Michael on the Mount of Olives. Judgement would follow.[128] The *Prophecy of the Tiburtine Sibyl* had a wide dissemination, appearing in several Latin manuscripts of the time as well as being translated into Anglo-Norman verse by Philip de Thaon and dedicated to the empress Matilda, daughter of Henry I.[129]

One of the most feared of future events was the coming of Antichrist, 'the son of perdition', the Beast of Apocalypse, who would tyrannize over the world before the End. He was awaited with apprehension. Various dates were given for his arrival. In the year 1210 the prior of Dunstable had a vision in which two Jews announced to him that Antichrist would be born in forty years' time.[130] On his way to Palestine in 1190, Richard I took the opportunity to visit the famous Italian prophetic teacher, Joachim of Fiore, and have a discussion with him about the Book of Revelation and the coming of Antichrist. Joachim believed that Antichrist had already been born, in Rome, and would go on to become pope. Richard was puzzled, for the traditional teaching was that Antichrist would be born in Babylon of the tribe of Dan. Debate among the assembled leaders and prelates was vigorous but inconclusive. Roger of Howden, the Yorkshire cleric who was with Richard's army and reports this meeting in his *Chronicle*, supplements the account with a long treatise giving the older teaching on Antichrist.[131]

---

[127] BL Cotton Vespasian B xxv, fo. 144.

[128] Ernst Sackur, *Sibyllinische Texte und Forschungen* (Halle, 1898), pp. 177–87.

[129] Philip de Thaon, *Le Livre de Sibile*, ed. Hugh Shields (ANTS 37; 1979); lines 1207–12, p. 89, for the dedication.

[130] *Ann. Dunst.*, p. 33.    [131] *Gesta Ric. I* 2, pp. 151–5; R. Howd. 3, pp. 75–86.

The coming of the End was a topic that fascinated Roger, and the passage about the king's meeting with Joachim is not the only place in his writing that the subject surfaces. The Book of Revelation describes a vision in which Satan, 'the dragon, the ancient serpent', is bound for a thousand years, 'and after that he must be freed for a little while'. In 1201, according to Roger of Howden, 'our doctors preached that the ancient dragon had been loosed' and that 'the thousand years was up and the devil released'. If the devil had been able to do so much harm when bound, reflected Roger, how much would he do now that he was free? Moral reform was the proper response, so that, 'when Christ comes as judge at the end of the world, he may make us partakers of eternal joy'.[132]

Joachim's teaching was clearly of interest in England, for not only Roger of Howden but also his contemporary Ralph of Coggeshall, a Cistercian like Joachim. Joachim's interpretation of the Book of Revelation, in Ralph's paraphrase, was that the opening of the sixth seal, initiating the period of history in which Antichrist would rule, would take place in 1199. The reign of Antichrist would occur in his own lifetime, for Antichrist was already living, a young man in Rome. Prophecies describing his birth in Babylon were to be taken metaphorically, with Babylon standing for Rome. Ralph judiciously left a decision on the truth of this doctrine to 'our successors', but obviously felt it made sense. The spread of Islam, particularly, was preparing the way for Antichrist. Saladin was the fifth great persecutor, Antichrist the sixth.[133] Alongside a general sense that the world was old and that Judgement could be soon, there were thus specific prophecies that the reign of Antichrist would come within the lifetime of the present generation.

## 2. THE WORLD

### Nature

Although the world was ruled by God and shot through with marvels and prodigies, 'Nature' was a familiar, indeed a central, concept in the thinking of the period. Anselm maintained that all events could be divided into three classes: those that depended solely upon God's power, those that were produced by nature and those that sprang from the will of a created being. The resurrection of the dead and the parting of the Red Sea are examples of the first category, the growth of the trees and plants of the second, building a house of the third. In summarizing his argument, he explicitly postulates a natural course of events:

Therefore, since everything happens either by the will of God alone, or by nature

---

[132] R. Howd. 4, pp. 161–3.     [133] R. Coggesh., pp. 67–70.

through the power God has implanted in it, or by the will of a creature, and those things that are done, not by created nature, nor by the will of a creature, but by God alone, are always marvellous, it is clear that there are three orders of event, the marvellous, the natural and the intentional.[134]

Anselm's concept of the natural thus excludes deliberate human (and possibly animal) actions. This might lead to difficulties: a man throwing a ball was part of the 'intentional' order of things, the ball falling to the ground part of the 'natural'. Nevertheless, Anselm here presented a systematic theory which had an important place for Nature.

The idea of a natural order was given even sharper definition by John of Salisbury, who spoke of 'the law of Nature'. This he defined as 'a series of causes'. He considered the natural order to be a comprehensible system of physical causal chains. Nature is 'a series of causes from which this material world takes its being'. It is true that 'the order of causes is dependent on the divine will', but this does not mean that it is unpredictable or random: 'there is nothing that lacks rational order' [*ratio*]. John thus pictures a natural realm that was intelligible, perceptible, and ordered.[135]

Such a concept of Nature was not uncommon. The uniformity and regularity of the natural world was, however, frequently breached. Miraculous cures were one of the most important components of the cult of the saints. Portents and wonders disrupted the usual course of nature. In 1222, for instance, a monk of the Cistercian abbey of Waverley in Surrey noted that 'dragons were seen by some people, flying here and there through the air; some people also saw them fighting each other'.[136]

These unprecedented and unusual things had to be fitted into the model of the universe alongside the order of nature. Although they had the common characteristic that they caused wonder, a distinction could be made between natural marvels and miracles. 'We call something a marvel', wrote Gervase of Tilbury, 'if it is beyond our knowledge, even if it is natural.' A miracle he defines as 'something supernatural that we ascribe to divine power'.[137] Hence amazing phenomena could be classified as either miraculous or marvellous. Although both stimulated astonishment, they belonged to different orders of event.

Gerald of Wales employs this distinction in the structure of his *Topography of Ireland*. Part Two of the work deals with both 'the prodigious works of playful Nature' and also 'things done by the saints through their extraordinary merits truly miraculously'. The first twenty-seven chapters are devoted to tidal phenomena, petrifying wells, fish with golden teeth, and the

---

[134] Anselm, *De conceptu virginale* 11 (*Op.* 2, pp. 153–4).
[135] John of Salisbury, *Entheticus*, lines 603–30, ed. Ronald E. Pepin, *Traditio*, 31 (1975), pp. 127–93, at p. 155.
[136] *Ann. Wav.*, p. 297.       [137] Gerv. Tilb. 3, pref., p. 960.

like. Then he marks the change of subject: 'now let us turn to miracles'. A fish with golden teeth and St Kevin's miracles were equally 'contrary to the course of Nature and worthy of wonder', but the source of the marvels was Nature, even if they did not follow the usual course of Nature.[138]

If this natural world stimulated amazement by its frequent oddities and wonders, its ordinary, usual course could also be appreciated. The beauty of sunsets or fertile landscapes was often remarked. The idyllic note rings out clearly in the following description of Rievaulx, written by one of its monks:

The valley is surrounded and enclosed by a circlet of high hills, clothed in many different kinds of trees. They provide the sweet solitude of secluded retreats and offer the monks a sort of second paradise of wooded delight. Rippling fountains send down their waters from the high rocks into the depths of the valley and, as they run first through small and narrow passages and then spread out into wider channels and water-courses, they whisper a soft sweet murmuring sound and join their notes into a lovely melody. The branches of beautiful trees rustle and leaves fall softly to the ground, singing together . . .[139]

The seclusion and harmony of this purely natural scene promise the chance of a return to Eden.

## The Physical Universe

This wonderful but comprehensible natural world had a similar harmony when viewed as a whole. The physical universe was spherical and consisted of concentric spheres, with the earth at its centre. The fixed stars and all of the celestial bodies had their own sphere, rotating around the centre of the universe, i.e. the centre of the earth. The earth was only a point in comparison with the universe as a whole, and many of the heavenly bodies were larger than the earth. The sun, the largest, was just over 166 times larger then the earth.[140]

Although the earth was small compared to the universe, it was large in relation to human beings. People were like 'ants on a ball'.[141] The globe was divided into five zones, freezing at the poles, intolerably hot in the equatorial zone, but temperate in between. The northern temperate zone, of course, had inhabitants. The question of whether the southern temperate zone, the antipodes, was inhabited was theologically controversial. If all humans descended from Adam and Eve, how could they have crossed the unbearable heat of the equator to reach the antipodes? Moreover, when Christ returned in

---

[138] Gerald, *Top.* intro.; 2. pref., 28 (pp. 7–8, 74–5, 113).
[139] W. Dan., *V. Ailred* 5 (pp. 12–13).
[140] Alex. Nequam, *DNR* 1. 8 and 2. prol. (pp. 44, 126).
[141] Alex. Ashby, *De modo pred.*, p. 916.

majesty at the Second Coming, how could he manifest himself to northern and southern hemispheres simultaneously? As Augustine's argument has been memorably summarized, 'how could Christ have died for antipodeans?'[142]

For those who did not believe in antipodeans, the inhabited world thus consisted of the land mass of the northern temperate zone. This was surrounded by sea and divided into three continents, Africa, Asia, and Europe. Its centre was Jerusalem. Asia was the size of the other two continents combined. A common schematic world map showed a 'T–O' pattern, made up of the three continents, the surrounding ocean and the waters separating the continents as shown in Figure 17.

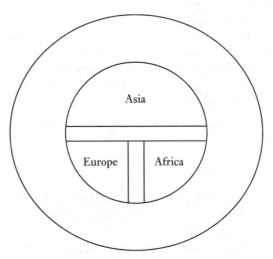

FIGURE 17. A 'T–O' world map

Twelfth-century England was in regular contact with some parts of this 'known world', especially continental Europe and the Mediterranean basin. Beyond that, the more distant regions of the Old World, such as black Africa, India, and China, were the source of exotic imports, like silk, ivory, and gold, and the realm of legend. Of the New World there was, of course, no idea, although the widely read *Voyage of St Brendan* told of mysterious islands in the Atlantic.

'The East', i.e. Asia, had the reputation of being vast, rich, and full of marvels. The wealth and fertility of India was fabulous. William of Newburgh, discussing the situation of the Holy Land, mentions that the Bible asserts the

    [142] J. K. Wright, *The Geographical Lore of the Time of the Crusades* (New York, 1925), p. 56, based on *De civitate dei* 16. 9 (*PL* 41, cols. 487–8).

special place of Palestine, but considers that this cannot mean it is the richest and most fertile part of the world, 'unless what is recorded about India be false'. If God had wished the Chosen People to enjoy the most fertile land on earth, that would have been where he would have placed them.[143]

The East was also where Nature was most playful, producing oddities and wonders of all kinds. A twelfth-century English manuscript, now in the Bodleian Library in Oxford, contains fifty illustrations of these 'Marvels of the East'.[144] They include two-headed snakes, men with dogs' heads, elephants, cannibals, centaurs, black men, unicorns, and parrots who can say 'hello'. The geographical location of these natural marvels is vague— 'beyond Babylonia'—and the real geography is psychological. There is inversion (bearded women), outrage (cannibals), fantasy (dog-heads), as well as dreams of unimaginable wealth: gem-bearing trees and mountains of gold, even if guarded by serpents. Classical mythology made a contribution to this rich mixture, in the form of satyrs and centaurs, while some of it was obviously based on real, if much mediated, knowledge.

A new element was added to the European picture of Asia in the twelfth century with the birth of the legend of Prester John. He was supposedly the ruler of an enormous, rich, and Christian kingdom that lay beyond the Islamic world. In a letter purporting to be written by Prester John and sent to the Byzantine emperor, his kingdom is described. There are seventy-two tributary kings, all kinds of exotic animals and marvellous peoples, such as pigmies, dog-heads, and giants, a river that flowed from Paradise, precious stones, a fountain of youth, a sea of sand, and a river of stones, beyond which lived the Ten Lost Tribes of Israel, also tributary to Prester John.[145]

Prester John was taken seriously. Pope Alexander III wrote to him in 1177 and the text of this letter was inserted into several English chronicles.[146] There grew up the hope that an alliance with this powerful eastern Christian ruler could lead to a giant pincer movement against Islam. In 1221 Ralph of Coggeshall recorded, 'Rumours spread throughout Christendom that King David, also known as Prester John, had advanced from India with a huge army and conquered Persia, the land of the Medes and many other Muslim lands and provinces, and that he had threatened the caliph of Baghdad that he would conquer him and the whole pagan world unless he converted to Christianity.'[147] These hopes were not to be realized. The huge army that came out of Asia in the thirteenth century was to be very different—the Mongols.

[143] W. Newb. 3. 15 (1, pp. 250–1).

[144] MS Bodley 614, reproduced in *Marvels of the East*, ed. M. R. James (Roxburghe Club, 1929).

[145] The essential texts and studies are assembled in Charles F. Beckingham and Bernard Hamilton (eds.), *Prester John, the Mongols and the Ten Lost Tribes* (Aldershot, 1996).

[146] *Gesta Hen. II* 1, pp. 210–12; R. Howd. 2, pp. 168–70; R. Diceto, *Ymag.* 1, p. 440.

[147] R. Coggesh., p. 190.

## The Peoples of the Earth

All human beings were descended from Adam and Eve. The various races, however dissimilar in appearance, were thus kindred. The kin had, however, divided into branches long ago. One of the most frequently held theories was that the different peoples of the earth could be classed into three groups, each descending from one of the three sons of Noah. Henry of Huntingdon, following Bede, describes the division of the world among them. Shem received the area from Persia eastwards, containing 406 peoples and 27 different languages, Japheth the area west of this, with 200 peoples and 23 languages, and Ham received Africa with 394 peoples and 22 languages. The different races in the world thus totalled 1,000, the different languages 72.[148] The number of different languages neatly corresponded with the 72 apostles sent out by Christ according to the gospel of Luke (Chapter 10, in the Latin Vulgate version).

Language was one of the primary, primordial, and fundamental marks of a people, as is made clear by Henry of Huntingdon's comments on the Picts.[149] One can read about them in old books, he says, but they and their language have disappeared so completely 'that it now seems like a fable that mention of them is found in old writings'. The extinction of their rulers and the people itself, the passing away of the Pictish stock and language, should, according to Henry, inspire us to love heavenly and enduring things and shrink from earthly and transient things. Even if the destruction of their kings and their race is not remarkable, what is truly astonishing is the disappearance of their language, 'that God created, among the rest, at the origin of languages'. The 'origin of languages' dates to the building of the Tower of Babel. Before the dispersal of the peoples that followed from that hubristic act, Hebrew was the only language.

The idea of the descent of various peoples from the three sons of Noah could be integrated with that of individual progenitors who gave their name to the different nations, Scots descending from Scotia, the wife of Gael, Britons from Brutus, etc. This genealogical approach to race could, if the ancestors were tied in with Noah and his sons, lead to a complete family tree of all humanity. William of Malmesbury gives the line of descent of the kings of Wessex (and hence the Angevin kings) from Noah, via Woden, the forefather of 'the kings of many peoples'.[150]

The physical environment in which people lived helped to shape their character. The French abbot Peter of Celle was of the opinion that *levitas*, the lack of intellectual soundness, characterized the English, since they have fantastic imaginations, dream a lot, and regard their dreams as true visions. The

---

[148] H. Hunt., p. 504.    [149] H. Hunt. 1. 8 (p. 24).
[150] W. Malm., *GR* 2. 116 (1, pp. 120–1); OMT edn., p. 176.

explanation is their watery island environment, which makes their brains humid.[151] The theory of climatic influence was particularly important to Gerald of Wales. He thought the quick-wittedness and loquacity of the Welsh could be explained by the nature of their original homeland, 'the hot, sun-burnt shore of Troy', while the English were cold and reticent, having come originally from chilly Germany.[152] Large-scale characterizations of racial psychology could be based on differences in physical environments: 'Because the air is subtler in the East, the people there are smaller in body but cleverer. Hence they conquer by poison rather than by strength and excel in skill rather than in fighting.'[153] Perhaps Gerald's most ingenious application of the theory was his idea that the devil cunningly adapted his temptations to the natural proclivities of the inhabitants of different regions. Since Europeans were cold, and hence avaricious, Satan suggested they become heretics and refuse to pay tithes, while to hot, and hence lustful Arabs, he suggested the attractions of polygamous Islam.[154]

Relations between the different peoples were characterized by hostile and ignorant stereotypes in the twelfth century as much as in the present day. The popular foreign notion of the English was of drunkards with tails. Where the idea of the tails came from is unclear, but it was widespread. The Sicilian Greeks among whom the English crusaders camped in the winter of 1190–1 called them 'tailed Englishmen' in derision.[155] The English responded in kind. Irish were barbaric, Normans proud. 'To be a German in comprehension' meant to be mentally slow.[156]

At the outer limits of racial consciousness lay black people. Scarcely known in England except as frightening figures in the romances or as oddities in such works as the *Marvels of the East*, African negroes raised the question of the limits of humanity, as is revealed in a short passage by the early thirteenth-century theologian Thomas of Chobham. He is discussing the power of the Church to define what was and what was not a valid marriage and admits that the limits of its authority in this matter were not fully clear. For example, it was uncertain whether the Church could decree that marriage could not take place between a white man and a black woman.[157] Thomas selected this example not because interracial marriage was a topical issue in England in John's reign but because it seemed to him an extreme limit of the imaginably permissible. Yes, both blacks and whites were human, hence it might seem that they could contract valid marriages; yet such a union verged on the outrageous and an ecclesiastical prohibition was thus not implausible.

---

[151] Peter of Celle, ep. 171 (*PL* 202, col. 614).    [152] Gerald, *Descr.* 1. 15 (pp. 192–3).

[153] Gerald, *Top.* 1. 37 (p. 71).    [154] Gerald, *Prin.* 1. 18 (p. 70).    [155] R. Devizes, p. 19.

[156] Robert of Bridlington, *The Bridlington Dialogue: An Exposition of the Rule of St Augustine for the Life of the Clergy*, ed. and tr. a religious of C.S.M.V. (London, 1960), p. 66.

[157] T. Chobham, *SC*, p. 192.

The teaching that we are all sons of Adam and daughters of Eve sometimes stumbled on the rocky protuberances of deep racial prejudice.

## 3. THE CHAIN OF BEING

### Angels and Demons

According to Peter of Cornwall, prior of Holy Trinity, Aldgate (1197–1221), three kinds of creatures possess vital spirits: those that have no bodies (angels), those that have bodies but whose spirit survives the body (human beings), and those whose spirit dies with the body (animals).[158] The hierarchy of living beings was thus threefold: angelic, human, animal. We shall see that there were also elusive creatures who did not quite fit into this simple schema, but it can serve as a typical and orthodox expression of the chain of being, as seen by a learned man of the period.

Because of the existence of angels, human beings were not the high point of created life. There were intelligent creatures above them and superior to them. Angels had a more subtle essence, a higher location, a more intimate familiarity with God, and a greater intellect than man.[159] They were divided into nine orders, each with a special role: 'the angelic citizens, enjoying eternal light, are distinguished by their merits and duties'. In descending order, the grades were seraphs, cherubs, thrones, dominions, principalities, powers, virtues, archangels, and (mere) angels. The principalities, to take an example, were responsible for the changing patterns of political power on earth.[160]

Devils and demons were, of course, originally angels and continued to possess many of the powers that were part of the angelic nature. It was possible, for instance, to employ witchcraft to sink an enemy's fleet, 'by the work of the devil, who can influence the physical elements very much through the power of his angelic nature'.[161] The fallen angels were still angels. Likewise, their knowledge far outstripped that of human beings. 'Demons have great knowledge of natural affairs,' explained Thomas of Chobham, 'both through the subtlety of their nature and the length of their days, so that they know the thoughts of men from certain external signs much more subtly and evidently than men do themselves.'[162] This was one of the reasons that demons might appear to have knowledge of the future, as discussed above (pp. 646–7).

---

[158] Peter Cornw., *Liber rev.*, fo. 3ᵛ.      [159] Gerald, *Top.* 1. 13 (p. 41).

[160] Alexander Nequam, *De laudibus divinae sapientiae* 1, lines 69–228, in Alex. Nequam, *DNR*, pp. 358–62.

[161] W. Newb. 3. 6 (1, p. 231).      [162] T. Chobham, *SC*, p. 474 (drawing on Augustine).

Although the theologians knew that angels did not have bodies, they also conceded that they might appear in corporeal form, as did demons. There are many stories of encounters with angels and demons and dozens of representations of them in the painting and sculpture of the period. Angels are depicted simply, as beardless human figures with wings (seraphs had three pairs). More gusto is evident in pictures of devils. Those on the Guthlac Roll of the late twelfth century have enormous ears, feathered wings, claws, hooked noses pointing up or down, and shaggy pelts. Those in the St Albans Psalter are similar, with wings, hides, clawed feet, large animal–like ears, and hooked noses. At this period devils still have feathered rather then bat-like wings, and horns and tail are optional. Painters clearly enjoyed portraying them. There is even a story of the devil remonstrating with an artist for depicting him as 'so foul and horrible'.[163]

Devils were also frequently encountered in animal form. A man from Kelloe in county Durham, who had gone out drinking with the village priest, was harassed on his way home by a pack of black dogs. These were no ordinary animals. When the drinker reached home he peered out of his window and saw a huge black dog. This leapt into his mouth and possessed him. Various remedies were applied in vain to restore him to himself, before the holy water of St Cuthbert achieved the desired exorcism.[164] The hermit Bartholomew of Farne was tempted on his remote island by the devil appearing in the shape of a mouse, lion, bull, ape, and cat.[165] Devils were presumed to be lurking everywhere and the natural elements needed to be exorcized before they could be safely used for sacred purposes. Baptism itself was an exorcism, with the priest addressing the following words to the devil in the baby: 'I command you, unclean spirit, to leave and depart from this servant of God!'[166]

Both angels and demons were deeply concerned with human beings:

The former display endless care for our well-being, the latter are always lying in wait for us; the former strive to bring us to their own regions, the latter endeavour to cast us into the lake of everlasting misery; the former gird us about with the wall of their protection, the latter make fierce attacks upon us, to compel us to surrender.[167]

A clash between demons and angels over a human soul that was witnessed by its terrified object took place around the sickbed of William of Corbeil (later to be archbishop of Canterbury). As he lay gravely ill in a house at Dover, a crowd of hideous demons rushed in and sat around him, gloating over what they would do to him. William then realized a lady was by his side and she told the demons they could not have him, 'for Michael, Gabriel and

---

[163] O. Cheriton, *Parabolae* 73 (p. 293).   [164] Reg., *Libellus* 17 (pp. 32–7).
[165] Geoffrey of Durham, *V. Bartholomaei Farnensis* 12, in Simeon, *Op.* 1, pp. 295–325, at p. 305.
[166] *Magd. Pont.*, p. 177.   [167] Alex. Nequam, *DNR* 1. 3 (p. 22).

Raphael will fight you for him'. The dispirited demons slunk off, but soon a much larger and more determined crowd came back. 'They appeared', reminisced William later, 'as ugly and terrifying as the ones you see painted on walls. They came to me wildly, armed with spears, pronged forks, tridents, iron forks, clubs and axes.' Once again, however, the lady—who was, of course, the Virgin Mary—told them that Michael, Gabriel, and Raphael would fight them and they eventually went off, grumbling 'we won't fight against them'. Mary disappeared and the three archangels entered. Their stature and beauty astounded William. When he recovered, to show his gratitude for the help he had received from the angels, those 'guardians assigned to us for our salvation', he frequently celebrated the 'mass of the angels'.[168]

William was defended by the three most well-known names in the angelic hierarchy. It was also believed that individuals might have a guardian angel permanently protecting them. When the pious Yorkshire peasant, Ketell of Farnham, forgot on one occasion to make the sign of the cross before sleep, he would have fallen into the power of two savage demons had not 'the man's angel', in the form of a shining young warrior, intervened.[169] 'It is a great comfort to human frailty', reflected an English priest on the Second Crusade, 'that everyone has a guardian angel assigned to him'.[170] There was need for such constant care, for the attention of the demons was equally unremitting and their hostility unquenchable. The devil was often simply termed 'the old enemy', while the word 'fiend' comes from the Old English *feond*—adversary, foe (modern German *Feind*). For good or evil, human beings were not alone.

## Animals

### Domesticated Animals

In the twelfth century humans and animals lived on intimate terms. Indeed, the presence of domesticated creatures was a sign of human habitation: to a wanderer in a forest the sound of dogs barking and cocks crowing showed 'where one could find a settlement'.[171] This intermingling occurred in towns as well as villages. One of the dangers faced by sick people begging in the streets of Salisbury was that the wandering pigs and dogs might harm them.[172] Archaeology has confirmed this picture of humans and animals on close terms, for many of the peasant dwellings of the period clearly housed both the family and some at least of the livestock under one roof. Affection grew up naturally between humans and the animals with whom they spent so much time. A story attributed to court raconteur Walter Map describes a rich

[168] Alexander of Canterbury, *Dicta Anselmi* 52, ed. R. W. Southern and F. S. Schmitt, *Memorials of St Anselm* (Oxford, 1969), pp. 266–8.
[169] W. Newb. 2. 21 (1, pp. 152–3).        [170] *De exp. Lyxb.*, p. 147.
[171] Marie de France, *Le Fresne*, lines 144–6 (*Lais*, p. 38).        [172] *Can. Osmund*, p. 39.

man going out in the evening, with a servant holding a light, to visit his oxen, 'going to each of them, shaking up their food, running his hand along their backbones with warm encouragement, instructing each to eat by its own name'.[173]

Domesticated animals fell into various categories that overlapped only slightly. There were those that worked for you, notably oxen and draught horses; there were those that were eaten, such as pigs, sheep, beef cattle, and fowl; there were those that hunted with you, like superior horses, dogs, and trained birds of prey. The only animal that fell into more than one class was the ox, that could be eaten once its working life was over (although it would be tough). Indeed, one of the reasons oxen were preferred to horses as plough beasts was that their value could be much more nearly recouped from sale for slaughter.

In twelfth-century England the common (although not universal) human distinction was maintained between domesticated herbivores, that were eaten, and domesticated carnivores, that were not. Dogs and cats, the latter only semi-domestic, were familiar in human dwellings but not in cooking pots or on tables. Cattle and sheep were eaten, although they might be raised primarily for their labour, their milk, or their hides and fleeces—not to mention their dung. The largest domesticated herbivore, however, the horse, was taboo. The Christian missionaries of the early Middle Ages had attempted to stop the Germanic peoples from eating horseflesh and a clause from a legatine council held in Mercia in the 790s shows that this crusade reached England.[174] Evidence from the twelfth century suggests that horse-meat was eaten only in abnormal circumstances. Starving garrisons under siege might have recourse to this desperate measure. The knights besieged in Carham (Wark) in 1138 killed, salted, and ate their horses and the rebels garrisoning Rochester in 1215 were forced to eat their warhorses. If we can believe the Welsh chronicler describing the hungry English army besieging Degannwy in 1211, it was not only the besieged who might have to descend to this level. 'It was a luxurious feast', he wrote, 'for them to have the flesh of their horses.' The context shows that these are exceptional situations and, in the last case, we may have a merely rhetorical flourish.[175]

Sheep may have been the commonest animals in England in this period (see above, pp. 306–8), but the records suggest that more care and attention were given to those companions of the aristocracy, the horse, hound, and

---

[173] Map, appendix (p. 515).

[174] *Councils and Ecclesiastical Documents*, ed. A. W. Haddan and W. Stubbs (3 vols.; Oxford, 1869–78), vol. 3, p. 459.

[175] R. Hexham, p. 171; R. Wend. 2, p. 149 (Paris, *CM* 2, p. 625); *Brut (RBH)*, p. 191; cf. the comments of John Langdon, *Horses, Oxen and Technological Innovation: The Use of Draught Animals in English Farming from 1066 to 1500* (Cambridge, 1986), p. 263 n. 43.

hawk. One sign of this attention is the multiplicity and complexity of terms used for types of horse or hound. Horses were differentiated into chargers, hunters, palfreys, and rounceys, as well as the humbler draught-horses, pack-horses, and farm-horses. Differences of function were reflected in price, with farm-horses valued at around 3s. 4d. in the second half of the twelfth century, while the knightly warhorse would cost between 30s. and 60s., with isolated examples reaching 10 marks (£6. 13s. 4d.).[176] The most expensive warhorse was thus worth 36 times as much as the average farm-horse. Such distinctions between kinds or breeds are not only economic facts, but argue also that humans dealing with the horse must have had a particularly developed and nuanced vocabulary and set of categories for those animals. Similarly, hunting dogs were classified as greyhounds, running-hounds, lyam-hounds (trackers), spaniels, etc. The complexity of the categorization is a consequence of the intensity of human attention.

A related issue is the practice of naming individual animals. This can be viewed in more than one light. On the one hand, only certain types of animal are usually given individual names—one names one's horse, but not usually the 200 sheep in the field. The practice thus picks out certain species for treatment almost on a par with humans. On the other hand, animals are usually given names that are distinct from those given to human beings. Hence individual naming simultaneously brings humans and (some) animals closer and distances them. Unlike sheep and like people, dogs and horses can be called by individual names; yet the names they are called by are not human names.

It is not surprising, given both the nature of the practice and the nature of the evidence, that the recorded animal names are those of aristocratic hunting beasts. Around the year 1200, in order to secure his office as usher to the earl of Chester and the land that went with the position, Ranulf of Merton gave to the earl 'two greyhounds [lepores] called Lym and Libekar'.[177] King John's horses were well known enough for an offer to be made to the king of 'a good hunter, like Liardus, the king's hunter'.[178] John's favourite gerfalcon (the great northern falcon) was called Gibbun. In 1215 the king not only found the time to seal Magna Carta, but also took care to send off 'three gerfalcons and the gerfalcon Gibbun—we have none better than him' to be placed in the mews.[179] His son, Henry III, continued these interests. When he was young, Henry had gerfalcons called Refuse and Blakeman, which were given special attention, even meriting a mention in the annual royal audit.[180]

[176] Hallam, Agrarian Hist., p. 748; R. H. C. Davis, The Medieval Warhorse: Origin, Development and Redevelopment (London, 1989), p. 82; PR 25 HII, p. 83; PR 10 RI, p. 38.

[177] Chester Charters, no. 271, pp. 269–70.    [178] PR 12 John, p. 93.

[179] Rot. litt. claus. 1, p. 192.

[180] PR 3 HIII, p. 92; PR 4 HIII, p. 149; PR 5 HIII, p. 74; Rot. litt. claus. 1, pp. 400, 401, 407, 412.

It is not always clear what these names mean. *Gibbun* may be connected with the medieval French *giboier*, 'to hunt with falcons', although it is possibly derived from the word for 'hunchback'. *Refuse* could be 'one who flies back' or 'one who refuses' (definitely a later technical hunting term). *Blakeman* is English, and means 'dark-haired man', and is, exceptionally, also recorded as a human personal name. These names were clearly used for purposes of identification ('a good hunter, like *Liardus*') but also probably for address. Contemporary learned belief was that of all animals, dogs alone recognize their names, but riders and falconers doubtless ignored this in practice.[181] Nor, as the story from Walter Map quoted above shows, did landlords disdain naming their oxen and calling them by name.

Naming is but one sign of the affective link that might tie humans and individual animals. Human-canine relations were particularly idealized. 'Dogs,' wrote the court cleric Gerald of Wales, 'more than any other beast, love and recognize human beings. Sometimes they even refuse to go on living when their master dies and they do not fear to engage in mortal struggle for him.'[182] Gervase of Tilbury was equally enthusiastic: dogs 'are possessive about those they love and, loving their master and home, they guard them out of a conscious and careful love'.[183] The emotional bond is especially evident in the case of pets, animals kept for companionship and entertainment, without any role as food, labour, or even hunting comrade. There is some, but slight, evidence for pet-keeping in the twelfth century. The Cistercian abbot Ailred of Rievaulx criticized monks and nuns who kept tame animals simply for pleasure. Cranes and hares, does and stags, magpies and crows 'have nothing to do with monastic poverty and only feed the eyes of the curious'.[184] Significantly, Ailred's list does not include dogs or cats, which were primarily working animals at this time.

## Captive Animals

In a sense all domesticated animals were captive animals, but the strong sense of the word may be kept for those animals who were chained and barred. Among these was the bear, the most important of the non-indigenous animals that were sometimes imported for entertainment. Bear-baiting had taken place in England since the Anglo-Saxon period, for before the Conquest one of the duties of the inhabitants of Norwich was to provide the king with 'a bear and six dogs for the bear'.[185] Doubtless the bear was imported from Scandinavia. The practice of bear-baiting continued in the twelfth century. In his description of the sports of Londoners, written in the 1170s,

---

[181] e.g. Oxford, Bodleian Library, MS Ashmole 1511, fo. 25.
[182] Gerald, *Itin.* 1. 7 (p. 70).   [183] Gerv. Tilb. 1. 9 (p. 891).
[184] Ailr. Riev., *Speculum caritatis* 2. 24 (*Op. asc.*, p. 99).   [185] *DB* 2, 117 (Nfk. 1. 61).

William fitz Stephen mentions the baiting of boars, bulls, and bears by dogs as a winter entertainment.[186] Some bears, however, may have been kept as permanent curiosities rather than for baiting. In 1175 money was paid to 'the king's bear and bear-keeper', who were at Nottingham, and there was also expenditure on the repair of the bear's chain; the following year money was paid out for their expenses in travelling from Nottingham to Winchester.[187] A trained bear with its keeper is represented in a drawing from a Rochester manuscript of around 1120. The bear is muzzled and on a leash, while its keeper beats it with a stick as it makes a valiant effort to learn the alphabet.[188]

The Tower of London is famous for its history as a state prison. In this period its captives also included animals. This is where king John kept his lion, and the royal accounts record payments to its keepers and the costs of an iron gate and chain for it.[189] Such imported animals were, of course, expensive rarities. Kings were the only ones rich enough to indulge their curiosity and exhibit their power by gathering beasts from distant lands. Henry I had a passion for exotic animals and created a menagerie at the royal palace at Woodstock, where he kept the lions, leopards, lynxes, and camels that he acquired from foreign rulers. Amongst them was a porcupine, sent by William of Montpellier. The chronicler William of Malmesbury saw it there and described its quills, 'more than a palm in length, sharp at both ends, like a goose feather where the plumage ends but a little thicker, and speckled black and white'.[190] The broadening of the knowledge of natural history went hand in hand with the display of the king's international status.

### Animals of the Wild

If humans encountered domesticated animals in a variety of roles, as food, labour, companions, and entertainment, they saw wild animals in a much simpler way—as prey. The mammals and fowl of the English countryside were all hunted. None of them hunted humans in turn. Not all animals were hunted to be eaten; some were wanted for their fur, some were hunted down as vermin. The wide range of hunted creatures is illustrated in the rights granted to Thomas of Milton, warden of Inglewood Forest in Cumberland from 1222 to 1265. He was permitted to hunt 'hare, fox, wild cat, badger, otter, marten, and squirrel' within his bailiwick; only the royal beasts—deer and boar—were excluded.[191]

---

[186] W. f. Stephen, *V. Thomas* 17 (p. 11).     [187] PR 21 HII, p. 29; PR 22 HII, pp. 90–1.

[188] Cambridge, Trinity College MS O. 4. 7, reproduced in *Engl. Rom. Art*, no. 42, p. 107; T. S. R. Boase, *English Art, 1100–1216* (Oxford, 1953), pl. 7c; compare his pl. 7a, a similar illustration from a contemporary Canterbury manuscript.

[189] PR 13 John, pp. 109–10; PR 14 John, p. 44.

[190] W. Malm., *GR* 5. 409 (2, p. 485); OMT edn., p. 740.

[191] *Calendar of Inquisitions Miscellaneous* I (London, 1916), no. 471, p. 156; Raymond Grant, *The Royal Forests of England* (Gloucester, 1991), p. 104.

It is possible to piece together a picture of the variety and distribution of wild animals in England in this period. The largest predator surviving in twelfth-century England was the wolf. The evidence of place names suggests that wolves had once been common in Anglo–Saxon England, since there are over 200 places named after wolves, like Woolley ('wolves' *leah*, or wood') and Woolmer ('wolves' *mere*, or lake'), distributed most densely in the upland regions,[192] and twelfth-century references show that wolves were still not at all unusual in the English countryside and could be a danger to livestock. Alexander Nequam, in a work written in the 1180s, advises the country-dweller to have traps for catching wolves and to retain an oxherd and shep-herd 'because of wolf attacks'.[193] The use of wolf-traps is borne out by a reference to their purchase in the Peak District in 1167 and the reality of the threat by a mention, in 1209, of two colts on the bishop of Winchester's manor of Marden in Hampshire that were eaten by wolves.[194]

Financial incentives were offered to those willing to undertake the haz-ardous task of ridding the countryside of wolves. By John's reign (1199–1216) the bounty paid for catching a wolf was the substantial sum of five shillings. In December 1209 the doorkeepers Richard Luverez (the name means 'wolf-catcher') and Odo were given fifteen shillings for two wolves captured at Gillingham (Dorset) and one at Clarendon, both places royal hunting-lodges.[195] In May 1212 the king authorized payment of five shillings to Stephen of Guildford, servant of Master Ernaldus of Auckland, a clerk in royal service, for the wolf his dogs had captured at the royal lodge of Free-mantle, and in the following November the doorkeepers Norman and Willekin Dogget received ten shillings for two wolves they had caught in the forest of Treville in Herefordshire.[196] Clearly the king's attendants were catch-ing wolves in the royal hunting grounds of the south and west, in ones or twos, at varying seasons of the year, and earning a generous bonus for doing so.

More permanent establishments were also maintained specifically to deal with wolves. A description of the royal household drawn up in the 1130s refers to the king's wolf-hunters (*luparii*), who received a daily payment for themselves, their horses, men, and dogs, as well as an annual sum for pur-chasing horses; they were to have a pack of 24 running-hounds and 8 grey-hounds.[197] From 1166 to 1209 the sheriff of Worcester paid an annual retainer of three shillings to 'the huntsman who catches wolves'.[198] In 1225 it was

---

[192] C. Aybes and D. W. Yalden, 'Place-Name Evidence for the Former Distribution and Status of Wolves and Beavers in Britain', *Mammal Review*, 25 (1995), pp. 201–26.

[193] Alex. Nequam, *Ut.*, p. 111.

[194] PR 13 HII, p. 140; *The Pipe Roll of the Bishopric of Winchester 1208–1209*, ed. Hubert Hall (London, 1903), p. 36.

[195] *Rot. lib.*, p. 144.    [196] Ibid., pp. 233, 246–7.    [197] *Const. domus regis*, p. 135.

[198] PR 13 HII—PR 12 John, *passim*.

reported that William de Leveriz (probably another 'wolf' name) held his land at Cowesfield (Wilts.), from the king 'for the service of catching wolves in the king's forest'.[199] Fostered in these diverse ways, through the royal household, local payments, and service tenures, the fight between human beings and wolves, England's fiercest and second fiercest mammals, went on.

The extinction and arrival of animals can sometimes be traced. Beavers, for instance, seem to have died out in England by the twelfth century. According to the Anglo-Saxon place name evidence, they had never been very common, with only 20 places having beaver names.[200] Gerald of Wales, writing around 1191, explicitly states that there are no beavers in England, and that they are extremely rare in Wales and Ireland.[201] The correlation between the disappearance of beavers and increasing density of human settlement is well established. By the later Middle Ages beaver pelts, along with the fur of other cold-forest animals, were a major import into western Europe from north-eastern Europe.

One of the most important additions to the fauna of England during our period was the rabbit.[202] Although the hare is native to England, rabbits were originally restricted to Spain and spread only gradually to other parts of Europe. This prolific and edible mammal reached the islands off the south and west coast of England by the late twelfth century. The earliest written record comes from the Scilly Isles in 1176, in a document whereby Richard de Wyka granted to Tavistock abbey 'all my tithes from Scilly, and expressly those from the rabbits, which I had kept back unjustly because I did not think tithes were given from such things'.[203] Rabbits are then mentioned on Lundy Island between 1183 and 1219. The earliest mainland reference appears to be a grant of land by Simon le Bret to the canons of Waltham (Essex) dating to the period 1187–94, in which he mentions that he once had a rabbit warren (*cunicularium*) there.[204] The next mention of rabbits in England occurs in a grant made by king John in 1209, allowing William Picot to hunt roe-deer, hare, rabbit, pheasant, and partridge on his lands in Lincolnshire.[205] The first English illustration of a rabbit is that in the bestiary in Fitzwilliam Museum manuscript 254, dated to the 1220s.[206] For a long while rabbits were a rarity. It is no surprise that when Alexander Nequam, writing in the 1180s, lists the

[199] *CRR* 12, p. 171.

[200] C. Aybes and D. W. Yalden, 'Place-Name Evidence for the Former Distribution and Status of Wolves and Beavers in Britain', *Mammal Review*, 25 (1995), pp. 201–26.

[201] Gerald, *Itin.* 2. 3 (pp. 114–15) ('Loegria' is a pedantic term for England).

[202] See Elspeth Veale, *The English Fur Trade in the Later Middle Ages* (Oxford, 1966), app. B, pp. 209–14, 'The Rabbit in England'.

[203] H. P. R. Finberg, 'Some Early Tavistock Charters', *EHR* 62 (1947), pp. 352–77, at p. 365.

[204] *Early Waltham Charters*, no. 450, p. 308.        [205] *Rot. chart.*, p. 185.

[206] Fo. 22ᵛ; Francis Wormald and Phyllis Giles, *A Descriptive Catalogue of the Additional Illuminated Manuscripts in the Fitzwilliam Museum* (2 vols.; Cambridge, 1982) 1, pp. 178–84.

animals that might be caught in the country, he refers to hares, fallow deer, roe-deer, and red deer, but does not mention rabbit.[207] They were first served at the king's table at Christmas, 1240. Rabbits continued to be an expensive food in the later thirteenth and early fourteenth centuries, costing four or five times as much as chicken.

As the references already cited from royal grants make clear, the freedom to hunt wild animals was not a birthright. Indeed, after 1066 England had an extremely intrusive and oppressive system for regulating hunting rights. In areas designated 'Forest', the king had a monopoly on hunting deer and boar. No one living in these areas was to have a bow and arrows or hunting dogs. Woodland could not be cleared. A special court, applying special law, the Forest Law, met in the Forest to deal with Forest offences. The punishment of mutilation is mentioned in the legislation regarding the Forest, although in records of actual cases heavy fines are usually the worst punishment. Even so, the disruption that might follow an accusation under Forest Law could be great. When venison was found in the house of Hugh the Scot in Shropshire in 1209, he fled to the refuge of the church. He confessed to the foresters that he had killed a hind (a female red deer). Unwilling to leave sanctuary, he stayed in the church a month and then escaped disguised as a woman. He disappears from the court records as proceedings for outlawry are about to begin.[208]

One unexpected consequence of the Forest Law regime that the Norman kings imposed upon England, and of the hatred that it inspired, was a new level of self-consciousness about the place of wild animals. The pressures of the Law brought to the minds of its critics questions about the ownership of wild animals and about the relative value of human and animal life. Roman Law taught that, until captured, wild animals were nobody's property (*res nullius*) and that, by the law of nations (*ius gentium*), they belonged to whoever captured them, whether the capture took place on the huntsman's own land or that of someone else.[209] This teaching was familiar to the learned men of the twelfth century. In his diatribe against hunting and, especially, the cruelty of the English Forest Law, John of Salisbury appeals to this principle:

Some people do not fear to ruin a man on account of a beast . . . human presumption dares to claim for itself things that are wild by nature and become the property of whoever captures them . . . you had heard that the birds of the air and the fish of the sea are common to all, but those that are hunted, wherever they fly, belong to the royal estate.[210]

His outrage had some foundation. The Forest Law went far beyond the

---

[207] Alex. Nequam, *Ut.*, p. 112.
[208] *Select Pleas of the Forest*, ed. G. J. Turner (Selden Soc. 13; 1899), p. 9.
[209] *Institutes* 2. 1. 12.      [210] J. Salisb., *Policr.* 1. 4 (1, pp. 30–1).

protection of the king's hunting on his own land. 'Forest' was an area defined legally. It was not a particular kind of natural terrain, nor need it be royal demesne. Hence the Forest Law, with its fierce assertion of the monopoly of the king's right to hunt deer and boar, applied to the farms, grazing land, and commons of many landholders within the Forest. While neither Roman Law nor Forest Law gave any privilege to the landowner in matters of hunting, the former asserted that anyone could hunt on the land, the latter prohibited the landowner from hunting even on his own land.

The Forest Assizes of 1184 and 1198 prescribe blinding and castration as a punishment for those who take deer or boar within the Forest and describe this as the practice also of the time of Henry I.[211] Offenders seem sometimes to have suffered capital punishment. For the critics of Forest Law this was a cruelly inappropriate equation of human and animal life. One passionate critic of Henry II made this unjust estimation of the relative weight of human life a main charge against him: 'In revenge for irrational wild animals, which ought by natural law to be available to all in common, he had either punished by death or cruelly mutilated in their limbs human beings, who employ reason, are saved by the same blood of Christ and share the same nature in equality.'[212] Here the Roman Law doctrine that wild animals are free to all is harnessed to the biblical tradition of man's especial place in Creation, as made in the image of God. The argument now left the sphere of property rights and turned on the relative significance of humans and animals. As the Canterbury monk, Nigel Wireker, put it:

Although man is created in the image of Him who made all things from nothing, kings regard the beasts of the earth more highly than man and think of the human race as more vile. How many wretches have they hanged on the gallows for taking the flesh of wild animals! Sicilian tyrants could command nothing worse than the death of a human being for killing a wild beast.[213]

The wild woods were, in some ways, the least free places in England.

## Animals of the Imagination

Some of the most remarkable animals of twelfth-century England were found neither in the fields nor in the woods but in books. This is the great age of the bestiary.[214]

---

[211] Gesta Hen. II 1, p. 323; R. Howd. 4, p. 63.
[212] Vis. Eynsham, p. 348.      [213] Nigel, Spec. Stult., lines 2563–70, p. 88.
[214] See, in general, M. R. James, The Bestiary (Roxburghe Club; 1928); F. McCulloch, Mediaeval Latin and French Bestiaries (Chapel Hill, NC, 1960); Francis Klingender, Animals in Art and Thought: To the End of the Middle Ages (London, 1971), pp. 382–97; Xenia Muratova, 'I manoscritti miniati del bestiario medievale: origine, formazione e sviluppo dei cicli di illustrazioni. I bestiari miniati in Inghilterra nei secoli XII–XIV', in L'Uomo di fronte al mondo animale nell'alto medioevo (Settimane di Studio del Centro Italiano di Studi sull'Alto Medioevo 31, 2 vols.; 1985), vol. 2, pp. 1319–62, with plates I–XXXVII;

The bestiaries that were produced in twelfth-century England contain descriptions and usually illustrations of a variety of animals, as many as a hundred or more in the elaborate versions made in the later twelfth century. Some of these creatures are familiar, like the fox and boar, or even domestic, like the dog; others, such as the lion and elephant, are exotic and are represented in conventional forms that were certainly not based on direct observation; others still are clearly fabulous, being either impossible hybrids, such as griffins, or creatures of legend, like the unicorn. The text accompanying the illustrations tells something of the habits (real or legendary) of the creature and concludes with a moral lesson or theological application. So, for instance, the entry about the beaver tells the story that it is hunted for the medicinal properties of its testicles and, in order to save its life, castrates itself and throws them in front of the hunters. This was moralized in the following way: 'similarly anyone trying to follow God's commandments and live chastely cuts off from himself all vices and shameless deeds and throws them before the devil. Then he sees that they have nothing of his and goes off in confusion.'

There was a long tradition behind the bestiary of twelfth-century England. The starting point is a work known as the *Physiologus*, produced by a Greek author in the early centuries of Christianity, in which real and legendary creatures of the Mediterranean world are described and interpreted as symbols of aspects of the Christian faith. The *Physiologus* was later translated into Latin, circulated, and copied during the Carolingian Renaissance and eventually imported into England. During this long process of transmission, the text was augmented by additional material, drawn from such authors as the ancient natural historian Solinus; St Ambrose, who had written a *Hexaemeron*, describing the work of Creation; and the seventh-century Christian encyclopedist Isidore of Seville. The bestiary text is thus a compilation and, because different passages were added at different times and places, no two versions are identical. Four 'families' of bestiary texts have been identified, according to the material they incorporate. Nevertheless, there is still a large amount of common material in the different manuscripts termed bestiaries. The earliest bestiary from England is a Bodleian Library manuscript, which dates from the 1120s.[215] At exactly this same period the French poet, Philip de Thaon, composed his vernacular *Bestiaire* for Queen Adeliza, wife of Henry I.[216] Thereafter, the bestiary was to flourish in England,

---

Willene B. Clark and Meradith T. McMunn (eds.), *Beasts and Birds of the Middle Ages: The Bestiary and its Legacy* (Philadelphia, 1989); Wilma George and Brunsdon Yapp, *The Naming of the Beasts: Natural History in the Medieval Bestiary* (London, 1991); Debra Hassig, *Medieval Bestiaries: Text, Image, Ideology* (Cambridge, 1995); Ron Baxter, *Bestiaries and their Users in the Middle Ages* (Stroud, 1998).

[215] MS Laud. misc. 247.

[216] Philip de Thaon, *Bestiaire*, ed. Emmanuel Walberg (Lund, 1900).

especially from the later twelfth century when spectacular luxury illustrated examples were produced.

The beautiful illustrated bestiaries of twelfth-century England were obviously not zoological treatises, based on observation and intended for practical use. They were celebrations of the variety and strangeness of the created world and often began with the passages from Genesis in which God created animals, birds, and fish and Adam named them. The moral or allegorical lesson was central. One could learn from animals. God had created them with a message for us. Their arresting idiosyncrasies were not simply wonderful quirks of the natural world but also had moral or mystical significance.

Manuscript Ashmole 1511 in the Bodleian Library at Oxford is a perfect example of the opulent bestiaries produced around the year 1200.[217] It is about 12 inches by 8 inches in size and is illustrated throughout with rich paintings on a background of gold leaf. Its text belongs to the so-called 'Second Family' and treats the animal world systematically, dealing first with land creatures, mainly mammals, then birds, and finally reptiles. Some 200 animals (and plants) are named, some with full descriptions, others with a mere mention. A vivid preface is provided by illustrations of the Creation. 'In the beginning God created the heaven and the earth', the text begins, and we have several almost full-page illustrations of God going about his work, fashioning the fish, birds, and reptiles on the fifth day and the land animals and man on the sixth. Then follows the scene of Adam naming the animals. They come, lion and stag, cat (holding a mouse), and hare, dutifully to receive their names, while Adam, enthroned and fully clothed, holds his hand raised in a commanding gesture. Lacking the power of speech, the animals cannot name themselves. It is a human prerogative to give order to the animal world by labelling and distinguishing. In words taken, like much else in the bestiary, from Isidore of Seville, the scene is described: 'It was Adam who first named all the animals, giving a name to each one according to the natural condition it served in the present arrangement of things.'[218]

The first animal described is the lion, the king of the beasts. We then encounter the elephant with its castle on its back, the self-castrating beaver, the unicorn that can be captured only by a virgin—'our Lord Jesus Christ is the unicorn in the spiritual sense'. There are some very naturalistic illustrations, of creatures such as the bat and owl, alongside images of the mermaid (siren) and phoenix. The spirit of Isidore's etymological enthusiasms is maintained: cats are called cats because they *cat*ch mice (*catum a captura vocant*). A powerful tradition and a powerful imagination alike can be sensed

[217] *Bestiarium: Vollständige Faksimile-Ausgabe im Originalformat* (MS Ashmole 1511) (Codices selecti 76; Graz, 1982); *Bestiarium: die Texte der Handschrift MS. Ashmole 1511 der Bodleian Library Oxford in lateinischer und deutscher Sprache*, ed. Franz Unterkircher (Interpretationes ad codices 3; Graz, 1986).

[218] Isidore of Seville, *Etymologiae* 12. 1. 1, ed. W. M. Lindsay (2 vols.; Oxford, 1911) (no pagination).

in the painting. The entry on the tiger tells how the beast, that is 'speckled, strong and wonderfully swift', will pursue a hunter who takes its young, but can be tricked if the hunter throws down a mirror. Seeing the image, it thinks the small tiger in the mirror is its cub and tries to suckle it and meanwhile the hunter escapes. The illustration in Ashmole 1511 shows a mounted knight in mail-coat and helmet with nose-guard, girded with a sword, carrying off a tiny tiger cub. The tigress is depicted as a blue beast covered with red and white speckles, with a long tail and a sheep-like face, with curly hair on top and longish ears pointing outwards.

The case of the crocodile is representative of the unusual blend of natural history, moralization, theological ingenuity, and visual creativity to be found in the bestiary.[219] There are two main entries dealing with this creature, one under its own name and one treating of its enemy the *hydrus*, a kind of water-snake. The first passage begins, characteristically, with a citation from Isidore, telling us that crocodiles are called crocodiles because they are crocus-coloured (*croceus*, 'yellow'), that they are huge, tough-skinned quad-rupeds found in the Nile, equally at home on land and in the water, and armed with fearsome teeth and claws. They lay eggs, that are tended by both the male and female, they are preyed on by a kind of sawfish and move only their upper jaw. Much of this material Isidore had himself taken from the classical tradition of animal lore going back to the *Natural History* of Pliny the Elder, a vast encyclopaedia of the first century AD. The bestiary contains the additional remark that crocodile dung is used by aged whores as rejuvenating cream, although its effects are only temporary. Under the heading *hydrus*, the crocodile figures as the victim of this water-snake, which covers itself in lubricating mud, slides down the crocodile's throat and, destroying its intestines, comes out intact from the crocodile's body.

Both passages are vividly illustrated and the crocodile is recognizably the same beast in each drawing (Plate 14). It is a huge yellow quadruped with long legs and talons, sharp, dagger-like teeth, and a spiky ridge along its back that continues into its tail. There is no hint here of the low reptilian posture of the actual Nile crocodile. In the first scene the creature is eating a man head first, in the second it lies on its back dead, while the serpentine *hydrus* entwines itself through the corpse, entering its mouth, emerging from a hole in its neck, re-entering the crocodile's body and finally coming out of a huge gap in its underside. Both passages are given a symbolic application. In the first case the crocodile stands for hypocrites. Just as the crocodile spends its nights in

---

[219] Wilma George and Brunsdon Yapp, *The Naming of the Beasts: Natural History in the Medieval Bestiary* (London, 1991), pp. 97–9; F. McCulloch, *Mediaeval Latin and French Bestiaries* (Chapel Hill, NC, 1960), pp. 106–8; George C. Druce, 'The Symbolism of the Crocodile in the Middle Ages', *Archaeological Jnl* 66 (1909), pp. 311–38.

the water and its days on land, so hypocrites 'live lecherously but neverthe-less love to be said to live holy and just lives'. The movement of the upper jaw signifies their sanctimonious exhortations, which they themselves ignore in practice, the short-lived ointment made from the crocodile's dung symbol-izes the way 'many evil people are praised by the inexperienced and raised up in the favour of this world for the wickedness they have done, as if it were an ointment, but when the strict judge sets in motion his anger against the evils that have been committed, then all this pleasant praise vanishes like smoke.' The hydrus story is interpreted in a theological rather than a moral sense: 'death and hell are represented by the crocodile, whose enemy is Jesus Christ. For he assumed human flesh and descended into hell, destroying its insides and leading out those who were unjustly held there.' The story of the croco-dile and the hydrus is thus an emblem of the harrowing of hell, when Jesus descended into hell after the crucifixion and led out Adam and the other righteous men and women who had been waiting there since their deaths. The ancient natural history that serves as the foundation of this account of the crocodile, the ingenuity of the moral and theological interpretations, the creative visual imagination, are all characteristic of the treatment of animals in the bestiary tradition.

While there was clearly a traditional series of interpretations, the moral or theological significance given to bestiary animals was not completely immut-able. Certain traits and allegories might be found in one set of texts but not in another, while an ingenious commentator could come up with his own symbolic expositions. Thus, for instance, the idea that the crocodile cries when it devours men—the origin of the phrase 'crocodile tears'—is in Philip de Thaon's *Bestiaire* and in Alexander Nequam's *De naturis rerum*, where it is put in pithy rhyming Latin: 'crocodrillus hominem vorat et plorat' ('The crocodile weeps when it devours a man').[220] The idea does not crop up, how-ever, in the main bestiary texts produced in twelfth-century England. Nequam's interpretation of the fact that the crocodile moves only its upper jaw is also very different from that in the usual bestiary text. After explaining that eating is a common image for bible reading and that scripture should inspire us with both hope and fear, he announces that the crocodile's upper jaw represents hope and the lower fear. People who have fear without hope are driven to despair, but people who have hope but not fear presume too much, expecting everything to go well. 'These presumptuous types are designated by the crocodile . . . they eat, as it were, only with the upper jaw, for their hopes are overconfident, not being corrected by fear.' Such elaborate and singular interpretations could be the subject of admiration. One of the enthusiasts for the elaborate allegories of animal life to be found in Gerald

---

[220] Alex. Nequam, *DNR* 2. 101 (p. 185).

of Wales's *Topography of Ireland* was Baldwin of Ford, archbishop of Canterbury. Where, he asked Gerald, had he got his 'theological moralizations and allegories'? Was it from the standard exegetes and commentators? Gerald replied, not completely truthfully, that he had devised them himself. 'Indeed,' said Baldwin, 'you and they must have had the same inspiration!'[221]

It is difficult to say much about who actually saw and read bestiaries, for there is not often sufficient evidence to establish where and for whom they were produced.[222] One exception is the deluxe manuscript Pierpont Morgan 81, which was given in 1187 by Philip, canon of Lincoln, to the Augustinian priory of Worksop in Nottinghamshire 'for the edification of the brethren'.[223] Illustrated bestiaries produced in the 1220s were owned by the Benedictine priory of Holy Trinity, York, the Augustinian priory of Newark at Albury in Surrey, and Rochester cathedral, while the Cistercians of Holm Cultram in Cumbria had a twelfth-century copy of Philip de Thaon's unillustrated *Bestiaire*.[224] Perhaps the typical 'audience' for the great English bestiaries would have been a group of monks or canons clustered around a lectern, entertained and charmed by the illustrations and listening earnestly to the moral and theological symbolism, possibly mentally noting these allegories for use in any preaching or homiletic work they themselves might undertake.

Bestiary images were actually used in sermons and other edifying literature. In his treatise on the perfect monk, Baldwin of Ford, who was a Cistercian abbot before he became archbishop of Canterbury, makes the following remarks when commenting on a biblical passage that mentions ivory: 'They say that ivory is elephant bone. The elephant is an animal constructed on a framework of bones so strong and steady that it can carry war machines and fortifications built on its back. Just so is the fortitude of the saints, which has, like ivory among bones, the surpassing glory of solidity, strength and beauty.'[225] Although Baldwin was to end his days in Palestine on the Third Crusade, he spent most of his life in the west and south of England and it is very unlikely that he had seen an elephant when he wrote this. Pictures of elephants, however, he clearly had seen, and the bestiary tradition invariably

---

[221] Gerald, *Spec. duorum*, pp. 170–2; Gerald, *De jure et statu Menevensis ecclesiae* 7 (*Op.* 3, pp. 334–5); Gerald, *Epistola . . . de libris a se scriptis* (*Op.* 1, p. 410).

[222] Xenia Muratova, 'Bestiaries: An Aspect of Medieval Patronage', in Sarah Macready and F. H. Thompson (eds.), *Art and Patronage in the English Romanesque* (London, 1986), pp. 118–44.

[223] Inscription *ad edificationem fratrum* on fo. 1ᵛ.

[224] MSS Oxford, St Johns 61; Bodleian Library, Bodley 602; BL Royal 12 F xiii; BL Cotton Nero A v; for provenance, see N. R. Ker, *Medieval Libraries of Great Britain: A List of Surviving Books* (2nd edn.; London, 1964).

[225] Baldwin, *Sermo* 1. 31 (*Tractatus* 16), *Op.*, p. 14 (*PL* 204, col. 568); the biblical reference is Lamentations 4: 7.

depicted elephants bearing castles on their backs. The illustration in Ashmole 1511 (although later than Baldwin's time) shows an elephant surmounted by a castle and four armoured knights, one of whom controls it by a chain through the tip of its trunk. An image of this type was obviously in Baldwin's mind. What is certain is that Baldwin was not interested in elephants as living creatures. On the whole he uses imagery from the bestiary very rarely.[226] Sparked by a biblical mention of ivory, he thought of elephants. The picture that would spring to his mind was not based on a visit to the zoo but on a depiction of the elephant and castle lodged in the back of his mind. He would know this either from perusing a bestiary or from looking at carvings or paintings derived from the bestiary. He 'knew' that elephants were strong enough to carry castles because bestiary lore permeated the learned culture of twelfth-century England.

Baldwin need not have obtained his image of the elephant from a book, for bestiary animals were frequently depicted in stone. A striking example is the twelfth-century church at Alne, ten miles north of York, where the arch of the south doorway is decorated with carved animals which can be identified not only by their iconographic features but also by the carved labels identifying them as 'fox', 'panther', 'eagle', and so on. They are in classic bestiary poses, the fox, for instance, lying on its back and pretending to be dead in order to lure down birds that it then catches as prey. In this way bestiary imagery could reach a wider public that did not necessarily have access to the big books.

The moralization of animals occurs in places other than the bestiary. Animal fables also used animal characters to make a moral point, and writers working in England in this period, such as Marie de France and Odo of Cheriton, present stories of the wolf, fox, lion, and lamb to drive home simple lessons.[227] A fox sees a reflection of the moon in a pool and thinks it is an enormous cheese. He laps away at the water to get to the cheese and eventually bursts. 'Many people aspire to have all their wishes, beyond what is right and fitting. This is their downfall.'[228] Such bland admonitions have little to do with the actual nature of the animal in question (although fables do attribute to foxes and other animals a taste for cheese that seems no longer one of their attributes). Sometimes, however, the matter is more pertinent. A wolf, meeting a dog and observing how well fed he is, is persuaded to go with him and obey his master too. On the way, however, he notices the collar and chain the dog is wearing. 'Brother,' he says, 'there is something remarkable around

---

[226] John Morson, 'The English Cistercians and the Bestiary', *Bulletin of the John Rylands Library*, 39 (1956–7), pp. 146–70.

[227] Joyce E. Salisbury, *The Beast Within: Animals in the Middle Ages* (New York, 1994), p. 134, fig. 4, lists animals in their fables in order of frequency.

[228] Marie de France, *Fables* 58 (p. 166).

your neck—though I don't know what it is.' When the dog explains the conditions of his life, the wolf declares, 'I'll never wear a chain. While I can chose, I'd rather be a free wolf than live in luxury with a chain. You go into town, I'm off to the woods!'[229]

## The Line Between Animal and Human

When they considered the distinction between humans and (other) animals, the learned men of the twelfth century had as a starting point the two major inherited traditions of the medieval world, the classical and the biblical. The classical approach was to categorize humans as a kind of animal, though one distinguished by reason and other attributes. The standard introductory text of Aristotelian logic, used in the schools throughout the Middle Ages, stated, 'When we are asked what man is, we answer "Animal". Animal is the genus of man.'[230] The biblical tradition had a different emphasis: humans were created in God's image, created separately from the animals and given dominion over them. 'Once everything had been created and ordered, last of all man was made, as lord and possessor, who was set over everything.'[231]

This biblically inspired tradition stressed the subordinate position of animals, and indeed of the whole of non-human creation. Learned men taught that 'every creature in the world was created solely for human beings'.[232] 'The sun does not shine for itself but for man.'[233] One of the characteristics of a 'brute beast' was that it was 'by nature prepared to serve'.[234] The animals' fate was tied up with that of humanity. As a consequence of man's Fall, the animals too had become 'weak and fleeting'.[235] In the paradisical state, all creatures, including human beings, were vegetarian and the beasts obeyed man—'the lion would comply with human commands as readily as the dog'. The domesticated animals that still serve man are a reminder to him of his glory before the Fall, while the midges, gnats, and fleas that persecute him make him constantly mindful of his lapse.[236]

One of the common features of saintliness was the power to restore sympathy between humans and animals, even animals of a wild or revolting kind. Such a rebirth of Eden was seen—at least temporarily—when the hermit Godric of Finchale moved into uncultivated country in county Durham:

Not only was he not afraid of the company of slimy serpents, but he even let them curl around his feet and legs. Serpents of horrific size lived with him for two years,

---

[229] Marie de France, *Fables* 26 (pp. 94–6).

[230] Porphyry, *Isagoge*, tr. Boethius, ed. L. Minio-Paluello, *Aristoteles Latinus* 1, 6–7: *Categoriarum Supplementum* (Leiden, 1966), p. 8.

[231] Peter Lombard, *Sententiae in IV libris distinctae* 2. 15. 5, ed. Rome, 1971 (Spicilegium Bonaventurianum 4), vol. 1, p. 402.

[232] W. Dan., *V. Ailred* 10 (p. 19).      [233] Alex. Nequam, *DNR* 2. 156 (p. 249).

[234] Gerald, *Top.* 2. 23 (p. 110).      [235] W. Dan., *V. Ailred* 10 (p. 19).

[236] Alex. Nequam, *DNR* 2. 156 (pp. 249–51).

coming and going as they wished. When a fire was lit in the hut, they stretched themselves out toward the warmth and—as far as they were able—made appreciative noises. They seemed to have laid aside their natural wildness and to have become tame and willing to be handled.

Eventually—perhaps to the modern reader's regret—Godric expelled his reptilian pets because they disturbed his meditations.[237]

Alongside this vision of man as lord of creation, even if one who had perversely sacrificed many of the prerogatives of his lordship, the classical tradition offered the alternative, naturalistic idea of a chain of being, in which man had a place. In this chain of being, animals had a position between plants and man. Plants surpassed inanimate rocks and stones, that could not move by themselves and were dependent on gravity, by having a 'quasi-vital force' that enabled them to grow, even though they lacked sensation. Animals surpassed plants by having sensation and being able to move from place to place. They also possessed the ability to recognize their own habitations and to recollect past experiences. This was because they had the power to form images (*vis imaginaria*). Indeed, in some respects their powers of this kind were superior to those of more rational beings: 'for where reason dominates, the capacity to deal in images declines'. Man was nevertheless the peak of the terrestrial hierarchy, marked out as 'the most worthy of all earthly creatures' by reason, an upright stance, and speech.[238] In one sense, this way of thinking was just as anthropocentric as the biblical view; yet it integrates humans more thoroughly, by stressing the continuum of created being and explicating characteristics that humans shared with beings lower down the ladder.

There was sometimes debate about the exact nature of the mental powers that animals possessed, a topic that was obviously important in defining the differences between man and beast. In his dialogue, *Natural Questions*, the early twelfth-century scientist Adelard of Bath asked 'whether beasts have minds'—or, perhaps, 'whether beasts have souls', for the word he employs (*anima*) had that meaning too.[239] He comments that ordinary people and philosophers differ on this issue, the former being certain that beasts do not have minds (or souls), the latter being equally sure they do. Adelard's nephew, who is the figure in the dialogue used to advance erroneous views, argues that animals 'do indeed have the power of sensory perception but they have no judgement or understanding concerning the things they perceive'. Adelard responds with the example of dogs, who seek some things out and avoid others, hence showing the power of judgement, and who can discriminate when following a scent: a dog 'has in his mind a kind of picture: "this is

---

[237] Geoffrey of Durham, *V. sancti Godrici* 1 (*AASS*, 5 May, p. 72).

[238] Gerald, *Top*. 1. 13 (pp. 40–1).

[239] Adelard of Bath, *Quaestiones naturales* 13, ed. Martin Müller (Beiträge zur Geschichte der Philosophie des Mittelalters 31/ii; Münster, 1934), pp. 15–18.

the one I should follow, this is another one, different from the first" '. Such an ability goes beyond mere perception, it is a power of making distinctions that can only inhere in the mind.

More people appear to have agreed with Adelard's nephew than with Adelard. Animals and humans were seen to be distinguished by the superior mental capacities of the latter. The numerous medieval representations of animals engaging in human activities imply not that there was much doubt about the line between man and beast but rather the opposite. The carving of the fox playing the harp on the doorway of Barfreston church in Kent or the animal musical ensembles carved onto the capitals of the Canterbury cathedral crypt show, of course, not that twelfth-century people believed that animals could perform on musical instruments but that they could not and hence depictions of them doing so were droll. Animals do not have the alphabet. That is why the image of the bear learning to pronounce 'A', mentioned earlier, is funny (or sad). Marie de France has a story of a wolf laboriously learning 'ABC', but then thinking it spells 'lamb'.[240] Just as they lacked the alphabet, and perhaps linked to that lack, animals had no history. It is, the historian Henry of Huntingdon asserted, 'knowledge of past events that distinguishes rational beings from brutes'.[241]

Yet this confidence about the division between human and animal is not the whole story. Areas of overlap, concerns about seemingly rational behaviour by animals and worries about creatures that seemed to span the boundaries suggest a more animated sense of the relative place of humans and animals in the world. Interest of a special kind was shown in apes, because they seemed to resemble human beings. Indeed, according to medieval etymological science, apes were given the name 'ape' (*simia*) because they were *simi*lar to humans. Alexander Nequam tells of wandering jesters with apes that were trained to leap and dance and even, astride dogs, to imitate knights at a tournament.[242] Humans were given names derived from animals: in twelfth-century Canterbury one finds a William Herring, Gervase Hog, and Ailred Snake.[243] Heraldry was a form of association of animal symbol and human dynasty, sometimes with a pun on the name. The seal of Alice Capra ('goat') shows her standing on a goat.[244]

Beyond these associative and symbolic fusions was the question whether the physical boundary between humans and animals could be crossed. Could the blood of humans and brute beasts be intermingled in hybrids? Could humans turn into animals and animals into humans?

---

[240] Marie de France, *Fables* 82 (p. 216).    [241] H. Hunt., prol. (p. 4).

[242] Alex. Nequam, *DNR* 2. 129 (pp. 209–11).

[243] Cecily Clark, 'People and Languages in Post-Conquest Canterbury', *Jnl Medieval History*, 2 (1976), pp. 1–33, at pp. 18–19.

[244] Birch, *Seals*, no. 6606.

The family tradition of earl Waltheof, who was executed by William the Conqueror in 1076 and from whom the later earls of Huntingdon and Northampton, as well as the kings of Scots, descended, relates that Waltheof's ancestor had been a bear. Waltheof's father Siward (a well-attested historical figure) was, according to the family saga, the son of a noble Dane called Beorn Bearson, distinguished by the possession of bear's ears. Beorn's great-grandfather Ursus ('bear') was born, 'contrary to the usual pattern of human reproduction', from the union of a noblewoman and a white bear.[245] (Since the present British royal family descends from Waltheof, we have here a startling claim about their distant ancestry.)

Such a claim of animal descent is unusual. It is, in any event, a more characteristically Scandinavian story than an Anglo-Norman one and points to Siward's Viking ancestry. Perhaps the rarity of such animal descent legends is connected with the absence of large clan groupings in the aristocracy of Norman and Angevin England. Yet, however odd, it is a story that was copied out, in Latin, at the Benedictine abbey of Crowland, where earl Waltheof lay buried. His ursine descent did not stop the monks claiming that he was a saint.

More common than aristocrats with an animal pedigree were sad hybrids supposedly resulting from bestiality. Sexual intercourse between humans and animals was, in the circumstances of close proximity that prevailed in the medieval period, probably more common than today. The Old Testament provisions regarding the severe punishments for such acts were incorporated into the canon law texts. Among them was the requirement that the beast involved be killed—'not on account of its fault, for the fact that it is a beast excuses it from that, but in order not to stir up memory of the crime'.[246] Deformed or misshapen progeny were interpreted as the offspring of such intercourse.

The most extreme breach of the wall between human and animal was shape-changing, the transformation of humans into animals and vice-versa. The process is vividly illustrated in a manuscript of Boethius' *Consolation of Philosophy*, dating to 1120–1140.[247] A picture of Ulysses' men turning into beasts is accompanied by a learned discussion, perhaps originally composed a generation before the manuscript was produced, of whether such changes can in fact take place. Different nutrition affects animals differently, the anonymous author argues. Feeding men certain kinds of food turns them into asses, pigs, etc. 'Hence one must believe that these kinds of transformations are not fables but fact.'

[245] *Gesta antecess. Waldevi*, pp. 104–5.

[246] Gerald, *Top.* 2. 24 (p. 111), drawing on Augustine, *Quaestiones in Leviticum* 74 (*PL* 34, col. 709); Ivo of Chartres, *Decretum* 9. 108 (*PL* 161, col. 686).

[247] MS Glasgow, University Library, Hunter U. 5. 19 (279), fo. 45ᵛ, reproduced in *Engl. Rom. Art*, no. 32, p. 102; cf. Margaret Gibson (ed.), *Boethius: His Life, Thought and Influence* (Oxford, 1981), pp. 296–7.

The most widely reported transformation was man into wolf. As the well-travelled courtier Gervase of Tilbury noted, werewolves were not uncommon in England: 'in England we have often seen men transformed into wolves at the changing of the moon. The French term this kind of man "gerulf", while the English say "werewolf".'[248] Gervase advances this point quite casually and incidentally, while supporting the claim that women often change into snakes. The shift from human to animal form is the subject of two of Marie de France's *Lais*. *Bisclavret* is the story of a werewolf ('Its name is *bisclavret* in Breton; the Normans call it *garwaf* '), who must spend three days a week as a wolf, living in the forest, devouring men. It hides its clothes before assuming the shape of a wolf and, if anyone takes them away, it cannot return to human form, human dress thus forming the gateway to humanity. The *lai Yonec* is about a lover who comes to a woman in the form of a hawk before being transformed into a handsome knight. She insists that he take communion before she becomes his lover, since, presumably, he might otherwise be a demonic trickster.

One werewolf tale provoked a full discussion of the boundaries and criteria of humanity. Gerald of Wales tells the story of the people of Ossory in Ireland who had been cursed by the local saint, Natal, so that two of them at a time had to spend seven years in the woods in the shape of wolves. Gerald says that an episcopal synod in Meath considered the case of a priest who had given the viaticum to one of these werewolves and that this assembly indeed asked him for advice on the subject. The story leads him on to the question whether such a creature should be considered a brute animal or a human being. Since these werewolves were able to talk and reason, they scarcely seemed brute animals but 'who would attribute human nature to a four-footed animal, that goes prone on the ground and does not have the power of laughter?'. There was a practical side to the question: would someone who killed these creatures be committing homicide? In discussing this issue, Gerald was able to draw on the views expressed by St Augustine in his *City of God*. Augustine held the basic premiss that any rational, mortal animal, however unusual in form, was human and of common descent with all other humans. Metamorphosis of one shape into another, such as lycanthropy, was, of course, within God's power, but many cases were purely specious. Drawing on his words, Gerald writes that 'demons and wicked men can neither create nor truly transform species but they can change the appearance of the things that God has created, if he gives them permission. In this way things may appear to be what they are not.' The human senses can be deluded by phantasms and magic.[249]

[248] Gerv. Tilb. 1. 15 (p. 895); cf. modern French 'loup-garou'.
[249] Gerald, *Top.* 2. 19 (pp. 101–7), drawing on Augustine, *De civitate dei* 16. 8, 18. 17 (*PL* 40, cols. 485–7, 573–4).

Gerald's comments show the enduring influence of the definition of man propounded in classical logic. The distinctive trio of sentience, rationality, and mortality constituted the essence of humanity. Such features as the ability to laugh and an upright posture were only secondary characteristics, properties. Hence humanity could come in a fairly wide variety of physical shapes. It was the rationality of the creature that was important. Moreover, because of God's power to effect genuine changes in Nature and the ability of demons and magicians to delude the senses, both real and apparent transformations from one species to another were possible. Here was the intellectual foundation for a view of the world in which men might well turn into wolves.

While men and women of the twelfth century used animals—ate them, hunted them, made them work—they also obviously thought through them, working out, in ways not always consistent, what it meant to be human by defining what it meant to be an animal. As St Ambrose had put it in his *Hexaemeron*, an important source for the bestiary text, 'we cannot fully understand ourselves unless we first know about the nature of all the animals'.[250]

## 4. BEINGS NEITHER ANGELIC, HUMAN, NOR ANIMAL

Even if the exact distinction between animal and human was sometimes a matter for debate, most people, both learned and unlearned, employed the categories. 'Animal' and 'human' were recognized as two major classes of being. The nature of angels and demons, moreover, was thoroughly explored by some of the most sophisticated analytical minds of the time. To that extent, their place in the cosmological scheme was also clear. There were, however, other beings to be met with in the wide world who did not fit into this triad of sentient beings—animal, human, or angelic/demonic—creatures that, while not certainly human or animal, were not demons in the sense that the theologians used the term.

One day in the reign of Henry II the servant Richard, of North Sunderland in Northumberland, who had gone out at his master's bidding to cut reeds for thatching, encountered three handsome youths, who were dressed in green and rode green horses. One of these 'supposedly human figures' pulled Richard up behind him and carried him off: 'and so Richard was led into the wilderness by the fantastic spirit, so that he might be tempted, or rather, if possible, retained by the devilish assembly.' The place he came to was very beautiful, with a lofty mansion, a king, and a crowd of all ages. They ate oaten bread and drank milk. When they offered to Richard a green drinking horn full of what appeared to be new ale, he decided not to drink, 'for he remembered the conversations he had heard when he was still among men and what

---

[250] Ambrose, *Hexaemeron* 6. 2 (*PL* 14, col. 243).

general opinion related about this sort of thing'. He resisted all their invitations to remain with them and was eventually returned to the spot whence he had been taken, but deprived of the power of speech as a punishment for his refusal (the miraculous restitution of his speech was, in fact, the occasion for this story being written down).[251]

The green-clad figures move in an ambiguous world. They are certainly not human, but nor do they seem to be diabolic in the sense of wicked fallen angels intent on doing harm to human beings, even though the word 'devilish' (*diabolicus*) is used once. Their setting is idyllic and pastoral. When describing their simple diet, the author of this story even talks of their 'eating and drinking what was before them, according to the Lord's commandment', with a reference to Jesus' words in Luke 10: 8. The servant Richard, who undergoes the experience, clearly identifies his abductors with creatures of whom he has already heard talk. His refusal to drink presumably stems from the belief that to take food with the fairies (if that is what they are) is to renounce all chance of ever returning to the world of men.

Such hazardous figures, many in human form but not human, were to be found throughout twelfth-century England. A Yorkshire peasant, returning home one night after drinking with a friend in a neighbouring village, and hearing singing and cheerful talk from a tumulus, saw a whole crowd feasting inside. When offered a drink by the underground revellers, he, like Richard of North Sunderland, was careful not to touch it, but, pouring out the contents, escaped with the cup. This fairy cup, 'of unknown material, unusual colour and unfamiliar shape', ended up as a curiosity in the royal treasury.[252] Other, odder creatures existed. Some are familiar in modern story, like the mermaids, with their long blond hair and their bare breasts, who sat on rocks and lured sailors with their sweet songs. Others are long forgotten: the 'Grant' or 'Giant', a long-legged, bright-eyed creature in the form of a year-old foal, whose appearance warns of a forthcoming fire in the town or village where it is seen; the 'Portuni', diminutive beings with wizened faces, who wear tiny clothes, like human company and enjoy toasting frogs on the fire. They offer help around the house and are in general beneficent except for one trick—they accompany solitary riders at night and then snatch the reins and guide the horse into a bog, dashing off laughing.[253]

These unusual creatures had to be placed in the interstices of the mundane world. Walter Map stressed the way the fairy folk seek to keep themselves secluded in secret habitations.[254] Some were invisible, like the 'fantastic spirit' called Malekin, who haunted a house in Dagworth in Suffolk and wore a cape

---

[251] H. H. E. Craster, 'The Miracles of St Cuthbert at Farne', *Analecta Bollandiana*, 70 (1952), pp. 1–19, at pp. 14–16.

[252] W. Newb. 1. 28 (1, pp. 85–6).     [253] Gerv. Tilb. 3. 61–2, 64 (pp. 980–1).

[254] Map 2. 12 (p. 156).

of invisibility.[255] Other uncanny creatures lived in the world's unknown spaces—under the sea, like the aquatic man caught in the waters off Suffolk, under the ground, or even above the clouds.

Stories of an underground country were numerous. A pigherd in the Peak District, following a wandering sow down into a cavern, found fields being harvested beneath the ground and was able to recover his animal from the subterranean reeve.[256] Gerald of Wales even recorded some words of the language supposedly spoken in the underground kingdom—it was similar to Greek.[257] The most remarkable story relates how, at the mouth of a cave near Woolpit in Suffolk, the local inhabitants found two children, a boy and a girl, human in every aspect except their colour—green. Their speech was incomprehensible. Brought to the house of a neighbouring knight, the children lived on a diet of beans, but the boy soon pined away and died. His sister, however, throve. As she grew accustomed to a more varied diet, her skin turned from green to pink, she learned to speak English, and was baptized. She was then able to tell her story: she said that all the inhabitants of her own region were green, and that they never saw the sun, but were lit by a kind of twilight glow. She and her brother had been tending their flocks and had entered a cavern. Then, hearing the ringing of bells, they had followed the sweet sound until it brought them out of the cave where they had been found, almost unconscious from the brightness of the sun and the warmth of the air.[258]

Just as there were worlds below, so there were worlds above. Gervase of Tilbury tells the story of how a crowd emerging from church after service saw an anchor coming down from the sky. From above, hidden in the clouds, came the sound of sailors trying to haul it up. Eventually one of these sailors climbed down the anchor rope, 'hand by hand, using the same technique as we do'. The unfortunate aerial mariner was seized by the church-goers and, 'suffocated by the moistness of our denser air, died in their grasp'.[259] Human-like enough to sail ships and fashion anchors, these sailors nevertheless had a respiratory system that confirmed they were not 'us'.

The problems of categorization that such creatures presented are illustrated by the case of the wild man caught by fishermen in their nets off the Suffolk coast. Ralph, abbot of the Cistercian monastery of Coggeshall, who tells the story, writes that the sea-man 'presented a human appearance in every part of his body'. Nevertheless, he was a natural, unsocialized creature, happy to eat raw fish, showing no signs of reverence in church and sleeping and rising with the sun. Nor did he speak, even when hung upside down and tortured—a piece of scientific experimentation that throws a sad light on the

---

[255] R. Coggesh., pp. 120–1.     [256] Gerv. Tilb. 3. 45 (p. 975).     [257] Gerald, *Itin.* 1. 8 (pp. 75–8).
[258] R. Coggesh., pp. 118–20; W. Newb. 1. 27 (1, pp. 82–4) has the important variation that the underground land is Christian, even though the children still undergo baptism in their new home.
[259] Gerv. Tilb. 1. 13 (p. 894).

humanity of twelfth-century humans. Fortunately, the wild man eventually escaped back to the sea. Reflecting on this incident, Coggeshall cannot decide 'if he was a mortal man or some fish in human form or a wicked spirit lurking in the body of a drowned man'.[260] The abbot is thus seeking to fit an oddity into the categories of being—human, animal, diabolic—that were familiar to him and theologically orthodox. His friend, Gervase of Tilbury, was rather more willing to admit the existence of grey and uncertain areas. When dealing with the 'Portuni', he begins, 'England has certain demons', but then qualifies himself at once: 'I say demons, but do not know whether I should say "forms of secret and unknown origin".'[261]

Gervase's almost despairing vagueness—'forms of secret and unknown origin'—is necessary because there was no consistent terminology for describing these creatures who hovered on the edge of humanity. The vernacular word 'elf' was used at the time, but only rarely. Nor is there a single common word in twelfth-century Latin that can be translated as 'fairy'. The closest is the term *fatalitas*, employed three times by the court writer, Walter Map, but, it seems, only by him. One of his stories concerns a knight who came across an assembly of beautiful women dancing at night in a woodland hall. They were 'larger and taller than our own women'. Falling in love with one of them, the knight eventually won her as his wife. William the Conqueror, king at the time, heard of this wonder and summoned the couple to London, to learn the truth for himself. The woman's extraordinary appearance was, says Map, 'a great proof of her fairy nature'.[262] Her *fatalitas* is thus demonstrated by her physical form, which was unlike that of 'our own', i.e. human, women. The word obviously has much the same meaning as the English word 'fairy' (which is not recorded until the fourteenth century) and, in fact, stems from the same root. It remains, however, a coinage of one author whose work survives in a single manuscript.

Yet, although there was no simple all-embracing formulation that writers of the twelfth century could use to label green children from below the earth, diminutive household sprites, beautiful ladies dancing by night in woodland halls, and other fleeting and uncanny creatures, they were clearly considered to belong together and are not merely a category invented by modern historians and scholars. The evidence for this is that writers like Ralph of Coggeshall and Gervase of Tilbury group their stories about such beings together. Coggeshall follows the story of the man from the sea with the tale of the green children, an account of giant teeth, and other huge bones proving the truth of 'what is read in old histories about the bodies of giants' and finally the report of the spirit Malekin. Moreover, he introduces the story of the green children with the words, 'another wonderful thing, similar to that just mentioned,

---

[260] R. Coggesh., pp. 117–18.          [261] Gerv. Tilb. 3. 61 (p. 980).          [262] Map 2. 12 (pp. 154–8).

occurred . . .' Dwellers in underground lands and creatures from the sea, giants and invisible spirits, all belonged together in the abbot's mind. Gervase of Tilbury has a series of chapters on the Portuni, the Grant and mermaids. William of Newburgh, likewise, passes on from the story of the green children to 'other, equally wonderful and marvellous things that happened in our own time', including the story of the midnight feast in the tumulus. It is their rarity and their unknown cause that makes 'things of this type' remarkable.

If such beings thus constituted a class in the eyes of contemporaries, there was still no agreed explanation of their origin and nature. One possibility was that they were not completely real, another that they were demonic, a third that they were real beings of a category not otherwise known. In any case, the reality of these uncanny events and strange creatures was to be established by the same criteria of evidence as applied to the ordinary world, that is, by reliable witnesses or first-hand experience. William of Newburgh, after telling the story of the cup stolen from the banquet in the tumulus, comments: 'this, and things like it, would appear incredible, if their reality were not supported by trustworthy witnesses.'[263] Gervase of Tilbury promises that the marvels he recounts will not be like those told by 'the lying tongues of minstrels', but will be 'a reliable account of what we have gathered from the old authorities or have confirmed by our own eyes and that can be checked any day'.[264] Exceptionally, Gerald of Wales, suspending judgement regarding the underground land, is willing to place it among the things that 'should neither be forcefully asserted nor denied'.[265] Such an agnostic position was rare, when faced with the word of respectable men and the plethora of physical reminders, like the fairy cup from the tumulus or the anchor from the sky that was preserved in the church where the events had taken place.

The natural tendency of the ecclesiastics who wrote down these stories was to interpret them in the light of Christian demonology. If the marine man was not genuinely human, or simply animal, opined Ralph of Coggeshall, then he might be an evil spirit in a drowned man's body. William of Newburgh thought a demonic explanation of these oddities the most likely one, though he was willing to concede that some things were simply beyond explanation:

it is not surprising that wicked angels can cause these things, by a certain capacity of the angelic nature, if the superior power permits them, either by sleight of hand and illusion, as in the case of the nocturnal feast in the tumulus, or in reality . . . by these means men are caught up in a fruitless amazement . . . as for the green children, who came from out of the ground, there must be a hidden explanation, beyond the power of our weak understanding to uncover.[266]

---

[263] W. Newb. 1. 28 (1, p. 86).        [264] Gerv. Tilb. 3, pref., p. 960.
[265] Gerald, *Itin.* 1. 8 (p. 78).         [266] W. Newb. 1. 28 (1, pp. 86–7).

The question of agency and origin—what power was at work here?—was linked with the question of intention—what did these beings want with us? In this connection, a long tale of Walter Map's is very revealing.[267] It tells of a baron's son who goes down in the world and ends up as a beggar. One day a huge and hideous figure appears suddenly before him and promises him the recovery of his fortune if he submits to his lordship. The baron's son is naturally sceptical: 'Who are you?' he asks, 'Was it not you who expelled us from the Garden through your persuasion of Eve?' The reply that the spirit gives is, in essence, a long attempt to draw a distinction between evil spirits and those, such as he claims himself to be, that are harmless.

The crucial passage begins, 'You should make a distinction between the harmful and the harmless and not condemn them equally.' The spirit argues that, at the fall of Lucifer, there were spirits who were carried along unthinkingly, rather than helping or consenting to the Devil's rebellion. Unlike the great demons who wish to destroy mankind, these harmless spirits exercise their powers in a light-hearted way: 'We are skilled in jokes and tricks, we devise illusions, we shape mental images, we construct apparitions, so that the truth is concealed by a deceptive and ludicrous semblance. We can do anything that tends to laughter, nothing that leads to tears.' Such beings are what the ancients called 'demigods'—fauns, dryads, and the like. Because of their long experience and their spirit nature they have predictive powers, knowing 'the causes of all things'. 'Because of this knowledge and our kindness, we are good counsellors and, if God permits, great helpers.' As it turned out, he was lying about who he was in an attempt to draw the young man to damnation, but, regardless of the sincerity of this particular spirit, his account offers a clear proposition: there are harmless, potentially helpful spirits, who are to be identified with the rustic deities of the ancient world, and who create illusions among human beings. Much of the uncanny could be accounted for in this way.

Relations between human beings and non-human beings in human form could be of the most intimate kind. The fairy wife has already been mentioned, and sexual contacts across the barrier between the two types of creature seem to have been common. In 1144 a maiden in Dunwich in Suffolk was pestered by an unwanted suitor: 'One of those whom we call fauns and *incubi*, who are lecherous and often assault women, turned himself into the shape of a very handsome young man and came to her unawares.'[268] The courting of this demon lover was assiduous but eventually unsuccessful. Other unions, though, bore fruit. Walter Map tells how the fairy bride and her human husband in the time of William the Conqueror had a son named Alnoth, a religious man and benefactor of the church. Such an outcome surprised him.

---

[267] Map 4. 6 (pp. 314–40, esp. 318–22).   [268] T. Monm., *V. William* 2. 7 (p. 80).

'We have heard of *incubi* and *succubi*,' writes Map, 'and of the perilous intercourse with them, but we have rarely or never read in old accounts that this produced heirs or offspring who ended their days well.' The existence of *incubi*, demons or woodland spirits who mated with women, was supported by the authority of St Augustine, the greatest of the Fathers of the Church.[269] Their exact nature is the subject of a passage in Geoffrey of Monmouth's *History of the Kings of Britain* which deals with the parentage of the magician Merlin : 'between the moon and the earth there live spirits whom we call incubus demons. In nature they are part human and part angel. When they wish they assume human form and copulate with women.'[270] Here is an explicit, if unexplored, formulation of the nature of these beings: part-human, part-angel, inhabiting the airy region.

The minds of the men and women of England in our period thus had room for a variety of beings that did not fit neatly into the orthodox and established trio of man, beast, and (good or bad) angel. There was nothing 'popular' about such beliefs, except in the sense that they were widespread. The knightly class was deeply involved with these strange creatures: the Suffolk marine man was in the ungentle care of a local knight, Bartholomew of Glanville, who was custodian of the royal castle of Orford and subsequently sheriff; the green children were brought to the household of the knight Richard of Calne and the girl was in his service for many years; the 'fantastic spirit' Malekin was to be found in the house of Osbern of Bradwell, who is specifically termed 'sir' or 'lord' (*dominus*) in Coggeshall's account and is likely to be the same person as 'Osbert of Bradwell' who held rights in the appointment of the parish priest of Bradwell.[271] Strange breeds and spirits were thus just as much at home with the gentry as with the peasantry.

Similarly, a learned education did not make one less likely to believe in such beings. The clergy were as deeply enmeshed as the gentry. These tales were recorded by ecclesiastics trained in Latin literacy. Ralph of Coggeshall was a Cistercian abbot, William of Newburgh an Augustinian canon. The story of the underground country below the Peak District was told by the prior of the Augustinian house of Kenilworth. Walter Map studied at the schools of Paris, the capital of Latin higher education at the time. Their Latin reading told them of fauns and nymphs, their religious education made clear to them God's infinite power. The strange creatures that flitted across the borders of the human and the mundane world were not beyond the bounds of possibility. Below the Essex fields, within the Yorkshire barrows, and beyond the Suffolk shore were creatures who lived an alien life of their own.

---

[269] Augustine, *De civitate dei* 15. 23 (*PL* 41, cols. 468–71).
[270] Geoff. Monm., *HRB* 6. 18 (107), p. 72; followed by Gerv. Tilb. 1. 17 (p. 897).
[271] *Feet of Fines for the County of Norfolk . . . 1201–1215, for the County of Suffolk . . . 1199–1214*, ed. Barbara Dodwell (PRS n.s. 32; 1958 for 1956), no. 550, pp. 264–5.

# Chronology of Political Events

| | |
|---|---|
| 1066 | Norman Conquest |
| 1070 | Lanfranc consecrated archbishop of Canterbury (29 Aug.) |
| 1075 | Rebellion of three earls against William I |
| 1086 | Domesday inquest |
| 1087 | Death of William I at Rouen (9 Sept.) |
| | Coronation of William II at Westminster (26 Sept.) |
| 1088 | Unsuccessful rebellion against William Rufus (Spring/summer) |
| 1093 | Anselm consecrated archbishop of Canterbury (4 Dec.) |
| 1097 | Anselm leaves England (8 Nov.) |
| 1100 | Death of William II in the New Forest (2 Aug.) |
| | Coronation of Henry I at Westminster (5 Aug.) |
| | Anselm returns to England (23 Sept.) |
| 1101 | Robert, brother of Henry I, invades England but makes terms in the Treaty of Alton (Aug.) |
| 1106 | Henry I conquers Normandy and captures Robert at Tinchebray (28 Sept.) |
| 1107 | Compromise on ecclesiastical investiture and homage (3 Aug.) |
| 1119 | Henry I routs Louis VI at Brémule (20 Aug.) |
| 1120 | Henry I's son, William, drowned in the wreck of the White Ship (25 Nov.) |
| 1124 | Henry I's forces defeat the Norman rebels at Bourgtheroulde (26 Mar.) |
| 1128 | Marriage of Henry I's daughter, Matilda, and Geoffrey of Anjou (17 June) |
| 1135 | Death of Henry I at Lyons-la-Forêt, Normandy (1 Dec.) |
| | Coronation of Stephen at Westminster (22 Dec.) |
| 1138 | Defeat of Scots at Battle of the Standard (22 Aug.) |
| 1139 | Empress Matilda and Robert of Gloucester land in England (30 Sept.) |
| 1141 | Battle of Lincoln and capture of Stephen (2 Feb.) |
| | Defeat of Matilda's forces and capture of Robert of Gloucester at 'the rout of Winchester' (14 Sept.) |
| 1152 | Marriage of Henry of Anjou and Eleanor of Aquitaine (18 May) |
| 1153 | Treaty of Winchester acknowledges Henry of Anjou as Stephen's heir (6 Nov.) |
| 1154 | Death of Stephen at Canterbury (25 Oct.) |
| | Coronation of Henry II at Westminster (19 Dec.) |
| 1164 | Archbishop Thomas Becket flees to France (2 Nov.) |
| 1169 | Anglo–Norman mercenaries land in Ireland (May) |
| 1170 | Murder of Becket (29 Dec.) |
| 1171 | Henry II lands in Ireland (17 Oct.) |

1172     Henry II's oaths to legates at Avranches (27 Sept.)

1173     Widespread rebellion against Henry II begins (Mar.)
Royalist forces defeat earl of Leicester at Fornham (17 Oct.)

1174     Capture of William, king of Scots, at Alnwick (13 July)

1183     Death of Henry the Young King (11 June)

1189     Death of Henry II at Chinon (6 July)
Coronation of Richard I at Westminster (3 Sept.)

1190     Massacre and mass-suicide of Jews of York (16 Mar.)
Richard I leaves Vézelay on Third Crusade (4 July)

1191     Richard I marries Berengaria in Limassol (12 May)
Richard I reaches Acre in the Holy Land (8 June)
Capitulation of Acre to crusaders (12 July)
Richard I's victory at Arsuf (7 Sept.)

1192     Richard I sails from Acre (9 Oct.)
Richard captured by the duke of Austria in Vienna (20 Dec.)

1194     Richard I's crown-wearing at Winchester (17 April)

1199     Death of Richard I at Chalus (6 Apr.)
Coronation of John at Westminster (27 May)

1204     Fall of Rouen to Philip Augustus (24 June)

1208     Interdict proclaimed on England (24 March)

1214     Interdict lifted (2 July)

1215     Magna Carta issued (15 June)

1216     Louis of France lands in Kent (21 May)
Death of John at Newark (18–19 Oct.)
Coronation of Henry III at Gloucester (28 Oct.)

1217     Royalist victory at Lincoln (20 May)
Royalist victory at sea off Sandwich (24 Aug.)
Peace of Kingston between Henry III and Louis of France (12 Sept.)

# The Sources

WRITING IN LATIN

More written material was produced in Latin than in any other language in this period. It is fortunate that there exist some first-rate guides to the Latin sources for medieval England:

Edgar B. Graves (ed.), *A Bibliography of English History to 1485* (Oxford, 1975) deals with both primary sources (documentary and narrative) and secondary works published before 1970.

A. G. Rigg, *A History of Anglo-Latin Literature 1066–1422* (Cambridge, 1992) discusses 'literary' works, including anonymous pieces.

Richard Sharpe, *A Handlist of the Latin Writers of Great Britain and Ireland before 1540* (Turnhout, 1997) deals with all named writers. When an author is simply named below, full details will be found in Sharpe's magisterial work of reference.

The list of abbreviations in the *Dict. Med. Latin* serves as a very full guide to sources of all types.

A useful anthology of material will be found in *English Historical Documents* 2, ed. D. C. Douglas and George Greenaway (2nd edn.; London, 1981); 3, ed. Harry Rothwell (London, 1975).

## Narrative histories

Some of the narrative histories are discussed in Chapter 12. The indispensable guide is Antonia Gransden, *Historical Writing in England*, 1. *c.550–c.1307* (London, 1974). Many of the most important chronicles are still only available in the Victorian editions of the Rolls Series, although new critical editions are continually being produced, especially in the series Oxford Medieval Texts, which also includes a facing-page English translation. The most frequently cited histories and chronicles in this volume are:

*Abingdon Chron.*; *Ann. Dunst.*; *Ann. Wav.*; *Ann. Wint.*; Barnwell Chron.; *Battle Chron.*; *De exp. Lyxb.*; Eadmer, *HN*; Flor. Worcs.; Gerald, *Exp.*; Gerv. Cant.; *Gesta Hen. II*; *Gesta Ric. I*; *Gesta S. Alb.*; *Gesta Stephani*; H. Hunt.; Hugh Chanter; *Hyde Chron.*; *Itin. reg. Ric.*; J. Hexham; J. Worcs.; Joc. Brak.; *Lib. Eliensis*; Orderic; R. Coggesh.; R. Devizes; R. Diceto, *Ymag.*; R. Hexham; R. Howd.; R. Torigni; R. Wend.; *Ramsey Chron.;* S. Durh., *HDE*; S. Durh., *HR*; S. Rouen, *Draco*; W. Malm., *GP*; W. Malm., *GR*; W. Malm., *HN*; W. Newb.

## Hagiography

There are hundreds of saints' lives, miracle accounts, and records of translations (ritual relocations of saints' relics) that survive from this period. Those used most extensively in this book are:

*About contemporaries*
Ad. Eyns., *V. Hugh*; *Bk. Gilbert*; Eadmer, *V. Anselm*; J. Ford, *V. Wulfric*; Joc. Furn., *V. Waltheof*; *Mir. Wulfstan*; Reg., *V. Godric*; T. Monm., *V. William*; *V. Christina*; W. Cant., *Mir. Thos.*; W. Dan., *V. Ailred*; W. f. Stephen, *V. Thomas*; W. Malm., *V. Wulfstan*

*About older saints*
Goscelin, *Hist. Augustine*; *Mir. Erkenwald*; *Mir. John Bev.*; Philip, *Mir. Fridesw.*; Reg., *Libellus*

## Letter Collections

Important letter collections include Osbert, *Letters*; J. Salisb., *Letters*; Foliot, *Letters*; P. Blois, *Letters*; *Episotlae Herberti de Losinga*, ed. Robert Anstruther (London, 1846); the Becket correspondence in *Becket Mats.* 5–7 (a new edition anticipated in OMT).

## Theological and Devotional Literature

Anselm is the most famous theologian connected with England, although the bulk of his religious works were written in Normandy before he became archbishop. Ailred of Rievaulx, Alexander Nequam, Baldwin of Ford, Gilbert Crispin, Odo of Canterbury, Peter of Cornwall, Stephen Langton, Thomas of Chobham, and William de Montibus produced works of doctrinal, pastoral, or contemplative significance.

## Other Literature

Humanist men of letters include Gerald of Wales, Gervase of Tilbury, John of Salisbury, Walter Map. Geoff. Monm., *HRB*, was the most successful Latin literary work—if it is not to be included in the section on 'narrative histories' above. The courtesy book, D. Beccles, is discussed in detail in Chapter 11 above, Saewulf's account of his pilgrimage in Chapter 9.

**Poetry:** Geoffrey de Vinsauf, Godfrey of Winchester, Joseph of Exeter, Lawrence of Durham, Nigel Witeker, Reginald of Canterbury, Serlo of Wilton.

**Scientific works:** Adelard of Bath, Alfred of Shareshill, Daniel of Morley.

**Dial. scacc.** is an Angevin administrative handbook.

## Records of the Royal Government and Courts

*Domesday Book*
The first printed edition was *Domesday Book*, ed. Abraham Farley (2 vols.; London, 1783; 2 supplementary vols., ed. H. Ellis, 1816, containing, *inter alia*, the 'Exon Domesday'). Farley's text was reproduced, county by county, with translation, in *Domesday Book*, ed. John Morris *et al.* (39 vols. plus 3 index vols.; Chichester,

1975–92). Citations in this book are to volume and folio of DB with the reference numbers of the Morris system added in brackets.

DB is also available in the Alecto facsimile, along with translation, maps, and commentary: *Great Domesday: Facsimile*, ed. Ann Williams and Robert Erskine (7 cases; 1986–92); *Great Domesday Book*, ed. Ann Williams, R. W. H. Erskine, and G. H. Martin (31 vols.; London, 1987–92); *Domesday Book: Studies*, ed. Ann Williams and R. W. H. Erskine (London, 1987).

*ICC* contains two of the so-called 'Domesday satellites'.

For an extensive specialized bibliography, see David Bates, *A Bibliography of Domesday Book* (Woodbridge, 1985).

### Royal Charters and Acts to 1200
Prior to the reign of John, the royal government made no attempt to keep a record of the charters and other documents that it issued. Hence they survived, if at all, in the archives of the recipients, and must be painfully reassembled from hundreds of diverse sources. The series *RRAN* undertook to do this for the Norman period. The first volume, dealing with the charters of William I and William II, was particularly unsatisfactory. *Regesta regum Anglo-Normannorum: The Acta of William I, 1066–1087*, ed. David Bates (Oxford, 1998), magnificently makes good part of this deficiency.

A project is in progress to produce an equivalent work for the charters of the Angevin kings. Early fruits are such volumes as *Acta of Henry II and Richard I*, ed. J. C. Holt *et al.* (List and Index Soc., Special ser., 21, 27; 1986–96). For the Angevin lands in France, there is *Rec. actes Hen. II*.

### Diplomatic Documents
Pierre Chaplais (ed.), *Diplomatic Documents Preserved in the Public Record Office*, 1. *1101–1272* (Oxford, 1964).

### Exchequer Rolls
**Pipe Rolls** (Public Record Office class E372) record the annual audit of the debts owed to the Crown by the sheriffs and others. After a solitary survival from 1130, the continuous series begins in 1156. Pipe Rolls are referred to by regnal year, e.g. PR 19 HII means the Pipe Roll for the nineteenth year of Henry II (1172–3).

The following were edited by Joseph Hunter for the Record Commission:

PR 31 HI: *Magnum rotulum Scaccarii . . . de anno tricesimo-primo regni Henrici primi* (1833)

PR 2, 3, 4 HII: *The Great Roll of the Pipe for the Second, Third and Fourth Years of the Reign of King Henry II* (1844)

PR 1 RI: *The Great Roll of the Pipe for the First Year of the Reign of Richard I* (Rec. Comm.; 1844)

The other Pipe Rolls, from PR 5 HII on, are published by the PRS, 1884– . PR 8 RI is missing and the duplicate Chancellor's Roll was printed instead. PR 15 John is lost. The first PR for the reign of Henry III is PR 2 HIII.

**Receipt Rolls** (E401 and E370) record money paid into the Exchequer. Fragments survive from 7 HII (1161); the earliest roll is edited with a facsimile, *The Receipt Roll of the Exchequer for Michaelmas Term, 1185*, ed. Hubert Hall (London, 1899); they often list Jewish receipts separately.

**Exchequer Liberate Rolls** (E403 and E1200A) record the Liberate writs that ordered the issues of money from the Exchequer. The series begins in 1220 (4 HIII).

**Memoranda Rolls** (E159, E368, and E370) contain notes about debts, accounting, etc. at the Exchequer. The two earliest are 1 John, ed. H. G. Richardson (PRS n.s. 21; 1943), and 10 John, ed. R. Allen Brown (PRS n.s. 31; 1957 for 1955); the series commences in 1217.

## Chancery Rolls

From John's reign the royal government adopted the practice of enrolling copies of the charters and letters that it issued (see discussion above, pp. 199–201).

**Charter Rolls** (C53), which record solemn grants or confirmations of lands and rights by the king, begin in 1199. Those surviving from John's reign (1–2, 5–7, 9–10, 14–18 John) are printed in *Rot. chart.* There are no Charter Rolls for the period 1216–25 during Henry III's minority.

**Patent Rolls** (C66), recording royal letters patent, sent out open with the seal pendant, begin in 1201. Those surviving for John's reign (3–10, 14–18 John) are printed in *Rot. litt. pat.*, and those from 1216–25 in *Pat. Rolls HIII 1*.

**Close Rolls**, recording royal letters close, sent out folded and sealed, begin in 1200. The earliest are classified as Liberate Rolls (C62). Those surviving for 2, 3, and 5 John are printed in *Rot. lib.*, pp. 1–108, with a fragment in *The Memoranda Roll (1 John)*, ed. H. G. Richardson (PRS n.s. 21, 1943), pp. 88–97. The series of Close Rolls proper (C54) begins in 1204. The Close Rolls surviving from 6–9, 14–18 John and those for the period 1216–25 are printed in *Rot. litt. claus.*

**Fine Rolls** (C60), also called Oblate Rolls in the early years of John's reign, recording payments offered to the king for grants and favours, begin in 1199. Those surviving for 1–3, 6–7, 9, and 15–18 John are printed in *Rot. obl.*, those for the reign of Henry III in *Excerpta e rotulis finium in turri Londinensi asservatis (1216–72)*, ed. Charles Roberts (2 vols., Rec. Comm.; 1835–6).

**Rolls of the Exchequer (or justices) of the Jews** (PRO class E9): the only surviving rolls for our period, those for 1218–20, are calendared in *Calendar of the Plea Rolls of the Exchequer of the Jews* 1 (1218–1272), ed. J. M. Rigg (Jewish Hist. Soc. of England; 1905), pp. 1–55, and printed in Cole, *Docs.*, pp. 285–332.

## Rolls of the Chamber

**Misae Rolls** (E101/349) record the expenses of the royal household; two survive from John's reign (11 and 14 John): *Rot. lib.*, pp. 109–71; Cole, *Docs.*, pp. 231–69.

**Praestita Rolls** (E101/325) record cash advances made to royal officers and others; three survive from John's reign (7, 12, and 14–18 John): Cole, *Docs.*, pp. 270–6; *Rot. lib.*, pp. 172–253; ed. J. C. Holt, in *PR 17 John and Praestita Roll 14–18 John* (PRS n.s. 37; 1964 for 1961), pp. 89–100.

*Legal Records: Court Rolls and Feet of Fines*
Records of the the Central Courts and the itinerant justices survive from 1194 onwards.

**Plea rolls and essoin rolls (i. e. excuses for non-attendance) of the Bench and the court coram rege** (PRO KB26) from 1194 to 1225 are mainly to be found in *CRR*. Others are printed in *Placitorum in domo capitulari Westmonasterii asservatorum abbreviatio* (Rec. Comm.; 1811); *Rotuli curiae regis* (1194–1200), ed. Francis Palgrave (2 vols., Rec. Comm.; 1835); *Three Rolls of the King's Court*, ed. F. W. Maitland (PRS 14; 1891); *PBKJ*; *The Memoranda Roll (10 John)*, ed. R. Allen Brown (PRS n.s. 31; 1957 for 1955), pp. 69–118.

**Eyre rolls and Assize rolls** (JUST 1) survive from 1194; David Crook, *Records of the General Eyre* (London, 1982), gives a full and meticulous account of all eyre records in manuscript and in print. He does not deal with assize records. Two assize rolls relate to our period: *The Earliest Northamptonshire Assize Rolls*, ed. D. M. Stenton (Northamptonshire Record Soc. 5; 1930), pp. 99–163 (1203); *Earliest Lincs. Ass. Rolls*, pp. 235–77 (1206).

**Rolls of the Forest eyre** of 1209 (E32) are printed in *Select Pleas of the Forest*, ed. G. J. Turner (Selden Soc. 13; 1899), pp. 1–10.

**Feet of Fines** (CP25/1) are file copies of agreements between parties made before the king's justices; *Fines sive pedes finium*, ed. Joseph Hunter (2 vols., Rec. Comm.; 1835–44) prints those from 1195 to 1214 from nine counties; all those prior to 1198 are printed in PRS 17, 20, 23; most of those for 1198–9 in PRS 24; others in PRS n.s. 27, 29, 32; local record socs. have printed many; the PRO maintains a list of published feet of fines.

*Fiscal and Feudal Surveys*
Several local surveys of landholding survive from the reign of Henry I, possibly connected with assessment for geld:

The Northamptonshire Survey: tr. J. H. Round, *VCH Northamptonshire* 1, pp. 357–92.

The Lincolnshire or Lindsey Survey: facs. ed. James Greenstreet (London, 1884); tr. C. W. Foster and Thomas Longley, *The Lincolnshire Domesday and the Lindsey Survey* (Lincoln Record Soc. 19; 1924), pp. 237–60.

*The Leicestershire Survey*, ed. C. F. Slade (Leicester, 1956).

In the 1160s a revised version of DB for Herefordshire was drawn up: *Herefordshire Domesday*, ed. V. H. Galbraith and James Tait (PRS n.s. 25; 1950 for 1947–8).

Various royal inquests into knights' fees and other free tenures were undertaken in the Angevin period, notably in 1166 and in John's reign. The returns are printed in *RBE*, *Liber niger scaccarii*, ed. Thomas Hearne (2 vols., 2nd edn.; London, 1771) and *The Book of Fees* (2 vols. in 3; London, 1920–31). The results of a similar inquest into widows and wards in the king's gift held in 1185 are in *Rot. dom.*

## Law Books and Accounts of Pleas

*LHP* are a private legal compilation from *c.*1115, Glanville a record of the workings of royal justice from *c.*1188. Other twelfth-century law-books are printed in

Liebermann, *Gesetze* 1, pp. 527–675 (*Quadripartitus, Instituta Cnuti, Leges Edwardi Confessoris*, etc.).

Van Caen., *Lawsuits*, contains editions and translations of texts describing lawsuits prior to the beginning of plea rolls in 1194.

## Non-Royal Charters

Of all types of source, non-royal charters have the largest proportion of unprinted material. Thousands of charters, either in single-sheet originals, cartulary copies, or antiquarian transcripts, survive. They can be grouped by the issuer, the recipient, or the topic they deal with. Examples of printed collections from a single issuer are the royal charters already discussed, the episcopal documents such as *EEA* discussed below (p. 702), and the charters of individual aristocratic families, such as *Chester Charters, Gloucester Charters, Mowbray Charters*, and those in the appendix to Stringer, *Earl David*. Other instances are 'Charters of the Earldom of Hereford', ed. David Walker, *Camden Miscellany* 22 (Camden, 4th ser., 1; 1964), pp. 1–75; *Charters of the Redvers Family and the Earldom of Devon 1090–1217*, ed. Robert Bearman (Devon and Cornwall Rec. Soc., n.s. 37; 1994).

Most cartularies are essentially collections of charters for a single recipient. They are discussed below.

Examples of charters selected by topic—either geographical area or theme—are *Borough Charters, Bury Docs., Danelaw Docs.*, and *EYC*. A great store-house of monastic charters is provided by the *Monasticon*.

### Cartularies

In 1991 it was estimated that of at least 760 cartularies surviving from medieval England, around 125 were in print: John S. Moore, 'The Anglo-Norman Family: Size and Structure', *ANS* 14 (1991), pp. 153–96, at p. 184. The earliest is Heming's: *Hemingi Chartularium Ecclesiae Wigorniensis*, ed. Thomas Hearne (2 vols.; Oxford, 1723). It is closely followed by the *Text Roff.*

The essential guide is G. R. C. Davis, *Medieval Cartularies of Great Britain* (London, 1958), which gives details of over 1,300 cartularies (many of course have been published since Davis compiled his list).

## Feudal Surveys

Like the king, other lords were interested in keeping track of their feudal tenants:

*The Domesday Monachorum of Christ Church Canterbury*, ed. D. C. Douglas (London, 1944).

Peterborough: *Petr. Chron.*, pp. 168–75.

## Estate Surveys

Important surveys of demesne and tenant resources are, in chronological order:

*Bury*, 1087×1098: *Bury Docs.*, pp. 1–44.

*Caen* manors in England, 1106×1127–1223/4: *Caen Custumals*, pp. 33–104.

*Burton*, 1114–1126: Burton Surveys.

*Peterborough*, 1125–8: *Petr. Chron.*, pp. 157–68.

*Shaftesbury*, perhaps *c*.1130 and *c*.1180: BL Harley 61, fos. 37–89.

*Leighton (Beds.)*, 1154×1157: Robert Richmond, 'Three Records of the Alien Priory of Grove and the Manor of Leighton Buzzard', *Bedfordshire Historical Record Soc.* 8 (1924), pp. 15–46.

*Aylesbury and Brill (Bucks.)*, *c*.1155: G. H. Fowler, 'Extents of the Royal Manors of Aylesbury and Brill, circa 1155', *Records of Buckinghamshire* 11 (1926), pp. 401–5.

*Ramsey*, *c*.1160–1216: *Ramsey Cart.*, 3, pp. 241–316.

*Worcester*, 1164×1168: *The Red Book of Worcester*, ed. Marjory Hollings (Worcs. Hist. Soc.; 1934–50), pp. 30–8, 57–60, 82–6, 108–11.

*Glastonbury*, 1171–1201: Trinity Coll., Cambridge, MS R. 5. 33, fos. 110$^v$–116bis$^v$; *Liber Henrici de Soliaco abbatis Glastoniensis: An Inquisition of the Manors of Glastonbury Abbey, 1189*, ed. John E. Jackson (Roxburghe Club; London, 1882).

*St Paul's, London*, 1181, 1222: *Domesday of St Paul's*, ed. William Hale Hale (Camden Soc. 69; 1857), pp. 1–107, 109–17, 140–52.

*Durham*, 1183: *Boldon Book, Northumberland and Durham*, ed. D. Austin (Chichester, 1982, supplementary vol. to DB, ed. John Morris).

*Templars*, 1185: *Templar Records*.

*Evesham*, late twelfth century: BL Harley 3763, fos. 72–82$^v$; BL Cotton Vespasian B xxiv, fols. 22$^v$–73.

*Ely*, 1222: BL Cotton Tiberius B ii, fos. 86–259.

## Manorial Accounts

The earliest surviving series of manorial accounts are those from the estates of the bishop of Winchester, beginning in 1208. Two are in print:

*The Pipe Roll of the Bishopric of Winchester 1208–1209*, ed. Hubert Hall (London, 1903).

*The Pipe Roll of the Bishopric of Winchester 1210–1211*, ed. N. R. Holt (Manchester, 1964).

## Miscellaneous Surveys

The Winton Domesday, ed. Frank Barlow, in Biddle, *Winchester*, pp. 31–141, contains two surveys of Winchester, one of *c*.1110, one of 1148.

*The Kalendar of Abbot Samson*, ed. R. H. C. Davis (Camden, 3rd ser., 84; 1954) is a list of dues from the Liberty of Bury St Edmunds compiled by abbot Samson (1182–1211).

## The Church

### Papal Correspondence

Papal Registers commence in 1198; before that time papal letters, like royal letters and charters, have to be assembled from the archives of recipients. Important collections are Holtzmann and Kemp; Walther Holtzmann (ed.), *Papsturkunden in England* (3 vols., Abhandlungen der Gesellschaft der Wissenschaften zu Göttingen, Philologisch-Historische Klasse, N. F. 25, 3. Folge 14/15, 33; Berlin and Göttingen, 1930–52).

### For the pontificate of Innocent III:

*The Letters of Pope Innocent III (1198–1216) concerning England and Wales: A Calendar with an Appendix of Texts*, ed. C. R. Cheney and Mary G. Cheney (Oxford, 1967).

*Selected Letters of Pope Innocent III concerning England*, ed. C. R. Cheney and W. H. Semple (NMC; 1953).

### For Honorius III:

*Calendar of Entries in the Papal Registers relating to Great Britain and Ireland: Papal Letters* 1, ed. W. H. Bliss (London, 1893), pp. 40–117.

### For the legate Guala:

*The Letters and Charters of Cardinal Guala Bicchieri, Papal Legate in England, 1216–1218*, ed. Nicholas Vincent (Canterbury and York Soc. 83; 1996).

### *Councils*

All relevant material is superbly edited in *Councils and Synods*.

### *Episcopal acta*

The series *EEA* is intended to print or calendar all documents issued by bishops between the Norman Conquest and the first surviving relevant episcopal register.

### *Libri Vitae*

Lists of names to be commemorated survive from three monasteries in this period:

**Durham:** *Liber vitae ecclesiae Dunelmensis*, ed. J. Stevenson (Surtees Soc. 13; 1841), facsimile ed. A. Hamilton Thompson (ibid. 136; 1923).

**Thorney:** BL Add. 40,000, fos. 1$^v$–12.

**New Minster, Winchester/Hyde:** *Liber Vitae: Register and Martyrology of New Minster and Hyde Abbey*, ed. W. de Gray Birch (Hants. Record Soc.; 1892); *The Liber Vitae of the New Minster and Hyde Abbey Winchester*, ed. Simon Keynes (Early English Manuscripts in Facsimile 26; 1996).

### *Monastic Customs*
Lanfr., *Const.*

### *Liturgy*
Not many published liturgical texts can be assigned to this period. Those that can include:

### *Magd. Pont.*
*The Missal of New Minster, Winchester*, ed. D. H. Turner (Henry Bradshaw Soc. 93; 1962).

Francis Wormald (ed.), *English Kalendars before A.D. 1100* (Henry Bradshaw Soc. 72; 1934); *idem* (ed.), *English Benedictine Kalendars after A.D. 1100* (2 vols., Henry Bradshaw Soc. 77, 81; 1939–46).

For a general guide, Andrew Hughes, *Medieval Manuscripts for Mass and Office* (Toronto, 1982).

## WRITING IN ENGLISH

As discussed in Chapter 10, this period saw a low point in the production of writing in English. The only important original historical narrative in English is the *ASC*, that concludes in 1154. Around 1200 literary English begins to revive, with such works as Layamon's *Brut* and the *Ormulum*, discussed above, and *The Owl and the Nightingale*, ed. E. G. Stanley (London, 1960). Although the present text of *Ancr. Wisse* dates to *c.*1230, it was probably originally composed earlier. It is not usually easy to assign a precise date to writing in English in the medieval period, especially at this time, and many lyrics, romances, and sermons could be either from this period or slightly later.

There are several anthologies of Early Middle English:

*Early Middle English Texts*, ed. Bruce Dickins and R. M. Wilson (Cambridge, 1951).

*Early Middle English Verse and Prose*, ed. J. A. W. Bennett and G. V. Smithers (2nd edn.; Oxford, 1968).

*Medieval English Prose for Women*, ed. Bella Millett and Jocelyn Wogan-Browne (Oxford, 1990).

*The Cambridge History of the English Language* 2, ed. Norman Blake (Cambridge, 1992), includes some discussion of texts from this period.

## WRITING IN ANGLO-NORMAN

Problems of dating writing in Anglo-Norman are compounded by the problems of localization. It is often impossible to tell whether a particular work was composed on one side of the Channel or the other. There is thus no hope of establishing a reliable list of works written in French in England in the period 1075–1225. A few literary products can be assigned to a particular time and place, as in the case of Hue de Rotelande, discussed on pp. 498–500, but there is a large and uncertain penumbra of more elusive material.

M. D. Legge, *Anglo-Norman Literature and its Background* (Oxford, 1963) is a classic survey. The bibliography in the *Anglo-Norman Dictionary*, ed. Louise W. Stone and William Rothwell (London, 1977–92), provides a list of written material in Anglo-Norman from all periods, while the series ANTS prints Anglo-Norman texts of all types.

The most important histories in French are Fantosme and Gaimar, the most significant poetry by Marie de France (if one accepts that she was a single individual and that she wrote in England). There is a good guide to printed editions of Anglo-Norman hagiography in J. Wogan-Browne, '"Clerc u lai, muïne u dame": Women and Anglo-Norman Hagiography in the Twelfth and Thirteenth Centuries', in

*Women and Literature in Britain, 1150–1500*, ed. C. Meale (Cambridge, 1993), pp. 61–85, at pp. 75–8 (n. 4). Four romances are available in English translation in Judith Weiss, *The Birth of Romance: An Anthology* (London, 1992).

## MATERIAL OBJECTS

### Archaeology

General introductions include:

Helen Clarke, *The Archaeology of Medieval England* (London, 1984).

John Steane, *The Archaeology of Medieval England and Wales* (London, 1985).

The journal *Medieval Archaeology* provides a good guide to current archaeological activity.

Introductions to the exploration of field and village include:

Christopher Taylor, *Fieldwork in Medieval Archaeology* (London, 1974).

Leonard Cantor (ed.), *The English Medieval Landscape* (London, 1982).

### Architecture

*King's Works* is a classic survey of royal building. Nikolaus Pevsner's series The Buildings of England describes medieval buildings along with those of other periods. On one specific type of building, Peter Fergusson, *Architecture of Solitude: Cistercian Abbeys in Twelfth-century England* (Princeton, 1984).

The British Archaeological Association Conference publishes annual volumes on individual cathedrals, etc., e.g. *Medieval Art and Architecture at Worcester Cathedral* (1978); *Medieval Art and Architecture at Exeter Cathedral* (1991).

D. J. Cathcart King, *Castellarium Anglicanum* (2 vols.; Millwood, NJ, 1983) provides bibliography for every castle in England and Wales.

### Art

*Engl. Rom. Art* provides a rich general introduction and bibliography.

T. S. R. Boase, *English Art 1100–1216* (Oxford, 1953) is useful.

The Bayeux Tapestry has been reproduced on more than one occasion: by F. M. Stenton (London, 1957), D. M. Wilson (London, 1985), Wolfgang Grape (Munich, 1994).

English illuminated manuscripts of the period are surveyed in volumes 3 and 4 of the series *A Survey of Manuscripts Illuminated in the British Isles*: C. M. Kauffmann, *Romanesque Manuscripts, 1066–1190* (London, 1975); Nigel Morgan, *Early Gothic Manuscripts, 1. 1190–1250* (London, 1982).

### Sculpture:

George Zarnecki, *English Romanesque Sculpture, 1066–1140* (London, 1951).

George Zarnecki, *Later English Romanesque Sculpture, 1140–1210* (London, 1953).

Lawrence Stone, *Sculpture in Britain: The Middle Ages* (2nd edn.; Harmondsworth, 1972).

## Coins

J. J. North, *English Hammered Coinage*, 1. *Early Anglo-Saxon–Henry III, c.600–1272* (3rd edn.; London, 1994).

## Seals

P. D. A. Harvey and Andrew McGuinness, *A Guide to British Medieval Seals* (London, 1996); Birch, *Seals*.

# Index of Persons and Places

# Index of Subjects

adultery 267, 454, 559–60, 568–9, 586–7, 610

advowson 123, 223, 409

Advent 38, 443, 485, 565, 639

Afterlife 603–12

aids (financial levy) 65, 121, 163–4, 224, 231, 232–3, 344

alms 381, 453, 455, 457–9, 591, 602, 604, 612, 615, 638, 647

anchoresses, anchorites, *see* hermits

angels 41, 126, 440, 450, 453, 470, 478, 520, 530, 531, 562, 664–6, 687, 690, 692

   *see also* Gabriel; Michael; Raphael (in Name Index)

apes 665, 683

Apocalypse 656–7

Arabic language 482, 499, 520–2, 589

Arabic learning 520–2, 589, 648–9

Arabic numerals 520

archdeacons 145, 378, 384, 388–9, 390, 400, 488

archers 21, 86, 240, 254, 258, 261, 264

   *see also* crossbowmen

archives, records 43–4, 48–9, 123, 129, 143, 158–9, 164–5, 166–7, 174, 194–200, 207, 215–16, 219, 220, 222, 236–7, 242–3, 266, 271–2, 297, 302–3, 304–5, 307, 321–2, 333, 351, 354, 367, 383–4, 439, 485, 492–3, 544, 553, 558, 569, 571–2, 573, 575–6, 583–4, 626–7, 639, 667–8, 672–3

   *see also* Domesday Book (in Name Index); Pipe Rolls

armour 55, 189, 206, 214, 235, 238, 241, 252–4, 256, 267, 499, 593, 609–10

arms (heraldic), *see* heraldry

arms (weapons) 167, 206, 234, 241, 250, 252–4, 262, 263, 265, 267–8, 324, 476, 490, 593

   *see also* archers; crossbowmen

assemblies, *see* councils

astrolabe 520, 648

astrology 520, 522, 647–50

badgers 670

banns 553

baptism 125, 355, 356, 359–60, 377, 378, 380, 381, 387, 404, 427, 442, 443, 444, 449, 454, 479, 483, 535–6, 540, 541, 542, 545, 546, 665, 688

   *see also* names

barley 304–5, 314

barons 202–7, 209, 212–14, 216, 219–22, 224–6, 227, 228, 230, 236, 239, 245, 246, 247, 261, 262, 273–4, 278, 280, 322–3, 333, 337, 338, 339, 362, 407–8, 436, 437, 486, 505, 539, 548–9, 562, 568, 599, 616, 648, 691

   of London 342, 344

bastardy, *see* illegitimacy

battle, trial by, *see* ordeal, trial by

bears 248, 575, 669–70, 683, 684

beer 134, 142, 184, 236, 314, 365, 422, 536, 579

Bench, court of the, *see* Common Pleas

bestiaries 45, 497, 527, 672, 674–80, 686

bishops 31, 64, 93–4, 125, 126–7, 133, 143–6, 167, 194, 239, 262, 265, 354, 387–412, 426, 437, 461–2, 473, 479, 488, 493, 495, 503, 510, 528, 567, 569–70, 589, 599, 603, 615, 616, 647, 652

   appointment of 17, 63–4, 395–402, 406–7

   burial of 595–9

   *see also* Bangor; Bath and Wells; Carlisle; Chester; Chichester; Coventry; Durham; Elmham; Ely; Exeter; Hereford; Lincoln; London; Norwich; Rochester; St David's; Salisbury; Selsey; Thetford; Wells; Winchester; Worcester (bishops of) (in Name Index)